FOUR CENTURIES OF
DUTCH-AMERICAN RELATIONS

FOUR CENTURIES OF
DUTCH-AMERICAN RELATIONS
1609–2009

EDITED BY

HANS KRABBENDAM
CORNELIS A. VAN MINNEN
GILES SCOTT-SMITH

SUNY
PRESS

Published by State University of New York Press, Albany

© 2009 Roosevelt Study Center, Middelburg, the Netherlands

For information, contact State University of New York Press, Albany, NY
www.sunypress.edu

Book design René van der Vooren
Print and binding Prosperous Offset International Ltd.
Production Ryan Morris
Marketing Michael Campochiaro

Library of Congress Cataloging-in-Publication Data

Four centuries of Dutch-American relations, 1609–2009 /
edited by Hans Krabbendam, Cornelis A. van Minnen, and Giles Scott-Smith
p. cm.
Includes bibliographical references and index.
ISBN 978-1-4384-3013-3 (hardcover: alk. paper)
1. United States — Foreign relations — Netherlands
2. Netherlands — Foreign relations — United States.
I. Krabbendam, Hans, 1964–. II. Minnen, Cornelis A. van, 1956–.
III. Scott-Smith, Giles, 1968–.
E183.8.N4F68 2009
327.730492 – dc22
2009018821

CONTENTS

2

THE NINETEENTH CENTURY

CONTENTS

3
THE PERIOD OF THE WORLD WARS 1914–1945

CONTENTS

4

THE COLD WAR AND BEYOND
1945–2009
Politics and Security

5

THE COLD WAR AND BEYOND
1945–2009
Economics and Society

CONTENTS

11

6

THE COLD WAR AND BEYOND
1945–2009
Culture

12

CONTENTS

13

ACKNOWLEDGMENTS

The publication of this volume has a history of its own going back to the fall of 2005. As a research institute devoted to the study of U.S. history and Dutch-American relations, we were already looking ahead to the four hundredth anniversary of Henry Hudson's famous 1609 voyage and pondering how we might contribute to its celebration. It soon became clear that the ideal way to do so would be to compile, for the first time, a comprehensive history of bilateral relations between the Netherlands and the United States. Many books exist that touch on this subject — none had so far covered the whole terrain, and 2009 would be the perfect moment to produce such a book. As inspiration we had Detlef Junker's recently published two-volume *The United States and Germany in the Era of the Cold War, 1945–1990: A Handbook* (New York: Cambridge University Press, 2004).

With this in hand, we invited a number of eminent Dutch historians and American studies scholars to the Roosevelt Study Center in the spring of 2006 to discuss and develop the plan, and from this meeting we were able to finalize the scope and range of the book, the specific topics to be covered, and the prospective authors. During the fall of 2007 a series of seminars was arranged in Amersfoort, Leiden, The Hague, and Middelburg to discuss with the authors of each section the first drafts of their essays. By late 2008 the final versions of the essays had been edited and the last details of the manuscript were prepared.

We are very grateful to all the contributors listed in the book. A special word of thanks is due to the authors of the introductory essays of each section: Doeko Bosscher, Wim van den Doel, Willem Frijhoff, Duco Hellema, Jaap Jacobs, James Kennedy, and Bob Reinalda. They not only contributed an essay but also provided valuable editorial commentary for each section. We want to commend our copy editor, Margriet Lacy, who for over a year worked with a high standard of professionalism and good cheer on the more than ninety essays. It was a great pleasure to work with her. We would also like to thank the Taalcentrum-VU in Amsterdam for their assistance with some of the texts.

From the start of the project we were enthusiastically supported by our publishers Geert van der Meulen of Boom in Amsterdam and James Peltz of State University of New York Press in Albany, NY. We thank them and Boom's editor Aranka van der Borgh, who skilfully guided the manuscript through the various stages of the publication process. We also thank Carol Inskip for providing the volume with an indispensable index.

The publication of this volume would not have been possible without the financial support of our sponsors. Many thanks are due to Delta N.V. in Middelburg, the Netherlands, the main sponsor, and to The Netherland-America Foundation in New York, the A.C. Van Raalte Institute of Hope College, in Holland, MI, and the Netherlands Ministry of Foreign Affairs in The Hague. We also want to thank the Province of Zeeland and the Royal Netherlands Academy of Arts and Sciences, the main sponsors of the Roosevelt Study Center, who made it possible for us to spend countless hours on this project. Last but not least we thank our colleagues at the Roosevelt Study Center and the members of the Board of Trustees and of the Academic Advisory Board for their unfailing support throughout this project.

The Editors

—

FOUR CENTURIES OF DUTCH-AMERICAN RELATIONS, 1609–2009: A MAJOR CONTRIBUTION TO ATLANTIC HISTORY

—

HANS KRABBENDAM, CORNELIS A. VAN MINNEN
& GILES SCOTT-SMITH

September 11, 1609 was a fateful day in the history of transatlantic relations. Some time after noon the crew of the Dutch East India Company ship the *Halve Maen* spotted land and recognized the potential for a "very good harbor protected from all winds." The precise location is unidentified, but this must have been somewhere between current-day Manhattan and Staten Island. The discovery encouraged entrepreneurs in the Netherlands, who had financed Henry Hudson's voyage in the *Halve Maen*, to invest in trade with North America. Seventeen years later, one of the most famous "land transactions" took place when Manhattan became an official Dutch colony. The deal was also a fateful occasion for the Munsee people in the region. Initial contacts had led not only to the exchange of gifts and the trading of goods, but also to sporadic violence.[1] These first encounters across the Atlantic encapsulate the nature of the Dutch-American relationship that would unfold over the next four centuries, a narrative marked by hopes, opportunities, expectations, transactions, conflicts, and cooperation.

Over this time span relations between the two have developed from imperial linkages and informal economic partnerships to the declaration of official treaties and alliances between sovereign states. The idea of "America" as the New World was alive before the first encounter took place, and its importance has changed over time from being an unspoilt paradise to an attractive area for commercial exploitation, an innovative industrializing nation, and lastly a superpower. During the same four centuries the Low Countries became a major commercial and financial center and an imperial power before adapting to being a modern independent state — as Joseph Luns used to say, the largest of the small nations. Throughout these developments, linkages between the two have been maintained. The intensity of the contacts has shifted over time according to context and circumstance, and the emphasis has altered according to whether political, economic, cultural, ideological, or religious interests were paramount. Commitments, expectations, disappointments, and missed opportunities crisscross and collide throughout, but mutual interest, curiosity, respect, and fascination have never been far away.

As one might expect through the impact of globalization, the general trend of Dutch-American relations has been one of gradual convergence. Yet there have been various dynamics at work here. The density of the contacts has obviously increased overall, but there have been highs and lows and it is not possible to refer to any particular "straight line" that sets out the relationship in simple terms. It is hard, for instance, to find a period when both states regarded each other as equal partners. Asymmetric power relations have always played their role in influencing contacts, notably during the intense period of colony building in the seventeenth century and, in the other direction, the expansion of American influence in the twentieth. After all, the pull of convergence began in the seventeenth century when the Dutch established trader and settler communities as part of the drive for overseas expansion by European maritime states. Part of the first wave of Western Europeans to settle the American eastern shore, the Dutch occupied a central position during the formative period of colonial America. Political expectations in the Netherlands rose at the outbreak of the American War of Independence, but apart from expressions of good will and important financial transactions no immediate close relationship developed.

At first glance it would be hard to speak of a convergence during the nineteenth century, when inward-looking agendas and protective trade regulations prevented large-scale contacts. The ruling elites in the Netherlands, accommodating themselves to a monarchical system, were repelled by the expansion of mass democracy in the U.S. As a result, one can even refer to a divergence between the Dutch in the Netherlands and those in New York. In contrast, ordinary Dutch citizens were attracted by the space and the image of freedom, and the impact of migration is essential for this story — a quarter of a million Dutch men and women crossed the Atlantic in search of a new life. These immigrants established themselves along a chain of settlements through the midwestern states of Michigan, Illinois, Wisconsin, and Iowa. Investments flowed across the Atlantic into American property, canals, and railroads. As a result the Dutch-American connection was given new value, and it was precisely during the nineteenth century that Dutchness acquired positive meanings in American society and became popularized within the fields of both high art and mass culture. Nineteenth-century New Yorkers used the Dutch colonial period to pride themselves on the commercial origins of their city, praising the purchase of Manhattan by Peter Minuit as the best business deal of the age and using it as justification for their own commercial plans and political aspirations.[2]

The agents of convergence have varied in status and importance over time, from individual travelers and migrants to transnational interest groups and multinationals. The protagonists of the first decades represented various nationalities — the crew of the *Halve Maen* itself consisted of a mix of sixteen Dutch and English sailors.[3] Particular causes such as religious beliefs and business opportunities have led to certain sections of society engaging in a transatlantic dialogue to a greater extent than others. The overall process has been eased since the late nineteenth century by the transportation and communication revolution, a growing cultural awareness, and the global expansion of American power and influence. As the American presence in Dutch life has become more and more apparent through the centuries, manifesting itself through all political, economic, and cultural channels, so the Dutch presence in the United States has become more diffuse, maintained in the form of traditions, artefacts, and festivals by those keen to uphold it as heritage. Dutch studies does exist in the U.S. university system, but its most prominent position, the Queen Wilhelmina Chair in Dutch Language, Literature, and History at Columbia University, has lost its prominent place, and outside the Dutch-American colleges it is only represented by language departments (usually as a subfaculty of German).[4] Partly due to this diffuseness, and partly due to the dominance of English-speaking culture, the Dutch contribution to the United States does not occupy a prominent position within that nation's consciousness. In recent years the move away from American exceptionalism in U.S. historiography has allowed for a greater appreciation of the intermingling of the history of the United States with that of other nations.[5] Now is the moment to reclaim the Dutch element to this story, in all its many forms.

Although the overwhelming influence of the United States through the second half of the twentieth century has tended to typify relations, the Netherlands has never been a passive beachhead for the latest initiative from across the Atlantic. Americanization is a complex phenomenon, and most will agree that it involves a selective appropriation of products, styles, and traits rather than a

19

simple acceptance of the Made in the USA label. The Dutch have contributed a great deal to the dimensions and workings of the transatlantic relationship, and have invested much in the transfer and interchange of goods, services, people, and knowledge over the ocean. Dutch migration has far outnumbered Americans coming in the other direction. There was no recognizable American community in the Netherlands until after World War I, and this has grown slowly from around five hundred in the 1920s to thirty-one thousand in 2008.[6] Three Dutch queens — Wilhelmina, Juliana, and Beatrix — have addressed joint sessions of Congress, while since 1782 only one U.S. president — George H.W. Bush — has made a state visit to The Hague.[7] Importantly, relations between the two nations have never been marked by violence, but they have shared plenty of enemies: the Spanish, the British, the Germans, the Japanese, the Chinese, the Russians, and now the Taliban. There have been clashes between the respective national interests, the most direct and notorious being when Franklin D. Roosevelt, who cherished his Dutch roots, set in motion the end of the Dutch colonial empire in the East. Yet the incident that led to the most serious diplomatic fallout is now long forgotten, namely the seizure of Dutch shipping in U.S. ports in the spring of 1918 due to a bitter dispute concerning the neutrality of the Netherlands during World War I.[8]

Despite the absence of a clear Dutch-American narrative, it is possible to distill a developing common bond that represents more than simple opportunism, and that has gradually led to the two nations recognizing a shared set of ideals, interests, and common goals. It is appropriate that they were brought closely together by World War II and thereafter entered a period of profound internationalism, the one ending more than a century of neutrality, the other rejecting a decade or two of isolationism and abandoning its avoidance of peacetime alliances with Europe. Since then the United States and its Atlanticist call have provided the Dutch with the perfect escape route from the ambitions of its larger European neighbors. The successful maneuvering of a Janus-faced Dutch foreign policy, somehow simultaneously European and Atlanticist, is surely one of the great diplomatic conjuring tricks of the modern era. For the U.S. the Netherlands has been an ideal ally in the middle of European affairs, although Dutch allegiance has generally been taken for granted and has rarely generated rewards from Washington. Not everything about the relationship has been smooth, and plenty of adaptation has been required (more by the Dutch, of course, than by the Americans). But the post-World War II period has also cemented the themes around which these two nations have been able to unite: a common commitment to free trade and cultural exchange, a profound belief in international institutions as a source of order, and a strong moral vision on world affairs.

20

This study has made use of a clear understanding of the Dutch nation. It is important to point out that the early settlements in the New World included Flemish and Walloon inhabitants, and the West India Company was led and financed by former citizens of the Southern Netherlands. At first sight this justifies the explicit inclusion of present-day Belgium into the narrative in order to provide comprehensive coverage. However, such an extension stumbles over the discontinuities in the story between 1648 and 1815, when the Seven United Provinces in the north formed a republic, while the southern provinces remained separate under Habsburgian and Napoleonic rule. What is more, language, religion, and trade fed the development of ties between the Northern Netherlands and the United States in ways that were not replicated in the south. After a brief and unstable union between 1815 and 1830, Belgium became independent and established its own diplomatic relations with the United States in 1835. From then on the Belgians steered a different economic course with America, and mixed Dutch and Flemish immigrant communities were rare. As a result, the argument for a separate Dutch-American narrative is a strong one.

Over the centuries America and Europe have used each other to construct their own identity,[9] and the Dutch-American relationship fits in this broader context. Anglo-American relations have followed a remarkable trajectory from the seminal War of Independence in the eighteenth to the so-called special relationship in the twentieth. Relations with Spain and France have been caught up in imperial competitions and rival worldviews. Two world wars have defined the German-American relationship. In contrast, the Dutch-American story is more subtle and diverse in the record it has left, and therefore all the more intriguing to identify and put on display. Some historians claim that the Dutch came too late to North America to establish a fully developed economic relation with the region, but even if this were true there is no doubt that a mere half a century was enough for them to leave a lasting cultural imprint.[10]

Others have made the claim that there was a *Dutch* Atlantic, within the context of a distinct Atlantic history. The concept of the Atlantic as a contained historical space is an adaptation of French historian Fernand Braudel's study of the nations bordering the Mediterranean as a single, connected civilization.[11] Using a similar appreciation for linkages and networks the Atlantic Ocean has also provided a form of geographical and social unity for the nations along its shores, although its coherence for this purpose is questionable.[12] The impact of the transatlantic slave trade, the multinational history of the American colonial period, and a postcolonial interpretation of the European empires all point toward the need for some kind of Atlantic history perspective, within which a Dutch network covering Europe, Africa, and the Americas occupied a strategic position.[13] The history of Dutch-American transatlantic ties should therefore

21

be placed within the broad bounds of an Atlantic grand narrative. In doing so, this book also contributes to the burgeoning field of transnational history, with its focus on cross-border interactions and exchanges that transcend the stiff narratives of national progress.[14]

There has been plenty of scholarly attention for the many and varied aspects of Dutch-American connections, but they have tended to be specialized studies and as a result fragmented in the picture they give. Scores of essays have uncovered unique events and examples of political, demographic, artistic, religious, and economic exchange, but up till now a comprehensive overview and assessment of the multiple interactions across the centuries has been lacking. American scholars are mostly intrigued by the New Netherland phase in New York's history and generally lose interest after U.S. independence, so that surveys of American history fail to follow the effects of this presence over a longer period.[15] Their Dutch counterparts often focus on immigration history and post-World War II matters.[16] The present volume exactly integrates the various inputs and streams that have shaped the bilateral history in a wider transatlantic setting over the full four centuries of contact. We believe that the result is a unique overview of the dominant themes that have connected the two nations through the centuries, along the way intertwining their respective national histories to highlight what has pushed them apart and what, importantly, has held them together. While accepting the problem of defining "Dutchness" and what it entails,[17] the 1609–2009 anniversary offers an ideal moment to not only recapture a space for the Netherlands in North America but also to illustrate in detail both the diverse array of activities and the common interests that have propelled relations through the last four centuries and into the future.

1   Donald S. Johnson, *Charting the Sea of Darkness: The Four Voyages of Henry Hudson* (New York: Kodansha International, 1993), 118; Paul Otto, *The Dutch-Munsee Encounter in America: The Struggle for Sovereignty in the Hudson Valley* (New York: Berghahn Books, 2006), 36-47.

2   David M. Scobey, *Empire City: The Making and Meaning of the New York City Landscape* (Philadelphia: Temple University Press, 2002), 90-91.

3   S.P. L'Honoré Naber, ed., *Henry Hudson's Reize onder Nederlandsche vlag van Amsterdam naar Nova Zembla, Amerika en terug naar Dartmouth in Engeland,*

1609 (The Hague: Martinus Nijhoff, 1921), xxiii note 1.

4   The most prominent Dutch-American colleges are in Michigan: Hope College in Holland, and Calvin College in Grand Rapids.

5   See Thomas Bender, *A Nation among Nations: America's Place in World History* (New York: Hill and Wang, 2006).

6   Centraal Bureau voor de Statistiek, available at http://www.cbs.nl/nl-NL/menu/themas/bevolking/publicaties/artikelen/archief/2008/2008-2599-wm.htm (accessed December 8, 2008).

7   The speeches by the Dutch monarchs took place as follows: Queen Wilhel-

mina, August 6, 1942; Queen Juliana, April 3, 1952; Queen Beatrix, April 21, 1982. The visit of President Bush took place on July 19, 1989 during a European tour. See Cornelis A. van Minnen, ed., *A Transatlantic Friendship: Addresses by Queen Wilhelmina, Queen Juliana, and Queen Beatrix of the Netherlands to the Joint Sessions of the United States Congress* (Middelburg: Roosevelt Study Center, 1992); "A Visit Too Long Delayed," *New York Times*, July 20, 1989.

8   The Netherlands was seen as being pro-German because of its refusal to choose sides in the war. One of the results of this episode was the establishment of the Netherland-America Foundation in New York to combat anti-Dutch feeling in U.S. society.

9   Stephen Fender, ed., *American and European National Identities: Faces in the Mirror* (Keele: Keele University Press, 1996), 11-20.

10   Jan de Vries, "The Dutch Atlantic Economies," in Peter A. Conclanis, ed., *The Atlantic Economy during the Seventeenth and Eighteenth Centuries* (Columbia: University of South Carolina Press, 2005), 18.

11   See Fernand Braudel, *The Mediterranean and the Mediterranean World in the Age of Philip II,* vol. 1 (New York: Harper-Perennial, 1975).

12   Alison Games, "Atlantic History: Definitions, Challenges, and Opportunities," *American Historical Review* 111.3 (2006): 741-757; Bernard Bailyn, *Atlantic History: Concept and Contours* (Cambridge, MA: Harvard University Press, 2005).

13   Some historians have objected to the term "Dutch Atlantic" because the western outposts of the Netherlands were overshadowed by the British and they were anyway of secondary importance in comparison with other imperial interests in Asia. Nevertheless the Dutch presence within all the transatlantic political, economic, and social networks was substantial, especially considering how the Netherlands was surrounded by more prominent powers, and this input should be acknowledged. See Pieter C. Emmer and Willem W. Klooster, "The Dutch Atlantic, 1600–1800: Expansion without Empire," *Itinerario* 23.2 (1999): 48-69.

14   See for instance Akira Iriye and Pierre-Yves Saunier, eds., *The Palgrave Dictionary of Transnational History* (New York: Palgrave Macmillan, 2009).

15   See Suzanne Sinke, "Making a National Story: A Textbook Example of Dutch American Life," unpublished paper presented at the Organization of American Historians convention, New York, March 29, 2008. Sinke found that most U.S. history texts let the Dutch briefly appear in North America to be absorbed by the British.

16   Extensive bibliographies can be found on the websites of the New Netherland Project (www.nnp.org) and the Roosevelt Study Center (www.roosevelt.nl). A chronological selection of collected essays are the following: J.W. Schulte Nordholt and Robert P. Swierenga, eds., *A Bilateral Bicentennial: A History of Dutch-American Relations 1782–1982* (Amsterdam: Meulenhoff, 1982); Robert P. Swierenga, ed., *The Dutch in America: Immigration, Settlement, and Cultural Change* (New Brunswick, NJ: Rutgers University Press, 1985); Rob Kroes and H. Neuschäfer, eds., *The Dutch in North America: Their Immigration and Cultural Continuity* (Amsterdam: VU University Press, 1991); H. Loeber, ed., *Dutch-American Relations 1945-1969: A Partnership, Illusions and Facts* (Assen: Van Gorcum, 1992); Joke Kardux and Rosemarijn Hoefte, eds., *Connecting Cultures: The Netherlands in Five Centuries of Transatlantic Exchange* (Amsterdam: VU Uitgeverij 1994).; D. Bosscher, M. Roholl, and M. van Elteren, eds., *American Culture in the Netherlands* (Amsterdam: VU University Press, 1996);

23

George Harinck and Hans Krabbendam, eds., *Sharing the Reformed Tradition: The Dutch-North American Exchange, 1846–1996* (Amsterdam: VU University Press, 1996); Johannes Postma and Victor Enthoven, eds., *Riches from Atlantic Commerce: Dutch Transatlantic Trade and Shipping, 1585–1817* (Leiden: Brill, 2003); George Harinck and Hans Krabbendam, eds., *Amsterdam-New York: Transatlantic Relations and Urban Identities Since 1653* (Amsterdam: VU University Press, 2005); Joyce D. Goodfriend, ed., *Revisiting New Netherland: Perspectives on Early Dutch America* (Leiden/Boston: Brill, 2005); George Harinck and Hans Krabbendam, eds.,

Morsels in the Melting Pot: The Persistence of Dutch Immigrant Communities in North America (Amsterdam: VU University Press, 2006); Joyce D. Goodfriend, Benjamin Schmidt, and Annette Stott, eds., *Going Dutch: The Dutch Presence in America, 1609–2009* (Leiden: Brill, 2008); Margriet Bruijn Lacy et al., eds., *From De Halve Maen to KLM: 400 Years of Dutch-American Exchange* (Münster: Nodus Publikationen, 2008); and special issues of *Tijdschrift voor geschiedenis* 121.3 (Summer 2008) and *Sociologie* 4.2/3 (2008).

17 Willem Frijhoff, "Dutchness in Fact and Fiction," in Goodfriend, Schmidt, and Stott, eds., *Going Dutch*, 327-358.

CHRONOLOGY OF DUTCH-AMERICAN RELATIONS

1602	United East India Company chartered by the States General of the United Provinces
1609–21	Twelve Years' Truce between the Dutch Republic and Spain
1609	Henry Hudson explores the Delaware Bay and the upper Hudson River
1614	The name New Netherland first appears in an official document; New Netherland Company licensed by the States General; fur trading post Fort Nassau
1618–19	Synod of Dordrecht
1621	End of Twelve Years' Truce; West India Company (WIC) chartered by the States General
1624	First colonists arrive at Nooten Island and Fort Orange (Albany)
1625	Willem Verhulst director of New Netherland; founding of Fort Amsterdam (later New Amsterdam)
1626	Pieter Minuit replaces Verhulst as director; purchase of Manhattan Island
1628	Piet Heyn captures Spanish silver fleet for the WIC; first Reformed church founded
1631	Beginning of patroonships
1632	Minuit replaced by Bastiaen Jansz Crol; Swaenendael destroyed by Indians
1633–38	Wouter van Twiller director of New Netherland
1638–47	Willem Kieft director of New Netherland
1639	WIC's monopoly of fur trade lifted
1643–45	Kieft's War with the Indians around Manhattan Island
1647	Petrus Stuyvesant becomes director general of New Netherland
1648	Peace of Westphalia ends the Dutch-Spanish Eighty Years' War; end of Thirty Years' War
1650	Hartford Treaty settles boundary dispute between New Netherland and New England
1652–54	First Anglo-Dutch War

1653	New Amsterdam receives municipal charter; Wall Street built as defense against threat of New England invasion
1655	Stuyvesant conquers New Sweden in the Delaware Valley; Indians around Manhattan attack New Amsterdam, Pavonia, and Staten Island in a conflict called the Peach War
1658–63	Esopus Indian Wars in New Netherland
1664	New Netherland surrenders to an English naval force led by Richard Nicolls, the first governor; name changes to New York
1665–67	Second Anglo-Dutch War
1665	Admiral Michiel Adriaansz de Ruyter's plans to retake New Netherland aborted
1672–74	Third Anglo-Dutch War
1673	New York captured by Dutch naval force; New Netherland restored as a Dutch colony
1674	New Netherland becomes New York again as a result of the Peace of Westminster
1688	Glorious Revolution; Dutch stadtholder William III ascends British throne as William I

1764	First Dutch Reformed minister in New York preaches in the English language
1772	The Protestant Reformed Dutch Church becomes independent from Classis of Amsterdam
1776–83	American War of Independence
1776	Dutch canons on the Caribbean island of St. Eustatius salute the American flag of the brig-of-war *Andrew Doria* (November 16)
1780–84	Fourth Anglo-Dutch War
1781	John Adams appointed as minister plenipotentiary to the Netherlands
1782	Dutch Republic recognizes American independence; commercial treaty signed
1792	Holland Land Company organized to speculate in land in western New York (liquidated in 1858)

1809	Publication of Washington Irving's *A History of New York, by Diedrich Knickerbocker*
1815	Kingdom of the Netherlands established; unification of Southern and Northern Netherlands
1830	Secession of Belgium

1830–31	Arbitration of King William I in the North-Eastern Boundary Dispute between the U.S. and the UK
1837–41	Presidency of Martin Van Buren
1846	First wave of groups of Dutch immigrants to the United States
1856	Publication of John L. Motley, *The Rise of the Dutch Republic*
1861–65	American Civil War
1865	Publication of Mary Mapes Dodge, *Hans Brinker, or the Silver Skates*
1873	Founding of the Nederlandsch-Amerikaansche Stoomvaart Maatschappij (NASM, or Holland America Line)
1898	Spanish-American War; Queen Wilhelmina ascends the throne
1899–1902	Second Anglo-Boer War

1901–09	Presidency of Theodore Roosevelt
1903	Dutch Chamber of Commerce opens in New York
1913	Vincent Van Gogh introduced in America in Armory Show, New York
1914–18	World War I
1919	The Netherlands joins League of Nations; the U.S. Senate votes American membership down
1919	Royal Dutch Airlines founded (KLM)
1919	Jazz music is discovered in the Netherlands
1921	Concertgebouw Orchestra's Willem Mengelberg conducts in New York
1924	Ford opens first plant in Rotterdam
1926	Willem de Kooning arrives in New York as a stowaway
1933–45	Presidency of Franklin D. Roosevelt; the New Deal and World War II
1940	Dutch army surrenders to Germany (May 15)
1941	Japanese attack on Pearl Harbor (December 7); U.S. enters World War II
1942	Queen Wilhelmina addresses the U.S. Congress
1944	Bretton Woods conference
1945	The Netherlands liberated by Allied forces (May 5), followed by liberation of Dutch East Indies (August 15)
1945	The Netherlands and the United States become charter members of the United Nations (June 26)
1948	Queen Juliana succeeds Queen Wilhelmina; General Assembly of the United Nations adopts the Universal Declaration of Human Rights
1948–52	The Netherlands receives financial and technical assistance through the Marshall Plan

27

1948–62	Second wave of Dutch immigration to the United States
1949	The Dutch East Indies become independent as Indonesia
1949	The Netherlands and the United States join NATO
1952	The Netherlands joins the European Coal and Steel Community (basis of the European Economic Community [1957]); Queen Juliana addresses the U.S. Congress
1953	Flood disaster in southern Netherlands; U.S. engineers provide assistance
1954	Rock 'n' Roll comes to the Netherlands
1956	Suez Crisis; Anne Frank play staged in the Netherlands
1958	First significant exhibit of examples of American modern art in Stedelijk Museum Amsterdam
1958	Introduction of economy fares in air transport
1961–64	Dutchman Dirk Stikker secretary general of NATO
1962	Founding of the American Chamber of Commerce in Rotterdam
1963	New Guinea is ceded to Indonesia
1971–84	Dutchman Joseph Luns secretary general of NATO
1975	Suriname becomes independent
1980	Queen Beatrix succeeds Queen Juliana
1982	Bilateral Bicentennial of Dutch-U.S. relations; Queen Beatrix addresses the U.S. Congress
1982-83	Antimissile demonstrations in the Netherlands
1989	Fall of Berlin Wall and end of Cold War; President George H. W. Bush visits the Netherlands (first state visit by an American president)
1991	First Gulf War
2001	Terrorist attacks on World Trade Center and Pentagon on September 11
2003	American invasion of Iraq
2004–09	Dutchman Jaap de Hoop Scheffer secretary general of NATO
2005	Hurricane Katrina hits New Orleans; Dutch assistance
2009	Celebration of Hudson 400 and publication of *Four Centuries of Dutch-American Relations, 1609–2009*

1

COLONIAL PERIOD AND EIGHTEENTH CENTURY

1609–1782

1

COLONIAL PERIOD AND EIGHTEENTH CENTURY

1609 – 1

——

THE DUTCH, NEW NETHERLAND, AND THEREAFTER (1609–1780S)

——

WILLEM FRIJHOFF & JAAP JACOBS

The Dutch Experience in Early America

On March 30, 1624, the Dutch West India Company (WIC) issued a *Provisional Order* of government for New Netherland, the area of North America that they claimed, corresponding roughly to the current states of New York, New Jersey, and parts of Delaware and Connecticut.[1] Dutch rule applied to all of the territory's inhabitants, regardless of origin, for forty years, until the provisional surrender of the Dutch colony to the English under Colonel Richard Nicolls on behalf of King Charles II on September 6, 1664 (August 27 in the old style still prevailing in England). From 1614, even before the WIC had established a formal colonial structure, this privately explored territory bore the name Nieuw Nederland (New Netherland).[2] Following the 1664 "takeover," the colony was renamed New York after its new owner, the Duke of York, the king's brother. At the Peace of Breda (July 1667), New Netherland was exchanged with England for Suriname. But the Dutch fleet recaptured the colony on August 9, 1673, following the next declaration of war by England (1672). Dutch government was restored, no longer under the authority of the almost insolvent WIC, but of the Amsterdam Admiralty. Fifteen months later, on November 10, 1674, the "restitution" period came to

31

1
—
COLONIAL PERIOD AND EIGHTEENTH CENTURY

1609–1782

an early end when the Dutch ratified the cession of their colony to the English that they had accepted in the Treaty of Westminster (February 19, 1674).

All things considered, this was a rather brief period of Dutch *rule*, spanning as it did barely two generations. It nonetheless laid the foundations for a new society, at first colonial, then independent. The original framework, modeled on Dutch roots, forms of government, and customs, evolved with the growing influence of other peoples and cultures: the natives, who from the beginning were indispensable partners in the system of trade that was the West India Company's main objective; the European settlers from other countries; and the blacks, brought from Africa as slaves, and who from the outset formed their own founding community within that colonial society.

The influence and significance of the Dutch, as a community of inhabitants, did not evaporate when Dutch rule came to an end. Under English rule and, indeed, until long after United States independence, the community that had formed under Dutch rule continued to conduct its collective life with a degree of autonomy. It followed customs that came from the Netherlands itself and were adapted in America in response to the needs of that specific community. Some principles of the original Dutch community were adopted by the American state. They characterize American values and standards, and are an abiding source of inspiration for human and citizens' rights.[3] Although Dutch rule ended, signs of the colony's Dutch origin survived in more lasting forms of Dutch law and Dutch culture (see Middleton's essay).[4] For some considerable time under English rule, Dutch *law* and jurisprudence continued to govern aspects of life in the colony, such as the local administrative agencies and forms of civil law that remained valid in the "Dutch" community, the descendants of the original "Dutch" settlers (see Shattuck's essay).

Long after the independence of the United States and the introduction of homegrown legislation and a legal system, Dutch *culture* was still influential in the everyday lives of many of the residents of these states, albeit with diminishing intensity. People in rural areas and the lower classes also continued to identify themselves as "Dutch" for far longer than the leading circles in New York City. Dutch culture manifested itself in the Dutch language, the Reformed Church, specific styles of building and furnishing, interior design, old-Dutch objects, customs, and stories, and old or reinvented Dutch traditions, such as Saint Nicholas' Eve and other reminiscences of Dutch family life (see Goodfriend's essay). The historical awareness of being descendants of the founders of the new state, regardless of their origin or race, and being the distant representatives of the national tradition of the Dutch, were the longest to endure. This can be seen clearly on the most basic level of cultural transfer, the family, with its group traditions, genealogical awareness, and myths of origin. It is not surprising that the first genealogical societies in the West were created as long ago as the early nineteenth century in the United States, and the awareness of belonging to an extensive and intricate kinship underpins many lasting forms of sociability and public representation. At the first census, in 1790, about one hundred thousand Americans (2.6 percent of the total population) were labeled as being of Dutch descent.

Various values of the Dutch cultural tradition were perceived by the English majority as a form of "otherness," and later appropriated by the community of Americans of Dutch descent as typically "Dutch." Examples included the Dutch traditions of political representation, republicanism, striving for equality under the law, democratic decision making, tolerance, and freedom of conscience, if not of religion. It does not matter whether there is any basis in historical reality to the notion that these values are the Dutch legacy to America, or whether it is a form of invented tradition or wishful thinking. Either way, they are the core of the sense of identity of the American Dutch. In a new context, outside the homeland, the core values of a cultural community are always formulated more sharply, and felt more emotionally, than at home.

In fact, there was tension from the outset between two major sectors in the New Netherland colony and its successors. One was the core of WIC employees together with the original settlers who benefited from the WIC regime. The other was formed by groups of inhabitants of different origin, history, and tradition, such as the natives and the colonists of diverse origin including many Dutch themselves, the African slaves, and later the English rulers. This tension was related to the special administrative traditions and power relations that also held sway in the European homeland. The Dutch Republic was a union of formally independent states that were both difficult to hold together and driven internally by a variety of factions seeking power and influence.[5] Hierarchical structures were of only modest importance in the political and social culture of the homeland, since decisions were usually reached through negotiation and consultation, and had to accommodate many forms of representation of interested parties. We can identify a corresponding situation in New Netherland. The art of controlling this tension through communal effort, and the resultant dynamism and opportunities for innovation, continue to characterize the former New Netherland region, and are possibly the most important legacy of the Dutch.

History and Memory of the Dutch   33

For more than two centuries the achievements and significance of the Dutch experience in America have been the object of complex, often contradictory, perceptions, which has produced an almost impenetrable tangle of history and

1

—

COLONIAL
PERIOD
AND
EIGHTEENTH
CENTURY

1609–1782

memory of the Dutch. Vilification and glorification have alternated at regular intervals to the present day, to which the often lively, sometimes even grim, discussions in historical narrative about the representation of New Netherland and New York clearly testify. Whereas some emphasize what they see as the essentially English origin of current New York, others rediscover the lasting meaning of the old-Dutch institutions and values, not only for the settlers and their offspring, but also for the political establishment of independent America.

At an early stage, the tension between history and memory prompted historical investigation of the colony's Dutch past. Washington Irving's highly influential *A History of New York by Diedrich Knickerbocker* (1809) acted as a catalyst. Irving drew his material from historical sources and the oral history of the Dutch-American tradition. When the educated public realized how little they knew of the state's Dutch past, the government commissioned the Dutch Patriot and New York immigrant Francis Adrian Van der Kemp to translate the seventeenth-century official government documents into English. Unfortunately, the twenty-eight volumes of the Dutch Colonial Records of the State of New York that Van der Kemp translated between 1817 and 1822 proved to be of poor quality and were burned in 1911. However, there was eventually to be a Dutch answer to the image created by Irving: the first history of the colony by the Middelburg patrician Nicolaas C. Lambrechtsen, completed in 1818 and published in English in 1841 by the New York Historical Society.[6] It would be another century and a half before a history of New Netherland was published in the Netherlands itself, and, unlike the great bulk of published material of the Dutch East India Company (VOC), that of the WIC remained largely unknown in the Netherlands.

The almost constant rivalry in trade and navigation between England and the Netherlands is reflected in the English cartoon tradition, with its caricatures of the Dutch competitor and opponent from as early as the seventeenth century. Irving adopted and standardized these caricatures, and in the nineteenth century they created a stereotype of the Dutch in America: a fat, lazy, pipe-smoking dullard, a merchant with trivial tastes and no breeding, a parsimonious capitalist, or an uncontrolled thug — in all respects the complete opposite of the active, expansive, cultivated, and self-assured English gentleman. It is because of these caricatures that no serious attention was given to the Dutch cultural tradition of former New Netherland for so long.

The variable perceptions of "the Dutch" have engendered many myths and much "invented memory," and to the present day have lent an anti-Dutch bias to the historiography of New York. But it goes without saying that they occasionally worked to their advantage. An example of this ambivalence is the concept of tolerance and the Dutch attitude to it. Practical tolerance is a time-honored Dutch value with roots as far back as the founding charter of the Dutch Republic, the Union of Utrecht (1579), but it is certainly not true that the New Netherland

community was always a model of tolerance toward other religions. Legal restrictions on the freedom of public worship were upheld in New Netherland, albeit that personal freedom of conscience was respected better than elsewhere,
and also expressly acknowledged as a value.

The perspective on "Dutchness" is in constant flux in the United States. The
seventeenth-century Dutch from New Netherland have since been succeeded
by more recent groups of Dutch immigrants in the Midwest and elsewhere,
whose conduct and image have caused a review of the notion of "Dutchness."[7]
New elements of the Dutch experience also emerge repeatedly in the states that
correspond to the former Dutch colony. The Dutch Revival in the early nineteenth century followed a phase of ethnification of the "Dutch" in the eighteenth
century. Later came Holland mania. The first really serious historiography of
New Netherland came about between the 1840s and the 1930s, as a result of new
research in the state and church archives, and the translations and substantial
publications of John Romeyn Brodhead, Edmund B. O'Callaghan, Berthold
Fernow, Edward T. Corwin, and later especially Arnold J.F. Van Laer, not to forget J. Franklin Jameson's much quoted edition of literary sources, the *Narratives
of New Netherland* (1909). Van Laer not only translated the state documents and
various series of Court Minutes, but also published the correspondence of the
Van Rensselaer family concerning policy and life in the Rensselaerswijck patroonship (around present-day Albany), which presented a complementary picture of colonial development.

Since 1974 the New Netherland Project, led by Charles T. Gehring and supported by the New York State Library in Albany, has been retranslating the old
documents into English to a higher standard. Together with a growing number of newly translated texts, the project is achieving a profound revitalization
of the history of New Netherland.[8] Simultaneously, professional historians on
both sides of the Atlantic are designing a new image of Dutch-American history
with fresh perspectives and new historical methods. For instance, for the early
modern period more attention is being given not only to ethnicity and gender,
visual representation, mentalities, and material culture, but also to political
representation, state formation, economic policy, and symbolic action in the
public space. A careful description of the period in which the Dutch played their
part in the creation of the area is therefore vital for a proper understanding of
the later history of former New Netherland. This is not in the least because the
Dutch experience still appears to provide material for today's debates about
America itself.

35

The historiography of New Netherland has surged forward in recent decades.[9] The nationalistic view of history also determined the oldest historical images of New Netherland. Until only a few decades ago, its population and culture
appeared much more Dutch than later research has shown. This image of ho-

1

——

COLONIAL
PERIOD
AND
EIGHTEENTH
CENTURY

1609-1782

mogeneity hindered a proper understanding of New Netherland's significance for the later, grand development of the English world around it. A subsequent image was that of a multinational settlement colony, which was accompanied by a greater importance of New Netherland for American history. This new image was compatible with New York's self-image of multiethnicity, as well as with new insights into the character of Dutch society in the Golden Age, as a migration community with a high melting-pot content.

The retention of a certain degree of Dutch *law* and Dutch *culture* after the English takeover put the original European population of the colony in a position to develop a Dutch ethnic sensibility, which again leveled the multinational character of the Dutch community. In the Hudson Valley, Long Island, and East Jersey in particular, this ethnification process led to the gradual adoption of the term "Dutch" as the name for the remaining group of colonists from the Dutch period of whatever origin, including Scandinavian, German, English, or French. The later immigrants from the Netherlands went along with this usage. "Dutch" has since become an ambiguous term that refers to diverse identities. In New Netherland with its population from many countries, "Dutch" originally referred to the colony's property. After 1664, the colonists' geographical origin became less important than their common origin in "Dutch" New Netherland and their belonging to a tightly interwoven network of descendants.

However, other differences also gained in importance, both inside and outside the Dutch community. Some examples are religion and language, along with Dutch varieties of civic culture and a specific Dutch-American historical tradition. The role of Dutch pietism in the First Great Awakening is well known, and the language of the colonial Dutch was long upheld in the religious practice of the rural churches, despite its gradual divergence from the standardizing language in the Dutch Republic (see the contributions by Van Lieburg and Noordegraaf). But differences also emerged between the Dutch of urban New York City and those of the extensive rural areas. It would therefore be wrong to take only the urban tradition of the Dutch of New York City as the criterion for the development of the whole Dutch community of former New Netherland. The administrative structure of New Netherland was more consistent with that of the rural areas of the Dutch Republic than the urban tradition of Holland, and it can be identified only to a limited extent in the later developments in rural America. It goes without saying that the tensions and contradictions that these developments sometimes evoke in America itself and elsewhere must also be seen against the background of a growing awareness of the rights of all population groups to a collective memory and their own history, and of the struggle for their recovery. These rights are not always mutually consistent.

Structure and Issues

This first part of the book covers the period from the arrival of the Dutch to American independence. It offers a balance of our knowledge about the ways in which New Netherland in its own time and later under English rule contributed to the special place of the Dutch in the history of early modern North America. This history begins around 1600 with the first perceptions of the natives, and continues until the independence of the states concerned, two centuries later. Of course, any balance requires choices to be made, and ours were guided by the topicality in the historiography and by the themes that are currently important in society. We present Dutch-American relations in the context of broader frameworks, such as the Atlantic world, the European background, and Dutch networks, and of wider issues, such as political, administrative, and legal institutions, economic trends, culture and religion, perceptions, and so on. The essays present broad and major lines of development, while avoiding excessively detailed dissertations. They do not set out to draw a comparison with the English colonies, but instead concentrate on New Netherland itself. The central aim was to document Dutch *rule*, Dutch *law*, and Dutch *culture* satisfactorily as the three different forms of influence of the Dutch on the historical forms of community in North America.

The most important message of this part of the book is that the colony of New Netherland was not an isolated, fully autonomous, or marginal area of the Dutch alone, but was integrated along many lines in the network of relationships between the continents and the states, the regions and the colonies, the peoples and the nations, the migration patterns of the early modern period, the goods flows of the economy and the culture, and the value systems of the Old and the New Worlds. New Netherland cannot be understood purely as a separate entity. Its history, development, and later significance must constantly be viewed in interaction, or in interference, with the world around it. Perceptions appear not infrequently to be just as important as objective historical data.

Although there were many and varied developments throughout the early modern period, some even extending far into the contemporary period, we can identify two turning points. The first was the takeover of the colony by the English in 1664, in a process that completed in 1674, and the second was the War of Independence in the 1770s and its immediate consequences for the structure of American society. Within these two periods we can observe developments on a shorter timescale. The period until the foundation of the WIC and the establishment of a sustainable colony in 1623–25 was characterized by exploration and the rise of new images and representations of America. Then, until 1664–74, we see the colony's expansion and consolidation under Dutch rule. From the

1

——

COLONIAL
PERIOD
AND
EIGHTEENTH
CENTURY

1609–1782

takeover until Leisler's Rebellion in 1689, the Dutch settlers developed a survival strategy, which used the opportunities provided by Dutch law and Dutch culture, to the extent that they were still enforced under the relatively open English rule (see the essay by Voorhees). This shaped a Dutch community that underwent a process of ethnification in the eighteenth century, in which the identity of the Dutch Americans gradually shifted away from Dutch culture toward American citizenship, which large numbers of them enthusiastically embraced at the time of independence. The *Articles of Confederation* of September 15, 1777 actually expressed appreciation for the historical Dutch example. However, ten years later, in the *Constitution* of September 17, 1787, the new state demonstrated its independence by distancing itself from that example (see Te Brake's essay). This marked the end of the era.

New Netherland

No one will ever know whether there would have been a New Netherland at all had the Englishman Henry Hudson not joined the Dutch East India Company in 1609 and sailed to the New World, remaining instead with the English, his previous employer (see Gehring's contribution). What is certain is that several factors worked in favor of the Dutch wish for expansion into new areas in the West: the perceptions of the American continent and its inhabitants (see Van Groesen's essay), technical developments in shipbuilding, the Dutch Republic's economic growth, the war with Spain, which extracted its wealth from South America, a flourishing Dutch cartography, the growing interest in science, and the need for minerals, not to mention the mental impact of the myth of the West and the frontier.[10]

In the eyes of the Dutch, the northeast coast of America was a "blessed country, where milk and honey flow."[11] All things considered, the exploration of this area owed much to coincidence and personal choices. Hudson and his ship *Halve Maen* were supposed to discover the northeast passage to China, but he deviated from his instructions and arrived in early September 1609 in New York Bay and the river that now bears his name. Rather than continuing his voyage, he returned to Europe after a brief exploration of the upper reaches of the river. The news and the products he brought home helped persuade individual merchants to back further exploration. In 1614, a merger of private interests and existing trading companies formed the New Netherland Company, a consortium of merchants dedicated exclusively to the fur trade. It envisaged no stable settlement on the American continent, even though the English in nearby Virginia and the French in New France had already done so. However, neither of them was then interested in colonizing New Netherland, and the 1620 landing of the Pilgrim Fathers to the northeast was some time in the future.

From the arrival of the first colonists on Governor's Island in 1623 and the establishment of public administration in 1624, a permanent colony was established on that territory under the authority of the Chartered West India Company, which took over the private trading posts. But this settlement was not preordained. It benefited from the coincidence that a group of Walloon Calvinists was interested in colonization overseas. The Company originally hesitated about its policy. The immigrants were distributed over several support centers scattered around the immense area, with a view to using these Dutch settlements to claim as much territory as possible as Company property. The WIC opted to consolidate the habitation only as a second thought. The first full director, Willem Verhulst (1625–26), whose several predecessors had control only for the duration of a voyage, started in 1625 on the construction of a fort and a rudimentary administrative center on the southern tip of Manhattan, which was called New Amsterdam. The next director, Pieter Minuit (1626–32), bought the eleven-thousand-acre island from "the wild people" for goods worth about sixty guilders (or twenty four dollars at the nineteenth-century exchange rate). The purchase was reported on November 5, 1626 in a letter from deputy Pieter Jansz Schagen to the States General in The Hague.

A feature of the colony for some considerable time was its bipolar structure. On one side was the administrative and trading center of the WIC on Manhattan with a wide hinterland on Long Island, the west, and the south, but plagued by a constant power struggle with its English neighbors in the northeast and southwest. On the other side was the ample Rensselaerswijck patroonship, which was an intensive colonization zone comprising a manor with seigniorial rights that was founded by a consortium of Dutch financiers led by the Amsterdam jewel merchant Kiliaen van Rensselaer. Rensselaerswijck's interests often differed from those of the WIC, but it also had more intensive, and usually better, contacts with the natives in the north, and occasionally with the French in New France (Québec).

This bipolar nature was attributable to a fundamental difference between the administrators of the Amsterdam Chamber, who were responsible for New Netherland, about how to interpret the charter of the WIC, which attempted to reconcile an explicit trading goal with the religiously tinted colonization ideal of a group of major shareholders. Accordingly, the WIC board split almost immediately into trading and colonial factions, which alternately gained the upper hand and determined policy. The motives for establishing the post in North America had more to do with immediate gain and trade competition with the other European powers than with rational considerations. The fur trade profits

39

1

—

COLONIAL
PERIOD
AND
EIGHTEENTH
CENTURY

1609–1782

originally envisaged by the WIC soon proved to be losses, and only private trading firms flourished. In fact, the location policy was mainly driven by the colonial faction, whose aim was to set up patroonships. The only one of these actually to enjoy lasting success was Rensselaerswijck, owing to its hybrid economy of fur trade and agriculture. It was to be a long time before the administrative center of New Amsterdam would acquire the contours of a real city. Even a real church, the traditional counterpoint to the fort in colonial cities, was not built until 1642, and then not in its own space where it could enjoy autonomy, but inside the fort.

This was in stark contrast to the other core WIC area in seventeenth-century America, Brazil, which it attempted to capture from the Portuguese from 1624 onward. There were military, political, and economic reasons for the WIC to devote far more attention to Brazil, or New Holland, than to New Netherland, and much more was invested there. Brazil stretched in the northeast of South America from Maranhão in the north to Pernambuco on the east coast.[12] The dominant factor there was the plantation economy for sugar, which could be made profitable in the short term only with slave labor, leading the WIC into an active slave trading role from the 1630s. Furthermore, the Portuguese had intensively colonized and Christianized Brazil. There was already an administrative structure, unlike New Netherland, where the WIC actually had a free hand and took only very limited account of the natives.

This is how New Netherland came to occupy a unique place in the Dutch Republic's overseas possessions. Other locations of the Dutch East and West trade were no more than simple trading posts until well into the eighteenth century. The settlement colony of Brazil soon had to be abandoned, and younger colonies, such as Suriname and Guyana, continued as plantation communities with scattered habitation. Despite its start as a trading support post, New Netherland was soon developed by the WIC and the free colonists into a sustainable settlement colony, with stable habitation centers and a growing internal autonomy (see the essay by Jacobs). The lack of a preestablished colonial regime, the existence of a wide range of natural resources, and rather quick links with the homeland, made it possible to shape the colonial community in a way familiar to the Netherlands. Were it not for the active input of the native tribes and the African slaves, New Netherland, with its characteristic mix of trading post and settlement colony, would have been more likely than the other Dutch colonies to acquire the countenance of a region of the homeland.[13]

But the conflict between the two factions stood in the way of a balanced development of the area. One group had an inward orientation, and another was disposed toward the Atlantic world, but no structural, organic cohesion developed between them. This contrast persisted through the subsequent centuries. The dynamic, multiethnic, and international life of New York City and

its quickly urbanizing environment was long in stark contrast to the rural development of upstate New York, around its antithesis Albany, and of New Jersey.
In these rural areas, the traditional culture, language, and Reformed religion
of the Dutch pioneers and founders thrived for more than a century after the
English takeover.

Minuit's successor, Wouter van Twiller (1633–38), was a weak leader, and his
directorship a chaotic interlude. Moreover, his links with his uncle, Rensselaer,
were probably too close for him to defend the WIC's interests adequately. Director Willem Kieft (1638–46) also lacked the necessary administrative experience.
He was an upper-crust Amsterdam wine merchant, with French trade experience,
and he took his position, rights, and privileges extremely seriously. The same
was true of Kieft's successor, Petrus Stuyvesant (1647–64), a Frisian clergyman's
son who left his theology studies to join the WIC. Stuyvesant had been appointed director of the WIC on the island of Curaçao before his appointment in New
Netherland, and because of this double function he was given the title of director general. Kieft was the first to bring administrative stability and the beginnings of social order. He started the exploration of natural resources and the
urbanization of the most important settlement, New Amsterdam. At the same
time, Rensselaer too was turning his hand to moral authority, religion, and civilization, by building a church in his patroonship and appointing a pastor. But
Kieft's wars with the natives in 1643 and 1644, partly because of his own rash
policy, ruined what had already been achieved, divided the Company servants
and the settlers into two directly opposing camps, and meant on balance that
his period of control was a failure.

A comparison with what happened at the same time in Dutch Brazil may
be illuminating. Count Johan Maurits van Nassau, governor from 1637 to 1644,
built his new capital city Mauritsstadt near Recife, including a princely palace.
While the still humble New Amsterdam was being weighed down by punishing
wars with the natives, Johan Maurits was turning his capital city into a center
of new urban culture, where science, art, and tolerance flourished. But he too
received insufficient support from the WIC, and in 1654 the Dutch lost Brazil
forever. The irony of history is that the Portuguese-Jewish colony that had bur-
geoned in Mauritsstadt settled in New Amsterdam after 1654 with permission
from the WIC, but against the will of both director general Stuyvesant and his
council and of the Reformed ministers. Toleration clearly had its limits among
the Dutch in America.

Despite the persisting struggles with the natives and the English neighbors,
New Netherland in Stuyvesant's period of control (1647–64) became a fully
fledged colony with a society that was well ordered in many respects. New settlements were founded and brought to fruition; public services, such as the office of
notary, were established; new pastors were installed in Manhattan, Beverwijck

41

1

—

COLONIAL
PERIOD
AND
EIGHTEENTH
CENTURY

1609–1782

(Albany), Breuckelen (Brooklyn), Long Island, and Wiltwijck (Esopus); care for the poor and the education system were improved, and a Latin secondary school founded.[14] The rather autocratic attitude of the director general was successfully counterbalanced by early forms of popular representation, such as the *Landdag* (Diet) and the Nine Men. In 1649, this representative body sent a delegation to patria, headed by a locally prominent lawyer, jonker Adriaen van der Donck (after whom Yonkers is named), to negotiate a radical change in the colony's legal statute. The proposal was for the administration of the colony to be taken over as quickly as possible by the States General from the WIC. This would have made New Netherland a Generality Land under direct rule of The Hague, as had happened in 1648 with States Brabant, Van der Donck's home.

However, the only tangible concession made by the WIC was the incorporation of New Amsterdam as a fully fledged city on February 2, 1653, through the establishment of a court of burgomasters and *schepens*. Nonetheless, this decision proved to be of great symbolic importance. New Amsterdam became the first chartered town with elected city self-government and a full urban culture. New Amsterdam was also effectively extracted from the supreme authority of the WIC. A small bench of justice was established in Beverwijck as early as 1652, and another fifteen towns gained one between 1642 and 1664 (see the essay by Jacobs). Finally, in the late 1650s a new patroonship was founded by the city of Amsterdam itself on the Delaware, called New Amstel. New Amsterdam's sophistication manifested itself in urban self-assurance. Just as in the homeland, city pride was soon expressed in a series of engravings with the perspective of the city surrounded by metaphors of prosperity.

Old and New Netherland

It is possible to identify three main interpretations of New Netherland. The old interpretation, still dominant in the Anglophone historiography of New York and the surrounding states, emphasizes the rapid adaptation of the colonial community to the New World, and, after the takeover, to the rule and culture of the English. There is a contrasting revisionist view that emphasizes the fundamental and sustainable Dutch character of the colony. While acknowledging the growing interaction with the English social world, along with the Dutch community's gradually declining autonomy, the gist of this view is still the autonomous development of Dutch culture, which imparted its own color to the community of former New Netherland.

Even more recent is the Atlantic perspective (see Klooster's essay).[15] It breaks the myth of the autonomous development of the continents and likewise makes light of the bilateral relationship between the Dutch Republic and New Netherland, pointing instead to the totality of links between all players in the Atlantic zone. Only a broad transatlantic network analysis of this kind can actually do justice to the role of the slave trade and the links between the individual colonies: those of the WIC, but also those of England, France, Portugal, Spain, and even Sweden. From 1639 until its incorporation into New Netherland in 1655, there happens to have been a Swedish colony on the Delaware, originally under Director Pieter Minuit, who had gone over to the Swedes. The Atlantic perspective also weakens the nationalistic Anglo-American and Dutch-American visions, in that the colonies' economies, social relationships, and cultures developed in their own, complex way, despite the natural links between administration and legislation and the homeland.

Right to the end, the WIC treated New Netherland as an area that, while commercially interesting, was not its greatest priority, and on which it expended only extremely limited resources. The war with Spain, one of the WIC's primary purposes when it was founded, remained remote from the North American territory, despite its profiting occasionally from the spoils of war and receiving the first captured slaves from this source. There were also few push motives for the inhabitants of the Dutch Republic to emigrate to New Netherland. At most, America offered pull motives, such as the craving for adventure that played a large part in the growth period of the Dutch economy. However, there never was a collective, mass migration of citizens from the Dutch Republic. The Dutch emigrants were mainly individuals with private interests in trade, agriculture, or a craft, not to mention those who simply remained in America in service of the WIC as officials, sailors, or soldiers. The political regime of the Dutch Republic was extremely moderate, and the social climate provided more opportunities for ordinary citizens to participate than in most other European states, with their usually rigid hierarchical structures and proclivity for absolutism.

The Dutch Republic had no religious minorities who could only hope to practice their faith by emigrating. Even though Roman Catholics and a few other Christian groups were occasionally repressed in the Dutch Republic, the freedom of conscience guaranteed under Article 13 of the founding charter of the Dutch Republic, the Union of Utrecht (1579), was consistently respected in a way viewed outside the Dutch Republic as particularly tolerant. In fact, the Europeans, inured to religious wars and religious coercion, also perceived this tolerance as extraordinary. Finally, living conditions in Dutch rural areas were not bad enough to necessitate urgent mass emigration to the New World. The occasional group of farmers and their families came only from the poorer rural provinces. But many colonists in the first decades were not of Dutch origin at all, and neither were many of the WIC's soldiers. These people gave the colony its multinational, mul-

43

1

—

COLONIAL
PERIOD
AND
EIGHTEENTH
CENTURY

1609–1782

tiethnic, and multireligious composition during Dutch rule, and its actual multilingual status, which it shared, *mutatis mutandis*, with the Dutch Republic in its own growth phase.

Relations between the communities of New Netherland and the homeland remain a crucial point of discussion. Besides a historical debate with historical arguments, it often also carries an emotional charge, because of the associated search for roots, the awareness of identity, and national pride. The question as to which society people want to identify with implies a choice for the values and the culture that are embodied in a certain historical community, such as that of the Dutch, the English, the Germans, or the French. Effectively, two questions are involved. The first is to what extent the structure of New Netherland as a country and as a society — in other words, physically and materially as well as in administrative and social, cultural, and mental terms — was modeled from the outset on that of the homeland. To what extent have the new physical living environment and the contact with other peoples, whether native or immigrant, modified and transformed the traditional structures and institutions, and imparted a new identity to them?[16]

Research of this kind is extraordinarily delicate because it is particularly difficult to evaluate from an American position the historical reality of the Dutch homeland, and it is equally difficult to assess from a Dutch perspective the factors that determine the American perception of the Dutch. Wrong conclusions, bad guesses, and even wishful thinking about the homeland's values, or the copying of social structures and cultural traditions, are potential pitfalls. Everywhere Dutch merchants and warriors pitched their tents, they created copies of their homeland and gave them familiar names: Batavia, New Holland, Mauritsstadt, Mauritius, New-Walcheren, Arnhemland, New Zealand. New Netherland was a logical extension to this list: New Amsterdam was modeled on old Amsterdam, and other towns likewise were given a Dutch inclination and homeland institutions. But, seen from abroad, this homeland acquired sharper contours than at home, and even sharper in a period of contrast with a different political ruler (the English king) or religious authority (the Anglican Church).

How Dutch were the Dutch of New Netherland indeed? Questions of this kind are always of the greatest importance for a nation's self-awareness. The question has been asked clearly, and answered in very different ways in recent decades, sometimes with great emotional charge. And occasionally it is simply not asked because it might cause an unwelcome dissonance in prevailing historical perceptions. A scientifically sound approach to the history of New Netherland and its successors would do well to recognize the clear competitive relationship between a Dutch-minded and an English-oriented history of New York, and more generally of New Netherland. Interest is reviving in publications and on the internet about Dutch roots and the Dutch history of the Big Apple and the surrounding states. This interest conflicts with New York's sometimes militant self-assurance as having been created from an English colony, which ignored any previous Dutch history. In a dialogue of the deaf of this kind, values such as citizenship, democracy, and tolerance are alternately put forward as originally Dutch or typically English.

The second question is the extent to which the mature community of New Netherland continued to reflect later developments in the homeland. How Dutch did the Dutch of New Netherland remain? In general terms, our answer would have to be: quite a lot. Besides the wic's own flow of trade, major Amsterdam firms developed the trade across the Atlantic, and the economic bonds were tightened and diversified (see Matson's contribution). In the social and cultural fields, too, New Netherland remained rather close to patria. The recognition of the Dutch Republic's independence in the Peace of Westphalia (1648) was followed by turbulent economic growth, cultural supremacy, and virtually limitless social opportunities. A process of consolidation ensued in many different areas.

For example, in the area of religion it marked the beginning of confessionalization. In the first decades of the Dutch Republic's history, following the revolt against Spain, and in the first phase of New Netherland's growth, the Dutch Reformed Church had been able to play a virtually universal role in society as the only public church. This supraconfessional role was now contested and gradually made way for a more limited position as one of several confessions, or religious communities. The Lutherans and the Quakers of New Netherland still fought in vain in the 1650s for their public right to exist, as did the Jews, but after the takeover by the English the Dutch Reformed Church soon lost its monopoly and was obliged to coexist with other confessions, just as had happened in patria (see Van Lieburg's essay). One of the key elements of the confessionalization process was a greater emphasis on the doctrinal and moral requirements for membership of the Reformed Church as a church of "pure believers." Together with a marked hardening of attitudes toward non-Europeans, such as the black slaves, this resulted in greater social segregation between the populations of European and African origins, and significantly more discrimination than in the colony's early years.

However, New Netherland differed fundamentally on two points from homeland society. As a trading colony it relied strongly at first on contact with the original inhabitants of the area, the native Indians, who assured the fur trade's success. In addition to trade, these contacts were also of great intercultural importance. Agriculture (corn), monetary exchange (sewant or wampum), and the material culture and lifestyles of Europeans and natives influenced each other in a way that made New Netherland into more than a mere copy of "Old" Netherland. Yet, the settlement colony of New Netherland differed profoundly

45

1

—

COLONIAL
PERIOD
AND
EIGHTEENTH
CENTURY

1609–1782

from the homeland in the import of slavery, which was forbidden in Europe it-self. This point led to heated discussions among Dutch Calvinists in the Dutch Republic. We can hear the echo of these doubts and the subsequent acceptance of slavery by the moral authority, the Reformed Church, in the changing atti-tude to the New Netherland slaves after the 1640s.

Although the introduction of slavery had more to do with the ups and downs of international politics than with economic necessity and a conscious politi-cal decision, it nonetheless developed in New Netherland on the same foot-ing as elsewhere in America. There no longer was any doubt about the right of enslavement or of a different, less harsh, Dutch attitude to slavery. Since New Netherland differed in these two respects from the European pattern, intercul-turality is a central theme of current research. The "memorial return" of the natives and the blacks in history is a clear sign of this. From the first decades the culture and society of New Netherland were formed in part by interaction with the natives (see Otto's essay) and with the blacks, whether enslaved or manu-mitted (see the essay by Heywood and Thornton). Ethnicity therefore does not refer solely to origin, but also has elements of culture, religion, and politics, and always has an intercultural dimension.

Despite, or perhaps because of, the interaction of coincidental factors and the colony's somewhat remote location relative to the WIC's normal trade routes, New Netherland quickly became a colony with its own identity and a growing autonomy, in both economic and sociocultural terms. This autonomy also manifested itself from 1650 onward in an ever accelerating expansion of the administrative infrastructure in accordance with the example of the homeland, as if it were already an independent region. The ultimate nonviolent takeover by the English was an unsurprising finale. The colony also differed strongly in this respect from the settlements in Brazil, Curaçao, and the Gold Coast, which continued to rely more heavily on contacts with the homeland and on the sup-port of the WIC and the States General, and which were actually also deemed to be of greater strategic, political, or economic importance. Perhaps we may call it a paradox of the history of New Netherland that this relatively marginal area in the homeland's international strategy managed to develop into one of the key areas in the global world order precisely because of conditions created in the homeland for economic growth, political organization, and sociocultural development.

46

1   General surveys of the history of New
Netherland before or after 1664 include
Oliver A. Rink, *Holland on the Hudson:*
An Economic and Social History of Dutch
New York (Ithaca, NY/London: Cornell
University Press, 1986); Joyce D. Good-

friend, *Before the Melting Pot: Society and Culture in Colonial New York City, 1664–1730* (Princeton, NJ: Princeton University Press, 1991); Jaap Jacobs, *New Netherland: A Dutch Colony in Seventeenth-Century America* (Leiden: Brill, 2005).

2 "Nieuw Nederland" was originally translated into Latin as *Novum Belgium*, as can be seen in old prints. This term, as was the fashion of the time, was derived from classical antiquity, and despite suggestions to the contrary has nothing to do with modern Belgium. It actually refers to the Republic of the Seven United Provinces in the Northern Netherlands, the precursor of the current Kingdom of the Netherlands. The Latin name of the Dutch Republic itself was *Belgium Foederatum*, which means the Confederation of Low Countries.

3 See, e.g., chapters 14 and 15 of Russell Shorto, *The Island at the Center of the World. The Epic Story of Dutch Manhattan and the Forgotten Colony That Shaped America* (New York: Doubleday, 2004), 284-318.

4 The information in parentheses refers to the various essays in this section of the book. For this long-term evolution, see "Holland in America," the introduction to Joyce D. Goodfriend, Benjamin Schmidt, and Annette Stott, eds., *Going Dutch: The Dutch Presence in America, 1609–2009* (Leiden/Boston: Brill, 2008), 1-23.

5 On Dutch political and social culture in the seventeenth century, see chapters 2 and 3 in Willem Frijhoff and Marijke Spies, *1650: Hard-Won Unity*. Original title: *Bevochten Eendracht*; English translation by Myra Heerspink Scholz (vol. 1 of the series Dutch Culture in a European Perspective) (Assen: Van Gorcum; Basingstoke: Palgrave Macmillan, 2004), 69-225.

6 N. C. Lambrechtsen, *A History of the New Netherlands*. Trans. by Francis Adrian Van der Kemp (New York: New York Historical Society, 1841).

7 Willem Frijhoff, "Dutchness in Fact and Fiction," in Goodfriend, Schmidt, and Stott, *Going Dutch*, 327-358.

8 See www.nnp.org.

9 For the state of the art of the historiography, see Joyce D. Goodfriend, "The Historiography of the Dutch in Colonial America," in Eric Nooter and Patricia U. Bonomi, eds., *Colonial Dutch Studies: An Interdisciplinary Approach* (New York: New York University Press, 1988), 6-32, and the other contributions to that volume; Joyce D. Goodfriend: "Writing/Righting Dutch Colonial History," *New York History*, 80 (January 1999), 5-28; Joyce D. Goodfriend, ed., *Revisiting New Netherland. Perspectives on Early Dutch America* (Leiden/Boston: Brill, 2005), in particular her introduction, 1-10.

10 For the cultural background, see Benjamin Schmidt, *Innocence Abroad: The Dutch Imagination and the New World, 1570–1670* (Cambridge: Cambridge University Press, 2001); Jan Willem Schulte Nordholt, *The Myth of the West: America as the Last Empire* (Grand Rapids, MI: Eerdmans, 1995).

11 From a poem by Jacob Steendam, in Henry C. Murphy, *Anthology of New Netherland, or Translations from the Early Dutch Poets of New York with Memoirs of their Lives* (New York: s.n., 1865), 30-31.

12 On Dutch Brazil, see C. R. Boxer, *The Dutch in Brazil 1624–1654* (Oxford: Clarendon Press, 1957); E. van den Boogaart, H. R. Hoetink, and P. J. P. Whitehead, eds., *Johan Maurits van Nassau-Siegen 1604–1674: A Humanist Prince in Europe and Brazil* (The Hague: Johan Maurits van Nassau-Siegen Stichting, 1979); Jonathan I. Israel, *The Dutch Republic and the Hispanic World, 1606–1661* (Oxford: Clarendon Press, 1981); Evaldo Cabral de Mello, *O Negócio do Brasil. Portugal, os Paises Baixos e o*

1

—

COLONIAL
PERIOD
AND
EIGHTEENTH
CENTURY

1609-1782

Nordeste, 1641–1669, 3rd ed. (Rio de Janeiro: Top Books, 2003).

13   However, use of the term "Province" should be avoided for the Dutch period because of the risk of confusing different definitions of the term. Each of the seven Provinces (*gewesten*) composing the Dutch Republic considered itself a sovereign state and enjoyed formal autonomy. The situation in the overseas colonies was completely different. Until 1664 New Netherland formally remained a "colony" of the WIC, under the ultimate authority of the States General.

14   See Janny Venema, *Beverwijck: A Dutch Village on the American Frontier, 1652–1664* (Hilversum: Verloren; Albany: New York State University Press, 2003).

15   See David Armitage, "Three Concepts of Atlantic History," in David Armitage and Michael J. Braddick, eds., *The British Atlantic World, 1500–1800* (Basingstoke/New York: Palgrave Macmillan, 2002), 11-27; Pieter C. Emmer, *The Dutch in the Atlantic Economy, 1580–1880* (Ashgate: Aldershot, 1998); Jan de Vries, "The Dutch Atlantic Economies," in Peter A. Coclanis, ed., *The Atlantic Economy during the Seventeenth and Eighteenth Centuries: Organization, Operation, Practice, Personnel* (Columbia: University of South Carolina Press, 2005), 1-29.

16   See, for example, Donna Merwick, *Possessing Albany 1630–1710: The Dutch and English Experiences* (Cambridge: Cambridge University Press, 1990); Shorto, *The Island at the Center of the World*.

IMAGES OF AMERICA IN THE LOW COUNTRIES UNTIL THE SEVENTEENTH CENTURY

—

MICHIEL VAN GROESEN

America's Early Impact

When Henry Hudson's ship *Halve Maen* arrived at the island of Manhattan in early September 1609, the New World was not quite so new anymore. Almost 120 years had passed since Columbus successfully crossed the Atlantic and explored the Caribbean, quickly reaching the conclusion that this was truly a new world unknown to both his contemporaries and to the ancient geographers he so admired. The sixteenth century had seen a flurry of European explorers attempting to — literally — strike gold in this newly found Eden. Their reports, peppered with information about natives unaware of Christianity and other elementary traits of civilization, had aroused feelings of bewilderment, cultural superiority, introspection, and greed, depending on the social position and the ethnic background of the Old World observer. Hudson, announcing the arrival of the young Dutch Republic on the North Atlantic scene, can be regarded as one of the last in a long line of discoverers, exploring such regions now known as Hudson Valley and Hudson Bay. Yet, America had already made an impact in the Low Countries well before Hudson. This essay will discuss how one of the most important maritime regions of sixteenth-century Europe, without entering the Atlantic fray, came to terms with the discovery of the New World.

The initial impression America made in the Low Countries was not different from elsewhere in Renaissance Europe. The sudden confrontation between classical learning and the first-hand experiences of navigators left many scholars perplexed. While some played down the significance of the discoveries and continued to rely on ancient geographical knowledge, others attempted to

49

1

——

COLONIAL
PERIOD
AND
EIGHTEENTH
CENTURY

1609-1782

blend the new experiences into their existing models of expectations. Erasmus of Rotterdam, the leading scholar from the Low Countries, was among those who quickly acknowledged the impact of the New World on the Old. In June 1517 he wrote a letter to Dukes Frederick and George of Saxony stating that "previously unknown lands are currently being discovered, of which nobody has been able to establish the limits, but which are certainly immensely large."[1]

By this time, the accession of Charles V as ruler of the Habsburg Netherlands and of Spain had united the fortunes of Castile, Portugal, and the Low Countries, and this political connection was to influence Netherlandish images of America for fifty years. Born in Ghent, Charles used his New World possessions to ensure the loyalty of noblemen, prelates, and other allies, not just in Spain but also in the Netherlands. He handed out American fiefs and benefices, offering for example the bishopric of Santiago de Cuba to his former teacher Jan de Witte of Bruges, and the island of Cozumel, off the coast of Yucatán, to the lord of Veere, Adolf of Burgundy. Whereas De Witte never considered going to the New World himself — he did collect the taxes that came with the Cuban diocese — Adolf of Burgundy did, planning an expedition to Cozumel in the 1520s. Due to bad living conditions in the Spanish port of San Lúcar de Barrameda in 1527, many of his group of colonists died before departure, and his two galleons never arrived in America. Meanwhile other Netherlanders reached the New World: Peter of Ghent, or Pedro de Gante as he was known in Spanish, acquired fame as one of three Franciscan missionaries sent to Mexico by Charles V in 1523, and his efforts to educate and Christianize the Aztecs are still celebrated today in Latin America.[2]

Descriptions of Voyages to America

None of these early operations, however, contributed to the perception of America in the Low Countries. Like Erasmus, the armchair travelers of the sixteenth century had to rely on printed and translated reports of adventure. Although the Spanish and Portuguese crowns went to great lengths to withhold information of their overseas ventures from potential rivals, their censorship regulations were no match for the curiosity of readers outside the Iberian Peninsula. Since Antwerp was one of the hubs of the European printing industry, readers in the Low Countries were in a good position to acquire information about the New World. Publishers and printers in the city on the river Scheldt, most notably Jan van Doesborch, issued reports of voyages to America in a number of languages, including Dutch. One of the first reports to make Renaissance Europe aware of the discoveries, the letters supposedly written by Amerigo Vespucci first appeared in a Dutch translation as early as 1506.[3]

Yet while inhabitants of the Low Countries welcomed other important translations like the Dutch edition of Hernán Cortés's exploits in Mexico in 1523, their knowledge of America remained sketchy, as factual works continued to compete for attention with established fictitious best-sellers like the narrative of John Mandeville. Through the Vespucci editions, some of Mandeville's fantasies even reentered the body of "credible" Americana. Only in the 1530s did the first comprehensive humanist accounts of the New World arrive in northern Europe. The Italian historian Peter Martyr's *De Orbe Novo* (1530) and Johan Huttich and Simon Grynaeus's collected work *Novus Orbis Regionum* (1532) signaled a shift to a more systematic understanding of the American continent. The collection of voyages by Huttich and Grynaeus in particular, first printed in Basel, was widely available in the Low Countries, as the inventories of humanist libraries there indicate.[4] Whether such scholarly literature also influenced navigators is questionable, but in 1563 Huttich and Grynaeus's collection was still considered sufficiently authoritative to merit a Dutch translation.

This edition, translated and augmented by the Antwerp humanist Cornelis Ablijn, neatly recapitulates the knowledge of America available to readers in the Low Countries in the middle third of the sixteenth century. Following the original editors, Ablijn included the narratives by Columbus and two of his pilots, Vespucci, Martyr, and Cortés, indicating that geographical knowledge about America had not significantly increased since the 1530s. More interesting than the reprinted early reports, however, was the preface Ablijn included in the Dutch translation. It was written in the form of a dedication to Prince William of Orange, stadtholder of Holland, Zeeland, and Utrecht, and announced that the narratives were meant to hold up a mirror to readers in the Low Countries. These readers were supposed to reflect on leading a life without material wealth like Native Americans, while monarchs, according to Ablijn, "could learn how to conduct themselves properly in times of war and peace, and how to deal with both obedient and rebellious subjects."[5] The New World further provided plenty of examples of the glory awaiting those who faithfully served their rulers, like Columbus, "who often put his life in danger for the sake of his monarch," and Vasco Nuñez de Balboa, who "discovered for his king a road between the two seas which could be used to transport gold and precious metals to him." Unfortunately, Ablijn explained, both men were not rewarded for their loyalty, as Columbus was taken into custody after all his services, while Nuñez de Balboa was beheaded after a faction struggle among the conquistadors.

Impact of the Dutch Revolt

1

COLONIAL
PERIOD
AND
EIGHTEENTH
CENTURY

1609-1782

Ablijn's dedication reveals two different sides of the representations of America circulating in the Low Countries in the 1560s. First, Spanish explorers like Columbus and even the rather thuggish Nuñez de Balboa were presented as icons, examples of "how courageously and manly the Spaniards had coped with great perils." This was the traditional exalted image of America in territories under Habsburg rule. Second, it warned against the backlash one could expect when standing up to a lawful ruler. It is very ironic that William of Orange, to whom Cornelis Ablijn addressed these words, would soon himself be leading a revolt against Phillip II, the king of Spain. This political conflict, possibly augured by Ablijn in an era of increasing tension, was to influence the representation of America from the late 1560s until well into the seventeenth century. The Dutch Revolt divided the Habsburg Netherlands into seven rebellious provinces in the north, known as the Dutch Republic and embracing Calvinism, and ten provinces in the Southern Netherlands that remained Catholic and loyal to Madrid. From the late 1560s onward, the Dutch constructions of America were therefore diametrically opposed to those in the southern provinces. The 1622 public celebrations in Antwerp for the beatification of Ignatius of Loyola and Francis Xaver, for example, which included representations of jubilant American Indians successfully converted by Jesuit fathers, were inconceivable in the United Provinces, where tyranny and avarice were the most familiar terms to classify Spanish conduct in the New World.

The construction of this so-called Black Legend of Spanish tyranny in the New World quickly gathered pace in the Dutch Republic after the outbreak of the revolt.[6] Carefully orchestrated propaganda depicted Spaniards as treacherous and, above all, greedy and cruel. "It is not for faith that [the] natives were murdered," the fiery Dutch pamphleteer Jacobus Viverius wrote in 1601, "but for the gold that rightly belongs to them."[7] The Black Legend in turn influenced the perception of Native Americans in the Northern Netherlands. Indians, in this view, were essentially innocent victims of Spanish tyranny in the New World, just like the Dutch rebels were at the receiving end of Spanish oppression at home. Many of the pamphlets distributing these images were based on Bartolomé de Las Casas' *Brevissima relación* (Seville, 1552), which was first translated into Dutch in 1578 and reprinted in 1596, 1607, and 1609, the year Hudson crossed the Atlantic. The third Dutch edition, titled *Spieghel der Spaenscher tyrannye, in West-Indien* (Mirror of Spanish tyranny in the West Indies), also sported seventeen copper engravings by Jodocus van Winghe graphically depicting the misbehavior of the conquistadors (see ill. 1). Illustrations like these were instrumental in disseminating the Black Legend. While the

1
Jodocus van Winghe, *Spieghel der Spaensche tyrannye*
(Amsterdam 1607) ill. 10.

ANTEHAC HVMANIS VESCENTES CARNIBVS INDI,
IAM DOMITI INVICTIS MITESCVNT CAESARIS ARMIS.

Los Indios, qui hasta aqui de carne humana   Les Indiens viuans de chair humaine,
Pacian, como fieros y indomados,   En cruauté incomparable à dire,
Con virtud, y con fuerça soberana,   Sont conuaincuz par la puissance hautaine
Los veys por Cesar ya domesticados.   VI   Des tresuaillans combattans de l'Empire.

2
Dirck Volckertsz Coornhert (after Maerten van Heemskerck),
The army of Charles V in America (1555).

Dutch Revolt continued, the technique of including engravings into printed books developed rapidly in the United Provinces. Hence, these images were at the forefront of the representation of America around 1600.

Visual Representations

These were, however, by no means the first and only iconographic accounts of America in the Low Countries. Earlier generations of artists had already attempted to visualize the new continent, and here, as with textual representations, the same demarcation line of the late 1560s can be observed. The Haarlem artist Dirck Volckertsz Coornhert, later also known as one of the champions of religious toleration in the Dutch Republic, designed an image in the mid-1550s that captured the multilayered imaginations of the discovery (see ill. 2). The Coornhert print, like other contemporary depictions of the New World in the Low Countries, intended to sing the praise of Charles V. Although at first glance the Indians appear to be the demonic, anthropophagous victors rather than newly subjected vassals, the poems at the bottom of the image, in both Castilian and French, reassure readers that the Spanish troops had succeeded in righting Indian ways. The Latin title of the subscription confirms that "[w]hile earlier, the Indians nourished themselves with human flesh, they have now been civilized by the invincible arms of the Emperor."[8] The uncontrolled behavior of the Indians emphasized in the image thus added an extra dimension to the achievements of the conquistadors.

In addition to these compositions before the revolt and to illustrations supporting the Black Legend, Netherlandish images can be divided into two more categories: illustrations focusing on the cultural and moral values of natives in the New World and allegorical impressions of America. Prints of the first category emphasized both the exotic and the uncivilized nature of the native population. The inhabitants were usually depicted wearing little more than feathers, a type of iconography that had its origin in some of the very first "reliable" pictures Europeans had seen of American Indians, designed in southern Germany in the early sixteenth century. These woodcuts, despite their exotic value, also presented a less attractive aspect of the Renaissance image of America: cannibalism. This habit was typically located in South America, most notably in Brazil, but could pop up elsewhere in the New World depending on the accuracy of the European artist. This image did not change significantly as Europe became more familiar with America. Ever since the early decades of the sixteenth century, and repeatedly reinforced by later reports, cannibalism was one of the cornerstones of Old World representations, including those produced and consumed in the Low Countries.

55

1

—

COLONIAL
PERIOD
AND
EIGHTEENTH
CENTURY

1609–1782

Allegorical prints and illustrations recycled some of the elements used for ethnological images. One tradition presented America as a personification, often depicted in conjunction with similar allegories of the other three continents. America, in contrast to the other three, was generally envisioned as a naked female figure, combining connotations of earthly paradise with unease about the perceived lack of civilization in the New World. The features included came to be synonymous with the stereotypical notion of America in the Netherlandish imagination: a continent with unsophisticated weaponry, like clubs, spears, and bows and arrows, unspoilt landscapes inhabited by exotic animals — often parrots, opossums, or armadillos — and barely disturbed half-naked humans covered only by feathers. The actual moment of discovery was sometimes chosen to add a narrative element to the composition, at the same time employing and enhancing the lasting reputation of Columbus (see ill. 3). Allegories made by the Antwerp artists Jan Sadeler, Maarten de Vos, and Johannes Stradanus were copied time and again. Since the personifications of America were politically and religiously "neutral," they reappeared in the rebellious provinces in the north, for instance in the decorated borders of world maps, a genre that was to flourish in the Dutch Golden Age.

The last decade of the sixteenth century saw an upsurge in the number of pictorial representations of America, with the Frankfurt publisher and copper engraver Theodore de Bry and his sons Johan Theodore and Johan Israel playing a key role.[9] Theodore, born in Liège, had developed his skills as an engraver in Antwerp before settling down among other Netherlandish *émigrés* in Frankfurt, the center of the early modern book trade. In 1590, he began publishing volumes of his monumental collection of voyages. This collection, which combined travel accounts translated into Latin and German with high-quality copper engravings, was to influence images of America across Europe for many decades. By 1602, nine luxurious folio volumes devoted to the New World had come off the presses, comprising canonical accounts by the likes of Thomas Harriot, Hans Staden, Jean de Léry, Girolamo Benzoni, Francis Drake, and José de Acosta. This nine-volume *America* series contained well over two hundred engravings — some derived from existing compositions, but many invented in the workshop of the De Bry family.

The illustrations of the De Brys influenced Dutch representations of America for the better part of the seventeenth century. Alongside graphic depictions of cannibalism in Brazil and Spanish atrocities in Mexico and Peru, the De Brys emphasized the pagan rituals of the natives across the New World. The volumes presented a juxtaposition, which was to infiltrate the iconography in the Dutch Republic, of civilized Christian adventurers from Europe and the unsophisticated heathen practices of the Native Americans. The first two De Bry volumes also distributed the first "naturalistic," sometimes even paradisiacal, images

3

Theodore Galle (after Johannes Stradanus),
The arrival of Columbus in America (ca. 1575?).

4
Theodore de Bry, 'Eating habits in Virginia', *India Occidentalis I*
(Frankfurt 1590) ill. 16.

of North American Indians. The engravings of the Roanoke colony in North Carolina and Florida, based on watercolors by the Englishman John White and the Huguenot Jacques Le Moyne de Morgues respectively, reveal another aspect of Indian life that is reminiscent of Cornelis Ablijn's preface of the early 1560s, and became to some extent typical for the Reformed representations of America.

The Algonquian and Timucua Indians of North America were presented as role models of frugality and moderation, inviting contemplation and reflection from European readers in a decade of extremely bad harvests and famine (see ill. 4). This construction was not so much the result of the ideology of the De Bry family, given that the publishers were inspired first and foremost by commercial objectives. It rather revealed the influence of the Oxford geographer Richard Hakluyt, whose intentions to stake English claims to Virginia corresponded with the Elizabethan attempts to attract settlers to the New World in order to develop a plantation society.[10] Closely cooperating with Sir Walter Raleigh, Hakluyt offered Thomas Harriot's travel account and John White's watercolors to Theodore de Bry. As a result, the praise for the moderation of Native Americans and the attractive prospect of establishing colonies of European settlers abroad made an impact beyond Tudor England.

Dutch Maritime Expansion and Cartography

For an enterprising merchant like Willem Usselincx, this combination of temperance and political and religious expansion was predictably appealing. Usselincx, a Calvinist who migrated to the Northern Netherlands after the Spanish army had recaptured Antwerp in 1585, pleaded with the States General in the Dutch Republic to unleash a similar initiative.[11] His efforts were repeatedly frustrated by leading regents like Johan van Oldenbarnevelt, who was reluctant to further antagonize Madrid. When Hudson left the port of Amsterdam in early 1609, Usselincx's pamphlets arguing the need for Dutch plantation settlements in the New World were nevertheless being heavily discussed. At the turn of the century, America had suddenly appeared on the horizon of the large Dutch mercantile fleet. As, in the 1590s, Iberian embargoes severely restricted trade contacts with Portuguese and Spanish ports, Holland and Zeeland merchants were prepared to sail to America themselves to satisfy their needs. Instead of obtaining salt for their fishing industry in Portugal, merchants from towns like Hoorn and Enkhuizen organized expeditions to the salt pans of Punta de Araya, off the coast of Venezuela. With increasing regularity, ships from the Zeeland island of Walcheren sailed directly to Brazil in pursuit of sugar, and Dutch privateers

59

1

—

COLONIAL
PERIOD
AND
EIGHTEENTH
CENTURY

1609–1782

raided Spanish ships in the Caribbean as part of the war effort, bringing home West Indian hides, pearls, and tobacco.[12]

Apart from the odd manuscript containing eyewitness accounts, these expeditions did not generate a new body of literature on America and those who stayed at home therefore continued to rely on published accounts often written by foreigners. Yet the explosive growth of Dutch maritime expansion to the Orient did encourage printers and publishers in Holland and Zeeland to issue more information on the overseas world, and on transatlantic voyages as well. The 1590s were crucial in this respect, as several "modern" treatises written abroad, like José de Acosta's *Historia natural y moral de las Indias*, were first translated into Dutch shortly before the turn of the century. The catalogue of the Amsterdam publisher Cornelis Claesz is the outstanding example in the United Provinces, offering a wide variety of national and international travel accounts and large maps of the overseas world in his bookstore close to the docks of the East Indiamen.[13]

Due to the unrivaled output of titles on overseas expansion, in the vernacular as well as in Latin, the private libraries of Dutch scholars around 1600 were exceptionally well stocked with books and other material concerning the New World. Humanists, for example, could satisfy their interest in the natural world: Carolus Clusius, the famous botanist of the newly founded university in Leiden, was a prominent European specialist on exotic herbs and plants, and used a large number of travel accounts to America in preparing his *Rariorum plantarum historia* (1601) and *Exoticorum libri decem* (1605). His friend Bernardus Paludanus, a physician in Enkhuizen, was one of northern Europe's leading collectors of rarities, treasuring a small number of American objects in his cabinet. Dutch and foreign visitors flocked to his *musaeum* to see his stunning collection of naturalia and artefacts, including "bones of a human who was eaten by the American cannibals."[14] And the geographer Petrus Plancius, a Reformed minister in late sixteenth-century Amsterdam, set up his own school of navigation and played a leading role in planning northern routes of exploration.

Yet the scholars who arguably made the greatest impact by applying their knowledge of the New World for practical purposes were cartographers. The two leading mapmakers of late sixteenth-century Europe, Gerard Mercator and Abraham Ortelius, were both born in the Low Countries. Of the two, Mercator was the more mathematically gifted. His world map of 1569 introduced a hemispherical projection in order to correctly represent the globe's curvature on a flat surface, allowing seamen to lay down a compass course as a straight line for the first time. Active as a mapmaker since the 1530s, Mercator is also credited with being the first cartographer to apply the term America to both the northern and the southern part of the continent. Ortelius used Mercator's findings for what is traditionally considered the first modern atlas. His *Theatrum Orbis Terrarum*

(1570) combined several of the representations of America that did the rounds in the Low Countries.[15] The title page of his work contained an allegorical image of America closely resembling the personification designed by Johannes Stradanus, while the explanatory texts to his map of America included some of the discourse of Las Casas that was to become so influential in the United Provinces. Although the *Theatrum* initially contained only one map of America, it was continually improved and augmented as the book went through more than twenty editions in various languages. Like most other scholarly output, cartographical knowledge survived the political troubles in the Low Countries largely unscathed, and Ortelius's maps of America remained highly influential for the activities of Dutch cartographers of the next generation, like Jodocus Hondius and Willem Jansz Blaeu.[16]

In 1602, the bookseller Cornelis Claesz used the available information to publish the first large wall map of America.[17] Well before Hudson set out for the New World, then, the new continent had already entered the houses of the regent and merchant families in Holland and Zeeland. Although the Englishman, in the service of the Dutch East India Company, is rightly regarded as the first "Dutch" captain to reach North American shores, he was in all likelihood very well informed on what to expect on the other side of the Atlantic. His expedition was instigated by regents who were extremely well versed in Europe's overseas expansion, had recently followed the Portuguese vessels to Asia, and had successfully cornered the trade in pepper, nutmeg, and cloves within ten years of their arrival. Early Dutch expeditions to America had suggested that, perhaps, similar riches could be attained there. In order to be successful, however, the Dutch had to move quickly: in 1607 English settlers had founded Jamestown in Virginia, while in 1608 French Huguenots had landed in Quebec. Maps produced in the United Provinces provided Hudson with the latest information on the routes to follow, while a multitude of printed texts and illustrations must have given him a relatively good idea of the societies he was likely to encounter. Since in North America he was almost certain to avoid running into the tyrannical Spanish enemy, he could try to establish friendly relations with uncivilized yet innocent Native American people and commence a profitable trade in furs. Through Dutch eyes, in 1609, America looked very promising indeed.

1   Letter of Erasmus to Frederick and
    George of Saxony, June 5, 1517, in
    P.S. Allen et al, eds., *Opus Epistolarum
    Des. Erasmi Roterodami* (Oxford:
    Clarendon Press, 1906-58), nr. 586.

2   *America. Bride of the Sun. 500 Years
    Latin-America and the Low Countries* (exh.
    cat., Antwerp, 1992); L. Sicking and R.
    Fagel, "In het kielzog van Columbus: de
    heer van Veere en de Nieuwe Wereld,

1

━━━

COLONIAL
PERIOD
AND
EIGHTEENTH
CENTURY

1609–1782

1517–1527," *Bijdragen en Mededelingen betreffende de Geschiedenis der Nederlanden* 114.3 (1992): 313-327.

3   For this edition and other early Americana, see the indispensable J. Alden and D.C. Landis, eds., *European Americana: A Chronological Guide to Works Printed in Europe Relating to America, 1493–1776*, vol. 1, *1493-1600* (New York: Readex Books, 1980).

4   J. Lechner, "Dutch Humanists' Knowledge of America," *Itinerario* 16.2 (1992): 101-113.

5   For the Ablijn quotations, see C. Ablijn, *De nieuwe weerelt* ... (Antwerp, 1563) [*3r], [*3r-3v], and again [*3r].

6   For this paragraph and the following, see B. Schmidt, *Innocence Abroad: The Dutch Imagination and the New World, 1570–1670* (Cambridge: Cambridge University Press, 2001).

7   J. Viverius, *Den spieghel van Spaensche tyrannie* (Amsterdam, 1601) [B2v].

8   Coornhert's print is titled *Antehac humanis vescentes carnibus Indi, iam domiti invictis mitescunt Caesaris armis.*

9   For this paragraph and the following, see M. van Groesen, *The Representations of the Overseas World in the De Bry Collection of Voyages (1590–1634)* (Leiden: Brill, 2008).

10 On Hakluyt, see P.C. Mancall, *Hakluyt's Promise: An Elizabethan's Obsession for an English America* (New Haven, CT: Yale University Press, 2006).

11 There is hardly any scholarly literature available on Usselincx. The most recent account of his life in English is J. Franklin Jameson, *Willem Usselinx, Founder of the Dutch and Swedish West India Companies* (New York: Putnam's Sons, 1887). In Dutch, Usselincx has fared little better; see C. Ligtenberg, *Willem Usselinx* (Utrecht: Oosthoek, 1915).

12 V. Enthoven, "Early Dutch Expansion in the Atlantic Region, 1585–1621," in J.C. Postma and V. Enthoven, eds., *Riches from Atlantic Commerce: Dutch Transatlantic Trade and Shipping, 1585–1817* (Leiden: Brill, 2003), 17-47.

13 G. Schilder, *Monumenta cartographica Neerlandica*, vol. 7, *Cornelis Claesz. (c. 1551–1609): Stimulator and Driving Force of Dutch Cartography* (Alphen aan den Rijn: Canaletto, 2003).

14 Th. H. Lunsingh Scheurleer, "Early Dutch Cabinets of Curiosities," in O. Impey and A. MacGregor, eds., *The Origins of Museums: The Cabinet of Curiosities in Sixteenth- and Seventeenth-Century Europe* (Oxford: Clarendon Press, 1985), 115-120.

15 M. van den Broecke, P. van der Krogt, and P. Meurer, eds., *Abraham Ortelius and the First Atlas: Essays Commemorating the Quadricentennial of his Death, 1598–1998* ('t Goy-Houten: HES, 1998).

16 K. Zandvliet, *Mapping for Money: Maps, Plans and Topographic Paintings and Their Role in Dutch Overseas Expansion during the 16th and 17th Centuries* (Amsterdam: Batavian Lion International, 2002).

17 Schilder, *Monumenta*, vol. 7.

THE DUTCH
IN THE ATLANTIC

—

WIM KLOOSTER

Dutch overseas expansion began in the late sixteenth century, when vessels from the Northern Netherlands embarked on explorations and commercial ventures outside Europe. While large ships went in search of the riches of the East Indies, smaller craft plied the different corners of the Atlantic Ocean, tapping markets in West Africa, the Caribbean, the northern coast of South America, and Brazil, and carrying back local products. Before long, commercial opportunities led to the foundation of trade posts and overseas settlements, which in turn intensified relations with Indians and Africans. This essay will sketch the outlines of these Atlantic activities in the period until 1800.

Although individual Netherlanders had settled in Spanish America in the first half of the sixteenth century, it was the revolt against Habsburg Spain that first induced the Dutch to cross the Atlantic independently. In 1569, the Sea Beggars, who formed the rebels' maritime arm, sought out the Isthmus of Panama for their depredations, albeit without causing much harm to Spanish shipping. This was a false start, however, for Dutch expansion into the Atlantic. The real lift-off took place in the 1590s, once again due, at least in part, to the war with Spain. Spain's King Philip II, who also ruled Portugal after 1580, ordered his officials to detain Dutch ships in Iberian ports in 1595 and 1598, halting the flow of Brazilian sugar to the Dutch Republic and forcing Dutch merchants to look for alternative sources of salt — a search that would lead them to Cabo Verde, Punta de Araya (Venezuela), St. Martin, and Curaçao. Such measures were a sore blow to merchants buying products from the Iberian empire in Seville and Lisbon and selling those in northern Europe. Some of them began looking for direct connections with the East Indies, especially the Moluccan spice islands, by chartering ships that were instructed to find passages to the East, not only replicating Vasco da Gama's southeastern passage, but also finding new routes north of Russia, by way of the Strait of Magellan, and north of the Americas.

The Dutch were latecomers in the Atlantic world, arriving long after the first Portuguese, Spanish, French, and English explorations. Perhaps inevitably, there-

1

━━━

COLONIAL
PERIOD
AND
EIGHTEENTH
CENTURY

1609–1782

fore, Dutch expansion was not completely original. Two available models were used, both deliberately and instinctively: those of Portugal and England. Although the Dutch were more experienced traders, Felipe Fernández-Armesto has pointed to the remarkable parallels between the Portuguese and the Dutch: both were peripheral European peoples with a small population, experienced in agriculture and fishing, and both practiced shipping and piracy in nearby seas before embarking on empire building.[1] The global empire run by the Portuguese commanded respect in the Low Countries. In Africa and Asia, the Dutch would copy many aspects of the Portuguese imperial system, from the fortified trading posts to the design of their ships to accounting practices. More than a few Dutchmen owed their expertise as mariners to their schooling on board Portuguese ships, while others had served Portugal in India. And those who had no such experience relied on Portuguese publications in their navigation and exploration.[2]

Portugal was not the only country on which the Dutch modeled themselves. Dutch plans for trade and war in the wider world were informed by the works of Richard Hakluyt, with their detailed knowledge of Spanish fortifications, population figures, and commercial opportunities. Dutch ships also followed in the wake of the English, whose Elizabethan privateers they admired. The Dutch expeditions to the Strait of Magellan, begun in 1598, would probably not have taken place if Francis Drake and Thomas Cavendish had not shown the way. And on their first trading ventures across the Atlantic, the Dutch preferred the more experienced English pilots, including Henry Hudson.[3]

An Empire of Goods

The initial focus of Dutch interest in the Atlantic world was West Africa, where linen, cloth, copper, iron, and other items of trade were exchanged for hides, gum, ivory, and gold. An estimated two hundred ships completed an African voyage between 1592 and 1607. By 1615, they arrived in Africa at a rate of sixty ships a year. An outgrowth of these commercial ties was the brief occupation of the islands of Príncipe (1598) and São Tomé (1599) in the Gulf of Guinea. While some ships sailed from Africa to Brazil before returning to Dutch home ports, a direct trade from Europe to Portugal's only American colony also took place. The Dutch commercial link with Brazil was transnational, with Portuguese intermediaries at work in Lisbon, Oporto, and Viana, and Dutch, Flemish, and Portuguese factors operating in Brazil.[4]

Although the war with the Habsburgs created opportunities for privateers, it was an obstacle for Dutch extractive and commercial activities in the Iberian colonies. Spain struck hard, for example, at the Dutch at the salt lagune of Araya

Florida

ATLANTIC OCEAN

Cuba

Hispaniola

Jamaica

St. Martin

Saba

St. Eustatius

CARIBBEAN SEA

Aruba   Curaçao

Bonaire

Tobago [New Walcheren]

Trinidad

Orinoco

Nova Zelandia •   • Stabroek

Fort Kijkoveral •

• Paramaribo

Essequebo

Demerara

Amazon

Dutch West India land claims and trading posts in
the Caribbean and the northern coast of South America.

1

━━━

COLONIAL
PERIOD
AND
EIGHTEENTH
CENTURY

1609–1782

in eastern Venezuela, leaving many salt rakers dead in attacks in 1605 and 1606. In these years, the Dutch attempted to extend their domestic warfare with the Habsburgs to other continents, eyeing São Jorge da Mina (later called Elmina) on the Gold Coast, the Portuguese headquarter in West Africa. After two failed attempts to conquer this fort (in 1596 and 1606), the Dutch returned to the Gold Coast (1612) and built a fort in Mouri to protect the lucrative gold trade. A foothold was thus established in Africa.[5] Their permanence on the African coast helped the Dutch conduct a lively trade in West Africa in the years ahead, accounting for 90 percent of the value of their overall Atlantic commerce.

After 1621, (trans-)Atlantic warfare continued, now under the auspices of the newly established West India Company (WIC), a counterpart of the Dutch East India Company (VOC). The foundation of the WIC had been discussed for a quarter century, but a critical mass of supporters had been lacking. That changed during the Twelve Years' Truce, which the Dutch concluded with Spain in 1609 after four decades of uninterrupted warfare. The truce years saw the politicization of a theological dispute about the meaning of predestination with implications for the future of the Reformed Church, which brought the Northern Netherlands to the brink of civil war. After Stadtholder Prince Maurits decided the feud in favor of the orthodox party by staging a *coup d'état*, it was clear that war would be resumed once the truce expired in 1621.

The WIC was thus established not simply to direct and coordinate the flow of trade in the Atlantic basin, but primarily to open new fronts against the Iberian enemies. The main weapon that it used in the early years was privateering. Hundreds of Portuguese and Spanish vessels were captured in the 1620s and 1630s, the most spectacular catch occurring in 1628 in Cuba, where a Dutch naval force under the command of Admiral Piet Heyn subdued the Spanish treasure fleet en route from Veracruz to Seville. The Company also launched numerous attacks on fortified places in Africa and the Americas. Tactics were simple: a surprise assault was followed by the capture of merchant ships, a bombardment of the fortifications, and the landing of troops that occupied the strongholds. This plan was seldom successful, but did enable the Dutch to seize Bahia (1624), the capital of Brazil, and Pernambuco (1630), the captaincy in northeastern Brazil where the Dutch were to remain until 1654. These tactics were not needed, however, to claim possession of lands on the coast of Guyana (Berbice, Essequibo) and various Caribbean islands, most of which were only nominally Spanish. When St. Martin, St. Eustatius, Saba, Aruba, Bonaire, and Curaçao became Dutch within one decade (1631–40), only at St. Martin and Curaçao did actual fighting occur with the Spanish enemy.

Nowhere was warfare more intense than in Brazil after the Dutch landing in Pernambuco. Between thirty-five and forty thousand Dutch soldiers and sailors were used in a war that seemed never-ending. In one battle outside Recife

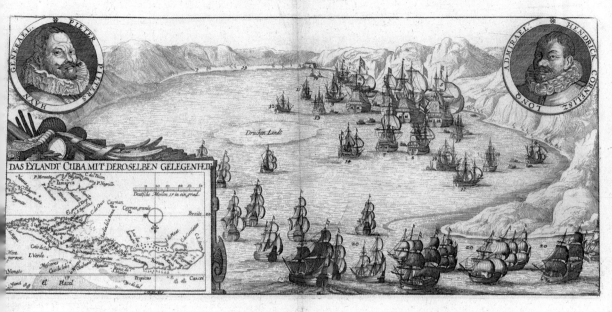

Abbildung /

Welcher Gestalt die Spanische Silberflotta von dem

Holländischen General / Peter Peters Hayn / an der Insul Cuba / in der Baya Matanca Anno
1628. erobert worden.

PIETER PETERS HAYN GENERAEL

HENDRICK CORNELISZ LONCQ ADMIRAEL

Drucken Lande

DAS EYLANDT CUBA MIT DEROSELBEN GELEGENHEIT

Erklärung der Ziffer.

1. Eine Batterey neben einem newen Werck.
2. Der Spanische Admiral.
3. Spanischer Vice-Admiral.
4. Spanischer Wachtmeister oder Schutz bey Nacht.
5. 2. andere Spanische Schiff.
6. 1. ander klein Spanisch Schiff.
7. Der General Peter Peters Hayn.

8. Der Admiral Heinrich Cornelius Lonq.
9. Der Vice-Admiral Pangras.
10. Zwey kleine Schifflein so die Wacht halten.
11. Das Schiff Stork.
12. Das Schiff Speermonde.
13. Das Schiff Harlem.
14. Der Holländische Wachtmeister oder Schutz bey Nacht.

15. Das Schiff Delphin.
16. Das Schiff Tiger.
17. Das Schiff Hollandt.
18. Das Schiff der Gülden Falck.
19. Ein breit Ufer an der See / da sich die Spanischen noch täglich erzeigen.
20. Die übrige Schiff so zu der Holländischen Flotten gehören.

A German print from 1630 depicting the capture by a West India Company fleet
(in the front) of the Spanish treasure fleet in Cuba in 1628. Featured are Piet Heyn (left)
and the second-in-command Hendrick Loncq (right). In 1630, Loncq would
command the Dutch force that conquered Olinda and Recife in Brazil, thus laying
the foundation for Dutch colonization.

1

—

COLONIAL
PERIOD
AND
EIGHTEENTH
CENTURY

1609–1782

(1649), more than one thousand Dutchmen perished in what was probably the most deadly Dutch military encounter in the Atlantic world. At stake was control of the sugar industry at a time when Brazil was the leading global producer. By the mid-1630s, the Dutch had achieved this goal, but at a high price. Many plantations had been destroyed in the course of the war and many others, now in Dutch hands, proved to be easy targets for Portuguese forces.

It was only at this stage that the need for slave labor made itself felt in Dutch America. As one Dutch observer wrote: "Without such slaves it is impossible to accomplish anything in Brazil; without them no sugar mills can operate and no land can be tilled." And he added, "it would be needlessly scrupulous if anyone had qualms about it."[6] Dutch merchants certainly had no qualms about entering the African slave trade. They now needed — preferably direct — access to African slave markets. Their conquest of Elmina and the other Portuguese colonies of Angola and São Tomé within a four-year span (1637–41) was therefore mostly motivated by New World concerns.

In 1654, the Dutch lost their war in Brazil, a fight that had been so costly that it contributed in no small way to the demise of the first West India Company. The Dutch eventually gave up all claims to their prize colony in exchange for the right to load salt for free in Portugal for a number of years. Dutch persistence in trying to maintain a presence in Brazil in order to control not only trade, but also production of sugar and tobacco, contrasts with the typical Dutch role in other parts of the Atlantic, where they opted for the role of intermediaries. That role suited a country with a small population base. In the mid-seventeenth century the Dutch were unmatched as carriers and financiers. Therefore, only a relatively small share of the Atlantic trade of the United Provinces involved the shipment of goods produced in their own colonies. Most products carried back were obtained through trade with Native American or foreign European settlements. The Dutch made the most of their commercial proficiency. The Dutch connection was vital in the Chesapeake, where they bought tobacco with linen, coarse cloth, and brandies. The Dutch participation in French colonial trade was even more significant, especially in the Caribbean islands of Martinique and Guadeloupe. In the British Caribbean, the Dutch role went beyond commerce. In Jamaica and Barbados they left their mark on architectural design, while the Dutch impact on Providence Island extended to the naming of places.[7]

After the fall of Brazil, Dutch slave traders also offered their cargoes for sale in foreign colonies, especially Spanish America. In the seventy years after 1658, they would ship approximately one hundred thousand Africans to Venezuela, New Granada (present-day Colombia), Cuba, and Panama. Only a minority of these slaves were imported from the Gold Coast. Most were embarked in the Bight of Benin and on the "Angolan" coast between Cape Lopo Gonçalves and Luanda. The tradition of Dutch intermediation would continue throughout the eighteenth century, when St. Eustatius and Curaçao functioned as regional distribution centers for a large variety of products. Suriname and Essequibo and its twin colony of Demerara provided a counterpoint, functioning as plantation societies in the same vein as Brazil, producing sugar, coffee, cacao, and cotton for the Dutch market and beyond. Still, much trade was conducted at these places by ships that hailed from British North America, especially New England. In Suriname, the North Americans accounted for 90 percent of all vessels arriving from ports in the western hemisphere. They exchanged horses, provisions, building materials, and household supplies for molasses and rum, but most enslaved Africans who arrived in the colony were supplied by Dutch ships. In all, an estimated one hundred sixty thousand slaves arrived in Dutch Guyana (including Suriname) in the period 1730–1803.[8]

The Dutch Atlantic was a world of commerce, an empire of goods. In contrast with the British Atlantic, it was not a route well traveled by passengers from the mother country nor an outlet for migrants, in spite of policies designed to attract those. The Walloons who sailed to New Netherland, where they were the first settlers, received a free passage, two months of free food supplies by the WIC, free land, and the right to trade with natives. Settlers of Brazil were given free passage and were exempted from tithes, initially for two years, then seven years, and one additional year for every child.[9] And still, few Dutchmen were eager to leave their native soil behind, although the colonies needed settlers badly, as several pamphleteers emphasized. The immigration of "free" settlers — those not in the employ of the West India Company — so the argument ran, did more to guarantee the survival of a colony than the colonial presence of soldiers. A free population would bring about economic activity, which in turn could finance colonial defense. Such arguments convinced the West India Company in the late 1620s to allow private individuals to develop lands within its jurisdiction by setting up settlements of fifty or sixty people within a period of four years. A number of these so-called patroonships were founded in North America, where Rensselaerswijck was the only one to survive the teething troubles. The Leeward Islands of St. Martin, St. Eustatius, and Saba were delegated to patroons shortly after the Dutch took possession, Tobago also functioned as a patroonship, and Berbice in Guyana was the private domain of the Van Pere family from Zeeland. The second West India Company, founded in 1674, gained control of all three Dutch Leeward Islands in 1680, and all other patroonships collapsed, with the exception of Berbice.

An obstacle to the permanence of Dutch overseas settlements was that return migration from Dutch America was substantial. Family duties, homesickness, and a variety of other circumstances could make migrants cross the ocean again. Many others put their luck to the test when they first migrated, trying to make a quick fortune and then return home. In New Netherland, the resulting colonial society was one in constant flux, with merchants and factors traveling back and forth between the Old World and the New, officials returning after their appointment had come to an end, and farmers and artisans going back as well if the Promised Land fell short of their expectations. Nor did return migration decline in the eighteenth century, when two-thirds of all migrants to Suriname repatriated.[10]

One group was less likely to return to Europe: religious minorities. Usually foreigners fleeing religious persecution and moving on after a short stay in the Netherlands, they wished to leave the Old World behind completely. Plans to settle religious refugees date back to the early stages of Dutch presence in the Americas, and the Dutch authorities initially considered Guyana to be an appropriate location for their settlement. The toleration of Jews led to the settlement by thousands of them, mostly Sephardim, in Dutch America. In Brazil they established the first synagogue of the New World, and after 1654 they came to make up one-third of the white population of both Curaçao and Suriname, the colony in Guyana captured from England in 1667. Hardly any Jews settled in New Amsterdam, although the arrival of twenty-three refugees from Dutch Brazil in 1654 is usually seen as the beginning of the Jewish presence in North America.

Relations with Africans and Indians

When the first Dutch expeditions left European waters, the natives of Africa and the Americas were as yet abstract beings, *tabulae rasae* on whom one could project hope, fear, and fantasy. Of all the fantastic traits attributed to Africans and Indians, cannibalism, at times in combination with exceptional longevity, was perhaps the most common. A Dutch ship that called at Allada (in present-day Benin) in 1622, was invited by the inhabitants to trade there, but declined in the belief that the local people were man eaters.[11]

Much like their English rivals, however, the Dutch soon entered into business relations with Africans and Indians, availing themselves of native "brokers," who traded and/or translated on their behalf, and native allies in the wars with other European colonizers. In the New World, Dutchmen were also left behind in or near Indian territories, while some natives were taken to the United Provinces and submerged in Dutch culture. In many parts of Africa, Dutch traders depended on the willingness of local rulers. Even on the Gold Coast, where they established long-lasting fortified trading posts, they were dependent on the protection from local African authorities, whom they had to shower with gifts and show the respect due from subjects. Dutch policy mainly consisted in concluding alliances and signing contracts that enabled them to acquire commercial monopolies and sovereign rights.[12]

The Dutch presence in West Africa remained small. Confined to about a dozen coastal forts, their overall number hovered around 350, most of them soldiers. Nor was the European population of Dutch America impressive. Even after substantial growth in the eighteenth century, all American colonies of the Dutch combined could only boast a white population of sixteen thousand by the year 1800.[13] In the plantation societies of Guyana, where many of them lived scattered along major rivers, the Dutch could therefore not ignore the natives. On the one hand, the expansion of the Dutch area under cultivation forced the natives into interior migration. On the other hand, Indians who tried to avoid the advancing Spanish missions left the interior and made their way eastward, seeking refuge with the Dutch. These natives were not merely pawns in the power struggle between Spaniards and Dutchmen. Both European nations may have claimed authority over vast, overlapping areas, but neither was effectively in control, for lack of substantial government centers, military presence, or sizeable settlements. Guyana thus remained Indian territory until the mid-eighteenth century, when the growth of the Dutch plantation system made relations with Spanish settlers more important than the ties with Carib Indians. Mules and horses bought from nearby Spanish territories drove the Dutch sugar mills, while the fisheries on the mouth of the Orinoco River provided food for the Africans who worked the fields.[14]

There was a conspicuous difference between Spanish and Dutch missionary zeal among natives and slaves. Aversion to the ease with which the Iberians "converted" heathens was actually an important reason for the Dutch to eschew native baptisms. True conversion, Dutch ministers emphasized, required the transfer of religious knowledge, which cost much time and effort. Such skepticism had not existed in the early days of Dutch expansion. In the 1640s, the Dutch introduced scores of Protestant catechisms in Angola and also sent many to the king of Kongo, who had them burned publicly.[15] Likewise, ministers in the Americas tried to deliver the natives from their "barbaric ways" by converting them both to Christianity and a "civilized" life. An economic motive also inspired these efforts, since civilization would mean that Indians had to dress themselves and thus form a potential market for Dutch textiles. Nevertheless, the number of native baptisms remained small, even in Brazil, where the Dutch found themselves governing fifteen thousand Indians. Their prior baptism by Roman Catholic priests prevented the Dutch in this case from proselytizing.[16]

In much of Dutch America, outright spiritual neglect or simply indifference characterized the Dutch attitude vis-à-vis African slaves. Planters certainly did

71

1

—

COLONIAL
PERIOD
AND
EIGHTEENTH
CENTURY

1609–1782

not encourage their slaves to attend church services. In Brazil they even made them work on Sundays, until the government banned that practice. Yet even the colonial authorities themselves saw slaves primarily as investments instead of fellow humans. Neglect meant that Protestant ministers concerned themselves in the eighteenth century almost exclusively with residents of European birth or extraction, leaving the salvation of black inhabitants to Roman Catholic priests, as in Curaçao, or the Moravian Brotherhood, as in Suriname and the Dutch Leeward Islands. The former were so successful in their pursuit that all free or enslaved Afro-Curaçaoans had become Catholic by the mid-eighteenth century, whereas the latter never reached the majority of Suriname's blacks.[17]

The nature of slavery was not necessarily harsher in Dutch America than in other societies based on plantation agriculture, although by the late eighteenth century 85 percent of its inhabitants were enslaved and Suriname had the dubious reputation to be the place where masters were the cruelest in the world. The exploitation of slaves did eventually cause major uprisings in Berbice (1763–64) and Curaçao (1795), but, ironically, failed to produce a revolt of any magnitude in Suriname. Instead, runaway slaves managed to carve out their own settlements in Suriname's interior, where they were able to resist Dutch arms. These maroons ultimately forced the government to recognize them as legal rulers of these territories, long before the abolition of slavery was discussed among Dutch policymakers.

In sum, inspired by Portuguese and English models, the Dutch burst onto the Atlantic scene in the 1590s as raiders and traders. After 1621, they captured various Iberian trading posts and settlements in Africa and the Americas, some of which would serve a purely commercial function, while others, such as Brazil and the Guyana colonies, produced cash crops for the European markets. Enslaved Africans provided most of the labor force in these plantation colonies, eventually making up the vast majority of Dutch America's population.

1   Felip Fernández-Armesto, *Before Columbus: Exploration and Colonization from the Mediterranean to the Atlantic, 1229–1492* (Philadelphia: University of Pennsylvania Press, 1987), 217.

2   Victor Enthoven, *Zeeland en de opkomst van de Republiek. Handel en strijd in de Scheldedelta, c. 1550–1621* (Leiden: Luctor et Victor, 1996), 241; Klaas Ratelband, *Nederlanders in West-Afrika 1600–1650. Angola, Kongo en São Tomé* (Zutphen: Walburg Pers, 2000), 33.

3   Peter T. Bradley, *The Lure of Peru: Maritime Intrusion into the South Sea, 1598–1701* (London: Macmillan, 1989), 12, 201-202.

4   Christopher Ebert, "Dutch Trade with Brazil before the Dutch West India Company, 1587–1621," in Johannes Postma and Victor Enthoven, eds., *Riches from Atlantic Commerce: Dutch Transatlantic Trade and Shipping, 1585–1817* (Leiden: Brill, 2003), 49-75.

5   John Vogt, *Portuguese Rule on the Gold*

Coast, 1469–1682 (Athens: University of Georgia Press, 1979), 148, 155-156, 164-165.

6 "Sommier discours over de staet vande vier geconquesteerde capitanias Parnambuco, Itamarica, Paraiba ende Rio Grande, inde noorderdeelen van Brasil," *Bijdragen en Mededeelingen van het Historisch Genootschap* 2 (1879): 257-317, here 292-293.

7 Charles Frostin, *Histoire de l'autonomisme colon de la partie de St. Domingue aux XVIIe et XVIIIe siècles. Contribution à l'étude du sentiment américain d'indépendance* (Lille: Université de Lille III, 1973), 31, 62, 65; Carl Bridenbaugh and Roberta Bridenbaugh, *No Peace beyond the Line: The English in the Caribbean 1624–1690* (New York: Oxford University Press, 1972), 313, 372.

8 Johannes Postma, "Suriname and Its Atlantic Connections, 1667–1795," in Postma and Enthoven, *Riches*, 287-322, here 299-305; Eric Willem van der Oest, "The Forgotten Colonies of Essequibo and Demerara, 1700–1814," in ibid., 323-361, here 353-357; Johannes Postma, "A Reassessment of the Dutch Atlantic Slave Trade," in ibid., 115-138, here 134, table 5.6.

9 Jaap Jacobs, *New Netherland: A Dutch Colony in Seventeenth-Century America* (Leiden: Brill, 2005), 98; José Antônio Gonsalves de Mello, ed., *Fontes para a história do Brasil holandês* (Recife: MinC – Secretaria da Cultura, 1985), 2:221.

10 Willem Frijhoff, *Wegen van Evert Willemsz. Een Hollands weeskind op zoek naar zichzelf, 1607–1674* (Nijmegen: SUN, 1995), 575 [translated as *Fulfilling God's Mission: The Two Worlds of Dominie Everardus Bogardus, 1607–1647* (Leiden: Brill, 2007)]; Victor Enthoven, "Dutch Crossings: Migration between the Netherlands and the New World, 1600–1800," *Atlantic Studies* 2.2 (October 2005): 153-176, here 168-169.

11 Robin Law, *The Slave Coast of West Africa, 1550–1750: The Impact of the African Slave Trade on an African Society* (Oxford: Clarendon Press, 1991), 120.

12 Henk den Heijer, *Goud, ivoor en slaven: Scheepvaart en handel van de Tweede West-Indische Compagnie op Afrika, 1674–1730* (Zutphen: Walburg Pers, 1997), 226.

13 Harvey M. Feinberg, *Africans and Europeans in West Africa: Elminans and Dutchmen on the Gold Coast during the Eighteenth Century* (Philadelphia: American Philosophical Society, 1989), 34-35; Enthoven, "Dutch Crossings," 158, table 2.

14 Alvin O. Thompson, "Amerindian-European Relations in Dutch Guyana," in Hilary Beckles and Verene Shepherd, eds., *Caribbean Slave Society and Economy: A Student Reader* (Kingston: Ian Randle Publishers; London: James Currey Publishers, 1991), 13-27, here 14, 17, 21, 22; Neil L. Whitehead, *Lords of the Tiger Spirit: A History of the Caribs in Colonial Venezuela and Guyana 1498–1820* (Dordrecht/Providence, RI: Foris Publications, 1988), 153-155.

15 Louis Jadin, *L'ancien Congo et l'Angola, 1639–1655, d'après les archives romaines, portugaises, néerlandaises et espagnoles* (Brussels/Rome: Institut Historique Belge de Rome, 1975), 973-974, 1070.

16 Frans Leonard Schalkwijk, *Igreja e estado no Brasil holandês, 1630–1654* (Recife: Governo de Pernambuco, Secretaria de Turismo, Cultura e Esportes, Fundação do Patrimônio Histórico Artístico de Pernambuco, Diretoria de Assuntos Culturais, 1986), 275 [in the English translation, *The Reformed Church in Dutch Brazil, 1630–1654* (Zoetermeer: Boekencentrum, 1998), quotation on 189].

17 Gert Oostindie, "Same Old Song? Perspectives on Slavery and Slaves in Suriname and Curaçao," in Gert Oostindie, ed., *Fifty Years Later: Antislavery, Capitalism and Modernity in the Dutch Orbit* (Leiden: KITLV Press, 1995), 143-178, here 163.

1

COLONIAL
PERIOD
AND
EIGHTEENTH
CENTURY

1609–1782

NEW NETHERLAND: THE FORMATIVE YEARS, 1609–1632

CHARLES T. GEHRING

Unknown to seventeenth-century explorers probing the waterways along the northeastern coast of North America, there were only two accesses to the interior of the vast land mass lying before them: the Saint Lawrence River valley and the geographical configurations of the Hudson and Mohawk river systems. Just by chance the United Provinces of the Netherlands gained control of the southern corridor, denying this lucrative trade route to the English for most of the seventeenth century. The Dutch Republic was able to claim this vast territory from Cape Cod to Delaware Bay through right of discovery made by Henry Hudson — an English navigator, sailing for the Dutch East India Company. In 1609 the appearance of Hudson in the river now bearing his name set in motion a series of events, which would establish the Dutch as a major force in the fur trade and competitor of the English in the New World.

Early Explorations

In 1607 and 1608 Hudson had made two northern voyages in the employ of the English Muscovy Company. His goal was to find a passage to the Far East by sailing north of Siberia. Such a breakthrough would have made it possible for commercial ventures to reach the riches of "Cathay" without the cost and risk of navigating in the hostile waters around Africa and in the Indian Ocean. Both failed to discover this fabled passage. Hudson's experience and enthusiasm, however, attracted the attention of the Dutch East India Company (VOC). He was given command of the Dutch-built ship *Halve Maen* with instructions to sail northeast in search of the elusive passage to the Far East, one that was possibly shorter, and one that was certainly safer. After encountering adverse weather

74

conditions and dangerous ice floes his crew expressed a near-mutinous desire to sail in safer waters. Contrary to VOC instructions Hudson turned his ship about, heading south by southwest. He failed to find the northern passage to Cathay but did succeed in opening an area of North America to the Dutch.[1]

Shortly after Hudson's explorations various commercial operations in the Netherlands were licensed by the States General to trade with the natives in the major waterways from Maine to Virginia. One of the most active trader-explorers in these early years was Adriaen Courtsen Block. Sailing for Lutheran merchants from Amsterdam, Block made three voyages from 1611 to 1614. For some time the island off the coast of Rhode Island still carrying his name may have served as his base of operations while exploring the coast of Connecticut. Other names of Dutch explorers also became associated with various landmarks, such as Cape May at the mouth of Delaware Bay, named after Cornelis Jacobsz May from Hoorn. It is interesting to note that in the early years of fierce competition between merchant cartels in the Netherlands, certain areas may have become associated with the ships that frequented them. In any case it is curious that two place names along the coast of Massachusetts — Vos Haven (Fox Harbor) and Craen Baij (Crane Bay) — coincide with the names of two ships, the *Vos* and the *Craen*, operating in the area in 1611–12 under the command of Jan Cornelisz May, also from Hoorn. These place names are recorded on Block's *Figurative Map* of 1614. As risky as it may seem to make these associations since foxes and cranes could have been found all along the coast, it is not a coincidence that further north, approximately at the mouth of the Kennebunck River, is the notation *Het Schip de Schildpadde*, "the ship the Turtle."

Block's initial voyage was apparently a follow-up to Hudson's explorations. Whereas Hudson had approached Manhattan from the south, Block was attempting to find the entrance to Hudson's river by following the coast of New England. According to Johannes de Laet's reading of Block's journal: "He sailed into every river and stream from Cape Cod westward, indicating clearly that he had the specific intention to find the river discovered by Hudson, which he succeeded in doing."[2]

By 1614 competition between traders had become so violent and bloody that the New Netherland Company was chartered as a monopoly to trade in the region in order to stabilize the situation. The first written reference to the place name Nieuw Nederlant (New Netherland) appears in a document of the States General concerning the chartering of traders on October 11, 1614. Under the terms of the Company, the trading cartel was permitted to finance four voyages within three years between the latitudes 40 and 45 degrees (from Barnegat Bay, NJ to Eastport, ME). The main base of operations became Fort Nassau on the upper Hudson (the Mauritius or North River), 150 miles north of Manhattan Island. The fort was built on Castle Island, now mostly occupied by the port

1
——

COLONIAL
PERIOD
AND
EIGHTEENTH
CENTURY

1609–1782

of Albany. It was 58 by 58 feet (interior dimensions), and was surrounded by a moat 8 feet wide. The moat and breastworks protected a trading house of 38 by 28 feet. Fort Nassau served as a focal point for trading activities in an area that was to become the most lucrative fur-trading operation in the Northeast. As the description and location of the fort are recorded on Block's *Figurative Map*, it can be viewed as road map for traders to this site on the upper Hudson.

Early Traders

Expeditions were sent from this post into the interior in search of mineral deposits and other natural resources to exploit. Not only would Fort Nassau serve as a trading post but it could also serve as a base of operations for further exploration. Sometime during the year 1614 a Fort Nassau trader named Kleyntie, "little man," accompanied by two compatriots, ventured westward into unexplored country, where they were captured by Indians and held for ransom. The following year they were rescued in the South River (present-day Delaware River) valley by the Dutch trader Cornelis Hendricksen van Monnickendam. Their adventures from Fort Nassau to point of capture, either along the Schoharie watershed or near the source of the Delaware River, and their eventual ransoming in the lower Delaware Valley gave Kleyntie insights into the configurations of the various waterways within New Netherland. The map upon which his expedition is reported shows awareness of the source of the South River extending far to the north into territory supplying furs to Fort Nassau. Dutch knowledge of the configuration of the various waterways within New Netherland is important for understanding later concerns regarding settlements on the three major river systems. In fact, as late as 1649 Petrus Stuyvesant, director general of New Netherland, expressed deep concern for keeping this waterway out of the hands of the English, who were still unaware of its strategic importance.[3]

When the New Netherland Company's charter expired in 1618, the territory was once again opened to cut-throat trading activities. As if to define the moment, Fort Nassau was washed away by a spring freshet the year before forcing traders to operate seasonally from aboard ship or from tents on shore. During this period of unregulated trading several events occurred worthy of note here. In 1622 it was reported that a chief of an Indian tribe in the Fresh River (present-day Connecticut) valley had made an agreement with Pieter Barentsz, indicating that he would trade with no one else. The chief gave as a reason that another trader by the name of Jacob Eelkens had held him on his yacht for ransom, threatening to cut off his head. The ransom of 140 fathoms of *sewant* or wampum was paid and his life was spared. Barentsz gained the chief's trust because he apparently was using less draconian methods in his negotiations.[4]

Assuming that the above report is accurate, this incident demonstrates that unscrupulous traders were employing brutal tactics to deprive the natives of sewant. Jacob Eelkens was also indirectly involved in another extortion attempt—possibly in the same year. An interrogatory sworn before a notary, twelve years later, revealed how Hans Jorisz Hontom had held a Mohawk chief for ransom aboard his ship.[5] After the ransom was paid (it was not noted whether sewant or furs were demanded) Hontom cut off the male organs of the chief, causing his death. Jacob Eelkens was supercargo aboard Hontom's ship. Although we are not sure that Eelkens condoned this action, we do know that he had previously threatened to remove another part of a sachem's anatomy in the Fresh River. Putting the brutality of these trading practices aside, it is important to note that as early as 1622 the Dutch traders had recognized the value of sewant, which was being produced by the Pequots. If these two incidents occurred in the same trading season of 1622, it is quite likely that Hontom and Eelkens had been busy acquiring sewant from the Pequots to take up the Hudson for use in acquiring furs from the Mohawks. Sewant became so essential in trading operations that it became known as "the source and mother of the whole beaver trade."[6] The Dutch had developed the ideal trading relationship in New Netherland—an exchange of Pequot sewant for Mohawk furs.

WIC Involvement

The chaotic situation created by private traders was not addressed until 1621 when the West India Company (WIC) was chartered as a trading monopoly similar in organization to the VOC. The WIC's area of operations extended from the west coast of Africa westward across the Atlantic and Pacific to the eastern edge of the Indonesian archipelago. New Netherland was one of its many interests, which included the Gold Coast of Africa, Brazil with its wealth of sugar and dyewood, and the salt-rich Caribbean islands. Although founded on June 3, 1621, the WIC needed almost two years to raise enough capital to finance its first attempt to take possession of its holdings in North America.

It is unclear when the first settlers arrived. According to Catelyntie (or Catherine) Trico, some set foot in New Netherland as early as 1623. Her deposition sworn out in 1688 states that she came over with Adriaen Jorisz Thienpont aboard the WIC ship *De Eendracht* (The Concord). Trico, who was from the small village of Pry in the county of Namur (in present-day Belgium), was part of a group of Walloons. Contrary to her memory, Nicolaes van Wassenaer records in his chronicle *Historisch Verhael* that thirty families (mostly Walloons) came over in 1624 aboard the 260-ton ship *Nieuw Nederlant*. Trico deposed that she, then eighteen years old, and three other women married at sea. Upon her arriv-

77

1

━━

COLONIAL
PERIOD
AND
EIGHTEENTH
CENTURY

1609–1782

al in New Netherland she was among eighteen families sent to the upper Hudson River valley. Two families and six men were sent to the Fresh River, probably to the place called Kievits Hoeck (Saybroeck Point) at the mouth of the river on the western bank; and two families and eight men were sent to the South River to occupy Fort Wilhelmus on High Island (today's Burlington Island, NJ). While sailing upriver Trico and her companions stopped at the Esopus (present-day Kingston, NY) to lighten their load by making use of some boats that had been left there the previous year by private traders. Trico also states that eight men were left behind at New York. In 1624 this would have been *Nooten* or Nut Island (present-day Governor's Island), where the Dutch built a fort and a windmill. Although it can be argued that her advanced age of eighty-three years may have clouded some of the details, her statement does accurately describe the early thinking of the WIC regarding settlements.[7]

It is evident from Trico's deposition that the first colonists were to be distributed among the remote trading posts on the three major river systems in order to serve as agricultural support communities and in the process lay claim to the three-river system of the Dutch possession. Nut Island off the tip of Manhattan was to serve as a point of assembly for transferring cargo from coastal-trading vessels to large ocean-going ships; a similar role was played by the island of Texel in the Netherlands. In 1625 Willem Verhulst came over as director of New Netherland with instructions to strengthen the trading posts and their related settlements, but he was ordered to focus on the post on High Island and to make it the center of the colony. It is unclear why the directors were drawn to this island in the Delaware River. It is possible that they had been looking for a major trading center deep in Indian country but, unlike Fort Orange, ice free the year around. The directors had apparently been misinformed about the Delaware. In fact, one winter it was reported that Indians coming from the west had been able to cross over the river on the ice to the Dutch trading post on the eastern shore (Gloucester, NJ). The freezing of the Delaware was no abnormality. It must be remembered that the period of the settlement of New Netherland coincided with the high point of the Little Ice Age from 1300 to 1850. In fact, it is reported that a traveler from New England was able to cross the East River on the ice to Long Island at the place of the *witte steen* (location of the present-day Whitestone Bridge). In the end it was not the decision of poorly informed directors but an incident at Fort Orange on the upper Hudson that determined the location of the center of New Netherland.[8]

Catelyntie Trico states that she lived at Fort Orange for three years but in 1626 returned to Manhattan. She does not indicate the reason for leaving her new home in the north; however, it is known that the local commander, Daniël van Crieckenbeeck, became involved in a war between the Mohawks and Ma-

78

hicans in the spring of 1626. When he and six of his soldiers accompanied a Mahican war party for an attack on the Mohawks, they were ambushed a short distance from the fort and thoroughly defeated. Crieckenbeeck and three of his soldiers were killed together with many Mahicans. The Mohawks were outraged that the Dutch, who had instructions to remain neutral in such conflicts, would betray them in this manner. Fortunately Crieckenbeeck's indiscretion coincided with the arrival of Pieter Minuit, who shortly after his arrival replaced Verhulst as director. It was also fortunate that someone as reliable and trusted as Pieter Barentsz was available; the same trader who had gained the confidence of the Pequots after the incident with Jacob Eelkens in 1622.

Barentsz was immediately dispatched to Mohawk country to discuss the unfortunate incident at Fort Orange. He was able to convince the Mohawks that it had been an unauthorized initiative on Crieckenbeeck's part and assured them that it would not happen again. Upon hearing the news of the disaster Minuit sailed immediately to Fort Orange. He had arrived in the colony the previous year and took on the assignment of exploring New Netherland from one end to the other for precious metals and other marketable resources. Minuit knew the land and the various Indian peoples better than anyone else in the colony at that time. He saw the dangers in the situation and realized that the outlying support communities were in peril of destruction. Minuit resolved the problem by purchasing Manhattan Island for sixty guilders worth of trade goods and moving most of the outlying families to this central location. Up till this time the island was being used to pasture cattle sent over the previous year. Apparently the Mohawks agreed with Barentsz to allow trading personnel to remain at Fort Orange but insisted that the families be removed; or they may have indicated that they could no longer guarantee the settlers' safety. At this time even the families from the Fresh River and High Island were withdrawn. Instead of retaining a presence at Fort Wilhelmus on High Island, the trading post was moved to a new location on the eastern shore of the South River (present-day Gloucester, NJ). The new trading post was christened Fort Nassau.[9]

By the end of Pieter Minuit's tenure as director in 1632, the configuration of settlements was complete. Trading posts had been established on two of the three river systems at Fort Orange and Fort Nassau; Dutch traders also maintained a presence at the mouths of the Connecticut and Housatonic rivers. Tensions between the Dutch and Mohawks had been reduced, making it possible to establish agricultural communities to support the trading operations. The change in atmosphere, since the Crieckenbeeck disaster, can be attributed to the Mohawk defeat of the Mahicans in 1628. As the Mohawks had become dominant on the west side of the Hudson and the primary supplier of furs to the Dutch, it was in their interest to allow the WIC traders to maintain their presence on the

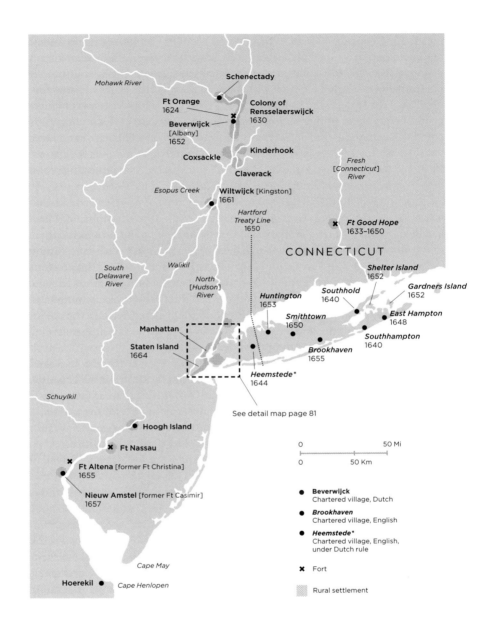

Mohawk River

Schenectady

Ft Orange
1624

Colony of
Rennselaerswijck
1630

Beverwijck
[Albany]
1652

Kinderhook

Coxsackle

Fresh
[Connecticut]
River

Claverack

Esopus Creek

Wiltwijck [Kingston]
1661

Hartford
Treaty Line
1650

Ft Good Hope
1633–1650

CONNECTICUT

South
[Delaware]
River

Walikil

North
[Hudson]
River

Shelter Island
1652

Southhold
1640

Gardners Island
1652

Huntington
1653

Smithtown
1650

East Hampton
1648

Manhattan

Staten Island
1664

Brookhaven
1655

Southhampton
1640

Heemstede*
1644

See detail map page 81

Schuylkil

Hoogh Island

Ft Nassau

Ft Altena [former Ft Christina]
1655

Nieuw Amstel [former Ft Casimir]
1657

0   50 Mi
0   50 Km

● Beverwijck
  Chartered village, Dutch

● *Brookhaven*
  Chartered village, English

● *Heemstede**
  Chartered village, English,
  under Dutch rule

✗ Fort

▦ Rural settlement

Cape May

Hoerekil   Cape Henlopen

New Netherland, 1664.

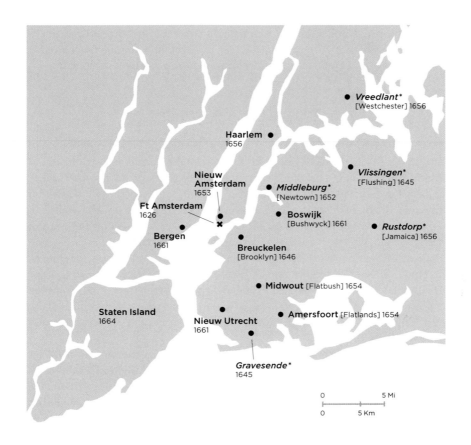

Vreedlant*
[Westchester] 1656

Haarlem
1656

Vlissingen*
[Flushing] 1645

Nieuw
Amsterdam
1653

Middleburg*
[Newtown] 1652

Ft Amsterdam
1626

Boswijk
[Bushwyck] 1661

Rustdorp*
[Jamaica] 1656

Bergen
1661

Breuckelen
[Brooklyn] 1646

Midwout [Flatbush] 1654

Staten Island
1664

Nieuw Utrecht
1661

Amersfoort [Flatlands] 1654

Gravesende*
1645

0   5 Mi

0   5 Km

New Amsterdam (Nieuw Amsterdam) and surrounding villages, 1664.

1

—

COLONIAL
PERIOD
AND
EIGHTEENTH
CENTURY

1609–1782

upper Hudson. Once again the Dutch could consider locating settlements in the proximity of the trading posts. However, an event far to the south occurred in the same year that would have ramifications on future means of settlement.

Short- and Long-Term Approaches

In 1625 the WIC suffered a series of setbacks that would retard exploitation of its interests from Africa to Brazil: failure to take the Portuguese stronghold of Elmina on the Gold Coast of Africa; repulse of its attack on the Spanish stronghold at San Juan, Puerto Rico; and most important, the loss of the city of Salvador in Bahia, Brazil, to the Portuguese. However, the taste of Brazil sugar would not be forgotten. When Piet Heyn captured the Spanish silver fleet off the coast of Cuba in 1628, WIC stock rose over two hundred points. This sudden increase in disposable income gave the Company the financial flexibility to consider means to colonize New Netherland and to mount another attack on Brazil. By 1632 the Dutch were in control of Recife and an expanse of territory to the mouth of the Amazon. Soon the profit from sugar and dyewood would attract most of the WIC's financial and human resources — all to the detriment of development in New Netherland.

This paucity of resources forced the WIC to consider other means of attracting settlers to New Netherland. Two factions among the Amsterdam directors of the WIC locked horns. The debate divided along two well-defined lines: One group wished to discourage colonization because the expense would eat into profits and the colonists would soon compete with the Company in the exploitation of the natural resources, again reducing income. They argued that a force of professional soldiers and well-formed alliances with the natives should be enough to maintain the security of the region; and, that the expense in resupplying the post would be offset by the increased cash flow. These directors were embracing a short-term strategy: "Take the money and run." Another group among the directors, however, promoted the position that by encouraging colonization and by establishing support farms in the proximity of the trading posts the region would soon become self-sufficient and immune to any disruption in the shipping. This was the long-term strategy: "Invest in the future." Self-sufficiency would eventually increase profits because it would no longer be necessary to send over so many supply ships or take up valuable cargo space better used to ship trade goods. The region also would flourish by natural increase, creating a population from which troops could be raised in emergencies. Best of all, a militia formed from the settlers would save the Company the expense of recruiting and maintaining a large force of professional European soldiers.

This argument sounded logical. However, it would cost large sums of money to ship over significant numbers of colonists, set them up on farms, and maintain them until they could become productive. The opposing directors argued that the expense would be prohibitive. Continued debate in the WIC concerning colonization resulted in a concession called the Freedoms and Exemptions (June 7, 1629). Rather than expend WIC capital the directors decided to privatize colonization.[10]

The patroonship plan of colonization allowed an investor (or group of investors) to negotiate with the natives for a tract of land upon which he was obligated to settle fifty colonists within four years at his own expense. In return the patroon was granted the rights of high, middle, and low jurisdictions, and held the land as perpetual fief of inheritance with the right to dispose of the colony by last will and testament. This scheme was in many ways similar to the Portuguese system of land development in Brazil, in which the Crown granted *donatários* (patroons) land called *capitanias* in return for colonizing and developing the region.

When in 1632 Minuit returned to the fatherland he left a colony struggling for its existence. Preoccupation with Brazil was draining much-needed support at this early stage of development. Instead of pouring in resources to secure this territory between New England and the tobacco colonies of Maryland and Virginia, the WIC was forced to resort to private investors to maintain a presence in this fur-bearing region. Although there was initial success in attracting colonists to private holdings such as Rensselaerswijck, Swanendael, and Pavonia, not much would change until 1654 when the Portuguese recaptured Dutch Brazil. The loss of Brazil would be New Netherland's gain. Colonists and material resources previously intended for Brazil would now find their way to North America.[11]

As disjointed as the early years were for this WIC possession, the process of extracting furs for the profit of the Company slowly established a presence that would develop into a viable colony. In 1609 Hudson had no notion that he was inadvertently laying claim to a region that one day would be populated by colonists from every corner of Europe.

1   S. P. L'Honoré Naber, ed., *Henry Hudson's Reize onder Nederlandsche vlag van Amsterdam naar Nova Zembla, Amerika en terug naar Dartmouth in Engeland, 1609* (The Hague: Martinus Nijhoff, 1921); and Donald S. Johnson, *Charting the Sea of Darkness: The Four Voyages of Henry Hudson* (Camden, ME: International Marine, 1993).

2   Johannes de Laet, *Beschrijvinghe van West-Indien* (Leiden, 1630), 101-104; Quotation translated by the author.

1

——

COLONIAL
PERIOD
AND
EIGHTEENTH
CENTURY

1609–1782

3   Charles T. Gehring, ed. and trans., *Delaware Papers 1648–1664*. New York Historical Manuscripts (Baltimore: Genealogical Publishing Co., Inc., 1981), 29.

4   Nicolaes van Wassenaer, *Historisch verhael alden ghedenck-weerdichste geschiedenisse, die hier en daer in Europa, als in Duytsch-lant, Vranckryck, Enghe-lant, Spaengien, Hungaryen, Polen, Sevenberghen, Wallachien, Modavien, Turckyen en Neder-lant, van den beginne des jaer 1621 … (tot Octobri des jaers 1632) voorgevallen syn* (Amsterdam, 1621–31), 4:39.

5   Charles T. Gehring and William A. Starna, "Dutch and Indians in the Hudson Valley: The Early Period," *The Hudson Valley Regional Review*, 9.2 (September 1992): 15ff.

6   Kevin A. McBride, "The Source and Mother of the Fur Trade: Native-Dutch Relations in Eastern New Nether-land," in Laurie Weinstein, ed., *Enduring Tradition: The Native Peoples of New England* (Westport, CT: Bergin & Garvey, 1994), 31-51.

7   Edmund Bailey O'Callaghan, *Documentary History of the State of New York*, 4 vols. (Albany, NY: Weed, Parsons & Co., 1849–51), 3:49-51.

8   A. J. F. Van Laer, *Documents Relating to New Netherland, 1624–1626* (San Marino, CA: The Henry E. Huntington Library and Art Gallery, Publications Americana, 1924); Charles T. Gehring, ed. and trans., *New York Documents, Council Minutes 1655–1656* (Syracuse, NY: Syracuse University Press, 1995), 8.

9   George Olin Zabriskie and Alice P. Kenney, "The Founding of New Amster-dam: Fact and Fiction," *De Halve Maen* 50.4 (January 1976): 5-6, 15-16; 51.1 (April 1976): 5-6, 13-14; 51.2 (July 1976): 5-6, 13-14; 51.3 (October 1976): 11-12, 13-14; 52.1 (Spring 1977): 11-12, 13-14.

10 Van Cleaf Bachman, *Peltries or Planta-tions: The Economic Policies of the Dutch West India Company in New Netherland, 1623–1639* (Baltimore: Johns Hopkins University Press, 1969).

11 Jaap Jacobs, *New Netherland: A Dutch Colony in Seventeenth-Century America* (Leiden: Brill, 2005); and A. J. F. Van Laer, *Van Rensselaer Bowier Manuscripts* (Albany: University of the State of New York, 1908).

MIGRATION, POPULATION, AND GOVERNMENT IN NEW NETHERLAND

━━

JAAP JACOBS

Introduction

Between the first arrival of settlers in the early 1620s and the English takeover of 1664, New Netherland developed from a small trading post of a few hundred colonists, led by a commander and a council, into a settlement colony of seven to eight thousand inhabitants, spread out over a large area, governed by local courts and a centralized provincial government of a director general and a council. While the beginnings were slow, in the 1650s the pace began to pick up as many new immigrants arrived. The institutions developed at the same pace. In a process of gradual maturation, New Netherland began to display distinctly Dutch features, both in the composition of its population and in its institutional organization.

Population

Although a small number of traders spent the winter at Fort Nassau on the upper reaches of the Hudson River in the 1610s, permanent colonization started with the decision of the West India Company (WIC) to counter claims of the English government to almost all of North America. It employed a group of Walloons to take up agriculture in what essentially was a set of scattered trading posts aimed at conducting the profitable trade in peltries, principally beaver skins, with the Indians. In 1629, New Amsterdam had three to five hundred inhabitants. Through the patroonship plan the population of New Netherland grew, albeit slowly, in the 1630s, for instance around Fort Orange, where Kiliaen van Rensselaer set up Rensselaerswijck, the only patroonship venture of any conse-

1

COLONIAL
PERIOD
AND
EIGHTEENTH
CENTURY

1609–1782

quence until the foundation of New Amstel. In 1640 the WIC relinquished its fur trade monopoly by not including it in a new set of Freedoms and Exemptions. By this time there may have been between fifteen hundred and two thousand colonists. Kieft's War with the Indians in the lower Hudson River area proved disastrous. Although casualties among the colonists were limited, a number of them decided to return to the Dutch Republic. News of the events dampened the enthusiasm of prospective settlers, thus bringing emigration to a standstill. It was not until 1650 that New Netherland attained a population size that exceeded that of before Kieft's War.[1]

The boom years of New Netherland started after the First Anglo-Dutch War ended in 1654. The loss of Dutch Brazil in the same year prompted the WIC to instigate a policy by which its returning employees from Brazil were granted land in New Netherland as compensation. In the ten years before the English takeover numerous new settlers arrived, some drawn to the fur trade in Beverwijck, others to agriculture, including the cultivation of tobacco, which by 1664 rivaled fur as the main export commodity. By that time New Netherland had an estimated seven to nine thousand colonists, divided over two major settlements, Beverwijck and New Amsterdam, two patroonships, Rensselaerswijck and the city-colony New Amstel on the Delaware River, fifteen towns with a court of justice, including the English villages under Dutch jurisdiction on Long Island, and several small settlements without jurisdictional powers as yet (see map, p. 80). The towns can be estimated at 100 to 150 inhabitants each, while the number at Beverwijck has been estimated at 897 in 1657 and 1,051 in 1660. Without a full demographic study, including a population reconstruction, today's estimate of the number of New Amsterdam's inhabitants in 1664 lies between 1,750 and 2,500, not including slaves and free blacks. In 1638 about 100 slaves worked in the colony, a number that grew to approximately 150 in 1655. In 1664 there cannot have been more than 250 in the whole of New Netherland and their number doubled with the arrival of the ship *Gideon* in August, with 291 slaves on board. In that year, Africans, both free and enslaved, made up 6 to 8 percent of the total population, with a concentration in New Amsterdam where it may have been 10 to 17 percent.[2]

In comparison with surrounding English colonies, New Netherland appears to have a low population count. But by Dutch standards, it was a great success as a settlement colony. After 1664, immigration stopped but natural growth continued. In 1790 about one hundred thousand people, 2.6 percent of the white American population, were of Dutch stock, a percentage well below that of English, Scotch, Irish, and German groups. In New York and New Jersey the percentages were 17.5 and 16.6 respectively, showing the extent to which the American Dutch had remained in the area that used to be called New Netherland.

Immigration

The European colonists in New Netherland had various backgrounds. Analysis by David Cohen of a sample of 904 immigrants shows that almost half of them were not born in the Dutch Republic. They originated primarily from German states, France, the Southern Netherlands, Schleswig-Holstein, and Scandinavian countries. Those who listed a place of birth within the Dutch Republic mostly came from Holland, Gelderland, and Utrecht.[3] These oft-quoted results need to be interpreted with caution, as geographical origin should not be equated with culture. Cohen's dataset was not obtained by random sampling for instance, and the well-to-do immigrants and their servants are not included. Also, the focus on transatlantic immigrants obscures two important groups: the English, who immigrated from the surrounding colonies, and the native-born New Netherlanders. The number of English in New Netherland seems to have been considerable, judging from the frequent occurrence of English names in court records. The effect of natural increase should not be underestimated either. Between 1639 and 1665 1,636 children had been baptized in New Amsterdam alone and even accounting for the high infant mortality rate of the early modern age, by 1664 roughly 15 percent of the New Netherland population may have been locally born.

On the whole, the population of the Dutch Republic had little incentive to go overseas. Some may have been drawn by a desire for adventure, to see foreign countries, or to spend a few years in the colonies with the intention to return with riches. Such pull factors existed in most European countries, but the Dutch Republic, especially Holland, lacked the push factors that fueled English migration: religious persecution and economic hardship. Compared with other European countries, especially England and France, the Dutch Republic was relatively tolerant and its economy was booming. It attracted economic and religious immigrants from the surrounding countries, such as the Pilgrims. Other immigrants were French Protestants (Huguenots) or refugees fleeing from the Thirty Years' War in the German states. The latter were recruited by the East and West India Companies as soldiers for the overseas ventures. Most soldiers in the 1630s and 1640s had little choice as to the colony in which they would serve the three or five years of their contract, but in the 1650s the WIC started a policy of recruiting soldiers specifically for New Netherland on a short contract, with the understanding that they would subsequently take up another occupation.[4]

Unlike the soldiers, most farmers and artisans in the 1650s were independent, making the transatlantic voyage with wife and children. Those with experience in dry farming were considered more suitable for New Netherland than

87

COLONIAL
PERIOD
AND
EIGHTEENTH
CENTURY

1609–1782

those who had farmed in the wetter provinces in the west. Therefore most of the farmers in New Netherland came from the sandy soils of the Veluwe in Gelderland or from Drenthe and Overijssel, which were still suffering from the war with Spain. The Van Rensselaer and Van Twiller families, for example, recruited their tenants and farmhands both from the local population of villages in Utrecht and Gelderland, where they owned land, and from the international labor pool in Amsterdam. There is clear evidence for both group and chain migration from Utrecht, Gelderland, and Drenthe. Tailors, carpenters, shoemakers, surgeons, masons, and coopers for the most part fall in the category of nuclear family migration in the 1650s.[5] Contract laborers were mostly male, hired for three to six years, with the younger men getting a longer contract and a lower yearly salary. Maidservants for domestic work made up about 20 percent of the contract laborers. Unlike the indentured servants who went to Virginia and other English colonies, Dutch contracts were nontransferable, but in cases of maltreatment servants were often able to persuade the New Netherland court to dissolve the contract.[6]

Two small immigrant groups are the merchants and the nonmilitary WIC servants. The first group was split between minor and major merchants. Minor merchants were dominant in the 1640s, after the Company relinquished the fur-trade monopoly. They were itinerant traders, originating mostly from North Holland above the IJ and West-Friesland. They traveled to New Netherland with trade goods in spring, conducted business with colonists and Indian traders in Beverwijck in summer, and returned to the Dutch Republic in the fall. In contrast, the major merchants resided in New Netherland. Most of them began their career as agents for one of the larger merchant houses in Amsterdam, which regularly sent them on overseas assignments to trade goods. Gradually these agents, who generally were from Haarlem and Amsterdam, started trading for their own profit. After New Amsterdam acquired city rights in 1653, they became the elite from which the members of city government were recruited. The last group of immigrants consisted of the nonmilitary personnel of the West India Company, such as clerks, commissaries, secretaries, schoolmasters, ministers, and of course the directors. Most members of this group had an Amsterdam background, with some exceptions, like Petrus Stuyvesant who was born in Friesland, or Cornelis van Tienhoven who came from the province of Utrecht. While this group remained small in size, it formed the governmental elite of New Netherland.

Government and People

Relations between the WIC officials and the colonists in New Netherland, as well as among the authorities in the colony, were rife with conflict. Several factors played a role: the difficulty for superiors in Amsterdam to intervene quickly due to slow communication; the gradual transition of New Netherland from a trading post to a settlement colony; and the incompetence of individuals and the incompatibility of characters. While these factors can be attributed to the specific situation of New Netherland as a colony, two overarching themes found their origin in developments in Europe: the church-state antithesis and the issue of popular or divine sovereignty. In varying combinations these causes determined the development and the outcome of the conflicts.

In contrast to what is often presumed, the highest West or East India Company official in a colony, whether going by the title of commander, commissary, director, director general, or governor general, did not wield exclusive power. Rather, he was the chief executive officer, whose decisions could be overturned by a majority vote in his council. Councilors were appointed by respective West India Company chambers in the Dutch Republic, sometimes with the approbation of the *Heren XIX* or the States General. In many cases, however, vacancies were provisionally filled on the spot, with the appointment being subject to later approval from patria.[7]

While this executive system proved to be adequate for trading posts or colonies in which the WIC maintained its trade and shipping monopoly, it turned out to be less suitable for settlement colonies in which Company officials were outnumbered by free burghers, not in the employ of the Company. Some of the later problems of New Netherland can at least partly be explained as emanating from the friction that arose during the colony's transition from a trading post to a settlement colony. The solution tried by both Director Kieft and Director General Stuyvesant was a model with medieval origins: the creation of advisory councils and, as a next step, the creation of subordinate bodies of local government with prerogatives in the sphere of criminal and civil justice. In the Low Countries the Estates and towns had used their growing commercial power over a large period of time to obtain specific rights, including the amalgam that is often called city rights, by granting or withholding agreement to extraordinary taxes requested by the overlord and intended to defray the costs of war. In New Netherland this development was mirrored, but it proceeded at a much faster pace, in a matter of twenty rather than two hundred years. The quick population growth as well as the awareness among both colonists and executives in New Netherland of the existence of this model of government accelerated its development.[8]

1

COLONIAL
PERIOD
AND
EIGHTEENTH
CENTURY

1609–1782

In its first years the colony was run almost like a fleet at sea. Ship captains such as Adriaen Jorisz Thienpont and Cornelis Jacobsz May were in charge of the string of four trading posts while their ships remained in the area. Soon after May departed for Europe in October 1624, Willem Verhulst took charge. By mid-1626 the council provisionally appointed Pieter Minuit in his place. Interestingly, the allegations raised against Verhulst—arbitrary government, favoritism, neglect of the Company's interest, corruption, self-enrichment—were similar to those voiced against some of his successors, sometimes with the added charge of drunkenness. Such claims should not be taken at face value, as they were often expressed by adversaries and denied by supporters of the official in question.[9]

Unsurprisingly then, Pieter Minuit's rule drew similar accusations as he became involved in several conflicts, most seriously with New Netherland's first minister, Jonas Michaëlius. This gradually led to the potentially more dangerous discussion on the ultimate source of moral authority in a small community like New Netherland: the director, whose position rested on the traditional view of government, in which secular authority was divinely sanctioned, or the minister, who did not wield worldly power but could appeal to religion as a higher moral power. In the end, the Amsterdam directors decided to recall both men in 1631.[10]

The conflict between Minuit and Michaëlius was exacerbated by the latter's affiliation with a militant, theocratic, and externally oriented movement within the Further Reformation that tried to establish ecclesiastical primacy and was especially prevalent in the first part of the seventeenth century. Michaëlius was replaced by Everardus Bogardus, who turned out to be at least as vocal. His first target was Minuit's successor, Wouter van Twiller, who received his share of the accusations. None of these allegations were proven, but in general Van Twiller does not seem to have had the required leadership qualities. As he returned to patria in 1637, the conflict did not get out of hand.[11]

This was different in the case of Willem Kieft, who is usually blamed for plunging New Netherland into the deepest crisis of its existence. Whether the decision to demand neighboring Indian groups to contribute to the defense of New Netherland was entirely his, or whether the directors in patria were in the know remains murky. It is clear, however, that when the Indians retaliated by killing a number of settlers, Kieft did not stop a group of colonists and soldiers who took revenge by carrying out a surprise attack on a group of Indians in Pavonia. The attack turned into a massacre in which about eighty Indians died, and sparked off a series of counterattacks that destroyed the properties of many and threatened the existence of the colony. It also started a long-lasting conflict on who was to blame for the disaster. As many colonists had lost everything, they turned against the West India Company and its representative Kieft and found minister Bogardus on their side. The antagonism between the two men turned ugly, with accusations of drunkenness, slander, and improper behavior flying between them. At the root of the conflict was the issue whether the church, with the minister as its main exponent was a higher source of moral authority than secular government.[12]

Kieft had at an early stage involved representatives of the population into the decision-making process by instituting advisory bodies, only to disband them when they exceeded their traditional prerogatives by meeting on their own accord and issuing advice on other matters than had been put before them. They added a new dimension to the conflict by requesting a form of local government. In itself, this request was neither unreasonable nor innovative, as some of the English villages in New Netherland had already obtained a local bench of justice. Yet in conjunction with the charge that the WIC officials and their policies were to blame for the situation in which the colonists found themselves, their request turned the conflict into a power struggle. Neither the States General nor the Amsterdam Chamber was keen on rewarding rebellious behavior, but it was obvious that some measures needed to be taken. Kieft was recalled and both he and Bogardus left the colony in August 1647 and lost their lives at sea.

Kieft's successor, Petrus Stuyvesant, faced the antagonism of the colonists that his predecessor had created, but was to a far greater extent than Kieft committed to the orthodox version of the Reformed Church. Like Kieft, Stuyvesant tried to involve the colonists by instituting an advisory body, in this case the Nine Men. The role of main spokesman was taken on by Adriaen van der Donck, patroon of Colendonck, present-day Yonkers. Initially, the director general and the council supported the Nine Men's effort to persuade the authorities in the Dutch Republic to provide more support to the colony, but relations turned sour when it became obvious that the Nine Men intended to request changes in government as well. Especially the plan to grant the patroons seats on the council would put Van der Donck personally in a powerful position.

Another bone of contention was local self-government for New Amsterdam, which was long overdue. The form this would take was obvious and none of the parties disagreed. It would be similar to the situation in patria: a small bench of justice with the addition of *burgemeesters* as urban executive officials and a *schout* as representative of the overlord, i.e., the WIC. Essential, however, was the extent of the prerogatives that the city government of New Amsterdam would be granted and who would be appointed to the first government. This depended on who made the grant: the West India Company or the States General. Timing therefore was of the essence.

In the summer of 1649 the settlers, against the wishes of the director general and the council, decided to send a delegation of three men, headed by Adriaen van der Donck, to the Dutch Republic. Their main goal was to persuade the

91

1

——

COLONIAL
PERIOD
AND
EIGHTEENTH
CENTURY

1609–1782

States General to provide far more assistance, as the WIC seemed to be unwilling or unable to do so. The first step, therefore, needed to be a change in the government of New Netherland, removing it from under the aegis of the Company and putting it directly under the jurisdiction of the States General, with more say for the colonists in local government. The delegation made its views known by publishing the *Remonstrance of New Netherland*, written by Van der Donck. The attempt came after several years of vehement criticism of the West India Company by both the general public and the States General for its conduct of the war against the Portuguese in Brazil. It is likely that the delegation was aware of this and tried to use the general opposition to the WIC to achieve its aims. But soon after the New Netherland delegation submitted its protests the political balance of power within the Dutch Republic began to change. By this time two members of the delegation had returned to America, leaving only Van der Donck as their spokesman in the Dutch Republic. As a result of the political turmoil and subsequent changes in the Dutch political situation, and because of the outbreak of the First Anglo-Dutch War, Van der Donck had no success whatsoever in advocating the political case of the colonists. Yet, his *Description of New Netherland*, which he wrote while in the Dutch Republic, may have stimulated immigration to the colony after its publication in 1655 and is one of the earliest and best-known accounts of New Netherland.[13]

Meanwhile, Stuyvesant had acted decisively in the colony. He had granted the Nine Men limited civil jurisdiction, to be carried out under the supervision of a council member. This took the sting out of the conflict and indicated the WIC's willingness to move toward creating a stable framework for relations with the New Amsterdam colonists. More important, the director general and the council had intervened, in late 1650, in the composition of the Nine Men, whose members were selected by cooptation. Instead of accepting their nomination, Stuyvesant and the council had appointed six new members more favorable to the Company. Of the members of the Nine Men from 1647 through 1650, none were left in office by 1652. This deliberate policy to purge the Nine Men of opponents of the WIC had created a new political atmosphere. It was now safe to grant New Amsterdam further prerogatives, and Stuyvesant and his council suggested as much to the Amsterdam Chamber in late 1651. After permission was granted in April 1652, the director general and the council proceeded to install the city government of New Amsterdam on February 2, 1653. Five of the members of the Nine Men of 1652 were appointed to the seven-man city government. Obviously, these measures did not ensure that no new conflicts would arise, but they did provide a recognizable institutional framework with traditional avenues for disagreements between provincial and local governments to be solved.

VERTOOGH

VAN

Nieu-Neder-Land,

Weghens de Gheleghentheydt,
Vruchtbaerheydt, en Sobe-
ren Staet desselfs.

IN 'sGRAVEN-HAGE,

Ghedruckt by *Michiel Stael*, Bouck-verkooper woonende
op 't Buyten-Hof, tegen-over de Gevange-Poort, 1 6 5 0.

Title page of Adriaen Van der Donck's
Remonstrance of New Netherland (1650).

Conclusion

The gradual development of New Netherland from a trading post to a settlement colony is the common element in the history of its population and its government. The number of colonists grew only slowly in the first decades and their geographical origin reflected the transient character of its community, as well as its Dutch origin. "There may well be on this island of Manhatte and in its environs, four or five hundred men of different sects and nations, the Director General told me he had eighteen kinds of languages," French Jesuit Isaac Jogues wrote in the early 1640s.[14] He does not indicate which eighteen languages or dialects, nor whether he thinks this diversity was a good or a bad thing. Neither do we know in what way Willem Kieft made this remark. Was there pride in this incipient cosmopolitanism, or exasperation at the unstable community of this "motley collection (few excepted) of various countries,"[15] as Stuyvesant called it fifteen years later? The often-made statement that only half of the settlers were Dutch needs to be nuanced, though, especially as the equation of geographical origin with ethnicity, culture, or even identity, is unwarranted.

As the population of New Netherland outgrew that of a regular trading post, its governmental development lagged behind. The West India Company and its officials in the 1640s had difficulty adjusting to their new role after the abolition of the fur-trade monopoly. With the exception of Breuckelen, all local governments created before 1650 were located in English villages on Long Island. After 1650 many villages received their own jurisdiction, while some settlements never reached the required size before 1664.

The conflicts that troubled the highest officials of the West India Company show a similar development from trading post to settlement colony, mixed with the religiously infused struggle over the ultimate source of moral authority. The early quarrels of Verhulst and, to a slightly lesser extent, Minuit are typical for trading posts in which superiors had no means of quick intervention. Van Twiller's and Kieft's problems show a more complex mix of factors, with religion taking center stage in the confrontation between Kieft and Bogardus. Stuyvesant inherited from Kieft the antagonism of the colonists, but managed to outmaneuver his main opponent Van der Donck and with the grant of city rights to New Amsterdam expanded the framework of local authorities under a central provincial government, based on a recognizable Dutch model with medieval origins.

95

1

—

COLONIAL
PERIOD
AND
EIGHTEENTH
CENTURY

1609–1782

1 Jaap Jacobs, *New Netherland: A Dutch Colony in Seventeenth-Century America* (Leiden: Brill, 2005), 47-48, 132-133, 293-294.

2 Henry A. Gemery, "The White Population of the Colonial United States, 1607–1790," in Michael R. Haines and Richard H. Steckel, eds., *A Population History of North America* (Cambridge: Cambridge University Press, 2000), 155-157; Jacobs, *New Netherland*, 312-313, 333.

3 David S. Cohen, "How Dutch were the Dutch of New Netherland?" *New York History* 62 (1981): 43-60.

4 Jaap Jacobs, "Soldiers of the Company: The Military Personnel of the West India Company in New Netherland," in Herman Wellenreuther, ed., *Proceedings of the 3rd Jacob Leisler Workshop* (Göttingen: Göttingen University Press, forthcoming).

5 D.J. Wijmer, J. Folkerts, and P.R. Christoph, *Through a Dutch Door: 17th Century Origins of the Van Voorhees Family* (Baltimore: s.n., 1992); cf. Greg Roeber, "'The Origin of Whatever is not English Among us': The Dutch-Speaking and German-Speaking Peoples of Colonial British America," in Bernard Bailyn and Philip D. Morgan, eds., *Strangers within the Realm: Cultural Margins of the First British Empire* (Chapel Hill: North Carolina University Press, 1991), 220-283.

6 Jacobs, *New Netherland*, 77-83.

7 Ibid., 99.

8 Jaap Jacobs, "'To Favor This New and Growing City of New Amsterdam with a Court of Justice': The Relations between Rulers and Ruled in New Amsterdam," in George Harinck and Hans Krabbendam, eds., *Amsterdam-New York. Transatlantic Relations and Urban Identities Since 1653* (Amsterdam: VU University Press, 2005), 17-29; Jaap Jacobs, "Dutch Proprietary Manors in America: The Patroonships in New Netherland," in Lou Roper and Bertrand Van Ruymbeke, eds., *Constructing Early Modern Empires: Proprietary Ventures in the Atlantic World* (Leiden: Brill, 2007), 301-326.

9 Jacobs, *New Netherland*, 107-108.

10 Willem Frijhoff, *Fullfilling God's Mission: The Two Worlds of Dominie Everardus Bogardus, 1607–1647* (Leiden: Brill, 2007), 407, 423; Jacobs, *New Netherland*, 109-110, 275-277.

11 Jaap Jacobs, "A Troubled Man: Director Wouter van Twiller and the Affairs of New Netherland in 1635," *New York History* 85 (2004): 213-232; Frijhoff, *Fullfilling God's Mission*, 422-434.

12 Jacobs, *New Netherland*, 135-139, 278-280; Frijhoff, *Fullfilling God's Mission*, 452-461, 472-523, 550-557.

13 Jaap Jacobs, "De frustratie van Adriaen van der Donck, kolonist in Nieuw-Nederland," *Historisch Tijdschrift Holland* 31 (1999): 74-85.

14 R.P.F. Martin, *Le P. Isaac Jogues de la Compagnie de Jésus, Premier Apôtre des Iroquois*, 4th ed. (Paris: Edouard Baltenweck, 1888), 345.

15 Jacobs, *New Netherland*, 92.

ECONOMIC NETWORKS OF DUTCH TRADERS AND THE BRITISH COLONIAL EMPIRE

———

CATHY MATSON

At the opening of the seventeenth century, British colonists were just beginning to set down roots in the western hemisphere, but Dutch traders already had a full generation of experience trading goods and slaves to the Spanish and Portuguese. That experience was primarily as worldwide carriers and creditors, not as colonizers. Between 1580 and 1650 the Dutch first traded along the coastline of Portuguese Brazil and then conquered Portuguese settlements, where they hoped to produce sugar and export it to Amsterdam, but they failed to mobilize sufficient capital to sustain the efforts. Other Dutch merchants initiated slave trading into the western hemisphere, though sales were almost exclusively to foreign settlements. And although Dutch merchants tried to conquer and settle Guyana on the South American mainland, this effort also failed to prosper.

Early British-Dutch Collaborative Networks

As world-famed carriers of goods and, since the 1620s, also of slaves, Dutch merchants were uniquely poised to form collaborative networks with British traders and settlers in the New World. Dutch ships frequented the earliest British colonies in North America, and after the West India Company's monopoly had weakened and crumbled in the 1640s, individual Dutch investors and merchants were able to increase their interests in Brazilian sugar, Caribbean tobacco, slaves, and North American commodities. From the 1660s, when the British islands in the Caribbean turned emphatically toward sugar production, down to the eve of the American Revolution, Dutch investors in the home country placed more money in the Caribbean carrying trade than in any other Dutch activities in the western

1

———

COLONIAL
PERIOD
AND
EIGHTEENTH
CENTURY

1609–1782

hemisphere, even though there were comparatively few Dutch plantations and sugar mills on the islands. These investors remained important intermediaries, using systems of informal and illicit networking to elude the formal rules of the British and French empires that sought to exclude the Dutch.[1]

In Virginia, competing independent Dutch and British merchants carried tobacco to their home countries. During the 1640s when the English Civil War disrupted transatlantic English commerce, the Dutch deepened their ties to the infant colony and in 1647 the Virginia Assembly declared the Dutch "free trade" of the utmost importance to the colony's survival. At least twelve Dutch ships called at Virginia in 1648, and similar numbers came during the next few years, despite passage of the first Act of Trade and Navigation in 1651. By then, Virginians traded at Curaçao as well, hoping to fill their vessels before crossing the Atlantic, though enforcing mercantile legislation required that British naval vessels actively seize Dutch ships at Virginia. In his capacity as director general of New Netherland, Petrus Stuyvesant attempted to negotiate an agreement with Virginia in 1653, one finally signed in 1660, that arranged for continued Dutch transport from Africa of slaves so necessary for Virginia's prosperity by then. Further Navigation Acts made this trade difficult, too, by requiring that all goods leaving British colonies go to England, though a number of Dutch merchants who resided in Virginia were able to continue a modest amount of trade to their home country, where tobacco prices remained more stable than in England.[2]

A few Dutch merchants in Amsterdam also secured special permission from the English Crown to trade occasionally at Virginia. For their part, British colonists on the eastern shore such as Stephen Charleton and John Stone traded at New Netherland before 1664 and crossed to Rotterdam with tobacco that was exchanged for Dutch wine, textiles, and earthenware. Eastern shore tobacco merchants of Dutch descent had connections with colleagues in other Dutch ports in the Atlantic world, including Edmund Scarborough, William Whittington, Argoll Yardley, and William Kendall, who shared voyages to New Netherland with merchant Jacob van Sloot. Augustine Heermans lived first in New Netherland and then in Maryland; from both places he established a strong trade with Amsterdam during the 1650s and 1660s. Mixed crews of Dutch and English sailors strengthened these ties, as did the marriage alliances crossing national and geographical boundaries. Heermans's wife Anna Varleth, New Netherland's Margriet Hardenbroeck, and Virginia's Susan Moseley conducted trade between British and Dutch colonies, both during the lives of their husbands and after their deaths. As in the Netherlands, women of Dutch descent moved freely in British colonies and owned property in their own names, defying the regulations of national boundaries regularly to secure necessary credit and goods.

2. The "Half Moon" in New York Harbor.
Copyright, 1909, by Stereo-Travel Co.

Replica of the *Half Moon* (*Halve Maen*) on the Hudson River in 1909.

1

—

COLONIAL
PERIOD
AND
EIGHTEENTH
CENTURY

1609–1782

Barbados was an especially fertile ground for transnational collaboration during the early and mid-seventeenth century. Here, the Dutch were instrumental in the island's transition from meager tobacco and cotton production to swelling sugar exporting and labor importing. Crosscurrents of knowledge about the technology of sugar production joined British and Dutch investors, and by the 1640s Dutch merchants were bringing sugar mills and processing equipment from Brazil to Barbados. The migration of a few Sephardic Jews after 1645 deepened these connections. By the time the Dutch were failing in Brazil, the Lesser Antilles became a primary outlet for slave sales being removed from Brazil.

From the outpost of early New Amsterdam Dutch settlers traded not only with their home country for necessary goods, but also with a number of similarly struggling British settlements in New England, Virginia, and the West Indies. From his extensive landholdings up the Hudson River, Kiliaen van Rensselaer preferred to export much of his grain to Virginia, where there were hungry buyers who also had tobacco ready for transport to Amsterdam. But furs were far more lucrative than agricultural exports for New Netherlanders, and from the 1620s to 1650s they were used to pay for a variety of imported clothing, housewares, and foods. Although the port city numbered only about two thousand residents in these early years, merchants and West India Company employees cleared at least thirty ships from New Amsterdam a year for the Netherlands and coastal British places. By the late 1640s, ships going to Virginia, Aruba, and Curaçao carried locally made beer and imported cloth and brandy, returning with tobacco, sugar, indigo, ginger, cotton, and dyewood. Eager colonists along the Delaware River were able to negotiate occasional stop-offs of these vessels in order to sell animal hides, tobacco, and small cattle. By the 1640s, Dutch and British colonists in the West Indies bought a variety of colonial and Amsterdam goods, and sold New Amsterdam traders slaves that were taken into Virginia, Maryland, and New Netherland. [3]

This trade remained limited, however, as long as New Amsterdam's merchants relied primarily on furs for exports, the quantities of which diminished steadily after the 1640s. In addition, trade held sway over a commitment to settlement. Compared to the British, the Dutch free working population was more reluctant to migrate because employment levels and wages remained high at home in the early seventeenth century. The British, by contrast, mobilized thousands of indentured servants and free farming families to move abroad. In addition, the great Dutch merchants continued to supply manufactured commodities to the colonists of North America and the West Indies, and used their advantages of larger ships and extensive credit in Europe to haul away staple goods such as tobacco, sugar, and cotton from the southern Atlantic. Then, too, the Navigation Acts of 1651, 1663, and 1664 limited the ability of New Amsterdam merchants to carry

British colonial goods across the Atlantic. British ships could no longer sail to the West Indies after purchasing goods in the Netherlands, and goods going to the British islands were required to travel in British ships, ensuring that planters got preference in their own home markets. In formal terms, the laws undermined connections between the Caribbean and the Netherlands. But informally, a few wealthy Dutch merchants who had the ability to mobilize capital, vessels, and commodities bypassed the northerly ports altogether and made the voyage directly from southern British colonies to Amsterdam through the seventeenth century.[4]

By the time Petrus Stuyvesant relinquished his seventeen-year leadership of New Netherland to the English in 1664, Dutch residents were already expressing fears about being overwhelmed by the British commercially. Rumors held that most of the colony's trade was "petty exchange" with New Haven, Hartford, Boston, and various Chesapeake inlets. In addition, New Amsterdam merchants complained that British merchants were flocking into their port, hauling away their goods, adding English fees and duties on commerce, and demanding payment in English sterling exchange rates. But the truth was somewhat more complicated than these ethnic tensions suggest. In 1664 there were about twenty "great traders" in the port city. Ten imported large quantities of dry goods from Holland and exported most of the region's furs. Seven of them handled most of the reexports of dyewoods, cotton, sugar, and tobacco brought in from the British Caribbean. Together, all of them enjoyed strong connections with Amsterdam and, to a lesser extent, Rotterdam families, from whom they acquired cloth, hardware, and extensive credit for international trade. Moreover, some seven to eleven ships cleared Amsterdam annually for the colony, and up to thirty more touched at the port on their way to additional markets. Augustine Heermans, Oloff Stevensz van Cortlandt, Govert Loockermans, Mathias and Balthasar de Haert brothers, Jacques Cousseau, Cornelis Steenwijck, and a few other wholesale merchants at New Amsterdam cultivated extensive networks of commerce to Curaçao, Amsterdam, St. Christopher, Barbados, and coastal British ports during the final days of Dutch control over the colony and well into the first years of English control.[5]

Another layer of "middling merchants," numbering at least seventy-five, operated in this transnational networking as well. Moreover, few Dutch merchants moved away when the colony became English, and many of them adapted their commerce to new conditions with success. For the most part, new rulers and changing jurisdictions over trade routes did not disrupt many economic patterns of trade, and ethnic Dutch and British merchants in New York City together argued against mercantile restrictions imposed by British authorities and jointly defended the interests of local consumers and farmers. Even as English immigration into the colony increased by the 1690s, persistent Dutch customs and trading networks fostered collaboration across imperial identities. Although there were far fewer merchants involved in these transnational networks by the time Queen Anne's War (1702–13) ended, a few large consolidated networks of eminent families, with kinship in both empires, kept up a visible presence through the 1750s.[6]

1

———

COLONIAL
PERIOD
AND
EIGHTEENTH
CENTURY

1609–1782

Dutch Trade Eclipsed by British

In short, in every seventeenth-century Dutch arena of commerce in the western hemisphere there were abiding networks with British merchants involving credit, goods, ships, and family alliances. But this transnational collaboration altered significantly by the end of the seventeenth century, even though it was hardly less important to British North Americans and Dutch traders. For one thing, the Dutch lacked truly diverse communities large enough to sustain export production and to mature developmentally, in stark contrast to the thousands of British bound servants and willing free workers surging into prospering colonies in the Caribbean and then on the North American mainland. Bolstered, too, by an ideology of producing in the New World and transforming its environment and native peoples into an image of productive development, British migrants set themselves apart from Dutch traders, who focused on the carrying trade. By the later 1600s British North American colonies also purveyed more of their own goods, and in more colonial-built ships. But the Low Countries remained an important secondary source of textiles for the growing colonial population (England took first place by the 1720s), and the Dutch remained an important market for southern rice and northern flour. Goods coming through Amsterdam from northern Europe, especially linen, often were imported into North America directly rather than going through British ports for payment of duties. As North American populations grew, demand for textiles grew apace, and these were comparatively cheaper as smuggled commodities from Rotterdam or Amsterdam than as duties goods from mercantile-controlled English ports. Merchants' ledgers show that textiles trading accounted for a continued vital presence of the Dutch in the Atlantic world during the 1700s.

The collaborative transnational carrying trade remained profitable for a small number of merchants in each empire well into the eighteenth century. After 1680 the balance tipped emphatically toward the British planters and merchants, who overtook the Dutch in the total value and volume of commercial exchanges between the western hemisphere and the home countries. Still, Dutch carriers remained indispensable partners with British planters in the deepening sugar and slave trade. Together, they developed sophisticated means to evade British mercantile enforcement. British planters at Barbados, and the Leeward Islands welcomed Dutch captains at their ports because they were able to provide goods and slaves at lower costs, as well as reliable transportation and marine insurance rates. Though the British islands became stable enough to take over more of their own slave and sugar trade, the slave trade from Africa to Curaçao was especially important for Dutch carriers, and formed a valuable line of contact connecting Dutch and British people in the Caribbean. British governors in the Caribbean clearly understood these relationships, too. They argued at first that eliminating mercantile regulations was the best approach to this illicit transnational collaboration, since it was occurring anyway and enriched everyone concerned. But failing such an official "free trade," many island planters and merchants simply worked outside the law, accepting the opportunities of doing business with Dutch captains and Amsterdam merchants, especially those who brought textiles, dishware, and indentured servants to needy colonists.

Evidence of persistent networks of Dutch and British commerce abounds. During the eighteenth century, New Yorkers found a variety of Dutch goods advertised in their newspapers and sold in local shops, including textiles, guns, tea, and other goods available at consistently lower wholesale prices than English firms offered. Merchants' letters often cited both English and Dutch prices, and Dutch firms still offered year-long credit terms, usually without interest, to North Americans. British colonists also shipped wine from the Azores, Madeira, and the Canary Islands to Amsterdam during the 1720s and 1730s, which paid for return cargoes of dry goods to mid-Atlantic cities. These same North American merchants often took West Indian sugar to London and Amsterdam, along with colonial ginseng and potash; for their return cargoes, Amsterdam brokers offered the best marine insurance on New York- and Philadelphia-bound vessels. By the 1730s many mid-Atlantic merchants sent goods to London, where sales of their cargoes earned them credit to be forwarded to Dutch creditors, who then outfitted shipments back to North America. The four Dutch firms of Jean de Neufville & Son, John Hodshon, Daniel Crommelin & Son, and Levinus Clarkson — all of whom had worked as commission agents in British colonies before settling down in Amsterdam — kept transnational contacts for decades in the eighteenth century. Their records are filled with instructions from British colonies to purchase vessels, discount bills of exchange, forward cargoes of West Indies goods, or make money transfers for British colonists.[7]

Smuggling directly into mid-Atlantic ports from Amsterdam and Dutch West Indies islands also represented a large quantity of this transnational trade. Governors reported "many vessels lurking" near North American beaches with "Holland goods" from Amsterdam or Curaçao. By the early 1700s, imports intended for North America that originated in Barbados or St. Kitts were technically legal shipments, but merchants of different nations took on many parcels

1

—

COLONIAL
PERIOD
AND
EIGHTEENTH
CENTURY

1609–1782

from foreign islands as well, including tea, lime juice, dried fruits, and sugar. They simply reported these goods as British; some stole into North American ports "under cover of night" to evade inspection and required import duties. Safe-conduct passes were relatively easy to acquire at Dutch West Indies ports. It was "common and practical," said some merchants, to sail for Amsterdam, then carry fish to southern Europe or salt and wine to the Newfoundland fisheries, and make a return voyage through Amsterdam without paying required duties at London or in North America. New Yorkers carried Carolina rice directly to Holland, or gunpowder, cocoa, and molasses from St. Eustatius, on a regular basis without posting necessary bonds or paying taxes. By the 1730s Dutch ships stopped at New York three or four times a year with loads of tea for which captains paid a fraction of the duties and used false documents to gain entry into British ports. A number of New York merchants sent captains all the way to Honduras for logwood that was carried, without paying duties or stopping at a British port, to Amsterdam.

Through the eighteenth century, Dutch Curaçao and St. Eustatius remained important way-stations for merchants of many nations. Networks of British and Dutch merchants also mingled across lines of national origins, language, and culture at Dutch Guyana, Essequibo, and Demarara, as well as at British Barbados, Jamaica, and the Leeward Islands. Numerous British planters owned great estates at Demarara, where the blended Dutch and British populations served them as merchants, shipbuilders, retailers, and financial intermediaries. As neutral carriers, the Dutch were able to profit in supplying food and construction products to the British and French settlements, even during wars. Reports of hundreds of ships docked at Curaçao and (after 1696) St. Eustatius lend support to historians' view that the Dutch regularly transported sugar, coffee, tobacco, indigo, and island wood for British planters. At the same time, North American merchants seized the opportunity to sail for Guyana and St. Eustatius when possible, building informal arrangements into regular routes of commerce between 1700 and 1750 that relied on the open flow of goods and people around the Atlantic basin outside the barriers of mercantilism.

St. Eustatius was a truly international crossroads of trade during the second half of the eighteenth century: not only a conduit between Amsterdam and the Dutch islands, it warehoused and marketed goods of all European empires, and increasingly those to and from the British colonies in North America as well. Through the 1700s the British Leeward Islands were important stops for ships outbound from St. Eustatius, which would have been illegal trade under most circumstances since Dutch shippers did not pay duties at those British islands. By the 1750s, Dutch ships still carried goods to and from the islands of all European empires in the Caribbean, but by then it was equally significant that ships of other nations shuttled to and from St. Eustatius in their own vessels and without the credit and services of Dutch merchants. Still, through the eighteenth century, reexports of foreign colonial goods from the Dutch islands to the Netherlands was a lifeline for Dutch merchants, and by the 1750s was probably more valuable than the exports of Dutch islands directly back to the home country.

Enduring Dutch Commerce in the Western Hemisphere

The Seven Years' War (1756–63) introduced new problems to these long-term networks of British and Dutch traders, most importantly the problem of English and North American privateers preying on both enemy and neutral vessels indiscriminately. But the most successful merchandizing during these years was by the mid-Atlantic merchants who had deepened their networks at St. Eustatius and Amsterdam earlier in the century. Some shuttled goods among the various foreign islands of the West Indies despite imperial orders to stop this trade and periodic embargoes imposed by one or another foreign nation. Using false papers, and changing flags as necessary, captains carried Dutch goods in French or British ships, entering ports of major West Indies islands by bribing port collectors and tide waiters. By the Rule of 1756, the British parliament designated any neutral Dutch carriers involved in trade with French ports to be enemy vessels during the war. But North American shippers systematically ignored the law in order to trade with the West Indies and profit from supplying troops with food and munitions. Only the long-distance trade directly between the British colonies and Amsterdam diminished for the time being. Then, once the war ended, the "Hollander trade" resumed and colonists welcomed the lower prices of goods originating in Amsterdam as opposed to London. Dutch tea, taken through West Indies ports, also entered northern American port cities in large quantities through the 1760s. In 1764, for example, three vessels sailed from New York to Newfoundland, then on to Amsterdam, returning to Rhode Island with untaxed linen, sailcloth, gunpowder, tea, and bricks for North Americans.[8]

Following the Seven Years' War, only a few consolidated networks of blended British and Dutch makeup continued the transnational carrying trade. But they played a vital role in the coming revolution, both commercially and ideologically. Colonial boycotts of English imports during the Imperial Crisis, especially when concerning the widely consumed item of tea, evoked older arguments made popular by the Dutch about the evils of overly taxed and regulated trade and the virtues of free and open commerce. Until 1775, the "Holland free traders" — North American merchants of English and Dutch descent who demanded free trade — spurred revolutionary thought and action in North Amer-

1

—

COLONIAL
PERIOD
AND
EIGHTEENTH
CENTURY

1609–1782

ica, though their ardor cooled thereafter. Appeals made by revolutionaries to cease drinking tea after March 1, 1775 brought worried correspondence from Dutch merchants who tried to exempt their own commerce in tea from the revolutionary nonimportation movement — to no avail.

Even when some delegates in the American Revolutionary Congress proposed in 1775 to import military supplies from Dutch sources, couching this typically clandestine trade in patriotic language, many delegates could not agree about "placing such trust in the Dutch men." In the breech, Dutch supplies were smuggled into American ports out of pressing necessity during the opening of the war. In late 1775, Congress imposed an embargo on all American trade with the British, thereby almost guaranteeing that merchants would seek markets with Dutch West Indies islands and the Low Countries. As guns and gunpowder were brought into the revolutionary states, flaxseed, flour, and rice were sent in payment to Dutch merchants in Amsterdam.

In more officially diplomatic ways, Dutch banker Jean de Neufville helped negotiate an agreement with the American Continental Congress starting in 1778, and soon revolutionaries welcomed the infusion of cash and credit offered as a Dutch loan. In appeals to their respective governments, both American and Dutch merchants sought to strengthen this commercial alliance, but most of them did not wait for official sanctions and simply continued to take goods across dangerous waters to demanding consumers. Trade between Americans and the Dutch at St. Eustatius during the Revolution was a source of British anxieties, and eventually, British belligerence. In 1781, British naval ships overtook the island, even as some 150 merchant ships were docked and loaded along the shoreline. In the confiscations that occurred over the next couple of months, merchants of many nations lost tremendous stocks of goods and ships. Account books documenting these losses are largely in the handwriting of merchants in the long-standing transnational Dutch-American trading networks.

1   See also the article by Wim Klooster, elsewhere in this volume. Additional references are D. W. Davies, *A Primer of Dutch Overseas Trade* (The Hague: Nijhoff, 1961); and Cornelis C. Goslinga, *The Dutch in the Caribbean and on the Wild Coast, 1580–1680* (Gainesville: University of Florida Press, 1971).

2   For this and the next paragraph, see April Hatfield, *Atlantic Virginia: Intercolonial Relations in the Seventeenth*

Century (Philadelphia: University of Pennsylvania Press, 2004); and C. A. Weslager, *Dutch Explorers, Traders, and Settlers in the Delaware Valley* (Philadelphia: Temple University Press, 1961).

3   See Cathy Matson, *Merchants and Empire: Trading in Colonial New York* (Baltimore: Johns Hopkins University Press, 1998); Dennis Maika, "Commerce and Community: Manhattan Merchants in the Seventeenth Century" (Ph.D.

dissertation, New York University, 1995); and Oliver Rink, *Holland on the Hudson: An Economic and Social History of Dutch New York* (Ithaca, NY: Cornell University Press, 1986).

4   Matson, *Merchants and Empire*, chapters 2-5.

5   Ibid., chapters 1, 3; Niels Steengaard, "The Growth and Composition of the Long-Distance Trade of England and the Dutch Republic before 1750," in James D. Tracy, ed., *The Rise of Merchant Empires: Long-Distance Trade in the Early Modern World, 1350–1750* (Cambridge: Cambridge University Press, 1990), 102-153; and G. M. Welling, *The Prize of Neutrality: Trade Relations between Amsterdam and North America, 1771–1817: A Study in Computational History* (Amsterdam: University of Amsterdam, 1998).

6   Matson, *Merchants and Empire*, chapters 3-6; Cathy Matson, "The 'Hollander Interest' and Ideas about Free Trade in Colonial New York: Persistent Influences of the Dutch, 1664–1764," in Nancy Zeller and Charles T. Gehring, eds., *A Beautiful and Fruitful Place* (Albany, NY: New Netherland Publishing, 1991), 251-268; and Charles Wilson, *Anglo-Dutch Commerce and Finance in the Eighteenth Century*, 2nd ed. (London: Longmans, 1966).

7   For this and the following two paragraphs, see Matson, *Merchants and Empire*, chapter 1; Rink, *Holland on the Hudson*.

8   For this and the following three paragraphs, see Matson, *Merchants and Empire*, chapters 6-7.

1

▬

COLONIAL
PERIOD
AND
EIGHTEENTH
CENTURY

1609–1782

108

THE WANING OF
DUTCH NEW YORK

▬

SIMON MIDDLETON

Introduction

By the early 1660s New Netherland's population of some eight thousand souls was dispersed among remote small holdings and a handful of villages scattered across Long Island and along the Hudson and Delaware rivers. More than half of New Amsterdam's fifteen hundred free male settlers, West India Company officials, and soldiers had arrived in the previous decade, many seeking opportunities in the increasingly prosperous seaport town. The wharf bustled with the comings and goings of sloops, barques, and larger ocean-going vessels: boatmen, porters, and carters unloaded cargoes of grain and furs from upriver settlements and tobacco dispatched by the planters of Virginia and Maryland; municipal officials scrutinized products for quality and levied whatever duties were payable to the Company or the town; packed in locally manufactured hogsheads and barrels, the colonial products were shipped to the Dutch Republic to be exchanged for the blankets, kettles, hatchets, and knives taken by the Indians in trade, and for household necessaries and luxuries retailed to the colonists. The reconciling of earlier disagreements between patroons, free settlers, and the West India Company had transformed the once misfiring colonial administration into a more or less harmonious provincial government. Under the watchful eye of Petrus Stuyvesant New Netherlanders balanced private pursuits with the public good and carved out a niche for the colony in the Company's Atlantic trade. In New Amsterdam, after years of uncertainty, the burghers celebrated their prosperity: the many fine houses built by local tradesmen, the envy of their English neighbors, and the three militia companies that defended the community.

The transformation of New Netherland from a handful of isolated trading posts to a dynamic settler society occurred incrementally and in response to the demands of the New World environment. One of the earliest and most telling demands had been for immigrants to secure the Company's claim to the land. It was to attract these settlers that the Company relinquished its monopoly of the fur trade and offered farmland on liberal terms to any who would come, drawing in hundreds of English Puritans from Massachusetts and Connecticut. Thus, as early as the 1640s New Netherland was a polyglot territory comprising immigrants from across northern Europe, a bare majority of whom hailed from the Netherlands. Given the Company's authority and the origin of most of the settlers, the colony's governance and institutions bore the unmistakable imprint of Dutch civic, Protestant, and republican mores. And yet the familiarity of Reformed religious practice and civic institutions to settlers from other northern European communities provided New Netherland with the foundation for a broad-based consensus. Despite the occasional flaring of dissent, mostly from the more zealous Puritans on Long Island, the colony developed into an inclusive community in which migrants from diverse backgrounds traded and established homes. The public culture of the Dutch Republic and the rights and privileges it guaranteed to individuals and communities operated as a centripetal force binding together settlers from disparate origins. This essay is concerned with the waning of this colonial adaptation of Dutch civic and republican traditions.

Economic, Political, and Ethnic Changes under English Rule

For even as the burghers of New Amsterdam celebrated their success, New Netherland attracted the attention of Englishmen envious of Dutch imperial success. In the spring of 1664 Charles II granted his brother James, the Duke of York, a charter for the territory comprising New Netherland. In May the duke dispatched Colonel Richard Nicolls and three hundred soldiers, who landed at the west end of Long Island and marched west to the ferry station across from New Amsterdam. The colonists quickly assented to Nicolls's lenient Articles of Capitulation; smaller detachments of English forces accepted the surrender of Beverwijck and, when they encountered resistance at New Amstel, plundered the settlement and sold its defenders into slavery in Virginia. However, the swift and easy conquest belies the fact that established Dutch institutions and practices remained influential for a long period. In spite of this, social, economic, and political changes over the longer term gradually supplanted the Dutch civic and republican culture and integrated New York into the British Empire. In part, this followed a determined effort by imperial overseers to Anglicize the newest North American colony. More often, however, change followed as the unintended consequence of the same commercial, demographic, and cultural processes that affected colonial communities throughout the English Atlantic. Even in

109

1

COLONIAL
PERIOD
AND
EIGHTEENTH
CENTURY

1609–1782

the thirty years after the conquest, for example, the export of farm produce to English and plantation markets supplanted the colony's exhausted trade in furs. Similarly, as migration from the Dutch Republic slowed and some among the Dutch left to establish farms and families in East and West Jersey, New York attracted immigrants from France, Germany, and especially England; the growing population also purchased more slaves, who comprised seven hundred of New York City's forty-five hundred residents by the 1690s. As the eighteenth century progressed New Yorkers became increasingly prominent players in an interdependent commercial empire, taking their bearings from English rather than Dutch political and cultural styles. Commerce, immigration, slavery, and European cultural influences had all played their part in New Netherland's early history. But it was in the century after 1664 that these factors gave rise to novel forms of social and economic inequalities and struggles that shaped the dynamic and contentious culture of the emerging Empire State.

Richard Nicolls and his successors were military men occupied with the defense of imperial borders and the movement of the French and hostile Indians to the north. Consequently, they relied on New York's merchant elite to manage trade and collect the duties needed to pay for the costs of government and the duke's emolument. The partnership produced winners and losers. Directing agricultural exports and imported goods through the main port at New York City bolstered urban trade and employment and provided for the easy collection of duties. The minimal amendments made to the existing municipal government reassured city dwellers of Nicolls's benign intentions. Provincial towns and villages, however, rankled under the centralization of authority and the favoring of the city. The clearest victors were the Dutch merchants — men such as Stephanus van Cortlandt, Cornelis Steenwyck, and the carpenter-made-good Frederick Philipse — who embraced English rule and reaped hefty financial rewards. The only threat to this mutually beneficial partnership came from a group of English traders who settled in the city following the end of the Third Anglo-Dutch War (1672–74) and who resented the advantages of their Dutch competitors. The rivalry soon passed, however, and as the imperial authorities pushed on with heavy-handed reforms intended to secure English rule in New York and the wider region, a powerful Anglo-Dutch oligarchy comprised of merchants and landowners such as Lewis Morris, Robert Livingston, Philipse, and Van Cortlandt tightened its grip on the provincial import and export trade. In 1689 the combination of overbearing governance, economic distress, and an international crisis sparked by the Glorious Revolution in England pitched the colony into a rebellion named for the man who emerged as its unlikely leader.

Leisler's Rebellion and its aftermath have long provided grist for the interpretive mills of students of the society and economy in early New York. It was once common to emphasize economic discontents arising from declining trade, rising taxes, and the engrossing of urban wealth by a well-connected merchant elite to explain the breakdown of royal rule; some even discerned an implied challenge to economic and political inequalities in the revolt.[1] There is reason, however, to question this attribution of socially leveling or ethnic motives to the rebels who focused on the defense of the privileges and autonomy of provincial communities and the Protestant religion. The protean quality of ethnic loyalties belies the confidence of claims made on behalf of monolithic "Dutch" and "English" identities. And the postrebellion turmoil, in particular, more likely reflected the reaction of the anti-Leislerian elite to the reorientation of provincial politics from an oligarchic Dutch to an English electoral model. Provincial merchants and landlords benefited from the patronage of the Tory Governor Benjamin Fletcher (1692–97), who restored royal rule and lavished land grants on favored counselors including Van Cortlandt, Philipse, and Lewis Morris. However, as the discredited opponents of the popularly supported Leislerian regime, this same elite lacked the constituency necessary to swing elections and control city and provincial government. Facing antagonists with overwhelming, if poorly organized, backing the elite resorted to the politics of prejudice. Accusing opponents of favoring Dutch over English interests, they generated a documentary trail of "ethnic conflict," which petered out once they secured the necessary electoral support in the early eighteenth century. In this respect, Leisler's Rebellion and its aftermath witnessed a struggle between middle-class working inhabitants whose survival depended, at least in part, on rights and privileges established during the Dutch era, and a class of ambitious merchants, landlords, and royal officials eager to deploy the emerging military-fiscal English state in pursuit of their ambitions. In the early eighteenth century Dutch and other residents dedicated themselves to commerce, electing to accommodate rather than contest the interests of this Anglicized provincial elite. In defiance of the passion for party politics that raged in Queen Anne's England and neighboring colonies, New York's elections were relatively lackluster affairs.

Provincial commerce grew in fits and starts: warfare between 1689 and 1697 produced economic stagnation; recessions followed a devastating outbreak of yellow fever in 1702 and the renewal of Anglo-French hostilities in Queen Anne's War (1702–13); hard times hit shipbuilding and provincial trade again in the early 1720s. In spite of these difficulties the colony prospered on the back of Europe's insatiable appetite for West Indian sugar and the concomitant demand for timber, food, and clothing to house and provision plantation slaves. In the city an influx of English and French traders augmented second- and third-generation merchant families, enhancing local contacts in London, Amsterdam, and Barbados. Englishmen such as Richard Willet and Caleb Heathcote and French Huguenots such as Stephen Delancey, Benjamin Faneuil, and Elias Boudinot

1

—

COLONIAL
PERIOD
AND
EIGHTEENTH
CENTURY

1609–1782

rubbed shoulders with sons of established merchant families including Adolph Philipse, Isaac de Peyster, and Jeremiah Tothill. Upriver, landowners such as the Morrises employed slave and tenant labor in agriculture and the Livingstons, Van Cortlandts, and Roosevelts all tried their hand at sugar refining and the production of naval stores. Marriage between prominent families and across ethnoreligious communities was common and ensured that the merchant and landed gentry retained control of the commanding heights of the economy. The broader provincial prosperity depended more on the activities of numerous lesser merchants and petty traders, who connected middle-class agricultural producers along the Hudson River and on Long Island through the port to other colonial and Caribbean communities. In the absence of a sufficient supply of coined money to support this complex and ramified trade, credit quickly became the lifeblood of the local and regional economy.

When registering for the freemanship or being assessed for taxes, the majority of New York City's free European workforce professed to follow a skilled occupation, frequently one of the core trades of tailor, blacksmith, brickmaker, carpenter, carter, mariner, cooper, or cordwainer. However, the uncertain market for colonial manufactures and easy availability of credit from merchants eager to secure the specie that came to the hands of artisans and farmers encouraged these middle-class residents to set up as petty dealers. Thus, builders bought and sold beer and brewers traded bricks and timber and, over time, the pursuit of marginal gain through commodity trades fostered a network of client-patron exchange and credit relations. The lure of an independent life was such that few could be persuaded to work for hire, leading to a shortage of laborers and wage inflation that the young Cadwallader Colden opined "overballances all the advantages which the country naturally affords." Labor shortages encouraged New Yorkers to turn to slavery. As early as the turn of the eighteenth century, 40 percent of urban households owned at least one slave, giving the city a demographic profile more akin to communities in the plantation Chesapeake than other coastal towns such as Boston and Philadelphia. African workers resisted the degradation of their labor, most notably in 1712 in an abortive conspiracy that sent shockwaves through the colony. In time, however, Europeans became accustomed to differentiating between the independence of free "white" laborers and the dependence and servility of "black" slave labor. By the early 1720s, according to Colden, the colonists' sense of their independence within the empire constituted the "surest tye she [England] has upon the affections of the people in the Plantations . . . where the native English are less in number than Foreigners French and Dutch." For the moment at least, the polyglot community "think themselves happy under the English Liberty."[2]

With the arrival of new settlers from diverse European and West Indian origins the proportion of the population who could claim Dutch ancestry diminished. The 1707 French invasion of the Rhineland inspired an exodus of refugees from the German Palatinate, some twenty-five hundred of whom came to New York. They were joined in their hunt for land and new lives by hundreds of families of Scots-Irish Presbyterians, descendants of those driven by poverty to settle the northern counties of seventeenth-century Ireland. Thousands more Roman Catholics, similarly stirred by straitened circumstances, migrated to America, some opting to settle in New York. By 1730 city slaves numbered almost twenty-five hundred, approximately one-fifth of the urban population. Dutch settlers clung on to their majority in isolated communities on Long Island, New Jersey, and up the Hudson at Albany. In the city, although visitors continued to remark upon Dutch buildings and influences, their share of the population fell below 50 percent. Equally noteworthy, while prominent merchants such as Rip van Dam, Abraham de Peyster, and Jacobus van Cortlandt prospered and their countrymen clung on to their dominance in certain occupations — especially coopers, smiths, masons, and cartmen — most residents of Dutch ancestry lived in the poorer neighborhoods, paid less tax, and held proportionately fewer public appointments than their more recently established English and French neighbors. One could point to a variety of factors to account for the diminishing Dutch influence: the exodus of ambitious families to the status-conscious Anglican congregation; the surge of Pietism (later, the Great Awakening) that undermined the liturgical formalism and vitality of the Dutch Reformed Church; the propensity to ethnic insularity that led, for example, Dutch artisans to recruit apprentices mostly from within their own community. Yet the likeliest explanation remains the sheer weight of numbers: by the third decade of the eighteenth century English residents comprised almost half of the city's population, and the proportion of those claiming Dutch ancestry had fallen to less than two-fifths; over the next twenty years this latter figure halved again to less than one-fifth.

New York's Economic Crisis and Its Consequences

It is common for historians to highlight crucial periods or decades in long-term social and economic developments. For eighteenth-century New York it was the 1730s and the impact of an extended commercial slump. The core problem was the rise of Pennsylvanian and Bermudian suppliers who competed with New Yorkers in the supply of foodstuffs to the plantation colonies. By the winter of 1730 all indices suggested that the city's maritime business was in crisis: the locally owned merchant fleet had shrunk to fifty vessels, fewer than half the number at the turn of the eighteenth century; imports of slaves and commodities had fallen to their lowest level in more than a decade; shipyards languished

1

———

COLONIAL
PERIOD
AND
EIGHTEENTH
CENTURY

1609–1782

for want of commissions and construction sites across the city fell silent. But what transformed this business downturn into a protracted slump from which the colony would not recover until the late 1730s was the collapse of the credit system that had hitherto provided the liquidity for urban, and therefore provincial, trade. By 1730 the majority of city families possessed minimal taxable assets and relied on petty trading, day labor, and credit to survive. Whenever commercial fortunes took a turn for the worse, or borrowers gave the impression of planning to leave town, nervous creditors trooped to court to recover what was owed. When a smallpox epidemic hit the city in 1731–32, claiming five hundred lives and forcing hundreds more to flee, the death or departure of a substantial section of the middle-class and borrowing sort sent shock waves through credit networks. Lenders scrambled to recover what they could, poor laws were liberalized to assist unfortunate debtors, and business confidence and investment collapsed bringing the economy to a standstill. News of the credit crunch and the 150 fashionable homes available for rent in New York City circulated as far away as Boston and Philadelphia.

The story of the decade's political machinations, pitting a greedy and arrogant governor against ambitious and unprincipled provincial politicians, is well known and oft-told. But in addition to high political drama, the decade also marked a watershed in the fortunes of the city's artisans, in which class interests trumped ethnic loyalties. In the early years of the recession city politics was awakened by workers' campaigns for protectionist measures such as the suspension of rawhide exports and an end to imports of barrels and bread. For the first time in thirty years, upriver and city politicians competed for the support of an animated urban constituency and the Dutch vote, particularly in the city's North Ward, was crucial to campaign against the hated governor, William Cosby. The Leislerians had been galvanized by fears for the security of civic rights and the Protestant faith. In the 1730s protestors marched in the name of popular rights and identified political corruption and market manipulation as the source of their woes. In a series of bitterly contested municipal and assembly elections urban workers, particularly the middle-class and poorer Dutch tradesmen, flocked to the opposition's ranks and railed against those who employed slave labor insisting that "Negroes may be supprest of having the Benefit of poor Laborers and Tradesmen."[3] When fortunes lifted toward the end of the decade, however, the better-off artisans, English and Dutch, abandoned the popular party for their erstwhile opponents. The crisis of the 1730s highlighted the diminishing influence of ethnoreligious loyalties over class priorities. It also introduced the language of radical English Whiggism to provincial politics and, although it was never the intention of its sponsors among provincial elite, in time this language would challenge the aristocratic government favored by those who thought of themselves as the "better sort."

Socioeconomic Impact of New York's Growth

Political contests in the colony's rural hinterland up the Hudson Valley, on Long Island, and across the river in New Jersey centered on the ownership and use of land. By 1710 a handful of English, Dutch, and Scottish landlords controlled great swathes of the region's choicest tillage, much of it bestowed in the aftermath of Leisler's Rebellion: the Livingstons boasted one hundred sixty thousand acres, the Philipses two hundred thousand, and the Van Rensselaers had parlayed their long-established patroon rights into more than one million acres; in New Jersey, Scottish Presbyterian landlords also managed large tracts. Eager to join the mushrooming trade in the supply of timber and farm products to Europe and the plantation colonies, landlords relied on tenants from diverse ethnoreligious backgrounds to cultivate their farms. But there was something far more important than wealth at stake in this relationship. By providing for the landlords' status and financial independence, the estates also backed their claim to constitute a governing gentry. As enlightened members of eighteenth-century society, the provincial elite agreed that all men were driven by natural appetites and passions, which only those of wealth and standing possessed the necessary virtue and refinement to overcome. Able to restrain the passions that drove ordinary men, the gentry employed their reason to discern the public good and govern well. This core assumption rationalized contemporary inequalities and justified the ideal of patrician rule over deferential plebeians. In the hands of the Delanceys, Morrises, and Livingstons these principles could be marshaled, conservatively, in justification of monarchical and, radically, in defense of colonial rights against an overbearing executive. What they could not bear was opposition from below and, in particular, the proposition that the plebs might also possess virtue and reason enough to participate in the appointment and scrutiny of those who presumed to govern them. It was against this ideological background, with its roots in early modern and classical political thought, that landlord and tenant struggled for control of the land.

   Although formally powerful and possessing considerable provincial influence, in practice the landlords depended a great deal on their tenants' loyalty and support. The ill-defined and porous character of colonial boundaries, particularly between New York and southern New England, provoked competitive claims to lands that were frequently subject to multiple patents and Indian sales stretching back many years. Such disputes weakened New York landlords' claims to remote and undeveloped lands unless settled by trustworthy tenants. The diversity of the tenant population also made for challenges to the authority of landlords from different ethnoreligious backgrounds: even as New Jersey's Presbyterian proprietors endeavored to recreate the hierarchical social struc-

115

1

—

COLONIAL
PERIOD
AND
EIGHTEENTH
CENTURY

1609–1782

ture of eastern Scotland, they were resisted by New England Congregationalists and members of the Dutch Reformed Church. Most important of all, the contest between landlords and tenants for control of agricultural production and the latter's sense of entitlement to land that they farmed, sometimes for generations, made for a fraught relationship. When tenants launched formal proceedings protesting against higher rents or restriction on the use of common land, landlords relied on their political connections to win the day. Yet their dependence on tenant loyalties also required a paternalistic approach, tolerating low yields and indebtedness and even suffering protests that flew in the face of deferential ideals from all but the most grievous of challengers. In this recurring struggle over land rights and in periodic rebellions prosecuted through the 1730s–1770s, the multiethnic tenants articulated a radical conception of landownership derived from use and improvement, and tied this popular ownership to equally novel claims for liberty and political representation of the common man.

In the 1740s and 1750s New York City boomed once again as city merchants and tradesmen agreed on contracts for the construction of new ships and provisioning of the imperial armies engaged in King George's War with Spain (1739–45) and the French and Indian War (1757–63). The profits from these and other ventures permitted wealthy New Yorkers to participate in the pursuit of a genteel lifestyle. They commissioned houses in the latest, Georgian style; they dressed in metropolitan fashions and socialized at concerts featuring popular composers such as Handel and Bach. It was not only the upper classes who developed a fascination for consumer goods and refined pursuits. The return of prosperity also encouraged artisans and shopkeepers to elevate ordinary activities — dressing, eating, and tea drinking — to new levels of sophistication. Gentility posited a clear demarcation between the refined and the rough. But it was a distinction that depended more on acquirable manners and possessions than on inherited estate. Consumption and the pursuit of gentility gave middle-class residents status and pleasure. It also gave them the freedom to fashion the self and, in so doing, subvert once fixed and rigid social hierarchies. Beneath this elite and aspirant middle-class sort, however, gathered a motley proletariat of mariners, servants, and slaves. They were more likely to dine on oysters and mussels harvested for free from the shore of the East River than the turtle soup and pastries of polite society. Between 1740 and 1770 ten thousand immigrants pitched up in New York City, double the number of arrivals since the turn of the eighteenth century. The influx of newcomers gave the city the highest rate of growth of any community in North America, just as a last great struggle for European control of North America provided them with jobs amid the ranks of wage workers and the laboring poor.

A portrait of a member of the eighteenth-century New York gentry with
Dutch forbears, Abraham Keteltas Beekman (1756–1816).

1

—

COLONIAL
PERIOD
AND
EIGHTEENTH
CENTURY

1609–1782

"War is declared in England — Universal joy among the merchants," wrote William Smith in his diary early in 1756. And all the evidence confirms Benjamin Franklin's assessment that the outbreak of the Seven Years' War made New York "immensely rich, by Money brought into it from all Quarters for the Pay and Subsistence of the Troops."[4] In 1750 the city's merchant fleet had comprised 157 vessels and a combined tonnage of 6,400 tons; twelve years later, on the eve of England's victory over the French, it had tripled to 477 vessels and 19,500 tons. In the first two years of the war provincial ships seized enemy cargoes valued at two million pounds. The growth of individual fortunes was no less staggering. In 1754 the twenty-two-year-old James Beeckman (great-grandson of Willem Beeckman, who in 1647 came to New Amsterdam aboard *The Princess,* with Petrus Stuyvesant) imported English goods to the value of fifteen hundred pounds sterling. Within a year, and following the designation of the city as "general Magazine of Arms and Military Stores," his imports rose to more than ten thousand pounds. On the strength of his new-found wealth, Beeckman commissioned the building of a stunning mansion, Mount Pleasant, on the East River close to modern-day Fifty-First Street. Yet the boom driven by military contracts also left sections of the laboring poor behind and, what was worst, raised the expectations of many more before decimating middle-class-family fortunes when the fighting moved south in the closing stages of the war. Even as Beeckman picked out the furniture from the latest English style for his new house, his neighbors from the middle and lower ranks contemplated unemployment, hunger, and revolt against an overbearing and heartless imperial regime.

Conclusion

In 1664 transplanted and adapted Dutch institutions and practices had bound together the vulnerable colony of New Netherland: notions of citizenship, community, and government and the colony's commercial, legal, and political culture all bore the imprint of the mores of the United Provinces. The familiarity of these civic and republican traditions to settlers hailing from other European communities and, perhaps more important, the security they promised encouraged a diverse and polyglot community to identify with Dutch privileges and liberties. The beginning of the end for Dutch New York came with the English conquest and the colony's subsequent absorption into the burgeoning British Empire. In some respects, such as the reform of provincial political and legal institutions, this was driven by a determined effort to Anglicize the colony. The effect of these purposeful imperial reforms, however, was outweighed by anonymous social and economic developments that fostered novel social distinctions of race and class and differentiated between the upper, middle, and lower classes. In the 1760s and 1770s, farmers in the Hudson Valley and New Jersey and artisans in New York City combined protests against material inequalities with calls for political reform and improved representation, driving New York into rebellion with likeminded patriots against the mighty British Empire. In isolated hamlets and farming families the influence of Dutch language and culture remained strong. By the eve of the American Revolution the vigor of the practices and traditions that once defined Dutch New York had waned to the point at which they survived only as nostalgia. Claims to particularistic and once determining Dutch privileges were drowned out by new, general, and increasingly louder cries on behalf of the universal rights of men.

1   Simon Middleton, *From Privileges to Rights: Work and Politics in Colonial New York City* (Philadelphia: University of Pennsylvania Press, 2006). Bernard Mason, "Aspects of the New York Revolt of 1689," *New York History* 30 (January 1949): 165-180; Jerome K. Reich, *Leisler's Rebellion: A Study of Democracy in New York, 1664–1720* (Chicago: University of Chicago Press, 1953).

2   "Mr. Colden's Account of the Trade of New York, 1723," in E. B. O'Callaghan and Berthold Fernow, eds., *Documents Relative to the Colonial History of New York*, 15 vols. (Albany, NY, 1856–87), 5:688.

3   *Journal of The Votes and Proceedings of the General Assembly of the Colony of New York* (New York, 1764), 1:723.

4   Edwin Burrows and Mike Wallace, *Gotham. A History of New York City to 1898* (New York: Oxford University Press, 1999), 168.

1

COLONIAL
PERIOD
AND
EIGHTEENTH
CENTURY

1609–1782

THE SOCIAL AND CULTURAL LIFE OF DUTCH SETTLERS, 1664–1776

JOYCE D. GOODFRIEND

Introduction

The history of the Dutch in America between 1664, when New Netherland was seized by the English, and the declaration of American independence in 1776, unfolded in the English colonies of New York and New Jersey. After the change in government, the great majority of New Netherland's settlers chose to remain in the communities they had carved out on Manhattan, in the Hudson Valley, and on western Long Island. Though they became subjects of the English Crown, they continued to speak Dutch, worship at the Dutch Reformed Church, and perpetuate Dutch customs. Many still thought of themselves as fundamentally Dutch for more than a century.[1]

The Dutch West India Company governed New Netherland for only forty years, but this was time enough for Dutch institutions to be planted in the territory and for the Europeans of diverse origins who made up the colony's population to grow accustomed to conducting their lives in ways reminiscent of the Netherlands. In the generations that followed the English takeover, farmers and artisans in rural areas and traders in Albany renewed the social patterns and cultural practices with which they were familiar. Even when they relocated to new towns in New Jersey at the turn of the eighteenth century, Dutch farmers displayed little eagerness for change, recreating agricultural communities resembling the ones they had left in Flatbush and Brooklyn. Only in the urban center of New York City, where English dominance was established more rapidly, did significant numbers of descendants of New Netherlanders depart from the ways of their ancestors.[2] There, close contact with the English in the economic and civic arenas led well-to-do and ambitious Dutch men to embrace key elements of English culture. Urban dwellers lower down the social scale and most women, however, tended to hold fast to Dutch traditions.

Factors Supporting a "Dutch" Way of Life

The way of life that took root in New Netherland and was elaborated in the later seventeenth century remained remarkably intact through the first two-thirds of the eighteenth century in all the areas of Dutch settlement outside New York City. The persistence of Dutch social forms and cultural practices in English territory for so many generations is attributable to several interrelated factors. Although often overlooked, the adoption of a hands-off policy by English authorities was crucial to this outcome. Efforts to promote Dutch conversions to Anglicanism through the agency of the Society for the Propagation of the Gospel in Foreign Parts (SPG) notwithstanding, English officials did not prevent the Dutch Reformed Church from expanding to meet the religious needs of the growing population of Dutch in New York and New Jersey. Nor did English authorities intrude into Dutch community life. Not faced with a coercive cultural policy, Dutch colonists could follow in the footsteps of their progenitors.

Given the latitude to control their private lives, worship in their own way, and educate their children, Dutch families opted to cluster in rural villages composed of people whose personal histories resembled their own. When the supply of land could no longer accommodate the numerous offspring of the residents of the agricultural communities on western Long Island at the turn of the eighteenth century, they moved to newly founded towns in northern and central New Jersey, where they reproduced the homogeneous Dutch communities in which they had been nurtured. Surrounded by like-minded people and insulated from English influence, Dutch farming families were free to perpetuate the customs and habits of their forbears.

The fidelity of latter-day New Netherlanders to the ways of their predecessors can also be traced to the virtual halt of immigration from the Netherlands to North America after English rule had been established along the eastern seaboard. Though trade continued between New York and Amsterdam and a few newcomers of Dutch origin trickled in from Europe and the Dutch colonies of Curaçao and Suriname, the Dutch settlers of New York and New Jersey were largely cut off from the society and culture of their ancestral land. During the century following the shift in government, their communities grew almost entirely by natural increase. Endogamous marriages led to the formation of large Dutch clans that became progressively more intertwined as the generations passed. When non-Dutch individuals were chosen as marriage partners,

121

1

—

COLONIAL
PERIOD
AND
EIGHTEENTH
CENTURY

1609–1782

they were incorporated into the Dutch family circles. The strong kinship bonds uniting families with origins in New Netherland strengthened the impulse to conserve the traditions that had taken root there.

This is not to say that the Dutch colonists of New York and New Jersey were entirely cut off from contact with the evolving culture of the Netherlands. Individuals corresponded with people in the homeland, but letter writing was largely limited to men — primarily merchants, ministers, and congregational lay leaders. Personal contact was rarer, though occasionally local ship captains and merchants voyaged to the homeland. For most colonists, exposure to the culture of the Dutch metropole was confined to interactions with people recently arrived from the Netherlands, such as ministers and traders, or reading imported printed material. In short, the flow of ideas across the ocean was sporadic and unpredictable.

Because communication with the United Provinces was neither routine nor sustained, especially in the eighteenth century, the provincial Dutch culture of New York and New Jersey was not systematically replenished by new currents of thought. Developing in relative isolation, it diverged from mainstream Dutch culture in Europe. Instances of Dutch Reformed clergymen arriving in densely settled Dutch neighborhoods of New York and New Jersey and finding that their language was largely unintelligible to residents who spoke what amounted to a Dutch dialect, graphically illustrate the deviation of Dutch-American culture from that of the Netherlands. Complicating the cultural profile even further, distinct versions of Dutch culture emerged in the Hudson Valley, on Long Island, and in New Jersey, the three main areas of Dutch settlement in the English colonies of North America, due to the limited contact between residents of these regions.

Family, Church, and Printed Materials

The primary agencies for the transmission of Dutch values over the generations in America were the family, the Reformed Church, and print culture. Each worked to perpetuate Dutch language, customs, and beliefs. Families were at the center of every Dutch colonial community in America. The nuclear family was the fundamental unit of economic production, the crucible of cherished relationships, and the site of religious devotion. It was where the fabric of Dutch-American identity was woven.

Though men were the titular heads of the often large families, women played a pivotal role in them as economic partners and managers of the domestic domain. Inheritance practices transplanted from the Netherlands supplied the legal basis for the power exercised by women in family governance, and custom reinforced their responsibilities in the area of child care.[3] Not least, women were the conservators of Dutch traditions. As cooks, they reproduced and elaborated the New Netherland diet that originated in the combination of Old and New World ingredients. As keepers of the household, they orchestrated the celebration of religious holidays such as *Pasen* (Easter) and *Pinksteren* (Pentecost). And as mothers, they instilled in their daughters and sons the language and religious beliefs that stood at the core of their identity as Dutch people.

Women were largely responsible for the fact that children of successive generations retained Dutch as their native language, since they taught them their ABCs along with the rudiments of Reformed doctrine. In the rural areas of New York and New Jersey, mastering the English language was not essential to gaining a livelihood. Since the family's economic well-being did not depend on the acquisition of English, the bits of English that adult males picked up in their interactions in the larger society remained superfluous in the family environment, where wives and mothers held sway. Even after sons and daughters had learned some English, private conversations continued to be held in Dutch.

Because Dutch was ordinarily spoken in the home, it also became the language of the involuntary members of many Dutch colonial families: enslaved Africans.[4] Slaveholding differentiated Dutch colonial families from their counterparts in the Netherlands, but the terms on which Dutch colonial farmers incorporated slaves into their households reflected the values of the homeland. By perpetuating a paternalistic model of family organization that, in their minds, mitigated the worst features of slavery, they assumed that they were not violating social norms. Dutch Americans shared their homes, work, meals, and values with the African Americans whom they claimed to own. The extent to which enslaved African Americans absorbed the elements of Dutch family culture remains debatable. Their proficiency in the Dutch language, observed by travelers and documented in advertisements for runaway slaves, leaves little doubt of the influence exerted on them by their masters. In the realm of religion, however, the evidence is mixed, since African Americans often were prevented from participating in Reformed Church rituals.

The Dutch-American home was a spiritual center, where prayers were said before meals, Biblical tiles lined the hearth, and the Great Dutch Bible, the *Statenbijbel*, occupied an honored place. Reading of the Bible as well as other religious works took place in the home. The Reformed faith was practiced by the family in the domestic arena but it also was displayed to the community every Sabbath at the local Reformed church.

The Dutch Reformed church was the centerpiece of most Dutch communities in New York and New Jersey. Under the governance of the Classis of Amsterdam until 1772, Reformed churches were the main conduit for communication with the fatherland. Here, men and women of Dutch families rehearsed the

123

1

———

COLONIAL
PERIOD
AND
EIGHTEENTH
CENTURY

1609–1782

doctrines established at the Synod of Dort and received guidance for conducting their daily lives. Dutch-speaking dominees delivered lengthy sermons, every Sunday, to remind their audiences that spiritual matters transcended material comforts. Though the style and message of some eighteenth-century preachers diverged from the orthodoxy typical of seventeenth-century sermon givers, and members of the laity became involved in heated church disputes, the overall experience of churchgoing was integral to the lives of Dutch Americans.

Catering as they did to Dutch families, Dutch Reformed churches were ambivalent in their treatment of blacks. Whether delegated to bring heated foot stoves to keep their mistresses warm in their pews or allotted time to witness worship from segregated seating, enslaved African Americans were kept at the fringes of congregational life. Although in the early years of New Netherland's history people of African descent had been included in New Amsterdam's Dutch Reformed church, where many were married and baptized, church policy had changed even before the advent of English rule, with the result that most African-American members of Dutch households were denied religious sanction for their major life events. Additionally, they were excluded from the church-sponsored catechism classes that taught Dutch children the fundamentals of their faith through lessons in the Heidelberg Catechism. There, schoolmasters employed by the congregation reinforced the language and beliefs boys and girls had imbibed at home.[5]

A minority of Dutch settlers in New York and New Jersey were Lutherans. In churches in New York City, Albany, the Hudson Valley, and New Jersey, they practiced their version of Protestantism assisted by the consistory of the Amsterdam Lutheran Church, which supplied them with bibles, hymn books, and catechisms in the Dutch language. Lutheran congregations also included African slaves, whom they treated more equitably than their counterparts in the Dutch Reformed churches.

The Dutch language was of vital importance to both Dutch Reformed and Dutch Lutheran worshippers in America. This was vividly illustrated in conflicts over the language of worship in both churches in mid-eighteenth-century New York City. When German immigrants attempted to introduce their language into worship, a hard core of Dutch Lutherans resisted mightily, eventually resulting in the formation of a German Lutheran congregation in the city. In New York's Dutch Reformed congregation, the initiative to call an English-speaking preacher came from acculturated gentlemen who feared the loss of members to other churches where English ministers presided.[6] They encountered substantial opposition from a cohort of ordinary Dutch men and women who argued passionately that language and faith were interlocked.

This debate over the language of preaching raised a crucial issue. Could one identify as Dutch in British America without speaking the language of the homeland? Members of the city's Dutch elite argued that introducing English-language preaching was a practical measure meant to ensure the perpetuation of the Dutch religious community in an English society. Accommodating to the majority culture was not surrendering the fundamentals of faith. It was selectively adopting aspects of English culture in order to sustain fundamental Dutch Reformed beliefs. The English faction carried the day with the support of the Amsterdam Classis, but not without earning the enmity of the Dutch traditionalists in the congregation.

Instruction in English was mandated from the beginning at Queen's College (later Rutgers University), the institution of higher learning sponsored by the Dutch Reformed Church, in New Brunswick, NJ. To compete with the other denominational colleges in British America, the founders realized that fluency in English was essential for its students. The 1770 college charter also stipulated that "all minutes of the meetings and transactions of the trustees, and all rules, orders and regulations, relating to the government of the … college … shall be in the English language."[7] If the Dutch language was to be a casualty in the search for educational parity, the price was deemed acceptable if the accumulated wisdom of generations of Dutch Reformed theologians was preserved and passed on.

For many descendants of New Netherlanders in eighteenth-century America, and especially those living in rural communities and Albany, jettisoning the Dutch language was akin to cultural suicide. Language was regarded as the repository of cultural beliefs. For these people, even acquaintance with the English language did not mandate losing Dutch as a primary language. Hearing Dutch in the family and at church were not the only sources of allegiance to the Dutch language. For America's Dutch men and women, the majority of whom were literate, reading printed books in Dutch was another means to reinforce their use of the language that had informed daily life in New Netherland.

Dutch-language books, most notably the Great Dutch Bible, were passed down in families and many still are extant. The transmission of Dutch books to successive generations was part of the cultural inheritance. Families affixed a high value to the family bible. When Dutch men and women made their wills, they frequently mentioned this massive volume, which contained not only the word of God but records of the family's vital events, thus making it one of the family's most important possessions. Since only one person, usually the eldest son, inherited the family bible, other sons were compelled to obtain copies of the book from Europe. To meet the continuing need of New York and New Jersey Dutch families, Great Dutch Bibles printed in the Netherlands were regularly imported into New York City through at least the 1770s, along with psalters, small volumes containing the psalms and the New Testament, which were carried to church.[8] The demand for Dutch books was not confined to bibles and

1

—

COLONIAL
PERIOD
AND
EIGHTEENTH
CENTURY

1609–1782

psalters. Newspaper advertisements placed by New York City merchants during the third quarter of the eighteenth century also mention catechisms, school-books, and song books, as well as various other titles, largely, but not exclusively religious in nature.[9]

Dutch books were not only imported from the Netherlands, they were printed in New York City beginning in the 1690s and continuing through the eighteenth century. The numbers were not large — Hendrik Edelman has identified ninety-two Dutch-language books and broadsides that were printed in New York between 1693 and 1774 — but the mere fact that they were published serves as a reminder that there was a readership for such works in New York and New Jersey.[10] While there were a few catechisms and an arithmetic textbook, many were theological works, often produced as part of ongoing debates among local dominees, and therefore of interest to their followers. The most popular genre was arguably the Dutch-language almanacs, which probably commanded the largest number of readers among the descendants of the New Netherlanders.

At the time of the American Revolution, many Hudson Valley Dutch were still not able to read English. In order to participate in the debate over the proposed new federal constitution, residents needed to have the document made available to them in their native language. A Dutch translation of the draft of the proposed United States Constitution was printed in Albany in 1788.[11] Dutch print culture played a substantial role in perpetuating traditional values in both urban and rural Dutch communities. With their attachment to Dutch culture reinforced through family, church, and print culture, the multiplying Dutch population of eighteenth-century New York and New Jersey remained anchored to the ways of the past.

Dutch Material Culture

The children, grandchildren, and great-grandchildren of New Netherland's settlers, with the exception of those in New York City, continued to live in what amounted to Dutch cultural preserves, islands in the midst of an expanding British society and culture. Traces of these circumscribed worlds can still be glimpsed across the landscape of the mid-Atlantic states in houses, barns, and burial places. Other examples of Dutch material culture have been conserved in museums, historical societies, and private collections. By supplementing these sources with descriptions of the settings of Dutch life drawn from eyewitness accounts, archaeological evidence, and lists of household possessions in inventories of estates, a reasonably complete picture of the material world of the descendants of New Netherlanders can be outlined.[12]

Kort-Begryp

Der Waare
Christelyke Leere,

Uit den *Heidelbergischen Catechismus* uit-getrokken, door·ordre der Christelyke Synode te Dordrecht Anno 1818 & 1619,

MET

Eenige verklaaringe over elke Vraage verrykt, voor den Leer-lievenden en Begeerigen tot

's Heeren H. Avontmaal.

't samengestelt door

GUALTHERUS DUBOIS,

Pred^t· in de N. duidsche Herv. Prot. Ge-meente te N. York.

En in de zelve ingevoert door Ordre der zelve E. Kerken-Raat.

Gedrukt te Nieuw-York bij William Bradford, in den Jaare 1712.

Dutch-language books such as this catechism written by New York's Reformed minister Gualtherus Du Bois in 1712 continued to be printed and read in New York for more than a century after New Netherland was ceded to the English.

1

COLONIAL
PERIOD
AND
EIGHTEENTH
CENTURY

1609–1782

Limning these Dutch communities in broad strokes reveals an image of Reformed churches, adjacent graveyards, dwelling houses, barns, and hay barracks. Buildings were constructed using time-honored techniques practiced by Dutch craftsmen, and displayed an array of architectural features emanating from the Netherlands. Experts differ on the degree of correspondence between New World structures and Old World models. Yet divergences in the appearance of exteriors and evidence of the adaptation of newer English styles did not necessarily signal the renunciation of core Dutch values.[13] Indeed, the overall impression of the built environment in regions with the heaviest concentration of Dutch families conveyed by travelers in the later decades of the eighteenth century was of its distinctiveness.

Dutch Reformed church buildings in rural precincts varied in appearance but remained the primary site of communal life for villagers. Adjacent to the church was the graveyard, where earlier generations of local families had been buried in accordance with Dutch funeral customs. Inscriptions carved in the Dutch language on their gravestones linked the latter-day kin of New Netherland's settlers to an ancestral land many had never seen. The Dutch graveyard, with its associations of family and homeland, was unparalleled as a site of memory for Dutch communities in the United States.

The interiors of the houses occupied by the descendants of the early Dutch in New York and New Jersey were even more revealing of cultural preferences regarding design elements, furniture, decorative arts, and silver. Dutch tiles lined the hearths, Dutch *kasten* held the family's clothing, scripture paintings by Dutch-American artists decorated the walls, and silver objects crafted by Dutch-American silversmiths graced the table.[14] The family bible, published in the Netherlands, was displayed in the great chamber and other Dutch books, usually of a religious nature, were found around the house.

The descendants of New Netherlanders who lived in rural communities of New York and New Jersey inscribed their chosen identities as Dutch men and women on the physical and cultural landscape of their locality. That these identities were not entirely congruent with those of their contemporaries in the Netherlands is less significant than the fact that American-born people whose ancestors had migrated from the Netherlands in the mid-seventeenth century continued to imagine themselves as Dutch a century after sovereignty over New Netherland had passed to the English. Their determination not to be absorbed into the swelling Anglo-American population surrounding them is striking, especially when contrasted with the more rapid adaptation of English ways of many of their brethren in New York City.

Concluding Remarks

The case of the many Dutch city dwellers, largely men of ample means or men with good prospects, who had taken steps to accommodate to English culture by the fourth generation, if not earlier, is more than just the exception that proves the rule. It anticipated an alternative path toward cultural identity that was traversed by increasing numbers of descendants of New Netherlanders in later years. Although some of the city's most prominent Dutch merchants cast their lot with the English and renounced any claim to Dutchness, many more urban Dutch did not believe that their sense of being Dutch was undermined by linguistic or cultural adjustments. Their conviction that a Dutch identity could be mediated through the English language paved the way for subsequent generations of New Netherland descendants who could no longer insulate themselves from the culture of their English-speaking neighbors.

Although the abundance of land in the mid-Atlantic region made possible the physical separation of Dutch and English districts and consequently fostered the creation of cultural zones in which Dutch customs could readily be perpetuated, the example of the minority of Dutch in New York City who fought so hard to maintain Dutch as the exclusive language of preaching in the Dutch Reformed congregation cautions us not to attach too much importance to geography in explaining the cultural conservatism of Dutch Americans. Even in areas where the Dutch were pressed into contact with the English, cultural transformation was far from inevitable.

Standard accounts of British America pay scant attention to the continuing Dutch cultural presence in the Middle Colonies. For too long, the so-called Anglicization model has shaped studies of Dutch cultural adaptation in the region, resulting in interpretations that take for granted the erasure of Dutch culture, whether rapidly or gradually. Overwhelmed by an assumption based on logic more than history — that once political power was ceded to the English, Dutch colonists would scramble to equip themselves to compete in the English world — many scholars have failed to appreciate the multiple contingencies that eventuated in the perpetuation of Dutch cultural dominion in large swaths of English territory for over a century. In October 1664, King Charles II of England, exultant over the recent seizure of New Amsterdam, described it as "a place of great importance to trade." He went on to boast, "The Dutch... built a very good town, but we have got the better of it, and 'tis now called New York."[15] But New York City remained a Dutch settlement in many ways for several decades.[16] And in Albany, as well as in the Dutch towns of the Hudson Valley, Long Island, and New Jersey, families with roots in New Netherland were still paying homage to the traditions of their home country at the outbreak of the American Revolution.

1

—

COLONIAL
PERIOD
AND
EIGHTEENTH
CENTURY

1609–1782

130

1   Alice P. Kenney, *Stubborn for Liberty: The Dutch in New York* (Syracuse, NY: Syracuse University Press, 1975).

2   Joyce D. Goodfriend, *Before the Melting Pot: Society and Culture in Colonial New York City, 1664–1730* (Princeton, NJ: Princeton University Press, 1992).

3   David E. Narrett, *Inheritance and Family Life in Colonial New York City* (Ithaca, NY /London: Cornell University Press, 1992).

4   Graham Russell Hodges, "Slavery and Freedom without Compensation: African Americans in Bergen County, New Jersey, 1660–1860," in Graham Russell Hodges, *Slavery, Freedom, and Culture among Early American Workers* (Armonk, NY/London: M.E. Sharpe, 1998), 28-58.

5   William Heard Kilpatrick, *The Dutch Schools of New Netherland and New York* (Washington, DC: s.n., 1912); Jean Parker Waterbury, *A History of Collegiate School* (New York: Clarkson N. Potter, 1965).

6   Joyce D. Goodfriend, "Archibald Laidlie and the Transformation of the Dutch Reformed Church in Eighteenth-Century New York City," *Journal of Presbyterian History* 81 (2003): 149-162.

7   William H.S. Demarest, *A History of Rutgers College 1766–1924* (Princeton, NJ: Princeton University Press, 1924), 76.

8   Robin A. Leaver, "Dutch Secular and Religious Songs in Eighteenth-Century New York," in George Harinck and Hans Krabbendam, eds., *Amsterdam-New York: Transatlantic Relations and Urban Identities since 1653* (Amsterdam: VU University Press, 2005), 99-124.

9   Joyce D. Goodfriend, "The Dutch Book Trade in Colonial New York City: The Transatlantic Connection," in James Raven and Leslie Howsam, eds., *Connected by Books* (forthcoming).

10 Hendrik Edelman, *Dutch-American Bibliography, 1693–1794: A Descriptive Catalog of Dutch-Language Books, Pamphlets and Almanacs Printed in America* (Nieuwkoop: De Graaf, 1974).

11 *De Constitutie, eenpariglyk geaccordeerd by de Algmene Conventie, gehouden in de Stad von Philadelphia, in 't jaar 1787: en gesubmitteerd aan het volk der Vereenigde Staaten van Noord-Amerika: zynde van ses derselver staaten alreede geadopteerd, namentlyk, Massachusetts, Connecticut, Nieuw-Jersey, Pennsylvania, Delaware en Georgia. Vertaald door Lambertus De Ronde, V.D.M.*: Gedrukt by order van de Federal Committee, in de stad van Albany, door Charles R. Webster in zyne vrye boek-drukkery, no. 36, Staat-Straat, na by de Engelsche Kerk, in dezelvede stad, 1788.

12 Roderic H. Blackburn and Ruth Piwonka, *Remembrance of Patria: Dutch Arts and Culture in Colonial America 1609–1776* (Albany, NY: Albany Institute of History and Art, 1988).

13 Joseph Manca, "Erasing the Dutch: The Critical Reception of Hudson River Valley Dutch Architecture, 1670–1840," in Joyce D. Goodfriend, Benjamin Schmidt, and Annette Stott, eds., *Going Dutch: The Dutch Presence in America 1609–2009* (Leiden/Boston: Brill, 2008), 59-84.

14 Kevin L. Stayton, *Dutch by Design: Tradition and Change in Two Brooklyn Houses* (New York: Brooklyn Museum, 1990); Peter M. Kenney, Frances Gruber Safford, and Gilbert T. Vincent, *American Kasten: The Dutch-Style Cupboards of*

New York and New Jersey, 1650–1800
(New York: Metropolitan Museum of
Art, 1991).

15 Charles II to Henrietta, Duchesse
d'Orléans, Whitehall, October 24,
1664, in Arthur Bryant, ed., *The Letters,
Speeches and Declarations of King
Charles II* (London: Cassell and Co.,
1935), 168.

16 Joyce D. Goodfriend, "The Dutch in
17th-century New York City: Minority
or Majority?," in Randolph Vigne and
Charles Littleton, eds., *From Strangers
to Citizens: The Integration of Immigrant
Communities in Britain, Ireland and
Colonial America, 1550–1750* (Brighton
/Portland, OR: Sussex Academic Press,
2001), 306-312.

1

—

COLONIAL
PERIOD
AND
EIGHTEENTH
CENTURY

1609–1782

DUTCH POLITICAL IDENTITY IN ENGLISH NEW YORK

—

DAVID W. VOORHEES

Dutch political identity in New York long outlasted West India Company Director General Petrus Stuyvesant's surrender of New Amsterdam to an English invasion force commanded by Col. Richard Nicolls on September 9, 1664. While the Hudson and Delaware River valley communities controlled by the Dutch now became the proprietary possession of the English James, Duke of York, the inhabitants' political perspective did not change as readily as did their allegiance. The liberal terms of capitulation granted by the English further reinforced people's ability to retain their identity. They were guaranteed their customary rights of property, inheritance, and liberty to practice their own religious beliefs. New York City and Albany retained their Dutch forms of government, and no changes were introduced into local administration except the adoption of English titles for public offices: mayor for *burgemeester*, sheriff for *schout*, and alderman for *schepen*. Nearly nine years later, on July 30, 1673, the English surrendered New York to an invasion force composed of nineteen Dutch warships. New York, New Jersey, and the Delaware again became New Netherland. A five-man council of war appointed Dutch marine captain Anthony Colve governor general and took over the provincial government. The change had little impact. Within seven months, the Treaty of Westminister restored New York to England and fifteen months later, on November 10, 1674, Dutch Governor Colve surrendered the administration to incoming royal Governor Edmund Andros.

Again, the English allowed the Dutch in New York to retain their customs and, as English imperial administration from London remained distant, the transition from Dutch to English political culture was gradual. The subsequent division of New York into counties in 1683 was not unfamiliar to the Dutch, whose fatherland consisted of duchies, counties, and lordships. English became the official language, but Dutch remained the primary language for many civil and ecclesiastical functions and most private affairs for the next century. Moreover, the retention of commercial and familial ties with the Republic kept Dutch cultural influences alive despite a dramatic decrease in immigration from the Netherlands after 1664.

Although the ethnic Dutch became a minority in New York, close contacts with the province of Holland, as well as Holland's position as an international exporter of culture in the early modern era, created an environment that encouraged Netherlandic customs to survive in the former West India Company province for generations after the conquest. A flourishing commerce, both legal and illegal, continued between Holland and New York that effectively evaded England's attempts to restrict it with various Navigation Acts. When in 1756, for example, the British parliament passed an act to stem the flow of smuggled goods on Dutch vessels, it created a crisis among New York merchants. New York imports of Dutch manufactured goods declined in relation to the import of English manufactured goods, but Dutch exporters adjusted to the transition by developing markets for new products, such as porcelains, paper, and gin. As a result of the continuing contacts with the Republic, a high rate of natural increase among Dutch-American women, and the heterogeneous complexion of Dutch culture, the Mohawk and Hudson River valleys, western Long Island, and East New Jersey remained strongly Dutch in culture throughout the colonial period.

Urbanism and Oligarchy

In the early modern Low Countries, towns dominated the countryside and merchant oligarchies dominated the towns. The Dutch brought with them to the New World this tradition of urban culture. The West India Company's grant of local governing rights to Beverwijck (present-day Albany) in 1652 and municipal rights to New Amsterdam (today's New York City) in 1653, as well as the various town charters granted by the Company, resulted in the re-creation of a way of life familiar in the Old World. With New York's incorporation into the English mercantile world, its urban cultures flourished, albeit in Dutch fashion. One example is the emergence of a *burgerlijke* urban patrician class after 1664. This followed the pattern of the province of Holland in the Dutch Republic. Society in Holland during the revolt against Spain had been porous, but by 1650 public offices in the major western Dutch cities had become closed through cooption to all but a small group of regent families of mercantile origins who controlled civic activities. English New York followed this Dutch metropolitan pattern as its social structure matured. Urban and provincial offices increasingly became dominated by a handful of interrelated mercantile families whose lifestyle remained comfortably middle class.[1]

133

1

—

COLONIAL
PERIOD
AND
EIGHTEENTH
CENTURY

1609–1782

The land-grant policies of James, as duke and king, ironically reinforced the Dutchness of New York's political landscape. In the Republic, multiple jurisdictions overlapped between provinces, towns, and manorial estates. James's establishment of manors with political privileges followed the pattern of similar estates in the Netherlands — a jurisdictional form that had been introduced into New Netherland with the patroonship plan in 1629 but a plan that had, with the exception of Rensselaerswijck and New Amstel, ultimately failed due to the expense of maintaining a private colony prior to 1664. The larger of these manorial patents included Rensselaerswijck, established in 1629 and repatented in 1685, Livingston Manor (1686), Philipsburgh Manor (1696), and Cortlandt Manor (1697). These manorial grants concentrated much of the best arable land in the Hudson River valley in the hands of a few mercantile families who, in Dutch regent fashion, derived their wealth from trade and continued to maintain their primary residences in urban centers.[2]

Outside the towns and manorial holdings, the English conquest had little impact on the rural population, except for the requirement that farmers secure new patents for their land. The English royal government left a considerable amount of autonomy to New York's villages and farming hamlets, a situation similar to that in the Republic. The Duke's Laws of 1665, written for New York's English communities and only gradually expanded throughout the province, contained a number of Dutch features. Among these were tacit indulgence in allowing various religious communities to exist other than the Reformed and plural nomination and partial retirement in public offices. The imposition of the English form of town government in the rural Dutch villages after 1675 thus did not represent a complete break with Dutch traditions. As late as the American Revolution, villages in the Hudson River valley were said to continue to follow "modes peculiar to the Hollanders." The consequence was a tangled web of governments, traditions, and jurisdictions in New York, which, as in the Republic, complicated decision making and resulted in an intercommunal bickering among New York regions that persists into the twenty-first century.[3]

Corporate Rights and Traditional Liberties

In the Dutch Republic, ancient privileges and traditional liberties acquired by communities as corporate rights resulted in decentralization and factionalism. Neither cultural, commercial, nor ethnic unity bound the Netherlandic people into a republic in the sixteenth century but rather their federation for military protection under the Union of Utrecht (1579). New York and East Jersey reflected this tradition of diversity and localism, and the political and social insular-ism of their Dutch communities was noted throughout the colonial period. It is most evident in New Yorkers' longstanding opposition to centralized governmental authority under the English and jealous guarding of the prerogatives granted to them in their town charters. The competition between Albany and Schenectady over the fur-trade monopoly, between New York City and Albany over the export-trade monopoly, and between New York City and upriver communities over the flour-bolting monopoly are a few examples. Monopolies, however, were only favored when they contributed to the order and stability of a community as a whole. Opposition to monopolies arose when they were found to benefit an individual at the expense of a community. Individual rights and liberties were thus tied to the corporate communal welfare and manifested in the concept of toleration.[4] The paradoxical nature of rural New York and New Jersey of being simultaneously insular and parochial while socially tolerant is a legacy of the Dutch tradition of corporatism.

Within New York's towns, special interest groups coalesced in Dutch fashion to pursue common goals. Individual rights were defended through the acquisition of communal privileges. Ever since the Middle Ages, Dutch trade guilds, for example, regulated and promoted specific craft interests within the community. Although the guild system never formally developed in New Netherland, beginning in the 1670s, at one time or another New York's bakers, boatmen, butchers, cartmen, coopers, shoemakers, and tanners combined to protect their collective rights.[5] Special interests became a fixture in eighteenth-century New York politics, which, because of the localized concerns of each group, fractured the promotion of a larger interest before the English Crown.[6]

A peculiar characteristic of colonial New York was the prominence in public affairs of the local militia company, or burgher guard. In the Low Countries, citizens' militias — the *schutterijen* — traditionally played a pivotal role in civic life. In the Dutch Republic, civilian military units, created to maintain order within the towns, would occasionally be employed in military tasks outside the city walls during times of crisis. They increasingly acquired also a more ceremonial role and active political capacity as the guardians of traditional liberties.[7] In similar fashion, the New York militia company served a more social and, as we will see, potent political role rather than solely that of a defensive unit. Indeed, the English mocked the New York militia companies as a burlesque of militarism.[8] Yet, attempts by English governors to diminish their autonomy through patronage in the appointment of officers were perceived by New Yorkers throughout the colonial period as a threat to good government and constitutional balances.[9]

1

—

COLONIAL
PERIOD
AND
EIGHTEENTH
CENTURY

1609–1782

Factionalism

The Dutch Republic's political divisions resonated in English New York. In the seventeenth century the Dutch body politic split into two factions. On one side were the supporters of the *raadpensionaris*, the principal representative of the town regents, loosely identified as the *Statenfactie*. Opposing them were the Orangists, supporters of the *stadhouder* or provincial military commander-in-chief, a post traditionally held by a prince of Orange. New York's political factions echoed these divisions as the close-knit kinship network that formed the mercantile elite — which included Bayards, Cuylers, Gouverneurs, Kierstedes, Leislers, Loockermans, Schuylers, Staatses, Stuyvesants, and Van Cortlandts — began to feud, fracture, and coalesce after 1675 into opposing camps.[10] The leaders of New York's late seventeenth- and eighteenth-century political factions emerged, as European factional leaders often did, out of elite intrafamilial networks in which cousins, brothers, and in-laws vied for public opinion and royal favor.

In the protracted disputes, political interests aligned in New York, as they did in the Republic, with theology. In the United Provinces, *Staatsgezinden* and Orangists took opposing sides in the doctrinal conflict between the followers of Utrecht University professor Gisbertus Voetius, who emphasized moral precisionism and the need for a personal conversion to Christ, and the followers of Leiden University professor Johannes Cocceius, who espoused a more liberal covenant theology. In this dispute, Orangists largely allied with Voetians while the *Staatsgezinden* largely allied with Cocceians. By the last third of the century this controversy colored every aspect of the Republic's political life and provided the ideological glue for factional disputes in late seventeenth-century New York.[11] The 1676 controversy over minister Nicolaes van Rensselaer is illustrative. James, Duke of York, had appointed Van Rensselaer, ordained as an Anglican, to the Albany Reformed pulpit. The Roman Catholic duke's act outraged the orthodox Reformed Dutch, who held to the rule from the Synod of Dort that a minister must be ordained in the Reformed Church and called by the congregation. The controversy came to a head in July 1676 when Jacob Leisler, a New York City Reformed Church deacon, circulated a four-point gloss criticizing a sermon by Van Rensselaer on original sin. In a critique that followed arguments within the Calvinist world, Leisler charged the domine with heresy for suggesting that only after Adam's fall did God decree the election or nonelection of individuals to salvation. The resulting dispute pitted Leisler against his Van Cortlandt and Bayard relations and presaged later political events.[12]

In the 1680s, Voetian-inspired Pietist movements swept through New York's Dutch, French, and English Reformed and Lutheran congregations, despite the opposition of the province's more urbane domines and ministers.[13] Tensions between factions increased as the Duke of York, now King James II, implemented centralizing governmental policies. The Roman Catholic king's patronage of a small group of wealthy New York merchants with offices and other perquisites fueled resentments. Orangist populist and antirepublican ideology emanating from Rotterdam, which city became after 1674 the primary focus for New York's continental trade, further inflamed the population. Paralleling popular support for the House of Orange in the Netherlands, Orangism and anti-Catholicism became a rallying cry for the opposition to Stuart policies in New York, while New York's Anglicizing Dutch elite was increasingly portrayed in terms of Holland's regents.

Leisler's Rebellion

The 1689 event known as Leisler's Rebellion illustrates the continuing influence of Dutch political culture in New York. In November 1688, William, Prince of Orange, stadtholder of several Dutch provinces, and son-in-law and nephew of England's King James II, invaded England with a force of twenty-one thousand men. The subsequent Glorious Revolution, which replaced the Roman Catholic King James with the Protestant William III and his wife Mary, James's daughter, on the English throne, set off rebellions in the American colonies. Revolt in New York broke out at the beginning of May 1689 on Long Island's East End, when the towns of Suffolk County, following Boston's example, overthrew James II's government. Rebellion spread across Long Island and up the Hudson River valley, where mobs ousted James's appointees and chose others to replace them. In pattern, the New York and East Jersey rebellions bear similarities to the 1672 Orangist uprisings in the Netherlands, when mobs played a significant role in the numerous towns where the magistrates were replaced by Voetian Orangists.[14]

The Dutch nature of the New York uprisings is evident in the central role taken by the militias. In the Republic, town militias, viewing themselves as representatives of the people, claimed a role in the election of new council members. In like manner, the militias in New York oversaw the changes in the government. When in June 1689 the New York militia captains organized themselves as a Council of War and called for a meeting of representatives from New York and East New Jersey to oversee the government, they followed the example of such Dutch towns as Dordrecht and Rotterdam. As in the Republic, cities in the New York convention were given a weighted influence by being allowed a larger share of the delegates. In late June the convention elected senior militia captain and wealthy merchant Jacob Leisler commander of the fort and, in August, commander-

Trainbands Signing Leisler's Declaration. The print was produced for
William Cullen Bryant, *Popular history of the United States, from the first discovery
of the western hemisphere by the Northmen to the end of the Civil War*, 4 vols.
(New York: Charles Scribner's Sons, 1876–1881) and was also sold separately.

in-chief of the province. This, too, followed Dutch precedent. In the Republic, fundamental law, natural rights, representative institutions, and popular sovereignty were important aspects of the political structure. When ruling elites were discredited in the seventeenth-century Netherlands, the loss of legitimacy caused a demand for change in those holding high offices and the restoration of the rights of local burgher communities. The provincial convention's election of Leisler thus fell within the Dutch political tradition of finding a leader to balance the power of the magistrates.[15]

When they rebelled in 1689, Dutch New Yorkers believed, as they interpreted the English system from a Dutch perspective, that they were acting within a proper constitutional and legal framework. Ever since the French invasion of the Republic in 1672, anti-Catholic hysteria had been building in New York, where reports from Europe of French Catholic atrocities inspired a fear of Roman Catholic violence. Yet, despite the Prince of Orange's declarations encouraging rebellion against the Roman Catholic James II, which had circulated in New York since January, New Yorkers were reluctant to act on them. This is because for those with a Dutch perspective, the defense of liberty was based on a constitutional framework of fundamental laws and a balanced system of institutions. The memory of these constitutional traditions restrained rebellion in New York and shaped its course. Political change had to follow legal principles. The militia, as the people's representatives, acted only after official confirmation of William's coronation had arrived and only after the constituted magistrates continued to refuse to affirm it. Also, in following the Dutch principle that they could not rule without the people's consent, the militia captains were prompted to call for the representative convention.

Drawing on Dutch republican ideology, Leislerians sought to restore the traditional balances in the government. They thus undertook a program to reclaim the corporate rights of the people, the abolition of monopolies, the abolishment of taxation without representation, and the right of the people to bear arms unrestricted, and sought the devolution of governmental authority to local communities.

The Pressures of Anglicization

Ironically, under the Dutch William III, Prince of Orange, as king of England, the Anglicization process in New York became fully implemented. In a judicial blunder, Leisler was beheaded for treason in 1691, only to be exonerated by parliament in 1695. New York's judicial system was reorganized in 1691 to follow English common law rather than Dutch Roman law, and a permanent elective assembly was instituted. With the death of William III as both king of England

1

——

COLONIAL
PERIOD
AND
EIGHTEENTH
CENTURY

1609–1782

and stadtholder of five Dutch provinces (not of Friesland and Groningen) in 1702, the Republic entered a second stadtholderless period, and Orange died as a political force in America. His memory lingered among New Yorkers and Jerseyites in the numerous places named Orange and Nassau found in the region.

The Republic's political divisions, nonetheless, continued to influence New York. By the 1720s, mercantile and agrarian interests hardened. One faction led by the Morris and Livingston families supported Dutch Reformed and Presbyterian interests and, known as the Country Party, reflected Orangist ideology; an opposing faction of mostly Anglican mercantile and manorial families including DeLanceys, Schuylers, Philipses, and Van Cortlandts, known as the Court Party, reflected the *Statenfactie*. In Dutch fashion, elites with fluid allegiances dominated. The two parties, supplemented by lesser factions throughout the province, disagreed on economic, constitutional, and religious issues, and the establishment of a college, today Columbia University.

New Yorkers clearly saw their political alignments in the terms of those in the Republic. When Robert Livingston called Leislerians "butter boxes and boors," or when Leislerians termed their opponents "grandees" and "Cocceians," they were using commonplace Dutch political labels. Seeing New York's factionalism as an extension of Dutch politics, one Leislerian pamphleteer reflected that the opposition had "scap'd being Dewitted by a sufficiently provoked People." The reference was to the brutal 1672 murders of Holland *raadpensionaris* Johan de Witt and his brother Cornelis by an Orangist mob in The Hague.

The continuing impact of Dutch events upon New York politics is seen in the wake of the Dutch Revolution of 1747, which placed Willem IV of Orange as stadtholder in all seven provinces. At the time of the revolution, the Dutch turned out an enormous literature looking back to the traditional balances of good government and the corporate rights of the people. Following the example of the Netherlands, New Yorkers and Jerseyites also looked to their Dutch traditions. Dutch Reformed and Presbyterian sermons and the lay press used the Republic as an important symbol and paradigm for colonial union and independence. American Dutch-language almanacs republished the 1581 Act of Abjuration (*Plakkaat van Verlatinghe*), by which the Republic had declared its independence from the Spanish sovereign, and the 1579 Union of Utrecht (*Verhandelinge van de Unie*), which increasingly became seen in the seventeenth century as the Republic's basic constitutional document. When New York Lieutenant Governor James DeLancey convened a congress of colonial delegates and Mohawk diplomats in Albany in June 1754 for the purpose of establishing an intercolonial alliance with the Iroquois, New Yorkers looked at the Union of Utrecht as a model for creating a common defense against the French.[16]

New York inherited unfettered commerce, freedom of conscience, the concept of toleration, and a republican political culture from the Dutch. The complex political alliances and intrafamilial feuds among New York's interrelated patrician families, the Presbyterian-Anglican rivalry, and the contest between commercial and landed interests were all reflections of political alignments in the Republic. The concept of individual liberties protected through corporate rights left a strong tradition in New York in the influence of special interests upon the shaping of governmental policies. Out of New York's factionalism emerged the seeds of America's modern party system in the nineteenth century.

1   Cathy Matson, *Merchants & Empire: Trading in Colonial New York* (Baltimore: Johns Hopkins University Press, 1998), 147-149, 271-273, 298-299.

2   For the development of oligarchies in New York see Alice P. Kenney, *The Gansevoorts of Albany: Dutch Patricians in the Upper Hudson Valley* (Syracuse, NY: Syracuse University Press, 1969), particularly the introduction.

3   Sung Bok Kim, *Landlords and Tenants in Colonial New York Manorial Society, 1664-1775* (Chapel Hill: University of North Carolina Press, 1978).

4   Patricia U. Bonomi, *A Factious People: Politics and Society in Colonial New York* (New York/London: Columbia University Press, 1971), 26-27.

5   Matson, *Merchants & Empire*, 102-103.

6   Allan Tully, *Forming American Politics: Ideals, Interests, and Institutions in Colonial New York and Pennsylvania* (Baltimore: Johns Hopkins University Press, 1994); Simon Middleton, *From Privileges to Rights: Work and Politics in Colonial New York City* (Philadelphia: University of Pennsylvania Press, 2006).

7   Allison Gilbert Olson, *Making the Empire Work: London and American Interest Groups, 1690-1790* (Cambridge, MA: Harvard University Press, 1992), 72-73.

8   Paul Knevel, *Burgers in het geweer: De schutterijen in Holland, 1550-1700* (Hilversum: Historische Vereniging

Holland/Verloren, 1994); J.C. Grayson, "The Civic Militia in the County of Holland, 1560-81. Politics and Public Order in the Dutch Revolt," *Bijdragen en Mededelingen betreffende de Geschiedenis der Nederlanden* 95 (1980): 35-63.

9   Donna Merwick, *Possessing Albany, 1630-1710: The Dutch and English Experiences* (Cambridge/New York: Cambridge University Press, 1990), 273.

10 Bonomi, *A Factious People*, 158-159.

11 For family connections see William Brower Bogardus, *Dear "Cousin": A Chartered Genealogy of the Descendants of Anneke Jans Bogardus (1605-1663) to the 5th Generation — and of her sister, Marritje Jans* (Wilmington, OH: Anneke Jans and Everardus Bogardus Descendants Association, 1996); For one view of the division among the elite see Firth Haring Fabend, "'According to Holland Custome': Jacob Leisler and the Loockermans Estate Feud," *De Halve Maen* 67 (Spring 1994): 1-8.

12 Henry C. Murphy, ed. and trans., *Journal of A Voyage to New York and a Tour in Several of the American Colonies in 1679-1680, by Jaspar Dankers and Peter Sluyter of Wiewerd in Friesland* (Brooklyn, NY: Long Island Historical Society, 1867), x-xii.

13 Lawrence H. Leder, "The Unorthodox Domine: Nicholas Van Rensselaer," *New York History* 35 (April 1954): 166-176;

1

———

COLONIAL
PERIOD
AND
EIGHTEENTH
CENTURY

1609–1782

Ernestine G. E. van der Wall, "Prophecy and Profit: Nicolaes van Rensselaer, Charles II and the Conversion of the Jews," in C. Augustijn, P. N. Holtrop, G. H. M. Posthumus Meyjes, and E. G. E. van der Wall, eds., *Kerkhistorische opstellen aangeboden aan/Essays on Church History Presented to Prof. dr. J. van den Berg* (Kampen: J. H. Kok, 1987), 75-87.

14   James R. Tanis, "Reformed Pietism in Colonial America," in F. Ernest Stoeffler, ed., *Continental Pietism and Early American Christianity* (Grand Rapids, MI: Eerdmans, 1976), 34-73; Martin H. Prozesky, "The Emergence of Dutch Pietism," *Journal of Ecclesiastical History* 28 (January 1977): 29-37.

15   Charles Howard McCormick, *Leisler's Rebellion* (New York: Garland Press, 1989); A. F. Salomons, "De rol van de Amsterdamse burgerbeweging in de wetsverzetting van 1672," *Bijdragen en Mededelingen betreffende de Geschiedenis der Nederlanden* 106 (1991): 198-219.

16   Martin van Gelderen, *The Political Thought of the Dutch Revolt 1555–1590* (Cambridge: Cambridge University Press, 1992), 286.

17   James R. Tanis, "The Dutch-American Connection: The Impact of the Dutch Example on American Constitutional Beginnings," in Stephen L. Schechter and Richard B. Bernstein, eds., *New York and the Union: Contributions to the American Constitutional Experience* (Troy, NY: Council for Citizenship Education, Russell Sage College, 1990), 22-28.

DUTCH JURISPRUDENCE IN NEW NETHERLAND AND NEW YORK

———

MARTHA DICKINSON SHATTUCK

On March 24, 1624 the first colonists employed by the Dutch West India Company (WIC) to go to New Netherland, took an oath of allegiance to the States General and the WIC after reading the twenty-one provisional regulations. The colonists were instructed to obey the orders and instructions of the WIC, given and yet to be given "in matters of administration and justice." They were also to practice only the Reformed religion, while allowing freedom of conscience, as was stipulated in Article 13 of the Union of Utrecht (1579). For the most part the regulations dealt with such things as residence assignment and requirements, supplies and payments, hunting rights — in other words, the settlement rules by which they were to live during their six-year contract. Instructions given to Provisional Director Willem Verhulst in January 1625 reminded him that the people were to "observe the tenor of the 37 articles of the *articulbrieff...*," which were instructions for maintaining discipline among Company employees "so te Water als te Lande" (on sea and land) and were to be in force despite any further details. Therefore, the Freedoms and Exemptions of 1629 required passengers to swear to the *Artijcul-Brieff*. However, it was the Further Instructions of April 22, 1625 given to Verhulst that presaged the arrival of Dutch jurisprudence to the new colony.[1]

Dutch Jurisprudence in the New Colony

In the Further Instructions the WIC spelled out the legal requirements, mandating that the ordinances and customs specifically of Holland and Zeeland, and the "common written law qualifying them," particularly regarding "the administration of justice, in matters concerning marriage, the settlement of estates,

1

COLONIAL
PERIOD
AND
EIGHTEENTH
CENTURY

1609–1782

and contracts" be enforced. Criminal justice, which had been administered under a variety of local and often confusing laws in Holland, was regularized under the adoption of the 1570 Criminal Justice and Procedure Ordinance of Philip II near the end of the sixteenth century. The WIC also sent over some placards issued by the States of Holland in 1587 regarding intestate estates. These laws, and the requirement that the council could not pass any new laws, ordinances, or new customs without first sending them to the Company for either approval or rejection, as well as the 1629 Order of Government issued by the WIC, would be augmented with the civil and criminal laws from Holland, the laws and ordinances of Amsterdam sent by the Amsterdam Chamber of the WIC, which was given oversight of New Netherland, and local laws and ordinances needed for circumstances not found in Dutch law, such as those involving Indians and slaves. This collective jurisprudence would govern the actions of the colonial council as well as the court system of governance up to, and in some instances beyond, the English conquest in 1664.[2]

For help in applying these laws the courts were sent copies of the Amsterdam ordinances, as well as legal reference books. Thus, patroon Kiliaen van Rensselaer sent his *schout* such books as Joost de Damhouder's *Praxis Crimineel* (*Practycke in criminele saecken* [Procedures in Criminal Matters]), Paul Merula's *Maniere van Procederen* (Civil Procedure of the Courts of Holland, Zeeland, and West-Friesland), and *Ars Notariatus*, which was the basic book on notarial practices, as well as Hugo Grotius's *Inleydinghe tot de Hollandsche rechtsgheleerdheyd* (Introduction to the Jurisprudence of Holland). Director General Petrus Stuyvesant, who frequently cited Damhouder, also supported many of his arguments by quoting from a variety of other sixteenth-century jurists as well as from Roman law, the statutes of Charles V, and the Bible.[3]

While the New Netherlanders were faithful to Dutch jurisprudence, there were some differences in the arrangements of authority. Instead of the Dutch Republic's decentralized approach, New Netherland had a centralized government. The director and council were appointed by the West India Company and their first responsibility was to protect its rights. The villages were not represented in the colonial government, although on three occasions advisory bodies were appointed in New Amsterdam, two of which were quickly dissolved when they proceeded to offer unwanted advice and requested reforms in local government. The *lantdagh*, a provincial assembly, was only called four times in the life of the colony, one of which was considered illegal as the council had not called it. It was also up to the colonial government alone to decide when and where to grant a patent and what rights would be given to the village. Although the villages could appeal local decisions to the council, according to a 1653 resolution of the States of Holland and West-Friesland, the right of appeal from judgments ended with the director general and council of New Netherland. However, a most effec-

MR. HUGO DE GROOT,
Raad en Pensionaris
te Rotterdam.

A. Schouman del. naar 't Origineel.   J. Houbraken fec.

J. Tirion excudit.

One of the important legal reference books in use in New Netherland
was Hugo Grotius's *Inleydinghe tot de Hollandsche rechts-gheleerdheyd*
(Introduction to the Jurisprudence of Holland).

1

——

COLONIAL
PERIOD
AND
EIGHTEENTH
CENTURY

1609–1782

tive form of popular influence used in the Republic and brought to New Netherland, was the use of petitions. Individuals or groups submitted them to influence the local and colonial administrations; to get changes in ordinances or request new ones; to request a license for a particular position; or to request that inhabitants stop playing golf in the streets, among many other concerns both large and small.

Once inhabitants in the various settlement areas reached twenty to thirty families, an inferior court of justice (*kleine banck van justitie*) could be chartered. Until such time, settlements from the more urban New Amsterdam to the rural areas on Long Island and along the North (Hudson) and South (Delaware) rivers were overseen by the director and council. All, that is, but the colony of Rensselaerswijck, a patroonship that was founded in 1630 on the upper Hudson River and held its own court. Notably, and unlike some of the local courts in Holland, major criminal matters, from murder and adultery to blood shedding and slandering the government, were sent to the colonial council for adjudication and punishment. Local magistrates could, and sometimes did, sit in with the council in those sessions. The local courts, which acted in administrative and legislative capacities, tended to affairs such as fights, threats, debts, slander and petitions, and local ordinances and appointments, although most villages were required to have the latter approved by the director general and council before they could be enacted. The *schout*, who functioned both as a sheriff and prosecuting attorney and was appointed by the director and council, presided over the courts. The director and council also selected the magistrates (*schepenen*) from a double number submitted by the sitting magistrates, who were often returned to the bench for another two years after retiring for a year.

Established at various times as increase of population determined, all village courts followed the same structure, laws, and ordinances and, under their charters, were admonished to observe both the laws of the fatherland and the ordinances and edicts of the director general and council. There were, however, some differences in the rights and privileges granted in the various charters. The five English courts under Dutch rule on the eastern end of Long Island, for example, were established in the early 1640s and contained dissidents from New England — people who were accustomed to the English town-meeting form of government. Due to few Dutch settlers and the need of the WIC to affirm ownership of the land, the first village to receive its charter in New Netherland was the English village of Hempstead in 1644. The council allowed the town-meeting format and the eligible voters could choose their own selectmen, but were required to submit their choices to the council for approval and final selection. Gravesend, which was chartered the next year, had, as did all the English towns, " ... libertie of Conscience according to the Custom and manner of Holland.... "

It could make its own ordinances, elect three of the "ablest, approved, honest men" as magistrates and present them to the director annually for confirmation. Unlike the Dutch villages whose *schouten* were appointed by the director and council, Gravesend could elect its own *schout*, who had the same power "as any *schout* in the villages of Holland," provided he had the director's confirmation. Depending on the size of the villages, three magistrates and one *schout* were the usual beginning complement of the courts.[4]

There was one notable exception to the court makeup of the average village. Chartered in 1652 by Director General Stuyvesant and the council, the Court of Fort Orange and Beverwijck (present-day Albany) was particularly important. Since the days following Hudson's discovery of the river the Fort Orange area was the colony's most productive and active fur-trading center. Second only to New Amsterdam in size and its extended rights and privileges, the Court of Fort Orange and Beverwijck was given five magistrates and a vice director who was also commissary of the fort and the *schout*. Isolated in a remote location during the five months that the Hudson River was blocked by ice, the court was trusted to handle on its own a variety of problems that came before it weekly. It was also given oversight of the several small settlements in the surrounding area, as well as the Esopus area farther downriver, until the newly named village of Wiltwijck received its own court in 1661. Moreover, a few criminal cases were sent from the council back to the Court of Fort Orange and Beverwijck for their adjudication, and some local ordinances and appointments of minor officials were made without the need for the director general and council's approval.

Although New Amsterdam was the capital of the colony, with the largest population, it was under the jurisdiction of the director and council, much to the general annoyance of the inhabitants who felt that rights and privileges that they would have had in Holland were denied them. Ultimately a municipal government was granted in 1653, with two burgomasters, five magistrates, and a *schout*, but they too had to present their nominations for burgomasters and magistrates to the director and council for selection. By 1664 the population had significantly increased in the colony as seen by the chartering of six new villages between 1660 and 1664. With these charters the colony then contained a total of sixteen villages, as well as the city of New Amsterdam and the patroonships of Rensselaerswijck on the upper Hudson River and New Amstel on the Delaware River.

A Period of Transition

1

—

COLONIAL
PERIOD
AND
EIGHTEENTH
CENTURY

1609–1782

Unfortunately, in August 1664 any hope for continued growth of New Nether-land was quickly dashed when English ships appeared off shore in a surprise attack during a time of peace between the two countries. The representative of the Duke of York, Richard Nicolls, demanded the surrender of the colony. Not surprisingly, the Dutch pressed for keeping what they saw as their rights in the agreement. Of particular interest were liberty of conscience in the matter of religion — a right that became urgent for the Reformed Dutch themselves with the establishment of an Anglican government in view — and the Dutch inheri-tance practice and customs. Contracts made before the surrender were to be determined in the Dutch manner and the men were not to be pressed to serve in war "against any Nation whatsoever." In true Dutch fashion, three magistrates from the Court of Fort Orange and Beverwijck bent on protecting their specific particularistic rights, not the least of which was the continuation of the fur-trade monopoly, negotiated their own agreement with Nicolls not long after the surrender articles were sent around to the villages.[5]

Although the English takeover was swift, the elimination of Dutch jurispru-dence was not. With a limited supply of English soldiers garrisoned at the widely separated forts in the 350-mile-long colony, Governor Richard Nicolls was care-ful not to impose at once the full impress of the Duke's Laws, named for James, Duke of York and Albany in whose name the colony was taken. In February 1665 these laws were promulgated only on Long Island and in parts of Westchester where, much to their distress, the English residents saw their hopes for par-ticipation in the new government dashed and also lost their right to have town meetings.[6]

Then, on June 13, 1665, Nicolls revoked the government of burgomasters and *schepenen* in New York City and the Duke's Laws replaced the Dutch. The gover-nor also appointed new officers — a mayor, five aldermen, and a sheriff —to re-place the Dutch burgomasters, *schepenen*, and *schout*. While only three of the aldermen appointed were Dutch, they were men of considerable standing in New Amsterdam. Olaf Stevensz van Cortland was appointed frequently to the post of burgomaster on the New Amsterdam court and Johannes van Brugh had served as a *schepen*. Cornelis van Ruyven was secretary to the colonial council. For the rest of the colony, Nicolls worked with the existing Dutch courts whose records were kept in the Dutch language and which continued to adjudicate ac-cording to Dutch law. As Albany's court minutes for the English period are only extant as of September 13, 1668, how much, if anything, of the Duke's Laws was used in the Dutch court between 1664 and that date is not known.

Little by little, however, bits of English law and process found their way into it and the other courts. Although the village of Schenectady had been given its own *schout* by the English in 1668, it remained under Albany's jurisdiction. In 1665 Governor Nicolls placed Rensselaerswijck under Albany's jurisdiction as well, thus creating the Court of Albany, Colony of Rensselaerswijck, and Schenectady. Under Nicolls' successor, Francis Lovelace, things began to change, however. In the Nicolls court, besides a *schout* there were five magistrates, two each from Albany and Rensselaerswijck and one from Schenectady. Those from Schenectady and Albany were chosen by the governor from double nominations submitted from sitting magistrates, as was the process under the Dutch. Rensselaerswijck's patroon, however, made his own nominations that were subject to the governor's approval. In 1671, responding to complaints that often the representatives from Rensselaerswijck did not make the court sessions, Lovelace added another magistrate for Albany, thus giving it and Schenectady a quorum. He also ordered that three of the magistrates, including the president, were sufficient to be a court to make decisions on the cases coming before it, which differed little from the Dutch process. The court did not convene every week as before, but the content and manner of handling the cases did not change. While the court reluctantly accepted Lovelace's replacement of the Dutch *schout* with the military commander of the fort, his 1672 implementation of a special court of Oyer and Terminer, and the empaneling of a jury to try a murder case in Albany appeared to cause no concern.[7]

Under Governor Lovelace more English jurisprudence and forms appeared, particularly in the Esopus area, including the village of Wiltwijck, renamed Kingston by the English, as well as the towns of Hurley and Marbletown. Kingston maintained its Dutch format and laws until September 1669 when Lovelace named a commission that made various appointments to the village government. Among them was the establishment of a magistrate and two overseers for Hurley and Marbletown with the requirement of using English laws. Not until October 1671, however, was implementation of the Duke's Laws started. At that time a justice of the peace was appointed, along with a court of sessions that was to meet only twice a year. By 1673 the residents of the Esopus area requested the colonial council for an English court of law.

This request had to wait as during the Third Anglo-Dutch War a Dutch fleet of a reported twenty-one sail arrived in New York harbor on July 28, 1673 and on the 29th several large frigates anchored at Staten Island. Governor Lovelace was in Connecticut and the fort was in sad shape with few men to defend it. The Dutch Council of War, comprised of commanders Cornelis Evertsen the Youngest and Jacob Binckes, appointed Anthony Colve provisional military governor to take over once they left to join the rest of the Dutch fleet. The Council of War

COLONIAL
PERIOD
AND
EIGHTEENTH
CENTURY

1609-1782

moved quickly to reestablish a Dutch government and the Dutch legal system throughout the colony. This time it included all of Long Island and the proprietary colony of New Jersey. The seven Jersey towns, including the former Dutch chartered village of Bergen, submitted to the Dutch government. Their rights and privileges previously granted were restored not only to them but also eventually throughout the colony. All had to submit *schouten*, magistrates, and burgomasters for approval.[8] As the colony was returned to the English in February 1674 under the Treaty of Westminster, the Dutch government lasted only fifteen months and formally ended with the arrival of Edmund Andros in November 1674. Governor Colve did his best to get Dutch rights protected, tendering Andros a list of proposals. Foremost among them was keeping their religion and inheritance practices, to which Andros agreed. Even so, Andros's proclamation on November 9 made clear the way things were to go. While he confirmed as legal the property and privileges granted by the former English government and any legal proceedings by the recent Dutch government, the Duke's Laws were put back in force.[9]

Firm English Control

On November 17, 1674 the New York Mayor's Court with its predominately English members found reading papers written in Dutch difficult and decreed that no such papers were to be brought into court or they would be thrown out, excepting the poor who could not afford a translator.[10] But this did not occur in Albany where the citizens — mainly Dutch, including many merchants and traders who were leading members of the community and many of whom served as magistrates — were still dominant. Although the Duke's Laws were in force throughout the colony and had finally been sent to the Delaware region under Andros, Albany was the last bastion of Dutch jurisprudence. Here the court was held once a month instead of every week, although extraordinary sessions appeared with frequency in between. In 1675 Albany's magistrates appointed constables whose duties were the same as in "New York and other English places."[11] Juries started to be used more frequently and justices of the peace were appointed by the magistrates, yet nominations for new magistrates were still sent in double numbers to the governor for approval. While Dutch institutions and customs still appeared both in the court records of Albany until 1685 and in the notarial records until 1696, the days of any Dutch jurisprudence were numbered. By 1683 Governor Dongan divided the colony into counties with courts of session and a court of Oyer and Terminer while allowing each town a court for small causes. In April 1684 Albany asked the colonial council for a mayor's court. Albany then was divided into six wards, and their leaders formed a six-person common council that, with the justices of peace, transacted administrative and legislative business while the magistrates administered justice under English law. Albany received its city charter from Governor Dongan in July 1686, ending the use of the Dutch language in its governmental records and marking the definitive end of Dutch jurisprudence in the colony.

The change to English law ultimately affected the lives of women, who under Dutch jurisprudence had greater rights and freedoms than women under English law. Single or widowed, they had the same rights as men, except for political rights. Married, unless women had an antenuptial contract that denied the husband any marital power, they were under the coverture of their husbands, but could run a business or trade with their husband's permission, which appeared to be given most generously in the commercial society of New Netherland. Thus, they appeared in court unaided and on either their own or on their husband's behalf gave and received powers of attorney to carry on all sorts of enterprises between New Netherland and patria; traded with the Indians, or with tobacco merchants in Virginia; were sued and took others to court. It took time, but inevitably these women's rights were diminished under English law. Their appearance in courts lessened after 1674 and they engaged much less frequently in trade or as independent entrepreneurs. By the end of the seventeenth century fewer and fewer women made joint wills with their husbands.

Dutch inheritance practices that the Dutch so earnestly requested and that were allowed when they petitioned for their rights from the English governors, were observed and accepted under the English. In order to write a valid will the Dutch had to execute it before a notary trained in inheritance laws of the Netherlands or before the court secretary. The English government licensed such notaries and secretaries until the 1690s. The inheritance practices differed considerably from the English, as married women could make their own wills or the more commonly used form, a mutual will with their husbands. In either case they could bequest land as well as personal property, unlike the English wife who could bequest personal property but only with the husband's permission. Under Dutch law the surviving spouse received half the estate and the children the other half, since the Dutch law did not entail the primogeniture, and debts incurred by one spouse or the other had to be paid by the survivor. Mutual wills also protected the children's inheritance by either the appointment of the orphan masters to oversee the minor children's inheritance until they came of age, or by naming a person, often the surviving spouse, to administer the will. Should the widowed spouse remarry, arrangements had to be made to protect the minor children's inheritances. While by the 1700s most of Dutch wills written in New York City were in English, some of the Dutch from the Esopus region and Albany kept the Dutch notarial format well into the mid-1700s. Even so, the English probate requirements for property in 1692 had to be approved

1

─────

COLONIAL
PERIOD
AND
EIGHTEENTH
CENTURY

1609–1782

by the governor or his representative. Indeed, probate reforms and centralization throughout the last two decades of the seventeenth century occurred in the same period that saw the fading use of the notarial and mutual wills.[12]

Dutch social customs and the presence of some of the early settlers and their descendants in colonial politics of their communities throughout the Hudson Valley region did not fade, but lasted well into the next century — and beyond in some areas. The only truly lasting piece of Dutch jurisprudence, however, was the *schout*. One part of the *schout's* duties was that of police officer and in that capacity he became known as the sheriff, the English name for the position. The other job of a *schout*, that of prosecutor, was incorporated into the English colonial form of government where it remains today as the district attorney.

1   A. J. F. Van Laer, trans. and ed., *Documents Relating to New Netherland, 1624–1626* (San Marino, CA: The Henry E. Huntington Library and Art Gallery, Publications Americana, 1924), Doc. A 1-9; The quotation is in the *Groot Placaet-Boek* (The Hague, 1658), 1:626.

2   Van Laer, *Documents*, Doc. D 16-18; See J. W. Wessels, *History of the Roman-Dutch Law* (Grahamstown, South Africa: s.n., 1908), 302; Philip's criminal ordinance is discussed in Dennis Sullivan, *The Punishment of Crime in Colonial New York: The Dutch Experience in Albany during the Seventeenth Century* (New York: Peter Lang Publishing, Inc., 1997), 28-29; Dutch jurisprudence is discussed in Martha Dickinson Shattuck, "A Civil Society: Court and Community in Beverwijck, New Netherland, 1652-1664" (Ph.D. dissertation, Boston University, 1993), chapter one; See also Jacob A. Schiltkamp, "On Common Ground: Legislation, Government, Jurisprudence, and Law in the Dutch West Indian Colonies: The Order of Government of 1629," *De Halve Maen* 70.4 (Winter 1997): 73-80.

3   Jaap Jacobs, *New Netherland: A Dutch Colony in Seventeenth-Century America* (Leiden: Brill, 2005); A. J. F. Van Laer, trans., Kenneth Scott, and Kenn Stryker-Rodda, eds., *Council Minutes, 1638–1649*. New York Historical Manuscripts: Dutch (Baltimore: Genealogical Publishing Co., Inc., 1974), 4:407-410, 415-417, 447-448.

4   For an example of the admonishment regarding laws of the fatherland and the director general and council, see E. B. O'Callaghan, comp. and trans., *Laws and Ordinances, 1638–1674* (Albany, NY: 1868), 407. The charters for Hempstead and Gravesend are in *Laws and Ordinances*, 42-46 and 53-57 respectively. For further discussion of the English towns on Long Island see Martha Dickinson Shattuck, "Heemstede: An English Town under Dutch Rule," in Natalie A. Naylor, ed., *The Roots and Heritage of Hempstead Town* (Interlaken, NY: Heart of the Lakes Publishers, 1994), 29-44, and Shattuck, "The Dutch and the English on Long Island: An Uneasy Alliance," *De Halve Maen* 68.4 (Winter 1995): 80-85.

5   For a list of the articles and the petition from Beverwijck see Peter R. Christoph and Florence A. Christoph, eds., *Books of General Entries of the Colony of New York, 1664–1673*. New York Historical Manuscripts: English (Baltimore: Genealogical Publishing, Co., Inc., 1982), 35-37, 49-50.

6   Robert C. Ritchie, *The Duke's Province: A Study of New York Politics and Society,*

1664–1691 (Chapel Hill: University of North Carolina Press, 1977), 33-36; For the problems of governance see 31-46.

7   Ibid., 40–42; A. J. F. Van Laer, trans. and ed., *Minutes of the Court of Albany, Rensselaerswyck and Schenectady, 1668–1673*, 3 vols. (Albany: University of the State of New York, 1926-1932), 1:326-328.

8   For a discussion of the restoration of New Netherland see Donald G. Shomette and Robert D. Haslach, *Raid on America: The Dutch Naval Campaign of 1672–1674* (Columbia: University of South Carolina Press, 1988), 123-196.

9   Ritchie, *The Duke's Province*, 96; Peter R. Christoph and Florence A. Christoph, eds., *The Andros Papers, 1674–1676*

(Syracuse, NY: Syracuse University Press, 1989), 14-15; Mary Lou Lustig, "Edmund Andros and the Dutch in New York, 1674-1681," *De Halve* Maen 69.4 (Winter 1996): 67-75.

10 Kenneth Scott, ed., *Minutes of the Mayors Court 1674–1675.* New York Historical Manuscripts. (Baltimore: Genealogical Publishing Co., Inc., 1983), 3.

11 Van Laer, *Minutes of the Court*, 2:16.

12 David E. Narrett, *Inheritance and Family Life in Colonial New York* (Ithaca, NY: Cornell University Press, 1992), 28; See particularly 12-68 for a full discussion of all aspects of Dutch inheritance customs and the process of their demise under English law in the eighteenth century.

1
━━

COLONIAL
PERIOD
AND
EIGHTEENTH
CENTURY

1609–1782

THE DUTCH AND THEIR RELIGION

━━

FRED VAN LIEBURG

Introduction

In 1620 a group of English dissidents sailed to North America—to stay for good—after twelve years in Holland. This classic rendition of the story of the Pilgrim Fathers illustrates the ambiguous position of the Dutch Republic in Europe at the time. On the one hand, the welcome the English separatists received in Holland can be interpreted as characteristic of this commercially oriented nation's tolerant attitude toward religious refugees. On the other hand, the Republic also fit the general pattern of confessional states that opted for a Protestant or a Catholic order after the sixteenth-century split in the Christian church. Countless individuals and groups left for North America when they no longer felt welcome in the dominant church or religiosity of their countries. In the seventeenth century these were primarily Puritans from the Church of England. Later, Huguenots from France and Lutheran Pietists from German and Scandinavian state churches abandoned the European continent.

A Colonial Church

It was against this religious backdrop that the Dutch Republic engaged in expansionist trade practices. Trade was the primary impulse for establishing colonies. The Dutch overseas trade companies were able to provide a secure political climate that was conducive to the formation of local daughter churches of the Dutch Reformed Church. These overseas churches were primarily engaged in providing pastoral care to people from highly varied social strata, including administrators, businessmen, and laborers. The permanent colony of New Netherland, however, was remarkable in that its social structure—even with regard to religion—closely mirrored that of the Dutch Republic.[1]

154

The public, normative religion was of course the Calvinist-Protestant version of the Christian faith, which is expressed in the Three Forms of Unity as established during the Synod of Dort in 1618–19. The government and the church in New Netherland had a relationship similar to that of their "parent" organizations back home. The highest authority was exercised by the West India Company (WIC), in religious affairs as well. Its headquarters were in Amsterdam. The norms for Christian society in the colony, the organization of the church, and the qualities of its spiritual leaders were determined by the Dutch Reformed Church. Church administration was conducted though classes, regional bodies of representatives from local consistories.

Although each branch of the WIC had the authority to consult with any classis on posting pastoral workers, the Amsterdam branch was to a great degree solely responsible for posts to the colony of New Netherland. Initially, the WIC worked together with the municipal council of churches of the city of Amsterdam. Starting in 1638 the WIC and the Classis of Amsterdam were delegated by a special committee for West Indian affairs, which had the authority to examine and appoint candidates. The first pastor to travel to Manhattan was a comforter of the sick, Bastiaen Jansz Krol (1595–1674). That was in 1624, and one year later he was given the authority to baptize children and perform marriages. In 1628 the first fully ordained minister, Jonas Michaëlius (about 1584–1638), arrived in the colony. He appointed a number of elders. The establishment of a consistory in New Amsterdam is considered to be the birth of the Dutch Reformed Church in North America.[2]

Evarardus Bogardus (1607–47), who succeeded Michaëlius as pastor, characterizes this pioneering phase in the religious history of New Netherland in many ways. Bogardus experienced profound religious inspiration at a Dutch orphanage and spent a couple of years at grammar school. Nevertheless, he chose not to pursue academic studies and instead sought an appointment as a comforter of the sick for the WIC. As a pastor he represented a group of laymen who had been admitted to the clergy by virtue of singular spiritual gifts. Bogardus was relentless in his efforts to give shape to a Calvinistic society on Manhattan Island. In response to a furious dispute with the governor, Bogardus sailed back to Amsterdam. His ship, however, struck upon a rock and sunk, taking all aboard to a watery grave.[3]

Initially, the New Amsterdam congregation met for services in the fort. A new church built of stone was completed in 1642 and ten years later a second benefice was established. Immigration figures continued to grow, resulting in increasing numbers of congregations outside the colony's capital. Churches were built in New Albany (Rensselaerswijck, 1642; Beverwijck, 1656), along the Hudson River (Wiltwijk, 1660), and on Long Island (Midwout, 1654; Breuckelen, 1660), among other places. In 1664 there were eleven congregations in total

1

━━━

COLONIAL
PERIOD
AND
EIGHTEENTH
CENTURY

1609–1782

that formed a regional organization under the aegis of the Classis of Amsterdam. This meant that local autonomy in the colony was given an impulse, which was in defiance of the wishes of the authorities back home.

Public Christianity

The congregations in New Netherland received protection from the authorities by virtue of their confession. Just as in the Republic, their charge was to carry out regular preaching duties, celebrate the sacraments, and maintain clerical discipline. Sunday worship services were held in Dutch, even though there were Germans and French in the congregation. Infant baptism was administered to the children of all Christians, whether or not they were members of the congregation. Holy Communion was reserved for those who had been accepted into the congregation after having been specially catechized and after having professed their faith, or based on an attestation of church membership elsewhere. The moral rectitude and creed of these communicant members were also subject to scrutiny and disciplinary measures by the pastor and the elders. The deacons worked together with the authorities to provide relief for the poor in this colonial society.

The first pastors in New Netherland were quite serious about including the heathen in the WIC's vision of expanding the Kingdom of Christ as part of the larger trade mission. What they encountered, however, was an impenetrable local tongue, a strange culture, and a high degree of animosity among the original population. It was decided in 1657 that preaching would never be productive as long as the native population was not part of the broader polity. Missionary work was difficult, however, even among slaves, who were part of colonial society in a formal sense. Many who had been brought from ex-Portuguese colonies in Africa had a Catholic background. Slaves who were brought into the fold of the Christian congregation were freed. This led to doubtful sentiments about their religious motivation. Pastors gradually required them to be better versed in religious matters, which led to a drastic decrease in the number of baptisms among black converts.

The governor and council, as well as local administrators, were quite busy simply maintaining order among the colonial population. The degree to which religious morality contributed to social cohesion and peaceful coexistence among the various segments of the population was a function of the subtleties of theory and practice. The sentiments of the dignitaries back in Amsterdam often served to complicate matters. The successive governors of New Netherland responded to the undisputedly Calvinistic character of the colony in different ways. After a period in which an open model of a Protestant regime for the en-

tire population had been in place, a more confessionalized state of politics followed under Petrus Stuyvesant (1592–1672)—himself a pastor's son—which
also broke through in the Republic after the Peace of Münster in 1648 and the
Grand Assembly of the States General in 1651. This process was too late, however, to have any real effect in either region.[4]

From time to time the colonial authorities issued proclamations to regulate
or ban certain undesirable, yet popular, forms of entertainment that could be
construed as "heathen," "godless," or "superstitious," such as goose hunting
or celebrating Fat Tuesday. Starting in 1625 many edicts were issued regarding
regulations for Sunday services. This series of edicts started with rules for commercial activities during church services and progressed to a general proclamation in 1663 that imposed a highly puritanical ordinance for twenty-four hours
of rest on the Sabbath. The administrators of the city of New Amsterdam found
most of the prohibitions by the colonial authorities to be far too oppressive.
This was the first clear divergence between the public monopoly and cultural
multiformity in the permanent colony.[5]

Practical Tolerance

Just as in the Republic, the Dutch Reformed religion was a publicly upheld affair, but no one was required to become a member of the Church. It is unlikely
that actual membership figures in New Netherland ever reached 20 percent of
the colonial population, even though there was certainly a larger group that regularly attended services. Freedom of conscience was upheld for other religious
creeds, as long as worship was conducted privately and quietly. Even Jews had a
place, despite resistance from the governor and the pastors. Thanks to the support of the WIC governors, a few dozen Jewish merchants were able to leave the
colony of Brazil, which had been lost, or could even emigrate from Amsterdam
itself, settle in New Amsterdam, and gather there in a local synagogue.

The authorities even turned a blind eye to the Sunday worship services of
non-Reformed Christians. Catholics and Mennonites were the Calvinists' most
prominent competitors, but these minority confessions were of little consequence in New Netherland. The few Mennonite immigrants formed informal
congregations in keeping with their low-profile interpretation of confession
and offices.[6] Catholics received the sacraments from itinerant priests or Jesuits who traveled in secrecy. Some of them had been ransomed from the native
population. The Jesuit martyr Isaac Jogues arrived in Manhattan in 1643/44
and received a hearty welcome, something that would have been unthinkable
in Holland. This can be seen as a demonstration of interconfessional solidarity
in the presence of the "wild heathens."

1

——

COLONIAL
PERIOD
AND
EIGHTEENTH
CENTURY

1609–1782

Religious dissent in New Netherland was best represented by the Lutherans, who from the beginning came not only from the Dutch Republic, but also from Germany and Scandinavia. Requests for public recognition of their confessional freedom began to backfire starting in 1694, however. Political and ecclesiastic officials in the colony and back home had to avoid any legal controversy in a question that needed to be dealt with through quiet diplomacy. Pastor Johannes Ernestus Gutwasser (16??–16??) came to New Amsterdam on the sly in the 1650s, hoping for "tolerance by connivance." He was sent back in 1659 by Petrus Stuyvesant. The latter did, however, permit the continued existence of a Lutheran congregation in New Sweden along the Delaware River, a colony he had taken from the English in 1655.

Quite a few English Puritans also lived in New Netherland. The colonies of New England were their most obvious destination in North America. This is where the distinguishing ideal of a covenant between God and the visible saints was made manifest. Ann Hutchinson (1591–1643), the prophetess who was excommunicated in Massachusetts because of her controversial ideas and religious activities, was given shelter by Dutch settlers on Manhattan, where she later became the unwitting victim of a violent uprising of the native population during Kieft's War. The English Puritans and the Dutch Calvinists were kindred spirits, to a degree. Pastor Bogardus was even the nephew of the most important translator of the writings of the Puritan theologian William Perkins (1558–1602). And one should also remember that soldiers in Massachusetts Bay refused to fight against New Netherland during the First Anglo-Dutch War in 1652–54.

The colonial authorities in New Netherland took firm action against conventicles, not to be confused with gatherings for prayer and worship in individual homes, which were allowed and even encouraged, along with bible study and study of the catechism. A 1656 decree (issued again in 1662 in English) was aimed at sectarian groups that threatened the unity of Christian society. Many liberal groups came into being during the period of nonconformism during the English Civil War. The adult baptisms that an English pastor conducted in the coastal town of Vlissingen (Flushing) in 1656 were especially detestable. The Quakers, who arrived on the scene in 1657, seemed even more dangerous. They were Christians who drew on an "inner light" and renounced all outward expressions of religion, including confessions, offices, and sacraments. Men and women were regularly arrested for conducting services or administering sacraments in the villages and towns on Long Island, where there was no Dutch Reformed pastor.

The Church under the English

The colony of New Netherland was taken over by the British in 1664. A sense of political realism encouraged the new masters to seek cooperation with the Dutch, who wielded great economic power. Things were not quite as easy the other way around, especially from a religious point of view. During Leisler's Rebellion (1689–91), which followed the short term of office of a Catholic governor, many Dutch Reformed colonists took his side, partly out of sympathy for the English Puritans. The ruling class, which even enjoyed the support of Dutch pastors, subscribed to the royalist/aristocratic ideals that went on to gain ascendancy during the reign of William III (1689–1702). Eventually, Dutch and English political solidarity was victorious in the British colony.

With regard to religious relationships, the regime change of 1664 implied a transformation from the public church of New Netherland into an ethnically oriented denomination under English rule. The Church of England took over the position of state church of course, but traditional freedom of conscience was maintained. The Dutch Reformed congregations were allowed to maintain their independent network under the supervision of the Classis of Amsterdam. Lutherans, who had been reluctantly tolerated, quickly took advantage of the new situation. Their congregation in New Amsterdam built a new church in 1669. They also acquired their own pastor and church council, which was under the supervision of the Lutheran church council in Amsterdam. The Lutheran church remained oriented toward the Dutch Reformed model, not only in language, but also in liturgy and organizational structure. French Huguenots had had a designated space for worship in the fort since 1668. In 1688 a church was built for them where they could worship in their own tongue.

The number of congregations in North America grew quickly from thirty-five in 1714, to forty-five in 1740, to nearly one hundred in 1772. This was partly due to natural population growth, but also thanks to the influx of new waves of immigrants: these were Calvinists who came not from the Republic, but from France and the German Palatinate, and who were welcomed into the Dutch Reformed Church based on their confession. Proportionately speaking, however, the Dutch and Dutch Reformed colonists were quickly surpassed in number by waves of Anglo-Saxon immigrants. Many people from England, Scotland, and Ireland settled in the colony, leading to a rich diversity of confessions: Catholics, Episcopalians, Presbyterians, Baptists, Quakers, and Methodists, who came later. In spite of this relative freedom of religion, the Church of England managed to maintain its dominant influence. It received support from London from the Society for the Propagation of the Gospel in Foreign Parts.[7]

159

To the Honourable

RIP VAN DAM. Esq

PRESIDENT of His Majestys Counsill for the PROVINCE of NEW YORK

This View of the New Dutch Church is most humbly

Dedicated by your Honours most Obedient Servt Wm Burgis

The middle church building built in 1729 to harbor
the many Dutch Reformed believers.

The greatest degree of multiformity was to be found in the city of New York, where ethnic Dutch residents went from being the majority to forming a minority around 1700. In 1729 the Dutch Reformed congregation moved to a new building (Collegiate Church), which could hold twelve hundred worshipers. The Anglican Trinity Church was stiff competition in the metropolis. This was not only because of the language issue but also due to the many mixed marriages and the fact that the Anglicans' more lenient stance toward lifestyle and doctrine was difficult to resist for many members of the Dutch Reformed Church. Outside New York the former Dutch villages in the countryside and along the coast retained their ethnic and cultural homogeneity for quite a while.[8]

During the first half of the eighteenth century, Dutch Reformed pastors once again began to feel the need to convert the heathen. This time, it was not a confessional duty imposed by a public church, but a pious ideal born of a Christian community. Preaching was done among the Mohawks on the frontier, especially in the Schenectady area, and basic Christian texts were translated. Although "Indians" were regularly baptized, the success rate of the Dutch missions should not be exaggerated, especially when compared to the spectacular results of the English missions.

Pietism and Evangelicalism

A trend of Pietism had begun to grow within the Dutch Reformed Church in the Republic after the victory of orthodoxy at the Synod of Dort (1618–19) and under the strong influence of English Puritanism. Both in preaching and in pastoral care, the emphasis was very much on the personal and social consecration of life, on the moral purity of church and clergy, and on the emotional conviction of the "true children of God." This Pietism was compromised in 1669–70 when the radical Calvinist Jean de Labadie (1610–74) left the Dutch Reformed Church. Peter Sluyter (1645–1722) was one of his followers. He came from the Dutch congregation in Wesel in the German Rhineland and traveled with the WIC to America to look for a suitable location for a Labadist colony, which he finally founded in Maryland (Bohemia Manor).[9]

Most followers of Reformed Pietism remained true to the public church, despite their criticism of moral decline. This applied to Jacobus Koelman (1631–95), a prolific author of inspirational works and translator of English "practisans," even after his politically motivated removal as pastor in the city of Sluis in Zeeland in 1674. He was called by the Dutch colonists in Nieuwer-Amstel in 1682, more than likely because of his Puritan identity, but also because of his expertise in confessional polemics. Koelman remained in Holland, but in 1683 his pupil Guiliam Bertholf (1656–1726) went to New Jersey with other residents of

1

—

COLONIAL
PERIOD
AND
EIGHTEENTH
CENTURY

1609–1782

Sluis. He impressed his spiritual peers with his skill as a lay pastor, was ordained in 1694 by the Classis of Walcheren (bypassing the Classis of Amsterdam), and spent more than three decades preaching in and around New York.[10]

Reformed Pietism seriously took off during the office of Theodorus Jacobus Frelinghuysen (1692–1747). He was educated in Reformed German satellite states of the Dutch Republic (Lingen and East Frisia) and arrived in America in 1720 to serve the congregations in the Raritan Valley. His theology was not particularly original: he propagated the spiritual heritage of Further Reformation authors such as Koelman and Wilhelmus à Brakel (1635–1711), whose popular and dogmatic *Redelijke Godsdienst* was widely read in New Netherland in the eighteenth century. Frelinghuysen was well known for his theatrical style of preaching, his emotionally charged ideas about belief, his criticism of orthodox formalism, and his penchant for eliciting intrigues, conflicts, and polemics.[11]

Frelinghuysen created a revival in the colonies that found its parallel — partly through personal contacts — in similar developments in the Dutch Republic. In America he inspired not only colleagues of his own denomination, but also young English Presbyterians like Gilbert Tennent (1703–64) and Jonathan Edwards (1703–58). He is even considered the forerunner of the First Great Awakening, partly because of his influence on the important Anglican revivalist pastor George Whitefield (1714–70). The Lutheran community in New York also had its share of tension between orthodoxy and Pietism as a result of developments back home in Germany. The transatlantic chain of revival movements paved the way for evangelicalism, which was indifferent to specific confessions and creeds and, besides combating tendencies of rationalistic liberalism, broke down the old frames of orthodoxy, replacing legal Christianity with religion of the heart.[12]

Church Self-Sufficiency

The religious polarization in the former Dutch colony was inextricably bound up with tensions resulting from dependence on the Classis of Amsterdam. Communication between the Old and the New World was laborious. Calling new pastors, providing counsel on ecclesiastical affairs, and settling disputes took tremendous amounts of time. Misunderstandings grew more common on both sides of the Atlantic. Church and WIC officials in Amsterdam persisted nevertheless in their resistance to an independent organizational structure for the American congregations. The libertine regents of the Republic, who had lost political sway in North America, wished to maintain authority of the churches there, which had become susceptible to spiritual and civil willfulness. It was only in 1737 that the Classis allowed an assembly of pastors to be formed that had the authority to provide counsel to the congregations and mediate in disputes.

Over the years, some pastors with a Pietistic orientation began to train young people to become pastors so that they could avoid the long and arduous process at one of the faculties of theology in Holland. They formed a majority in the assembly and in 1754 established their right to examine and ordain new pastors. The orthodox minority of the clergy in New York was displeased by this development. In 1757 the opposition joined forces in a Conference, which remained loyal to the Classis of Amsterdam. The traditionalists viewed ecclesiastic independence as a schism from the roots of culture and doctrine. They insisted on the classic Reformed values of uniformity and virtue. The accommodationists, however, claimed that religious and organizational autonomy was the only way to escape the paralysis caused by endless internal struggles and the fierce competition from English denominations.

This informal schism lasted until 1771. Reconciliation came during a communal synod, led by the American pastor John Henry Livingston (1746–1825), who had studied both at Yale College and at the University of Utrecht. He was a model for the new generation of evangelical, moderately enlightened pastors, the majority of whom were born in North America. One year later, the Classis of Amsterdam decided that it was time to transfer authority to the churches in America. This marked the independence of the Reformed Church in America (called the Hollandsche Gereformeerde Kerk van Noord-Amerika until 1867), which continues to this day. The Church was divided into five regions that gathered twice annually for Particular Assemblies and sent a delegation to the annual meeting of the General Assembly. The year 1772 also saw the end of the union between the Lutheran church in New York and the Lutheran consistory in Amsterdam.

Language and Identity

Factors that contributed to weakening the relationship between Holland and America included the dominance of English culture, the breakthrough of Pietism, and the independence of the Church. The deciding factor, however, was language assimilation. The Dutch language maintained its position as an important mother tongue for a surprisingly long time, not only in the domestic environment, but also in private conversation, in personal communication with God, and as a language of the Church and of education. Preaching, teaching, and religious reading were conducted in Dutch until well into the eighteenth century. The bulk of books imported from Holland consisted of bibles (the 1637 translation), books of psalms (the rhymed version by Petrus Datheen; its 1773

163

1

—

COLONIAL
PERIOD
AND
EIGHTEENTH
CENTURY

1609–1782

successor was of no consequence in America), catechisms for children (Petrus de Witte's edition in the seventeenth century; later, that of Abraham Hellenbroek), and books of sermons on the Heidelberg Catechism. In North America, Frelinghuysen and his Pietistic colleague Bernardus Freeman (1662–1743) were the only figures to publish a number of devotional works in Dutch.

In the course of the eighteenth century the dominance of the English language became too much for the ethnic/religious minorities. A battle over language was unavoidable for the descendants of Dutch immigrants, especially when it came to religion. The preservation of the Dutch language in church services was the cause of local conflicts and tensions between congregations and church authorities. After forty years of debate, the congregation in New York City was the first to switch to English-language services in 1763. Other congregations followed suit, often much later. An English translation of the Dutch Reformed liturgy was published in 1767. Curiously, the translation was based on a seventeenth-century edition intended for English Puritan immigrants in the Dutch Republic. An English edition of Abraham Hellenbroek's confirmation book was published by the Classis of New Brunswick in 1783.[13]

In the wake of the battle to preserve Dutch language and culture, Reformed orthodoxy and piety became iconic symbols of Dutch identity, with the Synod of Dort as a *lieu de mémoire*. Although new generations of Dutch Americans attempted to stay true to their spiritual roots, adaptation to and acceptance of the dominant evangelical culture was inevitable. Even the old Pietistic heritage had to succumb. A 1793 attempt by a New Brunswick publisher to release an English edition of the aforementioned standard work by Brakel was a failure. A translation of the catechism sermons by Johannes van der Kemp did make it into publication in 1810. Nevertheless, the religious climate in the Reformed Church in America had already been substantially affected by the Anglo-Saxon, Methodist, optimistic and, indeed, nationalistic piety that swept though American Protestantism in the Second Great Awakening.[14]

Conclusion

During the War of Independence (1772–76) the Reformed Dutch residents of the colonies were a strong political factor on the American side. In their old fatherland freedom of religion had been an important ambition for the revolutionary patriots, and later for the united citizens of a Protestant nation. The last Dutch-language sermon in the Reformed Church in America was spoken in 1833. At the time no one suspected that the history of 1620 would soon repeat itself. "A new body of Pilgrims has reached our shores from Holland, the land of our fathers, and the shelter in ages gone by to outcast from persecution," noted the *Christian Intellegencer* with surprise in 1847. A new chapter in American religious history had begun: a chapter whose parameters consisted of waves of immigrants, the establishment and division of free churches, and reinventions of the Calvinist past.

1   George L. Smith, *Religion and Trade in New Netherland, Dutch Origins and American Development* (Ithaca, NY: Cornell University Press, 1973); Jaap Jacobs, *New Netherland: A Dutch Colony in Seventeenth-Century America* (Leiden: Brill, 2005), chapter 5.

2   Gerald F. De Jong, *The Dutch Reformed Church in the American Colonies* (Grand Rapids MI: Eerdmans, 1978).

3   Willem Frijhoff, *Fullfilling God's Mission: The Two Worlds of Dominie Everardus Bogardus 1607–1647* (Leiden: Brill, 2007).

4   David Hackett, *The Rude Hand of Innovation. Religion and Social Order in Albany, New York 1652-1836* (New York/Oxford: Oxford University Press, 1991).

5   Willem Frijhoff, "Seventeenth-Century Religion as a Cultural Practice. Reassessing New Netherland's Religious History," in Margriet Bruijn Lacy et al., eds, *From De Halve Maen to KLM. 400 Years of Dutch-American Exchange* (Münster: Nodus Publikationen, 2008), 159-174.

6   A special case represents the Amsterdam merchant Pieter Plockhoy (ca. 1620–ca. 1700), settler at Swanendael (Horekill), Nieuwer Amstel, 1663–64. See Irvin B. Horst, "Pieter Cornelisz Plockhoy: An Apostle of the Collegiants," *Mennonite Quarterly Review* 23 (July 1949): 161-185.

7   Richard W. Pointer, *Protestant Pluralism and the New York Experience: A Study of Eighteenth-Century Religious Diversity* (Bloomington: Indiana University Press, 1988); Randall H. Balmer, *A Perfect Babel of Confusion: Dutch Religion and English Culture in the Middle Colonies* (New York/Oxford: Oxford University Press, 1989).

8   Joyce D. Goodfriend, *Before the Melting Pot: Society and Culture in Colonial New York City, 1664-1730* (Princeton, NJ: Princeton University Press, 1992).

9   Trevor John Saxby, *The Quest for the New Jerusalem, Jean de Labadie and the Labadists, 1610–1744* (Dordrecht/Boston: Martinus Nijhoff, 1987).

10 Firth Haring Fabend, *A Dutch Family in the Middle Colonies, 1660–1800* (New Brunswick, NJ: Rutgers University Press, 2000).

11 James R. Tanis, *Dutch Calvinistic Pietism in the Middle Colonies: A Study in the Life and Theology of Theodorus Jacobus Frelinghuysen* (The Hague: Martinus Nijhoff, 1967); Joel R. Beeke, ed., *Forerunner of the Great Awakening: Sermons by Theodorus Jacobus Frelinghuysen (1691-1747)* (Grand Rapids, MI: Eerdmans, 2000).

12 Fred van Lieburg, "Interpreting the Dutch Great Awakening (1749–1755)," *Church History* 77 (2008): 318-336.

13 Fred van Lieburg, "Pietism beyond Patria: A Dutch Religious Heritage in North-America," in George Harinck and Hans Krabbendam, eds., *Morsels in the Melting Pot: The Persistence of Dutch Immigrant Communities in North America* (Amsterdam: VU University Press, 2006), 43-54.

14 Firth Haring Fabend, *Zion on the Hudson: Dutch New York and New Jersey in the Age of Revivals,* (New Brunswick, NJ: Rutgers University Press, 2000).

1

—

COLONIAL
PERIOD
AND
EIGHTEENTH
CENTURY

1609–1782

DUTCH LANGUAGE
AND LITERATURE IN THE
UNITED STATES

—

JAN NOORDEGRAAF

Introduction

Few will be surprised to learn that the Dutch language was still used in North America after Petrus Stuyvesant's death in 1672. Less widely known is the fact that spoken Dutch remained in use far longer than people generally assume, although the production of literary texts appears to have been limited. From a linguistic perspective it is important to examine how Dutch developed in North America. Such considerations invite comparison with another language descended from a form of "colonial Dutch"—Afrikaans—but by necessity that subject remains beyond the scope of this essay.

What might have happened if, late in the summer of 1664, the Dutch had not handed New Amsterdam over to the English and had succeeded in repelling English attacks, is fascinating to consider. The United States might have become a colony of the Netherlands, with Dutch as its official language. Millions of Americans would have spoken Dutch instead of English. This flight of fancy is also tellingly illustrated in the widespread myth that, during the American Revolution, a single vote in the state of New York supposedly made the difference between "the whole of America" speaking Dutch rather than English. Actually, there are various versions of this myth: the same one-vote difference has been attributed to other languages.

The final loss of Dutch authority over New Netherland in 1674 did not spell the end of Dutch as a language in North America. In 1788, it was still of sufficient importance to warrant a swift translation into Dutch of the first constitution of the newly established United States, in hopes of drumming up support among the Dutch colonists.[1] When in the 1820s the Dutch pastor Gerardus Balthazar Bosch (1794–1837) visited Albany as well as Hoboken, NJ, and heard Dutch spoken wherever he went, he expressed surprise that "the Dutch language [had] survived in North America for so long." However, he went on to add that this Dutch had become so "poor, clumsy and coarse" that it would be no great loss if it were no longer spoken. People at the time estimated that this language death would occur around 1850. In fact, it did not take place until almost a century later, and Jaap van Marle recently stated that "during the first decades of the twentieth century there were still people around who were fluent in so-called Low Dutch."[2] Bosch's observations lead to questions on the development of the Dutch that was spoken in the colony of New Netherland during the first half of the seventeenth century to the variant that the he heard at the market in New York in 1825. Anyone who plans to study "older American Dutch," as it is referred to in the literature, will have to take into account that in the second half of the twentieth century a number of American-Dutch texts appeared that turned out to be falsifications, a phenomenon that, according to Van Marle, has also occurred in other languages. Another problem when studying the development of New Netherland Dutch (or *Laeg Duits* as it was called by later generations) is the size of the material that served as a basis for the most important study of American Dutch to date, a corpus of some two hundred "New York Dutch" documents that was analyzed in the early 1970s.[3] By current standards this corpus is modest. As regards literary language, most of what has been passed down to us consists of a number of poems from the second half of the seventeenth century and it is questionable whether their language use differed from that in the Netherlands at that time; in all likelihood it did not. Beyond this point, Dutch in North America, as far as we know, seems to have ceased as a language for literary expression.

American Dutch: Disappearance and Change

Since the foundation of the colony, Dutch — as the language of the West India Company — was used for administrative purposes, poetry, and religion. It continued to serve as the language of the pulpit in some areas until the early nineteenth century — the last standard sermon in Dutch was held in 1833. The years between 1640 and 1690 are regarded as the "formative years" of New Netherland Dutch: from 1640 on, the Dutch contingent that had settled in this new region was large enough to enable a new variant of Dutch to begin developing. Dutch in North America therefore had half a century to flourish and gain a firm foothold.[4]

Around 1664, the colony had between seven and eight thousand inhabitants, including a number for whom Dutch was not the native language, such as the British, the Germans, the Scandinavians, and the French. It is interesting to note that foreign employees of the West India Company were quick to switch to

1

—

COLONIAL
PERIOD
AND
EIGHTEENTH
CENTURY

1609–1782

Dutch, which was the lingua franca that offered them the desired access to the colonial social structures. As sociolinguistic research from recent decades has taught us, social status and prestige are far more decisive factors in constructing a language than the number of speakers. What is more, there was no competition with a widely spoken language such as French: contact with the northern French border territory of Québec remained infrequent. However, English remained the language of a significant minority in nearby areas such as Maryland, Virginia, and Massachusetts.

For the further development of New Netherland Dutch it is important to distinguish between New York City and the areas along the upper Hudson and lower Mohawk rivers. English rule became definitive in 1674 and as large numbers of English speakers settled in the former Dutch territory, the pressure from English first increased in the city, where much of the Dutch-speaking population became bilingual. The year 1730, for example, saw the publication of a small schoolbook for teaching English to speakers of Dutch. This slim volume appeared in New York, where we know that the signs of imminent "language death" were evident by the mid-1700s. The first minister to preach in both Dutch and English was a bilingual Scot by the name of Archibald Laidlie (1727–79). In 1763 he made the crossing from Vlissingen to New York City to become the first English-speaking pastor in the Dutch Reformed churches in America. Thus it transpired that Dutch gradually disappeared as a cultural language that was spoken and written for ecclesiastical and administrative purposes.

In two rural areas, however, speakers maintained Dutch as a domestic language: in Bergen County in northeastern New Jersey and in the heart of eastern New York State, around the Mohawk and Hudson rivers. Both varieties resembled each other closely. In this context, the language survived for almost a century after it had died in New York City, albeit in spoken form and only for informal communication about everyday matters. James Storms (1860–1949), a native speaker of New Jersey or Bergen Dutch, noted that when he was a young boy this form of Dutch was still "the prevailing and natural form of speech in many homes of the older residents when there were no strangers present."[5]

The nature of the Mohawk-Hudson variant of *Laeg Duits* in the seventeenth and eighteenth centuries has been described by Gehring, in his study mentioned above, on the basis of written material produced in Dutch during that period. He concludes that, where pronunciation was concerned, a remarkable amount of divergence was tolerated, but that divergence in word form was regarded as less acceptable. His study shows that the influence of English was already affecting various typically Dutch syntactic constructions. One should keep in mind that Gehring's conclusions are based on an analysis of written language, which was more closely related to written Dutch in the Netherlands than to spoken Low Dutch. This difference between written and spoken lan-

THE

English and *Low-Dutch*

SCHOOL-MASTER.

CONTAINING

Alphabetical Tables of the moſt Common Words in *English* and *Dutch*. With certain Rules and Directions whereby the *Low-Dutch* Inhabitants of *North-America* may (in a ſhort time) learn to *Spell, Read, Underſtand* and *Speak* proper *English*. And by the help whereof the *English* may alſo learn to *Spell, Read, Underſtand* and *Write Low-Dutch*.

By *FRANCIS HARRISON*,

School-Maſter. in *Somerſet-County*, in *New-Jerſey, America.*

NEW-YORK:

Printed and Sold by *W. Bradford*. 1730.

DE

Engelſche en *Nederduytſche*

SCHOOL - MEESTER.

BEHELSENDE

Verſchydene Tafelen, na de order van *A, B*, in gericht van de gemeenſte Woorden, in 't *Engels* en *Duytſch*. Met eenige Regels en Onderwyſingen, waardoor de *Nederduytſche* Inwoonders van *Nort America* in korten tyt de *Engelſche* Taal mogen leeren *Spellen, Leeſen, Verſtaan* en *Spreeken*. Ende de *Engelſche* in 's gelyks mogen leeren *Spellen, Leeſen, Verſtaan* en *Schryven*, in de *Nederduytſche* Taal.

Opgeſtelt door *FRANCIS HARRISON*, School-Meeſter, in *Somerſet-County*, in *Nieuw-Jerſy*, in *America.*

NIEUW-JORK:

Gedrukt en te Koop by *W. Bradford*. 1730.

Title pages of Francis Harrison (1693/4–1735), a "School-Master, in Somerset-County, in New-Jersey, America" published the first and only grammar written for Dutch-speaking inhabitants of North America in "Nieuw-Jork."

1

—

COLONIAL
PERIOD
AND
EIGHTEENTH
CENTURY

1609–1782

guage must have been considerable, as it was in the Netherlands, where a standard for written and spoken language use did not materialize until the nineteenth century. It is assumed that, due to the influence of English, New Netherland Dutch had changed considerably in the mid-eighteenth century. However, in order to reach firm conclusions, much more textual data with regard to the divergent forms in the phonological, morphological, and syntactical makeup of the language is needed. The availability of large text corpora, for example including letters written by authors without much schooling, would considerably aid further research using technological resources.

Anthony Buccini, discussing the rare accounts of Bergen Dutch, points to the noteworthy fact that this variant is still recognizable as Dutch, however much people around 1800 considered it "corrupted" (which brings us back to the experiences of the Reverend Bosch). However, Van Marle emphasizes that the ongoing influence of English must have left deeper traces, thereby giving Low Dutch a character all of its own. Thus Low Dutch, as a spoken variety of the language, did not disappear but went on to develop autonomously. As contact between the Dutch-speaking community of North America and the Netherlands quickly waned, particularly in terms of the gap between rural areas and intellectual life, there was no fresh impetus from the eighteenth-century scholars and writers in the Netherlands who were seeking to establish a standard Dutch language.

Putting Eighteenth-Century Language Description to the Test?

The first and only grammar written for Dutch-speaking inhabitants of North America was published in "Nieuw-Jork" in 1730 by the renowned printer and bookseller William Bradford: *De Engelsche en Nederduytsche School-Meester*, or in its English title, *The English and Low-Dutch Schoolmaster*. The writer of this bilingual book was Francis Harrison (1693/4–1735), who according to the title page was a "School-Master, in Somerset-County, in New-Jersey, America." Through his publication he aimed to achieve "The better Instructing of the Netherlanders, and the Dutch inhabitants of this Northern part of America in the English Tongue." In addition, the title page states that with the help of this book "the English may also learn to Spell, Read, and Understand and Write Low-Dutch." This work can therefore be characterized as a bilingual aid for Dutch learners of English and vice versa. The book's structure is traditional and synthetic, in that it starts with the "letters" and moves on to a chapter on syllables that takes up almost half of the book. The reader is provided many lists of words that consist of one or more syllables. One highly practical section contains all kinds of prayers and sample letters. Then follows an "abstract of English grammar" and the entire work concludes with a "table of Names, Dutch and English."[6] However, Harrison's book provides little in the way of concrete insight into American Dutch as used around 1730. For despite his claim in "To the Reader" that he never had "any Grounds … to the like purpose from which I might receive any furtherance or help herein," Harrison drew extensively from existing works. By far the most important source for his book was *Anglo-Belgica. d'Engelsche en Nederduytsche Academy* or *The English and Netherdutch Academy* (Amsterdam, 1677), a book for an English and Dutch readership written by English expatriate Edward Richardson: over 80 percent of the content of *De Engelsche en Nederduytsche School-Meester* is literally the same as Richardson's work, which was published half a century earlier and also features the term "Low Dutch." In short, almost the entire content of Harrison's work is taken from seventeenth-century sources. The most influential grammar in the Netherlands at the time was *Nederduitsche spraakkunst* (Dutch grammar), written by the Reverend Arnold Moonen (1644–1711). It was a bulky grammar that was published in 1706 and reprinted until the mid-eighteenth century. Yet there is no evidence that this work influenced *De Engelsche en Nederduytsche School-Meester*. The fact that contemporary grammarians from the Netherlands were working to construct a standard Dutch language, whatever the status of their endeavors, does not appear to have been a point of reference.

Harrison's work is a unique document on second-language learning. It does not, however, reflect language use among the Dutch in North America in the early eighteenth century. It simply contains seventeenth-century written language from the Dutch Republic. Nor can the process of language change be extrapolated from the book, while its rules of Dutch pronunciation do not constitute a reliable reflection of what was customary in New Jersey in the first quarter of the eighteenth century.[7] However, the very fact that a bilingual book such as Harrison's was published, indicates that there was a need for such a work in 1730 and tells us something about the ongoing process of linguistic accommodation in which the speakers of Dutch were involved: a number of them "found it increasingly necessary to communicate in English"[8] in order to keep up with their English-speaking compatriots in terms of political and socioeconomic status.

The Literature of New Netherland: Poets and Patriots

As was mentioned, the literary production of New Netherland was modest and has not been the subject of extensive research to date. The only New Netherland poetry to enter the canon consists of some verses by three seventeenth-century poets, anthologized by the American Henry Cruse Murphy (1810–82) as early as 1865. Murphy, who was minister resident for the United States in The Hague

1

———

COLONIAL
PERIOD
AND
EIGHTEENTH
CENTURY

1609–1782

from 1857 to 1861, was appointed a foreign member of Leiden's celebrated Maatschappij der Nederlandsche Letterkunde (Society for Dutch literature) in 1858 and became an expert on Dutch history and literature. The section in his anthology only features a small number of poems, inspired by these poets' residence in parts of New Netherland.[9] The fact that part of their poetic oeuvre was created elsewhere and is devoted to other themes is described in other surveys of Dutch literature.

The best-known of the three poets is Jacob Steendam (1615–72/73), a former comforter of the sick who had already gained a certain literary reputation before he arrived in New York in 1652. Within this context, two of his poems are worthy of scrutiny. *Klacht van Nieuw-Amsterdam in Nieuw Nederlandt tot Haar Moeder* (Complaint of New Amsterdam to her mother, 1659) sums up all the advantages offered by the new colony and appeals to the Dutch motherland to come to the colony's aid. His plea appears to have fallen on deaf ears, since he repeated it in *'T Lof van Nieuw Nederland* (Praise of New Netherland, 1661), in which he emphasizes the colony's abundance in almost biblical terms. It was an effective piece of propaganda for the young colony.

Henricus Selyns (1636–1701) served as a minister in the Dutch Reformed Church of Breuckelen (1660–64) and the First Reformed Church of New York City (1682–1701). In addition to Dutch poetry, he wrote verse in English and Latin. Only those poems in which Selyns wrote of a link with New Netherland are relevant to the present context, such as his *Bruydtlofs Toorts* (*Bridal Torch*, 1663). This text, which has recently been the subject of thorough literary-historical research, deals with wedding and war, and was written to mark the nuptials of the rector of the New Amsterdam Latin School, not long after a massacre "committed at Wiltwyck ... by the Indians."[10]

The third author whose poems are included in Murphy's seminal anthology is Dr. Nicasius de Sille (1610–74), a "man of no ordinary attainments in literature and science," as Murphy puts it: he came from a line of Dutch regents and had an academic background. Having arrived in New Amsterdam in 1654, he became Petrus Stuyvesant's first councilor. Later on, De Sille, a statesman through and through, acted as *schout* (sheriff) of New Amsterdam and held the positions of church warden, fire warden, and even the office of captain lieutenant for a time. When living at New Utrecht on Long Island, around 1660, he wrote *Description of the Founding or Beginning of New Utrecht*. His poem *Het Aerdtrijck spreeckt tot Syne Opquekers* (The earth speaks to its cultivators) contains a reference to New Utrecht, a place he liked very much.

While these three colonial poets have more or less entered the canon now that a selection of their poems has been included in a relatively recent anthology of seventeenth-century Dutch poetry, one looks in vain for an account of other types of literature.[11] Hardly anything coherent on American-Dutch litera-

Painting of Jacob Jacobsz Steendam (1615–73), poet and historian
in Amsterdam, New Amsterdam and Batavia.

1

—

COLONIAL
PERIOD
AND
EIGHTEENTH
CENTURY

1609–1782

ture from the late seventeenth and eighteenth century appears to have been published, not even on texts for special occasions such as wedding poems and odes. Only a few rare examples of eighteenth-century poetry have been selected for study. This may be due to the fact that a sufficiently thorough search has yet to be undertaken, or to the fact that very little literature was produced during this period. A comparison between colony and homeland at this time reveals that the social context in North America was not exactly favorable for the creation of a written culture in the Dutch language and exhaustive cultivation of language. This was, on the contrary, the case in the motherland, where sociable eighteenth-century writers met in hundreds of literary societies and theater visits were commonplace.

In 1825 the Reverend Bosch, quoted above, noted of the Dutch spoken around Albany and Hoboken that "books in the language are not to be found" and this would appear to be an accurate observation, at least with regard to literary works written in this variety of Dutch. As *Laeg Duits* was exclusively a spoken language, it possessed neither a literature nor a normative grammar with a generally accepted orthography.

The Gift of Dutch

In order to maintain adequate contact with Native Americans, it was important that a number of people acquire at least some knowledge of their languages. This learning process was by no means simple. Comforter of the sick Bastiaen Jansz. Krol was "well acquainted with the language," but in 1644 he told the Reverend Johannes Megapolensis (1603–70), a learned scholar who was preparing a vocabulary of "the Makuakuaas' language," that he thought the Native Americans "changed their language every two or three years." Megapolensis wanted to learn this "very difficult language" in order to be able "to speak and to preach in it fluently."[12] We also know the names of various other *taelsmannen* (interpreters). One of them was a woman, Sara Roelofs (1627–93), the eldest daughter of the legendary New Netherland matriarch Anneke Jans.[13] Sara was famed for her extensive knowledge of Native American languages, which she probably acquired during her childhood in Rensselaerswijck, where the white settlers had contact with Native Americans on a daily basis, primarily with Mohawks and Mahicans. Later, in May 1664, she acted as an interpreter for Petrus Stuyvesant at the peace talks with the Esopus Native Americans. Unfortunately, as far as we know, she did not embark on a grammar of any of these languages. However, we do possess a "Vocabulary of the Maquas," a glossary of Mohawk, drawn up by Harmen Meyndertsz. van den Boogaert during his foray into Mohawk Country in 1634–35. This glossary forms the basis for the list that Johannes de Laet used in the 1640s in his discussion with Hugo Grotius about the origins of the *gentium Americanarum*, the term he used to refer to the American peoples.[14]

Although there is scant evidence of Native Americans learning Dutch, in trading they did pick up a number of Dutch words, which they incorporated into their own language as borrowings. The languages of the Loup, Mahican, and the Munsee Delaware all contain words of recognizably Dutch origin. Most of them are domestic words and words for new items. For example, various Native American languages have adopted the Dutch word *poes* (pussycat): in Loup the word *puspus*; in Mahican *poschees* and *poschesh*, derived from the diminutive form *poesje*; and in Munsee Delaware *poosis*. Reduplication was a frequently applied morphological procedure: *kipkip* (chicken in Loup), *kuskusj* (*varken*/pig in Munsee Delaware), and *kitkit* (*kat*/cat in Mohawk). *Memekis* (Munsee Delaware for *schaap* or sheep) has a clear onomatopoetic value (see the Dutch *mekkeren*, which means to bleat). Mahican, now a dead language, borrowed *gónan* (*kool*/cabbage) and *kumkùmsch* (*komkommer*/cucumber), while Munsee Deleware borrowed *kómkòmes* (*komkommer*/cucumber) and *šelāš* (*salade*/salad). The Dutch traded *brandewijn* (brandy) with the Native Americans and this appears in Delaware as *brandywyne*.

It is widely known that the Dutch provided U.S. English with all manner of place and street names. But other Dutch elements can be found in the vocabulary of American English, words such as winkelhawk (from the Dutch *winkelhaak*), for example, in addition to better-known borrowings such as coleslaw, cookie, waffle, spook, and sleigh. The word *stoep* became stoop in American English, referring to a veranda or landing accessed by means of a narrow flight of steps. According to one American dictionary it was "formerly, a small porch with seats or benches, usually occupied by a pipe-smoking householder."

Concluding Remarks

In seventeenth-century New Netherland, Dutch was used for administrative purposes, poetry, and religion, and in some areas it continued to serve as the language of the church until the early nineteenth century. Some seventeenth-century New Netherland poets eventually came to be included in modern Dutch anthologies, and in the first decade of the twenty-first century they have become the subject of more extensive literary analysis.

Under the strong influence of English, the spoken variant of New Netherland Dutch developed into a sui generis variety of colonial Dutch. It is an established fact, however, that evidence of the general decline of Low Dutch could be observed as early as the 1750s. A contemporary grammar of this variety has never been passed down to us and, as other contemporary descriptions of the spoken

1

COLONIAL PERIOD AND EIGHTEENTH CENTURY

1609–1782

language are also conspicuous by their absence, the true shape of spoken Low Dutch in the period under discussion will probably remain unknown. The structural aspects of its written counterpart have become clear from the study of seventeenth- and eighteenth-century documents. Lastly, it should be noted that, in the final quarter of the twentieth century in particular, *Laeg Duits* has received the attention it deserves from linguists both in the Netherlands and elsewhere. In the line of recent European linguistic projects such as "language from below," further historical sociolinguistic research—possibly on the basis of a corpus of surviving informal correspondence and ego documents—might shed some light on the way in which spoken eighteenth-century American Dutch was constructed, and in particular how it continued to be used in rural areas.

1   Jan W. de Vries, Roland Willemyns, and Peter Burger, *Het verhaal van een taal. Negen eeuwen Nederlands* (Amsterdam: Prometheus, 2003), 268; See also the article by Joyce D. Goodfriend, elsewhere in this volume.

2   G.B. Bosch, "Eene zomerreis in Noord-amerika. II. Albany," *Vaderlandsche Letteroefeningen 1827*, section 2 (*Mengel-werk*), 275-276; Jaap van Marle, "Myths and Forgeries Relating to American 'Low Dutch,' with Special Reference to *Walter Hill's Notebook*," in Margriet Bruijn Lacy et al., eds., *From De Halve Maen to KLM: 400 Years of Dutch American Exchange* (Münster: Nodus Publikationen 2008), 321.

3   Charles Gehring, "The Dutch Language in Colonial New York: An Investigation of a Language and Its Decline and Its Relationship to Social Change" (Ph.D. dissertation, Indiana University, 1973).

4   Anthony F. Buccini, "New Netherlands Dutch, Cape Dutch, Afrikaans," *Taal en tongval*. Themanummer 9 (1996): 37. The subject of change and disappearance of American Dutch has been addressed, in recent decades, by researchers such as Buccini and Van Marle. See for example Anthony F. Buccini, "The Dialectical Origins of New Netherland Dutch," in Thomas Shannon and Johan P. Snapper, eds., *Dutch Linguistics in a Changing Europe. The Berkeley Conference on Dutch Linguistics 1993* (Lanham, MD: University Press of America, 1995), 211-263; Jaap van Marle, "American 'Leeg Duits' ('Low Dutch')—a neglected language," in P. Sture Ureland, ed., *Global Eurolinguistics. European Languages in North America—Migration, Maintenance and Death* (Tübingen: Niemeyer, 2001), 79-101; See also Charles Gehring, "The Survival of the Dutch Language in New York and New Jersey," *De Halve Maen* 58.3 (October 1984): 7- 9, 24.

5   See the introduction of James Storms, *A Jersey Dutch Vocabulary* (Park Ridge, NJ: Pascack Historical Society, 1964).

6   For an analysis of Harrison's work, see R.A. Naborn, "NT2 in New Jersey in 1730. Francis Harrisons *De Engelsche en Nederduytsche School-Meester* nader bekeken," *Voortgang, jaarboek voor de neerlandistiek* 21 (2002): 113-142.

7   Ibid., 134. Buccini, who was one of the few to formulate a serious response to Harrison's book and to draw conclusions on that basis with regard to pronunciation, did not recognize his Dutch source material. See Buccini, "The Dialectical Origins," passim.

8   Charles Th. Gehring, "Colonial Dutch,"
    in Jacob Ernest Cooke et al., eds.,
    *Encyclopedia of the North American
    Colonies* (New York: Scribner, 1993),
    3:21.

9   Henry C. Murphy, *Anthology of
    New Netherland or Translations from
    the Early Dutch Poets of New York*
    (New York: Bradford Club, 1865.
    Repr. Amsterdam: N. Israel, 1966); See
    also Elisabeth P. Funk, "De literatuur
    van Nieuw-Nederland," *De Nieuwe
    Taalgids* 85 (1992): 383-395, and the
    forthcoming anthology compiled by
    Frans Blom, *Nieuw Nederland. Repre-
    sentaties in poëzie en proza.*

10 Frans R. E. Blom, "Of Wedding and War.
    Henricus Selyns *Bridal Torch* (1663).
    Analysis, Edition, and Translation of
    the Dutch Poem," in *From* De Halve
    Maen *to KLM*, 185-200.

11 Ton van Strien, ed., *Hollantsche Parnas:
    Nederlandse gedichten uit de zeventiende
    eeuw*. (Amsterdam: Amsterdam Univer-
    sity Press, 1997).

12 Lois Feister, "Linguistic Communication
    between the Dutch and Indians in New
    Netherland, 1609-1664," *Ethnohistory* 20
    (1973): 33.

13 Willem Frijhoff, *Fulfilling God's Mission:
    The Two Worlds of Dominie Everardus
    Bogardus, 1607-1647* (Leiden: Brill,
    2007), 386-387; See also Hendrik
    Edelman, *Dutch-American Bibliography,
    1693–1794: A Descriptive Catalog of
    Dutch-Language Books, Pamphlets and
    Almanacs Printed in America* (Nieuw-
    koop: De Graaf, 1974).

14 J. A. Jacobs, "Johannes de Laet en
    de Nieuwe Wereld," *Jaarboek van het
    Centraal Bureau voor Genealogie* 50
    (1996): 120.

1

COLONIAL
PERIOD
AND
EIGHTEENTH
CENTURY

1609–1782

INTERCULTURAL RELATIONS BETWEEN NATIVE AMERICANS AND EUROPEANS IN NEW NETHERLAND AND NEW YORK

PAUL OTTO

Introduction

Interaction between the Dutch and their descendants in North America and Native Americans began in the 1610s. In the colonial period, this took place in the context of two successive colonies — New Netherland and New York. This essay explores Dutch relations with Native Americans during the whole colonial period.

Because of the placement of the Dutch colony in the geographical and cultural landscape of North America, Dutch-Native American relations were of importance not just to the colony's own history but to the broader history of the early American frontier. Several factors made it so — Dutch access to the fur trade, Dutch involvement in the manufacture and trade of wampum, and, most important, their trade partnership with Indian groups, particularly the Iroquois, who became quite significant in the late seventeenth- and eighteenth-century wars of empire between France and England. Dutch-Indian relations, however, have been frequently overlooked by historians, whose attention has focused on New England, New France, and the Iroquois. In fact, while certain aspects of Dutch-indigenous affairs are unique, many of the interaction patterns readily compare with New France and the New England colonies of northeastern North America.

Peoples and Boundaries

New Netherland was home to many different indigenous groups that were organized in a variety of ways including small kinship groups, villages, collections
of villages, and larger maximal groupings. These different groups represented
themselves by specific names by which the Dutch usually knew them and are
classified under broader terms that represent linguistic similarities and shared
cultural patterns, but none can successfully or accurately portray the complexities of native society before and after contact with Europeans. In the Delaware
Bay region lived diverse groups of Unami speakers (of the Algonquian language
stock) and in the New York Bay and lower Hudson Valley lived Munsee speakers. Both groups would later be known collectively as the Lenape or Delawares.
Living further inland from the Unamis were the Susquehannocks, speaking
an Iroquoian language, while native people up the Hudson River included the
Mahicans, another Algonquian language group. Contending with the Mahicans for access to the upper Hudson River were the Mohawks, the easternmost
tribe of the Five Nations Iroquois, which also included the Cayugas, Ononda-
gas, Oneidas, and Senecas all living to the west of the Mohawks. To the east of
the Munsees and Mahicans lived other Algonquian speakers including the Qui-
ripi, Mohegans, Pequots, Nipmucks, Narragansetts, and many others. While
the Dutch-Indian encounter encompassed all these groups, this essay focuses
primarily on the Hudson Valley interaction with the Munsees, Mahicans, and
Mohawks.[1]

Historical Overview

While European-Native American contact occurred everywhere on the Atlantic
coast throughout the sixteenth century, it was relatively limited in the New York
Bay and Hudson River region. Hudson's 1609 voyage led to the most significant
intercultural contact to date — meetings between the European mariners and
many native people for the first time, the exchange of goods, and some hostile
encounters as well — and to an active Dutch interest in the North American fur
trade in that region.

   Until 1624 trade was the main reason for interaction. Native residents regularly met and traded with private Dutch merchants who came to their coast-
lands and waterways. Representatives of each society ate together, found ways
to communicate with one another, and shared information and ideas. As some
traders stayed for longer periods, more intimate forms of contact took place.

1

—

COLONIAL
PERIOD
AND
EIGHTEENTH
CENTURY

1609–1782

The focus on the exchange of goods changed over time as native people's interest in European goods changed and grew. The Dutch, who like most Europeans had many naïve and false ideas about indigenous peoples, grew in their knowledge and understanding of them.

The Dutch-indigenous encounter expanded and evolved when the first European settlers arrived. Their permanent presence created a whole array of new encounters and challenges. New opportunities for and patterns of interaction emerged, as well as deadly diseases and increased conflict, especially in areas where European settlement was most intense. While no formal hostilities between the Dutch and the Mohawks took place, three wars with the Munsee occurred. The Munsee, who became marginalized in their trade with Europeans and increasingly lost control of their tribal territories, largely lost out on the encounter.[2]

Patterns of Interaction

It was in the economic realm that the Dutch and Indians made their most significant impact upon one another. Furs of beavers, otters, and other animals formed the principal element of trade. These were exported as well as used as a local medium of exchange. Another item used as currency was sewant as it was known to the Dutch and Indians of the Hudson Valley, or wampum, another Indian term, by which it is readily known today as it then was in New England. These strings of white and dark shell beads were products of the Long Island Sound and were greatly valued by the Indians of the north, particularly the Iroquois. The Dutch also traded for Indian products such as wild game and services (transportation in canoes, guidance in the woods, and labor in their fields and orchards).[3]

The exchange of goods took place wherever Dutch and Indian met, but the most economically important trade involved beaver furs and eventually centered on Fort Orange. It was regulated by the West India Company throughout the colony's history. At first, all furs to be exported had to be sold to the WIC through its officials. Eventually the fur trade was opened to all settlers but a duty on each fur had to be paid before export. The fur trade season lasted from June to August. Indians came to the settlement where they found eager traders among the Dutch (men and women, poor and rich). Many acted justly toward the Indians, but others were prone to unethical practices that included threatening, detaining, and striking Indians to discourage them from seeking better trade opportunities elsewhere. Some would meet Mohawks in the woods before they arrived at the settlement, seeking to monopolize their trade. Abuses also included the use of alcohol to cheat the Indians out of a fair price for their furs.

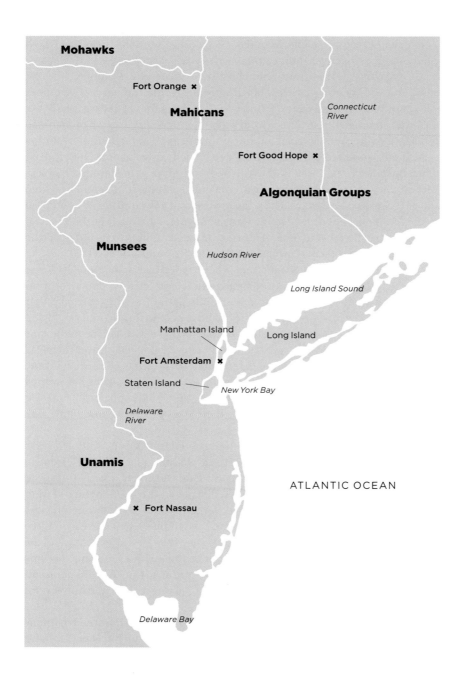

Mohawks

Fort Orange ✗

Mahicans

Connecticut
River

Fort Good Hope ✗

Algonquian Groups

Munsees

Hudson River

Long Island Sound

Manhattan Island

Long Island

Fort Amsterdam ✗

Staten Island

New York Bay

Delaware
River

Unamis

ATLANTIC OCEAN

✗ Fort Nassau

Delaware Bay

Native American tribes in the New Netherland region.

1

COLONIAL
PERIOD
AND
EIGHTEENTH
CENTURY

1609–1782

In payment native people accepted a wide range of items including baked goods, shirts, stockings, duffel cloth, awls, kettles, adzes, axes, knives, shoes, pipes, scissors, files, mirrors, lead cloth seals, mattocks, thimbles, buttons, bells, and sundry other articles. Most notoriously, the Indians also acquired guns, ammunition, and liquor. Native people utilized these goods in a variety of ways that spanned the spectrum from their intended purposes when manufactured by Europeans to outright modification and application to Indian purposes. It is often pointed out that alcohol debauched native people, and, indeed, much mischief came from its abuse. However, Indian people drank to excess because they associated affects of extreme intoxication with the much desired state of "spiritual" elevation. The trade in arms and ammunition was outlawed by the Company, but a clandestine trade had emerged already in the 1630s. It soon became clear that in order not to lose their customers to the English who were offering guns, the WIC would have to relax its prohibitions.[4]

While the Mohawks, Mahicans, and others traded furs to the Dutch at Beverwijck, the Indians in the vicinity of Manhattan Island continued to bring wampum for trade. Wampum was not just valuable to the Dutch as currency. Very early on the Dutch discovered its value to native people throughout the region and particularly to their fur suppliers in the north. In fact, before Europeans arrived in the Hudson Valley, wampum was being exchanged upriver to the Iroquois and others and was utilized ceremonially in a variety of particular functions including social, political, and diplomatic exchanges. After discovering that it significantly facilitated the trade in furs, the Dutch soon became middlemen in the trade in wampum, providing their Munsee- and Algonquian-speaking suppliers the same goods offered for furs.[5]

Suppliers of furs and wampum greatly benefited from these goods. However, as native people became accustomed to the availability and utility of European goods, many slid into a dependency upon them. Observers noted Munsee dependency on such goods and an increased focus on the manufacture of wampum. Iroquois dependence contributed to the reasons for their ongoing warfare with their neighbors. But the Iroquois, geographically removed from the territorial demands of European settlers, avoided the worst effects. Many of the Munsees, however, lost their lands through conflict with Europeans, became incorporated into the Dutch market economy, and were forced to abandon subsistence farming and social-based trade in favor of wager labor and industry for economic survival and material gain.[6]

The Dutch who first encountered Native Americans quickly formed opinions of them and made special designations for them, including *heiden* (heathen), *inwoner* (inhabitant), *natie* (nation), and *Indiaan* (Indian). The most commonly used term was *wilden,* unsatisfactorily translated into English as "wild men."

This term did not necessarily have racist connotations. Instead, it characterized their state with regard to the standards of Western civilization. Assessing native people as *wilden* buttressed other forces that contributed to the marginalization of native people. While theoretically it was possible to see Indians as potentially "civilizable," in practice Dutch colonial efforts did not include significant attempts to introduce Christianity and European civilization, and while native behavior was legislated for those who lived in or near settlements, little evidence exists to demonstrate that the Indians were embraced.[7]

As regular trading partners and indigenous occupants of the land, the Indians had an ongoing presence among the Dutch, which raises important questions about social interaction. In the earliest years of contact, there was miscegenation between Dutch men and Indian women, but no evidence of intermarriage. In a couple of recorded cases, the children of these liaisons received Christian baptism and married Dutch spouses, but most often, it appears, these offspring joined Indian society. Further, there are no recorded cases of adults "going native," During the Second Dutch-Munsee War, several Dutch captives were taken and while most were returned within a short time, two years later a few Dutch children still resided among the Indians and likely never returned to European society. Several individuals throughout New Netherland's history learned to speak Indian languages or at least trade jargons, and some gained a sympathetic understanding of Indian culture. These "cultural mediators" played important roles as translators and diplomats. On a broader scale, many Dutch adopted certain native agricultural practices such as fall brush-burning and the planning of corn and pumpkins.[8] As for the Indians, much of the changes related to the economic impact and to their struggle to maintain their territories and political sovereignty. But as native people, particularly the Munsees, lost territory and political and economic independence, some chose greater degrees of acculturation.

While missionary activity was not prominent and produced few results, it is inaccurate to say that the Dutch did not have an interest. Yet, several obstacles stood in the way of successful evangelism. In early discussions about the creation of the West India Company and then in WIC instructions to early New Netherland administrators, particular concern was voiced about conversion of the natives. Over the years the Amsterdam Classis repeated this concern and Kiliaen van Rensselaer expressed it in his appointment of spiritual guides to his patroonship. Ministers such as Jonas Michaëlius, Johannes Megapolensis, and Samuel Drisius declared their interest or made explicit efforts to evangelize.[9] The Dutch never sent ministers to New Netherland with the express purpose of missionary work. Those, like Megapolensis, who worked with the Indians, had many other duties to attend to. Furthermore, successful evangelism required

1

—

COLONIAL
PERIOD
AND
EIGHTEENTH
CENTURY

1609–1782

language ability and cultural sensitivity. Conversion to Protestant Christianity also required significant instruction before indigenous people could be baptized and admitted to the Lord's Table. Native Americans themselves did not understand the attraction of Christianity, saw the inconsistency between the colonists' behavior and the tenets of the faith, and connected the religion with the culture of those who invaded their territory, introduced brandy, and made war on them. By 1664, virtually no credible conversions had taken place among the Indians.

Since the Dutch soon established a permanent presence among the indigenous peoples, contests necessarily arose over everything from unfair trading to major conflicts over land use, ownership, and occupation. Due to the colony's bifurcated nature — European settlement among decentralized coastal peoples in the lower Hudson Valley and a trade outpost on the fringes of a powerful Indian confederacy in the north — diplomatic relations in each area sharply contrasted with one another. Except for an early conflict in the 1620s, warfare between Europeans and Indians never existed in the north while three significant conflicts took place in the south.

The Dutch soon learned that Indian people throughout New Netherland engaged in a variety of practices that could be described as "social reciprocity," which was most immediately identifiable in the giving and receiving of "gifts." Wampum often played a central role in these exchanges. Not always fully embraced by the Dutch, social reciprocity nevertheless continued to be important and could not be ignored when seeking diplomatic goals with native people. Colonial administrators who failed to engage in such Indian protocols often exacerbated the problems of the frontier, whereas individuals who successfully engaged in Indian social exchanges wielded significant influence. Among the Mohawk, Arent van Curler, employee of Kiliaen van Rensselaer from 1637 and his chief agent in the fur trade from 1641, rose to such prominence. Known by the Indians as "Corlaer," he frequently mediated between the two societies building upon the relations he developed as a trader. After his death, the Iroquois applied the name to successive governors of New York indicating his profound significance.[10]

Van Curler and other Dutch traders and negotiators established an important relationship first with the Mahicans and then with the Mohawks that formed the foundation for later colonial-Iroquoian alliances. These were metaphorically understood by the Indians, first as a "rope" that firmly secured the Dutch to the shores of the Mahican lands, and later as an "iron chain" that bound together the Dutch and the Mohawks, and later the English and the Iroquois. No mediator of the same prominence emerged to help negotiate conflicts between the Dutch and the Munsees. Furthermore, the strains of intercultural contact were greater on the lower Hudson. Here the Dutch began purchasing land from the Indians at least as early as 1626 with the transfer of Manhattan Island. Indian land cessations were likely seen by themselves more as short-term leases than anything else, but such territorial alienation meant the increase of European influence. Growing settlement increased opportunities for conflict and drew Indians further into the European economy. Such broader pressures were accompanied by smaller-scale conflicts such as stolen cattle or hogs, trampled crops, abuses in trade, exchanged blows, and even murder. Over time, the Dutch in the lower Hudson settlements found themselves surrounded by native people who had less and less to offer them as their own supply of furs diminished and the settlers' appetite for farmland grew. The particular reasons for each of the conflicts were unique, but as the intensity of colonization and settlement grew and expanded outward from the Manhattan Island epicenter, warfare followed. The First Dutch-Munsee War (1643–45) has traditionally been known as Kieft's War, which unfairly lays too much blame at the feet of one individual. The Second Dutch-Munsee War (1655) was called the Peach War because of the Dutch murder of one Indian taking peaches from a settler's orchard on Manhattan, but is better understood as resulting from the overreaction of the militia to the presence of a sizeable number of Munsee warriors on Manhattan Island. Finally, further to the north (modern-day Kingston) occurred the Third Dutch-Munsee War (1659–60, 1663–64) or First and Second Esopus Wars named after the Munsee band that was primarily involved. This war represented the classic conflict between an expanding settler population and an indigenous population whose territorial sovereignty is being threatened. While the Dutch suffered important losses in each of these wars, the impact upon native people was far more profound, significantly contributing to the loss of Munsee population, land, and political sovereignty.[11]

Post-1664 Relations

Despite the 1664 English conquest of New Netherland, contact between Dutch settlers and the native inhabitants continued and the Dutch ethnic presence remained significant, especially in Albany but also in Schenectady and other villages. No major wars or conflicts took place either on the lower Hudson or upper, but misunderstandings, beatings, murders could still occur. At the same time, more intimate and positive contact such as intermarriage and miscegenation, while never common, continued. Albany and the other northern settlements were still frontier settlements and stood in Indian country — the homelands of northern Munsees, Mahicans, and Mohawks. Much of the contact that

1

—

COLONIAL
PERIOD
AND
EIGHTEENTH
CENTURY

1609–1782

must have occurred in these areas has gone undocumented, but in missions, trade, and diplomacy the evidence reveals the continuing and prominent role of the Dutch.

Under English control Dutch communities continued to grow and expand, supporting the work of their Dutch Reformed ministers, some of whom added evangelization of the Indians to their responsibilities. Although by the end of the 1670s there is no concrete evidence of Christian conversions among the Munsees, traveler Jasper Danckaerts's observations reveal that some Indians had begun to adopt Christian concepts of a transcendent creator God.

Dutch evangelistic efforts especially among the Mohawk redoubled after Jesuit missionaries from New France began making headway throughout Iroquoia but especially in the Mohawk villages near Schenectady. Dutch ministers from Albany and Schenectady—Petrus Tesschenmaeker, Godfridus Dellius, and Johannes Petrus Nucella—evangelized among the Iroquois in the late seventeenth century. Bernardus Freeman arrived in Schenectady in 1700. Following the path paved by Dutch Calvinists, Anglican ministers later established churches among the Iroquois as well. Conversion to Christianity, whether Protestantism or Catholicism, was partly shaped by political considerations within Indian communities becoming divided in their sympathies between New France and New York, but without the efforts of these Dutch ministers, Protestant Christian influence among the Iroquois would have remained limited.[12]

Albany was not just the center of the fur trade in the north, but served as the official site for all commercial exchanges with the Indians. At first trade was open to diverse itinerant Europeans, but over the last third of the seventeenth century greater restrictions were introduced and such traders were ultimately prohibited from trading there altogether. As long as Albany was largely Dutch in its composition, it was they who made up the European traders.

The takeover by the English did lead to a cessation of the flow of goods from the Netherlands, but the shift from Dutch- to English-manufactured goods did not seem to disrupt the Indian trade as some had feared. The Iroquois continued to bring their furs to Albany, now in exchange for "English woolens" and "West Indian rum" among other English products. From 1664 to 1700, beaver exports declined overall, in part due to western warfare among the Indians, and exported pelts numbered from five to fifteen thousand annually compared to an estimated forty to fifty thousand in the 1650s. Demand for pelts also decreased during this time with the decline in popularity of the beaver hats in Europe. Nevertheless, the fur trade remained the core of Albany's economy.[13]

The goods the Dutch and other Europeans traded to native people largely remained the same ranging from smaller and less frequent items such as knives, awls, and tobacco, to larger and more common items such as cloth, blankets, wampum, alcohol, and arms. The trade and gifting of alcohol continued, with

mericanus ex
Virginia, Ætat: 23

W: Hollar ad vivum
delin: et fecit 1645

van hollar

"An American from Virginia," W. Hollar, 1645. This etching by Wenceslaus Hollar, a Bohemian artist living in Antwerp for much of the period 1644–1652, was based on a sketch done from life of an Indian he called a Virginian. Since the term Virginia often served the Dutch as a synonym for North America, including New Netherland, it is not impossible that this man was a Munsee and likely the native man sold to a pair of Dutch soldiers by Director Kieft for return to and exhibition in the Netherlands.

1

COLONIAL
PERIOD
AND
EIGHTEENTH
CENTURY

1609–1782

the same attendant problems. The trade in arms grew after 1664, especially as conflict between England and France and frontier warfare expanded. While Albany Dutchmen continued to take the lead as traders, it was a younger, more flexible group of "Anglicizers" who did so, while more traditionalist Dutch, some investing in Schenectady with hopes of gaining an edge on the fur trade, lost out.[14]

Dutch residents of Albany contributed in significant ways to frontier diplomacy in Anglo-Indian relations after 1664, and this role stemmed from the relationships created through missions and trade. In the late eighteenth century, these included individuals such as Peter Schuyler, Dirck Wessels ten Broeck, Evert Bancker, and Dominie Dellius. Also of importance was Robert Livingston, who was not Dutch himself but was raised in the Netherlands and later took a Dutch bride in the New World. Much like "Corlaer," they stood out because of their ability with native languages and cultures. But unlike the older Dutch traders with such expertise, these men were the new generation of "Anglicizers." Thus they brokered between three ethnic worlds — Dutch, English, and Indian, particularly Iroquois. Furthermore, Albany, as the official center of the fur trade, became the center of European-Indian diplomacy in the north.

These were the origins of what was later formalized as the "Albany commissioners" — a group of Europeans, mostly Dutch, who served as diplomats and mediators between English colonial governors and native leaders from the late seventeenth until the mid-eighteenth century. Continuing the alliance with the Mohawk metaphorically referred to as an "iron chain," the Albany commissioners helped forge the Covenant Chain alliance between the English and Iroquois, who referred to their connection as a "silver chain." In the minds of the Iroquois, Albany became the only legitimate place to renew the chain and undertake Euro-Indian diplomacy. Important agreements and congresses took place there throughout the late seventeenth and eighteenth centuries while the Albany commissioners were responsible for enlisting Mohawk and Iroquois warriors in several imperial conflicts.

This is not to say that the commissioners controlled the Iroquois or had unequal influence among them. The Iroquois themselves were divided into "anglophone" (courted by the Dutch commissioners), "francophone," and "neutralist" factions. Furthermore, as the Iroquois suffered increased pressures of European colonization and were no longer courted by the Albany commissioners as they had been in earlier decades, the commissioners received the brunt of their criticism. The Mohawks "were become the property of Albany people," complained the Mohawk sachem Hendrick, "they were their dogs."[15]

Dutch diplomats continued to predominate among the commissioners until 1757, during the Seven Years' War, when Irishman Sir William Johnson, who himself served for a while as one of the commissioners, became sole superintendent for Indian affairs of the northern colonies. This was not the end of of

Dutch negotiators on the Indian frontier, however. After the American Revolution broke out, the new United States created both a commission for Indian affairs and a continental army. Notably, it was Philip John Schuyler, of Albany-Dutch descent, who represented the United States to the Six Nations and thereby reestablished the role of Dutch Albany commissioners in Indian affairs and renewed the Covenant Chain first established between the Dutch and the Iroquois. In August 1776, Mohawk leader Abraham said "You informed us that the Council Fire which you had kindled at this place was kindled from a Spark brought from the great Council Fire antiently [sic] kindled by our ancestors at Albany."[16]

Conclusion

On the surface, there are obvious differences between Dutch-Indian relations as compared with French and English encounters in the colonial northeast. These stemmed from the unique nature and scale of the respective colonies. The New England colonies were heavily populated and necessarily made a major impact on the indigenous peoples through land acquisition, trade, environmental changes, missionary activity, and conflict and war. In New France, colonial efforts entailed far fewer colonists and relations with the Indians were shaped by France's *coureurs de bois* approach to the fur trade and its parallel "flying missions" approach to evangelism. In this regard, New Netherland might be seen as a hybrid of the two. In the lower Hudson River valley, where Dutch settlement was most intense, relations closely paralleled those of New England. At Fort Orange, the fur trade remained the focus of engagement with the Indians and, like New France (even though the approach to trade and missions differed for each colony), the area was spared the kinds of conflicts that engulfed New England and Manhattan Island.

But at least two additional observations should be made. All three colonies were similar in their general interaction with the Indians. What differed was not primarily something culturally distinct about the French, Dutch, or English, but the scope of their colonial efforts. In each colony one period of its history emphasized trade with the Indians, and those developments closely paralleled one another, while each also engaged in settlement efforts that were usually accompanied by conflict and violence even if the scale of such conflicts was much smaller in New France than in New England.

Second, we need to consider the cultural and natural landscape of America itself. Maps of the era show neatly drawn territorial claims by each of the nations with the names of native groups dotted throughout. Had native people made their own maps of similar scale, Europeans would have realized that the

189

1

COLONIAL
PERIOD
AND
EIGHTEENTH
CENTURY

1609–1782

peoples who lived there and the land they lived in had certain characteristics and a dynamic history that affected colonial efforts. In the case of New Netherland, a major facet of its unique position in the New World came from the dynamic presence of the Iroquois with their access to a huge bounty of furs and the river access—the Hudson and Mohawk—which brought together those Indians and their furs with the Dutch and their goods. The role of the Munsees at the mouth of the Hudson was an additional factor. They produced the strings of wampum beads so valued by the Iroquois and thus helped open the lucrative fur trade to the Dutch. In this way, the Dutch in New Netherland had unique access to the peltry bounty of America and formed the vanguard of Europeans who would, through the seventeenth and eighteenth centuries, seek out and form alliances with the Five Nations Iroquois.

1   Paul Otto, *The Dutch-Munsee Encounter: The Struggle for Sovereignty in the Hudson Valley* (New York: Berghahn Books, 2006), 2-6; See also 27-77.

2   Ibid., 78-162; Daniel K. Richter, *The Ordeal of the Longhouse: The Peoples of the Iriquois League in the Era of European Colonization* (Chapel Hill: University of North Carolina Press, 1992), 75-104.

3   Jaap Jacobs and Martha Dickinson Shattuck, "Beavers for Drink, Land for Arms: Some Aspects of the Dutch-Indian Trade in New Netherland," in Alexandra van Dongen, ed., *One Man's Trash is Another Man's Treasure* (Rotterdam: Museum Boymans Van Beuningen, 1995), 95-113.

4   Ibid., Otto, *The Dutch-Munsee Encounter*, 111.

5   Ibid., 58-59, 67-68.

6   Ibid., 66-68, 90, 169-170; Richter, *The Ordeal*, 86-87.

7   Otto, *The Dutch-Munsee Encounter*, 64-66; James Homer Williams, "Dutch Attitudes toward Indians, Africans, and Other Europeans in New Netherland, 1624–1664," in Rosemarijn Hoefte and Johanna C. Kardux, eds., *Connecting Cultures: The Netherlands in Five Centuries of Transatlantic Exchange*

(Amsterdam: VU University Press, 1994), 23-50.

8   "Representation of New Netherland," in J. Franklin Jameson, ed., *Narratives of New Netherland* (New York: Scribners, 1909), 340; Otto, *The Dutch-Munsee Encounter*, 70, 121, 139, 146, 175; Thomas E. Burke, *Mohawk Frontier: The Dutch Community of Schenectady, New York, 1661-1710* (Ithaca, NY: Cornell University Press, 1991), 147-150.

9   Otto, *The Dutch-Munsee Encounter*, 56, 85-85, 140-141; F. J. Zwierlein, *Religion in New Netherland: A History of the Development of the Religious Conditions in the Province of New Netherland, 1623–1664* (Rochester, NY: John P. Smith Printing Company, 1910), 266-275.

10 Daniel K. Richter, "Cultural Brokers and Intercultural Politics: New York-Iroquois Relations, 1664–1701," *Journal of American History* 75 (June 1988): 45-56.

11 Otto, *The Dutch-Munsee Encounter*, 106-162.

12 Richter, "Cultural Brokers," 52-53; Burke, *Mohawk Frontier*, 151-154; Mark Meuwese, "Dutch Calvinism and Native Americans: A Comparative Study of the Motivations for Protestant Conversion among the Tupís in Northeastern Brazil (1630–1654) and the Mohawks in

Central New York (1690–1710)," in James
Muldoon, ed., *The Spiritual Conversion
of the Americas* (Gainesville: University
of Florida Press, 2004), 118-141.

13 Jaap Jacobs, *New Netherland: A Dutch
Colony in Seventeenth-Century America*
(Leiden: Brill, 2005), 197-201.

14 Allen Trelease, *Indian Affairs in Colonial
New York: The Seventeenth Century*
(Ithaca, NY: Cornell University Press,
1960), 215-227; Richter, "Cultural
Brokers," 49-52.

15 "Conference between Commissioners
of the Colonies and the Indians, 5-14
October 1745," in E. B. O'Callaghan,
ed., *Documents Relative to the Colonial
History of State of New York* (Albany, NY:
Weed, Parsons and Company, 1855),
6:294.

16 Six Nations Reply to Schuyler's German
Flatts Treaty Speech, August 9, 1776,
Huntington Manuscripts 14187, Henry
E. Huntington Library, San Marino, CA.

1

—

COLONIAL
PERIOD
AND
EIGHTEENTH
CENTURY

1609–1782

INTERCULTURAL RELATIONS BETWEEN EUROPEANS AND BLACKS IN NEW NETHERLAND

—

LINDA HEYWOOD & JOHN THORNTON

Afro-Dutch relations in the Atlantic were the first non-Iberian sustained diplomatic and cultural contacts between Europeans and Africans, particularly in Central Africa, where the conquest of Angola in 1641 placed the Dutch more closely in contact with African cultures than any European power besides Portugal. The brief Dutch occupation of Portugal's Brazilian cities of Salvador in 1624-25 and even more their conquest of Recife from 1630 until 1654 also exposed them to African culture as it had developed in the Americas, enslaved Africans in Brazil representing a majority of the population in the area they occupied. Moreover, their settlement of New Netherland presented them with the challenge of integrating newly arrived Africans into their emerging colony. What stands out in all three sites is that the Africans with whom the Dutch had their deepest relations were almost all from Central Africa and had already been integrated into a complex network of intercultural relationships.

The Acquisition of Slaves

192

When Dutch merchants first reached the African coast in the last years of the sixteenth century, they entered into a wide variety of relations with many states stretching from Senegal to Angola. In West Africa the Dutch established a few trading posts and developed a range of commercial and diplomatic ties but did not trade in slaves until 1638.[1] Dutch initial relations with Central Africa, notably the Kingdom of Kongo, began with an exchange of letters and diplomatic relations in 1607. Here, however, the deep involvement of the independent kingdom with the Portuguese colony of Angola would increase not only the commerce and diplomacy but also deepen intercultural relations. The increasing hostility between Kongo and Portuguese Angola heightened Dutch interest there since Kongo, although Catholic, seemed a potential ally in the larger struggle between the Low Countries and the Spanish Empire. For example, when Portuguese forces invaded Kongo in 1622, Kongolese King Pedro II wrote to the States General proposing a joint military operation to drive the Portuguese from Angola, and the West India Company promptly sent a fleet under Piet Heyn to follow the operation up in 1624. Though the operation floundered, the alliance remained, and eventually led to a full-fledged military cooperation between the two that resulted in the Dutch taking of Luanda, Angola in 1641.

In all contacts before 1638, Central Africa, like West Africa, did not sell slaves to the Dutch. Instead, the latter acquired all the slaves they used in the Americas from privateering activities, first by privately funded voyages and then, after 1623, by the West India Company. Typically, Dutch operations involved the capture of Portuguese slave trading vessels — bound either for their own colony of Brazil, or for the Spanish territories in the Caribbean, Mexico, and Peru — which they sold illegally to Spanish residents, or later, took to emerging Dutch colonies, including, in 1628, to New Netherland.

Patterns of the Portuguese slave trade as they developed during the period of Dutch privateering focused increasingly on their colony of Angola as their supplier. Angola acquired many of its slaves through its own military activities in the region surrounding the areas occupied by Portuguese settlers, including the Kingdom of Kongo and other kingdoms, notably Ndongo. As many as 90 percent of the more than 370,000 slaves who reached Spanish and Portuguese possessions in the New World between 1600 and 1650 came on Portuguese ships from Angola.[2] According to West India Company records as used by Johannes de Laet, the Dutch managed to capture over 2,356 slaves in this way.[3] Not only did Dutch privateers capture slaves of predominantly Angolan origin on the high seas, but when they took Recife in Pernambuco (Brazil) in 1630 the existing slave population was also predominantly Angolan. Portuguese settlers in Pernambuco came by their slaves through the "contract of Angola" (an exclusive import arrangement), and a report of 1612 already noted that the majority of slaves in the region were from Angola.[4] Dutch intelligence about the slave trade to Brazil in 1620–23 found that all of the more than fifteen thousand slaves listed in Portuguese customs books as arriving in Pernambuco had Angolan origin.[5]

Given this background, it is not surprising that the vast majority of the slaves mentioned in Dutch records about New Netherland had Angolan origins. In the earliest records, slaves typically carried an ethnonym as their second name — for example, the "Negro Mayken van Angola" who appears in 1628, the earliest named African in New Netherland — and some 70 percent of the slaves

193

and freedmen who married or baptized their children in the church or appeared in court before the late seventeenth century bore this ethnic signifier. This situation of Angolan numerical dominance only began to change in 1655 when the first large contingent of West Africans arrived on the *Witte Paert*.

The African Cultural Background

1

—

COLONIAL
PERIOD
AND
EIGHTEENTH
CENTURY

1609–1782

The cultural background of the Africans played a vital role in the way in which they interacted with the Dutch. The people who were generally identified as Angolans in the various records of Portugal, Spain, and the Dutch Republic, came from a fairly broad stretch of the Angolan coast including the Kingdom of Kongo, the Portuguese colony in Angola (founded in 1575), and the interior African Kingdom of Ndongo, as well as lesser polities that lay between these larger kingdoms. Unlike West Africans, Central Africans had quickly accepted a great deal of European culture, and most notably Christianity, since the arrival of Portuguese sailors and missionaries in the late fifteenth century, possibly because it fit their local political dynamics better. The conversion of King Nzinga a Nkuwu of Kongo to Christianity and his baptism as João I in 1491 had marked the beginning of this phase in Central African history. For a century, Kongo had dealt with Portugal and worked to spread both Christianity and an Africanized form of European culture to its neighbors. Angolans had adopted not only Christianity but elements of Portuguese language, law, foodways, clothing items, and names.

Several features of this cultural interaction were readily visible to newcomers to the region, and the earliest Dutch visitors in the seventeenth century noted the prevalence of churches, rosary beads, and roadside crosses in Kongo. According to the German visitor Samuel Brun, sailing on a Dutch vessel to Soyo, Kongo in 1611, "they speak the Portuguese language fairly well … they make their prayers in Latin and Portuguese … they also have schoolmasters as in Spain, but only in Spanish and Portuguese, not in their own language."

The situation in the Portuguese colony of Angola and in Ndongo and its immediate neighbors was different. The penetration of Christianity was much less than in Kongo, though fairly substantial in the areas where Portugal established its authority firmly. Olfert Dapper, describing Angola as the Dutch found it during their seven-year occupation (1641–48), noted that "in recent years many of them, by the endeavor of the Portuguese Jesuits, have been brought from their idolatry to the Roman religion and baptized … every Sova [local ruler] has a priest in his Banza or village, to baptize children and celebrate mass."

There was a strong sentiment in favor of preserving the Catholic faith in Kongo in spite of the kingdom's hostility to Portugal. Dutch plans to convert the country to Calvinism took off after the occupation of Luanda, but met with de-

NETHERLANDS

ENGLAND

FRANCE

PORTUGAL

SPAIN

NEW NETHERLAND

VIRGINIA

Bermuda

Canary Islands

Cape Verde

Vera Cruz

Jamaica

Barbados

Providence
Island

Trinidad

Cartagena

Magarbonda

Sierra Leone

GOLD COAST

Allada

Calabar

São Tomé

WILD COAST

Amazon

MARANHAO

Kongo

PERU

PERNAMBUCO

Recife

Luanda

Salvador

BAHIA

BRAZIL

Rio de Janeiro

São Paulo

Buenos Aires

Places of Dutch interactions with Central Africa
and South America.

1

COLONIAL
PERIOD
AND
EIGHTEENTH
CENTURY

1609–1782

termined resistance, not just from King Garcia II who ordered an *auto-da-fé* of Calvinist books in 1645, but also among common people, as witnessed by the popular reaction to Dutch attempts to exclude Italian Capuchin missionaries who arrived in Soyo in 1645.

Following the fall of Luanda, the Dutch also formed an alliance with Queen Njinga and with Dutch assistance she triumphed over the Portuguese army in Angola in 1647, though was unable to dislodge them from their fortifications. In the wars between factions of the Kongo elite, and especially in the wars between the Dutch and Portuguese during the occupation of Luanda, thousands of Africans were captured, enslaved, and subsequently embarked to Dutch Brazil if taken by the Dutch or their allies, or to Portuguese Brazil if taken by the Portuguese, unless these ships were captured by Dutch privateers.

Dutch-Central African interactions were not restricted to Africa, nor to military and religious affairs. The Dutch entertained Central African diplomats in Brazil,[6] and also brought thousands of Central African slaves to Recife. In Brazil the Africans showed interest in Calvinism and attended Reformed Church services because Dutch authorities knew that they had been baptized.[7] The Reformed preacher Soler worked hard in Recife to convert the Catholic Afro-Brazilian population to Calvinism, and with the support of the Company built an annex to the church to hold African converts. However, their efforts were not entirely successful, since at the same time some five hundred Africans and Native Americans continued to attend Catholic services at the Portuguese church.[8] Nevertheless, Africans were drawn into the Calvinist church. Frans Schalkwijk noted that Africans accounted for 7 percent of all references in marriage and baptismal documents in Dutch Brazil.[9]

Interactions in New Netherland

Dutch interrelations with Africans in New Netherland were part of this larger history of diplomatic, cultural, and commercial environment. The first Central Africans, perhaps two dozen people, to come to New Netherland arrived around 1628, probably captured from a Portuguese ship outbound from Luanda off Trinidad by the *Bruin-Visch*, a Company privateer that stopped in New Amsterdam on August 29. They were soon joined by some fifty more Central Africans (twenty men and thirty women) captured by the *Bruin-Visch* from another Angola man near Ilha de Vespera de Paschoa in 1630. Others arrived in smaller lots, brought by Dutch and English privateers, as a few scattered references indicate, and ships continued to arrive in the same pattern through the 1640s. At best they numbered a few hundred, and made up less than one-third of New Amsterdam's population, a marked contrast to the situation the Dutch faced in Recife.

The majority of these Africans were held by the Company in New Amsterdam, though private owners in other parts of the colony also purchased a handful. The Dutch always considered the Africans to be slaves and often used the term *slaven* to describe them, along with other designations, unlike the English colonies, for which there are questions concerning the status of early Africans as slaves or indentured servants.

Despite their status as slaves, the Africans had close interactions with the Dutch and various other European settlers in the colony. The Company's Africans labored alongside settlers in a variety of tasks. They assisted in building the fort (finished in 1639), the windmill, saw mill, and the grist mill, engaged in community tasks such as clearing land and burning lime, and worked as additional labor at harvest. The women were also present in the colony: at least four worked for Stuyvesant in 1662, one of whom claimed to have been in the colony since 1628. Indeed, some of the Angolan women were engaged in housework as early as 1628 and they were well enough known that the pastor Jonas Michaëlius, seeking household workers after the death of his wife, noted that the "Angolan slave women are so thievish, lazy and useless trash." The Company slaves were mobilized to defend the colony against attacks by indigenous people as well. Some of the younger children born of African parents spent part of their early years living in settler households, as they were loaned out for fixed periods to Dutch proprietors under conditions similar to those for Dutch settlers who also apprenticed their children. The privately held slaves are less visible in the records, but they appear to have been fully integrated into the economy as farm workers, baker's assistants, and the like.

By the mid-1640s the Company contingent of slaves stood out as a distinct community. They had a substantial settlement, located near the "Kalckhoeck" (today's Washington Square Park), composed of separate houses, and generally called simply "the negros," or more specifically, "the negros residence," "the negroes houses," or even the "negroes' plantation,"[10] and this proximity allowed them to form close ties among themselves. Even though the settlement was compact, it was surrounded by Dutch properties and was probably not particularly separate from them, so that all the Africans and settlers would have mixed a great deal in their daily lives. The Africans were not isolated in the community either, for many labored alongside white settlers who had been condemned to do the same work the slaves did. Certainly the members of the community sued their Dutch neighbors in court for various infringements, including nonpayment of wages or wounding or harassing of their livestock. Court records show that Africans used the court, which also investigated cases of violence done against them or among themselves.[11]

The most important place where Africans and settlers interacted in a cultural sphere was in the Reformed Church, in New Netherland as in Recife. By 1639,

197

Francisco d'Angola, an early Boswijk farm owner.
The image is probably a mid-nineteenth-century draft
of images of old New York.

the time of the first extant baptismal and marriage registers in the colony, a substantial number of the Africans were already participating in the church's sacraments. In 1641, the consistory of the church of Manhattan noted that the "Negroes, living among the colonists, come nearer to [the right knowledge of God] and give better hope" than the indigenous people.[12] The consistory referred perhaps to the newly arrived, since at that time almost a third of the church's sacraments were administered to Africans and their children.

Africans in the colony baptized and were married in the church according to Dutch custom. The records reveal their naming patterns, which were an interesting combination of Central African and Dutch customs. Many Africans bore Iberian names, and some of them subsequently translated them into Dutch, for example Paulo Angola, Maria, Antonia Negrinne, Suzanna Congo, Manuel Congo, and Francisco d'Angola. In addition, their pattern of assigning names to their children by placing a second name that incorporated (or was) the father's given name was prevalent in Central Africa as well as in some parts of the Dutch Republic. Here a cultural convergence no doubt contributed in a small way to the strengthening of intercultural relations.

One reason why Africans frequented the church and resorted to the Dutch courts lay in the specific background of the Africans in New Netherland. The Company slaves, the freedmen, and the scattered Africans serving in private households had one thing in common: until 1655 they were all or almost all from Central Africa. This background with its engagement with European culture, and particularly its Christian and Catholic component, as well as the contact that the Dutch had with them in Angola and in Brazil, shaped the way in which they integrated into Dutch society in New Netherland. For example, the group of eleven Africans who petitioned for their freedom in 1644 said they had served the Company for eighteen or nineteen years, literally suggesting they came in 1626 or 1627 or were among the first to come to New Netherland. They had probably come on the *Bruin-Visch*, and their names, which included Paulo Angola and Symon Congo, show their Central African origins. The Angolans among them were probably enslaved in the troubled times during the war between the Portuguese and Njinga, when a situation of great chaos existed in the region, while Symon Congo was perhaps enslaved as a result of the warfare surrounding the deposition of Garcia I.

At the same time that the New Netherland Africans were petitioning for their freedom and baptizing their children in the church, the Company was also responding to questions about the status of Africans in Brazil. In 1645, in response to a request concerning the acceptance of Africans into the church in Brazil, where the pastors did not know their language, the directors decided that they should wait until the Dutch language took precedence over Por-

199

1

—

COLONIAL
PERIOD
AND
EIGHTEENTH
CENTURY

1609–1782

tuguese because then "all would be required to live according to our religion, custom and habits."[13] Such a situation never prevailed in Brazil, but it was soon the custom in New Netherland.

The Catholic beliefs of at least some of the Angolan slaves meant that they fit into a Christian society, and as they quickly accepted Calvinism they fell under the legal considerations of Calvinist doctrine concerning slavery. Calvinists had long considered the possibility that slavery was for non-Christians. Furthermore, the Dutch did not necessarily consider slavery as a lifelong or heritable condition in the early and mid-seventeenth century. Godefridus Udemans, who published a guide to proper Christian conduct for overseas operations in 1638, noted that normally only people who were taken in just wars, such as Turks, or sold by their rightful masters for a just price could be enslaved. He further noted that the customary time for servitude was seven years, but — more important — added that "legal slave men or women may be held in slavery as long as they do not willingly accept the Christian Religion: but as they themselves accept the sweet yoke of Our Lord Jesus Christ that Christian love they should be set free from the yoke of human slavery."

In addition to this theoretical background, employees of the Company had dealt with Africans who were a part of an Atlantic Creole community, as well as others from the same regions whom they called savages. In fact, in Brazil Company officials had returned a number of captives brought by Dutch shipping from Angola in 1642 because they concluded that the Africans were Christians of good birth and could read and would not be able to serve the Company as slaves.[14] On the whole, however, in Brazil as in New Netherland the Dutch relationship with Africans focused on their status as slaves, despite the latter's right to participate in the religious and community life of the colony.

Slaves or Servants?

Nevertheless, the Dutch directors in New Netherland remained conflicted about the status of their African slaves. In 1644 when, as noted above, eleven of the earliest Africans to arrive in New Amsterdam petitioned the government for their freedom, referring to their length of service and complaining that they had been promised freedom many times before, their request was perhaps implicitly based on their understanding of the seven years of servitude concept. Director Kieft accepted their petition, which seems to have allowed them to own land and be protected by the courts and other privileges of free people, but he did not in fact render them entirely free. The act of granting freedom still specified that they had to deliver agricultural tribute and that their children would remain serfs (*lijffeygenen*) of the Company.[15] Other settlers commented on the hypocrisy of the government's decision, noting in the remonstrance of 1649 that "some other Negroes here in the country have been made free on account of their long service, while their children remain slaves (*slaven*), against all natural law, by which anyone born of a free Christian mother, should notwithstanding be a slave, and obliged to remain in service," to which Kieft's successor, Petrus Stuyvesant, responded that in fact few of the children were actually enslaved. The "free Negroes" continued to be called upon to serve as a "company" of their own, for example in public works, where they are cited separately from other free citizens and the soldiers and servants of the Company. This last group certainly included a significant number of Africans who were not free. This compromise preserved the desire of the Company to have a bound and dependent labor force available for its public works, while complying with the law that required Christian slaves to be freed.

As new Africans with no Christian background entered New Netherland, the church adopted a harder and restrictive policy that limited access to Christianity to the enslaved. The issue of freedom for Christian slaves was thus set aside. The Dutch began acquiring non-Christian slaves directly on the African coast by purchase in 1638, thus beginning the period of the slave trade and gradually eclipsing privateering as a source of African workers. All the first slave traders carried their cargoes from various ports of the African coast, including West African ports such as Allada and Calabar, to Brazil, as indeed Company rules of 1650 specifically prohibited slaves to be carried to New Amsterdam from the West African trade. Nevertheless, in 1652, the Company decided to allow a trade with West Africa, and in 1655 the ship *Witte Paert* arrived in New Amsterdam with a large contingent of slaves from Allada. Many of them were subsequently sold to Virginia traders, and a list of their names reveals the new and different origins. Unlike Angola, the Lower Guinea coast, where Allada and Calabar were located, had no substantial Christian population and these slaves' desire for freedom would eventually lead to attempts to limit the freer associations between Africans and settlers that had characterized the early years of the colony.

Thus, in 1664, for example, Henricus Selijns refused to baptize the children of slaves, arguing that children could not be baptized if their parents were not also Christian, and contending that the parents had little understanding and faith and only sought baptism to free their children from material slavery. This may well have been directed against the large number of non-Christian West Africans who had more than doubled the African population of the colony, but the ruling would also affect the Central Africans, for the church also refused to acknowledge the Christian status of those who had been baptized by "papists" in Angola.[16] Over the years, the trend toward importing West Africans increased constantly as the African-descended population grew from 700 in 1698 to 5,867 in New York County in 1800.[17]

1

—

COLONIAL
PERIOD
AND
EIGHTEENTH
CENTURY

1609–1782

One of the many consequences of the close interrelationship between the early Africans and the Dutch settlers in New Netherland was the adoption of Dutch as their language, which remained among the older population even after the English takeover. Although it is less visible, later cultural practices that were recorded linked back to this early set of connections. Africans remained members of an ethnically closed Dutch community for years afterwards, in their clothing, customs, and folklore. A good many of the Afro-Dutch population moved away from their concentration in New Amsterdam to interior areas where there were more opportunities, often forming their own mixed-race communities, such as the Ramapo Mountain people. In particular, the celebrations of Pinkster, by the early nineteenth century largely associated with the Afro-Dutch population around Albany, represent an interesting fruit of this history.[18]

1   Linda Heywood and John Thornton, *Central Africans, Atlantic Creoles, and the Foundation of the Americas, 1585–1660* (New York/London: Cambridge University Press, 2007), 42-43; Most details and quotations found in this article can be located in this book.

2   Total volume from Herbert S. Klein, *The Atlantic Slave Trade* (Cambridge: Cambridge University Press, 1999), 210; For the percentages from Angola, Heywood and Thornton, *Central Africans*, 39-40.

3   Johannes de Laet, *Historie ofte Iaerlijck verhael van de Verrichtinghen der Geoctroyeerde West Indische Compagnie* (Leiden: Elsevier, 1644), appendix: 21.

4   Statement of Camara of Olinda and Pernambuco, November 28, 1603, "Correspondencia do Diogo Botelho," *Revista do Instituto Historico e Geografico Brasileiro*, 73 (1910): 24; "Razão do Estado do Brasil," fol. 3 and 82v, in Engel Sluiter, ed., "A Report on the State of Brazil, 1612," *Hispanic American Historical Review* 29 (1949): 523, 552 (ed. of Portuguese text only); see also fol. 11v on 528.

5   De Laet, *Historie,* book 7:192.

6   Johan Nieuhof, *Gedenkweerdige Brasi-*

liaensche Zee- en Lantreize (Amsterdam: Jacob van Meurs, 1682), 56.

7   Frans Leonard Schalkwijk, *The Reformed Church in Dutch Brazil, 1630–1654* (Zoetermeer: Boekencentrum, 1998), 146.

8   Vincent Joachim Soler, June 8, 1636, in B.N. Teensma, ed. and trans., *Seventeen Letters by Vincent Joachim Soler, Protestant Minister in the Service of the West Indies Company, Compiled and Written in Recife, Brazil between 1636-1643* (Rio de Janeiro: Index, 1999), fol. 9.

9   Schalkwijk, *The Reformed Church*, 151.

10 New York State Archives, Dutch Documents (hereafter NYSAD), Land Records GG 67, HH 11, GG 208; We read the original, and these references are marked in the English translation, Charles Gehring, ed. and trans., *New York Historical Manuscripts: Dutch. Land Papers,* vols. GG, HH, and II (Baltimore: Genealogical Publications, 1980).

11 For further discussion, see Jaap Jacobs, *New Netherland: A Dutch Colony in Seventeenth-Century America* (Leiden: Brill, 2005), 386-387.

12 See Willem Frijhoff, *Fulfilling God's Mission: The Two Worlds of Dominie Everardus Bogardus, 1607–1647*

(Leiden: Brill, 2007), 530-546, and Jacobs, *New Netherland*, 314-318.

13 Hendric Hamel, Adrien van Bullestrate, P. Jansen Bas, "Relatorio to XIX, 1645" in José António Gonçalves de Melo, ed., *Fontes para o Brasil Holandes.* 2nd ed., 2 vols. (Rio de Janeiro: s.n., 2004), 2: 274.

14 Process Verbal of the Recife Council, November 11, 1641; French translation in Louis Jadin, ed. and trans., *L'ancien Congo et l'Angola, 1639–1655, d'après les archives romaines, portugaises, neérlandaises et espagnoles*, 3 vols. (Brussels/Rome: Institut Historique Belge de Rome, 1975), 1:126.

15 NYSAD, Council Minutes, February 25, 1644, fols. 183-184.

16 C. Schulz, Pastor, 1661, in Hugh Hastings, ed., *Ecclesiastical Records of the State of New York* (Albany: 1901-05), 508.

17 *Final Reports: African Burial Ground, History Report,* 82, http://www.africanburialground.gov/FinalReports/ABG_HistoryReportFinal/.

18 Shane White, *Somewhat More Independent: The End of Slavery in New York City, 1770–1810* (Athens: University of Georgia Press, 1991), 95-106.

1

▬

COLONIAL
PERIOD
AND
EIGHTEENTH
CENTURY

1609–1782

THE DUTCH REPUBLIC
AND THE CREATION OF
THE UNITED STATES

▬

WAYNE TE BRAKE

Introduction

In the last third of the eighteenth century, the Dutch people and their government, the Republic of the United Provinces, played a variety of important, if also ambiguous, roles in the creation of the United States of America. To active proponents of a close Dutch-American relationship, like John Adams and Joan Derk van der Capellen, these two republics seemed like natural allies — as Adams described it in his "Memorial" to the Dutch government in 1781, "the originals of the two republics are so much alike, that the history of the one seems but a transcript of the other...."[1] In the years leading up to formal American independence, however, the Dutch found themselves in a very precarious position in European affairs, and establishing a durable relationship between the Dutch and American people and their governments was more easily imagined than accomplished. As it happened, the Dutch Republic was among the first states to recognize the United States of America, and in the early years of American independence the Dutch were the principal financiers of the new republic. But this story begins with illicit trade and unconventional politics on both sides of the Atlantic.

Unofficial Contacts through Trade

Following the Treaty of Utrecht, which ended the last of Louis XIV's wars with the Dutch in 1713, the Dutch Republic had consistently pursued a policy of strict neutrality in European affairs, which meant that the Dutch forfeited their former prominence amid the great military powers of Europe. Indeed, on the eve of the American Revolution, the British fleet boasted approximately ten times the number of warships in the Dutch fleet. Still, the Netherlands remained a prosperous center of international trade and finance, and under the umbrella of neutrality, Dutch merchants generally profited from military competition by supplying gunpowder, armaments, and naval stores to the various combatants. Meanwhile, during the eighteenth century, the island of St. Eustatius, one of the small Leeward Islands in the West Indian chain, became the focal point of Dutch trade, much of it illicit, throughout the Caribbean and with the English colonies of North America. This set the stage for the first important, if informal, Dutch contribution to the American War of Independence.

The relationship between the composite British monarchy and its North American colonies began to deteriorate in the wake of the Seven Years' War (1756–63) as the British government sought both to tax the colonies to support their defense and to enforce their mercantilist policies restricting intercolonial and international trade. Though the Stamp Act of 1765, which resulted in loud protests from the colonies, was repealed just a year later, it was followed by the Declaratory Act (1766), the Townshend Acts (1767), and the so-called Coercive Acts (1774), each of which occasioned ever more sophisticated protest from the colonies that culminated in the first Continental Congress in September 1774. Following the outbreak of hostilities in the spring of 1775, with the Battles of Lexington and Concord and the capture of Fort Ticonderoga, the second Continental Congress meeting at Philadelphia created the Continental Army with George Washington as commander in chief.

Desperately short of munitions and gunpowder, the American rebels built on their illicit trade contacts with the Dutch at St. Eustatius — there was a well-established contraband trade in molasses, rice, and indigo — to secure a critical supply of war materiel. Even before the outbreak of hostilities, the British were well aware of the flow of gunpowder through St. Eustatius to the American colonies, and despite British protests, Dutch merchants quickly became the most important suppliers of munitions to the American cause, some of which came directly from the port of Amsterdam. When the commander of Fort Orange actively prevented the British seizure of an American ship just off the coast of St. Eustatius in January 1776, the British admiral, James Young, complained bitterly that the "very pernicious traffic carried on between his Brittanic majesty's rebellious subjects from North-America and the inhabitants of St. Eustatia for gunpowder and warlike stores has been so general and done in so public a manner as to be no secret to any person in the West Indies islands."[2] Thus, it is perhaps fitting that following the American Declaration of Independence in July 1776, when the American brig of war *Andrew Doria* sailed into the harbor at

205

1

—

COLONIAL
PERIOD
AND
EIGHTEENTH
CENTURY

1609–1782

St. Eustatius on November 16, 1776, the Dutch commander of Fort Orange and the island's governor, Johannes de Graaff, offered the first ceremonial salute to a ship flying the red and white striped flag of the American Congress.[3]

Against the backdrop of this illicit trade in arms and munitions in support of the American cause, the Dutch government found itself in an increasingly precarious position. Even under the best of conditions, forming national policy could be a very cumbersome process in the loosely confederated United Provinces, which balanced provincial sovereignties and parochial interests within the States General while investing military leadership and considerable political patronage in the office of stadtholder. But with regard to the American War of Independence, the leaders of the Dutch Republic were deeply divided and Dutch national politics virtually paralyzed. On one hand, in the maritime provinces, and especially in the city of Amsterdam, people demanded protection for Dutch commercial interests and dreamed of new opportunities should the American rebellion succeed. On the other, the stadtholder, Prince William V of Orange, who was commander of both the army and the navy, considered England a natural ally and sought to avoid giving any offense to British interests. Thus, under pressure from the British ambassador, Sir Joseph Yorke, the Dutch government in 1775 announced an embargo of trade in contraband, naval stores, and even clothing with the American colonies, though this had no practical effect whatsoever. But when the British, citing a one-hundred-year-old treaty, asked for Dutch aid in mobilizing troops for combat in North America, the States General, citing Dutch neutrality, refused the request.

The Dutch Republic as an Example

Given the official paralysis of the United Provinces with regard to the American conflict, it may seem ironic that the Americans should look to the Dutch example when they drafted the Articles of Confederation in 1777. Still, the history of the "heroic" Dutch struggle against Spanish "tyranny" in the sixteenth century constituted a useful, if rare, precedent for those who resisted British tyranny in the eighteenth century. And for the first century of their independence, at least, the Dutch had demonstrated that a loosely confederated republic could more than hold its own on the international stage while enjoying unprecedented economic prosperity. The Union of Utrecht, drafted in 1579 in advance of the Dutch provinces' declaration of independence from their Spanish overlord in 1581, preserved the principle of provincial sovereignty while binding the diverse provinces of the Northern Netherlands in a perpetual union with a common currency, a common foreign policy, and unrestricted internal trade. The first national government of the new United States of America under the Articles of Confederation adopted these same general principles, with the possibly fatal exception of the common currency, and it was a loose confederation of North American states, not unlike the Dutch confederation, that prevailed in the American War of Independence from 1775 to 1783. Indeed, the fundamental similarity between the Dutch Union and the American Articles made John Adams' assertion in 1781 of parallel republican histories something more than fanciful rhetoric.

The War of Independence began with serious setbacks for the American rebels, including the loss of New York (1776) and Philadelphia (1777) to British occupation. But the surrender of British General John Burgoyne at Saratoga in October 1777 prompted the French, who had secretly aided the war effort for two years, to recognize the United States and join the American rebels. In February 1778, the Kingdom of France signed treaties of commerce and alliance with the United States of America, which greatly improved the prospects of the American cause. At the same time, the American Congress sought closer ties with the Dutch Republic, as an important center of European diplomacy as well as an international credit market, and to that end, as early as 1775 the Committee of Secret Correspondence quietly engaged Charles Dumas, a correspondent of Benjamin Franklin, to be an American agent in The Hague; not surprisingly, Dumas was instructed to send his correspondence to the American Congress via St. Eustatius. But as the war dragged on and as the need for loans to finance the war effort grew ever more urgent, in October 1779, the American Congress named Henry Laurens, a wealthy planter from Charleston, SC, and a former president of the American Congress, to be its envoy to the Netherlands with the task of concluding a treaty and securing, if possible, a Dutch loan. As it happened, Laurens never made it to the Netherlands: for personal reasons, he did not actually depart from Philadelphia until August 1780, and then the small packet boat on which he was traveling was captured by the British off the coast of Newfoundland. Laurens was arrested and brought to London, and the papers he threw overboard during his capture gave the British the official reason they used to declare war on the Dutch Republic in December 1780.

Among the papers that Henry Laurens attempted to destroy was a "preliminary" Dutch-American commercial treaty drafted two years earlier in the German city of Aachen. At the time of the French treaties with the United States in early 1778, Charles Dumas had been working feverishly in official Dutch circles and in concert with the French ambassador, the Duke de La Vauguyon, to secure a Dutch treaty as well. His effort came to naught, however, because of opposition from both the French foreign minister, the Count de Vergennes, ostensibly to preserve Dutch neutrality, and the Prince of Orange, who threatened to resign his office and leave the country rather than accept such a treaty. In the wake of this disappointment and without Dumas' knowledge, Engelbert van Berckel, the influential pensionary of the city of Amsterdam, facilitated contact between

207

1

—

COLONIAL
PERIOD
AND
EIGHTEENTH
CENTURY

1609–1782

an American agent, William Lee, and a Dutch financier, Jean de Neufville, who aspired to be an American financial agent in Amsterdam. After a first encounter in Frankfurt, Lee and Neufville met again at Aachen to finalize their draft treaty, which mirrored the provisions of the French commercial treaty with the United States; it had all the trappings of a formal treaty, though it bore the title, "A Preparatory Plan of a Treaty of Commerce of the Seven Provinces of Holland and the Thirteen United States of North America, to be Put on the Table of their High Mightinesses [the States General] in the event that England should recognize them as Free Nations."[4] Clearly this contingent document, drafted informally by an agent of a single Dutch city and ratified by neither state, had no official standing, but its embarrassing discovery was sufficient to propel the Dutch Republic willy-nilly into indirect involvement in the American War of Independence.

The Fourth English War

The British declaration of war on the Dutch Republic on December 20, 1780, began the last in a series of Anglo-Dutch wars that had begun in the mid-seventeenth century. The Fourth English War (1780–84), as it is known in Dutch history, was an unmitigated military and economic disaster for the Dutch, and it was also of no consequence in the outcome of the American War. In the first month of the war, January 1781, some two hundred Dutch ships were captured by the British, and the vital shipping of the Dutch provinces through the English Channel and on the North Sea was blockaded for the duration of the war. The British also immediately seized important Dutch trading posts in Asia as well as St. Eustatius, which effectively ended the illicit Dutch trade with the rebellious colonies. In the few actual battles that were fought before a ceasefire in 1783, the Dutch navy was generally humiliated, though a naval skirmish battle at Doggers Bank, which ended in a virtual draw, did briefly revive Dutch spirits. Not surprisingly, the Fourth English War also precipitated a domestic political crisis in the Dutch Republic, which resulted, among other things, in the recognition in the spring of 1782 of John Adams as minister plenipotentiary of the independent United States of America.[5] But the political path that Adams followed toward that critical outcome was unconventional, to say the least.[6]

John Adams, who was one of America's most indefatigable and unpredictable advocates in Europe, traveled to the Dutch Republic in August 1780 to test the prospects of a Dutch loan in advance of Henry Laurens' arrival. Adams quickly found, however, that these prospects were not good as long as the rebellious American colonies had no official standing, and the disastrous start of the Fourth English War did nothing to improve the situation. Following Laurens'

JOHN ADAMS. Gezant der
Noord-Americaſche Staaten,
in de Vereenigde Nederlanden.

John Adams, first American envoy to the Dutch Republic.

1

COLONIAL
PERIOD
AND
EIGHTEENTH
CENTURY

1609-1782

capture, Adams was named the official American envoy to the Dutch Republic, and in the spring of 1781, without being invited he submitted his diplomatic credentials directly to the States General against the strong objection of the French ambassador. When Dutch officials at The Hague refused even to receive his submission, Adams took the highly unorthodox step of publishing his "Memorial" to the States General in Dutch, French, and English and distributed it throughout the Dutch Republic. In taking this bold action, Adams signaled his collaboration with an unusual set of Dutch political actors who stood well outside the realms of diplomacy and traditional power, including Joan Derk van der Capellen, Jean Luzac, and François Adriaan van der Kemp, who worked tirelessly to popularize the American cause and to turn Adams into something of a celebrity in the Netherlands.

Joan Derk van der Capellen was an ardent proponent of domestic reform in the Dutch Republic who had been admitted to the nobility in the Provincial Estates of Overijssel in 1772, and he was single-handedly responsible in 1775 for preventing the loan of the so-called Scots Brigade — a contingent of British troops in Dutch service since the time of the Dutch Revolt — to Great Britain for service against the American rebellion. In this affair he had pioneered the political strategy of publicizing normally privileged or secret matters of state, but his principled support of the American cause also brought him into contact with important leaders of the Revolution like Jonathan Trumbull, governor of Connecticut, and William Livingston, governor of New Jersey, with whom Van der Capellen corresponded for years. In 1776, he also translated into Dutch the Englishman Richard Price's fervent defense of the American cause, *Observations on the Nature of Civil Liberty*. For a time, Van der Capellen even hoped that he might be appointed a spokesman in the Netherlands for the American cause, but by 1778 he had been suspended indefinitely from the Estates of Overijssel for alleged insults to his colleagues. Thus, when he first came into contact with John Adams, Van der Capellen was clearly a political outsider, as were Jean Luzac, the well-respected publisher of the *Gazette de Leyde*, and François Adriaan van der Kemp, a radical Mennonite pastor from Leiden, both of whom were very vocal defenders of the American cause and, like Van der Capellen, called themselves "Patriots."

In the context of the Fourth English War, the Dutch Patriots emerged as partisan critics of the stadtholder, Prince William V of Orange, whom they blamed for the disastrous course of the war and for the decline of the Dutch Republic in general. In the fall of 1781, Van der Capellen crystalized the partisan association of the American cause with Dutch "Patriotism" when he anonymously published his famous pamphlet *To the People of the Netherlands*, which was enormously successful despite being officially banned; at the end of this long-winded historical indictment of the princes of Orange, Van der Capellen called for the Dutch to organize themselves and to take up arms against Orangist tyranny, following the example of the American Patriots. For Adams to allow the American cause to be implicated in the partisan split between Patriots and Orangists was, of course, a very risky political gamble, but it finally paid dividends in the winter and spring of 1782, when the Patriots organized a popular political campaign demanding that local political leaders, who instructed the delegates to the provincial estates and, by extension, the States General, recognize John Adams as the American minister plenipotentiary. This proved to be a brilliant demonstration of the potency of bottom-up political initiative in a decentralized and aristocratic republic as, one by one, the seven provinces that constituted the States General supported recognition of the United States of America and instructed their delegates accordingly.

Official Recognition of the United States

On April 19, 1782, the Dutch Republic became only the second polity, after France, to recognize officially the independence of the United States of America, and this was followed by the formal signing of a Treaty of Amity and Commerce between the United States and the Dutch Republic at The Hague on October 8, 1782. The Dutch Republic named Pieter Johan van Berckel, brother of the Amsterdam pensionary who had instigated the infamous "preliminary" treaty in 1778, to be their first envoy to the United States, and in June 1783 a squadron of four Dutch ships set sail for North America bearing the first Dutch diplomatic mission to the new republic. Among the small official entourage that accompanied Envoy Van Berckel, in order to add luster to the arrival of the diplomatic mission, was a young nobleman, Carel de Vos van Steenwijk, from a well-known "Patriot" family in the eastern Netherlands, who carefully recorded the very difficult fifteen-week crossing — a violent storm broke up the squadron and eventually one of the badly damaged ships sank off Cape Cod with more than three hundred men on board — as well as their formal reception finally at Princeton, where the American Congress had moved because of political unrest in Philadelphia. Also on board one of the Dutch ships was a young "Orangist," Gijsbert Karel van Hogendorp, though because of his politics he was not allowed to travel on board the diplomat's vessel. Both De Vos van Steenwijk and Van Hogendorp traveled extensively in the U.S. over the next year, and were thus among the first systematic European observers of the new United States of America. While Van Hogendorp's long letters were filled with decidedly Orangist philosophical reflections on this new state and society — he was unimpressed by George Washington, for example — De Vos van Steenwijk's more formal journal was chockfull of practical details regarding the political structures of the new republic — he was

211

1

—

COLONIAL
PERIOD
AND
EIGHTEENTH
CENTURY

1609–1782

thrilled to meet Washington on several occasions — and especially the regionally specific opportunities for commerce, reflecting the dual nature of the Patriots' interest in North America.

John Adams remained the U.S. minister plenipotentiary to the Dutch Republic until 1788, though he was absent much of the time from 1782 onward and was in London instead.

Meanwhile, his Dutch Patriot allies very quickly turned their attention to domestic affairs, and the Patriots of Overijssel built on the success of the campaign for American recognition by launching a massive petition campaign in October that resulted in the reinstatement of Van der Capellen in the Provincial Estates of Overijssel on December 1, 1782. From there the Patriot reform movement built nationally, emulating in concrete ways the committees of correspondence and citizen militias that had fueled popular mobilization in North America from the Stamp Act Crisis onward. By 1785, the Patriots were able to strip the stadtholder of many of his prerogatives and to initiate constitutional reform processes in many cities and provinces. Despite his long absences, Adams continued to be very interested in, even impressed by, these political developments in the Dutch Republic. In 1786, for example, he was in Utrecht at the inauguration of new magistrates who had been elected democratically according to the provisions of a new municipal constitution. He later wrote to Thomas Jefferson, "We were present at Utrecht at the August Ceremony of Swearing in their new Magistrates. In no instance of ancient or modern History, have the People ever asserted more unequivocally their own inherent and unalienable sovereignty."[7] Eventually, the Patriots seized power in three of the seven sovereign Dutch provinces before Prussian military and British financial intervention restored the Orangist regime in late 1787.

Dutch Loans to the Young Republic

Though they were unsuccessful in establishing a democratic regime in the 1780s, the Dutch Patriots clearly learned much about revolutionary political change from their American allies, and in this general sense the American Revolution served both to precipitate and to inspire the Dutch Patriot Revolution. Unfortunately, what the Dutch advocates of an American alliance had most fervently hoped for — a spectacular expansion of trade between the two republics — failed to materialize as the Americans frequently reverted to their established networks of trade with Great Britain. Instead, the most tangible consequence of the 1782 alliance between the two republics was evident on the American side in the form of much-needed loans. In the spring of 1782, John Adams negotiated the issue of a first direct loan to the American Congress; the original

The installation of Pieter Johan van Berckel as the first
Dutch envoy in the United States (1783).

1

—

COLONIAL
PERIOD
AND
EIGHTEENTH
CENTURY

1609–1782

issue, through the banking houses of W. & J. Willink, N. & J. van Staphorst, and De la Lande & Fynje, was for three million guilders, which was later increased to five million.[8] Though the Dutch had been lending money to European states for more than a century, Dutch investors were worried about the precarious fiscal situation of the American Congress, which did not have the authority for direct taxation, and while the loan was issued at 4 percent interest, the Americans agreed to additional premiums and commissions that increased the effective cost to 6.65 percent, which was considerably higher than European states generally paid. In addition, this first American loan was slow to subscribe, perhaps because many Dutch investors were Orangists, but Adams' augmented loan was fully subscribed and available to the Congress by 1786.

Over time, the United States proved to be punctual in its annuity payments — apparently few investors knew that the Americans were taking out new loans to meet their existing payments — and new loans, in 1787 and 1788, were made at lower effective rates of interest. With the adoption of the new federal Constitution in 1789, however, the Amsterdam credit market took on new importance for the American republic. The new federal government, with its undeveloped taxing authority, assumed more than seventy million dollars of existing debt from the thirteen states, but in 1792, for example, the total debt charges were nearly twice the government's actual tax revenue. Thus, between 1790 and 1794, the American Congress raised loans of more than twenty-three million guilders in the Netherlands — most of it in Amsterdam but some in Antwerp as well — in order to keep up its debt payments until such time as tax revenues were sufficient to service debt obligations. These new and even larger loans, which were not paid off until 1809, were critically important to maintaining the fiscal solvency of the new American republic, but they also paved the way for substantial private Dutch investment in the American economy, especially in land development projects in upstate New York and Pennsylvania and in transportation infrastructure projects like the Erie Canal.[9]

Conclusion

In all, then, the Dutch people and the Republic of the United Provinces played a wide variety of roles, both symbolic and practical, in the creation of the United States of America. Though official Dutch recognition and alliance came late in the history of the War of Independence, the official reception of the first Dutch diplomatic mission in 1783 was, by all accounts, an important step in legitimating this new revolutionary state. Meanwhile, Dutch smuggling through St. Eustatius was critically important in supplying the American war effort in its early stages, and Dutch finance was essential to the solvency of the new state in its first decades of independence. Perhaps because these critical, even indispensable, Dutch contributions to American independence, far removed from the traditionally "heroic" military contributions of the French, were often seen to be legally suspect and/or basely profitable to Dutch merchants and investors, they have not always enjoyed the historical recognition they deserve. But, given these specific origins, it is not surprising that after more than two centuries of unbroken peaceful relations, the Dutch continue to be among the largest investors in the American economy.

1   C. F. Adams, ed., *Works of John Adams* (Boston: Little, Brown, 1856), 7:396-404.

2   Quoted in J. W. Schulte Nordholt, *The Dutch Republic and American Independence* (Chapel Hill/London: University of North Carolina Press, 1982), 39.

3   See further Barbara W. Tuchman, *The First Salute* (New York: Alfred Knopf, 1988).

4   See Schulte Nordholt, *The Dutch Republic*, 66.

5   See further David McCullough, *John Adams* (New York: Simon and Schuster, 2001).

6   See Wayne Te Brake, "Popular Politics in the Dutch Patriot Revolution," *Theory and Society* 14 (1985): 199-222.

7   J. Boyd, ed., *Works of Thomas Jefferson* (Princeton, NJ: Princeton University Press, 1954), 10:348.

8   James C. Riley, "Foreign Credit and Fiscal Stability: Dutch Investment in the United States, 1781–1794," *Journal of American History* 65 (1978): 654-678.

9   See also the article by Augustus J. Veenendaal, Jr.: 283-294.

2

THE NINETEENTH CENTURY

2

THE
NINETEENTH
CENTURY

—

FROM DISTANT IMAGES TO CLOSER RELATIONS: THE NETHERLANDS AND THE UNITED STATES DURING THE NINETEENTH CENTURY

WIM VAN DEN DOEL

Distant Images

At the beginning of what is sometimes described as the "long nineteenth century" the proclamation of the Batavian Republic in the Netherlands was celebrated with allegorical processions in which the Batavian, French, and American flags were emphatically shown together. For those present, it pointed up the fact that developments occurring in their own country were linked to a broader and history-making revolutionary movement. The American Revolution and its aftermath in the New World were far removed from their own circumstances, however, both in place and time. A few conservative political theologians pointed to America as an example of a place where — so it seemed — a perfect balance had been achieved between popular influence and aristocracy. The United States was, in the words of the political philosopher Johan Luzac, the land "where the Laws, having a most salutary effect of tempering the State, protect the Freedom of the Populace while also keeping them in order."[1] Rutger

Jan Schimmelpenninck — the man later appointed "grand pensionary" (*raad-pensionaris*) of the Batavian Republic — took an opposite stance, arguing that American structures of government should not enter into the Dutch political debate. How, after all, could the Netherlands possibly be compared with the United States? "Who would not immediately find himself lost in the immeasurable discrepancy in the expanse of their respective territories? Who would compare our Netherlands, our dot on the World Map, with a nation in which one single Region alone — Georgia, if I am correct — takes up a greater immensity of land than the entirety of the French Territory?" Besides, only time could tell how developments in the United States would unfold; the nation was still young and would encounter many obstacles on its path. "Onlookers awaited that moment when the swelling prosperity and astonishing accretion of people would give way to a battle of manifold interests." Only then, according to Schimmelpenninck, would "experience imprint thereon its Seal of approval, upon which that model, too, may be put forward with the force of authority."[2] And so the United States slowly dipped below the Netherlands' horizon.

In 1809 various newspapers in the United States — and specifically in New York — carried advertisements reporting the mysterious disappearance of a Dutch historian by the name of Diedrich Knickerbocker. In the ads, the owner of the hotel in which the Dutchman had stayed threatened to publish a manuscript that the man had left behind, should he fail to settle his account. Within the year Knickerbocker's *History of New York: From the Beginning of the World to the End of the Dutch Dynasty* was published and quickly became a bestseller. The man behind the ad campaign and the bogus Knickerbocker name was Washington Irving — not a Dutch historian at all, but an American author who had written the book as a satire and who painted an unflattering picture of the Dutch colonists in Manhattan. As Annette Stott points out in her article on "Images of Dutchness in the United States," Knickerbocker claimed that among New Amsterdammers "the very words of learning, education, taste, and talents were unheard of."

It was with Irving that the stereotypical and very persistent image of the lazy, pipe-smoking, gin-guzzling Dutch colonist was born. For many Americans, it formed their only mental picture of the Dutch, insofar as they were able to imagine the Netherlands and its inhabitants at all. In fact, at the beginning of the nineteenth century, the Netherlands' influence on the United States had grown liable to considerable erosion. The once so proud Republic had become a vassal of Napoleonic France and seemed to have little to offer to the New World. In 1801 the American government decided to recall its envoy to the Netherlands without naming a successor. The official reason given was that the American government wanted to cut spending, but it was clear that Washington held the not altogether unjustified view that the Netherlands' foreign policy was determined entirely by France. In response, the Dutch representative in the United States, Rogier Gerard van Polanen, chose to likewise quit his post, resulting in a cessation of diplomatic relations between the two countries.

It goes without saying that Dutch-American relations were reinstated after the French period, but not to any level of great consequence. Though the first American envoy to the Netherlands, William Eustis, was counseled upon his departure that The Hague was "a principal theatre of the most important negotiations in Europe," as Cornelis van Minnen describes in his article "Dutch-American Diplomatic Relations," the reality was altogether less inspiring. So, too, did the expectation of profitable trade with the United States that many Dutch citizens had fostered toward the end of the eighteenth century turn out to be a false hope. High American tariffs proved an enormous obstacle to the export of goods to the U.S. The result was a minimum of shipping traffic between the two countries during the first half of the nineteenth century, to which the poor state of the Dutch economy (and thus lack of export products for the American market) also contributed. Bilateral relations did not encounter complications of any significant interest over the course of the century either — the Netherlands being too dull and too insignificant, and the United States being too inwardly focused. Not even the election of the first Dutch-American president, Martin Van Buren, in 1836, was able to change this. Van Buren was a president nurtured on the politics of New York State, and his Dutch heritage exerted no influence in this respect. "There is no indication that Van Buren's politics or those of any other of the New York political elite of Dutch background in this period were influenced by the Dutch political tradition, as had been true in the eighteenth century," Firth Haring Fabend quite rightly surmises in her article "The Dutch-American Political Elite in New York State."

And so it may seem that the story of Dutch-American relations in the nineteenth century can be summed up in a few words: after a period of close relations around the time of the American Revolution, the Netherlands and the United States each went their own way, with no interest for respective developments in the other country and with no influence issuing in either direction. There would be no change in this relationship until the end of the century, when the United States developed into the center of the so-called Second Industrial Revolution that furnished the world with telephone and telegraph lines, vast railway networks, regular shipping connections, mass media including radio and film, and the first automobiles and aircraft. These were the same developments that transformed the United States into a nation that was unequivocally the most modern and potentially most powerful in the world, thereby not only arousing Dutch interest, but also luring Dutch immigrants to the New World.

Interest in Literature, Art, and Architecture

Yet this picture is too simplistic. Though it is undeniable that more intensive bilateral relations would not take shape until after the American Civil War, in fact a steady stream of original and translated fictional, historical, and travel literature about the United States found its way to the Netherlands during the first half of the nineteenth century. Amsterdam had its own English and American Reading Society, among whose members was the critic Everhardus Johannes Potgieter. Potgieter was the editor of *De Gids*, a magazine that published its first issue in 1837 and was led by perhaps the first true "intellectuals" in the Netherlands, who had set themselves the goal of raising the level of Dutch culture. In his book *Jan, Jannetje en hun jongste kind* (1841), he created a character that, in the eyes of many, was the embodiment of contemporary Dutch society: Jan Salie. Unlike his older brothers who engaged in lives of trade and sea travel, Jan Salie was a slow and sluggish youth. So it was off to the United States with him — a country of which Potgieter wrote admiringly: "America, that offers for every … refugee a refuge, for every … sorrow succor, for every … need fulfillment, and does not merely write on your pennants: *e pluribus unum* but in deed unites the most disparate forces into one great goal; the free, full development of all that is human — what a glorious performance you present, what further feats may the world not now expect of you!"[3] Fueled in part by Potgieter, *De Gids* sought to trace the development of American literature in all its minutiae. As such, its first year of publication included, for example, a review of the Dutch translation of *Three Years in North America*, a travel book authored by the Scotsman James Stuart.

Other magazines likewise carried discussions of American literary works. This led one such publication, *De Tijd*, to conclude in 1850 that even the best American writers "had not been able to break away from the influence of their European models," as Hans Bak cites in his article "The Reception of American Literature in the Netherlands." Yet this negative verdict did not stop C.M. Mensing, for example, from making a Dutch translation of *Uncle Tom's Cabin*, entitled *De negerhut: een verhaal uit het slavenleven in Noord-Amerika*, nor did it prevent the book from subsequently enjoying enormous success in the Netherlands.

In certain nineteenth-century American circles, too, interest in the Netherlands never faded entirely. Midway into the century, the American historian John Motley decided to pen a history of the Netherlands, focusing particularly on the era of the Dutch Republic. In 1851 he traveled to Europe to conduct his research, consulting archives in Dresden, Brussels, and The Hague. His *The Rise of the Dutch Republic*, which was published in 1856, as well as in numerous ensuing reprints, was fully in keeping with a period in which wealthy Americans had also begun collecting the paintings of the likes of Rembrandt, Hals, and Vermeer. As Stott observes, this led to a paradoxical situation in which "some Dutchophiles had no Dutch blood and some Dutch Americans had little interest in the Netherlands or its impact on American society."

It was in New York, more than anywhere else, that works by Dutch and Flemish masters of the Golden Age were being collected. The Metropolitan Museum and the homes of Henry Frick and Benjamin Altman alone exhibited over twenty paintings by Rembrandt, five by Vermeer, and dozens of others by a range of masters. They presented a view of the Netherlands that, though of course no longer an accurate reflection of the nineteenth-century reality, furnished a source of inspiration for a new generation of American painters such as John Singer Sargent, who copied the works of Frans Hals and later acquired the epithet "the Van Dyck of our times." What especially appealed to Americans, as Nancy Minty describes in her article "Artistic Affinities: New-World Painters Recast the Golden Age," were the values that the Netherlandish works seemed to exemplify: "Serious, solid, sincere — Dutch national characteristics — the characteristics of Dutch art."

Representations of a fantasy of the Netherlands were more important and more influential in the United States than was true knowledge. A case in point is the American architectural style that became popular toward the end of the nineteenth century, which stamped its characteristic features — such as gambrel roofs with curved eaves over the long ends of porches — on many houses on the American East Coast and was dubbed "Dutch Colonial Revival." Though houses of this description would have been impossible to find in the Netherlands, in the United States they were marketed under the label of "Dutch." By 1911, as Stott writes in her article "Dutch-American Material Culture," Americans could purchase prefabricated houses with names such as "The Amsterdam" and "The Rembrandt." Buyers could opt for "Dutch-style" dining rooms with a blue and white décor of "Delft" tiles and wallpaper bearing "Dutch" motifs. Stott continues: "Despite its kitsch quality to modern eyes, it appealed to Gilded Era Americans as a reflection of the refined tastes, material wealth, and democratic impulses they attributed to the Dutch Golden Age."

That nineteenth-century American travelers journeyed to the Netherlands with Motley's books on Dutch history or Mary Mapes Dodge's *Hans Brinker, or the Silver Skates* stored in either their luggage or their memories certainly did not help in promoting any more realistic images of the Netherlands. It also meant that American tourists concentrated their visits in such places as Volendam, Marken, and Katwijk, where, after all, the "real" Netherlands could still be observed at first hand. The Holland America Line further reinforced this image by publishing *A Journey Through Old Holland*, in which, as George Harinck and Augustus Veenendaal recount in their article "Transatlantic Transportation and Travelers' Experiences," the narrator falls asleep and enters a dream in which he joins a Dutch colonist on a tour of seventeenth-century Holland.

Throughout the nineteenth century most Americans therefore had only a vague conception of the Netherlands and the Dutch — or in any case one that had little to do with reality. Nevertheless, the Netherlands' influence on American art and architecture — however circuitous and asynchronous — should not be discounted. Though Dutch-American relations signified little on the surface, something of the Netherlands clearly did cross over into nineteenth-century American culture and take root there.

Immigration and Americanization

Not until the second half of the nineteenth century would there be an intensification of relations between Europe and the United States, with the Atlantic Ocean coming to function, more and more, as the inland sea of the Western world, traversed by goods and people in ever greater numbers. Connections were improving elsewhere in the world, too; trade relations between the United States and the Dutch East Indies received a powerful impetus, for example. As the nineteenth century drew to a close, the global economic system for which the major European trade companies had laid the rudimentary framework grew steadily in size and significance. Economies were drawn into worldwide networks, and none more so than the United States and Europe, together with Europe's colonial holdings.

Accompanying these developments was the mass migration of people between Europe and the New World. While there was at the same time a not inconsiderable flux of migrants both within Asia and from Asia to the New World, it was the movement of Europeans to South and North America that made the greatest impact. The United States received immigrants from a broad range of countries, and the 250,000 people who traded the Netherlands for the United States between 1820 and 1920 were entirely overshadowed by the 6 million Germans, 4.7 million Italians, 4.6 million Irish, 3.3 million Russians, 1.2 million Swedes, and 800,000 Norwegians. Compared with other European countries, far fewer people chose to emigrate from the Netherlands at all during this period: only 380,000 left their native country over the course of the entire century, which averages out to a mere 72 of every 100,000 residents. This put the Netherlands tenth on the list of Europe's emigrant nations, with only France, Belgium, and Luxemburg having lower percentages.

Far and away the largest group of nineteenth-century Dutch emigrants, nearly 90 percent in total, chose the United States as their destination, despite the

Netherlands' extensive colonial territories. The remaining 10 percent went to these colonies, Latin America, or South Africa. These Dutch emigrants knew exactly what they were looking for in their new homeland: land — either to start a farm or to expand upon an existing farming enterprise. Almost without exception, those who went to the United States came from rural regions. Of more particular statistical interest is the fact that they originated from a limited number of geographic areas in the Netherlands: in the period from 1820 to 1880, three-quarters of all Dutch emigrants came from only 134 of the country's 1,156 municipalities. The municipalities concerned were concentrated in Zeeland, on Goeree-Overflakkee, in the Peel, in the Achterhoek, and in the northern reaches of Groningen and Friesland. Every time the United States simplified procedures for acquiring land, there followed another exodus of Dutch farming families from these specific areas — and in fact a similar trend can be observed throughout Europe. The first great wave of migration to the United States took place in the mid-1840s, following the U.S. Congress's approval of the Preemption Act under President Andrew Jackson, which inaugurated a period in which large numbers of Native Americans were forcibly driven from their ancestral lands.

Opportunities for potential Dutch emigrants to obtain land in the United States thus abounded during the 1840s. But this in itself was not enough to induce Dutch farming families to undertake the journey across the Atlantic. Rather, what motivated many of these emigrants were the religious disagreements besetting the Dutch Reformed Church, which incidentally also drew attention from the United States. Though the full background of the conflict need not concern us here, it is worth noting that in the 1830s the schism ultimately resulted in a separatist (*afgescheiden*) church, whose leaders were imprisoned and prohibited from conducting services. Open persecution of the new religious community ceased in 1841, but for many years thereafter its members continued to be treated as second-class citizens who were prevented from founding their own schools, whose meetings were not only not acknowledged, but banned, and whose organization as the Christian Reformed Church would not be officially recognized by the government as a religious community until thirty years later. It was, as George Harinck writes in his "Religious Exchange in the Dutch-American Network," a situation that prompted even the General Synod of the Holland Reformed Church in North America to send a missive. Its writers described for their European brothers and sisters the happy existence of the Reformed churches in the United States: "enjoying liberties and privileges, without any vexation or compulsion ... she never experienced any persecution, and she never had one single martyr in this country."

The situation was made even worse for the separatists by the persistent economic depression of the 1830s and 1840s. The division of the Low Countries into the Netherlands and Belgium in 1830, combined with the costs of main-

225

taining a large military force because King Willem I refused to accept Belgian independence until 1839, had a detrimental effect on the Dutch economy. Dutch industry found itself scarcely able to compete with the more modern British and Belgian industries, a circumstance compounded by agricultural sector losses resulting from crop failures and the potato blight between 1845 and 1847. Small farmers working areas with sandy and clayey soil suffered the most, and with them the craftsmen and laborers who depended on agricultural production for their livelihood. In the province of Zeeland, the agricultural sector replaced a portion of its crop production with more labor-extensive stock farming, resulting in increased unemployment among agricultural workers. And in the sandy regions in the east, where farming had never been more than a marginal sector, many found themselves unable to meet their costs of living, a situation exacerbated by the growing population. It was within the groups of Dutch people living under these conditions that some came to believe it would be preferable to seek their fortunes elsewhere. For most, elsewhere became the United States.

Thanks to the concentrated and distinctive pattern of their settlement, and despite their relatively small numbers, the Dutch were able for a long time to preserve their own unique character and exist as discrete communities within American society. These immigrants were hardly typical representatives of the Dutch population, and Americans who believed that in visiting these Dutch settlements they had gained an understanding of society in the Netherlands were altogether mistaken. These immigrants only served to reinforce the mental pictures that American tourists had brought back with them from Volendam and Katwijk: that of a society that was agrarian and rigidly Calvinistic in nature, which did not mirror the real situation in the Netherlands at all. In fact, when viewed in the context of religion, Katwijk and Grand Rapids or Pella bore a closer resemblance to each other than, for example, Katwijk and nearby Leiden. Without question, Dutch immigration to the New World was unlike that of any other nationality. "Few immigrant groups clustered more than Hollanders," Robert Swierenga notes in his article "The New Immigration." "Their USA focus and clannish colonization created a choice environment in which to nurture and sustain a strong sense of 'Dutchness' for many generations." But it was a very specific brand of "Dutchness," and one that was steadily dying out in the Netherlands.

Ultimately, however, the Dutch communities were no less immune to the slow process of Americanization, which was propelled in part by the Reverend Albertus van Raalte and his congregation's decision to join the existing American Reformed Protestant Dutch Church. A subsequent second wave of immigrants were more adamant about upholding their heritage and chose to establish instead what would later become the Christian Reformed Church. The latter church was to maintain a more distinctively Dutch character, though naturally it could not avoid being influenced by the American society surrounding it. Of particular significance in this respect was the American Civil War. One of the effects of the war was that Dutch settlers now began to see themselves as full citizens of the United States. In other words, they came to regard the New World as their homeland.

The Civil War also exposed Dutch immigrant communities to aspects of American life that were entirely foreign to run-of-the-mill orthodox Calvinists. Dutch youth living in the Michigan settlements became increasingly "worldly" after the war; they patronized taverns with greater frequency and slowly freed themselves of the rigid straightjacket of Calvinist mores, thereby alarming conservative members of the community.

Impact of the U.S. Economy

The period between the end of the American Civil War and the beginning of World War I was one of the most turbulent chapters in United States history. The ruins of the conflict between North and South were to form the foundation of a new and powerful industrial nation that no other country in the world could afford to ignore. It was therefore no coincidence that the Dutch from now on began to trace developments in the United States with considerably more interest. Evidence of this increasing attention was manifested not only in expanded coverage in the Dutch newspapers, but also in activity on the financial markets. Whereas Dutch investments in the American economy had still been exceptionally low during the 1850s—a period of relative economic growth in the United States—this changed after the Civil War. There was enormous interest in U.S. railroad bonds, for example, which quickly climbed to become one of the top investment categories at the Amsterdam Stock Exchange. During the last decades of the nineteenth century, over one-third of Amsterdam's foreign investment funds were based in the United States, and nearly 90 percent of those American funds comprised railroad securities. In fact the first such bonds were already being offered in Amsterdam by the Illinois Central Railroad in 1857, but not until after 1868 did their values soar. "The American railroad corner of the Amsterdam Stock Exchange did become a strong center of trade," Augustus Veenendaal quite rightly concludes in his article "Dutch Investments in the United States."

Yet Dutch confidence in the American railroad was somewhat misplaced. Those at the head of the railroad companies were sometimes motivated only by thoughts of filling their own pockets, rather than profiting their shareholders and bondholders. In his guide to the American railroads listed on the Amsterdam Stock Exchange, entitled *Amerikaansche spoorwegen op de Amsterdamsche*

227

beurs, N. J. den Tex cautioned readers about American practices. "Let no one seek guarantees from those appointed as the Directors in America. One should take as a general rule," he advised, "that the Directors of the American railroads regard their seats on the Boards of Directors as being first and foremost an occasion for personal gain." Manipulation was rife in the American sale and construction of railway lines.

These abuses played out against the backdrop of an already ailing American economy: there was a negative balance of trade, the rapid opening up of the western frontier had resulted in a surplus of agrarian products, and the government treasury was anything but robust. The inevitable crisis came in September 1873. Many railroad companies found themselves unable to pay off their loans, and America's leading bank, Jay Cooke & Company—which had also financed the corrupt Union Pacific Railroad—was forced to close its doors. General panic ensued on Wall Street, with banks, investment firms, railroads, and other enterprises filing for bankruptcy. It would take more than six years for the United States to recover from this stock market crash.

The Panic of 1873 had serious consequences for Dutch investors, too. Many securities suddenly turned out to be entirely worthless, with losses amounting to over 129 million dollars in 1875. The Amsterdam Stock Exchange lost every shred of confidence it had had in the American railroads. "Our public appears unfamiliar with the golden mean and keeps reverting to extremes," noted the September 28, 1873 edition of the *Amsterdams effectenblad*. "In its intoxication two years ago it bought at high prices without concern for separating the wheat from the chaff, while now in its ludicrous anxiety it hastily throws everything overboard."[4]

The economic crisis in the United States led to a dramatic reduction in emigration from the Netherlands to the New World, though this would prove to be only temporary. With the American economy on the upswing again after 1880, the influx of Dutch immigrants resumed also. From 1873 they could make the trip on the Nederlandsch-Amerikaansche Stoomvaart-Maatschappij (Dutch-American Steamship Company), better known later as the Holland America Line. Before 1873, nearly all shipping connections between Europe and the United States had been foreign enterprises, and the Dutch shipping industry had been struggling since midcentury. The important mail route between New York, Le Havre, and Bremen did not call at any Dutch ports at all, and Dutch export products were shipped out mainly from Antwerp, whose port did have regular connections to and from the United States. The 1850s and 1860s marked a dim chapter in Dutch-American trade, in which no more than 1 percent of all U.S. exports were shipped to destinations in the Netherlands, while Dutch products constituted a mere 0.8 percent of total U.S. imports in the 1850s, and dropped to 0.56 percent in the next decade. The Netherlands' trade position was further jeopardized by the opening of a rail link between Antwerp and Co-logne — the Iron Rhine, as it soon became known. At the same time, however, there were signs of recovery. In 1860 the endless conflict between private par-ties and the government about who would take charge of the construction and exploitation of the railroads was finally settled. That year's Railway Act decreed that the state would build the rail tracks and that private companies would be able to exploit them. At last it would be possible to start on the expansion of the rail network, for which the Netherlands' East Indian assets would prove a useful boon. Compared to the country's 176 kilometers of railroad tracks in 1850, the total length of the Dutch rail network had expanded to 1,419 kilome-ters by 1870. In 1863 the Dutch decided to build a series of canals that would link Amsterdam and Rotterdam directly with the sea. Digging commenced for the North Sea Canal (Noordzeekanaal) to connect Amsterdam with IJmuiden in 1865, and Rotterdam's New Waterway (Nieuwe Waterweg) was begun in 1866; the two canals were opened in 1876 and 1872, respectively.

A whole host of initiatives were introduced to resuscitate the Dutch econo-my, many of them in Rotterdam. In an article that appeared in *De Economist* in 1869, Antoine Plate F. Jzn. pointed up the need for a regular steamship service between Rotterdam and New York. His recommendation found a receptive au-dience among such Rotterdam businessmen as Marten Mees and Lodewijk Pin-coffs, and in February 1871 the limited partnership of Plate, Reuchlin & Co. was established with a small fleet of two ships. On October 15, 1872 the company's first ship, the *Rotterdam*, set out for New York carrying ten cabin passengers, sixty immigrants (lower-deck passengers) and eight hundred tons of freight, ar-riving on November 5. But two ships were hardly sufficient to maintain a regu-lar service between New York and Rotterdam, so in 1873 the fleet was expanded with another two ships and relaunched on May 1 as the public limited liabili-ty company Nederlandsch-Amerikaansche Stoomvaart-Maatschappij (NASM). Yet the economic crisis of 1873 created huge obstacles for the new enterprise, and it was not until interest in transport to the United States revived after 1880 that the NASM's prospects seemed secure. The company strengthened its posi-tion by starting another line to Argentina in 1888, but it was the transportation of passengers to and from New York that proved the most lucrative. In 1889 its owners signed the lease on a pier in Hoboken, NJ, in a prime spot at the bot-tom of Fifth Street that the NASM would continue to use until 1963. Improve-ments were also made to its Rotterdam facilities. For many years, emigrants from Europe had had to settle for cramped portside hotels where hygiene levels often left much to be desired. Infectious illnesses such as cholera were a con-stant threat to passengers and thus an ever-present risk for the shipping en-terprises; all the more so since the United States applied stringent conditions on incoming immigrants' health. To address this situation, a group of Rotterdam residents led by Jonkheer Otto Reuchlin — the cofounder of Plate, Reuchlin & Co. — undertook to build an emigrants' hotel on the Wilhelminakade, to be leased to the NASM. The four-hundred-bed hotel on the quay was completed in 1893, and would serve for many years as the place where many of those seeking a new life in the United States would spend their last night in the Netherlands. When the NASM — which continued from 1896 on as the NASM/Holland America Line — celebrated its twenty-fifth anniversary, the directors could feel well satisfied. They had transported a total of around ninety thousand cabin passengers and over four hundred thousand lower-deck passengers — mostly immigrants — along with five million tons of cargo. The twenty-fifth annual report closed with the words "When one calls to mind ... what our Line has contributed to the development of traffic between our Native Country and the United States, then we may certainly ... express the conviction that we have been and shall more and more be for our Native Country that which was intended upon our foundation: a 'bridge across the ocean.'"[5]

Other factors besides immigration contributed to the significant rise in traffic between the Netherlands and the United States during the last decades of the nineteenth century. The latter's economy experienced strong growth in this period, and the Dutch economy also grew — more slowly, but surely — thanks in part to developments in Germany. The Ruhr Basin in particular had evolved to become a center of modern industry, helping secure Germany's position as one of the strongest economies on the European continent. As the gateway to the Ruhr region, the port of Rotterdam benefited from an enormous rise in commercial activity. "The role of the Netherlands as 'main port of Europe' still had to be invented, but it developed quickly: in 1910, while imports from the United States amounted to 295 million guilders, reexported American goods amounted to 102 million guilders," Jeroen Touwen concludes in his article "American Trade with the Netherlands and the Dutch East Indies."

Where trade between the Netherlands and the United States was concerned, expanding commercial activity in the Dutch East Indies from 1870 onward was of even greater significance. The Sugar Law and Land Law passed in that year put an end to the government's economic monopoly and rang in a period in which private initiative and capital took center stage, with a resultant boom in the colony's economy. A particularly important role in these developments was reserved for the so-called outer regions, or regions beyond Java. In 1863 Jacobus Nienhuys introduced the cultivation of tobacco on the Sumatra east coast, for example, which straightaway proved to have vast potential; the tobacco leaves were by and large shipped to the Netherlands, and from there distributed to various trade partners.

In fact, by 1890 tobacco had grown to become far and away the Netherlands' most important export product for the U.S. market, in spite of numerous attempts by the Americans to restrict its import. In 1890 alone over 9 million dollars worth of tobacco was shipped to the United States. Other statistics offer further evidence of an upward trend in Dutch-American trade. Dutch exports to the United States rose from a value of 1.3 million dollars in 1870 to 15.8 million in 1900, and apart from tobacco consisted chiefly of diamonds, flower bulbs, plants, and spices. In comparison, the Americans were exporting their goods to the Netherlands on a scale many times greater, growing from 6.4 million dollars in 1870 to 89.4 million in 1900. Clearly this was not exactly an even balance of trade; however, it should be noted that direct exports by the Netherlands from the Dutch East Indies to the United States added another 28 million dollars, whereas America exported hardly any products to the Indies itself. The single most important product to be exported directly from the Dutch East Indies was sugar. In 1900 it accounted for 87 percent of the total volume of sugar exports to the United States. However, when the Americans introduced higher tariffs to keep Indies' sugar off the U.S. market after the turn of the century, East Indian export figures declined accordingly.

This decline turned out to be a trend that not even the emergence of a new branch of industry, one that actually profited from developments in the United States, could avail. The industry concerned was the American automotive industry, whose demand for rubber provided a major impetus for cultivation of this raw material. It was thanks in part to this demand that, by 1914, some 240,000 hectares of farmland were being used for rubber cultivation in the Dutch East Indies, much of it on the Sumatra east coast. Even so, rubber production could not make up for the continuing uneven economic trade balance between the Netherlands and the United States: the 38.2 million dollars in goods exported by the Netherlands to America in 1913 paled in comparison to the latter's 125.9 million dollar export volume in the opposite direction — a figure that served to place the Netherlands fourth among American import countries.

Admirers and Critics

The success achieved by the United States during this period drew Dutch admiration, though almost never without an accompanying dose of criticism. One obvious admirer was the editor of *De Gids*, Charles Boissevain, who would travel to the United States in 1880 on behalf of the *Algemeen Handelsblad* newspaper. He was to author several enthusiastic reports describing his experiences and impressions during his stay, which were brought together in 1881–82 in the book *Van 't noorden naar 't zuiden. Schetsen en indrukken van de Vereenigde Staten van Noord-Amerika*. His reports evince a clear intent to counter negative stereotypes emphasizing American corruption and lack of refinement. Of course

231

the United States had its problems, like any country, but "those who paint or write must endeavor always to shine the light on the main issue, and," according to Boissevain, "the spittoon in the South and East, the revolver in the West, the abominable civic administration in New York, the gambling fever in Chicago, are not worth a place in the foreground. They are but shadows in the background that make the light brighter." The journalist was particularly impressed by the dynamic pace of American life, the energy of New York, the bustle of Chicago, and the endless expanse of the American prairie: "It is as though a map of eternity were being laid out before you." Boissevain believed the Netherlands would do well to follow the example set by the Americans, who had used their common sense and willpower to generate tremendous prosperity. Anyone willing to take the trouble to visit America would not be disappointed; it was nothing less than "an elixir of youth to go to America."[6]

If Boissevain's America was chiefly a source of inspiration for the modernization of the Netherlands, the America that inspired the late nineteenth-century socialist scholar Frederik van Eeden was altogether different. In 1898, Van Eeden started a colony near Bussum in the Netherlands that he named Walden, with the aim of bringing a better society within reach. According to Van Eeden, the two essential ingredients for an ideal society were communal ownership of land and cooperative division of labor. Its members would each occupy their own home on communal property, where they would lead frugal, modest lives and strive to develop their respective talents. Van Eeden's inspiration for the colony came after reading the American writer Henry David Thoreau's *Walden, or Life in the Woods*, published in 1854. Thoreau was an admirer of Ralph Waldo Emerson, himself one of the nineteenth century's foremost American thinkers and an adherent of transcendental philosophy. In his book, Thoreau described the two-year period during which he turned his back on the civilized world and led a solitary existence in a forest cabin on Walden Pond in Concord, MA.

Van Eeden first read *Walden, or Life in the Woods* in 1894, having borrowed a copy from Jacobus P. Thijsse; it was not until 1897, however, that he fell under its spell. Van Eeden identified with Thoreau's individualism and desire to abandon the materialistic world. He believed that the ideal society was within reach, that it could be molded, and was reinforced in this view by another work of American literature — Edward Bellamy's *Looking Backward*. This novel, which he also recommended to others, caused him to reflect that "We humans are omnipotent on the earth; the earth has a gentle nature, and so when one soul of the human race suffers from some lack, then it is completely and utterly the fault of mankind, and not of ineluctable fate."[7] In the end, Van Eeden founded Walden, a colony that was intended to spark a major cooperative movement, but that ultimately succumbed to incompetence, quarreling, and idealism in 1907.

The Walden fiasco did not dampen Van Eeden's enthusiasm, however. In seeking a means to realize his ideas he now turned his gaze to the United States, where the climate was exceptionally conducive to idealistic experiments. Between 1908 and 1909 he would make three separate visits to the United States and lecture there on various topics. Van Eeden's experience of his trips mirrored precisely those that the liberal Boissevain had reported nearly thirty years earlier. In her article "Dutch Social Reformers' Perceptions of American Reform," Maartje Janse quotes Van Eeden's words: "The Americans are willing to listen. They do not scoff at novelty like the people of the old countries. Americans have the enthusiasm and the spirit of progress." Yet their enthusiasm notwithstanding, few Americans were actually willing to embrace Van Eeden's ideals, even if his visits did coincide with the United States' so-called Progressive Era. His proposal to found what he christened the Co-operative Company of America, with responsibility for organizing cooperative settlements throughout the country, met with rejection by nearly everyone he approached; only a certain Hugh Mac-Rae, a banker and a real estate agent from Wilmington, NC, thought Van Eeden's plan had potential and so started a second Walden — the Van Eeden Colony — in the United States. But this experiment likewise failed: though eleven families had settled there in 1913, differences of opinion and poverty soon sent most of them packing. For Van Eeden it was enough to douse his interest in the United States. The American reality had proven unable to live up to his lofty expectations.

Scholars and Missionaries

Writers such as Van Eeden, political activists like Aletta Jacobs — who also visited the United States on multiple occasions — and various scientists played key roles in intensifying Dutch-American relations. As Pieter Hovens explains in his contribution, the missionaries and researchers who focused on Native American populations also had a hand in forging unique ties. The Amsterdam-born Dominican Theodore Van den Broek was one such missionary, who went to Wisconsin in the 1830s to work among the Menominee Indians and whose experiences there, published in the form of letters to *De Tijd*, convinced the newspaper's Catholic readership in and around Uden to join him in Wisconsin in the 1840s. With their migration the village of Little Chute took on a distinctly Dutch aspect, and the Menominee Indians were eventually forced to withdraw to a reservation. Other Dutch missionaries headed even farther west, with the Jesuits settling among the Blackfoot, Northern Cheyenne, Arapaho, Crow, and Sioux.

The missionaries were not alone in their interest in the original inhabitants of America; Dutch scholars, too, were drawn to conduct research among

233

the various tribes living there. The pioneer in this field was the anthropologist Herman ten Kate. As a student in Leiden, Ten Kate had studied such subjects as physical geography, Eastern and East Indian languages, and ethnology, and in 1878 attested his ongoing interest in the Indians in an article entitled "Amerikaanse toestanden" (American scenarios), in which he censured the American government's policy in respect of the Nez Percés and pleaded for more humane treatment of Indians in the Americans' westward push.[8] Having obtained the support of the Royal Dutch Geographical Society, the Royal Holland Society of Sciences and Humanities, and his father, Ten Kate departed for the United States in 1882. Three years later he published *Reizen en onderzoekingen in Noord-Amerika*, detailing his experiences there and the lives of the Papago, Mohave, Navajo, Apache, and Zuni.[9] Ten Kate was cognizant of the fact that he was observing a "vanishing race," stating in his book: "The solemn courage, the strength of once-mighty tribes is broken for ever, and 'civilization' has now almost everywhere taken over."[10]

At the beginning of the twentieth century the brilliant Dutch linguist Christianus C. Uhlenbeck would follow in Ten Kate's footsteps, though he set his sights on an entirely different part of the United States, investigating the Blackfoot together with his assistant J.P.B. de Josselin de Jong. The latter would publish the book *Blackfoot Texts from the Southern Peigans Blackfoot Reservation, Teton County, Montana* in 1914, but later became known mainly for his anthropological work on Indonesia. Uhlenbeck himself authored numerous works, including *An English-Blackfoot Vocabulary: Based on Material from the Southern Peigans* in 1930. Not only did Dutch researchers add to knowledge about the original inhabitants of America, the American experiences of the likes of Uhlenbeck and De Josselin de Jong also provided a valuable catalyst for work in the fields of linguistics and anthropology in the Netherlands.

Special Bonds

Nineteenth-century Dutch-American transatlantic relations were considerably more complex than they might at first appear. Influential in this respect were, on the one hand, the imagined historical Dutch prototypes that shaped American architecture and painting over the course of the century and created a vogue for Dutch culture among the New York and New England elite and, on the other, the rural Dutch emigrants whose by and large highly specific religious background imported an entirely different image of the Netherlands. Together they ensured that not only the Holland of Rembrandt and Vermeer but likewise the Holland of windmills, traditional costumes, clogs, and Reformed churches imprinted their legacy on the United States — in some respects more so than they ever did on the Netherlands. These migrations also helped wipe away the caricaturized image invented by Washington Irving in the early years of the century. And regardless of whether the then contemporary Netherlands was the land of Rembrandt and Vermeer or of the simple, hardworking migrants with roots in rural Holland, the impression that the Americans had formed of the Netherlands and the Dutch was a positive one.

Yet America was to be a more important example to the Netherlands than vice versa, though this was hardly surprising considering the mutual shifts in their relationship. In a reversal of the two countries' eighteenth-century roles, it was now the United States that was a "light in the distance," albeit that its impact on Dutch culture and the Dutch political and religious landscape remained limited. There was as yet no hint of Ten Kate's "American scenarios" in Dutch churches or Dutch politics: these would not come until much later.

These developments played out against a turn-of-the-century backdrop of strengthening relations between various regions, including between Europe and the New World. The United States, the Netherlands, and the Dutch colonies formed links in a dynamic global economy, in which Dutch investors backed American railroads, Americans imported ever-greater volumes of raw materials from the Dutch East Indies, and the Netherlands evolved into a multimodal transport hub. Yet the transportation revolution and the improved possibilities for maintaining contact with the Netherlands would do nothing to change the fact that the Dutch immigrant population in the United States was beginning to veer off on its own, progressively more American course. Even among orthodox Calvinists, church services were becoming markedly more American in character and American holidays were now being celebrated with wholehearted enthusiasm, causing many a minister to wring his hands in despair. After all, they had not broken with the Dutch Reformed Church and emigrated to the United States simply to be swallowed up in a "swelling tide of worldliness." And yet this is precisely what happened.

Even so, their perception of having an exceptional bond with the Netherlands would experience a powerful revival around the turn of the century. Spurring this revival were two events in particular: the first was the Second Boer War that broke out in 1899 and the second was the Anti-Revolutionary Party's leader Abraham Kuyper's visit to the United States in 1898 and 1899. By the 1880s the South African Boer republics had come to occupy a place of significance in the minds of many Dutch. There was a strong sense of cultural kinship with the Boers, who were themselves of course the descendants of seventeenth- and eighteenth-century Dutch colonists. Kuyper went so far as to declare that in South Africa a "New Holland has risen, with the old language, the old blood, with new fire and with new force." [11] British aggression against the Boer republics thus elicited great indignation. As such, when Transvaal Republic Presi-

235

dent Paul Kruger was brought to Europe aboard a Dutch warship in 1900, he was given a true hero's welcome in The Hague, accompanied by a general outpouring of anti-British sentiment. The response of Dutch immigrants in the United States was no different. The Dutch-American poet Henry van der Werp was inspired by these events to write his nationalistic poem "Aan mijn Transvaalsche Stamgenoten" ("To my Transvaal Clansmen"):

The British Lion, as ever keen for spoils,
Has struck his claw in Holland's blood again;
The prideful Brit, deaf to right and reason,
Would honor boldly risk for wicked gain.[12]

Everywhere where sizeable Dutch communities had settled, protest gatherings were held, angry telegrams were sent, and money was collected to aid the Boers. Often this was paired with impassioned renditions of the Wilhelmus — the Dutch national anthem — anthems of the Boer republics, and commemoration of the participants' Dutch heritage. In the words of Douma, "If the Civil War was a test to become American, the Boer War was a reassertion of Dutch ethnic identity."

Abraham Kuyper's arrival in the United States only served to fan such patriotic sentiments. Kuyper left for America in August of 1898 in order to give a series of lectures and receive the honorary doctorate that Princeton University had awarded him in 1896. Naturally the latter represented the highpoint of his trip; before an audience of more than a thousand students, Kuyper accepted his doctorate diploma from the university's president. Kuyper used his lectures at Princeton — the so-called Stone Lectures — to defend his interpretation of Calvinism, arguing that Calvinism went beyond a system of theological precepts and in fact comprised a worldview that upright Calvinists could apply in any societal sphere.

Whatever their significance, neither Kuyper nor the Boer Wars could reverse Dutch Americans' slow but steady withdrawal from the Netherlands and the Dutch language. As the last decade of the nineteenth century segued into the first of the twentieth, it became clear that the process of Americanization, having already been accelerated by the Civil War, was now unstoppable. Of course, this did not spell the end for Dutch-American relations — quite the reverse: the nineteenth-century revolutions in transportation and information not only simplified the carriage of goods and money across the Atlantic, they also prompted growing numbers of Dutch writers and journalists to satisfy their interests and travel to the United States. Many of them returned with enthusiastic stories lauding the scale, expansiveness, and vibrancy of America and, hoping to rouse the Netherlands from its torpor, hailed America as a role model. The United

States ultimately also became an object of serious study among Dutch scholars, as the example of Uhlenbeck and De Josselin de Jong shows. Such interest would continue to amplify during the twentieth century. Thus, Leiden Professor Johan Huizinga's decision in the summer of 1917 to start giving lectures on the United States can be seen as not only marking the conclusion of the "long nineteenth century," but also as hailing the beginning of a new period in Dutch-American relations.

1   J.W. Schulte Nordholt, *Voorbeeld in de verte. De invloed van de Amerikaanse revolutie in Nederland* (Baarn: In den Toren, 1979), 252-258.

2   Ibid., 257.

3   E.J. Potgieter, "Landverhuizing naar de Vereenigde Staten. Een brief uit Pella, door den Salamagundist," *De Gids*, 1855, 1:529.

4   *Amsterdams effectenblad*, September 28, 1873.

5   A.D. Wentholt, *Brug over den oceaan: Een eeuw geschiedenis van de Holland Amerika Lijn* (Rotterdam: Nijgh & Van Ditmar, 1973).

6   A. Lammers, *Uncle Sam en Jan Salie. Hoe Nederland Amerika ontdekte* (Amsterdam: Uitgeverij Balans, 2001), 47-58.

7   Frederik van Eeden, *Walden in droom en daad: Walden-dagboek en notulen van Frederik van Eeden e.a., 1898–1903, uitg.*

met inl. en comment. door J. S. De Ley en B. Luger (Amsterdam: s.n., 1980), 23-61.

8   *Omnibus* 10 (1878): 366-369.

9   H.F.C. ten Kate, *Reizen en onderzoekingen in Noord-Amerika* (Leiden: Brill, 1885). Translated into English by P. Hovens, with W.J. Orr and L.A. Hieb, eds., *Herman ten Kate's Travels and Inquiries in Native North America, 1882-1883*) (Albuquerque: University of New Mexico Press, 2004).

10 Hovens, *Herman ten Kate's Travels*, 179.

11 M. Kuitenbrouwer, *Nederland en de opkomst van het moderne imperialisme. Koloniën en buitenlandse politiek, 1870–1902* (Amsterdam: De Bataafsche Leeuw, 1985), 126.

12 Henry Stephen Lucas, *Netherlanders in America: Dutch Immigration to the United States and Canada, 1789–1950* (Ann Arbor/London: University of Michigan Press, 1955), 565-566.

IMAGES OF DUTCHNESS
IN THE UNITED STATES

—

ANNETTE STOTT

Images of Dutchness in American visual culture and literature during the nineteenth century differed radically between portrayals of the Netherlands Dutch and those of the American Dutch. Early in the century, it was the image of colonial Dutch Americans and their Hudson Valley descendants that dominated the representation of Dutchness in American art, literature, and popular culture. After 1855, and the publication of John Lothrop Motley's *The Rise of the Dutch Republic*, the image of the sixteenth- and seventeenth-century Netherlands Dutch gained ascendancy. By the end of the nineteenth century American views of the Dutch in the Netherlands and their views of the Dutch in America were merging. The stereotypes of Dutchness that prevailed in the early part of the century had been transformed into quite different stereotypes of Dutchness by the end of the century.

The Knickerbocker Image

Inspired by Washington Irving's popular *History of New York, from the Beginning of the World to the End of the Dutch Dynasty* (1809) and related tales, early nineteenth-century images of the Dutch often took on the comic dimensions of caricature. Irving, writing as Diedrich Knickerbocker, would influence American perceptions of the early Dutch settlers and their contributions to the making of the United States (or lack thereof) for the next one hundred years. Throughout the century, historians and writers of all sorts quoted Knickerbocker's observations on "the unutterable ponderings of Walter the Doubter, the disastrous projects of William the Testy, and the chivalric achievements of Peter the Headstrong," among other characters and incidents of New Netherland. According to Knickerbocker, the *Halve Maen*'s Dutch crew was "a patient people, much given to slumber and vacuity," while among the New Amsterdammers "the very words of learning, education, taste, and talents were unheard of." The first settlers smoked so much that they did not regulate their time by hours, but pipes, and "in this manner did the profound council of New-Amsterdam smoke, and doze, and ponder, from week to week, month to month, and year to year." Knickerbocker expounded at length on the girth of the New Netherlanders, explaining that the burgomasters "were generally chosen by weight" and that "an alderman should be fat [because] a lean, spare, diminutive body is generally accompanied by a petulant, restless, meddling mind ... whereas your round, sleek, fat, unwieldy periphery is ever attended by a mind like itself, tranquil, torpid, and at ease ... and surely none are more likely to study the public tranquility than those who are so careful of their own." Although he had less to say about Dutch women, he noted that "cleanliness was the leading principle in domestic economy," going on in wonderful exaggeration to explain that New Amsterdam's houses were so constantly inundated with washing water that some diligent Dutch housewives developed "webbed fingers like unto a duck."[1]

Irving's texts provided rich material for painters and illustrators. Washington Allston, John Quidor, Charles Leslie, Felix O. C. Darley, and John Whetten Ehninger are just a few of the artists who depicted scenes from the *Knickerbocker History* and from *Rip Van Winkle* (1819) and other tales of the Hudson Valley Dutch.[2] Faithful to Irving's comic view, they created visual stereotypes of portly, pipe smoking, gin-swilling Dutchmen sleeping in the shade, measuring land by laying trousers end to end, and making absurd political pronouncements. Even the stick-thin, serious Dutch character was treated as a figure of fun, a counterfoil to the rollicking type, while Dutch-American women barely made an appearance in the illustrations of this period.

Knickerbocker images gathered a similar, but separate popularity to that of the texts. Not only did the prints illustrate Irving's books, which appeared in new editions every few years, but they were bound and sold separately in portfolios and as individual framed prints. Paintings were exhibited, collected, and given away as prizes by the highly popular art unions of the early nineteenth century. On the whole, entertaining images of Irving's Dutch-American characters constituted the most broadly recognized representations of Dutchness among America's middle class in the first half of the nineteenth century.

Irving did provide a few hints that the traits he ascribed to the Dutch colonists were imported from the old country. He wrote, for example, that "Wouter (or Walter) van Twiller was descended from a long line of Dutch burgomasters, who had successively dozed away their lives, and grown fat upon the bench of magistracy in Rotterdam."[3] Most citizens of the Netherlands during this early period had no idea of the way American art and literature portrayed their colonizing ancestors. Irving's *History* had been translated into Swedish, French, and German before 1830, but it was never published in Dutch.[4] There is no ev-

239

idence that the book was distributed in the Netherlands or reviewed in Dutch publications.[5] Only those Dutch fluent in other languages could have read it.

Irving's brief, less than flattering portrayal of the Old World Dutch correlates with the general lack of interest that Firth Fabend has detected among some of Irving's contemporaries, Dutch-descended New York politicians who treated the Netherlands as an unworthy model for emulation. She suggests they may have found little to admire in a contemporary Netherlands ruled by France. Their own colonial forebears, on the other hand, excited the interest and allegiance of many New Yorkers who felt Dutch influence in the region was on the wane. Dutch and non-Dutch New Yorkers had joined forces to form the New-York Historical Society in 1804 with the purpose of preserving the early history of the city and state. In fact, it was to this society that Irving's alter ego proclaimed the *History* to be "respectfully dedicated, as a humble and unworthy testimony of the profound veneration and exalted esteem of the Society's sincere well wisher and devoted servant Diederich Knickerbocker."[6] Ironic hyperbole aside, the quest of a new nation to construct its own history and to invent a national literature and art based on that history provides part of the explanation for the insular focus.[7]

Throughout the nineteenth century, scholars and informed readers understood the *History* to be, in Irving's own words, "a work of humor," but recognition of its comic intent and imaginative inventions did not lessen its impact on American opinion of Dutch colonial history. Its very popularity, and that of Irving's imitators and illustrators, unconsciously molded public opinion into deep-seated stereotypes and myths.

The Old World Dutch

Although Irving's writings remained popular until the end of the century, they were superseded by a very different perspective on Dutchness around midcentury. John Lothrop Motley's history of *The Rise of the Dutch Republic* helped turn attention from the Dutch in America to the Dutch in the Netherlands. His interpretation of the Dutch as a heroic group of farmers and burghers defending their homeland against a foreign despot struck a sympathetic chord with the American public. Rather than fat, lazy, pipe-smoking dullards and wits, Motley portrayed the Dutch as courageous, independent, resolute, resourceful, and highly principled. "Their national industry was untiring; their prosperity unexampled; their love of liberty indomitable; their pugnacity proverbial," wrote Motley. "The women were distinguished by beauty of form and vigor of constitution ... their morals were pure and their decorum undoubted. The prominent part to be sustained by the women of Holland in many dramas of the Revolution would thus fitly devolve upon a class enabled by nature and education to conduct themselves with courage."[8] This characterization could hardly have differed more from Irving's. Motley drew parallels between the rise of the Dutch Republic in the sixteenth century and the rise of the American Republic in the eighteenth. The book went through multiple editions and was succeeded by other histories of the Netherlands. It became standard reading for the educated American, providing a solid foundation of respect for the Netherlands Dutch.

Yet Motley's story of a great Dutch struggle for unity and independence did not inspire American artists to take up brush and pen in the way that Irving's tales had. The lack of American illustrations created a void that the art of the old Dutch masters filled. In general, Americans considered the paintings of Holland's Golden Age to be authentic representations of Motley's heroic land and peoples. Although a small number of such paintings were already present in American collections as early as the 1830s, it was not until the second half of the nineteenth century, and especially after 1865, that wealthy industrialists and financiers began seriously collecting paintings by Rembrandt, Hals, Vermeer, and many lesser-known Dutch artists.[9] By the end of the century, curators found that Dutch pictures outnumbered all others in American collections of the old masters. In some respects, the acquisition of old Dutch master paintings also satisfied the longing for recognition and status among an American elite that suffered from the insecurity of being thought an unsophisticated provincial up-start by the Old World aristocracy. In Nancy Minty's words, the Golden Age redeemed the Gilded Era.[10] For those who could not afford to buy expensive oil paintings, magazine articles and reproduction prints, as well as oil copies of famous Dutch paintings were readily available. Exhibitions and books about Golden Age art also enjoyed great popularity with the American public. The art of the Netherlands joined Motley's histories in fixing American attention on the old Dutch Republic and helped rehabilitate popular opinion of Dutchness.

Irving's fiction and the illustrations that it inspired formed the early nineteenth-century American view of the New World Dutch as comic figures engaged in trifling historical incidents whose ineptitude caused them to lose their colony to the English. Motley's history and the old Dutch master paintings that seemed to support it, formed the midcentury view of the Old World Dutch as enterprising, civic-minded heroes fighting to preserve life, liberty, and prosperity, and winning against all odds. How could such disparate images of two Dutch peoples and cultures, separated only by the Atlantic Ocean, coexist in the nineteenth-century American mind? Could the transatlantic crossing really have

241

loomed so large as to reduce a heroic people at the height of modern economic, scientific, and cultural development to a cast of buffoons, and finally to ghostly figures haunting the Dutch-American landscape?

2

—

A Composite Image of Dutchness

The seeming opposition between American views of Dutchness in the Netherlands and Dutchness in North America did not last long, as evidenced by Irving-inspired images of the Dutch colonists later in the century. By the 1880s the more positive image of the Netherlands Dutch was having its effect on representations of Dutch Americans. Instead of rotund, drunken Dutch colonists, late-century artists depicted dignified Dutch-American burghers in the manner of Rembrandt and Hals. Illustrations in the later editions of Irving's *History* became more restrained, and many paintings attempted to portray events in colonial Dutch-American history without reference to Irving or any other literature.

Increasing exchanges between Americans and Netherlanders through business, trade, immigration, and tourism bolstered the improving American image of Dutchness. As travel became easier, American artists went abroad in droves to study old masters and sketch contemporary Holland. The differing images of the Netherlands Dutch and of Dutch Americans finally merged into a mostly positive amalgamation after 1880. Artists, including George Henry Boughton, Edwin Austin Abbey, and Walter MacEwen, painted historical scenes of New Netherland as well as contemporary scenes of the Netherlands using the same figures, costumes, and props from their sketchbooks for both. They blended the seventeenth, eighteenth, and nineteenth centuries into a seamless vision of Dutchness, one more in line with Motley's characterization than with Irving's. Tourists also traveled abroad, finding there confirmation of the beliefs that fiction, art, history, and travel literature had instilled in them. Popular speakers and amateur historians, especially the Scottish-American attorney Douglass Campbell and the Anglo-Saxon minister William Elliot Griffis, moved beyond Irving's colonial history or Motley's Netherlands history to make specific claims for the importance of America's Dutch roots. Without denying a strong English heritage, they declared it overdrawn, and set about "correcting" American history by refocusing on the Dutch contributions in New York and New Jersey. This was not an isolated phenomenon, but a fad of national dimensions. Holland mania swept the country from coast to coast.

Across the United States, Americans built Colonial Dutch Revival houses, decorated their interiors in pseudo-Dutch style, and read Mary Dodge's *Hans Brinker* to their children. American travelers and tourists continued to note negative traits — red-nosed topers, tobacco-smoking children, and fat placid women — but these images were far outweighed by the new characterization of the Dutch as a brave, clean, Protestant middle-class people with an admirable culture. Ironically, tourism contributed to new stereotypes at the turn of the twentieth century. Popularized in children's books, postcards, travel books, and advertisements for products from Rembrandt toothpaste to Dutch Masters cigars, the picturesque stereotypes of costumed Dutch men and women, tulips, windmills and wooden shoes became embedded in American ideas about the Netherlands, and by association, New Netherland and Dutch-American history. These positive, but regressive and distorted images would be embraced in the twentieth century by descendants of the nineteenth-century Dutch immigrants, who codified them in the ritual street cleaning, costumed parades, windmill booths, and wooden-shoe-carving demonstrations enacted in annual tulip festivals across Michigan and Iowa.

A comparison between two different, but equally mythical American icons of Dutchness — Rip Van Winkle in the first half of the nineteenth century and Hans Brinker in the second — may serve to highlight the changing image of the Dutch in America.[11] Irving's fictional character Rip Van Winkle descended from New Netherland colonists. He lived in a small town near the Hudson River just before the American Revolution. Rip was too lazy to farm, preferring to fish or take a nap. His affability knew no bounds, so he was well liked in the village where he could often be found drinking at the local inn. His family was not so complacent about Rip's shortcomings. The hen-pecked Rip meekly submitted to his wife's public nagging until he fell asleep for twenty years, returning (only after his wife's death) to tell a fantastic tale of Hudson's ghostly Dutch crew playing nine-pins in the mountains. In the context of early nineteenth-century gender expectations, Rip's inability to control his wife and provide for his family symbolized his failures as a man.

In contrast, Dodge's fictional hero Hans Brinker lived in a town in the Netherlands during the nineteenth century. Although only a boy, Hans took on the responsibilities of a man when his father suffered a debilitating accident. He worked hard to provide for his mother and little sister, whom he protected from various threats. Hans sacrificed his own dreams for those of others, and generally exhibited the highest ideals. His character was compounded by Dodge's inclusion of a story within the story, a fictional folktale about an unnamed Dutch boy who supposedly saved Haarlem through an act of selfless courage by sticking his finger in a leaking dyke until help arrived. The nameless boy became so closely associated with Hans Brinker that their identities merged.

243

For Dodge and her youthful readers, Hans Brinker embodied all that was good in Dutch national character, while for Irving and many of his readers, Rip Van Winkle symbolized the loveable, laughable qualities they attributed to the Dutch American. Just as Rip's laziness and lack of direction were rooted in Ir-

Allen B. Doggett, "Hans and Gretel Hear the Story of St. Nicholas,"
illustration (dated 1895) from Mary Mapes Dodge's *Hans Brinker or the Silver Skates*
(New York: Charles Scribner's Sons, 1905).

ving's *History*, Hans's sterling qualities grew from Motley's *Rise of the Dutch Republic,* which Dodge cited as the place where Americans "learn to revere the brave people" of the Netherlands. She intended her book to help reverse the Knickerbocker image by instilling in American children a reverential attitude that would, as she put it, "free them from certain current prejudices concerning that noble and enterprising people." In tune with those (including Edward Bok, editor of the *Ladies' Home Journal*)) who would eventually declare Holland the Mother of America, she also described Americans as "homeopathic preparations of Holland stock."[12]

The American Audience and Dutch Americans

With respect to the reception of the Dutch in America, the opinions discussed so far have been those of a generalized American public. It included people with no Dutch blood or allegiance, New Englanders as well as westerners, immigrants from throughout Europe, and Dutch Americans, in a large undifferentiated mix. The creators of the image of the Dutch in the early nineteenth century most often came from non-Dutch backgrounds. Irving was born in New York of English parents and lived for a time in England, so he combined Dutch and English cultural surroundings with a strong Anglo heritage. The artists who translated Irving into pictures were of mixed, but dominantly Anglo ancestry. At midcentury, Motley's Boston Brahmin heritage helped shape his interpretation of Dutch history.[13] Several of the later historians, notably Campbell and Griffis, also had non-Dutch ancestry, although they were undoubtedly influenced by living in New York in the former case and by associating with Dutch Americans and the Reformed tradition in the latter. Some Dutchophiles had no Dutch blood and some Dutch Americans had little interest in the Netherlands or its impact on American history. In short, it is practically impossible to separate people into ethnic or national identities that would clearly differentiate the Dutch from the non-Dutch American. Still, it is worth making an attempt to investigate the roles of Dutch Americans in the progress toward a more positive image and greater acceptance of Dutchness that seems to have taken place over the course of the nineteenth century.

There have always been Americans of Dutch heritage who promoted a positive image of the Dutch. Dutch Reformed publications inveighed against the early comic Dutch representations. Other New Yorkers countered Irving's spreading interpretation of Dutch-American history with a concerted midcentury campaign to dig out archival documentation of the Dutch. Funded by the state legislature, John Romeyn Broadhead brought many volumes of transcripts back to the United States from European archives, including Dutch documents.

245

These became the basis of several histories of New York published between 1846 and 1853 that took a different view of the Dutch period than had Irving's *History*. This effort paralleled the general looking back across the Atlantic to the Netherlands that occurred at midcentury (and after) in the efforts of Motley and collectors of old Dutch masters.

Dutch Americans and Dutchophiles joined together in history and heritage organizations where lectures and social activities often focused on the Dutch contribution to America. In 1835 a group of thirty-one New Yorkers, including Irving, founded the Saint Nicholas Society of the City of New York in order to preserve knowledge of the history and customs of the city's origins. Membership was limited to men of any national origins who could prove descent from a resident of New York before 1785. Although many were not of Dutch descent, they chose Saint Nicholas for the name of the club as a deliberate reference to the city's Dutch roots. Irving and his friends were also responding, in a lighthearted spirit, to the perceived challenge of the recently formed New England Society of New York. Many of the Dutch-descended New Yorkers who joined the New-York Historical Society and the Saint Nicholas Society were Irving's friends, at whom he poked gentle fun for their pride in their Dutch blood.

Near the end of the century, the City History Club and the Holland Society also contributed to a positive vision of the Dutch. Founded in 1885, the latter focused more exclusively on preserving and celebrating the history of New Netherland. Membership originally included only men descended in the direct male line of an ancestor who lived in New Netherland before 1675. The Society held dinners and entertainments for its membership, collected and commissioned art, compiled genealogies, and furthered historical knowledge. The City History Club developed a campaign to "Americanize" immigrant children in New York City by teaching them the history of the city from its colonial beginnings. But how much effect did the research and expressed opinions of nineteenth-century Dutch Americans have on mainstream history? Concentrated in New York, Pennsylvania, and New Jersey, how much of a role did they play in convincing Americans elsewhere?

Similar questions arise with respect to nineteenth-century Dutch immigrants. The fact that a new wave of Dutch immigration in the second half of the nineteenth century coincided with the shift in attention from New World Dutch to Old World Dutch, and from comic caricature to dignified and respectful representation, deserves investigation. Did the arriving Dutch immigrants, who spread out fairly rapidly from New York and New Jersey to Michigan, Wisconsin, Minnesota, Illinois, and Iowa, and then farther west to the Dakotas, Colorado, California, and Texas, play a role in this transformation? Did art or popular culture depict these new Dutch arrivals to the United States, and if so, in what guise? As white Protestant farmers and merchants, the majority of Dutch

A DUTCH HOUSEHOLD IN OLD NEW YORK.

The late nineteenth-century approach toward seeing the New Netherlanders
as serious and dignified. It is the frontispiece for Horace E. Scudder's children's story,
The Bodley Grandchildren and their Journey in Holland (Boston: Houghton,
Mifflin and Company, 1883).

immigrants fit established models of Americanness, in stark contrast to the larger numbers of immigrants arriving from southern and eastern Europe and from Asia. American resentment of these Catholic, "Celestial," and otherwise foreign "hordes" did not touch the Dutch immigrants. But to what extent was their relatively small presence a factor in the emerging celebration of Dutchness in the United States at large?

Further research is certainly called for before definitive conclusions are reached, but some observations may be made with assurance. The environs of New York and New Jersey, with New York City at its heart, remained the Dutch stronghold in America throughout most of the nineteenth century. By the last quarter of the century, New York City had attained national prominence as a commercial and cultural center and importance as a major port for international immigration to the United States. As a publishing center, it was well placed to disseminate views of the Dutch history in America, and did so. At least a few individuals of Dutch heritage, such as Edward Bok in Philadelphia, held powerful enough positions to wield real influence.[14] New York City was also a center for American art and illustrators. The Colonial Revival helped focus attention on all aspects of colonial America, including New Netherland, and a greater number of artists turned to this subject after the nation's centennial. Yet no great Dutch-American artist or author arose to counter Irving's influence or to take up Motley's cause. Given public skepticism of anything written by Dutch-born and Dutch-descended advocates about the theory of American institutions' Dutch origins, it was most likely Griffis, Campbell, and others perceived as standing outside the Dutch community who played the greater role in convincing non-Dutch Americans across the nation that the country's Dutch heritage was significant.

By the end of the nineteenth century, so many New Yorkers understood and valued the Dutch roots of their city and state that some laid claim to Dutchness, no matter what their personal ancestry might be. Thus, Francis Hopkinson Smith, a New York City artist, stood on the streets of Amsterdam and proclaimed himself a Dutchman by birthright, although he did not claim Dutch blood. This acceptance of Dutchness by non-Dutch Americans is similar to a trend that Fabend has noted among residents of New York and New Jersey who had no Dutch blood, but joined the Dutch Reformed Church and became accepted as Dutch by their Dutch-American neighbors.[15] Similarly, the Dutch-Renaissance-style public buildings that rose in tribute to New York City's Dutch roots at the turn of the twentieth century were no more associated with Dutch New Yorkers than New Yorkers from many other nationalities, but simply expressed shared identity in a city with Dutch origins.

Holland mania, when many Dutch and non-Dutch Americans embraced the Dutchness of America, lasted only a short time. The excessive nature of its claims and its minutely detailed arguments dwindled into surface stereotypes of advertisements and decorations. Ultimately, the twentieth century returned to seeing the Dutch as a fairly minor force in the American enterprise, one that had ended with the conquest of the New Netherland colony.

1   Washington Irving, *A History of New York from the Beginning of the World to the End of the Dutch Dynasty*, rev. ed., Home Lib. (New York: A. L. Burt, n.d.), subtitle, 58, 87, 100, 107 (in order quoted).

2   Annette Stott, "Inventing Memory: Picturing New Netherland in the Nineteenth Century," in Joyce D. Goodfriend, ed., *Revisiting New Netherland* (Leiden: Brill, 2005), 13-39.

3   Irving, *History*, 94.

4   *New York's Historia* (Stockholm: s.n., 1827), *Histoire de New-York* (Paris: A. Sautelet, 1827), and *Humoristische Geschichte von New York* (Frankfurt: Sauerländer, 1829).

5   I am grateful to Hans Bak who pointed out that no review is included in J. G. Riewald and J. Bakker, *The Critical Reception of American Literature in the Netherlands, 1824-1900* (Amsterdam: Rodopi, 1982). Elizabeth Paling Funk mentions a derogatory reference to Irving in an 1841 poem by E. J. Potgieter in "Knickerbocker's New Netherland: Washington Irving's Representation of Dutch Life on the Hudson," in George Harinck and Hans Krabbendam, eds., *Amsterdam-New York. Transatlantic Relations and Urban Identities since 1653* (Amsterdam: VU University Press, 2005), 144.

6   Irving, *History* (New York: Inskeep & Bradford; Philadelphia: Bradford & Inskeep, 1809), 1:a2. This dedication page does not appear in revised editions.

7   Judith Richardson, *Possessions: The History and Uses of Haunting in the Hudson Valley* (Cambridge, MA: Harvard University Press, 2003).

8   John Lothrop Motley, *The Rise of the Dutch Republic* (New York: A. L. Burt, n.d.), 1:79-80.

9   Walter Liedke, "Dutch Paintings in America," in Ben Broos, ed., *Great Dutch Paintings from America* (The Hague: Mauritshuis; Zwolle: Waanders, 1990).

10   Nancy T. Minty, "Great Expectations: The Golden Age Redeems the Gilded Era," in Joyce D. Goodfriend, Benjamin Schmidt, and Annette Stott, eds., *Going Dutch: The Dutch Presence in America, 1609–2009* (Leiden: Brill, 2007), 215-235.

11   Washington Irving introduced Rip Van Winkle as the subject of a short story in his book *The Sketch Book of Geoffrey Crayon* (New York: C. S. Van Winkle, 1819); Mary Mapes Dodge, *Hans Brinker, or the Silver Skates: A Story of Life in Holland* (New York: C. Scribner's Sons, 1865).

12   Dodge, *Hans Brinker* (Project Gutenburg, via NetLibrary), 8, preface, 7 (in order quoted).

13   Mark A. Peterson, "A Brahmin Goes Dutch: John Lothrop Motley and the Lessons of Dutch History in Nineteenth-Century Boston," in Goodfriend, Schmidt, and Stott, *Going Dutch*, 109-133.

14   Hans Krabbendam, *The Model Man: A Life of Edward William Bok, 1863–1930* (Amsterdam/Atlanta, GA: Rodopi, 2001).

15   Firth Haring Fabend, *Zion on the Hudson: Dutch New York and New Jersey in the Age of Revivals* (New Brunswick, NJ: Rutgers University Press, 2000), 8-13.

THE DUTCH-AMERICAN
POLITICAL ELITE
IN NEW YORK STATE

—

FIRTH HARING FABEND

Dutch Americans in New York State Government,
1783–1840s

After the Revolution, prominent Tory families fled to Canada or England, leaving the political ground to those who had supported independence. From 1783 and up through the 1840s, as they had before the Revolution, Dutch Americans, whether they were Jeffersonian Republicans (progressives) or Federalists (conservatives), played important roles in New York politics. Members of the New York State political elite born just before, during, or just after the Revolution were of the Bleecker, DeWitt, Schuyler, Van Alen, Van Buren, Van Cortlandt, Van Ness, Van Rensselaer, Van Schaick, Van Vechten, Verbryck, and Verplanck families, among others. Men in these families had distinguished careers in politics and public service, as a few examples will illustrate:

Philip Van Cortlandt (1749–1831), a notable patriot in the Revolution, served in the New York State Assembly and Senate from 1788 to 1793 and in the U.S. House of Representatives from 1792 to 1809.

William W. Van Ness (1776–1823), prominent in Federalist politics in Columbia County for decades, was a State Assemblyman in the early 1800s and served on the State Supreme Court from 1807 to 1822. Van Ness was a member of the powerful Council of Revision, which had veto power over legislation, and after Congress refused to renew the charter of the Second Bank of the United States in 1811, he was influential in obtaining the Merchants' Bank charter, as well as the charter of the Bank of America. In 1821, he was a delegate to the New York State Constitutional Convention to revise the 1777 Constitution. President James Madison appointed William W. Van Ness's first cousin William P. Van Ness (1778–1826) a federal judge in the Southern District of New

York, and he distinguished himself by coauthoring the first codification of the laws of the state.

Stephen Van Rensselaer (1764–1839), the eighth and last patroon of the now-million-acre Manor of Rensselaerswijck, served in both the New York State Assembly and Senate before becoming lieutenant governor for two terms (1795–1801). He was elected to the U.S. House of Representatives in 1822 and provided the swing vote that elected John Quincy Adams president in 1824. Van Rensselaer was appointed chancellor of the University of the State of New York in 1835 and served as president of the Erie Canal Commission from 1825 until his death.

Of those Dutch Americans active in New York State politics who lived into the second half of the nineteenth century, Solomon Van Rensselaer (1774–1852), nephew of the eighth patroon, served in the U.S. House of Representatives for two terms, but resigned to accept appointment as the U.S. postmaster in Albany — an important political sinecure in those days.

One final example, Gulian Verplanck (1786–1870) served in the New York Assembly from 1820 to 1823, in the U.S. House of Representative for four terms (1824–32), and in the New York Senate from 1837 to 1841. He was appointed to the Board of Regents of the University of the State of New York in 1826 and served from 1858 until his death as its vice chancellor.

When these men died off, however, their sons did not pick up the reins of power their fathers had laid down. Some chose other avenues to power and influence, as we will see, whereas some scions of the old Dutch settlers, particularly in rural backwaters, simply melded into the local scene where they led quiet, unassuming lives, their descendants hardly aware of their Dutch heritage.

First Dutch-American U.S. President:
Martin Van Buren

The most prominent Dutch American in the first half of the nineteenth century was Martin Van Buren (1782–1862). The eighth U.S. president, the first president born in the United States of America, and the first of non-British ethnic origins, Martin Van Buren was born a year after the Battle of Yorktown had effectively ended the war, and while the terms on which it would formally conclude were being worked out. The son of a farmer and tavern keeper, Van Buren had formal schooling only until the age of fourteen. He nevertheless rose from fence viewer in Columbia County and then surrogate to attorney general of New York State, to three terms in the New York State Senate, during which time he organized and led the so-called Albany Regency, the original political "machine." In 1821 Van Buren was elected to the U.S. Senate, and in 1828 he became gov-

251

ernor of New York State, a position he shortly resigned to become secretary of state under Andrew Jackson. Jackson subsequently appointed him minister to Great Britain, a post to which Van Buren's enemies in the Senate refused to confirm him. In 1832 he was elected vice president under Jackson, and finally president of the United States in 1836. He served one four-year term.

Martin Van Buren was proud of his Dutch roots and was the fifth generation of his family in America to marry endogenously. Of his four sons only one married outside the Dutch community. Regarding the significance to his political ideology of Van Buren's Dutch background, however, one finds little evidence. In his lifetime, while in Europe on other business, he made two trips to Buren, the home of his settler ancestors in the Netherlands. When president, he appointed his friend and neighbor, a member of the old Dutch stock, Harmanus Bleecker, as chargé d'affaires to The Hague, requesting at one point that Bleecker bring him back a "good Dutch cow" for his farm in Kinderhook, NY, where he resided after his presidency. He appointed his friend James K. Paulding (1778–1860), a man of letters fond of the Dutch and the author of *The Dutchman's Fireside* and *The Book of Saint Nicholas*, as secretary of the U.S. Navy. And in 1833 he accompanied Washington Irving, the famous or infamous "historian" of the Dutch in New York and New Jersey, on what Irving called his Dutch Tour of the Hudson Valley from Esopus (Kingston) to Jersey City.

But despite such examples of sentimental attraction to his ethnic origins, there is no indication that Van Buren's politics or those of any other of the New York political elite of Dutch background in this period were influenced by the Dutch political tradition, as had been true in the eighteenth century. (The Declaration of Independence is thought by scholars to have been influenced by Thomas Jefferson's acquaintance with the Dutch Republic's declaration of independence from Spain, the Oath of Abjuration of 1581, and the American Constitution by the Dutch Union of Utrecht, the de facto Dutch constitution.)[1] Of the members of the powerful Albany Regency that reigned in New York during Van Buren's rise, none was of Dutch background.

On this matter, an early biographer of Van Buren put it this way: "more than any other American, Martin Van Buren had succeeded to the preaching of Jefferson's political doctrines." Van Buren himself nurtured the idea that he was Thomas Jefferson's ideological successor and never at any time attributed his political philosophy to any European source. He followed Jefferson in distrusting the unlimited power of the executive branch and an expanding central government and in supporting the rights of the sovereign states, and he was imbued with Jefferson's ideal of a nation in which the common man, with the benefit of a free public school system, could be counted on to "judge as wisely and safely as the opulent, the cultivated, the educated." By the close of the American Revolution, this biographer wrote, "those who farmed the rich fields of Columbia county were pretty thorough Americans; their characteristics were more immediately drawn from the soil they cultivated and from the necessary habits of their life than from the lands of their Dutch forebears."[2]

There are several other possible explanations for the absence of Dutch political influence on Van Buren's thinking: First, the local scene in New York was turbulent during these years. One historian of the period has identified eighteen political parties in New York State during Van Buren's era, all busily fomenting partisan turmoil. (Of this exotic plethora, only the Democratic and Republican parties survived.)[3] Further, national issues of the day were compelling, and the minds of politicians were fully concentrated on home things, not foreign. These included the War of 1812, which was particularly controversial in New York State, the character and style of Andrew Jackson, the rise of the common man, the rise of the party system, patronage, sectional tensions, Indian problems, the nullification crisis, the opening of the Erie Canal, the expansion of the West, the Bank War, the real estate boom and bust, and the Panic of 1837–43.

And a third explanation: Americans, whether of Dutch background or not, were appalled by the happenings in Europe during the Napoleonic era and after it, especially in the United Republic of the Netherlands. In 1795, the Dutch Republic, bereft of most of its former military and naval strength, came under the administrative control of France as a virtual French protectorate. Holland's Golden Age and its brilliant political struggle to secure its freedom from Spain and its people's ancient rights and privileges soon became distant memories. Called first the Batavian Republic, from 1795 to 1806, then the Kingdom of Holland, from 1806 to 1810, the emphasis came to be on reorganizing the historic provinces into a united republic, while guaranteeing citizenship to all parts of the former provinces and equal status under the law to all religions. Despite these advances, however, the Netherlands was not "free." France demanded that the kingdom bear the expenses of its own government, as well as those of the French occupying forces, and pay financial tribute to Paris, while at the same time it prohibited the country from trading as it historically had. In 1810, Napoleon absorbed the Netherlands into his empire, and so it remained until 1813. In 1815 the Kingdom of the Netherlands was created.

As Van Buren put it at the time of the War of 1812, Americans were the "only free people on earth," unlike the peoples of the "old world."[4] In short, the inescapable conclusion for American political history in the first half of the nineteenth century is that European governments and institutions were not models for the American government and American institutions. Dutch-American relations would very much improve in time, but for the Dutch political elite in New York in Van Buren's lifetime, the Netherlands, the Old World itself, had disappointed and was not considered worthy of emulation.

Nearly half a century later, Van Buren was still of this opinion. Although the Netherlands had long since rid itself of French control and established itself as a constitutional monarchy, it was a monarchy, and until 1840 it was ruled by an enlightened despot, William I, who believed that power and the country's welfare best reposed in a strong leader, not in the people. The States General enacted laws as proposed by William's government, but it did not represent a sovereign people. In 1830, Belgium, which resented William's authoritarianism, declared its independence, and a decade later, the revolution complete, William sadly abdicated the throne in favor of his son, William II. It was not until the outbreak of the 1848 revolutions in Europe, however, that the Dutch got a British-style constitution that put the States General at the head of the government and made the monarch subordinate to it. But even this was not enough to satisfy the democratic principles of Martin Van Buren, who in 1856 scolded: "Among the various systems which have been devised and are now in force for the Government of mankind, it is in those only of England and the United States that adequate provisions are to be found for the security of personal liberty and the just rights of man."[5]

Dutch Americans Leave Politics

After the postwar generations had gone to their rest, and after the Van Buren era, the sons of former political leaders tended to find their niche not in politics but in finance, banking, and commerce on the one hand, and on the other hand in the fervent missionary, moral reform, and benevolent movements that characterized the so-called Age of Revivals.

Dutch-American absence from the political arena in this era is amply demonstrated in a "statistical list" of the New York Assembly in 1853. Of the 146 members of the Assembly, including the elected clerk, four deputy clerks, and two librarians, only sixteen members, or fewer than 11 percent, had either a father or a mother of "Holland ancestry." Of these sixteen men, only four, or slightly more than 2 percent, claimed Holland ancestry on both sides of their families: Nicholas Blauvelt, Peter G. Ten Eyck, Abram N. Van Alstine, and William Van Vranken, representing respectively Rockland, Rensselaer, Montgomery, and Schenectady counties — all old Dutch-American strongholds. On the other hand, Dutch Americans and those men and women who considered themselves "Dutch" by virtue of their membership in the Dutch Reformed Church, are found in great numbers in organizations established to work toward bettering society during this same period.[6]

Why did Dutch Americans desert the political scene at midcentury? Perhaps they wearied of the ever-querulous partisan politics in the New York of that

day. Perhaps they saw an opportunity to effect social change and public policy through action on another more amenable front. Or perhaps their absence
from politics was simply a factor of the migration of New Englanders into New
York State, which peaked in the years from 1783 to 1820. Whatever, many Dutch
Americans of the "elite" class turned from politics to the world of banking and
commerce, while another set, joined by clergymen and churchgoers of all denominations, trained their energies on the so-called Benevolent Empire, the
moral reform movement, Abolition, Temperance, and related efforts to improve society.[7] (Temperance and Abolition had their counterparts in the Netherlands, but the Benevolent Empire and the moral reform movement in America were shaped by circumstances peculiar to New York, namely the hordes of
illiterate immigrants pouring into the country at the time, and the forces of poverty and vice that accompanied the rampant immigration.)

In 1824, in a departure from the denomination's usual position of isolationism, the General Synod of the Dutch Reformed Church, endorsing Sabbath
schools as "mighty instruments for the advancement of the Kingdom," joined
the ecumenical American Sunday School Union (ASSU). By 1830, six thousand
schools belonged to the Union, led by sixty thousand men and women teaching
four hundred thousand students. The Sunday school was a powerful and innovative instrument not only of religious education but also of the socialization,
"civilization," and Americanization of the immigrant population. This institution on its own, however, was not strong enough to stem the forces of poverty
and vice, and by the late 1830s, governmental action was necessary to brush
up the common school system and to establish state-supported public schools
open to all. Church and state now had an urgent common goal to pursue, for before society could wield effective moral control of the increasingly motley, impoverished, vice-ridden population, it was clear that that population had to be
inculcated with American political ideology, history, traditions, and customs,
as well as with American religious, moral, and ethical values.

So evolved the moral reform and benevolent movements. Dutch Reformed
clergymen and laymen sat on the boards not only of the ASSU, but of the American Tract Society, the American Bible Society, the American Colonization Society, the American Temperance Union, the New York Female Moral Reform Society, the New York Society for the Relief of the Poor, and a host of other do-gooding, evangelical, and humanitarian institutions, all ecumenical in that they
were supported by all of the mainstream Protestant denominations with equal
enthusiasm. One historian listed 158 moral reform, benevolent, charitable,
and missionary societies, asylums, commissions, unions, associations, and
auxiliaries flourishing in the evangelical age. But a comprehensive list would
actually contain thousands of names if every such organization in America in
this era were included.[8]

2

———

In New York (and New Jersey) these groups comprising clergymen and laymen of all the Protestant denominations attempted to work with and through the state legislatures by lobbying to cast their desired reforms into law. As legal historian James W. Hurst put it, in the nineteenth-century United States, evangelical Protestantism influenced main currents of life, "sometimes with strong, if indirect, impact on law."[9]

But if it was logical, and comforting, to think that the widespread grassroots enthusiasm for social change could bring every desired change about through the law, the reality was that legislation was not the easy answer. Legislation proved to be effective in jumpstarting the public school movement. But then as now there were ideological objections to imposing morality by legislative fiat in other areas. For one example, when a law prohibiting alcohol was passed in New York State in 1855, the mayor of New York City refused to enforce it, and the following year it was declared unconstitutional. Vigorous efforts to keep the Sabbath holy did not get even so far as temperance law. A populace that demanded its Sunday railroad and steamboat excursions, games, saloons, beer gardens, and newspapers vehemently and successfully protested Sabbatarianism. Societal reform was not easily accomplished.

The Second Dutch-American U. S. President: Theodore Roosevelt

At the end of the century, another Dutch American rose to become president of the United States. Like Martin Van Buren, Theodore Roosevelt (1858–1919) was proud of his Dutch roots, and unlike many of his social class he maintained his relationship with the Dutch Reformed Church throughout his life. To what extent TR's Dutch Reformed background infused him with his pronounced sense of social justice and a vision of what a decent world should look like can only be guessed, but his father, a religious man, was an important link between the earlier moral reform and benevolent organizations and Theodore Roosevelt's own moral crusades. Although Theodore Roosevelt, Sr., was one of those Dutch Americans who eschewed politics for commerce, he was deeply involved in the mid-nineteenth-century attempts to ameliorate the deplorable social conditions of the day. "My father," TR wrote, "was the best man I ever knew. ... He was interested in every social reform movement, and he did an immense amount of charitable work himself. ... His heart was filled with gentleness for those who needed help or protection ... against a bully or an oppressor."[10]

U.S. President Theodore Roosevelt during his inspection of Yellowstone National Park in 1903.

➤

2

—

Theodore Roosevelt made the protection of Americans against corporate bullies and society's oppressors his own mission. His career in public service took off in 1889, when President Benjamin Harrison appointed him, at age thirty-one, to be civil service commissioner. For six years TR sought to reform, over bitter opposition, the deeply entrenched spoils system by which politicians delivered plummy offices and sinecures to political friends regardless of merit or prior service. It was his first crusade but hardly his last. As an agent for change, TR would come to possess for Americans a "spiritual power," as one contemporary, William Allen White, put it. (Religious imagery and rhetoric were often invoked when Roosevelt was spoken of.) His times would see, White went on, that "by his life and his works he should bear witness unto the truth."[11] The truth was that "monster trusts," as Roosevelt called them, were trampling on the rights of ordinary folks and perverting American democracy.

TR described his role as steward of the public welfare. As he put it, throughout his career, and especially in the presidency (1901–09), he "stood at Armageddon and battled on the Lord's side," taking on the trusts to set Americans free from economic inequality and injustice. By creatively broadening the power of the executive branch, without exceeding the limits of the Constitution, he brought the trusts under regulation, and by using volunteer unpaid commissions to study "land thieves and corrupt wrong-doers," he reformed the government and protected public lands and waterways for future generations.

TR's relationship with Edward Bok, the Dutch-born American editor of the *Ladies' Home Journal,* provided both men an opportunity to revel in their Dutchness and in their goals for America. "We must work for the same ends," Roosevelt told Bok. "You and I can each become good Americans by giving our best to make America better. With the Dutch stock there is in both of us, there's no limit to what we can do."[12]

During TR's first term as president, Bok published in his magazine an article to acquaint America, as he had TR, with the strong Dutch influences he discerned underlying American institutions, among them the public school system, freedom of religious worship, freedom of the press, the secret ballot, the office of attorney general, and, most important, Dutch influences on the Declaration of Independence and the U.S. Constitution.[13] But in his long litany he neglected to include the Dutch Reformed Church.

Yet if American institutions were able to be influential in making society a better place in the nineteenth century, it was in no small part a result of the efforts of the do-gooding Dutch Americans of New York and New Jersey who trained their energies on the power of pen, pulpit, and peroration to bring about social change. Their forebears had chosen politics as the way to improve society, but the nineteenth-century descendants of the Dutch settlers of New Netherland chose to order and reform their complex and complicated world according to their idea of what God wanted it to be. In Theodore Roosevelt, Americans had a president who combined the reformers' crusading zeal with his own keen sense of economic justice and equality as the hallmarks of democracy.

Roosevelt took up where the reformers had left off in attempting to improve America for the common man, giving him a "Square Deal" in the process. But beyond his reforms, his contemporaries believed that his greatest achievement was the movement for the conservation of the nation's natural resources. As the *New York Sun* wrote in 1904: "His greatest work was inspiring and actually beginning a world movement for staying terrestrial waste and saving for the human race the things upon which, and upon which alone, a great and peaceful and progressive and happy life can be founded."[14]

Americans were soon to have a third president of Dutch-American background, another Roosevelt who would be possessed with a vision similar to his distant cousin's.

1   James R. Tanis, "The Dutch-American Connection: The Impact of the Dutch Example on American Constitutional Beginnings," in *A Beautiful and Fruitful Place: Selected Rensselaerswijck Seminar Papers* (Albany: New Netherland Publishing, 1991), 353-356; Reprinted from Stephen L. Schechter and Richard B. Bernstein, *New York and the Union: Contributions to the American Constitutional Experience* (Albany: New York State Commission on the Bicentennial of the U.S. Constitution, 1990), 22-28.

2   Edward M. Shepard, *Martin Van Buren* (Boston/New York: Houghton Mifflin, 1888), 3, 8, 15.

3   Donald B. Cole, *Martin Van Buren and the American Political System* (Princeton, NJ: Princeton University Press, 1984), see index.

4   Ibid., 38-39.

5   John C. Fitzpatrick, ed., *The Autobiography of Martin Van Buren,* 2 vols. (Washington, DC: G.P.O., 1920), 2:483-485.

6   C.H. Maxon, Librarian, "A Statistical List of the Members and Officers of the Assembly of the State of New-York, No.

41, February 4, 1853," Cornell University Library, New York State Historical Literature Collection, on line.

7   Firth Haring Fabend, *Zion on the Hudson: Dutch New York and New Jersey in the Age of Revivals* (New Brunswick, NJ/London: Rutgers University Press, 2000; repr. 2005), chapters 3-8.

8   Ibid., 45.

9   James W. Hurst, *Law and Social Process in United States History* (Ann Arbor: University of Michigan Press, 1960), 13.

10   Theodore Roosevelt, *An Autobiography* (New York: Macmillan Company, 1913), 6, 9.

11   James MacGregor Burns and Susan Dunn, *The Three Roosevelts: Patrician Leaders Who Transformed America* (New York: Atlantic Monthly Press, 2001), 67.

12   Edward Bok, *The Americanization of Edward Bok: The Autobiography of a Dutch Boy Fifty Years After* (New York: Scribner's, 1920), 267.

13   Edward Bok, "The Mother of America," *Ladies' Home Journal*, October 1903.

14   Quoted in Roosevelt, *An Autobiography,* 407.

DUTCH-AMERICAN DIPLOMATIC RELATIONS

———

CORNELIS A. VAN MINNEN

Introduction

When the United States and the Dutch Republic established diplomatic relations in 1782, expectations were high. The United States not only needed recognition as a new nation but, even more, needed Dutch loans, and in securing these John Adams, the first U.S. diplomat to the Dutch Republic, was successful. Dutch merchants hoped the American market would bring new prosperity but during most of the nineteenth century import tariffs in both countries prevented a flourishing trade relationship. There was hardly any political work to do for the diplomats in each other's country and therefore they mostly became observers of another culture.

After John Adams officially left The Hague in 1788, his successors in the late eighteenth century, including his son John Quincy Adams in the 1790s, reported on the increasing influence of France on what was then called the Batavian Republic. In fact, the country became a satellite state of France and would be annexed by Napoleon in 1810. The overwhelming French influence made the U.S. government decide to close the American legation in The Hague in 1801. This was followed by the closing of the Dutch legation in Washington a year later. Diplomatic relations between both countries were reestablished in 1814.[1]

This essay briefly describes U.S. and Dutch foreign policy and its organization in the nineteenth century, and then reviews a number of U.S. and Dutch diplomats and their correspondence in order to get a flavor of the nature of Dutch-American diplomatic relations. Limited space does not allow a review of the consuls.[2]

American Foreign Service

Influenced by John Quincy Adams's reports from the Batavian Republic, George Washington formulated in his Farewell Address of 1796 the principles of American foreign policy: extend U.S. commercial relations but have as few political connections as possible. As President James Monroe's secretary of state, John Quincy Adams in 1823 further developed Washington's foreign policy in the Monroe Doctrine, which considered the western hemisphere as America's own interest. To Europe, hands off America, was the clear message. By virtue of its geographic remoteness America could remain aloof from European power politics and concentrate attention on the development of its own continent. This was the rule of U.S. foreign policy throughout the nineteenth century until the American intervention in World War I in 1917.[3]

In 1789 the U.S. Congress established the Department of State, headed by the secretary of state whose responsibility it is to advise the president on formulating and implementing foreign policy. The diplomatic ranks used by the United States in the nineteenth century were minister plenipotentiary, sometimes combined with the title of envoy extraordinary; minister resident; and, most frequently used, chargé d'affaires, which was the lowest rank. The U.S. adopted the rank of ambassador only in 1893. In 1800 the American Republic had six diplomatic representatives in Europe, including one in the Dutch Republic. In 1850 U.S. diplomats were posted in twenty-seven countries and in 1900 there were forty-two diplomatic missions.

Throughout the nineteenth century the Department of State was understaffed. This situation and the slow postal service made it difficult for diplomats and consuls to ask advice from Washington. The efficiency of the American foreign service was also seriously impeded by the meager compensation. Most U.S. diplomats and consuls had to rely on their own funds to maintain their positions on even the most modest level. In keeping with democratic simplicity Secretary of State William L. Marcy in 1853 issued the famous regulation that on official occasions American diplomats had to wear "the simple costume of an American citizen — that is, the conventional black evening clothes." This often caused confusion, and at the colorful European gatherings American diplomats were frequently taken for servants. Although attempts were made in the nineteenth century to reform and strengthen the foreign service, none of them succeeded. It was only in 1924 with the creation of the United States Foreign Service that the professional quality improved.[4]

2

—

American Diplomats in the Netherlands

In December 1814 President James Madison appointed William Eustis, a former secretary of war, as envoy extraordinary and minister plenipotentiary to the Netherlands. In July 1815 he presented his credentials to King William I. Secretary of State James Monroe in his instructions to Eustis underlined the friendly relations between both countries and considered The Hague an important listening post, which he described as "a principal theatre of the most important negotiations in Europe, for more than a century past and promised to become again, a very interesting one, in many circumstances." Monroe's expectation would not materialize. According to Alexander Hill Everett, the American chargé d'affaires in the Netherlands from 1819 to 1824, the country had lost its political importance and therefore he suggested his government close the legation. Everett used his time to write a book on the situation in Europe that included passages criticizing the role of the House of Orange in Dutch history and describing the Dutch kingdom as a nation in decline that would eventually disappear in the ocean. No wonder Everett made a bad impression in the Netherlands.

Everett was succeeded by one of America's first career diplomats, Christopher Hughes, who served in Europe for some thirty years, including twice in the Netherlands: from 1825 to 1830 and from 1842 to 1845. Hughes, whose letters are full of complaints about his low rank and salary and the high cost of living, described the Netherlands in the 1820s enthusiastically as "the most prosperous and happy, because the best governed country in Europe." He was also able to gather information for the State Department at receptions and dinners for the diplomatic corps. But during his second mission in the 1840s he frequently complained that there was little for him to do. Indeed, Hughes felt buried alive in The Hague and was glad to return to his native Baltimore.

Just before the secession of Belgium in 1830 King William I was asked by the United States and Great Britain to arbitrate the so-called North-Eastern Boundary Dispute, a dispute between both countries since 1783 about the border between Canada and Maine. The Dutch king gladly accepted this special request, and the United States sent William Pitt Preble, a prominent lawyer from Maine, in the position of envoy extraordinary and minister plenipotentiary. Initially, after he and the British ambassador, Sir Charles Bagot, had presented all the relevant documents on the dispute to the king, Preble was optimistic that the decision would favor the United States. However, because of the revolution in France and the revolt and subsequent secession of Belgium that year with the liberals praising the United States as an example, the conservative segment of the Dutch population became increasingly anti-American. Preble feared a negative result of the arbitration. In January 1831 William I told the American and British diplomats that the documents and arguments from both sides had made it impossible for him to agree with either view and therefore he had decided to propose an alternative boundary. Preble furiously protested the king's counterproposal. In his correspondence to his secretary of state he angrily suggested the American diplomatic representation in the Dutch kingdom be downgraded to one or two consuls. Back in the United States, Preble in the interest of his own state did everything he could to prevent ratification by the U.S. Senate of William I's counterproposal. The North-Eastern Boundary Dispute dragged on for another decade until the United States and Great Britain signed the Webster-Ashburton Treaty in 1842. Ironically, the area awarded to the United States in this treaty was smaller than the one called for by the Dutch king's compromise.[5]

In the period 1837–41 the United States for the first time had a president with Dutch roots: the Democrat Martin Van Buren. He appointed his old friend Harmanus Bleecker, of Dutch descent too, as U.S. chargé d'affaires to the Netherlands in 1839. Bleecker's knowledge of the language and history of the Netherlands soon earned him a place of honor in The Hague's social life. But it did not take long before his affection for the land of his forefathers cooled. In Bleecker's view monarchy and aristocracy were the principal causes of the "abuses, absurdities, frivolities, fooleries, servility, and superstition" he constantly witnessed. In correspondence with his friends at home Bleecker was fond of contrasting the "pitiful image" he sketched of the Old World with the "shining example" of America and its political institutions designed to promote "the greatest happiness." Yet he was prepared to accept justified foreign criticism of his country, such as the fact that several American states did not honor their financial obligations to Europe, the corruption and vulgarity in the U.S. Congress, and the lynchings described in the American press. But compared to Europe, the United States in Bleecker's opinion was "almost a paradise." While in the Netherlands, Bleecker seemed to have become more American and lost much of his affection for Europe and the country of his ancestors.

From 1831 to 1839 and, again, from 1845 to 1850 the U.S. chargé d'affaires in The Hague was Auguste Davezac, a missionary Jacksonian Democrat who reported thoroughly on political events, including the secession of Belgium and its aftermath in the 1830s and the growing demands of the Dutch middle class in the 1840s leading to the constitutional revision of 1848. After 1840 Davezac avidly supported Manifest Destiny and President James K. Polk's expansionist policy on the American continent as he saw the annexation of Texas, Oregon, and Mexico as proof of the vitality of the U.S. democratic system. He yearned for the day Europeans would cast off "the feudal yoke" and democracy would also triumph in the Old World but he was bitterly disappointed by the failure of the

U.S. Chargé d'Affaires to the Netherlands Harmanus Bleecker (1779–1849).
Unidentified photographer. Daguerreotype, ca. 1845.

Revolution of 1848. Upon returning to his "happy republic" in 1850 he was pessimistic about the prospects of freedom in Europe. In the Netherlands, however, he saw a bright spot and wrote that the liberal leader Johan Rudolf Thorbecke and his ministers presented "a consoling spectacle to the friends of freedom throughout Europe."[6]

The American Civil War hardly affected the friendly Dutch-American diplomatic relations and aroused very little interest and debate in the Netherlands. The American minister resident in The Hague in the years 1861–66, James S. Pike, observed that the gin industry in Schiedam, which lost some of its market to the United States, was the only segment of the Dutch economy pinched by the Civil War. Some differences arose between Washington and The Hague when a Confederate war vessel, the *Sumter*, was allowed to enter a bay near Willemstad, Curaçao, in July 1861 and a month later in Paramaribo, Suriname, leading American Secretary of State William H. Seward and Pike to question the neutrality of the Dutch. Another, more serious, incident was the invasion in May 1862 of the Dutch consulate in New Orleans by federal troops and the seizure of its archives and money in the vault. This led to a Dutch protest and after a federal investigation all items, including the money, were returned to the Dutch consul. A third incident was the seizure and auction of the Dutch vessel *Geziena Hillegonda* and its cargo, which in December 1864 had strayed accidentally into American territorial waters. This also led to some diplomatic friction. But in all three cases the U.S. government manifested a desire to satisfy the aggrieved party and maintained cordial relations with the Dutch government.[7]

Of Dutch stock, too, was Theodore Roosevelt's uncle Robert B. Roosevelt, who is credited with influencing his nephew to become a conservationist. Robert Roosevelt served as envoy extraordinary and minister plenipotentiary to the Netherlands from August 1888 to May 1889. His dispatches hardly included any perceptions or relevant information for the Department of State. This confirms that also in the late nineteenth century there was not much to do for U.S. diplomats in the Netherlands.

During the years 1913–17 President Woodrow Wilson dispatched another U.S. diplomat with seventeenth-century Dutch roots to The Hague: the author, educator, and clergyman Henry van Dyke. He was able to uphold a good relationship with the Dutch government and his most important task was to maintain the neutral rights of his country. At the opening of the States General in September 1915 he was the first U.S. diplomat to appear in a colorful gala uniform, like the other members of the diplomatic corps. The time of "the simple costume of an American citizen" dress code seemed to be over, as was, after April 1917, American neutrality.[8]

Dutch Foreign Service

Dutch foreign policy from 1815 until the adoption of the constitution of 1848 was in the hands of the king while the ministers of foreign affairs were his servants. Even if the king's power was reduced by the constitution and the role of his ministers and parliament increased, in the second part of the nineteenth century foreign policy still remained in the king's sphere of influence rather than parliament's. The promotion of free trade and neutrality and the determination to defend colonial possessions became the crucial pillars of Dutch foreign policy. These pillars were guaranteed and protected by powerful England, which would not accept that a continental power might incorporate the Netherlands or its colonies. Around 1900, though, British power was declining and, because of the Boer War in South Africa, England had become very unpopular in the Netherlands. Meanwhile, Germany became increasingly important for the Dutch economy. Although the Dutch government tried to maintain neutrality, in the years preceding and during World War I the country was regularly accused of pro-German sympathies.[9]

In the nineteenth century the Department of Foreign Affairs attracted little interest in the Netherlands and hardly required negotiations when a new cabinet was formed. It was characterized by aristocracy, traditionalism, routine, and a limited view of the Netherlands and the world. The ministers of the department only occasionally left a mark on policy.

William I's pretension that his kingdom ranked as a near-great power was reflected by having diplomats at more than twenty legations at foreign courts, including an embassy in London and Constantinople. After the Belgian secession from the Netherlands the country became a third-rate power and the king's foreign missions came under growing criticism from the Dutch parliament as top-heavy. The States General's parsimony between 1830 and 1850 led to a salary reduction averaging 25 percent. As a result, the Dutch diplomatic corps was increasingly underpaid after 1848 and was recruited from a single, aristocratic class with a conservative view on the world and few ties with trade, commerce, or industry. Furthermore, private income became a more important criterion for admission to the foreign service than personal merit.

The number of foreign missions, twenty at the start of the nineteenth century, was cut back to sixteen in 1850 and increased to twenty-two in 1914. After the 1820s the Netherlands appointed no ambassadors until World War II. Because of its commercial relations the number of Dutch consuls expanded during the nineteenth century, but the Department of Foreign Affairs showed little interest in the consular reports.[10]

Dutch Diplomats in the United States

In May 1814 the Dutch government dispatched François D. Changuion as envoy extraordinary and minister plenipotentiary to the United States. The principal aim of his mission was described in his instructions as the establishment of commercial relations between the two countries. He was warmly welcomed, including crowds cheering "Oranje boven," and presented his credentials to President James Madison in September that year. Soon, however, the Dutch government judged that the purely commercial relations with the United States did not require a full mission and within a year after his arrival Changuion was recalled. It was only in 1839 that a commercial treaty was concluded to establish reciprocal import duties on goods carried directly from country to country, irrespective of whether such goods were of native origin. Changuion's successors in Washington, J.W. ten Cate (1815–18) and A.J. Viscount de Goupy de Quabeck (1818–22), each served as chargé d'affaires but there was not much for them to do.[11]

The Dutch legation in Washington was not even occupied until in 1825 Christiaan D.E.J. Bangeman Huijgens, a former Dutch envoy to the Hanseatic Cities residing in Hamburg, was appointed envoy extraordinary and minister plenipotentiary and served until 1832. Bangeman Huijgens reported objectively about John Quincy Adams, for whom he felt little sympathy, but he had excellent contacts with his "brother Dutchman" Martin Van Buren, already before the latter became secretary of state. This probably was also the reason for his sympathy for President Jackson and his administration. He nevertheless regularly expressed his criticism of the American political and legal institutions. Bangeman Huijgens also reported on the descendants of Dutch colonists in New York State and was frequently invited to their activities. He hardly reacted to the deportation of Native Americans from Georgia to western territories nor showed sympathy for the situation of the African-American population. In 1832 he happily returned to the Netherlands.[12]

After Bangeman Huijgens the Dutch diplomats in Washington resumed the rank of chargé d'affaires until in 1854 it was upgraded to minister resident and from 1888 to envoy extraordinary and minister plenipotentiary. Bangeman Huijgens's successor, E.M. Adriaan Martini (1833–42), a former chargé in Brazil, in his dispatches frequently criticized the American democratic system. In his opinion American politicians in order to get the popular vote had become slaves of the political system, which, he thought, led to demoralization and was a clear lesson for democratic- and republican-minded people in Europe. The Jackson administration was in his view an example of people's sovereignty that ultimately would lead to violence, anarchy, or despotism. Martini's criticism was tempered by

2

—

his friendship with Martin Van Buren, although he regretted Van Buren's leadership of the "Ultra Democratic Party." He sincerely but vainly hoped President Van Buren would be reelected for another term.

Martini's successors, J.C. Gevers (1842–45) and F.M.W. Baron Testa (1845–54), both had an aristocratic background and, like Martini, viewed the United States through conservative lenses. In their dispatches they criticized its "vicious" political system and democratic institutions. Both were very skeptical about the wave of Dutch emigration to the United States in the 1840s and warned their government that many poor emigrants upon arrival became victims of abuses and ended in dire circumstances. Testa clearly observed that in the U.S. Congress the politicians' origins from the North, South, or West of the country had a bigger influence on their political opinion than party affiliation. Commenting on President Polk's expansionist policy toward Mexico, Testa wrote that the American character was impassioned by adventure and like a spoiled child was used to getting what it wanted. The conservative Testa not only regretted the revolutionary events taking place in Europe in 1848 but also the enthusiastic response these met with in the United States. In his view the American enthusiasm was based on ignorance of the European situation and on republican prejudices.[13]

The Dutch diplomats dispatched after 1848 were not very positive either about the United States. Theodorus M. Roest van Limburg, who served in Washington as minister resident from 1856 to 1867, had been an ardent liberal before 1848 and a Thorbecke supporter, but in the United States he became increasingly conservative and dismayed by the political reality of mass democracy. In his view the spoils system gave power to the mob and he saw Abraham Lincoln as the personification of this system. Roest van Limburg criticized Lincoln's Emancipation Proclamation and considered the liberation of the slaves a catastrophe. His letters leave the impression that he favored the aristocratic South. Only in the last winter of the Civil War, in 1864, did he predict that the South would be defeated. While complaining regularly about his low salary, he served for a decade in the United States. Although he was married to the daughter of Lewis Cass, an American general and Democratic statesman who provided him with useful information, Roest van Limburg never felt at home in the New World.[14]

From 1883 through 1899 the Dutch legation in Washington was led by career diplomat Wilhelm H.F. von Weckherlin, serving in the rank of envoy extraordinary and minister plenipotentiary. He reported, without showing much of his own views, on the debates in Congress and in the press on the annexation of Hawaii, the U.S. involvement in conflicts between Great Britain and Nicaragua and Venezuela, and American relations with Cuba in particular. He explained the sympathy in the U.S. Congress for the Cuban insurrectionists against Spain as based on the American hatred against monarchy and on jingoism and did not appreciate America's economic interests in Cuba. After the explosion of the U.S. battleship *Maine* in the harbor of Havana Von Weckherlin noticed that the public, influenced by the yellow press, was more belligerent than the government, which had to give in to the pressure resulting in the Spanish-American War of 1898. Von Weckherlin regularly criticized the American war effort and invasion in Cuba, and America's expansionist policy in general. Like his predecessors, he observed with dismay the influence of public opinion and of what he considered to be irresponsible politicians.[15]

Conclusion

After the creation of the Kingdom of the Netherlands in 1815 and the subsequent secession of Belgium in 1830 the political position of the Netherlands — and, as a consequence, the prestige of The Hague as a diplomatic post — declined during the remaining years of the nineteenth century. Also, Washington was not a post that was attractive to Dutch diplomats. The United States mainly focused on its own development on the American continent, and only at the end of the century did the country move its frontier overseas. The foreign policy of neutrality and aloofness of both the United States and the Netherlands and the small volume of trade relations made that both countries hardly played a role in each other's foreign policy. It is not surprising, then, that some diplomats advised their government to close their legation altogether and let consuls take care of the business of the limited trade relations.

As the diplomats had not much political work to do, they became primarily observers of another culture. In general, they did what they could to keep their governments informed about the political developments at their posts but they reported with a strong bias. There was clearly a difference in cultural perception: the American diplomats praised the democratic and republican system of their own country and criticized the shortcomings of the European system of monarchy and aristocracy, whereas the Dutch diplomats, usually with an aristocratic background and very conservative, abhorred the American system of "mob rule" and never felt at home in the New World. Both the American and Dutch diplomats had limited views on what was happening outside the small circle in which they lived. They usually were dependent on newspapers for their information. The slow postal service and the understaffing of their foreign offices made communication difficult and they regularly had to rely on their own judgment. In their performance they often felt handicapped by their low diplomatic rank and frequently complained about their meager salary. After a few years the diplomats from both sides usually were glad they could return home.

269

2

**THE
NINETEENTH
CENTURY**

1   On the late eighteenth-century U.S. diplomats in the Netherlands, see Cornelis A. van Minnen, *American Diplomats in the Netherlands, 1815–1850* (New York: St. Martin's Press, 1993), 15-21; On the Dutch diplomats in the United States in this era, see Jan Willem Schulte Nordholt, *The Dutch Republic and American Independence* (Chapel Hill /London: University of North Carolina Press, 1982), 252-263.

2   On the consuls, see Hans Krabbendam, "Capital Diplomacy: Consular Activity in Amsterdam and New York, 1800–1940," in George Harinck and Hans Krabbendam, eds., *Amsterdam-New York: Transatlantic Relations and Urban Identities since 1653* (Amsterdam: VU University Press, 2005), 167-181.

3   Van Minnen, *American Diplomats*, 2-3; Armin Rappaport, *A History of American Diplomacy* (New York: Macmillan, 1975), 45-46, 91-93.

4   William Barnes and John Heath Morgan, *The Foreign Service of the United States: Origins, Development, and Functions* (Washington, DC: Historical Office of the Department of State, 1961), 89, 146, 205, 349; Van Minnen, *American Diplomats*, 5-14.

5   Van Minnen, *American Diplomats*, 22-74, 108-117.

6   Ibid., 75- 107, 118-148.

7   Gerlof. D. Homan, "Netherlands-American Relations during the Civil War," *Civil War History* 31.4 (1985): 353-364.

8   On Henry van Dyke's diplomacy, see Hans Krabbendam, "Mooie woorden. Het geletterde leven van Henry van Dyke (1852-1933)," in E. F. van de Bilt and H. W. van de Doel, eds., *Klassiek Amerikaans. Opstellen voor A. Lammers* (Leiden: Universiteit Leiden, 2002), 115-120.

9   On Dutch foreign policy in this era, see Cornelis Boudewijn Wels, *Aloofness and Neutrality. Studies on Dutch Foreign Relations and Policy-Making Institutions* (Utrecht: HES Publishers, 1982), 29-75, 85-87; and Duco Hellema, *Buitenlandse politiek van Nederland. De Nederlandse rol in de wereldpolitiek* (Utrecht: Het Spectrum, 2006), 34-46, 64-73.

10 On the Dutch Department of Foreign Affairs and the Foreign Service, see Wels, *Aloofness*, 86, 118-129, 153-160; on the consular service, see ibid., 176-194.

11 J. C. Westermann, *The Netherlands and the United States. Their Relations in the Beginning of the Nineteenth Century* (The Hague: Martinus Nijhoff, 1935), 109-150, 323-328, and Peter Hoekstra, *Thirty-Seven Years of Holland-American Relations, 1803 to 1840* (Grand Rapids, MI: Eerdmans-Sevensma, 1916), 115-117, 166-172.

12 G. W. van der Meiden, "De brieven van de Nederlandse gezant Bangeman Huijgens uit Washington, 1825-1832" (Master's thesis, Universiteit Leiden, 1968).

13 The correspondence of the Dutch diplomats discussed above is deposited in the Archief Ministerie van Buitenlandse Zaken, 1813–1870, and in the Archief van het Gezantschap Verenigde Staten/Legatie Washington, 1814–1946, both in the Nationaal Archief (National Archives) in The Hague. On Gevers and Testa, see C. A. van Minnen, "Tussen Washington en Den Haag in een turbulente tijd. De berichtgeving van de Amerikaanse en Nederlandse zaakgelastigden en consuls in de periode 1845-1850" (Master's thesis, Universiteit Nijmegen, 1983).

14 J. W. Schulte Nordholt, "De brieven van de Nederlandse gezant in de Verenigde Staten tijdens de Burgeroorlog," *Tijdschrift voor Geschiedenis* 72 (1959): 206-225, also published as "The Civil War Letters of the Dutch Ambassador," *Journal of the Illinois State Historical Society* 44 (1961): 341-373.

15 Ben Schoenmaker, "Berichten uit de Bondshoofdstad. Politieke rapportage van de Nederlandse gezant te Washington, 1893-1917" (Master's thesis, Universiteit Leiden, 1987).

AMERICAN TRADE WITH THE NETHERLANDS AND THE DUTCH EAST INDIES

JEROEN TOUWEN

Introduction

Trade has been an important component of economic development, fostering industrialization by providing raw materials and allowing sales to distant markets. In the present globalized world, rich industrialized countries pressure poor countries to open their borders for imports. It is hard to imagine how rigidly today's rich nations protected their own economies during the period leading up to their industrial takeoff. This article analyzes trade relations between the United States and the Netherlands including its colonies in the Far East during the nineteenth and early twentieth centuries. We observe that during most of the nineteenth century the level of international trade was not very impressive and import tariffs abounded. Only when industrialization increased significantly and sought new markets, American exports to the Netherlands expanded. The demand for raw materials continued and led to increasing imports from the Dutch East Indies (today also referred to by some as colonial Indonesia) to the United States in the 1910s and 1920s.

By focusing on overseas trade we attain an interesting view on comparative economic development: when industrialization and modernization in the United States gained momentum, its exports of manufactured goods and wheat to the Netherlands increased, but Dutch exports to the United States remained rather traditional. Only the slight increase in exported capital goods such as iron products must have been significant for Dutch economic development. By contrast, the United States developed a booming trade with the Dutch East Indies as a result of its increasing demand for various raw materials, such as rubber. The Dutch economy profited more from this colonial trade than from exports to the United States from the mother country. In a sense, trade flows from the moth-

271

er country and the colony form each other's mirror image: the former imported, the latter exported. In part, this can be explained by the fact that the United States already was a more industrialized country than the Netherlands.

2

Up to 1860: Slow Trade

During the nineteenth century, up to the Civil War, the commercial ties between the United States and the Netherlands displayed little dynamism. Apart from trade in colonial goods such as coffee and sugar, which were reexported from Amsterdam, Dutch commerce was not impressive during the mid-nineteenth century. The Netherlands' main trading partners were Prussia (Germany), Belgium, and the United Kingdom. In fact, during the first half of the century the Dutch share in international trade with other western economies decreased due to its economic stagnation.[1] The relatively slow modernization of the German hinterland did little to stimulate trade. The Netherlands did not have a particularly strong trading relationship with the United States. In 1850, Dutch imports from the U.S. amounted to almost 4.5 million guilders (which was 2.5 percent of total imports), and exports to America consisted of roughly the same amount (contributing 3.4 percent to total Dutch exports).[2]

At that time, the United States was not really in a position to conquer European export markets or stimulate synergetic gains from intercontinental trade with Western Europe. High tariffs restricted imports into the American market, weakening commercial ties and invoking countermeasures of the trading partners. Moreover, the Napoleonic Wars and conflicts with Britain were not beneficial to overseas trade. Import tariffs played an essential role in funding the U.S. federal government, providing 90 percent of its tax revenues from 1789 to the Civil War.[3] The peak was reached in 1828 with the so-called Tariff of Abomination of 57 percent. Between 1830 and 1860 the average import tariff was roughly 15-30 percent. If strategic trade theory is correct in stating that import protection is beneficial to infant industries (an argument already made by Alexander Hamilton in the eighteenth century), this must have helped American industries such as the cotton textiles, which after the Civil War expanded dynamically. Tariffs, however, continued long after these export industries matured. In the "liberal era," between the Civil War and World War I, tariffs remained high: 30 percent in the 1870s and 1890s, and 20-30 percent on average after 1890.[4]

Industrialization and Trade Expansion, 1865–1930

The end of the Civil War in 1865 inaugurated a period of American economic expansion.[5] The Gilded Age created unprecedented prosperity and triggered industrialization. This attracted both immigrants and investors. American railroads formed an alluring investment to many Dutch investors, although it can be argued that it was rather the glamorous appeal of New World economic dynamism than a rational profit-oriented analysis that inspired investors to place their capital in the risky railroad funds, which experienced several crises.[6]

American economic expansion resulted in new export products, such as the notoriously cheap grain that washed over Western Europe in the last quarter of the nineteenth century. Innovation and technological spillovers were not so manifest in the Netherlands — quite unlike the situation in the decade after 1945, when the Marshall Plan (1948–51) stimulated the exchange of technology, resulting in spectacular catch-up growth in Western Europe's productivity levels. In the nineteenth century, the Dutch economy was dominated by agriculture and services, and industrial development followed its own, rather unhurried, trajectory. It did not seem to be prodded by American modernization — even though emigrants sent back their stories.

One such story, already conveyed before 1850, concerned an efficient type of plough employed on U.S. farmland. The American *Arendploeg* turned out to be quite suitable for working Dutch clay soil as well. As a result, several hundreds of them were imported.[7] This wonderful American invention did not, however, spark a widespread introduction of other technology in agriculture. It has been argued that the state of agricultural technology in the Netherlands was, in general, not so backward. The market strategy in the Netherlands was, however, geared toward optimization of existing methods rather than innovation and the adoption of foreign techniques. In several sectors, such as madder (*meekrap*) processing, this approach eventually led to a relative inferiority, in terms of quality, compared to industrial processing.[8] This was all the more important since pigments such as madder, *garancine,* and *colorine* formed one of the main export categories to the United States, together with raw iron, lead, tin, coffee, and sugar.

At the turn of the twentieth century, imports from the United States grew significantly. Cotton had been the leading export product in the nineteenth century, surpassing tobacco in 1803 and constituting circa 50 percent of American exports between 1830 and 1860. After the Civil War, other exports surged, so although the cotton export recovered from impediments related to the war (such as the Union blocking the Southern ports), it lost its primacy. By the beginning of the twentieth century, the United States had become the world's pre-eminent manufacturing nation. In manufacturing output, America's share in the world economy grew from 7 percent in 1860 to 24 percent in 1890, and to 39 percent in 1928.[9]

Imports into the Netherlands from the United States, which had been only 4 million guilders in 1850, grew to 284 million guilders in 1900, securing a third place in Dutch imports after Germany and England (see table 1). In the trade flow to the Netherlands, foodstuffs remained dominant (in contrast to the Dutch East Indies): Dutch imports from the United States included wheat, corn, flour, meat products, animal fats, vegetable oil, and only relatively small quantities of timber, iron, and cotton.

TABLE 1

Trade of the Netherlands with the United States, 1850–1940.

	Imports from United States	Share of total Dutch imports	Exports to United States	Share of total Dutch exports	Rank	
	million guilders	%	*million guilders*	%	*imports*	*exports*
1850	4	2.5	5	3.4	7	6
1860	11	3.7	5	2.0	7	6
1870	10	2.2	3	0.8	7	9
1880	81	9.7	16	2.5	4	5
1890	98	7.6	24	2.2	6	5
1900	284	14.4	65	3.8	3	4
1910	295	9.0	85	3.2	6	5
1920	526	15.7	77	4.5		
1930	211	8.7	49	2.8		
1940	135	13.2	12	1.8		

Note: Imports refer to imports destined for the Netherlands (*invoer tot verbruik*), excluding goods in transit. Exports exclude reexports of goods in transit (*uitvoer uit het vrije verkeer)*. Gold and silver are excluded.

Sources: Statistiek van den handel en de scheepvaart in het Koninkrijk der Nederlanden over het jaar 1846–1877; Statistiek van de in-, uit- en doorvoer, 1877–1916; Jaarstatistiek van den in-, uit- en doorvoer over 1917–1943; CBS (Centraal Bureau voor de Statistiek), *Zeventig jaar statistiek in tijdreeksen, 1899–1969* (The Hague: Staatsuitgeverij, 1970). Totals for 1850–75 from Statistiek van den handel en de scheepvaart 1875, vol. 2, 86. Values are in current prices.

The bulk of Dutch late nineteenth-century trade was still conducted with neighboring countries. For example, in 1870 the most important export partners of the Netherlands were Prussia (144 million guilders), England (exports of 106 million guilders), and Belgium (67 million guilders). The United States, with its high import tariffs and unsettled conditions because of the Civil War, occupied the ninth place in the rank order of Dutch export partners (even Russia ranked higher) (see table 1).

In 1870, exports from the Netherlands to the United States amounted to only 2.9 million guilders. These exports consisted of liquor such as rum (750,000 guilders), iron (327,000 guilders), lead (261,000 guilders), madder (467,000 guilders), and flax (72,000 guilders), as well as a range of smaller products such as barrels and casks, coffee, and pottery. In 1880, iron and iron-made products formed the major component of exports to the United States (8 million guilders out of total exports to the U.S. of 16 million guilders). In 1890–1910 kina formed the principal commodity shipped to the United States. Kina, or quinine, was used as a medicine against malaria and is produced from the bark of the cinchona tree that grows in tropical areas such as the East Indies. Kina exports to the United States amounted to 7.4 million guilders in 1890, 40 million in 1900, and 30 million in 1910. At the turn of the twentieth century, other exports to the United States consisted of raw iron, cheese, herring, coffee, sugar, cement, and tuff (*tufsteen*), all in relatively small amounts.

Imports from the United States were consistently higher than Dutch exports. In 1870, the U.S. occupied the seventh place in imports. That year the Netherlands imported cotton (4 million guilders), oil (2.8 million guilders), and tobacco (1.6 million guilders) from the United States, as well as a large range of smaller products, such as wheat, wood, palm oil, syrup, sugar, and paints. This resulted in total imports from the States of slightly more than 10 million guilders.

During the latter half of the nineteenth century, Dutch transit trade was substantial (15 percent of the volume of imports in 1880, 23 percent in 1900). This explains the presence of colonial goods such as sugar, coffee, and kina in the Dutch exports to the United States. During World War I the trading pattern changed: since access from the East Indies to the overseas Dutch market was difficult, new destinations were sought and found, and the Netherlands' role in the trade of colonial goods decreased.

Imports from the United States were primarily destined for local use, only 2.7 percent of the volume of imports was reexported in 1880 and 2.3 percent in 1900. The role of the Netherlands as "main port of Europe" still had to be invented, but it developed quickly: in 1910, while imports from the United States amounted to 295 million guilders, reexported American goods amounted to 102 million guilders.

The Agrarian Depression of 1882–96 was a mixed blessing. One result of American economic modernization and the expanding infrastructure (large-scale production, railroads, steam shipping) was the inflow of cheap American wheat in Western Europe from the 1870s onward. Although these imports harmed Dutch agriculture, the positive effect of decreasing wheat prices was that they allowed real wages to decrease, stimulating the structural transformation of the Dutch economy into a modern industrial nation.[10] Also, Dutch agriculture was forced to modernize and specialize in sectors such as meat, dairy products, and horticulture. In the long run, these effects were therefore beneficial to the economy. In 1880 the combined value of imports of various types of wheat, corn, rye, and flour amounted to circa 39 million guilders. In 1890 grain imports constituted 27 million guilders, in 1900 even 67 million guilders, and in 1910 about 40 million guilders.

In short, during the Gilded Age, imports from the United States into the Netherlands facilitated further economic development, by providing foodstuffs and manufactured goods. In return, the Netherlands did not manage to export much to the United States, except for rather traditional agricultural exports.

Colonial Inputs in the Early Twentieth-Century World Economy

The Dutch colony in the Far East, however, took on a more dynamic role as exporter to America. In contrast with the mother country, exports from the East Indies to the United States were significant, and consistently larger than imports. During the Cultivation System, coffee and sugar were sold on the world market, and when in 1870 the Agricultural Law was issued private enterprise gained a greater role in the Dutch colony, leading to an impressive expansion of exports.[11]

Until the 1910s, the main commodities exported from Java to the United States were coffee and sugar, plus a number of smaller agricultural and forest products, as well as some tin. In 1880, in the total package of exports to the United States, which amounted to 15.6 million guilders, a value of 11 million guilders concerned coffee (this was a large share of the total East Indies' coffee exports of 28 million guilders that year). Interestingly, a value of 6 million guilders of these coffee exports to America originated from Sumatra (total coffee exports from this region amounted to roughly 11 million guilders). This confirms that for the development of export agriculture in the Outer Islands, exports to the United States were more important than for Java. It foreshadowed developments in the twentieth century during which the islands outside Java became a very dynamic growth region.[12]

[:1893]

389—World's Fair, Midway Plaisance, St.,
in Java Village, Chicago, Ill., U.S.A.

The Javanese village at the World Fair in Chicago, 1893.
Stereophoto nr 389 of Keystone View Compagny Meadsville, Penn[sylvani]a.

In 1880, sugar exports to the United States consisted of 3.8 million guilders (total sugar exports were about 49 million guilders that year). In 1900, sugar exports to America had risen to 25 million guilders (of total sugar exports of 74 million guilders). That year, total exports from the Dutch East Indies to the United States amounted to 28 million guilders, which constituted almost 11 percent of the colony's total exports (259 million guilders). Coffee exports to America in 1900 had stuck at about 2.3 million guilders. Obviously, the United States was an important market for the late nineteenth-century Java sugar industry.

In the twentieth century, this trend continued: exports to the United States formed a considerable share of exports from the Dutch East Indies (see table 2). In 1920, sugar exports amounted to 174 million guilders, and second were coca leaves (48 million guilders worth shipped to the United States). Copra oil, gained from coconuts, was a new product that could be processed into products such as soap and margarine. In 1920, exports of copra oil to the U.S. consisted of 13 million guilders (and coffee amounted to only 9 million). Rubber was another relatively new but successful commodity in the export package: in 1930, rubber exports to the United States amounted to 70 million guilders (in total exports to America of 142 million guilders). Second in 1930 was palm oil (10 million guilders). In 1938, exports of latex rubber (Hevea Brasiliensis, *caoutchouc*) amounted to 46 million guilders, palm oil to 9 million, petroleum to 2 million, and in addition there was a range of smaller products.

In the first decades of the twentieth century there was a gradual increase in American companies in estate agriculture. As a result of World War I, when it was difficult to trade with the Netherlands, commercial emancipation from the mother country took place in the colony. After the war, colonial trade with the Netherlands did not return to its previous level and trading links with Asian and American partners intensified. American enterprise found its way to the colony: much of the rubber exports of the 1920s and 1930s actually came from American rubber plantations.

In the booming exports from the East Indies oil acquired a dominant place, especially from 1910 onward. Crude oil was drilled in several places in Sumatra, Kalimantan, and Java, and refined in five refineries. Although Standard Oil tried to compete locally, this American company was kept at bay by Royal Dutch and the colonial government. Its subsidiary the "Koloniale" (in full: the Netherlands Colonial Petroleum Company) only managed to obtain a few productive drilling places in Palembang (Sumatra), including a small refinery near Sungai Gerong as of 1913.[13]

Royal Dutch (amalgamated with Shell in 1907) dominated oil production. Its production company, the Bataafsche Petroleum Maatschappij (BPM), shipped little oil to the United States, though. For example, in 1930 oil exports to the U.S.

consisted of only 1.2 million guilders (of total exports to the United States of 142 million guilders and of total oil exports amounting to more than 170 million guilders!). Like tobacco, this important export commodity did not find a destination in America since the domestic industry provided these goods for the home market.

TABLE 2
Trade of the Dutch East Indies with the United States, 1850–1938.

	Imports from United States	Share of total Indonesian imports	Exports to United States	Share of total Indonesian exports
	million guilders	%	*million guilders*	%
1850	0.4	1.6	0.8	1.4
1860	0.3	0.5	0.9	0.9
1870	0.4	0.8	2	2.4
1880	8	4.7	16	8.7
1890	7	4.2	11	6.2
1900	3	1.4	28	10.8
1910	5	1.5	16	3.6
1920	163	14.6	198	8.8
1930	89	10.4	142	11.9
1938	60	12.3	89	13.5

Note: Until 1890, the United States was the sole provenance for imports from the American continent; as of 1900 the figures include a negligible proportion of South American trade; from 1910 on, the United States is listed separately from other American countries (see also Korthals Altes, *General Trade Statistics,* 76, 91). Data concern both trade on private and government account.

Sources: For 1850–70: W. L. Korthals Altes, *General Trade Statistics. Changing Economy in Indonesia,* vol. 12a (Amsterdam, Tropical Institute, 1991); For 1880–1900: Statistiek van de handel, de scheepvaart en de in- en uitvoerregten in Nederlandsch-Indië over het jaar 1880, 1890, 1900; For 1910–20: Statistiek van den handel en de in- en uitvoer-rechten in Nederlandsch-Indië over het jaar 1910, 1920; For 1930 and 1938: Jaaroverzicht van de in- en uitvoer van Nederlandsch-Indië gedurende het jaar 1930, 1938; Mede-deelingen van het Centraal Kantoor voor de Statistiek, no. 101, 178.

However, oil imports from America into the Dutch East Indies were traditionally much more important. In the nineteenth century, the oil trade mainly consisted of kerosene, which was used for lamps. In 1880, petroleum imports of roughly 63 million liters added up to 7.6 million guilders, by far the largest sector of all imports from the United States into the Dutch colony (8 million guilders). In 1890, oil again dominated imports — 67 million liters, worth 6.7 million guilders — and formed the largest sector of imports from America, which totaled about 7 million guilders. That same year, Russia was the second source for oil, providing 3.8 million guilders worth of it.

Oil remained the leader of total American imports until 1920. By then, in addition to 11 million guilders worth of oil, a value of 25 million guilders was spent on American automobiles. Consumption of kerosene (lamp oil) was replaced by gasoline. Other American industrial products finding their way into the Dutch East Indies in 1920 were fertilizer (17 million guilders) and machines and tools (10 million guilders). A remarkably large quantity of foodstuffs (vegetables, fruits, meat, and fish) was imported from the United States at that time: to the amount of 9 million guilders in 1920, and 13 million guilders in 1930. Machines and motorized vehicles remained a stable import flow over these years. Allegedly, American cars were better suited for the rough colonial roads than cars of European makes.

From the early 1870s to the early 1930s, the Dutch East Indies constituted an open and unprotected economy, without tariffs discriminating against imports from overseas.[14] This favored imports of American kerosene, cars, and tools. By comparison, the Dutch market was less accessible to products that could compete with domestic industry (although quite substantial import flows to the Netherlands developed nevertheless in the early twentieth century). Conversely, the American market was even less accessible to Dutch products.

Conclusion

During the first three quarters of the nineteenth century, the international trade of the Netherlands was not very dynamic. Modest levels of trade focused on neighboring countries. During the liberal era, after 1870, trade with the United States increased, but imports into the Netherlands clearly outweighed exports.

In many other regards, the relationship between the Netherlands and the United States had been traditionally strong: there were historical ties (such as the colony of New Netherland), America was a destination for numerous Dutch emigrants, and Dutch investors bought American shares and bonds. Why, then, did not a more flourishing trade relationship develop? The main answer lies in the protectionist character of the era before 1870. Considerable import tariffs existed in the period leading up to industrialization, both in the United States and the Netherlands. Another reason was that for raw materials and agricultural products, the cost of transportation to neighboring countries was much lower.

After the Civil War, American exports expanded as a result of the country's accelerating economic modernization. This led to new trade flows in addition to the traditional cotton exports. The introduction of steam shipping was beneficial to bulk exports of wheat and corn (and other foodstuffs) to Western Europe. Yet, other types of trade, such as in machines, were hindered by the fact that industrialization in both countries ran parallel. In this regard the United States was ahead of the Netherlands, which explains that a voluminous trade in processed foodstuffs and consumer goods found its way into the Netherlands in the 1920 and 1930s.

Trade of the United States with the Dutch East Indies displayed a more dynamic character because these economies complemented each other, rather than forming a rivalry. Nineteenth-century imports from the United States into the East Indies consisted predominantly of petroleum, while after 1910 increasing numbers of American machines and cars were sold. Exports to the United States were dominated by sugar and (before 1900) coffee. In the early twentieth century rubber became the major commodity that was shipped to the U.S. in enormous quantities, partly being produced on American estates in Sumatra. As the rubber and coffee trade formed a major incentive for economic development in the Outer Islands, the role of American trade can be considered to have been an important stimulus for the economic development of the Dutch East Indies.

During the late nineteenth century, the Dutch economy benefited from cheap wheat imports. Incentives originating from the United States to innovate or modernize were not strong, even though knowledge about the New World abounded.[15] As a nation with a modernizing economy, the Netherlands hardly profited from the expanding American market, but the developing economy of its colony did.

1   Jan Luiten van Zanden and Arthur van Riel, *Nederland 1780–1914. Staat, instituties en economische ontwikkeling* (Amsterdam: Balans, 2000), 108 [published in English as *The Strictures of Inheritance: The Dutch Economy in the Nineteenth Century* (2004), 108].

2   Specific data concerning Dutch-American trade are all from the trade statistics as specified in tables 1 and 2. We should be careful with the interpretation of values, since the Dutch foreign trade statistics of the nineteenth century used prices from fixed mark years to calculate values, and the distinction between regular exports and reexports is not reliable. However, for comparative and descriptive

2

———

purposes I decided to use these statistics, for lack of others.

3   Robert Whaples, "United States," in John J. McCuster, ed., *History of World Trade since 1450* (Detroit: Thomson Gale, 2006), 2:783-790.

4   Ibid., 786; Thomas Weisss, "United States: Antebellum Period," and Robert Whaples, "United States: Modern Period," in Joel Mokyr, ed., *The Oxford Encyclopedia of Economic History* (Oxford: Oxford University Press, 2003), 5:163-167, 167-174.

5   Gary M. Walton and Hugh Rockoff, *History of the American Economy*, 7th edition (New York: Dryden Press, 1994), 298, 372-375.

6   See the article by Augustus J. Veenendaal, Jr., elsewhere in this volume.

7   J.L. van Zanden, "Mest en Ploeg," in H. Lintsen et al., eds., *Geschiedenis van de techniek in Nederland. De wording van een moderne samenleving, 1800-1890* (Zutphen: Walburg Pers, 1992), 1:53-70, in particular 61-63; Van Zanden and Van Riel, *Nederland 1780-1914,* 254.

8   J.W. Schot, "Innoveren in Nederland," in Lintsen et al., *Geschiedenis van de techniek* 5:222.

9   Whaples, "United States," 787.

10 Van Zanden and Van Riel, *Nederland 1780-1914*, 360.

11 H.W. Dick, V.J.H. Houben, J.Th. Lindblad, and Thee Kian Wie, *The Emergence of a National Economy. An Economic History of Indonesia, 1800-2000* (Crows Nest: Allen and Unwin, 2002), 123-130; Anne Booth, *The Indonesian Economy in the Nineteenth and Twentieth Centuries. A History of Missed Opportunities* (London: Macmillan, 1998), 217.

12 L.J. Touwen, *Extremes in the Archipelago. Trade and Economic Development in the Outer Islands of Indonesia, 1900-1942* (Leiden: KITLV Press, 2001).

13 For a survey of the Dutch East Indies' oil industry, J.Th. Lindblad, "The Petroleum Industry in Indonesia before the Second World War," *Bulletin of Indonesian Economic Studies* 25.2 (1989): 53-77; Touwen, *Extremes in the Archipelago*, 143-150.

14 Booth, *The Indonesian Economy*, 216.

15 See for example George Harinck and Hans Krabbendam, eds., *Amsterdam-New York. Transatlantic Relations and Urban Identities since 1653* (Amsterdam: VU University Press, 2005).

DUTCH INVESTMENTS IN THE UNITED STATES

———

AUGUSTUS J. VEENENDAAL, JR.

Early Investments

The decline of Dutch political influence in New Netherland did not put an end to the commercial relations between the United Provinces and America. Indeed, trade in colonial products boomed in the eighteenth century and Dutchmen made large profits running arms and supplies from St. Eustatius to the American armies during the Revolution. Soon after the establishment of the American Republic the first federal loan was floated in Amsterdam in 1782, and more followed until in 1794, before the French armies overran the Dutch Republic, the total stood at eleven loans amounting to a total of 30.4 million guilders.[1] The federal government turned out to be a good debtor, paying interest on time. States such as Maryland, Ohio, and Pennsylvania, however, which had also borrowed in Amsterdam, proved to be less dependable.

Other Dutch investments in the U.S. before 1795 came in the shape of canal and river improvement schemes, such as the Potomac Canal, James River, and Connecticut River companies. Most did not give the promised return on the money and Dutch interest waned. Moreover, the unsettled nature of the European money markets after the French occupation did not help. Nevertheless, immediately after the Peace of Amiens, in 1802, between Great Britain and France, the Amsterdam house of Hope & Company became involved in raising the fifteen million dollars President Jefferson needed to buy the French North American colonies, the famous Louisiana Purchase. The London house of Francis Baring & Company handled the loan, but needed a partner, and Hope sold at least six million dollars of these American bonds on the Dutch market.[2] The First Bank of the United States was partly funded from Amsterdam, but more important was the Dutch share in the Second Bank of the United States of 1816, and at least nine million guilders were poured in from Amsterdam in 1840, secured by U.S. federal and state bonds.

One complicated case was the Chesapeake and Ohio Canal. The three cities of Washington, Georgetown, and Alexandria had guaranteed the construction costs of this canal and issued some 3.7 million guilders in bonds, with sections of all three cities as security. Amsterdam had taken all these bonds and when the canal went bankrupt, the creditors claimed the security. The thought that part of the capital city of the United States was about to fall into Dutch hands must have been so horrible that Congress stepped in and paid off the Dutch.

The Holland Land Company, established in 1792 in Amsterdam, was a grand scheme designed to buy land in western New York and Pennsylvania and settle it with Dutch and German farmers. Headquarters were set up in Batavia, NY, and an important settlement was founded on Lake Erie, called New Amsterdam, which later came to be known as Buffalo. More than five million acres were held, but the results for the investors were meager. Problems with squatters, legal complications, and a lack of communication between Amsterdam and the local managers hindered development. Yet it was not until 1858 that the Holland Land Company was finally dissolved.[3]

Most of these early transactions had been handled by well-established Amsterdam houses, which had developed a network of agents in America for their commission trade during the eighteenth century and now branched out into real estate and finance. But of all these "old" houses, only Hope & Company was to remain active in the field of American finance, together with their traditional London partner Barings.[4]

By 1850 almost all of the old U.S. federal and state bonds had been redeemed, the land and canal companies wound up, and Dutch investment in the United States in general was at a low point. The American Civil War provided a temporary surge in the sale of government bonds in the Netherlands. Again, the federal government turned out to be a dependable debtor. Confederate bonds, yielding a higher interest rate and generally secured not by government credit but by stocks of cotton in the blockaded Southern ports, never caught on in Amsterdam, in spite of active salesmanship of Confederate agents.

The Railroad Boom

Despite economic stagnation, the Dutch still had money to invest, part of which was "old" money accumulated in the eighteenth century. Additionally, new capital generated by the colonies and by the domestic industry became available in the 1860s. This surplus could find an outlet in low-renting but safe domestic government loans, but after the reorganization of the national debt by Minister F. A. van Hall in 1844, no new loans were issued until 1877.[5] British consols were also eminently safe, but again, their yield was low, 3 percent or less. Other countries, such as Spain and Portugal, promised a better rate, but their credit standing was much lower. More attractive were higher-renting Russian railroad loans, extremely reliable because they were generally guaranteed by the Czarist government. Even more remunerative but much less safe were American railroad loans. For all three types of investment a market existed, depending on the character of the prospective investor. A host of bankers and stockbrokers were active in this field, and Amsterdam firms such as Wertheim & Gompertz, Boissevain Brothers, Lippmann, Rosenthal & Company, and many others became household names. It was estimated that by 1914 as many as fifteen hundred stockbrokers — one for every four thousand Dutchmen — served the needs of the investing public.[6] A lot of this Dutch surplus capital was to find its way into American railroads.

The construction of railroads on a truly gigantic scale inaugurated a new era of foreign investment in the United States. From a total mileage of 9,201 in 1850, the American railroad network had grown to 30,626 miles ten years later. The Civil War caused a short delay in new construction, but by the end of the nineteenth century the mileage had grown to almost 200,000.[7] The enormous amount of money needed for an industry such as this was simply not available domestically, and American railroad builders had to look to the traditional European money markets, London and Amsterdam foremost. Of an estimated total of five or six billion dollars used for new railroad construction between 1865 and 1900, at least 33 percent came from Europe, probably more.[8] Great Britain was the leader, followed at a distance by the Netherlands, France, and Germany, in that order.[9] Most of this European capital consisted of long-term loans, with a fixed rate of interest and secured by a mortgage on the property. Shares were less popular, although those issued by some solid companies were widely held. Shares of less respectable railroads were often thrown in free as an incentive to persuade buyers to invest in a company's bonded debt.

Of course, the big attraction to Dutch investors was the potentially high yield, higher than anywhere else in the world. In the 1860s and 1870s interest rates of 7 or 8 percent were not uncommon, and coupled with a purchasing price of well under par (= nominal value), this could mean a yield of 10 percent or even more. But here was the snag: the railroads that promised the highest interest rates were generally not the most financially solid. Many of them amounted to nothing more than two streaks of rust on the ground, but the prospectus issued by the incorporators would only talk of prosperous towns and fertile land, waiting to be developed. Dutch bankers should, of course, have checked the soundness of such companies before recommending these securities to their customers, but during the early years of the boom they often failed to do so, despite the transatlantic telegraph cable that had been in use since 1855. After the economic crisis of 1873, when many of the more vulnerable companies went bankrupt, bankers did indeed become more careful, but many Dutch investors lost

285

2

—

sizeable sums. There was also an element of speculation in the trade of these bonds. Buying cheap and selling higher before the inevitable crash, was a risky sport for the more adventurous. The cautious investor was better off buying the more expensive but safe bonds of companies such as Illinois Central, with prices generally over par, but at little or no risk. Another, more psychological aspect may also have played a role: for Europeans America was the country where everybody could get rich, so why not join in by investing in one of these promising ventures?

Obviously, not all Dutch investments went into American "rails," but the American railroad corner of the Amsterdam Stock Exchange did become a strong center of trade. Of a grand total of 829 different — both domestic and foreign — securities listed in Amsterdam in 1893, as many as 154, or 18.57 percent, pertained to American railroads. Twenty years later, the total number had grown to 1,512, with 179 U.S. railroads, proportionally somewhat less, but still 11.83 percent.

By the end of the nineteenth century the focus slowly changed. Interest rates in the railroad sector were declining to less attractive figures of 3 or 3.5 percent, while in contrast, the new industrial corporations promised higher yields. United States Steel, Standard Oil, and other corporate giants offered a better deal, and trade in their securities became more popular. This did not mean an end to Dutch interest in American railroads, only a greater diversification. Moreover, the domestic industry of the Netherlands now offered good opportunities, while in the Dutch East Indies oil and agricultural companies were becoming ever more attractive. Nevertheless, railroads remained one of the leading, if not the leading sector of Dutch investments in the United States well into the twentieth century.

*The Character of Dutch Investments
in the United States*

The Dutch nearly always preferred a straight portfolio investment, without any attempt at actually controlling the company in question. Management of railroads that worked with a lot of Dutch capital was generally left to Americans, sometimes kept in check by the presence of Dutch or Dutch-appointed representatives on the board. In the 1880s Anthony G. Dulman, a New York merchant of Dutch extraction, was director of as many as seven such American railroad companies. But Dutch bankers and brokers also served on the boards of largely Dutch-owned railroads such as the Illinois Central, Chicago & North Western, or Missouri, Kansas & Texas companies. Their influence on the actual day-to-day running of the railroad in question must have remained small, though.

286

Sample of American railroad bonds owned by Dutch investors.

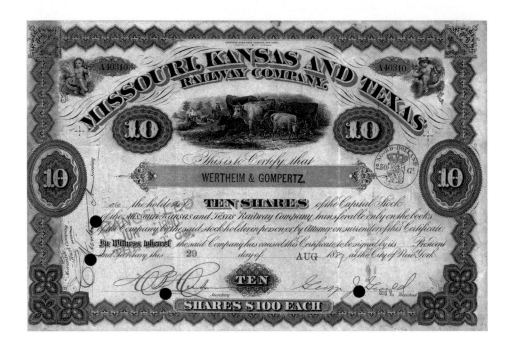

Sample of American railroad bonds owned by Dutch investors.

More personal involvement from the Dutch would become necessary when a railroad company went bankrupt. In such cases the company sought protection of the courts, and a judge appointed a receiver to manage the property until the court had sorted things out. As shares were hardly ever fully paid up, the courts generally assigned the railroad to the bondholders, who had provided most of the construction capital. Whenever the Dutch had a very large share in the bonded debt, it became customary to form a protective committee, with the banker who had introduced the securities in question taking the lead. The next step was to prove that the Dutch had indeed a majority, so a member of the committee would travel to America with the Dutch bonds to lay before the court. And when the court did indeed assign the railroad to the Dutch committee, they took steps to sell the road to an interested party, usually an American group or a neighboring railroad. The committees were generally not inclined to run "their" railroad themselves as they simply lacked the means to do so. Between 1860 and 1915 as many as forty-one such committees were set up, most of them exclusively Dutch, some with other European partners. Some were successful, but large losses had to be swallowed again and again, despite the efforts of the committees.

These were the days of unbridled competition, without a Securities and Exchange Commission to keep Wall Street in check. Of course, there were honest men on both sides of the Atlantic who wanted to do sound business, but swindling American promoters, shady financiers, and greedy businessmen who longed for a quick dollar at the expense of foreign capitalists, corrupt judges and politicians, gullible Dutch investors who dreamed of getting rich overnight, negligent brokers who failed to check the securities offered — they all played a role in the risky game of investing in American railroads. Frauds were all too common, and hard to prevent without personal involvement from the Dutch. American promoters usually set up a construction company as a vehicle for financing the road. They advanced some money to construct the line, in return for railroad bonds and land if a land grant was part of the deal. Before the expected crash came, they could dispose of the bonds and the land at a good price, leaving the hapless other bondholders with almost worthless securities. One of the most notorious examples of such a fraud was the case of the Kansas City, Pittsburg & Gulf. The promoter of this line, Arthur Stilwell, had, by a chance meeting with a Dutch merchant, obtained access to Dutch capital. But this time, the Dutch investors, before pouring in their millions, demanded a majority in the two construction companies involved. Thus, when the railroad went bankrupt in 1899, they still owned the assets of the construction companies, mostly valuable land along the line. And when the great Spindletop oil field in Texas was discovered, it turned out that part of it was on the Dutch-owned land![10]

289

Other Forms of Investment

Despite the overwhelming importance of railroad investment, there were other ventures that attracted Dutch capital. After the demise of the Holland Land Company, Dutch interest in land in America did not disappear completely. The biggest operation in this respect was the Maxwell Land Grant Company, that went back in time to the years when New Mexico was still under Mexican sovereignty. After the cession of the territories to the United States in 1848, Lucien Maxwell was confirmed in the possesion of a land grant, some two million acres altogether. In 1870 he sold out to a British-Dutch consortium that went bankrupt in 1874.[11] A new Maxwell Land Grant Company was then formed in Amsterdam, in hopes of settling the estate with Dutch farmers and stock breeders and developing the mineral holdings. As such, the company was not successful, despite several inspection tours of Dutch directors to the Maxwell headquarters in Cimarron, NM. On one of these trips, in 1883, a young Dutchman, Albert Verwey, served as secretary because of his knowledge of the English language. He was to become a famous poet and wrote one of his very first sonnets, "The Far West," while there. The Maxwell never became a pot of gold for the investors, but slowly the real estate was sold and the proceeds invested in shares of the Dordtsche Petroleum Maatschappij, a holding company of Royal Dutch/Shell. As such the Maxwell became popular on the Amsterdam Stock Exchange. One of the very few visual reminders of the Dutch presence in Cimarron is Verwey's signature in the guest register of the historic St. James Hotel.

There was, however, still another type of investment—more in the sphere of direct investment—where Dutchmen actually operated the companies they set up. The Maxwell had been an abortive attempt at such a business, but in the 1880s a new venture, the Dutch-American mortgage bank, became common. These banks were headquartered in the Netherlands, with an office in America under a Dutch manager. One of the first was the Northwestern and Pacific Mortgage Bank of Olympia, WA, founded in 1885, and others followed.[12] Most operated in states with agricultural potential such as Minnesota, Idaho, and especially Washington, where Spokane became the center with offices of at least five of these banks. They advanced money to farmers to improve their property, tried to settle Dutch farmers in the area, and generally did a lot to advance the state of agriculture. The extensive irrigation projects in the Yakima Valley, where a small group of Dutchmen started fruit growing, were among the more fortunate results of the activities of these banks.[13]

When oil became a much-sought-after commodity toward the end of the nineteenth century, Dutchmen soon found out that oil companies could be a profitable vehicle for investment—and not only the big companies such as

Royal Dutch/Shell or Standard Oil, but also those operating on a smaller scale. S.F. van Oss, a well-known Dutch financial journalist and writer, decided to enter this field himself early in the twentieth century. After some disappointments in Oklahoma railroads, he became aware of the vast oil potential of that young state. Acting upon the advice of a Dutch engineer, Martin Middelberg, he bought two existing firms in Oklahoma and grouped them together in the Oklahoma Petroleum Compagnie, incorporated in The Hague in 1908. Dividends were high, between 10 and 30 percent, and Van Oss continued by setting up other oil companies — all headquartered in The Hague and operating in Oklahoma. In 1911 he sold out at a profit to a French consortium, the Union des Pétroles d'Oklahoma.[14]

Government and Investment

The Netherlands government generally abstained from interfering in the flow of Dutch capital across the Atlantic. Dutch consuls in American cities did occasionally act at the request of Dutch holders of American securities, but always by means of mediation and advice, never through pressure of any kind. The official position of the Dutch government was not to intervene in "foreign, and sometimes risky, investments, and to expose itself thereby to international problems." Dutch investment in the United States was clearly considered to be for profit only, and the risks involved were to be borne by the investors, not by the government. Political or other reasons are not visible and the Netherlands government never used the enormous Dutch capital invested in the United States as a lever to foster its political or economic interests.

Conclusion

Estimates of all Dutch investments in the United States, both railroad and non-railroad, are hard to establish. Most probable is a maximum of worldwide Dutch investments of about two billion dollars by 1914, including four hundred million in Russian securities and five hundred million in American stocks and bonds, railroad and non-railroad.[15]

The craze for American "rails" in the Netherlands almost eclipsed all other fields of investment. Higher yields than anywhere else were possible in these railroads, and the enormous demand for capital was met by European investors, with the Netherlands always in second place after the British. Political reasons were largely absent, although some contemporary Dutch writers did argue that capital invested in the United States was not being used for the production of arms or the waging of wars, but for more peaceful goals, and therefore more favored than, for instance, investment in Russia or Austria. Dutch investors were not interested in the day-to-day operations of the railroads they had invested in. As long as interest and dividend were being paid they were content to leave management in the hands of Americans. And if the need for more direct control was felt, as in cases of bankruptcy, they took measures to protect their interests. Only around the turn of the century did Dutch interest in American railroads diminish as other American industries promised a better return on the money.

A transfer of technology from Europe — especially from Britain — to America, apart from the very first years in the 1830s, is not visible. In the opposite direction, American technology hardly influenced Dutch railway engineers, and the railway worlds of the Netherlands and the U.S. were vastly different. Only toward the end of the nineteenth century some influence can be traced in the fields of electrification and signaling. The Dutch were not very much interested in American politics as long as the country's financial stability was not threatened. But issues such as doubts about the monetary soundness of the country in the 1890s did disturb the market and held up the flow of money across the Atlantic for a short time. There hardly seems to be any link between Dutch immigration and investment. The states with the largest Dutch populations such as Michigan and Iowa did not attract substantially more Dutch capital, proportionally, than states or territories such as Kansas, Minnesota, Washington, or New Mexico. And although there were areas of investment other than railroads, the latter were so overwhelmingly important that it is easy to forget that other possibilities for gainful employment of surplus capital in the United States did exist.

What remains of this huge Dutch investment in American railroads are a couple of names of towns along some of the lines. The Kansas City Southern, with its enormous Dutch interest, provides the most visible proof. To name but a few: Amsterdam, MO; Mena, AR, named for Queen Wilhelmina who was expected to visit but never came;[16] De Queen, AR, named for Jan de Goeijen, the man who sluiced the Dutch millions into Stilwell's dream and whose name no American could pronounce correctly; Zwolle and DeRidder in Louisiana; and last but not least Nederland, TX, near the KCS terminus of Port Arthur, and also a settlement of Dutchmen from the East Indies, who introduced artificial irrigation to grow rice. And in rural Oklahoma the towns of Vanoss and Middleberg are clear proof of the Dutch involvement in the ill-fated Oklahoma Central Railway.[17]

1   P. J. van Winter, *Het aandeel van den Amsterdamschen handel aan den opbouw van het Amerikaansche Gemeenebest*, 2 vols. (The Hague: Martinus Nijhoff, 1927-33), 1:82-83; 2:197-222.

2   Martin G. Buist, *At Spes non Fracta: Hope & Co. 1770-1815* (The Hague: Martinus Nijhoff, 1974), 57-62, 188-190; K. D. Bosch, *De Nederlandse beleggingen in de Verenigde Staten* (Amsterdam: Elsevier, 1948), 35-36.

3   Paul D. Evans, *The Holland Land Company* (Buffalo, NY: Buffalo Historical Publications, 1924), and a short survey in Wilhelmina C. Pieterse, *Inventory of the Archives of the Holland Land Company 1789-1869* (Amsterdam: Municipal Archives, 1976).

4   Joost Jonker, *Merchants, Bankers, Middlemen. The Amsterdam Money Market During the First Half of the 19th Century* (Amsterdam: NEHA, 1996); Also Walter H. Salzman, *A Market to Explore. A History of Public-Private Partnership in the Promotion of Trade and Investment between the Netherlands and the United States* (Amsterdam: Netherlands Chamber of Commerce in the United States, 1994).

5   H. C. Wytzes, *En het geld verantwoordt alles. Een financiële geschiedenis van het Koninkrijk der Nederlanden* (Amsterdam: VU Uitgeverij, 2002), 38-48.

6   Augustus J. Veenendaal, Jr., *Slow Train to Paradise. How Dutch Investors Helped Build American Railroads* (Stanford, CA: Stanford University Press, 1996), 27.

7   Figures from John F. Stover, *American Railroads* (Chicago: University of Chicago Press, 1997), 205.

8   Melville J. Ulmer, *Capital in Transportation, Communications, and Public Utilities: Its Formation and Financing* (Princeton, NJ: Princeton University Press, 1960), 256-259.

9   Mira Wilkins, *The History of Foreign Investment in the United States to 1914* (Cambridge, MA: Harvard University Press, 1970); Dorothy R. Adler, *British Investment in American Railways 1838-1898* (Charlottesville: University Press of Virginia, 1970). A short overview is H. W. van den Doel, "'Het pandaemonium van alle booze geesten der heb- en geldzucht.' Nederlandse beleggers en Amerikaanse spoorwegen in de negentiende eeuw," in H. W. van den Doel and G. van Boom, eds., *In het verleden behaalde resultaten. Bijdragen tot de Nederlandse beleggingsgeschiedenis* (Amsterdam: Bert Bakker, 2002), 123-147.

10 It was estimated that no less than twenty-six million Dutch guilders (nominal value) had been invested in Stilwell's companies. The KCP &G was reorganized in 1900 as the Kansas City Southern, still with large Dutch holdings. See Augustus J. Veenendaal, Jr., "The Kansas City Southern Railway and the Dutch Connection," *Business History Review* 61.2 (Summer 1987): 291-316.

11 Jim B. Pearson, *The Maxwell Land Grant* (Norman: University of Oklahoma Press, 1961).

12 Jacob van Hinte, *Netherlanders in America: A Study of Emigration and Settlement in the Nineteenth and Twentieth Centuries in the United States of America* (Grand Rapids, MI: Baker Book House, 1985), 679-687.

13 Augustus J. Veenendaal, Jr., "Dutch Towns in the United States of America," in Robert S. Kirsner, ed., *The Low Countries and Beyond.* Publications of the American Association for Netherlandic Studies nr. 5 (Lanham, MD: University Press of America, 1993), 309-322.

14 Kenny A. Franks, *History of the Oklahoma Petroleum Industry* (Norman: University of Oklahoma Press, 1982); Augustus J. Veenendaal, Jr., "The Dutch Connection. Salomon Frederik van Oss and Dutch Investment in Oklahoma," *The Chronicles of Oklahoma* 65 (Fall 1987): 252-267.

15 All figures from Wilkins, *The History*, 156, and Veenendaal, *Slow Train to Paradise*, 171-175.

2

——

16 Queen Wilhelmina State Park on
Rich Mountain, near Mena, AR, still is
a famous resort. A large portrait of the
queen is part of the gateway.

17 Vanoss was named for S. F. van Oss
(1868–1949), Dutch financial journalist
and author, stockbroker, and founder of
the weekly *Haagsche Post*; Middleberg
was named for Gerrit A. A. Middelberg
(1846–1916), Dutch engineer and former
director of the Netherlands South
African Railway Company, who
inspected the Oklahoma Central Railway
in 1905 and again in 1907 at the request
of Van Oss. See Augustus J. Veenendaal,
Jr., "Railroads, Oil and Dutchmen.
Investing in the Oklahoma Frontier,"
The Chronicles of Oklahoma 63 (Spring
1985): 4-27.

THE NEW IMMIGRATION

—

ROBERT P. SWIERENGA

The Netherlands poet Everhardus Jan Potgieter plumbed the national mood in 1855 when he penned these lines: "Go to the United States, friends! ... Westward the Star points the way."[1] America was the land of rising expectations with plenty of "free land," while at home land was scarce, times hard, and the Golden Age only a distant memory. Some two hundred thousand compatriots — 75 percent of all overseas emigrants, followed Potgieter's advice and settled in the United States before Congress in 1921 closed the "golden door" with the first quota law. Yet, this was a comparatively low rate of only seventy-two per one hundred thousand average Netherlands population from 1820 to 1920. Except in a few villages, the Dutch never contracted "America fever," as did the Irish and Italians. Most Dutch stayed close to home and hearth, or they crossed into neighboring countries, notably Germany and Belgium. Among European nations, the Netherlands ranked only tenth in the proportion of its population that emigrated overseas in the nineteenth century, and in the United States the Dutch were seventeenth among foreign-born groups.[2]

Overseas migration from Western Europe to the United States, according to Brinley Thomas's classic work, *Migration and Economic Growth* (1954), rose and fell with the business cycle in the larger Atlantic economy. Peaks came during prosperous times, and the intervening troughs during depressions or wartime. Hence, secular migration trends tended to be similar across national boundaries. Dutch emigration had four major gulfs from 1840 to 1920, each lasting about a decade. The first, from 1847 to 1857, brought religious Seceders from the Hervormde Kerk (Reformed Church) by the thousands. Persecuted for their faith and penurious from the failure of the potato and rye crops, they sought a brighter future in a nation with religious liberty and cheap land. The second spurt, a lesser one, began after the American Civil War and continued to 1873. It attracted more farmers, as did the third peak — the greatest of all, which ran from 1880 to 1893, when an agricultural crisis thrust tens of thousands of farm workers off the clay soils along the North Sea coast due to mechanization

2

—

and land consolidation. The final upsurge, from 1903 to 1913, saw more immigrants end up as urban factory workers in the silk mills of Paterson, NJ, the Pullman shops in Calumet, IL, and the furniture factories of Grand Rapids, MI. The latecomers had little choice. By 1900, most land on the frontier suitable for homesteading was in private hands. Financial panics and hard times ended the first, second, and third migration waves in 1857, 1873, and 1893, respectively. From 1860 to 1865, the Civil War was the main deterrent, and from 1914 to 1919, World War I made crossing the Atlantic too hazardous.[3]

That free land was the magnet for Netherlanders is evident from the fact that 80 percent of all overseas emigrants hailed from the *platteland* (countryside) and 90 percent settled in the United States, until the mid-1890s when the government declared the frontier was "closed." This news sent many to the Dutch East Indies, and to a lesser extent, to Canada, South America, and South Africa. From 1900 to 1920, only 56 percent entered the United States, and most settled in large cities with jobs to offer. The "American-centeredness" of Dutch immigrants was in the upper range among northern European countries.

The Dutch provinces with the most emigrants before 1900 had relatively low population densities — Zeeland, Gelderland, Groningen, and (after 1880) Friesland — and, with the exception of Gelderland, were devastated by the agricultural depression of the 1880s. The interior sandy-soiled provinces of Overijssel and Drenthe never contributed much to overseas destinations. Neither did the culturally distinct Catholic provinces of Noord-Brabant and Limburg. Considerably fewer emigrants, relatively, left from the large and populous urban provinces — Noord- and Zuid-Holland and Utrecht. Collectively, this urban area with the major seaports and government center, contributed only one-fourth to the total emigration. Only after 1900, when the Dutch economy belatedly experienced an industrial "take-off," to use Walter Rostow's phrase, did emigration from the *Randstad* surpass that from the rural provinces. Many were civil servants, hardly typical emigrants, departing for Dutch colonies in the Far East and the Caribbean.

Scholars have long debated whether immigrants to the United States were "uprooted" or "transplanted," to use gardening images. Oscar Handlin, in his Pulitzer Prize-winning book, *The Uprooted* (1951), portrayed the mostly eastern European immigrants as being torn from their homelands by pogroms, wars, and brutal discrimination, and crammed into teeming tenements and sweatshops in New York and other East Coast cities. Were Handlin's ghettoized immigrants typical? Certainly not for the Dutch. John Bodnar's book, *The Transplanted* (1985), better describes their experience.

Whether Christian or Jewish, Dutch immigration was a folk movement. Families booked passage in religious groups and settled together in rural colonies and city neighborhoods, where they quickly reestablished cultural institutions and familial networks — churches and synagogues, schools, cemeteries, benevolent societies, social clubs, and ethnic businesses. Studies of the United States ship-passenger manifests show that 80 percent of Dutch immigrants from 1840 to 1880 traveled with immediate family members, mostly parents with children, sometimes joined by siblings, grandparents, uncles and aunts, and cousins. The familial Dutch migration surpasses that from Germany and Scandinavia by 15 to 30 points, but Dutch household heads were older than those from other northern European countries. The average age of the Dutch couples was thirty-eight years for husbands and thirty-six for wives. Unlike northern Europe generally, Dutch immigration shifted belatedly from a folk to a labor migration. After 1895, the proportion of singles climbed above 30 percent, reaching 50 percent briefly during World War I. As late as 1920, however, two-thirds of the Dutch still emigrated with immediate family members. Dutch immigration was definitely a "family affair." It was pre-industrial and rural, sustained by traditional clannishness and familial loyalty.

Occupations lend further support to the folk argument. Before 1880, two-thirds were farmers, farm laborers, and day laborers; one-fifth worked in pre-industrial crafts. Only one in twenty was an industrial worker. White-collar workers — professionals, business executives, clerks, and government officials — together comprised only 10 percent of emigrant households. Thus, 85 percent of the emigrants were blue-collar workers. The sluggish pace of Dutch industrialization adversely affected these rural craftsmen and farm laborers, and America held out the allure of cheap farmland and high-paying factory jobs. To use the common "push-pull" metaphor, the American "magnet" pulled Netherlanders more than Dutch "devils" pushed them out.

Settlement Patterns

The Dutch typified the "chain migration" that was common among northern European immigrants. The trailblazers sent back "bacon letters" urging family members to join them in a place where they could eat fat pork and white bread lathered in butter. The truth was that the pioneers were lonely and desperately wanted to rebuild the family life they enjoyed in the old country. They also needed confirmation that they had done the right thing by leaving the motherland. Thus, they offered to help kith and kin get a new start in a land of economic opportunity and personal freedom. The tens of thousands of these "America letters" almost guaranteed that fresh immigrants would follow family and friends. The private networks of communication also led to a high concentration of families from particular Dutch villages and cities settling in specific colonies and urban neighborhoods in America.

That migration was planned and not random is evident by microanalyses at the local level of nominal records in both countries. Dutch emigrants originated in a select few villages. Of the 1,156 administrative units (*gemeenten*) in 1869 — the equivalent of American townships — only 134, or 12 percent, provided nearly three-quarters of all overseas emigrants in the period from 1820 to 1880; 55 municipalities (5 percent) sent out one-half, and a mere 22 municipalities (2 percent) furnished one-third. The major source fields were in the eastern Gelderse Achterhoek and Veluwe; the northern sea-clay regions of Friesland and Groningen; the southwest islands of Goeree-Overflakkee (Zuid-Holland), and West Zeeuws-Vlaanderen, Walcheren, Schouwen-Duiveland, and Zuid-Beveland (Zeeland); and the southeast Brabantse Peel region centered in Uden.[4]

Dutch settlements in North America were equally concentrated. In 1870, after sixty to seventy thousand immigrants had arrived, 60 percent lived in only twenty-two counties in seven midwestern and mid-Atlantic states; and 38 percent resided in only forty-six townships and city wards. Few immigrant groups, if any, were as concentrated as the Dutch. The primary settlement field was within a fifty-mile radius of southern Lake Michigan from Muskegon, Grand Rapids, Holland, and Kalamazoo on the east shore, to Chicago, Milwaukee, Sheboygan, and Green Bay on the west shore. Secondary settlement areas lay in central Iowa, southeastern Minnesota, and the New York City region, including northern New Jersey.

Many Seceder pastors led their congregants to America, e.g., Albertus C. Van Raalte to Holland; Cornelius Vander Meulen to Zeeland; Seine Bolks to Overisel; and Marten Ypma to Vriesland, all in Michigan ; Henry P. Scholte to Pella, IA; and in Wisconsin, Pieter Zonne to Cedar Grove, Gerrit Baay to Alto, and Theodorus Van den Broek to Little Chute. This funneling process, like a megaphone, amplified Dutch visibility in America. Subsequently, the Dutch dispersed themselves over a wider area of the Great Plains and Far West in search of cheap farmland. But initially, few immigrant groups clustered more than Hollanders. Their U.S. focus and clannish colonization created a choice environment in which to nurture and sustain a strong sense of Dutchness for many generations. Rob Kroes rightly titled his book on the Dutch Calvinist colony of Amsterdam, MT, *The Persistence of Ethnicity*.

The initial colonies of 1847 — Holland and Zeeland, MI; Pella, IA; South Holland, IL; Milwaukee and Sheboygan, WI; and Clymer, NY — continued until 1900 to attract at least three-fourths of their compatriots. The Holland colony rapidly expanded across most of Ottawa and northern Allegan counties. The Michigan map by 1870 sported many Netherlands place names — Zeeland, Drenthe, Vriesland, Overisel, Groningen, Zutphen, Niekerk, North Holland, South Holland, New Holland, Harlem, Borculo, and Hardewyk. Pella spread into Yankee areas up to twenty miles distant. In 1847, Dutch neighborhoods also took shape in

Map of nineteenth-century Dutch settlements in the Midwest.

cities along the inland travel routes — New York City, Albany, Rochester, Buffalo, Cleveland, Cincinnati, Chicago, Grand Rapids, Kalamazoo, and St. Louis.

The key to the survival and growth of the successful colonies and ethnic neighborhoods was to have a vital Reformed church at the center of community life. Colonies that failed, such as Lancaster, NY, Friesland, MN, Friesland, SD, Muscatine, IA, and Franklin and La Crosse, WI, shared a common denominator: the lack of a viable church. In colonies and in large city neighborhoods, an ethnoreligious identity persisted for many generations where churches and Christian day schools provided the glue. Otherwise, the natural tendency to assimilate and disperse into the majority English culture inevitably broke the bonds.

A microlevel analysis of the migration streams reveals a surprisingly narrow focus. In Grand Rapids, MI, the quintessential Dutch-American large city where 40 percent of the population was of Dutch birth or ancestry in 1900, they were concentrated in twelve distinct neighborhoods, sorted largely by provincial or regional origins, e.g., a "little Groningen," a "little Friesland," or a "little Zeeland." The silk city of Paterson hosted 70 percent of all immigrants from Goeree-Overflakkee. Almost 90 percent of the emigrants from the wheat-growing regions of the Hoekse Waard (Klaaswaal and Westmaas) in Zuid-Holland and Vijfheerenlanden (Vianen) in the province of Utrecht settled in Pella. Half of all the emigrants from the province of Utrecht followed Scholte to Pella. Groningers went to Chicago, Muskegon, Kalamazoo, and Lafayette, IN, in large numbers.[5]

Frisians, always more independent-minded, scattered more than most; yet in the northern municipalities of Ferwerderadeel, Barradeel, and Kollumerland, 80, 70 and 60 percent, respectively, settled in Grand Rapids and Vriesland, MI. Emigrants from Het Bildt and Westdongeradeel preferred the "Frisian Hoek" at Pella. Mennonites from Gaasterland settled in Goshen, IN. Over 90 percent of emigrants from the province of Drenthe settled in the Michigan village of that name. The same proportion from the Overijssel villages of Staphorst, Hellendoorn, Den Ham, Nieuwleusen, and Zwolle went to west Michigan.[6]

Dutch immigrants in larger cities repeated the old-country pattern of living near kith and kin from the same province or region. In Cleveland, Gelderlanders kept to the west side of the Cuyahoga River, Overijsselers to the east side.[7] In Chicago, the Groninger Hoek on the west side contrasted with the Noord-Holland and Frisian character of Roseland on the south side, and the Zuid-Holland farming colony of South Holland in the far-southern reaches. In the celery fields of Kalamazoo, Overijsselers farmed the muck soils south of the city and Groningers the muck lands to the north. Studies of other cities would likely show similar residential patterns in the first generation. Over time, the provincial distinctions disappeared, and by the third generation a shared identity as Dutch held the groups together.

From the 1870s to the 1910s, Dutch immigrants seeking cheap farmland settled all across the northern Great Plains and West Coast as far as Lynden, WA,
and Hanford, CA. They often joined earlier Dutch immigrants or their adult children, who had ran out of room in the established colonies and planted daughter colonies farther west. The first families to settle at Amsterdam, MT, in the
early 1890s, for example, originated in a few municipalities in Groningen (Spijk
and Bedum) and Friesland (Dokkum and Ee).[8] They were joined by earlier immigrants who found land prices too high in the pioneer colonies, or farming too
difficult in semi-arid regions with grasshopper plagues and periods of drought.
Pella was a "beehive ready for swarming" by 1869 and energetic men set off to
plant new colonies in northwest Iowa. Within a decade, settlers there moved
further west across the Missouri River into South Dakota and into southwestern Minnesota.[9] In the 1870s, Dutch Catholics from Little Chute and De Pere,
WI, led by John Verboort, founded the first Dutch colony on the Pacific Coast, at
Verboort, OR. Reformed families from the area of Sheboygan, WI, in the 1880s
migrated westward to Sioux County, IA, and eventually to Lynden and Oak Harbor, WA, on the Puget Sound. Dutch celery growers on the muck lands of Kalamazoo, MI, in the 1920s were attracted to Hollandale, MN, when its ditched and
drained wetlands became available for celery production.

Catholic and Jewish Immigrants

Dutch Catholic and Jewish immigrants did not cluster in colonies to the same
extent as the Reformed, but some did settle near family and friends and organize nationality congregations and societies. Catholics, who made up one-fifth
of the Dutch immigrants, formed a number of colonies. Little Chute, WI, was
the seminal one in 1847, led by Father Van den Broek, which spawned satellite
settlements at De Pere, Hollandtown, and Appleton. Other Dutch Catholics
clustered in cities along the inland travel routes, where they found a welcome
at German-language parishes or founded Dutch-language parishes, as they did
on Cleveland's west side and in Cincinnati, in Bay City and Grand Rapids, MI, in
Kensington, IL, and in Benton Carver near Minneapolis.[10]

Most Catholic emigrants hailed from specific municipalities in Limburg
and Noord-Brabant and again chose very specific destinations. The Peel region
of Noord-Brabant, centered in the municipalities of Uden, Zeeland, and Boekel
— the major source area in 1847 — sent its emigrants to the Fox River Valley of
Wisconsin. In Limburg, those from municipalities north of Roermond joined
fellow religionists in Wisconsin, while those from municipalities south of that
city went exclusively to Carver County, MN. Catholics had a strong sense of localism, tradition, and family ties, and their priests discouraged congregants from

301

going to Protestant America, where they were at risk of being lost to the faith. Hence, they were underrepresented among emigrants. Catholics comprised 38 percent of the Netherlands population in 1849, but made up only 18 percent of the overseas emigrants before 1880. They were clearly adverse to long-distance moves. Economic forces also militated against emigration. Farmers in Noord-Brabant and Limburg were heavily engaged in the home production of textiles as part of the thriving industry of the region. Home industry augmented farm income and provided a greater measure of stability against fluctuating food prices. Many Catholic laborers also found temporary work in nearby German and Belgian factories.

In America, Dutch Catholics founded few colonies that survived more than one generation. As of 1870, less than one-third of Catholics lived in colonies, compared to three-quarters for Protestants. More than one-third of Catholics settled in cities and dispersed widely. By 1920, Dutch Catholics had founded only twenty-five congregations with Dutch-speaking priests, while Dutch Calvinists had founded five hundred congregations and most still worshiped in the Dutch language. Significantly, Catholics worshiped in a Latin liturgy common to all, and their churches were ubiquitous. The Dutch Reformed had to worship separately. In short, religion encouraged dispersal for Dutch Catholics and concentration for Dutch Calvinists.

Jewish immigrants, like Catholics, shared a common liturgy, either Askenazic or Sephardic. Religion thus gave Jews of all nationalities the freedom to settle anyplace with a consecrated cemetery and synagogue. When numbers warranted, of course, the various nationalities founded ethnic synagogues, whether English, Dutch, German, or Russian, just as did Catholics.[11] Dutch Jews began emigrating during the Napoleonic Wars, several decades earlier than Christians, and comprised 2 percent of nineteenth-century emigrants, which equaled their proportion of the total population. An estimated sixty-five hundred Jews settled in the U.S. between 1800 and 1880. Unlike Christians, who were primarily rural to rural migrants, Dutch Jews were urban to urban migrants. Most hailed from the *Randstad*, notably Amsterdam, and settled in large East Coast cities such as New York, Philadelphia, Baltimore, and Boston, or in Chicago and other Great Lakes cities, and in San Francisco and Los Angeles.

Dutch Jews were the forerunners of Judaism in the United States and led in the formation of cemeteries, synagogues, schools, and social organizations. As early as 1830, first-generation Dutch Jews comprised one-half of the Jewish families on New York's Lower East Side, and one-third on Philadelphia's northern and southern periphery and Baltimore's Fells Point district. The Frisian immigrant, the Reverend Samuel Myer Isaacs, long-time rabbi of Temple Shaarey Tefila in New York City, was renowned as the "father of the American [Jewish] clergy." The Reverend Simon Cohen Noot of Amsterdam led Bnai Israel, the largest and longest-lived synagogue in New York City. Noot, an educator of the first rank at midcentury, founded Jewish day schools in New York, Philadelphia, and Boston. Another Amsterdam-born rabbi, Jacob Voorsanger, served Temple Emanu-El in San Francisco, the largest and most prestigious on the West Coast, and mentored the brilliant Judah Magnes. The Peixotto and Magnin families became department store magnates in San Francisco.

The occupational profile of Dutch-Jewish immigrants mirrored that of American Jews generally and reflected their urban character. Most were self-employed shopkeepers, peddlers, brokers, and traders. Over time, however, the proportion of merchants declined and craftsmen increased, especially in the needle and tobacco trades. In the early decades, more than four-fifths were shopkeepers and brokers, but by 1870 more than one-half worked in clothing and tobacco sweatshops, and as diamond cutters and polishers on New York's Lower East Side.

Dutch Jews assimilated more rapidly than did Catholics and Calvinists. Many immigrated in a two-stage process, by way of London's East End ghetto, where they lived for a decade or more, and mastered the language and adopted English ways. The family of Samuel Gompers (1850–1924), famed labor leader and founder of the American Federation of Labor, is a typical example. The Gompers family, of Askenazi background, had lived in the Jewish Quarter of Amsterdam for generations. Samuels's grandfather and namesake, Samuel Moses Gompers, was an import-export merchant who traveled five or six times a year between Amsterdam and London. In 1845, amid hard times in Amsterdam, he moved his wife and six children to the Spitalfields district of London's East End, where many relatives had already relocated. Here Samuel was born, the son of Solomon, a cigar maker, and raised in a mixed Dutch and English culture. In 1863, Solomon emigrated to New York City, following family and friends. The Gompers family chain migration was special only in that they went via London, as did many Dutch Jews. The Dutch joined the wider Jewish mainstream of American commerce, but unlike German Jews, who had a penchant for Reform Judaism, the Dutch clung to Amsterdam's orthodox traditionalism. Like Dutch immigrants generally, they were family-oriented and looked to the extended family for assistance in migration, in business dealings, and for perpetuating the Dutch cuisine. Samuel Gompers, for example, always spoke glowingly of his mother's "Dutch kitchen."

Immigrant Entrepreneurship

Several Protestant businessmen rose to early prominence. Paulus Den Blyker of Noord-Holland invested in lands and homes in and around Kalamazoo and died a wealthy man, as did the Reverend Van Raalte, who platted and sold all the town lots in the Holland colony and died with a large estate.[12] Theodore F. Koch of Amsterdam, a dealer in railroad lands based in St. Paul, MN, sold more than one million acres in that state, many to Dutch immigrants. Koch developed the successful marketing technique of donating land in station towns and building churches, recognizing that Dutch Reformed immigrants gravitated to places with churches.[13] In Chicago Frisian immigrant Folkert Kuyper, who changed his name to Frank Cooper, in 1887 cofounded the Siegel-Cooper Department Store on State Street, which within a decade boasted of being "the largest retail establishment in the world."[14] Edward W. Bok (1863–1930), whose family immigrated to Brooklyn, NY, in 1870, for thirty years (1889–1919) held the editorship of the influential women's magazine, the *Ladies' Home Journal,* and from this "bully pulpit" helped shape mass culture in America. Bok was the most famous Dutch American in the early twentieth century.[15] In Grand Rapids, four interrelated families founded Christian book-publishing companies that gained national dominance: Eerdmans, Zondervan, Baker, and Kregel.

Conclusion

Dutch immigrants in America, like most ethnic groups, derived their sharp sense of identity from religion. In church and synagogue, they practiced the "communion of the saints" in ways real and symbolic, but none more than the Reformed immigrants, who made up 80 percent of all immigrants from the Netherlands in the nineteenth century. As a covenanted community, they clung together for worship, school, work, and play. The ethnoreligious "glue" dissolved first among second-generation Catholics and Jews, whose universal religious rituals attracted immigrants of every nationality. Because Reformed immigrants worshiped in the mother tongue, the third generation was the first to break the cultural mold, and many in the fourth and fifth generation still treasure their Dutchness, even if diluted by American ways.

1   E.J. Potgieter, "Landverhuizing naar the Vereenigde Staten," *De Gids* (1855).

2   Robert P. Swierenga, *Faith and Family, Dutch Immigration and Settlement in the United States, 1820–1920* (New York: Holmes & Meier, 2000), chapter 2. The actual number of immigrants from 1840 to 1920 might be as large as two hundred fifty thousand, because inadequate record-keeping systems by both national governments allowed thousands to migrate without civil functionaries recording them as such (ibid., 293-309).

3   Three general histories are Jacob van Hinte, *Nederlanders in Amerika: Een studie over landverhuizing en volkplanters in de 19de en 20ste eeuw in de Vereenigde Staten van Amerika*, 2 vols. (Groningen: P. Noordhoff, 1928), with an English edition by Robert P. Swierenga, gen. ed., and Adriaan de Wit, trans., *Netherlanders in America: A Study of Emigration and Settlement in the Nineteenth and Twentieth Centuries in the United States of America* (Grand Rapids, MI: Baker Book House, 1985); Henry S. Lucas, *Netherlanders in America: Dutch Immigration to the United States and Canada, 1789-1950* (Ann Arbor: University of Michigan Press, 1955); and Hans Krabbendam, *Vrijheid in het verschiet: Nederlandse emigratie naar Amerika, 1840–1940* (Hilversum: Verloren, 2006). A specialized account is Suzanne M. Sinke, *Dutch Immigrant Women in the United States, 1880–1920* (Urbana/Chicago: University of Illinois Press, 2002).

4   Robert P. Swierenga, "Exodus Netherlands, Promised Land America: Dutch Immigration and Settlement in the United States," in J.W. Schulte Nordholt and Robert P. Swierenga, eds., *A Bilateral Bicentennial: A History of Dutch-American Relations, 1792–1982* (Amsterdam: Octagon Books/Meulenhoff, 1982), 127-147.

5   David G. Vander Stel, "The Dutch of Grand Rapids, Michigan, 1848–1900: Immigrant Neighborhood and Community Development in a Nineteenth-Century City" (Ph.D. dissertation, Kent State University, 1983); Robert P. Swierenga, *Dutch Chicago: A History of the Hollanders in the Windy City* (Grand Rapids, MI: Eerdmans, 2002).

6   Annemieke Galema. *Frisians to America, 1880–1914: With the Baggage of the Fatherland* (Groningen: REGIO-Project Uitgevers, 1996).

7   Robert P. Swierenga, "Religious Diversity and Cultural Localism: The Dutch in Cleveland, 1840–1990," *Northwest Ohio Quarterly* 67 (Summer 1995): 1-29.

8   Rob Kroes, *The Persistence of Ethnicity: Dutch Calvinist Pioneers in Amsterdam, Montana* (Urbana/Chicago: University of Illinois Press, 1992).

9   Brian W. Beltman, *Dutch Farmer in the Missouri Valley, 1866–1950* (Urbana/Chicago: University of Illinois Press, 1996).

10 Yda Schreuder, *Dutch Catholic Immigrant Settlement in Wisconsin, 1850–1905* (New York/London: Garland, 1989); Henry A.V.M. van Stekelenburg, *Landverhuizing als regionaal verschijnsel van Noord-Brabant naar Noord-Amerika.* (Tilburg: Stichting Zuidelijk Historisch Contact, 1991); Henry A.V.M. van Stekelenburg, *"Hier is alles vooruitgang": Landverhuizing van Noord-Brabant naar Noord-Amerika, 1880–1940* (Tilburg: Stichting Zuidelijk Historisch Contact, 1996).

11 Robert P. Swierenga, *The Forerunners: Dutch Jewry in the North American Diaspora* (Detroit: Wayne State University Press, 1994).

12 Robert P. Swierenga, "Albertus C. Van Raalte as a Businessman," in Jacob E. Nyenhuis, ed., *A Goodly Heritage: Essays in Honor of the Reverend Dr. Elton J. Bruins at Eighty* (Grand Rapids, MI: Eerdmans, 2007), 281-317.

2

——

13 For the land dealings of Theodore F. Koch, see Robert Schoone-Jongen, "A Time to Gather, a Time to Scatter: Dutch American Settlement in Minnesota, 1885–1910" (Ph.D. dissertation, University of Delaware, 2007); and Robert P. Schoone-Jongen, "Cheap Land and Community: Theodore F. Koch, Dutch Colonizer," *Minnesota History* 53 (Summer 1993): 214-224.

14 Swierenga, *Dutch Chicago*, 663-665.

15 Hans Krabbendam, *The Model Man: A Life of Edward W. Bok, 1863–1930* (Amsterdam/Atlanta, GA: Rodopi, 2001).

DUTCH PIONEERS
AND NATIVE AMERICANS

—

PIETER HOVENS

Introduction: The Frontier and Indian Removal

When surveying the involvement of the Dutch in the history and development of the new American nation, one cannot but wonder about the specific role they played in the process of the westward-moving frontier, especially after the American Revolution, in the settlement of the West, and in the development of regions in which substantial numbers of emigrants from the Netherlands settled and rooted. Little attention has been paid to the encounters and relations between the Dutch newcomers and the Native American peoples in the nineteenth century when such contacts were most varied, numerous, intimate. Two main factors determined the character of Indian-Dutch relations in that century: federal Indian policy and regional conditions.[1]

Dutch investment into the development of the new nation was intensive, and thus influenced the future of the native peoples of the eastern states in an indirect but fundamental way. In 1803, during Jefferson's presidency, the Louisiana Purchase was funded primarily by Dutch financial institutions. As a consequence the territory of the U.S. doubled in size, the native tribes of the Plains came under American jurisdiction, the forced removal of eastern tribes to the west became possible, and expansionist ideology was invigorated, soon incorporating the whole North American continent from the Atlantic to the Pacific.

The Indian Removal policy was instituted in 1830 during the administration of President Andrew Jackson, and aimed at the forced resettlement of tribes from the eastern United States to the trans-Mississippi West, for a short time appropriately named Indian Territory. Soon, however, the perimeters of the territory began shrinking and finally were confined to what is now the state of Oklahoma. The Creeks faced the consequences first and were forcibly removed from Alabama in 1836. President Martin Van Buren, of Dutch descent, inherited and continued this policy during his 1837–41 tenure. During the fall and winter seasons of 1831–34 the majority of the Mississippi Choctaws were removed under the supervision of the army. The Chickasaws were forced from Mississippi to Indian Territory in the winter of 1837–38. Many Carolina Cherokees marched along their Trail of Tears to Indian Territory in 1838. The removal of the Seminoles was taken on next. Van Buren had to replace Indian Commissioner Carey Allen Harris at the War Department when this official proved to gain financially from Indian removal. Thomas H. Crawford, a reputable critic of graft in the Indian Office, took his place. Van Buren repeatedly drew upon his Dutch-American network to fill official positions, also in the Indian Service.[2]

The Upper Midwest: Immigration and Settlement

The Dutch immigrants who arrived in the United States in the 1840s settled primarily in Wisconsin, Michigan, and Iowa, on the western margins of the Eastern Woodlands, the region from where soon a new generation moved further westward to settle on the Plains and beyond. The Dutch settled sufficiently close to the frontier to experience, for at least a number of years, frequent encounters with Indians who had a hard time being forced to part with their land, not only physically and geographically, but spiritually and emotionally as well.

The Black Lake region of Alleghan County in southwestern Michigan became the focus of Dutch Secessionist settlers led by Reverend Van Raalte in 1847. This was the territory of the Ottawa Indians of Chief Waukazoo. Their main camp in this region was on Point Superior on the north side of Black Lake. Chief Macketenenessy (Black Hawk), Waukazoo's brother, camped above Big Rapids on the Muskegon River. The Ottawas secured their livelihood by hunting, fishing, and gathering. With the advance of white settlement, they became involved in the fur trade, trapped over a wide area in Michigan and adjacent areas, trading mostly at Arbre Croche. The title to their lands was extinguished by the Treaty of Chicago in 1821, in return for a small reservation and a perpetual annual payment in cash. In 1835 white colonists began to settle the Black Lake region, and when Michigan gained statehood two years later pressure was put on the Ottawas to vacate their lands and move to their reservation. Old Wing Indian Mission and School were established in the Black Lake region in 1838 by a Congregationalist minister, George Nelson Smith. Two years later many Ottawas perished in a smallpox epidemic, and dysentery took its toll in 1845.

In January 1847, Van Raalte purchased several lots in Ottawa County for Dutch immigrants and the new settlement was named Holland. He enlisted Indians to provide lumber for the construction of log homes. In the spring and summer a large contingent of Dutchmen arrived and took up residence in the area, some even occupying vacant Indian wigwams and cabins. A smallpox epidemic struck the Dutch colony that very first summer, and the Indians suffered great losses. Relations with the local Ottawas became especially strained: the Dutchmen's cattle and hogs were left roaming through the woods, plundering and destroying the corn, potato, and melon fields of the Indians, while sugar-making equipment was repeatedly destroyed by roaming livestock as well. Construction of log cabins had priority over fencing in the animals. Some efforts at containing the cattle and pigs were undertaken, but these were too limited to prevent frequent destruction of Ottawa gardens. In retaliation, the Indians felt free to plunder corncribs, pigsties, and smokehouses of Dutch settlers. Additional problems stemmed from alcohol abuse and resultant deviant behavior by the Ottawas, and internal strife between Indians favoring either Catholicism or Protestantism. Eventually, Chief Peter Waukazoo persuaded his people to resettle on their assigned reservation where they might rebuild their lives. They ceded their lands in the Black region to Van Raalte for $208 on June 24, 1848, and departed for their reservation on Grand Traverse Bay, accompanied by Reverend Smith. Soon the Dutch immigrants spread to satellite communities in the southwestern part of Michigan.[3]

In 1847 Reverend Scholte took his followers across the Atlantic to establish a new home in the Red Rock region of central Iowa. According to Scholte's sources, the Meskwaki (a.k.a. Fox) Indians had been removed to Kansas. On October 16, 1842, the lands west of the Red Rock Line had been opened to settlement. In Marion County, IA, Reverend Scholte found and purchased free and fertile lands, and founded Pella. The Dutch soon discovered, however, that Meskwaki Indians were still present in the area, a cause for some anxiety among the newcomers. Groups of Indians had stayed behind and tried to survive without any recognized title to land by traditional hunting, fishing, and the gathering of wild foods. Wildlife was still available but dwindling because of growing population pressure from white settlers. Deer and rabbits were the mainstay of the Indians' diet, which was complemented by fish, wild fruits, and nuts. The small-scale horticulture from which they had derived part of their staple food became virtually impossible. The influx of white settlers into Marion County immediately had its tragic consequences when a flue epidemic broke out in the winter of 1847–48 and many Indians died.

The Indians and Dutch settlers in central Iowa engaged in trade, the natives offering ponies in exchange for western foodstuffs and clothing. The history of encounters between Indians and Dutch settlers in Marion County is one of friendly relations, only marred by anxiety on the part of the settlers. Such anxiety was only too understandable, as the natives represented the fearsome wild men of the woods, so pervasive in European folklore. Moreover, they were heathens, given to idolatry, even devil worship, according to a common belief among Christians. Essentially, their humanity was cast in doubt. Moreover, the colonists realized that they were settling on former Indian lands, and that the previous occupants had been forced to accept unilaterally dictated treaty stipulations and removal. In some cases they had even been defeated in armed encounters. The immigrants had an inkling of how the Indians must have felt about their arrival and settlement, and this caused some trepidation. A *modus vivendi* emerged, though, and a pattern of peaceful intermittent contacts and social interaction ensued in which trade dominated relations.[4]

2

THE
NINETEENTH
CENTURY

The Dakotas: The Sioux Frontier

The Dutch emigrant communities in Michigan, Wisconsin, and central Iowa prospered. Soon all the available land was settled and cultivated, and land prices increased at a rapid pace. For newcomers, the only available option was to cast their eye further west: Dakota Territory. The main obstacle, though, for moving west was the mighty Dakota or Sioux Nation. These Indians defended their homeland against white encroachment vehemently. Although the Spirit Lake Massacre in 1857 led by Chief Inkpaduta in northwestern Iowa temporarily stopped settlers in their tracks, the Minnesota Indian Uprising in 1862 under Chief Little Crow was harshly quashed. Forty perpetrators faced public execution in Mankato. The Civil War (1861–65) only temporarily delayed the settlement of western Iowa, but from the mid-1860s settlers arrived in droves. The Dutch from Pella pioneered the northwestern corner of the state and founded Orange City, Hospers, and Sioux Center. Encounters between the Dutch and the Sioux in this region were intermittent and occurred mostly when bands of Indians journeyed away from their reservations to hunt, to trade, and to visit relatives farther afield. The settlers often had mixed feelings about the sudden appearance of such traveling Indian groups, fear and attraction competing with each other. However, the Indians were rarely troublesome, and on the whole no conflicts arose from such encounters. [5]

When northwestern Iowa filled up, Dutch-American farmers and newcomers from the Netherlands did move into Dakota Territory. From 1874 they became neighbors of the Yankton and Santee Sioux in Bonne Homme County. In 1882 Dutch Iowans established new communities in Douglas and Charles Mix County. From 1884 groups of Dutch and Dutch Americans settled on the eastern bank of the Middle Missouri River, on opposite sides of the South and North Dakota border in Campbell and Emmons Counties. They became neighbors of the Standing Rock Sioux who lived across the river.[6]

Indian-Dutch encounters in the Dakotas resulted from interethnic competition over resources. Both groups exploited the wild-food resources, game, bird eggs, and wild fruits, depleting resources from overuse. Indians and settlers gathered firewood and cut fence posts, for their own use and for trade. Occasionally, groups of Dutch settlers banded together and surreptitiously trespassed on reservations to cut wood on the banks of the Missouri River. Frequent encounters between the Indians and the Dutch settlers in the Dakotas resulted from mutually profitable trade. The Sioux offered ponies and horses, wild fruits, wild birds' eggs, fence posts and firewood, beaded moccasins, and carved tobacco pipes, as well as woolen coats, blankets (to be sewn into garments), and shawls issued by the government under treaty provisions. The settlers, in exchange, offered items valued by their Sioux trading partners: bread, milk, eggs, chickens, dogs, iron and copper kettles, and sometimes cash. Interethnic trading created hardly any problems and therefore continued for many years, and sometimes decades. In the recreational sphere Indians and Dutch settlers came together at powwows on reservations and during Fourth of July celebrations. Several Dutch settlers in the Dakotas supplemented their farming income by hauling freight for the army garrisons stationed at the forts on or near Indian reservations. Farmers also sold parts of their harvest to the forts where the garrisons needed to be fed, and to the Indian Department, which supplied the food rations to the Sioux. Thus, the Indian presence near the Dutch settlements was a major stimulus for the frontier economy.

The land rush resulting from the establishment of the Great Sioux Reservation soon was followed by settlers' encroachment on Indian land: they let cattle graze across reservation boundaries and planted corn on reservation soil. The Indians regarded this as breaches of treaties, and in 1890 frontier newspapers reported on a Ghost Dance, an imminent Indian uprising led by Sitting Bull. When he was accidentally killed during his arrest, colonists in the Dakotas panicked. Dutch and other settlers near the Sioux reservations left their homes and fled to the nearest railroad town where women and children boarded eastbound trains. On the Pine Ridge Reservation the army wiped out a Sioux encampment. The Indian unrest was quashed by what whites preferred to call the "Battle of Wounded Knee," but what in essence was a massacre.[7]

Allotment: On the Reservation

The General Allotment or Dawes Act of 1884 broke up communal tribal ownership of the land and furthered individual ownership and private enterprise as means of civilizing and Americanizing the Indians. Because of the small size of individual plots and the lack of knowledge necessary to make the land profitable, many individual Indians first leased, and later sold, their land to white farmers. In this way new white landowners came to settle on reservations and lived among the Indian population. A number of Dutch and Dutch Americans thus settled on reservations in Wisconsin, the Dakotas, and Montana. Often, the Indian and white families and communities kept their distance from each other. The loss of their traditional livelihood demoralized the Indians, frequently resulting in an anomic lethargy, so often described by early observers, including Dutch settlers.[8]

Indian Missions

The early American Republic was thoroughly Protestant, the legacy of almost two centuries of predominantly Anglo-Saxon immigration, settlement, and joint ruling by church and state. The new American Constitution clearly separated state and church, and soon after the American Republic gained independence the Catholic Church undertook initiatives to establish a foothold in the new nation. A number of Dutch and Flemish Jesuit priests crossed the Atlantic and several of them began missionary work among the Indian tribes of the trans-Mississippi West.

The Dominican Father Theodore Van den Broek was a Dutch pioneer of Indian missions in the nineteenth century, and in 1836 established the mission of St. John Nepomucene among the Menomini Indians at Little Chute in Wisconsin's Fox River Valley. The priest embarked on a civilization offensive, urging the Indians to give up their migratory existence based on hunting, gathering, and fishing and become sedentary farmers, living in permanent homes and settlements. By laying out a vegetable patch and establishing a small herd of livestock, he taught interested Indians to till the soil and tend animals the American way. Their children would go to school and receive instruction in academic subjects and vocational training. They and their parents would also attend religious instruction and services, before being baptized and becoming Christians. Despite the early success of the mission, the government moved the Indians to a remote reservation at Lake Poygan. A few Indian families remained behind and were joined by Dutch settlers, Van den Broek and Father Godhart catering to the spiritual needs of natives and settlers alike. The Fox River Valley remained attractive to Dutch settlers for several decades, and their numbers in the region gradually increased until 1900. Several of them were instrumental in developing a Catholic mission among the Oneida Indians, west of Green Bay, among whom Dutch priests labored.[9]

On the woodland-plains frontier, Dutch Jesuits began working among the Kickapoos, Potawatomis, and Osages in Iowa and Kansas during the 1830s and 1840s, and further west in the northern Rocky Mountains among the Kalispels, Flatheads, and Kutenais. In the upper Midwest the missionaries were especially successful among the mixed-blood Indians. In the latter part of the nineteenth

Christian Reformed Indian missionaries visiting a Zuni Indian home
in Zuni Pueblo, New Mexico, USA, ca. 1900.

century Dutch Jesuit fathers became involved with missions among the Indians of the northern Plains (Blackfoot, Northern Cheyennes, Arapahos, Crows, Sioux), and continued their involvement in Rocky Mountain missions (Coeur d'Alenes, Nez Percés). Catholic priests from other denominations were active among native peoples in Wisconsin, the Gulf states, Oklahoma, and the Pacific Northwest.

The Dutch Reformed Church has a long but interrupted history of involvement with Indian missions in North America. In the seventeenth century ministers in New Netherland tried to spread the gospel among the Iroquoian and Algonquian tribes in that area, albeit with little success. After the transfer of the colony to the British in 1664, the church concentrated on white settlers only. With the opening of the American West, the call for sending missionaries to the Indian tribes sounded increasingly louder. When the United Missionary Society was formed in 1816 with the express purpose of converting native peoples, the Dutch Reformed Church joined the new institution, and its support for Indian missions consisted of funding initiatives through collections. In 1867 the Dutch denomination in the U.S. was renamed and became the Reformed Church in America (RCA). The RCA supported President Grant's endeavor to rid the Indian administration of corruption and incompetence, and used the opportunity to propose suitable candidates as Indian agents for the Pima and Maricopa Agency and the Colorado River Agency between 1870 and 1880. In 1882 a Women's Executive Committee was organized within the RCA, and from 1895 funds and personnel, partly of Dutch-American background, were gradually made available to several Indian missions in Oklahoma.[10]

The Dutch Christian Reformed Church (CRC) was a relative latecomer to the field of Indian missions because it was a rather small denomination and needed to develop a sound basis for its own parishes first. In 1888 the Synod created a Board of Heathen Missions, but its attempt to establish a mission among the Rosebud Sioux failed. By 1896 sufficient support was available to begin a series of missions among the Navajos and Zunis in Arizona and New Mexico, employing Dutch and Dutch-American ministers and mission personnel. The CRC's work included the translation of religious texts into Navajo and the training of Navajo assistants for missionary work.[11]

In many cases the Dutch and Dutch-American missionaries endeavored to advance Christianity and a western "civilized" lifestyle by providing religious instruction to Indians of all ages, education to children, medical care, vocational training, and clothing and food in periods of hardship. The Indians valued these services because of the precarious economic and social living conditions on reservations in the late nineteenth century, exemplified by hunger, disease, and alcoholism. Financial support for many of these missions was provided by parishes in Dutch-American communities and in the Netherlands, and also by the U.S. federal government, which regarded the churches as a major pacifying and civilizing force.[12]

Researching and Collecting Indian America

Scientists, writers, and artists have played major roles in understanding the American West, and the imagery they created had an impact that is still felt today. Herman ten Kate was a scientific pioneer and spent two years of anthropological fieldwork and archaeological excavations among the Indian tribes of the American West in the 1880s. On the Plains and in the Far West he encountered tribes that were to some extent still engaged in war against white settlers and the American army. Others had recently surrendered or accepted white dominance grudgingly and were settling on reservations. Ten Kate's aim was to study the origin of and relationships among the American-Indian peoples, and to arrive at an understanding of the process and direction of tribal culture change and Indian-white relations. He published extensively on Native Americans in popular journals, informing a wider public about Indians and their victimization by the onslaught of white settlement, Christian missions, and government policy. He also pioneered studies of imagery of Indians in literature and art. His ethnographic collection of over four hundred specimens, curated at the National Museum of Ethnology in Leiden, is one of the earliest systematically aggregated by an academically trained anthropologist in North America and constitutes the basis of North American Indian collections in the Netherlands. The World Museum in Rotterdam, the Museon in The Hague, Groningen's University Museum, and the Zeeuws Museum in Middelburg have minor collections from a variety of sources.[13] In 1910 and 1911 Leiden Professor C.C. Uhlenbeck spent a total of six months on the Blackfoot Indian Reservation in Montana doing ethnolinguistic fieldwork for his seminal studies on Blackfoot and Algonquian. He was assisted in 1910 by J.P.B. de Josselin de Jong, who also did fieldwork among the Chippewas in Minnesota.[14]

The completion of transcontinental railroad lines across the United States and Canada opened up the interior for travelers and tourists in the 1880s. The Grand Canyon in Arizona, Glacier Country Park in Montana, and the Rocky Mountains in Alberta attracted rapidly increasing numbers of visitors, even before they officially became national parks. Indians who lived adjacent to or in the vicinity of the parks became an additional attraction. The Atchison, Topeka & Santa Fe Railroad, the Great Northern Railway, and the Canadian Pacific Railway gradually began using Indian themes in the design of their hotels and restaurants, and employed Indians as guides and entertainers and as low-skilled personnel. Dutch civil servants and entrepreneurs who worked or did business

2

———

in the Dutch East Indies increasingly chose to return home by way of North America when railroad travel became available as a comfortable and affordable alternative to a long ocean journey. They were the first tourists to come into contact with Navajos, Hopis, Zunis, Pueblos, Blackfoot, and Sioux Indians, taking home photographs and arts and crafts as mementos. The image of the American Indian that popular American and Dutch fiction had gradually romanticized around the turn of the century made for a receptive audience. Back home, travelers related their experiences with great enthusiasm to family and friends, inducing a new generation to see America and follow part of the moccasin trail.[15]

1   P. Hovens and G. Van Bussel, "Ouderlijke zorg: Indianen en blanken, 1776–1917," in E. v.d. Bilt and J. Toebes, eds., *Een samenleving op de rails: de Verenigde Staten* (Nijmegen: Sun, 1995), 90-121.

2   R. N. Satz, *American Indian Policy in the Jacksonian Era* (Lincoln: University of Nebraska Press, 1975), 21-23; R.M. Kvasnicka and H. J. Viola, eds., *The Commissioners of Indian Affairs, 1824–1977* (Lincoln: University of Nebraska Press, 1979), 17-27.

3   On the Dutch settling in Michigan and notes on their relations with Indians, Ch. Lorenz, *The Early History of the Black Lake Region, 1835–1850* (Holland, MI: Joint Archives of Holland, 1987); W. Van Appledorn, *Chief Waukazoo: From Roots to Wing* (Holland, MI: privately printed, 2001); Extensive bibliographic references in P. Hovens, "Moccasins and Wooden Shoes: Indians and Dutchmen on the Plains Frontier," in P. Fessler et al., eds., *Dutch Immigrants on the Plains* (Holland, MI: Joint Archives of Holland, 2006), 51-52.

4   Extensive bibliographic references to the history of Indian-Dutch interaction in Iowa in Hovens, "Moccasins and Wooden Shoes," 52.

5   A. S. Gardner, *History of the Spirit Lake Massacre* (Des Moines, IA: Mills and Co., 1885); Extensive bibliographic refer-ences to northwestern Iowa in Hovens, "Moccasins and Wooden Shoes," 52-53.

6   On the settlement of the Dutch in the Dakotas and notes on their relations with Indians, H. Van der Pol, *On the Reservation Border: Hollanders in Douglas and Charles Mix Counties* (Stickney: Argus Printers, 1969); Extensive bibliographic references in Hovens, "Moccasins and Wooden Shoes," 53.

7   See S. Vestal, *Sitting Bull: Champion of the Sioux* (Norman: University of Oklahoma Press, 1932); Ch. A. Eastman, *From the Deep Woods to Civilization* (Boston: Little, Brown and Co., 1916); Van der Pol, *On the Reservation Border*, 40-41, 267-272; J. Mooney, *The Ghost Dance Religion and the Sioux Outbreak of 1890* (Washington, DC: Fourth Annual Report, Bureau of American Ethnology, 1896).

8   Van der Pol, *On the Reservation Border*, passim; B. J. Van Balen Ankrum, *Raised on the Rez: Views, Visions and Wisdom of the West* (Freeman: Pine Hill Press, 1996); Further bibliographic references in Hovens, "Moccasins and Wooden Shoes," 54.

9   On Van den Broek's Indian mission and the settlement of Dutch in Wisconsin, H. S. Lucas, "De Reize naar Noord Amerika van Theodoor J. Van den Broek," *Nederlands Archief voor Kerk-*

geschiedenis 41 (1956): 96-123; F.H. Doppen, "Theodore Van den Broek: Missionary and Emigration Leader," *U.S. Catholic Historian* 3.3 (1983): 202-225; Additional bibliographic references in Hovens, "Moccasins and Wooden Shoes," 37-55; Also, P. Hovens, *Forest, Faith, and Field: Indians and Dutchmen on the Wisconsin Frontier* (forthcoming).

10   F. Zwierlein, *Religion in New Netherland* (Rochester, NY: J.P. Smith, 1910); Leroy Koopman, *Taking the Jesus Road: The Ministry of the Reformed Church of America among Native Americans* (Grand Rapids, MI: Eerdmans, 2005); P. Hovens, *Moccasins and Wooden Shoes: The Dutch Reformed Indian Missions in Oklahoma* (forthcoming).

11   J. Dolfin, ed., *Bringing the Gospel in Hogan and Pueblo* (Grand Rapids, MI: Van Noord Book Company, 1921); P. Hovens, "Kruistochten in Indiaans Noord Amerika: het Nederlands aandeel in missie en zending, 1840–1940," *De Kiva* 37.5-6 (2000): 157-162; P. Hovens, "Moccasins and Wooden Shoes: Dutch Jesuit Superiors at St. Stephen's Arapaho Indian Mission, 1890–1904," *Annals of Wyoming* 77.2 (2005): 12-29; J.H.M. Nijsten, *Mgr. J. N. Lemmens: Belevenissen van een Schimmertse missionaris tussen de Indianen* (Schimmert: Heemkundevereniging, 1992).

12   P. Hovens, *The Indian and the Cross: Dutch Missionaries in Native North America* (forthcoming).

13   P. Hovens, *Herman F.C. ten Kate (1858–1931) en de antropologie der Noord Amerikaanse Indianen* (Ph.D. dissertation, Radboud University, Nijmegen; Meppel: Krips, 1989); P. Hovens (with Anneke Groeneveld), *Odagot: Photographs of American Indians* (Amsterdam: Fragment Uitgeverij, 1992); P. Hovens (with W.J. Orr and L.A. Hieb, eds.), *Herman ten Kate's Travels and Researches in Native North America, 1882–1883* (Albuquerque: University of New Mexico Press, 2004); P. Hovens, ed., *North American Indian Art: Masterpieces and Museum Collections in the Netherlands* (forthcoming); A catalogue of the Ten Kate collection is scheduled for publication in 2008.

14   M. Eggermont-Molenaar, *Montana 1911: A Professor and his Wife among the Blackfeet* (Calgary: University of Alberta Press, 2005); P. Hovens, "C.C. Uhlenbeck: Blackfoot Culture and History. The Uhlenbecks' Ethnographic Collection," in I. Genee and P. Hinrichs, eds., *C.C. Uhlenbeck: His Life and Work* (Amsterdam: KNAW Press, forthcoming).

15   P. Hovens, *Indian Detours: Wooden Shoes on the Moccasin Trail* (forthcoming).

TRANSATLANTIC TRANSPORTATION AND TRAVELERS' EXPERIENCES

___

GEORGE HARINCK &
AUGUSTUS J. VEENENDAAL, JR.

Over the centuries there have been many kinds of travelers in the Atlantic world: explorers, sailors, settlers, and merchants. Tourists and journalists, on whom this article mainly focuses, were conspicuously absent until the nineteenth century. The growing number of these travelers from both sides of the Atlantic gradually created a better appreciation of each other and of each other's history and culture.

Traveling to America in the early nineteenth century was something not casually undertaken and an experience not easily forgotten. For well-to-do passengers a trip in a sailing ship across the Atlantic could be daunting, even when they could pay for fairly comfortable quarters and good food. For the less affluent emigrants the journey could be a nightmare. In bad weather a passage could easily last six weeks or more, food would become scarce, and sickness would prevail among the families huddled below decks. The gradual introduction of steam propulsion in the 1860s meant a general improvement for all classes of travelers, even for the poor emigrants. Still, in the later part of the nineteenth century, when the established steamship lines had attracted most of the traffic, steerage passengers — mostly emigrants from eastern Europe — had few comforts, although schedules were now more dependable. Once in New York, after the rigors of medical examination and immigration procedures, early Dutch emigrants had to board a steamer to Albany and from there a boat along the Erie Canal to Buffalo. Next, they went by ship across Lake Erie and Lake Huron to Chicago or Milwaukee, and from there by boat to Holland, MI, or overland to the Dutch settlements of Pella and Orange City, IA, and others. During these

The *Statendam*, one of the passenger ships of the Holland America Line.

travels they were exposed to all the hazards of accidents, robberies, fires, and general inconvenience.

In the later part of the eighteenth century Rotterdam had been a popular port for German emigrants, but that position had been lost early in the next century to Bremen and Hamburg. Later, Liverpool became the favorite port of embarkation for many European emigrants because of the availability of regular steam shipping lines such as the Cunard and Inman lines. For Dutch emigrants the Red Star Line sailing from Antwerp also became popular. The first Dutch company offering regular sailings from Rotterdam was the Nederlandsch-Amerikaansche Stoomvaart Maatschappij, incorporated in 1873 — later better known as the Holland America Line.[1] Thousands of emigrants from eastern Europe were carried by the HAL, and in Rotterdam a cheap hotel, a church, and a disinfection installation took care of these poor souls before they could board.

For all classes of travelers — emigrants, tourists and businessmen — the establishment of railroads in America, although certainly not perfect at first, meant a much better and cheaper way of travel. Every year more of the outlying parts of that vast country were opened up by the steam cars, and travel became less dependent on rivers, canals, and bad roads.

American Travelers in the Netherlands

Prior to 1865 American travelers rarely visited the Netherlands for pleasure. Most early visitors were diplomats of some sort and their families.[2] There were exceptions, though. The first record of an American tourist in the Netherlands was the account of Elkanah Watson in 1784. Other American visitors did not generally publish their experiences but sent their comments in letters home. Guidebooks on the Netherlands were available from the 1830s, with their emphasis on painters, on the history, and on the general quaintness of the country. The common opinion was fairly negative but the Civil War, which undermined Americans' confidence in their institutions and values, changed this. Another positive contribution was made by John Lothrop Motley's books on Dutch history, published in the 1850s and 1860s. In his trail several American historians emphasized the similarity, and consequently the inspiration to Americans, of the history of the Dutch Republic, once described as Europe's United States.[3] Another impetus for visiting the Netherlands was Mary Mapes Dodge's book *Hans Brinker, or the Silver Skates*, published in 1865. The small size of the Netherlands, its cleanliness, its wooden shoes, windmills, and tulips, all contributed to suggesting that this was an idyllic place. It was the perfect nation to fulfill American dreams at that time: distant and yet so near, alien and akin at the same time, and more democratic after the 1848 constitution.

After the Civil War, mass tourism to Europe started to blossom and the steamship lines carried Americans at the rate of four or five thousand a week to the old continent. In the early 1850s Thomas Cook had introduced "vacation packages," including tickets, sleeping accommodations, guides, and so on. In the 1880s the Holland America Line had a fleet of comfortable passenger steamers and the crossing time had been cut from sixteen to nine days. A second-class round trip cost $90, well within the means of the more affluent members of the American middle class.

On the European tour England, France, Germany, and Italy were the most popular destinations. Tourist travel to the Netherlands remained negligible until the 1880s, and if the country was part of a grand tour at all, it was often because the ship had docked in Rotterdam or Antwerp. Not more than a few days were spent in the region: Rotterdam, Delft, The Hague, Leiden, Haarlem, Amsterdam, and—at least until the 1870s—Broek in Waterland. Around 1900, approximately thirty thousand Americans visited the Netherlands annually, for pleasure and business.

American Travelers and Their Writings

American travel writers were few, mostly giving practical or business information and tips for seeing tourist places. However, by the 1890s, American publishers had discovered a market for travel books. By 1914 about two hundred American travel accounts had been published that included some information on the Netherlands. The country was the exclusive subject of fifteen of them, and filled at least 10 percent of the pages in a hundred others.[4] The most prolific author was the clergyman William E. Griffis, who traveled to the Netherlands more than ten times and published a dozen books on the country. The Pilgrims' revival movement played an important role in his writings, which included a well-known illustrated children's book, *Young People's History of Holland*.[5] A clear sign of the country's rising popularity in the United States was the inexpensive edition of Edmondo De Amici's *Holland and its People* by the New York publisher G.P. Putnam's Sons, which went through five printings in its first two years (1880–82). Rather than using analogies between Dutch and Italian cities, the American edition compared Amsterdam to New York and The Hague to Washington, DC.

This new interest in the Netherlands changed the image of the colonial Dutch as lazy dreamers and stupid humorists, as depicted in Washington Irving's absurd but wonderful legends of old Knickerbocker New York, published in 1809 and the best-known description of the colonial Dutch before 1880. In its place Douglas Campbell offered, for example, this much more positive image: "If an American of the present generation could go back to the Dutch Republic of two centuries and a half ago, he would find himself in a familiar land, because he would be among a people of the nineteenth century."[6] Campbell considered the ideas of seventeenth-century Holland essentially modern, as they correlated so well with ideas he saw operating in the United States.

The House of Orange, especially in its historic role, was also part and parcel of the knowledge of American travelers. They considered the Dutch to be liberty-loving people like themselves, they came to the Netherlands expecting to see their own democratic and republican values at work, and in this context held the House of Orange in high esteem as a safeguard of liberty. In many travel books Dutch sites were described as famous pictures from two centuries previous, ensuring that the reader would form a clear mental picture, and reinforcing the notion that the Netherlands was old fashioned and unchanging. This historical sense determined the American view, but the country could hardly meet these expectations. It was presented as a pastoral Eden and most guidebooks did not pay much attention to its actual conditions to correct this view — and if they did, they usually agreed with the popular image around 1900 of a land of windmills and wooden shoes.

Staying in the Netherlands for only a short time, many American visitors naturally misunderstood some of what they saw, and modernizations were easily overlooked. The Dutch cities facilitated this, for quite a few of them contained an old quarter dating back to the Middle Ages, and Amsterdam had its Jews in rags and its stagnating stinking green water in the canals. The reality of Amsterdam was often grim indeed, and the city was called a "vulgar Venice" by some visitors. Because of its cosmopolitan and industrial character Rotterdam failed to satisfy American expectations. The Hague was appreciated better, but to many visitors only Marken and Volendam were considered to be really Dutch.

Artists in particular had an idyllic view of the Netherlands and were attracted, too, by the closed communities that still existed despite modernization, such as Katwijk, Volendam, or Egmond. But the greatest of them all, the painter and etcher James Whistler, in 1883 went to Amsterdam and did picture the reality of a modern city. Most travelers were not artists, however. They came to see the original paintings of Rembrandt, Hals, and Ruysdael that they knew from their guidebooks, and they also more or less expected to see the living models outside the Mauritshuis and the Rijksmuseum. The Holland America Line promoted this historic view by publishing *A Journey Through Old Holland*, in which the narrator fell asleep and in his dreams toured the Holland of the old masters with a seventeenth-century Dutch-American colonist.

Although most American travelers were Protestants, only a few of them were interested in Dutch religion. The churches in Amsterdam were not appreciated very much, but the fact that Protestantism was the dominant religion certainly contributed to the positive view of the country. The Pilgrims formed a special attraction. The short period of their stay began to loom larger in American interpretations of Pilgrim history as the Netherlands became a more popular destination, and the Dutch readily invented some historic sites. There was a lively interest in places where the Pilgrims were said to have lived, like Brownists' Alley in Amsterdam, or John Robinson's house in Leiden, and the place in old Delfshaven where they were supposed to have departed for America, aptly renamed "Pilgrim Quay" in 1892. Griffis noted in 1914 that Americans had erected thirteen memorials in the Netherlands to their own historical roots there,[7] and Annette Stott remarked that "the importance of Holland for many tourists was its role in American history — which they now believed they could readily see in the land and people around them as they traveled through the Netherlands."[8]

Dutch Travelers in America

Shifting the focus back to early Dutch visitors to the U.S., a growth of travel literature in Dutch was noticeable in the 1850s. In view of the rigors of their early transatlantic journeys, it was not surprising that many of these travelers wrote about their experiences. And there was a demand for serious literature about America, about the American way of life, the attractions of the New World, and the opportunities for emigrants. All sorts of travelers described their experiences, but as most of the early Dutch emigrants had more important things on their minds, this group hardly ever penned down their stories in book form: generally, they only sent letters to family and friends back home and, later, sometimes had memoirs or reminiscences published in Dutch and Dutch-American newspapers.[9] Among the numerous travelers who did write books — mostly academics, journalists, and businessmen — a few deserve our attention here. They were people like J.R. Mees, a businessman who went to the U.S. in 1843, W.T. Gevers Deynoot, a member of parliament who traveled there in 1859, or C.A. Crommelin, who crossed the Atlantic in 1866.[10] Among later visitors were Charles Boissevain, editor of the Amsterdam newspaper *Algemeen Handelsblad*, and R.P.J. Tutein Noltenius, a civil engineer and financier who published his account in 1900.[11] There was one scholar among these authors: Hugo de Vries, the famous botanist who published no less than three books about his travels and experiences in America.[12] A late traveler to be mentioned was J.C. van Reigersberg Versluys, another civil engineer, who crossed the American continent to reach

323

his destination in the Dutch East Indies in 1917.[13] The Protestant dogmatician Herman Bavinck and the neo-Calvinist leader Abraham Kuyper, who traveled to the United States to receive an honorary degree from Princeton University, lectured at many educational and cultural institutions and published about their travels and inpressions,[14] as did the liberal Amsterdam minister P.H. Hugenholtz, Jr.[15]

Dutch Travelers' Background

All travelers-authors named here were well-to-do citizens who could afford a cabin in the ship and who had the means to travel around in America. They all were well educated and able to write down their stories in ways that would interest the Dutch public. But what were their reasons to go there at all, what motivated them to write about their experiences, and what did interest them most in this strange country? Were they looking for new ideas that could be applied profitably at home, or were they convinced of European superiority over the crude American civilization?

The case of Mees is fairly simple: he was a tobacco merchant and crossed the Atlantic to inspect the tobacco trade in America, which brought him to the plantations in the South that in his time were still worked with slave labor. As a member of the Dutch parliament, Gevers Deynoot was more interested in the political system, at the time of his visit in turmoil because of the clash of interests over the issue of slavery just before the outbreak of the Civil War. He was optimistic, however, about the almost limitless possibilities of the country and felt that once the slavery question was settled, America would have a bright future. Crommelin, himself a lawyer but a scion of an old established Amsterdam trading family with many business contacts in America, was interested in almost every aspect of the country. Because of his name he was received everywhere: all doors opened, from Newport, RI, to Savannah, GA, and as far west as St. Paul, MN. He was curious about the future of the plantation economy after the abolition of slavery, and very critical of the political system after the assassination of President Lincoln. He wondered about the virtuousness of American married women, about the prevailing corruption in the New York state and city governments, and about the position of former slaves drifting toward the northern industrial towns in search of work. He approved of the Pennsylvania cellular prison system and of the poorhouses of New York and Boston, but had his doubts about the quality of education in the New York schools.

Like Crommelin, Boissevain was also interested in almost every aspect of America and the Americans. And he also was welcomed almost everywhere, again because of his name. He described, for instance, the workings of the New York Stock Exchange for his Dutch public, and he apparently knew the Amsterdam Exchange price list by heart and informed his readers about the wisdom of investing in American securities. He also had some critical remarks about corruption in the political world and the quality of American democracy. The engineer Tutein Nolthenius, interested in the new building material concrete, wanted to see how it was being used in America. His family firm was financially involved in the Kansas City, Pittsburg & Gulf Railroad, which led him to inspect that line and describe in glowing terms the regions through which it passed. Of all these authors, Hugo de Vries was the only one involved in the world of universities and colleges. Of course, he visited places that were of interest to him as a botanist, but — as most of the others — also took in the usual sights, such as Niagara Falls and other popular attractions. De Vries described his botanic findings in detail, as well as the several universities where he gave lectures or received honorary degrees. But he also gave a very precise description of the effects of the great San Francisco earthquake and fire of 1906. Another, even less expected topic was Henry Flagler's railroad to Key West, opened shortly before De Vries's arrival in Florida. Van Reigersberg Versluys was mostly interested in industry and transportation, and his chief reason for traveling to the United States was unique. He was going to take up his job in the East Indies and because of the war in Europe and the danger of submarines and mines, he preferred the then still relatively safe crossing of the Atlantic over the passage of the Mediterranean or the long and tedious voyage around South Africa. He very much praised American industry, which was gearing up for war production, but made only a few comments about the American way of life.

Opinions Shared by Dutch Travelers

Despite their many diverse interests the Dutch travelers all agreed that the average American was friendly and hospitable, but generally shallow and avoiding difficult questions. And they were also critical of the American way of life, the unceasing quest for the dollar, and the unlimited belief in progress and future prosperity. They deplored the lack of common courtesy, the sometimes crude manners, and the lack of sophistication. They did admire the down-to-earth attitude of their hosts and the ease with which things were organized for them. Although Crommelin was critical of the free and easy attitude of most women, Bavinck and Kuyper appreciated female independence and assertiveness: "America is the country for women." All travelers were impressed by the vastness of the country, the size of public buildings, and the productivity of industrial complexes. The giant advance in technology in America had their sincere admiration, although some wondered whether too much was being made of the belief in technology.

325

The position of "colored people" was a topic found in every book about America. The travelers who came before the abolition of slavery were all opposed to the "peculiar institution," but Mees was much less negative about slavery than Gevers Deynoot and foresaw a labor problem when slaves would be declared free. De Vries had little to say about African Americans; he met them only in menial capacities, not in academic circles. Kuyper, too, met African Americans only as servants on trains and did not comment on the race issue. Crommelin and Boissevain, writing twenty years apart, condemned slavery on moral grounds and had much to say about the inferior position of the former slaves in the South and their lack of political and economic clout. Crommelin, though, when visiting black schools in New York City, was favorably impressed with their higher than expected quality, but a black church amused him only very little. Again, both he and Boissevain agreed that the continuing separation of the two races was a great problem that would have to be solved somehow before the country could really be unified. Equality between races had to be the cornerstone of a really democratic America. Apart from this, Boissevain and Kuyper were concerned about the enormous power of the moneyed classes. In Boissevain's opinion the "tender plant of democracy" could easily be trampled underfoot by the monopolists of big business and banking syndicates. The journalists among the travelers did not appreciate the sensational character of the press, but they had to admit: "…there is no working man who doesn't buy his daily paper." Kuyper, owner of a newspaper himself, was impressed by the large number of newspapers, the activity of the journalists, and the amount of advertising.

The Dutch heritage was another thing that interested most travelers. Some, of course, visited the Dutch settlements in Michigan and Iowa on purpose, but Crommelin, who did not, was pleasantly surprised to find a number of Dutch street names in Albany, NY. He also visited families living in old country houses of early settlers on Manhattan in what is now Yonkers, and in Hoboken, NJ, but had little to say about things Dutch in New York City itself. Impressed by the books of Motley, Griffis, and others, the Dutch travelers in the last quarter of the century repeated the opinion of these authors that "the sun of freedom over America [had] risen from the old-Dutch low countries."[16] Dutch influence on the early history of the United States was considered strong. When in America in 1898, Kuyper founded branches of the General Dutch Alliance to foster the Dutch-American cultural heritage. He visited Dutch communities in Michigan and Iowa, and lectured for Dutch-American clubs and societies. And in these circles he encountered a great enthusiasm for the House of Orange and the newly enthroned beautiful young Queen Wilhelmina.

Because traveling by train was the only practical way of seeing the country, almost all authors paid attention to the American railroad system, and most were positive. Although trains often were late and sometimes even overcrowded, they generally were comfortable and the splendor of the Pullman cars was much appreciated by our travelers. Apparently they accepted the frequent accidents as unavoidable.

Conclusion

The few early American visitors generally had a negative view of the Netherlands. Life there was quiet and slow, nothing really happened, and the people were phlegmatic and backward. Starting in the 1860s these narrow-minded feelings of superiority slowly gave way to a greater appreciation for the Dutch way of life. With the growth of mass tourism after the 1880s, American travelers were generally upper-middle-class tourists who visited the Netherlands as part of a grander European tour. Dutch quaintness was still a major selling point but Dutch art and history became part and parcel of American tourism. The role of the Dutch in American history — exaggerated or not — and the similarities in political and cultural development added up to the reasons for a visit, and by the end of the century ignited a popularity of Dutchness in certain circles.

Dutch travelers to America were much less numerous — mostly intellectuals, journalists, and businessmen who could afford to cross the Atlantic out of curiosity or for professional reasons. Sometimes severely critical, sometimes full of praise, all of them were interested in the American way of life, in the workings of the political system, in the religious diversity, in the growth of industry — in short, in almost all aspects of life in America. And despite the wide gap in interests between the average American and Dutch visitor, one aspect became common to both: the interest in the Dutch roots of American civilization and history.

1   A. D. Wentholt, *Brug over den oceaan. Een eeuw geschiedenis van de Holland Amerika Lijn* (Rotterdam/The Hague: Nijgh & Van Ditmar, 1973); Cees Zevenbergen, *Toen zij uit Rotterdam vertrokken. Emigratie via Rotterdam door de eeuwen heen* (Zwolle: Waanders, 1990); Hans Krabbendam, "Rituals of Travel in the Transition from Sail to Steam: The Dutch Immigrant Experience, 1840–1940," in Margriet Bruijn Lacy et al., eds., *From* De Halve Maen

to KLM: *400 Years of Dutch-American Exchange* (Münster: Nodus Publikationen, 2008), 269-287.

2   Pieter R. D. Stokvis, "The Dutch Experience of American Visitors during the Nineteenth Century," in Santiago Henriquez, ed., *Travel Essentials. Collected Essays on Travel Writing* (Las Palmas de Gran Canaria: Chandlon Inn Press, 1998), 111-132.

3   So did the American author William Elliot Griffis. See Annette Stott, *Holland*

2

—

THE
NINETEENTH
CENTURY

Mania: The Unknown Dutch Period in American Art and Culture (Woodstock, NY: The Overlook Press, 1998), 86.

4   See Erika van der Linden, "American Tourists in the Netherlands, 1784–1914" (Master's thesis, Katholieke Universiteit Nijmegen, 1990).

5   William E. Griffis, Young People's History of Holland (Boston: Houghton Mifflin, 1903).

6   Douglas Campbell, The Puritan, in Holland, England, and America. An Introduction to American History, 2 vols. (New York: Harper & Bros., 1892), 2:358.

7   For a complete list see William E. Griffis, "Thankful America," The Outlook 106 (January 10, 1914): 88-90.

8   Stott, Holland Mania, 101-102.

9   A useful survey of early travel literature is Pien Steringa, Nederlanders op reis in Amerika 1812–1860. Reisverhalen als bron voor negentiende-eeuwse mentaliteit. Utrechtse Historische Cahiers 20.1 (1999) [series published by the Vakgroep Geschiedenis of the University of Utrecht]. Many writings of emigrants have been published in Henry S. Lucas, Dutch Immigrant Memoirs and Related Writings, 2 vols. (Assen: Van Gorcum, 1955).

10   J. R. Mees, Dagboek van eene reis door Amerika 1843–1844. Ingeleid en van aantekeningen voorzien door B. Schoenmaker (Rotterdam, 1988); W. T. Gevers Deynoot, Aanteekeningen op eene reis door de Verenigde Staten van Noord-Amerika en Canada in 1859 (The Hague: Martinus Nijhoff, 1860). Crommelin's

1866 diary is located in the manuscript collections of the Minnesota Historical Society in St. Paul, and will be published in an English translation in the near future.

11   Charles Boissevain, Van 't Noorden naar het Zuiden. Schetsen en indrukken van de Vereenigde Staten van Noord-Amerika, 2 vols. (Haarlem: H. D. Tjeenk Willink, 1881–82); R.P.J. Tutein Noltheni us, Nieuwe wereld. Indrukken en aanteekeningen tijdens eene reis door de Vereenigde Staten van Noord-Amerika, 2 vols., 2nd ed. (Haarlem: H. D. Tjeenk Willink, 1902).

12   Hugo de Vries, Naar Californië (Haarlem: H. D. Tjeenk Willink, 1905); idem, Naar Californië II (Haarlem: H. D. Tjeenk Willink, 1907); idem, Van Texas naar Florida (Haarlem: H. D. Tjeenk Willink, 1913). Parts of these books and some of his letters home have been published by Erik Zevenhuizen, O Wies! 't Is hier zo mooi! Reizen in Amerika (Amsterdam/ Antwerpen: Atlas, 1998).

13   J. C. van Reigersberg Versluys, Amerika. Indrukken, aanteekeningen, opmerkingen (The Hague: Martinus Nijhoff, 1917).

14   H. Bavinck, Mijne reis naar Amerika, edited and introduced by George Harinck (Barneveld: De Vuurbaak, 1998); A. Kuyper, Varia Americana (Amsterdam /Pretoria: Höveker & Wormser, 1899).

15   P. H. Hugenholtz, Licht en schaduw. Indrukken van het godsdienstig leven in Amerika (Amsterdam: Tj. van Holkema, [1888]).

16   Kuyper, Varia Americana, 63.

RELIGIOUS EXCHANGE IN THE DUTCH-AMERICAN NETWORK

———

GEORGE HARINCK

Coming of Age in the United States

In June 1829 the General Synod of the Hollandsche Gereformeerde Kerk van Noord-Amerika (Dutch Reformed Church in America) sent a letter to the members of the Reformed Church in France in which it recalled the "suppression and persecution, more cruel than death" of their "unhappy brethren" in France after the revocation of the Edict of Nantes in 1685. The letter contrasted this European history of oppression with the freedom of the Reformed churches in the United States: "... enjoying liberties and privileges, without any vexation or compulsion ... she never experienced any persecution, and she never had one single martyr in this country!"[1]

This contrast aptly reflects the mentality of the young American Republic. Formally independent since 1776, it sought to grow and did so in a significant way through the purchase of the French territories in America from Napoleon in 1803, which doubled its size. After this deal, the United States no longer was an extension of Europe but a political as well as a cultural entity of its own. In this context, the perception of Europe as the continent of suppression, as opposed to the United States as the beacon of freedom, became popular. It was a contrast within the Atlantic frame. Newly positioned in history, the Americans "required the credit of origins and a past, and these they ascribed back to Europe, therefore reserving the new life and the great historical future for themselves."[2]

In order to acquire "credit of origins" the Dutch Reformed Church in America reached out to fellow European churches. One way was building relationships in France, another was fostering its Dutch roots. In 1836 the Reformed Church sent its first missionaries to the Dutch East Indies. In 1843 it offered the Dutch lay church leader and political activist Guillaume Groen van Prinsterer an honorary membership on its recently constituted Board of Foreign Missions and Board of Domestic Missions. And in the same year Rutgers College at New Brunswick, NJ — founded by the Reformed Church — awarded Groen an honorary doctorate in letters.[3] These were deliberate American acts of cultural rooting.

The Dutch had founded their Reformed Church in America in 1628 — the oldest denomination with a continuous ministry in the United States. But now, two hundred years later, it was the Americans' turn. In their French letter they explained their initiative: "We remember with great joy that the true church of Jesus Christ, our Lord, though spread over many countries, is 'one in Him.'" Within a century Christianity would develop into a world religion and the letter reveals that the American churches with their missionary and ecumenical zeal were ready.

An American Alternative for the Dutch

The letter to the French Reformed was translated into Dutch and published in 1830 by J. H. den Ouden, the Amsterdam publisher of the Dutch Réveil, a religious revival movement. The Dutch did not have an Atlantic perspective in those days and were, instead, absorbed by their national tribulations. The Americans boasted in their letter of their orthodoxy, praised the Synod of Dordt of 1618–19, and reported a revival in godliness over the past twenty-five years. Therefore, the letter was translated as an incitement to restore Reformed orthodoxy in the Netherlands.

Why was this restoration needed? In 1815 the Kingdom of the Netherlands had been created. It was a modern unitary state, partly based on Napoleonic principles. All denominations were subjected to and reorganized by the state, including the Nederlandsche Hervormde Kerk (Netherlands Reformed Church), which had accepted this subjection, hoping in this way to regain the privileged position it had lost in the Napoleonic era. And in a sense it succeeded. In the first half of the nineteenth century the Netherlands Reformed Church unofficially functioned as an established church.

But the freedom of the denominations was too restricted and the king's strict political regime in general frustrated the development of public life. The Catholics were the first to protest, followed soon by some Reformed Church members. They defended the church's independent position within the state and wanted the Dordt church order to be restored. The protest of the Catholics was a major impulse for the secession in 1830 of the southern provinces (present-day Belgium), where the population was predominantly Catholic. As a result, the Catholic population within the kingdom became a minority. Did this mean the former Protestant Dutch Republic should be restored? Two years later, in 1832, a cholera epidemic hit the country, which reinforced insecurity. Was this a hint from God that the Dutch had gone astray? Political uncertainty was mixed with religious commotion. Many pamphlets were published, contemplating the political and religious fate of the Netherlands — the American synodical letter was one of them. As a result of this turmoil the Réveil movement came to the fore. And in 1834 an orthodox Reformed section seceded from the Netherlands Reformed Church. Some traits of this revival movement resembled the Second Great Awakening (1800–1830s) in the United States, religiously typified by personal salvation experiences and socially by reform movements (temperance, women's suffrage, abolishment of slavery). The American Methodist preacher George Whitefield was known in Réveil circles and appreciated for his orthodoxy, and the Dutch movement was sometimes labeled "le Réveil méthodiste."

Was this a case of "religious transfer"?[4] More comparative research of the exemplary character of the Second Awakening for the Réveil movement in Europe is needed to determine the relationship. In 1805 Willem Bilderdijk, leader of the Réveil, still adhered to the traditional European perspective in his rejection of America as a country missing "toute culture d'esprit, toute science, et tout commerce d'étude."[5] But the translator of the letter recommended the Americans as "one of the most civilized peoples of the world." This was a new notion in Dutch orthodox circles and suggested that the orthodox Dutch Protestants should update their view of America. While in the Netherlands the members of the small Réveil movement protested against the ungodly spirit of their times, the freedom of the American Reformed people offered their European fellow Protestants an attractive perspective. It was, as their poet Isaac Da Costa wrote:

> And yet, America, no Christian must defame Thee,
> No Protestant must fail to see what precious seed
> Of piety and truth and faith Thou hast preserved.... [6]

In the 1830s and 1840s the Dutch Reformed Church in America focused in Europe on the Netherlands, drawn by stories about fines and persecution and quartering of troops imposed on the Seceders of 1834. The persecution of the French Reformed was history, but this revolt and this persecution were happening now. As soon as the Americans realized that the Dutch government reacted to this revival as the French had in 1685, they reached out in sympathy. In 1846 the Reverend J.N. Wyckoff of the Reformed Church in Albany, NY, offered a translation of a Dutch text, "Appeal to the Faithful in the United States," in which the Seceders called for help to fight against their religious suppression and lamentable social conditions. In identifying with these groups the Reformed Americans emphasized three points: these were people adhering to the Reformed faith, they had gone through trials and tribulations, and their difficulties were related to their secession from the established church — in short, "Here were persecuted Protestants who wanted to come to the land of the free."[7] From 1846 onward, many of them moved in groups to the United States, where they were welcomed and helped along to the Midwest by the Reformed Church in America. Many immigrants settled in Dutch communities. Soon, members of the Netherlands Reformed Church followed their example, and by 1857 some twenty thousand Reformed Dutch had emigrated to the United States.

Like other ethnic groups that came to America, Dutch immigrants — more than two hundred thousand between 1846 and 1914 — could turn to societies for protection and support. Among the organizations for Dutch immigrants the Reformed Church was the most effective. In part, the energy it invested in these people stemmed from its hope that newcomers would be instrumental in planting a western branch of the church. The Reformed had failed to move westward with the opening of the Mississippi Valley and Ohio in the 1810s. In 1841 two new western classes were formed, in Illinois and Michigan, but they did not really grow. The arrival of what the General Synod of 1847 — with a revealing sense of history — called "a new body of Pilgrims," was exactly the impulse the western branch needed.

Overall, nineteenth-century Dutch immigration to the United States is a Protestant story, but approximately 20 percent of the immigrants were Catholics. In general, the attitude of the Dutch Catholics toward a move to the United States was not as favorable as among the Dutch Protestants. The United States was a strongly Protestant country, where Catholics were "sectarians." And there was no American Catholic Church reaching out to their Dutch fellow believers. The Dutch clergy was worried emigrants from their parishes might lose their faith in a hostile America. For that reason they urged potential emigrants not to cross the Atlantic but choose European destinations instead, like Belgium or the Ruhr area in Germany, both predominantly Catholic. Dutch Catholics who nonetheless did come to the United States severed their ties with the Netherlands more quickly than did Protestant emigrants. Their church was not Dutch but international in character and many Catholics — with the exception of some Dutch Catholic communities in Wisconsin, for example — settled in the cities, where Americanization was harder to avoid than in the countryside.

U. S. Revivalist Efforts Abroad

In 1848 the Netherlands adopted a new, liberal constitution, introducing full separation of church and state, as well as parliamentary rule, and the distress over the loss of Belgium was replaced by a national zeal to strive for a second Golden Age. Churches and religions now were free to organize without the government's permission. The Netherlands Reformed Church had difficulty coping with the new situation and was disturbed by the rise of free churches and religious movements after 1848.

Full sympathy for American Christianity was only found in the margins of Dutch Protestantism. Inspired by the American Presbyterian Church historian Robert Baird, Secession leader Hendrik P. Scholte had been a proponent of separation of church and state since 1840 or so. During his stay in Europe in the 1830s (he originally came to support the French Protestants) Baird visited the Netherlands and made a plea for social reform — a novelty for American Christianity. His ideas were welcomed in Réveil and Secession circles, while others feared the effects of emotional and low-church American revivalism. The social impact of the new ideas on Dutch society was limited, compared to the United States. The Netherlands was a small country, where in public life the names of the small group of politicians were more important than the numbers of anonymous mass movements. And contrary to the United States, revivalism was not strongly rooted in the middle class. American practices were copied, but radical and theatrical elements were avoided, and the example of American women's active participation in society was not followed.

Yet, a certain American revivalist influence on Dutch society was undeniable in two of the earliest Dutch single-issue associations, both in part originating in the Réveil movement: the temperance and the antislavery movements. The Dutch temperance movement started in the 1850s and was advised by Baird. Tactics, ideas, and strategies were copied from the United States Inspired by religious ideals, moral issues entered Dutch politics. At first, Dutch parliament resisted curtailing the use of liquor. The American laws were judged "utterly severe and despotic in nature." But in 1881 the first law licensing the sale of liquor was passed.[8] The Dutch antislavery movement was stimulated by the Dutch translation of Harriet Beecher Stowe's *Uncle Tom's Cabin* (1852) in 1853. The book went through five printings within one year, and its evangelical message influenced public opinion on slavery profoundly. For many Dutchmen this book framed their first impression of America. Slavery was abolished in the Netherlands in 1863.[9] This organized civil action for social reform with an American flavor reflected the introduction of the moral and religious narrative in politics and promoted the development of Dutch democracy.

The Netherlands Reformed Church was not involved in Christian social action. Together with the Catholic Church (40 percent of the Dutch population), it was the small Seceder community that was the most dynamic religious force in Dutch society from the 1850s until the 1890s, when the socialist movement took over. Their fast-growing free church, with ninety thousand members (2.5

percent of the Dutch population) in the 1860s, had doubled in size by the 1890s. The Seceder Church best reflected the American dynamism effectuated by a close relationship between church and social action: they were financially independent, had their own theological school, were well organized with a strong lay influence, promoted a range of religious societies, and were at ease with a functional differentiation between church and state.

It was no surprise that this community had sympathy for the American Reformed churches — the Dutch Reformed Church and the stricter Christian Reformed Church, founded by Dutch Reformed immigrants in 1857. But none of the Dutch churches was open to a revivalist injection and genial Christianity. The Dutch did not appreciate "high pressure and mass conversion Christian evangels." Public expression of emotion or religion did not become a Dutch feature. The qualifications of American religion as childish, vulgar, or shallow ran continuously through Dutch travel accounts.

Some of this American revivalism came directly to the Netherlands, like the Church of Jesus Christ of Latter-day Saints, founded in 1830 in the state of New York by Joseph Smith, Jr. (1805–44); the Jehovah's Witnesses, founded in 1870 in Pennsylvania by Charles T. Russell (1852–1916); Pentecostalism, starting in 1907 with the black minister William J. Seymour (1870–1922) from Louisiana; and the Seventh-day Adventist Church, founded in 1863 in New England. These movements were related to the activist and transformational (postmillennial) Third Great Awakening (1850s–1900s). This revival greatly stimulated the Social Gospel and the missionary movements. Crossing the Atlantic, these "sects" had the same intention as the American Reformed in 1829: reaching out to the distressed European continent with a message of hope.

The Mormons visited the Netherlands from the 1840s on and founded their first congregation in 1862 in Amsterdam. The first Dutch edition of the *Book of Mormon* (1830) was published in 1890. In the 1870s the Seventh-day Adventist denomination reached Europe and in 1887 its first church in the Netherlands was founded. In 1907 Pentecostals opened their first church in Amsterdam. Russell visited the Netherlands in 1891, but a Dutch branch of the Jehovah's Witnesses was not founded until 1922.

The Dutch churches successfully excluded these new American groups from the domain of the classic confessional traditions: a Baptist was not as acceptable in the Netherlands as an Anabaptist. The "sects" did not win many Dutch souls and operated on the fringes of the religious market. Nevertheless, the American influence was discernible in the informal and personal strata of Dutch religious life. When the American-style Higher Life conferences with Robert Pearsall Smith, of the Holiness Movement, were organized in England (e.g., in Brighton and Keswick in 1875), some Reformed ministers from the Netherlands crossed the North Sea and were impressed: surely the Lord was in this place (Gen. 28: 16).[10] Another representative of the same movement was the American evangelist Dwight L. Moody (1837–99). Dutch church leaders opposed his sensational performances, but he made a name for himself from the 1870s on, and in 1888 an intimate story of his personal life was published in Dutch. This American way of religious personality building was imitated in the Netherlands with the publication, two years later, of a biographical sketch of Abraham Kuyper (1837–1920). This biography of a living politician and church leader marked the introduction of "the personality" in Dutch religion and public life.[11]

But the only example of real religious Americanization was the song, the vehicle of Methodism. "Poetry is the handmaid of piety," as John Wesley said, author of some 6,500 religious songs. The new-style revival songs — gospel hymns — Moody and his solo singer Ira D. Sankey used at their evangelistic crusades, and the negro spirituals sung by the Jubilee Singers of Fisk University in Nashville, TN, on their 1877 tour in the Netherlands were soon translated. From the 1860s on such hymns became popular, not within the walls of the church, but surely in Dutch religious life. About 10 percent of the published Dutch religious songs between the 1860s and the 1930s were gospel hymns ("Sankey liederen").[12] They were adopted in hymn books of evangelists like the well-known Johannes de Heer and are being sung to this very day.

Impressed by Moody's preaching, American students and other young men in the 1880s devoted themselves to mission. The Nobel Peace Prize-winner John Mott (1865–1955) organized the World Student Christian Federation (WSCF), with the watchword: "The evangelization of the world in this generation" (1888). The Dutch, too, responded to this drive. In this missionary movement lay the roots of the Protestant ecumenical movement that, not least thanks to Dutch initiatives, would result in the founding of the World Council of Churches in 1948 in Amsterdam. In 1891 the World's Conference of the Young Men's Christian Association was held in Amsterdam as well. In 1896 a Dutch branch of the WSCF was founded, the Nederlandsche Christen Studenten Vereeniging (NCSV), devoted to mission in a religiously indifferent student world. In the first decades of the twentieth century about one out of ten Dutch students joined the NCSV, and the association spurred a moral revival in the Dutch academic world.[13]

A Heliotropic Trajectory

335

The Protestant Dutch were influenced, but not conquered, by America's religious zeal, enthusiasm, and business-like approach. Yet, when confronted with American theology and church life and the national revival experienced from the 1860s on, they tended to emphasize their own religious particularities: their Calvinism or religious liberalism. The America-mindedness of the liberal Hugenholtz family was an exception. The clergyman F. W. N. Hugenholtz returned to the Netherlands in 1895 with a social and democratic Christian message. In 1877 his half-brothers Ph. R. and P. H. Hugenholtz founded the independent Vrije Gemeente (Free Congregation) in Amsterdam, inspired by examples of American Unitarian and Universalist congregational life.

In the 1870s the new religious-political movement of neo-Calvinists joined the Seceders in their appreciation for the American religious situation. This positive attitude originated in its leader, Abraham Kuyper. He was attracted by the American free churches and church-state relations. When he was heavily criticized for his militant orthodoxy and his social and political activism and "programs," Kuyper, like some Seceders thirty years before, considered group emigration to South Africa, but in the 1880s many of his followers went to the United States. There are similarities between Kuyper's neo-Calvinism and Walter Rauschenbusch's Social Gospel creed: "Whoever uncouples the religious and the social life has not understood Jesus." The neo-Calvinists appreciated the United States as a country in the Calvinist tradition, like Switzerland and England, instrumental in "driving the broad stream of the development of our race from Babylon to San Francisco." Kuyper emphasized that America had been placed in this "heliotropic" trajectory through Dutch Calvinism. This Dutch godfatherhood of America's national history was in line with the American hype of Dutchness at the end of the nineteenth century,[14] which facilitated Kuyper's successful American tour of 1898.

After neo-Calvinism had won substantial political, ecclesiastic, and academic influence in the Netherlands in the 1880s, quite a few Dutch-American immigrants looked back in envy. They had left for the "food and faith" that their homeland now seemed to offer in abundance: the Netherlands had revived. In the end, however, they opted for Americanization. In Kuyper's days, the Reformed Church in America had already accomplished this process by eliminating in 1867 the word "Dutch" from the denomination's official name. The Christian Reformed Church tried to avoid, or at least postpone, Americanization. Its intellectual culture was dependent on Dutch books and periodicals until World War I. The first generations of professors at their intellectual bulwark, Calvin College in Grand Rapids, MI, were educated in the Netherlands or steeped in Dutch culture. The Calvinistic revival in the Netherlands at the end of the nineteenth century spurred a continuing relationship between the Dutch commu-

Program for a lecture of Abraham Kuyper in Cleveland, November 15, 1898, organized by several churches in Cleveland, together with universities and colleges in Ohio.

Cleveland's Welcome to ❧ ❧ ❧
HOLLAND'S FOREMOST CITIZEN.

PROFESSOR ABRAHAM KUYPER, D. D., LL.D.

STATESMAN, THEOLOGIAN, LITERATEUR,

AT THE

Old Stone Church, Tuesday, November 15, 1898,

7:30 P. M.

nities in the United States and the Netherlands. The Reformed Church in America and the Christian Reformed Church eventually created their own American religious blend of the Reformed tradition.

Catholics, about 20 percent of the Dutch immigrants in the United States, did not have these problems of ambiguity. Their leaders were more interested in relations with international Catholicism than in supporting the Dutchness of emigrants. Joining the American parishes in the cities was emphasized, instead of founding new Dutch Catholic communities in the countryside.[15]

Conclusion

The Dutch-American religious exchange provides an argument for an Atlantic history. The new role of the United Sates after 1776 resulted in a shift in initiative from Europe to America. Americans started missionary projects worldwide. They helped the Dutch Seceders and, later on, exported their revivalist religion. Dutch Protestants welcomed America's freedom of religion and some projected the religious future of the world in America. The subsequent revivals in both countries and the mutual influence (with America as the dominant force) are striking, and the religious-intellectual transfer and mediating structures between the two countries deserve more research.

1   Brief van het algemeen synode der Hollandsche Gereformeerde Kerk van de Verenigde Staten van Noord-Amerika aan de leeraren, kerkenraden en leden der Gereformeerde Kerk in Frankrijk (Amsterdam: s.n., 1830), 13-14.

2   Malcolm Bradbury, *Dangerous Pilgrimages. Trans-Atlantic Mythologies and the Novel* (London: Penguin Books, 1996), 7.

3   Th. de Witt to G. Groen van Prinsterer, March 30, 1843, in G. Groen van Prinsterer, *Briefwisseling*, vol. 2, *1833–1848* (The Hague: Martinus Nijhoff, 1964), 511; See also 574, 603, and I. Ferris to Groen, June 15, 1842, ibid., 627; "Annual meeting of Board Trustees R.C. held July 25th 1843," in Minutes of the Board of Trustees of Rutgers College, 1840–1844, Special Collections, Alexander Library, Rutgers University, New Brunswick, NJ.

4   The expression "religious transfer" is analogous here to the expression "political transfer"; see the special issue on political transfer of the *European Review of History* 12 (2005): 2.

5   Willem Bilderdijk , "Helmstedt of Amerika," in Marinus van Hattum, ed., *Mr. W. Bilderdijk's briefwisseling 1798–1806* (Utrecht: Hes en De Graaf, 2007), 951.

6   I. da Costa, *Wachter! Wat is er van den nacht?* (1847) (translated by J.W. Schulte Nordholt), in "Perceived in Poetry. Poetical Images of America from Dutch Immigrants," in Rob Kroes and Henk-Otto Neuschäfer, eds., *The Dutch in North-America. Their Immigration and Cultural Continuity* (Amsterdam: VU University Press, 1991), 12.

7   See Albertus C. Hyma, *Albertus C. Van*

Raalte and His Dutch Settlements in the United States (Grand Rapids, MI: Eerdmans, 1947), 102; quote from 56.

8 Hans Krabbendam, "'A Plant of American Origin. Fit for Dutch Soil?' American Protestantism and the Dutch Reformed Temperance Effort, 1835–1935," in George Harinck and Hans Krabbendam, eds., *Sharing the Reformed Tradition: The Dutch-North American Exchange, 1846–1996* (Amsterdam: VU University Press, 1996), 57-78.

9 Maartje Janse, *De afschaffers: Publieke opinie, organisatie en politiek in Nederland 1840-1880* (Amsterdam: Wereldbibliotheek, 2007), 91-100, 124-127; Hanneke Hoekstra, *Het hart van de natie. Morele verontwaardiging en politieke verandering in Nederland 1870–1919* (Amsterdam: Wereldbibliotheek, 2005), 91-95.

10 Hans Krabbendam, "Zielenverbrijzelaars en zondelozen. Reacties in de Nederlandse pers op Moody, Sankey en Pearsall Smith, 1874–1878,"

Documentatieblad Nederlandse Kerkgeschiedenis 34 (May 1991): 39-55.

11 Witsius H. de Savornin Lohman, *Dr. Abraham Kuyper* (Haarlem: H. D. Tjeenk Willink, 1890). Published in the series *Mannen van beteekenis in onze dagen* that started in 1870.

12 Jan Smelik, *Eén in lied en leven. Het stichtelijke lied bij Nederlandse protestanten tussen 1866 en 1938* (The Hague: SDU uitgeverij, 1997), 170-177.

13 A. J. van den Berg, *De Nederlandse Christen-Studenten Vereniging 1896–1985* (The Hague: Boekencentrum, 1991), 312.

14 See Annette Stott, *Holland Mania. The Unknown Dutch Period in Art and Culture* (Woodstock, NY: Overlook Press, 1998).

15 See Henry A. V. M. van Stekelenburg, "Dutch Roman Catholics in the United States," in Robert P. Swierenga, ed., *The Dutch in America. Immigration, Settlement, and Cultural Change* (New Brunswick, NJ: Rutgers University Press, 1985), 64-77

DUTCH SOCIAL REFORMERS' PERCEPTIONS OF AMERICAN REFORM

MAARTJE JANSE

Introduction

In the nineteenth century many people, both in the Netherlands and the United States, manifested the desire to reform people and society at large, and believed that this was possible, provided the right strategies were employed. Reform causes included, but were not limited to, antislavery, antiprostitution, temperance, prison reform, housing reform, vegetarianism, protests against animal cruelty, vivisection, child abuse and child labor, the promotion of women's education, Christian education, Sabbath observance, women's rights, free trade, and world peace. The strategies used to further these causes ranged from founding organizations and organizing public meetings and lecturing tours, to the publication of tracts, periodicals, and novels. Furthermore, reformers put pressure on political candidates to vote in favor of change, and petitioned government to implement legislative reform.

The story of the interaction between nineteenth-century American and Dutch social reformers is not a straightforward love story. In many ways the countries were far apart. The fact that similar movements existed does not necessarily imply close ties between reformers on both sides of the Atlantic. It seems that for most of the century Dutch reformers were mainly interacting with British colleagues — as were the Americans. Through their British counterparts and through contacts with other reformers, they participated in a global culture. It was not until the last quarter of the century that Dutch and American reformers grew more fond of each other and engaged more frequently in direct exchanges of ideas and encouragement. In the earlier decades, American social-reform practices were known and discussed in the Netherlands, but often denounced.

This article focuses mainly on three Dutch reform movements: the temperance movement, the communal movement, and the women's rights movement, selected not because of their coherence, but because all of them had distinct ties with American counterparts, and praised as well as criticized the American example. Instead of giving an overview of the ideals and developments of these movements, which can be found elsewhere, the goal of this article is to trace the development of Dutch reformers' thoughts on American reform.

Why was it that in the first half of the nineteenth century American reform movements were not very prominent examples for Dutch reformers? While the Dutch public had some understanding of both British and American antislavery and temperance movements — the two most prominent social movements of these decades — they were generally looked upon with a frown. Most people found their style too theatrical and too enthusiastic, and felt uncomfortable about the massive popular support they were able to generate. In the Netherlands, for most of the nineteenth century, dealing with social and political questions was perceived to be a serious and difficult matter, in which not everyone was suited to participate. In the United States, this elitist notion of politics had been prevalent prior to the Revolution, but a more democratic attitude had gradually replaced it, in which public opinion, public debate, and general male suffrage (albeit for white men only) played major roles. Democracy was sustained to a large extent by Protestant Evangelicalism. The Second Great Awakening in particular provided a fertile foundation for nineteenth-century reform.

Even though the Netherlands had experienced a similar revolutionary era during the late eighteenth century, which had given birth to "modern politics" (with a national public debate in periodicals and societies), its legacy for the nineteenth century was almost the opposite of the North American one. As in many other European countries, it was followed by a restoration period in which extending suffrage and political participation in general became associated with the threat of more revolutions and more bloodshed. Together with the absence of a broad, popular, middle-class evangelical movement, this different legacy explains why the political cultures of the United States and the Netherlands during the 1830s were miles apart.

This was so much so that comparing, for example, the Dutch and American antislavery movements at first glance seems like comparing apples and oranges. In the United States, from the 1830s onward, antislavery advocates displayed intensely emotional appeals and built a dense associational network, in which around 1838 one hundred thousand people were said to participate — among them many women and black abolitionists, whose crucial contributions to the movement have been increasingly acknowledged in the past decades. They published abolitionist newspapers, gave antislavery lectures, organized mass petitions; some even founded a political party while others stayed away from politics, believing a spiritual transformation of the nation was the only way to salvation of the sin of slavery.[1]

The Dutch antislavery movement (1840–63) chose to be calm, cautious, and respectable. Partly because of the strategy to exclude women from membership, the Netherlands Society for the Abolition of Slavery, at its peak in 1857, counted no more than 670 members. Although seemingly different, this type of movement strongly reminds one of the American antislavery movement before 1832.[2] This is not to say that the Dutch movement stagnated in an early phase while the American movement developed fully — such a finalist approach does not do justice to the historical specificity of both countries and both movements. If we stop focusing mainly on differences and, instead, concentrate on the historical developments of the reform cultures in both countries, we may be able to better appreciate the changing relations between Dutch and American reformers.

Temperance Movement

In the 1830s and 1840s, Dutch temperance advocates admired the efforts of reformers abroad. Examples from the New World, together with British, Irish, and German ones, were inspirational during the founding phase of the first Dutch local temperance organizations.[3] Although there is no evidence that the 1836 visit of the famous American reformer Robert Baird, who was enormously influential in the German and Scandinavian countries, had any impact on the Dutch temperance movement,[4] in 1842, at the founding meeting of the Nederlandsche Vereeniging tot Afschaffing van Sterken Drank (Netherlands Society for the Abolishment of Hard Liquor, hereafter NVASD), the American example proved important. When the question arose whether a national reform organization of citizens could function without the explicit support of the government, the heated debate was decided when someone "proved from the example of North America and Britain that beneficial effects were to be expected from voluntary association of citizens, even without recognition or cooperation from the government."[5] What happened abroad was an eye opener for the Dutch reformers; it broadened their ideas of what they could contribute to society, independent from government. And, equally important, they could justify their actions by referring to reformers elsewhere.

Especially from the early 1850s on, one particular North American crusade against alcohol was to become the success story that inspired a politicization of temperance movements worldwide. In 1851 the eyes of temperance advocates all over the world were fixed upon the American state of Maine, where a law was passed that prohibited the sale of all alcoholic beverages. Other states followed Maine's example, and the American experiments with prohibition opened up new possibilities for onlookers overseas. Amsterdam temperance advocates eagerly wrote: "What has been obtained in so many American states by means of pure conviction of a well-informed and energetic people, ... is possible in *the Netherlands* as well."[6]

In 1852 the NVASD adopted the prohibitionist strategy. However, since prohibition was perceived as a radical measure, the organization had to convince the public of its calm, responsible, and respectable character. To that end, it contrasted itself to temperance movements abroad. They were denounced and even ridiculed by chairman Willem Egeling: "When I spoke of new means to extend our cause, I did not have in mind the American and English processions with standards and banners, nor the Temperance Festivals of the Germans with the roar of guns and merrymaking in the open air, nor the Cold Water Army of the Americans, nor the Bands of Hope of the German or English boys, who, like their fathers, parade in public. No! Such loud and ostentatious spectacles do not suit our respectable and dignified nation."[7] One tool that Dutch temperance advocates did adopt in the 1850s was that of holding "American and British *meetings*," which were livelier than the solemn *vergaderingen* had been.

Despite countless meetings and petitions, no Dutch Maine Law came into being, but in 1881 a Dutch Liquor Law was adopted, introducing both a (rather ineffective) licensing system and forbidding public drunkenness. Nor was the American nationwide Prohibition of 1919–33 followed by a similar one in the Netherlands. In the 1920s, however, it led to forceful pressure in favor of a "local option" (to give city councils the power to forbid the sale of liquor if three-quarters of the population requested so through a referendum) that was just barely stopped by the Dutch Senate (partly for unrelated, procedural reasons). The negative effects of America's Prohibition were now used against the Dutch attempts at legislation.

All in all, the Dutch movement was very different from the one in America. First, it did not promote total abstinence from all alcoholic beverages, as was common practice in British and American organizations from around 1840. Teetotalism was seen as fanaticism, which is why moderate consumption of beer and wine was condoned until the end of the nineteenth century. Second, American women played a pivotal role in paving the road to Prohibition, most notably through the Women's Christian Temperance Union, founded in 1873. Dutch women's organizations were remarkably absent — partly because in the Netherlands, women's rights and temperance had not become intertwined, as was the case in the United States. Third, Dutch churches did not unequivocally speak out on behalf of temperance and prohibition, as they had done in the U.S.

It seems fair to conclude that the American example played a vital role in founding, politicizing, and reinvigorating the Dutch temperance movement. In the end, however, Dutch (political) culture and society — hardly touched by the early nineteenth-century Evangelicalism that largely accounted for the

343

2

——

massive support among British and American women and churches — proved too different for the British and American example to have a stronger impact. This applies to Dutch antislavery as well.

Cooperative and Communal Movement

Around the turn of the century, when social needs became more pressing and a different cultural climate had developed in the Netherlands, the American example became increasingly alluring to some reformers. The story of the "American dream" of one of them offers insight into the particular attraction of the United States.

Frederik van Eeden (1860–1932), medical doctor and novelist, was a prominent figure in the literary and artistic Eighties Movement, whose followers were critical of the old bourgeois culture of their predecessors. Many of them focused on art for art's sake, but some wanted to renew society at large and expanded their literary criticism to social critique. Van Eeden, for example, served as a guiding figure in the Dutch communal and cooperative movement, a modernized version of the utopian socialist movements of the early nineteenth century. Its goal was to replace competitive capitalism by an alternative society based on mutual assistance and private landownership by autonomous communities. The underlying belief was that successful communitarian colonies would serve as examples and revolutionize society at large.[8]

Van Eeden had become a socialist not by reading theoretical works by Russian authors, but because of an American novel. Around 1890, he read Edward Bellamy's *Looking Backward 2000–1887* (1888), a utopian tale of the righteous and prosperous city that Boston had become in the year 2000. He was struck by "the clear common sense, the cheerful optimism of the American author."[9] Another American text prompted him to act upon his new-found ideals: Henry David Thoreau's *Walden, or Life in the Woods* (1854), which he read in 1898. Thoreau's account of his experiences living a secluded life in a simple cabin on Walden Pond, gave Van Eeden the incentive to put his ideals into practice: only a few months later he purchased an estate near Bussum to start his own colony, which, as a tribute to Thoreau, he named Walden.

Accordingly, the American history of the colonizing experiments of different religious and social groups — from the Shakers and Harmonists to the Owenites and Fourierists — became of special interest to Van Eeden. Since the seventeenth century European sectarian groups, on the run for the law or intolerance, had settled in the U.S., which offered both literally and figuratively the space that Europe lacked. But Van Eeden was critical of their inclination toward isolating themselves from the outside world, their strict asceticism and unworldly manners. It was the surplus of ideals and the lack of practicality, he believed, that had caused most colonies to fail. He wanted his colony to be practical, and, astonishingly for a socialist, looked at American business life for guidance. Van Eeden dreamed of passing onto the cooperative movement the optimism of both entrepreneurs and workers, their energy and spirit of enterprise, and most of all the efficiency of large-scale organizations. Nonetheless, Walden was declared bankrupt in 1907 due to mismanagement, lack of experience, and unwillingness of the workers to share the profits. Still, Van Eeden did not give up his plans. Yes, he had failed in the Netherlands, but believed more than ever he would succeed in the land of hopes and dreams.

Almost immediately after Walden's demise, he accepted an invitation for a lecturing tour in the United States. He wanted to spread the idea that domestic colonization could become a great success in modern times, if it was carried out in a businesslike manner, and he put his hopes in persuading a business tycoon of the caliber of Andrew Carnegie, whose *The Empire of Business* (1902) he had approvingly read, to make the cooperative movement a success. His finest hour came on March 8, 1908, when he addressed an audience of three thousand in New York's Carnegie Hall. His speech on "practical communism" was greeted with enthusiasm, as Van Eeden did not condemn big business as such, but suggested ways in which it could be used to reform society. His message resonated with the ideals of the Progressive Era and his unbound optimism matched that of his audience. Van Eeden enjoyed his tour. "The Americans are willing to listen," he wrote. "They do not scoff at novelty like the people of the old countries. Americans have the enthusiasm and the spirit of progress." On his three American tours in 1908 and 1909 he made many friends and acquaintances, among them the socialist writer Upton Sinclair, women's rights advocate Charlotte Perkins Gilman, and banker, landowner, and entrepreneur Hugh MacRae.[10]

It was by collaborating with MacRae that Van Eeden received another chance to carry out his reform plans: in Van Eeden Colony near Wilmington, NC, some twenty Dutch families came to work and live in the summer of 1911. This would be the ultimate test case for the modern, "American" approach to colonizing that Van Eeden had in mind. To his great disappointment Van Eeden Colony failed just as Walden had — shattering his American dream. But despite his disillusionment, he never fell out of love with the United States.

345

Women's Rights Movement

Aletta Jacobs (1854–1929) can be characterized as someone who did not just court American reformers but developed an equal relationship with them.[11] In

1904 the famous Carrie Chapman Catt (1859–1947) introduced her good friend Aletta as the first Dutch woman to graduate from university, finish her Ph.D., practice medicine, and then claim the vote for women and provide the incentive to found the Vereeniging voor Vrouwenkiesrecht (Association for Women's Suffrage). Like Van Eeden, Jacobs was on a lecturing tour in the United States. Likewise, she had been inspired by American reformers and was excited about American reform experiments, which gave women the right to vote in the states of Wyoming (1869), Colorado (1893), Utah and Idaho (1896). During her first travels through the United States Jacobs witnessed the election campaigns in Colorado and was impressed with the thorough inquiries women voters made into political matters. She concluded: "Yes, the American women, as a whole, are ahead of us by one or more generations. Wherever we still need to get hold of a position, they have obtained a firm footing."[12]

Pioneers of national movements often follow examples from abroad. As becomes clear from Mineke Bosch's recent biography of Jacobs, in the course of her life her activism was increasingly embedded in an international network. British and American women's rights advocates were her main sources of inspiration: she read about them, met them at international conferences, collaborated and corresponded with many, and developed intimate friendships with some. At home she boasted of her "connections with foreign pioneers of the women's movement, who are very experienced."[13]

Jacobs strategically employed their stories as exemplary models for other women. One of the first things she did after becoming president of the Vereeniging voor Vrouwenkiesrecht and editor of their monthly, was to publish a series of inspirational portraits of feminists abroad, starting with American activists Susan B. Anthony and, soon thereafter, Elizabeth Cady Stanton. To Jacobs, her friends Antony and Chapman Catt personified the American love of liberty that fueled the struggle for women's rights. Jacobs identified with them, to the point where even her autobiography *Herinneringen* (1924) follows that of Stanton and other American and British feminists, sometimes very literally.

Yet, Jacobs' relationship with American activists consisted of more than merely following their example. Through her personal contacts with reformers, she developed a relationship of equality with them. For example, she became very close to Carrie Chapman Catt, especially after they each lost their husband. The two women even traveled the world together. In 1906 they visited the Austro-Hungarian Empire as representatives of the International Woman Suffrage Alliance, and in 1911–12 they tried to urge women in South Africa, Egypt, Pales-

Aletta H. Jacobs (right) and Carrie Chapman Catt in the garden of the American Club in Hankou, China (1912).   ►

In the garden of the
american Club in
Hankou. 1912

tine, the Philippines, the Dutch East Indies, British India, China, and Japan to found chapters of the Society for the Advancement of Women.

On their trips, Jacobs and Catt together represented the "civilized world." The women's movement perceived itself to be internationalist by nature, but class, race, and nationalist identities were also at play. International ceremonies at conferences featured national flags, anthems, and performances, in national dress, of traditional songs and dances. The women in attendance not only represented womanhood in general, but their own country as well. In the case of the Netherlands, this was in accordance with a growing national pride. The Netherlands was no longer the world power it had been during its Golden Age, but its relative weakness was turned into a strength: the country emphasized its special guiding role in the world as a neutral, impartial guide for the bigger countries. Seen in this light, Catt and Jacobs' trip around the globe can be understood as a Dutch-American enterprise to enlighten the world.

Empowerment

The above suggests that between 1830 and 1914 ambivalence prevailed in the Netherlands regarding the "excessive" passion and enthusiasm with which zealous American reformers pursued their goals. We need of course to be careful not to jump to conclusions based on a handful of cases, but this conclusion seems to match the assessment the Dutch historian Lammers made of the perception of the United States in the Netherlands: criticism usually took precedence over praise.[14] While Dutch temperance advocates were empowered by the success of the American organizations and by the first American prohibition laws, they were put off by the dramatic style of these movements. Aletta Jacobs was critical of the "high-society ladies and disinterested toilers" she met during her American travels. And even Van Eeden, who expected so much of the United States, was highly critical of the way American values were employed in daily practice.

Their sometimes harsh criticism notwithstanding, Dutch reformers admired American values like individualism, love of democracy, freedom, and civil rights, as well as the American political system with a key role for public opinion and its high degree of political participation. The extended suffrage, combined with the "heightened morale of the masses," could force political leaders to act in ways "that seem to us unheard of and unimaginably generous." Above all, they praised the mindset of the American people: energetic, enthusiastic, willing to try something new and unusual. Van Eeden characterized America in 1909 as "the great country of experiments, where freedom is in the making, where there is no lack of energy, plenty of good-will and optimism, and a great number of able, well-intentioned men."[15] If nothing else, the openness to change and opportunities to experiment drew reformers from all over the world to the United States.

From midcentury onward, Dutch reformers were increasingly inspired by what happened in the U.S., a development that reached its height in the first decades of the twentieth century. In explaining why the balance slowly shifted toward appreciation and admiration, the role of personal contacts between reformers seems crucial. The cheaper fares of modern ocean liners made more, and more frequent, personal encounters possible — Aletta Jacobs crossed the Atlantic in 1914 on the superliner *SS Potsdam*. Hence, the exaggerated image they originally had of each other gave way to more accurate views. American lecturing tours transformed the perceptions Dutch reformers had of the U.S., and intimate friendships with American reformers made them love the country.

There is more, though, to account for the growing appreciation of American reform. In stating that American women were generations ahead of their Dutch sisters, Jacobs elaborated on an older theme in which the United States was envisioned as the youthful guide into the future for old Europe. The power of this general idea for Dutch reformers is clear. Just like the temperance advocates who pointed to Maine's prohibition laws, European advocates for women's suffrage pointed to American reforms as if looking into their own future. This made reform seem inevitable while making opposition look intolerably backward. As was emphasized earlier, the Dutch did find many faults in American society and were by no means eager to Americanize the whole of Dutch society; nevertheless, they followed what happened on the other side of the Atlantic with special interest, as history had proven that many developments would, sooner or later, surface in Europe too. Especially from the 1890s to the 1920s, when countless initiatives for national and municipal reform were developed in response to pressing social questions, the appreciation for American reform grew, simply because social reform was considered more important than it had been previously.

In addition, Dutch political culture was starting to resemble American political life much more closely. With the extension of the vote and the advent of "partisan" politics, an emotional and dramatic political style became common practice. In the meantime, the American culture of reform had also changed profoundly. From 1870, the evangelically based reform movements faded into the background, and the new wave of reform brought by the Progressive Era was much less inspired by religion. Its preoccupation with practical and businesslike reform made it much more accessible to the Dutch public.

349

One may argue that the self-images of both countries started showing similarities. Because of its size, economic success, and ambitions, the United States had always perceived itself as a leading nation, while the idea of the Netherlands as a neutral guide to the world powers was relatively new. At the begin-

2

—

ning of the twentieth century the United States and the Netherlands were in some ways equal partners in their reform efforts. Carrie Chapman Catt chose to travel the world with Aletta Jacobs, to show "less civilized" women the road to freedom. Also, American business tycoon Carnegie, so much admired by Van Eeden, selected The Hague as the seat for his Peace Palace, which was opened in 1913. And after President Woodrow Wilson received Aletta Jacobs — who was involved in the international peace movement as well — at the White House in 1915, he wrote that it "gave him great pleasure to meet so interesting a woman." In instances like these, the appreciation was mutual.

1   One of the best introductions to American antislavery is James Brewer Stewart, *Holy Warriors: The Abolitionists and American Slavery*, 2nd, rev. ed. (New York: Hill and Wang, 1997).

2   Richard S. Newman, *The Transformation of American Abolitionism: Fighting Slavery in the Early Republic* (Chapel Hill/London: University of North Carolina Press, 2002); For the Dutch antislavery movement see Maartje Janse, *De afschaffers: Publieke opinie, organisatie en politiek in Nederland, 1840–1880* (Amsterdam: Wereldbibliotheek, 2007), 51-127.

3   The following paragraphs are based on Janse, *De afschaffers*, 27-51, 129-172; Hans Krabbendam, "'A Plant of American Origin, Fit for Dutch Soil?' American Protestantism and the Dutch Reformed Temperance Effort, 1835–1935," in George Harinck and Hans Krabbendam, eds., *Sharing the Reformed Tradition: The Dutch-North American Exchange, 1846–1996* (Amsterdam: VU University Press, 1996), 57-78.

4   Janse, *De afschaffers*, 51 n. 111; see also Krabbendam, "A Plant," 58-59.

5   Janse, *De afschaffers*, 47.

6   Ibid., 142.

7   Ibid., 151.

8   Ronald G. Walters, *American Reformers 1815–1860*, 2nd, rev. ed. (New York: Hill and Wang, 1997), 39-75.

9   The following paragraphs are primarily based on Marianne Mooijweer, *De Amerikaanse droom van Frederik van Eeden* (Amsterdam: Bataafse Leeuw, 1996); Quotation on 21.

10   Mooijweer, *Amerikaanse droom*, 68.

11   The following paragraphs are primarily based on Mineke Bosch, *Een onwrikbaar geloof in rechtvaardigheid: Aletta Jacobs 1854–1929* (Amsterdam: Balans, 2005).

12   Ibid., 363.

13   Ibid., 246; See also Mineke Bosch (with Annemarie Kloosterman), ed., *Politics and Friendship: Letters from the International Woman Suffrage Alliance, 1902–1942* (Columbus: Ohio State University Press, 1990).

14   A. Lammers, *Uncle Sam en Jan Salie: Hoe Nederland Amerika ontdekte* (Amsterdam: Balans, 1989).

15   Mooijweer, *Amerikaanse droom*, 44, 47.

THE RECEPTION OF AMERICAN LITERATURE IN THE NETHERLANDS

——

HANS BAK

Just as the Netherlands was among the first to acknowledge the political reality of the new American republic, Dutch critics and reviewers were among the first to take note of the New World's nascent literature. Thus, even before a Dutch translation appeared in 1784, *De Algemeene Vaderlandsche Letteroefeningen* reviewed Crèvecoeur's *Brieven van een Amerikaansche Landsman.*[1] In the early nineteenth century, as American writers were struggling to prove that a person from the "wilds" of America could write with as much grace and substance as writers in the Old World, Dutch observers (often writing anonymously and within the circumference of the moral decorum governing Dutch magazine culture) closely monitored the emergence of a distinctly American literature. Though they mostly took this literature as a subsidiary branch of English writing and measured it by European standards, leading Dutch magazines generously opened their pages to sophisticated and substantial considerations of American literature.

In 1850 *De Tijd* published a first retrospective of the literary achievements of the New World at midcentury. Written anonymously, it posited the then current perception that American writing before independence had "no real literary value" but mostly concerned politics, law, and religion. But even the best American writers since then (Cooper, Irving, Longfellow) had "not been able to break away from the influence of their European models," and had mostly been marked by a "desire to imitate." Unlike Franklin, whose *Poor Richard's Almanac* was "an original product of American literature," and Emerson, whose thought and writings bore "the stamp of his native country," the greatly talented Edgar Allan Poe evinced but "little of the American national character."[2] Although, as we shall see, by 1850 other critics had discovered much that *was* distinctly American about the literature of the New World, the impression that American writing was at best second rate, modeled after British or European examples, and hence derivative, remained persistent through the nineteenth century. "The U.S. is still a British colony culturally," maintained Maurits Wagenvoort in *De Amsterdammer* as late as 1892.

The scope of what critics and magazines deemed worthy of notice was mostly delimited by what was translated into Dutch and by what was considered "work of merit" in the United States. As a consequence, the Dutch interest largely mirrored what was thought important by American critics or publishers and what was popular with American readers. Thus, the ten American writers who garnered most Dutch critical attention in the nineteenth century were Harriet Beecher Stowe (60 reviews) and James Fenimore Cooper (58), followed by Washington Irving (34), Henry Wadsworth Longfellow (27), Ralph Waldo Emerson (22), Walt Whitman (20), Nathaniel Hawthorne (19), Bret Harte (15), and Mark Twain and Louisa May Alcott (both 14).[3] Apart from the fact that even these authors were not always appreciated then for the reasons for which we appreciate them now, the ten include authors (Longfellow, Harte, Alcott) subsequently expelled from many a twentieth-century anthology of American literature, whereas others who later gained recognition or canonical rehabilitation were virtually invisible on the radar of nineteenth-century Dutch periodical criticism.

Irving, Cooper, Stowe, Hawthorne

The earliest consideration of an American author was an 1824 review of Washington Irving's *Sketch-Book*. The anonymous reviewer thought Irving "a pleasant, entertaining, instructive, and also a funny writer" but felt he could hardly be called an American Sterne (*177*). The early Dutch interest in Irving may well have owed something to his satirical treatment of Dutch colonial history in "Rip van Winkle," "Legend of Sleepy Hollow," and his pseudonymous *History of New York*. The latter, curiously, was not among the twelve books by Irving that appeared in Dutch translation between 1824 and 1842. A rather unappreciative and humorless 1835 review for *Het Leeskabinet* considered it one of Irving's least successful ones, marred by exaggeration and "an itch to be witty" (*209*). More popular were his travel books and biographies of Columbus and Spanish explorers. If for one critic Irving's American travel books gave Dutch readers an "invaluable" insight into "the American West, a wild and uninhabited region which is bound to play an important role in the expansion of North American civilization across the American continent" (*206*), another felt that Irving's "meticulous description of the inhuman cruelties perpetrated by the Spaniards on the native Indian population make quite clear that it might have been better if Columbus had never discovered America" (*187*). By 1838 Irving had passed the high point of Dutch appreciation: to E.J. Potgieter, editor of *De Gids*, he had become tedious after his "excellent" early works (*210*).

James Fenimore Cooper far outranked Irving in the quantity and quality of the Dutch critical response: between 1821 and 1845 twenty-two of his books appeared in translation, and in 1900 a six-volume edition of his complete works. If he was often compared to Sir Walter Scott, the Dutch particularly relished Cooper as a novelist of the sea.[4] Potgieter, momentarily blind to the presence of countless native tribes, proclaimed in *De Gids*: "Please do not cast up his wildernesses, his Savannahs, his forests at me; what are these but another ocean, interminable Spaces, where no human inhabitants left a trace of their presence."[5] But it was Cooper's *Leatherstocking Tales* (also adapted for the young) that singled him out as "a genuine representative of America, the land of freedom, where the new civilization coexists with the wilderness, where man is young and nature eternal, and where the settlers, separated from the other continents by the Ocean, have to depend on human solidarity and their own resources to achieve their aims" (*88*). As a historical novelist Cooper managed to make a "masterful use of the little that was at his disposal" (*42*), his "honest representation of America's War of Independence" receiving particular praise (*46*). Though critics found Cooper an essentially "moral writer" (if given to "tedious longwindedness"), his depiction of Indian warfare, morals, and customs met with ambivalence. *The Last of the Mohicans* seemed a "savage book" to *De Recensent*, providing "nourishment neither for the heart, nor for the mind" (*48*). *De Vaderlandsche Letteroefeningen* was more balanced — "We watch the Indians here as the paragons of physical perfection and poetic eloquence on the one hand, and of inhuman cruelty, relentless vindictiveness, hellish cunning and bloodlust on the other" — and recognized the symbolic importance of Natty Bumpo as "Cooper's most impressive creation, a rare embodiment of on the one hand European civilization and Christian virtues, and on the other physical prowess and hunting skills, matching those of the most keen-sighted and agile Indian" (*49*). The consensus was that Cooper was "one of the most brilliant men of letters of this century ... not only in the somewhat arid literary climate of his native country, but in all civilized countries" (*91*).

That moral astringencies were characteristic of the Dutch response is borne out by the reception of Harriet Beecher Stowe, twenty-four of whose books appeared in translation between 1839 and 1892. *Uncle Tom's Cabin* (1852) alone, easily the most popular of American novels, went through five translations — one of them, by C. M. Mensing, going through thirteen editions between 1853 and 1900 — and received a record number of fifteen reviews. The book's popularity reflected the strong Dutch interest in the morally contentious issue of the "cancerous disease" of slavery (*273*), and in Stowe's compassionate and Christianity-inspired campaign for its abolition. Several reviews discussed the history and humanly degrading conditions of American slavery, but it was a rare Dutch critic who ventured to suggest an application to the practice of slavery in "our colonies in the East," as did M. E. van der Meulen, a Frisian minister of the Dutch Reformed Church (*276*). Mostly, the moral, human, and Christian sentiments in Stowe's work met with strong and unqualified endorsement. If aesthetic deficiencies were noted — the use of "some very clever conjuror's tricks" in Stowe's playing with readers' "human and Christian feelings," a lack of complexity in the characterization (slave traders being represented as "black devils" and slaves as "black angels"), and a facile, tear-jerking plot (*268-269*) — still, these did not diminish its status as a "masterpiece" (*271*).

The popularity of *Uncle Tom's Cabin* also triggered a steady Dutch interest in Stowe's later works, like *Dred: A Tale of the Dismal Swamp* (1856), or books focused on the domestic lives of women and the nascent struggle for female emancipation, such as *Little Foxes* (1866) and *The Chimney-Corner* (1868). The critical response is revealing of (male responses to) the changes in women's position in Dutch society. Though Stowe's position on the women's movement was circumscribed by her Christian preference for the domestic as woman's natural domain, critics were teased into comparing the "issue" of female emancipation in the United States and the Netherlands. Thus, *De Vaderlandsche Letteroefeningen* noted that women's emancipation was pursued with "much more openness and energy" in America, "because there is nothing to hinder its growth. ... What really matters is how to control it properly, and this is not an easy task" (*308*).

"If Mrs. Stowe had had Hawthorne's pen, her book [*Uncle Tom's Cabin*] would have been even greater," *Het Leeskabinet* proclaimed in 1853. From the start Nathaniel Hawthorne's Dutch reputation was strong: he belonged "among the most distinguished writers of our time" and *The Scarlet Letter* was clearly "superior" to *Uncle Tom's Cabin* on account of "its originality and its grand design" — "Richness of sentiment, brilliant imagination, and especially a wonderful knowledge of the hidden reaches of the human heart are the rare qualities of Hawthorne's genius" (*143*). Hawthorne's Dutch reputation rested mostly on artistic and psychological grounds, and critics noticed early that the author was likely to have a limited appeal, mostly to the "cultured and educated" (*145*). Only six of Hawthorne's books were translated into Dutch between 1853 and 1860. Yet, he was one of the first American writers to earn a place in world literature: he was, proclaimed *Boekzaal der Geleerde Wereld*, "the North American Dickens" (*147*).

E.J. Potgieter on America and
American Literature

The Dutch critic with the greatest enthusiasm for Hawthorne was E.J. Potgieter (1808–75), founding editor and from 1837 to 1865 the principal force behind *De Gids*.[6] He saw Hawthorne as a kindred soul, sharing his sense of the magic of the ordinary as well as his presumed solitariness, admiring his literary persistence and integrity in the face of a lack of popularity. Potgieter's fascination culminated in his fine 1864 novella "Journey in the Rain."[7] Published in the year of Hawthorne's death, the text, incorporating elements from the newly published *Dolliver Romance* and Oliver Wendell Holmes's graveside speech, showed how *au courant* Potgieter's interest in American literature was. In the novella (set in what Hawthorne had termed "a middle ground of fact and fancy") Potgieter, traveling by train from The Hague to Amsterdam, is engrossed in reading Hawthorne when he finds an (imaginary) American seated across him. The ensuing conversation soon reverts to the American author who, in Potgieter's appreciation, truly grasped the mystery of art.

At a time when U.S. culture occupied at best a peripheral place in the minds of Europeans, few Dutch writers were as persistent in their enthusiasm for American literature as Potgieter. He sought to regenerate a flagging and anemic Dutch literature by urging a return to the spirit of the Golden Age, when the Netherlands was the illuminating beacon for the world in military accomplishment as well as commerce, art, literature, and science. Hence he looked with hope and confidence to young America where a nascent liberal democracy was fulfilling the role that the Netherlands once had and which he hoped might serve as a source of inspiration and emulation. Seeing in America "a challenge to the present, a prophecy of the distant future," Potgieter was not averse to the rhetoric of Manifest Destiny: he sent a transcription of Berkeley's poem, "Verses on the prospect of planting arts and learning in America," with its famous line, "Westward the course of empire takes its way," to his friend Conrad Busken Huet, and observed: "I believe that if I had three or six months time, I should go to the United States."[8] Revering the geniuses of Franklin, Washington, and Lincoln, he wrote poems in tribute to them, and kept a rose from Washington's grave, embossed in glass, as a relic in his room. Yet he also recognized there were blemishes on "the great white whole" of America: "Brave, dazzling, stalwart Beauty, who bear on your shield the arms of labor and liberty, why does there cling to your white robe the stain of Slavery, the blood of your African brother?"[9] He translated several of Longfellow's poems on slavery for *De Gids*, observing in 1851: "God's image carved in ebonwood has found a champion in Longfellow who will overcome the prejudice."[10] He was equally disturbed by the abuse of America's native peoples and in an 1837 review of a *History of Indian Tribes in North America* lamented the fate of "a race which had only the wilderness as a witness and, accordingly, as the grave for its heroic deeds, a race which approached the altar of civilization only to be butchered upon it" (*348*).[11] Like many international observers, Potgieter also mistrusted American materialism, the all-pervasive "love of money."

Potgieter never actually visited the United States. His was an imaginary America, formed by impressions gained from its literature and the histories and travel reports that circulated in his day. A member of an English and American Reading Society in Amsterdam, he was an avid reader of American journals like *North American Review* and *Atlantic Monthly*, and wrote about American books only a short time after they appeared in the U.S. Not only did he introduce Cooper and Irving to the Netherlands, he also drew attention to lesser-known writers such as N.P. Willis, James Kirk Paulding, Thomas Chandler Haliburton, David Crockett, Henry Dana, and Catherine Maria Sedgwick. And he was a sympathetic but (like Hawthorne) not uncritical student of the Transcendentalists. He disliked Poe for his extreme aestheticism, was silent on Whitman, and greatly appreciated Longfellow — but in general, he felt, the American taste in poetry was hampered by "a practical, a didactic, a religious *purpose*."

Longfellow, Twain, Whitman, Emerson, Alcott

Few shared Potgieter's strong enthusiasm for American life and letters. More representative perhaps was the anonymous critic for *De Vaderlandsche Letteroefeningen* who in 1857 exclaimed "America! What art thou?" and evoked it as enigmatic and riveted with contradictions: a country where immigrant dreams were as often fulfilled as disappointed, where freedom was celebrated but slavery reigned, where human rights were respected and violated, where an empire was built on sin, cunning, and deceit as well as on a new hope for Christianity. It was "a land where literature seems to be silenced by the thunder of steam engines, while at the same time it produces geniuses who can rival if not surpass the most celebrated of Europeans in novelty of form and power of ideas" (*216*). Nor did Potgieter's admiration for Longfellow go unchallenged. Although he was widely regarded as "the greatest poet of the United States of America" (*237*), Charles Boissevain felt that his fame was "out of all proportion to his poetic talents." It was mostly due, he wrote with venom in *De Gids* in 1869, to the fact that "the public prefers graceful, elegant mediocrity to the brutal power of great geniuses. What the public loves are platitudes, eloquently expressed, inspired by a religious, Christian creed and refined and rounded off by an unmistakable talent." Longfellow was "effeminate, sentimental, and weak" — above all, his work lacked passion (*229*).

E. J. Potgieter (1808–75).

Boissevain had visited Longfellow during a two-month trip to the United States as a reporter for the *Algemeen Handelsblad*.[12] A journalist with literary aspirations, he was an editor of *De Gids* (1872–88) who, like Potgieter, held the Dutch seventeenth century up as an invigorating model, as opposed to the state of malaise of Dutch culture in his days, and saw in America a new source of energy and vitality. Indeed, the spirit of the Dutch Golden Age seemed alive and well in the New World, from the "restless competition, iron power of the mind, and sturdy diligence" he found in New York, to the rough but rich business entrepreneurs he met in the "magical" city of Chicago. Although he shared the racial condescension of his time, was disturbed by the political scandals and corruption, as well as by the "unthinking barbarity" with which Americans destroyed their natural resources, he remained a firm believer in America's resilience and its pragmatic ability to solve such problems.[13]

By the late nineteenth century, as Wagenvoort noted, Americans were still so "impregnated with [their] inferior taste that they [were] unable to recognize their own masters" (*358*). This certainly applied to two unmistakably American authors, Mark Twain and Walt Whitman. Though as many as thirteen books by Twain appeared in Dutch translation between 1877 and 1900, reviewers remarkably failed to take note of the works valued most highly today (*The Adventures of Huckleberry Finn*, *Life on the Mississippi*). Their verdict of Twain was marked by a persistent moralism and a curious inability to appreciate the distinctive quality of his humor. If they recognized that here was an "original" American genius, they often had difficulty liking what they saw: American characters and conditions seemed simply *too* different from Dutch life and identity. Thus, *De Tijdspiegel* thought that *Roughing It* "[failed] to increase our liking for this wondrous, rough country in which everything is big, even the crimes" (*24*). Speaking out on *The Adventures of Tom Sawyer*, *Het Leeskabinet* rather dourly objected that "we, in the Netherlands, are not familiar with the kind of strange adventures and daring exploits" of American boys, and added: "Love stories of boys and girls of ten to twelve years old are unknown luxuries here." Indeed, the book might be "harmful to our youth," in that it would "dangerously excite" their imagination rather than "teach them discipline, industry, accuracy, obedience, and similar virtues" (*28*).

No wonder that the Dutch were slow to appreciate Walt Whitman. Though a first edition of *Leaves of Grass* had appeared in 1855, Dutch critics remained largely silent on "the good gray poet" until his death in 1892. An obituary in *De Amsterdammer* recognized that Whitman wanted to be "the creator of a national literature which looked for its models at home, not in England," but also thought his poetry "too controversial, too unusual in form and content, to be accepted and appreciated by the public at once" (*336*). The two critics who did most to illuminate Whitman's achievement were Maurits Wagenvoort and W.G. van Nouhuys. Wagenvoort had fallen under the spell of *Leaves of Grass* during a visit to the United States in 1892, and, feeling that the poems epitomized "all the admirable, awe-inspiring, and perplexing things I have seen in America," had embarked on a first Dutch translation. Knowing that Whitman was "grossly underestimated" in both America and Europe, he was prepared to encounter derision as a translator of reputedly "obscene" verse. As he refused to "bowdlerize," it took him five years to find a Dutch publisher for his (inaptly titled) *Natuurleven* in 1898 (*327*). Meanwhile he had embarked on a crusade to generate appreciation for Whitman in four sensitive if idolizing essays, published (under a pseudonym, Vosmeer de Spie) in *De Kunstwereld* in late 1894 (*340-343*). More discriminating criticism was offered by W.G. van Nouhuys in two essays for *De Gids* in 1894, which he later expanded into a monograph, *Walt Whitman*, in 1895 (*338-339, 344*). Both Wagenvoort and Van Nouhuys were able to see beyond the charges of "immorality" and "untamed primitivism" and recognized Whitman's larger aims, thus giving a broadminded reception to a poet who continued to be controversial.

The situation was different for Ralph Waldo Emerson, Whitman's great inspirer, whose essays were repeatedly noticed in the Dutch highbrow press between 1853 and his death in 1882. M.A.N. Rovers, an important Dutch champion of Emerson, devoted a long chapter to him in his *Mannen van Beteekenis in Onze Dagen* (1880), considering him "one of the great geniuses of our time" (*116*). Most Dutch critics and reviewers (many of them theologians or ministers) rather effortlessly accommodated Emerson as a morally high-minded thinker in a European line including Montaigne, Goethe, Swedenborg, Coleridge, and Carlyle, even as they recognized his innate Americanism.

Louisa May Alcott, whose *Little Women* (1868) went through seven editions in the two-part Dutch translation (*Onder Moedervleugels* en *Op Eigen Wieken*) between 1876 and 1895, likewise received a warmly sympathetic reception, mostly, one suspects, because her moral didacticism and Christian sentiment were congenial to a large Dutch reading public. With twenty of her titles appearing in translation, all deemed "eminently suitable for girls" (*3*), her popularity approached that of Harriet Beecher Stowe. While Stowe and Alcott were virtually the only female "domestic" or "sentimental" novelists whose works received broad attention, an exceptional article in *De Portefeuille* for 1891 introduced Dutch readers to a plethora of women novelists many of whom would only be appreciated again a century later: besides Anne Bradstreet and Phyllis Wheatley, the essay referred to some twenty-five American women writers, including Susanne Rowson, Lydia Maria Child, Catharine Maria Sedgwick, Margaret Fuller, Elizabeth Stoddard, Rebecca Harding Davis, and Helen Hunt Jackson.[14]

Generally speaking, however, the attention of Dutch critics and reviewers was mostly reserved for authors whose works were popular or in the limelight in the United States, or who could easily be accommodated to a Dutch literary taste governed by a predominantly orthodox, moralistic view of art. Even *De Nieuwe Gids*, founded in 1885 by adherents of the Beweging van Tachtig (Eighties Movement) like Frederik van Eeden, Willem Kloos, and Albert Verwey, was, despite its promise of a spirit of renewal in Dutch letters, mostly silent on American literature.[15] If lesser-known writers like Bellamy, Cable, Harte, and Howells received a modest share of attention, "classic" writers like Poe, Thoreau, and Melville were given relatively short shrift, while Charles Brockden Brown, Kate Chopin, Stephen Crane, and, remarkably, Henry James (none of whose books were translated into Dutch before 1900) remained outside the ken of Dutch reviewers altogether. Frederick Douglass's autobiography, translated into Dutch from the German, received one brief mention in *De Recensent* (*281*); Harriet Jacobs went completely unnoticed. Most of these authors would not be properly appreciated in the U.S. until far into the twentieth century, and here, too, the Dutch interest would follow suit. Thus, Melville and Dickinson did not enter American modernist literary consciousness until the 1920s and a first Dutch translation of *Moby-Dick* was not realized until 1929, by J.W.F. Werumeus Buning, while Simon Vestdijk published his splendid personal testimony to Emily Dickinson in *Forum* in 1933.

Conversely, the resonance of Dutch literature in the United States during the nineteenth century was modest to nonexistent. Notable exception was the chapter that Longfellow devoted to the poetry of Jacob Cats, Joost van den Vondel, Willem Bilderdijk, Hendrik Tollens, and some twenty other Dutch poets in his anthology *The Poets and Poetry of Europe* (1845). It is perhaps one of the ironies of Dutch-American literary ties in the nineteenth century that Louis Couperus was the one Dutch author who attained significant visibility in America, with fifteen of his books appearing in the New World after 1892,[16] while the American author whom he resembled in more ways than one — Henry James — remained conspicuously invisible in the literary world of the Netherlands.

1   See Arianne Baggerman, "De vele
     gedaantes van een boer uit Pennsylvania:
     Nederlandse reacties op Crèvecoeur's
     Letters from an American Farmer,"
     *Mededelingen van de Stichting Jacob
     Campo Weyerman* 26.3 (2003): 142-157.
2   "De Amerikaansche Letterkunde van
     dezen Tijd," *De Tijd* 11 (1850): 129-134.
3   Data derived from J.G. Riewald and
     J. Bakker, *The Critical Reception of*

*American Literature in the Netherlands,
1824–1900. A Documentary Conspectus
from Contemporary Periodicals* (Amsterdam: Rodopi, 1982). The one comprehensive survey of translations to date,
the book lists and summarizes reviews
from most major Dutch periodicals, but
omits newspaper reviews and excludes
popular literature such as Horatio
Alger's novels. References in italics are

to reviews as numbered by Riewald and Bakker.

4   Richard Henry Dana's *Two Years before the Mast* (1840) was likewise praised by Potgieter and Albert Verwey (*92*, *94*).

5   "John Fenimore Cooper op Reis," *De Gids*, 1837, 2:69-74. Translation by author.

6   For my discussion of Potgieter I am indebted to Henry Zylstra, "A Mid-Nineteenth-Century Dutch View of American Life and Letters," *PMLA* 57.4 (December 1942): 1108-1136; See also A. Lammers, *Uncle Sam en Jan Salie: Hoe Nederland Amerika ontdekte* (Amsterdam: Balans, 1989), 13-16, and Olf Praamstra, "E.J. Potgieter's and Conrad Busken Huet's Views of the United States," in J.C. Prins et al., eds., *The Low Countries and the New World(s). Travel, Discovery, Early Relations* (Lanham, MD: University Press of America, 2000), 157-165.

7   "Onderweg in den regen," *De Gids*, 1864, 4:427-453.

8   Huet did not share his friend's enthusiasm for the U.S., but in his scant references to the New World displayed a tenor of anti-Americanism that prefigured Menno ter Braak's later "rejection" of the United States. Huet was appalled by the behavior of American tourists in Europe and felt that the rise of democracy inevitably inaugurated the decline of an aristocratic civilization: the spirit of democracy was essentially a "Yankee-spirit" and could but lead to a "tyranny of fools." See Praamstra, "E.J. Potgieter's

and Conrad Busken Huet's Views," 157-165.

9   "Landverhuizing naar de Vereenigde Staten," *De Gids*, 1855, 1:529-530. Written in response to two letters from Reverend Scholte's Dutch settlement at Pella, IA, the essay entailed a reconsideration of the causes of Dutch emigration to the U.S.

10 "Salmagundi," *De Gids*, 1851, 1:670.

11 This quotation and the one at the end of the next paragraph are in Zylstra, "A Mid-Nineteenth-Century Dutch View," 1116 and 1129.

12 See his *Van 't Noorden naar 't Zuiden: Schetsen en Indrukken van de Vereenigde Staen van Noord-Amerika* (Haarlem: H.D. Tjeenk Willink, 1881-82).

13 See Lammers, *Uncle Sam*, 47-58, for a more extensive treatment of Boissevain's travel account.

14 Helen Gray Cone, "De vrouw in de letterkunde van de Vereenigde Staten van Noord-Amerika," *De Portefeuille* 12 (1891): 342-345, 370-382, 445-446, 450-453.

15 Toward the end of the century Frederik van Eeden was inspired by Thoreau's *Walden* (1854) and Edward Bellamy's utopian novel *Looking Backward* (1897); See Marianne Mooijweer, *De Amerikaanse droom van Frederik van Eeden* (Amsterdam: Bataafsche Leeuw, 1996), 30-33.

16 Gerda van Woudenberg, "Couperus and His American Readers," *Dutch Crossings* 36 (1988): 73-92.

ARTISTIC AFFINITIES: NEW-WORLD PAINTERS RECAST THE GOLDEN AGE

——

NANCY T. MINTY

By the close of World War I, the United States — and New York in particular — had become the outpost for Dutch and Flemish seventeenth-century painting in the New World. Fifth Avenue alone, from the Metropolitan Museum down past the mansions of Henry Frick (1849–1919) and Benjamin Altman (1840–1913), yielded over twenty paintings by Rembrandt, five Vermeers, and about a dozen each of Van Dyck and Hals, updated attributions notwithstanding.[1]

This bounty was featured at the Hudson-Fulton exhibition (Metropolitan Museum of Art, 1909), a dual celebration of the centenary of Robert Fulton's inauguration of steam power and the three hundredth year since Henry Hudson's arrival in America. The Dutch section of the exhibition included about 150 Golden Age paintings culled from America's newly minted collections, with nearly forty Rembrandts, twenty Hals, and six Vermeers. Indeed, as noted by one reviewer, the selection afforded "a somewhat astonishing revelation of America's recently acquired wealth of masterpieces."[2]

Shared Affinities

How were the reverberations of this insatiable taste for Rembrandt et al. manifested in the larger artistic community — among painters in particular — outside the lavish galleries of Gilded Era collectors? The Dutch aesthetic and the morality it evoked permeated the period, as seen for example in the American

362

1 William Merritt Chase, *The Patrician*, 1875, oil on canvas, 21¾ x 18".

➤

artist William Merritt Chase's (1849–1916) contemporary painting *The Patrician*, 1875 (Minneapolis Institute of Arts), a tribute to the conventions of Netherlandish portraiture (figure 1).

In a consideration of Golden Age influences on Gilded Era artists the concept of a shared "artistic affinity" prevails,[3] even though the periods are separated by centuries. The "Dutch" sensibility — moral, cultural, aesthetic — that nineteenth-century Americans perceived (and misperceived) was deemed both familiar and exemplary. This sensibility and its emulation penetrated the closely integrated arts community. If a given painter did not know a particular critic or collector, he or she inevitably had an acquaintance that did — six degrees of separation. This is not to say that Chase was dining with the plutocrats, Frick and the like. However, the activities of the collectors, their advisors, and the critics (often artists themselves) and the lives of painters in their studios overlap and intersect, interweave, and connect.

Consider one pivotal figure, the portraitist John Singer Sargent (1856–1925), the "American Van Dyck" (as christened by the French sculptor Auguste Rodin, 1840–1917). How was he enmeshed in the American community that targeted Dutch and Flemish painting? In 1897 he painted the portrait of Henry Gurdon Marquand, whose wife he had portrayed ten years earlier (Metropolitan Museum of Art and Princeton University Art Museum), at the precise moment when Marquand was assembling a collection that he bequeathed to the Metropolitan Museum in 1889. This groundbreaking gift included significant Dutch and Flemish paintings: Vermeer's *Woman with a Water Pitcher* (the first Vermeer to come to America), Rembrandt's *Head of a Man* (the first Rembrandt for the museum), Hals' *Portrait of a Man*, and Van Dyck's *Portrait of James Stuart*. Further, Sargent executed the portrait of another Hollandophile American collector, P. A. B. Widener, in 1902 (National Gallery of Art), rendering him in a manner reminiscent of Van Dyck's most sober likenesses. At this time, Widener already owned a couple of Van Dyck's works. He and his son would eventually amass eight, building a "Van Dyck room" at their mansion where Sargent's portrait of the elder Widener hung alongside the aristocrats of Genoa, as Van Dyck had painted them centuries before.

Throughout the nineteenth century and beyond, the ethos of the American artistic community — be it that of philanthropic collectors, critics, or the painters themselves — centered on the redemptive potential of art. This concept informed the actions of every public-minded collector, from the earliest efforts of individuals like Robert Gilmor, Jr. (1774–1848) — who secured intimate Dutch cabinet paintings by the little masters — through Frick et al., who captured the vaunted masterpieces. The supporting rhetoric expressed a consistent message, steeped in the Christian notion of spiritual amelioration, and articulated in a review of 1848:

[G]reat Works of Art ... refine and spiritualize thousands, dead to all
other softening influences ... . [S]uch amusements for our labouring
population ... will draw them away from gross and corrupting habits
and inspire them with pure and elevating aspirations.[4]

Little wonder, then, that Dutch art, weighted as it was in New World interpretations with moral and technical virtue, became the model for those who aspired
to "elevate" the viewer. In American criticism, the vocabulary used to praise the
technique and effects of Dutch painting was interchangeable with a description of personal virtue, with terms like chaste, immaculate, and integrity figur-
ing most prominently. The confusion or conflation of a school of painting with
a perceived national character is unequivocally expressed in a headline of 1899:
"Serious, solid, sincere — Dutch national characteristics — the characteristics of
Dutch art."[5] Of course, Americans were not alone in this belief. The lead had come
from Eugène Fromentin's *Les Maîtres d'Autrefois*, whose ideas were absorbed
by Charles Caffin, a prolific New World critic in his *Story of Dutch Art* (1909):

With morality such as this conspicuously abroad in the community, it
would have been strange if [Holland's] artists had not reproduced it ...;
if to directness and sanity of vision they had not brought a scrupulous
artistic conscience, that resulted in integrity and thoroughness of crafts-
manship.

This apparent morality, with truth and naturalism as the corresponding artistic
hallmarks, confirmed the values of the American community that cast itself in
a similar light. The rhetoric of our enthusiasts of the Golden Age, replete with
references to faithful, unadorned representation, reads much like the guidelines American artists were setting for themselves. Chief among them was Asher B. Durand (1798–1886), a father of the American landscape school. In 1855
Durand proclaimed: "[A]ll Art is unworthy and vicious which is at variance with
Truth."[6]

In addition to the virtue that accrued to the Dutch school as a whole, Americans encoded the work of iconic painters, namely Rembrandt (1606–69), Hals
(ca. 1582–1666), and Vermeer (1632–75), with the current stereotypes. Predictably, Rembrandt loomed largest, as the misunderstood and profound genius.[7]
His significance to American artists resided in the mystique of his paintings and
especially in the legacy of his prints. Frans Hals, affectionately referred to as
"Frank" by some Americans, represented the *louche*, bad boy of Dutch art who
transformed questionable subjects with the brilliance and dash of his brush.
Vermeer's reputation in the New World was equal to his perceived technique
— immaculate — and his disciples were many.

365

Nearly every American artist discussed here was exposed to the Dutch and Flemish masters abroad. For the first generation in the early 1800s, the Grand Tour was mandated as part of a civilized education, and later in the century a residency period in Europe was expected.[8] Further, from about 1870 onward, American artists could draw on the burgeoning collections of old masters at home, not to mention the photographic reproductions that began appearing in local journals and newspapers.

Prints must also be considered as carriers of influence, especially in the early nineteenth century. Long before American collectors had established an aggressive reputation in the paintings market, they had become print amateurs, amassing collections of encyclopedic scope. The impetus behind these collections, with several running into the tens of thousands of specimens, was the idea that the fledgling collector would never have a chance to acquire the coveted master works of European painting — a concept that quickly became obsolete. The Bostonian Francis Calley Gray (1790–1856) was one of the earliest print enthusiasts, accruing over four thousand, with many Dutch examples. Later, James Claghorn (1817–84) of Philadelphia dominated with his collection, exceeding twenty thousand impressions.

Further, the print collector was generally a bibliophile, with an extensive library including art books with reproductions — additional potential models for artists. Finally, these enthusiasts showed a propensity for "Grangerism" or extra-illustration whereby a book would be expanded to multiple volumes with inserts of prints, sometimes numbering into the thousands. Since such activities and collections were never exhaustively recorded they are largely untraceable today and unidentifiable as specific sources of influence.

Durand, Mount, and Edmonds

A survey of nineteenth-century American painting offers dozens of examples of Dutch influence, as for instance the early *Still Life*, ca. 1815 (Museum of Fine Arts, Boston), by Charles Bird King (1785–1862), or the domestic interiors of Thomas Hicks (1823–90). One may argue a generic Dutchness, but precise models or prototypes are elusive. However, a look at three painters who flourished around midcentury and belonged to one artistic circle reveals direct channels of influence from the Golden Age. The landscapist Asher B. Durand (1796–1886) and the genre painters William Sidney Mount (1807–68) and Francis William Edmonds (1806–63) were all acquainted with the New York business partners

2 Asher B. Durand, *Kindred Spirits*, 1849, oil on canvas, 44 x 36". ➤

3

Anonymous, after Jan Both, *The Woman Mounted on a Mule*, ca. 1854.

Luman Reed (1787–1836) and Jonathan Sturges (1802–74), collectors of Dutch seventeenth-century and American paintings, as well as prints and illustrated books.

Durand is revered as a founder of the Hudson River School, characterized as a uniquely American phenomenon; thus, it seems near heresy to suggest that he might have worked directly from Dutch models. In 1840, he embarked somewhat belatedly on the Grand Tour, under the patronage of Sturges for whom he was to purchase prints and make copies after the old masters. One such work, now lost, was made after Metsu's *Soldier and Girl*, 1660/61, at the Louvre. Rembrandt's *Self-Portrait*, 1660, at the Uffizi also provided a model for Durand, in his *Self-Portrait (after Rembrandt)*, 1840 (Wadsworth Atheneum Museum of Art, Hartford).[9]

If we consider Durand's post-European vision, as for example in his *Hudson River*, 1847 (Fenimore Art Museum), we detect the obvious influence of Claude (1600–82), an inspiration repeatedly acknowledged by the artist himself and one that recurs in the scholarship. Further, Aelbert Cuyp (1620–91) and John Constable (1776–1837), two additional declared favorites, are credited as sources. During this period Durand painted a number of vertical landscapes, striking for their naturalistic detail. The most celebrated is his *Kindred Spirits*, 1849 (Crystal Bridges Museum of American Art, Bentonville) (figure 2), commissioned by Sturges as a memorial to Thomas Cole (1801–48), seen at right, Durand's mentor and America's foremost landscape painter. It is a portrait of America's champions of nature, including the poet William Cullen Bryant (1794–1878) at left, and a portrait of Nature herself. Here the artist fuses national identity with the indigenous wilderness and her greatest proponents. Is it sheer temerity to link an icon of American painting—a paean to the landscape itself—to a foreign prototype? I believe that Durand, a reproductive engraver and a print collector himself, must have known Jan Both's etching *The Woman Mounted on a Mule*, ca. 1630–52 (Bartsch 205), one of four such prints by the artist, when he envisioned his *Kindred Spirits*. That this type of imagery was current in America is signaled by the fact that this precise print was published in an article on Both in a New York journal of 1854 (figure 3).[10]

Two more prints from the same series by Both (Bartsch 206, 207) seem to provide the general compositional formulae for a couple of Durand's other vertical paintings, *The Beeches*, 1845 (Metropolitan Museum of Art) and *Forenoon*, 1847 (New Orleans Museum of Art). A critic of the latter (along with its pendant) touched precisely on their contrived appearance: "Perhaps the most striking fact in them is that they are not so much made from Nature as from patterns collected and prepared beforehand."[11] Further, Durand's monumentalization of the trees and his fascination with their surfaces—bark, branches, and leaves—recall the vertical paintings of the Dutchman Adam Pynacker (1622–73), whose

369

work he would certainly have seen in his travels. However, while we may detect a shared affinity for the mysteries of the forest and an obvious pleasure in the rendering of detail, no direct prototype may be discerned.

William Sydney Mount was an innovator in American genre painting as Durand was in landscape. Since Mount never visited Europe, though, he relied primarily on prints as sources. While Dutch models are the focus of this study, Mount et al. also looked to British art — an intermediate conveyor of Dutch influence — most notably to the Scottish painter David Wilkie (1784–1841), an emulator of the Golden Age aesthetic, and much admired in America.[12] Two of Mount's early and intimate interiors suggest a close reliance on the conventions of Dutch genre, both in subject and composition: *The Sportsman's Last Visit*, 1835 (The Museums at Stony Brook) and *Courtship*, 1836 (Nelson-Atkins Museum of Art, Kansas City). This type of imagery proliferated in American genre painting, in part because of Mount's success, and provided a "Dutch" compositional and spatial framework, as seen in the works of his closest follower, Francis W. Edmonds.

Edmonds had employed motifs from Dutch painting even prior to his Grand Tour, as for example in his *Epicure*, 1838 (Wadsworth Atheneum). When he visited Europe, in part with Durand, he further imbibed Dutch genre through several copies, such as his *Peasant Meal*, 1841 (private collection), after Frans van Mieris. His subsequent oeuvre exhibited his debt to the compositional conventions of Dutch genre, i.e., the open window and the "Dutch box," pictorial devices that would proliferate in later American interiors.[13]

Influence of the Great Dutch Masters

The next wave of influence began around 1870, just as American collectors sought out the coveted masterpieces of the Dutch school rather than its minor cabinet paintings. They targeted monumental portraits with "pedigrees" (read aristocratic provenance) and prestige — the names Rembrandt, Hals, and Vermeer. As these masterpieces made their westward journey across the Atlantic, American artists were going the opposite way, to train at the European academies and the galleries of the Dutch masters. William Merritt Chase and Frank Duveneck (1848–1919) were at the fore, taking up residence in Munich in the early 1870s.

Each artist's respective portrait of the other — Duveneck's *William Merritt Chase*, ca. 1876 (Philadelphia Museum of Art) and Chase's likeness of Duveneck, reproduced in an etching of 1879 by William Unger — tells of the debt to Hals in different ways: Duveneck's tenebrist painting assumes Hals' brushwork and his palette while Chase's print pastiches his props (clay pipe and broad-brimmed hat), pose, and mood.

The almost comically derivative nature of the etching nearly replicates the *tableaux vivants* that were, in fact, staged by the artists, as shown in a contemporary photograph of Chase, ca. 1876 (Parrish Art Museum, Southampton, NY), where the smoking rake appears in hat, white ruff, and velvet breeches. While these entertainments were light-hearted, they do convey a sense of identification with the master on the part of the players, an idea put forth by a contemporary critic: "[T]hey [Chase et al.] go to the galleries and study Rubens or Hals or Rembrandt ... and they meet at night in some old Bavarian tavern to talk of their art over pipes and beer."[14]

Duveneck's absorption of Hals' aesthetic is one of the purest examples of Dutch influence in American painting.[15] During his most Halsian period his reliance on the old master was quite literal, as for example in the *Whistling Boy*, 1872 (Cincinnati Art Museum). Nonetheless, he also paid homage to Van Dyck in likeness such as the *Portrait of Ralph Curtis*, 1872 (private collection).

Chase assimilated Hals' technique with more subtlety. When we look again at his *Patrician*, 1875 (Minneapolis Institute of Arts) (figure 1), we might detect Hals or Van Dyck. We might well see both. Nonetheless, even in full maturity Chase acknowledged his early debt to the old master in his depiction of a print of Hals' *Malle Babbe* displayed on the wall of his famous atelier in *The Studio*, ca. 1880 (Brooklyn Museum of Art). The *Malle Babbe*, the Berlin painting of a witch, was so admired by Americans that she could have been called Hals' poster girl.

John Singer Sargent also partook of Hals. Around 1880, he made at least two oil sketches after Hals' *Officers of the St. George Civic Guard*, 1627 (Frans Halsmuseum), and a full version of his *Regentesses* (Hals, Frans Halsmuseum; Sargent, Birmingham Museum and Art Gallery).

In spite of Sargent's early debt to Hals he achieved his greatest fame as the Gilded Era Van Dyck. The influence is direct yet not literal, as seen in a striking comparison of Van Dyck's *Lady Borlase*, 1638 (Kingston Lacy) and Sargent's *Mrs. Henry White*, 1883 (Corcoran Gallery of Art). Sargent takes the formal vocabulary of his model, transforming the technique and contemporizing the spirit. Furthermore, as with Chase, the assimilation of influences is so complete that one encounters paintings that bespeak Dutchness yet defy precise classification, as for example, *The Four Doctors,* 1905–06 (Johns Hopkins University School of Medicine). It takes liberally from Van Dyck — think of his imposing portraits of Genoese aristocrats — a little from Hals' group portraits such as the *Regents of the Old Men's Almshouse*, 1664 (Frans Halsmuseum), and perhaps a smattering from Rembrandt, as in his *Syndics*, 1662 (Rijksmuseum).[16]

It is with James McNeill Whistler, Sargent's elder, that we come to Rembrandt, whose spirit seduced American painters but whose influence was strongest in the production of prints — spawning a widespread etching revival. By way of introduction, Rembrandt's *Self Portrait*, 1659 (National Gallery of Art) and Whistler's *Arrangement in Gray: Portrait of the Painter* (Detroit Institute of Arts), painted around 1872 — the precise year that Rembrandt's example was exhibited in London, where Whistler resided — offer a provocative comparison.[17] In 1885 Whistler named Rembrandt the "high priest of Art" and throughout the American's etched oeuvre he paid homage to his mentor. Early on, Whistler took inspiration from the compositions of the master, as in his *Venus* (Kennedy 59), firmly based on Rembrandt's *Jupiter and Antiope*, 1647 (Bartsch 285). Later, though, as he mastered the painterly etching techniques pioneered by Rembrandt, he adhered to an aesthetic while he broke new ground, as seen in a comparison of Whistler's *Lady at a Window* (Kennedy 138) and Rembrandt's *Jan Six*, 1647 (Bartsch 285).

With Vermeer we glimpse the end of the nineteenth century. In the late 1880s the first autograph work arrived in America, the *Woman with a Water Jug* (Metropolitan Museum of Art). Several more followed, and the painter was venerated in a monograph by the American painter Philip Hale, first published in 1913. Americans have been bewitched by Vermeer ever since, witness the line-ups snaking around Washington's National Gallery during the exhibition of 1995–96.

The many early American reinterpretations of Vermeer lack the sophistication of the assimilations of Dutch influence seen in Chase, Sargent, or Whistler. Led by Thomas Wilmer Dewing (1851–1938), Vermeer's American disciples were somehow too literal and yet too contemporary, as for example in Dewing's *Necklace*, 1907 (Smithsonian American Art Museum), seen in juxtaposition to Vermeer's *Woman with Pearl Necklace*, ca. 1664 (Staatliche Museen, Berlin), the presumed inspiration.[18] Edmund Tarbell (1862–1938), William MacGregor Paxton (1869–1941), and Frank Benson (1862–1951) offer more examples — somehow pastiche-like and sentimental — missing the immaculate character that Americans so admired in Vermeer. It seems that Vermeer's New World followers were so transfixed by the perfection of their muse that they could neither truly assimilate it nor free themselves.

While it is clear that the Gilded Era was fully and manifestly in the thrall of the Golden Age, what about our own era, arguably as gilded as the first, or even more so? New York enters this century, as it did the last, with unprecedented wealth and a frenzied art market, and we preserve the ties: Mark Tansey's *Innocent Eye Test*, 1981 (Museum of Modern Art), a riff on Potter's famous *Bull*, and Devorah Sperber's *After Vermeer 1*, 2003–04 (private collection), multimedia applied to the old master, offer fresh insights on a favorite aesthetic.[19]

1 In the present context the label "Dutch" is used anachronistically to signify both the Dutch and Flemish schools of painting since they were generally elided as one and labeled "Dutch" by Americans through the nineteenth century. For the purposes of this study the Gilded Era (and earlier) attributions will stand.

2 Kenyon Cox, "Dutch Paintings in the Hudson-Fulton Exhibition," *Burlington Magazine* 16, part 3(1909): 293; On the American taste for Dutch art, see Ben Broos, *Great Dutch Paintings from America* (exh. cat., The Hague/San Francisco; Zwolle: Waanders 1990–91), notably the essay of Walter Liedtke; See also Nancy Minty, *Dutch and Flemish Seventeenth-Century Art in America, 1800–1940: Collections, Connoisseurship and Perceptions* (Ph.D. dissertation, New York University; Ann Arbor: UMI, 2003), and Peter C. Sutton, *A Guide to Dutch Art in America* (Kampen: J.H. Kok; Grand Rapids, MI: Eerdmans, 1986).

3 Barbara Novak applies this concept in "Asher B. Durand and European Art," *Art Journal* 21 (Summer 1962): 251.

4 From the *Democratic Revue* (August, 1848) as excerpted in the *Catalogue of the Pictures Forming the Collection of the Works of the Old Masters ...* [collection of Gideon Nye] (New York: Old Art Union, 1858).

5 Alfred Trumble in *The Art Collector* 9.11 (April 1, 1899):1.

6 Excerpted from a letter published in *The Crayon* 1 (January 3, 1855): 2.

7 On the Rembrandt cult, see Alison McQueen, *The Rise of the Cult of Rembrandt: Reinventing an Old Master in Nineteenth-Century France* (Amsterdam: Amsterdam University Press, 2003); Catherine Scallen, *Rembrandt, Reputation and the Practice of Connoisseurship* (Amsterdam: Amsterdam University Press, 2004); and Esmee Quodbach, "Rembrandt in America: The Politics of Taste in Old Master Collecting"

(Ph.D. dissertation, Utrecht University, forthcoming).

8 For a view of the influence of nineteenth-century Dutch painters on their American contemporaries who studied in the Netherlands, see Annette Stott, "Dutch Utopia: Paintings by Antimodern Artists of the Nineteenth Century," *Smithsonian Studies in American Art* 3.2 (Spring 1989): 46-61.

9 While the school and Durand's general debt to, and affinity for, the conventions of Dutch landscape are certainly acknowledged in the literature — see, most recently, Barbara Dayer Gallati's and Linda Ferber's articles in Linda Ferber, ed., *Kindred Spirits, Asher B. Durand and the American Landscape* (exh. cat., Brooklyn/Washington/San Diego: Brooklyn Museum of Art, 2007) — specific Dutch prototypes for Durand's most important landscapes have not been identified.

10 *The Illustrated Magazine of Art* 4.20 (1854): 129.

11 Anon., 1847, quoted in Ferber, *Kindred Spirits*, 149.

12 See Deborah J. Johnson, ed., *William Sidney Mount: Painter of American Life* (exh. cat., New York/Pittsburgh/Fort Worth: The American Federation of Arts, 1998), and Henry Nichols Blake Clark, *The Impact of 17th C. Dutch and Flemish Genre Painting on American Genre Painting* (Ph.D. dissertation, University of Delaware; Ann Arbor: UMI, 1982).

13 See Henry Nichols Blake Clark, in *Francis W. Edmonds: American Master in the Dutch Tradition* (exh. cat., Fort Worth/New York: New York Historical Society, 1988), figures 32, 34, and Catherine Hoover, "The Influence of David Wilkie's Prints on the Genre Paintings of William Sydney Mount," *American Art Journal* 13.3 (Summer 1981): 4-33.

14 Kenyon Cox, "William M. Chase, Painter," *The Metropolitan Museum of Art Bulletin* 12.2 (February 1917): 26.

2

—

THE
NINETEENTH
CENTURY

15 On the taste for Hals, see Frances S.
Jowell, "The Rediscovery of Frans Hals,"
in Seymour Slive, ed., *Frans Hals* (exh.
cat., Washington/London/Haarlem;
London: Royal Academy of Arts, 1989),
61-86; See also Ronald Pisano, *William
Merritt Chase 1849–1916: A Leading
Spirit in American Art* (exh. cat., Seattle:
Henry Art Gallery, 1983), and Michael
Quick, *An American Painter Abroad:
Frank Duveneck's European Years*
(exh. cat., Cincinnati: Cincinnati Art
Museum, 1987).

16 Richard Ormond and Elaine Kilmurray,
*John Singer Sargent: The Complete
Paintings*, vol. 3 (New Haven: Yale
University Press, 2003), no. 492: note the
influence of Hals and Rembrandt; See

also pp. 3-4 and 14 for a more general
discussion of Van Dyck and Sargent.

17 Katharine Lochnan, *The Etchings of
James McNeill Whistler* (exh. cat., New
York/Toronto; New Haven: Yale Univer-
sity Press, 1984); Andrew McLaren Young
et al., *The Paintings of James McNeill
Whistler* (New Haven, CT: Yale University
Press, 1980).

18 See Susan Hobbs et al., *The Art of Thomas
Wilmer Dewing: Beauty Reconfigured*
(exh. cat., Brooklyn/Washington/
Detroit: Smithsonian Press, 1996).

19 For a postmodern reading of Tansey's
painting, see Annette Stott, *Holland
Mania: The Unknown Dutch Period in
American Art and Culture* (Woodstock,
NY: Overlook Press, 1998), 256-257.

DUTCH-AMERICAN IDENTITY DURING THE CIVIL WAR AND THE BOER WAR

—

MICHAEL DOUMA

Like other European immigrant groups in nineteenth-century America, the Dutch pointed to their colonial presence in the seventeenth century, to their democratic values, and to their contribution to America's wars as ideological justifications for their American identity. According to Norwegian historian Orm Overland, immigrants often used these three types of myths (foundational, ideological, and sacrificial) in combination, forming the backbone of their calls for acceptance. Dutch immigrants commonly employed foundational and ideological myths, while less frequently alluding to their sacrifices in war. For the Dutch, wars have been times of intense debate, reflection, and questioning in which long pent-up emotions surface, sometimes in excess, sometimes betraying old prejudices.

Dutch Americans were not always unified about the decision to go to war or to support one warring faction against the other. In the American Revolution, for example, the New York Dutch split into patriot and loyalist camps. Many conflicts to follow, whether at home or abroad, pressed later nineteenth-century Dutch immigrants in America to again identify their loyalty.

This essay discusses the effects of the American Civil War, the Anglo-Boer War, and the Spanish-American War on the consciousness of the Dutch Americans. Dutch identification with the United States was strengthened in the Civil War, and despite some resistance, Americanization of Dutch immigrants continued apace through the century. Dutch ethnic identification, however, required a more active and self-conscious effort. The Dutch-American reaction to the Boer War demonstrates how Dutch ethnicity and American national identity formed a sometimes uneasy union.[1]

The American Civil War

During the Civil War, about 97 percent of the Dutch in America lived in the Northern states. While these immigrants held slavery in ill repute, they had almost no experience with blacks and there were few outspoken abolitionists in their ranks. For much of the country, the war was about the interrelated issues of slavery, states' rights, and the preservation of the Union. While not blind to these concerns, the Dutch had other motivations to fight, both patriotic and practical. Indeed, the war laid the foundations of a new level of patriotism as it offered the chance for the immigrants to identify with a new fatherland. In supporting the war, Dutch Americans argued that love and loyalty to country outweighed the implications of new taxes, the loss of loved ones, and the uncertain future of a divided country.

The Dutch men who took up arms had come to the United States as the young children of Calvinist and Catholic families. Most were used to hard work on the farm; some were familiar with the working conditions of cities like Grand Rapids and Chicago. Some thought the war was a grand adventure; others had fled the Old World to avoid conscription. As the draft threatened the Dutch colony of Pella, IA, 138 persons, just over 6 percent of the city's inhabitants, fled to California and Oregon, only to return after the war.[2] In general, the war was a coming-of-age experience, which helped bring the small Dutch communities into closer contact with greater America. From the pulpit of the First Reformed Church in Holland, MI, the Reverend Albertus Van Raalte cast his unflinching support for Lincoln and the Union while proudly watching two of his sons march off to war. Pella's founder, Hendrik Scholte, also backed the Republican administration. While Pella gave a small plurality to Lincoln in the 1864 election, Holland voters chose his opponent, the Democrat George McClellan. By 1868, however, Holland and Pella became Republican and Democratic cities, respectively, and have remained so to this day. Although Dutch Catholics in Wisconsin voted almost entirely Democratic in the 1860s, they showed similar patterns of early volunteerism followed by resistance to the draft. When the war ended, the Dutch soldiers all around returned home to become business leaders, politicians, and progressive-minded thinkers who often challenged local orthodoxy. The historian Herbert Brinks has argued that Dutch-American soldiers, by participating in the war, became "more unreservedly American than their relatives and friends on the home front."[3]

But prowar sympathies were far from universal. Willemien Schenkeveld found that the Dutch were underrepresented in the Union military, both nation-

Dirk Van Raalte, one of Reverend Albertus Van Raalte's two sons who fought for Lincoln and the Union in the Civil War. ➤

ally and locally in west Michigan. In 1861, 50 men of an eventual 410 by war's end volunteered for military service from the Holland area. In Holland Township, WI, a similar scenario played out with about forty men raising their hand to heed Lincoln's call for a volunteer army. In the fall of 1862, when the draft threatened to take a quota of soldiers from the Holland, MI, area, more Dutchmen volunteered, following the original fifty. The fact that Dutch soldiers volunteered before being drafted has caused historians to view the Dutch immigrants as considerably patriotic. But volunteerism among them was not overwhelming, and it often fell short of the local quotas. Those who did volunteer may have done so for reasons other than patriotism. By joining before being drafted, volunteers not only saved other loved ones from the draft and fulfilled social pressures to contribute to the war cause, but they also earned an enlistment bonus of up to $65. Those who fought and survived the war found their finances in better shape than those who paid to avoid service. The government conscription agents who had to be repeatedly paid off were no better than tax collectors, thought the Dutch-American correspondents of soldier Willem Roon, who was from Vriesland, MI. In addition to the cash incentive, volunteer service was appealing because there was a good chance to fight alongside other local soldiers in Dutch units such as Company 1 of the 25th Michigan Infantry Regiment. On the whole, the contribution of the Dutch in the Civil War should not be celebrated as an example of exceptional patriotism, but recognized as a practical compromise between personal, familial, and community self-interest on the one hand, and national, patriotic goals on the other.[4]

Sources from the period point to a number of peculiar developments about the way Dutch-American soldiers and families interacted with their new fatherland. On the Dutch-American home front, in Wisconsin, Illinois, Iowa, New Jersey, and New York, women led efforts to send bandages, homemade foodstuffs, and books to their local soldiers. Pella, which had sent sixty-three of its own men to war along with an additional forty-five from the surrounding area, led the state of Iowa in voluntary contributions to the war effort.[5] A midwestern regional network of Dutch-language correspondence and newspapers served during the war to keep soldiers and their families informed on current events, while simultaneously providing information to fuel pro- and anti-war positions. The war years should be seen not only as a period of Americanization, but also as a time of increasing interconnectivity between Dutch settlements.

Dutch soldiers like Jan Nies of Holland, MI, penned weekly letters home to his dear family. These letters serve to illustrate the nature of the Dutch-American web. From the front, Nies sent mail by express train all the way to Grand Rapids, but his handwritten letters then had to travel by wagon to Holland. Letters containing cash he commonly addressed to Aldred Plugger, a businessman in Holland whose store also operated as a bank and a local exchange for all news coming from or going to the front. While Nies had little choice but to put his faith in the U.S. mail service, with the possibility that letters containing cash would be stolen, he knew that everything would be all right as soon as his money arrived in the hands of his hometown Hollanders. This was a network of ethnic trust, and Nies was just one of many Dutch soldiers who put his faith in it.[6] Since the soldiers wrote in Dutch they knew that no one else but the intended audience was likely to decipher the script or understand the contents of the letters. In many cases, recipients saved these prized letters from the front, evidence of the important ties of friends and family.

Thrown into a foreign environment, Dutch soldiers sought the comforts of home to maintain a feeling of the familiar. They took advantage of chaplain services and sought Sunday leave to attend church if their company set up camp within proper distance from town. Away from home and family, the soldiers confronted a strange and harsh world where their Calvinist (or Catholic for some) faith and morals were challenged. Soldier Willem Roon (mentioned above) repeatedly received warnings from his Michigan and Wisconsin correspondents to stay away from sinful activities. A Dutch Calvinist would have been well aware of the sinfulness that surrounded him. The camps were godless, Roon said. In his letters home he mentioned attending church; once he even mentioned the specific verse that a sermon was based upon. When his unit moved further south, Roon made a trip to Cincinnati where he was elated to meet a certain Dominee Reijd, another Dutchman. Like others, Willem was comforted by the familiar and needed to hear of the reassurance of salvation for believers.

The destruction wrought by war also impacted Dutch-American perceptions of gender roles. Their husbands away at war or killed, the horses and mules stolen by the passing armies, women across war-torn Appalachia and Dixie had no choice but to plow their own fields. This was a strange sight for a Dutch soldier, but not completely foreign. After all, Dutch-American women regularly worked in the garden or tended to barn animals, and if extra help was needed to bring in the harvest they often lent a helpful hand. But heavy physical labor was uncommon for Dutch-American women. In this time of necessity, female labor took on a new character. "Here it is no wonder at all if one sees a women plowing, cutting wood, or doing any other manly work," Jan Nies told his mother.[7] The Civil War years did indeed see a rise in the number of female farm workers. Despite the introduction of reapers, mowers, and other machines, the labor shortage in Northern fields was acute and women naturally helped fill the demand. A root cause of avoiding the draft—the Dutch case included—was to stay home and help on the farm.

379

A complete narrative of Dutch-American involvement in the Civil War has yet to be written. It is perhaps easier, as the tendency has been, to write about

2

—

individual contributions to a war effort than to write more broadly about how war shaped Dutch Americans. The study of Dutch Americans in the Civil War betrays this bias and exhibits a larger scholarly neglect. While some have covered the Civil War, these researchers tend to write about the more popular romantic and strategic elements of the war. And although a few letter collections have been published, Dutch-American researchers have no scholarly publication or interpretation of letters to compare to Wolfgang Helbich and Walter D. Kamphoefner's work on German-American Civil War letters, *Deutsche im Amerikanischen Burgerkrieg*.[8] Such a published collection of Dutch-American Civil War letters with accompanying translations and interpretations could reach a larger audience than previous works and, among other uses, would be helpful in comparing Dutch soldiers to those of other ethnic groups.

An additional promising avenue of study would be to trace the legacy of the Civil War in the minds of Dutch Americans, from former soldiers' participation in veterans organizations like the Grand Army of the Republic to the use of old soldiers as standards of morality, bravery, and patriotism. For example, after the U.S. declaration of war on Germany in 1917, Holland, MI, held a prowar rally in which local Civil War soldiers were presented as the epitome of patriots. Civil War veteran Gerrit Van Schelven, a trustworthy old-timer who had served as alderman, postmaster, and justice of the peace, in addition to holding a number of other respectable positions, was one of the chosen speakers for the event. As the accepted local authority on all matters historical, Van Schelven spoke about the undoubting patriotism and courage of the boys of '61.[9] By then, the memory of the war had become a black-and-white morality tale, a story of good and evil with the Dutch Americans unequivocally on the side of the former. A new generation had to follow suit, buy war bonds, and volunteer to fight the Kaiser.

The Boer War

Nearly thirty-five years, or two generations, passed after the Confederate surrender at Appomattox before the Dutch Americans again had to choose their loyalties in war. The South African Boer War (1899–1902), which, pitting the Dutch-descent Afrikaners against British forces, was unique in that while Dutch Americans were not physically involved in the fighting, the war questioned ethnic identity. The most significant synthetic works on Dutch-American history correctly treat the Boer War as a rallying call, leading to turn-of-the-century rejuvenation in Dutch pride, an arousal of "ethnic consciousness." Yet, few attempts have been made to work in the primary sources of the period. As with the Civil War, research on the Dutch-American reaction to the South African Boer War has been centered on west Michigan. Building on the pioneering work on this subject by Henry Ippel, further research on the reaction of Holland, MI, to this war revealed that the war gripped the attention of the city to the degree of the Civil War or, later on, World War I, but exceeded them on an emotional level. Hollanders displayed strong pro-Boer sympathies, wrote petitions, raised funds, held rallies, and spoke of Dutch nationalism. Their sympathetic attachment to the Boers was based on common ethnic ties and reinforced by traditional Dutch enmity with England. All local newspapers, regardless of party politics, supported the Boers and displayed deep interest in the historical development of this rough and somewhat exotic kin. The Dutch-language *De Grondwet* with a substantial circulation in other Dutch-American communities helped spread the message of support beyond west Michigan.[10]

To understand its relative importance in the Dutch-American mind, the Boer War must also be considered in relation to the Spanish-American War, which, running simultaneously, received far less attention in the Dutch-American press. In the Netherlands as well, the South African crisis was a political headline as Dutch politicians debated coming to the aid of South African President Paul Kruger amid his many calls for foreign intervention. Disturbed by the growth of British power, the officially neutral Dutch government was content with the U.S. victory over Spain in the Far East, but worried that the U.S. implementation of the Monroe Doctrine in the Caribbean might extend too far. For that reason, Dutch newspapers opposed the U.S. invasion of Cuba. Yet the Netherlands' Dutch later justified Spain's colonial losses by positioning themselves as moral superiors in the proper management of colonies.[11] Through print media and word of mouth, the political unease in the Netherlands filtered back to Dutch-American circles.

Perhaps the Dutch Americans were not much interested in the war with Spain because few local soldiers from their flock were sent to fight and the war's impact on the home front was insignificant compared to that of the Civil War or World War I. Writing in the 1940s, Ray Nies (from Holland, MI, and the son of the aforementioned Civil War soldier of the same last name) offers a glimpse into the mind of his octogenarian Dutch-American grandmother, who was exceptionally interested in the war's result. The comic element of this woman's reaction to the war emphasizes the generational changes in Dutch-American sympathies. Nies remembers how his grandmother went out and told all the people she met,

381

"Now shall those devilish Spaniards catch it! Now they will be punished!"
She certainly displayed her animosity against the Spaniards that day. It was evident that the occasion brought back to her mind the stories that she

had heard when a child in The Netherlands; stories of murder, torture, and burnings at the stake. That war was over long before she was born, but no doubt, ancestral memories were at work that day.[12]

2

——

This quotation illustrates the lingering attitudes of an elderly generation, but Nies employs it in a joking manner. With Americans fighting a war in Cuba and the Philippines, Dutch Americans could be secure in the belief in American victory while exponentially more concerned with a war in far-off South Africa and the imposing calamity and loss of life there.

Thus, while Dutch Americans had relinquished their enmity with the Spanish, they also actively reinforced international ties with their Dutch-Afrikaner kin. There are hints that Dutch-American support for the Boers was similar or even stronger outside Holland, MI. Peter Van Schaak, president of Chicago's Algemeen-Nederlands Verbond, an international Dutch-language and cultural society founded in 1895, claimed to have forty-eight men who were going to go fight alongside him in South Africa. He planned to pick up more soldiers in other Dutch cities. In addition to its Chicago chapter and its base in New York City, the Algemeen-Nederlands Verbond had branches in Boston, Holland and Zeeland, MI, Pella, IA, Fulton and Roseland, IL, and Minneapolis. The Chicago-Dutch relief effort for the Boers was mild compared to the effort of Chicago's Swedish Americans to aid the famine in their old country. Nevertheless, the war was certainly the most important foreign policy issue among Chicago's Dutch Americans, and it even provided the Dutch youth organizations of the city a cause to rally behind at their meetings. The Dutch in Chicago were particularly displeased with the pro-English policies of Theodore Roosevelt, a fellow Dutch American who made occasional, often unannounced, visits to Chicago's Dutch churches.[13]

Outside Chicago, few Dutch Americans volunteered for action. A handful of Dutchmen left Iowa to fight in South Africa, but the Dutch in west Michigan apparently did not follow. Nevertheless, in cities of Dutch influence in Iowa (Orange City, Pella, Sioux Center) there were also aid meetings, petitions, and public expressions of sympathy for the Boers. A correspondent of *De Grondwet* from Orange City wrote that "nearly the entire populace here is for Transvaal."[14] *De Grondwet* asked the citizens of Holland, MI, to consider how they would respond to an inquiry of an Iowa Dutchman who intimated that surely that larger Dutch-American city (Holland) had done more for the Boers than tiny Orange City, IA.

Pro-Boer ideas spread from Chicago throughout the Midwest and to the Canadian border. Other immigrant groups, each with a historical reason for disliking English policies, joined in the commotion. These developments worried British officials who warned the U.S. government that Dutch and Irish societies were planning raids on British possessions in Canada. In Canada itself, Dutch populations were proportionally smaller and even less able to influence their government's pro-English policies. For a small group of Dutch immigrants in Manitoba, however, opposition to the Boer War provided the decisive motivation to found their own Christian Reformed Church and abandon any attempts at religious cooperation with other Canadian denominations in the province.[15]

Research concerning Dutch-American involvement in the war should be taken up from within South Africa. How many Dutch Americans arrived there, did they stay long enough to fight, and what became of them? Perhaps more so than any other topic, the Boer War offers a chance for historians of Dutch America to think in international terms. Although there never existed a Dutch World in the same sense as historians speak of a British World or British Empire, this did not prevent the Dutch from speculating on the possibility. Dutchman R.P.J. Tutein Noltenius imagined a Dutch World when he made a turn-of-the-century trip through America. "Our land," he wrote, "can not be better served than by the going out of many: because one never completely leaves: one stays connected to the mother country. Truly, it would be different with our brothers in South Africa if the Dutch voice sounded powerfully elsewhere than just in the low land by the sea. And maybe the time is not far that we ourselves will need foreign supporters."[16]

Nearly all Dutch Americans opposed their government's pro-English policy in South Africa. While protest against the government was officially repressed in the Civil War (think of Lincoln's retraction of habeas corpus) and popularly denounced during World War I, Dutch Americans took up an unfamiliar position during the Boer War, as a minority group protesting the policies of a Republican government that they had voted for overwhelmingly. If the Civil War was a test to become American, the Boer War was a reassertion of Dutch ethnic identity. But the latter war was more than that. It also highlighted a problem in holding to multiple identities. Could one be patriotic and opposed to federal foreign policy? For the Dutch Americans at the turn of the century, necessity demanded such.

What can we learn from these nineteenth-century conflicts? In the Civil War, Dutch Americans discovered a new patriotism, but many remained ambiguous about their support for the Union. In the Boer War, however, their support for the Boers was nearly unanimous. Could Dutch ethnic pride override national identity? I would argue that the American identity of Dutch Americans had been established by the end of the Civil War and was constantly reinforced through the century to satisfy those keen on assimilation. Dutch ethnic identification, however, required a more concerted effort. While the Civil War left a legacy of self-reflection about the place of Dutch Americans in the United States, the memory of the Boer War faded rather quickly. As the attachment to Dutch ethnicity weakened, the American character of Dutch immigrant children and

383

grandchildren became more secure. Later generations were schooled in American ways, and the Dutch Afrikaners became as obscure a memory to them as the Spanish Inquisition had been to their parents by the time of the Spanish-American War. Wartime experiences reinforced a sense of Dutchness but, more substantially, they added new elements to Dutch-American identity, further distinguishing the immigrants, through their shared experiences, from the Dutch in the old country.

1   Orm Overland, *Immigrant Minds, American Identities: Making the United States Home, 1870–1930* (Urbana: University of Illinois Press, 2000); Hans Krabbendam, "Dutch-American Identity Politics: The Use of History by Dutch Immigrants" (Holland, MI: Van Raalte Institute, 2003).

2   Brian Beltman, "Civil War Reverberations: Exodus and Return among the Pella Dutch during the 1860s," in Hans Krabbendam and Larry J. Wagenaar, eds., *The Dutch-American Experience: Essays in Honor of Robert P. Swierenga* (Amsterdam: VU Uitgeverij, 2000), 117-142.

3   Herbert J. Brinks, "Dutch American Reactions," *Origins* 6.1 (1988): 17; Hans Krabbendam, *Vrijheid in het verschiet: Nederlandse emigratie naar Amerika, 1840–1940* (Hilversum: Verloren, 2006), 273-276; Jacob van Hinte (Robert P. Swierenga, ed. and Adriaan de Wit, trans.), *Netherlanders in America: A Study of Emigration and Settlement in the Nineteenth and Twentieth Centuries in the United States of America* (Grand Rapids, MI: Baker Book House, 1985), 439.

4   Willemien M. Schenkeveld, "The Colony and the Union: Dutch-American Reactions to the Civil War (1861–1865)," in Rob Kroes and Henk-Otto Neuschäfer, eds., *The Dutch in North-America. Their Immigration and Cultural Continuity* (Amsterdam: VU University Press, 1991); Douwe R. Bouma, P. Peesk, and

P. Hoekstra (Vriesland, MI) to Willem Roon, December 24, 1863, Willem Roon Collection, Joint Archives of Holland, MI.

5   Van Hinte, *Netherlanders in America*, 433.

6   Ray Nies Collection, Holland Museum Archives, Holland, MI (in particular, see Nies's letter from Camp near Cleveland, TN; March 28, 1864); Walter Weener of Holland, MI, provides another example in his letters of May 22 and 23, 1862 (recently acquired, unaccessioned collection, Joint Archives of Holland, Holland, MI).

7   Suzanne Sinke, *Dutch American Women in the United States, 1880–1920* (Urbana: University of Illinois Press, 2002), 57-58, 128; Ray Nies, letter from Camp near Cleveland, TN, April 3, 1864, Holland Museum Archives.

8   Wolfgang Helbich and Walter D. Kamphoefner, eds., *Deutsche im Amerikanischen Burgerkrieg: Briefe von Front und Farm 1861–1865* (Paderborn: Ferdinand Schuningh, 2002); Published collections of Dutch-American Civil War letters include Janice Van Lente Catlin, ed., *The Civil War Letters of Johannes Van Lente* (Okemos, MI: Yankee Girl Publications, 1992).

9   *Holland City News*, July 4, 1917.

10 J.W. Schulte Nordholt and Robert P. Swierenga, eds., *A Bilateral Bicentennial. A History of Dutch-American Relations 1782–1982* (Amsterdam: Octagon Books/Meulenhoff, 1982), 144; Henry Ippel,

"The Anglo-Boer War: Dutch American Reaction, 1899–1903," *Origins* 11.2 (1993): 30; Michael Douma, "The Reaction of Holland, Michigan to the Boer War, 1899–1902" (Hope College, unpublished paper, JAH H03-1515).

11 Nico Bootsma, "Reactions to the Spanish-American War in the Netherlands and in the Dutch East Indies," in Sylvia L. Hilton and Steve J.S. Ickringill, eds., *European Perceptions of the Spanish-American War of 1898* (New York: Peter Lang, 1999), 35-52.

12 Ray Nies manuscript, available at Holland Museum Archives.

13 *De Grondwet*, December 26, 1899; Robert P. Swierenga, *Dutch Chicago: A History of Hollanders in the Windy City*. (Grand Rapids, MI: Eerdmans, 2002), 156, 460, 533-534.

14 *De Grondwet*, January 9, 1900.

15 *Holland City News*, December 29, 1899; *New York Times*, January 1, 1900; Timothy Nyhof and Catharina de Bakker, "The Dutch Community in the Kildonans (1893–1911), the English Churches and the Boer War," *Canadian Journal of Netherlandic Studies* 26.2 (Fall/Automne 2005).

16 R.P.J. Tutein Noltenius, *Indrukken en aanteekeningen tijdens eene reis door de Verenigde Staten van Noord-Amerika*. (Haarlem: H.D. Tjeenk Willink, 1900), 280.

2

DUTCH-AMERICAN
MATERIAL CULTURE

—

ANNETTE STOTT

The history of Dutch-American architecture and artifacts between the Revolutionary War and World War I may be categorized in three broad periods. During the first period, 1780–1830, some Dutch-American families held onto the objects and practices of their ancestors while creating newer forms that blended elements from many sources and yet were called Dutch Colonial. The second period, roughly 1830–70, represents a transitional era during which most old Dutch families in the East abandoned the last vestiges of colonial traditions, and a new wave of Dutch immigrants brought modern industries to isolated regions of the Midwest. In the third period, 1870–1914, attention to Dutch culture in America shifted from Dutch Americans to the general public as Dutch Colonial architecture was revived in a modernized form that appealed to the vast middle class, and stereotypical Dutch motifs came into fashion on a broad range of domestic objects. Both the definition of Dutch-American material culture and the audience for it changed during this long century.

1780–1830

The buildings and objects associated with Dutch-American culture groups had already gone through a long and erratic evolution before the Revolutionary War. Dutch colonists had discarded their cupboard beds in favor of English bedsteads, modified jambless fireplaces for greater fuel efficiency, and modernized the *kas* into such a tasteful and efficient linen cupboard that English neighbors sometimes adopted it. This pattern of abandonment, adaptation, and cultural exchange continued after the war.

By 1780, a style of vernacular architecture had emerged that was so strongly associated with the rural Dutch farming communities of New York, New Jersey, Delaware, and the Minisink region in Pennsylvania that it acquired the name

386

Dutch Colonial. This type of house attained its greatest flourishing during the postcolonial period between 1780 and 1830.[1] Most architectural historians today believe that it originated in the early eighteenth century, after the demise of New Netherland, but they do not agree as to its exact antecedents. Distinguishing external features included one or more end-wall chimneys, a gable roof with overhang or a gambrel roof with short, shallow upper slopes and long sweeping lower slopes, often ending on one or both sides of the house in flared eaves sheltering a veranda porch. One or two doors led from the veranda into rooms of nearly square proportion with visible ceiling beams. Some of these houses retained the "Dutch door" with its top half swinging free of the bottom half.

Architectural historian David Cohen has identified four distinctive subgroups of this style: brick houses laid up in Dutch cross bond (at least until 1800 when common bond began to dominate) in the upper Hudson River valley; grey fieldstone houses in the middle Hudson and upper Delaware valleys; red sandstone houses in northern New Jersey and Rockland County, NY; and wood frame houses in western Long Island and Monmouth County, NJ.[2] The Long Island Dutch Colonial often featured shingled exterior walls, a technique most likely borrowed from Anglo neighbors. All four regions had adopted English floor plans or combined aspects of Dutch and English plans to attain the preferred symmetry and center focus of the Georgian or Federal style by about 1800.

As historians look deeper into each of these regions, they are finding considerable variety and some distinctive preferences, but relatively little relation to architecture in the Netherlands. Investigating buildings in Marbletown, NY, Thomas Ryan found the three-room Hudson Valley farmhouse normally identified as Dutch to be the most common house type in 1800, but identified six additional plan types in this ethnically diverse community. Lacking any correlation between plan and ethnicity of owner, he concluded that all the ethnic groups contributed to the formation of a "truly regional architecture … far removed in time and space from their northern European roots."[3] In an important chronological study of the architecture of Bergen County, NJ, historians Brown and Warmflash note that people of Dutch origin comprised only 40 percent of the county's population in 1800 when the sandstone Dutch Colonial house with overhanging gambrel roof became ubiquitous in the county.[4] The so-called Dutch gambrel roof has been variously ascribed to English, Dutch, French, and Belgian origin or to pure American invention.

Ironically, architectural historians have demonstrated that perhaps the most authentically Dutch aspect of so-called Dutch Colonial architecture is the least visible. The building construction method used for timber-framed houses and outbuildings was the Dutch H-bent system. A pair of solid upright timber posts, connected from two to four feet below their tops by a horizontal anchor beam, formed an "H" shape. These H-bents lined up to define bays down the length of

387

the building. Builders attached the exterior siding to the posts, then applied dried brick or other infill between posts for insulation, and finally plastered over the interior walls, leaving the framing timbers visible only on the ceiling. H-bent construction is consistent among the Dutch-built rural frame houses of the Middle States. Neighboring Anglo farmers generally used different framing devices.

The Dutch Colonial style is best understood as an amalgam of continental European and English ingredients transformed in North America by local geography and necessity. Whether or not it had any counterpart in the Netherlands, it became an important part of what Americans considered to be Dutch and a defining aspect of rural Dutch-American life at the end of the eighteenth and dawn of the nineteenth centuries.

Dutch barns also provided a distinctive visual feature in the Dutch-American landscape. Using H-bent construction, knee walls, and long sloping roofs, the most typical Dutch barn form is believed to derive from the aisled house-barn found in the eastern provinces of the Netherlands. Its broad central "nave" served as a threshing floor onto which large central doors opened from the gable ends. Side aisles housing livestock were accessed from small doors on the façade that butted up against the outside walls. Unlike house construction, the bents supported only the roof, which continued in a single slope across the side aisles, creating proportions that are especially wide in relation to the height of the barn. The early research of John Fitchen, followed by that of members of the Dutch Barn Preservation Society, has identified several types and subgroups among these barns.[5]

Dutch-American farmers also used some distinctive agricultural equipment that they and their neighbors adopted and improved upon over time. The Dutch plow consisted of a cast-iron pyramidal-shaped plowshare with a wooden moldboard to turn the earth into the furrows, one or two handles, and sometimes wheels to ease its passage as a team of horses pulled it along flat lands. Historian Peter Cousins has traced the origins of the American "Dutch plow" to an agricultural region along the coast of northern Belgium and the province of Zeeland. It was not abandoned for newer plows until about 1810 in rural New York and 1840 in New Jersey. One variation may even have developed into the Connecticut plow that was manufactured well into the middle of the century. Similarly, the sith and mathook, used by Dutch- and German-American farmers for harvesting grain during the late eighteenth century only gave way to the American scythe and cradle in the early nineteenth century.[6]

The versatility of the long-bodied Dutch farm wagon pulled by two horses kept this vehicle in use, despite the ridicule of some English neighbors. Using painted side boards, cross benches, and canvas draped over flat wooden hoops, farmers converted their wagons from hauling hay during the week to conveying the family to church on Sundays. It has been speculated that the Dutch farm wagon provided a prototype for the covered wagons made famous in western wagon trains.[7]

The persistence and transformation of Dutch material culture continued through the first three decades of the nineteenth century on a steadily diminishing trajectory. Dutch features were retained longest in places where Dutch language and religion remained strongest, often, but not exclusively, in rural areas. They disappeared fastest in urban areas where the pressing proximity and intermingling of many culture groups, as well as increasing real estate values and modernizing trends, motivated the adoption of new tools and fashions, and the razing of older buildings. This makes it hard to identify the last remnants of colonial Dutch influence on material culture in the city. Perhaps the high stoop on New York City row houses and the facing high-backed benches on porches in smaller cities are vestiges of the Dutch *stoep*. Art historian Joseph Manca argues that the American porch, generally, derives from Dutch practice.[8] But the desire of post-Revolutionary War Americans to create architecture and design that conveyed their new identity as a unified and unique nation made the retention of distinctive ethnic design elements less attractive and contributed to the fading of the Dutch Colonial style.

1830–70

About the time that recognizable Dutch material culture was disappearing from common use in the East, a new wave of immigrants began to settle in the Midwest, bringing their mid-nineteenth-century Dutch possessions and sensibilities with them. A similar, but much more rapid process of cultural transformation took place over the next several generations among these new Dutch Americans. Even those who settled on the eastern seaboard in areas of former cultural Dutch hegemony often adopted outward expressions of their new American identity quite rapidly.

In some midwestern cities, merchants imported Dutch goods and craftsmen established traditional manufacturing businesses. For example, a couple from Groningen, Jan and Grietje Kolvoord, began a small furniture-making enterprise in Holland, MI, in 1849. Two other Dutch immigrants, Jan Slag and Andries Steketee, each formed boat-building concerns in the same town around 1850, launching a local industry.[9] The extent to which furniture and boats represented Dutch design, distinctive from those built by non-Dutch competitors, requires additional investigation.

389

It appears that Dutch material culture was in abeyance nationwide through the middle decades of the nineteenth century, except in these small pockets of new Dutch settlement and among some older families and historical societies attempting to preserve Dutch artifacts and buildings. It was not until the 1870s and the emergence of the Colonial Revival that new forms of American architecture and material culture became widely identified as Dutch. Even then, the Dutch was a minor strand within a cluster of styles largely inspired by English precedents, and it harked back not to New Netherland, but to the late eighteenth- and early nineteenth-century Dutch Colonial style that had lain dormant for just fifty years.

1870–1914

The Colonial Revival has been recognized as emerging out of a post-Civil War desire to celebrate a (theoretically) reunited nation's roots. It gained major impetus with the country's centennial in 1876, the 1890 census-based closing of the western frontier, and the 1893 World's Columbian Exposition, which showcased colonial architecture and artifacts. Historians have explored the political and cultural motivations of the style; its relationship to modernism and progressivism as well as to antimodernism and conservatism; the breadth of its manifestations in literature, architecture, and painting; its class associations; its symbiosis with the nascent preservation movement; and its relationship to colonial-era styles. All of these studies help illuminate what was originally called the Modern Dutch Colonial and was renamed Dutch Colonial Revival in the twentieth century.

Peter Kaufman identifies the T.H. Munroe House in East Hampton, Long Island, as the first Dutch Colonial Revival house in America.[10] Designed by Isaac Henry Green and completed in 1888, it contained the hallmark gambrel roof and overhang of the original Dutch Colonial style. While others may disagree about the "first," it is generally accepted that the Modern Dutch Colonial style emerged and enjoyed its earliest success in areas historically associated with Dutch culture groups. It took two forms: remodels of old Dutch colonial buildings, including windmills, in which an attempt was made to match the original building's character, and newly designed buildings that united modern practicality with a visual continuity to Dutch Colonial houses in the neighborhood. In the case of Green, who was born and raised on Long Island in a family that inherited land from one of the original patroonships, this historic Dutch association was reinforced by the appearance after the Civil War of immigrants from the Netherlands who settled in his home town, Sayville. Green's uncle owned the land on which they settled, and issued their mortgages from his bank; when Green became president of the bank he also became involved with this modern Dutch element in the community. Green established his architectural practice in Sayville and worked in several styles, including the Modern Dutch Colonial, but his reputation did not develop very far beyond New York.

Credit for popularizing the Modern Dutch Colonial must go to another architect, Aymar Embury II. He lived in a traditionally Dutch region of New Jersey before moving to Long Island and maintained an architectural practice in New York City. From 1900 on, he studied colonial structures, designed modern variations, and wrote for the general public on such topics as New Netherland farm houses and Dutch roads and their houses. His first book, *One Hundred Country Houses: Modern American Examples* (1909), contained chapters on New England Colonial, Southern Colonial, Dutch Colonial, and Spanish Mission revivals, among others. In 1913 he summarized what he had learned in *The Dutch Colonial House: Its Origin, Design, Modern Plan and Construction*, a guide that championed the Modern Dutch Colonial as the most appropriate form for middle-class and small rural houses, due not only to its physical properties, but to philosophical associations with what he understood to be shared Dutch and American values.

Embury and other architects accepted that the physical relationship between their houses and the originals was superficial at best. Modern Dutch Colonial houses were usually larger and airier, with plans better suited to late nineteenth-century life styles. They almost always included dormers for more light and comfortable second-story living, often featuring a shed dormer across the entire façade. Those built of wood used standardized, milled lumber in modern American construction techniques. The gambrel roof remained the style's most common and easily identified hallmark.

The proliferation of publications and photographs, together with broad nationalistic associations between the seventeenth-century Netherlands and the United States, helped propel the Modern Dutch Colonial beyond the Middle States. When architect George Palliser published his 1906 catalog of 150 modern house plans for Americans, 9 had names with national references, including 2 American and 7 Dutch (e.g., Modern Dutch Cottage, Dutch Colonial Style, Dutch Colonial Home). As part of the Colonial Revival, the Modern Dutch Colonial became a nationally recognized and patronized style employed by many architects. By 1911, Sears Roebuck began advertising mail-order houses in a wide range of Colonial Revival styles, including gambrel-roofed models with names such as The Amsterdam and The Rembrandt. Modern Dutch Colonial was purely American in its use and appearance, yet the very fact that everyone continued to name it Dutch suggests the extent to which aspects of America's Dutch heritage had become mainstream. Dutch Colonial architecture (original and revival) bracketed the nineteenth century and may constitute the single most widely recognized physical manifestation of Dutch-American identity during this century.

In a separate, simultaneous architectural development, a number of late nineteenth-century New York City and area buildings, from skyscrapers to churches, fire houses, and libraries, adopted aspects of Dutch and Flemish Renaissance architecture. Common features included steep roofs, stepped or shaped gables, contrasting colors of brick and stone, large many-paned windows, and decorative patterns of glazed brick (see, for example, illustration om page 393). Regionally prominent architects employed it for public buildings in towns along the Hudson and Delaware rivers to reflect the former Dutch character of the locale. Yet the style was also featured in national architecture magazines and building manuals. As more people recognized the diversity of America's roots it became more popular as a symbol of national heritage.

A different fashion for ornamental brick effects developed in the Midwest among middle-class Dutch-American builders and masons who worked primarily for Dutch-American patrons. For example, the Dutch immigrant brick maker Jan Hendrik Veneklasen and his sons established a brick-manufacturing business in and around Holland, MI, at midcentury that eventually provided both light cream and dark red bricks for the region. In the 1870s and 1880s local masons used these bricks to construct houses with bands of ornamental geometric patterning under the eaves, on gable ends, around door and window openings, and along string courses. Michael Douma cites the origins of such patterned brickwork in Dutch buildings in the Netherlands, possibly the very house in which Veneklasen grew up.[11]

The connections between the Michigan and New York ornamental brick modes are still murky. Both may simply derive from building practices in the Netherlands or there may have been a modern dialogue between the East Coast and Midwest. By about 1895, the fashion for polychromatic brick houses was waning in Michigan. It lasted a bit longer in New York and nationally where the motivating factors for its use were broader, including a Beaux Arts-inspired fashion for architectural references to northern European Renaissance architecture.

Another form of material culture identified as Dutch but employed nationwide was furniture produced in Chicago and Grand Rapids, MI. Most of this furniture had little or no origin in Dutch design. The West Michigan Furniture Company began manufacturing reproduction French and English period furniture in 1889. They used a logo of a Dutch woman standing before silhouetted windmills to indicate its fabrication by Dutch-American craftsmen. By 1900, about half of Grand Rapids' seven thousand furniture workers were of Dutch birth or descent. They labored in a mechanized mass-production system where owners and designers often came from English and German backgrounds.[12]

Other Michigan furniture makers specialized in modern forms that partook of the Arts and Crafts, Mission, and Craftsman aesthetic. Some of this furniture

LEGIATE · CHURCH · BUILDINGS · WEST · END · AVENUE · NEW · YORK.   R · W · GIBSON   B · WALES · N · Y ·

Robert W. Gibson, architect. Collegiate Church and School of New York, 1892, NYC.
From a reproduction in *The Architectural Record*, March 1895.

Chatles P. Limbert, *A Library in Limbert's Holland Dutch Arts and Crafts 'Flanders,'* from catalog #114, no date. The furniture was made in Holland, Michigan, and this would be very early 20th century.

also became associated with Dutchness because recent Dutch immigrants made it and marketers chose to advertise it as distinctively Dutch. Charles P. Limbert's Holland Dutch Arts & Crafts furniture provides an excellent example of this phenomenon. A third-generation Pennsylvanian of unknown ancestry, Limbert followed in his father's footsteps as a furniture salesman. By the early 1890s he was making and selling furniture in Grand Rapids, often employing Dutch immigrant workmen. He traveled to the Netherlands and on his return developed designs loosely based on Dutch furniture forms. In 1906, he moved the Charles P. Limbert Company to Holland, MI, which allowed him to add the word Holland to his marketing of Dutch-made Arts and Crafts furniture. Some of it featured images of stereotypical Dutch windmills and costumed figures.

Whereas the primary consumers of earlier Dutch-American products appear most often to have been of Dutch descent, the turn-of-the-century furniture makers shipped all over the country to Americans of every culture. Berkey and Gay, Grand Rapids-based furniture makers with a show room in New York City, specialized in antique reproductions and, like many manufacturers of the time, named some of their lines Dutch or Belgian in a bid to capitalize on Americans' interest in things Dutch. These reproductions not only took part in the general enthusiasm for the colonial — a word that referred to anything American between the European discoveries of the continent and about 1830 — but they also participated in a major shift that occurred in the conceptual and physical location of Dutch material culture in the United States during the late nineteenth century. A fabricated mythic Dutchness began to inform objects that included Dutch-motif household decorations, souvenirs from vacations in the Netherlands, and American-manufactured products from paint and household cleanser to cocoa and cigars that were packaged and advertised to identify with this picturesque notion of Dutchness. Only a few of these things were created by or for Dutch Americans.[13]

In a novel twist, a few American manufacturers exported products to the Netherlands and then used that image to market their product in the United States. Singer Sewing Machine Company not only sold its sewing machines to the Dutch, it launched a global advertising campaign that used pictures of women sewing on Singer machines in every corner of the world, including the island of Marken and the town of Volendam. Americans collected these advertising cards, which became part of Dutch Americana.

An example of the way in which an increasingly artificial Dutch material culture informed mainstream America's eclectic taste was the fashion for Dutch dining rooms.[14] A blue and white décor, antique or modern Delft tiles, fabrics and wall paper with Dutch motifs, ceramics featuring Old Dutch Master reproductions, and antique Dutch cupboards were all one needed to produce a pseudo-Dutch interior. Despite its kitsch quality to modern eyes, it appealed to

Gilded Era Americans as a reflection of the refined tastes, material wealth, and democratic impulses they attributed to the Dutch Golden Age.

2

———

THE
NINETEENTH
CENTURY

Summary Remarks

At the beginning of the nineteenth century, Dutch-American material culture consisted primarily of a combination of Dutch/Anglo-derived architectural and furniture forms and Dutch-made heirlooms (furniture, silver, jewelry, family bibles), all concentrated in traditionally Dutch areas of New Jersey, Delaware, Connecticut, New York, and Pennsylvania. By the end of the century, notions of Dutchness had become attached to broader spectrum of goods, no longer necessarily made or used by Dutch Americans. Instead, a vocabulary of iconic images identified as Dutch by the non-Dutch appeared on objects, advertisements, and buildings throughout the country. Dutch-American material culture had moved from the domain of Dutch-heritage families to that of every American, and it was more often defined by its appearance than the ethnicity of its primary users.

1 John R. Stevens, *Dutch Vernacular Architecture in North America, 1640–1830* (Hurley, NY: Society for the Preservation of Hudson Valley Vernacular Architecture, 2005).

2 David Steven Cohen, *The Dutch-American Farm* (New York/London: New York University Press, 1992).

3 Thomas R. Ryan, "Cultural Accommodations in the Late-Eighteenth-Century Architecture of Marbletown, New York," in Carter L. Hudgins and Elizabeth Collins Cromley, eds., *Shaping Communities: Perspectives in Vernacular Architecture* (Knoxville: University of Tennessee Press, 1997) 6: 147.

4 T. Robins Brown and Schuyler Warmflash, *The Architecture of Bergen County, New Jersey: The Colonial Period to the Twentieth Century* (New Brunswick, NJ: Rutgers University Press, 2000), 47.

5 John Fitchen, *The New World Dutch Barn: The Evolution, Forms, and Structure of a Disappearing Icon*, 2nd edition, edited

and updated by Gregory D. Huber (Syracuse, NY: Syracuse University Press, 2001).

6 Peter H. Cousins, *Hog Plow and Sith: Cultural Aspects of Early Agricultural Technology* (Dearborn, MI: Henry Ford Museum, 1973).

7 David Steven Cohen, "Dutch-American Farming: Crops, Livestock and Equipment, 1623–1900," in Roderick H. Blackburn and Nancy A. Kelley, eds., *New World Dutch Studies: Dutch Arts and Culture in Colonial America, 1623–1900* (Albany, NY: Albany Institute of History and Art, 1987), 185-200.

8 Joseph Manca, "On the Origins of the American Porch: Architectural Persistence in Hudson Valley Dutch Settlements," *Winterthur Portfolio* 40 (Autumn 2005): 91-131.

9 Geoffrey Reynolds, "Built along the Shores of Macatawa: The History of Boat Building in Holland, Michigan," in Robert P. Swierenga, Donald Sinnema,

and Hans Krabbendam, eds., *The Dutch in Urban America* (Holland, MI: Association for the Advancement of Dutch-American Studies, 2004), 94-107.

10   Peter Kaufman, "The Dutch Colonial Architectural Revival on Long Island," in Joann P. Krieg, ed., *Evoking a Sense of Place* (Interlaken, NY: Heart of the Lakes Publishing, 1988), 55-60.

11   Michael J. Douma, *Veneklasen Brick: A Family, a Company, and a Unique Nineteenth-Century Dutch Architectural Movement in Michigan* (Grand Rapids, MI: Eerdmans, 2005), 12-17.

12   Christian G. Carron, *Grand Rapids Furniture: The Story of America's Furniture City* (Grand Rapids, MI: Public Museum, 1998).

13   Annette Stott, *Holland Mania: The Unknown Dutch Period in American Art and Culture* (Woodstock, NY: Overlook Press, 1998).

14   Annette Stott, "The Dutch Dining Room in Turn-of-the-Century America," *Winterthur Portfolio* 37 (Winter 2002): 219-238.

3

THE PERIOD
OF THE
WORLD WARS

1914–1945

3

THE PERIOD
OF THE
WORLD WARS

—

TOWARD A COMMUNITY OF INTERESTS: THE NETHERLANDS AND THE UNITED STATES BETWEEN THE WORLD WARS

—

DOEKO BOSSCHER

During the interwar period (1918–40), relations between the United States and the Netherlands were relatively untroubled. Prior to World War I, a foundation had already been laid for more intensive communication, and after 1918 diplomatic relations between the two countries were further strengthened. The community of Dutch settlers had earned respect in the United States and their contribution to American society was seen in a positive light. The trading links — which to a large extent centered on the Dutch East Indies — were proving ever more fruitful. The following essays, which take in the interwar period and the two World Wars by which it is defined, therefore describe a period of *rapprochement*. Beneath a relatively uneventful surface, the conditions were steadily being created for the strong alliance that emerged after 1945. As these essays argue, a clearly observable shift in the Dutch view of the United States took place around 1930. In Dutch eyes, the United States gradually went from being an impressive potential world power that was nevertheless relatively unimportant to the Low Countries to gaining full recognition as the powerhouse of an American Century. The various aspects of this change form the main theme of this introductory essay.

3

——

THE
PERIOD
OF
THE
WORLD
WARS

1914–1945

An Improvement in the Netherlands' Image

As will be explained later in this volume, although World War I had inflicted some damage on Dutch-American relations, this friction was quickly forgiven and forgotten. From 1918 onward, opposing interests were few and far between. With the approach of World War II, the values to which the two countries jointly subscribed only gained in significance. The Netherlands still cherished its neutrality ("independence"), a stance that had met with little appreciation in the United States in the years 1917–18. But now that the Americans themselves had rejected participation in the League of Nations and had opted for detachment ("isolationism"), any basis for frowning upon Dutch neutrality had largely evaporated.

Cultural exchange gradually gathered momentum, albeit sparsely and with the proviso that "exchange" was perhaps too weighty a word, in light of the countries' unequal status. How did the peoples of these two nations see each other during the interwar period? Where the American view of the Dutch was concerned, a positive development had been under way since the final decades of the nineteenth century. It was generally known that a number of the founding fathers who had shaped the United States had taken their inspiration from the desire for freedom demonstrated by the Dutch Republic, and this knowledge engendered respect. The cultural output of the Netherlands' Golden Age, particularly in the field of painting, met with growing appreciation. During the first half of the nineteenth century, the immigrants who formed America's own Dutch community, its citizens of Dutch descent, had suffered from the negative image that arose during the period when the British and the Dutch regarded each other as rivals, both internationally and within the United States.[1] But at the end of the century, the prevailing ideas about "the Dutch" increasingly merged into a single, more positive image.[2] As mentioned, the Netherlands' neutrality during World War I led to a measure of bitterness and inflicted a certain amount of damage on this largely favorable opinion. As Cornelis van Minnen relates, years would go by before these wounds healed entirely. Ultimately, appreciation survived the minor crisis in relations. The Dutch, whether far away in Europe or nearby in the U.S., remained relatively unaffected by the climate of xenophobia that seized the United States after 1918. Those Dutch people who had since become Americans, as white country dwellers with a keen sense of enterprise, were viewed more favorably than those whose physical characteristics, beliefs, or political persuasions were regarded as difficult to rhyme with the concept of the "real America." The fact that there had been a difficult relationship with the British Americans in a distant past paled in comparison to the contribution the Dutch had made to the development of the country.[3] Besides, they were few enough in number not to form any kind of threat.

During World War I itself, relations between the two countries were not particularly cordial, at least not at the diplomatic level. As Hubert van Tuyll mentions in his contribution, the Americans had the mistaken idea that Dutch neutrality actually masked pro-German leanings. In fact, The Hague's main worry was the prospect of German reprisals if the Netherlands were to create the impression of siding with the British and the Americans. Accordingly, Dutch policy was characterized by circumspection. When the Allies demanded the use of cargo holds in Dutch ships and began commandeering any ship they could lay their hands on when their demand was rejected, a major outcry erupted in the Netherlands. Surely President Woodrow Wilson, famous for his moving speeches about enforcing international law and other worthy causes, had now shattered his image as a man of morals? Van Tuyll concludes that, at least in part, this Dutch outrage was more for show than it was real. By railing indignantly against this move, the Dutch were making sure they did not give the Germans a pretext for occupying all or part of the country. The American diplomats understood the precarious position of the Netherlands and looked the other way on occasions where it made practical sense for the Dutch to bow a little to German pressure.

After the war, relations improved again fairly quickly. Fortunately, The Hague did not incur blame in connection with the German Kaiser's decision to flee to the Netherlands and take up residence in Huis Doorn, the stately home where he remained until his death during World War II. Belgian attempts to win back Zeeuws-Vlaanderen, an area that remained part of the Netherlands in the partition of 1839, did not therefore win U.S. backing as the Dutch government had feared. Even the diplomats at the U.S. State Department who had shown the most embittered response to the Netherlands' "cowardly" neutrality bit their tongues. The United States was careful not to indulge in what would have been a form of victor's justice. The cultural affinity and shared interests between the two countries were already too far developed to permit this.

Decline in Immigration

After World War I, the number of Dutch immigrants to the United States declined. Between 1901 and 1910, forty-eight thousand people from the Netherlands had set sail to start a new life on the other side of the Atlantic.[4] They were part of an enormous influx during that period, the absolute peak in the history of immigration to the United States when no fewer than nine million persons

403

3

—

THE
PERIOD
OF
THE
WORLD
WARS

1914–1945

found their way to American shores. In the decade thereafter (1911–20), another forty-three thousand Dutch people followed their example, with a surge in the years leading up to 1914. During the war, which the United States did not enter until April 1917, immigration was beset with practical difficulties, quite apart from the restrictions imposed by the U.S. government. This was especially true for the years 1917 and 1918. Anyone who embarked on the ocean crossing had to brave a number of risks.

After 1918, there was a major decline in cultural openness and in the number of immigrants. Wars tend to make the people of a country more conservative and more inclined to safeguard the ethnic and cultural "purity" of their domain.[5] In the U.S., this tendency gave the Ku Klux Klan the opportunity to rage against the supposed dangers that were threatening "America's own." Given the circumstances, there was plenty of scope for racism and xenophobia. Insecurity was partly fueled by the consequences of the Russian Revolution in 1917. Many were gripped by fearful visions of the revolutionary, anticapitalist violence that the world had witnessed in Russia sweeping across their own continent. This "Red Scare," which surfaced during World War I but reached its peak in the years immediately afterwards, contributed greatly to the repression of "foreign elements" and the emphasis on American values.[6] Needless to say, immigration policy did not remain unaffected by such sentiments. A movement had already arisen to curb the admission of Asians (particularly the Japanese and Chinese) but now migrants from certain parts of Europe suffered a similar fate. The First Quota Law of 1921 took a close look at an immigrant's country of origin and limited the number to be admitted each year to 3 percent of the number of their fellow nationals represented in the total population of 1910. This automatically gave preferential status to the more "trusted" nationalities. On the basis of the Second Quota Law (known as the Johnson-Reed Act), which came into effect in 1924, immigration from regions other than northwestern Europe was squeezed out even more, either openly or implicitly. Not only did this new law operate on the basis of an earlier benchmark year (1890 instead of 1910) but Congress also lowered the quota from 3 to 2 percent. On balance, the candidates from southern, central, and eastern Europe were granted a far more restricted quota with regard to absolute numbers.

Although Dutch emigrants benefited from a relatively favorable quota, their number fell to twenty-seven thousand in the period between 1921 and 1930. The further drop in numbers in the years that followed had nothing to do with new waves of xenophobia or a fear of communism in the United States, but with the economic turmoil of the Great Depression. In the aftermath of Black Thursday on October 24, 1929, the U.S. economy rapidly went from bad to worse. The United States had no desire to welcome newcomers and discouraged them rather than trying to attract them. As a result, in the decade leading up to World

War II, the number of Dutch people emigrating to the United States was 70 percent lower than in the previous decade. In relation to the total number of immigrants still coming to the United States, the share of northwestern Europeans remained steady or even increased. Among the declining numbers of those who sporadically made the crossing, the Dutch — along with Germans and Scandinavians — encountered the fewest obstacles.

The decline in U.S. immigration was not only the result of the restrictive measures imposed by Washington. The country's appeal to potential immigrants was also on the wane. Not surprisingly, the trials and tribulations of the U.S. economy had been noticed in the Netherlands. The number of remigrations (people returning to their homeland) increased. It was inevitable that the willingness among the Dutch to leave for a new country suffered as a result. People were no longer sure whether they would be heading for a better life or jumping out of the frying pan and into the fire. Those who nonetheless made the effort to enter the U.S. formed a hard core of determined folk. Individuals were more strongly represented than those making the crossing with their whole family. They were quick to adapt and were soon absorbed into the masses.

Vague Impressions on Both Sides

For the Dutch, the United States was a far-off country, with the magical appeal of every land that lies beyond the horizon. Could lessons be learned from the social experiments that were taking place there, such as Prohibition — the general ban on alcohol that was in place between 1920 and 1933? A number of anti-alcohol lobbies in the Netherlands, from both the Left and the Right of the political spectrum, were encouraged by this development. But it was far from easy to transform enthusiasm for such a revolutionary measure into deeds; the image that people were able to form of the situation in the United States remained too vague to serve as a basis for action. The handful of Americans who took an interest in the true nature of the Netherlands had the same problem. The only mode of transport between the two countries was by ship and even the quickest ocean voyage took at least six days. And in any case, such an endeavor was the exclusive province of the privileged classes. The growing stream of well-to-do Americans who embarked on a grand tour of Europe with their Baedeker in hand only included the Netherlands in their itinerary if they had a particular reason for doing so.[7] Promotional brochures distributed by organizations such as the Holland America Line, bearing titles like "It costs so little to see so much in Tulipland," did little to change this.[8] Many of the Dutch who undertook the ocean voyage did not do so under their own steam. They were mostly sent by a Dutch company or government body, or in rare cases traveled at the invitation of an

3

—

THE
PERIOD
OF
THE
WORLD
WARS

1914–1945

American organization. Transatlantic tourism was far from being the norm, although it did gather momentum in the course of the 1930s. In this regard, it is worthwhile noting that most highly educated Dutch people at the time spoke better German than English. Some were also more fluent in French. In that respect, too, a voyage to the United States was a major undertaking. It was only through cultural "Americanization" after World War II that a basic knowledge of English became more or less commonplace in the Netherlands.

It will come as no surprise to discover that the people of the United States had only the vaguest of notions about the Netherlands. In size and population, the U.S. was an elephant to the Dutch mouse. Why should the United States concern itself with the affairs of a speck on the map called the Netherlands, which was virtually irrelevant in terms of world politics? Hans Krabbendam's biography of Edward Bok and Cornelis van Minnen's biography of Hendrik Willem van Loon have revealed more about the image of the Netherlands in the United States.[9] Editor-in-chief of the *Ladies' Home Journal*, Bok (1863–1930) made an effort to promote Dutch cultural heritage, not least by launching a series of publications on "Great Hollanders." Prolific writer Van Loon, who also features in one of Van Minnen's contributions to the present volume, found time in his busy literary schedule to write extensively on Dutch culture and the Netherlands in general, including a book on Rembrandt. He succeeded in reaching a wide audience. Of course, Van Loon and Bok were not alone in seeking to bring the Netherlands to the attention of the Americans. Another noteworthy contribution was made by Adriaan Barnouw, holder of the Queen Wilhelmina Chair at Columbia University in New York City. But for all that their industrious efforts achieved, they did not succeed in giving the average American a clear perception of the Netherlands. Even the fact that Franklin D. Roosevelt, an American who openly took pride in his Dutch heritage, moved into the White House in 1933 had no more than a superficial influence on raising the profile of the Low Countries. The Netherland-America Foundation (NAF), founded as early as 1921 to stimulate bilateral contact between individuals and companies, also turned out to have little effect.

What else is there to be said about "hyphenated Americans" of Dutch origin within this context? In general, they were busy integrating into American society. While they sought to maintain their own identity, insofar as circumstances allowed, the fact that they were relatively few in number meant that remaining entirely true to their cultural roots was never going to be a realistic prospect. Their adaptability ensured that, as already stated in relation to the immigration restrictions after 1918, they were seldom seen negatively in the immigration debate and therefore had a low profile. This is not to say that they did without their own newspapers, such as *De Utah Nederlander* published in Salt Lake City between 1914 and 1935 under the editorship of Willem Jacobus DeBry. But could they be considered enthusiastic ambassadors for the Netherlands? No, that was not really their style. During the war, Van Loon complained about the lack of support he received from his many "compatriots" in Michigan. As a group, he found them very inward looking. First and foremost they were orthodox Christians, eager to achieve social success in their new environment. Any identification with the Netherlands was subordinate to this.

More Active Diplomacy

The Americans could well afford to have only the faintest of notions about the Netherlands, or even complete ignorance for that matter. The reverse was far from true. It was abundantly clear that, in peacetime as well as wartime, the international influence of the United States was growing day by day. It is true that U.S. foreign policy in the interwar period had a relatively low profile, though to describe it as "isolationist" would be something of an overstatement. Yet for the Netherlands, a great deal depended on remaining friends with the United States: even if the giant was in repose, it remained a giant. Gradually, Dutch foreign policy started to develop something that began to resemble a policy on America. Other considerations aside, this gave the Netherlands an additional counterbalance in relation to its European neighbors. Great Britain had fulfilled a similar role for some time, but excessive dependence on the British was equally undesirable. The Dutch business community had its own interests to defend. Dutch exports mainly consisted of cheese, fish, plants, flower bulbs, diamonds, and tobacco. Largely because of import tariffs imposed by Washington, the proportion of industrial products in the overall exports to the U.S. was small (not exceeding 21 percent until the financial crisis broke out), especially compared to the proportion of such products in exports to the rest of the world.[10] From 1929, exports to the United States fell dramatically, only to revive somewhat in the late 1930s when the U.S. economy began to climb out of depression. In practice, efforts to step up exports were largely a private matter and were partly channeled through the Dutch Chamber of Commerce in the United States, with varying degrees of success. The government did play a part in this respect, but only took up this task professionally from 1933 when the Ministry of Economic Affairs set up a department of trade promotion. In their consultations with the U.S. government, the Dutch repeatedly displayed a reluctance to lower their own import restrictions in exchange for greater export opportunties. The Americans were looking to attain the status of most favored nation, but given the inequality in trade volume, The Hague was afraid that such a concession would be a reckless move. During the late 1930s in particular, Dutch foreign policy lacked decisive leadership. Under the auspices of Andries Cornelis Dirk de Graeff, who held the post of foreign

407

3

——

THE
PERIOD
OF
THE
WORLD
WARS

1914-1945

minister between 1933 and 1937, the realization dawned that relying entirely on the League of Nations would not be wise; after failing to prevent Italian aggression in Ethiopia, the League's prestige was at a low ebb. However, the Netherlands was not yet ready to give up its neutrality and take the logical next step of seeking strong democratic partners for protection. Instead, the government took refuge in the notion of an even stricter neutrality. Its illusory nature became abundantly clear in May 1940.

The various versions of neutrality that the Netherlands explored did not exclude increasingly active diplomacy toward the United States, and it was primarily the future of the Dutch East Indies that encouraged this approach. In the aftermath of World War I, the Netherlands held its breath: a neutral country had to wait and see whether, in the euphoric flush of victory, the conquering nations would be tempted to view the possessions of outsiders as the spoils of war, the ill-gotten gains of those who had reaped the benefits of conflict without lifting a finger to aid the war effort. Partly because of the relatively favorable perception that American diplomats had of the Netherlands' governance of the Dutch East Indies, this turned out for the best. As Frances Gouda explains in her essay, a comparison between the United States' running of the Philippines and the administration of the Dutch East Indies turned out to the Netherlands' advantage. It should be added that this comparison mainly focused on economic gain as opposed to the fate of the population. U.S. observers had an idealized impression of Dutch respect for the governmental traditions of the indigenous people. The system of indirect rule that formed the basis of Dutch colonial government left a great deal of feudal injustice intact, but the result appeared to be far preferable to what the British, for example, had achieved in India.

As time went on, however, the persecution of nationalists by the Dutch administration in Batavia began to trouble the United States. The Americans decided early on to grant the Philippines independence, not least because their colonial foray had not proved very profitable. After Franklin Roosevelt came to power in 1933, the United States made the moral assumption that the same fate should be bestowed on all the colonies of the world.

A number of other factors made American observers more critical of the Dutch regime in the East Indies. The onset of economic depression in 1929 shed a starker light on the colony's economy, as the colonial governors saw themselves compelled to put the Netherlands first. Countries such as the United States, which until then had been free to participate in the exploitation of the colony's riches, were disadvantaged in a way that was entirely at odds with the American creed of free trade. Gouda also describes the effect that mounting tensions between Japan and the United States had on Dutch-American relations. This put a greater focus on the strategic position of the Dutch East Indies, not only its geographical significance but also its production of raw materials such as oil, rubber, and tin. The United States became seriously concerned that the Dutch East Indies were virtually unprotected against Japanese military aggression. Especially after the outbreak of war in Europe, which led everyone to fear the worst about what was to come in Asia, cabinet members such as Cordel Hull (Roosevelt's secretary of state from 1933 to 1944) proclaimed that under no circumstances the Dutch colony should be allowed to fall into enemy hands. Among the countries that exported strategic goods to the United States, the Dutch East Indies ranked in the top ten in monetary terms.[11]

Although the Netherlands did what it could to raise the colony's defenses, no one expected that they could withstand the onslaught of the Japanese war machine. After the attack on Pearl Harbor in December 1941, the Netherlands immediately declared war on Japan, in the knowledge that an invasion of the Dutch East Indies would only be a matter of time. In March 1942, a crushing defeat at the hands of the Japanese had become reality and Batavia capitulated.

Beyond Asia the mild differences of opinion between the United States and the Netherlands on policy centered on issues very different from raw materials and the political emancipation of indigenous peoples. Partly because of the presence of the International Court in The Hague, the Netherlands was a supporter of the League of Nations. Nevertheless, the Dutch kept a close watch on their neutrality, which was termed "independence" after World War I. As Michael Riemens explains, the Netherlands did its utmost to limit the domination of the major powers within the League to prevent the organization from becoming paralyzed by political wrangling. For its own sake, the Netherlands was keen to steer clear of international political waters as much as possible. From November 19, 1919 on, when the U.S. Senate proclaimed its final "no" to the League of Nations, the United States adopted a bluntly negative stance toward the organization rather than a constructively critical one. After Republican Warren G. Harding became president in 1921, nothing more could be done to change the United States' unwillingness to contribute toward Woodrow Wilson's ideal. A decision that could initially be seen as resulting from a kind of industrial accident in Congress was now written in stone. Although the United States did play a role in some of the League's committees, either as a discussion partner or an observer, it kept a clear distance from more important bodies such as the Court of International Justice. The 1930s brought a tragic solution to the problem of the League's authority. Japan and Germany withdrew in 1933, with or without international pressure, and in 1939 the Soviet Union was expelled for its aggression against Finland. Without the active membership of these major players, the organization became a paper tiger.

3

—

THE
PERIOD
OF
THE
WORLD
WARS

1914–1945

Cultural Influence

The influence of the United States' culture on the Netherlands was much great-er than that of its foreign policy. The phenomenon of mass culture began to make its impact felt across the world in all kinds of ways and the Netherlands was no exception. More often than not, mass culture meant American cul-ture. Countless publications have documented the rejection of this aspect of America by Dutch intellectuals. The writings of many commentators who had visited the United States or who had intensive experience of American mass culture were shot through with a measure of arrogance, rooted in a European sense of superiority. For a writer such as Van Mourik Broekman, the notion of "American culture" was almost a contradiction in terms. In an essay that went on to become famous — or indeed notorious — Menno ter Braak haughtily dis-missed Hollywood's film production in no uncertain terms. While his protest focused mainly on the American film as a symbol of American mass culture, be-tween the lines it was possible to discern a rather pedantic view of America it-self. A similar pedantry held most of the Dutch intellectual elite in its grasp. It stemmed from prejudice and cultural shortsightedness, as very few believers in European cultural superiority actually had first-hand experience of the United States. In hindsight it is almost comical to observe the extent of this knee-jerk rejection of American culture in a country that, after Hilter's rise to power in Germany in 1933, had or should have had other things on its mind.

Commentators were quick to jump to the conclusion that America had lit-tle to offer Europe as a role model. But there were two academics who formed a favorable exception to the rule that the upper echelons of Dutch culture nec-essarily turned up their noses at all things American: Johan Huizinga and Arie den Hollander. They at least made the effort to inform themselves first hand and this personal encounter alone forced them to take a more balanced view. Huizinga only began to study the United States in depth during and immediate-ly after World War I. His timing was logical given the enormous influence that the Americans exerted after they entered the war. His conclusions were critical but not without respect or even a degree of awe. He was concerned about the fact that organizational and practical principles had begun to lead a life of their own in America, separate from or in some cases even at odds with its culture. The long journey that he undertook in 1926, and that took in a large portion of the country, partly confirmed his negative assessment but also offered new and more optimistic perspectives. Ambivalence set the tone. He decried shocking vulgarism alongside inspiring idealism. Den Hollander set out on his journey with a less prejudiced view and returned home with a balanced assessment to report his findings in the press and elsewhere. After World War II, as holder of the first Dutch chair in American studies at the University of Amsterdam, he went on to become a true pioneer in this field.

The rejection of American culture by a host of intellectuals — in the present context it might even be justified to refer to them as snobs — in no way hampered the success of all kinds of cultural expressions that had their origins in the United States. Extensive evidence of this rapid rise can be found in the contribution by Drukker and De Rijk on material culture and product design, and in Herman van Bergeijk's article on architecture and urban planning. Interior planning and design were greatly influenced, more so than disciplines relating to the building's exterior, where European tradition held sway for longer. The interest among certain young architects in innovators such as Frank Lloyd Wright, ultimately met with a muted reception. Van Bergeijk cites the power of lobbies and artistic trusts as one of the roots of this conservatism. Dutch attempts to bring the United States into contact with European architectural styles fell on equally deaf ears. There was a mutual reluctance to see the traditional approaches of the other as relevant or appropriate to one's own situation. However, this mutual exclusion in architecture formed an exception. As mentioned, there were areas where the other's ideas were warmly welcomed. For example, the Dutch kitchen increasingly began to take on more of an American look. In this development it appears that the efficiency of the industrial production process in the United States, based on principles of scientific management, played a greater role than aesthetic considerations.

American domination was much more apparent in the entertainment sector, most notably film and popular music. Karel Dibbets and Thunnis van Oort point out the stark contrast between the view of Hollywood held by certain intellectuals and the appreciation of the general public, which felt no desire to whine about the drawbacks of "reprehensible commercialism." Many cinemas were given American names such as "New York," indicating a firm belief in the pulling power of U.S. culture. This did not mean that European films always had to bow to their American counterparts. The popularity of German and French cinema remained high throughout the interwar period. In his article, Kees Wouters describes the moral panic in certain Dutch circles prompted by jazz and swing music and the "shameful" dances associated with them. The process of Americanization continued effortlessly in the face of deliberate repression, with some authorities even attempting to invoke the law, but in many ways the rejection of U.S. influence was a projection of more general unease about modern society.

411

And then, of course, there was literature. The article by Hans Bak encompasses many authors whose work found its way to the Netherlands. Bak notes that the first American successes were primarily reserved for those writers whose views confirmed critical European perceptions of the United States. If Upton

3

—

THE
PERIOD
OF
THE
WORLD
WARS

1914–1945

Sinclair's vision of his own society had not been grist to the mill of Dutch critical opinion, his success would surely have been less pronounced. In the decades
that followed — those around World War II — irony and social critique were no
longer grounds for special recommendation. As the United States came to the
fore on the world stage, a growing group of reviewers and readers abandoned
the preconceived notion that American literature was merely a pale shadow of
its European counterpart. And once three Americans had been awarded the Nobel Prize for Literature — Sinclair Lewis being the first in 1930 — this position
became especially difficult to defend.

The question of whether the Netherlands also influenced American culture
in the interwar period is easy to answer. Any such influence was unarticulated
and diffuse. The only serious example, and a modest one at that, can be found in
Frits Zwart's essay on classical music. Conductor Willem Mengelberg achieved
some success with his propaganda for Gustav Mahler in the United States, although a number of critics soon tired of his "Mahleritis." However, bringing
Dutch music into the spotlight was an impossible task.

A Democratic Role Model?

If, during the interwar period, the United States did not quite become the very
embodiment of the future, it certainly represented a possible future. It was a future some welcomed, while others resisted with all their might. But what about
the image of American democracy? As a society structured along religious and
ideological lines that ran through all social classes, and therefore almost by definition an inward-looking society, the Netherlands was not overly impressed by
the brand of direct democracy practiced in the United States. This directness
in the United States is often linked to a local or regional orientation, while the
social pillars (*zuilen*) in the Netherlands operate with national representatives
of the elite as the primary spokesmen. Although there was participation within
each pillar, the phenomenon of passivity or obedience, identified as a key feature by political scientist Lijphart, automatically excluded the notion of a referendum democracy. The main aim of the pillar was emancipation: each group
sought to obtain greater influence on government policy and attract more resources from the state coffers. The elite determined what was best for the group
from an emancipatory point of view. In response to each change in the political landscape, whether as a result of constitutional reforms or other developments, each group carefully weighed up the pros and cons before adopting its
own standpoint.[12]

In this way the Netherlands decided on a far-reaching constitutional change
during World War I (adopted in 1917 and implemented in 1918) that went against

the grain of an important lesson in the U.S. system: electoral districts were re-placed by proportional representation. What was assumed to be logical in the United States was far less so in the Netherlands. The principle of proportional-ity offered the complex society of minorities (Protestants, Catholics, liberals, so-cial democrats) that made up the Netherlands, the opportunity to benefit from the increasing influence of the state, according to simple rules of shared justice. The new electoral system showed for the first time how strong the support for each party was, as each vote, no matter where it was cast, counted toward the big picture. According to the now clearly defined cultural, religious, and political bal-ance of power, the blessings of government intervention (education, social provi-sions, subsidies and the like) could be distributed pro rata among the population. The distribution of income — and its levels — that the state gradually began to take upon itself could now be carried out along fairer, more proportionally clear-cut channels.

In the discussions surrounding the system change, all parties were optimis-tic about their chances. They each hoped that, on balance, it would bring them more seats in parliament. But as it turned out, the Rooms-Katholieke Staatspar-tij (RKSP; Roman Catholic State Party) was the main beneficiary.[13] Whatever its consequences, the transition to proportional representation was a clear exam-ple of a development that flew in the face of the American model and where the United States could at most be regarded as a negative example. Developments in the Netherlands also reflected a major difference in how the state was per-ceived: it was not an entity that should be kept at a distance, come what may. Paradoxically, the government and the various social groups put up with one another extremely well, notwithstanding all the talk by the latter about the need to keep state power in check. Given their autonomy within their own circle, the groups ensured that there was a healthy degree of pluralism; in terms of wealth and welfare, the state supplemented the groups to exactly the desired level. This well-considered balance gave Dutch politics "the best of both worlds."

In the United States, however, the marginal role accorded to the state from the very beginning has never really changed. When the nation was founded in the last twenty-five years of the eighteenth century, "American" primarily stood for "free." The government was subject to restrictions from the very start. There was a strong emphasis on individual land rights, and identification with the community primarily took shape within a local, regional, or cultural unit: the town or city, the county or state, an ethnic group or a church. Pluralism was just as much a core concept as it was in the Netherlands, since everyone determined their own fate as far as possible within a self-appointed context, political or oth-erwise. But while Dutch pluralism voluntarily made the state a key player, the U.S. version continued to view it as a necessary evil, as the discussions on isola-tionism and the New Deal demonstrated.

413

The New Deal

3

—

THE
PERIOD
OF
THE
WORLD
WARS

1914–1945

The Netherlands did not feel the effects of the Great Depression until after many other countries, including the United States. But once it hit, the consequences were ultimately more serious and protracted than elsewhere. While unemployment peaked around 1932 in most neighboring countries, in the Netherlands it only reached its height in 1936.[14] Who was responsible for this prolonged process in the Netherlands? A number of historians have been fairly successful in their efforts to exonerate the policy of the Dutch government under the leadership of Hendrikus Colijn, who became prime minister in May 1933. Nevertheless, the current consensus among experts centers on the fact that maintaining the gold standard until 1936, one year after neighboring Belgium had abandoned it, had a very negative influence. The strong guilder had a disastrous effect on exports and meant that companies in the Netherlands could not compete on the world market. A number of protectionist measures aimed at safeguarding Dutch production against imports resulted in a dramatic rise in the cost of living. This, combined with efforts to keep wages as low as possible in order to boost exports to some extent, led to widespread impoverishment.

Quite apart from the question of whether Colijn and his cohorts can be substantially blamed regarding their actual policies, their lack of empathy is most striking. In her contribution, Janny de Jong places great emphasis on the importance of hope as a way of making life's trials bearable. While Herbert Hoover in the United States certainly did his part to overcome the economic malaise, he fell short when it came to offering people a hopeful vision of the future. Roosevelt did succeed on that front and it was for that very reason that he won the elections of 1932 and was reelected in 1936. He also went on to win the support of the people in 1940 and 1944, albeit in different circumstances and partly for different reasons. Rhetoric such as "I pledge you, I pledge myself, to a New Deal for the American People" struck an entirely different chord in comparison to gloomy warnings about tightening one's belt and hoping things would not get worse.[15] Roosevelt's credo was to reject fear as a "nameless, unreasoning, unjustified terror which paralyzes needed efforts to convert retreat into advance."[16] With this message he captured the hearts of the people, and he reinforced this effect by immediately matching his words with deeds and setting to work with formidable energy. Colijn and his advisors took a dim view of such activism — and in particular of the rhetoric that accompanied it — in light of the major ideologies with which Europe was being confronted at the time. These were closer and more threatening to the Netherlands than they were to the United States. The dividing line between revolutionary communism and the reforming zeal of social democracy had yet to become clear in the international arena and, bearing this in mind, it would be far from appropriate to look back with the benefit of hindsight and blame the Dutch prime minister for refusing to take the plunge.

World War II

From May 10, 1940, the Netherlands was suddenly a nation at war, very much against its will. In contrast to 1914, Germany had shown itself to be no respecter of neutrality. Facing the prospect of a war with Britain, in which an offensive on the British Isles would be inevitable, the Germans saw occupation of the Netherlands as a necessity. After June 1941, when Hilter invaded the Soviet Union, the Dutch government in exile in London found itself allied with Stalin. At the end of that year, after Pearl Harbor, an unmistakable community of interests had been formed with the United States. At a much earlier stage, Roosevelt had realized that the United States would not be able to stay out of the war, but strong isolationist forces stood in the way of the Wilsonian politics that he saw as necessary. The Netherlands was understandably overjoyed at the United States' entry into the war. Van Loon, whom we mentioned earlier, was one of those who had tried in vain to influence public opinion in his adopted fatherland with the publication of his book *Invasion* (1940), which styled itself as "an eyewitness account of the Nazi invasion of America."[17] After the shock of Pearl Harbor, a host of FDR's political opponents revised their position, some of them with an admission of blame. The Republicans were drawn into the newfound spirit of internationalism. Nowhere was this more apparent than in the title of Wendell Willkie's best-selling book *One World*.[18]

Both countries had hard lessons to learn (particularly with regard to preparedness and the formation of alliances) but the Netherlands was affected more deeply by the transition. Thanks to its extensive colonial possessions, the Dutch had long been able to cling to the notion that theirs was not a small and helpless nation but a medium-sized or even major power that deserved to be treated as such. However, these possessions turned out to be extremely vulnerable. The colonial empire crumbled in the blink of an eye, first at the hands of the Japansese and subsequently in the face of a powerful wave of Indonesian nationalism. The latter was given the benefit of the doubt by the international community. The Netherlands itself had to rely on large-scale assistance from other nations for its liberation, after which it took years to recover economically. In economic terms too, outside aid was indispensable, particularly from the United States in the shape of the Marshall Plan. In his contribution, Albert Kersten describes the details of this learning process in harrowing terms that are all too fitting. On the Dutch side, indignation gave way first to disillusionment and eventually to resignation.

3

—

THE
PERIOD
OF
THE
WORLD
WARS

1914–1945

During the war, there were a handful of fleeting moments when the Netherlands briefly thought its prominent status might be recognized. During Queen Wilhelmina's visit to the United States in the summer of 1942, the government in exile had the impression that its wishes had received a sympathetic reception, but this soon turned out to be an illusion. Even if FDR was well disposed toward the Netherlands, at heart the United States had little sympathy for colonial empires and followed its own path. A prolonged and complicated battle between a pro-British and a pro-American faction developed within the Dutch cabinet. The former maintained that, while Britain and the Netherlands had been rivals for centuries, the British at least had their own highly regarded colonial tradition. On that score the Netherlands would have little to fear from the British and could even count on a measure of support. The latter faction foresaw that Britain would be in no position to help the Netherlands restore its empire in the postwar era. They argued that it was therefore better to seek *rapprochement* with Washington, despite the risks that this entailed. The Dutch foreign minister, Eelco van Kleffens, was married to an American. Partly inspired by his familiarity with his wife's country, he opted for close ties with the United States. However, his legalistic approach to international politics often clashed with the American vision, which was more concerned with the balance of power than with abstractions such as justice. This led Van Kleffens to initially reject the idea that a new international organization should make a distinction between the major powers (which would exercise their authority in what would eventually become the Security Council) and the rest. With his haughty and unrealistic approach, he was fighting a rearguard action. Given the circumstances, the Netherlands was bound to feel increasingly marginalized. Yet the lack of understanding on the part of the Americans was more the expression of rapidly changing geopolitical circumstances than a lack of empathy.

Free

Even the liberation of the Netherlands took place on the margins, or, in Wim Klinkert's words, it was "the byproduct of a military strategy geared toward defeating the Nazis." In order to reach Germany and deliver the final *coup de grâce*, the Allied troops had to go through Limburg, Brabant, and Gelderland. The first area of Dutch territory was liberated on September 12, 1944. Liberation then steadily spread northward, as the Germans no longer considered it worthwhile deploying large numbers of troops in much of Limburg. During Operation Market Garden in late September 1944 the United States deployed over twenty thousand parachutists in what was the most important American contribution to the further military operations in the Netherlands. However, the Germans fought tooth and nail to defend Arnhem and the surrounding area. This led to the fail-ure of British Field Marshall Montgomery's plan to capture the bridges across the Rhine by Arnhem and push through to Berlin before winter. It meant that the western Netherlands had to endure a period of extreme hardship before the Germans finally capitulated in May 1945.[19]

In the remaining months of the war, the Americans fought on in the west-ern part of Brabant and spread out across other locations, but by and large it was the British and the Canadians who took it upon themselves to liberate the Netherlands step by step. U.S. bombers did carry out air strikes on a large num-ber of German positions, claiming the lives of many civilians in the process. The repeated calls by Queen Wilhelmina and her government to save the Dutch people from starvation by speeding up the Allied advance toward the western cities were not heeded because of other priorities. The Americans could have made the difference if they had wanted to, but the logic of the war drove them eastward.

The British and the Canadians were also compelled to sacrifice civilian lives, for instance during the liberation of Zeeland. In order to make Antwerp acces-sible to Allied shipping, all of Walcheren was flooded, drowning many people and causing untold damage to property. There are, therefore, no grounds for laying particular blame at the door of the Americans, but to regard them — as people sometimes have done — as the ultimate liberators as opposed to the British or Canadians, is also an inaccurate representation of the facts. Klinkert points out that over half of the military victims on the side of the Allies were British, followed by the Canadians and only then the Americans, with a figure of 8 percent. This inclination to raise the Americans to the highest level of hero-ism appears to have been a projection of Dutch regard for the nation on which it would have to rely in so many respects in future. From being a distant friend, the United States had become a partner with a major presence in an extremely imbalanced relationship. The Netherlands demonstrated an understandable tendency to see its new best friend/partner/ally as it wanted to be seen, to rein-force America's view of itself.

Conclusion

The history of Dutch-American relations in the interwar period featured many instructive, revealing, inspiring, and painful moments for the Netherlands. But a remarkable lack of urgency in revising established prejudices continued long after 1918. The idea that American culture and all that the United States stood for could be criticized with impunity and from a safe distance was still very deeply entrenched. It was only around 1930 that the landscape began to

417

3

——

THE
PERIOD
OF
THE
WORLD
WARS

1914–1945

change. Tensions began to build in Europe, especially in response to the collapse of the Weimar Republic and the determination of Germany's new leaders to renege on the Treaty of Versailles. The Great Depression put political relations in a host of countries on a knife edge, both on the domestic and international front. Slowly but surely the Netherlands began to abandon its view of the United States as a major power that was nonetheless irrelevant and arbitrary. The benefits to be gained by seriously analyzing and working toward *rapprochement* with this distant friend became increasingly clear. The American Century turned out not to be a flight of fancy or a propagandandist exaggeration; there was more than a grain of truth to this phrase. America held the key to world economic improvement. Only America could guarantee European security in the face of the Cold War, for which the stage had been set during the final months of World War II. The concept of security that played a central role in this respect encompassed not only Dutch territorial interests but also its cultural integrity. The Netherlands' image of itself became more modest, but did not wither away. After all, if Germany, France, and Britain all found themselves sheltering under America's protective umbrella, why should the Netherlands be ashamed of its new relationship?

1   To read about the prejudice against the "British" Americans that prevailed in the Netherlands, see J.C.H. Blom, "Slavernij en Yankee. Nederlandse openbare meningsuitingen over de Amerikaanse burgeroorlog," *Tijdschrift voor Geschiedenis* 85 (1972): 205-223.

2   See, for example, Willem Frijhoff, "Dutchness in Fact and Fiction," in Joyce D. Goodfriend et al., eds., *Going Dutch. The Dutch Presence in America, 1609–2009* (Leiden: Brill, 2008), 327-358.

3   Joyce D. Goodfriend et al., "Holland in America" [Introduction], in Goodfriend et al., eds., *Going Dutch,* 1-23.

4   The immigration figures mentioned here and later on come from *Historical Statistics of the U.S., 1789–1945* (U.S. Bureau of the Census).

5   Michael Lemay and Elliott Robert Barkan, eds., *U.S. Immigration and Naturalization Laws and Issues. A Documentary History* (Westport, CT: Greenwood Press, 1999), 48.

6   A. Mitchell Palmer, Woodrow Wilson's attorney general, became notorious for the "Palmer Raids" (hunting down "anarchistic" individuals and groups). Many hundreds of suspects were simply sent back to their country of origin, the Soviet Union.

7   Before the start of the Great Depression, the number of American visitors to Europe had grown to a quarter of a million per year. See Walter H. Salzmann, "Bedrijfsleven, overheid en handelsbevordering. The Netherlands Chamber of Commerce in the United States, Inc., 1903–1987" (Ph.D. dissertation, Universiteit Leiden, 1994), 84.

8   Salzmann, "Bedrijfsleven, overheid," 85.

9   Hans Krabbendam, *The Model Man: A Life of Edward William Bok, 1863–1930* (Amsterdam/Atlanta, GA: Rodopi, 2001); Cornelis A. van Minnen, *Amerika's beroemdste Nederlander. Een biografie van Hendrik Willem van Loon* (Amsterdam: Boom, 2005), and *Van Loon:*

Popular Historian, Journalist, and
FDR Confidant (New York: Palgrave
Macmillan, 2005).

10   Salzmann, "Bedrijfsleven, overheid,"
72-73.

11   Ellen van Zuyll de Jong, "The American
Stake in Netherlands India," *Far Eastern
Survey* 9.13 (1940): 145-153.

12   For an introductory article on the
structure of Dutch society, see D.F.J.
Bosscher, "Good Old Pillarisation:
An Attempt at (Re-)Evaluation," in
F.R. Ankersmit and H. te Velde, eds.,
Trust: Cement of Democracry? (Leuven
/Paris/Dudley, MA: Peeters, 2005),
89-108.

13   The change meant that the surplus of
Catholic voters in the south suddenly
became a national phenomenon. This
is why the RKSP gained most when the
Netherlands abandoned its electoral
districts.

14   Jan Luiten van Zanden, *Een klein land in
de twintigste eeuw. Economische geschiedenis van Nederland, 1914–1995*

(Utrecht: Het Spectrum, 1997), 151-156.

15   It was with these words that FDR accepted
the Democratic nomination for the
presidency at the party convention in
Chicago on July 2, 1932.

16   Inaugural address, March 4, 1933.

17   H.W. van Loon, *Invasion. Being an
Eyewitness Account of the Nazi Invasion
of America* (New York: Harcourt, Brace
& Company, 1940). A number of other
"allohistories" (or "what-if histories")
were also published (Marion White,
Alfred Bester, Fred Allhoff), but it took
a national trauma on the scale of Pearl
Harbor to change the mood of the
nation.

18   John S. Odell, "From London to Bretton
Woods: Sources of Change in Bargaining
Strategies and Outcomes," *Journal of
Public Policy* 8.3/4 (1988): 287-315, here
300-301.

19   Food shortages during the "hunger
winter" claimed between thirty and forty
thousand lives, according to official
estimates.

3

—

THE
PERIOD
OF
THE
WORLD
WARS

1914–1945

DUTCH-AMERICAN RELATIONS DURING WORLD WAR I

—

HUBERT P. VAN TUYLL

The Netherlands and the United States entered and left the World War I era with similar views in international affairs but experienced frictions that temporarily weakened their relationship.

Introduction: The United States and the Netherlands on the Eve of War

Before World War I, the diplomatic and strategic relationship between the United States and the Netherlands was limited, excepting issues pertinent to Asia. Neither country wished for war in Europe. The peace conferences held at The Hague symbolized Dutch commitment to neutrality and peace, a preference that American statesmen shared. Influenced by these events, Andrew Carnegie even built his famous Peace Palace in The Hague. Americans, however, were reasonably aware of the increasingly threatening situation between 1905 and 1914, and even the Netherlands' position was of some, if mostly unofficial, interest. In 1910 the Dutch government embarked on the construction of fortifications at Vlissingen, commanding the Scheldt River approaches to Antwerp. Belgian, French, and British officials and journalists complained that this was done at German instigation, and these charges were echoed in the American press.

Of far greater importance, however, was the position in Asia. The Unites States had no objection to the Netherlands' control of the Dutch East Indies, but both were greatly concerned about the expansion of Japan (and, to a lesser extent, Britain) into the region. Fear of losing the colonial connection led the Dutch to develop a telegraph net with the Germans that utilized American-held islands to circumvent the British-controlled networks. This was achieved after overcoming both political and technical difficulties, including the opposition of American anti-imperialists to participation in such multinational venture.[1]

A Shared Vision, 1914–16

The outbreak of war did not strain relations because both countries had similar wartime goals, albeit for different reasons. Both declared neutrality. For the Netherlands, American neutrality was comforting. A great power with whom all combatants needed to curry favor seemed committed to international legal protection for neutrals. The theoretical and practical positions were, in reality, quite different, but this only became clear to the Dutch in 1917 when the United States entered the war. America maintained neutrality from a position of strength. It could function economically even if foreign trade or investments were disrupted. For the Netherlands neither was the case; it was a commercial nation and its finances were intricately woven into the international web:

Stocks of outward foreign direct investment in 1914[2]

	% of G.D.P
Netherlands	85
Britain	65
France	20
Germany	20
United States	5

Neutrality had also evolved differently. In both countries, it had begun as a function of strategic weakness, but this factor had grown for one while it had disappeared for the other. American neutrality was linked to isolationism, a belief that was nonexistent in the Netherlands. The American commitment to the "rights of neutrals" was more a function of the country's experiences during the French Revolution/Napoleonic Wars than of any abstract belief. Perhaps these differences explain why the U.S. rejected Foreign Minister John Loudon's attempt to create a bloc of neutrals (echoing the eighteenth-century League of Armed Neutrality).

The differences did not appear significant in 1914. Both desired neutrality. After the invasion of Belgium, the two countries would cooperate to move relief supplies to Belgium. There was also shared concern for the situation in Asia.

Dutch Minister of Foreign Affairs John Loudon.

The situation in the Dutch East Indies was dangerous, especially after Japan's August 15 ultimatum to Germany demanding that Berlin hand over its colony in China. Japanese expansion was definitely feared. Loudon had no difficulty obtaining an expression of shared concern from U.S. Under Secretary of State Robert Lansing.

Dutch-American relations also benefited from personal diplomacy. Loudon had enjoyed a successful stint as envoy in Washington, and he developed a close relationship with Henry Van Dyke, American envoy in The Hague (1914–16). His relationship with the notoriously anti-German Van Dyke was significant because the American had close ties to President Woodrow Wilson and had served under him at Princeton University. The views of Van Dyke and his son, also present in The Hague, are instructive because Loudon is one of the few figures who earned their unqualified admiration. This was no small matter because the Dutch envoy in Washington, W. L. F. Ch. van Rappard, caused problems through his openly pro-German attitude, at one point endangering the delivery of munitions purchased in Washington.

America Enters the War

In the long run, American belligerency (April 6, 1917) may have benefited the Netherlands. Had Germany won, it would have completely surrounded and probably dominated its smaller neighbor. In the short run, however, America's participation in the war was an unmitigated disaster. In some Dutch circles it was even seen as a greater threat than Germany's declaration of unrestricted submarine warfare. The latter endangered trade with Britain, but the former deprived Dutch-flag vessels of a "safe haven" and the protection of a fellow neutral. Dutch assumptions that Wilson would maintain his sympathy for the rights of neutrals proved false. The American government believed that the best protection for the neutrals was an Entente victory. Public opinion, if not belligerent, had long left neutrality behind anyway.

The Netherlands expected the American declaration of war. Woodrow Wilson's vigorous response to the sinking of the *Lusitania* in 1915 indicated that he would protect the passage of American people and goods across the Atlantic. The Dutch assumed that Wilson did so in order to protect the rights of neutrals, especially since the president was viewed as an idealist. Wilson's outlook particularly appealed to Loudon, who had Washington experience. As it turned out, the president shared many of Loudon's views about a proper international order. None of this mattered, however, in the short run. Once the United States entered World War I, Wilson ceased to champion the rights of neutrals. After April 6, 1917, not a single great power remained neutral.

423

3

—

THE
PERIOD
OF
THE
WORLD
WARS

1914–1945

American belligerency had other consequences as well. The Netherlands had painstakingly constructed a system to regulate its international trade that would be acceptable to both camps. After the American entry, this system unraveled. Neither Britain nor Germany had to tolerate free trade to curry favor with a neutral America. The system's most famous component, the National Oversea Trust Company, declined rapidly. The Netherlands also had to assume more responsibility for Belgian relief as the American envoy there, Brand Whitlock, obviously could not remain.

The Relationship in Crisis

The pressure on commerce became severe. With American support Britain could afford to be less flexible. By August 1917, the Netherlands was effectively under blockade. While at least one Dutch author conceded that American actions were simply a function of military necessity, this was hardly an argument that Wilson could make in public, it being the same argument used by German Chancellor Theobald von Bethmann-Hollweg to justify the 1914 invasion of Belgium. Ties to the Dutch East Indies became feeble; there were no more telegraph lines through neutral territory, and the British could now safely claim the right to stop and inspect Dutch vessels headed there. As the U.S.-supported Entente made more demands, the Germans did the same. Soon there would no longer be any diplomatic room between the demands of the belligerent alliances; each would insist on concessions that the other would not accept. Yet outright refusal risked war.

This point was nearly reached in the spring of 1918. For some time, the Entente-U.S. alliance had been demanding the use of Dutch merchant vessels. This did not much affect the vessels' owners, as many of their ships were periodically idled anyway due to the submarine threat. Sailing in Allied convoys created risks but also promised rewards. From a national perspective, however, ceding vessels to the belligerents was anathema. It would worsen food shortages at home, and create a crisis abroad. The cession of Dutch-flag merchant vessels to the Allies would undoubtedly lead to demands from the Central Powers for compensating benefits (as indeed happened).

The threat to Dutch shipping developed slowly, and initially came mostly from the British. In February 1917, two weeks after the United States had broken relations with Germany, the Foreign Office informed the Dutch government that Dutch vessels could not leave British ports until previously agreed-upon food shipment targets were met. The U.S. also restricted Dutch sailings from its ports. In May 1917, Britain seized Dutch-owned vessels flying the British flag, and in June added Dutch-flag vessels with British owners.

Although the June action was legally questionable, the ownership made the situation sufficiently ambiguous that the Dutch were not forced to issue a major protest. In 1918, however, a far more drastic action would completely alter the Netherlands' position. On March 20 and 21, the United States and the United Kingdom seized 135 Dutch vessels then in their ports. The 450,000 tons of shipping represented a third of the Dutch merchant fleet, and other ships entering American and British ports could expect the same fate. This action — and Germany's response — must not be seen in a vacuum. The Allies had pressured the Dutch government for months, but neither Loudon nor Prime Minister P.W.A. Cort van der Linden felt able to concede because of the anticipated German reaction and believed it was safer to await a seizure. A more important part of the background, however, was that both alliances were fighting for their lives. In early 1918, Germany gambled everything on a series of offensives on the Western Front that came stunningly close to success. No belligerent was in a mood to accept legalistic Dutch arguments.

Still, the seizure had to be justified because the Entente nations claimed to be protectors of the small nations and of international law. Wilson especially had emphasized principles and laws as the foundation for all his actions. He argued that the Dutch lacked the "free will" to make an agreement regarding the vessels because of German threats to sink them in case they were made available to the Entente, and that the ships were stuck uselessly in port (a disputed point).[3] Lansing's State Department did better, digging out an obsolete legal concept, *jus angariae,* the "right of angary." In maritime law this means that a sovereign may compel a vessel to engage in a public purpose, such as carrying troops and supplies.[4] This is what Wilson was referring to on March 21 when he claimed the "indisputable rights as a sovereign."[5]

The U.S. president's actions and language caused outrage in the Netherlands, and not only because of the seizure itself. Losing control of the ships might have been the main issue. Wilson, however, was long viewed as an exponent of international law and the equality of nations, and his recycling of an ancient and obsolete legal principle to justify what was no more than a militarily necessary theft, described as "the most spectacular single act of force employed by the United States against the neutrals," struck the Dutch as hypocritical. This may explain why anger was directed more at the Americans than the British, even though the latter remained unpopular because of their behavior in the Boer War. The Dutch government issued as powerful a legal protest as it could without actually claiming a neutrality violation. The protest also accused the American action of being "in conflict with the traditional friendship between the two countries."[6]

The protest had no immediate result in the Entente capitals other than annoyance, although U.S. officials were somewhat sympathetic. American Envoy

425

3
___

THE
PERIOD
OF
THE
WORLD
WARS

1914–1945

John Garrett conceded that the Dutch felt "maltreated" and "humiliated" and the State Department began working to improve relations before the war ended. However, the protest was not really aimed at the U.S. and its Entente allies at all. The primary "customer" was Germany, which might see the seizure as a *casus belli* on which the Netherlands had failed to act. This would entitle the Germans to demand further concessions, or even to occupy the Netherlands.

Germany did make demands. At the insistence of army commander General Erich Ludendorff, these included the shipment of sand and gravel to Belgium via Dutch territory, and the use of Dutch rail lines across Limburg. The demands were actually made on the same day as the ship seizures; the latter merely gave the Germans more ammunition against the Dutch and caused Ludendorff to become more inflexible, even moving troops to the Dutch border as a prelude to invasion. Eventually the pressure became so great that the Netherlands made concessions — but not before Loudon consulted the Americans. His communication to Wilson went unanswered, but this was deliberate. Wilson wished to act as if the transshipments of sand and gravel were a purely domestic Dutch matter. This was not the case, as the materiel was being used for military purposes. The United States and its allies understood, however, that a firm position would force the Netherlands to take a hard line against Germany, which could lead to invasion; and no Allied troops were available to assist the Dutch. The Allies only issued tepid objections to the Netherlands' concessions. This was a moment when the Dutch were grateful that Wilson had not adhered to a strictly legally principled stance.

End Game

The unraveling of the German position in the summer and fall of 1918 created an entirely different situation for the Netherlands and a fundamentally different relationship with the U.S.-Entente combine. As German forces retreated, the necessity of simultaneously appeasing two enemies disappeared. However, the Dutch would now have to deal with a victorious alliance whose demands could not be limited by reference to the putative reactions of the other side. Two events aggravated the situation. First, the Dutch government, disoriented and distracted by the threat of domestic revolution, allowed eighty thousand (disarmed) German soldiers to go home via Dutch Limburg. Second, the German emperor fled to the Netherlands.

Both of these situations created problems for the Netherlands that persisted well after the armistice of November 11. The Limburg passage was more serious with regard to U.S. relations. Foreign Minister Herman A. van Karnebeek, who was new, had compounded the situation by issuing justifications that were

not believable and, as it turned out, not true. To American observers, the "explanations of the Dutch were lame." Later this would cause the United States, like
Britain, to demand a number of concessions for the movement of men and supplies via the Rhine. Here, the U.S. position differed little from that of its allies.
Fortunately, the same was not true regarding the Kaiser, as the president was
opposed to demands for extradition. One American diplomat expressed the
view, quite representative of thinking in American circles, that the Netherlands
"had too much honor to think of" extraditing the Kaiser, and that "Holland has
made the world its debtor by refusing to surrender the Kaiser."[7]

Moving toward Peace

This American attitude regarding the Kaiser was important because, had the U.S.
stood monolithically with its allies at Versailles, the Netherlands would have
been in a perilous position, given Belgium's annexation plans of parts of the
Dutch southern provinces. There were plenty of friction points, even such relatively unimportant ones as the location of the peace conference and the League
of Nations. Requests to have these in The Hague were rejected, reportedly because Wilson "wanted nothing to do with Carnegie and his peace palace."[8] If
the United States were even tolerant toward Belgian annexationism — and some
U.S. diplomats appeared friendly to the idea — the peace settlement could be
worse than the war for the Netherlands.

   This did not happen. Several reasons can be advanced to explain why the
Netherlands received American support. Wilson, Lansing, and presidential confidant "Colonel" House all had reservations about the Belgian demands. Intensive Dutch diplomacy (see below) played a major role. Finally, the United States
and the Netherlands shared similar long-term perspectives. Wilson's call for a
new international order resonated with the Dutch, and their sympathy played
well with the president. The Dutch used this to great effect during the struggle
at Versailles over the future of the Scheldt River, Antwerp's lifeline, which runs
through Dutch territory. By proposing that the entire matter be referred to the
League of Nations, Dutch diplomats were making a calculated appeal to the
Americans, the League's prime sponsors.

The Specter of Belgian Imperialism

Unfettered access to Antwerp was not the only Belgian objective. There was also
interest in annexing Zeeuws-Vlaanderen, on the south bank of the Scheldt, and
southern Limburg, which Belgian nationalists argued had been "lost" in the

3

—

THE
PERIOD
OF
THE
WORLD
WARS

1914–1945

agreements of 1839, under which the Netherlands finally recognized Belgium. There were strategic, economic, and historical arguments undergirding the Belgian claims, but these would not matter unless the major powers supported them.

The Dutch feared they might. The Netherlands was not popular in the Entente, viewed by some (particularly the French) as having promoted Germany's cause. (This atttitude has not disappeared completely, as on October 15, 1998 the former French Minister for European Affairs Alain Lamassoure stated: "Seen from Paris, a Dutchman is a German.") Concern over the outcome was so great in The Hague that Van Karnebeek even called upon his predecessor to go to Paris because of his experience with the Americans. A common expression was that "our only protection lies with Wilson." Getting in to see the president proved difficult. Wilson claimed not to have time, which may even have been true. Loudon did eventually see him, however, and apparently used his charm effectively, Wilson allegedly being "especially susceptible to his charming manners and engaging conversation."[9] However, it may not be with the president himself that the most significant diplomacy occurred. There were numerous contacts with House, who sympathized with Belgium, and more significantly, Lansing. The latter became increasingly hostile toward the Belgians and helped ensure that the final commission established to study the issues between the two larger low countries could consider "neither a transfer of territorial sovereignty, nor the creation of international servitude." (The latter language blocked any forced transfer of sovereignty over the Scheldt.) More than one scholar has suggested that the greater experience of the Netherlands in international affairs played a significant role in the outcome.[10]

Conclusion

While frictions lingered after the war, their practical impact on Dutch-American relations was not great. Here and there slight evidence existed of anti-Dutch attitudes, exacerbated by the continued presence of the Kaiser and occasional republication of the (false) story that the Netherlands had abandoned the defense of Limburg. While the Kaiser's asylum was better known to Americans, it was not really all that important. Wilson never favored extradition.

Besides, there were several factors that militated toward a return to "normalcy." First, the international ideals of the Wilson administration, especially those involving international law and international organization, resonated well in the Netherlands. This is obvious from the fruitful conversations between Wilson and Loudon, among others, where common ground was quickly established. Second, as the war hysteria in America declined it became less impor-

428

tant to Americans whether this or that country had leaned toward the Central Powers. Even at Versailles the very pro-Entente Lansing had moved to protect the Netherlands from Belgian annexationism. Third, the two countries shared a common concern about the future balance of power in the Pacific. Not that America was totally solicitous toward the Dutch position; aside from criticisms of Dutch colonial management, the U.S. had supported at Versailles the seizure of the German-Dutch telegraph network in the Pacific, which represented a considerable investment in regional communications for the Dutch.

Thus, in general the post-Versailles era represented a rapid normalization of relations between the Netherlands and the United States. Among the efforts from the Dutch side to improve relations was the expanded funding for the Queen Wilhelmina Chair in Dutch studies at Columbia University which, in the decades that followed, contributed to a better understanding between both countries.

1   U.S. perceptions of the Dutch empire, and Dutch fears of Japanese aggression, are examined further in Frances Gouda's essay in this volume.

2   "One World," *Economist,* October 18, 1997, 80.

3   Edgar Turlington, *Neutrality: Its History, Economics, and Law,* vol. 3, *The World War Period* (New York: Octagon, 1976 [first published in 1936]), 96-97; Charlotte A. van Manen, *De Nederlandsche Overzee Trustmaatschappij. Middelpunt van het verkeer van onzijdig Nederland met het buitenland tijdens den wereldoorlog 1914-1919* (The Hague: Martinus Nijhoff, 1935), 4:247-249.

4   M.W.F. Treub, *Herinneringen en overpeinzingen* (Haarlem: H.D. Tjeenk Willink, 1931), 367; *Black's Law Dictionary,* 4th ed. (St. Paul: West, 1968), 112-113.

5   Turlington, *Neutrality,* 95; Efraim Inbar and Gabriel Sheffer, eds., *The National Security of Small States in a Changing World* (London/Portland, OR: Frank Cass, 1997), 1.

6   C. Smit, *Tien studiën betreffende Nederland in de Eerste Wereldoorlog* (Groningen: H.D. Tjeenk Willink, 1975), 142-144;

Treub, *Herinneringen,* 367-368; Turlington, *Neutrality,* 96; Reuters report attached to De Marees van Swinderen to Loudon, April 25, 1918, in C. Smit, *Bescheiden betreffende de buitenlandse politiek van Nederland 1848-1919, Derde Periode 1899-1919* (The Hague: Martinus Nijhoff, 1957-64), part 5, *1917-1919,* 473-474, # 462.

7   James Brown Scott, "The Trial of the Kaiser," in Edward M. House and Charles Seymour, eds., *What Really Happened at Paris: The Story of the Peace Conference, 1918-1919* (New York: Charles Scribner's Sons, 1921), 231-258 and answers to questions in appendix; quotations on 240, 241, 246.

8   Balfour to F. Villiers, October 8, 1918, in Kenneth Bourne and D. Cameron Watt, general eds. *British Documents on Foreign Affairs: Reports and Papers from the Foreign Office Confidential Print,* part 2, *From the First to the Second World War,* series 1, *The Paris Peace Conference of 1919,* M. Dockrill, ed. (Frederick, MD: University Publications of America, 1989), 6:124, # 38; Ernst Heldring diary entry, April 19, 1919, in Smit, *Bescheiden ... 1917-1919,* 1039-40, #1027.

3

THE
PERIOD
OF
THE
WORLD
WARS

1914–1945

9 Townley to Earl Curzon, February 20, 1919, in Bourne and Watt, *British Documents,* part 2, series 1, vol. 6, 128-129, # 42.

10 See, for example, Sally Marks, *Innocent Abroad: Belgium at the Paris Peace Conference of 1919* (Chapel Hill: University of North Carolina Press, 1981). Recommended further reading on this article's topic: Hubert P. van Tuyll van Serooskerken, *The Netherlands and World War I: Espionage, Diplomacy, and Survival* (Leiden: Brill, 2001); Maartje Abbenhuis, *The Art of Staying Neutral: The Netherlands in the First World War, 1914–1918* (Amsterdam: Amsterdam University Press, 2006); Marc Frey, *Der Erste Weltkrieg und die Niederlande: Ein neutrales Land im politischen und wirtschaftlichen Kalkül der Kriegsgegner* (Berlin: Akademie Verlag, 1998).

DUTCH PERCEPTIONS OF AMERICAN CULTURE AND PROMOTION OF DUTCH CULTURE IN THE UNITED STATES

———

CORNELIS A. VAN MINNEN

During the interwar years the United States was a faraway country for most Dutchmen. The cultural elite were skeptical about what was perceived as American mass culture, materialism, and mediocrity, and there was by no means a widespread and warm Dutch interest in developments in the United States. For most Americans the Netherlands was a country outside their scope too, but some Dutch Americans tried, not without success, to put the Netherlands on the mental map of their fellow Americans.

Dutch Perceptions of American Culture

Only very few Dutch people realized during the Great War and its aftermath that the United States was going to play a major role on the world stage. Symptomatic of this situation was the limited interest among Dutch career diplomats in an appointment at the Washington legation, which they perceived as a very unattractive and expensive post. The correspondent of the *Algemeen Handelsblad* in the United States, Daniël J. von Balluseck, was concerned about this and wrote in 1922 that in a short period of less than five years four diplomats had arrived and left the Washington mission, causing a lack of continuation in representing the Netherlands there. He regretted that the Dutch government almost had to beg potential candidates to accept the position. Considering the increasing importance of the United States, Von Balluseck was of the opinion that the

3

—

THE
PERIOD
OF
THE
WORLD
WARS

1914–1945

Netherlands could no longer afford to send second-rate people to the American capital but should send only those who would represent the best the country had to offer. In 1918 the Dutch-American historian Hendrik Willem van Loon had already expressed the same concern, and he had pleaded for the establishment of a Holland Institute in New York to help change the negative image the Dutch had in the United States at that time. From the U.S. involvement in World War I on, in April 1917, the Dutch were depicted in the American press as pro-German war profiteers. Even after the war had ended, these negative feelings still persisted around 1920 and in Van Loon's view the Dutch government had never even tried to improve that image.

In the early 1920s Dutch Minister of Foreign Affairs Herman A. van Karnebeek was dissatisfied with the lack of quantity and quality of the diplomatic dispatches from Washington and demanded an improvement. It came with the appointment in 1922 of the experienced diplomat Andries C.D. de Graeff and his successor in 1927, Jan H. van Roijen. But the Dutch diplomats at the Washington legation in the 1930s were conservative aristocrats who had no sympathy at all for the United States and its people and profoundly disliked Roosevelt's New Deal policy. They considered the federal government's deficit spending to fight the Depression and massive unemployment a form of state socialism that should not serve as an example to the Netherlands. When in 1939 the Dutch government dispatched Dr. Alexander Loudon to Washington, the legation finally had the right person that Von Balluseck and Van Loon had been asking for. In 1942 the Dutch legation was upgraded to an embassy, and by that time more and more people were aware that for its democratic survival the Netherlands had become dependent on the country that so few people had been interested in during the 1920s and 1930s.[1]

Of course, there were during this period a number of Dutch travelers to the United States who were interested in the country and who published their observations in books and articles. But they were often skeptical about American culture and thought European culture was far superior to what they saw in the United States.[2] An outstanding writer about the United States was the Leiden University historian Johan Huizinga. America's new role on the world stage in the Great War in 1917 — from a neutral country to a decisive player — made Huizinga lecture on U.S. history in the academic year 1917–18, and subsequently he published his book *Mensch en menigte in Amerika*. In its preface he wrote: "We know much too little about America. True, many a traveler back from America sets down his impressions in a book, but by their very nature such writings lack the historical background necessary for understanding the present." Studying the history of the United States had pleased him unexpectedly, for he had anticipated not "to find in it any of the things by which the grandeur of the European past holds us in its grasp." This had changed, however, when he began his research: "And I found myself stimulated and fascinated as seldom ever before; it was as if something of America's spiritual élan is transmitted to anyone who takes the trouble to understand the spirit of the country."

In 1926 Huizinga had the opportunity to visit the United States. It was the time when the Jazz Age was in full swing and the sky seemed the limit for the American economy. Huizinga published his impressions of his two-month tour in *Amerika levend en denkend.* His judgment in this book is not essentially different from his views on the United States in his first book. He expressed his admiration but also his objections. He was clearly ambivalent and in the foreword of this second book he wrote: "America flings you from one hour to another between acceptance and resistance." At the end of the volume he concluded that among his fellow European travelers, "there rose up repeatedly this pharisaical feeling: We all have something that you lack; we admire your strength but do not envy you. Your instrument of civilization and progress, your big cities and your perfect organization, only make us nostalgic for what is old and quiet, and sometimes your life seems hardly to be worth living, not to speak of your future." It is remarkable that at this time of strong nationalistic feelings in Europe, travelers visiting the United States, including Huizinga, perceived themselves in the first place as Europeans. What bound them together were feelings of European cultural superiority toward the United States. Huizinga especially dreaded the spread of manifestations of American culture across Europe, such as materialism, mediocrity, the mechanization of society, and the supremacy of economic forces and ideas.[3]

The influential Dutch writer and critic Menno ter Braak abhorred America less than "America," the symbol *par excellence* of mass culture as opposed to the elitist culture he himself represented and which he wanted to protect from the creeping tide of mass culture and vulgarity. Ter Braak was especially annoyed with American movies that Dutch theaters were increasingly showing: by the late 1930s more than half of the major sound films came from the United States, but as eager as the public at large was, just as averse was the Dutch elite to American cinema. In Ter Braak's view these movies were only commercial, based on vulgar taste and, contrary to European films, seldom pioneering and hardly showing any artistic creativity. As he explained in his 1928 essay "Why I reject 'America,'" Europeanism meant a quasi-monastic sphere of silence and reflection, an immersion in art, literature, music, and philosophy without material gain, as opposed to Americanism: the American attitude that everything had to be useful, efficient and should lead to material profit. Ter Braak felt no need at all to visit the United States.[4]

433

Ter Braak's attitude of cultural superiority toward the U.S. was far from original and echoed the opinion of Dutch liberal clergyman M.C. van Mourik Broekman. In his 1914 book, which was based on a trip to the United States and en-

3

—

THE
PERIOD
OF
THE
WORLD
WARS

1914–1945

titled *De Yankee in denken en doen. Karakterteekening van het Amerikaansche leven*, he wrote: "When I begin to speak about civilization, and put together the two words American civilization, I think a knowledgeable person of American life will smile. If he has a delicate sense of hearing, he will experience a feeling of pain, because those two words grate each other and make a crunchy noise. American civilization; the further advanced the civilization the less American it will be, and the more American the civilization, the worse the condition of the civilization will be." In Van Mourik Broekman's perception "America was materially the richest but intellectually the poorest country in the world" and in its civilization he only saw "emptiness and poverty." He thought that the American population in general was not very artistic and he wondered what great musician the country with its millions of inhabitants had bred. Asked by an American what his opinion of the country was, he had replied, "America is big, but not great." In his 1926 book *De geschiedenis van Amerika. Van Hollandsche kolonisatie tot dollarland* Van Mourik Broekman called on his fellow countrymen to resist the American cultural influences that had already contaminated the Netherlands more than most Dutchmen realized.[5]

Among the Dutch travelers to the United States during the interwar years were a number of scientists who attended conferences, gave lectures at various universities, and reported on their travel experiences. Their focus was especially on the American higher education system and they often observed that American universities, both in their research projects and their teaching programs, had stronger ties with daily practical life than was the case in the Netherlands. In general, most of them — even Johan Huizinga — were enthusiastic about this aspect of U.S. higher education. The two most interesting reports on the American university system were written by the Utrecht professors of chemistry Ernst J. Cohen and Hugo Rudolph Kruyt. Cohen, who in 1926 lectured, among other places, at Cornell University and the University of Chicago and who traveled the country extensively from coast to coast, admired the way Americans dealt with research and education. His volume *Uit het land van Benjamin Franklin* is one of the most informative books on academic America in the interwar years. Cohen's colleague Kruyt, who had also lectured at various places in America's Midwest and the Northeast, published a brochure in 1931, entitled *Hooge School en Maatschappij*. In it he endorsed the American system of higher education where the relationship between university and society in his view was much stronger, and therefore much more appreciated than in the Netherlands, and where vocational education was intertwined with university education. At the time many doubted whether American universities should serve as an example to the Netherlands but in the years after World War II several of Kruyt's ideas about higher education would be implemented. Dutch scientists, thus, expressed themselves generally in more positive terms about the U.S. university system than the way in which representatives of the cultural elite, such as Huizinga and Ter Braak, wrote about American mass culture in general.[6]

In the early 1930s, when the devastating effects of the October 1929 stock-market crash had plunged America into the Great Depression, the young Dutch sociologist Arie N. J. den Hollander — after World War II to become the first Americanist at the University of Amsterdam — studied the position of poor rural whites in the U.S. South, the poverty-stricken region that President Franklin D. Roosevelt in 1938 would describe as "the Nation's No. 1 economic problem." The result of his field research and study of literature was a hefty dissertation, which he defended with honors at the University of Amsterdam. After his return to the Netherlands Den Hollander published a series of articles in the *Algemeen Handelsblad*, in 1933 and 1934, on a variety of aspects of American life, including Indians, black hobos, lynchings in the South, and life on Georgia plantations. In July 1935 he published, in the same newspaper, five interesting articles on the New Deal in which he explained the background of the economic crisis and the political dilemmas. The *Algemeen Handelsblad* also featured a captivating series of articles by its then editor-in-chief Daniël von Balluseck on Roosevelt's America, which he wrote during his tour of the United States between November 1937 and April 1938.[7]

Intelligent views on the United States as published by Den Hollander and Von Balluseck, however, were scarce in the Netherlands. Newspapers and periodicals like the *Algemeen Handelsblad* and *De Gids* published only occasionally on America and were only read by the elite. For the majority of the Dutch population developments in the New World took place outside their view, and few people read the publications written by the intellectuals discussed above. In the popular illustrated family magazines there also was a general lack of interest in the United States. Research on 1920s Dutch magazines has shown that American phenomena such as the Prohibition, the Red Scare, the Sacco and Vanzetti case, and the Ku Klux Klan received little or no attention. The image of the U.S. emerging from these Dutch magazines in the 1920s is that of a country of oddities and inventions, of skyscrapers and natural splendor, of gangsters and movie stars, of corruption and materialism. But analyses of U.S. society were lacking. This hardly changed in the 1930s when the Depression and widespread unemployment were more on people's minds than faraway developments in the United States. Even if the social democrats were interested in Franklin Roosevelt's New Deal policy, as was shown by their daily *Het Volk*, the Social Democratic Labor Party was not part of Prime Minister Hendrikus Colijn's coalition cabinet and the New Deal never became a topic of prime interest on the Dutch political agenda or in parliamentary debates.[8]

Promotion of Dutch Culture in the United States

3

—

THE
PERIOD
OF
THE
WORLD
WARS

1914–1945

If the United States was in general a faraway country for the Dutch, what cultural presence did the Netherlands have in the United States? In other words, were there any persons and/or organizations, apart from the Dutch diplomats in Washington, who made any effort to explain the Netherlands and its history and culture to an American audience? Yes, indeed. Established in 1885, the Holland Society of New York continued to perpetuate the memory of the Dutch West India Company colony of New Netherland and organized a wide range of activities for the descendants of New Netherland colonists. In the 1920s as many as twenty-six local branches of the Holland Society were organized outside the New York metropolitan area, though most of them remained concentrated in what had been New Netherland, and the Society's scholarly publications continued to expand with the printing of additional church and other seventeenth-century records. In 1922 the Holland Society's newsletter, *de Halve Maen*, made its appearance: it kept the members informed about activities and began to publish articles on the settlement of New Netherland. At the Society's fiftieth anniversary in 1935, the banquet address was delivered, via amplified telephone, by Society Trustee Franklin D. Roosevelt, and Dutch Minister H.M. van Haersma de With read Queen Wilhelmina's personal message of congratulations. Proud of his Dutch roots, President Roosevelt had been a member of the Holland Society since 1910. He was especially interested in Dutch colonial architecture and during his presidency he saw to it that the Dutch architectural style and the construction material of fieldstone were not only used to build post offices in Hyde Park, Poughkeepsie, and Rhinebeck, but for his retreat Top Cottage and the Franklin D. Roosevelt Library as well.[9]

Roosevelt was also active in the Netherland-America Foundation (NAF) and from 1921, the year the NAF was founded, through his election as president of the United States in 1932, he served as its vice president. The objective of the NAF was and is to advance educational, literary, artistic, scientific, historical, and cultural relationships between the two countries and to work toward mutual understanding. The NAF's first president, from 1921 to 1924, was Edward Bok, the famous Dutch-born editor of the *Ladies' Home Journal* and philanthropist whose 1920 book *The Americanization of Edward Bok: The Autobiography of a Dutch Boy Fifty Years After* had been a bestseller. Bok saw the Netherlands' cultural heritage as the main instrument to generate interest in the United States and launched a series on "Great Hollanders." Authors in this series were Johan Huizinga with a biographical portrait of Erasmus, British historian Frederic Harrison, who reprinted his book on William the Silent, and Adriaan J. Barnouw, who contributed a biography of the Dutch poet Joost van den Vondel. Although

436

these books were generally well received, the series as a whole did not meet its goal: to make Holland a household word in the United States. Indeed, as the Dutch diplomat Andries C. D. de Graeff desperately exclaimed soon after his arrival in Washington in 1922: "The lack of knowledge about the Netherlands in the United States borders on the unbelievable."[10]

In order to promote the study of Dutch language, literature, and history in the United States a group of Dutch businessmen and scholars founded the Queen Wilhelmina Lectureship at Columbia University in New York in 1913. The first lecturer was the American literary scholar of Dutch descent Leonard Charles van Noppen. His successor in 1919 was Adriaan J. Barnouw, who had taught Dutch and history at a grammar school in The Hague and English at the University of Leiden. In 1923 the lectureship became a professorship and Barnouw served in that capacity with great enthusiasm until his retirement in 1948. He did not limit his activities to Columbia University. As he once wrote, he served as translator, information desk, impresario, cultural attaché, and literary agent all in one. He lectured at many places across the United States and was frequently invited as after-dinner speaker. He also published several books on Dutch literature, history of art, and contemporary Dutch society, which were mainly geared to the public at large. For the Netherland-America Foundation Barnouw wrote his numerous and famous "Monthly Letters" from 1924 until 1961, covering a multitude of topics dealing with Dutch history, culture, and contemporary affairs that were also widely read and appreciated by Americans outside the circle of NAF members. In 1940 he was cofounder and president of the Netherlands-America University League and served as a mentor to Dutchmen who were attempting to make a career for themselves in the intellectual or academic life of the United States. Although Barnouw took American citizenship, he remained completely loyal to both his country of adoption and his country of origin. A selection of the "Monthly Letters" made by Barnouw himself was published in one volume in 1969, a year after his death. On both sides of the Atlantic he was honored as a cultural ambassador of the Netherlands to the United States. Living up to the expectations of the founders of the Queen Wilhelmina Lectureship, Barnouw had made it "a centre of influence, whence, by means of lectures, in several parts of the United States, a more accurate and extensive knowledge regarding Holland and its inhabitants is being prepared."[11]

Even if the contributions to strengthening Dutch-American relations and to spreading knowledge about the Netherlands in the United States made by Edward Bok and Adriaan Barnouw were remarkable, the most famous Dutchman in the U.S. from the 1920s until his death in 1944 was Hendrik Willem van Loon. Born in Rotterdam in 1882 and raised in The Hague, he left for the United States at age twenty to study at Cornell University and to work as a journalist. His breakthrough came in 1921 with his bestseller *The Story of Mankind*, which was highly

3

——

THE
PERIOD
OF
THE
WORLD
WARS

1914–1945

praised by the historian Charles A. Beard but trashed by Johan Huizinga, who saw in the book's popularity in the United States "a bad omen for our civilization." Van Loon made a name for himself in the United States as a popular historian, journalist, radio commentator, and illustrator. Through his numerous publications — including more than forty books on history, art, geography — he reached millions of readers, not only in the United States but all over the world as several of his books were translated into more than twenty languages. His mission was to acquaint ordinary people with history and art, especially with Dutch history and culture, and he wanted to make the Americans "Dutch-conscious." His circle of friends included Albert Einstein, Thomas Mann, Princess Juliana, and Franklin and Eleanor Roosevelt, who frequently invited him as their guest to the White House and to their estate in Hyde Park.

Among Van Loon's books about the Netherlands were *R.v.R.: The Life and Times of Rembrandt van Rijn* (1930) and *An Indiscrete Itinerary or How the Unconventional Traveler Should See Holland* (1933). He also tried to explain the United States to his former countrymen in two series of articles published in *De Groene Amsterdammer* in the 1920s, because in his opinion the United States was *terra incognita* in the Netherlands. In a number of these articles he criticized the Netherlands for being too complacent and out of touch with the modern world. From 1928 to 1931 Van Loon lived in the picturesque small Dutch town of Veere, where he wrote his biography of Rembrandt and which in the following years back in the United States served as a source of inspiration for his drawings and books, most notably his bestseller *Van Loon's Lives* (1942). In numerous articles and radio broadcasts in the 1930s and in his books *Our Battle* (1938) and *Invasion* (1940), he served as a Cassandra to warn the American public of the dangers of Nazi Germany. When in May 1940 the Germans occupied his native country Van Loon organized and chaired the Queen Wilhelmina Fund. During the war years he helped, as a one-man charitable organization, numerous European — including Dutch — refugees. His short-wave radio broadcasts to the Nazi-occupied Netherlands were a beacon of hope for his former countrymen.

Franklin Roosevelt described Van Loon upon his death in March 1944 as "my true and trusted friend" and the *London Times* wrote that he was "one of the most engaging products of the marriage between Holland and the United States." Adriaan Barnouw had no doubt that "Holland had in him her most eloquent spokesman in America." In his efforts to make the United States "Dutch-conscious" Van Loon served as a unique cultural bridge between the Netherlands and his adopted country. Indeed, for many Americans Hendrik Willem van Loon and the Netherlands were synonymous from the 1920s through the 1940s, and they would agree with Van Loon's assertion, "I put Holland on the map, and that's the simple truth."[12]

Hendrik Willem van Loon with Eleanor Roosevelt,
probably at Hyde Park, NY, in 1936.

3

THE PERIOD OF THE WORLD WARS

1914–1945

440

1   On the Dutch diplomats in Washington during the interwar years, see A. Lammers, *God Bless America. Zegeningen en beproevingen van de Verenigde Staten* (Amsterdam: Uitgeverij Balans, 1987), 52-73; On the negative image of the Dutch in the United States during and after World War I and Hendrik Willem van Loon's attempts to improve that image, see Cornelis A. van Minnen, *Van Loon: Popular Historian, Journalist, and FDR Confidant* (New York: Palgrave Macmillan, 2005), 63-64, and, more extensively, Van Minnen, *Amerika's beroemdste Nederlander. Een biografie van Hendrik Willem van Loon* (Amsterdam: Boom, 2005), 98-100, 106-109.

2   A survey of travel reports is offered by Bob de Graaff in his article "Bogey or Saviour? The Image of the United States in the Netherlands during the Interwar Period," in Rob Kroes and Maarten van Rossem, eds., *Anti-Americanism in Europe* (Amsterdam: Free University Press, 1986), 51-71.

3   J. Huizinga, *Mensch en menigte in Amerika. Vier essays over moderne beschavingsgeschiedenis* (Haarlem: H.D. Tjeenk Willink, 1918); Huizinga, *Amerika levend en denkend. Losse opmerkingen* (Haarlem: H.D. Tjeenk Willink, 1927). Both books have been translated into English as, respectively, *Man and the Masses in America* and *Life and Thought in America* by Herbert H. Rowen and published in one volume: Johan Huizinga, *America: A Dutch Historian's Vision, from Afar and Near* (New York: Harper & Row, 1972); Quotations on 3-4, 229, 283, 312, 314.

4   M. ter Braak, "Waarom ik 'Amerika' afwijs," in *Verzameld werk* (Amsterdam: Van Oorschot, 1950) 1:255-264; On Menno ter Braak and American movies, see M.L. Mooijweer, "Menno ter Braak en de filmbeelden van Amerika," in K. van Berkel, ed., *Amerika in Europese ogen. Facetten van de Europese beeld-vorming van het moderne Amerika* (The Hague: SDU uitgeverij, 1990), 124-134.

5   M.C. van Mourik Broekman, *De Yankee in denken en doen. Karakteeteekening van het Amerikaansche leven* (Haarlem: H.D. Tjeenk Willink, 1914), 226-266; Van Mourik Broekman, *De geschiedenis van Amerika. Van Hollandsche kolonisatie tot dollarland* (Amsterdam: Nelissen, 1926), 171; Quotations translated by author.

6   E.J. Cohen, *Uit het land van Benjamin Franklin* (Zutphen: Thieme, 1928); H.R. Kruyt, *Hooge School en Maatschappij* (Amsterdam: s.n., 1931); K. van Berkel, "De amerikanisering van de Europese universiteit. Het begin van de discussie in Nederland (1900–1940)," in Van Berkel, *Amerika in Europese ogen*, 135-160.

7   A.N.J. den Hollander, *De landelijke arme blanken in het Zuiden der Vereenigde Staten. Een sociaal-historische en geografische studie* (Groningen: J.B. Wolters' Uitgeversmaatschappij, 1933); On Den Hollander's and Von Balluseck's articles in the years 1937-38, see A. Lammers, *Uncle Sam en Jan Salie. Hoe Nederland Amerika ontdekte* (Amsterdam: Uitgeverij Balans, 1989), 131-137, 193-194.

8   On the Dutch popular magazines in the 1920s, see Joop Toebes, "A Country Too Far Away. Images of the United States in the Dutch Illustrated Press in the 1920s," in Doeko Bosscher et al., eds., *American Culture in the Netherlands* (Amsterdam: VU University Press, 1996), 24-42; On the Dutch social democrats and the New Deal, see Peter Zoetmulder, "Een grootsche proefneming? Nederlandse sociaal-democraten over het Amerika van Roosevelt," *Spiegel Historiael* 23.2 (February 1988): 80-89.

9   David William Voorhees, *The Holland Society: A Centennial History 1885–1985* (New York: The Holland Society of New York, 1985), 72-101; On Franklin Roosevelt's Dutch roots, see Frank Freidel,

"The Dutchness of the Roosevelts,"
in J.W. Schulte Nordholt and Robert
P. Swierenga, eds., *A Bilateral Bicentennial. A History of Dutch-American Relations,1782–1982* (Amsterdam: Meulenhoff, 1982), 149-167.

10 Hans Krabbendam, *The Model Man:
A Life of Edward William Bok, 1863–1930*
(Amsterdam/Atlanta, GA: Rodopi, 2001),
170-176; Quotation of A. C. D. de Graeff
in Van Minnen, *Amerika's beroemdste
Nederlander*, 109.

11 G. Kalff, *A New Holland-America Line.
The Queen Wilhelmina Lectureship for*

*Dutch Literature and History in the United
States of America* (Oosterbeek: s.n.,
1920); Quotation on 18; Adriaan J.
Barnouw, *Monthly Letters of the Culture
and History of the Netherlands* (Assen:
Van Gorcum, 1969); On Barnouw's life
and work, xiii-xxxv.

12 Van Minnen, *Van Loon*, passim; Quotations on 3, 95, 205, 261; Van Loon's life
and work as well as Dutch-American
relations in this era are more extensively
dealt with in Van Minnen, *Amerika's
beroemdste Nederlander*, passim.

3

———

THE
PERIOD
OF
THE
WORLD
WARS

1914–1945

AMERICAN INFLUENCES ON DUTCH MATERIAL CULTURE AND PRODUCT DESIGN

———

J. W. DRUKKER & TIMO DE RIJK

Introduction

Shortly after the end of World War I, the United States entered the age of high mass consumption, the level of economic development where standards of living have risen to the point where large groups of the population can, to some extent, afford to buy luxury durables.

At the close of World War I, Dutch real product per capita was slightly more than half the American figure (see figure 1).[1]

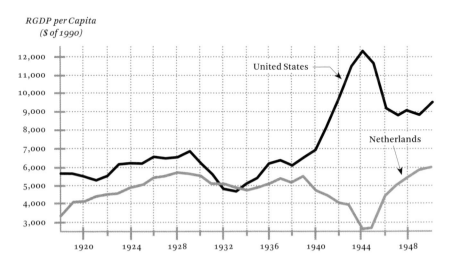

FIGURE 1
Real Gross Domestic Product per Capita, United States vs. the Netherlands, 1918–50.

If one accepts a certain threshold level of real product per capita as the closest quantitative proxy of the qualitative concept "high mass consumption," and if one sets this threshold somewhat arbitrarily at $6,000 (1990 price level), the conclusion is that it was not until the 1950s that Dutch society reached the level of material welfare that Americans already enjoyed in the 1920s. And although the product gap tended to become smaller in the course of the interwar years, the Netherlands was poor compared to the United States during most of this time.

One would expect wonder, admiration, a vivid curiosity, possibly mixed with some envy, with respect to this early *défi américain*, in Dutch writings, but the opposite is true. Both in contemporary publications and in retrospect, Dutch interest in the material culture of the United States, in general terms and as an example of modern product design in particular, has been slight. Dutch publications on the importance of American design, and on the ideas and professional practices of designers in the world's largest and richest industrial nation, are a fraction of those on the European modernist design culture.[2] Yet, to conclude from this that American influences on Dutch material culture in these years were faint, would be entirely wrong. In fact, there was hardly any country other than the United States that had such a deep and lasting impact on Dutch material culture, but the omnipresent ambivalence of Dutch intellectuals toward the civilization of the New World presents in retrospect a truly distorted picture.

The purpose of this article is to correct this perception. First, we will try to explain why American influences remained almost invisible in official writings. Then we set out, by concentrating on more popular texts, to reconstruct how, in what ways, and in what particular fields the American way of life crept almost unnoticed into the daily life of the Dutch.

U. S. Design through Dutch Eyes:
Concealed Admiration and Open Suspicion

In the 1920s and 1930s the Dutch attitude toward the United States did not differ much from the one that prevailed elsewhere in Europe: it was decidedly ambivalent. On the one hand, the United States was admired as a nation of enterprising pioneers and reckless daredevils who were prepared to take great risks in business and commerce in order to achieve what so far had proved impossible in Europe.[3] On the other hand, it was considered a land of barbarians, a nation of second-class Europeans who had been ejected or had fled from the Old World, and of colonists who had failed to make a go of things in the cradle of civilization. A good example of this ambivalence may be found in Dutch perceptions of

443

3

——

THE
PERIOD
OF
THE
WORLD
WARS

1914–1945

the American woman. Following the lead given by the popular press in reports of modern mechanized homes, the American household was portrayed as efficient and forward looking. But admiration went hand in hand with resentment and envy of the American housewife who was seen as overly organized, too rational, and who was, at any rate, devoid of culture and good taste.

Early twentieth-century American design was invariably regarded with at least a degree of suspicion. European design critics saw Americans as rough and uncivilized people who were dependent on tradition-steeped Europe for cultural matters. The opposite view, holding up the United States as an example to European artists and designers, seemed at that time almost impossible. Up to 1920, few designers or architects in the Netherlands had ever taken the trouble to embark on a proper study of American culture. A notable exception was the preeminent Dutch architect H.P. Berlage, who in 1911 undertook a now famous journey to the United States.[4] In Chicago he saw the architecture of Louis Sullivan and Henry Richardson, with which he was already familiar from his readings and which inspired some of his own work. Prior to his trip Berlage had indirectly heard about the young architect Frank Lloyd Wright, whom on his return — having seen Wright's work at first hand — he introduced to his young team as "the most talented architect in America."[5] But Berlage was an exception, and although he was kindly disposed toward American design, he nevertheless concluded that it was too far removed from the European tradition, so that American examples and American architectural principles were scarcely of any use to the European architect. Yet, even though Berlage did not praise Wright or any other American architect as a source of inspiration, some of the younger architects working in his office regarded Wright's work as important, without a doubt belonging to the, then new, modern canon.

One of them was Henk Wouda, who, after having worked for Berlage from 1910 to 1912, settled as an architect and interior designer in The Hague and was asked to set up the design department of H. Pander & Sons, the largest furniture manufacturer in the Netherlands. The small department was established as early as 1917, which made Pander effectively the first major Dutch furniture maker for whom it was a strict requirement that modern and original furniture be designed by his own young design staff.[6]

Right from the start of his employment at Pander's, Wouda was profoundly impressed by the work of Frank Lloyd Wright, which he came to know through the illustrations in the German Wasmuth publication *Ausgeführte Bauten* of 1910. This is evident in one of Wouda's first interiors, designed with W. M. Dudok in 1920 for the villa Sevensteijn in The Hague (figures 2a and b). The linking of open spaces and the use of tall chairs and Japanese lamps in the dining room were conceived directly from examples by Wright. It is interesting to note, however, that neither here, nor in relation to other relevant interiors, Pander

2a
Frank Lloyd Wright, interior Robie House, Chicago, 1906–09.

2b
Henk Wouda, hall and dining room, villa Sevensteijn,
The Hague, 1920–21.

3

—

THE
PERIOD
OF
THE
WORLD
WARS

1914–1945

and Wouda ever referred in public to the American inspiration of their work, whether in the many advertising campaigns in, for instance, the widely read interior magazine *Thuis* (At home), in model homes, or in the many reviews in professional journals. Where Pander was happy to discuss the Ideal Home Exhibition in London and frequently cited French influences when promoting his products, he never mentioned the far more obvious American signature in his furniture designs. Evidently, to the Dutch furniture industry American culture was not considered to be very helpful in marketing.

The "American System" and Scientific Management in the Netherlands

Whereas the United States was regarded as primitive when manifestations of high culture and good taste were at stake, the country was seen much more positively in questions of economic and technical modernization. The organization of American factories, offices, and shops, for example, was highly influential in Europe, including the Netherlands. But even in these fields where American technology was without any doubt clearly superior to its European counterpart, admiration was in no way unanimous. To see why, we have to go back in time a bit.

At the Great Exhibition of 1851 in London, Europeans were for the first time introduced to a new—American—industrial production technology: the assembly of prefabricated, mass-produced, interchangeable parts. Mass production of complicated products, such as fire arms or machinery, required a particularly precise standardization of their parts with, at that time, extremely small tolerances. The only way to achieve this was the development of a "scientific" design discipline, based on measurement and precise technical specifications, in which the United States excelled. In Europe these achievements were greatly admired, and during the second half of the nineteenth century and the first decades of the twentieth they became collectively famous as "the American System." Yet, enthusiasm was restricted to the realms of purely technical products, like machinery and equipment. Due to the dominating influence of the Arts and Crafts movement, with its scorn for division of labor, specialization, and modern mass-production technology in general, household products like clocks or furniture, produced according to the American System, were seen as tasteless and "cheap," despite their technical brilliance, and far inferior to European products made in the tradition of refined, high-quality handicraft.

In the early twentieth century, the scientific approach to production technology spread from products to people: the rise of "Taylorism" or "Scientific Management." Again, the new ideas and new methods of organizing factory labor were of American origin. And again, European and, more specifically, Dutch attitudes were profoundly ambivalent. In general, it did not take much time for government officials and employers to recognize the possibilities that Scientific Management offered to increase efficiency. They quickly embraced the system and put it into practice. During the interwar years, large state-controlled companies in the Netherlands, like PTT (Post, Telegraph, and Telephone Company) and the national railway company, were thoroughly reorganized according to Scientific Management principles. Simultaneously, a real boom manifested itself in a sector that had been virtually unknown before: management consulting agencies, like Raadgevend Bureau Berenschot, minutely imitating American examples, both in their organization and their approach. At the same time, Taylorization of factories, for instance in the large Dutch textile industry in the region of Twente, met with suspicion and even open resistance from labor unions and socialist political parties. In their eyes, a clearly capitalist invention claiming, among other things, to improve working conditions of factory workers could, almost by definition, not be trusted.

There was, however, an exception to this ambivalence, and strangely enough, exactly in the place where one would expect romantic, antirational sentiments of the Arts and Crafts variety to be dominant: the household, or more precisely, the kitchen. Scientific Management had spread to the household in the work of Christine Frederick, but her ideas were popularized in Europe by Grete Schütte-Lihotsky, a radical socialist architect of Austrian descent who was associated with the equally radical socialist Bauhaus movement. So, the modern, rationalized, American kitchen was imported into the Netherlands in socialist disguise, and as such unanimously heralded by both left- and right-wing politicians as a wonderful means to liberate women from tedious household work. The first mass-produced modern kitchen in the Netherlands was designed for Bruynzeel by Piet Zwart, whose political views were very close to Schütte-Lihotsky's. Even a quick glance at his 1937 kitchen (figure 3b) reveals, however, that he was actually far more influenced by luxurious American examples than by the extremely severe *Frankfurter Küche* of 1926 that had been the great success of his political ally.

Promoting Electricity the American Way

Perhaps one of the best examples of the American influence on Dutch daily life is the way in which the use of electricity in the household was promoted. These efforts are best exemplified by the marketing activities of the city of Amsterdam's electric company, which in the Netherlands, if not in the whole of Europe, was considered a pioneer with regard to the electrification of public buildings and transportation, street lighting, and dockyard cranes, in addition to the

447

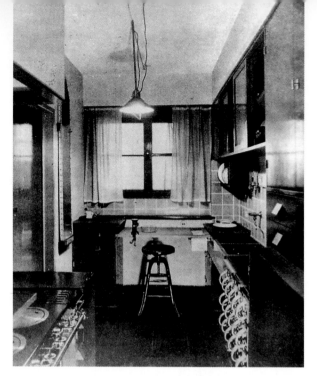

3a *Frankfurter Küche* by Grete Schütte-Lihotsky (1926).

3b First modern Dutch kitchen by Piet Zwart for Bruynzeel (1937).

household. Around 1920 city authorities were proudly proclaiming the slogan "Amsterdam, the most electrified city in the world."[7] This may have been boasting, but it was hardly an idle boast. The shortage of good-quality coal for home heating during World War I, in particular, had led the city council to invest a considerable sum in order to provide almost every household in the city with electricity. And although Amsterdam led the way, other cities such as Rotterdam, The Hague, and Utrecht, as well as some regional utilities, followed closely. Some large but sparsely populated (and relatively poor) parts of the Netherlands, such as the provinces of Overijssel and Drenthe (in the east) and Zeeland (in the southwest), remained without electrical connections during the 1920s. In 1932 these regions, too, were connected to electrical networks, a development that resembles the situation in Germany and Belgium.

As the 1920s and early 1930s progressed, the authorities in Amsterdam made efforts to increase consumption of electricity by stimulating the production of appliances which it was then able to sell at cost.[8] To ensure the success of this plan the municipal electric company, and in particular its visionary director W. Lulofs, openly looked for inspiration to the United States, where in some parts of the country and in some of its major cities electricity consumption had rocketed, thanks mainly to high penetration levels of all sorts of household appliances. During the so-called efficiency days of 1934 — an initiative of the Dutch Institute for Efficiency — Lulofs claimed that between 1924 and 1934 Amsterdam had reached the level of electricity use in the United States. Lulofs was particularly interested in the 20 percent share of consumption by the electric refrigerator, an appliance that was at that time still a curiosity in Europe, including the Netherlands.[9]

To give the people of Amsterdam an enticing view of the future, the company now held up to both the city fathers and its customers the glittering picture of American households and American levels of electricity consumption, going so far as to encourage electric cooking and, after 1938, with a direct reference to the United States, the use of metal electric washing machines and refrigerators. At the Bouw- en Architectuur-Tentoonstelling (Building and Architecture Exhibition) of 1935, not only the most eye-catching kitchens were supplied with American electrical household appliances, but the model kitchen of Amsterdam's electric company, too, was cast from an American example (figure 4).

Streamlining, Styling, and Streamlined Style 449

The scorn with which American material culture sometimes was met by the Dutch cultural elite, was most clearly visible when it had to do with traditional products that were steeped in an often centuries-long European design tradi-

4
American-styled, chromium-plated household appliances
at the Bouw- and Architectuur-Tenstoonstelling (Building and Architecture
Exhibition) of 1935.

tion, such as furniture. When it came to more mundane products, such as kitchen layouts and appliances, criticism was considerably less strong, as we saw in the previous section. For modern (electrical) products with little or no European tradition of their own — refrigerators, radio sets, vacuum cleaners, and the like — disdain for American design turned into enthusiasm, admiration, and almost uncritical imitation. To see why, we first have to look shortly at the development of American design itself.

It may seem a bit paradoxical, but the Great Depression, which in the U.S. had even more disastrous consequences than in Europe (see figure 1), led to a boom in American product design, since American manufacturers tried to improve the competitiveness of their products in the large American market by developing new and modern designs. In the space of a few years, between approximately 1933 and 1935, a number of designers developed a completely new style in product design, which not only proved attractive to customers, but was also easy to make, modern in appearance and, above all, seen by the whole world as uniquely American: streamlining.[10] Appropriating the universal fascination with speed in the Western world and turning it into an American style of design came to a temporary climax with industrial designers such as Raymond Loewy, Norman Bel Geddes, Walter Dorwin Teague, and Henry Dreyfuss.

In the U.S., however, the use of streamlining and the symbolic value of the new aesthetic came in for immediate and sharp criticism. In the influential *Art and the Machine* (1936) by Sheldon and Martha Cheney, the authors distinguished between the functional streamlining of locomotives and airplanes on the one hand and its purely commercial application on the other, rejecting the latter in scornful terms:

> The streamline as a scientific fact is embodied in the airplane. As an aesthetic style mark, and a symbol of twentieth-century machine-age speed, precision, and efficiency, it has been borrowed from the airplane and made to compel the eye anew, with the same flash-and-gleam-beauty reembodied in all transportation machines intended for fast going. If, since 1933, the term has threatened to become an abomination by its ill-considered application to short fiction and false teeth, wastebaskets and underwear, that is only another of the evidences that we still have superficial stylists eager to capitalize the new slogan and misapply the new idiom, and make of them a fad of the moment ... .[11]

451

Thus, even before streamlining had well and truly put itself on the map, the U.S. was engaged in a substantive, morally shaded debate about streamlining and the streamline style (figures 5a and b).

5a Functional streamline: Zeppelin.

5b Non-functional streamline style: pencil sharpener.

Streamlining in the Netherlands

Despite all the criticism of streamlining — even in the country of origin — it nevertheless received an enthusiastic reception in the Netherlands. As long as it was reserved for strictly functional use, i.e., for purposes relating to the need for speed, it is hardly surprising that even steadfast functionalists who otherwise were among the most ardent critics of this despicable, glamorous design from the U.S., saw in streamlined cars and locomotives a representation of a new scientific age, and for that reason heralded it with great enthusiasm. Among them was the modern architect J.B. ("Han") van Loghem, a radical socialist, who as early as 1933 devoted a favorable article in the avant-garde architectural journal *De 8 & Opbouw* to research carried out by the American designer Norman Bel Geddes.[12] Van Loghem's enthusiasm was exclusively based on the functional aspects of the streamlined form, and he completely neglected the stylistic claims Bel Geddes also made in this context.

It was not just in designers' circles, however, that streamlining was considered something new and fascinating. After reading Bel Geddes' writings, motoring journalist A.P.M. Moussault, who wrote for the magazine *De Groene Amsterdammer*, observed:

> I have been looking at a treatise published by the "Institute of Aero-Dynamic Research" and another brochure entitled "Horizons" containing excerpts of a work of that title written by Norman Bel Geddes, and truly, after I had read through these interesting documents I was no longer quite so enthusiastic in saying "You bet!" when I wondered if we were satisfied with our cars. In fact I am now exceedingly dissatisfied, for it has become apparent to me that the coachbuilders of our automobiles could have made something quite different from what they did ... .[13]

This was written on the occasion of the Amsterdam Motor Show of 1934, where streamlined production cars such as the famous Chrysler Airflow made their European debut. As a result, even high-quality European automobiles looked suddenly hopelessly outdated (figures 6a and b).

The early launch of the new Airflow model at the Amsterdam show was a clear sign in itself that American motor manufacturers treated the Netherlands as a conveniently sized pilot market. The Amsterdam show also had an important function as a trendsetter among all the larger motor shows in other European countries, a position that it was not to lose until well after World War II. Just outside Amsterdam the Ford Motor Company established a large plant

3

——

THE
PERIOD
OF
THE
WORLD
WARS

1914-1945

from which a sizeable part of the continent was supplied with models designed for the European market.

As long as streamline was applied to airplanes, zeppelins, ocean liners, and submarines, Dutch designers could effortlessly reconcile American design with their own European, avant-garde canon of functionalism, but as soon as the same style was used for pencil sharpeners, staplers, and electric heaters ("Objects that are, in an orderly household, not supposed to fly through the air," as one critic put it), they severely condemned the streamline style as "ludicrous," "snobbish," or "expensive." In this respect, the car apparently was double-edged: someone like Moussault could, as a simple journalist, be filled with admiration, while other, more highbrow design critics looked upon it with utter disdain. Such was the view of Otto van Tussenbroek, an influential designer and design critic who as a strict rationalist was greatly irritated, precisely by the same — in his view, nonfunctional — styling that had enchanted Moussault and that he observed in the new streamlined American cars. Very conscientiously, he traveled in his own car from his houseboat south of Amsterdam to the show in order to subject the Airflow's design to a closer inspection. Afterwards, he cynically wrote in *De Groene Amsterdammer*:

> Some designers, as if by intuition but without any adequate scientific basis, and indeed without even plausible reasons, have given their cars a "streamline" which was often ... somewhat ludicrous, but the snobs eagerly took possession of it, and no wonder: it was nice to be seen and noticed when one drove up in the eccentric vehicle and one could be certain that wherever one left the thing outside, town or country, one would find admirers crowding round the machine, greatly impressed with its expensive and unusual aspect .... [14]

Architect and critic J.J. Vriend joined the debate in 1936, when he compared the art of engineering, which was the basis for the anonymous shapes of ocean liners, a popular subject among modern architects during the interwar years, with the streamlining of cars. Summarizing the debate, as so often in his publications, he allowed artistry to take precedence over engineering:

> The thirst for beauty has always been the master of mankind, and has taken its often initially primitive design to a higher plane. In its early stages the motor car had anything but a "clean" shape. That was something that it could only acquire when, practically speaking, all technical requirements had been conquered; it was the demands of aerodynamics that brought it the "streamline." And then it emerges that in the final analysis it was not the "pure" engineer who determined its ultimate shape .... [15]

454

6a Peugeot (1934).

6b Chrysler Airflow 8, 6-Passenger Coupe (1934).

3

The debate between the scientific legitimation of aerodynamic shapes on the one hand and status-oriented styling arguments on the other, had now also sparked off in the Netherlands. Moreover, it had begun with a vehicle as the subject of discussion.

THE
PERIOD
OF
THE
WORLD
WARS

1914-1945

1   A. Maddison, *Historical Statistics of the World Economy, 1–2003 AD* (Groningen: Groningen Growth and Development Centre, University of Groningen, 2007), Table 3, GDP per capita (International Geary-Khamis dollars of 1990).

2   The most conspicious examples are Eleonora S. Bergvelt et al., eds., *Industry & Design in the Netherlands 1850–1950* (Amsterdam: Stedelijk Museum, 1985), and Gert Staal and Hester Wolters, eds., *Holland in vorm: Vormgeving in Nederland 1945–1987* (Amsterdam: Stedelijk Museum, 1987).

3   Among many publications, see especially R. Kroes, *If You've Seen One, You've Seen The Mall: Europeans and American Mass Culture* (Chicago: University of Illinois Press, 1996).

4   For the interest taken in America by Dutch architects in general and Berlage in particular, see Fons Asselbergs et al., *Americana, 1880–1930* (Otterlo: Rijksmuseum Kröller-Müller, 1975); The introduction by Leonard K. Eaton was reprinted in English in Jan Molema, *The New Movement in the Netherlands, 1924–1936* (Rotterdam: 010 Publishers, 1996), 153-159; The only fairly well-known Dutch architect traveling to the United States (in 1912) was J. de Bie Leuveling Tjeenk, who later (1924–25) was responsible for the selection of the Dutch contribution to the International Exhibition in Paris.

5   See especially A. van der Woud, "Variaties op een thema: 20 jaar belangstelling voor Frank Lloyd Wright," in Asselbergs, *Americana*, 28-40.

6   Timo de Rijk, *De Haagse Stijl: Art Deco in Nederland* (Rotterdam: 010 Publishers, 2004), 65-80.

7   Anon., *De ontwikkeling van de electriciteitsvoorziening van de gemeente Amsterdam* (Amsterdam: s.n., 1935), 35.

8   See A. Forty, *Objects of Desire. Design and Society 1750–1980* (London: Thames & Hudson, 1986), 182-206.

9   W. Lulofs, *Rationeele electriciteitslevering in Nederland* (Purmerend: s.n., 1935), 41-43.

10 For an overview, see D. J. Bush, *The Streamlined Decade* (New York: Braziller, 1975).

11 Sheldon Cheney and Martha Candler Cheney, *Art and the Machine. An Account of Industrial Design in 20th-Century America* (New York: McGraw-Hill, 1936), 97-98.

12 J. B. van Loghem, "Stroomlijnen," *De 8 & Opbouw*, 2.6 (1933): 46-48.

13 Quotation from A.P.M. Moussault, "Automobieltentoonstelling van de RAI. De auto van morgen," *De Groene Amsterdammer*, February 10, 1934.

14 Otto van Tussenbroek, "De schoonheid der auto's. Een beschouwing over aesthetische lijn," *De Groene Amsterdammer*, February 17, 1934.

15 Quotation from J.J. Vriend, *Nieuwere Architectuur. Beknopt overzicht van de historische ontwikkeling van de bouwkunst* (Amsterdam: Moussault, 1936), 69-70.

AMERICAN INFLUENCES ON DUTCH ARCHITECTURE AND URBAN DESIGN

———

HERMAN VAN BERGEIJK

Much has been written about twentieth-century Europe's fascination with the United States. We know that many European artists first experienced American art during the Armory Show held in New York in 1913. Amsterdam architect H. P. Berlage's trip to the New World in 1911 is of course equally well known; the lectures he gave upon his return drew large crowds, and his subsequent publications included not only articles, but also an illustrated book detailing his experiences. A lesser-known fact, however, is that the Netherlands, with its institutionalized denominational divisions, responded with interest not only to America's architectural forms, but likewise to its spatial policy structures and national planning administration. As a progressive and democratic power, the United States was seeking to plan out its landscape on a nationwide scale. Dutch architects observed America's endeavors during the 1920s and 1930s with a keen eye. This interest was not solely displayed by modern, radical Dutch architects, but in fact extended to those who were more conservative as well — a fact generally ignored until now.

Skyscrapers and Space

The post-World War I period saw the United States emerge to become a model on the architectural front. What many considered most striking was the technical progress that was seen to be putting its stamp on every aspect of life. It is almost impossible to overestimate the influence of Fredrick Winslow Taylor, Frank Gilbreth, and Henry Ford on the conceptualization of technology and economics. Even a European of the likes of Johan Huizinga fell under the spell of America. In 1918 he published the first of his two books on the country that

457

3

—

THE
PERIOD
OF
THE
WORLD
WARS

1914–1945

he described as being defined by its immense contradictions. He was fascinated by its power and efficiency, never more so than during his trip to the United States in 1926. Huizinga's perspective on the New World resembled that of an architect, as is reflected in this observation: "The big city is no longer a place to live but a mechanism, a machine for the movement of traffic, transportation, and communication. It has become completely dynamic. It does not serve primarily to give a person a particular place to live but rather to enable him to move, physically or intellectually, inside and outside the city. Its essential organisms are the means of travel, elevators, telephones, radio stations, the press, and adding machines. Houses only form the skeleton."[1] But Huizinga was a scholar, not an architect, and what he wanted was to understand and to see beyond the surface. America confused him. Just like every other visitor to this country, he saw the vastness of its space, and of its appropriation of that space. He visited many universities and spoke to countless scientists, but to architects never. Huizinga's observations are fully equal to those of a true expert. In Chicago, he commented on the "rash of houses," leading him to conclude: "Alas Chicago, to be a city of the world you would have to have better connections and be less cumbersome and complex." To New York he dedicated many pages, also noting its problems: "Some streets [are] like someone who has just begun to grow a beard. If they all become skyscrapers, it may turn out well. Then they will be true grand canyons." In the capital city of Washington — as elsewhere — he remarked on its spaciousness. Indeed, it is that very spaciousness that defines America.

Whereas space is a luxury for the Dutch, it is a given for the American. This is not to refute the fact that many American inner cities cope with a terrible lack of space. The skyscraper was to be one of the answers to this problem. There was a contradiction here — one that was remarkable and marked even in the characteristically contradictory age of twentieth-century modernism — of waste on the one hand and proliferation of space on the other. In the United States an exceptional balance seemed to have been reached. Both sides of this balance, space and congestion, attracted interest in the Netherlands. The idea of spatial experience fed a growing debate. Skyscrapers held an understandable appeal to the imagination of any architect; but whereas America focused on the technical, structural, and administrative hurdles, the Netherlands was more concerned with the question of skyscrapers' architectural — that is to say aesthetic — character. Ultimately, the latter approach was responsible for the failure to recognize the integral relationship between the city plan, or "grid," and the skyscraper. Contemporary Rotterdam is the prime example: the total lack of coordination between high-rise construction and urban planning has borne disastrous fruits, with buildings encroaching on public spaces that are laid out according to any number of varying design principles. Actual unifying elements are scarce.

The 1922 design competition sponsored by the *Chicago Times* and covered by several periodicals, and in which various Dutch architects were also to take part, further heightened interest in multi-story building. Here, too, the emphasis lay on the outward architectural form. It was a foreigner, the Fin Eliel Saarinen, who won, but the actual construction was awarded to an American agency — a clear case of protectionism. The Dutch had little hope of competing with Saarinen's rigid monumentality, despite the array of stylistic approaches encompassed in their designs. Nevertheless, the competition put high-rise building squarely on the agenda of many an architect. They saw untold opportunities for its application in the Netherlands, though the number of stories rarely rose above ten.

New Concepts in Urban Design

Even before the skyscraper had become the preeminent phenomenon of American architecture, H.P. Berlage was calling attention to the intriguing building trend taking shape in the United States. This was an architectural form without reference to any historical tradition. The Americans emphasized functionality and efficiency, and their attitude toward the design of certain buildings bordered on the scientific. Hospitals, schools, and other public buildings became emblematic of American functional architecture. This status was further cemented when, in its 1913 yearbook, the German Werkbund (work federation) took the modern American factory as its exemplar for a new style of architecture. Walter Gropius put the style on a level with the monuments of ancient Egypt. America had made its mark, and the yearbook inspired many civic administrators who read it, to take business trips to other American cities in order to gather their own insights. Dutch factories like Hoogovens, Bruynzeel, and Van Nelle were cast in the American mold, and hardly a new building project got off the ground without a preliminary research trip to the U.S.

It was thanks to Frank Lloyd Wright, H.P. Berlage, and the 1915 Panama Pacific International Exposition in San Francisco that awareness of American architecture really took hold in the Netherlands. The well-known Wasmuth edition showcasing Wright's work became a treasure trove for young architects such as Jan Wils, Dirk Roosenburg, and Jan Duiker.[2] Berlage crystalized the significance of the developments in the U.S., stating the need for society to divest itself "of a sentimental preference for the beauty of the old European cities, and come to accept that which is posited by modern life. People must have an expec-

3

—

THE
PERIOD
OF
THE
WORLD
WARS

1914–1945

tation and likewise a belief in the future and in so doing look to Nietzsche — to the chance of an 'Umwertung aller Werte.'" According to Berlage, it was not in the factory but, rather, in the store and the office building that modern architecture would first reveal itself. While it is true that Willem Kromhout's Dutch pavilion in San Francisco barely received mention in the Dutch press, World War I and America's role in it nevertheless ensured a growing spotlight on the new continent.

The problem of public space was a particular point of interest among Dutch urban planners. The urban-planning conference held in Amsterdam in 1924 served to boost awareness of the importance of a system of regional planning. Among the assembled company of leading international figures, America presented itself — in the persons of Clarence Stein, the British business émigré Thomas Adams, Henri V. Hubbard, and others — as a country that had worked out its own elaborate perspectives on urban building and planning. New York was held up as a complex entity whose expansion was modulated by means of exacting laws. C.B. Purdon referred to the heart of the matter in his assertion that Henry Ford was "the greatest factory organizer that has ever lived. I think we may learn something from him to apply to city organization."[3] At the same time, the conference's most important feature was that it brought together respected representatives of the discipline — the old guard — and the up-and-coming younger generation, which was a departure from the major urban-design expositions held in Europe until then. For the older generation, urban design meant building cities using residential building material; in the Netherlands Berlage was their most vocal spokesperson. The younger generation of urban planners saw mobility as key, and demanded a strict separation of functions. Adherents included Th. K. van Lohuizen, J. M. de Casseres, and H. Cleyndert, with the latter two displaying a particularly marked interest in America. De Casseres was active in regional planning, while Cleyndert was to pursue nature and green space, with America as a steadfast example. Both wrote for the *Tijdschrift voor Volkshuisvesting en Stedebouw* (Journal for Public Housing and Urban Planning). Van Lohuizen was primarily engaged on the academic front, and issued a positivistic plea for empirically grounded investigation: the "survey." Statistics would be a crucial component, since interpretation of numbers would lay the groundwork for the design process. Van Lohuizen gained recognition principally through his close collaboration with Cor van Eesteren in the development of the General Expansion Plan (Algemeen Uitbreidingsplan) for Amsterdam in 1934.

Alphons Siebers

In 1927 the Dutch architect and urban planner Alphons Siebers traveled to the United States and reported in Dutch magazines and journals on his experiences, which included a visit to the West Coast. Siebers, who had previously worked on Rotterdam's urban development plan, was particularly impressed by American landscape architecture.[4] As an advocate of a more cautious approach to the natural beauty of the landscape, he was quickly labeled a preservationist architect. Writing of New York, he observed: "Manhattan has everything a person can think of, even heavy industry has not yet withdrawn entirely. The process of creating order from such chaos is something altogether different from the measured pace at which European cities are developed. It entails a colossal struggle between the spirit of organization and the unruly elements."[5] Siebers' American stay of nearly one year included visits to the major cities and to such luminaries as Henry Adams and Frederick Law Olmstead. He had received a grant from the Laura Spelman Rockefeller Memorial, whose Dutch representative was Johan Huizinga, to study the work of the Regional Planning Association of America.[6] He used the initial period to spend days on end in the Russell Sage Foundation Building, a skyscraper that housed an excellent urban-design library, before setting off to see America by car. His motives, which he expressed in English, are illuminating: "To put it short, the American city has been affected and is being planned for the automobile to such an extent that this vehicle must be used by anybody who is after the study of its physical appearance. Though the automobile by far has not affected the European city to the same extent, even in Europe the automobile has become an indispensable instrument in the hands of the city-planner. Seeing the profitable use of air pictures and air maps being made in city-planning, one might be induced to say the same of airplanes, though I do not think this argument would go very far and I would hardly venture to suggest that the Rockefeller Memorial place airplanes at the disposal of its fellows."

Shortly after his arrival in New York, Siebers reported that "[its] streets tend to be ugly, dirty and messy." It reminded him of Rotterdam. Throughout his stay in America he corresponded with various people in the Netherlands, including Theo van Lohuizen, who had plans to work in the U.S. for a while should opportunities in the Netherlands dry up. Van Lohuizen expressed his regret "that people like those Americans, who would sacrifice so much to science, tend to do things with such a lack of precision, almost like dilettantes. Those studies about New York, such as … [here Van Lohuizen refers to regional planning studies by Adams and to the Regional Plan of New York and Its Environs] concerning which you also write, the economic study, and the one about traffic are excellent

3

—

THE
PERIOD
OF
THE
WORLD
WARS

1914–1945

insofar as all sorts of issues are taken up that have never previously been dealt with; yet never do they get through to the heart of the problem. Of course they will outgrow these things, but it is regrettable nevertheless." He asked whether Siebers had "gained any impressions of the city manager system. Given the way city administration has evolved here, it holds surprisingly great appeal." In a later letter Van Lohuizen expanded on his views about urban design as a discipline, speaking from a scientific perspective in much the same way as Huizinga had done in his books describing America. He divided the urban designer into two, driving a wedge between the scholar and the designer, thereby introducing a far-reaching trend that has continued to find unfortunate expression in many projects even to this day. The "natural" symbiosis that had existed within the single individual up until 1800 became fragmented, particularly during the twentieth century, into an artificial plurality of functions.

Siebers also corresponded with the then secretary-director of the Netherlands Institute for Public Housing and Urban Development (Nederlands Instituut voor Volkshuisvesting en Stedebouw), Dirk Hudig. Hudig read the articles Siebers published in the Institute's own journal and in the *Algemeen Handelsblad* (which included articles on American urban development), and wrote: "When I think of America, the question that intrigues me most is not what America is going to do with European notions but, rather, what America itself can contribute to the growth of our emerging new culture."[7] This viewpoint also explains Siebers' enthusiasm for an exhibition on Wright's work, which he recommended in a letter to Berlage. The idea held too little potential for Berlage, though, and he referred Siebers to the Opbouw, an architectural society chaired at the time by J. J. P. Oud. [8]

The most notable of Siebers' American articles appeared in the journal *Städtebau*, which Werner Hegemann published in association with the *Wasmuths Monatshefte für Baukunst*.[9] While Siebers hoped to write more for Hegemann's journal, the latter found the article about high-rise building too superficial ("nicht inhaltreich genug"). For progressive architects — a group in which Siebers cannot be included — high-rise building was a theme that had to win no matter what, since it was meant to serve as the poster child of their ideals. As such, New York was to be the leading exemplar of a dynamic society and a modern metropolis.

Other Contacts between the Old and the New World

In 1924, the same year of the Amsterdam conference and one year after his successful lecture that interpreted dynamic architecture as a compromise between Amsterdam and Rotterdam types, Erich Mendelsohn left the Netherlands for a trip to the United States that would last several months. He had been commissioned by the German publisher Rudolf Mosse to write a book about modern American architecture, which was to be illustrated with his own photographs. The published volume ultimately also included many photographs of work by the Danish architect Knud Lønberg-Holm. The latter had visited Oud in the Netherlands and kept up a correspondence with both Oud and Cor van Eesteren long after he moved to the United States; he was, in the words of the architectural historian Manfred Bock, "the link between Holland and America." Mendelsohn's name was certainly familiar in the Netherlands, and he sent reports of his experiences to friends, acquaintances, and family in Europe. Frank Lloyd Wright had become his undisputed hero and he felt that New York, with its "vital energy, space, and traffic," was the concentrated embodiment of all of America.[10] In subsequent years he would publish a variety of pieces on America, thus further solidifying his role as mediator between the Old and the New World. Mendelsohn was one of the first to believe that architecture itself could be an advertisement. His buildings for the business sector were to be conspicuous commercial signposts within the urban environment, and his *Amerika. Bilderbuch eines Architekten*, published in 1926, was one of the first books on modern architecture to apportion greater significance to images than to text.

In 1929, J.G.Wattjes, editor-in-chief of the journal *Het Bouwbedrijf* and friend of Jan Wils's, stated his belief that American architecture was lagging far behind that of Europe. Its only truly original contribution had been the tower block. No mention was made of Frank Lloyd Wright. Nor did he give any consideration to urban development, though it was precisely in this area that major changes were taking place in 1929. The stock market crash in October of that year did not only have economic and social implications, but led to a shift in politics as well. Confidence in a new world and a better future for everyone was extinguished in a single breath. Technology and its significance became a topic of debate. Government was asked to assume a regulatory function and to encourage investments. Unemployment was to be countered by means of large-scale new projects. New Deal politics provided the framework for setting up the Tennessee Valley Authority in America, which was to have consequences for the supply of power and regional planning alike. Major projects were launched in the Netherlands, too, under the auspices of legislation on the Zuiderzeewerken (land reclamation projects in and around the then Zuiderzee) that had been passed in 1918. In no time at all, drainage of the Dutch Wieringermeer flood plain was completed.

Nevertheless, efforts to introduce modern — that is to say European — architecture in the United States persisted. In 1932 the Museum of Modern Art hosted *The International Style*, an exhibition masterminded by the erratic and unpredictable American architect Philip Johnson, who was a close friend of J.J.P. Oud's. Johnson's ally in "operation MoMa" was the architectural histori-

463

3

—

THE
PERIOD
OF
THE
WORLD
WARS

1914–1945

an Henry Russel Hitchcock, author of the first monograph on Oud. In their later careers, each of these two men would come to assume positions of absolute authority in their respective fields. Oud himself was never to set foot on American soil, Johnson's 1931 request for the Dutch architect to design a house in Pinehurst for his mother notwithstanding. We can be sure that the conception Oud formed of America owed much to his aforementioned correspondence with Knud Lønberg-Holm, who, in countless letters — often accompanied by illuminating photographs — described for Oud's benefit the incredibly diverse facets of American architecture and the American city.

Two Outsiders: De Casseres and Bromberg

As an outsider in the world of Dutch urban design who early on in his career had succeeded in making various enemies in Netherlands Institute for Public Housing and Urban Development circles, J.M. de Casseres had little choice but to carve out his own niche. What he wanted, first and foremost, was to forge stronger links between the fields of planning, urban development, and geography. His energetic approach often got people's hackles up, and his book *Stedenbouw* (Urban design), published in 1926, was not particularly well received. De Casseres felt that urban design was too heavily grounded in artistic concerns and insufficiently based on sociological considerations. He observed that things were different across the Atlantic. In May 1938 he left for the U.S. with the notion of possibly settling there. He was impressed by Rexford Tugwell, who had been serving President Roosevelt since 1932 as an important advisor on the implementation of several New Deal programs, especially the Resettlement Administration. By the time De Casseres arrived Tugwell chaired the New York City Planning Commission, and De Casserres hoped to be able to collaborate with him.[11] As this idea could apparently not be materialized, he returned to the Netherlands after several months and subsequently wrote numerous articles about America, together with a book entitled *Het andere Amerika* (The other America), which appeared in 1939. That was also the year of the World's Fair in New York, with a Dutch pavilion designed by D.F. Slothouwer. Of all the entries submitted in a closed competition Slothouwer's winning design was certainly the least controversial. Rather than choosing a design that was truly representative, the Netherlands made a selection based on purely financial considerations.

De Casseres had already returned to the Netherlands by the time of the Fair, where his book became a bestseller. In it, he presented a view of the New World that did away with the standard, clichéd view of America — that of a barbaric, uncultured empire under the iron rule of big money. He also emphasized the country's abundance of space, even going so far as to attribute American cour-

Cover illustration of J. M. de Casseres, *Het andere Amerika*
(Amsterdam: Arbeiderspers, 1939).

3

—

THE
PERIOD
OF
THE
WORLD
WARS

1914-1945

age to that fact. As Europe descended into fascism and Nazism, De Casseres held America up as its shining counterexample. Yet, the book's great success ultimately was not enough to put him among the leaders of postwar reconstruction in the Netherlands.

Another person to set his sights on America—to which he temporarily migrated from the Netherlands during World War II—was Paul Bromberg.[12] He was an advocate of modern architecture and his various books all bear the clear stamp of his American experiences. His *Amerikaansche architectuur* (American architecture), published in 1946, is a catalogue of his knowledge about architecture and the building industry in America. The book closes with the observation that building in the United States "technologically speaking is further developed than in our country; on the organizational front, too, there is much for us to learn." While his books were certainly popular, he was never to gain a position of any great consequence. The Netherlands' artistic trusts and lobbies had each claimed their piece of the pie long before then, and all that remained for strangers who chose to venture outside the customary religious and political frameworks were the few stray crumbs that fell to them from the traditionalists and modernists. Not much has changed.

1 Johan Huizinga, *Amerika levend en denkend. Losse opmerkingen* (Haarlem: H.D. Tjeenk Willink, 1927), 17; Translation by Herbert H. Rowen in Johan Huizinga, *America: A Dutch Historian's Vision, from Afar and Near* (New York: Harper & Row, 1972), 235.

2 The key work about the impact of the Wasmuth publication is Anthony Alofsin, *Frank Lloyd Wright. The Lost Years, 1910–1922. A Study of Influence* (Chicago/London: University of Chicago Press, 1993); For more on Wright's influence in the Netherlands, see H. van Bergeijk, ed., *Amerikaanse dromen. Frank Lloyd Wright in Nederland* (Rotterdam: 010 Publishers, 2008).

3 C.B. Purdom, "The Development of Satellite Towns in Connection with the Regional Plan," in *International Town Planning Conference Amsterdam 1924* (Amsterdam: Van Munster, 1924), 118.

4 His publications included *De oogen open: wordt Rotterdam een goed gebouwde stad?* (Rotterdam: Vereeniging voor Stadsverbetering Nieuw Rotterdam, 1926).

5 Quoted in A. van der Woud, "Hoogbouw in de Lage Landen," in Fons Asselbergs et al., eds., *Americana, 1880–1930* (Otterlo: Rijksmuseum Kröller-Müller, 1975), 44.

6 The A. Siebers Archives in the Netherlands Architecture Institute (NAi) also contain several cards and letters from Huizinga; Siebers' trip is extensively documented.

7 Letter from Hudig, dated September 21, 1927, in Siebers Archives, NAi; Siebers also wrote for the Rotterdam newspaper *De Maasbode* during his American journey.

8 See Berlage's letter dated October 8, 1927, in Siebers Archives, NAi.

9 Alphons Siebers, "Die karrierte Stadt," *Städtebau* 9 (1929): 237-246; Earlier that year he published an article, "Butte und Longview. Planlosigkeit und Höchst-

leistung," in the same magazine
(1:26-32).

10 See Erich Mendelsohn, *Briefe eines
Architekten* (Munich: Prestel, 1961), 60.

11 See Koos Bosma, *J. M. de Casseres.
De eerste planoloog* (Rotterdam: 010
Publishers, 2003), 33.

12 For Bromberg, see Monique Teunissen,
*Paul Bromberg. Binnenhuisarchitect
en publicist (1893–1949)* (Rotterdam:
010 Publishers, 1987).

3
—
THE
PERIOD
OF
THE
WORLD
WARS

1914–1945

THE RECEPTION OF AMERICAN LITERATURE IN THE NETHERLANDS, 1900–1950

—

HANS BAK

For most Dutch readers in the first quarter of the twentieth century America was at best of peripheral interest, an increasingly powerful but young and strange country that, situated across a vast ocean, was developing in "modern" ways often considered undesirable and inferior. American literature — though it had produced important and unmistakably "American" writers like Cooper, Hawthorne, Stowe, and Twain — was still mostly thought of as derivative and immature, a pale copy of the best of European, especially English, writing. In the years before 1925 this bastion of European cultural and literary superiority appeared as yet inviolable. Dutch critics, if they were interested in foreign literatures at all, mostly focused on French, German, or English writers, and paid scant attention to what writing from America penetrated to Dutch shores, often via British publishers or through German translations.

This changed between 1925 and 1940, as in the wake of America's rise to world prominence, newspapers like *Nieuwe Rotterdamsche Courant* (NRC) and periodicals like *De Stem* and *Boekenschouw* were stepping up their interest in American books, reflecting the mounting recognition that the U.S. was producing a literature worthy of attention in its own right. In 1928 Leopold's publishers in The Hague launched an Amerikaansche Bibliotheek (American library), intended "to bring the best of the new American literature" to Dutch readers. In early 1933 Eugene Jolas's decision to publish his expatriate magazine *transition* from The Hague was taken as a sign that the Netherlands, following France, was becoming a center for the distribution of American avant-garde writing: "In this way very welcome literary relations of practical usefulness are coming into being between the Netherlands and America." The Nobel Prizes for Sinclair Lewis in 1930 (the first American to receive the award), for Eugene O'Neill in 1936, and for Pearl S. Buck in 1938, were unmistakable symptoms of the growing international stature of American literature, a process of recognition that, interrupted by the war years, would reach an ebullient height between 1946 and 1949. In 1950 *De Gids* published a double "American issue," acknowledging the new global importance of the U.S. and granting that American writing could vie with the best of Europe.[1]

For most Dutch readers between 1900 and 1950 it was the contemporary American novel that served as the primary window on American life and culture; the interest in American drama and poetry was relatively scant. If the American film was often taken as exemplary of the vulgarizing effect of American mass culture, the serious (unlike the popular) novel was held up for judgment by the severest standards. As Perry Miller, who taught at the University of Leiden in 1949–50, noted: "The novel is, on levels that really count, a more vital factor in Europe's image of America than the moving picture."[2]

Before World War II the attitudes of Dutch writers toward America ran the full gamut from fervent adulation to sharp rejection. Typically, "Amerika" served as the projection screen for social, political, and literary hopes or anxieties about the destiny of Dutch, and European, culture. America's rise to industrial, military, and political power inspired paradoxical responses of endorsement and dismissal, depending on whether one saw the U.S. primarily as threat or promise. Some saw it as both. Thus, after the failure of his utopian community Walden, the novelist, psychotherapist, and social reformer Frederik van Eeden hoped to find in America the idealistic open-mindedness and organizational wizardry for a second try. Over against an anemic and cynical "old" Europe, America seemed "the land of Life, of Movement and of Hope." In 1908 and 1909 he made three trips to the U.S., seeking to make the arrangements for Van Eeden Colony. "I feel in America precisely as if the lid of my box has been lifted," he observed. "All that Dutch heavy-handedness blows away here. Life here is spacious, large and royal, and I feel for the rest of my life as much American as Dutch." Van Eeden's messianic optimism soon clashed with a disillusioning practical reality, and, after Versailles, his ambivalence intensified, yet in 1926 he still believed that America was "the country and the people of which we can expect most."[3]

In 1927 the young Flemish writer and historian Marnix Gijsen published his travel impressions in *Ontdek Amerika*. America, he noted, had evolved from an "outpost" to "the material center of the world." With youthful impetuosity it was now ready to show the way to "old, threadbare Europe" and to exert its spiritual and cultural influence. Yet Gijsen was unsure whether this was a blessing or a curse: he recurrently measured Europe by American and America by Euro-

469

3

—

THE
PERIOD
OF
THE
WORLD
WARS

1914–1945

pean standards, exposing the strengths and deficiencies of each. His nuanced and balanced impressions thus revealed a typical ambivalence: he felt both an elated fascination and a deep-seated European skepticism.[4]

No such ambivalence was to be found in the famous essay in which Menno ter Braak "rejected" America. One of Holland's leading critics, he remained mostly silent on American literature. Not so Theun de Vries, communist critic, novelist, and editor of *De Vrije Katheder*, who came down harshly on capitalist America, but did so with euphoric enthusiasm for its literature. He, too, virulently lashed out against the corruption and power of American capital, religious hypocrisy, and cheapening mass entertainment, scoffing that in America democracy appeared in its "most banal, dishonorable form… power and greatness for the strong, subservience and modern slavery for the weak." Yet, he felt, despite its "monstrous contradictions," America had produced a splendid literature, "monumental even, virile in the best sense, broad and fertile like the plains of the Midwest, filled with refined subtleties, mercilessly sharp, trenchant in its analysis of character, never tired and uncertain, never pessimistic — in short, in all respects heartwarmingly young." If De Vries rejected America, he embraced American literature.[5]

Such attitudes toward America also infused the considerations of American books, which were often (naively) taken as trustworthy representations of life in the U.S. Many Dutch observers were inclined to read American literature as a confirmation of their preconceptions, at best as a challenge to them. Even when aimed at dispassionate critical evaluation, their reviews often betrayed a subtle, ironic condescension, an undertone of anti-Americanism that served to foster a cherished sense of cultural superiority.

Thus, Dutch critics seemed to prefer American books that expressed a critical or satirical vision of U.S. culture and society. Social realists and naturalists like Jack London, Theodore Dreiser, Upton Sinclair, and Sinclair Lewis were well known and widely read, while H.L. Mencken was relished for his biting critique of the American "booboisie." Younger writers like John Dos Passos, James T. Farrell, Erskine Caldwell, and John Steinbeck were appreciated for their critical exposure of injustices and inequalities in American society, though reviewers often were uncomfortable with the bleak pessimism and lack of redemptive vision in their novels. Before 1930 the Dutch interest in American fiction appeared to be sociological as much as aesthetic, but considerations of artistic merit became more prominent as the century went on. The literary deficiencies of Dreiser, Sinclair, and Lewis were more sharply noted, while the American contribution to international modernism was acknowledged, if not without hesitation or skepticism. Dos Passos was criticized for experimental devices like the Newsreel or the Camera Eye. Ernest Hemingway and William Faulkner were early felt to be in a league of their own, but Hemingway's greatness was much debated and his stylistic innovations discredited as well as praised. For all his complexities Faulkner was early recognized as a writer of superior depth and stature. Henry Miller, too, was highly valued for his virulent criticism as well as his literary qualities. From the late 1920s Dutch reviewers displayed a strong interest in the fate of African Americans and closely followed the emergence of the "New Negro" writing.

Edith Wharton and Willa Cather received serious critical attention, but Sherwood Anderson (one of the few Americans written on by Ter Braak) remained controversial. Whereas Kay Boyle was positively reviewed, Gertrude Stein was barely taken note of until her death in 1947. Edna Ferber and Fannie Hurst were curiously overappreciated, while Margaret Mitchell (*Gone with the Wind*) and Pearl Buck (*The Good Earth*), both bestselling popular novelists, were mostly deemed beneath notice by professional critics, even though a Dutch translation, *Gejaagd door de wind*, with illustrations by Anton Pieck, went through twenty editions between 1936 and 1940. Likewise, popular writers like Zane Grey and Edgar Rice Burroughs, while outselling Hemingway and Faulkner, were recurrently dismissed as manifestations of an objectionable popular culture.[6]

Before 1940, while the interest in earlier writers like Hawthorne, Poe, Twain, and Whitman persisted, Henry James and Herman Melville were scarcely noticed. Their importance would not be fully recognized until after 1945. Thomas Wolfe, too, did not appear on the radar of Dutch criticism until after World War II, while the significance of F. Scott Fitzgerald was not fully recognized until about 1950: a first Dutch translation of *The Great Gatsby* did not appear until the late 1940s. Zora Neale Hurston remained virtually unnoticed until the 1960s.

Sinclair, Lewis, Dreiser

The most widely read American writer of the early twentieth century in the Netherlands (as in Europe and the world)[7] was Upton Sinclair—thirty-five of his books were translated between 1907 and 1953; *The Jungle* (*De Wildernis*) had gone through seventeen editions by 1949. A close friend of Van Eeden's, Sinclair was valued because of his scathing exposure of the corruptions and injustices in American industry and politics, though later novels raised doubts about the accuracy of his reportage and Sinclair was considered less a literary artist than a zealous sermonizer and propagandist. In 1929 *Haagsch Maandblad* referred to him as "the describer, critic, and prophet of what interests the old world most in the new: the epoch of modern industrialization, realistically described and intellectually interpreted." *Boston* (1928), his novel on the Sacco and Vanzetti case, was typically relished by C. Houwaard, in *De Stem*, as "a picture of damna-

471

3

—

THE
PERIOD
OF
THE
WORLD
WARS

1914–1945

ble Americanism" — "America is a land of plutocracy in its most offensive form, of servitude and injustice, of soul-violation and murder of the spirit, of venality and humbug, Hollywood and jazz."

The appeal of Sinclair Lewis lay mostly in the wit and fierceness of his social satire, his critique of the materialism and spiritual barrenness of America, and its "Babbitts" feeding anti-American sentiment. A flood of critical attention followed the award of the Nobel Prize to Lewis in November 1930. The award was largely taken as a sign of the changing status of American writing in the world: whereas in 1928 A. Perdeck had observed that "from a purely aesthetic point of view, America has as yet contributed very little to the glory of English letters," five years later NRC unambiguously noted that "*The Scarlet Letter, Moby Dick, Tales* of Poe, *Leaves of Grass*, and *Huckleberry Finn*, [were] works which placed America in the ranks of nations that produced great literature."

Hendrik Willem van Loon was one of several who thought the award should have gone to Theodore Dreiser. In *De Gids* Jeanne van Schaik-Willing ebulliently celebrated Dreiser as "the Lucifer of American literature, the great equal and counterpart to Dostoevsky, the Moses who beat upon the American rock to release the source of belles letters."[8] Between 1927 and 1933 Dreiser was widely regarded as "the greatest living American writer." Despite his stylistic infelicities and massive detail, he too was relished for his exposure of the hypocrisies and contradictions of American society. While Theun de Vries declared him the "Zola of America," many were disturbed by his pessimistic determinism, and religiously oriented critics berated him for his "limited conception of man and his spiritual inadequacies."

Harlem Renaissance

Nowhere were the inconsistencies and injustices embedded in the American ideals of liberty and equality more glaringly apparent than in the postslavery fate of African Americans. The emergence of the "New Negro" and the Harlem Renaissance in the 1920s and 1930s was intently followed by Dutch critics, partly from a moral or sociological curiosity, partly from an interest in the artistry of black cultural expression and its perceived influence on American culture at large. In 1927, Marnix Gijsen noted the impact of blacks on the spiritual and cultural life of America, "no longer as the subject of romantic commiseration or caricature, but directly and immediately." Black songs and spirituals were "the best in art America could point to," he felt, though he thought it ironic that "America, which once prevented the negro from eating his ice-cream where he bought it, now twists and contorts itself willingly to the music of its former slaves." Between 1928 and 1934 A. Perdeck reviewed, for NRC, novels by Carl

Van Vechten, Claude McKay, Walter White, Langston Hughes, and Jessie Fauset, while in *De Stem* he sharply exposed the "race question" as a disturbingly hypocritical aspect of American life and culture. He praised the work of Cullen, Hughes, and McKay, yet seemed ambivalent about the desirability of a distinctly black aesthetic. P. Verhoog fully recognized its legitimacy. In 1935, in *NRC*, he noted the post-Emancipation emergence of a black tradition of expression rooted in slave songs, spirituals, and blues. Verhoog was aware of precursors like Phyllis Wheatley, Fredrick Douglass, and Booker T. Washington, and even discussed lesser-known writers like Rudolph Fischer, George S. Schuyler, and James Weldon Johnson.[9] By the mid-1930s, then, a Dutch reader of *NRC* could be remarkably well informed about contemporary African-American writing.

The work of Richard Wright did not reach the Netherlands until after the war. A translation of *Native Son* (1940) came out in 1947, of *Black Boy* (1945) in 1948. As Dutch critics were well aware, Wright's work had received a warm welcome in France. Theun de Vries was intrigued by Wright's embrace of Sartre's existentialism but felt that in doing so Wright had taken a backward step as a revolutionary writer. For W. F. Hermans, Wright's work was above all *littérature engagée*: hardly new or revolutionary in technique, yet the compelling product of an "artist" who never succumbed to a black-white portrayal of black-white relations.[10]

Hemingway, Faulkner, Steinbeck, Miller

The critical reception of Hemingway, Faulkner, Steinbeck, and Miller straddled the war. With Dutch hearts and minds turned toward the problems of resisting and surviving German occupation, literary matters in wartime were marked by Nazi censorship and paper shortage. The import of foreign literatures stalled (barring illegal printings by De Bezige Bij), the production of translations was severely curbed, and American books received scant or no attention from Dutch critics until after 1945.[11]

Ernest Hemingway was reviewed from the mid-1920s on, but Dutch critics found him difficult to fathom and to categorize. Hemingway's style — functionalist, understated — was recognized as new and influential, but many had trouble seeing the moral significance of his effort to control the chaos and emptiness of modern life. Thus, *A Farewell to Arms* (translated in 1933) was greeted by A. den Doolaard as "one of the best war novels," yet he concluded uneasily that "whoever rejects Hemingway's hopeless pessimism must still admire the way in which he expresses it." Ralph Kreemers in *Boekzaal* felt the novel had "unquestionable literary worth" yet was "horribly degrading" from a moral perspective. *For Whom the Bell Tolls* (1940) was not translated and reviewed until

473

3

___

THE
PERIOD
OF
THE
WORLD
WARS

1914–1945

after Dutch liberation, but then many embraced the book as possibly Heming-way's best. Max Nord thought it superior to Malraux's *L'Espoir* and pronounced Hemingway "the greatest living novelist." Annie Romein-Verschoor felt he had rivaled the nineteenth-century Russian masters, while for Max Schuchart Hem-ingway's novel showed that "American novel art is ahead of the European in many respects and offers more possibilities." The author's postwar reputation peaked with *The Old Man and the Sea* (1952), which won him the Nobel Prize in 1954. Though the book was among his most popular ones — a Dutch translation went through three editions in its first year — critics like Schuchart felt that Heming-way had "never really redeemed the great promise of his early work."

The originality and genius of William Faulkner were quickly recognized, even in the 1930s, when he was scantily appreciated in the U.S. Often the Dutch were earlier in reviewing his works than the French, who were mostly given credit for "discovering" Faulkner's importance.[12] Though he was not widely read, he was closely monitored by a small circle of writers and critics, who felt Faulkner's notorious complexity represented life more faithfully than Heming-way's understated simplicity. Many could more readily appreciate Faulkner's ethical concern than Hemingway's nihilism, and recognized that his con-cerns transcended southern regionalism. Jos Panhuysen in *Boekenschouw* felt Faulkner's complexity was "completely justified" to express his "bewildering realization of inescapable and incomprehensible evil."

After 1945, Dutch critical interest in Faulkner soared, yet the precise nature of his contribution continued to be hotly debated. Simon Vestdijk upbraided the American critic Malcolm Cowley for reducing Faulkner to "a historical nov-elist, a modern Walter Scott" of the South; his real distinction lay in "an astonish-ing and undeniably subjective sense for dramatic-psychological conflict." W.F. Hermans distinguished "two Faulkners" — one "an American regional writer," the other "an almost European writer, whose work is appreciated by Europeans for its metaphysical quality." For Hermans, it was Faulkner's hypnotizing, op-pressive, sensual "atmosphere," rooted in the "bad but indissoluble marriage" between black and white, which fascinated Sartre and Vestdijk, and which ex-plained why Faulkner could never be popular in America.[13] When Faulkner re-ceived the Nobel Prize in 1949, he was pronounced "one of the great American writers, or rather, one of the very greatest of modern literature."

John Steinbeck was perhaps the most popular American writer in the 1940s. Nearly all of his books appeared in translation, reaching twenty editions by the early 1950s. In 1939 E. van Hall-Nijhoff considered Steinbeck one of "the most promising and vital American writers" and thought *The Grapes of Wrath* (1939) might have the political and social influence of *Uncle Tom's Cabin*. The book reached the Netherlands just as war broke out, yet it was translated and re-viewed. Steinbeck's popularity continued through the war, despite Nazi censorship: a translation of *Of Mice and Men* appeared in 1941, while in 1945 *The Moon is Down* was printed illegally by De Bezige Bij and circulated widely in the last days of occupation. Despite his popularity, his critical reputation remained controversial, Gerard Walschap ardently defending Steinbeck, Hermans feeling he was a second-rate author at best. Vestdijk thought Steinbeck demonstrated the bankruptcy of the "behavioristic" novel, a typically American genre, but bound to be superseded by film.

No writer enjoyed a European reputation more diametrically opposed to his American one than Henry Miller. *Tropic of Cancer* (1934) and *Tropic of Capricorn* (1939), both published in Paris, were freely available in Dutch bookstores, but banned in the U.S. on the grounds of obscenity. Ignored in his home country, Miller was celebrated in the Netherlands as one of the greatest of living novelists. *Kroniek van Kunst en Cultuur* in 1936 thought his work belonged to "the most important which American literature has brought forth in recent years." After the war, *Litterair Paspoort* ranked his books "among the most remarkable products of modern American literature." Yet Miller caused controversy, much of it revolving around "the problem of pornography." The *Groene Amsterdammer* was uncomfortable with his obscenity and lack of "inner morality," while Van Kranendonk felt Miller's sexual frankness was "vulgar and dirty" as well as "unbearably monotonous." But Paul Rodenko argued the necessity for the use of obscenity, Pierre Dubois felt that Miller's pornography was functional, and Hermans thought he was "the healthiest man in our society." For Vestdijk, finally, Miller was "one of the greatest writers of his time," who presented his "incurable and naïve erotomania" with humor and "a sheer moralistic accent which betrays the author's American descent." Miller was "above all an American with an unhappy love for his country."[14]

The Postwar Upswing (1946-49)

Liberation not only generated a widespread curiosity about American lifestyles and values, it also opened the gates to a dammed-up critical interest for American writers in Dutch literary periodicals. Symptomatic was the ample attention that *Litterair Paspoort*, launched in 1946 by Adriaan Morriën as a magazine dedicated to "books from the old and new world," in its first years devoted to American literature, both old and new: it featured essays on Emily Dickinson, the postwar revaluation of Melville and James, and the renewed interest in the "lost generation." It reviewed new books by Miller, Robert Penn Warren, Vladimir Nabokov, Anaïs Nin, and Norman Mailer, and discussed the latest tendencies in American writing. The postwar interest in American literature was markedly better informed, and American literature was now generally reviewed with

475

3

—

THE
PERIOD
OF
THE
WORLD
WARS

1914–1945

more sophistication and historical awareness, by critics and writers of greater prominence and distinction: the fact that Hermans, Vestdijk, and Rodenko, as well as Michel van der Plas, Jacques den Haan, Willem de Geus, Adriaan Morriën, and Jos van der Steen recurrently entered the fray testified to the enhanced stature of American writing in the Netherlands after 1945.

If Dutch critics were highly skeptical about the influence of U.S. commercialism on "serious" American writing in what John Vandenbergh called this "Age of the Digest" and the Gallup Poll — the new phenomenon of "pocket books," or paperbacks, was greeted with ambivalence and Adriaan van der Veen spoke in a derogatory way of "the American cultural factory"[15] — still, by 1947 there was widespread recognition that one could no longer dismiss American literature as "infantile" or America as "cultureless." Symptomatic was the appearance of A.G. van Kranendonk's two-volume *Geschiedenis van de Amerikaanse literatuur* (published by G.A. van Oorschot in 1946–47), the first comprehensive history of American literature in Dutch. Van Kranendonk's study signaled both the culmination point of the Dutch reception of American literature in the first half of the twentieth century and the starting point of serious academic scholarship on American writing in the Netherlands.

By the late 1940s the Dutch had come to acknowledge that American literature had changed from a mere "branch factory" of English writing to "one of the great world literatures in its own right." Its contemporary writers were recognized as challenging and influential players in the international literary field. The altered appreciation, as Malcolm Cowley noted in 1948, was "not merely a secondary result of the growth in economic and military power of the American nation." It was also an "independent" development that testified to a change in the intrinsic quality of American literature, which after 1910 had produced a "second flowering" comparable to the American Renaissance of the mid-nineteenth century.[16]

1   Dirk Coster, "Amerikaansche Literatuur," *De Stem* 8 (1928): 894-899; V. Pearce Delgado, "Amerikaansche Letteren," *Het Vaderland*, February 5, 1933; "Verantwoording," *De Gids* (1950), 81-82.

2   Perry Miller, "Europe's Faith in American Fiction," *Atlantic Monthly* 188 (December 1951): 52.

3   Quoted in Marianne Mooijweer, *De Amerikaanse droom van Frederik van Eeden* (Amsterdam: De Bataafsche Leeuw, 1996), 105, 119, 229.

4   Marnix Gijsen, *Ontdek Amerika* (Brussel /Bussum, 1927), 7-15 (translation mine).

5   Theun de Vries, "Amerika in de Amerikaanse roman," *De Stem* 18 (1938): 587-89 (translation mine).

6   Peter Oppewall, "The Critical Reception of American Fiction in the Netherlands, 1900–1953," (Ph.D. dissertation, University of Michigan, 1960), 1-330. To date

*Gezicht op New York, 1699,
door Peter Schenk*

PROF. A. G. VAN KRANENDONK

GESCHIEDENIS
VAN DE AMERIKAANSE
LITERATUUR

EERSTE DEEL

MET 20 ILLUSTRATIES

AMSTERDAM
N.V. UITGEVERS MAATSCHAPPIJ G. A. VAN OORSCHOT
MCMXLVI

Title page and frontispiece of A. G. van Kranendonk's
Geschiedenis van de Amerikaanse literatuur, vol. 1, the first comprehensive
history of American literature in Dutch.

3

——

THE
PERIOD
OF
THE
WORLD
WARS

1914–1945

Oppewall remains the one comprehensive attempt to chart the Dutch reception of American fiction in the first half of the twentieth century. Jan Bakker has analyzed the reception of Hemingway in *Hemingway in Holland, 1925–1981* (Amsterdam: Rodopi, 1986). Unless indicated otherwise, all quotations in the ensuing are from Oppewall, passim, in his translation.

7   See Malcolm Cowley, "American Books Abroad," in Robert E. Spiller et al., eds., *Literary History of the United States* (New York: Macmillan, 1948), 1374-1391.

8   Jeanne van Schaik-Willing, "Theodore Dreiser," *De Gids* 1 (1931): 282-299.

9   Gijsen, *Ontdek Amerika*, 77-80; A. Perdeck, "Donkere tinten in de Amerikaansche letteren," *De Stem* 13 (1933): 193-197 (translation mine); P. Verhoog, "Neger-literatuur in Amerika," *NRC*, February 26 and 27, 1935.

10 Theun de Vries, "Existentie of revolutie," *Vrije Katheder* 7 (1947): 490-491, 508-509, 524-525; W. F. Hermans, "Korte besprekingen," *Litterair Paspoort* 2.11 (1947): 12.

11 Fred Batten, "Het buitenlandse boek in bezettingstijd," *Litterair Paspoort* 1.1 (January 1946): 6-7, 16.

12 Oppewall (182) notes that at least ten of Faukner's novels were reviewed in the Netherlands before, or simultaneous with, considerations in France.

13 Simon Vestdijk, "William Faulkner, Amerikaanse schrijver van de zuidelijke staten," *Het Parool*, March 13, 1948, 7; "Erotische driehoeksmeting," *Criterium* 6.5 (1948): 304-311; W.F. Hermans, "De twee Faulkners," *Litterair Paspoort* 4 (1949): 60-62.

14 Jacques den Haan, "Enkele notities over Henry Miller," *Litterair Paspoort* 1.2 (1946–47): 10; Simon Vestdijk, "Henry Miller: Onkruid dat niet vergaan zal," *Algemeen Handelsblad*, July 15, 1950 (translation mine).

15 John Vandenbergh, "Amerikaans proza," *De Gids* (1950), 130-140; Adriaan van der Veen, "De Amerikaansche cultureele fabriek," *Criterium* 2 (1947): 265-272.

16 Cowley, "American Books Abroad," 1391; See Malcolm Cowley, *A Second Flowering: Works and Days of the Lost Generation* (New York: Viking, 1973).

AMERICAN MOVIES REACH THE NETHERLANDS

———

KAREL DIBBETS & THUNNIS VAN OORT

American Cinema and Dutch Audiences

In June 1927 a group of young Dutch intellectuals formed the Nederlandsche Filmliga (Dutch Film League), an association that screened artistic films and published the periodical *Filmliga*.[1] Here cofounders Menno ter Braak, Leo Jordaan, and others propagated their ideas about film art that influenced contemporary and later generations of Dutch critics and filmmakers. A rigorous distinction was made between film as an art form and the movie theater as a site of reprehensible commercial amusement. Hollywood was explicitly labeled as the latter. According to Jordaan, the struggle for quality film was "a struggle against 'Americanism'—against the senseless and mindless transplant of the insipid, childish mentality and the overflowing energy of a young, and newly-marketed culture onto our old, experienced and weary state of mind."[2] In this respect the Filmliga movement did not deviate from the negative views held by most members of the Dutch cultural elite on commercial entertainment as a synonym for Americanization.

This uneasiness, however, was not shared by the large audiences that American cinema had won over in the Netherlands after World War I, just like in most other parts of the European market. While outside the Dutch borders the war raged, the emergence of American movies had become noticeable in the Netherlands. Charlie Chaplin, for instance, started to gain some popularity during the war years, although he was sometimes mixed up with (now forgotten) stars with a similar appearance, such as Billie Ritchie.[3] American cinema competed with French, Italian, and Danish films during these years. It was mainly after the war had ended that the now globally dominant position of the American film industry became evident on the Dutch screens. The war had had a devastating effect on the European film industries, with the notable exception of Germany's, which rapidly evolved from an insignificant position before 1918 into the

479

3

———

THE
PERIOD
OF
THE
WORLD
WARS

1914–1945

biggest competitor of American films in the Dutch market. The American film companies had used their advantage over the European competition to professionalize and upscale the industry.[4] Feature-length films and sensational serials with high budgets and equivalent production values could be turned out at a reliable, high rate. During the 1920s American and, in second place, German films dominated the Dutch theaters. With the introduction of talking pictures around 1930 the American market share dropped temporarily in favor of German film because the Dutch audience was more familiar with the German language. Subtitling solved this problem and Hollywood recovered and kept its leading position until the outbreak of World War II. In the meantime, the Dutch became accustomed to American voices in the cinema.

Still, the Dutch market was hardly worth the attention of the major Hollywood studios. Universal opened a Dutch branch in 1918, the other studios timidly opened branch offices several years later: Fox in 1923, Famous Players-Lasky in 1924, and First National in 1925. One year later two branches had already closed their doors. The Dutch market probably was too small to support the overhead costs of separate branch offices. American films were predominantly distributed by Dutch subcontractors. The most important Dutch distributor was Loet C. Barnstijn, active in the film trade since 1915. Barnstijn had gained prominence because he had secured important deals with American distributors. His brother Jack (Jaap) was a crucial contact in New York in gathering information and maintaining business relations overseas. Barnstijn visited the United States regularly to obtain distribution licenses. In the Dutch media and trade press he presented himself as a Dutch mogul, modeled after Laemmle and other business celebrities working behind the Hollywood scenes. His abundant advertising campaigns were seen as "typically American" compared to less conspicuous competitors.

The impact of American movies on Dutch society is as obvious as it is tricky to pin down exactly. Over the years Hollywood added a continuous stream of joy and suspense in a rich variety of stories and thrills to the pale diet of local pastime. This new and colorful dimension was as much appreciated as it seemed exotic to the general public, almost like a forbidden fruit. Its spectacle helped make the cinema a popular venue, but not on the same scale as in the Unites States or in any other European country. In fact, the frequency of movie-going per capita in the Netherlands has always been among the lowest in the Western world. The same goes for the number of movie theaters per capita. Picture palaces with a capacity of three thousand seats or more have never been built in the Netherlands; only a few venues could accommodate twelve hundred spectators. It is fair to say that cinema has remained a relative outsider in Dutch culture and that the impact of American movies has been less profound in the Netherlands than elsewhere.

Western movie star Tom Mix was greeted by huge crowds of fans
at his arrival in Amsterdam on April 25, 1925.

3

—

THE
PERIOD
OF
THE
WORLD
WARS

1914–1945

The modest interest in movie-going diverges from international trends but is less atypical when compared to regions instead of nations. In the United States significant differences exist between New York and, for instance, Kentucky with respect to movie-going frequency, theater density, and audience preferences.[5] Kathryn Fuller argues in her study of American small-town audiences that the centralized production and marketing of Hollywood before 1940 ran into local opposition against "sophisticated" movies ostensibly made for metropolitan audiences.[6] The "city movie" became a term of abuse in rural areas. It may make more sense to compare Dutch film culture to Kentucky or Ohio than to New York. The huge popularity of "unsophisticated" cowboy heroes like Tom Mix and Buck Jones in Rotterdam and Amsterdam during the 1920s seems to support this view. Their success matched the reputation of stylish, "sophisticated" stars like Rudolph Valentino and Gloria Swanson.

Yet, a resemblance to rural America should not divert our attention from important differences. Dutch exhibitors were keen to call their venues "Chicago," "New York," or "Cinema Parisien," which were unpopular names in the American countryside. More significantly, American movies had to compete with their European rivals in Dutch cinemas, and audiences could choose from a rich selection of foreign movies. Fan culture became a truly cosmopolitan experience of American, German, and French movie stars. Stimulated by the film industry, the popular press published gossip and photographs of international glamour, and its readers discussed the latest fad over lunch perhaps. It is hard to find specific information on Dutch movie fans and their preferences. Their numbers were barely large enough to support a small fan magazine over a longer period, *Cinema & Theater*. We do know, however, that Anne Frank, hidden away in an attic in Nazi-occupied Amsterdam during World War II, covered the wall of her room with pictures of Shirley Temple, Norma Shearer, and Ginger Rogers.

American Cinema and Dutch Film Production

Initially, there was only a very modest movie production sector in the Netherlands, which was similar to the situation in most other small countries. While the influence of Hollywood was obvious in film exhibition, one could argue that Dutch film production until 1940 was modeled after German rather than American cinema. Technical equipment and professional vocabulary came from Germany and France. The studio style and popular themes of Dutch films were closer to German than to American filmmaking. Dutch production history includes numerous examples of Dutch actors or film directors moving to Germany. After 1933 a wave of immigrants from Nazi Germany brought professional skills with them and began to stimulate new productions. Some of these profes-

TABLE 1

Top ten of the most popular feature films in the Netherlands until 1940[7]

	Country of Origin
De Jantjes (1934)	Netherlands
Pygmalion (1937)	Netherlands
Ben-Hur (1925)	United States
Hygien der Ehe (1922)	Austria
Modern Times (1936)	United States
It's in the Air (1938)	United Kingdom
La Maternelle (1933)	France
Bright Eyes (1934)	United States
One Hundred Men and a Girl (1937)	United States
Boystown (1938)	United States

sionals would soon move to the Unites States to continue their careers in Hollywood, including Herman Kosterlitz (Henry Koster), Detlev Sierck (Douglas Sirk), and Eugen Schüfftan.[8] One of the rare Dutch feature films with an explicit reference to the United States is *American Girls* (1919), a vehicle for the popular singer Louis Davids, who played eleven parts in it. The action took place in Amsterdam and the girls mentioned in the title seemed to fit the stereotype of the spoilt daughters of an American millionaire.[9] The — now lost — film appears to have reflected an older, quickly fading image of America, just before the breakthrough of a glamorous Hollywood cinema.

It comes as a surprise, therefore, that national film production managed to outstrip Hollywood in popularity during the 1930s. The list of the ten most popular movies seen before 1940 (table 1) is headed by two Dutch films, *De Jantjes* and *Pygmalion*, only to be followed by American pictures like *Ben-Hur* and *Modern Times*.

Censorship

If movie-going had any effect on political discourse at all, it has usually been attributed to Soviet cinema and its revolutionary propaganda. Hollywood, however, could also be seen as a risk to national security. In 1918, at the end of World War I, when a call for revolution reverberated in the Netherlands as well as elsewhere in Europe, several theaters responded by showing *The Bigger Man* (U.S., 1915), with its title translated as *Kapitaal en Arbeid* (capital and labor). Out of fear that this social melodrama might stir tensions by depicting inflammatory

483

3
—

THE
PERIOD
OF
THE
WORLD
WARS

1914–1945

class conflict, the movie was prohibited by local authorities in The Hague. Similarly, *Gabriel over the White House* (1933) could not be shown since it disseminated propaganda for dictatorship according to the censorship board.

Hollywood has been subject to a process of selective appropriation in the Netherlands as much as in the United States.[10] While American movies have been quite successful in Dutch cinemas, we may wonder whether some aspects of Hollywood were received with more enthusiasm than others. Censorship serves as a key indicator. In addition to fear of eroticism and violent behavior, religion became an object of grave concern for the national board of censorship. Its Catholic and Protestant members were keen to spot religious issues and ban them from Dutch movie theaters. For instance, *Dr Jekyll and Mr Hyde* (1931) was prohibited on grounds that the movie contravened the Catholic tenet against influencing the soul by means of chemical substances. *The Green Pastures* (1936) also met with considerable opposition. This famous musical about Heaven as seen through the eyes of black children was at first banned altogether, though after a year of legal disputes spectators of fourteen years and older received permission to watch the movie. Prime Minister Hendrikus Colijn and his orthodox Protestant party tried to reverse the latter verdict in parliament without success. Still, Colijn's brother was able to ban the biblical musical from the town where he held the office of mayor.

Shirley Temple may serve as a final illustration of what Hollywood was up to when promoting its most successful stars in the Netherlands. "Shirley mania" erupted in 1936 with the release of *Curly Top* featuring this child starlet. A local exhibitor in Utrecht, the fourth largest Dutch city, used the occasion to generate publicity for his Flora Theater by offering a prize for the best Shirley Temple look-alike. Over three hundred mothers and their dolled-up children showed up for the contest on April Fool's Day. This was not different from similar events in the United States (or elsewhere for that matter), including perhaps a local journalist's observation that "the majority of the contestants looked as much like Shirley as a flea resembles an elephant."[11] More remarkable was the fact that children under fourteen years of age were not allowed to enter a movie theater in Utrecht because of the very strict regulations in effect there. And so Utrecht's youth could not experience Shirley Temple on the silver screen, but only through their mothers' zeal to dress them up. American cinema was able to operate in a distinctive Dutch context in ways not intended or expected by the original American producers.

1   For more on the Filmliga, see Ansje
    van Beusekom, *Kunst en amusement.*
    Reactie op de film als een nieuw medium
    in Nederland, 1895–1940 (Haarlem:
    Arcadia, 2001); Céline Linssen, Hans
    Schoots, and Tom Gunning, *Het gaat om*
    de film! Een nieuwe geschiedenis van de
    Nederlandsche Filmliga 1927–1933
    (Amsterdam: Bas Lubberhuizen, 1999).

2   Quoted from and translated by Rob
    Kroes, "The Reception of American
    Films in the Netherlands: The Interwar
    Years," *American Studies International*
    28.1 (October 1990): 37-48.

3   Ivo Blom, *Jean Desmet and the Early*
    Dutch Film Trade (Amsterdam: Amster-
    dam University Press, 2003), 264.

4   Kristin Thompson, *Exporting Enter-*
    tainment: America in the World Film
    Market, 1907–34 (London: British
    Film Institute, 1985).

5   Gregory A. Waller, *Main Street Amuse-*
    ments. Movies and Commercial Enter-
    tainment in a Southern City, 1896–1930
    (Washington, DC: Smithsonian Institu-
    tion Press, 1995), 194-196; See also
    Robert C. Allen, "Relocating American
    Film History," *Cultural Studies* 20.1
    (2006): 48-88.

6   Kathryn Fuller, *At the Picture Show:*
    Small-Town Audiences and the Creation

7   of *Movie Fan Culture* (Washington, DC:
    Smithsonian Institution Press, 1996),
    98-114.

7   Computed from data in Cinema Context,
    the online encyclopedia of film culture
    and its history in the Netherlands,
    http://www.cinemacontext.nl. Box office
    figures of individual movies are not
    available for this period.

8   Kathinka Dittrich, *Achter het doek. Duitse*
    emigranten in de Nederlandse speelfilm
    in de jaren dertig (Houten: Het Wereld-
    venster, 1987), 65.

9   The film is lost, but an elaborate script
    has survived. Geoffrey Donaldson, *Of Joy*
    and Sorrow. A Filmography of Dutch Silent
    Fiction (Amsterdam: Stichting Neder-
    lands Filmmuseum, 1997), 181.

10 Richard Maltby, "Sticks, Hicks and
    Flaps: Classical Hollywood's Generic
    Conception of Its Audiences," in
    Melvyn Stokes and Richard Maltby,
    eds., *Identifying Hollywood's Audiences*
    (London: British Film Institute, 1999),
    23-41, here 30.

11 Quoted from Bert Hogenkamp, "A Curly
    Top, a Royal Engagement and a Local
    Bylaw: Cinema Exhibition and Innova-
    tion in Utrecht in 1936," *Film History* 17
    (2005): 139-147.

3

THE
PERIOD
OF
THE
WORLD
WARS

1914–1945

THE NETHERLANDS AND CLASSICAL MUSIC IN AMERICA

——

FRITS ZWART

Introduction

Around 1900, musicians hoping for work in America were at a distinct advantage if they had a European pedigree. Soloists had an especially difficult time securing engagements if they lacked European references. In the nineteenth century Europe was the worldwide center of music, a position that it maintained for much of the twentieth century as well. Americans in the nineteenth century went to great lengths to import this culture: many Europeans, for example, were members of American orchestras of the period. The Dutch contribution to this trend was relatively limited, however, and this article will investigate why.

Dutch composers have failed to leave their mark on the American musical experience and only a few Dutch performing musicians have had a significant impact as representatives of the Netherlands. Numerous Dutch musicians did move permanently to America, but they quickly absorbed the "indigenous" culture. Prominent Dutch musicians performed in leading American theaters and concert halls, but did not create a specific Dutch school. Opportunities were available, though. Willem Mengelberg (1871–1951) was a Dutch musician and conductor who spent years propagating his musical ideals in New York. He was tireless in his efforts to support the music of Gustav Mahler and he promoted both American composers and Dutch music. During his first performance in America, in 1905, he conducted masterpieces from the canon of classical music.[1] It took another fifteen years before he returned to New York, where he spent half a season during each of the next ten years.

During the same period America's influence on the classical music experience in the Netherlands remained negligible. This lack of an American presence can be explained by the fact that there already was a culture of classical music — concentrated in Amsterdam — that could measure up to the other great cities of the world. The interpretation of American music — music by composers living in the U.S. — was not a part of that culture. Works by George Gershwin and Aaron Copland, for example, were not played by the Concertgebouw Orchestra until long after World War II. American jazz and spirituals were wildly popular, but both genres are outside the scope of this essay. Nevertheless, it is worth noting that Willem Mengelberg and Georg Schneevoigt, the conductor of the (The Hague) Residentie Orchestra, were practically the only ones among "classically schooled musicians" who were truly enthusiastic when Paul Whiteman's orchestra came to the Netherlands for three concerts in the summer of 1926.

European Prestige

Because of their status, leading American orchestras (New York, Philadelphia, Boston) were able to attract numerous European musicians, who in fact dominated these orchestras. This trend was facilitated by the preference shown by conductors such as Willem Mengelberg and Arturo Toscanini for hiring musicians they knew from Europe. American musicians had to earn European prestige. Spending time in cities of note like London, Paris, or Berlin was certainly a great advantage. "Europeanizing" one's name could also be beneficial. Around 1900, a young, Paris-trained pianist from Texas by the name of Lucy Hickenlooper was warned by an influential impresario: "If you played like Liszt and Rubinstein rolled into one, I could do nothing for you without European notices."[2] Lucy changed her name to Olga Samaroff (1882–1948) and went down in music history as a great American pianist.

Classical music composed in America had little influence on the development of American culture while music of current or popular interest in Europe was quickly adopted instead — for example the music of composers such as Richard Wagner. Yet, after 1920 interest in American composers began to grow thanks to the efforts of a number of European conductors, including Bruno Walter, Willem Mengelberg, Frits Busch, and Arturo Toscanini.

Dutch Music and Dutch Musicians in America

Music by Dutch composers or other composers living in the Netherlands can best be categorized as insignificant when considered in an international scope. Of all Dutch composers, only Jan Pieterszoon Sweelinck (1562–1621) received some international recognition in the twentieth century. The 1951 publication

3

—

THE
PERIOD
OF
THE
WORLD
WARS

1914-1945

of *The American Symphony Orchestra* contains a survey of European music that was influential in America; Dutch music is not represented at all.[3] Willem Mengelberg's efforts to introduce Dutch music in New York had been doomed to failure.

European immigrant population concentrations in urban America were able to meet ethnic musical needs. New York City's Stadttheater primarily staged German operas. The Russian Symphony Orchestra Society was established in New York in 1904 to advance Russian musical culture. It did so by introducing, for example, the pianists Sergei Rachmaninoff, Alexandr Scriabin, and Joseph Lhévine, as well as the violinist Mischa Elman, all of whom went on to acquire worldwide fame.

Dutch immigrant communities lacked both the size and the musical tradition to be able to follow these examples. Nevertheless, quite a few Dutch musicians came to America between 1850 and 1940. Some stayed, others were on concert tours. They added luster both to the musical culture and to the land of their birth. Louis Victor Saar (1868–1937) was born in Rotterdam and educated in Germany. In America, he was associated with the Metropolitan Opera, the National Conservatory, and the College of Music in New York. Bernard Wagenaar (1894–1971) left the Netherlands in 1921 and found work with the New York Philharmonic Orchestra. Wagenaar is mentioned in a number of American surveys of music in which he is considered an American composer.[4] John Broekhoven (1852–1930) was born in the Dutch town of Beek and taught counterpoint at the College of Music in Cincinatti.[5] Hans Kindler (1892–1949) came from Rotterdam. He became the solo cellist of the Philadelphia Orchestra in 1914 and founded the National Symphony Orchestra (NSO) in 1931. Willem van Hoogstraten (1884–1965; violinist and conductor) was born in Utrecht. He was the conductor of the New York Philharmonic's summer concerts in Lewisohn Stadium from 1922 to 1939, and also served as associate conductor in the orchestra's regular season from 1923 to 1925. Van Hoogstraten conducted the New York Philharmonic's concerts in the period between Josef Stransky and Willem Mengelberg. He also was the conductor of the Portland Symphony Orchestra in Oregon from 1925 to 1937.

This brief summary shows that many musicians assimilated; their national origins were no longer important. Van Hoogstraten alone returned to Europe regularly, making him one of those musicians who were quite successful in the U.S., whether on tour or engaged by the great opera houses. Two others in this category were Anton van Rooy and Jacques Urlus. The world-famous Dutch baritone Van Rooy (1870–1932) sang with the Metropolitan Opera in New York from 1898 until 1908. He was involved in the first American production of Wagner's opera *Parsifal* in December 1903 (conducted by Alfred Hertz) and also sang in the first U.S. performance of Richard Strauss's opera *Salomé* in January 1907 (two years after the world premiere in Dresden). Jacques Urlus (1867–1935) was one of the most famous Dutch tenors. In 1912 he went on tour to New York and Boston, and the following year he performed with the Metropolitan Opera under Toscanini. He sang in New York every year until 1917. In 1923–24 he went on yet another American tour, this time with a German opera company.[6]

Willem Mengelberg in New York

The most famous Dutch musician in America was, without doubt, Willem Mengelberg. He was born in Utrecht, but his parents were of German descent and he spent part of his studies at the Cologne Conservatory. Once Mengelberg became chief conductor of the Amsterdam Concertgebouw Orchestra in 1895, he quickly turned it into one of Europe's leading ensembles. He attracted top international musicians to perform with the orchestra, including the conductors Richard Strauss, Gustav Mahler, and Arthur Nikisch, soloists such as the pianists Feruccio Busoni and Sergei Rachmaninoff, and the violinists Fritz Kreisler and Jacques Tibaud. Mengelberg's efforts turned Amsterdam into a musical city of international renown. He was also able to provide composers with a podium where they could present their new music to the world: in addition to Strauss, Mahler, and Busoni, these included Schönberg and Reger, to name but a few. In 1920 Mengelberg celebrated his twenty-fifth anniversary with the orchestra. To commemorate the event, he conducted Mahler's entire symphonic oeuvre in less than fourteen days, a feat that caused an international stir.

In November 1905 Mengelberg conducted for the first time the orchestra of the Philharmonic Society, in New York's Carnegie Hall. Starting in 1921, he conducted the second half of the National Symphony Orchestra's season. S.A.M. Bottenheim, who occasionally served as Mengelberg's private secretary, was partly responsible for convincing him to consider the appointment in New York. The disastrous political and economic situation in Germany provided Mengelberg with enough reason to end his work in Frankfurt, where he conducted from 1908 to 1920, and seek out new challenges in America. He made up his mind and left for America in January 1921. (Several years before, his colleagues and friends Richard Strauss and Gustav Mahler — the latter had worked for a number of years in New York — had already discussed the wisdom of a move with him.)

Accompanied by the ship's jazz band, the first-class passengers (including Mrs. R.A.D. Cort van der Linden, who penned the poem below) on board his ship sang to him and he even received a welcome wreath from a little girl dressed in a traditional Dutch costume. One thing was clear: this son of the Kingdom of the Netherlands was coming to conquer America.

489

Here comes the Conqueror
His name's on every tongue
Into America
He comes like none have done

The honour of a Kingdom
That of a gracious Queen
A Diplomatic Mission
Upon his right arm leans

He's conquered all Europa
From near and far he's hailed
He's brought men near to heaven
When everyone has failed

And when they hear the Conqueror
They'll bow and ever say
That Mengelberg's a DANDY
And shout hurray!!! hurray!!!

Mengelberg was facing a great challenge: he had to introduce himself to America as a representative of the culture of the Netherlands, but even more so as a celebrated conductor with experience throughout the countries of Europe. Many European musicians of international acclaim had preceded him. At the end of his first season he wrote, without much humility: "I have won. I am now number one in America too. And across from me were Toscanini with his Scala Orchestra, Stokowsky from Philadelphia, etc. Truly great conductors."[7] Two Dutch daily papers, the *Nieuwe Rotterdamsche Courant* and *De Telegraaf*, kept a close watch on him and regularly reported on his exploits in America.

The conductor received a great deal of attention and praise from the American press after his first concerts. *The Standard* expressed amazement at his "control over the musicians that has been acquired in a surprisingly short time." The *New York World* called him "a great conductor." The *New York Evening Post* wrote that Mengelberg's talent could be compared to that of great names like Arthur Nikisch and Felix Weingartner. The critic Max Smith (a friend of Arturo Toscanini's) wrote: "No other conductor in recent years, save Toscanini, who is in a class by himself, has achieved such notable results as Mr. Mengelberg on this occasion. ... It now remains to be seen whether the public will stand by a

491

◄ Willem Mengelberg receiving his honorary doctorate from Columbia University, 1929.

3

—

THE
PERIOD
OF
THE
WORLD
WARS

1914–1945

musician of Mengelberg's calibre, a musician whose coming ought to be hailed with hosannas." The press could hardly be more enthusiastic.[8]

America welcomed Mengelberg as one of those great European conductors who came from a long and rich tradition. He was well known in America for his curious interest in the music of Mahler. His energetic and nearly perfect interpretations, though often a bit unorthodox, always caught the public's eye and ear. His engagement with the NSO was an attempt to revive the orchestra, which had been suffering recently. After Mengelberg's appointment, the orchestra's board quickly came to the conclusion that the effort was a success from an artistic point of view, albeit that ticket sales and hence the general financial situation failed to improve. It was clear, though, that Mengelberg was able to train the orchestra, which initially was mediocre, and turn it into a successful ensemble in just three months.

The orchestra's financial situation nevertheless became so dramatic that it was decided to merge Mengelberg's NSO with the orchestra of the Philharmonic Society, which had reached a state of perfection under Josef Stransky, according to the press. Mengelberg looked at the bright side of the situation and said to journalists: "I told them I wished to make it a new Philharmonic, a bigger and better band than New York has ever heard."[9] The result was that an impressive 70 percent of the NSO members remained, while only 30 members of the Philharmonic retained their chairs. The new orchestra took the old Philharmonic Orchestra's name and was expanded to 120 musicians. According to Howard Shanet, the chronicler of the New York Philharmonic, Mengelberg turned the Philharmonic into a completely new orchestra in just a couple of years.[10]

Programming: Mahler

Mengelberg's programming choices in New York were the same as his choices elsewhere: they were based on his personal preferences. In 1922, however, it was decided that Lawrence Gilman would have to approve Mengelberg's programs on behalf of the board. This decision resulted from the fact that the board was often at odds with Mengelberg's choices. Ticket sales and cost containment played an important role. Some pieces required extra expenditures, such as the cost involved in hiring extra musicians to cover all the parts, and healthy finances were essential to the orchestra's survival. Mengelberg's attempts to program as much Mahler as possible led to tensions with the board, which discouraged performances of his music due to the overwhelmingly negative press. In October 1922 Gilman wrote to Clarence Mackay, chairman of the board of the New York Philharmonic Society: "I am glad to be able to report that Mr. Mengelberg has kept his Mahleritis under such heroic control."[11]

The critics' enthusiasm pertained especially to the promise and progress the orchestra was showing, not to its programming. During Mengelberg's second and fourth concerts in New York, on January 13 and 15, 1921, Mahler's First Symphony failed to garner any positive reactions. This lack of appreciation was not due to unfamiliarity with his music; rather, people simply did not want to hear it. The First Symphony had been performed less than a month earlier, on December 31, by Joseph Stransky and the Philharmonic Society Orchestra, and would be played again on January 20. Nevertheless, the American press shared a common sentiment with regard to Mahler's music: "for the most part a bore," wrote the *New York Tribune*. The *World* found the piece to be interminably long. The German-language *New York Staatszeitung* stood alone in its enthusiasm. In spite of the cool response to Mahler's music in New York, Mengelberg's performances received more positive reviews, generally speaking, than those of Stransky, and Mengelberg's valiant efforts to promote Mahler were enough reason for the critic of the *Musical Leader* to write that the music "deserves a place in current orchestral repertory."[12]

The newspapers gave Mengelberg plenty of opportunity to express his views. Regarding his plans for New York, he said: "I wish I could give all the symphonies of Mahler in New York. ... it has become one of the international musical centres. Once we thought Paris the only centre. Then we added Berlin and London. Now we count in New York, and Amsterdam, too. ... I hope I can convince you some time that a Mahler score is intelligible in every note. I admit, you see, that Mahler is difficult, but I hold nevertheless that he wrote with perfect clearness and that he had a great variety of things to say."[13] Considering the poor reviews, however, we must conclude that Mengelberg's statements failed to have much impact at all. He conducted the Fourth Symphony in February, 1921. The majority of New York music critics were unimpressed. Writing in the *Tribune*, Henry Krehbiel, Mahler's strongest critic, summarized his antipathy toward the music thus: "No; we cannot accept Mahler as a great symphonist, despite the passing moments of beauty which his works offer. As a melodist he is sometimes ingratiating, because of his reflection of folk tune; as a harmonist he is frequently labored and unnatural; as a writer for orchestral instruments he is often ingenious and delightful; as an architect he seems without sense of symmetry, proportion or coherency — or, at least, indifferent to these qualities which are essential in every art."[14] Yet, Mengelberg did exactly as he had promised: he devoted a part of each season to attempting to win over the New York audience for Mahler, the composer who had once been engaged as conductor of the orchestra of the Philharmonic Society. By performing one piece per season on average Mengelberg introduced Mahler's oeuvre to New York, and although he did not have the honor of being the first proponent of Mahler's music, he was without doubt the composer's most fervent advocate in New York.

3

———

THE
PERIOD
OF
THE
WORLD
WARS

1914–1945

American Composers

Mengelberg was more than just a proponent of Mahler. He also performed music by American composers during his first season in New York, and he did so with greater frequency starting in 1926 when Arturo Toscanini (1867–1957) joined the orchestra. Ernst Bloch (1880–1959) was one of the composers whom Mengelberg quickly got to know in America and whose compositions he immediately appreciated. Bloch's name was mentioned to him upon his arrival in New York. It was Bloch himself, however, who took the initiative and managed to gain access to Mengelberg's hotel suite. Bottenheim later recalled: "Mengelberg was touched by Bloch's pluck and was thrilled that Bloch had come to see him. He listened to what this gifted artist — who was much younger — had to say. He immediately became friends with the composer, whose oeuvre had thus far been unknown to him."[15] A couple of weeks later, in February 1921, Mengelberg conducted Bloch's *Schelomo* for cello and orchestra. The solo was played by the orchestra's Dutch solo cellist, Cornelis van Vliet. In a January 1921 interview with *Musical America*, Mengelberg called Bloch and Charles M. Loeffler true representatives of the American school of composition.[16]

Dutch Music

Mengelberg tried to introduce Dutch music to the audiences in New York a number of times. Critics were utterly unimpressed by this music that Mengelberg apparently held in such high regard. He conducted the New York premiere of the overture to *Cyrano de Bergerac* by Johan Wagenaar on February 24, 1921. In an interview Mengelberg said that Wagenaar was part of the Dutch "promising school of young composers," along with Bernard Zweers, Alphons Diepenbrock, Cornelis Dopper, Gerard von Brucken Fock, Willem Pijper, and Henri van Goudoever.[17] He was stretching things a bit, for Zweers was born in 1854, Wagenaar and Diepenbrock in 1862, Dopper in 1870, and Von Brucken Fock in 1859. The only true members of a young generation were Pijper, born in 1894, and Van Goudoever, born in 1898. The *New York World* called Wagenaar's work a "soso composition, moving at a leisurely gait and easy to listen to." Mengelberg tried again with the overture to *De Getemde Feeks* (*The Taming of the Shrew*) by Wagenaar, but the press was equally unenthusiastic. In 1922 he introduced music by Diepenbrock (overture to *De Vogels* [*The Birds*]), Dopper (*Ciaconna Gotica*), and Van Goudoever (Suite for Cello and Orchestra). "Falling Hollanders … of such dullness … the three misfits," wrote one critic.[18] The American composer Deems Taylor wrote in the *New York World*: "Mr. Mengelberg played three Dutch compositions that triumphantly refuted the oft repeated assertion that Americans write the feeblest music in the world." Diepenbrock's "amiable" music received the mildest press. Van Goudoever's music was treated especially harshly. It was called music in the style of Victor Herbert and unworthy of the merits of the Philharmonic. Every critic was convinced that modern Dutch music could safely be ignored if Mengelberg's choice of works was representative of the state of the art in the Netherlands. Mengelberg remained unmoved. He continued his performances of Dutch music: the *Piet Hein Rhapsodie* by Peter van Anrooy in 1923, the *Symphonische Elegie* by Rudolf Mengelberg in 1925, Julius Röntgen's *Old Dutch Dances* in 1926, Von Brucken Fock's *Impressions du Midi* in 1927, and Wagenaar's *Taming of the Shrew* and Dopper's *Ciaconna Gotica* in reprise, also in 1927.

Conclusion

The Dutch contribution to American musical culture was limited. There were but a few Dutch musicians who stood out in the context of the American musical experience and Willem Mengelberg was the most noteworthy among them. He made a name for himself through his efforts to improve the orchestras of New York so that they would match the competencies of the world's leading ensembles. His performances were thoroughly rehearsed and highly professional.

1   Frits Zwart, *Willem Mengelberg (1871–1951). Een biografie 1871–1920* (Amsterdam: Prometheus, 1999), 174-181.

2   David Ewen, *Music Comes to America* (New York: Allen, Towne and Heath, 1947), 68.

3   John H. Mueller, *The American Symphony Orchestra: A Social History of Musical Taste* (Bloomington: Indiana University Press, 1951), chapter 5, "National Sources of Orchestral Repertoire," 253-285.

4   Claire R. Reis, *Composers in America* (New York: Macmillan, 1947), and Nicolas Slonimsky, *Music since 1900* (London: Dent, 1937).

5   Earl Chateau, *Histoire de la musique symphonique aux Etats-Unis* (Strasbourg: Librairie Universitaire d'Alsace, 1933), 106.

6   J. Urlus, *Mijn loopbaan* (Amsterdam: Van Holkema en Warendorf, 1929).

7   Mengelberg to Mrs. Oyens, letter of March 28, 1921, Mengelberg Archive (MA), Netherlands Music Institute (NMI), The Hague.

8   *The Sun,* January [?], 1921; *The Musical Courier,* January 20, 1921; *The Standard,* January 17, 1921; *New York World,* January 12, 1921; *New York Evening World,* January 12, 1921; *The New York American,* January 14, 1921; *Evening Post,* March 23, 1921.

9   *Evening Post,* March 23, 1921.

3

━━━━

THE
PERIOD
OF
THE
WORLD
WARS

1914-1945

10 Howard Shanet, *Philharmonic: A History of New York's Orchestra* (New York: Doubleday, 1975), 246-247.

11 Lawrence Gilman to Clarence Mackay, letter of October 17, 1922, New York Philharmonic Archives.

12 *New York Tribune*, January 14, 1921; *Brooklyn Eagle*, January 14, 1921; *New York Staatszeitung*, January 14, 1921; *Musical Leader*, January 27, 1921.

13 *Christian Science Monitor*, January 8, 1921.

14 *Tribune*, February 9, 1921.

15 S.A.M. Bottenheim, "Autobiografie," 127, unpublished manuscript, NMI.

16 *Musical America*, January 15, 1921. Mengelberg performed works by other American composers, including S. Bucharoff, J.Ph. Dunn, P. Ferroud, P. Gallico, S. Gardner, R. Goldmark, H. Hadley, H. Hanson, A. Loeffler, E. Macdowell, J. Powell, V. Rieti, E. Schelling, J. Deems Taylor, and E. Withorne.

17 *Musical America*, January 15, 1921.

18 *Brooklyn Eagle*, March 31, 1922.

THE INTRODUCTION OF JAZZ IN THE NETHERLANDS

——

KEES WOUTERS

When the United States entered World War I in 1917, pianist and bandleader James Reese Europe was awarded the army rank of lieutenant and given the task of forming an orchestra to play for the troops overseas. In February and March 1918, he traveled some two thousand miles through France and performed in over twenty cities. Both the troops and the civilian population went crazy over Jim Europe and his all-black 369th Infantry Band, better known as the Hell Fighters. Apart from the usual marches, classic overtures, and Sousa's "Stars and Stripes Forever," they played rags and tunes like the "Memphis Blues" in full swing and, what's more, their music became known under a new label: jazz. Thanks to the Hell Fighters and other military bands such as Lt. Will Vodery's brass band and Lt. Tim Brymn's seventy Black Devils, France became the starting point for jazz in Europe.

Initially the Dutch, who did not participate in World War I, were kept in the dark. In 1918, they were still unfamiliar with the word "jazz," but this changed in 1919 when at various dance schools "Jes," "Jas," or "Yasz" was introduced as a new American dance. In 1920, the English orchestra The London Five played in The Hague and in that same year Amsterdam dance instructor James Meyer founded the first Dutch professional jazz ensemble, James Meyer's Jazzband, under the direction of pianist Leo de la Fuente. A year earlier, Meyer had traveled to England to seek inspiration in the modern ballrooms.[1] Through his orchestra, and especially through the BBC radio programs broadcast from the Savoy Hotel in London, the English ballroom dances became popular in the Netherlands. And when, starting in 1919, the first American dance records became available, the American ragtimes became a great success as well. A postwar dance craze erupted with great intensity. The reveling public was in an electrified mood. Fed up with the Wiener Damenkapelle, the salon orchestras, and the

3

———

THE
PERIOD
OF
THE
WORLD
WARS

1914–1945

melodies of Johann Strauss and Franz Léhar, the public demanded "jazz" music. Instead of "Tango Tea" at Pschorr in Rotterdam, people wanted to dance. One fashionable dance after another was introduced: the shimmy, the Charleston, the Black Bottom. Pschorr was rebuilt into a mecca for dancers and a six-foot replica of the Statue of Liberty, under the banner "Welcome to New York," formed part of the décor.[2] String sections added a drum equipped with a horn and an enamel pan, which was enough to qualify as a jazz band in those days. But this did not last very long. To alleviate the absence of a horn section, saxophonists, clarinetists, and trumpet players were recruited from military bands. Older musicians, string players, and pianists received remedial training in various wind instruments. For those who could make the transition from Suppé to "Alexander's Ragtime Band" and from violin to saxophone, there was plenty of opportunity to work.

This was especially the case for the younger generation who formed their own jazz ensembles. In 1924, the Original Victoria Band was founded in Breda under the direction of Theo Abels and two years later The Original Ramblers, with Jack and Louis de Vries, Theo Uden Masman, and Kees Kranenburg, first appeared. The brothers Willebrandts formed their orchestra in 1929. Amateur jazz practice took place especially in the more affluent quarters of society, notably the student world. Here English was spoken and enough money was available to buy records and expensive musical instruments. At many a university or grammar school one could hear the sounds of a school band. In Leiden, for instance, the fraternity orchestra Minerva was founded in 1925, and in Wageningen students of the Agricultural College were united in the Ceresband. Beginning in 1924, The Queen Melodists, a combination of well-to-do citizens and students with Theo Uden Masman and later on Melle Weersma at the piano, played in The Hague.

The arrival of American music caused much consternation among different groups in society. The enthusiasm of the often young jazz fans contrasted with the reserved attitude of especially the older generations. Yet despite all the criticism and obstacles, various societal and technological developments made it impossible to stop the Americanization of entertainment music in the Netherlands.

The Anti-Jazz Party

During the first postwar years the daily press hardly paid any attention to jazz music. This changed when in the summer of 1926 the American orchestra of Paul Whiteman came to the Netherlands. Its three concerts — two in the Kurhaus in Scheveningen and one in the Amsterdam Concertgebouw — had long been sold

Interior of dancing Pschorr at the Coolsingel in Rotterdam.

3

—

THE
PERIOD
OF
THE
WORLD
WARS

1914–1945

out and received generally ecstatic responses. The daily newspaper *De Maasbode* wrote, "Here jazz enters into a spiritual entente with the old world." "Unquestionably astonishing," wrote the *Nieuwe Rotterdamsche Courant,* "a delightful and colorful polytonal movie in sound." The newspaper *Het Vaderland* recognized in the orchestra a "Mengelberg-like ensemble ... a beautiful organism, in which each link acted in a perfect way. In the full strength of this ensemble one finds a dash of daring, a dash of humor, a dash of the glowing beauty of a tiger."[3]

The symphonic jazz of Whiteman (*Rhapsody in Blue*), interchanged with syncopic dance music and jazz-like arrangements of composers like Liszt and Wagner, was more in line with the European music vocabulary than the polyrhythm of the Original Dixieland Jazz Band (ODJB) from America, which introduced the improvised "classical jazz" in Europe during its visit to England in 1919. It looked as if with Whiteman's performance jazz music had suddenly become respectable.

Many classical composers and musicians, however, regarded the new music as a barbaric invasion, a threat to art. As carriers of the centuries-old musical tradition of the Western world they felt a responsibility to raise their voice against the invading, improvising competition. In the October 1926 issue of *De Muziek,* the official organ of the Federation of Dutch Musicians Organizations, composer and music critic Matthijs Vermeulen wrote: "Jazz is rubbish and a caricature of the modern orchestra, the orchestra of Debussy, Strauss, Mahler, Schoenberg; garbage arranged by half-grown musicians for the purpose and accommodation of public frolic. And do not think to reverse the roles! Whoever thinks that his instrumentation can benefit from jazz is twenty years behind in the evolution of music."[4] Composer Willem Pijper fully agreed with him: "Vermeulen put his finger on it excellently: 'old garbage scraped together from all pre-war dumps.'"[5]

Such criticism of jazz often concealed fear and dissatisfaction with postwar societal changes. This is quite obvious in the article "Jazz," which Karel Mengelberg, a student of Willem Pijper's, wrote in October 1927: "When people realized how hollow their nationalistic and moralistic phrases were, as the troops returned from the battlefields and the tanks of the revolutionaries rolled through the streets of the metropoles, jazz began, licentious, without a 'general music theory,' wild and loud. In overcrowded pubs jazz bands roared without interruption. Negroes, who from a musical point of view were equally animalistic and licentious, set the tone — in the literal sense of the word. We believe, however, that people will soon grow tired of this 'syncopated parade march.' In secret many actually curse jazz, but in the struggle with the syncopated spirit of the age, they end up losing in most cases."[6]

For many, World War I had raised doubts about the supremacy of Western civilization. All of a sudden, traditional values and faith in progress no longer went unquestioned. In addition to cultural pessimism and uncertainty, people became acquainted with a new, unknown American culture, with the Charleston, the Black Bottom, the foxtrot, and with jazz music.

At first, jazz in the style of King Oliver and the ODJB was heard and performed only in a small circle of connoisseurs, but the new dances quickly became popular with a much broader audience. Whereas the aforementioned representatives of the classical music world felt particularly threatened by the arrival of jazz music, educators, ministers, and youth leaders were above all opposed to the modern American dances. They considered the dance hall a breeding place for spiritual decay, symptomatic of a degenerated, disoriented society, where traditional value systems as presented by the Christian churches or socialism, had lost their influence.

According to socialist crusaders against moral decline, jazz and the quick-step formed part of a bourgeois pseudocivilization. On the occasion of Whiteman's performance, music critic Paul F. Sanders wrote in the socialist daily *Het Volk* of June 24, 1926, of "a thoroughly American evening." Among all appreciative reviews, he was the only one to cast a negative judgment. He regarded "the sexual atmosphere in the music" as an expression of a barbaric culture: "triumph of technique, a narcotic for exhausted businessmen, who seek a brainless diversion." The members of the Arbeiders Jeugd Centrale (the largest socialist youth organization) also went to battle. They too, instead of fighting the class enemy, began a campaign against the "easygoing pleasure seekers of our civilization in decay." In countless booklets, brochures, and pamphlets the spokesmen for the AJC condemned banal talking, loitering in smoky cafés, superficial flirting, smoking, drinking, and going to sultry dance halls. Instead of doing step and shuffle dances, people should be out folk dancing.[7]

In their denunciations Catholics sometimes reached quasi-poetic heights. In his 1927 pastoral Lenten letter the bishop of 's-Hertogenbosch, Monsignor Diepen, warned in what was still a calm tone against "the new paganism," with "its widespread modern dances." A year later, however, jazz was according to priests in the city of Utrecht "frivolous, indeed passionate dance music ... intended to bring the dancers into an intoxicated state of sensuality. ... Certainly we do not exaggerate when we maintain that our modern pagan dances are an abyss of sin. Where people dance, men become dazed and women encounter their downfall; one cannot dance on earth and one day enjoy the blessings of heaven."[8] In the educational brochure series entitled "For Honor and Virtue," we find the answer to the question: "Where have people learned the new dances? People have learned them from savage tribes. They dance like Kaffirs, waggling and wobbling like geese."[9]

The Protestant population was also admonished. In "Many questions-one answer," an educational publication from the 1930s, the dangers of gymnastics

501

3

—

THE
PERIOD
OF
THE
WORLD
WARS

1914–1945

were discussed: " … it looks a lot like dancing … and we do not want anything to do with dancing. Thank goodness Christian virtue still resists this."[10]

A similar attitude with regard to dancing and jazz could be detected among the Dutch national socialists. In *De Stormmeeuw,* the monthly magazine of the Nationale Jeugdstorm, one finds the same calls for character building and the same rejection of youths who have succumbed to the lure of mass culture (smoking, jazz, and makeup) as in the brochures and pamphlets of all the other youth organizations. During a membership drive in November 1934, the *stormers* addressed: "the youth for which Holland is waiting. Not the youth that is already written off. Those who have become old through jazz, and grey due to cocktails."[11]

National socialists, composers and musicians of classical music, Protestants, Roman Catholics, and reds, all cursed the arrival of the new American entertainment culture. Their moral indignation reverberated throughout the press. While most Dutch reporters had an open mind toward the new music of Paul Whiteman in June 1926, soon moral judgments and tendentious reviews gained the upper hand. A report on modern dancing in the *Haagsch Maandblad* of January 1927 observed with dismay that the dance pairs executed all kinds of motions "of which the origin lies in the erotic, maddening arousal of barbaric Negro tribes and wherein brute primal instincts of both sexes attempt to celebrate themselves."[12]

The Society for the Advancement of Good and Inexpensive Reading Material even went so far as to publish a travel account under the title "the raging saxophone." A fragment reads: "A few shrill, shrieking tones of the trumpet, a highpitched cry of distress of the saxophone, and then … through the open space of the hall shook and vibrated the bodies of the men dressed in smokings and the slim frames of the women … in their eyes lay something of the primal desire, of the primal instinct: the mating craze. And the five shiny black magicians filled the aristocratic party hall with an infernal, pagan rhythm."[13]

Time and again, jazz music and modern dances were associated with barbarism, primitive, primal instincts, and eroticism. The entertainment industry responded to this negative portrayal by imposing restrictions on the appearance and behavior of the musicians. During a concert both professionals and amateurs had to behave in an exemplary manner. Dress, hairstyle, presentation, everything had to be flawless to guarantee a respectable and civilized impression. After all, critics of all persuasions were lying in wait and therefore dance hall and bar owners kept a watchful eye to make sure that, despite the arrival of the new music, decency was maintained, if only for appearances' sake. No excessive drinking, no provocative hot dance music, for the slightest jarring note was enough to alarm the police and to risk losing one's license to sell liquor or have live music.

Despite these precautions, intervention at a national level followed anyhow. At the initiative of the Tucht-Unie (Discipline Union), an organization committed by its statutes "…to fight licentiousness and to beautify public life," a "committee concerning public entertainment" was installed, which in 1927 requested governmental action against modern dancing. The Discipline Union's paper, *de Gong,* warned those youngsters who succumbed to "dances originating with wild Negro tribes. It should be made clear that all these perverse gyrations, all this shuffling back and forth and jerking and shaking and twisting and licking one's lips quasi-gracefully and messing and wrangling, all this leads towards the forbidden act."[14]

The request was met and in 1930 a government commission was installed, which one year later presented a final rapport. The modern dances constituted a moral threat to young people, so the conclusion went. "Demoralization has penetrated from all countries involved in the war. Its ways of expression however, are mainly American." Jazz music and swing dances from the United States mirrored the superficiality of American social life. As the most important cause for this development the committee mentioned advanced mechanization and the division of labor, which had led to "the impoverishment of life and extremely superficial contacts with fellow human beings," all this at the expense of older organic structures like family, school, and church. "In such an incoherent mass as the American one, union has to be achieved in the instinctual realm and this is what determines the essence of American culture, a mass product, whether one tries to find it in the daily press, in music, or in film." "Negroes" set the tone and rhythm in American music, because they disposed of the greatest instinctual energy. There was a "contagious enjoyment of life," suited preeminently to create a daze in which it was easy to live for those for whom a deeper consciousness of life was too difficult. The committee saw in all this an enormous danger against which Europe should arm itself. It noted in Western Europe a decline of "a life of deeper meaning" toward a "life of primitive stimuli" and warned against those who cherished American "libertarianism" and who promoted the "Americanization of Europe." America was depicted as a naive country where, with primitive means such as "cries" and "yells" and raising the Stars and Stripes, an artificial kind of national enthusiasm was being aroused. "Those who in Europe pluck the strings of the instinctual life in the mode of American 'culture' without being able to provide a union, will only create one piece of confusion out of Europe, in which war, and civil war shall give expression to fierce whipped-up instincts."[15]

3

———

THE
PERIOD
OF
THE
WORLD
WARS

1914-1945

Fans and Musicians

Both in the government committee's report and in the responses from the classical music world, the churches, and the press, fear of an American mass culture to which domestic norms and values would be sacrificed, dominated. The counterpart of this camp of cultural pessimists was a rich tapestry of jazz and swing fans. They were to be found among intellectuals and cultural avant-gardists such as Piet Mondriaan and Theo van Doesburg, both members of the Stijl group. The hard core, however, consisted of a small group of primarily male grammar school, *gymnasium,* and university students of middle-class origin who, through gramophone-record-listening sessions, lectures, study sessions, and self-made music, dedicated all their free time to jazz.

At the Kennemer Lyceum in Overveen drummer Eddy Crommelin, together with a couple of school friends, decided to follow Belgian and French examples and founded a Dutch Hot Club (NHC) in 1932. Soon after starting in Haarlem, NHC branches appeared in Amsterdam, Nijmegen, Utrecht, Den Helder, and The Hague. These different branches were united in the Dutch Jazz League (NJL) and closely related to *De Jazzwereld* in which all NJL news was published. *De Jazzwereld* was a monthly magazine, founded in 1931 by Ben Bakema, better known as Red Debroy, who at that time was only sixteen years of age and played the alto in the Kennemer Lyceum band. The first edition came out in August and proved to be a great success. Every month the subscribers were kept up to date about the latest records and in a regional survey the whole national jazz landscape, from Heiloo to Valkenburg and from Groningen to Bergen op Zoom, was accurately mapped out.

The 1930s witnessed a tremendous increase in export of American and English music. As a result of the steadily growing number of households with a radio and the availability of better and less expensive record players, more people than ever before came into contact with jazz and especially its popular variant: swing. Soon various broadcasting companies employed permanent radio orchestras. The year 1935 saw the formation of the AVRO Decibels under the direction of Eddy Meenk, with Sem Nijveen, Maurice van Kleef, and arranger Klaas van Beeck. A year later The Ramblers formed the VARA Dance Orchestra. In 1935 the VARA organized its first Jazz Week with, among others, the Jack de Vries Internationals and record programs presented by the two *Jazzwereld* editors, Bob Schrijver and Mr. C. Poustochkine. Afraid of losing members, the Dutch broadcasting organizations were careful not to program all-too-controversial hot jazz, because this style was not appreciated by the broader audience. Therefore, the radio orchestras played in the more modest, polished English big band style, which was sometimes even interchanged with waltzes and ballroom

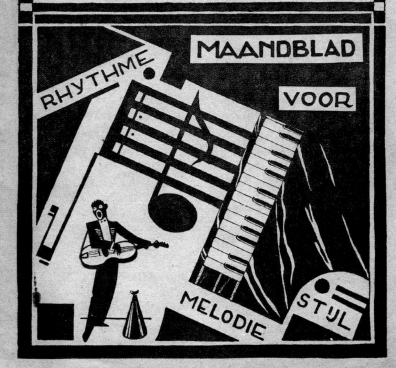

Cover of the monthly *De Jazzwereld*.

3

———

THE
PERIOD
OF
THE
WORLD
WARS

1914–1945

tunes (John Kristel), or with a mixture of cabaret songs and Dutch clog dances (Boyd Bachman). Nevertheless, the musicians themselves generally favored the American arrangements. Ernst van 't Hoff, Dick Willebrandts, Melle Weersma, Jack de Vries and The Ramblers all preferred the American repertoire.

Through radio broadcasts and guest performances of American musicians, this American jazz repertoire reached the Dutch public directly, unfiltered by European arrangements. Duke Ellington and his orchestra played the Scheveningen Kurhaus in July, 1933, featuring Cooty Williams and Johnny Hodges. That same year in November Louis Armstrong gave two concerts in the Netherlands, and in 1934 he came again, as did Cab Calloway and his orchestra. Willy Lewis, Benny Carter, Arthur Briggs, and Bill Coleman regularly returned as guests. In 1935, Coleman Hawkins was touring with Jack Hylton's English orchestra when the Nazis refused him entry into Germany because of the color of his skin. He stayed behind in the Netherlands and in the following years he often performed with The Ramblers, appearing as guest soloist. Together with drummer Maurice van Kleef and American pianist Freddy Johnson, who worked in the Netherlands from 1934 onward, he made numerous recordings. Their concerts were frequently broadcast by the VARA and AVRO radio broadcasting organizations. Furthermore one could hear the orchestras of Stan Brenders, Fud Candrix, and Jean Omer on Belgian radio. Radio Luxembourg regularly scheduled jazz music as well. But it was the BBC that gave the English orchestras of Harry Roy, Bert Ambrose, Jack Payne, and specially Jack Hylton the greatest popularity in the Netherlands. Their smooth, polished dance music, in which the arrangements were often more important than the improvisations, struck the popular fancy most.

Swing bands in Jack Hylton's style thrived on the popularity of the new American dances from the period after World War I. These dances had originated in the black ghettos of the big American cities, but during the twenties the Federation of Dutch Dance School Teachers, following the example of their English colleagues, restyled them and made them sufficiently "respectable" to meet the taste of a large audience. The same applied to swing dancing. Soon after Charles Lindbergh's successful flight across the Atlantic in 1927, a new dance style was introduced in the Savoy Ballroom in Harlem, on which occasion the dance partners took turns throwing each other through the air, flipping around each other's hips, and tossed to and fro—all this with a stoic facial expression. These people were "cool," dancing the Lindy Hopp. The film industry, revue theaters, and night clubs in the United States recruited the Harlem hoppers or white imitators like Fred Astaire and turned the Lindy Hopp into an American export product, which during the 1930s became known on the European market under the name of its music: swing. Hollywood movies like *Dancing Lady* (1933), *Born to Dance* (1936), *Swing High Swing Low* (1937), *On the Avenue* (1938), and especially *Broadway Melody* (1936–38), all featured the tempestuous "swing." This way, both swing dancing and swing music gained enormous popularity, particularly among the young.

The average age of the audience in the big-city dance halls was slightly over twenty, but during jazz concerts in local bars, at school parties, or in private clubs, such as The Wanderers Hotclub in The Hague where the *swing nozems* acted like madmen on the dance floor, most visitors were considerably younger. Generally, girls dominated the dance floor. During concerts or gramophone-record-listening sessions, when there was no opportunity for dancing, the audience consisted mainly of boys.

The fact that during the 1930s jazz and especially swing dancing were continuously discredited and equated with moral corruption, cultural barbarism, and the mores of uncontrolled, primitive Negro tribes, eventually created considerable confusion. This was especially the case among the jazz fans in the NJL and among the young editors of *De Jazzwereld*. Many of them could not separate themselves from the moralizing tutelage of the established authorities. When push came to shove, they did not have the courage to break with the adults and in their quest for self-justification and recognition they often resorted to a defensive posture. The vast majority of the young, however, listened carefree to The Ramblers, the Swing-Papa's, or Jack Hylton's orchestra. It was the popular dance music of the 1930s and 1940s which, through the new media, reached an unprecedented number of people.

Since the 1920s the critique of jazz and swing music had been dominated by a feeling of cultural superiority. That feeling was expressed in moral terms, which revealed in particular a fear of the unknown, the primitive, and the erotic. The United States' role in World War II led to a radical revision of this "primitive America" image. Jazz was no longer a primitive cultural expression of an uncivilized, naive people, but the music of conquerors and liberators. The old ethics of respectability suddenly had to make room for a higher moral code. Syncopes, swing, and improvisations were no longer associated with the sensations of the lower torso, but represented liberty, individualism, and vitality. By insisting on the prewar objections to jazz music, people identified themselves with the enemy, but by playing a Nat Gonella or a Benny Goodman record on a birthday party, one demonstrated that one was on the "right" side. It was a musical-political statement.

Partly because of the war the predominant view on jazz changed: its Americanness became a positive asset for many Dutchmen, but the traditional critique of jazz would nevertheless remain influential until the mid-1960s.

507

3

—

THE
PERIOD
OF
THE
WORLD
WARS

1914–1945

1 Herman Openneer, "Pianist Leo de la Fuente," *NJA Bulletin* 1 (September 1991): 4.

2 Jacques Klöters, *Honderd jaar amusement in Nederland* (The Hague: Staatsuitgeverij /Amsterdam: Unipers, 1987), 157.

3 Quotations from F.B. Hotz, "Een scheut tijger-glanzende schoonheid," *Vrij Nederland,* Color Supplement, August 2, 1986, 8. These and all subsequent Dutch quotations in this article have been translated by the author.

4 Matthijs Vermeulen, [no title], *De Muziek,* October 1926.

5 Willem Pijper, "Moderne Muziek," *De Muziek,* February 1927.

6 Karel Mengelberg, "Jazz," *De Muziek,* February 1927.

7 Ger Harmsen, *Blauwe en rode jeugd* (Nijmegen: SUN, 1975), 186-187.

8 Michel van der Plas, *Uit het rijke roomsche leven* (Utrecht: Ambo, 1965), 199, 201.

9 D.A. Linnebank, *Moderne amusements-problemen* (Roermond/Maaseik: Centraal Bureau van "Voor Eer en Deugd"/L.L. Romen & Zonen, 1934), 1.

10 A.C. de Gooyer, *Het beeld der vad'ren* (Baarn: Ambo, 1964), 187.

11 "Jeugd van Nederland," *De Stormmeeuw,* November 1934.

12 Henri Morel, *Haagsch Maandblad,* January 1927.

13 Simon Koster, *De razende saxofoon* (The Hague: N.V. Maatschappij tot Verspreiding van Goede en Goedkoope Lectuur/Wereldbibliotheek, 1931).

14 Quoted from Rudolf Dekker et al., "De vergeefse stormloop tegen zeden-verwildering en kattekwaad," *NRC Handelsblad,* May 16, 1984.

15 *Rapport der Regeerings-Commissie inzake het Dansvraagstuk* (The Hague: Staatsuitgeverij, 1931), 9-13.

THE UNITED STATES AND THE NETHERLANDS DURING THE GREAT DEPRESSION

——

JANNY DE JONG

The Great Depression of the 1930s was a crisis on a world scale. It triggered governments worldwide to intervene in their national economies. Though execution and the ideas underlying intervention certainly were not uniform, the dominant reaction was to find national solutions to problems that had an international scope. It is the aim of this essay to compare the ways in which the United States and the Netherlands tried to handle the economic crisis.

The New Deal policy that the Democratic President Franklin Roosevelt introduced, became famous and at the same time was highly controversial, in the United States as well as abroad. In the spring of 1933 Roosevelt started his first term as president. Almost at the same time the Dutch political leader Hendrikus Colijn formed his politically broad-based "crisis cabinet." In the Netherlands Colijn's name is still remembered for his conservatism and the severe economic retrenchment policy. But does that mean that measures like the New Deal never were considered in the Netherlands? How in fact did the Dutch react to the challenge of the New Deal?

Happy Days?

"Happy days are here again" was the campaign song the Democratic presidential candidate Roosevelt chose in 1932. Selecting that popular song was provocative since times were anything but happy. The 1929 crash of the New York stock market had started a period of economic distress that laid bare fundamental weaknesses in the country's economy. From 1929 to 1932 personal incomes de-

3

—

THE
PERIOD
OF
THE
WORLD
WARS

1914–1945

clined by more than half and unemployment rose from 3 to 25 percent of the labor force. A huge number of banks, factories, and mines closed, and farms were sold. The failure of no less than 40 percent of the American banks set off a chain reaction around the world.

On balance, 1929 was the key year for the retreat from globalization and for the disintegration of the world economy. In the 1930s autarky, instead of cooperation and consultation, was the key word. At the time, no powerful international economic organizations like the International Monetary Fund and the World Bank, nor a United Nations existed of course. The League of Nations had little power. The United States for one, though the institution was a brain child of President Woodrow Wilson, had refused to join it and retreated into isolation after World War I. This is not to say that the League was unimportant; subsidiary bodies concerned with the regulation of, for instance, labor standards certainly did useful work. Although attempts were made to counter the worldwide economic problems on a global scale — for example, at the 1933 London economic and monetary conference — these all failed.

The general response to the economic crisis was to maximize national production, and therefore employment, by minimizing imports. In other words: tariffs and quotas were imposed. In 1924 the U.S. had already adopted tight quotas for immigrants, especially barring poor ones who might be susceptible to socialist and communist ideology. In order to balance the national budget, taxes were raised and public spending was lowered. Thus, a negative spiral was created because people had less and less money to consume. Internationally the turn to national economies and to autarky meant that states became more expansionist, either by acquiring more territory (Germany, Italy, Japan) or by further exploiting existing colonial empires (Great Britain, France), or by developing land empires (Soviet Union, the United States). Roosevelt's New Deal policy, for instance, can be seen in this last perspective because it involved the federal government in large projects such as the building of big dams for the purpose of irrigation and hydroelectricity.

The experience of World War I, when official planning boards took the place of the free market to ensure the participation of the whole society in the war effort, had shown that governments could successfully intervene in economic management through their mobilization of resources and people. World War I was a "total war"; the difference between soldiers and civilians became blurred and the whole country was involved in the war effort. While this was a breakthrough everywhere, it particularly was so in the United States where the idea of a free market and a hands-off policy traditionally loomed large. When propagating the New Deal policy, Franklin Roosevelt did not hesitate to remind Americans how in 1917 the combined efforts of economic, industrial, social, and military resources had been mobilized to battle the Central Powers. The New Deal meant to do the same, only this time the enemies were poverty and huge unemployment at home. The program has often been summarized by the "three Rs": relief, recovery, and reform. In American history it was revolutionary not only because the federal government took an active role in relief assistance but because attempts were made to restructure the basis of the national economy and to introduce a social security system.

"It Could Be Much Worse"... The Importance of Hope

According to a persistent myth Roosevelt's predecessor, Republican President Herbert Hoover, had abstained from devising plans for economic recovery. He did make plans. In fact, during World War I it had been Hoover who had devised international food and relief programs. The problem with his plans and actions when president was that they did not work as intended, or were adjusted before taking effect. Hoover's name became associated with sham and hollowness. The shantytowns that sprang up near the city dumps and railroad tracks, for example, were "Hoovervilles." Counterproductive also were Hoover's personal appearance and political style, and most of all his failure to inspire hope in the years to come. At one point during the election campaign he told an audience of the possibility that the situation could grow much worse: "It could be so much worse that these days now, distressing as they are, would look like veritable prosperity."[1]

That hardly was the message one wanted to hear. On the surface, the contrast with the Democratic candidate, the optimistic Franklin Roosevelt, could hardly have been greater. In reality this was less a question of substance than of form. Not everything went smoothly for Roosevelt either. While he was still campaigning to win the Democratic nomination, big business, out of fear of his proposed government intervention, bluntly opposed him, as did the largest newspaper chains. Organized labor stayed aloof in 1932. Nonetheless, Roosevelt's optimism and his promise to counterattack the distress proved catchy. This was also true of the phrase "New Deal" that Roosevelt used in his acceptance speech at the 1932 Democratic national convention in Chicago. Although it was not a new phrase and was only intended by his advisors as political rhetoric, as a sort of throw-away line, Roosevelt's statement: "I pledge you, I pledge myself, to a New Deal for the American People," immediately worked as a highly influential wake-up call.[2] "New Deal" referred to the sudden change that is possible in a card game when new cards can flip bad luck into the opposite. Likewise, Roosevelt maintained that it was possible to reshuffle wealth and resources.

Roosevelt was brilliant in using the relatively new medium of radio to put his views and plans across. It was in an April 1932 radio address that he referred

511

3

—

THE
PERIOD
OF
THE
WORLD
WARS

1914–1945

to the so-called forgotten man. That image stuck. Plans were needed "that build from the bottom up and not from the top down, that put their faith once more in the forgotten man at the bottom of the economic pyramid." In November 1932 he was elected by a landslide. Interestingly, from the start Roosevelt had made no secret of the fact that the program of the New Deal was in its scope a large experiment and certainly not a systematic, nor necessarily a consistent, policy. "It is common sense to take a method and try it," he said, for instance, in May 1932. "If it fails, admit it frankly and try another. But above all, try something." Though pragmatic, the New Deal was not a mix of various approaches. Roosevelt rather moved from one tactic to another.[3]

New Deal: The First Hundred Days and What Came Next

When Roosevelt assumed the office of president on March 4, 1933, the position of the United States' banks was weak. On the day of his inauguration the uncertainty about what the promised New Deal would mean in terms of economic and monetary policy resulted in a lower level of gold cover in the Federal Reserve system than the statutory 40 percent requirement. In his famous inauguration address, with the legendary line, "the only thing we have to fear is fear itself," Roosevelt stated several times that immediate action was now needed. He acted promptly indeed. Various measures in the first hundred days of his presidency such as an Emergency Banking Act and an Economy Act aimed to restore confidence in the banking system and stabilize prices. On April 19 Roosevelt took the gigantic step to float the dollar.[4] Relief and recovery were the purpose of other measures such as the establishment of a Federal Emergency Relief Administration, a Civilian Conservation Corps, a Civil Works Administration (1934), and of course the inauguration of the Tennessee Valley Authority (TVA), which built dams and hydroelectric stations in the whole Tennessee River basin and became one of the world's largest irrigation and power stations.

Roosevelt's second term started with an attempt to balance the budget by cutting expenditures and raising taxes, but when a recession followed in 1937, it was an impetus for new measures to stimulate economic growth, progress, and mass consumption. The idea that consumption could be considered as a method to stimulate growth resembled Keynesian economics but the American program was not built on Keynes' ideas.

The above is only a very brief account of the interventionist measures taken by the first two Roosevelt administrations. In fact, the New Deal never really controlled the monetary and economic field and was not consistent. This was once described as "the car of economic progress in the hands of an enthusiastic but inexpert driver; it either goes too furiously fast or it brakes too joltingly."

But at least the government tried, and tried hard. The programs cost the federal government more than eleven billion dollars, and 35 percent of the population received public aid or social insurance in the 1930s. Yet despite all the hard work, the huge sums of money spent, the substantive job creation, and the positive effect on consumer spending, the economic distress was not solved. The United States would only return to full employment by early 1942, federal war expenditures creating the main push factor. But whether this also meant prosperity is doubtful.[5]

Experiments and Dutch Political Culture

American politics in the 1930s overtly expressed action, movement, energy, and experiments. This attitude stood in stark contrast to Dutch politics in these same years. Hendrikus Colijn, the prominent Protestant politician of the 1930s whose name almost became a synonym for this period due to the fact that he led four cabinets, was seen, and saw himself, as the solid leader who would not flinch from his duty to govern even if it involved taking strong, unpopular actions. That he had been an army officer and used to giving orders, reinforced his rock-solid appearance. In election campaigns the image of Colijn as an unyielding leader, capable of steering the Netherlands in times of rough weather and heavy storms into the quiet and safe harbor was propagated. One of the most famous election bills in the Netherlands shows Colijn, dressed in raincoat and southwester, as helmsman.

The Dutch sociopolitical landscape in these years was dominated by a phenomenon that political scientist Arend Lijphart has described as pillarization. Basically, political parties, unions, youth organizations, the press, and education were organized along ideological lines.[6] The introduction of universal suffrage in 1917–19 and a voting system based on proportional representation had resulted in the decline of old liberal parties, while strengthening the political subcultures of Catholics, orthodox Protestants, and social democrats. Although liberals used to propagate the idea that they were truly national and nonpartisan, they in turn felt compelled to organize themselves in a secular pillar. Additional smaller groups and parties existed as well, like the communists or the right-wing national-socialist movement. An important consequence of the four-part division of Dutch society was that socioeconomic tensions were covered by larger ideological rifts. The tendency to settle economic differences by compromise was especially strong in the Protestant and Catholic pillars because their electorate did not have a homogenous socioeconomic background.

The economic crisis had made itself felt relatively late in the Netherlands, namely in 1930 and 1931. It began in agriculture, from which it spread to indus-

513

'sLANDS STUURMAN

STEMT H.COLIJN
Nº 1 VAN LIJST 27

try and services. To battle the international drop of prices, the government as well as employers were in favor of wage and relief cuts. Also, because of the international orientation of the Dutch economy, it was considered of the utmost importance that international monetary relations be settled properly. The leading opinion in the Netherlands was that the gold standard would have to form the basis of such a system. Depending heavily on international trade, autarky of course was no option for a small country like the Netherlands.

In the years 1923–25 drastic measures to return to the gold standard at prewar value had been taken when Colijn was minister of finance. When he became prime minister in May 1933, he once again propagated serious cutbacks. But he was also very much a champion of international agreements, especially on monetary matters. In June 1933 he went to London to chair the Economics Commission of the international London Monetary and Economic Conference, where he understood his task, as one Dutch newspaper wrote, in "a dictatorial fashion, as expected."[7]

International Failure and National Solutions

The conference in London opened on June 12, 1933 and was attended by delegates from sixty-six nations. Tripartite currency talks, conducted by experts from the United States, Great Britain, and France, had already started. When on July 1 Roosevelt flatly rejected the results of these discussions, out of fear that the earlier depreciation of the dollar would be harmed, he caused the conference to fail. In his inaugural address he already had stated that his first priority was a sound national economy; international trade relations were secondary. Roosevelt's veto of the agreement on the stabilization of currencies, made public on July 3, created quite a stir. In America his so-called bombshell was praised and even somewhat bombastically called a "new declaration of independence": foreign powers should not interfere with, or worse, even dictate American policies! Needless to say, the reaction in Europe was different. Though Secretary of State Cordell Hull skillfully contrived to prolong the talks in order to save face, it was clear that eventually the conclusion could be no other than that the efforts had resulted in a complete fiasco.[8]

Casting an eye on the unhappy story of the 1930s and 1940s with the wisdom of hindsight, this bold American refusal has been criticized vehemently. Because no country was willing or able to act as an economic hegemon — Great

◄ Political helmsman Hendrikus Colijn steering the Dutch through bad weather (election poster, 1925).

Britain was too weak and the United States retreated into isolation and refused responsibility—the world economy broke down. Devising international measures to battle the economic crisis would be very far off.

The domestic consequence of the failure to reach an international understanding in 1933 was that the Dutch cabinet now had to resort to means that it would rather not have used, such as protection of the home industry and a cautious tariff policy. Of course, the success of this approach depended also on what importing countries would do: after all, they could adjust their import tariffs.

3

THE
PERIOD
OF
THE
WORLD
WARS

1914–1945

Pragmatism instead of Planning?

During his years as prime minister, six in all, Colijn remained a staunch defender of classic liberal socioeconomic policies. The most important issue in the Dutch government's monetary policy was to continue to observe the gold standard, and therefore to maintain a policy of a strong guilder. A balanced budget ranked second on the list of goals in the 1930s, which was of course far from unique, nor basically wrong. Although there was a debate in the public domain on the wisdom of the refusal to devalue the guilder in 1933 and 1934, where proponents pointed to the fact that the gold countries Belgium, France, Switzerland, and the Netherlands were worse off than England and Sweden, the government, especially Colijn, did not recoil. Ironically, it was precisely the Dutch role in the international economy that had dictated the government's stance: the fear was that the international reliability of the guilder would suffer if the connection to the gold standard were severed. Moreover, the private saver would be hurt.[9]

The question whether Dutch policymakers considered unemployment curable in itself, is difficult to answer. It is certain that the policies pursued were inconsistent and contradictory. The agricultural policy, for instance, led to higher prices while the aim of the retrenchment measures was to reduce price levels. Indeed, though economizing on expenditure was a top priority, spending on social services actually rose substantially, as did the national debt.[10] Here we find perhaps the biggest difference with the situation in the U.S. The Roosevelt administration repeatedly expressed its concern about the social and economic distress, while the Dutch governments in theory preached economizing, and forgot to show the Dutch people that they also cared for the "forgotten man" whose discontent and unease grew. The rather harsh official reaction to an uproar in 1934, which took place in the Amsterdam working-class Jordaan in response to a proposed 10 percent cut in social security benefits, showed that the government would react violently if put to the test. Military police and heavily armed soldiers were called in to restore order, causing the death of six people and dozens wounded.

In 1935, the Dutch Social Democratic Party and a federation of labor unions developed a substantial, wide-ranging program to battle the economic distress. Large public meetings were organized to promote their Labor Plan (Plan van de Arbeid), and an explicit attempt was made to inspire hope in the future. Even though Jan Tinbergen — who in 1969 would win the Nobel Prize in economics and who was among those who devised the program — had pointed to the New Deal to support his opinion that substantive investments in public works were necessary, it was not the American policy that formed the main source of inspiration, but rather the Belgian economic Plan du Travail that the social democrat H. de Man had proposed in 1933, as well as Swedish reform programs and liberal ideas promoted in Great Britain.

European socialists and social democrats at the time saw the U.S. as the bulwark of capitalism and therefore not as the first model to copy. Remarkable was that inspiration did work the other way around, for instance in a visit by an American New Deal administrator to European countries in order to evaluate housing and social security projects in 1934.[11] In Europe, few thoughts seem to have been spent on the question whether the American experience could form a democratic model to pursue in economic reforms. That it was democratic at all even was disputed by the Dutch embassy in Washington, which from 1934 was led by a conservative aristocrat who used strong language to put his opinion across that Roosevelt's New Deal policy was comparable to a form of state socialism. In his view, the American president showed an abhorrent tendency to employ "dictatorial" methods in order to introduce his programs.[12]

In the 1930s all sorts of economic plans and reforms were available from which to choose: a communist version in the Soviet Union, a corporatist one in fascist Italy, and as of 1933 a program of the national socialists in Germany. Perhaps that is precisely the reason why the Dutch government defended a pragmatic policy and explicitly denounced any economic planning in whatever form. Furthermore, as Colijn said in parliament in February 1936, the "dangerous experiments abroad" had produced no positive results. What was the point of building sandcastles if people in the end would have to be disappointed? Another politician considered the lack of enthusiasm for the government's policy even as a promising and confidence-building sign because it showed the government's immunity to any reproach of being unpopular and its dedication to wage the war against the economic crisis.[13]

Although Colijn argued that the Dutch results were not worse than those abroad, it is indisputable that in the Netherlands the highest level of unemployment occurred in 1936, at a time when it was decreasing in comparable countries. This gave rise to economic and historic studies on why the crisis in the Netherlands lasted exceptionally long. The main bones of contention were the question whether the Dutch stubbornness to keep to the gold standard while

3

—

THE
PERIOD
OF
THE
WORLD
WARS

1914-1945

other countries did not, was the principal cause or whether structural shortcomings and characteristics of the Dutch economy were responsible. After all, the Depression was not caused by monetary factors alone. One thing is certain, however: when France and Switzerland finally devalued their currencies, the Dutch had no choice but to follow, and when this decision was made in 1936, recovery started. The government really had postponed devaluation too long.[14]

Public Works but No New Deal

Public works formed the backbone of the American New Deal policy. Although the same remedy for unemployment was used in the Netherlands, it was in no way a copy of the American example and even preceded it. The Dutch government saw the measures as temporary relief, not as a way to restructure the economy. The fact that unemployed who were living on welfare were sometimes forced to work in labor camps did not contribute to a positive view of these measures. In 1936 a modest attempt was made to counter criticism when a book, starting with an introduction by the minister of social affairs, pointed to the public works' accomplishments and to the large sums of money spent on them. It was greeted with joy in the usually rather dry and fact-ridden journal *Economisch-Statistische Berichten*, which devoted an entire issue to elaborating on the large scale of the projects and massive government expenditures.[15]

But one swallow does not make a summer and the fact remains that the 1930s in the Netherlands are remembered by no one for restoring hope and confidence. Insufficient attention was given to the bad effects of welfare on the morale of the unemployed. The dominant images of this period are long lines of unemployed waiting to collect their daily stamp on their social security card. The fact that this impression is one-sided and oversimplified is true but hardly relevant. In America another image prevails. In 1948 historian Arthur M. Schlesinger, Jr., admittedly an admirer, stated that Roosevelt's solutions in the New Deal were arguably incomplete. But he considered that unimportant in comparison to what the New Deal did do, namely give America renewed hope and confidence.

The Dutch political atmosphere in the 1930s was predominantly conservative and down to earth. That the lack of enthusiasm for the Dutch socioeconomic policies even was presented as a good sign, expresses the remarkable insensitivity to what the man in the street experienced. Dutch political leaders missed an opportunity when they refused to learn the lesson of hope from the American New Deal policy.

1   Richard Norton Smith and Timothy
     Walch, "The Ordeal of Herbert Hoover,
     Part 2," *Prospect* 36.2 (Summer 2004),
     http://www.archives.gov/publications/
     prologue/2004/summer/hoover-2.html

2   Davis W. Houck, *Rhetoric as Currency.
     Hoover, Roosevelt, and the Great Depres-
     sion* (College Station: Texas A&M Uni-
     versity Press, 2001), 84-87, 131, 162-163;
     Steven Neal, *Happy Days Are Here Again:
     The 1932 Democratic Convention, the
     Emergence of FDR - and How America
     Was Changed Forever* (New York: Harper-
     Collins, 2004).

3   Radio address, April 7, 1932, and address
     at Oglethorpe University, May 22, 1932,
     http://newdeal.feri.org/speeches; James
     R. Moore, "Sources of New Deal Eco-
     nomic Policy: The International Dimen-
     sion," *Journal of American History* 61.3
     (December 1974): 728-744.

4   Patricia Clavin, *The Great Depression
     in Europe, 1929-1939* (Basingstoke/
     London: Macmillan, 2000), 157-158;
     Jonathan Alter, *The Defining Moment.
     FDR's Hundred Days and the Triumph of
     Hope* (New York: Simon & Schuster,
     2006), 207-211.

5   Quoted in F.A.G. Keesing, *De conjunc-
     turele ontwikkeling van Nederland en de
     evolutie van de economische overheids-
     politiek 1918-1939* (Utrecht: Het Spec-
     trum, 1947), 309; William E. Leuchten-
     berg, *The FDR Years. On Roosevelt and
     His Legacy* (New York: Columbia Univer-
     sity Press, 1995), 255-256.

6   For a further explanation of the notion
     of pillarization in Dutch politics and
     society, see the introductory essay of this
     section by Doeko Bosscher.

7   "Colijn houdt van opschieten," *Het
     Vaderland,* June 16, 1933, Avondblad A, 1.

8   Rodney J. Morrision, "The London
     Monetary and Economic Conference
     of 1933: A Public Goods Analysis,"
     *American Journal of Economics and
     Sociology* 52.3 (July 1993): 307-321, here

     310; Jeannette P. Nichols, "Roosevelt's
     Monetary Diplomacy in 1933," *The
     American Historical Review* 56.2 (January
     1951): 295-317, here 316.

9   Herman Langeveld, *Schipper naast God.
     Hendrikus Colijn 1869-1944*, vol. 2,
     1933-1944 (Amsterdam: Balans, 2004),
     69-227; P. de Rooy, *Werklozenzorg en
     werkloosheidbestrijding 1917-1940.
     Landelijk en Amsterdams beleid* (Amster-
     dam: Van Gennep, 1979), 137-138.

10   J.C. Siebrand and N. van der Windt,
     "Economic Crisis and Economic Policy
     in the Thirties and the Seventies," *De
     Economist* 131.4 (1983): 517-547, here
     535; P.W. Klein, "Depression and Policy
     in the Thirties," *Acta Historiae Neerlan-
     dicae. Studies on the History of the
     Netherlands* 8 (The Hague: Martinus
     Nijhoff, 1975): 123-158, here 128-129.

11   http://newdeal.feri.org/workrelief/
     hop08.htm; Alan Lawson, *A Common-
     wealth of Hope. The New Deal Response
     to Crisis* (Baltimore: Johns Hopkins
     University Press, 2006), 122-123.

12   H.W. van den Doel, "Nederland en de
     Verenigde Staten," in H.W. van den Doel
     et al., *Nederland en de nieuwe wereld.*
     (Utrecht: Het Spectrum, 1992), 268-270,
     and the essay by Cornelis A. van Minnen
     elsewhere in this section.

13   *Proceedings of the Dutch Parliament,
     First Chamber (Handelingen der Staten-
     Generaal)*, 1935-1936, February 5, 1936,
     237-238; February 7, 1936, 269-271.

14   J.W. Drukker, *Waarom de crisis hier
     langer duurde. Over de Nederlandse
     economische ontwikkeling in de jaren
     dertig* (Amsterdam: NEHA, 1990);
     J.L. van Zanden, *De dans om de gouden
     standaard. Economisch beleid in de
     depressie van de jaren dertig* (Amster-
     dam: VU uitgeverij, 1988).

15   *Economisch-Statistische Berichten* 21
     (December 9, 1936): 888-907, review by
     v.d.V. [H.M.H.A. van der Valk], 907.

3

—

THE
PERIOD
OF
THE
WORLD
WARS

1914–1945

AMERICAN DIPLOMATIC PERSPECTIVES ON THE DUTCH EAST INDIES

—

FRANCES GOUDA

Introduction

In the interwar years, U.S. Foreign Service officers' descriptions of the political and economic conditions in the Dutch East Indies can be interpreted as a barometer of shifting American visions of the nature of Western imperialism in Southeast Asia in general and of Dutch colonial governance in the Indonesian archipelago in particular.[1] During the 1920s, their reports expressed mostly admiration for the efficient and profitable Dutch management of the archipelago. In the early 1930s, however, American diplomats became more critical of the Dutch colonial government's repressive policies toward native politicians. During this decade, they routinely condemned Dutch tendencies to incarcerate Indonesian nationalists without due process of law. Toward the end of the 1930s, when Japan's military menace in the Pacific was a palpable foreign policy concern, American judgments about Dutch rule changed yet again. At this anxious time, U.S. Foreign Service officers began to incorporate both positive and negative evaluations in order to make a realistic assessment of the Dutch East Indies as a credible American ally in a potential geopolitical clash with Japan, while acknowledging at the same time the legitimacy of the Indonesian nationalist movement.

A variety of factors affected the United States' changing visions of the Dutch East Indies in the interwar years. First, America's own colonial experience in the Philippines played a distinct role in Washington's evaluations of the imperial policies of other Western nations in Southeast Asia. A second influence on U.S. diplomatic assessments was linked to the necessity to protect the considerable investments in such American enterprises as oil extraction and refineries as well as rubber and tobacco plantations in colonial Indonesia. During the 1930s, the new social-democratic commitments of President Roosevelt's New Deal and the more liberal ideology of his State Department began to color U.S. perspectives on the Dutch East Indies. Throughout the interwar years, however, American observers continued to be influenced by popular if romanticized impressions of Dutch history. In the public imagination, the picture of the Netherlands was a highly positive one, embodied in "good citizenship, stubborn courage, industry, resourcefulness, and cleanliness."[2] As a result, American diplomatic observers in Southeast Asia combined a pragmatic political and economic agenda with more ambiguous cultural clichés.

The 1920s: The Lucrative Dutch East Indies
Compared to the Costly Philippines

Initially, U.S. diplomats posted in Batavia, Medan, and Surabaya praised Dutch colonial society as a steady fountain of profitability for Dutch or foreign investors. Often, American Foreign Service officers compared the Dutch East Indies with the nearby Philippines. As Consul General Charles A. Hoover wrote in 1925, "the Philippines are a mere incident in the life of the United States, while the continued possession of the [Indonesian] islands is essential to the very life and prosperity of the Netherlands." Hoover made a simple point. The role of colonial overlord of a string of islands in Southeast Asia was a new and unaccustomed one for the United States. In the public arena, the U.S. intervention in the Philippines was legitimized by appealing to an evangelical sense of mission or the notion of Manifest Destiny.[3]

But the simplicity of Hoover's remark was deceptive. He implied that the possession of the Filipino nation was only tangential to Americans' patriotic pride, whereas control of the Indonesian archipelago constituted an essential feature of the Netherlands' national identity. Besides, as far as America's economic wellbeing was concerned, the Philippines represented a financial drain rather than an economic asset, whereas the Dutch East Indies, in contrast, constituted a veritable treasure trove not only for a small European democracy but also for American entrepreneurs. In comparison to the infrastructural expenditures of the Dutch government in Indonesia, the U.S. administration in the Philippines spent, proportionally, almost three times as much on education, social services, and public works. In 1929, for example, the American commitment of capital to the Philippines amounted to eighty million dollars, a figure that grew to ninety-two million in 1936. During the same years, the U.S. private sector invested sixty-six million (1929) and seventy million (1936) in the Dutch East Indies in moneymaking enterprises.[4] After all, as soon as Americans were ensconced in their new position as colonial masters after the turn of

3

—

THE
PERIOD
OF
THE
WORLD
WARS

1914-1945

the century, they went to work with indomitable optimism. While serving as the first U.S. governor of the Philippines during the period 1901–04, future President William Howard Taft had championed a policy of "benevolent assimilation" and improvement of the welfare of the Filipino people. And within a short time, U.S. colonial caretakers in the Philippines could boast of a lengthy list of accomplishments, such as the construction of longer roads and better sewers than any colonial power in Asia. American disbursements for improved medical care enabled the Filipino population to double in size between 1900 and 1920. The U.S. government also established an educational system based on the American model, emphasizing individual skills and creativity among Filipino students. Yet, at no time did the Philippines represent either a real benefit or a genuine threat to the lifeblood of the American nation.

Ambivalence about America's role as colonial master had emerged soon after its conquest of the Philippines. As a telltale sign of his political reversal concerning the wisdom of America's imperialist control of this archipelago, President Theodore Roosevelt raised the possibility of Filipino independence as early as his State of the Union address in 1908. Less than a decade later, Democratic Congressman William Atkinson Jones, having consulted the Filipino politician Manuel Quezon, drafted a congressional act that bore his name and stipulated that independence should become a reality as soon as Filipinos could establish a "stable government." After the U.S. Congress voted in favor, the act was signed into law by President Woodrow Wilson in August 1916. In doing so, the American political establishment accepted the ephemeral character of the relationship between mother country and her colonial possession. It also fostered the loyalty and cooperation of such nationalist organizations as the Filipino Partido Nacionalista, because the Jones Act proposed a feasible timetable for future independence. In reality, however, Americans were just as interested in garnering financial profit in their colonial possession as their Dutch neighbors in the Indonesian archipelago. Hence, it was likely that the precocious U.S. efforts to draft a blueprint for Filipino independence resulted from the sober calculation that the Philippines would remain an economic burden rather than emerge as a wellspring of material benefits for the mother country.

In the eyes of U.S. diplomats in Southeast Asia and Europe, a contrasting situation obtained in the Dutch East Indies because the prosperity of the Netherlands was "almost wholly dependent on the colonies," as American diplomat Richard Tobin, who served in the U.S. embassy in The Hague, argued in 1927. Tobin reported that the situation of the Indies was a subject of anxiety among all sectors of Dutch society because "the loss of the colonial possessions might result in financial as well as political ruin" of the Netherlands. Nonetheless, the nationalist agitation in British India in the late 1920s had not caused alarm among the Dutch because they were convinced that their country had governed its colonial empire "with more wisdom than the British and more vigor than the French." This wisdom and vigor, one of Tobin's colleagues in Batavia, Henry P. Starrett, had noted a few years earlier, resided in a form of government that was "paternal and therefore not in any sense democratic." A *New York Times* journalist, Nicholas Roosevelt, who was a scion of the famous FDR family, suggested in his book, *The Philippines: A Treasure and a Problem*, that the Dutch always tried to improve the welfare of the natives and never interfered with their traditions and superstitions. While the average American or Englishman, he claimed, had little patience with habits that were impractical albeit deeply rooted in the practices and cosmology of various ethnic groups in either the Philippines or India, "the Dutch accept it and make the most of it."

It was likely that Consul General Hoover, who served in Batavia when Nicholas Roosevelt published his comparative ruminations concerning the nature of colonial rule in 1925, would have agreed. In the same year, Hoover had written that the present government of the Dutch East Indies was the heritage of a long history of judicious policies. He tried to impress upon his superiors in the State Department that the Netherlands engaged in only the most even-tempered efforts to govern their multiethnic subjects in the archipelago "with a minimum expenditure of blood and treasure," and that the Dutch administration constituted a remarkable accomplishment. Hoover conceded that this form of colonial government required "a toleration of features which were distasteful to the progressive, liberty-loving Dutch, but which had become fixed in the very lives of the apathetically conservative people of these islands." In their efforts to cure their lassitude, Hoover lauded Dutch colonial civil servants for encouraging the participation of a growing number of natives in the affairs of local government, while carefully respecting *adat* in "all matters not regulated by Dutch legal codes." He added that experiments of this nature had not been "brilliantly successful" in other countries where people still functioned at a low level of development, but in the Dutch East Indies "the system of training for the responsibilities of self-government may be more intelligently directed than where it is attempted to clothe a people with powers of whose proper use they have not the slightest conception."

Only an occasional American disagreed with these fawning accounts, in part because during the 1920s American diplomats in Southeast Asia were not yet overtly worried about the strategic importance of the Indonesian archipelago. At that stage, the incipient military aggression of Japan and its eventual thirst for oil were still elusive political factors. Thus, the operative words in their congratulatory assessments of Dutch colonial policies in the 1920s were intelligence, paternalism, and especially thoroughness—a characterization that would prompt many a Dutch civil servant, planter, or businessman in the Indies to smile in agreement and burst with pride. Conversely, some critics of the Dutch colonial

523

3

—

THE
PERIOD
OF
THE
WORLD
WARS

1914–1945

enterprise — ranging from committed Dutch socialists to Indonesian nationalists — dismissed these positive judgments as evidence of Americans' desire to stay in the Dutch East Indies government's good graces in order to safeguard the profitability of U.S. oil, rubber, and tobacco ventures.[5]

Trade between the United States and colonial Indonesia soared during the 1920s; American imports in 1920 amounted to 167 million dollars, while American exports to the Dutch East Indies totaled 59 million dollars and continued to grow throughout the decade.[6] In 1924, several American companies managed plantations and furnished about 20 percent of the archipelago's gross rubber production, which represented a capital investment of 41 million dollars, whereas approximately 45 percent of the total rubber exports from the east coast of Sumatra in the 1920s was destined for the United States to supply the flourishing automobile industry in Detroit.[7] As the annual statistics of the international Rubber Growers Association revealed about the distribution of the world's aggregate production of rubber, only British Malaya supplied more latex to the international market than the Dutch East Indies.[8]

Although not the leading foreign investors in colonial Indonesia — the British and Franco-Belgian stakes in the economy were greater — they comprised about 7 percent. Until the outbreak of World War II, Americans continued to purchase crucial raw materials from the Dutch East Indies, despite the fluctuations imposed by the Great Depression. Hence, amidst a range of other valuable commodities, the U.S. bought 48.7 percent of Indonesia's rubber and 8 percent of its tin production and the lion's share of quinine, palm oil, cigar wrappers, and Javanese tea and coffee. The aggregate value of Indonesian exports to the U.S. would reach an all-time high of 242 million dollars in 1941.[9]

Inevitably, these impressive trade figures influenced the attitudes of U.S. diplomats in Batavia, who were charged with sheltering American political interests in the archipelago. Although they could not help noticing the growth of the Indonesian nationalist movement, they hardly raised objections to Governor General Dirk Fock's "high-handed authoritarianism" in the face of popular nationalist agitation in the early 1920s.[10]

The 1930s: Growing Criticism of the Dutch Colonial Government

This situation would soon change. The Great Depression struck the Indonesian landscape like a bolt of lightning — dotted as it was with plantations producing cash crops that were exceedingly sensitive to price levels on the world market. The economic downturn of the 1930s quickly reduced the generous financial revenues generated by Indonesia's fertile soil to a mere trifle. The Depression, meanwhile, was caused in part by the U.S., where the intoxicating celebration of the free forces of capitalism ended abruptly in October 1929, with the Wall Street crash. A protectionist response followed in colonial economies consisting of higher tariffs, production quotas, and preferential trade agreements. These new measures were designed to safeguard the interests of the mother countries. Such monopolistic impulses, in turn, generated anxieties in the United States about its dearly beloved principles of free trade. The Smoot-Hawley Act, however, had erected around the U.S. one of the highest tariff walls in the world, and Washington's concerns with free trade focused unilaterally on America's unfettered access to markets throughout the world.

During the 1930s, a new political vocabulary began to inflect American diplomats' reports to the State Department in Washington, DC. They dispatched more astute analyses of Dutch East Indies society that struck an infinitely more critical tone. In the face of newly recognized political and economic hazards in the Pacific, American diplomats in the field and policymakers in Washington started to perceive the Dutch East Indies government not only as oppressive and greedy but also as being overly lax in its preparation to defend the archipelago against foreign aggression. Despite Indonesia's strategic location and the archipelago's possession of abundant petroleum and other mineral resources — which would be crucial if Japan were to mount an armed assault on the rest of Asia — Dutch military readiness to defend Indonesia, according to American analysts, revealed a pathetic sight. The U.S. government, meanwhile, continued to prepare for the eventual independence of the Philippines. Dutch governance in Indonesia began to pale in comparison to America's infinitely more charitable colonial enterprise in the Philippines.

The Great Depression undermined social and economic conditions in many parts of the world and it also exerted a devastating effect on Indonesia's export-driven economy. Between 1929 and 1933, the total value of Dutch East Indies exports plunged from 1,488 million to 525 million guilders. Although rubber prices had started their gradual downward slide already in 1925, the market price for tin, quinine, sugar, coffee and tea plummeted with breathtaking speed in just a few years.[11] In addition, the Depression also jeopardized the hefty earnings U.S. oil companies had garnered in the archipelago during the 1920s. U.S. Foreign Service officers in colonial Indonesia began to articulate harsher judgments. The chronological proximity of the appointment of the new governor general, Bonifacius Cornelis de Jonge, in 1931, on the one hand, and the Republican Party's loss of the American presidency after controlling it for twelve years, on the other, exerted an indelible impact.

525

Once the Roosevelt administration was ensconced in power after the presidential inauguration in mid-January 1933, a concern with social justice became part of America's political grammar, in both domestic and foreign policy.

3

——

THE
PERIOD
OF
THE
WORLD
WARS

1914–1945

Moreover, the passage in the U.S. Congress of the McDuffie-Tydings Act in 1934, which decreed the unequivocal independence of the Philippines in ten years, was yet another expression of such shifts in attitude. An additional influence on the quality of political reporting in the 1930s may have been the delayed effect of the Rogers Act of 1924, which had reorganized the United States Foreign Service and was designed to attract better-trained personnel, men who would display the intellectual ability to conduct diplomacy in an expert manner.[12]

During the Great Depression, efforts to protect the United States' economy from foreign competition abounded and the strict new Tariff Act was followed by further measures. As soon as he was in office, President Roosevelt embraced a dynamic agenda of economic intervention and protective social legislation. At the same time, the imperialist practices of a variety of European nations became the object of ethical scrutiny and, in some instances, moral censure. Because the Depression ravaged the lives of millions of Americans, many had grown more aware of the social inequalities and injustices of a society in which the wealth of a blessed few was juxtaposed with the material misery of the majority. It therefore seemed logical also to question why a handful of Europeans lived in luxury, while millions of Asian men and women were forced to labor from sunrise to sunset for a wage worth a little more than a daily bowl of rice. Some segments of the U.S. population began to make a connection between the large number of downtrodden Americans, who had to scramble for food and shelter in Hoovertowns, and the legions of Asians whose toil did nothing but feed the already robust bank accounts of British, French, and Dutch colonizers. Many articles interrogated the moral legitimacy of European imperialism in general and Dutch colonialism in particular. John Gunther's widely read book *Inside Asia* included a chapter entitled "Dutch Treat," and the gist of his story was that "the Indies tail is what wags the Dutch dog," because the Dutch nation "sucks all the wealth" out of its colonial possession in Southeast Asia.

In 1931, as B.C. de Jonge began his tenure as penultimate governor general, the gold rush of the 1920s had been relegated to the realm of nostalgia, while Japan's ominous presence began to hover in the background. The Great Depression had caused the "phantasmagorical" prosperity of the Indies to evaporate with mind-boggling speed. In American as well as Indonesian eyes, it was curious that manufacturers in colonial Indonesia could not even produce the most humdrum necessities of daily life, such as "textiles, paper, bicycle tires, plates, or cups." Widespread suffering among the native population came in the Depression's wake. Since consumer goods imported from Japan were less expensive than similar European-made products, U.S. Consul General Kenneth Patton reported in 1933 that it created "a sympathetic feeling for Japan" among Indonesians and tended to destroy "the community of interest" with the Dutch.[13] As a result, Americans' growing moral objections to the worst excesses of colonial rule were moderated by a broadening concern with Japan's ascendancy in Asia.

In addition to Japan's burgeoning threat, Governor General De Jonge's conservative regime also provoked a new awareness among American diplomats that the stoic self-confidence of the colonial government had been rattled, due to the chorus of nationalist voices demanding to be heard. Ironically, De Jonge's arbitrary suppression of native politicians actually made American observers more sensitive to the aspirations of the nationalist movement. For example, in 1935 the U.S. consul general, Walter Foote, offered the opinion that De Jonge's despotic regime had forced native politicians to regroup and rethink their strategies, since any Indonesian nationalist, whether suspected of communist sympathies or not, was now "at risk of being summarily banished," purely as a preemptive measure. The colonial administration had designated certain prisons and internment camps for those it perceived as the most dangerous demagogues, who were summarily incarcerated without a formal trial. In an earnest attempt to disentangle the intricate web of Indonesian political parties and the varying degrees of radicalism they espoused, U.S. Foreign Service officers in the 1930s began to report on the nationalist movement with greater frequency. In order to walk the political tightrope between the residual anticolonialism of the Roosevelt administration and the celebration by some Indonesian nationalists of the motto "Asia for the Asians" under Japanese tutelage, American diplomats in Batavia routinely mocked the Dutch government's exaggerated tendency to conflate nationalism with communism. American diplomats blamed the governor general's antagonism toward the nationalist movement for actually aiding and abetting the "crystallization" of native political parties. They faulted the Dutch colonial government for interpreting all sentiments in favor of independence, whether or not they revealed any affinity with communist organizations, as "entirely seditious." Any such act of disloyalty warranted the government's use of its unrestrained "police state methods" and constituted a legitimate "ground for the arrest of its sponsors at any time."

On the whole, American observers rejected the idea of a pervasive communist plot and they no longer touted the thoroughness, wisdom, and intelligence of the Dutch colonial civil service, as their predecessors during the 1920s had done. Instead, they expressed their disapproval of Dutch violations of due process of law and the capricious infringement of the civil rights of all critics of the colonial regime. U.S. Foreign Service officers notified the State Department that the Dutch colonial regime had subverted the advisory character of the Volksraad (People's Council) by converting it into nothing more than an "organ of opposition," which eventually reduced this council to a "laughingstock" in Europeans' eyes. U.S. diplomats denounced the governor general's "police state" or "authoritarian" methods and commented on the fact that some pro-

527

American aviator Amelia Earhart and U.S. Consul General Walter Foote,
Batavia, Java, ca. 1937.

gressive Dutch residents of the Southeast Asia colony now referred to the colonial administration as "the fascist government." They criticized the government's restrictions on the right of assembly and condemned censorship of the press; they held these decrees responsible for "driving the native political movement underground and into secrecy," and predicted that sooner or later the Indies government would find itself facing a "powerful movement which can't be controlled by mere ordinances." Of course, in a mere ten years, they were proven right.

Conclusion

When B.C. de Jonge's tenure as governor general was about to end in 1936, the appointment of his successor was disclosed; the choice had fallen on a man with what John Gunther called "the jawbreaking name" of Jhr. Dr. A.W.L. Tjarda van Starkenborgh Stachouwer. As soon as the news broke, the U.S. consul general noted that the new governor general's reputation was a "very liberal" and "scrupulously honest" one. The State Department could thus anticipate a more enlightened and humane policy toward the native population in economic as well as political matters, although the consul general added that one of his informants had allegedly told him that "too much honesty is bad" for the Dutch East Indies, whereas "political liberalism and humanitarianism are fatal." By 1937, American Foreign Service officers in the Indonesian archipelago were already subjecting the new governor general to less personal criticism than they had heaped upon his predecessor — and they relished the fact that his wife was born and educated in the United States. But they continued to raise moral objections to the Indies government's encroachments on the freedom of the press and the civil liberties of Indonesian nationalists.

At the same time, geopolitical tensions in Asia were growing and the United States would need Dutch military cooperation if a war with Japan were to engulf Southeast Asia. As a result, American reporting on the Dutch East Indies became more temperate as the 1930s drew to a close. The possibility of Japanese aggression had settled in the minds of policymakers in Washington as the most significant factor in Asia; in this context, Indonesia's sophisticated oil industry would be a prime target for Japan's imperialists. As a consequence, the State Department became preoccupied with Japan's economic and political intrigues in colonial Indonesia. Foreign policy analysts in the Roosevelt administration also began to worry about the Dutch East Indies' inadequate military defenses in the event of a Japanese attack. In sum, between World Wars I and II American diplomatic visions of the Dutch East Indies had fluctuated between admiration for the economic *mise en valeur* of the archipelago and criticism

529

3

—

THE
PERIOD
OF
THE
WORLD
WARS

1914–1945

of the Dutch government's arbitrary suppression of the Indonesian nationalist movement. Throughout the interwar years, however, U.S. geopolitical and
economic interests had guided American assessments of the Dutch East Indies.
When Japan's potential belligerence began to hover in the background, the traditional fellow feeling between the United States and the Netherlands reasserted itself in order to prepare for the political and military alliance required to
face the ominous danger.

1   Based on diplomatic records of the U.S.
    State Department as cited in chapters
    3 and 4 of my *American Visions of the
    Netherlands East Indies/Indonesia:
    US Foreign Policy and Indonesian
    Nationalism, 1920–1949* (Amsterdam:
    Amsterdam University Press, 2002).

2   Frank Freidel, "The Dutchness of the
    Roosevelts," in Robert Swierenga and
    J.W. Schulte Nordholt, eds., *A Bilateral
    Bicentennial. A History of Dutch-American
    Relations, 1782–1982* (Amsterdam:
    Octagon Books/Meulenhoff, 1982), 156.

3   Stanley Karnow, *In Our Own Image:
    America's Empire in the Philippines* (New
    York: Random House, 1989), 189; See
    also Richard Barnet, *The Roots of War*
    (New York: Atheneum, 1972), in which
    he notes that America's "imperial creed
    rests on a theory of lawmaking … and
    organizing the peace," 21.

4   Theodore Friend, *The Blue-Eyed Enemy:
    Japan Against the West in Java and Luzon,
    1942–1945* (Princeton, NJ: Princeton
    University Press, 1988), 16.

5   D.M.G. Koch, in *Verantwoording.
    Een halve eeuw Indonesië* (The Hague/
    Bandung: s.n., 1956), 174, used the
    term "banker for Western capital"
    to describe the Indies government.

6   Robert MacMahon, *Colonialism and
    the Cold War. The United States and the
    Indonesian Struggle for Independence,
    1945–1949* (Ithaca, NY: Cornell Univer-
    sity Press, 1981), 45-46.

7   Glenn D. Babcock, *History of the United
    States Rubber Company. A Case Study in*

    Corporation Management (Bloomington:
    Indiana University, 1966), 172-188;
    F.J.J. Dootjes, "Deli: The Land of
    Agricultural Enterprises," *Bulletin of
    the Colonial Institute of Amsterdam* 2
    (1938-39): 130.

8   A.G.N. Swart, "Het aandeel van de
    Indische rubber in de wereldproductie,"
    *Jubileumuitgave De Indische Gids,
    1879-1929* 51.1 (January 1, 1929):
    292-293.

9   Gerlof D. Homan, "American Business
    Interests in the Indonesian Republic,
    1946-1949," *Indonesia* 35 (April 1983):
    125, cites these figures.

10 Takashi Shiraishi, *An Age in Motion.
    Popular Radicalism in Java, 1912-1926*
    (Ithaca, NY: Cornell University Press,
    1990), 232.

11 G. Gonggrijp, *De sociaal-economische
    betekenis van Nederlands-Indië voor
    Nederland. De Nederlandse volkshuis-
    houding tussen de twee oorlogen* (Utrecht
    /Brussels, 1948), xv, 11-17; Colin Barlow
    and John Drabble, "Government and the
    Emerging Rubber Industries in Indone-
    sia and Malaysia, 1900-1940," in Anne
    Booth et al., eds., *Indonesian Economic
    History in the Colonial Era* (New Haven,
    CT: Yale University Press, 1990), 191.

12 "The Rogers Act of 1924," in *Encyclopedia
    Americana* (New York: s.n., 1992), 580.

13 Margono Djojohadikusumo, *Herinne-
    ringen uit drie tijdperken* (Amsterdam:
    Nabrink, 1970), 70, and Gonggrijp, *De
    sociaal-economische betekenis,* 10, both
    use the term *"schijnwelvaart."*

THE NETHERLANDS, THE UNITED STATES, AND THE INTERNATIONAL POLITICAL CULTURE

—

MICHAEL RIEMENS

Following World War I the principal context for Dutch-American diplomatic relations changed dramatically. The megacatastrophes of the years 1914–18 and the diplomatic revolution of the Paris Peace Conference in 1919 resulted in a general transformation of the "international political culture" (the shared ideas, assumptions, and practices of normal interstate relations). Western political leaders introduced a new style of international politics and diplomacy, making greater use of the media to transmit populist sentiments and display charismatic qualities. Overall, the driving force for these initiatives was the loud popular outcry for peace, which demanded "no more wars!" This essay covers the particular experience of Dutch and American leaders, such as President Woodrow Wilson and Dutch Foreign Minister Herman A. van Karnebeek, as they traversed this new political environment and dealt with its most striking creation: the League of Nations. While Wilson was a pioneer in this field, single-handedly seeking to alter the practice of international relations, Van Karnebeek offers an interesting example of a more traditional diplomat learning fast and adapting to the new rules of the game. The differing styles of these two men are used to highlight the different approaches of the United States and the Netherlands toward international affairs during the 1920s and 1930s.

The New Style of International Diplomacy

Woodrow Wilson's decision to attend in person an international conference abroad—which no other American president had ever done—was the principal

3

—

THE
PERIOD
OF
THE
WORLD
WARS

1914–1945

reason why the Peace Conference following the "War to End All Wars" became a summit of democratic politicians, rather than a gathering of professional diplomats. There were additional reasons, related to developments during the war.

First, traditional diplomacy had a bad reputation among people in general, who associated it with secrecy and opacity and held it responsible for the catastrophic events of the summer of 1914. Second, the need to make speedy decisions in wartime led to frequent consultations between the Allied political leaders and the principal ministers concerned. The problems confronting them were simply too big, too numerous, too technical, and too urgent to be dealt with solely through normal diplomatic channels. In 1917 the Supreme War Council was established, whose nucleus was formed by the Allied political leaders who directed and decided the grand strategy of war. Third, the principal leaders during the war had little respect for professional diplomats. They dominated their foreign ministers, were confident of their own abilities as negotiators, and preferred to work through unofficial agents and think tanks. Thus, Wilson charged his friend Colonel Edward M. House in 1917 with the American preparations for the impending Peace Conference. To this end, House invited several academics from a number of prestigious U.S. universities to serve as external advisors to the Inquiry. Several of the Fourteen Points originated in this think tank (which went on to form the Council on Foreign Relations in 1921). At the Peace Conference, House acted as Wilson's chief deputy and he even took charge during the president's absences in February, March, and early April 1919. In the UK, where the Political Intelligence Department formed the British counterpart to the Inquiry, David Lloyd George preferred to listen to members of his secretariat, especially his private secretary, Sir Philip Henry Kerr, and to the secretary of the War Cabinet, Sir Maurice Hankey, who consequently left their mark on the foreign policy of Great Britain and the peace treaties. The prime minister even allowed his confidants to negotiate in Paris at the highest level. It was Kerr, for instance, who drafted the major portion of the Allied response to the German counterproposals of May 29, 1919.

Remarks from contemporaries make clear that people thought a new style of international politics and diplomacy had come into being: it was described as "new diplomacy," "open diplomacy," "democratic diplomacy," "diplomacy by conference," and even "diplomatic revolution." This did not mean, however, that the old style of politics had evaporated. Governments still used balance-of-power mechanisms, the European Concert returned in the League of Nations Council, and the Paris Ambassadors Conference supervised behind closed doors the enforcement of the Versailles Treaty. The new international political culture of the 1920s, therefore, formed a mixture of old and new forms, ideas, formulas, and practices. It had a character of its own, which was different from

its pre-1914 predecessor and different from the one that followed. One of its engines was the shared passion for peace of the electorates.[1]

The new power of the media was a crucial element in these developments.
Talks at the summits always took place in a white glare of publicity. The high-
profile meetings offered world leaders the opportunity to appeal directly to recalcitrant parliaments and expanded electorates back home, which exerted
pressure on them as never before. The rhetorically gifted and sometimes even
charismatic political leaders were in the full democratic spotlight at center
stage. They knew it and used it with theater-like performances.

The 1919 Paris Peace Conference

The Paris Peace Conference was profoundly different from earlier such meetings. The international public sphere had not only expanded in geographical
terms, but also in the number of topics of international concern. The defeated powers were not allowed to attend, nor was the new revolutionary regime in
Russia invited. Contemporaries believed that for the first time in Europe's history the peoples' voices would be heard in the corridors of power. The Council
of Ten, which consisted of the political leaders of the United States, Great Britain, France, Italy, and Japan, together with their foreign ministers, served as the
supreme authority. Additionally, there were seventeen committees and forty-
one subcommittees, which in a short time held more than sixteen hundred
meetings, many of them chaotic. Wilson was obsessed with secrecy in Paris. He
did not trust anybody and each night placed the most important documents
in a safe that he locked personally. Few people were allowed to see these documents. The more than five hundred journalists who were eagerly waiting for
news, were furious when they discovered that "open covenants openly arrived
at" did not mean that the negotiations were held in public. In mid-March 1919
Wilson, Lloyd George, Georges Clemenceau, and Vittorio Orlando decided to
withdraw from the outside world. As Council of Four (or even Council of Three
after Orlando walked out) they drafted the peace treaty with Germany. Their
proceedings were informal, chaotic, and often acrimonious. Wilson was forced
by his European colleagues to compromise his ideals. Nevertheless, a new form
of international political culture was emerging.

In the French capital the victors also discussed plans for a world order with
new rules and ultimately created one. In the future, international peace would
be organized through the League of Nations. The Covenant establishing the
League formed the first part of all the peace treaties. The aims of the world organization were to promote international cooperation and to achieve international peace and security. The League of Nations was to be an association of sov-

3

—

THE
PERIOD
OF
THE
WORLD
WARS

1914-1945

ereign states that pledged themselves, through signing the Covenant, not to go to war before submitting their disputes with each other, or with non-member states, to arbitration or inquiry. Its organization included a Council, an Assembly, and a Secretariat. Autonomous but closely connected to it were the Permanent Court of International Justice and the International Labour Organization. The Covenant also spoke of, among others, economic, social, and health matters. The cooperation between states was unprecedented. The passion for peace had never before found expression in an intergovernmental organization of such importance.

The Netherlands and the Paris Peace Conference

After the armistice, the Netherlands found itself diplomatically isolated. The Allies treated the country in an unfriendly, sometimes even hostile way because it had not borne the burdens of the war, but instead profited economically from it. The Hague was criticized for being pro-German in the war years. The admission of the former German emperor and the refusal to surrender him, and, subsequently, the permission for unarmed German forces to retreat via Limburg fostered anti-Dutch sentiments.

During the preparatory phase of the Paris Peace Conference the new minister of foreign affairs, Herman A. van Karnebeek, showed great energy when official information from the Allied and Associated capitals remained forthcoming. Like Wilson and Lloyd George, he hired nonprofessional advisors, such as captains of industry Hendrikus Colijn and Ernst Heldring, professors Cornelis van Vollenhoven and Gijsbert W. J. Bruins, and the *De Nieuwe Courant* correspondent Leo Faust, whose task it was to gather information in London, Washington, and Paris on territorial questions, the League of Nations, and related matters, in order to get the view of the Netherlands accepted and counteract the hostile feelings toward the Dutch. As a result, Van Karnebeek arrived well prepared in May 1919 in the French capital, where he succeeded in counteracting the Belgian demand for annexations of Dutch territory. Through Reneke de Marees van Swinderen, the Dutch envoy at the Court of St. James, he also knew that he could count on the very important support of the South African Jan Christian Smuts, who was a member of the British War Cabinet. From the start Paul Hymans, the insistent Belgian minister of foreign affairs, was fighting a lost cause. Van Karnebeek, countering Belgian demands, made an excellent impression by courting his audience in the language of the new, postwar era that focused on peace.

Following this successful exercise in conference diplomacy, Van Karnebeek went on to defend key Dutch interests elsewhere. One important example is the

023   011

Dutch Minister of Foreign Affairs Herman A. van Karnebeek (center, wearing
a Homburg) and Dutch delegation on their way to the Conference on the Limitation of
Armaments in Washington, November 1921.

3

—

THE
PERIOD
OF
THE
WORLD
WARS

1914–1945

Conference on the Limitation of Armaments held in Washington from November 12, 1921 to February 6, 1922, the first of several attempts at naval disarmament after the Great War. It was also an attempt to stabilize the unsettled situation in the Far East and provide for the development of an independent Republic of China. At the end of the conference the U.S., Britain, Japan, and France signed the Four Power Treaty guaranteeing each others' rights to possessions in the Pacific and agreeing to mutual consultations in the event of territorial disputes. The Five Power Treaty (including the four mentioned above plus Italy) provided for a ten-year moratorium on the construction of capital ships, and limited the size of their naval armaments. With the Nine Power Treaty the U.S., England, France, Japan, Italy, Belgium, the Netherlands, Portugal, and China guaranteed the independence and territorial integrity of China and proclaimed the principle of the Open Door Policy.[2]

Van Karnebeek, who was highly critical of America and its political culture, obtained his greatest success as foreign minister at the Washington Conference: the Great Powers reaffirmed and reinforced the Dutch colonial position in the Far East, without making any demands on The Hague. In the 1920s he frequently took part in international summits, although he often considered the results disappointing and complained about the lack of preparation and the ever-present time pressure. The Dutchman also disliked the new diplomatic style of openness.

The United States and the League of Nations in the 1920s

Officially, life began for the League of Nations on January 10, 1920, when the Treaty of Versailles came into effect. Its birth coincided with the near-fatal blow of America's refusal to ratify this treaty and its defection from the peace settlement, including the League of which Wilson had been one of the key architects. According to the U.S. president, the League was "a living thing" and he expected and wanted it to evolve over time. In the fight in the U.S. Senate over the Versailles Treaty, pride, temper, clumsiness, prejudice, and partisanship on the part of both parties, and of both Wilson and Henry Cabot Lodge, all played a role and in the end produced a disaster. Wilson's defeat broke the heart of the world.[3]

The question of American participation in the League was decisively settled, or so it was portrayed, with Warren G. Harding's landslide victory in 1920. The new Republican administration declared in public that the world should abandon all hope that the U.S. would ever join the League, and the State Department even refused to answer League inquiries. Yet, individual American citizens did work with the League: for instance, John Bassett Moore who served as a judge of the Permanent Court of International Justice, Norman Davis who acted as chairman of the Committee that negotiated the Memel Statute, and Jeremiah Smith who was appointed League Commissioner in Hungary.

After the Washington Conference the State Department began to entertain the possibility of corresponding, with infinite precaution, with the League's secretary general, Sir Eric Drummond. In May 1922 an American official was permitted to accept appointment as a member of the League's Health Committee. Later that year the astronomer George Ellery Hale became a member of the Committee on Intellectual Co-operation. After he fell ill, he was replaced by Robert Millikan, the 1923 Nobel laureate in physics. Secretary of State Charles Evans Hughes sent an unofficial observer to the Opium Committee in 1923 and allowed the American minister to Switzerland to establish direct contacts with League officials to convey informally the American point of view without committing Washington in any way. The idea of membership or the assumption of financial responsibility was taboo. Secretary General Drummond hoped that the participation of official and unofficial American representatives in the League's technical and humanitarian work would lead to future political links. Even after Anglo-American private bankers and financiers untied the "Gordian Knot" of reparations in 1924 and American money was mobilized through the Dawes plan for European purposes, the Calvin Coolidge administration rejected any political commitment to the economic arrangements it had promoted. Whenever Harding, Hughes, or Coolidge spoke of the League, they were careful to treat it as an essentially European affair. Though it was not expressed in such terms, they wanted to keep it away from the western hemisphere. Successive American governments, however, were interested in joining the Permanent Court of International Justice, which was established in The Hague in 1922. In 1923 Senate isolationists blocked Hughes' campaign for American membership, which was carried on by every U.S. president from Harding to Roosevelt.

The League of Nations contributed to the stabilization and recognition of juridical norms and parliamentary forms in international politics. From the mid-1920s leading statesmen and ministers of foreign affairs of the Great Powers, like Sir Austen Chamberlain, Aristide Briand, and Gustav Stresemann, became regular visitors to Geneva where they discussed and settled the affairs of Europe. These were also years of international peace and economic prosperity. From 1925 onward, the U.S. was present at all conferences on questions concerning armaments. The American delegates took part in the discussions, but remained aloof whenever the subject of political conditions that would facilitate disarmament came up. In 1927 the U.S. also agreed to participate in the work of the League's Economic and Financial Organization. At the end of the decade, the League of Nations had become part of the international landscape and the "Geneva system" was working.

3

—

THE
PERIOD
OF
THE
WORLD
WARS

1914–1945

The optimism of these years also found expression in a new American contribution toward a peaceful international system. In August 1928 the Kellogg-Briand Pact, or the International Treaty for the Renunciation of War as an Instrument of National Policy, was signed in Paris. The Pact aroused great hopes and was extremely popular because it was conceived and brought to life by the people and government of the United States. Ultimately, sixty-two nations ratified the treaty. For contemporaries this "pious declaration against sin" symbolized a new development in American foreign policy, a new sense of responsibility to contribute to the holy cause of peace. The Pact directed that its signatories renounce war as an instrument of national policy, and that the settlement of disputes should never be sought except by peaceful means. However, it provided no measures of enforcement, which was typical of the kind of "peace diplomacy" conducted during this decade.

The Netherlands and the League of Nations
in the 1920s

After the war, the Netherlands' foreign policy was restructured. In Van Karnebeek's words, it changed from a "policy of neutrality" to a "policy of independence." The Netherlands joined the League, albeit without much enthusiasm. When The Hague learned that Belgium would send a delegation — that would be anti-Dutch — to the First Assembly and that other countries would send their ministers of foreign affairs, Van Karnebeek decided that he would personally lead the Dutch delegation, even though he did not consider the League to be very important. In Geneva the Dutch minister attracted attention during the debate on the secretary general's report on the Council's work.

Because he personally wanted to ensure that his fellow countryman Bernard Loder was chosen for the Permanent Court of International Justice (he subsequently became its first president), Van Karnebeek went to the Second Assembly.[4] There, he was unexpectedly offered the chairperson's gavel, which he accepted. He made an excellent impression as chairman, especially in his opening words and closing speech, in which he spoke eloquently in the vocabulary of the new international political culture. In later years he was seen in Geneva as one of the League's elder statesmen. In 1932 Van Karnebeek was even sounded out about his availability for the post of secretary general, which he declined.

At the meetings of the Assembly the Dutch delegates contributed to the juridification of international relations. Maintaining its sovereignty, liberalizing trade, and avoiding involvement in the Great Powers' conflicts were of prime importance to The Hague. Thus, it was not surprising that the Dutch delegation was vehemently opposed to a potential expansion of the Council's authority because it was a political organ dominated by the Great Powers. For the same reason the Netherlands rejected both the Draft Treaty of Mutual Assistance of 1923 and the Geneva Protocol for the Pacific Settlement of Disputes of 1924. Van Karnebeek was also highly critical of multilateral intellectual cooperation. In 1924, the Dutch government even protested in Geneva against a brochure on universities in the Netherlands. The League's secretary general personally involved himself in the case because he feared negative consequences for the Committee on Intellectual Co-operation and the Secretariat.

An interesting example of Dutch idealism in Geneva was that in 1923 the Netherlands brought a complaint of the Six Nations Iroquois Indians against Canada to the attention of the League, suggesting that the circumstances were such as to endanger world peace. The Canadian and British governments protested against this interference in domestic affairs, after which the Dutch no longer supported the Six Nations.

Van Karnebeek's successor, Frans Beelaerts van Blokland, took a conservative line in Geneva. With regard to the Kellogg-Briand Pact his first reaction was to wait and see. The fact that the United States was involved played an important role in the Dutch government's decision to join eventually, on July 12, 1929.

The United States, the Netherlands, and the League in the 1930s

The Geneva system came to a standstill in the 1930s as a result of the onslaught of revisionist powers. Shortly before, global economic depression in combination with a financial crisis had set in. In September 1931 Japanese troops invaded Manchuria, after which China appealed to the League of Nations under Article 11 of the Covenant and to the U.S. as a signatory to the Kellogg-Briand Pact. During this crisis the American secretary of state, Henry A. Stimson, maintained close contact with the League. In January 1932 he notified Japan that there would be no recognition of any illegal situation arising out of violations of the Kellogg-Briand Pact. Stimson's nonrecognition doctrine contained no threat of sanctions and failed to impress the Japanese. It received only lukewarm support from the League Council. The Netherlands refused to take sides in the Far Eastern conflict. The Hague found a stable Japan a far more attractive prospect than a nationalist and revolutionary China, and it saw the Japanese as an important check on indigenous nationalist movements in its colony. When in February 1933 the Assembly found Japan guilty of violating Chinese sovereignty, the Japanese delegation left the meeting. The next month, Japan gave notice of its withdrawal from the League, thus dealing a heavy blow to the system of collective security. Interestingly, however, Japan continued to have representation on

3

—

THE
PERIOD
OF
THE
WORLD
WARS

1914-1945

the League's committees and within the Secretariat for a number of years afterwards. The Manchurian crisis overlapped with the World Disarmament Conference (1932–34). The latter's collapse meant an even bigger blow to the League's prestige and to the hopes of its supporters. In October 1933 Adolf Hitler pulled Germany out of the conference and out of the League itself. A third blow was the failure of the World Monetary and Economic Conference in London (1933), which was torpedoed by President Franklin D. Roosevelt.

Around the mid-1930s a new European war seemed likely. Under Hitler, German foreign policy became more openly revisionist. The Nazi leader defied the Versailles Treaty with the reintroduction of military conscription and in 1936 sent German troops into the demilitarized Rhineland zone, against which the League appeared powerless. An even bigger threat to the League was Italy's aggression in Abyssinia in 1935–36. The League members unanimously condemned the invasion, but their slow and half-hearted application of economic sanctions—which left out the crucial item of oil—did little except showing once more the League's ineffectiveness. The American reaction to the Italian-Abyssinian conflict was that the State Department issued a neutrality proclamation embargoing the sale of arms, but not raw materials, to either side. Soon, American exports of oil, copper, and steel to Italy rocketed up.

In the mid-1930s The Hague began to realize that Hitler Germany posed a serious problem to the country's security. The Dutch government took part in the economic sanctions against Italy, which, however, were revoked in July 1936 at the Special Session of the Assembly. At that meeting, the Netherlands and six other small European countries declared that they henceforth would regard the sanctions provisions of Article 16 of the Covenant as optional rather than mandatory. From then on the Dutch distanced themselves increasingly from the League's political activities. The Dutch government acknowledged that the world organization had failed to create a working system of collective security. It believed, however, that the League's functional and technical work should be maintained or even extended. For instance, in the final years before the outbreak of World War II the Netherlands did become an active supporter of multilateral intellectual cooperation.[5] In response to the German attack on Poland in September 1939, the Dutch government declared that the country would remain neutral. In May 1940 German troops invaded the Netherlands, after which the government fled to London and continued to fight. Notwithstanding Roosevelt's sympathy for the Allies and his dislike of Hitler, the U.S. stayed technically neutral until December 1941. But the hopes for a new international political culture that had been so prevalent following World War I, were clearly in ruins.

1   Michael Riemens, *De passie voor vrede:
    De evolutie van de internationale politieke
    cultuur in de jaren 1880–1940 en het
    recipiëren door Nederland* (Amsterdam:
    De Bataafsche Leeuw, 2005); Zara
    Steiner, *The Lights that Failed: European
    International History 1919–1933* (Oxford:
    Oxford University Press, 2005).

2   Benjamin D. Rhodes, *United States
    Foreign Policy in the Interwar Period,
    1918–1941: The Golden Age of American
    Diplomatic and Military Complacency*
    (Westport, CT: Praeger, 2001), 43;
    Riemens, *Passie*, 163-167.

3   John Milton Cooper, Jr., *Breaking
    the Heart of the World: Woodrow Wilson
    and the Fight for the League of Nations*
    (Cambridge: Cambridge University
    Press, 2001).

4   Michael Riemens, "Nederlandse steun
    en toeverlaat bij het Volkenbonds-
    secretariaat: Joost Adriaan van Hamel
    (1880–1964)," in Duco Hellema,
    Bob de Graaff, and Bert van der Zwan,
    eds., *In dienst van Buitenlandse
    Zaken. Achttien portretten van ambte-
    naren en diplomaten in de twintigste
    eeuw* (Amsterdam: Boom, 2008). 47-59,
    272-273.

5   Remco van Diepen, *Voor Volkenbond en
    vrede. Nederland en het streven naar een
    nieuwe wereldorde 1919–1946* (Amster-
    dam: Uitgeverij Bert Bakker, 1999);
    Michael Riemens, "La coopération
    intellectuelle multilatérale dans l'entre-
    deux-guerres vue des Pays-Bas," in
    l'Organisation des Nations Unies pour
    l'éducation, la science et la culture,
    *60 ans d'histoire de l'UNESCO. Actes du
    colloque international, 16–18 novembre
    2005, Maison de L'UNESCO, Paris* (Paris:
    UNESCO, 2007), 93-96; Michael Rie-
    mens, "'Towards a League of Minds':
    Intellectuele samenwerking in het kader
    van de Volkenbond," in Bob de Graaff
    and Duco Hellema, eds., *Instrumenten
    van buitenlandse politiek: Achtergronden
    en praktijk van de Nederlandse diploma-
    tie* (Amsterdam: Boom, 2007), 87-96.

3

—

THE
PERIOD
OF
THE
WORLD
WARS

1914–1945

DUTCH COMPANIES IN THE UNITED STATES AND AMERICAN COMPANIES IN THE NETHERLANDS

—

FERRY DE GOEY

The international level of foreign direct investment (FDI) declined between 1918 and 1940 because of the disruptive effect of World War I, increasing protectionism, and the severe economic crisis following the Wall Street crash of October 1929.[1] The Netherlands and the United States, however, followed a slightly different path. After World War I, both countries became creditor nations while most private companies recorded huge profits during the war. The availability of cheap capital and large financial reserves stimulated cross-border investments.

Dutch Companies in the United States

The Dutch have a long history of foreign investments, including in the United States.[2] At the beginning of the twentieth century, the Netherlands was the biggest per capita investor in the U.S. Well-known Dutch investors before 1914 included the Dutch-British combine Royal Dutch/Shell, light bulb manufacturer Philips, and the shipping company Holland America Line, but also many smaller companies like Van Houten (chocolate) and Van Berkel's Patent (slicing machines), besides a large number of mortgage banks. Philips gave up the U.S. market for patent reasons in 1916 and maintained only a small presence in America during the interwar period.

Dutch investments in the United States in 1914 are estimated at $650 million. Almost 80 percent was classified as portfolio and barely 20 percent ($125 million) was in direct investments (see table 1). During the interwar period, the level of portfolio investments (mainly land holdings, government bonds, and railways shares) decreased relative to direct investments, while the over-all amount of Dutch investments in the U.S. steadily rose, in contrast to inter-national developments. Three companies — Royal Dutch/Shell, Unilever, and (from 1929) ENKA/AKU made considerable direct investments between 1918 and 1940. In 1937, they alone accounted for approximately 95 percent of all Dutch investments of this type in the United States.[3] Competition in the U.S. was strong and the consumer market was, from a Dutch perspective, huge and grow-ing rapidly. This required large investments in manufacturing, management, and marketing right from the start. As a result, not all Dutch direct investments in the U.S. were successful. This is evident from the investment history of mar-garine producer Jurgens (before his company became part of Unilever) and of aircraft manufacturer Fokker.

Royal Dutch/Shell

The most important Dutch investor in America was Royal Dutch/Shell, headed from 1901 until 1936 by H. W. A. Deterding (1866–1939).[4] In 1907, Royal Dutch merged with the British "Shell" Transport and Trading Company to form Roy-al Dutch/Shell. The most important event in the oil industry before 1914 was, however, the dissolution of Standard Oil in May 1911 into many smaller com-panies. The chief enterprise to emerge from this process was Standard Oil of

TABLE 1
Dutch foreign investment in the U.S., 1914–41 (millions of U.S. dollars)

	1914		1929	1934		1939	1941	
	Amount	%	Amount	Amount	%	Amount	Amount	%
Portfolio	525	80.8		461	67.3		320	48.8
Direct	125	19.2		224	32.7		336	51.2
Total Dutch	650	100	400	685	100	888	656	100
Total World	7,090		4,700	4,943		6,247		
Dutch share	9.2%		8.5%	13.9%		14.2%		

Source: M. Wilkins, The History of Foreign Investment in the United States, 1914–1945
(London/Cambridge, MA: Harvard University Press, 2004), 9, 72, 365, 442.

3

—

THE
PERIOD
OF
THE
WORLD
WARS

1914–1945

New Jersey (later called Exxon). The breaking-up process of Standard Oil took many years to complete, but it offered opportunities for investments in the U.S. by non-American oil companies, including Royal Dutch/Shell.

Until 1905, Royal Dutch had only minor interests in the United States, but that changed after Standard Oil began selling gasoline in the Netherlands (see below). Deterding decided, "purely as retaliation," to begin exporting gasoline to Standard Oil's home market and set up a retail company in 1910. This resulted in fierce competition between both companies. From 1912, Deterding steadily increased investments in the U.S., including exploration, production, and retailing. Royal Dutch/Shell's first American oil refinery, located in Martinez, CA, started production in 1915. March 1917 saw the completion of the refinery in Cushing Fields, OK, and in the same year construction began for a large refinery in St. Louis, MO. Royal Dutch/Shell acquired, among many other companies, the Valley Pipeline Company, Dundee Petroleum, and California Fields, and later merged these into the Roxana Company (from 1928: Shell Petroleum). On the West Coast it established the Shell Company of California and on the East Coast Shell Union Oil Corporation (a merger with Union of Delaware in 1924). To counter anti-Shell sentiments (stimulated by Standard Oil's public relations campaigns), Deterding allowed American investors to play a role in these subsidiaries. Other subsidiaries included Shell Pipe Line Corporation (1914), Shell Development Company (1926), and Shell Chemical Corporation (1929).

By the early 1930s, Royal Dutch/Shell had thus evolved into a vertically integrated oil company in the United States, controlling operations downstream (exploration, drilling) and upstream (retailing). The economic crisis did slow down investments, but after 1934 the American economy showed signs of recovery and Royal Dutch/Shell further expanded its business, including a new factory for grease oil in Wood River, IL. By 1939, Shell Oil USA, the American holding company, was a major oil company and the Shell trademark a familiar sight along the highways.

A Failed Joint Venture: Anton Jurgens and Kellogg Products Incorporated

In 1876, margarine producer Jurgens & Co. (from 1906: N.V. Anton Jurgens' Vereenigde Fabrieken) visited the United States as a contributing member to the Dutch exhibition at the Centennial in Philadelphia.[5] U.S. demand for margarine was very limited, because of the low price of butter and extra taxes on margarine. Margarine producers needed to obtain a special license, while several states introduced laws banning the addition of artificial coloring agents to make margarine look like butter.

In 1912 Spencer Kellogg & Sons Inc., an American linseed oil producer from Buffalo, NY, at that time headed by Spencer Kellogg (1856–1944), visited Anton Jurgens' (1867–1945) headquarters in Oss. They proposed to build a large margarine plant, but Jurgens hesitated because he considered the American market for margarine too small for large-scale production. During World War I, however, consumption in the U.S. increased rapidly and both companies founded a 50-50 joint venture, Kellogg Products Incorporated (share capital of $2.5 million). Kellogg was responsible for managing the factory, while Jurgens offered technical assistance.

Spencer Kellogg & Sons later built two more factories on their own account: one for linseed oil and another for soap (both using the same raw materials as margarine). Kellogg then proposed a new, larger margarine factory in Chicago. Jurgens rejected the plan because the plant in Buffalo still operated at a loss. In his opinion, management at Buffalo and quality controls remained unsatisfactory, while the sales organization performed poorly. Matters worsened during the short economic recession of 1920. In 1922, Jurgens sold his share in the joint venture and the Buffalo margarine plant was shut down the following year.

Jurgens' main rival in the Netherlands, Van den Bergh Fabrieken N.V., followed a different investment strategy in the United States. In 1920, they bought the almost bankrupt margarine producer Stefenson Incorporated at Poonten (near New York). Van den Bergh also acquired a 25 percent share in the Lipton Tea Corporation in 1927. This more cautious approach seems to have been more profitable than Jurgens' strategy of Greenfield investments.

Jurgens and Van den Bergh merged in November 1927 to form the Margarine Union, and in 1929 this company merged with the British company Lever Brothers to become Unilever. Lever Brothers' American investments reintroduced Jurgens in the U.S. Since the turn of the century Lever Brothers had owned soap factories in Cambridge, MA, Philadelphia, and Vicksburg, MS. In the 1930s, Unilever built new factories in Chicago (edible oils), Baltimore (soap), and New York, while Boston became the home of the company's American headquarters. Before World War II, Unilever succeeded in becoming one of the largest margarine and soap producers in the United States.[6]

The Fokker Aircraft Company: Exiting
a Lucrative Market

Anthony ("Tonny") Fokker (1890–1939) earned his reputation as a German aircraft manufacturer during World War I. After the war, he transferred his factory to Amsterdam and founded the N.V. Nederlandsche Vliegtuigfabriek (1919).[7] Fokker always believed that America, because of its size, offered great opportu-

3

—

THE
PERIOD
OF
THE
WORLD
WARS

1914-1945

nities for the aircraft industry. As early as January 1920, he opened a small sales office in New York, the Netherlands Aircraft Manufacturing Company. Three years later, Fokker established his own manufacturing company, the Atlantic Aircraft Company, at Hasbrouck Heights, near New York. An important customer in this early period was the United States Army. In response to the growing "buy American mood" in the 1920s, Fokker decided to give his subsidiary a more American appearance and invited a number of local investors. These included, among others, Universal Airlines and Pan American Airways (Pan Am). Americans also sat on the board of directors, while Tonny accepted a post as chief engineer. The Air Corps Act of 1926 required the company to become mostly American-owned and American-managed, or it would risk losing its lucrative contracts with the U.S. military. Tonny Fokker therefore created a holding company—the Fokker Aircraft Corporation (1925)—and successfully applied for American citizenship. Major American shareholders in the new holding were the investors Frank Ford, George Davis, and Lorrilard Spencer.

Charles Lindbergh's successful nonstop Atlantic crossing in 1927 promoted a strong interest in the aircraft industry. The Fokker Aircraft Corporation was able to issue new shares in 1928, totaling $2.2 million. The major shareholder and president in the corporation now became Western Air Express, owned by James A. Talbot, also CEO of Richfield Oil Corporation. One year later, however, Alfred Sloan, Jr., CEO of General Motors (GM), bought a 40 percent share in Fokker Aircraft Corporation in order to compete with Ford, which had developed into a major aircraft manufacturer.

The New York stock market crash in October 1929 led to the cancellation of many orders and as a result Fokker Corporation's annual report showed a large deficit that year. GM decided to strengthen its grip on the company and increased its shareholding to 50 percent, while Tonny Fokker held only 20 percent in "his" company. In fact, he soon discovered that he no longer controlled the company and GM demoted him from his position as chief engineer. The new company name was General Aviation Company, but disaster struck in March 1931. A Fokker aircraft crashed in Kansas, killing all six passengers including Knute Rockne, the famous football coach of Notre Dame University. GM and Tonny Fokker formally broke off their association in late 1931. In the following months, General Aviation Company closed all remaining Fokker factories, while Tonny devoted his attention to the factory in Amsterdam. Thanks to his American contacts, Fokker became the sole agent for the marketing of Douglas and Lockheed aircrafts in Europe.

American Companies in the Netherlands

During the interwar period American investments abroad increased by more than 300 percent. Investments in Europe grew at an even faster pace. The gross nominal value of U.S. capital invested abroad in 1914 was $3,514 million (of which $709 million in Europe) and $11,491 million in 1938 ($2,386 million in Europe).[8] American companies wanting to invest in Europe faced a politically, economically, and culturally fragmented market requiring all sorts of adjustments. During the 1928 Olympic Games in Amsterdam the Dutch could taste their first bottle of Coca-Cola. Translating the slogan "Refresh yourself" proved, however, very difficult because in Dutch it meant "Wash your hands." This did not stop Coca-Cola from investing in the Netherlands and in 1930 it established the N.V. Nederlandsche Coca-Cola Maatschappij, a sales office and production plant in Amsterdam.

The level of American direct and portfolio investments in the Netherlands before 1900 remained small. Before World War I, Singer Company, Mobil Oil, Pure Oil, Texaco, and Standard Oil had set up sales offices in the Netherlands. These oil companies also owned storage facilities in the ports of Rotterdam, Amsterdam, and Vlissingen. After the war, the number of U.S. companies investing in the Netherlands steadily increased. These included, besides Coca-Cola, American Milk Products, General Electric, Westinghouse, Bell Telephone Manufacturing Company, ATT, RCA, Western Union Telegraph Company (Amsterdam), Gulf Oil, Du Pont, Eastman Kodak, Goodyear, B.F. Goodrich, Firestone Tire and Rubber Company, and the Boston Blacking Company.[9]

TABLE 2
U.S. direct investments in Europe and the Netherlands, 1919–40 (millions of U.S. dollars)

	1919	1929	1936	1940	1943
Europe total	694	1340		1420	
Netherlands (excl. Dutch East Indies)	c. 25	43.2	18.8		59.6
Dutch share	3.6%	3.2%			

Sources: F. Stubenitsky, *American Direct Investment in the Netherlands Industry. A Survey of the Year 1966* (London: Routledge, 2001), 46; For the year 1936, P. D. Dickens, *American Direct Investment in Foreign Countries–1936* (Washington, DC: Department of Commerce, Economic Series No. 1, 1938), 9; And M. Wilkins, *The Maturing of Multinational Enterprise: American Business Abroad from 1914 to 1970* (Cambridge, MA: Harvard University Press, 1974), 31, 56, 181.

3
—

THE
PERIOD
OF
THE
WORLD
WARS

1914–1945

Table 2 summarizes the development of American FDI in the Netherlands between 1919 and 1943. American FDI in the Netherlands increased from $25 million in the early 1920s to $43.2 million in 1929 (or 3.2 percent of total U.S. investment in Europe). The most important investors were the major petroleum companies. In 1929, they had invested almost $12.1 million in the Netherlands. Besides, American companies had made substantial investments in the Dutch East Indies, which amounted to $66 million in 1929, including more than $30 million in oil production and refining by Standard Oil. The economic crisis of the 1930s did have a negative impact on American FDI in the Netherlands, but not all industries suffered equally. The book value of U.S. direct investment shrank to $18.8 million in 1936, but grew again to $59.6 million in 1943.[10]

Standard Oil and the American Petroleum Company

From the beginning of the oil industry in the early 1860s, Standard Oil dominated the Dutch market using local agents in the ports of Rotterdam, Amsterdam, and Vlissingen. In the 1880s, Standard owned large storage facilities for petroleum (lamp oil).[11] In 1891, Standard set up a sales company for the Belgian and Dutch markets, the American Petroleum Company (APC; from 1938: N.V. Standard Amerikaansche Petroleum Compagnie). At first, the APC continued to sell petroleum *en gros* to Dutch wholesalers, but several years later it decided to take an interest in the retail trade. To this end the N.V. Maatschappij tot Detailverkoop van Petroleum "De Automaat" was founded. The APC thereafter established other sales firms, the main examples being the N.V. Maatschappij Pétrolifère (1910) and the N.V. Petroleumhandel "Holland" (1922). Both were typical Standard Oil "fighting companies" to thwart the interests of competitors. They mounted "stunt" campaigns concerning the price of gasoline, kerosene, and other oil products. The introduction of cheap electric light bulbs forced Standard Oil to develop new consumer products, such as gasoline for automobiles.

In 1906, APC's "De Automaat" started selling gasoline under the brand name of "Motor Spirit." Fierce competition with Royal Dutch/Shell ensued, lasting several years until they formed a price cartel. These cartels proved to be not very durable because "outsiders" (independent oil producers) offered gasoline at lower prices. Following international arrangements in 1925 and 1929 (Achnacarry), both companies made new cartel agreements in the Netherlands including several "outsiders." All oil companies in Rotterdam relocated their storage and production facilities to the (First) Petroleum Harbor in 1935. Standard Oil developed plans to build an oil refinery at the new site, but World War II frustrated the completion of the project until the 1950s.

Oilman of APC Petroleum is tapping petroleum from oil tin on wooden hand cart. The oilman and his customer are both wearing South Beveland (Province of Zeeland) traditional costumes.

3

—

THE
PERIOD
OF
THE
WORLD
WARS

1914–1945

Ford Motor Company in Rotterdam and Amsterdam

As early as 1903, Ford appointed an agent in the Netherlands.[12] The N.V. Ford Motor Company of Holland, a sales office in rented premises in Rotterdam, was officially established on March 6, 1924. The British and Belgian plants supplied the Dutch subsidiary with assembled cars, trucks, and tractors. Sales in the Netherlands went extremely well: at least 40 percent of the cars sold in 1926 were Fords (passenger cars and trucks). On March 4, 1928, the company changed its name to N.V. Nederlandsche Ford Automobiel Fabriek, giving it a more Dutch appearance. Following Henry Ford's wishes, the board of commissioners included several Dutchmen. Ford's policy was instigated to counter latent anti-Americanism, mainly by leftist intellectuals, in the Netherlands in the 1920s, and to attract additional foreign capital.

Since the tenancy contract lasted only until 1929, Ford requested from Rotterdam's mayor and aldermen that the company be allowed to rent or purchase an industrial site in the harbor. Finding a suitable site proved very difficult, but eventually a factory was built in the western part of the city. Henry Ford, on his visit to Rotterdam on October 3 and 4, 1930, found the, by then nearly finished, factory too small for the Dutch market. He also disliked the location since it did not connect directly with water as he had instructed. Because no other proper site was available, Ford decided to build a new, larger assembly plant in the port of Amsterdam in 1931 and closed down the Rotterdam factory.

Although assembly-line work was still the exception in the Netherlands, Ford had no trouble finding sufficient laborers because the company paid high wages and unemployment was on the rise. The number of employees at Ford Amsterdam grew from three hundred in 1932 to six hundred in 1946. Before 1940, the plant produced nearly four thousand units per year, mainly passenger vehicles and trucks for the European market. This made Ford the largest car manufacturer in the Netherlands.

Maurice Boas and IBM

In 1911, Hollerith's Tabulating Machine Company merged with Computing Scale Company of America and International Time Recording Company. In 1924 the combined Computing-Tabulating-Recording Company (CTR), based in New York, was renamed International Business Machine Corporation (IBM). IBM first established itself in the Netherlands through an agency agreement at the beginning of the 1920s: M.C. Boas and L. Fles & Company.[13] The two agents decided to jointly import and rent out Hollerith machines, but their collaboration ended in 1925 because the costs of financing the expensive Hollerith machines were too high for Fles. Boas, however, continued and obtained the sole rights to represent IBM in the Netherlands. The agency changed its name to M.C. Boas, Agent voor Holland en België der Tabulating Machine Company en International Time Recording Company, shortened to Firma Boas.

In the 1930s, Firma Boas developed a business that represented a greater volume per head of the population than any other IBM agency in Europe. As a result, the firm, which had forty-five employees, became an official subsidiary of IBM's new European headquarters in Geneva in 1936. Boas engineers could take the necessary international IBM courses and the company established a small punch-card factory in Amsterdam. In 1938, IBM's Board in New York nominated Maurice Boas "World Leader," as he was the most successful manager of the business outside the U.S. However, World War II forced Boas, being of Jewish descent, to migrate to the United States. During the war, Firma Boas became N.V. Watsons Bedrijfsmachine Maatschappij.

Hollywood Movie Studios and the
Nederlandse Bioscoop Bond

The film industry was one of the fastest-growing industries in the 1920s and 1930s. Before World War I, the major American movie studios developed the "Hollywood studio system": a wholly vertically integrated movie business. After the war, they expanded overseas, including the Netherlands. Despite competition from European movie makers (particularly Germany and France) and language difficulties, American movies held a market share of about 50-60 percent in the Netherlands.[14]

The main business of the British and Continental Trading Company (established in 1920) was the distribution of American films in the Netherlands. United Artists (UA) acquired the company in 1928 and renamed it N.V. United Artists Corporation of Holland. They appointed Loet C. Barnstijn (1880–1953), an important figure in Dutch movie history, as their CEO. Bartel Wilton, the son of a famous Dutch shipbuilder, began distributing and screening American movies in 1920. He represented Metro Goldwyn Mayer (MGM) until, in 1929, that company founded its own sales office: N.V. Metro Goldwyn Mayer Filmmaatschappij. Other American movie producers followed UA and MGM, including Fox Movies (1923), Paramount (early 1920s), Columbia (1927), Warner Brothers (1932), and RKO (1937).

After establishing their distribution offices, the American film producers attempted to integrate forward in screening, but Dutch movie-theater owners

551

3

—

THE
PERIOD
OF
THE
WORLD
WARS

1914–1945

were able to frustrate their plans. Together with Dutch movie distributors they had founded, in 1921, the Nederlandsche Bioscoop Bond (NBB), which became a powerful pressure group. During the economic crisis, the NBB was able to limit the number of newly built movie theaters, particularly in the large cities. This policy also affected direct investments by American companies. In 1935, MGM proposed to open a new movie theater in Amsterdam, but the company met with fierce opposition from the NBB and ultimately did not implement the plan. The American movie studios were thus unable to pursue the same strategy in the Netherlands as they had previously done in the United States, and remained distribution offices until the 1950s.

Concluding Remarks

During the interwar period, the Netherlands was the third-largest investor in the United States, while the U.S. was (probably) the largest investor in the Netherlands. In absolute terms, Dutch direct (and portfolio) investments in the U.S. were substantially larger than American direct investments in the Netherlands. Dutch investments, however, were mainly in oil, chemicals, and food, while American companies also included new consumer industries, such as cars, tabulating machines, and movies. A small number of Dutch companies accounted for the majority of FDI in the United States, while a range of U.S. companies invested in the Netherlands, although these also included some large investors (e.g., the oil industry). Dutch companies in the United States struggled in a large integrated and competitive market, while the survival of American companies in the Netherlands depended on successful adjustments to a wholly different environment. This period thus saw many instances of successful FDI, but also failures followed by exit strategies.

1   G.G. Jones, *Multinationals and Global Capitalism: from the Nineteenth to the Twenty-First Century* (Oxford: Oxford University Press, 2005), 20-31.

2   F.M.M. de Goey, "Dutch Overseas Investments in the Very Long Run (c. 1600–1990)," in R. van Hoesel and R. Narula, eds., *Multinational Enterprises from the Netherlands* (London/New York: Routledge, 1999), 32-61.

3   Mira Wilkins, "Dutch Multinational Enterprises in the United States: A Historical Summary," *Business History Review* 79 (Summer 2005): 193-274; K.E. Sluyterman, *Dutch Enterprise in the Twentieth Century. Business Strategies in a Small Open Economy* (London/New York: Routledge, 2005), 92-100.

4   J. Jonker and J.L. van Zanden, *From Challenger to Joint Industry Leader. A History of Royal Dutch Shell* (Oxford: Oxford University Press, 2007), 1:229-244, 414-491.

5   F.J.M. van de Ven, *Anton Jurgens Hzn*

*1867–1945. Europees ondernemer,
bouwer van een wereldconcern* (Zwolle:
Waanders, 2006).

6 G. Jones, "Control, Performance, and
Knowledge Transfers in Large Multi-
nationals: Unilever in the United States,"
Business History Review 76 (Autumn
2002): 435-479; Ben Wubs, "Unilever
between Reich and Empire 1939–1945.
International Business and National
War Interests" (Ph.D. dissertation,
Erasmus University, 2006), 27-44.

7 M. Dierikx, *Fokker: A Transatlantic
Biography* (Washington, DC: Smithsonian Institution Press, 1997).

8 A. Maddison, *The World Economy* (Paris:
OECD Publishing, 2006), 101.

9 F. Stubenitsky, *American Direct Investments in the Netherlands Industry*
(London: Routledge, 2001); F.A. South-
ard, *American Industry in Europe*
(London: Routledge, 2000).

10 Mira Wilkins, *The Maturing of Multinational Enterprise: American Business
Abroad from 1914 to 1970* (Cambridge,
MA: Harvard University Press, 1974),
31, 56-58, 181; The increase between
1936 and 1943 resulted to a large extent
from the migration of Jewish refugees
from Germany; See J. Hagedoorn and
R. Narula, "Evolutionary Understanding
of Corporate Foreign Investment
Behavior: U.S. Foreign Direct Investment
in Europe," in R. Narula, ed., *Trade
and Investment in a Globalising World*
(Amsterdam: Pergamon, 2001),
156-185.

11 F. de Goey, "Henri Deterding, Royal
Dutch/Shell and the Dutch Market
for Petrol," *Business History* 44.4
(Winter 2002): 55-84.

12 F. de Goey, "Ford in the Netherlands,
1903-2003. Global Strategies and
National Interests," in H. Bonin, Y. Lung,
and S. Tolliday, eds., *Ford. The European
History 1903–2003* (Paris: Éditions
P.L.A.G.E., 2003), 2:233-267; F. de Goey,
"De assemblagefabriek van Ford in
Rotterdam (1924–1931). Lokale overheid
versus een multinational," *NEHA-Jaar-
boek voor economische, bedrijfs- en
techniekgeschiedenis* 63 (2000): 166-195.

13 F. de Goey and B. Wubs, "US Multinationals in the Netherlands in the 20th
Century: The Open Gate to Europe,"
in H. Bonin and F. de Goey, eds.,
*American Companies in Europe (1890–
1980): Strategy, Identity, Perception
and Performance* (Geneva: Droz, 2008),
149-185.

14 K. Dibbets, "Het bioscoopbedrijf tussen
twee wereldoorlogen," in K. Dibbets and
F. van der Maden, eds., *Geschiedenis
van de Nederlandse film en bioscoop tot
1940* (Weesp: Het Wereldventer, 1985),
231-271; K.H.F.M. Dibbets, *Bioskoop-
ketens in Nederland: ekonomiese koncen-
tratie en geografiese spreiding van een
bedrijfstak, 1928–1977* (Amsterdam:
Universiteit van Amsterdam, 1980);
Information on American movie studios
is from the Cinema Context database,
http://www.cinemacontext.nl.

3

—

THE
PERIOD
OF
THE
WORLD
WARS

1914–1945

554

DUTCH-AMERICAN RELATIONS DURING WORLD WAR II

—

ALBERT KERSTEN

Introduction

In November 1939, Franklin D. Roosevelt extended an offer of hospitality to the Dutch royal family. It met with a friendly response from Queen Wilhelmina, who considered accepting on behalf of Princess Juliana and her children. This exchange was the start of a sporadic correspondence between the two heads of state, which would continue until 1944.[1] For Wilhelmina, it was unthinkable that she would leave the Netherlands while her subjects fought on. She ended up spending five years in exile in London, though, which was the center of Allied politics in the early years of the war. Crown Princess Juliana left for Canada with her children in May 1940; staying in the United States was not an option due to its neutral status. Nevertheless, the ties between the House of Orange and the Roosevelts did intensify. Prince Bernhard paid regular visits to the Roosevelts at the White House and Princess Juliana often spent the summer with her children in upstate New York, where the president came to see her. Political ties were also strengthened. In August 1942, Queen Wilhelmina became the first Dutch monarch to pay an official visit to Washington, where her speech to Congress made a considerable impression. She described the Allied democracies as indomitable forms of government that constantly renewed themselves, in contrast with the enemy: "the autocrat, incapable of rejuvenating himself, … every day nearer to his end, his regime doomed to die with him." Wilhelmina described the suffering of the Dutch in the occupied territories in Asia and Europe, as well as their resistance. She went on to express her belief that the answer of the American people would have been the same. The queen referred to the Atlantic Charter and the United Nations Declaration as the foundation for future peace, but stated emphatically that "first of all there is a war to be won." She reminded Congress of the first Dutch salute to the American flag in 1776: "that ancient partnership we see revived today. ... United we stand, and united we will achieve victory."[2] It was the ultimate expression of Allied solidarity.

While the close personal ties and the shared wartime objective held by President Roosevelt and Queen Wilhelmina formed a solid foundation for relations between the two countries, they did not reflect the diplomatic reality. World War II was a turning point. Even though the Netherlands was the second-most important foreign investor in the U.S. and materials from the Dutch East Indies (present-day Indonesia) were vital to U.S. industry, political relations had been anything but intensive. Until May 10, 1940, the *Pax Britannica* was a cornerstone of the Netherlands' international position. In hindsight it seems obvious that the *Pax Americana* would be the Netherlands' new security anchor, but for contemporaries this was less self-evident. The 1940–45 period was a chastening time for the Dutch government and people as they made up for lost time in the arena of international power politics, after over a century of voluntary neutrality. The Netherlands experienced firsthand what it meant to be involved in a major conflict. It had to come to terms with the relativity of its status as a small European country with extensive colonial possessions, but without sufficient military resources, and was plunged into a crash course in international power politics. The nature of this transition came to the surface in the Netherlands' relations with the United States.

Dutch Overseas Territories

The occupation of territory in Europe also raised questions about the fate of the overseas territories. The British government stationed troops to reinforce the defense of the Netherlands Antilles and Shell's oil refineries. Japan immediately showed great interest in the Dutch East Indies and their raw materials, while the German occupier also tried, albeit without success, to add the Netherlands' Asian assets to the spoils of war. Governor General A.W.L. van Starkenborgh declared the Dutch East Indies neutral and only agreed to trade talks with the Japanese in mid-June 1940 after the capitulation of the French. In the eyes of the world, the government in Batavia entered into negotiations with a Japanese delegation, but behind the scenes British and U.S. advisers were hard at work to prevent the Dutch from making concessions in agreements on the supply of strategic goods. Eventually the negotiations failed in midyear 1941 without Japan being able to increase its strategic supplies from the Dutch East Indies. At the same time, trade with the United States intensified, particularly in the very same strategic raw materials. But while the governments in the Dutch East Indies and the Netherlands were able to exert some influence in this respect, it

555

was mainly the business community and manufacturers' organizations for materials such as rubber and tin that encouraged such developments.

The Dutch government was seriously worried about the Japanese threat and attempted to obtain guarantees from Great Britain for a joint defense against a Japanese offensive. But military resources were scarce. Churchill was only willing to give such a guarantee after he had secured a joint defense commitment from the United States. Against the wishes of Van Starkenborgh, Anglo-Dutch staff meetings began in November 1940, and in February 1941 American-British-Dutch-Australian (ABDA) top-secret staff talks on military cooperation were held in Singapore. The result was a far-reaching contingency plan. The stationing of undercover liaison officers followed, but joint staff exercises were out of the question until Roosevelt would make the political decision to enter the war, a move for which he lacked domestic support at the time. He took this step on December 5, 1941, but it was too late to ensure any real implementation of the plan. Military cooperation also failed to get off the ground in the ensuing months that led up to the capitulation in March 1942. ABDA Command, located at Allied headquarters in Bandung, closed its doors at the end of January 1942, shortly before Japan launched its offensive on the Dutch East Indies. This sparked a great deal of ill feeling among the colony's civil and military authorities, who felt betrayed by their allies and could not appreciate the need for a retreat on the Australian line of defense due to the lack of Allied military strength.

Washington's tendency to act entirely in accordance with its own insights and without consulting its Dutch ally proved to be a hard lesson for the Netherlands, one which also applied to the political front. In the Dutch legalistic reasoning it was self-evident that the Netherlands should occupy a place alongside the United States and Great Britain in strategic decision making on the war against Germany and Japan. Dutch Minister of Foreign Affairs Eelco N. van Kleffens, who combined legalistic thinking with incisive political analysis, was determined to travel to Washington as soon as possible at the start of 1942, when news reached him of the first results of the talks between Churchill and Roosevelt. The Netherlands had signed the United Nations Declaration as a matter of course, but Van Kleffens also wanted a say in Allied planning. Roosevelt offered the Netherlands a seat on the Pacific War Council, but that was not enough. After attending a single meeting, Van Kleffens was convinced that the Council was a body where no real decisions were made. He demanded a seat in the Combined Chiefs of Staff (CCOS), but Roosevelt refused, offering participation in an advisory capacity. Van Kleffens "resisted and … obtained 'participation' on an equal footing" for issues pertaining to the Netherlands, such as the liberation of the Dutch East Indies and Dutch territory in Europe, or the deployment of the Dutch merchant navy.[3] Although Van Kleffens had won his point, in its actual workings the CCOS remained closed to the Netherlands. In the end, this

3

———

THE
PERIOD
OF
THE
WORLD
WARS

1914–1945

President Franklin D. Roosevelt and First Lady Eleanor Roosevelt with
Queen Wilhelmina of the Netherlands at the White House, Washington, DC,
August 5, 1942.

3

—

THE
PERIOD
OF
THE
WORLD
WARS

1914–1945

only underlined the Dutch sense of marginalization. It was a stark confrontation with reality, even if Roosevelt did his best to sweeten the pill. A few months later he proposed stepping up diplomatic relations to the ambassadorial level, thereby fulfilling a long-cherished Dutch wish. Queen Wilhelmina's official visit and her speech to Congress gave the impression that the Netherlands was an important ally. Yet, all in all, Roosevelt's sympathy for the Netherlands did not provide much in the way of political results.[4]

U.S. Hegemony

After the Japanese occupation of the Dutch East Indies, the Netherlands had far more dealings with the U.S. government. This was due in part to the United States' responsibility for the conduct of the war in the Far East. All Dutch armed forces there came under the command of General MacArthur. The recapture and liberation of the Dutch colony was in his hands. Acting Governor General J.H. van Mook built a good relationship and held direct consultations with him to lay the groundwork for the restoration of Dutch rule. MacArthur used his influence in Washington to have a marine brigade and the Dutch East Indies' air force trained in the United States. U.S. involvement was not only limited to the Netherlands' colonies in Asia. As early as September 1941, Roosevelt proposed deploying a 1,600-strong U.S. force to protect the bauxite mines in Suriname, which provided 65 percent of the raw materials for the U.S. aviation industry. This unleashed a fierce discussion within the Dutch cabinet, during which the deep-seated reflexes of neutrality and the forces of loyal Allied cooperation battled to gain the upper hand. Opponents of Roosevelt's proposal wondered whether it was the start of a permanent U.S. occupation and the loss of Suriname. The government decided it had no choice but to "abandon our pride in this matter" and gave its consent.[5] A few months later, U.S. troops also took it upon themselves to protect the refineries on Curaçao and Aruba. Westminster and Washington arranged this takeover without any consultation, which irked the Dutch government.[6]

The first two years of the war presented the Dutch government with a steep and difficult learning curve. This manifested itself most clearly in Dutch relations with the United States, partly due to the incongruence in the international position of the two countries, and partly due to the Netherlands' lack of familiarity with the American world. Until 1940, Dutch politicians had mainly looked to Great Britain and had grown to know and rely upon world politics British-style. While Britain could not count on automatic acquiescence from the Netherlands, there was an implicit trust between the two countries: both were colonial powers, geared toward international trade and both demonstrated a certain pragmatism. It was much more difficult to empathize with the American mindset. Van Kleffens and the minister for the colonies, H.J. van Mook, were convinced that the Dutch government had to shift its focus to the United States and should extricate itself from its ties with the British government. They regarded the U.S. as the new leading international power and recognized the necessity of putting the Netherlands on the map in the United States. At the start of the war, moves to set up a Netherlands Information Bureau in New York were already under way: contact was sought with the American press. A far greater challenge lay in convincing other Dutch ministers to turn their gaze across the Atlantic. Visits to America were seen as one way of bringing about a change in their mentality. Within the government, a certain tension remained between a pro-American camp led by Van Kleffens and Van Mook and a pro-British camp. This was most noticeable when the decolonization of the Dutch East Indies was being formulated.[7]

Van Kleffens' reorientation toward U.S. leadership occurred in 1941–42. His marriage to an American gave him a sense of familiarity with the American mentality. In his analysis of the international situation he observed that the technological progress of the arms race and the rise of air power had robbed the Netherlands of the capability to defend its territory independently. It could only continue to do so by cooperating with other democratic countries. Since Great Britain was no longer capable of safeguarding the balance of power in Europe, it was up to the United States to shoulder this responsibility. Given that country's traditional aversion to Europe and its general tendency toward isolationism, achieving this would not be easy, but it was absolutely essential if new German and Japanese aggression was to be prevented. Van Kleffens believed Washington would be prepared "and indeed desire, to contribute to attaining this important object," i.e., leadership of the postwar international security organization.[8] He feared a return to isolationism once the war came to an end. Roosevelt was convinced of the need for his country to play a leading role in the postwar world and adopted the "one world" approach. Global cooperation was his credo and the four Great Powers — the U.S., Great Britain, the Soviet Union, and China — were to take the lead.

Van Kleffens considered this approach misguided. In his view, the League of Nations had proven that global cooperation did not work, since in crisis situations there were not enough common interests to motivate states to take joint action. He did, however, believe that regional bonds existed and that regional security organizations should therefore form the basis for an international network. As he saw it, the United States and Great Britain, as powers with global interests, should take part in every organization and carry responsibility for peace and security. As a power with territories in various parts of the world, the Netherlands should be part of four organizations and be recognized implicitly

559

3

—

THE
PERIOD
OF
THE
WORLD
WARS

1914–1945

as a middle power.[9] Van Kleffens availed himself of the opportunity to discuss his plan with Roosevelt during Queen Wilhelmina's official visit. The monarch had cherished high expectations, but the talks on future peace announced by Roosevelt failed to materialize. The president showed himself to be a master of the anecdote, but important issues remained unaddressed. At Wilhelmina's request, he listened to Van Kleffens' proposal but "with nothing more than a degree of superficial attention" and without responding to the substance at all. He advised Van Kleffens to discuss the matter with Secretary of State Cordell Hull, Under Secretary Sumner Welles, and Vice President Henry A. Wallace. It was clear to Van Kleffens that Roosevelt was focused on the conduct of war and that his priorities did not lie with postwar issues. This did not, however, stop Roosevelt from expounding miscellaneous views on such issues as international food production, international cartels for raw materials, the total disarmament of Germany and Japan, and the partial disarmament of all other states with the exception of the Great Powers. Roosevelt also complained about "the old-fashioned ideas of the British, with their focus on balance-of-power politics and their lack of imagination," but did not present a consistent plan of action. It was a source of hope that Roosevelt — despite his anticolonial course — was in favor of restoring Dutch authority in the East Indies. Yet, Van Kleffens was not overly impressed. To him the U.S. president remained a spinner of yarns.[10]

This did nothing to alter the fact that the Dutch government had no choice but to follow the Anglo-American lead in the preparations for the postwar international order. All governments were hard at work developing their plans, including those for their own state and society, and the Netherlands was no exception. A readiness to embrace international cooperation and a rejection of the inward-looking nationalist 1930s approach to tackling problems characterized all this planning. For the Netherlands as a trading nation, it was crucial that the U.S. government should be geared toward liberalizing international trade by breaking down trade barriers and doing away with preferential treatment.

The first real test for the allies was the United Nations Food and Agriculture Conference in Hot Springs, VA, in May 1943, an initiative greeted with some skepticism. After two weeks of talks, the first blueprint for an international body, the Food and Agriculture Organization, was on the table and agreement on the basic principles had been reached. The conference was an important step in Dutch-American relations because the Dutch delegation set the tone for action at follow-up conferences on organizing the postwar world. The Netherlands was a conscientious advocate of international cooperation in many different areas and supported the U.S. initiative for this reason. Much to the satisfaction of the Dutch, their country was part of the conference's Steering Committee and the Dutch contributions to methods of increasing food production and protecting producers' rights also met with support. Both of these developments reinforced the sense that the Netherlands was an important international player. This feeling did not last long, however. The American plan for the United Nations Relief and Rehabilitation Administration (UNRRA), presented to the allies in midyear 1943, was the first expression and application of Roosevelt's Four Policemen concept. It reserved a leading position for the four Great Powers and elicited a furious response from Van Kleffens, who slammed the notion of a central committee of the Great Four as a structure suited "to [a] German model but not suitable for the United Nations." He bemoaned the fact that not a single European power was included.[11] With this criticism, Van Kleffens launched a determined battle for an uncompromising application of the principle of equal treatment for the smaller allies and against a privileged position for the Great Powers. It was a battle doomed to fail. Although Van Kleffens received support from Australia and Canada, which also claimed a status as middle powers on the basis of their wartime contributions, this failed to produce results at the UNRRA and later at the United Nations. The Netherlands finally agreed to the Central Committee of the UNRRA and to the veto rights of the Great Four in the United Nations Security Council. Van Kleffens' position was primarily determined by his legalistic approach to international relations and his partial blindness to power politics. His recalcitrant stance put a strain on Dutch relations with U.S. authorities without producing material gains.

Toward a New Relationship

The architecture of the postwar world order was not the only important aspect of relations with the United States. At a bilateral level, the war gave rise to a range of new issues that formed the basis for talks and sometimes also for differences of opinion. One protracted example of the latter concerned the U.S. government's decision, on May 10, 1940, to freeze all assets and receivables of Dutch persons and legal persons in German-occupied territory. Only weeks later, the first measure taken by the Dutch government in exile was to lay claim to all assets outside the occupied territories owned by Dutch persons and legal persons living under occupation in the Netherlands. These two measures created an insoluble political problem. The governments found pragmatic solutions in individual cases, but it was Washington that determined the path and the pace of any transfers. This was not the only problem regarding the implementation of Dutch and U.S. regulations. Dutch merchant navy personnel were subject to an injunction to continue sailing, but a conflict of interest arose in cases where sailors deserted in American ports and went to work for U.S. companies for higher wages. Washington resisted moves to try offenders before a Dutch

561

3

—

THE
PERIOD
OF
THE
WORLD
WARS

1914–1945

court in London, but did agree to cooperate in tracking them down and putting them to work in the Allied merchant navy. Agreements on carrying out Dutch measures for purposes of warfare were usually established fairly smoothly.

There was, however, no evidence of smooth sailing in cases where the Dutch government attempted to set its own course outside U.S. strictures. After the founding of the UNRRA, the Netherlands wanted to continue its own relief program, an ambition that Washington had no intention to support. When the Dutch government tried to obtain a loan from the Treasury to finance reconstruction in the Netherlands, Washington was not responsive. The United States was less rigid in its response to Dutch demands to be involved in the preparations for the Allied liberation expedition and in regulating the transitional administration. Washington reached an agreement with the Dutch government regarding the exercise of its sovereign rights by the Allied forces. The Civil Affairs Agreement of May 1944 was of great significance to the government in exile because it was proof of the inviolability of its own sovereignty.

Bilateral consultation had the effect of broadening and intensifying relations between the two countries. In May 1940, the Netherlands' official representation in Washington was still a modest post with three diplomats and one naval attaché. By mid-1944 it was home to sixteen accredited diplomats. Ambassador Alexander Loudon, stationed in Washington since 1939, had the reputation of not being the easiest of men: he suffered from poor health and could be impatient and demanding. Thanks partly to his marriage to an American, Loudon had access to an outstanding network of contacts, which even reached the White House in the person of Justice Felix Frankfurter. The staff grew with the addition of young diplomats and experts. The cementing of relations was most clearly illustrated, however, by the special missions that operated independently of the embassy. One of these was the Netherlands Purchasing Commission, a government center set up as early as 1940 that worked for both the Dutch East Indies and the London-based government. At the instigation of the government in exile, an operation was started in the fall of 1940 to stockpile food provisions for the Netherlands after its liberation. Many purchases were made in the Dutch East Indies but once the Japanese occupation began, purchasing in North and South America was led by the Food Purchasing Agency in New York. In the summer of 1942, the Economic, Financial and Shipping Mission was established and given the task to coordinate the activities of the aforementioned organizations and to study the United States' outlook on the postwar world. The purview of this mission partly overlapped with that of the embassy, as did the authority of the Military Mission that was installed a short time later. Thus, demarcation disputes became inevitable. Loudon was afraid of being marginalized in his dealings with U.S. authorities. Van Kleffens was able to prevent this by tightening the reins on the missions. This steady growth in the Netherlands' official presence in the United States was a unilateral process, an expression of the exponential increase of America's importance to the Netherlands. There was no evidence of a similar development in the opposite direction. U.S. Envoy George A. Gordon remained in The Hague until the end of May 1940; the appointment of a member of the American ambassadorial staff in London as chargé d'affaires for the government in exile followed by mid-August 1940; in March 1941 Roosevelt appointed an envoy extraordinary, Colonel Anthony J. Drexel Biddle, Jr. The Netherlands' significance to the United States in the Far East was demonstrated by the appointment of Stanley K. Hornbeck, head of the Far Eastern Division of the State Department, to the post of ambassador at the end of 1944. In addition to a small number of diplomats, the embassy was mainly staffed by attachés for the armed forces, an obvious choice in a period of liberation operations.[12]

Conclusion

The liberation of the Netherlands did not mean the end of the war; the prospect of a period of warfare in the Far East loomed, and in the liberated Netherlands the government began preparing its troops to do their part to free the Dutch East Indies from occupation. Effective cooperation between the Netherlands and the United States had developed in the region. The allocation of the Dutch East Indies to the newly formed British-zone South East Asia Command (SEAC) on August 15 cast a shadow, however, over the elation at Japan's surrender. Once again this was a decision made by the British and the Americans, without so much as a nod to the Netherlands. This appreciation of Dutch-American relations at the end of World War II was nothing new. The Netherlands' economic and financial might as the world's second colonial power carried hardly any weight in the world of international relations and it was the United States that ultimately called the shots, in its role as the strongest member of the alliance against Germany and Japan. Yet, this period brought more than just a harsh introduction to international power politics. It also gave rise to the shared struggle for the protection of democracy and humanitarian values, a common goal that Queen Wilhelmina and President Roosevelt both expressed and represented.

1   Cees Fasseur, *Wilhelmina. Krijgshaftig in een vormeloze jas* (Amsterdam: Balans, 2001), 268-269; Albert E. Kersten, "Wilhelmina and Franklin D. Roosevelt: A Wartime Relationship," in Cornelis A. van Minnen and John F. Sears, eds., *FDR and His Comtemporaries. Foreign Perceptions of an American President*

3

—

THE
PERIOD
OF
THE
WORLD
WARS

1914–1945

(New York: St. Martin's Press, 1992), 85-96.

2 A.E. Kersten and A.F. Manning, eds., *Documenten betreffende de buitenlandse politiek van Nederland 1919–1945. Periode C: 1940–1945* (The Hague: Martinus Nijhoff/Instituut voor Nederlandse Geschiedenis, 1976–2004) (hereafter *DBPN C*), 5:219-221.

3 *DBPN C*, 4:263.

4 Albert Kersten, *Buitenlandse Zaken in ballingschap. Groei en verandering van een ministerie 1940–1945* (Alphen aan den Rijn: A.W. Sijthoff, 1981), 136-139; H. Daalder, "Nederland en de wereld 1940–1945," *Tijdschrift voor Geschiedenis* 66 (1953): 170.

5 *DBPN C*, 3:290-293.

6 *DBPN C*, 4:74-75, 83, 100-101, 109-112, 239-240.

7 See the article by Frances Gouda elsewhere in this volume.

8 *DBPN C*, 4:599-603, here 602.

9 Albert Kersten, "Van Kleffens' plan voor regionale veiligheidsorganisaties," *Jaarboek van het Departement van Buitenlandse Zaken 1980–1981* (The Hague: Staatsdrukkerij, 1981), 157-164.

10 *DBPN C*, 5:58-61, 67-68.

11 *DBPN C*, 6:569.

12 Data in enclosures 2 and 3 of *DBPN C*, vols. 1-8.

CROSSING BORDERS: AMERICANS AND THE LIBERATION OF THE NETHERLANDS

———

WIM KLINKERT

The Americans Are Coming!

America looms large in the Netherlands' collective memory of the liberation at the end of World War II. After all, the great military operations in Western Europe took place under American leadership. An American, General Dwight D. Eisenhower, commanded the Allied coalition that fought its way from the beaches of Normandy to the streets of Berlin. Even more impressive was the figure of President Franklin D. Roosevelt, who sadly died just before the war's end. We find the names of these great men immortalized throughout the Netherlands. The country is also home to the vast American military cemetery in Margraten, which became the final resting place for thousands of American soldiers starting in November 1944. Yet, many of the brave men buried there were actually killed in action in Germany. They were laid to rest in the Netherlands because the American military does not believe in burying its war dead on enemy soil.[1] When we take a closer look at military actions in the Netherlands, it is important to note that the role played by American troops during World War II seems to be great and impressive, but was in reality fairly limited, both on land and in the air. What were the reasons?

The Ground War

The Allies' objective in Western Europe was clear: to destroy the German military might. Everything was centered around that one, crucial goal. Europe's geography meant that it would be necessary for the Allies to pass through Dutch terri-

3

—

THE
PERIOD
OF
THE
WORLD
WARS

1914-1945

tory. The liberation of the Netherlands was not a chief concern, but merely the byproduct of a military strategy geared toward defeating the Nazis. National borders were of no importance in determining the course of military action. For this reason, it is not strictly accurate to speak of "the liberation of the Netherlands" as a distinct military objective. Furthermore, Eisenhower had divided his coalition army into two forces: one made up of British and Canadian soldiers under Bernard Montgomery, and another comprised of Americans, led by Omar Bradley. Montgomery was responsible for the left (western) flank that covered almost all Dutch territory and was to enter Germany via the Netherlands.

British-American plans for the liberation of Western Europe had been in the pipeline since 1942. After several years spent gathering forces and coordinating strategy, the decision to take action was finally made in early 1944. That spring, a large force of British, Canadian, and American troops was to land on the beaches of Normandy in a bold opening move, followed by a slow, steady march to the Rhine. The advancing troops would fan out in a broad front stretching from the Netherlands to Switzerland and would be divided into three forces, two of which — the 21st Army Group under Montgomery and the 12th Army Group under Bradley — would operate from Normandy. This split was determined by the positions of the armies during the Normandy invasion, which, in turn, rested on a coincidence: the majority of American troops had been stationed in southwest England, which made it easier to transport them to the westernmost beaches. The Allied military strategists planned for the American troops to push on through Belgium and, via Aachen, to Germany's industrial heartland, the Ruhr Valley, which they were expected to reach in May 1945.[2]

But war seldom goes according to plan. Things got off to a slow start in the hedgerows of Normandy, yet the German opposition soon disintegrated. At this point, the only thing that hindered the Allied advance on the Ruhr Valley was a shortage of fuel. Eisenhower ordered the U.S. Army XIX Corps to take control of what would be the first major German city to fall into Allied hands: Aachen. This assignment required the 30th Infantry Division to enter Dutch territory. On September 7, 1944, this division was positioned near the famous Waterloo battlefield. Three days later, their progress slowed by fuel shortages, they were forced to halt their advance in the Maastricht-Liège sector to the west of the Meuse River, on Belgian soil. There had been no contact with the enemy for nearly a week, as the German army was busy regrouping in the south of the Netherlands and along the Siegfried Line.

The Meuse was the Nazis' last line of defense before Aachen. On September 10, American troops mounted an attack on the river between Maastricht and Visé. The German opposition quickly gave way, and the first American ground troops set foot on Dutch soil at 10:00 a.m. on September 12, 1944, just south of Maastricht.[3] One week later, the Americans reached the Siegfried Line. South Lim-

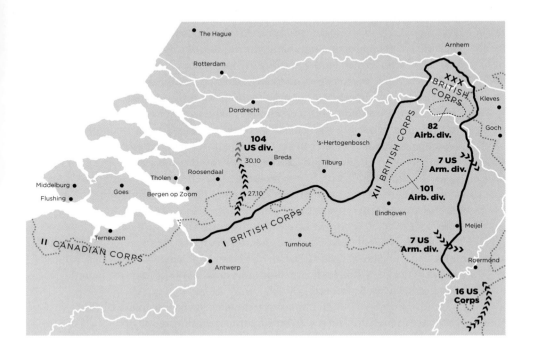

The Hague

Rotterdam

Arnhem

XXX
BRITISH
CORPS

Kleves

Dordrecht

82
Airb. div.

Goch

104
US div.

's-Hertogenbosch

30.10

Breda

Tilburg

7 US
Arm. div.

XII BRITISH CORPS

Middelburg

Tholen

Roosendaal

101
Airb. div.

Flushing

Goes

Bergen op Zoom

27.10

Eindhoven

Meijel

7 US
Arm. div.

I BRITISH CORPS

Terneuzen

II CANADIAN CORPS

Turnhout

Roermond

Antwerp

16 US
Corps

U.S. Army and Airborne Divisions and the liberation of
the southern Netherlands, 1944–45.

3

—

THE
PERIOD
OF
THE
WORLD
WARS

1914-1945

burg had been relinquished to the Allies with little struggle. The real work facing the American troops still lay ahead: they had to break through the Siegfried Line and seize Aachen. It was a struggle that would drag on until October 21.[4]

American troops remained in South Limburg until August 1945. The region became a "rest and recreation area" for the troops engaged in heavy combat just across the German border and those who had been engaged in the Ardennes since December 1944. As a result, South Limburg became the most "American-ized" part of the country. Along with the troops came headquarters, logistics depots, training grounds, and recreational facilities. The recreational facilities, in particular, tended to worry local Dutch authorities, but the people of South Limburg relished the chance to become acquainted with American popular music and dance, as well as such typically American luxuries as chewing gum and nylon stockings. Hollywood stars, including Marlene Dietrich and Fred Astaire, came to Maastricht to entertain the troops and the local population. The quartering of American troops in Dutch homes further served to bring the two groups into close contact. While the Dutch Military Authority was officially in charge of the region, the real power lay with the Americans, in the form of U.S. Civil Affairs. Leo Paul Senecal, who headed the Maastricht division of U.S. Civil Affairs until August 1945, was even given honorary citizenship of Maastricht and later had a street named after him.

The liberation of South Limburg by the Americans took place during a critical phase in the Allied forces' strategic campaign. During the first weeks of September 1944, the Allies were suffering from "victory disease." The German forces had been so thoroughly routed in the previous months that the Allies were convinced the end of the war was in sight. Montgomery argued that the Allies should take advantage of this momentum with a rapid advance to the Rhine. Under his command, troops would cross the Rhine at Arnhem and encircle the Ruhr area to the north, dealing what he felt would be a deathblow to the German army. By September 3, plans were already in place to deploy the 82nd and 101st U.S. Airborne Divisions, who were at that time stationed in England, to seize a series of bridges over major Dutch waterways. The next day, Eisenhower transferred command of these divisions to Montgomery.

On September 10, Montgomery received the go-ahead for Operation Market Garden, the largest airborne drop in history, and the most extensive U.S. military deployment ever on Dutch soil. On September 17 and in the days that followed, more than twenty thousand American troops parachuted into the south of the Netherlands. Their objective was to capture the bridges the advancing British army would need for its advance on Arnhem. At this critical juncture, Eisenhower stood behind the British field marshall. He, too, believed that it would be a swift victory.[5]

The dramatic events surrounding Operation Market Garden still capture the public's imagination.[6] Ultimately, the operation to secure the bridge at Arnhem failed, ending instead in weeks of fighting in the south of the Netherlands in which the American airborne troops were involved to no small degree. Montgomery, who intended to go ahead with his invasion of the Ruhr Valley despite this setback, established a base of operations in the Dutch city of Nijmegen, roughly fifteen kilometers (ten miles) south of Arnhem. At this time, in late September, he still had the support of Eisenhower, who even obliged Montgomery by shifting the dividing line between Montgomery's troops and those of Bradley northward. This ensured that the British units would advance onward from Nijmegen while the U.S. XIX Corps, who had previously liberated South Limburg, were left to mop up the remaining pockets of German resistance to the south of the British line of advance. U.S. army units, such as the 7th Armored Division, consequently became mired in protracted battles in the swampy Peel Marshes of North Limburg, with little success.

Eisenhower still believed in Montgomery's ability to push on eastward toward the Rhine while continuing efforts to clear access to the Belgian port of Antwerp. In early October, however, he began to have doubts. Montgomery had won few clear victories, and Antwerp's port was still inaccessible to the Allies. In the Peel Marshes to the south, U.S. troops remained unable to break through German defenses. Eisenhower urged Montgomery to rethink his strategy, but the latter, dangerously close to insubordination, refused. The crisis finally ended on October 16 when Eisenhower issued Montgomery direct orders to abandon his attempts to cross the Rhine and redirect all efforts to opening up the port of Antwerp so that it could be used as a logistics base for further Allied operations. The previous dividing line between the British and American troops was restored. Bradley's 12th Army Group turned over operational control to the British and Canadian 21st Army Group.

As mentioned, the Allied advance through northern France and Belgium proceeded much more quickly than planned, resulting in serious logistical problems. Badly needed supplies had to be brought ashore across the beaches of Normandy and transported over crumbling remains of Europe's infrastructure. The resulting chronic supply shortages meant that large-scale offensives such as Market Garden could only proceed if resources were diverted from other areas. Alternative resupply points, such as canal ports, had all either been too severely damaged to be usable or were still in German hands. British troops had managed to capture the port of Antwerp nearly intact on September 4, but it remained inaccessible as the Nazis still controlled the approach to the port, the Scheldt Estuary, which was in Dutch territory. Montgomery had ordered his Canadian forces to secure the banks of the Scheldt. It was too great a task for

3

—

THE
PERIOD
OF
THE
WORLD
WARS

1914–1945

the Canadian troops alone, but Montgomery refused to send in reinforcements at the expense of his advance toward the Rhine. Only in mid-October, after the Rhine mission had failed completely, did Montgomery give in to Eisenhower's demands that he make the opening of the Scheldt his highest priority. He appealed to the Americans for help, as during Operation Market Garden and the battles in the Peel Marshes. This assistance arrived in the form of the 104th Infantry Division, who were active under Montgomery in the western part of the Dutch province of North Brabant in late October-early November 1944. Within several weeks, the German forces had been driven out of Zeeland and most of North Brabant, leaving the Allies at last free to make use of the port of Antwerp.

The liberation of the Netherlands came to a virtual standstill in the winter of 1944–45. In the months since September 1944, the Allies had managed to clear the south of the Netherlands of all German troops, though they had not yet succeeded in crossing the Rhine from Dutch soil into Germany and would fail to do so for the remainder of the war. They were likewise prevented from advancing northward within the Netherlands by the system of rivers and canals bisecting the country, which proved to be a formidable natural obstacle made even more effective by German intervention. The Allies' supply problem had eased up slightly with the opening of Antwerp's port, but German opposition along the borders of the Third Reich was fiercer than ever.

This is how the winter of 1944–45 began for the Allies. On December 7 a group of high-ranking generals, including Eisenhower and Montgomery, met in Maastricht, where Montgomery stubbornly maintained that he should be the one to lead the Allied forces and that his original strategy, consisting of a concentrated thrust across the Rhine into Germany, was far superior to Eisenhower's plan. Afterwards, he vented his frustration at being overruled in a letter to the British secretary of state for war, Sir James Grigg: "The American plan for winning the war is quite dreadful; it will not succeed, and the war will go on. If you want to end the war in any reasonable time you will have to remove Ike's hand from the control of the land battle ... ."[7] But he was wasting his breath. The American military and political leaders had no intention whatsoever to increase Montgomery's role.

The events of that winter proved more dramatic than anyone could have imagined. The brutal Ardennes Offensive (Battle of the Bulge) pushed the front line back nearly to South Limburg. Though they suffered heavy losses, the Allies were ultimately able to put a stop to this desperate gamble on the part of the Germans. By January 1945, the German army was on the retreat, more exhausted than ever. This enabled the Allies to make their first major inroads into Germany's western front starting in February 1945. Montgomery was still pushing for command of an Allied offensive focused at the heart of Germany, north of the Ruhr Valley. In his opinion, this offensive should receive top priority, while the U.S. troops' advance from the south would be of secondary importance. Eisenhower refused these terms, but did allow Montgomery to launch an offensive in the direction of the Rhine, codenamed Operation Veritable, on February 8.

Montgomery's British and Canadian troops marched out of Nijmegen and pushed on through the Rhineland. It was a long, hard, bitter fight. American units based in South Limburg soon joined them. This American offensive, known as Operation Grenade, involved advancing northward across the Ruhr River. Approaching from the east, via German territory, the Americans reached the Dutch cities of Roermond and Venlo on March 1, 1945. The local Dutch population, which certainly had not expected its liberators to come from the east, was even more surprised to see that the 784th Tank Battalion was comprised of black soldiers. This experimental battalion had been formed at the insistence of General Lesley McNair and First Lady Eleanor Roosevelt, who sought to prove that African Americans were just as capable of serving their country as whites. The fact that the U.S. military could ill afford to exclude such an important source of manpower undoubtedly also played a role in the commission of this and other black units.[8]

The Air War

Starting in 1942, the United States Army Air Forces participated in large-scale strategic bombing operations over Germany. Britain's Royal Air Force (RAF) Bomber Command was responsible for carrying out extensive nighttime air raids on German cities and industrial targets. The role of the American bombers was to attack these same targets by day, with more emphasis on industrial areas and also on elimination of enemy Luftwaffe aircraft. Dutch territory was naturally excluded from these operations. The accuracy of the Allied air strikes left much to be desired, however. American sorties twice dropped bombs on the Dutch side of the border, thinking they were targeting German cities. The first of these cities to be hit was Enschede, on October 10, 1943, while on February 22, 1944, American bombs killed nearly eight hundred civilians in Nijmegen, in one of the deadliest bombardments to take place on Dutch soil.

Other Allied bombardments in the Netherlands were aimed at taking out infrastructure. Targets included the port of Rotterdam, the railways and rail yards surrounding Utrecht, and airfields, all of which were of strategic importance to the Nazis. One particularly catastrophic incident took place on March 4, 1943, when Allied bombers aiming for the port of Rotterdam instead hit a number of densely populated residential neighborhoods. In the following months, unsuccessful bombardments on a power plant in Velsen and the Fokker aircraft facto-

571

3

—

THE
PERIOD
OF
THE
WORLD
WARS

1914–1945

ry near Amsterdam cost hundreds of civilian lives. These disasters led the Allies to reconsider their strategy in the summer of 1943. Instead of aiming for risky urban targets, they began limiting bombardments primarily to airfields, which were part of the Luftwaffe's defenses against Allied bombing missions en route to Germany. The Allies succeeded in damaging a number of these airfields sufficiently to make them unusable to the German forces.

A number of bombings also took place as part of the Allies' Transportation Plan, which sought to destroy routes used by the Nazis to move troops to the coast of France. The Transportation Plan was part of preparations for the invasion of Normandy, formally known as Operation Overlord, which took place on June 6, 1944. The town of Roosendaal, an important railway junction in the south of the Netherlands, was bombed as part of this plan on May 31, 1944. There, too, Allied bombs scattered widely, killing dozens of civilians.

The various air strikes carried out by American forces above Dutch territory were all done in an effort to put a stop to the Nazis and to erode the German will to sustain hostilities. The Netherlands, with its strategic location between Germany and the United Kingdom, did not remain unscathed.

Famine in the Western Netherlands —
Can We Count on the Americans?

American troops were not active in the northern and western parts of the Netherlands. Allied strategy, and ultimately orders from Eisenhower himself, played a crucial role, though, in the events that took place in these areas during the final weeks of the war. The Allies' reluctance to leave the southern Netherlands and head northward toward the major cities in the western part of the country, together with the lack of food transport to this region, resulted in an emergency situation in terms of food supply. By early 1945, the four million people in this part of the Netherlands were literally starving to death. The Dutch government in exile appealed to Allied Command to take action to liberate this area, but their pleas fell on deaf ears. The terrain was unsuitable for large-scale military operations, and the German occupying forces could easily retaliate by flooding large tracts of land, which was in fact already taking place on a smaller scale. Furthermore, Allied troops were completely committed to destroying the German army, which at that point had retreated almost entirely onto German soil. The western Netherlands lay, quite simply, in the wrong direction.

In March 1945, Eisenhower, aware of the extremely precarious food situation, acknowledged that a military operation was not the solution. Earlier that year, in January, Queen Wilhelmina had made an urgent appeal to President Roosevelt: "… the people in North Western Holland are facing physical destruction. It is now the duty of the Netherlands Government to ask for urgent military action for the purpose of driving Germans away from Holland. They feel that this is a reasonable and necessary request."[9] But her efforts were in vain. The Allied strategists limited themselves to preparing for food distribution after the surrender of Nazi Germany. Food drops could not be scheduled any sooner, as all available planes were engaged in air raids in Germany at the time. Strangely enough, the Nazis themselves suggested the solution to this impasse. They would allow emergency food airlifts on condition that the Allies agree to a ceasefire within the Netherlands. Eisenhower accepted these terms on April 23, 1945. He immediately announced to the starving people of the Netherlands, via the BBC and the Dutch radio station Radio Oranje, that food drops were scheduled for April 29. The strategic bombing offensive against the German forces was officially halted. Favorable weather conditions that day contributed to the success of this initial food airlift. The next day, Eisenhower began negotiations with the German occupying forces in the Netherlands to allow the food aid to continue on a larger scale. The sheer humanitarian need of the Dutch population outweighed the moral repugnance of negotiating with the Nazi regime.[10]

The Balance Sheet

Between September 1944 and May 1945, thirteen thousand Allied soldiers lost their lives on Dutch soil: 52 percent were British, 8 percent American. The great majority of American casualties — 62 percent — occurred in the last two weeks of September 1944, during Operation Market Garden and its aftermath.[11] Air combat above the Netherlands proved even deadlier for American forces, with nearly four thousand U.S. lives lost. Of the 3,850 Allied planes shot down in Dutch air space, one-fifth were American.

What did the liberators and the liberated think of one another? To what extent did prejudices or a common cultural background influence their impressions? Did the Americans behave differently from British or Canadian soldiers? Were the Dutch even concerned about the nationality of their liberators? These questions have not yet been examined thoroughly. The scant information available on the subject largely concerns British and Canadian troops, who liberated the majority of the Netherlands. They were stationed in the country for a longer time and wrote down many of their experiences in regimental histories. Things were different for the Americans.[12]

One of the major determining factors in the impressions the Americans and the Dutch formed of one another was geography. Fall 1944 was unusually cold and wet, and neither the swamps of northern Limburg nor the heavy clay of western North Brabant provided ideal conditions for fighting. In addition, the

3

—

THE
PERIOD
OF
THE
WORLD
WARS

1914–1945

Dutch countryside, with its wide, open spaces, offered little cover and made it almost impossible to move without being seen.[13]

Another factor that influenced the two groups' experiences of one another was the fact that very few American soldiers had the chance to get to know the Dutch population. Most of the units were deployed in the Netherlands for only a short time, during which they were engaged in combat. This was particularly true of the divisions that took part in Operation Market Garden, as well as the 7th Armored Division who were brought in from Metz, in France, and immediately put into action. This division remained in the Netherlands for only three months, while the 104th's presence lasted just seventeen days. The exceptions to this rule were the troops stationed in South Limburg who, as mentioned, did stay longer.

The Americans generally had a good opinion of the Dutch, though there was some plundering of civilian property. U.S. troops were touched by the enthusiastic and appreciative response of the liberated Dutch people. Donald Burgett of the 101st Airborne Division remembers how the Dutch were quick to associate the United States with Henry Ford and Chicago gangsters: "So much for the influence of our American movies."[14] American troops were impressed with the language skills of the Dutch, noting that they spoke much better English than either the Belgians or the French. The troops were supplied information about the Netherlands by means of U.S. government brochures.

The actions taken by the Allies were determined by strategic considerations. Military strategy, in turn, determined when and if Allied troops were to pass through Dutch territory. The Dutch government had no say whatsoever in the matter. Regular calls for American reinforcements by Montgomery also brought U.S. troops onto Dutch soil, as did his continual requests to redraw the dividing lines between his troops and the Americans in the interest of his advance toward the Ruhr Valley. Montgomery, who despised Eisenhower and had no faith in his ability to command, favored a single, concentrated thrust over Eisenhower's "broad front" strategy. His ambition spurred him to seek command of the Allied offensive — and preferably of the 12th U.S. Army Group — and proved a decisive factor in the course of the war. To the Dutch, however, this was all irrelevant; they welcomed their liberators with open arms. Looking back on the liberation of the Netherlands, it is clear that the Americans still occupy a prominent place in the Dutch collective memory. This may be due in part to the dominant role that the United States came to play in the Netherlands in the areas of the economy, culture, and the military in the years immediately following the war, which helped the Americans distinguish themselves from the other Allies in the minds of the Dutch.

1 There are currently more than eighty-three hundred graves in the cemetery, as well as a monument listing the names of eleven hundred soldiers missing in action. At the request of families, roughly 60 percent of the deceased have been repatriated to the United States for reburial.

2 Carlo d'Este, *Decision in Normandy* (London: Robson Books, 2000), 72, and Dwight D. Eisenhower, *Crusade in Europe* (New York: Permabooks, 1952), 240.

3 H. Loeber and G. H. Sprenger, eds., *De Amerikanen en de bevrijding van Nederland* (Amsterdam: Bataafsche Leeuw, 1986), 11-20.

4 The battles that took place in South Limburg are described in detail in Charles B. MacDonald, *The Siegfried Line Campaign* (Washington, DC: Office of the Chief of Military History, Department of the Army, 1963), 96-115.

5 Richard Lamb, *Montgomery in Europe 1943-1945* (London: Buchan & Enright, 1987), 206-217.

6 Cornelius Ryan, *A Bridge Too Far* (1974) and the 1977 Richard Attenborough film of the same title.

7 Cited in Lamb, *Montgomery in Europe*, 301.

8 Ulysses Lee, *The Employment of Negro Troops* (Washington, DC: Office of the Chief of Military History, Department of the Army, 1966).

9 Cited in Ben Schoenmaker and Christ Klep, eds., *De bevrijding van Nederland 1944-1945* (The Hague: SDU uitgeverij, 1995), 278.

10 Eisenhower, *Crusade*, 454, 458-459.

11 Schoenmaker and Klep, *De bevrijding*, 317-333. More recent studies of American soldiers' experiences in Europe, such as Stephen Ambrose's *Citizen Soldiers* (1997) and Peter Schrijvers' *The Crash of Ruin* (1998), only discuss the Netherlands in passing.

12 Except for the 101st Airborne Division, whose September–October 1944 battles in the Netherlands featured prominently in Stephen Ambrose's book *Band of Brothers* (1992) and the TV series by Steven Spielberg and Tom Hanks (2001). Joe Mann, the most famous American GI in the Netherlands, who belonged to this division, has a monument dedicated to him in the town of Best. Two museums are devoted to the American war contribution: Wings of Liberation in Best, and the National Liberation Museum in Groesbeek.

13 See Dick Winters, *Beyond Band of Brothers* (New York: Berkley Caliber, 2006), 157.

14 Donald R. Burgett, *The Road to Arnhem* (Novato: Presidio, 1999), 52.

575

4

THE
COLD WAR
AND
BEYOND

1945–2009

POLITICS
AND
SECURITY

4

THE
COLD WAR
AND
BEYOND

1945–2009

POLITICS
AND
SECURITY

———

THE POLITICS OF ASYMMETRY: THE NETHERLANDS AND THE UNITED STATES SINCE 1945

———

DUCO HELLEMA

Political relations between the Netherlands and the United States since 1945 have been determined to a large extent by the great movements that took place in postwar world politics. Unlike the United States, the Netherlands has not been able to influence these movements and could only play a role of any significance on specific occasions. For the Netherlands, foreign policy was a matter of adapting as best as possible to the radically changing international circumstances following World War II. While the United States rose to world power and pursued global foreign policy and security goals vis-à-vis the Soviet Union, the Netherlands tried to defend more specific and limited interests.

Postwar Dutch governments, nonetheless, accepted and even welcomed the new leading role of the United States. For different reasons, they considered American hegemony over Western Europe, at least in principle, a state of affairs that was advantageous to Dutch interests, and as a result they generally advocated Atlantic unity and solidarity. The Netherlands even earned itself a reputation for staunch Atlanticist, pro-American loyalty. That does not mean that the Netherlands easily conformed to the role of a small and docile northwestern

579

4

—

THE
COLD WAR
AND
BEYOND

1945–2009

POLITICS
AND
SECURITY

European ally, as Dutch interests sometimes collided with American concerns. Frustrations and resentment were present over the decline of international status and the loss of the Dutch East Indies. Now and then, there was unease when U.S. foreign policy did not seem to take the interests of Western European allies into account. Moreover, during the 1960s and 1970s a leftist critique of U.S. actions in parts of the non-Western world, such as Vietnam and Chile, would to a certain degree affect the relations between the two nations.

The American-Dutch relationship was above all characterized by asymmetry. The United States was clearly much more important for the Netherlands than the other way around. For many in the Netherlands, the United States was, at least during the first postwar decades, a shining light. Sometimes, the Dutch felt neglected compared to other partners or interests. Sometimes, they seemed to overestimate the attention and sympathy the United States could provide for a small ally. And sometimes, notably in more recent years, the Netherlands, and Dutch foreign and prime ministers, have behaved like well-educated and disciplined members of the Atlantic family — an example for others — expecting to be rewarded for their loyalty as a result.[1]

Stalemate (1945–48)

After World War II world political relations were dominated by two major developments, decolonization and the start of the Cold War. Moreover, international relations took shape within the framework of various new international and multilateral organizations, which significantly changed the character of diplomacy and foreign-policy making compared to the prewar years. In these first postwar years, the struggle for independence in Indonesia and the reconstruction and security of Western Europe were at the forefront of the relationship between Washington and The Hague.

However, the most important international organizations that were to guide Dutch foreign-policy making during these years, NATO and the European Economic Community (EEC), did not yet exist. The Netherlands had joined several new international, or even global, institutions, such as the International Monetary Fund and the United Nations. The United Nations and related institutions were still based upon the wartime, anti-Nazi coalition, and included the Soviet Union and the Eastern European states. The Cold War, and in particular the process of Cold War bloc formation, had not yet started. Some commentators, such as Hans Daalder, have argued that the Dutch prewar foreign policy of neutrality seemed to be resumed, although Eelco van Kleffens, foreign minister in the wartime government in exile, had already concluded in 1942 that neutrality would not be an option in the postwar world.[2]

INTRODUCTION
THE POLITICS OF ASYMMETRY

As the political leader of the Catholic People's Party (KVP) stated in October 1946, the fate of the Netherlands depended on two crucial questions, Indonesia and Germany. Both questions indicate that the Netherlands tried to reestablish its prewar position as colonial power and as trading partner of Germany. The Dutch government deployed almost its entire armed forces in the Dutch East Indies in an effort to regain control over the rebellious colony, which shows that at that time fear of Soviet expansion did not determine Dutch military policy. However, the new postwar realities would determine the outcome of the Dutch military efforts. Ultimately, the United States would play a central role in the settlement of the conflict between the Netherlands and the Republic of Indonesia.

The Dutch government in exile was already aware of the fact that the United States had little sympathy for the postwar continuation of European colonialism. This was one of the reasons why Queen Wilhelmina in 1942 had promised the colonies self-determination. The Dutch government could nonetheless not accept the independence of Indonesia, which Sukarno and Hatta proclaimed in 1945, and refused to negotiate with these leaders because it considered them as traitors who had collaborated with the Japanese.

At first, the United States did not play a decisive role in the Dutch-Indonesian conflict and there were no clear signs that the Americans wanted to stop the Dutch from regaining control. Total Dutch forces deployed in the Indies reached a total of 140,000 toward the end of 1948, a remarkable mobilization considering that the country was still recovering from the hardships of German occupation.

As the struggle in the Dutch East Indies continued, American unease grew. Until 1948 the United States, like Britain, aimed at a compromise, culminating in the agreement signed by the Dutch and the Indonesians in January 1948 on an American warship, the U.S. *Renville*.[3] However, after the Indonesian Republic, which controlled the most important parts of the colony, suppressed a communist rebellion in September 1948, the United States government began to favor quick and complete Indonesian independence. The logic of the Cold War now began to dominate American policymaking. The second Dutch "police action" of December 1948 (effectively a full-scale military offensive aimed at destroying the power center of the Indonesian Republic on the island of Java) met with sharp American criticism and the UN Security Council ordered the Netherlands to end all hostilities. Early in 1949 the Truman administration made it clear that military aid to the Netherlands would be suspended if the Dutch government would not obey the Security Council resolutions. The American position irritated the Dutch, and not in the least Foreign Minister Dirk U. Stikker. The Hague felt that the United States in fact betrayed the Netherlands by forcing the Dutch government to accept a rapid independence of Indonesia. This obser-

4
——

THE
COLD WAR
AND
BEYOND
1945-2009

——

POLITICS
AND
SECURITY

vation was correct, although in retrospect the historian can only conclude that the days of Dutch colonialism in Southeast Asia were over anyway and that American pressure probably saved the Netherlands from a long and hopeless military conflict with the Republic of Indonesia, as Frey concludes in his essay.

Regarding Germany, the Netherlands was also confronted with new postwar international realities. As with Indonesia, the Dutch government first tried to tackle the problem of Dutch-German relations independently. The first postwar Dutch cabinets pursued contradictory goals. On the one hand, the Dutch wanted to resume trading relations, which were considered of vital importance for reviving the economy of the Netherlands. On the other hand, they wanted substantial compensation for the losses and damages inflicted during the years of German occupation, for instance through the (temporary) acquisition of German territory. Moreover, they wanted guarantees against possible renewed German aggression.

Again, the United States played a decisive role. Dutch-German trading relations were liberalized in 1948, but acquiring substantial German territories or economic concessions was out of the question. German access to Marshall aid and the American proposal of September 1950 to admit West Germany to NATO (which would ultimately be realized in 1955) were welcomed in The Hague. In this way, the Federal Republic was embedded in a multilateral structure led by the United States, guaranteeing both the liberalization of Dutch-German trading relations and Dutch security against a possible renewal of German aggression.[4]

The Formation of the Postwar World Order (1948–58)

At the start of the twenty-first century some commentators view the decades of the Cold War with a certain nostalgia, when Dutch foreign policy was still based upon firmness and certainties. Such nostalgia ignores the insecurity, the conflicts, and the uncertainties that existed in Western Europe during the Cold War, not least in the years when the political and military division of the continent took shape. The military structure of NATO had to be built in the early 1950s, and this was no easy matter. For several years, the problem of West Germany's military contribution and the efforts to create a European Defense Community dominated transatlantic diplomacy.

With respect to these problems and conflicts the Netherlands always took an Atlanticist stand, as Megens points out in her contribution. Successive Dutch cabinets were of the opinion that Dutch interests were best served by the formation of a political and military alliance that would link the United States to Western Europe. This was considered of vital importance, not only as a counterweight against Soviet expansionism but also because American hegemony would stabilize political relations within Western Europe itself. Moreover, the Americans had taken the lead in liberalizing the West European economies and forcing a level of policy coordination within the framework of the Organisation for European Economic Cooperation (OEEC). The Hague not only accepted but welcomed American leadership and Atlantic unity.

With the exception of the Dutch Communist Party (CPN), all political parties supported this Atlantic orientation. In many ways this was a logical extension of the prewar anticommunist tradition. The Dutch government had not recognized the Soviet Union until 1942. Dutch loyalty to NATO and the United States was not just a matter for the political parties on the right, such as the conservative liberal Volkspartij voor Vrijheid en Democratie (VVD) and the Christian-democratic parties; the social-democratic Partij van de Arbeid (Labor Party) also became a political cornerstone of Dutch Atlanticism (see the contributions of Koedijk and Zuijdam). Willem Drees, the social-democratic prime minister from 1948 until 1958, did not assume the Soviet Union would actually attack the Netherlands, and was therefore reluctant to raise the Dutch defense budget. However, he feared communist manipulation if postwar economic recovery would be slow, and like many others he strongly believed Western Europe's recovery needed American protection and guidance.

This is not to say that there were no differences of opinion and conflicts between Washington and The Hague. On the contrary, the country that supposedly played the role of an exemplary, loyal ally of the United States — as for instance Alfred van Staden has claimed — had several political and diplomatic confrontations with Washington during the 1950s.[5] Most of these conflicts concerned the former colonies and the relationship between the West and the non-Western world. The Dutch would never be able, as Frey writes, "to turn a colonial conflict into a battlefield of the Cold War." On the contrary, American policymakers would inevitably come to the conclusion that a continuation of such colonial conflicts endangered the interests of the Free World.

This was already clear during the negotiations that led to the signing of the NATO Treaty in 1949. They coincided with the apotheosis of Indonesia's decolonization, and Foreign Minister Stikker tried, unsuccessfully, to get American support for the Dutch position in the Far East by threatening not to sign the NATO Treaty. The Dutch ambassador in Washington, former Foreign Minister Van Kleffens, was instructed to "drop a hint, that the Netherlands without its ties with Indonesia, had little interest in an Atlantic alliance, because the Netherlands had lost its possibility of existence."[6] It proved to be an empty

583

4

—

THE
COLD WAR
AND
BEYOND

1945-2009

—

POLITICS
AND
SECURITY

threat and Stikker duly signed the treaty, but the incident indicates clearly that Dutch resentment over the loss of its colony did have an effect on Atlanticist attitudes.

Relations with Indonesia remained of prime importance for The Hague. At first, the Dutch had high hopes for the Dutch-Indonesian Union established during the Round Table Conference that had led in December 1949 to the independence of Indonesia (or, rather, to the Dutch acceptance of Indonesia's independence). The Netherlands held on to West New Guinea until 1962 and was still, in the words of the conservative Foreign Minister Joseph Luns, a "Southeast Asian power." This had an impact on Dutch-American relations in other ways. During the war in Korea (1950–54), the Netherlands reluctantly supported U.S. military actions because of concerns over its potential consequences for Dutch interests in Southeast Asia. According to historian De Moor, "the ties with the Asian countries, above all Indonesia, were of central importance in Dutch foreign policy in 1950."[7]

The integration of Dutch military forces into the structure of NATO created problems for the Netherlands' overseas ambitions. The Dutch Defence White paper of 1950 announced the build-up of a full-fledged Dutch navy, a goal that was questioned by NATO's supreme commander Dwight D. Eisenhower and NATO's Standing Group. The Dutch chiefs of staff, however, were of the opinion that the Standing Group did not understand and appreciate the role of the Netherlands as a maritime power and its overseas obligations. In the end, NATO accepted the Dutch position, and even though financial constraints in the early 1950s prevented the realization of the naval expansion plan, a modern aircraft carrier, the HMS *Karel Doorman*, was acquired, and a considerable amount of American financial and technical support was provided via the Mutual Defense Assistance Program (MDAP).[8]

Concerning German rearmament, the Netherlands supported Secretary of State Dean Acheson's proposal of September 1950 to accept West Germany, under certain conditions, as a member of NATO. The Dutch government, including Foreign Minister Stikker, was unhappy with French plans for a European Defense Community (EDC) and for integration of West Germany's armed forces into a European army, although the United States had endorsed these ideas. At first, the Netherlands only participated in the EDC negotiations as an observer, a position that did not change despite American pressure. The Netherlands was one of the first countries to ratify the EDC Treaty, but this was a gesture to please the United States. When the French Assembly turned the EDC Treaty down in 1954, and the Federal Republic was admitted to NATO instead, be it under strict conditions, a feeling of relief prevailed in The Hague.[9]

By 1955 the formation of the Western military bloc seemed complete, but tensions would soon follow. During the Suez crisis of 1956, which resulted in serious differences of opinion within the Atlantic Alliance between the United States on the one hand and France and Great Britain on the other, the Dutch government, and above all Foreign Minister Joseph Luns, firmly rejected the American point of view. The Eisenhower administration wanted a political solution to the crisis, which was a product of Egypt's nationalization of the French-British Suez Canal Company. The Netherlands, led by Luns, recommended that the Western countries confront radical non-Western leaders, placing Egypt's Nasser in the same category as Indonesia's Sukarno, who had unilaterally revoked the 1949 agreements between the Netherlands and Indonesia. Luns therefore sympathized with the French-British-Israeli military intervention. The Dutch role surprised policymakers in Washington. When the National Security Council discussed the position of the Western European allies regarding Suez, Secretary of State John Foster Dulles concluded that only the Netherlands — this time, not a loyal ally of the U.S. — had sided with France and Britain.[10]

The Dutch standpoint regarding Suez was closely related to the ongoing postcolonial conflict between the Netherlands and Indonesia, but there was more to it. Luns took the view that the United States, by giving in to the ambitions of Afro-Asian leaders such as Nasser, Nehru, and Sukarno, betrayed the interests of Western European countries, and of the Western world as a whole. This view also applied to East-West relations, which at that time were characterized by an American-Soviet *rapprochement* known as "the Spirit of Geneva" or "peaceful coexistence." Western impotence vis-à-vis the Soviet military intervention in Hungary in November 1956 was imputed by Luns to be linked to this "misleading" peaceful coexistence. After the dramatic events of 1956 many in The Hague hoped that the United States would from then on again be prepared to defend Western interests in an unambiguous way.[11]

There are no reasons to underestimate the level of Dutch resentment toward the United States at this time. The Dutch government supported the British and not the American standpoints during one of the most serious crises in the history of the Atlantic Alliance. As the British ambassador in The Hague reported to the Foreign Office in April 1957: "How fortunate we are to have in Dr Luns, a Minister of Foreign Affairs, who from reasoning and temperament alike, is so habitually disposed to share the standpoint of Her Majesty's Government."[12] The Americans were well aware of Dutch frustrations. In January 1955 the U.S. ambassador to the Netherlands, H. Freeman Matthews, warned his superiors in Washington that "in the long run it may gravely affect our future relations and materially reduce Dutch confidence in our integrity and leadership — and consequently their willingness to follow us."[13]

Nevertheless, although Dutch faith in the United Nations was also undermined, the Netherlands continued to advocate Atlantic unity and American leadership when it came to issues related to the defense of Western Europe. In

585

4

—

THE
COLD WAR
AND
BEYOND

1945–2009

—

POLITICS
AND
SECURITY

1958, the Dutch government readily accepted the deployment of American nuclear weapons on its territory. This deployment was based upon a two-key arrangement, which meant that the American president had the ultimate decision-making power regarding the use of these weapons. In the area of nuclear technology the Dutch had also accepted American leadership instead of pursuing cooperation with the Norwegians.[14]

The West New Guinea Crisis
(1958–62)

Just as the Netherlands seemed to have accepted American hegemony economically, politically, and militarily, another period of crisis opened up concerning West New Guinea. Toward the end of the 1950s, relations between the United States and the Western European allies were changing. The economic reconstruction of Western Europe began to bear fruit. The years of absolute American dominance, symbolized by Marshall aid and the MDAP, were over and Western European self-confidence began to grow. The six member states of the European Economic Community had been able to create a successful economic alliance. Against this background, various European-American conflicts arose, among other things over the control of nuclear weapons. Decolonization conflicts, particularly in Algeria, Belgian Congo, and West New Guinea, also complicated European-American relations,

During 1958 and 1959, Dutch worries over the security of West New Guinea had begun to grow because of the ongoing build-up and modernization of Indonesia's armed forces. Luns tried to persuade the United States and Great Britain to guarantee the security of West New Guinea against a possible Indonesian attack, and both the Americans and the British had been prepared to put some diplomatic pressure on the Indonesian government. Both allies had thereby accepted a certain responsibility for the stability in the region and for a nonviolent solution to the conflict. But concrete military guarantees, as the Dutch wanted, were out of the question. The Americans even refused to sell extra military equipment for the defense of West New Guinea.

As the Dutch-Indonesian conflict became more and more embittered, not in the least as a result of the militant Dutch approach, the American willingness to support the Netherlands decreased further. This became clear when the Dutch government in March 1960 decided to send reinforcements to West New Guinea. On May 31, 1960 the aircraft carrier HMS *Karel Doorman* and two destroyers departed from Rotterdam to show the world, and of course Jakarta, that the Netherlands would defend its sovereignty over West New Guinea. In Washington the news about this form of gunboat diplomacy was received with very mixed feelings. Dutch-American relations became strained not in the least because the *Karel Doorman* carried military equipment (especially fighter planes) that had been acquired by the Netherlands within the framework of the MDAP, and technically they were not to be used for non-NATO purposes without American consent. The Indonesians duly accused the United States of endorsing colonialist actions.[15]

When in May 1960 news reached The Hague that President Eisenhower wanted to visit Indonesia, emotions ran high. Ambassador J.H. van Royen was instructed to voice a strong protest against this potential visit to Jakarta, and on May 17 he told a State Department official that the Dutch government would consider such a visit a "slap in the face." "The Netherlands would feel constrained to re-examine its policy towards the United States and the result might even be a re-orientation of that policy," Van Royen stated. These were strong words that greatly irritated President Eisenhower, and he instructed Secretary of State Christian Herter to reply a few days later that Van Royen's protests had been "excessive in tone." It was up to the American president himself to decide which countries he wanted to visit, and "the use of phrases such as a reevaluation or reorientation of Dutch policy vis-à-vis the US was most disturbing".[16]

Dutch-American differences of opinion sharpened when the Democratic President John F. Kennedy came to power in January 1961. Ambassador Van Royen warned The Hague that the new American administration would not support the Netherlands in case of an Indonesian military invasion of West New Guinea (as if any American administration had ever had the intention of doing so). The Hague concluded that the Dutch government was losing ground and in September 1961 presented the so-called Luns Plan, which argued for a continuing Dutch presence in West New Guinea under UN auspices to prepare the population for self-determination. The proposal failed to gain a two-thirds majority in the UN General Assembly. The Dutch government was now pressured by the Kennedy administration to directly negotiate with the Indonesians, without any preconditions, something the Dutch had always refused. Ultimately the Dutch were forced to accept almost all of the Indonesian demands, and on January 1, 1963 the Dutch flag was lowered. On May 1, 1963 West New Guinea was handed over to Indonesia.

The fall-out for Dutch-American relations caused by West New Guinea was quite severe. When the Cuban crisis reached its apotheosis in October 1962, Foreign Minister Luns — then on vacation in Portugal — refused to return to The Hague, declined to issue a public declaration of support for the United States, and left the crisis to the internationally inexperienced Prime Minister De Quay. This meant that the Netherlands again, during a world crisis, just as in 1956, refused to side with the United States.[17] And that was not all. In 1963 Luns rejected President Kennedy's request for a Dutch military contribution to the war effort

4

—

THE
COLD WAR
AND
BEYOND

1945–2009

—

POLITICS
AND
SECURITY

in South Vietnam. Other Western European allies would also reject the American requests, but Luns's argument was remarkable. According to his own recollection, he told Kennedy: "Do you think that, after we have, under great pressure, withdrawn 12.000 men, 16 warships, and our fighter planes — and afterwards our entire administration — from the Far East, that I could appear before the Dutch parliament with the notification: we have decided to send a battalion of marines to support the Americans in Vietnam?"[18]

A Loyal Ally (The 1960s)

The 1960s were, at least after the Cuban crisis, a period of relative stability between Moscow and Washington, with both superpowers apparently wanting to bring their military rivalry under control, for instance by establishing a direct telephone line between the White House and the Kremlin. In Europe, relations between East and West seemed to be stabilizing as well. In 1967 NATO accepted the findings of the Harmel Report, which asserted that in addition to military defense East-West détente was also part of the alliance's responsibilities. The Warsaw Pact intervention in Czechoslovakia of August 1968 and the ongoing conflicts in parts of the non-Western world, such as Vietnam, did not obstruct this East-West *rapprochement*.

As far as Dutch foreign policy is concerned, the 1960s can be described as the "heyday of Atlanticism." Regarding the differences of opinion and conflict within NATO and the EEC, the Netherlands was a solid advocate of Atlantic unity and American leadership, as Van der Harst's essay demonstrates. Foreign Minister Luns would become one of the most effective opponents of French President Charles de Gaulle and his attempts to transform the EEC into a political union more independent from the United States. In contrast, Luns argued that the EEC should not develop into a political and military alternative to NATO, and this was one of the reasons why the Netherlands strongly supported British accession to the EEC. Although no Dutch troops were sent to Vietnam, the Dutch governments (and Luns in particular) backed the American interventions in Southeast Asia. With respect to other conflicts in the non-Western world, for instance the Israeli-Palestinian controversy, the Netherlands followed the American standpoints as well.

Robert Kagan's reproachful conclusion that life was easy for the Western European countries, being protected by American military power, is also applicable to the Netherlands.[19] Although the Netherlands duly contributed to the Allied defense effort it was relatively sheltered from the major conflicts in world politics and its military capacities were never really tested. And as East-West relations became more stable, the chances that Dutch armed forces would be tested in fact decreased. These circumstances meant that the prewar policy of aloofness and neutrality was, be it under completely different circumstances, in certain respects continued.

During the 1960s, this comfortable position as part of the *Pax Americana* was complemented by a certain "Americanization" of Dutch society. The arrival of American television programs and other products of American mass culture, films and music, and scientific influences, all had an important long-term influence on the Netherlands and on Dutch-American relations. Yet one of the contradictory aspects of this Americanization, particularly concerning its impact on youth culture, was that in the second half of the 1960s the younger generations began to defy the United States. Just as elsewhere in the Western world, Dutch youth — long haired, wearing blue jeans, and listening to American and British pop music — began to question the existing political order, and not in the least the pro-American orientation of Dutch foreign policy. This criticism was clearly stimulated by the war in Vietnam. At first the Dutch government was not impressed by this growing opposition (see Van der Maar), but gradually the gap between government policy and public opinion began to widen. It was against this background that Luns eventually stepped down as foreign minister, and in 1971 he became secretary general of NATO.[20]

The Radical Decade (1968–79)

During the first half of the 1970s the United States ran into serious difficulties. Defeat in Vietnam was imminent, the oil crisis hit the American economy hard, the Watergate scandal undermined the credibility of the presidency, and various political and economic problems hindered American-European relations. Just like in other parts of the world, in Western Europe the influence and status of socialist-oriented parties and movements were on the rise. Political developments in the Netherlands fit this pattern, with criticism of NATO and the United States increasing. In May 1973 the most progressive government in Dutch parliamentary history, led by the social-democratic leader Joop den Uyl, took office.

Somewhat surprisingly, the foreign policy of Den Uyl's cabinet, which was formed during the protests and indignation resulting from heavy U.S. bombings of North Vietnam, turned out to be the opposite of the widespread opposition to the United States and NATO of previous years. At first, policymakers in Washington, and not least Henry Kissinger, viewed the new Dutch government with skepticism and mistrust. Yet the Den Uyl cabinet, and its Foreign Minister Max van der Stoel, turned out to be more loyal to the United States than most commentators expected.

4

—

THE
COLD WAR
AND
BEYOND

1945–2009

—

POLITICS
AND
SECURITY

The first international crisis that the cabinet had to confront was the Israeli-Arab Yom Kippur War in October 1973 and the subsequent oil crisis. During the early days of the conflict the Netherlands, in great secrecy, delivered a considerable amount of ammunition and spare parts to Israel (especially for the Israeli Centurion tanks). Diplomatically Van der Stoel tried to support Israel as much as he could, and the Netherlands, along with the United States, was faced with an Arab oil embargo that at first seemed to pose a serious threat to the Dutch economy (not least because the European allies refused to introduce emergency allocation procedures to help out). Actually, the embargo against the Netherlands was not effective because of the oil companies' response (notably Shell) and the availability of Dutch natural gas. As a result the country survived quite well.

In reaction to the Arab export restrictions and price increases, France and to a lesser extent also Great Britain propagated a more independent Middle Eastern and energy policy. The Den Uyl cabinet refused to endorse the French and British proposals and instead followed a clearly liberal Atlantic course. It brought Van der Stoel the appreciation of Secretary of State Kissinger, and the Americans were even prepared to support the Netherlands, in case of an emergency, with extra oil supplies. This was probably an empty promise, but nonetheless it is significant that the Den Uyl cabinet pursued a more Atlanticist policy than center-right cabinets had done during comparable crises in 1956 and 1962.[21]

In the area of defense policy, things were not so different. The colorful Defense Minister Henk Vredeling, a social democrat like Den Uyl and Van der Stoel, was received by the military elite with suspicion, not in the least because the cabinet announced a reduction in the defense budget. It soon turned out that Vredeling was determined to maintain an Atlanticist outlook, symbolized in particular by the costly purchase of American F-16 fighter jets. Although the cabinet advocated nuclear weapons reductions and U.S. troop limitations in Europe, it did not want to contribute to a weakening of NATO's position vis-à-vis the Soviet Union and the Warsaw Pact. As Van der Stoel wrote at the time: "Every surrogate ... for the American security guarantee ... was both less reliable and destabilising."[22]

The loyalty of the Den Uyl cabinet also showed itself during the Conference on Security and Cooperation in Europe (CSCE). This East-West conference, a remarkable product of the years of East-West détente, started in July 1973 and lasted until August 1975, when the Helsinki Final Act was signed by a long list of Western and communist states. Van der Stoel feared the CSCE could be seen as a Soviet diplomatic victory. Although the Den Uyl cabinet recognized the relevance of détente, it emphasized that détente could only last when based upon a liberalization and democratization of the Soviet system. Therefore, during the CSCE process the Dutch constantly tried to raise the issue of human rights, sometimes with such idealistic zeal that it apparently annoyed Secretary of State Kissinger, as Baudet points out.

An exception to this Atlanticist norm was the policy of Jan Pronk, the young social-democratic minister for development cooperation. Pronk would cause annoyance in Washington by granting development aid to Mozambique, Cuba, and Vietnam, which was to receive no less than one hundred million guilders. According to the Americans, Cuba and Vietnam belonged to the communist bloc and should be subjected to an economic embargo. Dutch aid to these two countries, which also led to widespread misgivings in The Hague and at the Foreign Ministry, was ended soon after Pronk's resignation in 1977.

The Second Cold War
(1979–89)

Toward the end of the 1970s, and certainly at the beginning of the 1980s, the United States recovered from the crises and defeats of the previous period. The advance of the communist states and anti-Western forces in the non-Western world stagnated. Within the Western countries themselves social-democratic and reform movements began to lose ground, while neoliberal and conservative parties stepped forward with new fervor. The electoral victory of Ronald Reagan in 1980 was a remarkable moment in this development. The fall of the progressive Den Uyl cabinet in 1977 and the return of a center-right coalition, led by the Christian-democratic leader Dries van Agt, also confirmed this trend. But Dutch public opinion (and some members of parliament) did not find it easy to accept this political reversal. As a result, much discontent and frustration were directed to particular issues such as the neutron bomb and cruise missiles.

In December 1979 NATO decided to deploy cruise missiles in Western Europe, and the massive public opposition that this generated was a last expression of the rebellious spirit of the 1970s (see Righolt). It brought the center-right Van Agt cabinet and its successors into great difficulties, not in the least because the Christian Democratic Party (CDA) was divided on this issue. In December 1979 the cabinet was not able to mobilize a majority in the Second Chamber in support of the NATO decision to deploy forty-eight missiles on Dutch territory. These circumstances forced Van Agt to visit a series of NATO capitals, including Washington, in order to explain the predicaments of the Dutch government. During his conversation with Carter, Van Agt assured the American president that the Netherlands would never impede joint decision making within NATO. It was a promise that soon turned out difficult to keep. Again and again, the Dutch government was forced to postpone a final decision on missile deployment.

591

4

—

THE
COLD WAR
AND
BEYOND

1945–2009

—

POLITICS
AND
SECURITY

In November 1985 the center-right coalition led by the pragmatic CDA politician Ruud Lubbers decided to force the issue. The coalition of the liberals (VVD) and the CDA now managed to close ranks and support the government. This marked the end of a delicate phase in the history of postwar Dutch-American relations. Although Dutch prime ministers and ministers of foreign affairs and defense had always tried to make a loyal and solid impression, the concept of Hollanditis (that is to say, renewed Dutch neutralism) gained world fame. In the end the predictions of a new, contagious neutralism would prove to be exaggerated. But the protests burdened bilateral relations for much of the 1980s.

During this Second Cold War the expressly Atlanticist Minister of Foreign Affairs Hans van den Broek (1982–93) tried to improve the image of the Netherlands as a loyal NATO ally as much as he could. This did not preclude differences of opinion, of course. Just like other Western European capitals, The Hague had to get used to the hard and apocalyptic rhetoric that President Reagan used against communism and the Soviet Union. Van der Stoel (again briefly foreign minister during 1981–82) distanced himself from the tough and uncompromising attitude of the U.S. toward the Polish regime of General Wojchek Jaruzelski, and Van Agt canceled his participation in an American television spectacle, "Let Poland be Poland." But once Van den Broek became minister of foreign affairs the Dutch position toward Poland also hardened, and by the mid-1980s the Netherlands was uncompromising when it came to Polish-European Community relations and maintaining European Community (EC) sanctions against Jaruzelski's regime. As had been the case with the CSCE, Van den Broek's policy was oriented toward a reinforcement of Atlantic unity and American leadership. Furthermore, he did not declare himself openly against Reagan's Strategic Defense Initiative (SDI). As in the 1960s, Van den Broek's Atlanticism went hand in hand with a certain reluctance regarding plans to give the EC more political and military tasks.[23]

The Post-Cold War Era

Van den Broek's reappointment as foreign minister in Ruud Lubbers' third coalition (1989-94) symbolized the continuity of Dutch Atlanticism. Van den Broek was a strong advocate of an active Dutch military contribution to the U.S.-led first Gulf War against Iraq in 1991, and he criticized European attempts to prevent war by continuing diplomatic negotiations. In February 1992 he called for the American military presence in Western Europe to be maintained, since the year 1919 had taught Europeans an important lesson whereby American isolationism initiated "a chain of events in Europe" fed by national rivalries and sociocultural divisions.[24]

During the mid-1990s Van den Broek's successor Hans van Mierlo seemed to reorient Dutch foreign policy in a more European direction. However, this European reorientation did not persevere, not least due to the difficult and slow political evolution of the European Union and its weakness toward the crises in former Yugoslavia. As a result, at the end of the twentieth century the Dutch role in world politics was still remarkably oriented toward the United States, especially in the field of security. The Netherlands eagerly supported and joined U.S.- or NATO-led military operations, including deploying a squadron of F-16 fighter jets for the heavy bombardment during spring 1999 of Slobodan Milosevic's Yugoslavia. This loyalty was maintained after the terrorist attacks on the United States in September 2001. At first Prime Minister Wim Kok responded reluctantly to the tragic events in Washington and New York, calling on the American government to react in a "dignified" way. The Dutch government even hesitated to accept the NATO Council's decision to invoke article V of the Treaty, which states that an attack on one of the member states will be considered as an attack on all. But one week later, Kok declared that the terrorist acts of September 11 had been a declaration of war against the whole Western world and that the Netherlands was therefore also at war. [25] When American and British forces started their military offensive against Afghanistan, the Kok coalition stated that the Netherlands fully supported the campaign as a legitimate form of self-defense. Moreover, the Dutch government quickly offered troops for the International Security Assistance Force (ISAF) and the American antiterrorist campaign Enduring Freedom, both in Afghanistan.[26]

This pattern repeated itself before and during the war against Iraq in March 2003. The Dutch government supported the American preparations for war. Foreign Minister Jaap de Hoop Scheffer, for instance, endorsed the American point of view that an allied attack on Iraq did not need an extra Security Council resolution. He rejected the French and German attempts to prevent war and to continue negotiating with Saddam Hussein's regime. Prime Minister Jan Peter Balkenende publicly supported the American claims regarding Iraqi weapons of mass destruction. Again, the Netherlands did not participate in the actual invasion of Iraq (at least not openly), but, just as in 2001, supported the American war effort indirectly. Again, the Netherlands was one of the first allies to offer troops for the occupation of Iraq after the war was declared over.

Dutch loyalty to the United States and NATO seemed to be rewarded when, in December 2003, De Hoop Scheffer was appointed secretary general of NATO. This expression of gratitude seemed appropriate. More than ever, the Netherlands had been prepared to side with the United States. During the 1990s the Dutch army was reorganized into a true expeditionary force that could be deployed anywhere in the world. In the meantime, following the tragedy of Srebrenica, for which many in the Netherlands blamed the inefficiency of the UN, the

593

Dutch government strongly preferred participating in "green" missions led by NATO or NATO allies, as Klep argues.

4

———

THE
COLD WAR
AND
BEYOND

1945–2009

———

POLITICS
AND
SECURITY

Conclusion

It is an accepted observation that during the Cold War the Netherlands acted as a loyal ally of the United States. In certain respects this is correct. However, there were also many conflicts, differences of opinion, and hesitations. The asymmetrical power relation between a superpower and a small ally has not always been as simple as it might seem, particularly concerning decolonization and the relationship between the West and the non-Western world. The intensity of disagreement on these issues was remarkable for a loyal ally, and it influenced the Dutch position during the Korean War (although the Netherlands, reluctantly, did send a military unit), Suez, and the Cuban crisis.

Even though some commentators suggest that Dutch Atlanticism weakened during the radical 1970s, it was the "most progressive" Den Uyl coalition that supported the United States during another moment of Atlantic discord, the Yom Kippur War and the oil crisis of 1973. The policy of Foreign Minister Van der Stoel and Defense Minister Vredeling was explicitly oriented toward maintaining and reinforcing Atlantic unity. The opposition to the cruise missiles occurred during a phase of mostly center-right coalitions.

The loyal ally thesis is clearly too simple and further research is certainly necessary to clarify the U.S.-Dutch relationship, both during the Cold War and afterwards. More than during most of the Cold War period, Dutch foreign and security policy is currently oriented toward the United States. This is curious, because a widely accepted explanation for Dutch Atlantic loyalty — the Soviet threat — has lost its relevance. The days of Joseph Luns and his sometimes remarkable diplomatic assertiveness are long gone. Nonetheless, the Dutch government has put aside its traditional military passivity that was in certain respects prevalent during the Cold War. Dutch governments support America's military activism and are prepared to fight alongside American and NATO allies, although it is not always obvious which Dutch interests or humanitarian ideals are at stake to justify this.

1   See Duco Hellema, "De politieke betrek-
    kingen tussen Nederland en de Verenig-
    de Staten 1945-2005," *Tijdschrift voor
    Geschiedenis* 121.3 (2008): 284-296.

2   See for instance H. Daalder, "Nederland
    in de wereld, 1940-1945," *Tijdschrift
    voor Geschiedenis* 66 (1953): 170-201.

3   For the decolonization of the Dutch East
    Indies, see the work of J.J.P. de Jong,
    especially *Diplomatie of strijd. Het
    Nederlands beleid tegenover de Indone-
    sische revolutie 1945–1947* (Amsterdam
    /Meppel: Boom, 1988), and *De waaier
    van fortuin. Van handelscompagnie tot
    koloniaal imperium. De Nederlanders in
    Azië en de Indonesische archipel 1595–
    1950* (The Hague: SDU uitgeverij, 1998).

4   For the postwar Dutch-German rela-
    tions, see Friso Wielenga, *West-Duits-
    land: Partner uit noodzaak. Nederland
    en de Bondsrepubliek 1949–1955*
    (Utrecht: Het Spectrum, 1989).

5   See A. van Staden, *Een trouwe bond-
    genoot. Nederland en het Atlantisch
    bondgenootschap (1960–1971)* (Baarn:
    In den Toren, 1974). How Atlanticist
    the Netherlands' position actually was
    during the Cold War decades remains
    a matter of some controversy, and
    Van Staden's thesis of Dutch unambi-
    guous Atlantic loyalty has come in for
    some criticism.

6   Quoted in C. Wiebes and B. Zeeman,
    "Stikker, Indonesië en het Noordatlan-
    tisch verdrag. Of: hoe Nederland in de
    pompe ging," *Bijdragen en mededelingen
    betreffende de geschiedenis der Neder-
    landen* 100 (1985): 237.

7   J.A. de Moor, "Aan de Amerikanen
    uitgeleverd. Nederland, de Verenigde
    Staten en de oorlog in Korea, 1950–
    1953," in J. Hoffenaar and G. Teitler,
    eds., *De Koude Oorlog. Maatschappij en
    krijgsmacht in de jaren '50* (The Hague:
    SDU uitgeverij, 1992), 175-176.

8   See Ine Megens, "American Aid to NATO
    Allies in the 1950s. The Dutch Case"
    (Ph.D. dissertation, Rijksuniversiteit
    Groningen, 1994), 103ff.

9   See J.A. Schoneveld, "Tussen Atlantica
    en Europa. Over de opkomst en onder-
    gang van de Spagaat in de Nederlandse
    buitenlandse politiek" (Ph.D. disser-
    tation, Universiteit Leiden, 2000), 53ff.

10 Duco Hellema, "Backing Britain. The
    Netherlands and the Suez Crisis,"
    Diplomacy and Statecraft 4 (1993): 37-59.

11 Duco Hellema, "The Relevance and
    Irrelevance of Dutch Anti-Communism.
    The Netherlands and the Hungarian
    Revolution," *Journal of Contemporary
    History* 30 (1995): 169-187.

12 Mason to Selwyn LLoyd, nr. 92, 3 April
    1957, FO, 371/130933, National Archives,
    London.

13 Foreign Service Despatch Freeman
    Matthews to State Department, nr. 551,
    5 January 1955, RG 59, Box 3429,
    756.00/1-555, National Archives,
    Washington, DC.

14 See Jaap van Splunter, "Kernsplijting
    en diplomatie. De Nederlandse politiek
    ten aanzien van de vreedzame toepas-
    sing van kernenergie, 1939–1957"
    (Ph.D. dissertation, Universiteit van
    Amsterdam, 1993).

15 See Duco Hellema, *De Karel Doorman
    naar Nieuw-Guinea. Nederlands machts-
    vertoon in de Oost* (Amsterdam: Boom,
    2005).

16 Hellema, *De Karel Doorman*, 102.

17 See Jeroen Ploeg and Peter van der Vlies,
    "Zal dat oorlog geven? Nederland en de
    Cuba-crisis, oktober 1962," in Duco
    Hellema and Toby Witte, *"Onmachtig
    om te helpen." Nederlandse reacties op
    de socialistische dreiging* (Amsterdam:
    Het Spinhuis, 1995), 65-79.

18 Quoted in M. Kuitenbrouwer, *De ont-
    dekking van de Derde Wereld. Beeld-
    vorming en beleid in Nederland, 1950–
    1990* (The Hague: SDU uitgeverij, 1994),
    92.

19 Robert Kagan, *Balans van de macht. De
    kloof tussen Amerika en Europa* (Amster-
    dam: De Bezige Bij, 2003), passim.

20 For the Vietnam issue see Rimko van
    der Maar, *Welterusten mijnheer de*

595

4

—

THE
COLD WAR
AND
BEYOND

1945–2009

—

POLITICS
AND
SECURITY

president. Nederland en de Vietnamoorlog 1965–1973 (Amsterdam: Boom, 2007).

21 See Duco Hellema, Cees Wiebes, and Toby Witte, *The Netherlands and the Oil Crisis. Business as Usual* (Amsterdam: Amsterdam University Press, 2004).

22 M. van der Stoel, "Verantwoord veilig-heidsbeleid," *Internationale Spectator* 24 (1975): 163; See also Frank Zuijdam, *Tussen wens en werkelijkheid. Het debat over vrede en veiligheid binnen de PvdA in de periode 1958–1977* (Amsterdam: Aksant, 2002).

23 Paul Rusman, "De laatste Koude-Oorlogsstrijder. Hans van den Broek (1982–1993)," in Duco Hellema, Bert Zeeman, and Bert van der Zwan, eds., *De Nederlandse ministers van Buiten-landse Zaken in de twintigste eeuw* (The Hague: SDU uitgeverij, 1999), 269-281.

24 *NRC Handelsblad*, February 10, 1992.

25 *NRC Handelsblad* and *de Volkskrant*, September 19, 2001.

26 For the Dutch contributions to peace missions and humanitarian interven-tions see C. Klep and R. van Gils, *Van Korea tot Kabul. De Nederlandse militaire deelname aan vredesoperaties sinds 1945* (The Hague: SDU uitgeverij, 2005).

THE NETHERLANDS, THE UNITED STATES, AND ANTICOMMUNISM DURING THE EARLY COLD WAR

—

PAUL KOEDIJK

A Reluctant Choice

Anticommunism and antitotalitarianism became two of the defining themes in the relationship between the Netherlands and the United States during the Cold War, in a way that seems to have been stronger than what may be observed in bilateral American relationships with other European allies of that period. This is not entirely surprising. Both themes were very much present in the Netherlands before the outbreak of World War II and could be found across broad strata of Dutch society. The nature and roots of anticommunist attitudes were diverse and ranged from a religiously inspired disgust for a "godless" ideology, to the fear of a threat to economic individualism and, finally, to the conviction that communism would lead to the end of individual liberty itself. To this can be added elements like the loss of huge investments as a result of the Russian Revolution in 1917 and, last but not least, the deeply felt grudges of the Dutch royal family about the murder of the Romanovs to whom they were related through blood lines. Regardless of its different sources, anticommunism was therefore one of the few ideological common denominators among the different pillars in Dutch society (Protestant, Catholic, socialist, and liberal). From this perspective it is no surprise that the Netherlands government (meanwhile in exile) did not recognize the Soviet Union until 1942, being one of the last countries to do so.

The recognition of the USSR was forced by the circumstances of war and was but one expression of the need to rethink and redefine Dutch foreign policy in relation to an uncertain postwar world order. Traditional neutralism had failed

597

4

—

THE
COLD WAR
AND
BEYOND

1945–2009

—

POLITICS
AND
SECURITY

but it was not clear what kind of policy should take its place. From 1942 on-ward the Dutch government in London understood that somehow the United States would have to be involved permanently in the future of postwar Europe. In the occupied Netherlands the underground newspapers expressed similar opinions. Opinion polls shortly after the war also indicated that 65 percent of the Dutch population considered the United States to be the major factor in guaranteeing lasting peace in Europe.[1]

Yet, until late 1947 both the Dutch government and large segments of Dutch public opinion still held the position that the Netherlands should avoid mak-ing a choice between the United States and the Soviet Union. Although it would prove to be only temporary, Dutch anticommunism seemed to have lost some of its sharpest edges as a result of sympathy for the Soviet contribution to the de-feat of the Third Reich as well as out of respect for the communist contribution to the Dutch resistance movement. At the same time, in spite of the immense gratitude for the "Yankee liberators," there was a lot of skepticism, expressed in cultural, economic, and political terms, about the United States, which, more-over, had also become a nuclear power. The fact that the Americans themselves did not seem to have a clear notion yet of their new role as a major power contrib-uted to the uncertainty. Public opinion was divided on the issue, some commen-tators stating as early as 1946 that a choice in favor of the U.S. was "self-evident" because the conflict with the Soviet Union was in essence a "clash of worldviews," just as much as it was of "an imperial order."[2] Others still supported the, what would prove to be short-lived and unrealistic, option for a European "Third Way." This alternative was defined by some of its proponents as a kind of social-demo-cratic European "bridge" between the extremes of American capitalism and So-viet communism. Such a Europe would serve ideologically, politically, and eco-nomically as a "third superpower" between the U.S. and the USSR, instead of be-ing a bridgehead for either one of them. This idea remained alive for some time, also because it was used as a slogan to "sell" the Marshall Plan to Western Europe-an labor: "Neither Wall Street nor Stalin," in the famous words of Walter Reuther, the leader of the anticommunist American Federation of Labor (AFL).

The denial of the Netherlands government, backed up by segments of pub-lic opinion, that it had made any choice between East and West was in a way an echo of the old politics of neutralism. This wishful thinking that a choice exist-ed was still present when the Truman Doctrine was presented in March 1947. This doctrine was the expression of a new anticommunist consensus that had emerged in the United States and would evolve naturally into the Marshall Plan. Anticommunism from that moment on was an established theme of American foreign policy.

The Truman Doctrine effectively demanded that everyone make a choice be-tween "totalitarianism" and "democracy." Reactions in the Netherlands were diverse and in some cases ambivalent. To some Truman's speech stated the obvious, although many still shied away from its practical consequences. For example, while the Dutch social democrats would in just a few years time become strong supporters of American Cold War policies, according to a poll only 39 percent of them were in favor of America's military-economic support for Greece and Turkey in March 1947, which was the first practical effect of the new doctrine. Interestingly, in the eyes of Dutch media and opinion leaders it was the communist response to the announcement of the Marshall aid — the founding of the Kominform in September 1947 — that was considered as a defining moment finalizing the division between East and West and determining that everyone would have to take sides. The subsequent events in Prague in March 1948 with the communist takeover were seen as a mere confirmation of this division.

On the diplomatic level, the international situation in 1948 and the ensuing security issues for the Netherlands prompted the Dutch government and the majority of public opinion to finally accept a reorientation of its foreign policy. A further impetus for this shift was given by the independence of Indonesia in 1949, causing the Netherlands to lose its "world role." This change was reflected in the signing of the Brussels Treaty in 1948, to be followed by the North Atlantic Treaty in 1949. However, although Dutch policy changed radically in the years 1948–49, it was not the linear process that has been suggested in the mainstream historiography. Neither was it caused exclusively by issues of the Cold War. Just recovering from five years of Nazi rule, the focus was still very much on the future of defeated neighbor Germany, and as long as this "German issue" was not resolved between the new superpowers, the Dutch government remained reluctant to take sides. For a long time, a German military revival remained the predominant fear guiding Dutch foreign policy in Europe.

In terms of the emerging Cold War, the major danger in Dutch eyes was not as much a military attack by the Soviets, but home-grown, Soviet-supported communism acting as a potentially treacherous fifth column within the Netherlands itself. At the political level, this attitude resulted in a reluctance to raise military expenditures at the cost of improving the standard of living of the population, the latter being regarded as a major antidote against a growth of support for the Communist Party of the Netherlands (CPN). This view was also held by the social democratic Prime Minister Willem Drees, who would continue to express — be it not in public, but in private to American diplomats — his skepticism about the likelihood of a Soviet attack on Western Europe, even after the outbreak of the Korean War in 1950.[3]

4

—

THE
COLD WAR
AND
BEYOND

1945-2009

—

POLITICS
AND
SECURITY

American "Labor Diplomacy" and the Netherlands

It is worth noting that the first serious Dutch-American alliance with the aim of combating communism preceded official Dutch foreign policy by several years. Dutch trade unions, in particular the socialist-oriented Nederlands Verbond van Vakverenigingen (NVV), were apparently quicker to understand the looming realities of the postwar world. Many of their leaders had been hardened while fighting communism in the international trade union movement and held no illusions as to what would happen with the Soviet Union as a new superpower. Strong prewar contacts with American colleagues, like the American Federation of Labor (AFL), put the NVV in an advantageous position to profit from the mutual anticommunist agenda.[4]

As early as February 1945, NVV representatives discussed in London with their AFL counterparts the forthcoming struggle against communism in a liberated but devastated Europe. The established vision of the AFL, that of an ultimate struggle between "free" and "totalitarian" or "slave" nations, became the prevailing outlook of the whole American effort in the labor field in Europe. In the course of 1947, following the proclamation of the Truman Doctrine, the United States started its so-called labor diplomacy, aimed at strengthening in particular social democratic parties and labor unions in Western Europe. It was an expression of the growing American understanding of the fact that the European noncommunist Left would play an important, and possibly even decisive, role in the reconstruction of Western Europe, which required the containment and, if possible, defeat of the communist danger.

The AFL was on board much earlier and one of its responses was the promise of financial support to trade unions like the NVV, for which in this particular case the means were deposited in a Swiss bank. From late 1945 onward other donations would follow, aimed at helping the resurrection of a powerful NVV. In 1947, for example, the union received a sum of one hundred thousand dollars through the Dutch ambassador in Washington.[5] Dutch trade unionists were very much aware of the American self-interest involved in the Marshall Plan. Nevertheless, in the eyes of the NVV leadership, anticommunism was actually the predominant motive behind the plan in the first place, something they easily identified themselves with and which serves as one of many illustrations of the fact that Dutch anticommunists knew exactly what kind of "tune" the Americans were trying to call.

The NVV maintained excellent contacts with the Marshall Plan's European Cooperation Administration mission in the Netherlands. Dutch trade union leaders regularly coordinated activities with the mission and received propaganda material as well as information about the activities of the communist-influenced World Federation of Trade Unions (WFTU), where a power struggle with communist unions, foremost over the issue of support for the Marshall Plan, would eventually lead to a breakup. The NVV also satisfied requests by the American occupational authorities in Germany to reestablish contacts with the German trade unions with the intent to offer them support in rebuilding their organizations.

American confidence in Dutch noncommunist labor showed itself in the endorsement of E. Kupers as chairman of the committee to promote contact among European trade unions with regard to the Marshall Plan. Also with American support, another Dutch union leader, J.H. Oldenbroek, became the first secretary general of the International Committee of Free Trade Unions (ICFTU), which was established after the inevitable breakup of the communist-dominated WFTU. Philip Kaiser, Truman's assistant secretary of labor for international affairs, even arranged a visit with President Truman, who managed to impress Oldenbroek with his profound knowledge of Dutch maritime history.[6]

From the early 1950s onward there were also close relations between various American institutions, particularly the U.S. embassy, and the Partij van de Arbeid (PvdA). The Dutch social democrats were interesting in many ways. Until 1958 they were a major factor in coalition cabinets. Their anticommunism was fierce and fed by a physical sense of threat: Party Chairman Koos Vorrink privately told American Ambassador Matthews he expected to be killed should there be a communist takeover.[7] Contrary to most of its sister parties in Western Europe, the PvdA managed to quench whatever leftist opposition there was in its ranks. And last but not least, PvdA politicians were very active in international organizations, like the Socialist International, where they criticized relentlessly any neutralist and anti-Atlantic tendencies, especially within the British and West German socialist parties. PvdA attendants at international conferences, in particular Alfred Mozer, international secretary of the PvdA since 1948, regularly supplied the Americans with confidential reports about the inner wheelings and dealings of both the International and its constituents. In this, they acted most of the time in full accord with American policies, even if their motives were sometimes slightly different. As one American observer wrote in 1955: "It has been commented that the Dutch Labor Party is perhaps the only 'socialist' party in Europe that could hold a congress to discuss foreign policy without in some degree castigating the United States and its policies."[8]

U.S. diplomats gave their full support, providing information and, if necessary, logistics. Mozer, who openly supported Christian-democratic Chancellor Adenauer for his Atlanticist policies, made lecture tours in West Germany sponsored by the so-called America Houses. Another internationally active social democrat, M. van der Goes van Naters, closely cooperated with American diplomats in attempts to block Chinese membership in organizations like the Inter-

601

Alfred Mozer (1905–79), international secretary of the Dutch Labor party
in the 1950s, was an important source for U.S. diplomats on opinions within the
European socialist movement.

national Parliamentary Union.[9] One of his colleagues, Frans Goedhart, eventually became the driving force behind the organization of the pro-Taiwan lobby in Western Europe. Goedhart in particular, himself a former communist and resistance fighter, developed a range of close ties with different American, or American-sponsored, agencies and organizations that were active in the field of combating communism by developing activities aimed at the Soviet-dominated peoples of the Eastern bloc. Some of these activities, like Radio Free Europe, later turned out to be part of a program of covert operations organized by the CIA and its Office of Policy Coordination (OPC). Goedhart, like other old hands of the resistance, suspected these ties existed, but accepted and even welcomed them as inevitable in what he considered to be a struggle to the death.[10]

Skepticism of American Leadership

The preponderance of the fight against communism affected Dutch-American relationships in several ways. Support for American policies was not slavish but based on a deeply felt sense of mutual interest. At the same time it was laced with skepticism about American leadership. Illustrative of this fact is the position of J. M. (Joop) den Uyl, a prominent PvdA member and a future prime minister in the early 1970s. Late in 1953, he made a visit to the United States in the Foreign Leader Program, an exchange program run by the State Department and aimed at cultivating favorable relations with foreign elites.[11] Den Uyl, at that time the director of the PvdA's scientific bureau, was regarded by the U.S. embassy in The Hague as an important contact and, just like Mozer, he became in the course of the 1950s a valuable and above all friendly source for the Americans, with important connections both in the Netherlands and elsewhere in Europe. People such as Den Uyl, Mozer, and other high-ranking PvdA politicians were not only sources of knowledge but also useful channels through which American points of view and information could be injected into the Dutch political process in general and into PvdA party politics in particular. There was no doubt about the fervor of their anticommunism, nor about their generally unequivocal support for the basic tenets of American foreign policy. The contacts were therefore carefully fostered by the Americans. As important "opinion leaders," several PvdA leaders would receive invitations to private dinner buffets at the homes of American diplomats — some actually being covert CIA personnel — in The Hague.

603

As far as Den Uyl is concerned, his cooperative attitude and warm relationships with American diplomats during the height of the Cold War did not stem directly from his trip to the United States in 1953. On the contrary, to him the visit — in the heyday of McCarthyism — proved to be an eye opener of a kind

4

—

THE
COLD WAR
AND
BEYOND

1945–2009

—

POLITICS
AND
SECURITY

probably not envisaged by his hosts. In a private letter to Mozer, written in Knoxville, TN, Den Uyl confided that his visit, which was near its end, had made him conscious once again of the urgency of European unification. The trigger had been his realization of "the danger of American supremacy." His personal acquaintance with the "Wild-West way of making domestic and foreign policy over here," had given him "the cold shivers." According to Den Uyl, "it is a rather useless phrase but if ever a nation was *not* prepared for 'world leadership,' it would have to be the United States ... ."[12] This critical position of a leading member of the party that dominated Dutch coalition governments from 1945 until 1958 seems to illustrate a more general Dutch attitude toward the United States during the early Cold War.

The Dutch critique of a perceived lack of American leadership would be heard repeatedly, in particular during the Eisenhower administration. After Stalin's death in 1953 and the ensuing thaw in the Cold War, both Dutch officials and opinion leaders would criticize the United States for letting itself be lured to sleep by the Soviets. They also directed criticism at any sign that the United States accepted the de facto division of Germany and the Soviet occupation of eastern Europe. The memory of five years of (Nazi) occupation made the Dutch very sympathetic to "occupied peoples" and explains a great deal about the role of individuals like Goedhart in promoting the cause of the many American- (sometimes CIA-) sponsored organizations that claimed to represent these oppressed peoples. It also explains the emotional reactions of the Dutch against communists at the time of the Hungarian uprising in 1956 and the anger at the refusal of the Western world, led by the United States, to actively support the Hungarians.

Anticommunism the Dutch Way

There was one conspicuously anticommunist, American-sponsored activity during the Cold War in which the Dutch hardly played any role at all. The Congress for Cultural Freedom (CCF), set up in secret by the CIA, drew little interest in the Netherlands. Attempts at founding a Dutch section failed, and apart from occasional contributions to some of the CCF's many magazines, the Dutch were mainly absent. Various factors have been mentioned to explain this absence, such as the lack of a strong tradition of intellectual debate in the Netherlands and the ambivalent and often negative perception of American society.[13] But

Vrede en Vrijheid (Peace and Freedom) was an anticommunist organization active in the Netherlands during the 1950s. This poster, used during election time, reads "Choose Communists for Terror and Slavery."

4

—

THE
COLD WAR
AND
BEYOND

1945-2009

—

POLITICS
AND
SECURITY

one major reason may be that the Dutch preoccupation with the fight against communism had a distinct character that did not fit in well with the soft-boiled activities of the CCF, which were mainly aimed at an intellectual elite.

Just as a major characteristic of the Dutch resistance against the Nazis had been the emphasis on ideas and counterpropaganda, as expressed in numerous underground newspapers, the fight against communism was basically seen as one between fundamentally different belief systems. This led to a ban on communists in public functions in 1951 and to attempts to ensure the ideological "immunization" of the population in order to reduce the potential recruiting ground for a communist fifth column. It is therefore probably no coincidence that Dutch individuals as well as the Dutch internal security agency (the Binnenlandse Veiligheidsdienst or BVD) played an important role, even on a European scale, in waging the psychological war against communism, thereby supporting both overt as well as covert American activities in the same field. One example is the Dutch section of the Western European Peace and Freedom Movement, a covert operation by the CIA's OPC, which from 1952 onward directed crude anticommunist propaganda particularly at blue-collar workers in Western Europe. Vrede and Vrijheid, as the movement was called in the Netherlands, was actively and secretly supported by the BVD as well as the major Dutch trade unions and newspapers; the editors of these socialist, Catholic, and Protestant papers allowed some of their journalists to participate in the activities, such as the provocative campaigns against the communists during the 1952 general elections, in which the equation of fascism with communism appeared as the major propaganda theme.

This "negative anticommunism" as it was called, did not satisfy Dutch anticommunists in the longer term. Their reservations coincided with the generally critical Dutch attitude toward McCarthyism in the United States. Although the Dutch could hardly be accused of being soft on communism, many of them — in particular (as elsewhere in Western Europe) among highly educated layers of society — actually considered the strand of anticommunism practiced by Senator Joe McCarthy, who for a few years seemed to get free rein to pursue his "witch hunts," a danger because it promoted counterproductive "anti-anticommunism." Anticommunist countermeasures based on the premise of the theory of totalitarianism were increasingly being regarded as inadequate, as discussions within the PvdA in 1950 already indicated.

Therefore, in the course of the 1950s, with covert support of both the CIA and the BVD, attempts were made to develop a more sophisticated approach to fighting communism, which would acknowledge its appealing "positive" side and its obvious successes: the shock of Sputnik in 1957 as well as the impressive cultural display of the Bolshoi Theater and other Russian groups touring through Western Europe could not be ignored. This need for a more fundamental response to communist propaganda led to the founding of organizations, based in the Netherlands but active worldwide, that focused on so-called positive anticommunism; a combination of active promotion of Western democratic values and an informed discussion about the practice of communism based on intelligence material secretly provided by the CIA and other Western agencies.[14]

Conclusion

The examples given cover the most prominent channels where Dutch-American cooperation occurred in fighting communism up until the late 1950s. The close cooperation of the Americans with Dutch social democrats in fighting communism and promoting Atlanticism diminished after the PvdA was forced out of the coalition government in 1958. Yet, all these examples highlight the significance of the Netherlands as a close and willing ally for the United States. The specific character of the hard-line, highly ideological, and at the same time practical Dutch attitude toward fighting communism throughout society was quite useful for many American institutions seeking reliable international partners during the Cold War.

1   J.C.H. Blom, "Jaren van tucht en ascese. Enige beschouwingen over de stemming in Herrijzend Nederland (1945-1950)," in P.W. Klein and G.N. van der Plaat, eds., *Herrijzend Nederland. Opstellen over Nederland in de periode 1945-1950* (The Hague: Martinus Nijhoff, 1981), 151.

2   Commentator G.B.J. Hiltermann's statements in *Elseviers Weekblad*, September 28, 1946.

3   See J.A. de Moor, "Aan de Amerikanen overgeleverd. Nederland, de Verenigde Staten en de oorlog in Korea, 1950–1953," in J. Hoffenaar and G. Teitler, eds., *De Koude Oorlog. Maatschappij en krijgsmacht in de jaren '50* (The Hague: SDU uitgeverij, 1992), 163-177.

4   Comments on the NVV are largely based on Henk Sporken, "Een trouwe bondgenoot van de 'vrije wereld': het NVV, het Marshall-plan en de internationale

vakbeweging," *Cahiers voor de politieke en sociale wetenschappen* 2.1 (February 1979): 49-93.

5   Sporken also reports that the AFL had already funded the NVV in 1945 with a sum of 135,000 guilders, of which 50,000 was earmarked for "the financing of the press" (p. 53). However, the exact sums, and their timing, are still difficult to clarify precisely.

6   Philip M. Kaiser, *Journeying Far and Wide. A Political and Diplomatic Memoir* (New York/Toronto: Charles Scribner's Sons, 1992), 133-134.

7   Memorandum of conversation, April 2, 1948, Enclosure to despatch no. 202, April 5, 1948, RG 59, Decimal file, box 6417, National Archives, College Park, MD.

8   Amembassy Foreign Service Despatch 688, February 11, 1955, "Labor Party

4

—

THE
COLD WAR
AND
BEYOND

1945-2009

—

POLITICS
AND
SECURITY

Conference on Foreign Policy," RG 59, Decimal file, box 3429, National Archives, College Park, MD.

9   See, for example, Amembassy The Hague Foreign Service Despatches 208 and 224, "Interparliamentary Union Conference," October 11 and 16, 1956, RG 84, Hague Post Files, Confidential general records 1956–1958, box 9, National Archives, College Park, MD.

10 On Goedhart, see Gerard Mulder and Paul Koedijk, *Lées die krant! Geschiedenis van het naoorlogse Parool 1945–1970* (Amsterdam: Meulenhoff, 1996), in particular 389-394.

11 See Giles Scott-Smith, *Networks of Empire: The US State Department's Foreign Leader Program in the Netherlands, France, and Britain 1950–1970* (Brussels: Peter Lang, 2008).

12 "…wat me de urgentie van de Europese eenheid opnieuw bewust heeft gemaakt is vooral *het gevaar van de Amerikaanse overmacht*. Als je de wild-west manier meemaakt waarop hier binnen én buitenlandse politiek wordt gemaakt, krijg je de koude rillingen. Het is een vrij nutteloze frase, maar als er ooit een volk *niet* rijp was voor 'wereldleiderschap' dan is het het Amerikaanse…" (translated into English by the author), J.M. den Uyl to A. Mozer, December 15, 1953, PvdA archive, corr. Mozer, P10, nov.53-feb.54, U-2, International Institute for Social History, Amsterdam.

13 See Tity de Vries, "The Absent Dutch: Dutch Intellectuals and the Congress for Cultural Freedom," in Giles Scott-Smith and Hans Krabbendam, *The Cultural Cold War in Western Europe 1945–1960* (London: Frank Cass, 2003).

14 See Paul Koedijk, "Van 'Vrede en Vrijheid' tot 'Volk en Verdediging': Veranderingen in anti-communistische psychologische oorlogsvoering in Nederland, 1950–1965," in B. Schoenmaker and J.A.M.M. Janssen, eds., *In de schaduw van de muur. Maatschappij en krijgsmacht rond 1960* (The Hague: SDU uitgeverij, 1997), 57-81.

DECOLONIZATION AND DUTCH-AMERICAN RELATIONS

▬

MARC FREY

For decades, there was a widespread feeling in the Netherlands that the United States had forced the Dutch to relinquish their colonial empire in Southeast Asia. Politicians, the media, and the public at large felt betrayed by a country that the Dutch had traditionally held in the highest regard. In the mid-1950s, 22 percent of the Dutch argued that American intervention in Indonesia had left a "very unfavourable impression." For somewhat different reasons, dissatisfaction about decolonization persisted in the United States as well. Frustrated by Indonesian politics, President Dwight D. Eisenhower in 1954 asked his National Security Council: "Why the hell did we ever urge the Dutch to get out of Indonesia?"[1]

Colonialism and decolonization were the single most divisive issues in bilateral Dutch-American relations in the two decades following World War II. No other colonial power was affected so negatively by American policies to the same degree as the Netherlands. But did the United States really force the Netherlands to consent to the transfer of power in Indonesia? Did Washington influence developments in Indonesia, and if so, to what extent? And how did the Netherlands and the United States respond to subsequent colonial crises?[2]

Colonialism already came to play an important role in bilateral Dutch-American relations during World War II. President Franklin D. Roosevelt believed that colonialism had contributed to international tensions in the prewar period, and he felt that the war effort of democracies against fascism and totalitarian states entailed a sincere commitment to freedom and national self-determination, not only in Europe but everywhere. Roosevelt and his advisers further believed that a global economic order without imperial preferences, closed colonial markets, or metropolitan supervision would provide equal opportunities for everyone, thus alleviating tensions and conflicts worldwide. The colonial

4

THE
COLD WAR
AND
BEYOND

1945–2009

POLITICS
AND
SECURITY

powers were well aware of the American critique of colonialism. The Dutch government in exile did not make any plans, though, to reform its colonial empire in the future.

Regaining Control of the Indies

In view of the destruction caused by the German occupation and the war, the overwhelming majority of the Dutch believed that the colonies should contribute to the reconstruction of the "motherland." Economists J. B. D. Derksen and Jan Tinbergen argued late in 1945 that prior to the war 14 percent of the Dutch national income had derived from economic interaction with Indonesia. Economic rationales went hand in hand with an understanding of power. Many felt that without an empire, the Netherlands would no longer be the smallest of the significant powers of Europe but a second-rate power devoid of any influence. European reconstruction and fear of "Denmarkization" thus fueled the determination to reoccupy and recolonize Indonesia.[3]

Reoccupation, however, proved difficult. The Japanese had successfully exploited widespread notions of anticolonialism and had removed many vestiges of Dutch rule. In 1944, they had promised independence to the Indonesians, and on August 17, 1945 the Indonesian nationalist leader Sukarno duly proclaimed his country's independence.[4] The first Dutch administrators did not arrive until one month later, accompanied by British and British-Indian troops who had been assigned to manage the immediate postwar situation in the archipelago. The commanding general, Sir Philip Christison, recognized that some form of cooperation between the government of the Indonesian Republic and the returning Dutch colonial administration would be necessary. The nationalist government was popular, and Christison was not sure about the loyalty of his Indian troops in case they were ordered to take action against the Indonesians. From the beginning, then, the continuation of Dutch rule in Indonesia depended on outside actors.

Protracted British-mediated negotiations between the Indonesian nationalist movement and the Dutch led to the signing of the so-called Linggadjati Agreement in November 1946. Following additional negotiations, the agreement, subsequently signed in March 1947, stipulated the de facto sovereignty of the Indonesian Republic over Java, Madura, and Sumatra, continued Dutch control over the other islands, a federated Indonesian state, and a Dutch-Indonesian union with a common foreign and trade policy. Both sides, however, felt uneasy about the agreement: the Indonesians regarded it as a first step toward the complete transfer of power; the Dutch government took the agreement as the basis for continued Dutch influence in Indonesia.

Until Linggadjati the dominant external actor had been Great Britain. The United States had stood on the sidelines. At first, Washington provided some military assistance to the Dutch. But by mid-1946 the American government and media felt that the uncompromising Dutch insistence on the continuation of colonialism gradually forced moderate Indonesian nationalists into the communist camp. Under these circumstances, Washington turned down a Dutch request for a loan of one hundred million dollars to the Dutch colony.[5] In The Hague this response was perceived as unfriendly, all the more so because the Americans insisted that the Dutch continue negotiations with the Indonesians. The U.S. government strongly believed that only a just compromise could defuse tensions between colonizers and colonized. Moreover, by early 1947 Washington was increasingly alarmed about the prospects of communist encroachments in Southeast Asia. In Indochina conflicts between the French and the Vietnamese communist nationalists had turned into a war, and in China Mao Zedong's armies were on their march toward victory. Linggadjati was thus greeted in the United States as a promising development. Positive perceptions about Dutch policies, however, soon turned into frustration.

The Dutch government had signed Linggadjati only under pressure from Britain and the United States and upon the advice of Lieutenant Governor General Hubertus van Mook, who had been in favor of a bifurcated policy of negotiations with the Republic and a *divide et impera* policy vis-à-vis the traditional aristocracy. But at home the coalition government was under pressure from practically all sides to demonstrate toughness. With the exception of the tiny communist party, all political parties strongly supported a continuation of colonial rule, and the media followed the politicians. Moreover, there were immediate economic as well as military reasons for an end to negotiations. By mid-1947 the Dutch had built up their military capabilities in Indonesia and had shipped approximately one hundred thousand men to the other end of the world, at the staggering cost of one billion guilders. The military was strongly of the opinion that this investment had to be recovered, and it promised that it would sweep deep into the plantation areas of Sumatra and Java, thus making sure that products could be harvested, marketed, and taxed.[6] Following an ultimatum to the Indonesian Republic to fulfil certain demands, the Dutch cabinet authorized military action. Starting on July 20, 1947, the offensive, euphemistically dubbed "police action" (*politionele actie*), achieved a quick tactical victory. Within a week, the western and eastern parts of Java, Madura, and key areas of Sumatra came under Dutch control. But this did not translate into a strategic victory.

On the ground, the administration in large parts of Indonesia collapsed, guerrilla activities increased significantly, and security in the countryside suffered. In the international arena, the Netherlands was strongly criticized. In-

611

4

—

THE
COLD WAR
AND
BEYOND

1945–2009

—

POLITICS
AND
SECURITY

dia and Australia called on the United Nations Security Council, and the United States, acting upon this initiative, sponsored a resolution that called upon the adversaries to conclude an immediate armistice. Moreover, Washington offered to mediate in the conflict. This was a clear setback for Dutch diplomacy, as the Security Council and the United States perceived the Indonesian Republic as an actor equal to the Netherlands. Despite frantic Dutch diplomatic efforts to prevent the United Nations from debating Indonesia, the Security Council passed another resolution (August 18, 1947) that called for the establishment of a United Nations Good Offices Committee (GOC) to mediate in the conflict. Dutch efforts to recolonize Indonesia, considered by The Hague to be an internal affair that could be settled eventually by military force, had become an international problem in which the major allies were neutral, while the United Nations functioned as a kind of watchdog.

The GOC, chaired by Frank Graham (president of the University of North Carolina), arrived in Jakarta in October 1947. Both the Indonesians and the Dutch accused each other of frequent violations of the ceasefire, and it was quite apparent that the constitutional setup of the Linggadjati Agreement was not effective. Graham and the State Department worked out a proposal that foresaw eventual independence for Indonesia. This was a perspective the Dutch government would not entertain. Prime Minister Willem Drees was so infuriated that he termed the proposal a "meaningless document." Severe American pressure, however, made Drees and his colleagues change their minds. The State Department argued that an agreement would have a "decisive influence" on the distribution of Marshall Plan aid.[7] This brought the Dutch back to the negotiating table. On January 17, 1948 a new document, the Renville Agreement, was signed. It reflected, above all, American conceptions of decolonization: the prospect of eventual independence coupled with a period of "apprenticeship," that is, long-term cooperation between a European power and a newly independent country.

The agreement, however, was never carried out because of irreconcilable interests. The Netherlands demanded to remain the ultimate arbiter of Indonesian affairs, while the Republic wanted complete independence without strings attached. Toward the summer of 1948 these positions became even more pronounced. After the parliamentary elections in July, the new Dutch cabinet decided to centralize decision making on Indonesia in The Hague, and the new minister of overseas territories, the Catholic Emmanuel Sassen, argued that the Netherlands should not comply with anyone's wishes and pressures anymore. The Hague also sponsored a secret propaganda campaign in the United States to convince journalists and politicians of Dutch sincerity and to denounce Indonesian nationalists as communists. The specter of communism did indeed resonate in the United States, but for different reasons.

In the midst of increasing tensions and sprawling lawlessness in Indonesia, local communists staged a revolution in Madiun (central Java). Republican troops suppressed the uprising within days and many communists were killed. News of these events transformed American perceptions of the Indonesian Republic and of the conflict in general. While the newly founded Central Intelligence Agency sent its first adviser to the Indonesian nationalists, Undersecretary of State Dean Acheson and other top diplomats felt that the disturbing element in the Indonesian equation was no longer the colonial conflict itself but the colonial power. The Dutch, George Kennan argued, created chaos, and the only actors who could establish a noncommunist order in Indonesia were the nationalists.[8] From December 1948 on, the United States consciously and deliberately sought to end Dutch colonialism in Indonesia.

The Second "Police Action" and American Pressure

Meanwhile, the Dutch government decided to ignore world opinion and authorized a second military offensive. This time, politicians and the military were convinced that Dutch military action would wipe out the nationalists and put an end to the Republic. The archipelago was a matter of national interest, and the government believed that only continued colonial rule, legitimized by the modernizing impulses of a developmental colonialism, would pave the way for independence in the distant future. The Dutch offensive, again dubbed "police action," began on December 19, 1948 with one hundred forty thousand troops.[9] The military quickly achieved its objective; by January 5 all strategic places on Sumatra and Java were occupied, Indonesian leaders Sukarno and Hatta imprisoned.

Militarily, the operation was a success. Politically, it was a disaster. In Indonesia itself, administrators who had been loyal to the colonial power criticized the operation and ceased to cooperate any longer. In the international sphere the outcry was equally loud. The United States immediately called on the UN Security Council to demand a ceasefire (December 24, 1948). Subsequent resolutions, with which the Dutch did not comply either, called for the release of imprisoned politicians, general elections, and the transfer of sovereignty to a federal Indonesia within one year. Finally, the UN Good Offices Committee was upgraded to a UN Commission for Indonesia and its powers enlarged.

While Dutch media accused world opinion and American public opinion in particular of deep misunderstandings, a minority in the U.S. Senate demanded a freeze on all Marshall Plan aid to the Netherlands. State Department officials were equally enraged. For Kennan, Dutch policies amounted to "adventurism." The "fastest possible" transfer of power was "absolutely necessary" in order

613

4

—

THE
COLD WAR
AND
BEYOND

1945-2009

—

POLITICS
AND
SECURITY

to preclude a communist Indonesia and end instability and chaos.[10] The already strained Dutch-American relations reached an all-time low in the spring of 1949. When Foreign Minister Dirk Stikker visited Secretary of State Acheson on March 31, he was told that the United States might suspend economic aid and cancel the Military Assistance Program for Western Europe. The American message was clear: the Dutch were no longer allowed to jeopardize American and Western long-term interests.

American pressure was important in finally bringing about a fundamental change in Dutch policies; some authors contend it was instrumental.[11] Equally important, however, were military and political developments in Indonesia. The Dutch military was confronted with increasing guerrilla activities. By late spring in 1949, the conflict resembled the large-scale "dirty war" going on in Indochina. Some estimates put the number of Indonesian casualties at one hundred fifty thousand. Dutch casualties were rising as well. While from 1945 to December 1948 a total of 1,251 soldiers had died, casualties in the following six months amounted to 1,275, most of them draftees. This was a death rate the country could not sustain for long. A loss of control in the countryside, a fundamental lack of legitimacy, and international pressure went hand in hand to force the Dutch government to change its policies.

In the ensuing negotiations that culminated in the transfer of power on December 27, 1949, Dutch-American relations improved considerably. For somewhat comparable reasons, both countries were interested in the speedy reintegration of Indonesia into the world economy. The Americans wanted access to Indonesia's raw materials and markets. The Dutch wanted to save their investments in plantations, trading houses, banking, and so forth, and they wanted to reestablish normal trade relations as soon as possible. American mediation facilitated a compromise in three main areas. First of all, the projected Dutch-Indonesian Union would be a symbolic one, without joint responsibilities. Second, the Indonesians would have to pay a substantial amount of money to the Netherlands to cover prewar debts, but less than The Hague had demanded (a total of 4.3 billion guilders or 1.3 billion dollars). Third, the heavily contested issue of the status of West New Guinea was deferred to Union deliberations. In the final analysis, the United States prepared the ground for an advantageous retreat by the Dutch. Further military operations would have been costly, bloody, and ultimately futile. Moreover, the continuation of the impasse in Indonesia would have aggravated domestic tensions and the international isolation of the Netherlands. The majority of the Dutch as well as politicians and the media had a different opinion. They believed the United States had robbed them of something that rightfully belonged to them. This feeling of betrayal by the United States informed Dutch positions on colonialism and on American policies vis-à-vis colonialism in the 1950s and early 1960s.

The Round Table Conference in The Hague, August 1949, which led to
the granting of independence to Indonesia on December 27.

Suez and New Guinea

4
—

THE
COLD WAR
AND
BEYOND

1945–2009

—

POLITICS
AND
SECURITY

616

By the mid-1950s, Dutch expectations of close cooperation with independent Indonesia had ended in disappointment. The Union, which had been defunct from the beginning, was terminated by Indonesia in 1956, and most of the remaining Dutch and Dutch-Indonesians had left the country. More and more, Indonesian President Sukarno in particular came to personify a type of politician Western elites did not like. With his anti-Western rhetoric, his assertive nationalism, and his insistence on a transfer of power in West New Guinea, Sukarno became heartily disliked in the Netherlands.[12] When another Third World leader, Egypt's Gamal Abdel Nasser, provoked an international crisis, public opinion in the Netherlands as well as the Dutch government readily redirected their ill feelings toward Sukarno onto this other seemingly boisterous leader.

The Suez crisis began with the nationalization of the Suez Canal Company by the Egyptian government in July 1956. The main shareholders, Britain and France, immediately embarked on a course of confrontation. Diplomacy could not diffuse the crisis, and in October Paris and London issued an ultimatum, with which the Egyptians did not comply. The result was a combined Israeli-French-British invasion of Egypt and the occupation of the Canal Zone. During the crisis the United States had strongly criticized Nasser's actions. But the occupation was seen as a classic case of imperialist gunboat diplomacy. American anger over the outright colonialist behavior of its closest allies grew when the Soviet Union took advantage of the negative publicity of the Suez crisis to crush a nationalist noncommunist uprising in Hungary. The Eisenhower administration called on the United Nations Security Council, participated in a protest resolution of the General Assembly, and froze all payments to Britain. The Europeans felt humiliated, but had to withdraw. Suez symbolized for the last time America's desire to end colonialism as Washington made clear that it no longer tolerated any outright old-style imperialist policies.

During the crisis, the Dutch position, one of unwavering verbal support for Britain, was represented by Foreign Minister Joseph Luns, a Catholic diplomat who still had difficulties adjusting to a world in which former colonized territories played a more important role than age-old European countries. On several occasions, Luns lectured American diplomats on the righteousness of British and French policies. His prescriptions were not regarded as constructive, and Americans were slightly embarrassed about Luns's anachronistic attitudes. When Jakarta nationalized all Dutch businesses in Indonesia late in 1957, the U.S. government declined to issue a joint protest, as Luns had desired. By that time, however, the CIA had become deeply involved in a massive clandestine effort to support Sumatran rebels and to bring about the breakup of Indonesia.[13]

Indonesian leader Sukarno meets with President Eisenhower
at the White House, October 6, 1960.

4

—

—

The problem of West New Guinea also played a prominent role in Dutch-American relations during the second half of the 1950s. Both Indonesia and the Netherlands tried to gain American support for their respective positions, and because Washington did not want to jeopardize relations with either one of them, it remained neutral and argued that the two parties involved should find a compromise. By 1960, West New Guinea had assumed a symbolic meaning far out of proportion to its actual importance. The Sukarno regime had made the transfer of sovereignty the centerpiece of its program, while the Dutch government presented itself as the spokesperson of the indigenous population (which was never seriously consulted about its preferences). Both sides escalated the conflict. The Dutch sent a squadron of warships along with its sole aircraft carrier to West New Guinea; Indonesia severed diplomatic relations with The Hague.[14] Moreover, infiltrations and ambushes by Indonesian soldiers increased. Even more strongly than the previous government, the Kennedy administration considered West New Guinea a stumbling block for any improvement in American-Indonesian relations. The prospects of a military conflict were real. Five thousand Dutch troops guarded the territory, and the Indonesians had command over fighter jets and transport planes (acquired in 1960 from the United States and the Soviet Union). In this situation the Kennedy administration opted in favor of Indonesia and the anticommunist leadership of its army, Washington's sole remaining partner in the country, and against the Australians and the Dutch. Following a trip by Robert Kennedy to The Hague, the United States confronted the Dutch government in April 1962 with the so-called Bunker plan. Pending a temporary United Nations administration, it foresaw the transfer of sovereignty of West New Guinea to Indonesia within two years. After ten years, the Papuans should decide about their nationality in a referendum. In view of the increasing tensions in South Vietnam, Dutch objections were sidelined by Washington, and an agreement was signed in August. The Dutch flag was lowered on December 31, 1962. For Jakarta, this symbolized the successful conclusion of decolonization. For The Hague, ironically, the loss of territory paved the way for the acknowledgment of Indonesia as one of the leading nonaligned nations and as a country where Dutch development assistance was needed and appreciated.[15]

Conclusion

Dutch colonial interests and American superpower interests clashed in the crises over Indonesia and West New Guinea. In both instances, the Dutch were not able to turn a colonial conflict into a battlefield of the Cold War. Washington believed that continued Dutch control of the territories would only spread communism, rather than contain it. Colonialism, policymakers asserted, endangered the construction of the "Free World." For the Americans, stabilizing the periphery of the American empire in the Pacific implied support for forces that the United States associated with the future. Concrete economic interests did not play a significant role in this context. Rather, what mattered was the belief that a world without colonial protectionism would contribute to the development of the global capitalist order. But decision makers were equally aware of the limits of this vision. What could be pursued vis-à-vis the Dutch did not seem feasible in the case of the French in Indochina. France, as the most important continental ally, had at its disposal many more resources, policy options, and autonomy than the Netherlands. And while the Indonesian nationalist movement had demonstrated its resistance against communism, the Vietnamese struggle for independence was conducted mainly by communists.

Tensions in Dutch-American relations and a bitter media coverage in the Netherlands were only temporary and without lasting impact. Eventually, the United States' role as a broker of decolonization at times of deadlocks and tensions proved beneficial. Thanks to American intervention, the Netherlands, unlike France, did not get embroiled in bloody and protracted wars. This, in turn, cleared the way for much greater involvement in Europe and European integration in the 1950s.

1   "Public Opinion in Western Europe.
    Attitudes towards Political, Economic
    and Military Integration" (Amsterdam:
    International Institute of Public Opin-
    ion, January 1953), Record Group 306,
    Entry 1008, Box 2, National Archives II,
    College Park, MD; Discussion at the
    226th Meeting of the National Security
    Council, December 1, 1954, Eisenhower
    Papers, Ann Whitman File, National
    Security Council, Box 6, Dwight D.
    Eisenhower Library, Abilene, KS.

2   Robert J. McMahon, *Colonialism and
    Cold War. The United States and The
    Struggle for Indonesian Independence*
    (Ithaca, NY: Cornell University Press,
    1981); Frances Gouda with Thijs Bro-
    cades Zaalberg, *American Visions of the
    Netherlands East Indies/Indonesia.
    US Foreign Policy and Indonesian Nation-
    alism, 1920–1949* (Amsterdam: Amster-

    dam University Press, 2002); Marc Frey,
    *Dekolonisierung in Südostasien. Die
    Vereinigten Staaten und die Auflösung der
    europäischen Kolonialreiche* (Munich:
    Oldenbourg, 2006).

3   J. B. D. Derksen and Jan Tinbergen,
    "Berekeningen over de economische
    betekenis van Nederlandsch-Indië voor
    Nederland," *Maandschrift van het
    Centraal Bureau voor de Statistiek* 40
    (1945): 210-216; H. W. van den Doel,
    *Afscheid van Indië: De val van het Neder-
    landse imperium in Azië* (Amsterdam:
    Prometheus, 2001); J. J. P. de Jong,
    *Diplomatie of strijd: Een analyse van het
    Nederlandse beleid tegenover de Indone-
    sische Revolutie, 1945–1947* (Meppel:
    Boom, 1988).

4   William H. Frederick, *Visions and Heat:
    The Making of the Indonesian Revolution*
    (Athens: Ohio University Press, 1989);

4

—

THE
COLD WAR
AND
BEYOND

1945–2009

—

POLITICS
AND
SECURITY

Anthony Reid, *The Indonesian National Revolution, 1945–1950* (Hawthorn, Australia: Longman, 1974).

5   J. J. P. de Jong, "The Netherlands, Great Britain and the Indonesian Revolution, 1945–1950," in Nigel Ashton and Duco Hellema, eds., *Unspoken Allies: Anglo-Dutch Relations since 1780* (Amsterdam: Amsterdam University Press, 2001), 179-202; Dean Acheson to Walter Foote, October 1, 1946, in *Foreign Relations of the United States 1946*, vol. 8, *The Far East* (Washington, DC: Government Printing Office, 1971), 845-846.

6   "Nota van minister van oorlog, Fiévez, aan leden van de raad voor militaire aangelegenheden," April 21, 1947, in S. L. van der Wal, P. J. Drooglever, and M. J. B. Schouten, eds., *Officiële bescheiden betreffende de Nederlands-Indonesische betrekkingen 1945–1950*, 20 vols. (hereafter NIB) (The Hague: SDU uitgeverij, 1971–96), 8:346ff; "Notulen van de vergadering van de ministerraad," May 28, 1947, ibid., 9:63-73.

7   Willem Drees diary entry, January 5, 1948, NIB, 12:455ff; Van Kleffens to Foreign Minister C.G.W.H. van Boetzelaer van Oosterhout, January 9, 1948, NIB, 12:483-485.

8   Kennan to Marshall, December 17, 1948, Record Group 59, Lot 64D563, Box 18, National Archives, College Park, MD.

9   Petra M. H. Groen, "Militant Response: The Dutch Use of Military Force and the Decolonization of the Dutch East Indies, 1945–50," *Journal of Commonwealth and Imperial History* 21 (1993): 30-44.

10 "United States Policy Toward Southeast Asia," PPS/51, March 29, 1949, in Anna Kersten Nelson, ed., *The State Department Policy Planning Staff Papers 1947–1949*, 3 vols. (New York: Garland Publications, 1983), 3:32-58.

11 Pierre van der Eng, "Marshall Aid as a Catalyst in the Decolonization of

Indonesia, 1947–49," *Journal of Southeast Asian Studies* 19 (1988): 335-352; McMahon, *Colonialism and Cold War*, 293; Cees Wiebes and Bert Zeeman, "United States 'Big Stick' Diplomacy: The Netherlands between Decolonization and Alignment, 1945–1949," *International History Review* 14 (1992): 45-70.

12 Hans Meijer, *Den Haag-Djakarta. De Nederlands-Indonesische betrekkingen 1950–1962* (Utrecht: Het Spectrum, 1994).

13 Duco Hellema, "Backing Britain: The Netherlands and the Suez Crisis," *Diplomacy & Statecraft* 4.1 (1993): 37-58; Duco Hellema, *Zesenvijftig. De Nederlandse houding ten aanzien van de Hongaarse revolutie en de Suezcrisis* (Amsterdam: Mets, 1990), 100-166, 236-240; Frey, *Dekolonisierung*, 224-234; Audrey R. and George McT. Kahin, *Subversion as Foreign Policy. The Secret Eisenhower and Dulles Debacle in Indonesia* (New York: The Free Press, 1995).

14 C.L.M. Penders, *The West New Guinea Debacle: Dutch Decolonisation and Indonesia, 1945–1962* (Honolulu: University of Hawai'i Press, 2002), 279-328; Duco Hellema, *De Karel Doorman naar Nieuw-Guinea* (Amsterdam: Boom, 2005), 75-162.

15 J. J. P. de Jong, "Onder ethisch insigne. De origine van de Nederlandse ontwikkelingssamenwerking," in J. A. Nekkers and P. A. M. Malcontent, eds., *De geschiedenis van vijftig jaar Nederlandse ontwikkelingssamenwerking 1949–1999*, (The Hague: SDU uitgeverij, 1999), 79-81; Maarten Kuitenbrouwer, *De ontdekking van de Derde Wereld. Beeldvorming en beleid in Nederland 1950–1990* (The Hague: SDU uitgeverij, 1994), 45-46.

BILATERAL DEFENSE COOPERATION IN AN ATLANTIC PERSPECTIVE, 1945–1970

───

INE MEGENS

World War II brought an end to Dutch neutrality, a central tenet of Dutch foreign policy for over a century. In the context of the emerging Cold War the Netherlands took the side of the West. In military matters all attention initially focused on the conflict in Indonesia, but after 1949 Dutch defense policy developed a clear Atlantic preference. During the war the United States had come to the rescue of Europe and the Dutch government wanted to secure a permanent involvement of the U.S. in Europe. Within the North Atlantic alliance the Netherlands would display a great trust in the United States and this brought the country the title of America's most faithful ally, a concept that has dominated the discussion on Dutch foreign policy since it was introduced in 1974.[1] Only much later did researchers argue that colonial resentments were still noticeable in Dutch foreign policy in the 1950s, and that Foreign Minister Joseph Luns remained very bitter about the lack of American support to maintain New Guinea as Dutch territory.[2] But Luns, foreign minister for nineteen years, did not let this detract from his Atlanticist disposition, and in 1971 he became NATO's secretary general. The fact that there have been three Dutch secretaries general of NATO is taken by some in the Netherlands as proof of the privileged position of the Dutch as America's staunchest ally.[3] When it is really important the Dutch government takes sides with the United States in matters of defense, despite the fact that public opinion is often more critical of American foreign policy. However, in the early days of the Cold War the Dutch warmly welcomed American support for European defense, and the dominant position of the United States within the alliance was undisputed in the eyes of the general public.

The Formation of NATO and Defense Planning

4

———

THE
COLD WAR
AND
BEYOND

1945–2009

———

POLITICS
AND
SECURITY

622

In the first postwar years the Netherlands had tried to reoccupy Indonesia and sent more than one hundred thousand men abroad to combat the nationalists. Therefore hardly any troops were available to protect the Dutch homeland and the chiefs of staff had no defense plans ready. In 1948 the Europeans took the first steps toward the establishment of a union for collective self-defense. President Harry Truman pledged full support for this initiative. Opinions differed on the form this commitment should take: military assistance, a unilateral American security guarantee, or a formal treaty. The French insisted on a formal treaty and during the negotiations the U.S. government yielded to this demand. It took a long time to complete the North Atlantic Treaty because President Truman faced significant domestic opposition.[4] Apart from adherents of isolationism, who opposed any long-term commitment to other countries, several U.S. senators pressed for more efforts from the Europeans themselves and feared the pledge to assist the allies in case of an armed attack would impinge on their constitutional authority to declare war. The treaty was finally signed in Washington on April 4, 1949 by representatives of twelve states, among them the Dutch minister of foreign affairs, Dirk Stikker. While in Washington for the final round of negotiations, Stikker felt pressured by the American government, which threatened to withhold military support to the Netherlands prior to a settlement with Indonesia, and he doubted whether it would be wise to join the Atlantic Pact under this coercion. However, not signing it was not a viable option.[5] Later that same year the Dutch government recognized the independence of Indonesia, after which planning for defense could start.

These initial plans led to the creation of an army corps with three divisions. The Dutch chief of staff, General Hendrik Kruls, considered four divisions the absolute minimum to defend Dutch territory. The cabinet, however, considered even three divisions too ambitious and financially unacceptable. Repatriation and demobilization of the armed forces from Indonesia would burden the defense budgets for years to come. There were huge shortages of military equipment and there was a great need for professional soldiers. According to the minister of defense, Wim Schokking, the costs of the acquisition of military equipment as well as the lack of trained personnel necessitated a gradual build-up of the armed forces, and American assistance was indispensable for realizing the establishment of the Dutch military.

Membership of the North Atlantic Treaty in April 1949 did not bring about any immediate change in Dutch defense policy. The stalemate between the cabinet and the military authorities continued. This, in turn, caused friction with parliament, which considered the government irresolute. Because of this criti-

cism Schokking resigned in the fall of 1950. Relationships with the military authorities did not improve. The reproaches were mainly aimed at General Kruls.
There were differences of opinion on essential measures for defense, but it was
as much a dispute over competence and public behavior, because Kruls made
no attempt to disguise his criticism of the government.

The United States and Military Aid

Meanwhile, international consultations had started among the member states
of the North Atlantic Treaty. The United States had promised to furnish military
equipment to the allies on the condition that they agree on a common defense
plan. This was incorporated in a clause in the Mutual Defense Assistance Act
that would be the basis for the bilateral treaties of the U.S. with its allies. Some
preliminary work had been done by the European countries themselves, and
during the winter of 1949–50 the basic concept for the defense of the North Atlantic Treaty area was agreed upon in just three months. Mutual aid and self-
help constituted the principles for organizing collective self-defense among
the allies. Common action and coordinated planning had to be undertaken on
the principle that each nation would contribute in the most efficient manner
and would assume those tasks for which it was best suited. General Omar Bradley, chairman of the Standing Group, who considered some European forces
like the Dutch aircraft carrier *Karel Doorman* merely hobbyhorses, argued that
traditions had to give way to reality. Under his chairmanship the military authorities further developed the concept of balanced collective forces. National
defense efforts should be subordinated to an overall point of view and the European allies should concentrate their efforts on land forces. The Dutch, however,
claimed a role in the defense of the lines of communication across the Atlantic
Ocean, and through skilful diplomatic maneuvering they were successful in the
end. At the same time, the inclusion of these tasks in NATO defense planning
made the Dutch navy eligible for U.S. military assistance. The destroyer escorts
and minesweepers they received as end item assistance enabled the Royal Navy
to concentrate on its ocean-going fleet without jeopardizing the projected comprehensive naval build-up.

The United States used military aid as a means to speed up defense planning but soon noticed a tendency among its European allies to await results in
NATO planning. Therefore, the U.S. encouraged NATO bodies to make greater
efforts and tried to use military aid as an enticement for cooperation. At the
same time, however, the U.S. government obstructed the work of these committees by refusing to submit adequate information on its own defense planning.
The allies accepted a division of labor as well as the exclusion of American nucle-

623

ar weapons from planning in a NATO framework. After the Korean War broke out in June 1950 the United States repeatedly called for larger defense expenditures from its European allies.

The Dutch showed some reluctance to support the Americans in Korea because they were afraid their full support would deteriorate their relations with Indonesia. Initially, they only sent one naval vessel, while later on a detachment of volunteers was sent to Korea. The Dutch government also objected to the policy General Douglas MacArthur was pursuing during the war, and even considered expressing its displeasure by introducing a resolution in the UN Assembly because it thought the decision to cross the 38th parallel would provoke China into a counterattack. Besides, the Netherlands had been one of only a few Western countries to recognize the People's Republic of China earlier that year and preferred negotiations to end the conflict. The Americans put great pressure on the Dutch before they gave in and agreed to a UN resolution that marked the Chinese as the aggressors.

American pressure was also one of the reasons that brought about a substantial increase in the defense budget. Even after the outbreak of the Korean War the Dutch government did not think a Soviet attack in Europe was an urgent matter. Nevertheless the defense budget was increased and in The Hague further increments were under discussion. In January 1951 General Dwight Eisenhower visited the Netherlands in his capacity as the newly appointed supreme allied commander in Europe. He made no secret of his criticism of Dutch defense planning and the continuing lack of a sense of urgency. In the following months a consensus grew on the figure of 1.5 billion guilders for the annual defense budget, almost twice as much as before. In March 1951 the new defense minister, Cees Staf, presented a memorandum to parliament that comprised a plan for the future development of the armed forces. Expanding the Royal Army to five divisions, as promised to NATO, was central. From the beginning it was obvious that the plan would require a great effort from the Dutch and that American military assistance was welcome and in some respects even a necessity. Up to 1960 defense expenditures would be the largest item in the national budget of the Netherlands. Apart from expenditures for personnel and operating costs for materiel, the budget included large amounts for new investments. In financial terms, American military assistance almost fully matched these investments.[6]

The impact of U.S. military aid on the Dutch armed forces was apparent in other aspects, too.[7] The war in Indonesia had cost the lives of many soldiers and

625

◄ The steamship *Traute Sarnow* arrives in Rotterdam and delivers the first three Centurion tanks to the Dutch army in January 1953. The tanks, constructed in Britain for West European forces, were part of the military build-up under the Mutual Defence Assistance Program.

4

—

THE
COLD WAR
AND
BEYOND

1945–2009

—

POLITICS
AND
SECURITY

most of the military equipment had been left behind. Equipment planning for the Royal Army had to start from scratch, while new training regimes were required for both new conscripts and veterans of the Indonesian campaign. Rebuilding the armed forces would primarily come about with equipment granted under the military assistance program. As the materiel was not readily available, however, the execution of the plans proceeded slowly. Moreover, the plans were repeatedly adjusted according to American demands, for instance because U.S. officials attached great value to the state of readiness of troops or advised against the delivery of certain items under the military assistance program. Of the three military services the Royal Army received by far the largest share of aid, and the adaptations this required were more complicated than for the other two services.

Apart from help by way of military equipment, American guidance in the field of training and organization was very influential in the early period of the Cold War. The air force gained most from the training offered by the Americans in the United States, as there were hardly any training facilities in the Netherlands itself. The Dutch army organization changed from a British model to an American structure to organize its staff work as well as its army units. As a consequence of the military assistance provided by the United States the daily routine in the armed forces changed completely. Military authorities were convinced the American way of equipping, training, and planning was generally more efficient. The mobility of infantry divisions increased and greater firepower was allotted to lower-echelons units. U.S. officers were deployed as instructors, to supervise the use of end items or to give advice on organizational or technical difficulties. At the working level a close cooperation emerged between the American military advisors stationed in The Hague and their Dutch colleagues. Dutch military, in particular the younger ones, were only too willing to accept American advice.

The Americans thought some elements in the Dutch defense plans, such as the fleet plan or the territorial troops, were too ambitious and not in accordance with NATO planning. Dutch military authorities, though, attached great value to the territorial units to defend their home territory, as NATO's strategy at the time was based on the Rhine-IJssel line that left part of the country undefended. The only sanction the American government could impose on a policy by its allies that it disliked was to withhold equipment from these forces, which it did in this case. This demonstrates that military aid fell short of enforcing consent when it came to issues the Dutch considered to be of national interest. The Netherlands took great care not to force the issue with the U.S. because a close relationship with the Americans in the area of defense was too precious to disrupt and military assistance was only one element in the country's pro-American policy.

Suez and New Guinea

In the early 1950s the Dutch government had welcomed America's willingness to deploy more troops on the European continent, and it was also eager to carry through German rearmament in the framework of the North Atlantic alliance. The Netherlands showed a distinct preference for NATO here and only reluctantly joined the talks about the French proposal to establish a European army as a way to incorporate the German forces. The treaty to establish a European Defence Community failed to materialize and the Federal Republic of Germany then joined NATO as its fifteenth member state. As the Dutch government had advocated the Atlantic framework all along, it was particularly happy about the end result.

By the mid-1950s the alliance had developed into the main platform for transatlantic consultations on defense as well as an international military body for operational planning and training. The United States, although firmly embedded in the alliance, emphasized it had global responsibilities and continued to push the Europeans to take more responsibility for their own defense. By that time the situation in Europe had stabilized somewhat, and the change in Soviet policy after the death of Stalin even allowed President Eisenhower, along with the British and French, to meet Soviet leader Nikita Khrushchev in Geneva to diminish international tensions. Prior to the Geneva summit the representatives of the European allies had been informed, but they were not consulted and some allies believed that political consultation in NATO deserved more attention. The Netherlands at this point was not particularly concerned, nor had it ever before insisted on increased cooperation in nonmilitary affairs as Canada or Norway had done repeatedly. In December 1956 the report of the Three Wise Men that recommended to broaden NATO's nonmilitary aspects and to initiate consultation in the planning stage, was readily accepted by the representatives of all member states, including the Netherlands.[8] Two months earlier, France and Egypt had joined Israel and invaded Egypt to secure the Suez Canal, without the United States' knowledge. The Eisenhower administration showed its contempt for this action in no uncertain terms and forced the three countries to agree to a ceasefire and, eventually, to withdraw from Egypt. This time the Dutch sided with their European partners and rejected the American policy. Foreign Minister Joseph Luns thought the nationalization of the Suez Canal was only one more example of nonobservance of the law by Third World countries and the American attitude in this respect had been too tolerant. For the transatlantic alliance the Suez crisis had severe repercussions as the relationship between the three major allies deteriorated. An improvement in con-

627

4

—

THE
COLD WAR
AND
BEYOND

1945-2009

POLITICS
AND
SECURITY

628

sultation procedures, as advocated by the committee of the Three Wise Men, was out of the question.

The ministerial meetings of the North Atlantic Council, however, offered an excellent opportunity for all member states to put forward specific demands or draw attention to certain issues. From 1958 onward Luns used these meetings repeatedly to point to the deteriorating situation in New Guinea, to press his allies to condemn the Indonesian infiltrations, and to impose an arms embargo on Indonesia. Most of the time his colleagues merely took notice of the Dutch information and expressed some sympathy, but Luns failed to obtain actual support. In all other respects the alliance was a determining factor in Dutch defense thinking, and the 1960s have rightfully been called the prime time of Atlanticism in Dutch foreign policy.[9]

Nuclear Strategy

At the end of the 1950s the initial phase of the build-up of the armed forces in the Netherlands had come to an end. The Soviet Union still outnumbered the Western alliance in troops, but the introduction of nuclear weapons in Europe offered an adequate substitute and force goals were revised downward. For the Dutch army the minimum force requirements were reduced to one army corps with three divisions while each division was cut back in equipment and composition. Nuclear weapons offered a cheaper substitute and were welcomed for that reason by the European countries, as all of them had difficulties to keep up the high defense budgets established in the aftermath of the Korean War. Apart from the United States, only the United Kingdom at the time possessed nuclear weapons in the West. The issue of nuclear weapons control would be a major stumbling block among the allies in the early 1960s.

In Europe doubts emerged whether the United States would use its nuclear weapons to safeguard the defense of the European continent and risk nuclear disaster on its own territory. These doubts met with no response in the Netherlands, certainly not in the government, which gave its unqualified consent to the deployment of American nuclear weapons on Dutch territory. In 1960 the first of these weapons arrived; ultimately the armed forces would have six different weapon systems capable of firing nuclear weapons. The first generation of nuclear weapon delivery systems, Honest John missiles for the army and Nike Hercules missiles for the air force, were provided under the U.S. military aid program. They remained in American custody and only the U.S. president could authorize the launching of these tactical nuclear weapons.[10] To that end the American soldiers watched over the storage sites, along with Dutch conscripts

who guarded the outer rings of the sites and the immediate neighborhood. Nu-
clearization of the armed forces also led to further professionalization, as pilots
and other military personnel were trained in the United States and common
NATO exercises took place on a regular basis. Even the navy became an advocate
of the alliance after the loss of New Guinea in 1962. It was the only branch of the
Dutch armed forces that at an earlier stage had shown some reticence with regard to NATO because, in its estimation, the North Atlantic Treaty area was too
limited and did not protect the Dutch colonies, nor the commercial interests of
the merchant fleet. From the early 1960s onward the main defense task of the
navy was to fight the growing threat of Soviet submarines. As a result, it managed to avert budgetary reductions, even if capital ships such as the aircraft carrier and heavy cruisers would be taken out of service in due time.[11]

Unlike other European countries, the Dutch government was confident the
Americans would defend the European continent with nuclear weapons if necessary. It preferred to limit the number of countries with nuclear weapons and
was less concerned than some political parties and part of the general public
about West German nuclear ambitions. In January 1963 Minister of Defense
Simon Visser stated in parliament that the government had "absolute and
full confidence in the American guarantee that the nuclear power of the United States [was] meant to defend the territory of the treaty area" (absoluut en
volledig vertrouwen in de Amerikaanse toezegging, dat het nucleaire potentieel
van de Verenigde Staten voor de verdediging van het gehele verdragsgebied be-
stemd is").[12] It was the government's first public statement of this kind and a
clear reaction to the political unrest in Western Europe.

Earlier that same month French President Charles de Gaulle had vetoed
British membership in the European Economic Community and simultaneously rejected the American offer to buy nuclear Polaris missiles. De Gaulle had
criticized the idea of military integration before and was convinced that NATO
needed to undergo radical changes. In September 1958 he had proposed a reorganization of the alliance; a trilateral committee of the U.S., the UK, and France
should develop strategic plans and give the French a say in nuclear weapons
control. These French proposals held little appeal for the Dutch government,
but in the spring of 1963 it could not ignore the crisis in the alliance. For the moment a direct confrontation with France was avoided and discussions within
the alliance on the need for reform intensified. On the political level, Luns did
not consider changes necessary; he repeatedly expressed his satisfaction with
the structure of the alliance.[13]

629

4

—

THE
COLD WAR
AND
BEYOND

1945–2009

—

POLITICS
AND
SECURITY

Resolving Difficulties in the 1960s

In the military domain the debate focused on the plan to establish a nuclear multilateral force (MLF) that should be commonly owned and have a mixed crew of various nationalities. The Americans offered to equip the vessels with nuclear missiles and some U.S. officials held out the prospect for a greater European voice in the matter of control. As far as the Dutch cabinet was concerned, there was no need to create a European nuclear force or formulate a separate European defense policy. In the end, political expediency prevailed over the military objections as well as the government's own doubts, whereupon the Netherlands joined the international negotiations on a multilateral force. For over two years the MLF would dominate transatlantic relations, but the core issue of control over the launching of nuclear weapons was never resolved.

The ambivalent and reserved attitude of the Dutch toward the multilateral force resembles their position in the early 1950s on the European Defence Community. When it was really important the Dutch preferred the Americans over their European allies and put their trust in the American nuclear guarantee to defend the continent. In the eyes of the Dutch, military capabilities in Europe were inadequate, while the political will and decision-making structures on the European level were missing, too. The Dutch recognized American leadership within the alliance and were confident the U.S. would be vigorous in its efforts to protect European security, if necessary. At the same time they were always first to point to the equality of all members in an alliance of sovereign states and fully endorsed the European wish to get a greater say in the American nuclear decision-making process.

After the collapse of the MLF project and France's withdrawal from NATO's military structure, political consultation was improved within the alliance and it emerged from the crisis of the mid-1960s as a stronger organization.[14] In 1967 NATO established the Nuclear Planning Group, a small committee with only seven members who quickly agreed on guidelines for the use of tactical nuclear weapons. For nonnuclear powers it offered a platform to discuss nuclear matters. The Netherlands had played an active role in amending the initial American proposal in order to improve the position of the smaller allies, and seized the opportunity to participate in nuclear defense planning with both hands. Simultaneously, the Dutch government continued to try to meet defense and financial commitments adopted at the highest level in the alliance. In spite of growing criticism at home, basically this Atlanticist attitude would prevail from the late 1960s onward.

1   Alfred van Staden, *Een trouwe bondge-noot: Nederland en het Atlantisch bond-genootschap 1960–1971* (Baarn: Anthos, 1974).

2   Alfred Pijpers, "Dekolonisatie, com-pensatiedrang en de normalisering van de Nederlandse buitenlandse politiek," *Internationale Spectator* 45.2 (1991): 62-71.

3   The other two have been Dirk Stikker (1961–64) and Jaap de Hoop Scheffer (2004–09).

4   Lawrence S. Kaplan, *NATO 1948. The Birth of the Transatlantic Alliance* (Lanham, MD: Rowman & Littlefield Publishers, 2007).

5   Cees Wiebes and Bert Zeeman, "Belgium, The Netherlands and Alli-ances, 1940–1949" (Ph.D. dissertation, University of Leiden, 1993).

6   Ine Megens, *American Aid to NATO Allies in the 1950s. The Dutch Case* (Amster-dam: Thesis Publishers, 1994), 154-159.

7   Ibid., 197-200; Jan Schulten, "The Impact of the United States on the Dutch Armed Forces," in Hans Loeber, ed., *Dutch-American Relations 1945–1969. A Partnership. Illusions and Facts* (Assen/Maastricht: Van Gorcum, 1992), 76-105, here 94-95.

8   The Three Wise Men (Halvard Lange, Gaetano Martini, and Lester Pearson) were appointed by the North Atlantic Council in 1956 to examine ways for the alliance to strengthen its cohesion. See John Milloy, *The North Atlantic Treaty*

Organization 1948–1957: Community or Alliance? (Montreal: McGill-Queen's University Press, 2006).

9   Duco Hellema, *Neutraliteit en vrijhandel. De geschiedenis van de Nederlandse buitenlandse betrekkingen* (Utrecht: Het Spectrum, 2001), 218-221.

10 Pieter de Geus, *Staatsbelang en krijgs-macht. De Nederlandse defensie tijdens de Koude Oorlog* (The Hague: SDU uitgeverij, 1998), 98-104.

11 Jan Janssen, "Driestromenland in optima forma: identiteit, taken en organisatorische inbedding van de krijgsmachtdelen rond 1960," in Ben Schoenmaker and Jan Janssen, eds., *In de schaduw van de muur. Maatschappij en krijgsmacht rond 1960* (The Hague: SDU uitgeverij, 1997), 236-252, here 241-242.

12 Meeting of January 29, 1963, *Proceedings of the Dutch Parliament, Second Chamber (Handelingen der Staten-Generaal)*, 1962-1963, 585.

13 Anna Locher, "A Crisis Foretold. NATO and France, 1963–66," in Andreas Wenger, Christian Nuenlist, and Anna Locher, eds., *Transforming NATO in the Cold War. Challenges beyond Deter-rence in the 1960s* (London: Routledge, 2007), 107-129, here 116.

14 Andreas Wenger, "Crisis and Oppor-tunity: NATO's Transformation and the Multilateralization of Détente, 1966–1968," *Journal of Cold War Studies* 6.1 (2004): 22-74.

THE
COLD WAR
AND
BEYOND

1945–2009

POLITICS
AND
SECURITY

4

THE UNITED STATES, THE NETHERLANDS, AND THE ESTABLISHMENT OF THE UNITED NATIONS

PETER R. BAEHR

Introduction

Both the United States and the Netherlands have a history of involvement with international organizations.* In the case of the United States, Woodrow Wilson's idealism was thwarted by the Senate's refusal to accept the League of Nations treaty. After World War I there was a widespread opinion in the United States that it should not again become involved in what were considered "European wars." A majority in the Senate saw the League of Nations as an institution dominated by European powers such as Britain and France, which would not necessarily work for the interests of the United States. This policy changed with President Roosevelt's decision to enter World War II. In 1941 he formulated his famous four freedoms: freedom of speech and expression, freedom of worship, freedom from want, and freedom from fear.[1] Thus a number of important human rights became explicit goals of American foreign policy.

By the end of World War II the power of the United States had grown so much that it became the dominant power in the world — to some extent checked by its rival, the Soviet Union. During the war plans had been developed in the State Department for the creation of a new, worldwide international organization, the United Nations. This new institution, the planners in the State Department thought, would be dominated by the United States, as was in fact the case during the first years of its existence.

The Netherlands has, on the whole, been a supporter of both the League of Nations and the United Nations. But this does not mean that its expectations

* I thank Leon Gordenker for his critical comments on an earlier version of this article.

for both these organizations were the same as those of the United States, and the Netherlands had quite specific concerns when it came to deciding on the framework and outlook of the United Nations during World War II.

The Origin of the United Nations

Long before victory in World War II was on the horizon, the idea took root among the leaders of the Allied powers that the postwar world would require a general international organization. It would help maintain the reestablished peace and much more. As Woodrow Wilson made the creation of the League of Nations a U.S. aim for World War I, so too did Franklin Roosevelt and Winston Churchill work toward the formation of the United Nations.

Four months before the United States joined the battle, the British prime minister and the American president discussed war aims in August 1941. The result was the Atlantic Charter, the first open statement of principles about the postwar world. In line with FDR's four freedoms, Churchill and Roosevelt favored restoration of independence to those states that had lost it to German aggression. They rejected territorial gains for their own countries. They mentioned that "pending the establishment of a wider and more permanent system of general security," governments that threatened aggression should be disarmed. Although Churchill preferred a clear statement that an effective international organization was desirable, Roosevelt was held back by fear of a negative reaction from the United States Senate.

In the succeeding months a series of conferences and intense planning, especially in the United States and the United Kingdom, gave shape to a postwar world organization. On January 1, 1942, twenty-six governments, including the Netherlands, signed the Declaration of the United Nations, which set out principles for a "wider and more permanent system of general security." They viewed the Atlantic Charter as a common program for the Allied states and pledged mutual support in the war effort.

The Dutch Plan for a Regional Security Organization

The Netherlands was not always a fervent supporter of the creation of a new worldwide international organization. Although a member of the League of Nations, Dutch faith in that organization had been shaken by its inability to deal effectively in 1936 with the German reoccupation of the Rhineland and Italy's aggression against Abyssinia. The Netherlands government reverted to its age-old policy of neutrality—in vain, as the German attack in May 1940 and its subsequent

633

4

—

THE
COLD WAR
AND
BEYOND

1945–2009

—

POLITICS
AND
SECURITY

occupation of the country demonstrated. For a while, the Dutch government in exile in London tried to maintain a position of being a middle power, mainly on the basis of its colonial empire in the East and West Indies.[2] This ended, however, with the Japanese occupation of the Dutch East Indies in early 1942.

Since the summer of 1941, Dutch Foreign Minister Eelco van Kleffens had had informal contacts with his Belgian and Norwegian colleagues, Paul-Henri Spaak and Trygve Lie (later the first UN secretary general), about postwar problems and their solution. In a meeting in March 1942, Van Kleffens developed his views on political-military cooperation among the three states.[3] Modern warfare with its new developments in weaponry made defense by small states, acting on their own, impossible. Small states, such as the Netherlands, Belgium, and Norway, acting together in cooperation with other nonaggressive European states, should interest the United States in helping maintain their security. He took up a concept earlier developed by Trygve Lie to involve the United States and Great Britain in the defense of the European continent: states bordering the Atlantic Ocean should create an organization to secure together that ocean and those states. Faced with criticism from some of his ministerial colleagues, Van Kleffens argued that a worldwide organization could not guarantee the required security because it would lack a common political foundation. The Netherlands' interest required, he believed, clusters of countries that had a common direction.[4]

In the spring of 1942 Van Kleffens produced a more definitive plan in which he acknowledged that the League of Nations had achieved some results in solving certain economic and social questions, but had completely failed in dealing with important political matters. The world consisted of aggressive as well as nonaggressive nations, of large and smaller nations, and a universal organization could not serve as the foundation stone for the maintenance of international order. What was needed were international arrangements among "powers of good will, the great powers … being concerned in all, or several regions, whereas the smaller states … would take part in those regions where their interests are directly involved."[5] Participation by the United States in each of the future arrangements was of the greatest importance. An organization focusing on the Atlantic Ocean region would assure security in that area. Next to the United States and Great Britain, the Netherlands, Belgium, and Norway would become part of this North Atlantic security arrangement, while France, Spain, and Portugal would also be considered. Similar regional organizations would have to be established for the Southern Atlantic, the Pacific, and the Indian oceans, and for the Baltic and Mediterranean seas. Because of its colonial possessions the Netherlands was to become a member not only of the North Atlantic security arrangement, but also of the Pacific, the Indian Ocean, and the Southern Atlantic. The member states would grant entry to each other's naval and air forces and make their own arrangements for their territorial defense. The United States and Great Britain would act as international policemen in the area, whereas that status was to be denied to the Soviet Union.

Van Kleffens received some positive reactions from the United States and also from the Norwegian Minister Trygve Lie, who had a number of specific comments. However, Belgium's Foreign Minister Paul-Henri Spaak dissociated himself completely from the plan. He believed that the postwar political, economic, and social problems required an integrated approach. He did not think that regional security arrangements would work in view of possible rivalries between the various arrangements. This brought an end to the plan, as it meant that no common continental European proposal could be submitted to the Great Powers. It also ended the Netherlands' aspirations to be considered a middle power rather than a small one.[6] It was only with the greatest effort that the Netherlands and Norway succeeded at the San Francisco Conference to include in the UN Charter a reference to possible regional security arrangements.[7]

Further Preparations for the United Nations

The planning for a postwar organization quickly evolved in 1943. It began in earnest in the foreign ministries of several governments and above all in Washington.[8] The foreign ministers of the three leading Allied powers, the United Kingdom, the United States, and the Soviet Union, drafted the Declaration of Moscow, which sought to create a general international organization as soon as possible. Some further progress was made at the Teheran Conference of 1943, attended by Churchill, Roosevelt, and Stalin, followed by the Dumbarton Oaks Conference in Washington, DC, in 1944. The discussions were primarily based on drafts submitted by the U.S. State Department. At Dumbarton Oaks representatives of China, the Soviet Union, the United Kingdom, and the United States formulated the governing principles of the United Nations. Among them was the name, United Nations, to proclaim the intention of continuing peacetime cooperation on the basis of the common purposes of the war.

The disagreement over membership and the Soviet demand for sixteen votes for the component republics of the USSR ended when Roosevelt proposed giving a vote to each of the then forty-eight United States. Yet the Ukrainian and Byelorussian Soviet Socialist republics, never before identified as sovereign states, did get votes. Stalin argued that this advantage was offset by Washington's influence in Latin America. The list of "sponsoring powers" of the United Nations was expanded from the Big Three of Yalta to include China and France, both to have permanent seats on the Security Council. Invitees to the founding conference at San Francisco would include all states whose governments had declared

4

—

THE
COLD WAR
AND
BEYOND

1945–2009

—

POLITICS
AND
SECURITY

war on the Axis powers before March 1, 1945, and had signed the Declaration of the United Nations of January 1, 1942. Related to membership was the question of voting, a principal agenda item at Yalta. Except on procedural matters, the five Great Powers had to agree unanimously in the Security Council in order that a resolution be adopted. This right of veto was the principal signature of their great power status.

As for colonies, Churchill was assured at Yalta that no part of the empire would be put under UN control without British consent. Great Britain, or any country, could voluntarily put a colony under the supervision of a trusteeship system. This would also apply to former mandates of the League of Nations (seized from Germany and Turkey after World War I) that had not gained independence, and to additional territories that might be taken from Germany and Japan. Administration of other colonial territories would remain as before.

Within an hour of taking office after Roosevelt's sudden death on April 12, 1945, President Harry Truman announced that the founding conference for the UN would be held as planned. Accordingly, the United Nations Conference on International Organization opened on April 25, 1945, in San Francisco, presided over by U.S. Secretary of State Edward Stettinius.

The San Francisco Conference

In what was probably the most public diplomatic conference for that time, 260 representatives of 50 nations attended the conference that met in the San Francisco Opera House. As with earlier diplomatic conferences, each governmental delegation had an equal vote. But as in the past, everyone understood that without the concurrence of the Great Powers no real results could be booked. The debates took place in a plenary session, four main committees, and twelve subcommittees, all of them aiming at finding ways to resolve issues.

Issues there still were indeed, despite the lengthy preparations at Dumbarton Oaks and the subsequent agreements at Yalta. At the same time, the San Francisco Conference had solid, careful drafts on which to base its deliberations. In addition to the still lingering differences among the Great Powers, two cleavages that sometimes involved overlapping groupings of states became evident. One of these was between small and large states; the other between colonial and noncolonial states. The small powers became more persuasive whenever the major powers disagreed among themselves. The noncolonial powers usually sought to make the colonial powers, some of which were small states, more accountable for their policies. Generally the smaller states tried to strengthen the powers of the General Assembly, in which they had the advantage of numbers and equality, against the more exclusive Security Council.

Edward R. Stettinius, secretary of state of the United States and
chairman of the U.S. delegation, signs the United Nations Charter, June 26, 1945.
President Harry Truman is on the left.

4

—

THE
COLD WAR
AND
BEYOND

1945-2009

—

POLITICS
AND
SECURITY

Nowhere did the divergent tendencies among the great and small surface more visibly than in committee sessions that dealt with the Security Council. The smaller states resisted the provision for great power unanimity in the Council. In a memorandum on the Dumbarton Oaks proposals for a United Nations Organization the Netherlands and other small powers objected to the veto of the five permanent Security Council members.[9] They were, however, unsuccessful in these efforts. The major powers made clear that for them it was a matter of a world organization with a veto or no world organization at all.[10] The Big Five told the other states that there could be no semi-major power status for the Netherlands or other Allied nations.

Regarding the colonial issue, two categories of territories were defined. The new drafts distinguished territories placed under UN supervision or trusteeship from the rest of the colonial world. All colonies except those placed under trusteeship were to be known as non-self-governing territories. The trusteeship system was less controversial because of familiarity with the League of Nations mandates system and because it extended only to old mandates or new ones identified voluntarily. Even so, the U.S. Navy insisted that a special category of strategic trust territories be created for the Pacific islands that the United States had extracted from Japanese control. These supposedly had strategic value; their supervision was therefore made a duty of the Security Council, not the Trusteeship Council and the General Assembly. The general aim for the territories in the trusteeship system, unlike that of the other colonies, was independence.

The Netherlands was not very successful in its efforts to introduce more specific references to international law in the Charter. The widespread support for keeping the seat of the International Court of Justice — one of the six main organs of the United Nations — in The Hague was a small consolation prize. All in all, the Netherlands government was at first not very enthusiastic about the new organization.[11]

The vote of approval for the completed Charter of the United Nations came on June 25, 1945. Representatives of fifty nations formally signed it the following day. The U.S. Senate passed the treaty by a vote of 89 to 2 on July 28.[12] After the Permanent Five and a majority of the signatories had ratified it, it entered into force on October 24, 1945. The new General Assembly met for the first time on January 10, 1946, in London.

The planners in the State Department had played a crucial role in the establishment of the new organization. Thus it was by no means a coincidence that both the organizing conference (San Francisco) and the headquarters of the United Nations (New York) were located in the United States. It symbolized the fervor with which from the outset the Americans supported the new organization.

When the UN Charter came up for ratification in the Dutch parliament, both the government and several members of parliament expressed misgivings about the results of the San Francisco Conference. They wondered whether the new organization would be strong enough to uphold international law against the Great Powers. Still, the government considered it better to join without great expectations than to stay out.[13] One encouraging aspect was that, unlike the League of Nations Covenant, the UN Charter contained specific articles on human rights. Indeed, one of the principal purposes of the organization is to achieve international cooperation to promote and encourage respect for human rights and fundamental freedoms for all without distinction as to race, sex, language, or religion.[14]

Conclusion

The United States was originally a greater supporter of the United Nations than the Netherlands, and saw the new organization as a major instrument of its foreign policy. The Netherlands would have preferred a system of regional security arrangements, but, given the international situation at the end of World War II, some kind of international cooperation was a foregone conclusion. In the case of the United States, its enthusiasm for such cooperation depends greatly on the extent to which it is able to dominate the organization. Its initial enthusiasm for the new organization has waned over the years. With the expansion of UN membership mainly coming from states in Africa and Asia, doubts have grown over the years in the United States — in particular in Congress — as to the wisdom of its membership.

The most fundamental difference between the policies of the two countries in the United Nations seems to be that the United States' attitude is primarily based on its domestic priorities, while the Netherlands — with the exception of its approach to its colonial empire — became far more internationally directed. Both strongly supported the adoption of the Universal Declaration of Human Rights, although the Netherlands was unsuccessful in its efforts to have a reference to the divine origin of human rights included (the USSR and other states strongly opposed the inclusion of such language).[15]

Major differences between the two countries occurred at the founding conference in San Francisco about UN Security Council veto rights, which was clearly a dispute over the interests of a large state as opposed to those of a smaller state, and about Indonesian independence and the future of West New Guinea.

4

—

THE
COLD WAR
AND
BEYOND

1945–2009

—

POLITICS
AND
SECURITY

1 See M. Glen Johnson, "The Contributions of Eleanor and Franklin Roosevelt to the Development of International Protection of Human Rights," *Human Rights Quarterly* 9 (1987): 19-48.

2 Cees Wiebes and Bert Zeeman, "Belgium, the Netherlands and Alliances, 1940–1949," (Ph.D. dissertation, Leiden University), 1993), 56; See also p. 58: "The colonies were the main asset of the government, but also its main worry."

3 Albert E. Kersten, "Van Kleffens' plan voor regionale veiligheidsorganisaties, 1941–1943," *Jaarboek van het Departement van Buitenlandse Zaken, 1980–1981* (The Hague: Staatsdrukkerij, 1981), 157-164, here 158.

4 Ibid., 159.

5 Ibid., 160.

6 See Bert Zeeman, "Jurist of diplomaat: Eelco Nicolaas van Kleffens (1939–1946)," in Duco Hellema, Bert Zeeman, and Bert van der Zwan, eds., *De Nederlandse ministers van Buitenlandse Zaken in de twintigste eeuw* (The Hague: SDU uitgeverij, 1999), 139-151, here 146; See also Wiebes and Zeeman, "Belgium, the Netherlands," 68.

7 United Nations Charter, article 52.

8 United States Department of State, *Postwar Foreign Policy Preparation 1939–1945* (Washington, DC: Government Printing Office, 1950); Ruth B. Russell, *A History of the United Nations Charter* (Washington, DC: The Brookings Institution, 1958); Townsend Hoopes and David Brinkley, *FDR and the Creation of the UN* (New Haven, CT/London: Yale University Press, 1997).

9 Suggestions presented by the Netherlands government concerning the proposals for the maintenance of peace and security agreed on at the Four Powers Conference of Dumbarton Oaks. Reprinted in S. I. P. van Campen, *The Quest for Security: Some Aspects of Netherlands Foreign Policy, 1945–1950* (The Hague: Martinus Nijhoff, 1957), 163-179.

10 Russell, *A History*; See also United States Department of State, *Charter of the United Nations: Report to the President on the Results of the San Francisco Conference* (Washington, DC: Government Printing Office, 1950).

11 Cees Wiebes, "De oprichting van de Verenigde Naties 50 jaar geleden: het dagboek van minister Eelco van Kleffens over de conferentie in San Francisco, 11 april–7 juni 1945," in D. A. Hellema, C. Wiebes, and B. Zeeman, eds., *Jaarboek Buitenlandse Zaken: Tweede jaarboek voor de geschiedenis van de Nederlandse buitenlandse politiek in de twintigste eeuw* (The Hague; SDU uitgeverij, 1995), 74; Christ Klep and Richard van Gils, *Van Korea tot Kabul: De Nederlandse militaire deelname aan vredesoperaties sinds 1945* (The Hague: SDU uitgeverij, 2005), 31ff.

12 See Stephen C. Schlesinger, *Act of Creation: The Founding of the United Nations* (Boulder, CO: Westview Press, 2003), 263-279.

13 J. J. C. Voorhoeve, *Peace, Profits and Principles: A Study of Dutch Foreign Policy* (The Hague: Martinus Nijhoff, 1979), 200; See also Van Campen, *The Quest for Security*, 19-20.

14 See Peter R. Baehr and Leon Gordenker, *The United Nations: Reality and Ideal*, 4th ed. (Basingstoke: Palgrave Macmillan, 2005), 100-101; Thomas G. Weiss, David P. Forsythe, and Roger A. Coate, *The United Nations and Changing World Politics*, 2nd ed. (Boulder, CO: Westview Press, 1997), 132.

15 For an excellent account see Johannes Morsink, *The Universal Declaration of Human Rights: Origins, Drafting and Intent* (Philadelphia: University of Pennsylvania Press, 1999); See also Mary Ann Glendon, *A World Made New: Eleanor Roosevelt and the Universal Declaration of Human Rights* (New York: Random House, 2001).

DUTCH AND U.S. ASSESSMENTS OF EUROPEAN POLITICAL INTEGRATION

JAN VAN DER HARST

Introduction

The Netherlands' European policy in the 1950s and 1960s was first and fore-most one of remarkable consistency: a limited number of policy concepts and orientations shaped the Dutch government's stance on European integration throughout the two decades. These overarching themes, which apart from con-sistency lent a certain predictability to the country's policy toward Europe, can be summarized as: discouragement of hegemonic power aspirations on the part of the bigger European Community (EC) members (France and Germany in particular), support for regional trade liberalization, and reluctance toward Eu-ropean unification in the political domain. In the latter area Atlanticism — the bond with the United States and Britain — prevailed.

During the period under discussion, the scope and content of Dutch Europe-an policy were restricted by the demands of NATO membership in general and the country's security dependency on the United States in particular. The per-ception that, at the end of the day, only U.S. conventional and nuclear military power could safeguard the country's territorial integrity against threats from abroad made foreign policy makers judge political developments in Europe in the context of their possible consequences for Dutch-American relations and the cohesion within the multilateral Atlantic cooperation framework. Europe-an options threatening to damage such cohesion were discarded for that very reason. For the benefit of its own diplomatic flexibility, the government pre-ferred hegemony of a geographically remote superpower to what was perceived as less credible leadership but more immediate domination by France and/or Germany in a militarily independent Europe. This is not to say that NATO loyal-ty and the primacy of the transatlantic linkage were unassailable determinants:

4

—

THE
COLD WAR
AND
BEYOND

1945–2009

—

POLITICS
AND
SECURITY

they were called into question several times, especially when they threatened to damage the country's self-image as a middle-sized power with colonial interests. In the late 1940s and early 1960s, The Hague's Atlanticist faith was rocked when the U.S. government forced it into adaptive acquiescence by insisting on decolonization of the Dutch East Indies and New Guinea. However, during the intervening period (1950–62) the rare manifestations of bilateral tensions were the exceptions that proved the "NATO first" rule.

The above analysis has particular validity for the realm of foreign, security, and defense policies, which — in relation to Europe — are presented here under the common denominator of "political integration." In the area of economics and trade, The Hague opted for a predominantly regional-European framework to promote its interests. After the early postwar failure of global trade liberalization within GATT, Foreign Minister Jan-Willem Beyen paved the way for Dutch involvement in a Western European customs union, which later evolved into the common or internal market. The country's approach to European integration thus provided for a clear distinction between the economic and political domain: The Hague promoted the former, and obstructed — or at least discouraged — development of the latter. This was the official policy set out by the government. The Dutch parliament was more inclined to follow a European-federalist approach (including support for political integration), but in the foreign policy area the government was definitely in the driver's seat.

Two case studies have been singled out to analyze the Dutch and American assessment of political integration on the European continent: the Pleven plan for a European army, under discussion during the early 1950s, and the Fouchet plan for a European Political Union (1961–62). The two plans constituted the most far-reaching attempts to make foreign policy and defense integration in the EC work during the period under discussion. It appears that at crucial moments the Dutch government was more inclined to prioritize and cherish the Atlantic relationship than foreign policy elites in Washington.

Pleven Plan

The Hague's stance on the European Defense Community (EDC), or Pleven plan as it was initially called, serves as an eminent example of Dutch Atlanticist convictions in the early postwar period.[1] The EDC was a French initiative, launched in October 1950, to make West German rearmament feasible and acceptable within the controllable framework of a European army. The French government had become alarmed following a U.S. proposal (Acheson plan) in the summer of 1950 aimed at rearming the Germans in the context of NATO.

Paris feared that within NATO the German army would be given too much lee-way to develop into an independent institution, prone to escape control and su-pervision by the allies. It was only five years after World War II, and government and public were by no means convinced that the German danger had totally disappeared. Aiming to forestall the possible revival of a German *Wehrmacht*, Prime Minister René Pleven presented a proposal for a supranational Europe-an army, consisting of units of different nationalities. In reality, Pleven was just the spokesman; in the background the renowned Jean Monnet and his team played a crucial part in formulating the plan.

The initial reactions to the Pleven plan were decidedly negative. The Dutch government understood that the French initiative would boil down to the es-tablishment of a European pillar within or even outside NATO, hence under-mining American leadership, weakening the Western alliance, and conse-quently jeopardizing Dutch national security.[2] Moreover, The Hague felt that the Pleven plan would needlessly delay German rearmament. Against the back-ground of an evolving Cold War, Dutch military authorities strove for a "for-ward defense" as far to the east as possible — on the river Elbe in Germany — in order to repel a possible Soviet-led communist attack far away from the home country. The immediate deployment of German infantry soldiers was deemed an indispensable condition for realizing such a strategy. Military officers also felt that the proposed method of integrating national army units in European divisions was grossly impracticable and would never work on the battlefield, given the various differences in language, culture, and habits.[3] It was obvious that Monnet and his team, when drafting the proposal, had not taken account of military expertise.[4]

The Dutch opposition was shared by many others, and the plan was bound to fail. Even the French military immediately spoke out against it, preferring the NATO solution for German rearmament instead. In light of such wide-spread misgivings, it is no small wonder that the European army plan soon *did* get a firm place on the international agenda and indeed *would* dominate the discussions in the European capitals and in Washington for the next four years. This was mainly caused by the U.S. change of mind in the summer of 1951. From initial opponents, President Harry Truman and Secretary of State Dean Acheson were converted into supporters of the French plan, for several reasons. First, ever since the end of World War II Washington had been looking for ways to promote European unification, in order to get rid of extreme forms of dam-aging nationalism in the Old World. The Americans felt disappointed that the Organization for European Economic Cooperation (OEEC) and the Council of Europe had failed to make the desired supranational leap ahead, and in 1950 hailed the Schuman plan for coal and steel and the Pleven plan for defense as

643

4

—

THE
COLD WAR
AND
BEYOND

1945-2009

—

POLITICS
AND
SECURITY

steps in the right direction. On this matter, Truman and Acheson were strongly influenced by their Europe advisers William Tomlinson, John McCloy, David Bruce, Robert Bowie, and others.[5]

Second, after the war the U.S. had maintained a substantial number of troops in the western part of Germany and this number was expected to increase after the start of the Korean War (June 1950) and the implementation of NSC-68. The question raised in Washington was how long such a large-scale deployment overseas would be sustainable, both in domestic-political and financial terms. As a matter of fact, it was hoped that the European army would lead, in the short run, to a fairer method of burden sharing and provide, in the long run, an opportunity to bring (some of) the GIs back home.[6]

Third, it had become clear that the French government refused to accept any other solution than its own European army plan, and Washington realized that French collaboration was an absolute condition for a credible build-up of a postwar continental defense, especially in the context of a politically marginalized Germany and an absent Britain. French diplomacy, guided by the Monnet lobby in Washington, emphasized that the Pleven plan would help solve several problems simultaneously: it would bring about German rearmament, develop European integration, increase the chances of a responsible French policy on the continent, and, last but not least, contain German power aspirations.

The American change of mind proved decisive. From then on, the NATO solution for German rearmament was put on ice and the European army plan was the only concept left on the negotiation table. For some governments this development was hard to accept. The Netherlands, for one, joined the negotiations, but only reluctantly and after a long period of hesitation. In February 1951, at the start of the discussions, The Hague only sent observers and it was not until the fall of the same year that the delegation was upgraded to the status of full participant. Considerable American pressure was needed to convince the Drees government that Washington truly supported the French EDC project and considered a European solution along these lines indispensable for making German rearmament acceptable. Loyal to the superpower's wishes The Hague overcame its misgivings, adopted a critical but constructive stance during the negotiations, and signed the EDC Treaty in May 1952.[7]

Moreover, early in 1954, the Netherlands was the first among six participating countries to ratify the EDC Treaty. This had partly — but only to a small extent — to do with a more positive perception of the European army concept. As before, a majority in the cabinet still considered the EDC an unattractive phenomenon — an instrument used by the French to delay German rearmament — and instead kept prioritizing the Atlantic solution. In this respect, the Drees government proved more NATO-minded than the new American administration of President Dwight Eisenhower (inaugurated in January 1953) and Secretary of

State John Foster Dulles who, in their integrationist enthusiasm, were so convinced of the desirability of an EDC that they came to see the European army as an end in itself, namely as a keystone of the integration process, rather than as a means to the end of German rearmament.[8] The Dutch government showed much less enthusiasm, but was nonetheless prepared to speed up ratification.

This was done mainly out of pragmatic, if not opportunistic, considerations. The Hague noticed that from early 1953, after the rise to power of the Mayer government in France, Paris was looking for ways to get rid of the treaty. Prime Minister René Mayer was dependent on Gaullist support for his political survival and it was evident that the Gaullist movement fiercely opposed the supranational EDC. Many in the Dutch political establishment sensed that from that moment on the EDC was virtually "dead." Seen from this perspective it was not harmful at all to speed up the ratification procedure at home, which, as a concomitant advantage, helped portray the Netherlands as a constructive and reliable partner in the international arena.[9] Connected to this was the outspoken U.S. support for fast-track ratification. Secretary of State Dulles, encouraged by Congress, had made it clear that he would reward a cooperative stance by the European partners and punish noncompliance, in the form of a policy of "agonizing reappraisal." The continued need of U.S. support — in the form of army equipment and offshore orders — for the country's defense build-up and economic reconstruction provided the Dutch government with an extra motive to stimulate a positive decision on EDC. However, when the French Assemblée pronounced its ultimate, negative verdict on the European army there were hardly any regrets in the Netherlands. Neither did The Hague show overt signs of panic or nervousness about the vacuum the aborted EDC left behind. Unlike the British government, which vented serious concerns about the possibility of an American retreat from Europe, the Dutch never really believed that Dulles would enforce his threat.[10]

Eventually, after five years of delay and confusion, the NATO solution for German rearmament carried the day, with French support. In 1955, the Acheson plan of September 1950 was by and large accepted. Ironically, the Dutch government took far greater pleasure in the final outcome than foreign policy makers in Washington.

Fouchet Plan

During the 1960s French President Charles de Gaulle's attempts at restoring French *grandeur* on the world stage were looked upon with scorn in The Hague. The Dutch analysis was similar to that of the Pleven plan: Parisian initiatives aiming at a collective Western European foreign and security policy could cre-

4

—

THE
COLD WAR
AND
BEYOND

1945–2009

—

POLITICS
AND
SECURITY

ate leverage for French claims at codirecting NATO, and consequently result in undesired competition with American leadership and a weakening of Western defense against the Soviet threat. The primacy of Atlanticism was decisive in making the Dutch torpedo negotiations about the Fouchet plan (1961–62) and, more generally, led to initiating and supporting policies aimed at isolating France.

It all started in the fall of 1958 when de Gaulle, soon after his inauguration, launched a proposal for the formation of a Political Standing Group within NATO, a triple directorate, consisting of the U.S., the UK, and France. In the French view, the directorate should concern itself with the alliance's daily affairs and be given exclusive control over nuclear matters. The proposal was rejected instantaneously by Washington and London, and was never placed officially on NATO's Council agenda. Nevertheless, The Hague had become alarmed by what was seen as a highly inopportune move by the French president, potentially damaging to both the Atlantic alliance and the position of the smaller members. In this respect, the immediate Anglo-American refusal was only partly reassuring; new French steps in the same direction were anticipated.

As a matter of fact, de Gaulle's next move occurred in 1959 when, in the context of the European Community of the Six, he proposed regular meetings of the foreign ministers to explore ways of reaching an intensified form of political cooperation. A year later, the EC heads of government endorsed a committee, to be led by the French ambassador to Denmark, Christian Fouchet, to consider the matter in further detail. By November 1961, Fouchet and his committee produced a draft treaty for a "union of states" that included four key institutional components: a council of heads of government or foreign ministers, which would meet regularly and make decisions by unanimous agreement; a permanent secretariat, based in Paris and composed of senior officials of the foreign affairs departments of the member states; four permanent intergovernmental committees, which would take care of foreign affairs, defense, commerce, and cultural affairs; and a European assembly, composed of members appointed by the national legislatures. The ultimate aim of the Fouchet plan, inspired by de Gaulle, was the creation of a European Political Union (EPU) on an intergovernmental basis.

Obviously, The Hague's European philosophy differed widely from that of the French president. First of all, the De Quay government (successor of the Drees government) reiterated the traditional notion that NATO should remain the dominant forum for coordinating Western Europe's foreign and security policies. Foreign Minister Joseph Luns said that a reinforcement of political cooperation between the Six was only possible in a setting that would respect the communitarian framework, rather than the intergovernmental structure de Gaulle and Fouchet had pleaded for, "which was bound to lead to a French

Officials from the European Coals and Steel Community (ECSC) visiting
President Eisenhower in Washington DC, June 4, 1953.
From left to right: Jean Monnet (France, chairman of the High Authority of
the ECSC), President Eisenhower, Frank Etzel (West Germany, vice-chair).
Standing, from left to right: Secretary of State John Foster Dulles, Dirk Spierenburg
(Netherlands), David E.K. Bruce (U.S. representative with the ECSC), and
William Rand (Director of the Mutual Security Agency).
Up to the mid-1960s Monnet often had better access to the top levels of the
Washington policy-making establishment than the Dutch government.

4
—

THE
COLD WAR
AND
BEYOND

1945–2009

—

POLITICS
AND
SECURITY

policy for the whole of Western Europe." Recent French behavior in NATO had demonstrated that Paris was unwilling to discuss its internal and external problems with the allies, and the creation of new EPU institutions was not expected to change this. Also, as Luns pointed out, the council of heads of state or government, advocated by de Gaulle, would create domestic constitutional problems — because of the formally weak position of the Dutch prime minister in foreign affairs — and the proposed ministerial committees were expected to undermine the authority of both the European Economic Community and the European Commission. Instead of installing new institutions, the Six should adhere to the Treaties of Rome and avoid a wider political and economic division of Europe. For the latter purpose, the Dutch delegation in the Fouchet committee strongly pleaded for British participation in the negotiations. From The Hague's perspective, UK involvement, both in EPU and EC, was a *conditio sine qua non* for whichever Dutch commitment to foreign policy cooperation might evolve.[11]

During the negotiations on the Fouchet plan (which emerged in various versions), the Dutch desiderata were brought together in a compromise proposal, in which meetings of the heads of state or government were described as feasible if NATO-related issues were excluded from the agenda and each meeting were accompanied by parallel consultations within the framework of the Western European Union (thus allowing for British participation). Since discussing NATO-related issues in an EPU framework had been the dominant incentive behind the French proposals, the first condition alone sufficed to make the Dutch "compromise" unacceptable for the Paris government.[12]

For a long time, the Dutch position in the Fouchet negotiations was one of complete isolation. The Benelux countries were divided on the issue, Germany and Italy supported the earlier versions of the plan, and de Gaulle and Federal Chancellor Konrad Adenauer developed a close personal relationship, which seemed to be to the detriment of the smaller EC members. Even Monnet's Action Committee, which — together with the Dutch government — strove for a supranational organization of Europe (including a strong position for the Commission), was prepared to accept the Fouchet scheme for intergovernmental political *cooperation*, as long as it did not interfere with the *integration* method used in the EEC. Monnet made the diagnosis that de Gaulle's ideas could help Europe advance toward a federation by passing through some kind of "European confederation." This might be needed as the interim stage of evolution toward the new Europe, since no adequate framework existed in which the Six could jointly tackle political questions. It might also convince the European citizens that unification was not solely geared toward economic prosperity but also had a political dimension. Monnet envisioned two methods to be at work simultaneously: the integration method and another method for political, educational, and defense questions. He saw great potential in letting these two evolve together.[13]

For the same reasons, the Kennedy administration was for a long time supportive of the EPU plan. In November 1961, the Department of State wrote that the "US continues to feel that any moves toward integration are desirable and what we know of proposed French draft appears to us to be useful to this end."[14] Although President Kennedy's grand design for Europe was clearly far different from de Gaulle's international political thinking — the U.S. scheme of a Western bloc, encompassing an American senior partner and a European junior partner, clashed with France's preferences for a French-led third-force Europe — he was prepared to give the EPU the benefit of the doubt, thereby following the advice of Monnet's Action Committee. During the Kennedy administration Monnet still had a strong influence on U.S. policies toward Europe, mainly through Undersecretary for European Affairs George Ball, a convinced integrationist. At the time, Monnet's *entrée* in Washington was much easier than in The Hague. This would change, for good, under Kennedy's successors Lyndon Johnson and Richard Nixon, who gave Europe a lower priority in their foreign policy strategies.

However, the tactics used by Monnet and Ball clearly had their limits. De Gaulle's proposals for a confederation could only be accepted as long as there was a realistic hope that they could eventually lead to some kind of unified European government. They could *not* be accepted if they were specifically targeted toward preventing the emergence of a supranational Europe.[15] In this respect, the unfolding of the Fouchet negotiations was deemed highly disappointing. In January 1962, another amended version of the plan provided proof of de Gaulle's radical ideas on European integration and Atlantic cooperation. In this version the supranational EEC was made subservient to the EPU, an attempt by de Gaulle to modify, if not the letter, then at least the substance of the Treaties of Rome. The revised plan gave economic authority to the Political Union and, thus, fundamentally threatened the position of the supranational European Commission. Furthermore, the French proposal lacked an explicit reference to the NATO framework, while at the same time holding open the possibility of discussing NATO-related issues in the EPU.

Such an anticommunitarian EPU text was unacceptable to both Monnet and the Americans. In the Netherlands, Luns was relieved to see that the international positions on EPU slowly but surely changed in his favor. Eventually — in April 1962 — the Fouchet plan was removed from the negotiation table. This was a major diplomatic success for the Dutch government, although one achieved with extreme difficulty.

Conclusions

4

—

THE
COLD WAR
AND
BEYOND

1945–2009

—

POLITICS
AND
SECURITY

650

An analysis of the Dutch and American positions toward the Pleven plan of the 1950s and the Fouchet plan of the 1960s offers intriguing insights into the evolution of Atlantic relations during this period. Notwithstanding the diverging contents of the two plans (e.g., supranational versus intergovernmental, integrationist versus Gaullist) and the different national and international contexts, the respective Dutch and U.S. stances on the two plans give evidence of a striking degree of continuity. In both cases, The Hague seemed more inclined to stick to the primacy of Atlantic relations and to an undiluted central position for NATO in Western defense than Washington. In the early 1950s, the Drees government rejected the supranational EDC and only reluctantly gave in to American pressure to participate in the negotiations. Likewise, a decade later, Foreign Minister Luns became the main antagonist of the intergovernmental Fouchet plan. We find ourselves in the heydays of Dutch Atlanticism: it was the time just between vicious quarrels with Washington over the granting of independence to Indonesia (1949) and the transfer of sovereignty over New Guinea, culminating in the announcement of the U.S.-sponsored Bunker plan in April 1962 — the same month of the end of the Fouchet negotiations.

In its ambition to orient its security policies exclusively toward the United States, the Netherlands was frustrated by the lukewarm reactions coming from the other side of the Atlantic. In the European-political sphere, The Hague oftentimes positioned itself as being *plus atlantique que les Américains*, a reproach made by Gaullist politicians in France. In both the Pleven and the Fouchet plan, the Eisenhower and Kennedy administrations sought to appease France, realizing that a structural defense of the European continent was unthinkable without a committed contribution from the French government and army. Both times, Washington operated in close collaboration with the group around Jean Monnet. In the period 1950–62, the link between Monnet and Washington was considerably more intimate than between Monnet and The Hague. Unlike Monnet and Kennedy, who initially gave de Gaulle's EPU plan the benefit of the doubt, Luns refused to go along with the French president for fear of damaging the position of both NATO and EEC.

The 1960s witnessed fundamental changes in the international environment. During the Johnson administration, the traditional alliance between the Monnet committee and the U.S. East Coast establishment weakened, together with decreasing American support for European integration. Toward the end of the decade, de Gaulle's resignation paved the way for British entry into the European Community, a long-awaited objective of the Dutch government. From then on, the Netherlands showed itself more compliant on the issue of foreign policy cooperation in Europe, which eventually took shape in the European Political Cooperation (EPC) framework. Simultaneously, the bilateral and multilateral ties with the U.S. loosened under the influence of the Vietnam War, the Watergate scandal, and the collapse of the Bretton Woods international financial system.

1   J. van der Harst, *The Atlantic Priority. Dutch Defence Policy at the Time of the European Defence Community* (Florence: European Press Academic Publishing, 2003); See also A.E. Kersten, "Niederländische Regierung, Bewaffnung Westdeutschlands und EVG," in Militärgeschichtliches Forschungsamt, ed., *Die Europäische Verteidigungsgemeinschaft. Stand und Probleme der Forschung* (Munich: Oldenbourg, 1985), 191-219.

2   Code telegram Stikker, October 24, 1950, II, 921.331, EDC, box 7, Ministry of Foreign Affairs (MFA), The Hague.

3   Memorandum General Mathon, April 20, 1951, EDC 36, box 3, Ministry of Defense (MD), The Hague.

4   F. Duchêne, *Jean Monnet. The First Statesman of Interdependence* (New York: W.W. Norton & Co., 1994), 229.

5   R. Dwan, "The European Defence Community and the Role of French-American Elite Relations," in M. Dumoulin, ed., *The European Defence Community, Lessons for the Future?* (Brussels: P.I.E.-Peter Lang), 69; T.A. Schwartz, *America's Germany. John J. McCloy and the Federal Republic of Germany* (Cambridge, MA: Harvard University Press, 1991), 222-225.

6   M. Cresswell, "Between the Bear and the Phoenix: The USA and the EDC," in Dumoulin, ed., *The European Defence Community*, 222.

7   "Résumé van de Ambassadeursconferentie over het Europese leger," August 28, 1951, II, 921.331, EDC, box 7, MFA; Memorandum Stikker, September 24, 1951, box 8, ibid.; See also H.F.L.K. van Vredenburch, *Den Haag antwoordt niet. Herinneringen van Jhr. Mr. H.F.L.K. van Vredenburch* (Leiden: Martinus Nijhoff, 1985), 447-463. Van Vredenburch was the leader of the Dutch delegation at the negotiations on the European army plan.

8   See, e.g., The Secretary of State to the Embassy of France, March 26, 1953, Foreign Relations of the United States (FRUS) 1952-1954, vol. 5 (1), 781-782; July 15, 1953, FRUS 1952–1954, vol. 5 (1), 797-798.

9   Telegram Ambassador Chapin to the Department of State, July 8, 1953, FRUS 1952–1954, vol. 5 (1), 795.

10 K. Ruane, *The Rise and Fall of the European Defence Community. Anglo-American Relations and the Crisis of European Defence, 1950-55* (New York: St. Martin's Press, 2000), 175; MFA, II, DMA, 13 inv. nr. 16, Code Telegram Beyen, July 14, 1953.

11 A.G. Harryvan, "In Pursuit of Influence. Aspects of the Netherlands' European Policy during the Formative Years of the European Economic Community" (Ph.D. dissertation, EUI Florence, 2007), 144 and 150.

12 Ibid., 150; "Stand van zaken Parijse studiecommissie inzake plannen De Gaulle," April 27, 1961, II, GS, 913.10, 1890, MFA; Notulen Ministerraad (Minutes, Council of Ministers), April 7, 1961, April 17, 1961, April 28, 1961, May 26, 1961, Nationaal Archief (National Archive), The Hague.

13 P. Winand, *Eisenhower, Kennedy and the United States of Europe*, 2nd ed. (New York: St. Martin's Press, 1996), 257-258.

14 Circular Telegram from the Department of State to Certain Missions, November 3, 1961, FRUS 1961–1963, vol. 13, 48-49.

15 Winand, *Eisenhower, Kennedy*, 252-257.

4

___

THE
COLD WAR
AND
BEYOND

1945–2009

___

POLITICS
AND
SECURITY

DUTCH LEFT-WING POLITICAL PARTIES AND NATO

___

FRANK ZUIJDAM

At the end of the 1970s, U.S. Secretary of State Henry Kissinger referred to Prime Minister Joop den Uyl as "the most truly Marxist," and it was not meant as a compliment.[1] Although the remark was not entirely serious, it does illustrate the doubts that existed about the reliability of social democrats as allies, particularly as far as military affairs were concerned. Labour in the UK and the SPD in West Germany were other examples of social democratic parties that were, on occasion, out of step with the Americans. The United States therefore took a close interest in the position taken by the Partij van de Arbeid (PvdA, the Dutch Social Democratic Party) on peace and security issues, and even more so because the PvdA was often part of the governing coalition and thus able to influence the Netherlands' policy in this area. In this essay, the position vis-à-vis the United States of the parties on the left of the political spectrum will be analyzed in more detail, in order to assess to what extent they continued to see the Netherlands as a "loyal U.S. ally" during the decades following World War II.

The PvdA versus the Small Left-Wing Parties

After World War II, the Netherlands faced the task of formulating a new security policy. Following a period of uncertainty and latent neutralist thinking, the Dutch joined the Brussels Pact (1948) and the North Atlantic Treaty Organization (1949), and security strategy became centered around a close alliance with the United States. Predictably, the Communistische Partij van Nederland (CPN, the Communist Party of the Netherlands) was vehemently opposed to NATO membership. During the parliamentary debate on the subject, Henk Gortzak attacked the idea bitterly: "What is proposed will turn our young men into a battalion of mercenaries in the pay of American imperialism." According to Gort-zak, Dutch membership of NATO boiled down to little more than a "submission to Wall Street."

The PvdA also had its reservations. In particular, the party was disappoint-ed that the "Third Way" — a socialist alternative between capitalism on the one hand and communism on the other — was proving less feasible than hoped.[2] In the words of Jaap Burger, the PvdA let it be known that it was preferable to be "a bridge [between communism and capitalism] than a [U.S.] bridgehead in Europe." Burger also had doubts about the ideological basis of NATO. He considered its democratic principles difficult to reconcile with the inclusion of "clearly undemocratic countries" such as Portugal. The PvdA also supported the other political parties in their criticism of the American attitude toward de-colonization in Indonesia. Yet, despite all this, the PvdA ended up supporting NATO membership.[3]

Although this support seemed to spring mainly from the realization that the Netherlands had little choice, rather than from any great enthusiasm for a pro-American policy, the Americans need not have been concerned about the loyal-ty of the social democrats during the 1950s. The party seemed to miss no oppor-tunity to declare its allegiance to the collective defense of the West. Specifically under the leadership of hardliners such as Jacques de Kadt and Frans Goedhart, a policy of strength was pursued. The party believed that a policy of uncompro-mising resistance to the Eastern Bloc was the best guarantee for world peace. Protected by a strong defense policy, the West would simply await the collapse of the communist system. De Kadt and Goedhardt would tolerate no talk of *rap-prochement* with the Soviet Union. They believed that the PvdA should pay no heed to the "panic-stricken pacifists," and the "ragbag of suggestions such as summits, disarmament and nuclear-free and American-free zones" was to be firmly resisted.[4]

The positions of the political parties of the left solidified during the early 1950s. The CPN proved itself a loyal follower of Moscow and as such dissociat-ed itself from the *Pax Americana*. The party was to maintain this line for many years to come. The PvdA, however, was keen to present itself as thoroughly anti-communist and a "loyal ally" of the U.S. Only a small number of social demo-crats consistently opposed the PvdA's Atlanticist policy. There were also various groupings within the party that wanted the PvdA to express antimilitary senti-ments in parliament, but the party leadership rejected any such ideas, referring to these groups as "rats gnawing at the party's foundations." After the ideas of this Third Way had been repeatedly rejected by the PvdA, its adherents opted to establish a new party based on the principles of antimilitarism and socialism. The result was the founding of the Pacifistische Socialistische Partij (PSP, the Pacifist Socialist Party) on January 26-27, 1957.

4

—

THE
COLD WAR
AND
BEYOND

1945–2009

—

POLITICS
AND
SECURITY

The establishment of the PSP meant that there was an alternative home for disillusioned socialists or Marxists who did not feel comfortable in the other parties of the left. The PSP soon grew to include ten chapters and around four hundred members. The party's manifesto was somewhat equivocal. Its aspirations were kept deliberately general, while demands such as unilateral disarmament and Dutch withdrawal from NATO were carefully avoided. But this vague manifesto did not stop the PSP from presenting itself as the conscience of the socialist movement in the Netherlands. Under the slogan "socialism without the atom bomb," the party suggested that the PvdA was contradicting its principles by combining support for nuclear weapons with an allegedly socialist program. The PvdA, of course, was strongly opposed to such "coarse demagogy."

The Nuclear Question

At the NATO summit of December 1957, the Netherlands agreed to the U.S. proposal to base tactical nuclear weapons in the territory of its European partners. In 1959, the two countries concluded an agreement on this issue, and the following year the first nuclear warheads arrived in the Netherlands under the veil of strict secrecy. One important motivation for agreeing to the U.S. plans was that it was a way of holding defense expenditure down. The third Drees cabinet (comprising the PvdA and the Christian parties KVP, CHU, and ARP) also wanted to contain the spread of nuclear weapons, and by accepting U.S. nuclear warheads it hoped that further nuclear proliferation among the larger European countries — West Germany in particular — could be prevented. Another advantage of the arrival of nuclear weapons was that the strategic line of defense shifted further eastward, toward Germany. Significantly, the bilateral treaty was simply announced to parliament, and not put to a vote. Most political parties did not object to this course of action, and the CPN's and PSP's demands for a public debate on the issue were rejected. A motion against the possible arrival of nuclear weapons was neither put to a vote. Nor did the Dutch people themselves appear concerned about the arrival of such weapons, and the issue hardly featured in public debate.

Although parliament did not want to debate the stationing of nuclear weapons on Dutch soil, there was some concern about the build-up of nuclear armaments. Particularly on the left, calls for reflection were growing, the establishment of the PSP being one expression of this. Within the PvdA, too, the nuclear arms race became an "urgent and overriding" issue that repeatedly surfaced in the late 1950s: "The ability to manufacture nuclear weapons, the testing of nuclear weapons and the stationing of nuclear-missile bases on European territory mean that we, as humans, are increasingly compelled to examine our consciences on the question of where all this will lead humanity."[5]

From the late 1950s onward, the issue of nuclear weapons was intensely debated by various committees within the PvdA. However, the party was also careful to ensure that it remained "suited for government": it avoided utopian visions, concentrating on realistic steps that might bring controlled East-West disarmament closer. The PvdA put forward proposals for a ban on nuclear testing, the control of nuclear proliferation, and limitations on the development of national atomic arsenals. More generally, the party argued for more contacts of all kinds between East and West, and followed disarmament talks between the U.S. and the Soviet Union with great interest. A small minority of nuclear pacifists within the party wanted to try out new ways of achieving these objectives, and called for unilateral nuclear disarmament. The risk involved in such a course of action was acceptable, they believed, because the communist challenge had to be thought of in socioeconomic terms rather than in military terms. However, these pacifists held a marginal position within the party.

There was genuine concern about the nuclear arms race on the part of many within the PvdA and this led to the eventual abandonment of the hard line taken by De Kadt and Goedhardt. This change of course was also influenced by international developments such as the cautious reengagement of the Soviet Union and the U.S., the role of nuclear weapons in allied defenses, and the debate on nuclear weapons in other countries.

A Conditional Ally

From the mid-1960s onward, the left-wing debate on peace and security underwent a significant change. The postwar security doctrine based around NATO came under criticism from a new political generation, affecting the foreign policy outlook of the PvdA. The formation of Nieuw Links (New Left) within the party in 1966 led to more vocal opposition to "Cold War dogmas." It was argued that NATO ought to approach the Warsaw Pact to organize a European summit, the ultimate aim of which would be to achieve a demilitarized zone in Europe over as large an area as possible. New positions on "Iberia" also emerged, including the argument that undemocratic Spain should not be permitted to join NATO, while dictatorial Portugal should not be allowed to remain a member. If Spain were to join or if Portugal could stay, the Netherlands ought to withdraw from the alliance. More generally, Nieuw Links saw the Netherlands as being overly subservient to the U.S. These standpoints were further energized by the Vietnam War, which served as a catalyst for criticism of the Atlantic alliance. By

655

1967–68, opposition to the war was being expressed in public demonstrations and also in parliament, albeit mainly by the smaller left-wing parties.[6]

Nieuw Links was eventually able to insist on its idea of "conditional membership" of NATO at the 1975 party congress. After a party-wide debate on peace and security, it was decided at this congress to link Dutch membership of NATO to a set of conditions that were to be met in the foreseeable future. One of the demands was that a reduction in tactical nuclear weapons be put on the table during negotiations with the Soviet Union. If this was not forthcoming by 1979, the Netherlands should unilaterally remove all nuclear weapons from its territory. Other conditions included a unilateral declaration on the part of NATO that it would never be the first to use nuclear weapons, and a ban on the Netherlands' armed forces from participating in nuclear-related operations. However, the left-wing radicals within the party were not able to enjoy the success of this resolution for long. In 1977, when a "NATO evaluation committee" concluded that NATO had only met a handful of the conditions, the party was not willing to actually follow through on the consequences of the strict conditions it had agreed to. Nobody wanted to face the consequences surrounding the end of Dutch membership in NATO.

During the mid-1960s, two new parties that shared some opinions on foreign policy with Nieuw Links appeared on the left of the political spectrum. In 1966, Democraten 66 (D66) was established. The party presented itself as a modernizing movement whose aim was to "explode" the old political order. In the foreign policy section of its first manifesto, the party argued for "overturning outmoded assumptions and thought patterns" and for détente between East and West.[7] Accordingly, the party supported the diplomatic recognition of East Germany and opposed the spread of nuclear weapons. The second new progressive party on the scene was Politieke Partij Radicalen (PPR, the Radical Party), which came about when progressive dissidents from the Catholic KVP and the Protestant ARP split from their respective parties. The PPR considered the greatest threat to all life on earth to be "the unpredictable possibility of a war involving biological, chemical, or nuclear weapons." In order to minimize this "real danger," the party favored putting Dutch membership of NATO up for discussion and believed that the Netherlands should initiate discussions on the establishment of a nuclear-weapons-free zone in central Europe.

From the end of the 1960s onward, the PvdA, PPR, and PSP agreed on a Progressief Akkoord (PAK, Progressive Agreement) that ensured that they would coordinate their political positions in opposition to the other political parties. In 1971 D66 replaced the PSP in the Akkoord, and the new group went on to share, in part, the same election manifesto in 1971 and 1972. This manifesto included many of the points mentioned above, such as efforts to promote détente between East and West and the question of Spanish and Portuguese membership

4

—

THE
COLD WAR
AND
BEYOND

1945–2009

—

POLITICS
AND
SECURITY

of NATO. The parties remained supportive of continued Dutch membership of NATO, but they wanted this membership to be used more clearly to promote both a relaxation in East-West relations and the advance of democracy in other countries.

Defense Policy: Making Less Go Further

Like NATO membership, the level of the Netherlands' defense spending also became a subject of heated discussion. During the late 1960s, the U.S. urged the Netherlands to increase its defense expenditure. The coalition government under Piet de Jong (1967–71) was favorably disposed to this proposal, and in 1970 Defense Minister Van Toom (VVD, Liberal Party) announced that defense spending ought to rise from 3.8 to 4.2 percent of the national income. Yet in 1971 the cross-party Van Rijckevorsel Committee, formed to produce recommendations on defense spending, failed to arrive at a consensus. The majority favored an increase in defense spending to 4.25 percent of the national income, while a minority agreed with the position of the PvdA that existing levels of spending should be maintained. Many social democrats felt that the Netherlands could no longer maintain three full-fledged branches of the armed forces, and that it should instead consult with its NATO partners in order to establish a more specialized division of labor within the alliance. By investing in smaller units equipped with modern technology, the Netherlands could still play a key role in Western defense, and it would not necessarily increase costs. On the contrary, standardization, specialization, and a clear allocation of tasks within NATO could actually reduce Dutch defense spending. The PvdA calculated that through a more efficient defense policy, around 1.5 billion guilders could be saved in four years. The other progressive parties also supported a reduction in defense spending.

Due to the premature demise of the Biesheuvel cabinet, the defense issue fell to the Den Uyl cabinet (comprising the PvdA, KVP, ARP, D66, and PPR) to deal with. This was the "most left-wing cabinet ever," which during its period in office (1973–77) aimed to reduce defense spending by 1.5 billion guilders. On May 21, 1974, the cabinet put its proposals to its NATO partners, who found no merit at all in the Dutch plans. The Germans viewed them as "very, very alarming." The Belgians, meanwhile, thought it was rather brave of the Dutch "to present such a calamitous plan in public," and the Americans were "bewildered and worried."[8] Concerned by the strong criticism its plans had provoked, the Dutch government made a number of concessions. The NATO allies remained critical, but in the Netherlands the defense budget was passed by parliament without significant criticism.

Dutch Prime Minister Joop den Uyl and U.S. President Gerald Ford
share a lighthearted moment during Den Uyl's visit to Washington DC,
May 14, 1975.

The debate over defense expenditure resurfaced again surrounding the need to replace the Starfighter combat aircraft. However, the extra costs involved had been provided for within the defense budget and the cabinet eventually chose the U.S.-built F-16. Clearly, it was in America's interest that the Netherlands should choose an American-built model and the U.S. maintained close contact with decision makers in The Hague. Dutch politicians on the left were remarkably forthcoming in informing the Americans of every detail of their deliberations, with Defense Secretary Bram Stemerdink (PvdA) acting as a particularly useful informant.[9]

The purchase of the F-16 led to passionate debate within the largest of the governing parties, the PvdA, because the party found it difficult to come to terms with the cabinet's decision. The parliamentary party believed that opting for more advanced equipment would only intensify the arms race, in addition to putting excessive strains on government finances. The party council even argued that the Starfighter did not need replacing at all, and even if it were absolutely necessary, it should certainly not be replaced with an American model. The U.S. "would in any case use the money to overthrow democratically elected governments." However, Defense Minister Henk Vredeling (PvdA) refused to be swayed by the party rank and file, and PvdA members had to resign themselves to defeat on this issue.[10]

From Hollanditis to Normalization

By the late 1970s a new phase opened up in relations between the Dutch left and U.S./NATO issues as the issue of cruise missiles came to dominate the debate. Under the leadership of the Interkerkelijk Vredesberaad (IKV, the Interdenominational Alliance for Peace), there was widespread opposition to the U.S. proposal to station forty-eight cruise missiles on Dutch soil. With the slogan "Help rid the world of nuclear weapons, starting with the Netherlands," the IKV was able to mobilize large segments of the population around its moral antinuclear argument. Hundreds of thousands protested against cruise missiles in large demonstrations in 1981 and 1983, while some 3.75 million signed a petition.

In doing so, the opposition movement brought public opinion to bear on the government. Under pressure from the protests, the Christian-liberal coalition cabinet led by Dries van Agt (1977–81) was forced to rethink its unconditional acceptance and decided to wait for the conclusion of the nuclear disarmament negotiations between the U.S. and the Soviet Union before making a final decision. In December 1981, the second Van Agt cabinet (this time comprising the CDA, PvdA, and D66) postponed the decision again. The coalition

4

—

THE
COLD WAR
AND
BEYOND

1945-2009

—

POLITICS
AND
SECURITY

led by Ruud Lubbers that followed in 1982 then postponed it for a third time, and it was not until November 1984 that this cabinet gave the U.S. the go-ahead to station new nuclear weapons on Dutch territory. The Americans never, in fact, took up this offer because they signed an agreement with the Soviets under which all medium-range nuclear weapons were to be removed from Western Europe.

The peace movement could count on the support of all the left-wing parties, including the PvdA. The party threw itself heart and soul into the issue and soon committed itself to a position that came down to "no, no, and once again no."[11] The nuclear issue was used by the party leadership to try to force a division between the other centrist and rightist parties in order to open up the electoral field and ensure a PvdA victory at the polls. The consistency of the PvdA position even led Mint-Jan Faber, the IKV's secretary, to talk of a "left-wing Staphorst" in the sense of a committed opinion closed off to debate (Staphorst is famous for being a very strict Reformed Church community). Yet this highly principled position instead prevented any prospects for participation with other parties in government, and the PvdA was unable to force the breakthrough it sought.

Beginning in the mid-1980s, a change in attitudes toward peace and security took place. In the face of East-West détente and later the collapse of the Warsaw Pact, the polemics surrounding peace and security understandably declined. Evidence of this change came in 1991, when the Lubbers government (a coalition of Christian democrats and the PvdA) decided to make two frigates and Patriot missile batteries available to the U.S. during Operation Desert Storm. This decision found broad support within parliament, with only Groen Links (Green Left) voting against.[12] The parliamentary leader of Groen Links, Ria Beckers, feared that the Gulf War would result in many civilian casualties and asked parliament whether the cure was not worse than the disease. She believed that all diplomatic means ought to be exhausted before supporting a war that would result in "thousands of dead, countless wounded and refugees, an environmental disaster and total regional disruption," but her views were not shared by the PvdA members in the coalition government.[13]

During the 1990s and beyond, the Netherlands remained a loyal ally. In 2003, under the leadership of the Christian democrat Jan Peter Balkenende, the Netherlands was one of only a few countries from among the older NATO members to support the U.S. attack against Iraq. Yet parliament was divided on the issue, with the PvdA and Groen Links (both in opposition at that time) repeatedly declaring that they would not support the unilateral actions of the U.S. and the UK. PvdA leader Wouter Bos said that the Netherlands should be careful not to become involved in the "rogue-state doctrine" of the U.S.[14] However, when the party joined the Christian democrats under Balkenende to form a new cabinet in early 2007, this position was abandoned as part of the coalition agreement. Under the motto, "we agree to disagree," the PvdA accepted that it would put aside its differences of opinion over the war. Nevertheless, others on the left — most notably the big winner of the 2006 elections, the Socialist Party — continued to insist on a parliamentary inquiry into Dutch involvement.[15]

Conclusion

We can characterize the basic relationship of the Netherlands with the United States in the area of peace and security as that of a loyal ally, and this standpoint was basically shared by the larger parties on the left such as the PvdA and D66. The PvdA leadership in particular has always presented itself as strongly pro-Atlantic, although there has certainly been opposition to this from within the party over the years. During the 1950s, the PvdA was careful to ensure that its anti-militarist dissenters did not get the upper hand. From the mid-1960s on, though, this dissent was no longer containable. Under pressure from Nieuw Links the doctrines of "rigid Cold War rhetoric" were subjected to vigorous debate. Certainly by the 1970s, what had previously been thought of as marginal positions had become relatively mainstream, and criticism of foreign policy, which until the mid-1960s had been confined to the margins of social democracy, came to be heard more widely in left-wing intellectual circles. This process culminated in the mass protests against cruise missiles during the early 1980s.

The increasing criticism of defense policy doctrines must partly be seen against the background of the wider cultural revolution of the 1960s. Until the mid-1960s, peace and security had been the domain of a small elite of experts among whom there was a high degree of consensus. From the mid-1960s on, foreign policy was "demystified," and public opinion became more important in considerations of foreign policy. Linked to this from the mid-1960s onward was the "domesticization" of foreign policy, whereby foreign policy positions were adopted in order to achieve certain goals at home, or within a particular political party. For example, adopting radical positions proved an effective means of taking on the party's old guard or of demonstrating an oppositional identity. Foreign policy also proved fertile ground for the left-wingers to polarize the political debate. Peace and security became an area in which political divisions could be emphasized relatively safely, in hopes of wrong-footing the other parties on the center/right. The cabinet run by the PvdA leader Joop den Uyl (1973–77) was forced to maneuver carefully between its Atlanticist tendencies and the demands of its radical party members in order to maintain an internationally acceptable foreign policy course. The combination of social democratic opposition and public opinion also played a role during the cruise missile crisis of the 1980s.

661

4

▬▬

▬▬

From the end of the 1980s onward, however, the underlying pro-Atlanticism of the post-World War II era was clearly visible again. Despite all the polemics, the Netherlands' loyalty to the Atlantic partnership was never really called into question by the PvdA or D66.

1   M. van Traa, "Er is nog meer buitenland dan de NAVO," *Roos in de Vuist* 3.8, 10, 11 (1977).

2   On the Third Way see F. van den Burg, *De Vrije Katheder: Een platform voor communisten en niet-communisten 1945–1950* (Amsterdam: Van Gennep, 1983).

3   *Proceedings of the Dutch Parliament, Second Chamber (Handelingen der Staten-Generaal),* 1948–1949, 2637.

4   J. de Kadt, "Politiek of paniek. Antwoord aan Tolbeek en Tinbergen," *Socialisme en Democratie* 15 (1958): 113-115.

5   W. Banning et al., *5 stemmen over een brandend vraagstuk. Enige artikelen van democratisch socialisten over het vraagstuk van de atoombom* (Amsterdam: Partij van de Arbeid, 1958).

6   See Rimko van der Maar, *Welterusten mijnheer de president. Nederland en de Vietnamoorlog 1965–1973* (Amsterdam: Boom, 2007); D. Hellema, P. van Eekert, and A. van Heteren, *Johnson moordenaar! De kwestie Vietnam in de Nederlandse politiek 1965–1975* (Amsterdam: Mets, 1986).

7   H. van den Doel, H. Lammers et al., *Tien over rood. Uitdaging van Nieuw Links aan de PvdA* (Amsterdam: Polak & Van Gennep, 1996), 7-10.

8   J. Hoffenaar, "De baby is er! De defensienota van 1974 en het gevecht over de toekomst van de krijgsmacht," in J. Hoffenaar, J. van der Meulen, and R. de Winter, eds., *Confrontatie en ontspanning. Maatschappij en krijgsmacht in de Koude Oorlog 1966–1989* (The Hague: SDU uitgeverij, 2004), 51.

9   See Ko Colijn and Freke Vuijst, "De Holland-Amerika-Lijn," *Vrij Nederland*, May 13, 2006, 12-20, and "De Holland-Amerika-Lijn (2)," *Vrij Nederland*, May 20, 2006, 19-23.

10 Frank Zuijdam, *Tussen wens en werkelijkheid. Het debat over vrede en veiligheid binnen de PvdA in de periode 1958–1977* (Amsterdam: Aksant, 2002), 283.

11 Remco van Diepen, *Hollanditis. Nederland en het kernwapendebat, 1977–1987* (Amsterdam: Bert Bakker, 2004).

12 Groen Links was the result of a merger in 1990 of the CPN, PPR, PSP, and the Evangelische Volkspartij (Evangelical People's Party).

13 *Proceedings of the Dutch Parliament, Second Chamber (Handelingen der Staten-Generaal),* 1990-1991, 2638.

14 M. Hulshof and T. Wallaart, "Den Haag staakt het vuren," *Vrij Nederland*, March 29, 2003.

15 See G. Scott-Smith, "Testing the Limits of a Special Relationship: US Unilateralism and Dutch Multilateralism in the Twenty-First Century," in J. Dumbrell and A. Schaefer, *America's Special Relationships: Foreign and Domestic Aspects of the Politics of Alliance* (London: Routledge, 2009).

EMBASSIES AND AMBASSADORS IN THE HAGUE AND WASHINGTON

——

GILES SCOTT-SMITH & BERT VAN DER ZWAN

Since World War II, diplomatic relations between the Netherlands and the United States have been as one would expect between close allies. The commitment of the governments of the Netherlands to NATO under U.S. leadership, and their support for the Bretton Woods international economic regime of the IMF, the World Bank, and the GATT/WTO, ensured a broad consensus between the two nations on the level of macropolicy. Nevertheless, there have been issues that caused serious disagreement between The Hague and Washington, disrupting the usually solid ground of common interests and values. This essay discusses the different ways in which the respective embassies in these two cities functioned within the bilateral relationship. Embassies are required to fulfill the objectives of their nation's foreign policy and to act as the official "eyes and ears" in following local developments. The difference in power has naturally caused a contrast in the ways the embassies operate, and this is also reflected in the seniority and type of diplomats who were posted to run them.

The Americans in The Hague:
Dilettantes and Diplomats

One might expect that the function of the U.S. embassy in The Hague would be little more than a bystander in relation to the generally smooth passage of bilateral relations. Instead, it has proved itself to be a center of influence within the Dutch scene, at times led by an ambassador determined to have an impact on local policymakers. Monitoring and engaging with opinion "on the ground," the embassy has always been an active presence in Dutch politics. There has been a major division between types of ambassador posted to The Hague. Po-

4

—

THE
COLD WAR
AND
BEYOND

1945-2009

—

POLITICS
AND
SECURITY

litical appointments, often involving those whose only merit for the post was their financial or organizational contribution toward a winning presidential candidate's campaign, have been interspersed with professional diplomats, sometimes from a high level. Interestingly, since World War II four ambassadors have left their post early, two of them (John S. Rice and William J. Dyess) due to their inability to deal with awkward issues affecting Dutch-American relations at the time.

The first four postwar ambassadors — Stanley K. Hornbeck, Herman B. Baruch, Selden Chapin, and H. Freeman Matthews — were all foreign service professionals, reflecting the needs of U.S. foreign policy during the late 1940s and the 1950s to secure and maintain close diplomatic relations with Western Europe. Chapin was something of a *cause célèbre* on his arrival in The Hague in 1949 due to his being declared persona non grata by the Hungarian communist government earlier that year. Freeman Matthews in particular was a senior diplomat, having been present at both the Yalta and Potsdam conferences and serving as deputy undersecretary of state prior to his posting to The Hague. Significantly, the first political appointee, Philip Young, did not arrive with a favorable reputation. Young was certainly capable, having previously been Eisenhower's personnel advisor, but his role "in connection with dismissals from government service during the era of McCarthyism" as chairman of the Civil Service Commission brought some criticism from the Dutch press.[1] In fact, following Matthews only four of the next fifteen ambassadors would be foreign service professionals (William R. Tyler, Robert J. McCloskey, William J. Dyess, and L. Paul Bremer III).

The traditional post-World War II closeness of the two countries around political, security, economic, and business issues was disrupted three times by major policy frictions: the independence of Indonesia in the 1940s, the annexation of New Guinea by Indonesia in the 1960s, and the difficulties surrounding the placement of cruise missiles on Dutch soil in the 1980s. In each case the U.S. embassy needed to function as an arbitrator and in some instances as an enforcer to express the will of Washington. There is no doubt that Dutch-American relations were strained by the Indonesian issue, and the embassy, faced with this discontent on a daily basis, emphasized the need to understand this back in Washington. Ambassador Herman Baruch wrote to Secretary of State Dean Acheson in March 1949 the widespread opinion that the "Netherlands government, through its Foreign Minister has on several occasions been strongly pressured by [the] US during Indonesian crisis. This feeling...will die hard despite traditionally and fundamentally friendly feelings between two nations and their people." Baruch's successor, Selden Chapin, also reported to Acheson at the end of 1949 that most Dutchmen "feel that whether we like it or not, we have assumed some obligation [toward] assisting the Netherlands to overcome some of the economic difficulties arising from that settlement." Similar concerns continued to be sent to Washington through the 1950s. But the main role of the embassy in this situation could only be to try to explain the American position, a matter not made easier by the fact that unclear messages of support on the New Guinea issue had been given by Secretary of State John Foster Dulles.[2]

During the New Guinea affair in the early 1960s the U.S. ambassador was John Rice, the former chairman of the Democratic Party Committee in Pennsylvania, who received the posting as a reward for his efforts in John F. Kennedy's election campaign. Rice was not prepared for the political demands that the New Guinea issue was generating and was therefore "extremely dependent, quite overly dependent" on his embassy staff.[3] Samuel de Palma, embassy political officer from 1961 to 1963, has since recounted how the unpopular task of pressing the Dutch to withdraw from the colony was delegated down to the political section of the embassy when it should have been the ambassador's role. As a result de Palma admitted later that "it undercut our position by assigning the issue to my level. ... I am sure [the Dutch] couldn't have been overly impressed." Rice was certainly no match for Joseph Luns, and it is clear that the State Department did not have great faith in the ambassador's abilities. Some foreign service officers have since commented on whether a more forceful ambassador could have had a stronger impact in changing Dutch policy.[4] Rice eventually resigned in early 1964, a year before the end of his posting.

The Professional Diplomats:
Tyler and Bremer

William Tyler's arrival as U.S. ambassador caused some uncertainty among the Dutch. They had already hosted one senior diplomat in Freeman Matthews, but somehow Tyler's appointment, considering he had been assistant secretary of state for European affairs from 1962 to 1965, seemed to indicate serious problems with the U.S.-Dutch relationship. Tyler's oral history interview later pointed out one main reason for his going to The Hague: "I went to the Netherlands because I asked to go to the Netherlands. ... I had special reasons for being interested in the Netherlands, because [although] a small country [it] is a wonderful listening post for the rest of Europe, because of the fact that its a small country [with] a centuries-old experience in international commerce, trade, and involvement in other parts of the world."[5] This comment indicates the often overlooked importance of the Netherlands for U.S. interests. The Dutch commitment to and involvement in international organizations in general more than compensates for its relatively small size and power as a nation-state. Subse-

665

U.S. Ambassador to the Netherlands William R. Tyler arrives at the royal palace
to present his credentials to Queen Juliana, June 1965.

quent ambassadors such as J. William Middendorf II and Dyess have also pointed out how this gave the Netherlands a special place in U.S. diplomacy (alongside
Britain).[6]

In 1983 L. Paul Bremer III came to The Hague in order to manage what had
become a difficult period in Dutch-American relations. The constant need of
successive Dutch coalition governments to postpone a decision on the placement of cruise missiles caused a strain in relations with the administration of
President Reagan, where an understanding of the delicacies of the Dutch position was not always present. Bremer's predecessor had been William Dyess, who
despite having a long career in the field of diplomacy and international information policy had tried too hard to intervene in the local debate to ensure a positive
outcome. In contrast, Bremer introduced a more subtle "two-level" strategy. The
first level involved studying closely the Dutch political scene to understand the
main ideological and religious cleavages, followed by a gradual process of building blocks of support for deployment within parliament. The second level was
to direct resources toward Dutch society at large, since a positive vote in parliament would be "easier if people in the countryside were not seeing America completely as a demon force." During Bremer's posting the embassy made full use
of its public diplomacy capabilities to influence Dutch political and social opinion and solidify mutual support for close relations. Between 1953 and 1999 this
was largely the responsibility of the United States Information Agency (USIA),
which provided briefings and explanatory material on U.S. foreign policies and
developed contacts with (higher) educational establishments. It also coordinated an array of exchange programs, ranging from the binational Fulbright
Program for university students and lecturers, the prestigious Harkness and
Eisenhower fellowships for established scholars, and the International Visitor
Leadership Program or IVLP (begun in 1950 as the Foreign Leader Program) for
up-and-coming and influential individuals in public life. Bremer made full use
of the IVLP and was personally involved in applying it according to the needs of
U.S. foreign policy objectives. Overall, these kinds of activities cannot change
policy in the short term but they can, over the longer term, certainly strength-
en the sociocultural bonds between nations. Some ambassadors have sought
to directly influence Dutch policy by these means, most notably Clifford Sobel
when he was looking to secure support for the Joint Strike Fighter agreement
between 2001 and 2004. But due to the close working relations between the two
countries, such examples have been rare.[7] Bremer would later offer the san-
guine remark that "where there was a disagreement it usually was a genuine
disagreement … but it wasn't that there was somebody looking to pick a fight.
… [S]ometimes in France you get the impression that the French are basically
looking for a fight with America as a way to prove themselves, [but] that was not
the case [in the Netherlands]."[8]

The Dutch in Washington: Dealing with Informality

4

—

THE
COLD WAR
AND
BEYOND

1945-2009

—

POLITICS
AND
SECURITY

The United States is the Netherlands' most important ally, and as a result, in contrast to the Americans in The Hague, Washington is the most important bilateral posting in Dutch diplomacy and a prestigious location for Dutch diplomats. This major contrast clearly has an impact on how the respective embassies engage in foreign policy, and who is chosen to act as ambassador.

It is possible to illustrate the expectations of the Dutch vis-à-vis the United States by means of a revealing event. In 1964, Carl Schürmann succeeded Herman van Roijen—something of a legend in Dutch diplomatic circles—as ambassador in Washington. When Schürmann went to present his credentials at the White House on July 7, 1964, he was received (at far too low a level in his opinion) by only the third deputy of the assistant secretary of state for European affairs, and the White House ceremonial official hissed that he was not to bring up any official business with the president. Inside the office, President Lyndon B. Johnson confined himself to smiling politely and saying nothing, and seven and a half minutes later Schürmann was standing outside again. Moreover, both Johnson and his ceremonial official forgot to present him with the (standard) reply to his letter of credence. After having carefully pointed out the omission to the ceremonial official, Schürmann finally received the document later that evening. However, he found its contents to be utterly unacceptable and more or less an expression of contempt for the Netherlands. It scarcely mentioned his predecessor Van Roijen, who had spent nearly fifteen years in Washington as the diplomatic linchpin of Dutch-American relations. There were no special words for the close relationship between the United States and the Netherlands. Worst of all, the cordial salutations of the Netherlands were flatly ignored and not answered with a request to reciprocate them to the queen, as was usual. Schürmann was livid. In a "top-secret" coded telegram with an extremely limited distribution list, he announced that he intended—as cautiously as possible—to discover whether this was "extreme carelessness and bad manners" or a deliberate affront. He received personal backing for this from Minister of Foreign Affairs Joseph Luns. Within a few days Assistant Secretary of State William Tyler apologized that it was purely "stupidity and carelessness." Tyler added confidentially and by way of explanation that the State Department could not manage to run the letter of credence ceremony with the necessary decorum because President Johnson was simply not interested. Secretary of State Dean Rusk subsequently invited Schürmann to a meeting to resolve the misunderstandings, where Rusk again confirmed that there was absolutely "no question of any intent," apologized on behalf of the president, and offered to write a personal letter to Luns. Schürmann, now mollified, politely declined the need for such a letter and the incident was over.[9]

The reaction of Schürmann (and Luns) indicates the type of diplomatic decorum that was expected by the Dutch. Successive ambassadors in Washington in the postwar period were drawn from the top ranks of the Dutch diplomatic corps. Nevertheless, the demands for etiquette as displayed by Schürmann have declined over the years. In November 1997 Joris Vos presented his credentials to President Clinton in a ceremony that lasted all of three minutes. On his way out a White House ceremonial official put two boxes of presidential M&Ms (signed by the president) in his wife's purse, saying they were "for the kids."[10] Vos saw the amusing side to this, and found it typical of the relaxed American manners that prevailed at the White House ceremony. By 1997 there was no urge to cause a diplomatic incident, even if it did feel as if the Netherlands was receiving extra candy for good behavior.

In contrast to their U.S. counterparts in The Hague, the Dutch ambassadors have all been career diplomats, and by no means minor ones. The first two after World War II, Eelco van Kleffens and Herman van Roijen, were former ministers of foreign affairs, which made their relationship with their respective ministers rather complicated. Since then exacting criteria for selection have been applied: extensive diplomatic experience in overseas postings (preferably in both bilateral and multilateral environments) and extensive knowledge of diplomatic machinery in The Hague. Thus, at least three of the ambassadors posted to Washington in recent times (A.P.R. Jacobovits, J.M. Vos, and B.J. van Eenennaam) had previously occupied the post of director general of political affairs at the Ministry of Foreign Affairs in The Hague, traditionally the most prominent political advisor to the minister.

Dutch Atlanticism

There has certainly never been any doubt about the pro-Atlantic orientation of the Dutch ambassadors. In fact, it would not be going too far to say that many of them have been more pro-Atlantic than the ministers they were serving. The argument between Minister Dirk Stikker and Ambassador Van Kleffens about the signing of the NATO treaty in April 1949 is a good example. Stikker wanted to insist on American support in the Security Council for Dutch policy in Indonesia as a condition for signing, but Van Kleffens succeeded in persuading him to abandon this, in his opinion, disastrous policy.[11] Again, during the first half of Joseph Luns's long tenure at the Ministry of Foreign Affairs (1952–71) there was constant friction between the minister and his ambassador, Van Roijen, about

669

4

—

THE
COLD WAR
AND
BEYOND

1945-2009

—

POLITICS
AND
SECURITY

Atlantic themes. Few would deny that Luns was a far from obedient ally of the United States during the late 1950s and early 1960s. His stubborn opposition to American policy during the Suez crisis in 1956 and his stance on the drawn-out question of New Guinea in the years thereafter both led to public differences of opinion with Van Roijen. Admittedly, their disputes had a personal element, but basically they sprang from different views on the direction of Dutch foreign policy. In Van Roijen's opinion, showing greater willingness to bend to America's position was a question of simple realism. However, his position was fundamentally anticolonialist and did not subscribe to Luns's efforts to use what was left of the Netherlands' colonial influence to carve out a more independent role in world politics.[12]

Van Roijen's convictions stemmed partly from his years of experience in the U.S. capital. He must have found it rather frustrating that so few were prepared to listen to his views, which — as he saw it — clearly reflected the interests of the Netherlands. Not everybody in his homeland agreed. During the Suez crisis the Dutch paper *De Telegraaf* accused Van Roijen of being an "agent" of the United States after he visited The Hague declaring that he had come to restore confidence in the Atlantic partnership.[13] Over time, even Luns became an exemplary ally as the 1960s progressed, at least to the extent of presenting himself in such a way that his appointment as secretary general of NATO in 1971 met with American approval — a prerequisite to holding that post. But his departure as minister that same year also seemed to mark a turning point. A new period began after Dutch society changed, among other things, its obedient attitude toward elitist foreign-policy making during the 1960s. Criticism from within that society placed governments and ministers under ever greater pressure when formulating foreign policy, and this criticism was often directed at the United States.[14]

Dutch ambassadors in Washington regularly had to deal with opinions emanating from their home country that provoked amazement, to say the least, in the United States. On issues ranging from Vietnam and cruise missiles to the prisoners held at Guantanamo Bay and the invasion of Iraq, public opinion put the Dutch government under pressure to oppose American policies. This "domesticization" of foreign policy regularly led to tension between the two countries, despite U.S. awareness of the Dutch government's limited room to maneuver. At the Dutch embassy in Washington, the task became increasingly one of reporting on insights and information gathered from a broad range of local contacts. How successfully this was done is still open to question.

Jan Meesman, ambassador in Washington from 1990 to 1993, explained in an article on the character of modern Dutch diplomacy exactly what this has meant for Dutch diplomatic representation in the United States. One of his most important observations was that the Netherlands' diplomatic weight is so limited relative to the United States that it can often afford to take positions that bear little relation to reality. For the Netherlands, paying lip service to an idealistic policy position is easy because this will seldom have serious repercussions. One of Meesman's former bosses put it this way: "We have no foreign policy — we are too small for that. This gives our parliament greater freedom to ask critical questions." Many Dutch-American tensions of the past decades can be traced back to this cynical observation, in Meesman's opinion. It often makes the job of the Netherlands' embassy in Washington — as well as in other countries — rather difficult. Meesman concludes:

> What all these issues have in common is that although our antennas in the outside world do pick up the signals, those listening back at home allow other considerations to prevail. We are not forced to face the facts. Policy ambitions in The Hague — including unrealistic ones — seldom provoke much reaction outside our borders. Since reactions from abroad are often too little, too late, the significance of those signals is underestimated and only recognized after a considerable delay, or not at all.[15]

Fiascos such as the embarrassing episode surrounding Ruud Lubbers' failed candidacy for the post of secretary general of NATO in 1996 have been a direct result of the phenomenon described above, according to Meesman. The U.S. vetoed this appointment. If politicians in The Hague had listened more carefully to the embassy in Washington, they would have known this in advance.

Conclusion

The position of the respective embassies in The Hague and Washington presents an interesting set of contrasts, reflecting the realities of asymmetric power between the two countries. All in all, it appears that the room to maneuver enjoyed by the Dutch ambassador in Washington has undergone a steady decline since Van Roijen's days, not only because the ambassador must try to explain The Hague's occasional idealism, but especially because the overall influence of the ambassadorial position in a changing diplomatic environment has declined. Representing a small country in the capital of a superpower, albeit a traditionally close and even special ally, will of course create specific problems. These problems are only exacerbated when the small country's expectations of its own role are high and have continued to rise, which is true in the case of the Netherlands. Yet if the relative weight of the Dutch ambassador in Washington has undergone a decline, the function is still highly sought after among the small number of diplomats eligible for the position. The role remains, accord-

671

4

—

THE
COLD WAR
AND
BEYOND

1945-2009

—

POLITICS
AND
SECURITY

ing to Vos, the first prize of the Dutch foreign service. In contrast, the influence of the U.S. embassy in The Hague has often been affected by the personality and approach of the ambassador. The Dutch complain about the merits of political appointees and always prefer an effective professional who better reflects the close ties between the two countries. Nevertheless, the high quality of the embassy's foreign service personnel as a whole has generally been considered sufficient compensation.

1   Chapin was implicated in the show trial of Cardinal Mindszenty due to his previous contacts with the accused. See "Transmittal of Hungarian Press Accounts," February 16, 1949, Personal Files of US Diplomats in the Netherlands, State Department Decimal File 123, Reel 1: 1945–1959, microfilm collection, Roosevelt Study Center, Middelburg (hereafter RSC); Ambassador Freeman Matthews to Secretary of State, March 12, 1957, ibid.; On Young, the Civil Service Commission, and McCarthy see David Caute, *The Great Fear: The Anti-Communist Purge under Truman and Eisenhower* (New York: Simon & Schuster, 1978).

2   Baruch to Acheson, March 31, 1949, 711.56/3-3149, State Department Decimal File, RG 59, National Archives, College Park, MD; Chapin to Acheson, November 17, 1949, Personal Files of American Diplomats in the Netherlands 1910-1959, Reel 1: 1945-1959, RSC; On Dulles and Luns see Albert Kersten, "Het vodje van Dulles 1958-1962: Amerikaanse steun of een dagdroom van Luns?" (*afscheidscollege* [last professorial lecture], Leiden University, October 14, 2005).

3   Fisher Howe, deputy chief of mission, (unedited) interview with Charles Stuart Kennedy, February 3, 1998, CD-Rom: "Frontline Diplomacy," Oral History Program, Association for Diplomatic Studies and Training (hereafter ADST).

4   Samuel de Palma, interview with Thomas Stern, January 22, 1990, ADST; J. Robert Schaetzel to George Ball, April 10, 1961, 756.1, State Department Decimal File, RG 59, microfilm collection of RSC, Reel 1: 1960–63; Manuel Abrams (economics counselor, The Hague, 1962-66), interview with Charles Stuart Kennedy, January 16, 1990, ADST.

5   William R. Tyler, interview with Charles Stuart Kennedy, November 17, 1987, ADST. American diplomats said similar things about the value of being posted to The Hague during the nineteenth century; See Cornelis A. van Minnen, *American Diplomats in the Netherlands 1815–1850* (New York: St. Martin's Press, 1993).

6   J. William Middendorf II, interview with Charles Stuart Kennedy, July 28, 1993, ADST; William J. Dyess, interview with Charles Taber, March 29, 1989, ADST.

7   In fact, Dutch public servants have been accustomed to sharing inside information directly with the U.S. embassy as a matter of course in their close relations; See Ko Colijn and Freke Vuijst, "De Holland-Amerika Lijn," *Vrij Nederland*, May 13, 2006, 12-20, and "De Holland-Amerika Lijn (2)," *Vrij Nederland*, May 20, 2006, 19-23.

8   L. Paul Bremer III, interview with Doeko Bosscher, July 8, 1998, Washington, DC. For a fuller account of the program see Giles Scott-Smith, *Networks of Empire: The US State Department's Foreign Leader Program in the Netherlands, France, and Britain 1950–70* (Brussels: Peter Lang,

2008); Giles Scott-Smith, "The Ties That Bind," *De Groene Amsterdammer*, February 1, 2008.

9   See coded messages Schürmann 490, July 9, 1964 and 491, July 10, 1964, Confidential Files 1955-1964, inventory number 2017, Ministry of Foreign Affairs Archives, The Hague; Coded message Schürmann 509, July 16, 1964, ibid. The July 9 message was personally addressed to Minister Joseph Luns, State Secretary De Block, and Secretary General Van Tuijl van Serooskerken.

10 See coded message Vos 808, November 13, 1997, chronological series of coded messages Washington — The Hague, Ministry of Foreign Affairs Archives, The Hague. Bert van de Zwan would like to thank Joris Vos for the enjoyable and informative conversation in Brussels on November 28, 2007.

11 Bert Zeeman, "Legist or Diplomat. Eelco Nicolaas Van Kleffens (1939–1946)," in Duco Hellema, Bert Zeeman, and Bert van der Zwan, eds., *De Nederlandse ministers van Buitenlandse Zaken in de twintigste eeuw* (The Hague: SDU uitgeverij, 1999), 149.

12 See Duco Hellema, "The Thesis of the Loyal Ally: Dutch Foreign Policy in the 1950s," *Internationale Spectator* 46 (February 1992): 94-99; Cees Wiebes and Bert Zeeman, "Dutch Diplomacy during the Days of Fear. Jan Herman van Roijen (1946)," in Hellema, Zeeman, and Van der Zwan, eds., *De Nederlandse ministers*, 158-161.

13 See Duco Hellema, *1956. The Dutch Attitude towards the Hungarian Revolution and the Suez Crisis* (Amsterdam: Jan Mets, 1990), 239-241.

14 See A. van Staden, "American-Dutch Political Relations since 1945. What Has Changed and Why?," in J.W. Schulte Nordholt and R.P. Swieringa, eds., *A Bilateral Bicentennial. A History of Dutch-American Relations, 1782–1982* (Amsterdam: Meulenhoff, 1982), 88; H.W. van den Doel, "'Every Continent Will Go Its Own Way.' The Netherlands and the United States during Both World Wars," in H.W. van den Doel, P.C. Emmer, and H.Ph. Vogel, *The Netherlands and the New World* (Utrecht: Het Spectrum, 1992), 305.

15 J.H. Meesman, "The Hague Does not Listen," in A. van Staden, ed., *Contemporary Diplomacy: Indispensable Link or Superfluous Luxury? Positions on Diplomacy*, special edition, *Internationale Spectator* (The Hague: Clingendael Institute, 1997), 18-23.

DUTCH-AMERICAN INTELLIGENCE RELATIONS

4

BOB DE GRAAFF

In Dutch historiography there is debate about the extent to which the Netherlands has been a loyal ally of the United States in the post-World War II era. Although the Dutch often followed U.S. international policies closely, there were digressions at certain moments, especially regarding the decolonization process of Indonesia and Netherlands New Guinea. As in other Western nations, it is accepted in the Netherlands that intelligence services are allowed to operate in ways that diverge slightly from current government policies. There is general agreement that by following official policies too closely secret services would become (too) powerful political instruments, forcing them to make the same mistakes as their governments. Policies of secret services should be more consistent over time and remain more or less autonomous. Furthermore, intelligence services are sometimes used to conduct behind-the-scenes diplomacy that does not necessarily fall in line with official foreign policy. Whereas such considerations might suggest that loyalty to the U.S. might apply even more to the Dutch intelligence (and security) service(s) than to Dutch foreign policy as a whole, one should also take into account that a nation's secret services are real instruments of national sovereignty, meaning that policies of alliance might have a limited impact on their conduct. This article will offer a brief history of Dutch-American intelligence relations since World War II, especially through what is known as intelligence liaison, and will try to establish the smoothness, or lack thereof, in these relations.

The Postwar Dutch Intelligence Community and
Its Liaison with the CIA until the 1960s

After the liberation in 1945 an internal security service was set up in the Netherlands, with the initial help of Canadian Field Security. After its first turbulent postwar year, when its main task was to track down remnants of the German intelligence and security services, things settled down a bit and finally from 1947 on there was an internal security service (Binnenlandse Veiligheidsdienst or BVD) under the jurisdiction of the minister of the interior. It was modelled on the British organization MI5 and fulfilled counterintelligence functions similar to those of the counterintelligence part of the FBI.

In 1946 the Dutch government turned its foreign intelligence agency, which had been set up by the government in exile in London, into a peacetime organization, the Buitenlandse Inlichtingendienst (BID), which in 1972 was renamed Inlichtingendienst Buitenland (IDB). Both organizations, together with the intelligence services of the armed forces, which were formally integrated into one Military Intelligence Service in 1987, were geared toward the exigencies of the Cold War. This was also true of a top-secret stay-behind organization, called Intelligence and Operations (I&O), which would be involved in acts of sabotage, propaganda, and information gathering if the Netherlands were occupied by troops of the Warsaw Pact.

In May 1948 the first CIA representative was stationed in The Hague. That it took so long after the war to establish such a liaison was due to the fact that the U.S. authorities, sensing the close relationship between the BVD and MI5, insisted on exclusivity. In the end, however, the American government had to accept that the Dutch refused to give in on this point. Very soon the CIA, code-named "Karel" by the Dutch intelligence authorities, took pride of place among the allied services with the BVD, by supplying financial and technical assistance in return for generous access to BVD intelligence regarding Soviet and Chinese intelligence organizations. The same applied to the relations between the CIA and the BID.[1] The CIA equipped the Dutch with automatic pistols and ammunition, cars, funds to hire additional staff, and provided tools for illegal tapping operations. CIA technical and financial support amounted to approximately 10 percent of the BVD budget throughout the 1950s. Although Dutch intelligence staff were also trained in the UK and West Germany, many BVD personnel got CIA training. In return, there was constant intelligence sharing between the Dutch intelligence and security services and the American, British, and later also German and Israeli services. However, due to the greater capacities of the U.S. intelligence community, the Dutch were dependent on the CIA's willingness to provide information other than on a quid pro quo basis. This resulted in larger flows of information when the U.S. government wished to influence Dutch policies, whereas at other times the Dutch would have liked to learn more from their transatlantic allies.

675

Frequently there were joint operations, allocated operations (each of the services executing an agreed-upon part), or parallel operations against the same target.[2] An example of an allocated operation was the wiretapping of Soviet and East

Villa Maarheeze, the location of the Foreign Intelligence Service
(Inlichtingendienst Buitenland) of the Netherlands during 1946–94.

Bloc embassies with technical means provided by the CIA. The BVD would turn the taps over to the CIA, which returned the translated transcripts to the Dutch, who used them for counterespionage and counterintelligence purposes.

Not everything went smoothly, however. The BVD chief, Louis Einthoven, was a rather strongheaded man, who did not like to be patronized or humiliated by CIA operations in the Netherlands about which he was not informed. When he had the impression that the Americans were not generous enough from their side, he paid them back in similar vein. After several such confrontations in the early 1950s, the BVD started providing the CIA with periodic reports and held monthly meetings with CIA staff in the Netherlands. Soon DCI Allen Dulles commended the Dutch for the excellent quality of their reports[3] and Einthoven was, together with MI6 chief Dick White, held in high esteem at CIA headquarters in Langley.[4] According to the Agency the BVD was of much higher quality than most Western European services, especially with regard to the degree and level of penetration of the Dutch communist party and the maoist movement in the Netherlands. Throughout the latter half of the twentieth century, while joint and allocated operations against the Soviet bloc and China abounded, the BVD remained very sensitive concerning CIA operations in the Netherlands.[5] It objected, for instance, to a CIA proposal for black propaganda through a left-wing Dutch magazine, to the idea of filming Indonesian Foreign Minister Subrandio in a compromising situation during his visit to the Netherlands, and to the American wish in 1958 to wiretap the Egyptian embassy. The CIA's help was welcomed, however, in the screening of hundreds of Hungarian refugees who were to be accepted by the Netherlands in 1956, and a bugging operation against the Chinese embassy in The Hague proved to be real goldmine for both the BVD and CIA until the Chinese detected the microphones in December 1963.

After Einthoven retired in 1961 his successor wanted the BVD to be less dependent on CIA funding, and by the mid-1960s this way of funding the Dutch security services was terminated. The BID/IDB had a much smaller staff than the BVD. While the latter counted almost seven hundred staff members by the end of the 1950s, the BID/IDB never made it above approximately seventy employees and was considered a shoestring operation by the CIA.[6] During the late 1940s and the 1950s the BID had legal officers stationed in Paris, Stockholm, Berne, Vienna, Ankara, Madrid, and other capitals. They were a source of friction with the regular embassy staff and after several years these posts were all abolished. The BID relied mainly on some agents in place in established circles in Western European nations, as the policies of these nations regarding, for instance, Western European integration and NATO were of much more concern and easier to detect than the policies of the Soviet bloc.

However, in collaboration with the Navy Intelligence Service, the BID conducted combined operations with the CIA through the use of legal travelers to

677

4

————

THE
COLD WAR
AND
BEYOND

1945-2009

————

POLITICS
AND
SECURITY

Soviet bloc nations. Of the two Dutch services, the BID was the more forthcoming one as the Dutch navy still held a grudge against the Americans because of Washington's policies at the time of the Dutch-Indonesian confrontations.[7] Another field in which the BID and the Dutch Navy Intelligence Service operated together was the interception of diplomatic and other foreign communications.

It was in this field that there almost was a breakdown in Dutch-American relations. Close cooperation between the American intercepting organization and Dutch experts, dating back to World War II, turned liaison by the Dutch into espionage against their major ally. On Ocober 9, 1954 Joseph Sydney Petersen, a cryptologist of the National Security Agency (NSA), was arrested for handing over top-secret documentation to a Dutch counterpart.[8] Among these documents was information about the breaking of Dutch codes by the U.S. authorities. The latter accused the Dutch of foul play.[9]

This affair soured Dutch-American relations in cryptology for a long time, but since both governments downplayed the incident, it hardly affected overall intelligence relations. The liaison with the Dutch services was considered to be a boilerplate agreement: the Dutch handed over almost all intelligence that they thought to be worthwhile to the CIA.[10] This also applied to the information provided by a highly placed source of the Dutch in the Indonesian government, who provided information on Sukarno and on Indonesian plans regarding both communism and New Guinea. Between 1957 and 1962 the CIA helped fund this valuable operation. With the aid of the CIA the BID also hired safes in a bank in Holland, MI, between 1951 and 1965, to store documents that would help a Dutch government in exile continue functioning in case the Netherlands were overrun by Warsaw Pact troops. In 1965 the Dutch emptied the safes in this bank, but the practice was continued somewhere else in the U.S.[11]

The 1970s and 1980s: Downs and Ups

Up until 1970 the BID had little analytical capacity. After an analysis section staffed by academics became part of the restyled BID (IDB from 1972), the newly appointed staff showed dissatisfaction with the information the Dutch were given by the CIA. Partly as a result of this new attitude, partly as a result of the dismissive attitude of the then head of the IDB, and partly because of infighting among the IDB staff, relations between the IDB and CIA cooled down during the 1970s. Before he left for The Hague in 1974, CIA station chief Howard Bane was told in a briefing by the Agency's desk for Western Europe that any effort at closer cooperation with the IDB was useless and worthless.

However, in the following decade these relations improved. The IDB and CIA cooperated in the field of political intelligence and on intelligence gathering regarding science and technology, for which the Dutch received directives not only from the CIA but also from the American Defense Intelligence Agency. At the time, the IDB reports and analyses were considered to be of very good quality, especially given the small size of the IDB staff. This small size turned out to be even an advantage in some cases: IDB analysts always had all-round expertise, whereas CIA personnel sometimes suffered from overspecialization and compartmentalization.[12]

Relations between the CIA station in The Hague and the BVD were, as always, much better, as the BVD (much larger than the IDB) offered higher-quality information. There was friction, though, in the early 1970s when a CIA officer, against instructions of his own station chief in The Hague, recruited a member of the Dutch Labor Party. Nevertheless, the BVD was still highly regarded by the CIA as one of the better Western European secret services.[13] Cooperation between the CIA and the Dutch intelligence community was also close at the time of several Moluccan terrorist hijackings of trains and occupations of buildings in 1975 and 1977. These events were a deviation from the usual calm in The Hague. During the occupation of the French embassy in 1974 the CIA supplied the Dutch authorities with technical equipment to listen in on the members of the Japanese Red Army, and provided guidance about possible scenarios for a liberation action. In 1975 the CIA delivered listening devices that could be used in adjacent rooms of the Indonesian consulate where Moluccans held some of the consulate's employees hostage, and at the time of the train hijackings the CIA was helpful in finding ways to smuggle listening devices into the trains.

Small problems arose, however, because of the American insistence on information about Cuban activities in the southern part of Africa. As was mentioned above, an intelligence agency must, to a certain extent, operate independently of its government because otherwise it may become too politicized. Yet, when sailing a course of its own an intelligence organization must also observe certain limits in a democracy. The IDB was stretching these limits in the 1970s. In 1971 its head, C.J. Hagen, objected to a draft of a royal decree regulating the tasks of the Dutch intelligence services, because he could not agree with wording according to which the services would perform their duties in accordance with the law and the European Convention for the Protection of Human Rights and Fundamental Freedoms. Such a restriction would hamper offensive intelligence gathering, which, in the opinion of the intelligence chief, violated by definition human rights and human dignity. The government should not forget that Cold War was war, too. And a restriction like the one proposed in the decree would ridicule the intelligence service in the eyes of its foreign partners.

679

4

———

THE
COLD WAR
AND
BEYOND

1945–2009

———

POLITICS
AND
SECURITY

To placate the IDB chief, the Dutch government deleted the reference to the European Convention from the decree but embedded it in its commentary on the law.

More practical problems were caused by the always difficult relation with Dutch diplomats abroad. An effort by the IDB to convince the Ministry of Foreign Affairs of the necessity to enlist Dutch diplomats for its tasks was courteously turned down. And a suggestion that the IDB might establish informal diplomatic relations with the PLO was rejected outright. The operative work suffered and the only reason why Labor Prime Minister Joop den Uyl did not dissolve the IDB, was the argument that foreign intelligence services, especially the CIA, would then have free reign in that field of activity.

Meanwhile the CIA became concerned by the activities of one of the IDB employees, Piet Gerbrands, who in defiance of the Ministry of Foreign Affairs' unwillingness to involve diplomats had started the so-called residence project in which several Dutch diplomats sent him secret information. The CIA's counterintelligence chief, James Angleton, whose professional paranoia became less and less professional over time, suspected Gerbrands' activities to be possibly inspired by the KGB. However, a CIA investigation eventually yielded no negative results regarding Gerbrands.

In other respects the IDB was sailing in heavy weather as well, mainly because of the peculiarities of its head, Hagen. He was a very religious man and the CIA station chief in The Hague had to get used to the fact that every meeting with Hagen began with a Bible reading. Hagen was very unusual in the usually open context of Dutch-American relations and he was known to distrust the CIA. He did not allow his staff to attend parties organized by the CIA station chief. The intelligence relation between the CIA and the IDB was a one-way street at the time, the CIA giving materials without getting anything in return, not even comments on the reports it handed over, for instance, about the regime change in Portugal and the situation on the oil markets. Neither did Hagen show any enthusiasm for CIA offers to conduct joint operations against Rhodesia (Zimbabwe), the Middle East, Indonesia, or Portugal.

One piece of information the CIA would have liked to receive from Hagen was his knowledge of South Africa. However, unlike the CIA, the South African intelligence community was mainly at the receiving end in its relations with the IDB. Contradicting the official anti-apartheid policy of the Den Uyl cabinet, the IDB sent much information about South African anti-apartheid fighters to their South African counterparts for ideological, historical, and political reasons. It did not dare send the scarce information that was received in return to the Dutch Ministry of Foreign Affairs, rightly fearing that the Dutch diplomats would create havoc over this defiance of Dutch foreign policy. This close cooperation with South Africa lasted well into the 1980s in spite of protests by the IDB's chief analyst.

Meanwhile, during the first part of that decade relations between the CIA and the Dutch intelligence community were extremely tight when several plans were made for joint operations in the former Dutch colony of Suriname, which had made a swing to the political left after a military coup in 1980.[14]

The Demise of the IDB

In 1992 Prime Minister Ruud Lubbers decided to discontinue the IDB as of January 1, 1994 after frictions among the staff had endangered its security. Simultaneously, the stay-behind organization I&O was abolished. Probably because the IDB had proved its worth to the Americans at the time of the first Gulf War, the CIA was the only foreign service to protest its termination. It was hoped that the BVD could maintain the connections the IDB had formerly had with other intelligence agencies. It soon became apparent, though, that the absence of a Dutch intelligence service led to a substantial reduction of foreign information reaching the desks of the Dutch intelligence community. Therefore, it was eventually decided to transform the BVD into a combined intelligence and security service (Algemene Inlichtingen- en Veiligheidsdienst) when in 2002 it began to operate under a new act. Nevertheless, the intelligence branch has remained by far the smaller component of the organization, which since the terrorist attacks of September 11, 2001 has grown from just over five hundred to approximately fifteen hundred staff members.

Conclusion

It turns out that after a cumbersome take-off Dutch-American intelligence liaison became well established. The Dutch intelligence services were just as loyal an ally as their various governments, or even more so. Much depended, however, on the views and attitudes of the heads of services, who could at times insist on Dutch sovereignty or display a lack of interest. As a general rule, the Netherlands was out of bounds for U.S. operations of which the Dutch security service was not informed beforehand. As long as intelligence was gathered through liaison, however, everything went smoothly. Incidents like the so-called Petersen affair did not have a lasting effect on the otherwise very close relations.

4

—

THE
COLD WAR
AND
BEYOND

1945–2009

—

POLITICS
AND
SECURITY

1   Dick Engelen, *Geschiedenis van de Binnenlandse Veiligheidsdienst* (The Hague: SDU uitgeverij, 1995); Bob de Graaff and Cees Wiebes, *Villa Maarheeze. De geschiedenis van de Inlichtingendienst Buitenland* (The Hague: SDU uitgeverij, 1998), 322-323.

2   Bob de Graaff and Cees Wiebes, "Intelligence and the Cold War behind the Dikes: The Relationship between the American and Dutch Intelligence Communities, 1946–1994," *Intelligence and National Security* 12.1 (January 1997), 45; De Graaff and Wiebes, *Villa*, 99-100.

3   De Graaf and Wiebes, "Intelligence," 46; De Graaff and Wiebes, *Villa*, 107-108.

4   Bob de Graaff and Cees Wiebes, "Hand- en spandiensten. De CIA en het 'rode' kabinet-Den Uyl," *NRC Handelsblad*, November 21, 1998.

5   De Graaff and Wiebes, *Villa*, 110-111, 328-329, 334.

6   De Graaff and Wiebes, "Hand- en spandiensten."

7   De Graaff and Wiebes, *Villa*, 111.

8   See Bob de Graaff and Cees Wiebes, "Codes van vertrouwen. Bondgenoten lazen jarenlang geheime diplomatieke en militaire berichten van Nederland," *NRC Handelsblad*, June 29, 1996.

9   De Graaff and Wiebes, "Intelligence," 50-51.

10 De Graaff and Wiebes, "Hand- en spandiensten"; De Graaff and Wiebes, *Villa*, 333.

11 De Graaff and Wiebes, *Villa*, 161, 212-213.

12 De Graaff and Wiebes, "Hand- en spandiensten"; De Graaff and Wiebes, *Villa*, 118, 285, 334-335, 337.

13 De Graaff and Wiebes, "Hand- en spandiensten"; De Graaff and Wiebes, "Intelligence," 55-56.

14 De Graaff and Wiebes, *Villa*, 248-249, 266-267, 278, 305, 313, 333, 335, 340-341, 357.

DUTCH-AMERICAN RELATIONS AND THE VIETNAM WAR

———

RIMKO VAN DER MAAR

Introduction

According to the American historian James Kennedy, the Netherlands changed more radically than any other Western European country in the 1960s.* "Until the end of the 1950s, foreign observers widely regarded the Netherlands as a quaint, 'old-fashioned' society, steeped in the traditions and conventions of a previous age," he writes.[1] Just ten years later, this picture could not have been any more outdated. The Netherlands had become a prosperous nation with a tolerant and progressive climate that attracted attention and caused astonishment abroad. Domestic politics had also become more animated. As a result of an accelerated process of depillarization and secularization, the traditional religious, social democratic and liberal parties had lost the backing of the supporters they had once been able to count on as a matter of course, and were forced to compete with newly established parties for unaffiliated voters.

Historians remain divided about what caused the rapid changes in the Netherlands. Kennedy claims that they were advanced by moderate elites who abhorred conflict and believed it was better to channel the subsequent influx of modern developments than to resist them, as was happening in other Western countries. The Dutch historian Hans Righart related the changes to the clash between the prewar generation and the postwar protest generation, both of which were in crisis due to rapid material changes.[2] Other causes can be given as well, causes that in principle apply to other countries too, such as the advent of a transnational youth culture, the inability of the political order to anticipate new de-

683

* I am grateful to Alana Gillespie for translating this article.

4

—

THE
COLD WAR
AND
BEYOND

1945–2009

—

POLITICS
AND
SECURITY

velopments, the spread of television, and particularly important to this contribution, the emergence of new international public concerns.[3]

One of the most prominent of these concerns was the war in Vietnam. Just
as in other Western countries, this war was an important impulse for raising social and political awareness in the Netherlands. The unprecedented symbolic
character of the conflict is particularly notable in this respect. The prolonged
American military presence and the intensified bombing of North (and South)
Vietnam created an image of an immoral superpower employing ultramodern
military means to impede an impoverished peasant people's struggle for independence. Correct or not, this image contributed to criticism of U.S. authority,
encouraged opposition to domestic power relations, led to a reconsideration of
the communist threat, and increased solidarity with Third World countries.

This essay concerns the Vietnam War debate in the Netherlands and seeks
to determine to what extent the social criticism affected Dutch-American relations. Along with other NATO allies, in 1965 the Dutch government expressed
its support for the American military intervention in Vietnam. At first this went
undisputed, but when social criticism of U.S. policy in Vietnam grew, the Dutch
government came under increased pressure.[4]

Escalation and Polarization

Ton Regtien, the best-known Dutch student leader at the time, described the
onerous and complex Vietnam War debate as "[a] debate about interpretations
that's gone on for years, about the right word in the right place, about truth
and lies."[5] Throughout all the confusion and emotion of the discussions, one
question kept cropping up: was the American government setting up a blockade
against international communism or did Vietnam have an internal social conflict that in principle did not warrant U.S. involvement? In the early stages of the
conflict many people adhered to the former interpretation. Because so little was
known, most people trusted the American government's judgment. Moreover,
it was taboo to doubt the U.S. because of its role in the liberation of Europe and
the reality of the Cold War.

The consensus quickly began to unravel, largely because of the continual
bombing of North Vietnam. The Dutch government began receiving letters from
concerned citizens, the media published critical articles, and politicians began
openly to express doubts about the efficacy of the bombing. The critique was not
merely rooted in humanitarianism, but was also related to a discussion that had
been developing for some time about the relationship between the global North
and South.[6] For years, pacifist groups as well as social democratic and Protestant circles had argued that enduring peaceful coexistence between East and

684

West was only feasible if the social problems in Third World countries could be solved. However, it was those countries' own business to decide on the approach and in the postcolonial era the West could only contribute to the solution by offering development aid. In the context of such an interpretation, the U.S. was actually using violence to prevent a process of social revolution against a South Vietnamese regime known for its corruption and authoritarianism.

After a year of agitation and doubt, the debate had become entangled in the growing social and political unrest in the Netherlands and the tone was more trenchant. The year 1966 has been called calamitous because of the social upheaval that arose in reaction to the closed and pillarized political establishment. The marriage of Princess Beatrix and Claus von Amsberg in March 1966 had been a particular point of contention. In an already volatile Amsterdam, the fact that the successor to the throne would marry a German who had been a member of the Hitler Youth and served in the Wehrmacht caused many people to speak out against the government.[7] That same month the Labor Party (PvdA) and the Catholic People's Party (KVP), which had formed the Cals government along with the Protestant Anti-Revolutionary Party (ARP), lost the Provincial Council elections.

More and more, the Vietnam War began to be used as a means of putting pressure on the establishment. This was evident in the Vietnam demonstrations in Amsterdam, at which the predominantly young demonstrators regularly provoked the police and judicial authorities by shouting the slogan "Johnson murderer!," thus "offending" a "friendly head of state." The changing social climate was also evidenced in left-leaning media commentary, where support for the American intervention was branded conservative and "right-wing." Furthermore, in May 1966 the board of the Labor Party presented an open letter to U.S. Ambassador William R. Tyler. Influenced by the recent electoral loss, the board distanced itself from the Cals government's pro-American stance, calling in the letter for the cessation of the bombing of North Vietnam. The incident caused quite some commotion but eventually fizzled out because the parliamentary group of the Lower House and the PvdA ministers did not support the letter.

Despite the intensifying debate, it is important to note that in this period criticism of the American military presence in Vietnam was not yet hostile (with the exception of the radical protests, mainly in Amsterdam) because of the high esteem the Dutch felt for the United States. The critique that was expressed tended to be accompanied by the claim that American politicians and intellectuals also had their doubts about the U.S. military action. Many critics took for granted that the American government had sent troops to Vietnam with the best of intentions (namely, to fight communism). It was now up to loyal allies such as the Netherlands to persuade the U.S. to begin peace negotiations.

Protest demonstration against the war in Vietnam, on the Leidseplein, Amsterdam, July 1, 1966.

However, the Cals government was not prepared to do this. Foreign Affairs Minister Joseph Luns supported the U.S. not only out of anticommunist convictions, but also because he thought it was in the best interest of the Netherlands. The Vietnam War threatened to spread discord among NATO allies due to France's persistent opposition. Luns's candid support for America's Vietnam policy was greatly appreciated in Washington.[8]

Model Ally

In 1967 the escalating Vietnam conflict and the political tensions in the Netherlands again proved to be a volatile combination. The Vietnam debate would even create conflict between parliament and the new government, led by the Catholic former Minister of Defense Piet de Jong. His cabinet took office as a result of the elections that followed the demise of the Cals government in the fall of 1966. The elections had been dominated by an intense struggle between the PvdA and the KVP, both of which lost to newcomer Democrats 66 (D66), a left-wing liberal party and the biggest winner. This confirmed that the traditional parties were losing touch with voters. Still, the new government was extremely opposed to North Vietnam. This position clashed with a large segment of public opinion that held the American government responsible for prolonging the conflict with the continual bombing of North Vietnam. In May 1967, amid great media attention, about ten thousand people of all ages and backgrounds gathered for a demonstration demanding an end to the bombings.

De Jong, who had personally seen to the reappointment of Luns as minister of foreign affairs, saw the Vietnam War purely in terms of the East-West opposition. In his view, not only was the U.S. right to intervene because of the rise of China, but it was improper for NATO allies to denounce one another publicly. As the Netherlands was not officially involved in the conflict, he considered critique of the U.S. bombings "cheap" and "one-sided." According to him, North Vietnam was frustrating a peaceful settlement by rejecting American peace proposals and infiltrating South Vietnam.

A widely supported parliamentary motion calling for an end to the U.S. bombings was cause for discord between parliament and the government. The motion was a response to public unrest, but was politically motivated by the governing parties' desire to use their own motion to gain an advantage over the PvdA. It was also linked to a growing demand in parliamentary circles in general for a greater say in foreign affairs. Members of parliament of different political stripes felt that Luns and De Jong had an uncompromising view of international relations because of their strong anticommunist feelings.

687

4
—

THE
COLD WAR
AND
BEYOND

1945–2009

POLITICS
AND
SECURITY

However, the government resisted parliament's increasing interference. On the initiative of the prime minister, Luns announced that the government would only present the tabled Vietnam motion to the American government as the *opinion* of the Lower House. The proposed compromise kicked off a six-month power game between parliament and the government. Luns eventually managed to end the controversy in February 1968 by agreeing to a proposal to approach several countries about making an international appeal for peace. The plan never came to fruition because President Lyndon Johnson announced on March 31, 1968 that the bombing of North Vietnam would for the most part be stopped and that peace negotiations would be initiated.

The growing criticism of the U.S. in the Netherlands did not affect Dutch-American working relations. On the contrary — despite making frequent references in diplomatic discussions to what he felt had been an anti-Dutch attitude during the New Guinea affair in the early 1960s Luns tended to agree, as previously noted, with the American government on Vietnam. He met regularly with Ambassador Tyler and Secretary of State Dean Rusk to discuss how the increasing criticism in the Netherlands could be kept in check. Ambassador Tyler's commitment and involvement in this matter are particularly noteworthy.[9] In early 1968, he even reported to Washington that the Vietnam War might very well lead to a cabinet crisis in the Netherlands. While this did not actually happen, Vietnam did indeed dominate the political agenda, but the governing parties were not willing to allow it to dissolve the cabinet.

Despite the good relations, the State Department became annoyed with the Dutch government in 1968. It could not understand why Luns of all people would busy himself so sedulously in pursuing a peace appeal when a few "well-publicized démarches" would have sufficed. Evidently, Washington reasoned, the political pressure on Luns was so great that he was determined to carry out parliament's instructions successfully by any means. When he abandoned the international appeal midway through 1968, the American government was relieved. The incident had not damaged Luns's sympathetic image in Washington. By 1968, he was one of only a few European statesmen who continued to support the U.S., and a year and a half later, in May 1970, the Dutch government was the only NATO ally to openly express understanding for President Richard Nixon's decision to invade Cambodia in order to shut down the North Vietnamese bases there. The American government characterized the Netherlands in the international press as a "model ally," while it ignored the fact that the De Jong government's position was widely criticized in the Netherlands.

U.S. Secretary of State Dean Rusk and Dutch Foreign Minister Joseph Luns
at the opening of the NATO conference in The Hague on May 12, 1964 .

4

—

THE
COLD WAR
AND
BEYOND

1945-2009

—

POLITICS
AND
SECURITY

Pragmatism under Schmelzer

Dutch-American relations changed in the early 1970s and a pragmatic period ensued. This was because of changes in international relations as well as internal developments in the Netherlands. Atlantic relations had become awkward after Nixon took office and Henry Kissinger was appointed national security adviser in 1969. The European NATO members were piqued by the fact that the American government was making decisions that would have consequences for Europe without even consulting them. For instance, Nixon and Kissinger sought *rapprochement* with the Soviet Union and China during these years without conferring with their European allies.

The Vietnam War was also becoming a greater obstacle between the U.S. and Western Europe. This was a direct result of the change in perception of the conflict that occurred in 1969. Peace negotiations in Paris and the gradual withdrawal from Vietnam of American troops made the conflict no longer — or at least less symbolically — a clash between the West and communism. This meant that the Western European allies now had (even) less sympathy for the U.S.'s preoccupation with Southeast Asia. Their lack of understanding became greater after the resumption, in the early 1970s, of the American bombing of North and South Vietnam, which provoked outrage and protest throughout the world.

Meanwhile, the center-right Biesheuvel government took office in the Netherlands, with the Catholic Norbert Schmelzer as the new minister of foreign affairs. This government differed from its predecessor in its approach to foreign policy. In accordance with recent international developments, Schmelzer announced that he intended to plot a more independent course in the Atlantic alliance — among other things — by organizing a European security conference. As a former parliamentarian, he was also determined to take domestic views of foreign politics more into consideration than Luns had done. For Schmelzer, this was the way to correct the discrepancy that had arisen between public opinion and government policy. Criticism of the American bombings was more widespread during the 1970s than it had been in the 1960s, and Schmelzer was sympathetic to it. Yet, he did not think that the U.S. government should count its losses and get out of South Vietnam as soon as possible. Rather, just like his predecessor, Schmelzer worried that the U.S., after conceding defeat, would shirk its responsibilities in Europe. In his opinion, "peace with honor" for the U.S. was also in Europe's best interest. Nonetheless, Schmelzer did not feel that expressing criticism was inappropriate; it just had to be formulated in such a way that it could not give Washington reason to doubt the friendly ties between the Netherlands and the U.S.

But the American government was less tolerant of criticism than he had expected. In the spring of 1972, at the behest of parliament, Schmelzer began investigating the possibilities for diplomatic recognition of North Vietnam. Washington voiced serious objections. A parliamentary majority believed that ending North Vietnam's diplomatic isolation would be a positive contribution to a peaceful solution. The American government considered this nonsensical and claimed that Hanoi would only accept the offer of diplomatic recognition in order to further complicate negotiations with the U.S. Schmelzer initially wanted to persevere, but once Nixon and Kissinger became involved, he changed his mind and decided to postpone recognition.

In December 1972, Schmelzer collided with the American government on the issue of the Christmas bombings in North Vietnam. The resumption of bombings led to a wave of protest in the Netherlands, as it did in most Western countries — a truce had seemed close at hand but the bombing continued over Christmas. All major Dutch newspapers denounced it and protest demonstrations took place all over the country, culminating in a national demonstration in Utrecht on January 6, 1973, supported by all major political parties with the exception of the Party for Freedom and Democracy (VVD), and drawing fifty thousand to one hundred thousand people.

The furor over the Christmas bombings encouraged Schmelzer to lodge an official protest with the American government. This was a remarkable decision, as it was the first time the Dutch government had done so. Schmelzer was motivated by his concern about the growing anti-Americanism in Dutch society and the destructive effect the bombings could have on NATO's reputation. He believed that a protest might be able to temper the negative sentiment and was also frustrated that the American government had in no way informed its European allies of the circumstances of the bombings. All of this led him to believe he had no choice but to denounce them.

The U.S. government, however, did not see it that way. Under pressure from the new escalation in Vietnam the State Department declared that criticism from its allies undermined the American position, was damaging the very precarious negotiations with North Vietnam, and was worse for the Atlantic alliance's reputation than the actual bombings themselves. Secretary of State William Rogers told the Dutch government that he had expected his "long-time ally" to show more support and greater confidence in the U.S.

Impressed by the severe American response, Schmelzer explained to the Dutch cabinet that it had never been his intention to damage Dutch-American relations. But he continued to emphasize how important he thought it was to listen to what he called society's "emotions." Before resigning his post in March 1973 he decided to go ahead with the diplomatic recognition of North

691

4

———

THE
COLD WAR
AND
BEYOND

1945–2009

———

POLITICS
AND
SECURITY

Vietnam in order to make it possible to extend aid to that country. The U.S. government objected again, but Schmelzer felt that postponing it any longer would only weaken the reputations of NATO and the U.S. in the eyes of the general public. Besides, diplomatic recognition was considered less controversial by then because of the peace treaty the United States and North Vietnam had signed in Paris two months earlier.

Normalization under Van der Stoel

Following the Labor Party's decisive election victory, the Den Uyl government took office in May 1973. This coalition government of the three progressive parties — Labor, D66, and the Radical Political Party — along with the ARP and the KVP, brought a temporary end to the dominant position of the *confessionelen* (various Christian and Christian-democratic parties) in Dutch politics. Enthusiastically welcomed in some circles, this government became known as the most left-wing cabinet the Netherlands has ever had.

It was fortunate for the new government that American troops had already retreated from South Vietnam in early 1973. This helped prevent a painful confrontation with the United States. Given the blatant criticism expressed by the three parties that until recently had been in the opposition, it would have been unimaginable for the government not to have condemned a prolongation of the American presence in South Vietnam. The Paris peace agreements allowed it to shift its attention to other international issues, such as the process of European integration, North-South relations, the Arab-Israeli conflict, and the enforcement of human rights.

Once it became evident that the Paris treaty was not going to hold, the Den Uyl government was expected to take a stand. It turned out to be an ambivalent one. On the one hand, the new minister for foreign affairs, Labor's Max van der Stoel, maintained the course set by his predecessor. He was open to domestic criticism regarding South Vietnam and the (financial) support it received from the U.S. On the other hand, as an Atlanticist he was very keen on maintaining good relations with the U.S. Van der Stoel envisioned the Dutch stance as "critical and loyal."[10] When his own party repeatedly pressed for recognition by the Dutch government (as the first in the world) of the National Front for the Liberation of South Vietnam, he refused. As critical as he was of the regime in Saigon, he felt that under international law it was wrong to recognize a communist front organization that represented only a small part of the South Vietnamese people.

Opposing him was the young, progressive minister for development cooperation, Jan Pronk (also of the Labor Party). He made it no secret that his sympathy lay with the Vietnamese communists. In contrast to Van der Stoel, who believed in quiet diplomacy, Pronk saw development aid as a means of pressure. He openly stated that he absolutely did not want to provide bilateral aid to South Vietnam, but he did decide to give fifteen million guilders to North Vietnam. Pronk also generously supported many Dutch private initiatives for aid to North Vietnam. His commitment clashed with the more formal position of Van der Stoel, who regularly complained that the young minister's political stance was infringing upon his own territory too frequently.[11]

A year after the fall of Saigon in 1975, the Dutch government held out the prospect of one hundred million guilders for the unified communist country of Vietnam. In doing so, the Netherlands clearly distanced itself from the U.S., which was boycotting the unified Vietnam. However, this did not affect Dutch-American relations. From a worldwide perspective, after 1973 the Vietnam War had become too much of a rear-guard conflict for it to have a major impact. Furthermore, Van der Stoel remained dedicated to the Atlantic course. This came as a relief to Washington, which had been somewhat hesitant when the Den Uyl government had taken office. The subject of the one hundred million guilders was not raised during the extensive talks between Van der Stoel and Secretary of State Kissinger in August 1976.[12] Provided that Atlantic relations remained the mainstay of Dutch foreign policy, Washington was willing to accept that the Netherlands had chosen a different path for development aid.[13]

Conclusion

Consideration of the period 1965–75 shows that the Dutch government's attitude to American leadership was more reserved in the mid-1970s than in the 1960s. The change can be partially attributed to growing criticism of the United States' Vietnam policy within Dutch society, coupled with increased interest in and sympathy for Third World countries and Vietnam in particular. However, the transformation in international relations that took place at the end of the 1960s was also very important. Détente, the problems between the U.S. and Western Europe, and the U.S. withdrawal from Vietnam were all factors that allowed the Dutch government to adopt a more independent position.

Still, the margins for criticism were narrow, as became apparent when the United States put the Dutch government in its place following Schmelzer's protest against the Christmas bombings in 1972. This incident made clear that in times of difficulty, the U.S. government expected complete loyalty from its small ally. The average citizen, according to Schmelzer, did not always see the actual reality of the unequal relationship between the U.S. and the Nether-

693

lands. Looking back on the situation he said, "Mainly intellectuals and young people are very committed. But they are not aware of what goes on in secret diplomacy."[14]

4

—

THE
COLD WAR
AND
BEYOND

1945-2009

—

POLITICS
AND
SECURITY

1   James C. Kennedy, "Building New Babylon: Cultural Changes in the Netherlands during the 1960s" (Ph.D. dissertation, University of Iowa, 1995), 4.

2   Hans Righart, *De eindeloze jaren zestig. Geschiedenis van een generatieconflict* (Amsterdam: De Arbeiderspers, 1995).

3   See K. Schuyt and E. Taverne, *1950. Welvaart in zwart-wit* (The Hague: SDU uitgeverij, 2000), 379-383.

4   Unless otherwise stated, this essay is based on my published Ph.D. dissertation, *Welterusten mijnheer de president. Nederland en de Vietnamoorlog 1965–1973* (Amsterdam: Boom, 2007).

5   Ton Regtien, *Springtij. Herinneringen aan de jaren zestig* (Houten: Wereldvenster, 1988), 143-144.

6   See Maarten Kuitenbrouwer, *De ontdekking van de Derde Wereld. Beeldvorming en beleid in Nederland, 1950–1990* (The Hague: Staatsuitgeverij, 1994).

7   Righart, *De eindeloze jaren*, 211-216.

8   See Rimko van der Maar, "Dutch Minister for Foreign Affairs Joseph Luns and the Vietnam War (1963–1971)," in Ch. Goscha and M. Vaïsse, *La Guerre du Vietnam et L'Europe* (Brussels: Bruylant, 2003), 103-117.

9   See Giles Scott-Smith, "A Serious Business: The State Department's Foreign Leader Program in the Netherlands under Ambassador William R. Tyler 1965–1969," *Dutch Crossing* 28.1-2 (2004): 3-26.

10 Maarten Kuitenbrouwer, "Een realistische idealist," in Duco Hellema, Bert Zeeman, and Bert van der Zwan, eds., *De Nederlandse ministers van Buitenlandse Zaken in de twintigste eeuw* (The Hague: SDU uitgeverij, 1999), 243-255, here 248.

11 Ibid., 252; See Frank Zuijdam, *Tussen wens en werkelijkheid. Het debat over vrede en veiligheid binnen de PvdA in de periode 1958–1977* (Amsterdam: Aksant, 2002), 312-315.

12 Dutch Ministry of Foreign Affairs Archives, 1975-85, Code 9 (classified documents), inventory number 1121, various coded messages, August 12, 1976.

13 In January 1979, after the Vietnamese invasion of Cambodia, the American government insisted the Dutch government temporarily halt the aid. See Duco Hellema, "Wisselende perspectieven. Nederland en Vietnam na 1976," in J. Kleinen et al., eds., *Leeuw en draak. Vier eeuwen Nederland en Vietnam* (Amsterdam: s.n., 2007), 213-233.

14 "Een gesprek met Schmelzer," *Het Vrije Volk*, February 1, 1973.

THE NETHERLANDS, THE UNITED STATES, AND THE HELSINKI PROCESS, 1972–1989

━━━

FLORIBERT BAUDET

In October 1973 the Dutch deputy minister of foreign affairs, Peter Kooijmans, visited Washington for discussions with George Springsteen, the U.S. assistant undersecretary for Western Europe. Part of the meeting centered on the Conference on Security and Co-operation in Europe (CSCE) that had recently started in Geneva, and in this context Springsteen reproached the Dutch for their lack of realism. Five days earlier, the Netherlands had filed a proposal that should guarantee (or rather, reestablish) the right to self-determination of the peoples in Eastern Europe,[1] indicating that the long-term aim was to emancipate the region from Soviet domination. This aim was difficult to reconcile with U.S. policy under President Nixon, who strove to improve relations with the Soviet Union. In the declaration issued on the occasion of the signing of the ABM Treaty, in May 1972, the United States seemed to recognize the Soviet concept of peaceful coexistence and the division of Europe.[2] The Dutch proposal was diametrically opposed to this concept. A Soviet-dominated Eastern Europe was a fact of life, Springsteen held. Kooijmans retorted that this only proved the importance of the Dutch proposal.

The incident produced the immortal phrase "Dutch cabaret," coined by Henry Kissinger, who for several reasons disliked the CSCE and opposed including human rights in international diplomatic talks. Some time afterwards, when Max van der Stoel, the then minister of foreign affairs, visited Moscow, Soviet leader Brezhnev frankly told him that he did not appreciate Dutch cabaret. Kissinger's derogatory characterization had struck a chord at the Kremlin.

This article will focus on some aspects of Dutch-American relations with regard to the CSCE, with emphasis on the period after 1975. In that year the Final

4

—

THE
COLD WAR
AND
BEYOND

1945–2009

—

POLITICS
AND
SECURITY

Act was signed and it was agreed that the implementation of its contents be reviewed every three years or so. This happened at three subsequent conferences: in Belgrade in 1977–78, in Madrid between 1980 and 1983 (with interruptions), and, finally, in Vienna from 1986 until 1989. At this last conference, East and West made much progress and it may be seen as a prelude to the historic events of 1989. The central question to be considered here is whether the Netherlands was an example for the United States. As will become clear, this question, although seemingly somewhat exaggerated, is quite justified.

From the diplomatic incident just described it might be concluded that before the signing of the Final Act the Netherlands and the United States thought very differently about the importance of CSCE. To some extent this is true. Although some Dutch politicians were hoping for a lasting détente between East and West, the Dutch foreign ministry was skeptical about this. "We are too realistically minded" ("Daar zijn wij te nuchter voor"), said a high-ranking civil servant.[3] The foreign ministry had a strongly ideological mindset according to which one could not safely deal with the Soviet Union. It would have preferred to stay out of a conference on security issues but because most NATO allies wanted to take part, the Netherlands had to as well. Foreign Ministers Norbert Schmelzer (Catholic Party, 1971–73) and Max van der Stoel (Labor Party, 1973–77, 1981–82) expected little from the conference, yet felt that whatever was agreed to should never be interpreted as a victory for the communists. It was the Soviet bloc that wanted a conference. Therefore it served no purpose to present proposals that were readily acceptable to the East. On the contrary, if Moscow wanted détente it should prove its good intentions by making substantial concessions to satisfy crucial Western demands. This feeling inspired intransigence and tough negotiating tactics, which gave credence to the Soviets' frequently voiced suspicion that the Netherlands intended to sabotage détente between East and West.

For political as well as financial reasons the Netherlands did have an interest in negotiations on mutual and balanced force reductions (MBFR), and it wanted CSCE to have a strong military dimension as well. Détente was indivisible. Furthermore, tangible results such as verifiable force reductions and substantial confidence-building measures (CBMs) would be concrete proof that the Soviets meant business. The Hague, however, did not expect the Soviets to grant quick concessions so here, too, it raised the stakes. A direct link between CSCE and MBFR did not materialize and talks about the latter soon became deadlocked. As a result, CSCE became more important to The Hague and bolstered the desire for a substantial result, such as an outright condemnation of the Brezhnev Doctrine. The CBMs also gained importance.

The U.S. had a different approach. Civil servants at the State Department shared many of the Dutch ideas. They, too, wanted to condemn the Brezhnev Doctrine and like their counterparts in The Hague felt CSCE should serve to

U.S. Secretary of State Henry Kissinger meets the press with Dutch Foreign Minister
Max van der Stoel during Kissinger's visit to the Netherlands, August 11, 1976.

4

———

THE
COLD WAR
AND
BEYOND

1945–2009

———

POLITICS
AND
SECURITY

drive a wedge between Moscow and its satellites.[4] Henry Kissinger vehemently opposed this. As mentioned above, he questioned the wisdom of CSCE, but primarily for practical reasons. It was a forum for thirty-five states, including such small ones as Luxembourg, the Vatican, and Malta, and any one could block decisions. Kissinger did not like *Kleinstaaterei*. CSCE, he disparagingly remarked in 1975, was a kindergarten. He also was prone to acting without prior consultations with the allies, which was cause for arguments within NATO.[5] Kissinger preferred direct talks with Moscow. He believed the Soviet Union essentially to be a normal state with legitimate interests. In his opinion, recognition of the status quo was an important prerequisite. Subverting it, as the Dutch proposal implied, would lead to destabilization and endanger arms control negotiations.

The Dutch distrusted Kissinger's penchant for unilateralism. In fact, they feared a *détente à l'américaine* about as much as they feared a *détente à la russe*. This distrust was fueled by uncertainty about the American commitment to European security. Would the United States for the sake of the old continent really risk the destruction of its own cities? Also, as a small state surrounded by three strong states that traditionally had dominated Europe, the Netherlands wanted a strong American role within NATO. Kissinger, however, seemed to sacrifice the smaller allies to London, Bonn, and Paris. There was a wide consensus on the Atlantic community of values that lay at the basis of NATO, but by the early 1970s even Washington's most loyal followers had grown somewhat skeptical, exactly because the United States under Nixon and Kissinger had opted for *Realpolitik*. The Netherlands wanted the Americans to lead the alliance in accordance with its ideological foundations. Still, loyalty to the Americans was never really in peril, not even when protests in the Netherlands against cruise missiles made the headlines around the world and Hollanditis seemed the latest epidemic.[6]

After Helsinki

In August 1975, the Helsinki Final Act was signed. This was of course a compromise but in Principle VIII it reaffirmed the right to self-determination of the citizens of the East European states. The Brezhnev Doctrine was incompatible with most of the Principles of the Final Act. Human rights had become a legitimate issue in international relations, as Principle VII held that people had the right to know their rights and act upon them. Taken together, Principles VII and VIII formed a program for political change in Eastern Europe. The Soviets claimed victory but in reality "Helsinki" would prove to be a defeat for them.

Arguably the most important stipulation of the Final Act was that its signatories had to reconvene regularly to review the implementation. Not only did this transform détente into a process — détente could no longer be proclaimed, it had to be proven — it also led to a discussion in the West: How was it to stimulate implementation? Would the people of Eastern Europe have a part in the process?

NATO now developed the concept of the margin of tolerance. By putting pressure on the Eastern European regimes, it would be possible to expose differences of opinion between them and Moscow, be it in form or in volume. The West could stimulate this, and in so doing gradually weaken Moscow's hold over Eastern Europe.[7] It remained unclear, however, how best to proceed. This question became urgent with the formation of such groups as the Moscow Helsinki Monitor Group and Charter '77, which demanded that their governments grant them the rights they had reaffirmed at Helsinki. Should the West support or ignore these groups? Important as they were, no one in Western Europe wanted to make human rights the only criterion for détente.

Meanwhile in the United States a new president had come to power who seemed willing to do exactly that. Carter's idealism returned the moral dimension to American politics and so contributed to regaining much of the confidence that had been shattered by the Vietnam War — even though it would be dealt additional blows as a result of Carter's policies, a clear proof of the fact that it was difficult to combine human rights standards with interests such as national security.

In the summer of 1977, around the time NATO came up with the margin of tolerance, Carter appointed Patricia Derian to the position of assistant secretary of state for human rights and humanitarian affairs. This was the culmination of a development started in the early 1970s in which Congressmen Donald Fraser, Henry Jackson, and Dante Fascell had played important roles. They, and others, strove to give human rights a prominent position in American foreign policy when Kissinger tried to exclude them. Carter followed in their footsteps.

In December 1977 Derian held talks with several Western diplomats. She explained the new American approach to human rights and said that although until then there had been few negative effects, the Americans were willing to pay a price for their ideals. Countries could not treat their citizens as they pleased. Cliff Brody, an aide to Derian, explained that the new American policy owed a lot to the Dutch example.[8] Whether this is true is difficult to establish, but this view differed fundamentally from the mocking "Dutch cabaret" comment of the Nixon-Kissinger era. In all probability the new policy owed much more to the activities of Congress and pressure groups. As it was, the Netherlands also had its problems in promoting human rights in its foreign policy. Quite often these had to give way to economic or strategic considerations.

While Derian and her aides were considering how to implement American human rights policy and in the process also studied the Dutch experience,

699

4

THE
COLD WAR
AND
BEYOND

1945–2009

POLITICS
AND
SECURITY

CSCE's first review meeting opened in Belgrade. This conference took place when relations between East and West had become tense, partly because of the continued violation of the Helsinki agreements by the communist regimes. The American delegation leader, Arthur Goldberg, parted with established diplomatic practices when he harshly and openly criticized these violations. The other participants, the Netherlands included, increasingly took issue with Goldberg's approach. Nonetheless, the Netherlands criticized the abuse of psychiatry in the Soviet Union and the oppression of signatories of Charter '77 in Czechoslovakia.[9]

Eventually, East and West parted in March 1978 with the promise to try again in September 1980. The Dutch delegation leader, Ambassador Jo van der Valk, blamed the ideological zeal of the Americans for the conference's failure. Foreign Minister Christoph van der Klaauw was duly summoned to parliament to defend these remarks. No, Van der Klaauw explained, the ambassador had been quoted incorrectly; no, his remarks did not reflect the opinion of the Netherlands government.

That summer, the arrest and sentencing of three Russian dissidents inspired The Hague to temporarily freeze its relations with the Soviet Union. The Soviets were not impressed — in fact, during this episode they claimed that bilateral relations were "better than ever before" — but apparently The Hague felt compelled to do something. This step was at least partly aimed at the Dutch opposition parties that — erroneously — believed "charm bomb" Van der Klaauw to be a weak albeit sympathetic minister who, in stark contrast to his predecessor Van der Stoel, had no interest in human rights issues. Other countries, including Great Britain, took similar steps. The Americans, however, did not break off relations. Episodes like these, and skepticism about Van der Klaauw, contributed to parliament's demand for clarity about the position of human rights in Dutch foreign policy. Politicians wanted to know in what circumstances the Netherlands would take steps, and what these steps might be. The result was a government paper that endeavored to clarify the cabinet's position.[10] In the United States, involvement from the legislature resulted in the formation of a human rights desk and, subsequently, the establishment of the position of assistant secretary of state for human rights and humanitarian affairs. In the Netherlands no such institutional changes occurred. It was not until 1983 that a task group was formed to advise the foreign minister. That same year the government created the Advisory Council on Human Rights, which consisted of external experts, while a human rights ambassador was appointed in 1999.

Reagan and U.S. Policy

Carter's hesitant reaction to a number of domestic and international crises cost him his reelection in 1980. Before the election, several people in Reagan's entourage indicated they saw human rights as a "partisan issue" that the Republicans would immediately do away with.[11] In reality, and in part because of the Democrats' continued pressure, after Reagan assumed office U.S. policy did not change much. The human rights bureau was without a director for almost a year, but human rights retained their place in the country's foreign relations as the White House now made a distinction between authoritarian and totalitarian regimes. Although not democracies, countries in the first category *did* respect several Western core values such as freedom of religion and free enterprise, and were more likely to become democracies in the long run than the totalitarian regimes of the communist world. By introducing this distinction it seemed possible, at least in theory, to promote human rights without endangering the West's alliances with noncommunist authoritarian regimes.[12]

This new approach received support in The Hague, at least from those desks that were focusing on East-West relations. As in the Carter era, in practice the Americans steered a pragmatic-principled course vis-à-vis Eastern Europe. The presidential policy papers on Eastern Europe (PD-21 [1977] and NSDD-54 [1982], respectively) do not differ fundamentally: countries that had either a liberal communist regime or leaders who tried to steer away from Moscow were encouraged. Countries that had neither were put under pressure and frequently criticized. Even if analyses differed at times, the Netherlands did basically the same.

At the same time, this approach led to dissatisfaction among those civil servants who were tasked with the Netherlands' policy concerning the United Nations and development cooperation. They feared that the new American approach, and the Dutch one that resembled it, would result in harmful politicization of human rights. As things stood, it already was fairly easy to accuse the West of selectivity. The attitude of Reagan and his "Mr. human rights," Elliot Abrams, seemed to justify this fear. The Dutch foreign ministry's NATO and Eastern Europe desks were also concerned with this approach, as they themselves had expressed during talks with Derian in 1977. But of more imminent concern was the fact that an outright politicization of human rights could endanger the realization of the long-term goal of Dutch policy with regard to Eastern Europe, namely the gradual loosening of the Soviets' hold over these parts and liberalization of the region. Human rights policy should contribute to a safer world, not to escalation of the Cold War. But how could one tell the one from the other?

4

—

THE
COLD WAR
AND
BEYOND

1945–2009

—

POLITICS
AND
SECURITY

This dilemma was manifest during the Polish crisis that started in summer 1980 when, after a protracted series of strikes, the Polish communists agreed to the establishment of a free trade union. The continued existence of the communist regime was at stake, even more so because the party did not seem able to cope with the crisis. In Moscow, but equally so in the West (including in The Hague), this situation led to increased concerns over Europe's stability. President Carter warned the Soviets against the military option, but the Soviets too preferred Polish troops to stabilize the country. In December 1981 martial law was declared and many Solidarity members and other critics of the regime were interned.

The West unanimously decided to boycott Poland. However, the U.S. and the West Europeans found it very hard to agree on the range of the boycott and the preconditions under which to end it. No doubt spurred by its large Polish community, the United States demanded tough measures. In Western Europe and especially in the Federal Republic of Germany fears grew that a hard-line reaction would only serve to intensify the Cold War, while it would not help the Poles. An overtly politically motivated reaction to violations of human rights and of the Helsinki Final Act would solve little and would in fact be counterproductive. Among the Europeans the Netherlands was closest to the Americans. The Hague did not recall its ambassador from Warsaw, as Washington had done, but it refrained from engaging in political contacts for the time being and made it clear that these would only be resumed if the Polish authorities would free the political prisoners and engage in a dialogue with the opposition. Until then, economic help would not be forthcoming either.

When contacts were finally resumed in the fall of 1984 it was only after the other Western Europeans had done so, and after the U.S. no longer opposed Polish IMF membership. The Netherlands continued its highly critical stance toward developments in Poland. It tried to engage its European partners in a hard-line approach toward Warsaw, in which it sometimes was successful. It also expressed its support for the opposition. In 1987 Hans van den Broek was the first Western foreign minister to meet with Lech Walesa. Four weeks later, U.S. Vice President G.H.W. Bush did the same, and that meeting had of course a greater impact.[13]

The Dutch approach seems to support the popular view that the Netherlands was the most "Atlantic" European member of NATO. Yet, The Hague was quite unhappy with the U.S. stance. It sympathized with Washington's tough line, but Reagan's dramatic and theatrical reaction—he supported the call from Pope John Paul II to place a candle in the window to express solidarity with the Poles—was unpopular. The Hague feared that such symbolic gestures did not serve the interests of the Polish people; it also feared a further deterioration of East-West relations.[14] Therefore it was decided to enter a resolution with the United Nations' Human Rights Commission. One reason for the Dutch to take the lead was that the Americans might enter one. Given that they were politicizing human rights (at least according to some in The Hague), it was probable that an American resolution would be blocked. So the Netherlands took the initiative, which twice resulted in a condemnation of the Polish regime. This apparent "depoliticization" of human rights of course *was* political in nature: it was the first time a communist regime was condemned.

Another issue on which opinions in Washington and The Hague differed was Jewish emigration from the Soviet Union. This issue contributed a lot to the emerging focus on human rights in the United States (such as the Jackson-Vanik Amendment, which linked granting Most Favored Nation status to the Soviet Union to its emigration policies). The Netherlands, however, had been asked by Israel in 1967 to represent its interests in Moscow. Dutch policymakers felt this task precluded outspoken reactions to Soviet (mal-)practices in this regard. To the horror of the Dutch, American diplomats castigated the Soviets during the CSCE conferences in Belgrade, Madrid, and Vienna, and no doubt also in bilateral contacts. Even so, the Netherlands made a tangible contribution: up to 1991 its embassy in Moscow would hand Israeli entrance visas to some six hundred thousand Jews who had been allowed to leave the Soviet Union.

Most of the emigrants used these Israeli visas to travel to the United States. Jerusalem did not like this and tried to force the emigrants to settle in Israel. Washington then changed its regulations so that U.S. customs would accept entrance visas for the U.S. only. The Hague, however, objected that the Israeli efforts violated the emigrants' right to choose where to live or apply for asylum.[15]

Conclusion

From this brief overview it transpires that Washington gradually changed its opinion of the Netherlands' human rights policy. After the mid-1970s reports no longer contain disparaging remarks such as "Dutch cabaret." But it is difficult to tell whether there really was a Dutch example in Washington's CSCE policy after Carter's accession. It does not seem plausible. The politicians who in the United States promoted attention for human rights drew inspiration from American idealistic traditions, which they felt should be reflected in the country's foreign relations. Some of those traditions were close to ideas that were prominent in the Netherlands. This did not mean that the two countries had identical policies. Their interests, views, and opportunities differed too much. In Europe, the Netherlands was the strongest propagator of the Final Act's human rights paragraph because it was seen as a precondition for a truly lasting peace in Europe. This attitude resembled the views that shaped American policy from Carter onward.

The view — as put forward by a Dutch foreign ministry official — that the U.S. took the lead and the Dutch simply followed in its footsteps, is incorrect. But so is the opposite view. The characterization "Dutch example" is only found once in documents relating to Dutch policies on Eastern Europe. The two countries acted together where it served their interests and when their ideas converged, but they basically pursued their own policies. There were, and still are to this day, differences of opinion between The Hague and Washington, especially concerning (the existence of) social rights and the death penalty. Such differences warrant further research into the importance (if any) of human rights in Dutch-U.S. bilateral relations.

4

——

THE
COLD WAR
AND
BEYOND

1945-2009

——

POLITICS
AND
SECURITY

704

1   Unless stated otherwise, information is taken from Floribert Baudet, *"Het heeft onze aandacht." Nederland en de rechten van de mens in Oost-Europa en Joegoslavië, 1972–1989* (Amsterdam: Boom, 2001); For the proposal, see Igor Kavass et al., eds., *Human Rights, European Politics, and the Helsinki Accord. The Documentary Evolution of the Conference on Security and Co-operation in Europe* (Buffalo, NY: William S. Hein & Co, 1981), 3:121-122.

2   "Basic Principles of Mutual Relations between the United States of America and the Union of Soviet Socialist Republics," Moscow, May 30, 1972.

3   Alfred van Staden, *Een trouwe bondgenoot* (Baarn: In den toren, 1974), 154.

4   James Goodby, *Europe Undivided. The New Logic of Peace in US-Russian Relations* (Washington, DC: U.S. Institute of Peace Press, 1998), 52-55.

5   Floribert Baudet, "'Im Osten nichts neues.' Nederland en de militaire dimensie van het CVSE-proces," *Militaire Spectator* 174.3 (March 2005): 125-130.

6   See Frank Zuijdam, *Tussen wens en werkelijkheid. Het debat over vrede en veiligheid binnen de PvdA in de periode 1958–1977* (Amsterdam: Aksant, 2002), and Remco van Diepen, *Hollanditis. Nederland en het kernwapendebat 1977–1987* (Amsterdam: Bert Bakker, 2004); Beatrice de Graaf, *Over de Muur. De DDR, de Nederlandse kerken en de vredesbeweging* (Amsterdam: Boom, 2004).

7   Baudet, *Het heeft onze aandacht*, 145-146.

8   Internal memorandum 77/16, December 15, 1977, file 1249, Directorate of Atlantic Cooperation and Security 1975–1984, Dutch Ministry of Foreign Affairs Archives.

9   Peter Baehr et al., *Human Rights in the Foreign Policy of the Netherlands* (Amsterdam/New York: Intersentia, 2002); Bert Bomert, *Nederland en Oost-Europa. Meer woorden dan daden. Het Nederlands Oost-Europabeleid geanalyseerd binnen het kader van het CVSE-proces, 1971–1985* (Nijmegen: Centrum voor Vredesvraagstukken, 1990), 102.

10 Ministry of Foreign Affairs of the Netherlands, "Human Rights and Foreign Policy, Memorandum Presented to the Lower House of the States General of the Kingdom of the Netherlands, 3 May

1979," *Proceedings of the Second Chamber of the States General (Handelingen der
Staten-Generaal)*, 1978–1979, 15 571,
nos. 1-2.

11 Washington to The Hague, February 13,
1981, file 1252, DACS 1975-1984, Dutch
Ministry of Foreign Affairs Archives.

12 This approach was adopted from the
influential article by Jean Kirkpatrick,
"Dictatorships and Double Standards,"
Commentary (November 1979), 34-45.

13 Baudet, *Het heeft onze aandacht,*
162-163.

14 Toby Witte, "Met een kaars voor het
raam. Nederland en de Poolse crisis
van 1980–1982", in Duco Hellema and
Toby Witte, eds, *"Onmachtig om te
helpen." Nederland en de socialistische
dreiging* (Amsterdam: Het Spinhuis,
1995), 131-142.

15 Petrus Buwalda, *They Did Not Dwell Alone*
(New York: Praeger, 1997).

4

—

THE
COLD WAR
AND
BEYOND

1945–2009

—

POLITICS
AND
SECURITY

706

DUTCH-AMERICAN
RELATIONS DURING THE
SECOND COLD WAR

—

HANS RIGHOLT

One of the Weakest Links?

Between 1977 and 1985, the planned modernization of NATO's nuclear arsenal in Europe became a highly divisive issue in Dutch society and politics. As the public outcry against the introduction of "the neutron bomb" was followed by massive protest rallies against the placement of nuclear-armed American cruise missiles on Dutch soil, successive Dutch governments were forced to postpone a decision on deployment for nearly six years.

In scholarly works on Dutch foreign policy the Dutch resistance against nuclear force modernization is generally seen as the culmination of a period that started with the Vietnam protests of the late 1960s, in which the traditional Dutch loyalty vis-à-vis NATO and the U.S. was replaced by a more critical attitude.[1] According to some, the Dutch had even earned themselves the reputation of being one of the weakest links within the NATO chain at the time.[2]

Most notably at the level of government, the above analysis seems to overstate the extent as well as the importance of the changes that took place in the Dutch attitude and policies toward the U.S. and NATO during the period under consideration: despite the more critical attitudes of especially the younger part of the population, the Dutch governments remained as loyal as could be expected. This was true during the late 1960s, when the conservative long-time Foreign Minister Josef Luns simply refused to convey parliamentary criticism of the Vietnam War to the U.S. government. It was also true in 1973 when the most left-wing government in Dutch history, during what is generally considered an absolute low point in European-American relations, fully supported Israel and the U.S. during the October War. Whether it was also true during the late 1970s and early 1980s will be considered below.

The Waning of Détente?

Just as 1973 is considered a low point in Atlantic relations, 1975, with the official recognition in Helsinki of the Russian sphere of influence, has been termed the high point of détente. In the U.S., however, a growing number of critics started to feel their government was giving away the store. While Washington had been preoccupied with Vietnam and had seriously cut its defense budget afterwards, the Soviets had kept increasing theirs, so that by 1975 — aside from their conventional superiority — they owned about the same number of nuclear warheads as the U.S. Moreover, it seemed the Soviets were capitalizing on their military build-up by supporting proxy forces in the Third World, like the North Vietnamese, who in 1975 overran South Vietnam, or Fidel Castro, who sent Cuban troops to Angola.

In the lead-up to the 1976 presidential campaign, President Gerald Ford was already advised to refrain from mentioning the word détente. By using that tactic he just managed to fight off Californian Governor Ronald Reagan during the Republican primaries, but in a television debate with Democratic candidate Jimmy Carter, he got so mixed up that he even denied there was such a thing as a Russian domination of Eastern Europe. In the end, the legacy of Vietnam and Watergate and the assault on the détente policies of the Nixon/Ford/Kissinger team proved too much to overcome, and Ford ended up narrowly losing the November 1976 elections to Carter.[3]

In his inaugural address Carter underlined his global support for human rights and even promised to work toward the ultimate elimination of all nuclear weapons. For the center-left Dutch government of Joop den Uyl, with its foreign policy emphasis on human rights and the reduction of the role of nuclear weapons, a period of good working relations with Washington seemed to lie ahead, especially after Den Uyl's Labor Party (PvdA) won the May 1977 elections. Things turned out differently, however.

As early as 1976 the Soviets had started to deploy new and improved intermediate-range nuclear weapons aimed at Europe: the SS-20s. Quite a few Europeans, and many of the American critics of détente as well, saw this as a serious threat since these tactical nuclear weapons fell outside the scope of either the SALT negotiations on limiting strategic nuclear arsenals or the MBFR talks on reducing conventional forces in Europe. To them it meant that the USSR was circumventing these negotiations, and was creating a situation in which it could blackmail Western Europe politically.

At the same time, the Russians seemed not at all intent on honoring the human rights provisions they had agreed to in Helsinki. Relations between Brezhnev and Carter soured almost immediately, as a result of Carter's belief that ne-

4

—

THE
COLD WAR
AND
BEYOND

1945–2009

—

POLITICS
AND
SECURITY

gotiations on SALT II could go hand in hand with American criticism of Soviet human rights violations. Likewise, during the spring of 1977, Dutch Foreign Minister Van der Stoel's visit to Prague was cut short by the Czechoslovak government as a result of a meeting he had set up with a member of the Charter '77 group of Vaclav Havel.[4]

The Neutron Bomb

By late 1977 an almost uninterrupted twelve-year period of center-right rule commenced in the Netherlands. Back then, this was not self-evident at all, however. Den Uyl's PvdA had won the parliamentary elections handsomely, gaining ten seats in the 150-member house, thus defeating the Christian democrats (CDA) by fifty-three to forty-nine seats. But negotiations for a new coalition government dragged on for almost six months, and an overbearing Den Uyl finally ended up driving the CDA into the arms of the conservative Party for Freedom and Democracy (VVD). With a combined seventy-seven seats this first Van Agt cabinet owned an extremely narrow majority in parliament, and it would have to deal with the opposition of a frustrated PvdA. Since the CDA consisted of the three major religious parties of old that were still in the process of merging in order to stop their electoral decline, there was a lot of instability and political infighting in this major governing party, too. In the ranks of the Protestant Anti-Revolutionary Party (AR) seven parliamentarians had leftist, even pacifist, inclinations. They had favored a coalition with the PvdA and now vowed to be loyal to the center-right government only if they could do so with a clear conscience. These "loyalists," as they were called, would play a key role in the political debates on security of the late 1970s and early 1980s.[5]

A first such debate had emerged during the summer and fall of 1977, when the U.S., despite Carter's professed nuclear pacifism, tried to get allied approval for the eventual introduction into the NATO arsenal of the Enhanced Radiation Reduced Blast Weapon (ERW), a nuclear grenade that would be able to immobilize Soviet tank formations without damaging the surrounding civilian areas. Unfortunately, the ERW soon became known to the public at large as the weapon that killed people and left buildings standing: the neutron bomb.

As the ERW would have to be used at the frontline, which meant in Germany, West German Chancellor Helmut Schmidt was put in a difficult position by this American initiative. The left wing of his socialist party (SPD) was adamantly opposed to the introduction of a nuclear grenade, believing it would lower the threshold for a nuclear war in Europe. But Schmidt himself was a strategic realist who had great worries about the Soviet military build-up. He was inclined to support the U.S., but needed international support in order to sell such a decision at home. He therefore stipulated that at least one other continental European NATO member should join Germany in introducing the ERW. The Netherlands was thought of as one of the more likely candidates.

While negotiations for a new government dragged on, the Den Uyl government could get away with not taking a clear standpoint on ERW, but as soon as the Van Agt government was installed in December, a position had to be taken. Although Prime Minister Van Agt was determined to set out on an unconditional, pro-Atlantic course, he immediately encountered some serious opposition as protest rallies organized by the electorally marginalized radical left to "Stop the Neutron Bomb" were joined by the PvdA and various church groups. Within the ranks of the CDA both the "loyalists" and Defense Minister Kruisinga denounced the introduction of the ERW. As Van Agt and his Minister of Foreign Affairs Van der Klaauw tried to push their support for the ERW, Kruisinga even resigned in March 1978.

By this time, Jimmy Carter was struggling with some moral doubts of his own, and when it became clear that Europeans were trying to postpone a decision until after the U.S. had produced the ERW, he decided to cancel its development. Why produce a weapon that was of use only in Europe, without European consent to deploy it there, he reasoned. For the struggling Dutch government this provided a welcome relief. But Helmut Schmidt was furious. The German chancellor had put his political life on the line in order to support the U.S., and now all of a sudden Carter had cold feet. Many Washington officials were equally surprised and annoyed by Carter's handling of the situation. If nothing else, the ERW would have been an ideal bargaining chip. It could have been traded for tanks in MBFR, or even for the SS-20s. Now these options were lost. As the ERW affair turned into a debacle, allied discussions about countering the SS-20 threat were gaining momentum.[6]

The Euro-Strategic Balance

By 1977, U.S. defense specialists had already been contemplating for years how to make use of the emergent cruise missile technology, and they had finally come to the conclusion that the cruise missile should in time take over the nuclear tasks of the air force. This way, manned aircraft, that were anyway much too vulnerable to a nuclear surprise attack, could be made available for conventional tasks, for which they were badly needed. At the same time, people like Georgia Senator Sam Nunn saw the cruise missile as an excellent replacement for much of the aged stockpile of U.S. short-range tactical nuclear weapons in Europe. But as long as the cruise missile had not reached the production phase, this was not more than speculation.

4

———

THE
COLD WAR
AND
BEYOND

1945–2009

———

POLITICS
AND
SECURITY

A trigger was provided, however, by a speech that Helmut Schmidt gave in London, in October 1977, in which he briefly warned against the disturbance of the balance of nuclear forces in Europe. This Euro-strategic balance, as Schmidt called it, was a new concept, although it did not just drop from the skies in 1977. Europeans had been insecure about the American nuclear guarantee for a long time. What the Schmidt speech did, however, was to drive home to the U.S. government the notion that without a Europe-based counter to the ss-20s both the Russians and the Europeans could indeed calculate that the U.S. might not be willing to risk Boston over Amsterdam. And so consultations with the Europeans on what would become known as Intermediate-Range Nuclear Forces (INF) started at the end of 1977 and lasted throughout 1978.

This time the U.S. government clearly took the lead in the decision-making process. The initial European reaction was quite positive. After the neglect the European NATO allies felt they had suffered during the Vietnam era, when especially the Nixon administration had failed to consult them on almost anything, the U.S. now finally seemed ready seriously to commit itself to the Atlantic partnership again. "Thank God, the Americans are back," a high-ranking Dutch official reportedly exclaimed when he heard of the American initiative. In Washington, people realized quite clearly, however, that the initial European excitement might not last. Once Washington had decided by late 1978 that allied consensus would have to be reached within a year's time, Undersecretary of State for European Affairs David Aaron commented: "There's a lot of happy faces in Europe now, but just wait till we tell them what number of missiles, and in which countries."

Toward a Two-Track Decision

As a result of a summit in Guadeloupe between American, German, British, and French heads of government in January 1979, the allied defense specialists in the so-called High Level Group (HLG) began finalizing their conclusions. The outlines of the program soon became clear: by December 12 a unanimous decision would have to be made on the placement of a total of two hundred to six hundred INF in as many European NATO countries as possible.

Again, Schmidt had stipulated that at least one other continental country should join West Germany in stationing INF. With France not being militarily integrated in NATO, the Greek-Turkish relation being too complicated, Portugal being too far away, Luxembourg simply being too small, and the Scandinavian countries historically being opposed to stationing nuclear weapons on their soil during peace time, the pressure was on Italy, Belgium, and the Netherlands to join the UK and Germany in accepting the deployment of cruise missiles.

Even so, considering the strength of the Italian communist party and the strong opposition to nuclear weapons that the ERW affair had triggered in both Belgium and the Netherlands, U.S. officials were concerned that one or more of these countries might fail to come through. Partly to make the program more resilient to this sort of political attrition, they chose to push for the high number of 572 missiles, of which Belgium and the Netherlands would have to take 48 each. This way, if these countries indeed failed to participate, NATO's intermediate-range force would still create a credible deterrent to Moscow's much larger INF, if only by way of linking NATO's conventional defense to America's strategic forces.

To protect allied consensus, the U.S. tried to make concessions where this was possible. In response to German and Dutch wishes, it was decided that at least an equal amount of the older short-range missiles should be withdrawn. Another, more difficult, concession had to do with arms control negotiations with the Russians. Europeans, and again especially the Germans and the Dutch, had insisted that negotiations with Moscow on INF should be initiated right away. Although they feared this might inadvertently lead to a "negotiations first" approach, which would give the Soviets the power to frustrate the implementation process, the Americans finally caved in. And so it was decided that the modernization track and the negotiation track would run parallel to each other.

During the spring and summer David Aaron was sent on a couple of European tours to convince the allies that this time the president was utterly committed to the program. These bilateral consultations were also meant to give the allies a last chance to influence the U.S. proposal before it would become set in concrete after introduction in the IILG. For the center-right Dutch government, no matter how inclined it was to staunchly follow the American lead, it seemed clear that it would be impossible to get a majority in parliament: relations with the leftist opposition were completely polarized, and within the CDA the "loyalists" would never vote in favor of a positive decision either. Possibly hoping the storm would once again blow over, the Dutch government passed up this last opportunity to influence the final proposal by telling Aaron they would have to await the recommendations of the HLG before they could politically address the deployment program at home. Although Americans appreciated the dire political situation for the Dutch government and were confident that "the doughty Dutch" would join the program as soon as they had found the political leeway to do so, they still felt the Dutch government was making a serious mistake by sticking its head in the sand.[7]

711

Once the final HLG recommendations came out in October, it became crystal clear that the cruise missile issue was there to stay and could not be avoided any longer. In a last-ditch attempt to avoid a cabinet crisis, Defense Minister Scholten and CDA Party Chairman Ruud Lubbers shot off a whole range of un-

4

⸺

THE
COLD WAR
AND
BEYOND

1945–2009

⸺

POLITICS
AND
SECURITY

coordinated and totally unacceptable policy alternatives, like proposing to cut the number of 572 missiles in half—without even then being able to guarantee Dutch participation.

In the end Prime Minister Van Agt had to explain to the various allied heads of government that the Netherlands would have to postpone a decision on deployment for two years, by which time the matter would be revaluated on the basis of progress made in the arms control negotiations with the Russians.

Obviously, the allies were annoyed by this Dutch reservation. But as long as the Dutch only postponed and did not out of hand reject deployment, they seemed to be able to live with it. One important reason was that, to everyone's surprise, the Italians had immediately agreed to fulfill their role in the deployment program. Having been left out of the Guadeloupe summit earlier that year because of their Eurocommunist credentials, they now passionately wanted to reclaim their place at the "big boys" table. On December 12, 1979 the Dutch reservation was included in a secret, unpublished clause attached to the decision document, which was signed by all member states.[8]

A Continuing Stalemate

Having its hands tied by parliament on the deployment issue, the Dutch government could not have done much more in December 1979 in the way of supporting NATO's two-track program than to sign it and postpone a decision on deployment until after the next elections. In the meantime it could hope for a positive outcome of the arms control talks between Washington and Moscow, or a better election result in 1981. Neither would materialize, however. The Soviet invasion of Afghanistan in late December 1979 gave the death blow to the détente process. The chance of negotiations with the Russians leading to anything in the foreseeable future seemed to decrease even more after the election of Republican hardliner Ronald Reagan in November 1980. Moreover, during the Dutch parliamentary elections of 1981, the center-right governing coalition lost its majority, making PvdA membership in the next cabinet all but unavoidable.

During negotiations for a center-left second Van Agt government it was decided, however, that INF was such a divisive issue that it could not be addressed. In late November 1981 the first massive protest rally of the Dutch peace movement took place, as an enthusiastic crowd of over four hundred thousand took to the streets of Amsterdam. In December the government decided to postpone a decision on deployment for another two years. For the Americans, this was a somewhat comforting thought as their major concern had been to avoid a Dutch "no" in these difficult political circumstances.

Queen Beatrix of the Netherlands addresses a session of Congress
during her visit to the United States to celebrate two hundred years of bilateral
diplomatic relations, April 21, 1982.

4

—

THE
COLD WAR
AND
BEYOND

1945–2009

—

POLITICS
AND
SECURITY

The spring of 1982 saw some striking acts of anti-Americanism in the major Dutch cities, as popular criticism of U.S. involvement in Central America reached a high point after the shooting of four Dutch journalists by the military junta of El Salvador. When memorial crosses were placed in front of the American consulate in Amsterdam, Ambassador Dyess even threatened to close the consulates in the big cities, stating that the American diplomatic mission could not "operate in an environment like a circus." In these circumstances it was a good thing for Dutch-American relations that the struggling center-left government headed by Van Agt was soon replaced by a much more viable center-right coalition under the leadership of his successor, Ruud Lubbers. The appointment of Hans van den Broek as the new minister of foreign affairs looked especially promising, as his strong Atlantic outlook seemed to hark back to the heyday of Dutch Atlanticism during the 1960s. But he, too, had to take the "loyalists" within the CDA into account.

In late October 1983 the Dutch peace movement organized a second major protest rally. This time, at the high point of the second Cold War, the atmosphere was grim. In September the Soviets had shot down a civilian Korean airliner and on October 25 the U.S. had invaded Grenada. In Germany, Italy, and the UK the first new missiles were about to arrive according to schedule. Still lacking a clear majority in parliament, the Dutch government had to postpone a decision on deployment once more.

By early 1984 a few things had changed, however. First of all, now that the first missiles had arrived in Germany, there was no longer the risk of a Dutch or Belgian "no" seriously upsetting the deployment program. At the same time the Reagan administration, possibly with an eye on the forthcoming elections, began creating a better atmosphere for arms control negotiations with Moscow. The Dutch government felt it was now opportune to try to force the issue. In June 1984 a skilful compromise was crafted: if the number of Russian SS-20s were to increase by November 1985, the Dutch would allow the deployment.

In October 1985, in a last attempt to turn the tide, the Dutch peace movement managed to collect nearly four million signatures against cruise missiles in the Netherlands. It was to no avail. Intelligence showed that even under the new leader, Michael Gorbatsjov, the USSR had further increased the number of SS-20s. There would be no backtracking this time. Even the Belgians had endorsed deployment during the summer, and although there was pressure to await the results of the Washington summit between Reagan and Gorbatsjov later that month, the Dutch government finally gave its consent in early November. However, because of the INF treaty that was signed by Gorbatsjov and Reagan in 1987, the missiles never arrived in the Netherlands.[9]

One of the Weakest Links?

If we take into account the fact that the Dutch governments of the second Cold War period were among the few allied governments to stand by the U.S. on issues like Iran, Afghanistan, and the Middle East, it seems clear in retrospect that they remained as loyal as could reasonably be expected. And although the cruise missile issue might have been handled more vigorously at times, it is difficult to see how the outcome of even that most critical issue could have been much better. During the late 1970s and early 1980s a number of international and domestic circumstances combined to create a stalemate in Dutch politics on NATO's nuclear force modernization that could only be broken once most of these circumstances had started to shift by early 1984.

At the level of public opinion there may have been some reason to view the Dutch as a weak link in the NATO chain, but then only as one of many weak links. Antinuclear protests were widespread in most other member states, including the U.S. Notwithstanding the genuine fear of a nuclear holocaust, the Dutch peace movement was to a degree also a product of the polarization in Dutch politics: some 90 percent of the participants in the mass demonstrations voted for left-wing parties. Support for NATO membership remained high in the Netherlands: throughout the entire period 75 percent of the population was in favor.[10]

Last but not least, the political and military effects of the Dutch reservation remained small. Politically, the Dutch position never seriously endangered the NATO consensus on INF deployment. Despite opposition in their own country, the Germans went ahead with deployment on schedule. A Dutch "no" that might have upset affairs in the other basing countries before the fall of 1983 was never considered an option. Militarily, the Dutch reservation was of no importance at all, as the Americans had already reckoned with it in their choice for a high number of missiles. The Dutch attitude toward NATO and the U.S. during the 1970s and early 1980s was therefore in no way an aberration.

1   A. van Staden, "De rol van Nederland in het Atlantisch bondgenootschap. Wat veranderde en wat uiteindelijk bleef," in N.C.F. van Sas, ed., *De kracht van Nederland. Internationale positie en buitenlands beleid* (Haarlem: Becht, 1991), 219-231.

2   W. Laqueur, "Hollandits: A New Stage in European Neutralism," *Commentary* 72.2 (August 1981): 19-26.

3   D.H. Allin, *Cold War Illusions* (London: Macmillan, 1994).

4   F. Baudet, *"Het heeft onze aandacht." Nederland en de rechten van de mens in*

4

———

THE
COLD WAR
AND
BEYOND

1945–2009

———

POLITICS
AND
SECURITY

Oost-Europa en Joegoslavië, 1972–1989
(Amsterdam: Boom, 2001).

5 P.G. Kroeger and J. Stam, *De rogge staat er dun bij: Macht en verval van het* CDA *1974–1998* (Amsterdam: Balans, 1998).

6 G. Lundestad, *The United States and Western Europe since 1945. From "Empire" by Invitation to Transatlantic Drift* (Oxford: Oxford University Press, 2005).

7 J.A. Thomson, "Evolution of U.S. Theater Nuclear Policy: 1975–1979" (unpublished RAND paper, June 1988). Having been on the staff of the Office of the Secretary of Defense from 1974 until 1977, Dr. Thomson was a member of the National Security Council staff at the White House between 1977 and 1981, where he was primarily responsible for defense and arms control matters related to Europe. As such, he was the American representative in the High Level Group. In 1981 he joined RAND and has been its president and CEO since 1989.

8 B. van Eenennaam, *Achtenveertig kruisraketten. Hoogspanning in de lage landen* (The Hague: SDU uitgeverij, 1988).

9 R. van Diepen, *Hollanditis. Nederland en het kernwapendebat, 1977–1987* (Amsterdam: Bert Bakker, 2004).

10 J. Joffe, "Peace and Populism: Why the European Anti-Nuclear Movement Failed," *International Security* 11.4 (spring 1987): 3-40.

AMERICAN AND DUTCH POLICIES TOWARD THE REORIENTATION OF NATO AFTER THE COLD WAR

———

BRAM BOXHOORN

Introduction

Two major events in Europe at the end of the twentieth century, German reunification (1990) and the disintegration of the Soviet Union (1991), caused great concern as well as confusion within the national and international political communities. The questions that arose were enormous. What new roles, if any, were left for organizations such as the UN, NATO, Organization for Security and Co-operation in Europe (OSCE), and the EC (EU)? Initially, the UN seemed the appropriate body to provide leadership when dealing with international disputes. After decades of deadlock in the Security Council because of the Cold War, new opportunities appeared on the horizon. The common stance of the Great Powers in the UN's Security Council during the Gulf War (1991) seemed to confirm this change.

Geography came back as a subject in (European) international relations. One of the most important questions was how to act toward Central Europe. What would the strategic *Neuordnung* in Europe after the Cold War look like? How could the resurgence of old historical patterns in Europe be prevented? What measures should be taken to include Central Europe and Russia in the international system? And, related to these questions, what were the roles of NATO and the EU in this new order? Did NATO still serve a useful purpose after the loss of a common threat? And did any common interest remain between the North American and European partners?[1]

The basic issues that NATO needed to address were at least threefold and closely related to each other. First, what would or should be its future core

4

—

THE
COLD WAR
AND
BEYOND

1945–2009

—

POLITICS
AND
SECURITY

tasks? Second, should it admit new members? And third, what reform measures were internally needed for its command structure, the so-called internal adaptation? Manifold studies were produced in NATO's headquarter in Brussels to this end. This was no easy task since NATO's intergovernmental structure prevents quick decision making when allies' opinions diverge. Quite appropriately, the Brussels decision-making process in the 1990s has been labeled a "battle for consensus" (Rob de Wijk). Opinions differed in particular on the question of potential new tasks, such as conflict prevention and crisis management (the so-called non-article V operations), as opposed to the "classical" task of collective defense, as worded in article V of the Washington Treaty.

The U.S. in particular advocated a major change in NATO's responsibilities, fearing that NATO could lose its legitimacy in the post-Cold War era should it stick solely to the article V assignment and refuse to take in new member countries. Because of the differences of opinion, NATO postponed making decisions by first choosing the bureaucratic approach and by founding new institutions. As a first practical result of this strategy the North Atlantic Cooperation Council (NACC, 1991) and the Partnership for Peace program (PfP, 1994) came into existence. The NACC became the first Euro-Atlantic consultation platform for NATO and (former) Warsaw Pact countries, together with other OSCE members.

The enlargement debate was closed in July 1997 when NATO agreed to invite Poland, the Czech Republic, and Hungary to begin accession talks. The issue of a potential new role for NATO was finally settled in a new strategic concept, the not-so-philosophical document that serves as a basic guideline for NATO's policies, approved during the NATO summit in 1999.

The Route to Enlargement

Soon after German reunification European political leaders discussed the prospects of enlarging the EU and NATO. In this way, the argument ran, Central Europe would profit from the stabilizing and pacifying effects of both organizations. These positive effects were appreciated and recognized not only by Western political leaders, but also by a new generation of Central European leaders. The failure of all major international institutions (OSCE, EU, UN) to deal effectively with the civil war in the former Yugoslavia contributed to the desire of Central Europe's political elite to seek closer contact with NATO, notwithstanding the Russian-German agreements at the time of German reunification about the undesirability of NATO enlargement in an easterly direction. This initial German self-restraint served as a sort of compensation for the "loss" of Russian influence in Central Europe. This "lesson" was ignored, however, by the new Central European political leaders, as Jonathan Eyal has rightly put it.[2]

Germany's new role as Europe's post-Cold War "medium-heavyweight power" (Timothy Garton Ash) soon came to the fore in the Yugoslavian crisis (1991–95). Germany's unilateral recognition of the former Yugoslav republics of Croatia and Slovenia in 1991 signaled the start of a series of unforeseen and devastating developments on the territory of the former Yugoslavia that were beyond the international community's control. The German government then slowly but steadily accepted the idea that integration of Central Europe into the EU and NATO was the only way to avoid difficult historical choices and to promote stability along Germany's eastern borders. German Defense Minister Volker Rühe played a key role with a groundbreaking speech at the International Institute of Strategic Studies in London in March 1993. While not having informed his own foreign ministry or his chancellor regarding his views, he strongly advocated NATO enlargement.

Rühe's speech subsequently inspired the American Senator Richard Lugar to address the issue.[3] Although it took some time before President Clinton dropped his predecessors' "Russia first" policy, once the American president had changed his mind he promoted the idea enthusiastically to his European colleagues. Clinton further pushed the issue, to the chagrin of many European allies, by openly announcing at the end of 1993 that "the question is no longer whether NATO will take in new members, but when and how."[4] A familiar pattern in transatlantic relations then developed in which the European allies, irritated by Clinton's announcement, regularly complained about a lack of consultation. However, the U.S. administration by that time feared that NATO enlargement would be linked with the simultaneous process of EU enlargement. Since the U.S. was not able to influence that discussion, it feared becoming sidelined within NATO should the principle of parallelism be applied. The U.S. thus followed basically its own agenda at its own pace. The central aspect in Clinton's approach involved not simply enlarging "old" NATO but enlarging a modernized NATO, by broadening the collective defense task to collective security missions, including some outside NATO territory.

Not all European allies embraced these ideas, though at the meeting of defense ministers at Travemünde in October 1993 Dutch Minister of Defense Relus Ter Beek (member of the Labor Party) declared himself in favor of NATO enlargement. For some time the official Dutch stance was, however, that the so-called royal way regarding enlargement needed to be followed. It implied that countries needed to become EU members before being allowed into WEU and NATO. On November 12, 1993 the Dutch government still argued that allowing even a limited number of Central European countries into NATO could have a destabilizing effect. The whip of the Dutch Liberal Party (VVD), Frits Bolkestein, was most passionately opposed to NATO enlargement. His major argument was that it would unnecessarily provoke Russia, and he introduced a resolution in

719

4

—

THE
COLD WAR
AND
BEYOND

1945–2009

—

POLITICS
AND
SECURITY

parliament in March 1997 to the effect that "NATO enlargement under the present circumstances must be rejected." By that time, however, the political tide in parliament had changed and a large majority, including the major opposition party — the Christian democrats — rejected the resolution. A prominent detail in the parliamentary debate was that Bolkestein's party was a member of the "purple" coalition government (Liberal-Labor). Thus, Minister of Defense Joris Voorhoeve (a member of Bolkestein's party) defended the pro-enlargement position on behalf of the government.[5]

But even in the Pentagon many critical voices could be heard, particularly in view of the announced budget cuts (the so-called peace dividend) and the expected extra costs for the alliance in case of future enlargement.[6] Besides, not everyone was convinced of the strategic merits. The legendary George Kennan was fiercely opposed and did not mince his words in public discussions.

The relationship with Russia was indeed of particular importance. The February 1995 NATO study on enlargement stated that Russia should never be granted a *droit de regard* on NATO decisions, but acknowledged at the same time that the Russian "voice" should be allowed to be heard in Brussels. Evidently, this view echoed Chancellor Kohl's stance on further developing the relationship with Russia, combining enlargement with Russian *rapprochement*. It would take years of negotiations and political bickering between Russia and the U.S. and Germany before agreement on a special consultation mechanism between NATO and Russia was reached. The final breakthrough occurred during the American-Russian summit in Helsinki, in March 1997. The Foundation Act of May 1997 established a Joint Permanent Council between NATO and Russia.[7]

The Foundation Act paved the way for the final stage of NATO enlargement. The initial skepticism of France and some of its European friends gave way to a wave of enthusiasm, with the result that more candidates appeared on the shortlist than the U.S. had suggested. France proposed Romania since it was considered to be a francophone country and thus might support France in the alliance. Italy introduced Slovenia as a candidate. The argument that the southeastern Balkan countries were underrepresented played a crucial role in the diplomatic talks. The stakes ran high at the NATO summit in Sintra, Portugal (May 1997).[8] But in the end the "beauty contest," in Madeleine Albright's words, came to a halt. France could not make a convincing case for "super enlargement," not being a full member of the alliance and having declared itself unwilling to pay an extra *franc* for enlargement. At Madrid (July1997), after heavy political bickering, a compromise formula was found. Helmut Kohl played the role of honest broker between France and the United States. Dutch Prime Minister Wim Kok gave him his support at a crucial stage in the final discussions among the political leaders.[9] Poland, the Czech Republic, and Hungary would be invited to join

NATO, while the alliance would recognize Slovenia, Romania, and the Baltic countries as aspirant members.

Transforming NATO's Core Tasks and Fora

While the debate over NATO enlargement developed in and outside government circles on both sides of the Atlantic, history unexpectedly struck back: Europe became again the cruel scene of much bloodshed. The disintegration of Yugoslavia ended in a brutal civil war that neither UN Blue Helmets nor the EU were able to bring to an end. The European leaders again turned to Washington to come to their aid. As NATO for the first time in its history became involved in military actions, the *International Herald Tribune* commented that "the United States today is again Europe's leader."[10] Needless to say, these events completely dominated the discussions on NATO's new role as a security organization. It is argued therefore that the events following Yugoslavia's disintegration determined the outcome of the new strategic concept, signed in Washington in 1999. Practice or common policies thus preceded theory.

This was anything but clear when NATO published its first post-Cold War strategic concept in November 1991. In it, the philosophy of the famous Harmel report (1967), the two-tier concept of dialogue and defense, was slightly extended with the task of cooperation.[11] Dialogue and cooperation translated into the establishment of a wide range of new institutions to achieve the new goal. As mentioned earlier, the NACC (1991) was the first in this series of new bodies. Soon becoming obsolete, it was replaced by the Euro-Atlantic Partnership Council in May 1997. The name itself, Euro-Atlantic, alluded to the fact that allied members, full or associated, no longer needed to have or feel a direct geographical bond with the Atlantic Ocean. Hence any European country, however defined, could join. Three years later the Partnership for Peace program (PfP) was founded, an initiative of the United States. Seen by some critics as a compromise substitute for enlargement, it consisted of a practical series of cooperation projects between NATO and former Warsaw Pact members, as well as with those of the OSCE. The Netherlands would become an enthusiastic member of PfP with a broad range of common exercises and practical initiatives toward the former Warsaw Pact members.

The Mediterranean dialogue (1994) became another forum for cooperation, in which six Mediterranean countries (Egypt, Israel, Jordan, Mauritania, Morocco, and Tunisia) participated. An important relationship also developed with Ukraine, one of the major successor states of the Soviet Union. The NATO-Russian dialogue was the fourth pillar in this series of dialogues and coopera-

4

—

THE
COLD WAR
AND
BEYOND

1945–2009

—

POLITICS
AND
SECURITY

tion, but it should be emphasized that this one came about as an intrinsic part of the negotiations of NATO enlargement.

In the early 1990s discussion among the allies turned to ways in which the nature of NATO's military capabilities and command structure could be altered in view of changing global political realities. One did not need a crystal ball to foresee that the concept of flexible response, aimed at the former Soviet Union, was out of date and that future conflicts would be entirely different from those envisaged during the Cold War. From the changing security situation in Europe —with more, but diverse and unpredictable, risks to stability—arose the need to create highly flexible units that could perform their tasks far away from allied (European) territory. The new forces that were required should vary according to the situation and be highly mobile. As a consequence, standing armies, formed on the basis of conscription, were ideally to be replaced by professional armies. The transformation of the Dutch armed forces in the 1990s is exemplary for these new requirements. It followed the international pattern of downsizing. Furthermore, a number of bills were introduced in parliament to transform the armed forces into a professional, expeditionary army, also outside NATO territory.[12]

At the same time, NATO opened its doors to cooperation with other international players. It declared itself ready to support WEU-led operations and develop the concept of a European Security and Defence Identity (ESDI). Both arose from a growing need Europeans, France in particular, felt to play a more autonomous role in security questions. Besides, at the beginning of the 1990s there was considerable European uneasiness about a perceived selective U.S. engagement in Europe. The WEU, defined as the EU's defense component in the Maastricht Declarations, would in this plan develop into an informal European pillar of NATO. "Separable but not separate" was the key phrase to indicate that the alliance's assets had become available for WEU-led operations. Duplication of efforts between Europe and the alliance as a whole should be avoided.[13] The other side of this coin, however, was that the U.S. would continue to have a foot in the door in the WEU's decision-making process, deflecting the development of a much-feared "autonomous" European defense effort. In this context, Les Aspin, the U.S. secretary of defense, proposed the concept of combined joint task forces (CJTF) in October 1993, i.e., quickly deployable multinational military formations. The CJTF was developed in NATO to make possible coalitions that could be formed to assume "crisis management" duties, or more precisely, military interventions. In theory, this concept should also strengthen the possibility of greater, more independent, even fully European operations with the use of NATO assets, thereby meeting the demands of European voices to make serious work of the ESDI.

NATO Secretary General Jaap de Hoop Scheffer welcomes the Ukrainian Prime Minister Julia Timoschenko at NATO Headquarters, Brussels, January 2008.

Bosnian civilians receiving new identity cards, October 1997.

4

—

THE
COLD WAR
AND
BEYOND

1945–2009

—

POLITICS
AND
SECURITY

The Dutch minister of foreign affairs, Hans van den Broek, became actively involved in these discussion. But Prime Minister Ruud Lubbers also intervened personally when he deemed it necessary. In a February 1992 letter he argued, for instance, in favor of the possibility of NATO peace-keeping operations outside the NATO area. They both spoke out frequently in favor of a division of labor between a "mandate-issuing" CSCE on the one hand and WEU and NATO as executive organizations on the other.[14]

Interestingly, the need for CJTFs became clear before the concept was fully developed on paper. The Bosnian war (1991–95) turned out to be the figurative bridge too far for a solely European peace-keeping effort. In December 1994 the North Atlantic Council decided that the point of no return had been reached in Bosnia and that NATO should move forward. This decision to intervene put an end to the gradual erosion among NATO's allies about the question of when, where, and how to draw a line against the war atrocities in Bosnia.[15] The three NATO-led operations in the Balkans, IFOR (1995), SFOR (1996), and KFOR (1999), were conducted in the still rudimentary framework of the CJTF. The Dutch armed forces actively took part in all three operations, with a sharp increase of numbers after December 1995 (end of UNPROFOR and start of IFOR). This increase is especially remarkable given the cruel scenes at Srebrenica (July 1995), a UN "safe haven." Some eight thousand male Muslim civilians were killed by Serb military units under the eyes of Dutch Blue Helmets who were not able to prevent the slaughter. The political lesson learned was that future military operations would be conducted only with NATO as a whole or in cooperation with a major (NATO) ally.

In NATO's strategic concept of 1991 crisis-management operations were still defined in the framework of article V, as a collective response and responsibility. This changed radically with the signing of the new strategic concept. The discussion among the allies on a new strategy was put on paper and approved during the 1999 NATO summit in Washington. The document repeated the alliance's broad approach to security and the need, in addition to its established collective defense role, to take on new tasks such as conflict prevention and crisis management in order to "enhance the security and stability of the Euro-Atlantic area." Hence, so-called article V and non-article V (military) operations were both officially part and parcel of NATO's political mission and would serve as its new post-Cold War legitimacy.

The new strategic concept also officially confirmed the alliance's intention "to promote wide-ranging partnerships, cooperation and dialogue with other countries in the Euro-Atlantic area." It was obvious that outreach to all countries in the undefined Euro-Atlantic area was much needed to promote and extend a form of stability. The partnerships would in practice also serve, and had served already in a number of cases, as a policy instrument for defense reform in the countries involved. NATO's enlargement would not stop, the declaration stated, since "no democratic country … will be excluded from consideration."

Many words were also used to address the need for enhancing the European dimension of NATO. The ESDI would continue to be developed, and this "process [would] require close cooperation between NATO, the WEU and, *if and when appropriate, the European Union*" [emphasis added]. This remark, although not an integral part of the strategic concept, was highly significant for two reasons. Historically, this marked the first time that NATO referred to, and apparently acknowledged, the EU as a (semi-)political-security organization. Second, this outcome not only satisfied France, and to a lesser extent Germany, but also revealed the Clinton administration's policy direction to engage the EU as a partner beyond the global economic domain.

Conclusion

The question of NATO's rationale or, to put it differently, the communality of interests among the allies was answered in response to the breakup of Yugoslavia. During the double crisis (Bosnia, Kosovo) the European military contribution was modest. Especially during the Kosovo crisis the American military delivered the bulk of the fighting power. The ten years of experience in the Balkans confirmed again the fact that American military and diplomatic support was indispensable for conflict management in Europe.

The American administration turned out to be most explicit with regard to NATO's role in the post-Cold War era. Senator Richard Lugar publicly started the American debate with his brief and apt formula that NATO should go out of area or out of business. This led to a heated political discussion among the members of the alliance on its transformation in the 1990s. The central question was what further role NATO could play in a post-Cold War world.

The political fight on enlargement in NATO, stemming from cooperation with the former adversaries after the "velvet revolutions" in the former Soviet-bloc countries, ended in 1997 when three countries were invited to begin accession talks, and with the adoption of a new strategic concept during the summit in Washington, DC (1999) that commemorated NATO's fiftieth anniversary and welcomed the three new members. In this strategic concept a compromise was found between, on the one hand, the classical task of collective defense and, on the other hand, new tasks in the field of crisis management and crisis prevention. In such operations "coalitions of the willing" (unlike traditional operations where NATO as a whole would engage) were introduced. Dutch views on enlargement initially differed from the American position, but they soon fell in line with German and U.S. views.

725

4

THE
COLD WAR
AND
BEYOND

1945-2009

POLITICS
AND
SECURITY

Partnerships were created to further extend NATO's influence in the newly defined "Euro-Atlantic" territory. This less precise geographical notion served a dual goal. First, it met the demand to expand alliance influence and, in NATO jargon, "to keep the door open" for new members. Second, it became shorthand for referring to shared common values in this area, emphasizing democracy, human rights, and the rule of law.

Looking back on NATO's reorientation in the 1990s, it is evident that the Balkan wars dominated transatlantic security relations. These wars were an unexpected occasion to legitimize the "new" post-Cold War NATO. As such, the Balkan crisis prevented a possible fragmentation of the alliance. For the Dutch, whose military quickly transformed from a Cold-War stance into an expeditionary force, the main lesson of the 1990s was drawn directly from this crisis and in particular from the devastating experience at Srbrenica: future military operations would be conducted with NATO or together with one of its major allies.

The alliance succeeded in reaching agreement on changing its core goals and organization, making use of its newly acquired experiences in three major military operations. This change could be accomplished only with heavy American intellectual input. This thinking emphasized, much faster than realized or acknowledged in Europe, the "de-Atlanticist" consequences of the end of the Cold War in the transatlantic relationship and American foreign policy in particular. These consequences were most directly experienced by Europe after 9/11.

1   The introduction is based on Bram Boxhoorn, "De NAVO en de Russische federatie'," in M. Spiering et al., *De weerspannigheid van de feiten. Opstellen over geschiedenis, politiek, recht en literatuur* (aangeboden aan W. H. Roobol)(Hilversum: Verloren, 2000), 33-42; and Bram Boxhoorn, "De NAVO en de Europese defensie. Een moeizame verhouding," *Marineblad* 114.7/8 (2004): 220-225. The question of NATO's rationale was not an entirely new one. It had already come up — surprisingly soon — after the Atlantic Treaty was signed in April 1949. In the mid-1950s the North Atlantic Council installed a group of "three wise men" to give advice on "the ways and means to improve and extend NATO cooperation in non-mili-

tary fields and develop greater unity within the Atlantic Community." Quoted in Rob de Wijk, NATO *on the Brink of the New Millennium. The Battle for Consensus.* (London/Washington, DC: Brasseys's, 1997), 1. They answered, in short, that "NATO must become more than a military alliance"; otherwise, "it would disappear with the immediate crisis which produced it." They recommended the development of an Atlantic community "whose roots are deeper even than the necessity for common defence."

2   Jonathan Eyal, "NATO's Enlargement: Anatomy of a Decision," in Anton A. Bebler, ed., *The Challenge of NATO Enlargement* (London: s.n., 1999), 22-35.

3   Ronald D. Asmus, *Opening NATO's Door. How The Alliance Remade Itself for a New Era* (New York: Columbia University Press, 2002), 31-34.

4   Eyal, "NATO's Enlargement," 26. Asmus's study clearly opposes Eyal's idiosyncratic views.

5   A peculiar incident in this context concerned the Dutch ambassador in Moscow, Baron De Vos van Steenwijk, who in a Dutch newspaper article openly criticized his own government's pro-enlargement policy. He only received an official reprimand.

6   The cost issue of enlargement played a much more important role in the debate in the U.S. than in Europe; for an American perspective, see Ronald D. Asmus et al., "What Will NATO Enlargement Cost?," *Survival* 38.3 (Fall 1996): 5-26.

7   The Council certainly was no milestone of reconciliation, as the outbreak of the Kosovo conflict in 1999 would underline. A more positive stance was taken by Karl-Heinz Kamp, "The NATO-Russian Founding Act. Trojan Horse or Milestone of Reconciliation?" *Aussenpolitik. German Foreign Affairs Review* 4 (1997): 315-324. For an analysis of the post-9/11 relationship, see Stephen Blank, *The NATO-Russia Partnership: A Marriage of Convenience or a Troubled Relationship* (Carlisle, PA: Strategic Studies Institute, 2006).

8   Asmus, *Opening NATO's Door*, 213ff.

9   Ibid., 247-248

10 Quoted in Richard Holbrooke, *To End a War* (New York: Random House, 1998), 103.

11 David S. Yost, *NATO Transformed. The Alliance's New Roles in International Security* (Washington, DC: U.S. Institute of Peace Press, 1998), 74.

12 Dutch defense expenditures entered a downward spiral, declining from 3.0 percent (1980–84) to around 1.6 percent of GDP in 2000.

13 Yost, *NATO Transformed*, 77-79. Also, the proliferation of weapons of mass destruction (WMD) became a NATO policy topic soon after the first Gulf War in 1991. For NATO and ESDI, see David P. Calleo et al., *NATO's New Strategy & ESDI. European Security in the New Millennium* (Maastricht: Cicero Foundation Press, 1999).

14 De Wijk, *NATO on the Brink,* 52-54.

15 For an elaborate discussion, see Dana H. Hillen, *NATO's Balkan Interventions*. Adelphi Paper 347. (Oxford: Oxford University Press, 2002).

4

—

THE
COLD WAR
AND
BEYOND

1945–2009

—

POLITICS
AND
SECURITY

PEACEKEEPING AND
THE WAR ON TERROR,
1989–2007

—

CHRIST KLEP

Since the end of the Cold War, Dutch defense policies and military operations have converged with American global power projection, possibly even more so than during the pre-1989 era. This convergence emerged in two areas especially: international peacekeeping operations and the war on terror. The global struggle against terrorism was initiated by the Bush administration following the attacks of September 11, 2001. In fact, the two peacekeeping operations that have dominated Dutch military deployment overseas in recent years — Afghanistan and Iraq — are rooted in the war on terror.

Since 2001 the Bush administration has implemented (be it out of sincere conviction or political opportunism) a neoconservative agenda with strong messianic overtones: the idea that Western liberal democracy could be exported— if need be, through military force and regime change. To this was added the concept of preemptive war.[1] The Bush administration did not believe that terrorists or terrorist states, possibly in possession of weapons of mass destruction (WMD), would respond to rational foreign policy instruments such as deterrence, negotiations, or the gradual raising of diplomatic or military pressure. Their irrationality justified preemptive action.

Meanwhile, in the years following the end of the Cold War, Dutch defense policy became almost entirely geared to peacekeeping operations all over the world. This reflected Dutch foreign policy in general. The Ministry of Foreign Affairs emphasized the positive aspects it considered inherent in peacekeeping operations: strengthening human rights, democracy, and Dutch international prestige and diplomatic clout. In turn, albeit with some initial reservations, Minister of Defense Relus ter Beek announced the transformation of the comparatively large, conscription-based armed forces to a downsized military organization consisting entirely of professional soldiers. Since 1993 peacekeeping operations have in fact become the mainstay of the Dutch armed forces. Military leaders accepted this development grudgingly, knowing they would have to dispose of some of their prized heavier equipment, like tanks and artillery. The armed forces were now no longer able to field a division. The basic unit of peacekeeping operations was battalion-size.

The central theme of this essay is the compatibility of Dutch and American defense policy and military operations, especially since the attacks of 9/11 and the subsequent war on terror. The starting point is the following argument: since the end of the Cold War successive Dutch governments and military authorities, faced with a wide range of uncertainties, have consistently conformed to American military leadership. Reasons for this choice will be set forth below. Suffice it to say that continuity in the American-Dutch defense relationship has outstripped the points of friction that developed or even intensified after 1989.

Points of Friction

Areas of friction will be dealt with first. From the Dutch perspective, clashes of opinion with the Americans concerned human rights and democracy promotion. To begin with, the Netherlands considers itself to be a pioneer and advocate of international law. The Hague, presented as the legal capital of the world, is home to several international courts and tribunals. Human rights figure prominently in Dutch foreign policy. Against this background, the Netherlands government felt uncomfortable with the negative fallout, in the area of international law, caused by the American war on terror and the occupation of Iraq. The lack of unambiguous consent by the Security Council for American-led interventions, like the 1999 operations against Serbia and the 2003 invasion of Iraq, did not help.

Following the regime change in Afghanistan (end of 2001) hundreds of captured Taliban and al-Qaida fighters were transferred to Guantánamo Bay, an American military facility in Cuba. According to the U.S. government, the Geneva Conventions did not apply to these fighters, meaning they would not be treated as prisoners of war. They were classified as "unlawful combatants," and were held for years without access to the American legal system until the Supreme Court upheld in June 2008 the rights of Guantánamo prisoners to challenge their detention in U.S. courts.[2] In Iraq, Saddam Hussein was removed from power in 2003. In the ensuing internal chaos and violence, news about breaches of international law committed by American troops proved persistent. Disturbing pictures from Abu Graib prison, depicting naked Iraq prisoners being tortured or receiving degrading treatment, shocked the world.

4

———

THE
COLD WAR
AND
BEYOND

1945–2009

———

POLITICS
AND
SECURITY

730

American infringements on human rights in Iraq, or as part of the global war on terror, affected Dutch foreign policy and military operations directly. In both Afghanistan and Iraq, Dutch troop contingents participated in stabilization forces: the NATO-led International Security Assistance Force (ISAF) and the Stabilisation Force in Iraq (SFIR) respectively. Both forces deployed once American offensives had resulted in regime changes in Kabul and Baghdad. This evoked sensitive questions. What would happen if Dutch troops arrested (suspected) al-Qaida or Taliban fighters? Dutch politicians and human rights activists sought assurances that these fighters would receive correct treatment in case they were handed over to Americans. This problem was especially prominent with regard to the Dutch special forces detachment that took part in the American-led operation Enduring Freedom (OEF), from 2005 onward. OEF is a no-holds-barred combat operation, aimed at liquidating any terrorist presence in southern Afghanistan. The Dutch government pledged that its soldiers would comply with the Geneva Conventions. The Dutch detachment was given authority to refuse any American command that would violate the laws of war.

Obviously, however, the level of secrecy inherent in OEF operations was high. This made it extremely difficult for outsiders — or even Dutch authorities — to determine the real situation on the ground in southern Afghanistan. Moreover, there were tenacious rumors about CIA transfers ("renditions") of suspected terrorists to secret prisons ("black spots") in Europe, Asia, and Africa. Minister of Foreign Affairs Ben Bot expressed his unease about these CIA activities. The Bush administration repeatedly assured him that no such clandestine facilities existed. In the fall of 2006, however, Bot received an unpleasant surprise when President Bush acknowledged that "a small number of terrorist leaders and operatives captured during the war have been held and questioned outside the United States, in a separate program operated by the Central Intelligence Agency."[3]

Similar Dutch unease about the human rights side of international peacekeeping operations and the war on terror surfaced elsewhere, for instance in a somewhat bizarre incident in Iraq and the resulting media and political aftermath. In November 2006 a leading Dutch newspaper, *de Volkskrant*, claimed that Dutch soldiers had been involved in the torture of Iraqi prisoners.[4] During interrogation these prisoners had allegedly been blindfolded and deprived of sleep, partly through the use of loud music and cups of water being poured on them. Apparently, no brute force had been used. Nevertheless, a "torture scandal" was born. Interestingly, a certain consensus emerged during the debate that followed the *Volkskrant* article: Dutch soldiers were simply not supposed to resort to tough interrogation techniques *at all*. Such behavior was seen as completely alien to Dutch soldiering abroad. The Ministry of Defense immediately issued orders emphasizing that all prisoners should be treated correctly.

Dutch forces in Operation Spin Ghar, Afghanistan, November 2007.
Engineers leave for a patrol with the 13th Infantry Battalion Prince Bernhard.

4

—

THE
COLD WAR
AND
BEYOND

1945–2009

—

POLITICS
AND
SECURITY

The Bush administration, in turn, harbored far fewer reservations about legal finesses. President Bush had made it clear that there was no middle course: "Every nation, in every region, now has a decision to make. Either you are with us, or you are with the terrorists."[5] Top U.S. government officials still rejected outright torture. They did admit, however, that interrogation techniques used on suspected terrorists might well, and in fact did, involve the use of physical or psychological force. The Dutch attitude toward fighting terrorism has been fundamentally different. First and foremost, most Dutchmen did not actually regard themselves as being "at war" with global terrorism. Nor have they looked at Dutch territory or Dutch assets as possibly representing high-value terrorist targets. The Dutch angle has been more gentle and cautious. The vicious murder of cinematographer and Islam critic Theo van Gogh by a young Muslim radical sent shock waves through society. This disturbing event expedited the adoption of a host of antiterrorism laws and measures. However, these were not primarily of a repressive nature. Dutch antiterrorism policy aims in the first place at preventing young Dutch Muslims from becoming (potential) terrorists, as part of a wider dialogue on how to best integrate minorities.

Characteristically, the new Dutch antiterrorism laws, though fairly numerous, have been applied quite moderately. Some measures were taken to improve collaboration between ministries and to streamline calamity responses. In line with UN and EU policies, certain organizations suspected of terrorist activities were forbidden and their bank accounts frozen. In general, however, the political and public debate on antiterrorist measures was marked — the initial shock of Van Gogh's assassination having subsided — more by concerns about possible encroachments on human rights than by fear of an imminent terrorist attack. This feeling was undoubtedly reinforced by the somewhat amateurish behavior of the small group of young people arrested for suspected terrorist activities. Antiterrorist laws received criticism as being invasive of privacy, fostering stigmatization of minorities, and burdening the already sensitive immigration debate. American demands that Dutch airline companies provide detailed information about passengers to U.S. authorities annoyed many in the Netherlands.

Furthermore, some American-Dutch friction has sprung from a related question: was it really possible to achieve quick and decisive results in building new democracies and fighting global terrorism through military intervention and nation building, especially if these attempts were based on an ambitious but ill-conceived neoconservative agenda? The reality on the ground was disturbing. Large-scale military operations against the Taliban and Iraqi forces ended quickly. Shortly thereafter, though, the U.S. and its allies became bogged down in the process of trying to rebuild what were in essence failed states. As of 2008 the Afghan and Iraqi transitions to more democratic political systems are weak and unstable. In Iraq, sectarian violence has increased, despite continuous American military efforts. In 2007 the growth of poppies in Afghanistan reached record levels. This was a clear indication that the international and Afghan war on drugs was failing. Nor has operation Enduring Freedom succeeded yet in driving Taliban and al-Qaida fighters from southern Afghanistan. This has badly undermined the work of Dutch ISAF troops in the southern province of Uruzgan. Their efforts were supposed to be aimed primarily at rebuilding the primitive and devastated society in that area, strongly emphasizing civil-military cooperation (Cimic).

Since the demise of the bipolar Cold War world, the U.S. has tried to avoid the impression that it was fighting its wars on a strictly unilateral basis, but it has consistently attempted to shape its own so-called coalitions of the willing, if only because working through the UN Security Council to obtain unambiguous mandates proved cumbersome. This, too, has caused certain strains in Dutch-American relations. In a telling March 2003 incident, during the American-led attack on Iraq, a Dutch liaison officer was invited to attend an American press conference. Before he knew what was happening, the unsuspecting officer was introduced to the audience as representing one of America's faithful allies: the Netherlands. In fact, the Dutch government had declared it would provide political but not military support. In another telling development, the Dutch government refused to extend its participation in the stabilization force SFIR in the southern Iraqi province of al-Muthanna after March 2005. The Dutch contingent had been committed for two years. Strong British (the Dutch had been operating in a British zone) and American pressure proved insufficient to persuade the Netherlands to keep the contingent deployed for another few months.

Occasionally, therefore, Dutch irritations about American behavior have been expressed. But of equal importance is the fact that the demands of diverse military operations have strained the capabilities of the Dutch armed forces to the limit. In 1993, the so-called ambition level had been set at four simultaneous peacekeeping operations at battalion level. In 2002 this level was scaled down to three parallel operations. The mission in Afghanistan especially exceeded estimates by a large margin. Wear of equipment turned out to be much higher than expected. The ministers of defense, foreign affairs, and development were at odds over who would pay the additional costs. In a closely linked development, the Dutch armed forces found it hard to recruit sufficient soldiers, especially for specialist branches like the engineer corps, medical corps, and military police. All of this reflected a lesson that many peacekeeping nations have been learning since the end of the Cold War: once initiated, these operations develop a dynamic of their own.

The Dutch government has worked hard to avoid the impression of being

733

4

___

THE
COLD WAR
AND
BEYOND

1945–2009

___

POLITICS
AND
SECURITY

America's lapdog, a negative image that stuck to Britain's Prime Minister Tony Blair. The Dutch desire to act independently, at least in the public image, was evident in both Afghanistan and Iraq where Dutch contingents were not commanded directly by Americans, but were integrated into international SFIR- or ISAF-command structures. The Netherlands government consistently emphasized that its soldiers were not part of an American-led occupation force. Their primary task was to provide security and assist the local population in rebuilding their war-torn societies. This fit with a specific "Dutch approach" aimed at winning the hearts and minds of the local population through patient negotiations and humanitarian assistance, and contrasted with the American way of doing things, which — to many Dutch observers — was more violent and aimed at protecting its own soldiers ("shoot first, ask questions later").

Uneasy It May Be: Further Convergence of American and Dutch Military Efforts

And so, on the one hand, we find Dutch unease about American breaches of international law and doubts as to whether American goals (i.e., rebuilding failed states and winning the war on terror) would be attainable. On the other hand, though, it was undeniably true that American leadership continued to be the main pillar of Dutch defense policy and military operations. Before 1989, Dutch tractability had never really been put to the test of de facto military operations on a larger scale.[6] This changed after 1989. The Netherlands could no longer avoid hard choices about the operations it was going to take part in. After all, consistently avoiding difficult international missions would have sapped the entire raison d'être of its military apparatus.

The Netherlands has contributed to nearly all major American military operations since 1989, with the exception of the first Gulf War (1990–91). No conscripts were committed to that conflict, but the Dutch government did support the American offensive, rejecting further diplomatic initiatives by France to postpone the attack against Iraq. The Dutch armed forces did contribute warships and air force assets, as well as a joint battalion of Royal Marines and engineers, to assist Kurdish refugees in northern Iraq (humanitarian operation Provide Comfort). Between 1993 and 1996 Dutch marines, military police, and warships joined U.S. forces in peacekeeping operations in Haiti. In the Balkans, Dutch F-16s joined NATO fighter aircraft in American-led bombing offensives against Bosnian-Serb forces (operation Deliberate Force, 1995) and the Yugoslav army (Allied Force in 1999, during the Kosovo crisis). After 9/11 the Netherlands supported the American attack against the Taliban regime in Afghanistan as a legitimate form of self-defense. With regard to the second Gulf War (2003), the Dutch government distanced itself clearly from antiwar states like Germany and France and interpreted Security Council resolution 1441 — which threatened Iraq with serious consequences if it did not fully disclose its WMD programs — as sufficient ground for military action. In both Iraq and Afghanistan Dutch troops assisted in what was essentially an American attempt at rebuilding failed states.

Why have Dutch authorities felt it necessary to join the United States so consistently? The principal reasons appear to be the lack of viable alternatives and a conscious (and perhaps equally emotional) preference to look at American armed forces as the standard to aim for. Concerning alternatives, no international security actor could equal American power or vigor. Dutch policymakers were patently aware of this, even if this power and vigor were rooted predominantly in Washington politics. In the immediate aftermath of the fall of the Berlin Wall, many believed the United Nations would at last assume a strong role in maintaining international security. Within a couple of years these hopes had evaporated. In Rwanda and the former Yugoslavia especially, the UN proved powerless. Blue Helmet peacekeeping forces were unable to prevent genocides in the Central African country (1994) and the UN "safe area" of Srebrenica in July 1995. The main criticism in the Netherlands was that the lightly armed Dutch peacekeeping unit (Dutchbat) in Srebrenica had been given an impossible task and was left stranded by the major powers and the UN, which did little to stop the Bosnian-Serb attack.

Leaving aside the matter of the justifiability of these reproaches, the UN became a favorite scapegoat and a synonym for indecision. It speaks volumes that the Netherlands did not commit itself to new major or risky UN peacekeeping operations. A Dutch infantry company did take part in the United Nations Peacekeeping Force in Cyprus (UNFICYP), but only for a fixed period of three years (1998-2001). This contribution was also motivated by the fact that UNFICYP had been a long-term (since 1964) and fairly low-risk operation, providing a buffer between Turkish Cypriots in the north and Greek Cypriots in the south. The Netherlands also participated in the United Nations Mission in Ethiopia and Eritrea (UNMEE) from 2000 until 2003. The backbone consisted of a Netherlands-Canadian battalion (NECBAT). Like UNFICYP, this was a "classic" buffer force, which would be withdrawn if the former warring factions went to war again. Interestingly, after pressure from Dutch parliamentarians, four Apache attack helicopters were added to the Dutch UNMEE contingent at the very last moment. However, for a number of reasons the heavily armed helicopters could not be fully deployed, their base in Djibouti being too far away from the area of operations to be useful for anything other than an immediate threat to NECBAT. The

735

4

—

THE
COLD WAR
AND
BEYOND

1945–2009

—

POLITICS
AND
SECURITY

communis opinio in the Netherlands was that the Apaches had mainly been deployed to provide a false sense of security, with the fate of Dutchbat in Srebrenica in mind.

All in all, Dutch authorities felt far more at ease with American leadership during peacekeeping operations. A NATO framework was preferred, such as the Implementation Force (IFOR, 1996) and Stabilization Force (SFOR, 1997–2004) in Bosnia-Herzegovina. Both IFOR and SFOR were tasked with enforcing the Dayton peace agreement, which imposed a political settlement on war-torn Bosnia-Herzegovina. Dutch troops were familiar with NATO's operational procedures and military culture. But the end of the Cold War had questioned the continuing purpose of NATO. The application of article V of the NATO treaty, after the terrorist attacks of 9/11, was a far cry from the treaty's original intentions. Out of necessity, the alliance changed direction, becoming a much broader organization aimed at promoting international security and cooperation. Increasingly, individual member states prioritized their national agendas and judged their commitment to NATO operations on a case by case basis, a sure sign that NATO had lost some of its coherence and sense of purpose.

In this changing and less stable NATO framework, the Netherlands was inclined to further strengthen bilateral military ties with the U.S. The continuing lack of a viable European defense alternative set the seal on this choice. During the first few years after the end of the Cold War, the Dutch government aimed at preventing a transatlantic disconnect by reinforcing European military capabilities, especially to execute peacekeeping and humanitarian operations. The Netherlands supported initiatives to create bilateral headquarters, like the German-Netherlands army corps in Münster. These headquarters took command of ISAF in Afghanistan for a period of six months in 2003.

However, European defense cooperation continued to be a slow and very laborious process. First, the main European powers remained at odds, both about defense policies in general and their support for specific military operations. For instance, France and Germany opposed the American attack on Iraq in 2003, while Great Britain, Italy, Spain, and many of the new eastern European allies actively supported President Bush's offensive. Differences of opinion about the future course of European defense have so far prevented the establishment of a genuinely European military headquarters.

Second, resources were scarce. Both NATO and the European Union launched plans for quick-intervention forces (NATO's Response Force and European Battle Groups). The result was that both organizations laid claim to the same NATO "toolbox." What is more, the contents of this military toolbox — such as strategic transport capabilities — were to a large extent American. The scope and chances of success of any large-scale European out-of-area operation would therefore always depend heavily on U.S. approval and cooperation. The only larger and longer-term European Union peacekeeping mission so far has been operation Althea (European Force, EUFOR) in Bosnia-Herzegovina since 2004, originally an almost perfect replica of the preceding NATO SFOR operation. Against the background of the now fairly stable situation in that region, EUFOR, which includes a small Dutch contingent, requires little military show of force.

Dutch skepticism about building a collective European defense structure was matched by doubts about the possibilities of initiating a concerted European fight against terrorism. Here, too, the Dutch government gave preference to bilateral arrangements with the U.S. This attitude appears to reflect a criticism often leveled against European military and antiterrorism cooperation in recent years: the widening gap between "softer" economic, monetary, and — to a certain extent — political integration on the one hand and "hard" military power on the other. The American lead in operational capabilities and military technology appears to be increasing further. Some observers explain this chasm by pointing to diverging European and American cultures, especially since 1989. Postmodern Europe invested heavily in bureaucratic-institutional structures, at the expense of state sovereignty and feelings of nationalism. This undermined attempts at creating a powerful and coherent European foreign and defense policy. The U.S., however, continued to be a strong modern state looking, as always, at military power as a legitimate extension of diplomacy. Contrary to this American "creed," Europe has grown unaccustomed to brute force and finds it difficult to apply military power against third states.[7]

The preference of Dutch governments for working with the U.S. in international military operations and the war on terrorism was, and continues to be, shared by the Dutch armed forces. The Dutch military — air force and navy especially — still considers its American counterpart as the standard to aim for. In recent years American armed forces have tended to rely even more heavily on high-tech equipment and less on sheer manpower. The Dutch military is convinced that lagging behind the Americans would soon relegate its forces to a place outside the world's military elite. The good performance of Dutch pilots in the Kosovo air war was seen by many in the Dutch air force as a confirmation that they did indeed belong to this elite. They would quote NATO's air commander in southern Europe, American General Michael C. Short: "The Dutch Air Force is a high-value Air Force, small but proud. Give those pilots an order, and they'll salute and reply: 'Yes boss, we'll be there!'"[8] Similarly, the successful participation of Dutch special forces in American-led operation Enduring Freedom was interpreted as passing an important operational test.

737

Conclusion

4

—

THE
COLD WAR
AND
BEYOND

1945-2009

—

POLITICS
AND
SECURITY

Since the end of the Cold War the United States has continued to provide the measure for Dutch security policy and military efforts. The strong emphasis on international peacekeeping and antiterrorism operations strengthened this preference. Dutch politicians and public opinion leveled heavy criticism against American breaches of human rights. They doubted whether President Bush's neoconservative goals (reshaping Iraq into a genuinely democratic state) would be attainable. However, neither the UN nor European defense initiatives ever became a credible alternative to the transatlantic bond. At the same time, the Netherlands is seen as a reliable ally by Washington. At decisive moments during peacekeeping operations and the war on terror the Dutch decided to join the American-led coalitions of the willing. This appears to be the trend for the future. "The U.S. is still our most important ally," confirmed Dutch Minister of Foreign Affairs Maxime Verhagen in 2007. "We're allies, because we share the most important values: democracy, freedom, human rights, [and] whichever way you look at it, America is a superpower and that's what you need if you want to effect these values: in the Middle East, Afghanistan, you name it."[9]

1   *The National Security Strategy of the United States of America*, Washington, DC, September 17, 2002, http://www.whitehouse.gov/nsc/nss.pdf (March 18, 2008).

2   "US Supreme Court Guantanamo Ruling," BBC News, June 12, 2008, http://www.news.bbc.co.uk/2/hi/americas/3867067.stm (June 16, 2008).

3   "President discusses creation of Military Commissions to try suspected terrorists," Washington, DC, September 6, 2006, http://www.whitehouse.gov/news/releases/2006/09/20060906-3.html (September 15, 2007).

4   "Nederlanders martelden Irakezen" (Dutch used torture on Iraqi's), *de Volkskrant*, November 17, 2006.

5   President Bush in his address to a joint session of Congress and the American people, Washington, DC, September 20, 2001, http://www.whitehouse.gov/news/releases/2001/09/20010920-8.html (August 15, 2007).

6   A possible exception can be made for the Korean War. Between 1950 and 1954 the Netherlands contributed successive infantry battalions and warships to the American-led international force under General MacArthur. The Korean War, however, would remain the only UN-sanctioned peace-enforcement operation during the entire Cold War.

7   Robert Cooper, *The Breaking of Nations: Order and Chaos in the Twenty-First Century* (London: Atlantic Books, 2003).

8   Quoted in *NRC Handelsblad*, December 18, 1999.

9   Interview in *NRC Handelsblad*, September 15, 2007.

5

THE
COLD WAR
AND
BEYOND

1945–2009

ECONOMICS
AND
SOCIETY

5

THE COLD WAR AND BEYOND

1945–2009

ECONOMICS AND SOCIETY

—

THE NETHERLANDS, THE UNITED STATES, AND THE DEVELOPMENT OF A POSTWAR INTERNATIONAL ECONOMY

—

BOB REINALDA

In 1944–45, the United States wielded its position as the world's leading political, military, and economic power to implement an institutional strategy for postwar global relations. In the Netherlands this raised the question of the extent to which Dutch and American economic interests actually concurred, and Dutch policymakers found themselves struggling to adapt to the new American policy. The turning point came when a small group of policymakers finally saw through to the crux of the institutional strategy and were able to utilize it to advance Dutch interests and to modernize the country's economy and society. The nation's business sector adopted the American model for higher industrial production capacity and innovated accordingly. Bilateral ties between the two countries were strengthened, in part through their common objectives of free trade and monetary discipline. At the same time, however, their partnership was complicated by European developments linked to the opposing notions of "Atlanticists" and "Europeans" as these functioned within the triangle of the U.S., the Netherlands, and European integration. While this divide characterized Dutch views for the duration of the postwar period, it did not hamper economic relations between the Netherlands and the U.S.

5

———

THE
COLD WAR
AND
BEYOND

1945-2009

———

ECONOMICS
AND
SOCIETY

U.S. Postwar Institutional Strategy in 1945

American political scientist John Ikenberry claims that in the aftermath of a major war, the strongest and single most dominant nation (the "hegemon") can take the lead in shaping the postwar international order. In view of the newly formed asymmetries of power, this order must be stable and mutually acceptable for strong and weak states alike. The hegemon assumes the principal role, since its pursuit of a legitimate order allows it to impose certain limitations on its own exercise of power and guide its behavior along predictable lines. Its surrender of the liberty to wield its power when and as it sees fit can be set down in jointly agreed-upon principles, rules, and institutional procedures. This *institutional strategy* may serve to ease the fear that smaller and weaker states have of domination and abandonment by the hegemon. "The more institutionalized the order, the more that participants within the order act according to defined and predictable rules and modi operandi."[1] Ikenberry describes the institutional order carried out under U.S. leadership from 1944 onward as "the most far-reaching of any postwar settlement in history." In the period between 1944 and 1951 industrially developed nations engaged in "a flurry of institution building … vastly greater in scope than in the past, dealing with issues of economic stabilization, trade, finance, and monetary relations."[2]

Experiences with European post-World War I developments played a central role in this institutional strategy. While economic recovery was certainly stimulated through the package of joint measures developed in 1919 by the victors, in hindsight they invested insufficient effort into the actual implementation of their cooperatively conceived policies. Problems such as war debts, external imbalances, currency issues, and structural balances hampered Europe's successful economic and, by extension, political recovery. "Generally speaking, Europe's economic and political fragility was ignored in the 1920s, probably more out of ignorance than intent."[3] And in the economic crisis of the decade that followed, Europe's persistent weakness was marked. In 1939, Europe was "in a much weaker state economically than it had been in 1914, with her shares of world income and trade notably reduced. Worse still, she emerged from the war in 1945 in a more prostate condition than in 1918, with output levels well down on those of the pre-war period." Thanks to the U.S., the post-1919 scenario was not repeated after 1945. "In part this can be attributed to the fact that in the reconstruction phase of the later 1940s some of the mistakes and blunders of the earlier experience were avoided."[4]

Opposing Outlooks and Dutch Resistance to U.S. Policy

The idea of a U.S.-led institutional economic strategy by the end of World War II was at odds with the Dutch prewar policy of neutrality and threatened its self-image as a "medium-sized" player in the international arena with no intention of allowing its economic freedoms to be curtailed by a global power like the U.S. Moreover, the economic recovery plans pursued by the U.S. and the other occupying forces in Germany took no account of Dutch national interests.

The Netherlands' security-related and economic contributions to the League of Nations were limited and made without conviction. Nevertheless, the transgovernmental contacts of Dutch politicians and high-ranking officials within the League's economic framework were deemed to serve a purpose. At the 1933 League of Nations' World Monetary and Economic Conference, the Dutch Prime Minister Hendrikus Colijn presided over the Economic Commission. Hans Max Hirschfeld, the influential director general of trade and manufactures in the Dutch Ministry of Trade, Manufactures and Shipping, also served on this commission from 1933 until 1940. Up until 1933 it had been the Ministry of Foreign Affairs that delineated the country's foreign economic policy, but from 1933 onward Hirschfeld's ministry took responsibility for this policy area, also within the League of Nations.

Hirschfeld was to be the key figure in Dutch foreign economic policy for a full twenty years, plotting the course the country was to take in relation to both Germany (pre-1945) and the U.S. (post-1945). Though Colijn's Netherlands supported the free trade objectives pursued by the League of Nations and so-called Oslo states (the Netherlands, Belgium, Luxemburg, Finland, Sweden, Denmark, Norway), Hirschfeld's ministry used its direct responsibility for conducting negotiations to take several definitive steps during the 1930s in framing a policy oriented toward Germany, including a trade agreement with Nazi Germany that Hirschfeld masterminded in May 1933. In fact, this represented a protectionist move on the Netherlands' part, one that inherently implied a rejection of any possible economic cooperation with the U.S. In 1937, the Oslo states continued their economic cooperation, but when Hirschfeld's ministry, backed by the Dutch business community, opted in favor of a continued German orientation, Colijn was unable to renew the agreement in 1938. When in 1939 cooperation between the Oslo states and the U.S. was in the offing — the latter under the direction of President Franklin Roosevelt and his Secretary of State Cordell Hull, increasingly intent on free trade — the Netherlands proved the only opponent.

The Dutch attitude toward the League of Nations and the United States during the 1930s did not bode well for its reception of American institutional strategy, and it was to be a long time before the Dutch government — which had tak-

743

5

—

THE
COLD WAR
AND
BEYOND

1945–2009

—

ECONOMICS
AND
SOCIETY

en refuge in London when the German occupation began in 1940 — came to understand the full import of the joint U.S./UK-led Allied cooperation. When sounded out about the Atlantic Charter in 1941, Foreign Minister Eelco van Kleffens warned that the Netherlands could not enter into any agreements that interfered with its free trade position. The Netherlands continued to cling to the idea that its colonial holdings and its trade volume qualified it as a medium-sized power. Thus, when the U.S. proposed plans for joint relief aid in the form of the United Nations Relief and Rehabilitation Administration (UNRRA) in 1943, the Dutch government in exile had difficulty reconciling itself with the fact that the major international powers would be at the helm. Insofar as it developed a more Atlantic orientation, it had strong reservations about a global security system led by an alliance of superpowers as framed in the United Nations (UN). Instead, it preferred a number of regional alliances to which the U.S. would grant its permanent support and in which the Netherlands would count as a medium-sized power. Thus, from the summer of 1943 onward, a new "European" economic orientation began to emerge alongside a military "Atlantic" orientation. In October 1943, Belgium, the Netherlands, and Luxemburg (the Benelux) concluded an agreement for future free movement of currency, followed in September 1944 by another agreement for the creation of a postwar customs union.

These reservations against American strategy notwithstanding, certain members of the Dutch administration were increasingly open to greater multilateral cooperation. Minister of Social Affairs Jan van den Tempel participated in the work carried out by the International Labour Organization, which had fled to North America in 1940. He supported this organization's push to counter the economic crisis through fundamental social renewal, encompassing full employment opportunities, social security for all citizens, and social democracy in economic relations. By contrast, the policy aims of the Dutch delegation to the Bretton Woods conference held in 1944 failed to be compatible with those of the U.S. and the UK. The delegation itself was headed by Jan Willem Beyen, who had served as vice chairman and then chairman of the Bank for International Settlements from 1935 to 1940 and in 1943 had participated in drawing up the Benelux Monetary Agreement. At the Bretton Woods meeting, where plans for creating the International Monetary Fund (IMF) and the International Bank for Reconstruction and Development (IBRD) were to be worked out, Beyen advocated a regional framework for postwar economic and monetary reconstruction. But his proposal was not viable in the face of the American preference for a global program. However, gains were made in the form of new contacts that made it possible for Beyen to negotiate postwar loans for the Netherlands in New York and Switzerland near the end of 1944.

The Dutch position was the same regarding the formation of the United Nations, where it also preferred regional over global cooperation. Dutch membership was by no means a foregone conclusion for Foreign Minister Van Kleffens, since plans for the UN, which became more tangible from early 1945 on, involved a large role for the major powers. Nevertheless, the Dutch ambassador in Washington, Alexander Loudon, deemed it wise to keep pace with developments and in June 1945 signed the UN Charter on behalf of the Netherlands at the UN Founding Conference in San Francisco. While Van Kleffens' defense of Dutch membership at a session of the provisional parliament was markedly unenthusiastic, the Charter was almost unanimously approved during the session's November 1945 vote. No one wanted a return to neutrality. Though collective security as mediated by the UN entailed potential paralysis under the rule of superpowers, the creation of regionally based security organizations was simply not feasible. Yet, the Netherlands had not yet accepted American institutional strategy.

Shift in Dutch Position and Significance of the German Economy

The Dutch retreat from impartiality was completed under Van Kleffens' successor, who viewed the UN's role in continuing Allied cooperation in a more positive light. When the East-West divide began to impede UN operations starting from 1947, Dutch Minister of Foreign Affairs Carel van Boetzelaer effectively ended Dutch neutrality. Triggering this shift was Dutch interest in the German economy, which arose not from any emotive desire to annex German territory to compensate for war damage inflicted by Germany (which was the main issue in Dutch politics at the time), but from the wish to repair trade relations with its eastern neighbor. Convincing the U.S. and other occupying powers of the wisdom of this approach required considerable effort. The Allies had ensured that trade with Germany was all but impossible, and Dutch economic interests were not paramount in their minds.

Van Boetzelaer, himself opposed to proposed annexation schemes, was able to convince parliament of the futility of broaching any such plans with the occupying powers in Germany. In November 1946 he had named Hirschfeld as his ministry's advisor for German affairs, ignoring questions concerning the latter's ongoing appointment as a high-ranking official during the entire German occupation. When the Dutch government fled to London in 1940, Hirschfeld stayed on as a top official and accepted responsibility for the economic sector under the German occupying authorities. After the war he was cleared of wrongdoing, given his

745

5

—

THE
COLD WAR
AND
BEYOND

1945–2009

—

ECONOMICS
AND
SOCIETY

administrative role during the "hunger winter" of 1944–45. It was Hirschfeld who convinced Dutch politicians that not annexation, but the German economy was the pivotal issue. Speaking at a hearing organized by the four occupying nations in late January 1947, he stated that the Netherlands was absolutely opposed to imposing any kind of serious obstacles against German heavy industry. To support this position, he pointed out the role that German industry could play in the inter-European economic cooperation he thought would soon become a reality.

Since the Netherlands wanted to avoid dependency on Belgium or France for its supply of steel, it demanded that the German steel industry be reinstated in the international market. Whereas France aimed to limit German power on all fronts, the Netherlands and Belgium were united in opposing severe restriction. At Hirschfeld's instigation and under Van Boetzelaer's guidance, the two countries joined with Luxemburg in developing a coordinated policy on Germany. This resulted, in 1947, in the Benelux Memorandum for the liberalization of trade relations and the signification of German economic recovery. The Netherlands subsequently used the Benelux alliance to present a stronger front during international negotiations on economic and military cooperation held in 1947 and 1948, in Marshall Plan assistance, and in discussions concerning the future of the West German occupied zones.

The U.S. Marshall Plan and Dutch Participation

When the Marshall Plan was launched in June 1947, the Netherlands had only limited reserves of gold and foreign exchange assets, thus narrowing the scope of its recovery and perspectives for international trade. It therefore had a strategic interest in the success of the U.S. initiative. In April 1948, the first American Marshall aid vessel docked in Rotterdam carrying a cargo of 4,000 tons of wheat, 380 tons of soybean oil, and supplies of agricultural equipment. Plagued by continuing shortages of food and production resources, the Netherlands welcomed the ship with a display of fireworks.

Two days after the Plan's launch, Hirschfeld and Ambassador Loudon came to Washington for a meeting with Undersecretary of State Dean Acheson. They offered their support for a proposal for Benelux leadership in elaborating the common European recovery program as stipulated by the U.S. But the Dutch administration's hoped-for role in preparations for the Marshall Plan conference among sixteen Western European nations in Paris failed to materialize, because the major European powers had already made various arrangements among themselves. It was not until September that the conference was able to present the desired cooperative European recovery program. The Netherlands subsequently participated in the American relief effort, viewing independent action on the part of the U.S. with less anxiety than it would have had vis-à-vis France or the UK. The restrictive occupation policy regarding trade with Germany continued to be a point of dissatisfaction for the Netherlands, however. Added to this was the fact that it would have to proceed with care in the UN if it wanted to avoid Security Council sanctions for its Indonesian policing campaign (*politionele actie*) of July 1947. Having successfully presented a coordinated front, the Benelux countries were drawn into discussions on the future of Germany held during the London conference that opened in February 1948. Here it was determined that the three Western-occupied zones would be combined into a single economic entity with a common currency, which would ensure the financial stability vital for economic recovery. Hirschfeld and the Benelux had minimal influence on this decision, but did see their wish for German participation in the reconstruction of Europe recognized. The issue was thus settled. The wheels of U.S. institutional strategy in this context began to turn and the Netherlands now perceived — in this case thanks to Hirschfeld — an opportunity to exert some influence within that strategy and to utilize it for its own benefit.

The loss of the Dutch colonies and the subsequent disintegration of the national self-image as a medium-sized world power, which had rested largely on its possession of Indonesia, weighed heavily in Dutch politics. At the same time, however, the loss of these colonial markets had a positive effect on the Netherlands' own economy by forcing it to modernize and adapt to the changed international economic relations. Here, too, American institutional strategy was decisive.

Initially, the Dutch approached the 1945 plans for the nation's reconstruction with the idea that salvaging colonial ties with Indonesia would put it in a better position to achieve an advantageous balance of trade with the U.S. —just as it had done before the war. After all, raw materials from Indonesia could help alleviate the shortage of dollars. Shortly after the war had ended, the Netherlands therefore launched efforts to restore economic relations. "Dutch exports to Indonesia increased substantially, to a considerable extent in response to the demands for commodities by the Dutch armed forces in Indonesia. Dutch imports from Indonesia also increased rapidly: from 20 million dollars in 1946 to 770 million in 1951, or 8 percent of total merchandise imports in that year."[5] Yet the Netherlands' final defeat in the colonial wars and Indonesian independence in 1949 brought an end to this economic relationship. The rapid advancements achieved by the Dutch economy during the first decades after the war proved that the Netherlands was very capable of building a solid economic foundation and of shifting its economic focus from its largest colony onto Europe and the United States. It is likely that the "loss" of Indonesia even helped strengthen the sense that the Netherlands now had to put its shoulder to the wheel. "The human capital that had previously been applied to the development of the economy of colonial Indonesia now benefited the mother country."[6]

5

The Dutch Contribution to the IMF, IBRD, and GATT

The Netherlands was among the cofounders of the IMF and the IBRD, despite the rejection of Beyen's earlier proposal. Minister of Finance Pieter Lieftinck, who thanks to the intervention of the Red Cross had been able to review the Bretton Woods agreement while detained as a prisoner of war in Germany, traveled to Washington at the beginning of 1946. There he was able to secure a loan of great value to the Netherlands, which provided a temporary influx of the foreign currency so vital for reconstruction. In 1947 the Netherlands took advantage of IMF credits and obtained an IBRD loan, and in 1948 turned to Marshall aid. The Netherlands was to use the IMF on only one single subsequent occasion, in 1957, thereafter acting as a creditor. Beyen, who had accompanied Lieftinck on his trip to the U.S., was appointed IBRD executive director for the Netherlands in 1946, and from 1948 served in the same capacity at the IMF. He was to hold these posts until 1952, when he was named minister of foreign affairs. Though Beyen ultimately left the IMF and IBRD disappointed about the lack of influence he had been able to exert, his personal dissatisfaction could not detract from the fact that the Netherlands had now risen to join the circle of nations that provided direct and substantive support to these financial institutions. This new status corresponded with the Netherlands' role on the executive board of the Bank for International Settlements, as well as its efforts to achieve the financial discipline needed for stable international trade.

The Netherlands' position within both these institutions, unlike that of the Americans, was characterized by a consistent preference for financial discipline, with safeguards to protect financial resources from being exhausted and a monetary approach to balance of payment problems. Having each experienced the crisis of the 1930s, the Netherlands and the U.S. shared a firm faith in fixed exchange rates and a strong regulatory role for their central banks — De Nederlandsche Bank and the Federal Reserve System, respectively.

During the war, disputes about the correlation between free trade and full employment had made it impossible for the U.S. and the UK to reach agreement on a multilateral strategy for postwar global trade. When the U.S. renewed its efforts to bring international free trade to the table at the UN in 1945, the Netherlands accepted the invitation to participate in preparations for an international trade organization, but it opposed U.S. policies. The Netherlands complained about British participation with five Commonwealth countries, while from the entire European continent only five countries were present, but the

748

U.S. rejected a Dutch proposal to include Norway. While the Dutch minister of finance preferred working closely with the United Kingdom, the minister of agriculture was in favor of joint Benelux action, given that he sought agricultural policy regulation based on national borders rather than the single market ideas endorsed by the U.S. In October 1946, at the London conference held to prepare the charter for an International Trade Organization (ITO), the Netherlands argued in favor of lifting trade restrictions, but unlike the U.S. it also emphasized the need for structure in the business sector, recognition of international commodity agreements, the rejection of cartels, and the establishment of a permanent body to settle disputes. The Netherlands was disappointed that trade in agricultural products would not be covered by the Food and Agriculture Organization (FAO). The Dutch argued strongly that decisions taken by the ITO must not prevent the FAO from achieving its goals. This standpoint was not shared by the U.S., which considered that the FAO's aim to introduce regulations would interfere with the practice of free trade. The following year saw the start of parallel negotiations for the General Agreement on Tariffs and Trade (GATT), resulting from the U.S. 1945 Reciprocal Trade Agreements Act, which left the U.S. government three years to conclude trade agreements with other countries. There, hoping to enlist the political support required for the success of its intended free trade program, the U.S. yielded and agreed to an exception for free trade within regional customs unions, by which the Netherlands would retain its system of special border regulations for the import and export of agricultural products with Belgium. The U.S. accepted that regional customs unions could operate outside the general rules of free trade because it needed to secure wide political support for an agreement on a free trade regime as a whole. Yet the draft text formulated at a renewed ITO charter conference held in 1947 made fewer provisions for free trade. This time the Netherlands supported the U.S. Ultimately the ITO foundered for lack of support, leaving the GATT as the only international trade mechanism whose rules and procedures had been accepted by the leading trade nations. With the conclusion of an additional protocol, the GATT entered into force and put in place a system for free trade.

From now on the Netherlands was a full-fledged player in the American institutional strategy with regard to trade. Sicco Mansholt, the Dutch minister of agriculture from 1945 until 1957, who had been the actual initiator of the GATT exception for free trade within regional customs unions proposed in 1947, called upon the exception when he was appointed as the EEC agricultural commissioner as of January 1, 1958 and became responsible for shaping EEC agricultural policy.

It was typical of Mansholt the politician that immediately after the end of the war he set about expanding his international network of contacts by meeting with colleagues from other countries and attending international confer-

749

5

———

THE
COLD WAR
AND
BEYOND

1945–2009

———

ECONOMICS
AND
SOCIETY

ences. Mansholt traveled to the U.S. on numerous occasions during the 1950s, always — to the Americans' delight — toting his photo and filming equipment and inviting Americans to visit the Netherlands. The U.S. administration — not only the Department of Agriculture but also the State Department — was very interested in Mansholt's, at the time progressive, vision on the integration of European agriculture. In his position as EEC commissioner Mansholt sought direct contact with American politicians to discuss plans for a common agricultural policy, discussing matters at the highest levels with President Kennedy and others in his administration.[7]

From the very outset, Dutch trade politics have been based on the GATT because it promoted free trade. After 1970, however, all trade policies were implemented within the framework of the EEC Commission which, within its so-called Article 113 Committee, provides for common policy development among, and assessment of negotiations on Commission policies by, member states.

Dutch and American Aims for Western European Economic Cooperation

American pressure for a joint European approach was successful in bringing about a European vision on international cooperation. In the Netherlands it was Hirschfeld who led the way. Early in 1948, he was named government commissioner for the European Recovery Program, with a support office installed in the Ministry of Foreign Affairs (hence, not in Economic Affairs). He ordered that all communication with the American authorities be conducted through his office alone. As a party to the design of the Marshall Plan's Organization for European Economic Cooperation (OEEC) early in 1948, Hirschfeld advocated that this organization should be a permanent institution, and recommended participation by the German occupied zones and a system of unanimous decision making. Following a tiresome negotiations process, the OEEC convention was signed on April 16. Though the Americans had planned to appoint Hirschfeld as secretary general of the OEEC, resistance from the UK, France, and the Scandinavian nations led him to withdraw his candidacy.

During the period spanned by the European Recovery Program (1948–51), the most urgent task was to draft proposals for the allocation of aid monies. Once the work of this program had come to a close, the OEEC specialized in conducting regular reviews of member states' economic development. In 1961 the OEEC made way for the broader Organization for Economic Cooperation and Development (OECD), which also carried out this statistical task. The Netherlands played a role in both the OEEC and OECD. Dutch Ministers of Foreign Affairs Dirk Stikker (1950–52) and Beyen (1952–56) represented Dutch interests in the OEEC, while Emile van Lennep was secretary general of the OECD from 1969 until 1984.

American criticism of the OEEC's poor functioning led to the appointment in 1949 of a so-called political conciliator — a post to which Stikker was named in February 1950. Almost as soon as the appointment had been made, however, the position quickly faded into the background, and Stikker subsequently acted as OEEC chair until 1952. As a result of the Korean War the aims of American aid changed. In July of 1950, Stikker launched a plan for what he (and the U.S.) saw as the imperative task of liberalizing the economies of Europe through the successive liberalization of various branches of commerce. The plan was calculated to stimulate the modernization of different branches of industry, as elaborated previously in Stikker's Dutch Memoranda on Industrialization.

That Stikker's initiative was received with little enthusiasm — including in the Netherlands — was in part because it followed hard on the heels of the French Schuman Plan, which in 1951 was to result in the supranational European Coal and Steel Community (ECSC), comprising six West European member states. U.S. support for the Schuman Plan was motivated primarily by the fact that it was a European initiative. Stikker was initially wary of the French plan. Whereas some believed that supranationalism would be capable of breaking through European protectionism, the Dutch administration, like Stikker, saw supranationalism as problematic. Ultimately it did join in talks surrounding the plan, but noted its reservations regarding supranationalism. Since the UK did not participate and France and Germany were keen to find partners, the Benelux was for some time able to inject a measure of political counter-pressure against the major nations and to forge a compromise with less supranationality. Eventually the ECSC created a framework for transparency and competition in the coal and steel sectors that was acceptable to the Dutch coal mines and steel industry (the former Hoogovens), despite such unfamiliar business practices as tariff publication and terms and conditions of sale. Even so, Stikker continued to have reservations about the ECSC's limited membership of only six states. This instance of Western European integration had a sequel in the agreements framed between 1952 and 1954 for a European Defense Community and a European Political Community, though both were destined to succumb to political disagreement.

In 1952, Stikker was succeeded in his role as minister of foreign affairs by Beyen, who had previously served as executive director of the IMF and IBRD and had recently returned from Washington. Though the latter's orientation was more European than that of his predecessor, he was by no means an advocate of European federalism. He had first-hand knowledge of American political relationships and recognized that the administration that had taken office under President Dwight D. Eisenhower in 1953 was less inclined to tie itself to Western Europe than the Truman administration had been.

5

—

THE
COLD WAR
AND
BEYOND

1945–2009

—

ECONOMICS
AND
SOCIETY

In the as yet unperfected European Political Community, Beyen saw a mechanism suited not so much to engender military-political cooperation as to establish an economic customs union with no internal tariffs and a single common foreign tariff. His "general" perspective on integration represented a rejection of Stikker's "sector-oriented" approach targeting branches of industry, the content of which not only met with resistance but was finally swept from the table entirely when French national politics put an end to the European Political Community in 1954. One year later, the tides turned again with the new proposals for European economic cooperation put forward by Jean Monnet and Paul-Henri Spaak. Their proposals aimed at greater integration of the traffic and energy sectors, and outlined a new community for atomic energy. Beyen responded with his own memorandum, countering sector integration with a general strategy of gradual economic integration (from customs union to common market). In May of that year a compromise between the two schemes was submitted to Germany, France, and Italy. As part of the drive toward general integration in the form of an economic community, this Benelux Memorandum argued for greater unity among economic sectors bordering the ECSC. It called for the creation of common institutions, a common market, and a gradual synchronization of social policy. The Benelux Memorandum contributed to the 1955 *relance européenne*, which in 1957 would lead to the Treaties of Rome establishing the EEC and the European Atomic Energy Community (Euratom).

Closely linked with American institutional strategy was the rise of a small group of Dutch politicians as institutional players in Western European integration. The Netherlands had joined the U.S. in advocating the further integration of Germany into Western Europe. Yet it was not the OEEC as engineered by the Marshall Plan that provided the basis for this institutionalization, but the three European communities as molded by "the six" Western European nations themselves. Both Stikker and Beyen drew on the opportunities inherent in these international institutions to develop their schemes for modernizing and expanding Dutch industry and for liberalizing European trade.

The Divide between Atlanticists and Europeans

The Netherlands regarded American involvement in Western European economic cooperation as key to preventing either Germany or France from rising to a position of European domination. Involvement by the Americans was not considered problematic from the Dutch perspective because the two countries shared certain core economic conceptions about, for example, free trade, liberalization, and monetary balance, thus forging a strong transatlantic partnership. At the same time, however, developments in Europe gave rise to an opposition between Atlanticists and Europeans. The former looked to the U.S. in matters of global security and economic development, while the latter focused on Western European integration in the guise of the three Communities.

From the European vantage point, the situation was further complicated by the fact that there was also a group of Atlanticists in Europe who favored an intergovernmental free trade association rather than supranational cooperation within the European Communities. In 1960, the UK and six other states had joined to form the European Free Trade Association (EFTA), motivated by tensions within the OEEC and the European Communities, and solidified by French President Charles de Gaulle's subsequent rejection of British membership in 1963 — a position that would remain unchanged for ten years. European cooperation thus existed in different forms: the OEEC, the Europe of "the six" (the European Communities) and that of "the seven" (the EFTA).

For the Netherlands, it was the European Communities that counted most. Their creation marked the introduction and establishment of European integration ideas in Dutch foreign politics, manifested in both its participation in French and German-led European cooperative endeavors and in a certain European idealism among politicians and high officials. Its simultaneous orientation on the U.S. for global security and economic development would henceforth take Dutch politics along two different paths: one toward Western European cooperation and the other toward Atlanticism. Though the two paths did not always run parallel, they did yield acceptable compromises.

Industrialization and Transnational Enterprise in the Netherlands and the United States

The Netherlands had had a slow start in industrialization, which progressed very gradually during the nineteenth century, with the small business owner remaining dominant into the 1920s. In the period starting after 1945, however, industrialization finally took off, with transnational businesses taking on a significance for Dutch economic growth unmatched in the rest of Western Europe. Having emerged in the period between 1880 and 1920, the Netherlands' major transnational corporations continued to expand until around 1970, offering steadily more job opportunities and steering toward long-term economic growth. From the 1970s onward, however, their relative importance diminished in the face of a fast-burgeoning service sector and the sometimes more dynamic character of smaller businesses. In 1950 there were 1.1 million people employed in Dutch industry — 467,000 (or 42.5 percent) of them in the six largest transnational companies: Royal Dutch/Shell, Philips, Unilever, DSM, AKZO, and Hoogovens. By 1960 this percentage had risen to 61.4 (785,000 of

753

5

—

THE
COLD WAR
AND
BEYOND

1945–2009

—

ECONOMICS
AND
SOCIETY

the 1,185,000 employed in industry), and by 1993 it was still 80.2 (770,000 of the 960,000 employed in industry).[8]

These transnational enterprises profited from the liberalization set in motion by the OEEC/OECD, the European Communities, the EFTA and, on the global level, by the GATT with its various trade rounds. They also benefited from the macroeconomic data furnished by these international organizations, covering both long-term trends and cross-country comparative studies.[9] The large Dutch transnational enterprises, which had had subsidiaries in the U.S. from before World War II, continued to do well there, and in 1988 U.S.-based Dutch business owners started the European-American Business Council as a platform for transnational enterprises to discuss issues surrounding bilateral trade and investment. The Dutch broadened their investments in the U.S. during the 1990s, at the same time carving out solid positions in the service sector and especially in banking, insurance, and other financial services, which included the 1999 merger between Aegon and Transamerica.

Before World War II, American investments in the Netherlands were limited. After 1945, however, these grew to the extent that, by the end of the twentieth century, the U.S. was the largest foreign investor in the Netherlands. Moreover, the latter was now the second-largest recipient of American investments in all of Europe (after the UK). For the Americans, the strong Dutch commitment to free trade made it the perfect ally within the EEC. The establishment of the American Chamber of Commerce in the port city of Rotterdam in 1962 created new opportunities for American businesses to reach both the Netherlands and the whole of the EEC. Completing the picture was the launch of the single European market in 1993, generating even more American interest in investing in the Netherlands and giving the U.S. another foothold in the single European market — a market that, with the gradual expansion of the EU, was steadily growing both in size and importance.

The shaping of transatlantic relations was not merely the preserve of politicians, but was also guided by the dialogue between politicians and business owners. At the beginning of the 1950s, the generation that had consciously experienced World War II began to voice concerns about Western European anti-Americanism and questioned whether the newly formed international institutions would be enough to withstand the Cold War. The result was the Bilderberg Group: an annual meeting between businessmen and politicians, well known because of the Dutch royal family's participation (Prince Bernhard and Queen Beatrix). Dialogue between the business sector and politicians had existed in various forms since the end of the nineteenth century, and included the conferences that led to the founding of the International Chamber of Commerce in 1919, the World Economic Forum in 1970 — set up by Europe's policy elite to demonstrate that Europe, too, was involved in tackling major problems — and the Trilateral Commission in 1973 (policy elites from the U.S., Europe, and Japan). Rather than having any decision-making authority or intent to conspire (the Bilderberg Group's secrecy notwithstanding), these bodies function as mechanisms that can grease the wheels when systems fail to run smoothly.

Modernization in the Netherlands: Productivity Enhancement,
Advertising, and Road Networks

The internationalization of the Dutch economy as promoted by American institutional strategy from 1945 onward translated into industrial and economic growth, but also brought fundamental changes in the behavior of both business owners and consumers. The articles by Inklaar, Schreurs, Mom, and Bosma cover various aspects of the U.S.-inspired modernization of the Dutch economy and society.

One of the tools employed to sell the "American model" were the Marshall Plan study trips, through which teams from various professions could visit the U.S. to take a look behind the scenes and glean insights that would benefit them at home. Americans take pride in demonstrating their achievements and have no qualms about letting outsiders take a look, though never without losing sight of their own interests. Frank Inklaar describes this aspect of Marshall aid as a vehicle by which the American recipe for modern national prosperity was presented and passed on to the Netherlands. In adopting this recipe, however, the Netherlands adapted it to its own needs, for example by putting the development of a cohesive system of social services before direct stimulation of individual prosperity, as was done in the U.S. While many visitors were doubtful about the American approach to communication between business leaders and the labor unions and found the Dutch system more effective, unfamiliar concepts like productivity enhancement and public relations were put into direct practice. The contributions by Schreurs, Mom, and Bosma help illustrate Inklaar's analysis. Their articles discuss advertising, road networks, and suburbia.

Wilbert Schreurs looks at the Dutch advertising world, which for a long time resisted the adoption of American practices. American advertising forms, which featured such sales-driven devices as strips and balloons, were not at all well received in the Netherlands, and it was not until the 1960s that American marketing thinking gained acceptance. Marking this decade were the American takeovers of Dutch advertising agencies, a Dutch drive for renewal, and an emerging creative revolution in the U.S. By the 1970s, Dutch ad agencies had professional-

755

5

—

THE
COLD WAR
AND
BEYOND

1945-2009

—

ECONOMICS
AND
SOCIETY

ized and were beginning to make an impact in the U.S. The fact that Dutch designers can achieve professional success in the United States was amply proven by Paul Mijksenaar, known for his clear signage systems for large airports.

Gijs Mom's contribution examines how the U.S. exerted its influence on Dutch conceptions of mobility in the years following the war. In the interwar period, American cars had been very common in the Netherlands. This changed with reconstruction, when Dutch consumers switched to European cars because American models were too expensive — though it should also be said that the popular German Opel was acquired by General Motors in 1929. After the war, an outgrowth of the Marshall Plan productivity trips allowed Dutch engineers to study traffic engineering at Yale University, returning with American insights that were to be applied in the Netherlands when the expansion of its road network became necessary in the 1960s. Reconstruction had come to a close by the end of the 1950s. and as the 1960s unfolded national prosperity and consumerism were becoming the norm in Europe. Unlike France, the Netherlands created a system of highways that remained linked to the national road network, with entry ramps at intervals of around twelve miles. According to Mom, the Netherlands' American-inspired freeway system represents a model of "selective borrowing" combined with specifically Dutch accents, characterized by the dominant urban bicycle culture, the extensive Dutch waterway system, and the residential zones with their new rules for car traffic.

In his contribution, Koos Bosma discusses the evolution of "suburbia." Initially, American and Dutch perspectives on urban development had little in common. Compared to the meandering American suburbs with their detached homes epitomizing the American Dream, the "Dutch Dream" consisted of straight streets, rows of houses and a stronger community ideal. During the 1970s, the Netherlands turned away from this fixed formula, with far-reaching changes being implemented in residential building and urban patterns. Bosma traces its convergence with the American model first during the 1970s, and again in the 1990s, while showing that the American model itself underwent far fewer changes. Of course, one important difference with the U.S. is the availability of cheap and convenient bicycle transport all over the Netherlands.

Thus, while converging tendencies can certainly be identified in terms of similar patterns and problems, distinct national accents and areas of expertise continue to play a role in bilateral relations. The article by Dirk Dekkers and Taco Westerhuis in this section compares the Dutch storm surge of 1953 with hurricane Katrina in 2005. They illustrate the two countries' distinct approaches to water management and discuss how these have contributed to bilateral provision of aid and recent Dutch-American cooperation. Today, water management is not only an attribute, but also — and equally — a Dutch export product, in much the same way that advertising, road networks, and suburban districts were for America.

Industrial Relations, Corporate Governance,
and Business Schools

The new economic dynamic would also effect changes in industrial relations, though these retained a unique character in at least one respect, encapsulated in the so-called polder model. This term refers to the Dutch landscape, with its polders that protect every member of the community from the surrounding water. After 1945, the Dutch labor unions were recognized by the government as "social partners," to be involved in national wage and economic policy formation. Balancing the unions' acceptance of reduced wages — as prompted by the guided wage policy of 1945–63 — was an extensive system for social security. This social partnership resulted in strong national cohesion. Within the system of Dutch pillarization, the different "pillars" and groups consistently felt themselves bound together by the same welfare state.

Over the course of the 1980s, however, changes effected by the economic recession of the previous decade and shifts in the economic order spurred the Netherlands to follow U.S. President Ronald Reagan's lead in pursuing far-reaching liberalization and reduced government regulation as a means of stimulating market growth ("Reaganomics"), which in turn affected industrial relations. In fact, this period marked a paradigm shift in the economy. The Keynesian theory that had provided the foundation for postwar relations was replaced by the neoliberalism of Milton Friedman. In their contribution, Hendrik van Dalen and Arjo Klamer compare Friedman's ideas with those of fellow Nobel Prize winner Jan Tinbergen. Whereas right up until the 1980s Tinbergen was the embodiment of Dutch economic thinking and the international development aid to which the Netherlands attached such importance, Friedman laid the basis for 1980s and 1990s global neoliberalism in the U.S. The same trend emerged in the UK, set in motion by the economist Friedrich Hayek — a man much admired by Prime Minister Margret Thatcher.

The Dutch welfare state, too, experienced the pressure of this turnaround in economic thinking and policy, and underwent various modifications — including cutting back the government's role in the economy — that left the system partly dismantled. At the same time, a series of major corporate bankruptcies in the 1980s drew attention to failing corporate management and failing supervision. Shareholders' desire to protect their interests led to an attack on legislation limiting these interests. "In their view, Dutch shares were undervalued

757

5

———

THE
COLD WAR
AND
BEYOND

1945-2009

———

ECONOMICS
AND
SOCIETY

as a result of oligarchic devices. This offensive resulted in the introduction (in 1989) of rules against the accumulation of such devices." This "revolution of the shareholders" was reinforced by emerging globalization and Reaganomics, "because it made capital highly mobile and firms much more dependent on the whims of the stock exchange."[10]

Both Europe and the Netherlands took steps to introduce a stronger functioning of the market (the former through the gradual introduction of the "Europe 1992" single market project). Set against the backdrop of the economic turbulence of the 1990s, the economic success of the Dutch cabinet appointed in 1994 under Prime Minister Wim Kok was a model for the rest of the world. The government's social partners (labor unions and employers) also joined in talks on economic policy and the changes that would be required, contributing to and approving key compromises. U.S. President Bill Clinton, in particular, lauded the Dutch polder model and in 1999 invited Kok for a visit to the United States to explain the concept that had there become known as the Third Way.

In 1998 the Netherlands Competition Authority (Nederlandse Mededingingsautoriteit) was founded to safeguard fair competition across all sectors. Similar independent regulatory authorities were formed in various individual sectors, such as the financial markets and the postal and telecom and health care sectors, while a European commissioner for competition in Brussels keeps an active eye on the danger of cartels (since 2004 the former Dutch Transport Minister Neelie Kroes — number 59 on the 2007 Forbes list of "The 100 Most Powerful Women" — has been holding this position). The creation of these new regulatory bodies helped boost the economic expansion of the 1990s. Yet ensuing new cases of mismanagement, accounting scandals at Enron and Arthur Andersen (and at Ahold in the Netherlands, also active in the U.S. through its U.S. Food Services division), perceived hostile takeovers, and disturbances provoked by private equity and hedge funds have damaged the initial push for liberalization and led to calls for greater government regulation of business. The subprime mortgage crisis of 2007 and 2008 brought to light just how little information government and regulatory agencies had about financial products marketed by banks and other financial institutions.

That the Netherlands sought to preserve certain "Dutch" values was also evident with regard to the introduction of business schools, as discussed in Peter van Baalen's article. The Nyenrode Business School, founded in 1945 within a framework of British educational ideals and Dutch plans for reform, was to develop into a typical American business school. But that development was a long process, and it took many years before business administration was recognized as a regular course of study in higher education. Though the Dutch business community was in favor of the American business school model, the immense disparity between the American and Dutch higher education systems as well as the criticism (in the U.S. and the Netherlands) vis-à vis American business schools at the time made it difficult to reach consensus, and the government did not grant official recognition of the degree for several decades.

Another aspect of labor relations is the collaboration between Dutch and American trade union organizations, which shared perspectives on the Cold War. The close collaboration achieved between trade union organizations in the postwar period was rarely bilateral in nature. Rather, it occurred in multilateral frameworks — primarily through the International Confederation of Free Trade Unions (ICFTU) and within the International Labour Organization (ILO) in Geneva. Tom Etty's contribution demonstrates that while the two countries shared a strong bond when it came to international politics, their respective positions on communism in relation to certain issues of national significance — such as South Africa and Indonesia — were poles apart.

Sixty Years Later

More than sixty years have passed since 1945, and the relationship between the U.S. and the Netherlands today is different from what it was before and just after World War II. American institutional strategy established stability in Europe, and Dutch concerns about international institutions and America's leading global position have long since subsided. Thanks to the efforts of that small group of officials and politicians who both gained experience with and insight into the functioning of international organizations (in some cases even before the war), as well as familiarity with American politics (Hirschfeld, Polak, Lieftinck, Mansholt, Beyen, Stikker, and others), the Netherlands was an early, active participant in the international organizations born of American institutional strategy, as it still is today. On some occasions the Netherlands was able to find strength in numbers, as within the Benelux and, more fundamentally, the EEC/EU. To this day, the international economic order remains institutionalized, and Europe has achieved a large measure of unification (with twenty-seven EU member states). Economic relations between the U.S. and the Netherlands are managed both bilaterally and through the EU, for example in the WTO in the case of trade relations. Certainly, differences between the two countries continue to exist, evident in different perspectives on agricultural subsidies in the WTO and on personal information and privacy matters in the EU. The Dutch sometimes accuse the Americans of pursuing inconsistent policies in, for example, setting priorities that are politically motivated, or failing to enforce monetary discipline or assume international leadership. This perception also applies to the position that the U.S. has taken in the IMF, IBRD, WTO, and G7. When it comes to the value of a free and open system of trade, however, the

759

U.S. and the Netherlands share the same outlook. Their bilateral economic relations consistently serve to reinforce the two countries' solid partnership, with the Netherlands as one of the largest investors in the U.S. (with 441,800 American personnel in Dutch businesses in 2005, compared with 184,300 Dutch personnel in American businesses)[11] and with the U.S. as the largest foreign investor in the Netherlands. The Dutch have an apt expression that serves to place such situations in their proper perspective: "how a small country achieves great things."

5

THE
COLD WAR
AND
BEYOND

1945-2009

ECONOMICS
AND
SOCIETY

1   G.J. Ikenberry, *After Victory. Institutions, Strategic Restraint, and the Rebuilding of Order after Major Wars* (Princeton, NJ: Princeton University Press, 2001), 53.
2   Ibid., 163.
3   Derek Aldcroft in J.L. van Zanden, *The Economic History of the Netherlands 1914–1995. A Small Open Economy in the "Long" Twentieth Century* (London: Routledge, 1998), xii.
4   Ibid., xiii.
5   Van Zanden, *The Economic History*, 23.
6   Ibid., 24.
7   J. van Merriënboer, *Mansholt. Een biografie* (Amsterdam: Boom, 2006), 124-126, 197, 299.
8   Van Zanden, *Economic History*, 37, Table 3.2.
9   In 1968 the sudden fear emerged in the Netherlands that a small group of leaders active in the largest enterprises and banks were holding the reins of Dutch economic and political life. This group, now known as the "Mertens' 200" (after the labor union leader who had ascertained this fact), formed a close-knit network that met in various contexts within the business community and government committees.
10 Van Zanden, *The Economic History*, 46.
11 D.S. Hamilton and J.P. Quinlan, *The Transatlantic Economy 2008* (Washington, DC: Center for Transatlantic Relations, 2008), 110.

THE MARSHALL PLAN AND THE MODERNIZATION OF DUTCH SOCIETY

——

FRANK INKLAAR

In their authoritative guide to postwar modernization in the Netherlands, *1950: Prosperity and Welfare*, Kees Schuyt and Ed Taverne assert that:

> Interaction between Americanization, technological innovation, and new planning and organizational forms were together the foremost impulse in the Dutch "economic miracle." At the same time, these factors stimulated far-reaching cultural changes that were the essence of Dutch society's modernization until the early 1970s.[1]

This essay posits that Marshall Plan aid was an important stimulus behind the Netherlands' accession into what Victoria de Grazia has termed the "irresistible empire": a consumer society empire for which America provided the model.[2] The Marshall Plan gave a specific orientation to the Dutch process of modernization, whereby it not only served as a vehicle for American economic aid to the Netherlands, but also — and above all — as one that tendered and transferred the American recipe for a modern welfare state.

The Marshall Plan

On June 5, 1947, U.S. Secretary of State George C. Marshall delivered a speech at Harvard University that would go down in history as the first step toward the Marshall Plan. Europe was still reeling in the aftermath of the war, and economic conditions there had deteriorated to the extent that, so Marshall asserted, social and political instability had become a real threat. Europe needed American help. Yet the solution lay in Europe itself; what was needed was a fundamen-

5

———

THE
COLD WAR
AND
BEYOND

1945-2009

———

ECONOMICS
AND
SOCIETY

tal change that would restore European confidence in the future. Marshall proceeded to call on the nations of Europe to join in formulating an inventory of desired aid, together with a plan for sustainable economic recovery. This would then provide the basis for American relief efforts.

It was true that Europe's economic conditions were exceptionally worrying at the start of 1947. While there had been considerable economic recovery during the first two postwar years, this recovery subsequently foundered in a poorly functioning market. Europe had the immense damage brought about by the war to contend with, with losses both material and human, as well as shortages of food, fuel, raw materials, and housing. To alleviate these problems Europe was in a large measure dependent on dollar economies, with the U.S. foremost among them. There were few export goods to offer in exchange, however, and the result was a severe shortage of dollars. And it was precisely those dollars —which the U.S. alone could supply—that were needed to fund the imports that would facilitate further recovery. Europe was facing an economic collapse that would cripple public morale and quite possibly sow the seeds of social and political turmoil.

The American decision to offer assistance was inspired by a combination of economic and political motives. Playing in the background were the ghosts of the aftermath of World War I, when economic instability had culminated in a worldwide crisis and political disaster. Of more immediate concern were the stirrings of conflict and Cold War with the Soviet Union. With the lessons of history fresh in their minds, the Americans made the decision to take up arms against the communist enemy on the economic front. A healthy economy was the precondition for political stability in Europe. Major economic problems could serve to benefit the cause of communist parties in, for example, France and Italy, as well as, ultimately, furthering possible Russian ambitions in Europe. And even despite the flourishing U.S. national market, the loss of its traditional trading partner, and thus of a key export market, was nevertheless certain to take a tremendous economic toll.

Vital in Marshall's view was that the solution to the crisis should not take the form of a one-sided response. The Americans had already lent considerable bilateral assistance to various European countries, but bilateral aid did not in any way solve the fundamental economic problem.

> Only within a regional, multinational European framework (including Germany) and in close partnership rather than through charity could permanent recovery emerge. Recipients had to be centrally involved in planning for their own assistance. Only Europeans could reconstruct and save Europe. The US had to perform as a catalytic agent in the process.[3]

Such assistance would not only have to address the specific problems of 1947–48, but also provide an impulse for pan-European economic reform in a way that would establish a solid foundation for sustainable economic recovery. It was within this framework that America propagated its own successful economic expansion model as providing the politically neutral recipe for prosperity.

> Marshall Planners were pushing strenuously for greater European production, productivity, and economic interdependence as antidotes to the poisons of class consciousness and class hatreds that circulated widely throughout European society. Indeed, they sought to foster new values among Europeans towards market forces, particularly towards the expansion of Gross National Product (GNP).[4]

Europe's economic growth would have to be rooted in high productivity, fed by a "mass production for mass consumption" economy. The American recipe for economic expansion looked to resolve tensions between employers and employees. It was in both parties' best interests to work together; both would be better served by economic growth. Employers would benefit from higher profits, while employees would gain material prosperity, manifested "...in the ownership of a home, a refrigerator, an automobile, a radio set; and the television set, too, has found a fixed place in the living room," as a training team of Dutch book printers recounted upon their return from a 1952 U.S. study trip.[5] Adoption of this recipe would, according to the Marshall Plan message, put European aid recipients on the same road to prosperity; or, in other words, "you too can be like us." And this message worked.

> Transatlantic inspiration to European policies of growth...came not only from what the USA gave or preached but also from what the USA was.... Both openly and discretely the wish to catch up with the USA became the ambition of governments and the public.... American affluence and American levels of consumption—motor cars, domestic gadgets, and all—were held up as rewards to come. In short, America's very presence provided an impulse to European growth and a measure of its achievements.[6]

The European Context

763

The Americans had a clear-cut vision of how to proceed, as expressed by Marshall himself:

5

———

THE
COLD WAR
AND
BEYOND

1945-2009

———

ECONOMICS
AND
SOCIETY

It would be neither fitting nor efficacious for this Government to undertake to draw up unilaterally a program designed to place Europe on its feet economically. This is the business of the Europeans. The initiative, I think, must come from Europe. The role of this country should consist of friendly aid in the drafting of a European program and of later support of such a program so far as it may be practical for us to do so. The program should be a joint one, agreed to by a number, if not all European nations.[7]

Drafting a plan with all European nations together proved impossible. Before long the Soviet-dominated countries withdrew, leaving sixteen countries to meet in Paris and attempt to create a comprehensive European recovery program. All they managed to achieve initially was an overlong inventory of national wish lists. This was not at all the kind of collaboration that the Americans had in mind. Moreover, the Americans also wanted the German occupied zones to be included in the aid program. Not without considerable U.S. pressure did the European nations finally present their European Recovery Program (ERP) in September 1947. While the proposal was anything but ideal, it did at least make some provision for coordination and collaboration in the form of the Committee on European Economic Cooperation (CEEC), made promises (albeit vague ones) for reform, included the occupied zones in West Germany, and required a sum that was within U.S. means. The proposal was by and large approved and finalized in the Economic Cooperation Act of April 1948, according to which the Western European economy would be injected with approximately thirteen billion dollars in aid over a period of four years. Further bilateral agreements laying down specific conditions for assistance were concluded by the U.S. with each of the European aid recipients.

American responsibility for implementation of the Marshall Plan was in the hands of the Economic Cooperation Agency (ECA), which had its offices in Washington and was headed by Paul Hoffmann, the president and director of the automobile manufacturer Studebaker. Acting on his behalf in Paris was his "special representative in Europe" Averell Harriman, who coordinated contacts with the aid nations and monitored aid operations. Each of the recipient nations was also assigned an ECA country mission, installed in the respective American embassies, from where they would conduct discussions on aid at the national level and report on the program's progress. At the European end, the Organization for European Economic Cooperation (OEEC) assumed responsibility from April 1948 onward for apportioning aid and for a range of reforms intended to liberalize trade and money transfers.

The American dream of European cooperation proved exceptionally difficult to mobilize in almost every respect. It was only when the participating nations perceived some definite national interest in working together that results could be achieved, such as with the liberalization of money transfers, although one laudable achievement was the reintegration of the West German occupied zones back into Europe. At the heart of the Marshall Plan aid program was a system that facilitated the importation of goods without the need to pay for them in dollars. The desired products and raw materials were prefinanced in the U.S. and subsequently exported to the aid-receiving nations. The importers deposited an amount equivalent to what would have been paid in dollars into a special blocked account — the counterpart fund — in their own national currency. Money in this account was earmarked for special projects that would improve that country's economic structure, pending American approval.

While the organizational framework was the same for each country, the outcomes were anything but equal. Naturally the economic and political problems that existed in each of these countries were uniquely their own, and each had its own political and cultural background:

> Marshall Planners, mostly avowed Keynesians, had to partner with Christian Democrats and royalists, along with Socialists and Labourites. In West-Germany, they allied with supply-siders committed to competitive, unregulated markets. In Great Britain, France, and Norway they made common cause with Socialists pledged to nationalize industries.[8]

In practice, the Marshall Plan proved exceptionally flexible. A comparison of what aid efforts achieved in the various countries demonstrated:

> ... the Marshall Plan's fundamental flexibility, its rejection of a one-size-fits-all approach, and its mixed results. While its grand intention was to promote a more cooperative and interdependent "New Europe," various relief, reconstruction, reform, and development programs encountered local resistance and failure as well as cooperation and success.[9]

The Marshall Plan and the Netherlands

The Netherlands was among the countries that in 1947 found themselves coming up against the limits of postwar economic recovery as a result of an enormous deficit in its balance of payments with the U.S. Many more dollars were needed to finance U.S. imports, which were in turn vital for further recovery. But the Netherlands had hardly any export goods that could bring those dollars in. It would have to resort to drawing on its dollar and/or gold supplies — a recourse

765

5

—

THE
COLD WAR
AND
BEYOND

1945–2009

—

ECONOMICS
AND
SOCIETY

rather to be avoided. Exacerbating the situation were the particularly harsh winter and dry summer of 1947, which necessitated the importation of additional fuel and food.

Marshall Plan assistance thus came as a boon, especially in that it served to resolve the severe dollar-shortage problem. Its long-term perspective of economic growth through industrialization and higher agricultural production capacity was also entirely in line with the Dutch political agenda. The same was true of the Marshall Plan's foreign policy implications: European cooperation — not least West Germany's integration into a strong European economy — would serve Dutch interests very well, and it was for this reason that the Netherlands worked so hard to put cooperation among Benelux countries on the agenda during Marshall Plan negotiations. The Netherlands played an active role in preliminary discussions and, in subsequent years, in the apportionment of funds. And it certainly reaped the rewards, in part because the amount of aid was made proportionate to balance of payment deficits. The Netherlands ultimately received 1,127 million dollars — or 109 dollars for every man, woman, and child — placing it among the leading aid-receiving nations. Three months after the arrival of the first aid shipment, on June 29, 1948, the Netherlands signed its bilateral agreement with the U.S. This agreement was to remain in force until July 3, 1953.

The Marshall Plan met with little protest from Dutch society. Among the political factions, only the communists declared themselves opposed. Public opinion was by and large positive, though there was a general sense that Marshall Plan assistance was not as altruistic as the Americans made it out to be. Public opinion polls showed that most Dutch people believed U.S. national economic interests to be the chief motivation. However, as long as American and Dutch interests continued to run parallel, there seemed no reason to object to offers of relief. Moreover, any doubts as to the benefits were quickly erased by a publicity campaign of, until then, unknown proportions.

Marshall Plan aid made it possible for the Netherlands to finance U.S. imports. Those to profit most were the food, textile, and aviation industries, as well as, to a lesser extent, the metal, steel, and chemical industries. And it was precisely these branches of industry that had been designated to lead the way with Dutch industrialization. While no single branch was literally "saved" by Marshall Plan aid (though the case could be made for the textile industry), it did provide a greater scope for other investments. Relatively smaller businesses were to profit most from the program.

The Marshall Plan effected its most notable results in areas financed by the counterpart fund. In their bilateral treaty the U.S. and the Netherlands agreed to apply these funds to promoting internal monetary and financial stability and to building production capacity by means of special projects. Whereas the Dutch preference tended toward the former initiative, the Americans wanted the positive publicity that special projects would grant. Ultimately a compromise was reached whereby a portion of the fund would be used to reduce the national debt, while another portion would go toward special projects, which generally had already been budgeted for anyway. A substantial sum was put into projects supporting Dutch reconstruction; war damage to buildings, roads, bridges, and canals was repaired, and industrial infrastructure was developed to standards commensurate with those of a modern nation. The modernization of the Netherlands became another focus for new initiatives, which included agricultural reform projects and projects to advance industrialization in economically disadvantaged areas. There was funding for a wide range of small projects besides, including the construction of the Velser traffic and rail tunnel and expansion of the Delft Institute of Technology and the Krasnapolsky Hotel in Amsterdam. The counterpart fund continued to provide financing until 1960.

Approximately 1 percent of the counterpart fund was used for "Technical Assistance" (TA). While not amounting to much on the financial scale, it was to be precisely these activities, aimed at boosting Dutch production levels, that turned out to be tremendously important in the long run. From the perspective of the Marshall aid planners, low labor productivity was one of the central factors holding back the various European economies. Raising this productivity was therefore key to achieving sustainable economic recovery. With this idea in mind, the ERP set the ambitious goal of raising labor productivity levels in participating countries by 15 percent over the program's lifetime (1948–51).[10] No one invested as much energy in the initiative as Hoffmann, who saw implementation of American business organization and labor relations concepts as a key means for driving Europe's productivity levels up. Europe was to be won over to this way of thinking by integrating provisions for Technical Assistance into the ERP. The objective was:

> to stimulate greater efficiency in industrial production through the introduction of American production techniques, styles of business organization, and labour-managment partnerships.[11]

Shaping a Technical Assistance program proved rather more difficult in practice, however. The solution finally came from England, where the Anglo-American Council on Productivity — a working group bringing employer and employee representatives to the same table — was founded in 1948. This group developed the Technical Assistance concept through the introduction of so-called productivity teams: teams of sector-specific employer and employee representatives that were to be given the opportunity to travel to the U.S. and study American production techniques. Their plan proved to be a good fit for the TA con-

5

———

THE
COLD WAR
AND
BEYOND

1945–2009

———

ECONOMICS
AND
SOCIETY

cept and had the additional advantage of providing excellent publicity. Over the course of 1949, the amounts budgeted for TA were raised substantially, ultimately claiming about 1 percent of the counterpart fund.

Following the British example (and at the urging of the ECA mission), the Netherlands set up its own TA working group in November 1948. Progress was slow at first. Most remarkable among the early U.S. visits, and generating a huge amount of publicity, was the visit by thirteen trade union leaders at the end of 1949. The trip report reads as something of a tribute to American industrial relations, mass production, and mechanization. It also put forth a call to organize sector-specific teams joining employers and staff for the purpose of study trips to the U.S., where they would be able to glean insights into American production techniques in their particular branch of industry. A popular edition of this report was issued under the title "Hoe werkt Amerika" (The Way America Works), with a staggering print run of 1,345,000 copies that were distributed free of charge to Dutch workers.

In 1950, the first Dutch productivity team representing the building industry left for the United States. Their American hosts evinced dissatisfaction at the TA team's activities, which they described as insufficiently coherent and lacking any truly effective policy for raising productivity across the board. From their perspective, the working group resembled nothing so much as a tourist-like study trip engaging in a handful of other activities on the side. To address these criticisms, the Contact Opvoering Productiviteit (Productivity Committee, COP) was established in 1950, creating an arena in which employers, staff, government, and specialized consultancy and research agencies could work together to launch, coordinate, and stimulate productivity initiatives in the Netherlands. The COP was expressly prohibited from actual involvement in the resulting projects and activities; its role was strictly limited to that of catalyst.

COP efforts initially centered on "here-and-now activities," as they were termed in the summary report *Vijf jaar COP* (The COP at Five Years).[12] These activities were geared toward generating the maximum amount of awareness of and publicity about the productivity concept, through such media as publications, conferences, exhibitions, filmstrips, and radio broadcasts. Also included were targeted, results-oriented study trips. In addition, American experts were to be contracted to come to the Netherlands for knowledge-sharing activities. By the mid-1950s the time had come for rooting productivity thinking in firmer ground. While the concept was certainly sufficiently known, there had been little motivation to apply it in practice. Generating awareness and publicity remained essential, as did the study trips and the visiting American experts. The COP also began to advance the organization of productivity centers (regionally and/or by sector) and working groups that would take on responsibility for specific productivity-enhancing activities. And, last but not least, it launched the

The Marketing Techniques Study Team on National Productivity Day,
The Netherlands, September 28, 1954.

5

—

THE
COLD WAR
AND
BEYOND

1945–2009

—

ECONOMICS
AND
SOCIETY

COP research projects. By the time the COP ceased its operations in 1962, it had spent a total of forty-two million guilders on productivity-boosting initiatives.

The study trip represented the most fundamental approach to the TA concept. Some thirteen hundred Dutch participants went on more than one hundred study trips to the U.S. under the auspices of either the COP or the European collaborative framework. About half of these trips were organized for the farming industry, one-third for the manufacturing industry — whether as productivity teams representing a given branch or set up to study such specific industrial problems as production engineering and personnel management — while the rest studied areas of general application. Interest in the U.S. had grown measure by measure until it aspired not only to penetrating the secrets of its high productivity levels but also to understanding the mechanisms driving America's modern consumer society. Consequently, there was a strong focus on the specific aspects of American society that might reveal these mechanisms (education, distribution, advertising, agricultural and other information services, and social intervention techniques such as the human relations approach in business and community organization).

Dutch visitors had a firsthand look at the "best practices" at work in American society, and were keen to adopt those that could benefit the Netherlands. This was the COP's objective, too. As such, a key feature of the study trips was the stipulation that each would be concluded with a report that was subsequently to be published by the COP. Trip participants were furthermore charged with disseminating their new knowledge and insights to their industry colleagues.

Modernization of the Netherlands

To what extent did Dutch modernization progress according to the American recipe as advanced by the Marshall Plan? Certainly we may conclude that the general principles for stable economic development and for economic growth as the force powering prosperity were fully embraced, and successfully so. The vital need for raising production capacity was likewise not merely acknowledged, but led to concrete measures. Yet implementation of American formulae occurred within a framework of a low-wage policy — a distinctly un-American situation. The view that economic growth would bring with it future prosperity for all was presented as a foregone conclusion. It was all just a matter of everyone first tightening their belts and rolling up their sleeves and the promise of the slogan "you too can be like us" would soon be fulfilled. It might even be asserted that a low-wage policy was able to subsist thanks precisely to this glittering vision of the future. It is here that we can discern the first Dutch inter-

pretation of the American perspective. This was in the priority that the government allocated to creating a system of social services over and above the direct
stimulation of individual prosperity.

America served as a source of inspiration for Dutch modernization efforts in
a general sense, certainly during the Marshall Plan era. The United States provided an instructive example of the modern affluent society, but this is not to say
that the Netherlands aspired to replicate the model in every detail. Dutch interest was reserved for only those features that could be utilized in a Dutch context.
In fact, very little was actually adopted. On the one hand, Dutch study teams were
impressed by, for example, the harmonious relations between American industry employers and their staff. The two parties worked together to achieve higher productivity, since both knew that it would be in their best interests to do so.
This was a lesson the Netherlands could benefit from. On the other hand, many
study teams were also quick to note that there were no lessons to be learned
from the way in which employer-employee communications were organized:
the Dutch system was exponentially better.

Thus, there never was any desire to copy, slavishly, all things American. Instead, the American example served as a source of inspiration driving Dutch society toward modernization — an inspiration that would continue to exert its
influence over a long period, and whose scope reached far beyond simply raising productivity levels in industry and agriculture. Productivity enhancement
was a vehicle that helped carry many more aspects of the American way of life
to the Netherlands, ranging from such distribution techniques as self-service
and supermarkets to social scientific theories about business organization and
community social work.

American examples were usually adapted to fit the Dutch context and conditions. As such, theories concerning community social work were remolded
to reflect the Dutch pillarized society. The supermarket made its entree in the
Netherlands, but was much smaller in scale and built not at the edge of the
city but in the new postwar suburban districts. In other instances, such as in
the case of the human relations approach in business management, American
models proved a seamless fit with established Dutch ideas. And some American models were simply noted and put down as irrelevant for Dutch society
— only to reemerge much later and in a modified guise when the need finally did
arise.

What the Marshall Plan offered the Netherlands was a model society. The
U.S. would not force its adoption, but the offer was nevertheless so "irresistible"
that it gained general currency. Acceptance did not mean wholesale copying,
however; the Netherlands was perfectly capable, after all, of forming its own
conclusions about what it did and did not want, and what it might want to adapt

771

to its own ends. Even so, the Netherlands clearly did become a party to that "irresistible empire," and Dutch society subsequently evolved into a modern welfare state — a welfare state inspired by the vision that America had proffered, certainly, but one that was not any less Dutch as a result.

5

—

THE
COLD WAR
AND
BEYOND

1945-2009

—

ECONOMICS
AND
SOCIETY

1 Kees Schuyt and Ed Taverne, eds., *1950 Prosperity and Welfare* (Assen: Palgrave Macmillan/Royal Van Gorcum, 2004) 57.

2 Victoria de Grazia, *Irresistible Empire. America's Advance through 20th-century Europe* (Cambridge, MA/London: The Belknap Press of Harvard University Press, 2005).

3 Barry Machado, *In Search of a Usable Past: The Marshall Plan and Postwar Reconstruction Today* (Lexington, VA: George C. Marshall Foundation, 2007), 7.

4 Ibid., 14.

5 COP, "Nederlandse boekdrukkers in Amerika" (1952), 28.

6 Frank Inklaar, *Van Amerika geleerd. Marshall-hulp en kennisimport in Nederland* (The Hague: SDU uitgeverij, 1997), 33; Cited in David W. Ellwood,

Rebuilding Europe. Western Europe, America and Postwar Reconstruction (London/New York: Longman, 1992), 226-227.

7 Robert C. Baron, ed., *Soul of America. Documenting Our Past 1492–1974* (Golden, CO: Fulcrum, 1989), 367.

8 Machado, *In Search*, 132-133.

9 Ibid., vii.

10 As of January 1952 the European Recovery Program (ERP) was succeeded by the Mutual Security Progam (MSP). See John Killick, *The United States and European Reconstruction, 1945–1960* (Edinburgh: Keele University Press, 1997), 96.

11 Inklaar, *Van Amerika geleerd*, 33.

12 COP, *Vijf jaar COP. Contactgroep Opvoering Productiviteit 1950–1955* (The Hague: s.n., 1955).

TRADING ECONOMICS ACROSS THE ATLANTIC: JAN TINBERGEN AND MILTON FRIEDMAN

——

HARRY P. VAN DALEN & ARJO KLAMER

It is a little superfluous for any foreigner to come to Rotterdam to lecture about economics at all. I feel a bit like a 17th century New England smuggler lecturing on seamanship to Admiral Tromp. The trade in economics nowadays is as much the other way: we send our young men to Rotterdam to learn, not our middle-aged professors to teach. Indeed some of our best middle-aged professors are named Koopmans and Houthakker! I suppose the logic of the situation is that I am not import at all; I am to be processed and re-exported, like cocoa beans.

Robert M. Solow in 1963 when visiting the Rotterdam School of Economics

With his usual wit and politeness Robert Solow — at that point in his career a rising star — pinpointed the main Dutch intellectual export product at the time: rigorous thinking in economic models. He may have been right. Today, the trade flow goes the other way as Dutch economists either go to the U.S. to be processed and reexported or have become accustomed to the American approach by importing American-style Ph.D. programs. Something in the standing of Dutch economics must have changed.

In order to account for the transfer of the comparative advantage in economics from the Netherlands to the U.S. we focus on the tales of two giants in economic thought. Both started their career in the 1930s, both would end up winning the Nobel Prize. One more or less personifies Dutch economics until the 1960s, and the other almost single-handedly changed American economics in the 1970s: Jan Tinbergen (1903–94) in the Netherlands and Milton Friedman (1912–2006) in the United States. Friedman was the father of what has be-

5

—

—

come known as the Chicago School of economics and Jan Tinbergen pioneered a style that would come to dominate the science of economics. Their tales reveal a great deal of the story of the transatlantic relationship between Dutch and American economics. It is a tale of how a small country can be big and how a large country is able to impose its values on the global community of economists and policymakers.

A Common Bond

Both economists shared a common interest in mathematics and economics. Friedman originally intended to be a mathematician, and later an actuary. It was Arthur Burns, future chairman of the Federal Reserve, and Homer Jones at Rutgers University who guided him to the field of economics. (Rutgers was, incidentally, founded by Dutch Reformed immigrants in 1766). Jones also helped him win a scholarship to pursue a master's degree in economics at Chicago. Friedman wanted to do economics because of the experience of the Great Depression; he was convinced that economists could help solve it. From 1937 to 1942 he worked at the prestigious National Bureau of Economic Research, later returning to the University of Chicago to become the icon of American economists propagating his all-American vision of a free market and a minimal government.

Jan Tinbergen first studied mathematics and natural sciences at the University of Leiden, where he became an assistant of the famous physicist Ehrenfest. The latter introduced him to most of the creative minds in physics, including his friend Albert Einstein. Even so, Tinbergen developed an interest in economics because of his socialist ideas. He very much wanted to solve the problems of society, and for the realization of that ideal economics seemed a better vehicle. But his knowledge of physics was not lost; he found that the way of thinking he had learned in physics was most pertinent to the study of economic problems as well. He was especially captivated by the idea that the rigor of mathematical and statistical methods could discipline policy decisions.

Tinbergen started his career as an economist at the Central Bureau of Statistics where he initiated research on the business cycle with a small group of like-minded mathematics- and statistics-oriented economists. Based on this research, he was commissioned to work for the League of Nations in Geneva to evaluate the many business cycle theories suggested by Haberler. The results marked a breakthrough in macroeconomic modeling and paved the way for the application of statistical methods to quantify parameters in calculating economic policies. The models were intended as instruments for economists to advise politicians. This later earned him, together with his more theoretically

Jan Tinbergen receives the Nobel Prize for Economics
from King Gustav Adolf of Sweden, 1969.

Milton Friedman, winner of the Nobel Prize for Economics in 1976, with freshly-printed dollar bills. The picture is taken from the television series *Free to Choose*.

oriented colleague and friend Ragnar Frisch, the first Nobel Prize in economics in 1969.

Accordingly, like Friedman Tinbergen saw economics as an instrument to solve social problems and like Friedman he believed that economics needed a strong empirical basis in order to fulfill its political role.

...Yet, Worlds Apart

With such similarities in motives and intentions, the differences between the two economists are all the more striking. They also prove critical for an explanation of the reversal in the trading of brain power across the Atlantic. Before Tinbergen appeared on the scene Dutch economists were liberals (or conservatives in the American frame of mind). This all changed during the Depression years when economists were fed up with classical economics and the dogmatism that permeated economic policy debates. Both Tinbergen and Friedman (and many other economists) wanted to see a free society, but each had distinctively different views on what a "free society" actually meant.

Tinbergen was thinking of freedom from want and misery and to that end he was prepared to compromise on freedom of choice. In fact, Tinbergen was very much an egalitarian *avant la lettre* who remained committed to defending social justice as a primary policy objective throughout his life. Friedman took quite a different stand and put freedom of the individual central; he would go to extremes in order to defend freedom of choice. As he explained in an interview in 1974:

> I start from a belief in individual freedom and that derives fundamentally from a belief in the limitations of our knowledge, from a belief that nobody can be sure that what he believes is right, is really right. I'm an imperfect human being who cannot be certain of anything, so what position involved the least intolerance on my part? The most attractive position is putting individual freedom first.

Tinbergen never displayed such doubts or thoughts about the use of knowledge. He was, deep down, the social engineer who was struck by the analogies between physics and economics and who saw possibilities on a macroeconomic scale to improve the efficiency of the national economy and, at a later stage, the world economy.

Both Tinbergen and Friedman were highly visible in their respective countries, not in the least because they did not shy away from policy problems. Friedman participated in discussions as an advisor to numerous government leaders and as

5

———

THE
COLD WAR
AND
BEYOND

1945–2009

———

ECONOMICS
AND
SOCIETY

a columnist in *Newsweek*. He never became involved, however, in the Council of Economic Advisers, the American agency that most resembles the Dutch Central Planning Bureau founded by Tinbergen. For Friedman, the spheres of science and policy had to be separated and his advice to policy-oriented economists was simple: "If you really want to engage in policy activity, don't make it your vocation. Make it your avocation. Get a job. Get a secure base of income. Otherwise, you're going to get corrupted."[1]

The manner in which Friedman gave policy advice also differed markedly from the way in which Tinbergen — or, for that matter, most economists — operated. Friedman thought that the public-interest characterization of government was basically flawed. Giving advice directly to government officials or politicians was "a waste of time." Economists could nonetheless exert influence on policy formation in three ways.[2] The first approach relied on persuasion and information: " … give the public a better idea of what is in the public's own interest." The second approach focused on analysis of institutional arrangements (such as constitutional changes) that would bring about the desired results instead of trying to influence policymakers directly. And a third way was to keep options open for times of crisis. He deemed that most policy advice did not seem tenable in good times but that the hearts and minds of politicians might be ready for drastic action during bad times.

In contrast, Tinbergen did assume that governments were defenders of the public interest and that merely appealing to the common good would be sufficient. Advising and educating policymakers directly was in his view the proper way to proceed. As a result, Tinbergen was heavily involved in Dutch and global policy activities throughout his entire career: the Central Bureau of Statistics,

TABLE 1
Most respected economists in the Netherlands and the United States

	Dutch economists	Dutch Ph.D. graduates	U.S. Ph.D. graduates	University of Chicago Ph.D. graduates
1	Jan Tinbergen	Jan Tinbergen	John M. Keynes	Robert Lucas
2	John M. Keynes	John M. Keynes	Kenneth Arrow	Adam Smith
3	John K. Galbraith	Paul Krugman	Paul Samuelson	Milton Friedman

Sources: H.P. van Dalen and A. Klamer, *Telgen van Tinbergen. Het verhaal van de Nederlandse econoom* (Amsterdam: Balans, 1996); H.P. van Dalen and A. Klamer, "Blood Is Thicker Than Water: Economists and the Tinbergen Legacy," in P.A.G. van Bergeijk et al., eds., *Economic Science and Practice* (Cheltenham: Edward Elgar, 1997), 60-91; A. Klamer and D. Colander, *The Making of an Economist* (Boulder, CO: Westview Press, 1990).

the League of Nations, the Central Planning Bureau, the Social Economic Council (SER), the United Nations, the OECD, and numerous other advisory bodies could count on his advice. Tinbergen would become the inspiring example for subsequent generations of Dutch economists as table 1 clearly shows.

The influence of Friedman on American economic thought is more difficult to determine as Chicago economists have always formed a special category. Stating that Friedman was by and large America's premier economist would deny the enormous diversity of opinion and schools of thought, past and present, in the U.S. Contrary to Tinbergen who virtually dominated Dutch economics in every respect, the Friedman influence on American economics reveals itself more through an attitude and approach than in policy views. For a better understanding it may be helpful to bring to the fore the main differences between the two economists (see table 2), who have become the archetypes for economists in the U.S. and Europe.

Friedman was the advocate of the individual freedom to choose, with a strong distrust for a government's helping hand. The invisible hand, the apt metaphor used by Adam Smith, to describe the process of price formation and resource

TABLE 2
Friedman versus Tinbergen

FRIEDMAN	TINBERGEN
Economist as advocate	Economist as a consensus seeker and engineer
Positive economics	Normative economics
Marshallian, partial equilibrium	Walrasian, general equilibrium
Microeconomic ("price theory") stories	Macroeconomic models
Informal, microeconomic stories	Formalized models and stories
Money matters	Money does not matter (that much)
Governments are fallible	Governments are adaptable
Meritocratic outlook	Egalitarian outlook
Markets do not fail	Markets fail
Realism of assumptions does not matter	Realism matters
"Invisible hand" government	"Helping hand" government
Public intellectual	Guardian of the public interest

5

—

THE
COLD WAR
AND
BEYOND

1945–2009

—

ECONOMICS
AND
SOCIETY

allocation should be allowed to work and government should at most assist in making the invisible hand work. Friedman would, however, never have proposed the complete elimination of government. As he stated clearly in *Capitalism and Freedom,* the basic roles of government in a free society are "to provide a means whereby we can modify the rules, to mediate differences among us on the meaning of rules, and to enforce compliance with the rules on the part of those few who would otherwise not play the game. The need for government arises in these respects because absolute freedom is impossible."[3] In 1995 he admitted: "I would like to be a zero-government libertarian," but he quickly added, "I don't think it is a feasible social structure."[4] Friedman's approach was closely connected to understanding the actual workings of markets. As he put it, "I was trying to explain the data, but not through models, not through multi-equation models, but through more informal stories—basically trying to appeal to microeconomic interactions."[5]

Tinbergen shared Friedman's orientation toward "what can be done" but being the social engineer he was, he wanted to think by means of mathematical models. Tinbergen was also an economist in the literal sense of the word in that he practiced economics (or rather, promoted economical conduct) not only in the world of models but also in his everyday life. Here, he completely fits Nelson's description of the economist of that time as the progressive neutral expert.[6] Efficiency in large and in small matters would get equal attention. Playful research did not enter Tinbergen's vocabulary, or as he put it in his own words: "One does not primarily study to contribute to the progress of theory: the primary motive is to be traced to the problems of the day, and to advise policymakers on how to solve the problems."[7] One could not imagine a better guardian of the public interest than Jan Tinbergen. Not for nothing did his colleagues call him Sint Jan (Saint John).

The differences also became quite apparent in the two economists' thoughts on developing countries. Tinbergen taught classes in Rotterdam on "development programming," not on development economics. As chairman of the United Nations Development Planning Committee he made a strong plea for Western governments to allocate 0.75 percent of their national income to development assistance. He was disappointed that most governments never fulfilled their promise, and this also shows that his model of government did not make room for the logic and behavior of self-serving politicians and bureaucrats. The Friedman view on these issues could not be more different. When asked in 1968 whether he approved of planned development, he responded: "I am not sure what planned development is. This expression is a contradiction in terms. If you have extensive central planning you won't have much economic development."[8]

Exporting the Tinbergen Model

Exporting the Tinbergen model of thought took place through intellectual migration. Students and colleagues such as Hendrik Houthakker, J.J. Polak, and, last but not least, Tjalling Koopmans were pivotal in the spread of knowledge. Polak became a prominent member of the International Monetary Fund (IMF), and Koopmans and Houthakker became members of the Cowles Commission, a group of mathematical economists that was headquartered in its early years in the lion's den: the University of Chicago. Houthakker went on to Stanford University and then to Harvard. During the years 1969–71 he served as a member of the Council of Economic Advisors in the Nixon administration after being a staff member during the Johnson administration.

Koopmans, who became the Cowles Commission's director in 1948, was a student of Tinbergen's and like Friedman and Tinbergen he had followed the same road to economics. Starting with mathematics at the University of Utrecht he soon switched to theoretical physics. But with the onset of the Great Depression Koopmans sought contact with socialist- and communist-oriented students. In July 1933 he wrote to Tinbergen, who was lecturing in Amsterdam, about his motives for switching to economics: " ... although in principle I find physics a beautiful field, I am too concerned with the social problem to be able to devote myself completely to theoretical physics. I therefore consider the possibility to use the mathematical development I possess in the study of economic and statistical problems."[9] Looking back, one can say that Koopmans and the other Cowles staff members transformed the macroeconomics debate into a hi-tech discussion about intertemporal decision making and stability in general equilibrium models. This would later help Robert Lucas form his views on economic growth, including his famous critique of large-scale macroeconomic models: he believed that they were not suited to predicting the effects of economic policy and gave too optimistic a view of the discretionary power of economic policymakers.

However, Koopmans' approach to economics proved to be too mathematical for other prominent economists at the University of Chicago. At first he had to cope with Frank Knight, a libertarian economist who did not think much of quantitative economics. Later, under the regime of Oscar Lange, the Chicago department became more open to the scientific approach advocated by Koopmans and his Cowles Commission. Friedman did not care for Koopmans as a person — he found him cold and authoritarian — and when Koopmans criticized the empirical work of Friedman's friend and mentor Arthur Burns and that of the National Bureau of Economic Research, calling it "measurement without theory," Friedman responded. To make the values of Chicago explicit he pub-

781

5

———

———

lished in 1953 his *Essays on Positive Economics*, which offered methodological guidelines for generations of Chicago economists and included the often-used phrase that "the realism of assumptions does not matter; it's only the predictive accuracy of a theory that counts."[10] To this day, economists continue to pay at least lip service to this work. A clash between Friedman and the Cowles Commission ensued and it led to the Commission's move to Yale University. There, Koopmans wrote an equally inspiring book of essays — *Three Essays on the State of Economic Science* (1957)[11] — to persuade his colleagues of the axiomatic approach to economics. What is more, Koopmans proposed to distinguish theoretical from empirical economics. Eventually, this actually happened, and one might say that Friedman won the battle but lost the war, at least that time.

In the early 1970s the pendulum began to swing in Friedman's free-market and antigovernment direction. Economists continued to follow Koopmans and Tinbergen, but — disappointed with Keynesian policies — gradually warmed up to Friedman's ideas. As a consequence, the Chicago department displaced the East Coast departments of MIT, Yale, and Harvard from center stage.

A Small Global World

Has the practice of economics changed due to intellectual migration? Undoubtedly it has. Hitler's rise and the outbreak of World War II brought about a fundamental shift in the geographical location of the research frontier. The United States became the dominant site where economic research took place, and this continues to be so. However, the most striking element of today's economics profession is that in spite of internationalization, fractionalization, and an explosion of publications the social world of economists seems to have become not only more integrated but smaller. What may have contributed to this smaller world is the dominant use of neoclassical language in economics. In Tinbergen's and Friedman's heydays the world could be divided into theoretical schools that hardly communicated with each other. Post-Keynesians, Marxists, Austrians, new Keynesians, (neo) institutionalists, monetarists, and new classicists competed with each other for the hearts and minds of students and policymakers. The diversity was great and cohesion within each group was strong but unproductive. What Friedman was saying hardly affected the debate among Keynesians because at that time Friedman was considered a crank by many of his colleagues.[12]

The key to making diversity work is the actual exchange of ideas. The use of one language — that of neoclassical economics — has contributed to true intellectual discussion. At its core one finds essentially the economics of Chicago and, deep down, of Friedman. The downside of the integration of different fields is that diversity of perspective and incentives for creativity have been lost. Perhaps the smaller world of economists also explains why the so-called Washington consensus — a market-oriented approach toward solving all major policy problems — has dominated economic policy circles around the world and has only recently come under attack as the practical consequences of deregulation and privatization appear on the radar of politicians. At some point in the recent past the only good economist seemed to be an economist with a general equilibrium view of the world. The Cowles Commission — or better, the Koopmans approach — was the proper way to do economics, and with the advent of Lucas, Edward Prescott, and Thomas Sargent Chicago was won over by this approach and Friedman seemed to be the man of the distant past.

Tinbergen's influence, by way of his Dutch associates, continues to be noticeable. But his approach had to be adopted by American economists in order to become dominant and in the process some of his ideals were lost. Even though American economists initially put their economics to the service of politicians, under the influence of Lucas and his Chicago colleagues their modeling became less policy-oriented. In the meantime, Dutch economists have increasingly adopted the American version of Tinbergen's economics. Like their U.S. colleagues, Dutch economists look to gain academic recognition and ignore the world of policy. This Americanization is also evident in the growing suspicion regarding government intervention in the economy among Dutch academic as well as government economists, and in their enthusiasm for the market as the solution to all kinds of problems.

The irony of our two icons is that they produced disciples who carried their initiatives too far and generated great expectations that did not materialize in the 1980s and 1990s. Koopmans carried forward the Tinbergen approach but lost contact with the real world and turned economics into an exercise of optimal resource allocation. Lucas — with Koopmans' help — pursued the Friedman approach to assume rationality in economic behavior, but he also lost touch with reality and grounded his models on superrational individuals. Both Tinbergen and Friedman regretted this development and in hindsight they may have been right. The Koopmans approach was constructed at a time of optimism, and the belief that all problems could be solved on a blackboard was understandable although not plausible. The Lucas approach was constructed in a period of pessimism, and the belief that every policy act was a waste of money was logical during times of stagflation and opportunistic politicians, but it ignored the power of institutions and the recognition that individual rationality is bounded by many other factors. In our age of diminished expectations it may turn out that the hi-tech economics of Koopmans and Lucas is ill-suited for today's economies and that a return to the pragmatism and rationality of Tinbergen and Friedman may offer the best solutions.

5

—

THE
COLD WAR
AND
BEYOND

1945–2009

—

ECONOMICS
AND
SOCIETY

1   Brian Doherty, "Best of Both Worlds"
    [interview with Milton Friedman],
    Reason Magazine, June 1995.

2   Milton Friedman, "Economists and
    Economic Policy," *Economic Inquiry* 24
    (1988): 1-10.

3   Milton Friedman, *Capitalism and
    Freedom* (Chicago: University of Chicago
    Press, 1962), 25.

4   Doherty, "Best of Both Worlds."

5   P. A. Samuelson and W. A. Barnett,
    Inside the Economist's Mind (Oxford:
    Blackwell Publishing, 2007), 122.

6   R. H. Nelson, "The Economics Profes-
    sion and the Making of Public Policy,"
    Journal of Economic Literature 25 (1987):
    49-91, here 52.

7   J. Passenier, *Van planning naar scanning.
    Een halve eeuw Planbureau in Nederland*
    (Groningen: Wolters-Noordhoff, 1994),
    58.

8   Lanny Ebenstein, *Milton Friedman.
    A Biography* (New York: Palgrave Mac-
    Millan, 2007), 150.

9   A. Jolink, *Jan Tinbergen. The Statistical
    Turn in Economics: 1903–1955* (Rotter-
    dam: Chimes, 2003), 78.

10 Milton Friedman, *Essays in Positive
    Economics* (Chicago: University of
    Chicago Press, 1953).

11 T. C. Koopmans, *Three Essays on the
    State of Economic Science* (New York:
    McGraw-Hill, 1957).

12 Arjo Klamer, *The New Classical
    Macroeconomics. Conversations with
    New Classical Economists and Their
    Opponents* (Brighton: Harvester Press,
    1984).

U.S. MULTINATIONALS IN THE NETHERLANDS: THE CASES OF IBM, DOW CHEMICAL, AND SARA LEE

—

BEN WUBS

Although U.S. foreign direct investments (FDI) in the Netherlands before World War II were not on a large scale, by the end of the twentieth century the U.S. had become the largest foreign investor in the Netherlands and the latter the second-largest recipient of U.S. FDI in Europe, after Great Britain. This article aims to provide a brief overview of American FDI activity in the Netherlands after World War II. Simultaneously, it makes an in-depth analysis of three major American investors in the Netherlands — Dow Chemical, IBM, and Sara Lee — and investigates why and how U.S. multinational companies (MNCs) chose to invest in the Netherlands particularly in the second half of the twentieth century. What strategy did U.S. MNCs use: greenfield investments, joint ventures, mergers, or acquisitions? What internationalization pattern did they follow? How important, in absolute and relative terms, was U.S. FDI during the period under consideration? How did American companies present themselves in the Netherlands? And, finally, did these MNCs easily adapt to the Dutch business environment?

Overview

After World War II, U.S. investment flows began to grow steadily. By 1950, the value of American FDI in the Netherlands amounted to $84 million and total investments were valued at $191 million. In the immediate postwar period, 34 new companies started their operations; by the end of 1950, 195 U.S. companies had affiliates in the Netherlands (see table 1).

5

—

THE
COLD WAR
AND
BEYOND

1945–2009

—

ECONOMICS
AND
SOCIETY

During the 1950s and 1960s, U.S. FDI in the Netherlands increased rapidly for two reasons. First, after World War II American companies, which had generally flourished during the war, were looking for new expansion possibilities around the globe. A recovering Europe appeared a good prospect. Therefore, U.S. investment in western European countries increased in that period, and within that general pattern the Dutch case was no exception. Second, at the beginning of the 1950s the Dutch government launched an industrialization program to transform the country into a modern industrial nation and overcome the potential problem of large-scale unemployment in the densely populated Netherlands. Part of the ambitious government program was to attract FDI, through a combination of investment subsidies, accelerated depreciation schemes, and fiscal measures.[1] Because the United States was one of the few countries with a capital surplus the Dutch government focused on U.S. MNCs.

Another factor in the Netherlands' attractiveness for U.S. FDI was its position within the European institutions following the Treaties of Rome in 1957. The Dutch commitment to free trade made it a perfect U.S. ally within the European Economic Community, and U.S. FDI grew rapidly during the 1960s and 1970s (despite growing anti-American sentiments because of the Vietnam War). It is no coincidence that an American Chamber of Commerce was established in Rotterdam in 1962 to represent the growing numbers of U.S. companies in

TABLE 1

Number and value of U.S. FDI position in the Netherlands (in millions of dollars)

	Total number of affiliates	Value of the investment in million U.S. dollars
1950	195	191
1963	223	446
1966	597	858
1977	836	4,534
1982	674	6,812
1990	848	19,120
1996	1,058	54,118
2000	1,216	115,429
2004	1,493	201,918

Sources: Until 1966: Frank Stubenitsky, *American Direct Investment in the Netherlands Industry* (Rotterdam: University Press, 1970), 46. For the years 1977 to 2004: U.S. Department of Commerce, Bureau of Economic Analysis (BEA), http://bea.gov/bea.

the Netherlands. At the end of the 1970s and the beginning of the 1980s, however, the advance of U.S. companies came to a halt. The number of affiliates decreased from 836 in 1977 to 650 in 1985, which was the absolute low point of the 1980s. Due to the second oil crisis, there was a general atmosphere of depression in the Netherlands. Unemployment figures rose rapidly and the investment climate deteriorated.

In response to the slump, the Dutch government pursued a moderate monetary policy and began to restructure and liberalize the economy in the 1980s. Its main target was to reduce unemployment, and it cut budgets and reduced social programs to lower the deficit. In addition, it began to privatize some major Dutch companies. The Ministry of Economic Affairs set up the Netherlands Foreign Investment Agency (NFIA) to attract FDI, and this agency established various offices in the home countries of the most important foreign MNCs, with the majority being in various U.S. cities.

The Dutch government's reorientation improved the climate for investment, and with the general upswing of the world economy in the 1990s the Netherlands regained its attractiveness for American companies. Once again, its position within Europe was an extra factor, because U.S. companies were keen to establish sites within the Single Market that was introduced in 1992, and the Netherlands was a prime location for doing so. From the early 1990s to the beginning of the twenty-first century the stock of U.S. FDI in the Netherlands increased tenfold; from around nineteen billion dollars in 1990 to over two hundred billion in 2004. In 2003, the United States invested as much in the

TABLE 2

Relative U.S. FDI position in Europe, 1950–2004

	UK	F	D	NL
	%	%	%	%
1950	48.9	12.5	11.8	4.8
1960	48.3	11.1	15.0	4.2
1970	40.0	12.9	21.4	7.5
1980	29.6	9.6	15.6	8.3
1990	34.0	8.9	12.8	8.9
2000	33.4	6.0	8.0	16.7
2004	27.7	5.3	7.3	18.4

Source: Calculations based on U.S. Department of Commerce,
Bureau of Economic Analysis (BEA), http://bea.gov/bea

787

Netherlands as it did in the whole of Asia. By 2004 the number of U.S. manufacturing and nonmanufacturing multinational companies established in the
Netherlands had grown to almost 1,500, representing more than one-quarter
of about 5,300 foreign operations in the Netherlands.[2] From 1950 to 2004, the
Netherlands' relative FDI position in Europe had increased from a mere 5 percent to more than 18 percent (see table 2).

5

THE
COLD WAR
AND
BEYOND

1945-2009

ECONOMICS
AND
SOCIETY

TABLE 3

Strategy of top 20 U.S. operations in the Netherlands in 2004 — sorted by number
of employees

Company	Strategy	Since	Number of employees
Deloitte	Federation	1968	7,300
DAF Trucks N.V. (PACCAR)	Acquisition	1993	6,000
Ernst & Young	Federation	1980	5,000
PricewaterhouseCoopers B.V.	Federation	1998	5,000
IBM Nederland N.V.	Greenfield	1940	5,000
Sara Lee International N.V.	Acquisition	1978	3,500
Nalco Europe B.V.	Acquisition	1968	3,000
Dow Benelux B.V.	Greenfield	1955	2,236
EDS International B.V.	Greenfield	1978	1,934
General Electric Plastics Europe B.V.	Greenfield	1971	1,800
IBM Consulting B.V.	Acquisition	2001	1,750
Philip Morris Holland B.V.	Greenfield	1969	1,750
Hewlett-Packard Nederland B.V.	Greenfield	1961	1,500
Aon Groep Nederland B.V.	Acquisition	1991	1,500
H.J. Heinz B.V.	Greenfield/ Acquisition	1958	1,500
Nike European Headquarters	Greenfield	1991	1,400
Cargill B.V.	Greenfield/ Acquisition	1960	1,350
Honeywell B.V.	Greenfield/ Acquisition	1934	1,300
Cordis Europa N.V.	Greenfield	1969	1,200
Eaton Electric N.V.	Acquisition	2003	1,200

Source: American Chamber of Commerce in the Netherlands, *Netherlands American Trade Directory
2005–2006* (The Hague: AmCham, 2004), and various web pages of the selected companies.

Tables 1 and 2 show a considerable relative and absolute expansion of the American FDI position in the Netherlands in the past decade. Although some of the expansion can be explained by an increase of U.S. investments in services and manufacturing, the greater part is explained by a tremendous increase of American holding companies in the Netherlands during the 1990s and the early 2000s (see last column of table 1). In 2004, about 34 percent of all U.S. foreign affiliates in the world could be classified as holding companies.[3] Due to its favorable tax climate the Netherlands in particular has attracted many of these U.S. companies. Moreover, it has attracted, in the same period, the most European headquarters of U.S. companies of all European countries (nearly 50 percent) because of its advantageous position in the European trade and traffic network.[4]

Investment Strategy

What investment strategy did American MNCs use in the Netherlands? Did they prefer greenfield investments, joint ventures, federations, mergers, or acquisitions?[5] According to the annual report of the American Chamber of Commerce in the Netherlands (AmCham) in 1968, the use of joint ventures instead of subsidiaries in full ownership was acceptable for the first investment, but not always practical for an MNC that needed maximum flexibility.[6] The advantage of a joint venture was that it involved participation in the national economy and was more likely to avoid national protests. This could also be done through the establishment of national companies.

As table 3 clearly shows, joint ventures (federations) formed only a small minority. The large auditing firms in table 3, however, are a special case because they had difficulties entering the European market. As a result, during the 1980s and 1990s international federations that included the largest Dutch and U.S. auditing firms were formed.[7]

The preferred strategy of the twenty largest U.S. MNCs in the Netherlands was greenfield investment. Acquisition of Dutch companies was also an accepted strategy, but often only after an initial greenfield investment. In addition, the lack of mergers between the larger U.S. companies and Dutch companies is noticeable. The latter can be easily explained by the fact that U.S. MNCs were generally much bigger than their Dutch competitors. Besides, the big Dutch MNCs like Royal Dutch/Shell, Unilever, Akzo, and Philips either had been the result of earlier cross-border mergers or had defended themselves effectively against foreign takeovers.

789

Three Cases

5

———

THE
COLD WAR
AND
BEYOND

1945-2009

———

ECONOMICS
AND
SOCIETY

We now explore the investment strategy and the path three major investors —IBM, Dow Chemical (Dow), and Sara Lee (SLC)—followed after their initial investment in the Netherlands. Although these companies clearly preferred either greenfield investments or acquisitions, the ways in which they pursued their internationalization strategies differed significantly. Each company demonstrates an individual strategy, depending on the period of time, the line of business, its internal organization, and its place of origin in the United States. The reactions of a company from the Midwest (Dow) to the Dutch business environment were different from those of an East Coast company (IBM).

IBM — IBM's internationalization pattern in the Netherlands matched perfectly with Johanson and Vahlne's model of the incrementally increasing commitments to foreign markets. At first the company appointed an agent in 1925 (Firma Boas). Then, a closer link was established when the agent was appointed as an official subsidiary of IBM's new European headquarters in Geneva in 1936. Next, the agent became a fully owned subsidiary in 1940 (N.V. Watsons Bedrijfsmachine Maatschappij). The subsidiary then invested in production facilities (e.g., punched cards, electric typewriters) when the limits to the export market had been reached. What is interesting in IBM's case is that the Dutch agent became the director of the full subsidiary. Moreover, in due time all general directors of IBM in the Netherlands were Dutch. In spite of the formation of IBM's World Trade Corporation, the aim of which was to coordinate business outside the U.S., the overall corporate policy was that the national organizations were staffed and directed by citizens of the countries in which they operated.[8]

IBM showed a great adaptability to the Dutch environment. IBM Nederland was closely linked with the processes of innovation in Dutch business and (semi-) government organizations. Simultaneously, the business was managed according to IBM's international corporate strategy. Since the late 1930s the Dutch company had been embedded in IBM's strong corporate culture. However, IBM's human resource management in the Netherlands was very compatible with the development of Dutch postwar labor relations. Thomas J. Watson had been a genuine supporter of Roosevelt's New Deal principles and this resulted in IBM's social policy, of which job security was a most distinguishing feature.[9]

The introduction of the personal computer at the beginning of the 1980s revolutionized the computer market. At first IBM missed the new development, then it decided that it had to act. Although IBM's personal computers were popular in the Netherlands, the company had problems adjusting to a different market. Clone suppliers were undercutting IBM's prices and returns on the highly competitive personal computer market sunk. In addition, sales of main frames fell. Furthermore, in 1985 the Amsterdam plant switched from producing electric typewriters to manufacturing printers, a move that proved unsuccessful.[10]

In 1992, for the first time in its entire history, the IBM Corporation was losing money, and in 1993 it suffered a loss of eight billion dollars. On the corporate level a cost-reducing program was started, mainly through staff retrenchments. The company had to give up its old policy of lifetime employment, and its corporate structure was altered. IBM Nederland was made responsible for IBM's corporate distribution and became a key distribution center for many products into Europe, the Middle East, and Africa. In addition, the Dutch company acquired consultancy and software firms. From the mid-1990s on, IBM moved from hardware to software and services. In 2005, IBM Nederland's major activities were Logistics and R&D. Until the 1990s the Dutch company enjoyed relative autonomy, but since the restructuring IBM has become more and more a global company with global sourcing, in which the Dutch affiliate is just one center of competence among many others.

DOW — Dow's internationalization pattern showed incremental characteristics as well. In 1955, it set up a central warehousing point in the Rotterdam port as a gateway to the European market. Two years later, Dow acquired Dobeckmum packaging firm, with production and marketing facilities all over Europe and headquarters in Amsterdam, which included a lurex fiber plant. By 1960, it had built a small latex plant near the warehouse in Rotterdam. In the early 1960s, however, Dow planned to build a major chemical complex somewhere in the Benelux.[11] The company from Midland, MI, selected Terneuzen, a small town in the province of Zeeland, on an estuary of the Westerschelde. The location had been chosen because it offered Dow an opportunity to develop an industrial complex well away from population centers, as it always had done in the U.S. Between the ports of Rotterdam and Antwerp, the plant had easy access to leading markets and supply sources. Its location on the Westerschelde allowed Dow to build docking facilities capable of handling transatlantic shipments. Simultaneously, the site was easily connected to the European rail and road networks. Dow's choice to build an industrial complex in the middle of nowhere rather than, for example, in the Rotterdam Botlek area is a good example of path dependence, because the Dow Company had built its first plant in the countryside in the Midwest and has always kept a preference for similar sites. In addition, the Dutch proactive industry policy at the time helped Dow decide to settle in Terneuzen. This policy involved the creation of employment in un-

791

The petrochemical multinational Dow Benelux B.V., located on
the Westerschelde near Terneuzen in the Netherlands.

derdeveloped areas in the Netherlands by actively attracting FDI. In 2006, the location was Dow's largest chemical complex in Europe, and Dow had become the largest foreign direct investor in the Netherlands.

Dow Chemical is a striking example of how MNCs keep their home practices largely in place when they undertake FDI operations.[12] Though it adapted itself to the Dutch legal system, the company always chose its own path where possible. For example, Dow's preference for a site in Terneuzen rather than Rotterdam can be partly explained by the company's dislike for Rotterdam's long-term land lease regulations. Ownership of the lot was an absolute condition for Dow, as it had been in the U.S. In labor relations Dow did not adapt to the Dutch collective arrangements either. When possible, it introduced its own compensation programs. From 1979 until this very day Dow has not signed Collective Labor Agreements (CAOs) with its employees.[13] Dutch trade unions have been powerless as a great majority of Dow's staff have signed individual labor agreements. Besides, arguing too much with the largest employer in the region would endanger too many jobs.

SARA LEE — The corporate internationalization strategy of Sara Lee (SLC) in the Netherlands was based on acquisitions. The exceptional way in which the Dutch family firm Douwe Egberts (DE) was acquired also showed an incremental pattern, although not in the sense of the other two cases. The incrementality of SLC's investment refers to the acquisition of ownership and control. Majority economic ownership was acquired quite early, in 1977; yet, full control was only secured twenty-five years later. Meanwhile, SLC — a company committed to the principle of decentralized management — shared control with its Dutch management, a Dutch supervisory board, and a special Dutch trust. The latter was established to control part of the voting rights within the SLC management apparatus in order to preserve the "identity, integrity, and Dutch character" of DE.[14] A memorandum on the role and responsibilities of the trustees — all respected and independent Dutch businessmen and politicians — comprehensively described how the Dutch character of DE should be preserved. Clearly, SLC adapted largely, and even formally, to the Dutch business environment.

The trustees, however, always applied these guidelines in a pragmatic way. In twenty-five years neither party, SLC or DE, ever sought changes that the other opposed. There always was a general consensus among the top managers in Chicago and Utrecht regarding the interpretation of the contract. What is interesting, however, is that the Americans ran the Dutch business at arm's length for a long time. The Dutch character of DE was even preserved contractually. In comparison, most American companies wanted much more control over their foreign affiliates. DE nonetheless was seen as a potential center for international management and the coffee business was highly profitable — the hands-off idea made sense at the time.

During the 1980s and 1990s DE was integrated in various stages into the strategy of the parent company, though for a long time the Dutch subsidiary continued to maintain some autonomy. Meanwhile, with major acquisitions in the Netherlands and other countries, SLC had become one of the larger American MNCs: by 1987 SLC's foreign assets amounted to more than 40 percent of its total assets. In 1989 DE was renamed Sara Lee/DE to emphasize the integration of both companies. Sare Lee/DE became an international holding company that administered an important part of SLC's international businesses outside the U.S. During the 1990s Sara Lee/DE was integrated more fully into the American parent corporation. The international holding company was managed by means of guidelines and control points. Meanwhile, the Americans had convinced their Dutch colleagues that SLC's numerous reward systems to motivate management to perform should be introduced in the Dutch subsidiary as well.

When in the early years of the twenty-first century SLC changed more and more into a centralized multidivisional organization, the particular legal construction in the Netherlands had outlived itself. As a result, in 2002 the Dutch trust was abolished. The headquarters in Utrecht became an international management center that had to run SLC's international businesses outside the U.S. In 2007 Sara Lee International's corporate governance structure in the Netherlands changed completely: its supervisory board and board of management were discontinued.[15] As a result, the transformation process was complete.

Conclusion

In the early 2000s the Netherlands had become one of the key hosts of U.S. MNCs in the world. Since the 1960s the U.S. had even become the most important foreign direct investor in the Dutch economy. After World War II, the industrializing Netherlands offered U.S. investors several attractive features, apart from its central geographical location in western Europe. These included a stable political and social climate, a welcoming government, an excellent infrastructure, well-developed international trading contacts, modern banking facilities, proficient language skills, and well-educated workers: in short, an excellent business environment for U.S. investors. Besides, as a result of its favorable tax climate the country has attracted many U.S. holding companies in the past decade.

Although there were differences among the investment patterns of IBM, Dow, and SLC, there were similarities as well. All three cases showed an incremental internationalization pattern in one way or another. Moreover, these U.S.

5

—

THE
COLD WAR
AND
BEYOND

1945–2009

—

ECONOMICS
AND
SOCIETY

companies introduced their own individual compensation programs based on individual performance. Until the 1980s this was unheard of in the Dutch business environment, which was mainly based on collective bargaining, independent of individual performance. Nevertheless, since the 1990s these individual reward systems have become more common in the Netherlands. Another similarity among these three cases was that the relative importance or autonomy of the Dutch subsidiary decreased in the course of the 1990s. National subsidiaries became business units of global companies. This was a result of a general trend in organizational structures of MNCs at the time and a response to the process of globalization. Increasingly, MNCs operated and competed on a global scale and in global markets. The need to have national headquarters in various countries decreased; instead, virtual headquarters began to manage the businesses in various regions — sometimes not even on a national level anymore.

1   Ministry of Economic Affairs, "Fourth Memorandum on Industrialization of the Netherlands" (April 1953), 10.

2   American Chamber of Commerce in the Netherlands, *Netherlands-American Trade Directory, 2005–2006*, xxviii-xxix.

3   Jennifer L.Koncz and Daniel R. Yorgason, "Direct Investment Positions for 2004. Country and Industry Detail," in *US Department of Commerce, Bureau of Economic Analysis: Survey of Current Business* (July 2005), 45.

4   Buck Consultants International, *Ontwikkeling vestigingsputronen Amerikaanse en Japanse bedrijven in Europa* (The Hague: Ministry of Economic Affairs, 1998), 17-24.

5   A greenfield investment is a form of foreign direct investment where a parent company starts a completely new venture in a foreign country.

6   Jay H. Cerf, *Attitude of American Business in Europe* (American Chamber of Commerce in the Netherlands, 1967).

7   Keetie Sluyterman, *Dutch Enterprise in the Twentieth Century. Business Strategies in a Small Open Economy* (London: Routledge, 2005), 233.

8   Jan Johanson and Jan-Erik Vahlne, "The Internationalization Process of the Firm — A Model of Knowledge Development and Increasing Foreign Market Commitments," *Journal of International Business Studies* 8 (1977): 23-32; James Connolly, "History of Computing in Europe" (New York: IBM World Trade Corporation [unpublished report], 1968), 54.

9   Rowena Olegario, "IBM and the Two Thomas J. Watsons," in Thomas K. McCraw, ed., *Creating Modern Capitalism. How Entrepreneurs, Companies, and Countries Triumphed in Three Industrial Revolutions* (Cambridge, MA: Harvard University Press, 1997), 371.

10 Huub Surendonk, *IBM Nederland N.V. 60 jaar* (Amsterdam: IBM, 2000), 61.

11 E.N. Barndt, *Growth Company. Dow Chemical's First Century* (East Lansing: Michigan State University Press, 1997), 373-374.

12 Richard Whitley, "How and Why are International Firms Different? The Consequences of Cross-Border Managerial Coordination for Firm Characteristics and Behaviour," in Glenn Morgan,

5

—

THE
COLD WAR
AND
BEYOND

1945–2009

—

ECONOMICS
AND
SOCIETY

Peer Hull Kristensen, and Richard Whitley, eds., *The Multinational Firm. Organising across Institutional and National Divides* (Oxford: Oxford University Press, 2001), 27-68.

13 Interview with the vice president of the Board at Dow Benelux, Ed de Graaf, March 8, 2006; Ferry Pot, "Continuity and Change of Human Resource Management. A Comparative Analysis of the Impact of Global Change and Cultural Continuity of the Management of Labour Relations between the Netherlands and the United States" (Ph.D. dissertation, Erasmus University Rotterdam, 1998), 163.

14 Anthony Fudge, *Consolidated Foods Corporation Douwe Egberts 1978/Sara Lee Corporation Sara Lee/DE 1998* (Hilversum: s.n., 1998), 23; "Memorandum on the Role and Responsibilities of the Stichting Administratiekantoor Douwe Egberts Consolidated and Its Trustees" (Utrecht: Sara Lee Archive Utrecht [SLAU], June 1977), 10.

15 Sara Lee Corporation, "Annual Report," 1987; Sara Lee/DE NV, "Jaarverslag," 1988-89; Sara Lee Corporation, "Annual Report," 2000; interviews with Corporate Secretary Sara Lee International bv, Albert Six, January–March 2007; Sara Lee, Management Information, "Plan tot herstructurering van Sara Lee International," March 20, 2007.

DUTCH MULTINATIONALS IN THE UNITED STATES: THE CASES OF PHILIPS, SHELL, AND UNILEVER

―――

MIRA WILKINS

This article traces the path of Dutch multinational enterprises (MNEs) following World War II.[1] "Dutch investment in America" is defined here as nonresident (in America) investment: that is, the headquarters remain abroad. Special attention is given to the major Dutch MNEs: Shell, Philips, and Unilever, which together throughout the period under consideration held the largest share of activities in the United States.[2] Some observations on the nature and uniqueness of Dutch business operations in the U.S. will also be given.

World War II

A June 1941 U.S. census identified 179 Dutch-controlled enterprises in the United States, the value of which came to 336 million dollars; the Dutch ranked third in this field after the United Kingdom and Canada. In 1940, a Foreign Funds Control group was set up in the United States, administered by the U.S. Treasury Department, and when the Germans invaded the Netherlands in May 1940 an executive order promptly froze Dutch properties in America to avoid their falling under German control. However, Shell and Unilever received licenses to continue to operate. Royal Dutch set up nominal headquarters in Curaçao and the administration of the American Shell business remained Anglo-American. The U.S. business of Unilever continued to be "controlled" from London. NV Philips activated its previously made plans to create a trust, and the Philips group headquarters were shifted to New York City. Most of the Dutch merchant fleet escaped the Germans, and in June 1940 the British took over whatever they could

5

THE
COLD WAR
AND
BEYOND

1945–2009

ECONOMICS
AND
SOCIETY

of the Holland America Line for operation in war service on the North Atlantic. Thus, at the time when the Netherlands was occupied by the Germans and while the U.S. was still neutral, adjustments were made in the legal arrangements applying to Dutch business operations in the United States.

During the war years Shell proved to be an innovative company meeting U.S. wartime needs. It pioneered in the development of 100-octane fuel for aviation; its subsidiary, Shell Chemical, was an important contributor to the U.S. synthetic-rubber program. Unilever's Lever Brothers made excellent wartime profits from its consumer-goods lines and expanded its business. Although some members of the NV Philips family remained in New York, the company's operations within the Netherlands persisted during the entire war. On January 9, 1942, the Philips Trust set up the North American Philips Company that strongly backed the U.S. war effort.

The Office of Alien Property Custodian considered vesting the U.S. properties of the Dutch rayon company Algemeene Kunstzijde Unie (AKU) during the war due to the company's German connections, and this did eventually happen in 1947. AKU properties with a "German history" were then sold in 1948 to the American-owned Beaunit. Thus, "AKU was exceptional among the Dutch multinationals.... Shell, Philips, and Unilever were all able to preserve all their U.S. properties at war's end."[3] AKU did retain its subsidiary American Enka, which had no German heritage. Other German connections caused problems. Royal Dutch/Shell had agreements with I.G. Farben. Philips participated in a web of international licensing accords that included German companies, and it had to convince the American authorities that it was a Dutch enterprise. On the whole, though, Dutch business in the United States emerged out of the war years intact and ready for expansion.

Dutch Business in America from 1950 to 1970

In terms of foreign direct investment in the United States, the Dutch maintained third place for several decades.

After the war NV Philips decided to keep its American company—North American Philips Company—at arm's length, insisting it was independent. There were several reasons for this. The Dutch government was extremely short of dollars right after the war, leading some to suspect that it might force the sale of Philips' U.S. assets to garnish much-needed currency. Second, it was considered wise to separate the parent NV Philips, with its wartime contacts with the Germans, from the American company. Third, Amperex (a subsidiary of North American Philips) had defense contracts, and this made it sensible to have the American firm independent of foreign control. Last, and perhaps most impor-

tant, were antitrust considerations. U.S. lawyers were suggesting to their foreign corporate clients that subsidiaries' independence was needed in order to
avoid accusations of their being party to cartels.

Lever Brothers and Lipton Inc. operated as separate companies (with separate management) in the United States. This created problems for the parent,
Unilever — which owned both of them 100 percent — especially as the acquisition of many new companies in the U.S. introduced coordination and control
difficulties. The U.S. headquarters of Lever Brothers moved from Boston to New
York City, where the subsidiary came to occupy an impressive newly built high-
rise on Park Avenue. But competition in the American market was fierce. The
U.S.-owned firm Procter & Gamble (P & G) was the market leader in cleaning and
hygiene products, with its laundry detergent Tide and toothpaste Crest. On top
of this, Unilever had in 1957 its first encounter with U.S. antitrust law, an experience that had a major impact on its business strategy (as similar experiences
did for Shell and Philips). Nevertheless, in 1970 the Unilever group of companies in America ranked among the most important foreign direct investments
in the United States.[4]

Following World War II Shell maintained its position as a giant integrated
oil enterprise in the U.S. Although part of a large multinational enterprise, it
had (like Lever Brothers) forged considerable independence within the global

TABLE 1
Foreign Direct Investment in the United States, 1950, 1970*

	1950	1970	Rank in 1970
United Kingdom	1,168	4,127	1
Canada	1,029	3,117	2
The Netherlands	334	2,151	3
Switzerland	348	1,545	4
Other European Countries	377	1,731	
Rest of the World	134	599	
Total	3,391	13,270	

* Level, at year's end, in millions of U.S. dollars.

Source: U.S. Department of Commerce, Foreign Business Investments in the United States (Washington,
DC, n.d. [1962]), 34; and Survey of Current Business (February 1973), 30. These are "stock," not "flow"
figures. The Total for 1950 is out by one digit due to rounding off in the original. Although the Dutch
rank in 1950 was fourth place, it rapidly moved ahead of Switzerland.

organization of its parent, and this became even more evident as parent and U.S. company officials sought to shape the image of the company as American, with American directors making decisions based on American interests. U.S. antitrust policy undoubtedly contributed to this move. While an oil antitrust case had been postponed during the war and dismissed without prosecution in 1951, it and other cases made the Dutch parent of Shell aware of the dangers. Then, in 1952, a staff report to the Federal Trade Commission on "the International Petroleum Cartel" alerted all the big oil companies to the hovering thundercloud of antitrust litigation. In 1953, when a civil lawsuit was filed against the five largest U.S. international companies, interestingly Shell was *not* a defendant. The final judgment in this case did not come until 1968, and throughout this period the shadow of the antitrust threat hung over the entire oil industry.[5]

From 1950 to 1970 NV Philips was also continuously affected by U.S. antitrust policies, particularly as a codefendant in several cases against General Electric (GE). Old agreements (cartel relationships) were clearly no longer allowed by U.S. regulators in postwar America. Philips wanted to keep GE at bay in the Netherlands, and was even concerned that the Marshall Plan would offer preferential treatment for U.S. companies in European markets. Indeed, it seems that Philips did not want to compete with GE (and RCA) in the United States for fear of retaliation by these two firms in Europe. Yet in diversifying its operations to avoid head-on competition with the U.S. giants, by 1970 North American Philips had become one of the largest "European-controlled" manufacturers in the United States, making a range of producer and consumer goods, including electric and electronics equipment and components.[6]

Other Dutch MNEs expanded their operations in the U.S. in this period. AKU merged in 1969 with Koninklijke Zout Organon to form AKZO, which included a controlling interest in International Salt, America's second-largest salt company. In the field of banking, in the Netherlands the Nederlandsche Handel-Maatschappij merged in 1964 with the Twentsche Bank, forming Algemene Bank Nederland (ABN), which possessed a New York branch. In the same year, the Amsterdamsche Bank and the Rotterdamsche Bank combined to form the Amsterdam-Rotterdam Bank (AMRO), and in 1968 AMRO participated in the formation of the European-American Banking Corporation (EABC) and the European-American Bank and Trust Company (EABTC) in New York. Thus, by 1970 both ABN and AMRO had modest direct investments in the United States. However, technological advances ended the role of one major Dutch MNE. After World

◄ Lever House, on Park Avenue, New York, built in 1951–52 as the headquarters for Lever Brothers, the U.S. wing of Unilever.

5

—

THE
COLD WAR
AND
BEYOND

1945–2009

—

ECONOMICS
AND
SOCIETY

War II the Holland America Line had resumed its transatlantic service, but the rise of air travel — by 1965 95 percent of transatlantic traffic was by air — forced the Line to discontinue its transatlantic passenger service in 1971. By 1978 it had fully diversified into the cruise-liner business and had moved its headquarters from Rotterdam to Stamford, Connecticut, thereby effectively becoming a U.S. company. Overall, by 1970 Dutch direct investment in the U.S. had risen to 2.2 billion dollars, which was much larger than U.S. direct investment in the Netherlands (1.5 billion dollars).[7]

Dutch Business in America from 1970 to 2008

In the early 1970s the devaluation of the dollar and the end of postwar capital export-control restrictions in major European countries made U.S. properties cheap for foreign investors. The reported level of Dutch direct investment in the United States at year's end throughout the twentieth century always exceeded that of U.S. direct investment in the Netherlands.[8] Most large (and some smaller) foreign MNEs — whether they were profitable or not within the U.S.

TABLE 2
Foreign Direct Investment in the United States, 1970, 2000*

	1970	2000	Rank in 2000
United Kingdom	4,127	277,613	1
Japan	229	159,690	2
The Netherlands	2,151	138,894	3
France	286	125,740	4
Germany	680	122,412	5
Canada	3,117	114,309	6
Switzerland	1,545	64,719	7
Other European Countries	765	157,636	
Rest of the World	370	95,854	
Total	13,270	1,256,867	

* Level, at year's end, in millions of U.S. dollars.

Source: Survey of Current Business (February 1973), 30; (September 2003), 67. In the 1970 column, the figures for "Other European Countries" and "Rest of the World" differ from those given in table 1, since more countries are named on this table. These are "stock," not "flow" figures.

market — regarded the United States as too significant within the global economy to be neglected.

Table 2 shows the leap in FDI in the United States between 1970 and 2000. By 2006 the Dutch, with 189 billion dollars, had dropped to fourth in the rankings behind the United Kingdom with 303 billion, Japan with 210 billion, and Germany with 202 billion dollars.

While many Dutch businesses invested in the United States in the years from 1970 to 2008, it is truly remarkable how the three leading Dutch enterprises (Royal Dutch/Shell, Unilever, and Philips) held on to their premier position. A 1976 U.S. Department of Commerce study found for 1974 that these three companies accounted for approximately 69 percent of Dutch holdings in the United States, while six (including AKZO, DSM, and Thyssen Bornemisza) made up about 83 percent.[9] The study pointed out that the Shell, Unilever, and Philips U.S. subsidiaries were major corporations in their own right as they did not depend on their parents for capital. DSM was undertaking new investments in the United States in the chemical industry; Thyssen Bornemisza had just made a large investment in Indian Head, Inc., a U.S. textile firm that soon became a conglomerate. As for AKZO, in 1994 it acquired the Swedish Nobel Industries and became Akzo Nobel; its U.S. business operations, way below the three frontrunners, became highly diversified. Akzo Nobel acquired ICI in 2007, obtaining in the process ICI's U.S. operations. After 1970 other well-known Dutch industrials gained a foothold in the United States, such as the brewer Heineken and the publishing houses Elsevier (which joined with the British company Reed International to become Reed Elsevier in 1993) and Kluwer (which became Wolters Kluwer after 1987, albeit still known in the United States as Kluwer). ABN AMRO, which formally came into existence in 1991, became an important player in the U.S., and by the 1990s it was joined by two financial services groups, ING and Aegon Group.

In 1974, the Royal Dutch/Shell Group alone held more than half the total combined book value of all Dutch holdings in the United States. While Shell Oil greatly expanded its oil (and chemical) activities in subsequent years and even moved into the coal industry, its relative position (in Dutch direct investments) became less significant as other Dutch firms expanded. Moreover, by the early 1990s, Royal Dutch/Shell's management had become dissatisfied with the performance of its American affiliate. Key assets were sold off (including those in coal), the workforce reduced, and Royal Dutch/Shell drew Shell Oil more closely into its global strategy. Nevertheless the latter maintained its importance. In 1997 Shell and Texaco announced a joint venture, which merged their midwestern and western U.S. refining and marketing activities and their total U.S. transportation, trading, and lubricants business. When Chevron took over Texaco in 2001 and the latter was forced (for antitrust reasons) to divest itself of certain gas stations, Shell acquired full control over those that had been part of its 1997

5

—

THE
COLD WAR
AND
BEYOND

1945–2009

—

ECONOMICS
AND
SOCIETY

joint venture with Texaco. By 2002, with twenty thousand stations and about 15 percent of the gasoline market, it was by far the largest gasoline retailer in the United States. In the early twenty-first century, it was paying new attention to the natural gas industry, which gradually had emerged as a core business, and it began to look into renewable energy sources (wind and solar energy).[10]

Between 1970 and 2008, the other Dutch (British-Dutch) giant, Unilever, also greatly enlarged its U.S. business by undertaking multiple acquisitions and introducing new product lines, particularly in food. Few Americans had any inkling that when they bought Dove soap, Calvin Klein cosmetics, Lipton Cup-a-Soup, Lawry's Seasoned Salt, Country Crock margarine, Hellmann's Real Mayonnaise, Ragu Spaghetti Sauce, or Ben & Jerry's Ice Cream they were purchasing the products of a British-Dutch multinational enterprise.[11] In 2004–05 Unilever transformed its management structure, abolishing the two-chairman structure (one for the Dutch and the other for the British company) and replacing it with a single nonexecutive chairman (the former chairman of the Dutch company) and a group chief executive. As in the case of Royal Dutch/Shell, the ramifications of this reorganization remain to be seen.

North American Philips had long existed as a trust but was still described in U.S. literature as an affiliate of the Dutch Philips. Its business interests in the U.S. grew, notably with the establishment of its PolyGram music group, a fifty-fifty joint venture of NV Philips and Siemens, in 1972. But more significant was the rising competition from Japan in the consumer electronics field. As noted, NV Philips had not wanted to enter certain core sectors in the United States, as it had hoped to keep General Electric and RCA out of Europe, but the Japanese presence in the U.S. and elsewhere transformed this business landscape. As a result, in 1974 North American Philips acquired the Magnavox Company, which manufactured one of the five leading color-television brands in the United States. In the same year it acquired National Components Industries, and in 1975 it took over Signetics, the sixth-largest U.S. producer of semiconductors. By the mid-1970s Philips operated various types of electronic plants all over the United States. Its constant search for innovation meant that it was also in a position to join with the Japanese company Sony to commercialize compact disks (CDs) in 1982.

Finally, in 1987 NV Philips ended the trust arrangement and North American Philips became a wholly owned subsidiary. Similar to Shell, the growing U.S. market demanded a consolidation of the corporate structure. In 1990, Philips employed more than fifty thousand people in thirty-one American states, and it claimed that its television business was the second-largest in the United States. A reversal of fortune in the 1990s led to further reorganization and five separate divisions were created: Philips Consumer Electronics, Philips Domestic Appliances and Personal Care, Philips Lighting Company, Philips Medical

Systems, and Philips Semiconductors, each with its own head office in a different location in the United States and dealing separately with the corporate center in Amsterdam. Yet despite drastic downsizing, Philips in 2004 still employed twenty thousand people in the United States. During subsequent years it "dumped" noncore businesses and continued to restructure. By 2007, however, it was embarking on a new acquisition spree.[12]

The most significant development of the 1990s was that banking, insurance, and other financial services occupied an increasingly important share of Dutch direct investments in the United States. In banking, ABN AMRO stands out. Created in 1991, it immediately acquired full control of the European American Bank (which had already become the largest foreign-owned bank in New York in 1974). By 1996 ABN AMRO had offices in Chicago, New York, Atlanta, Boston, Miami, San Francisco, and Los Angeles, and four years later it could claim total assets of 171 billion dollars in the United States. With its acquisition of Michigan National in 2000, ABN AMRO held ownership control of three of the ten largest foreign-owned banks in America. Yet the momentum of ABN AMRO's expansion in the U.S. failed to continue into the twenty-first century. In April 2007, ABN AMRO sold for 21 billion dollars to Bank of America its key U.S. property (the consolidated LaSalle Bank group in Chicago). In 2007 Royal Bank of Scotland, Banco Santander, and Fortis acquired the parent ABN AMRO, and the Dutch bank's few remaining U.S. assets were transferred to Royal Bank of Scotland.[13] Other relatively new major players in the U.S. financial services sector were the ING group and Aegon. Both expanded greatly, providing a wide variety of financial services, from banking to insurance products, and both were affected by the financial crisis in the United States in the fall of 2008.[14]

Dutch activity in the retail sector was for a short time important and dominated by the family firms C&A (Brenninkmeyer) and Ahold. These retailers had mixed fortunes, ultimately resulting in exits. By 2004, Brenninkmeyer had left the U.S. retail market entirely, while Ahold, having become the second-largest food retailer in the United States in 1999, ran into major financial difficulties due to the discovery in 2002 of overstated earnings at its major subsidiary, U.S. Foodservices. Retreats followed, but at the end of 2004 Ahold still had roughly fifteen hundred grocery stores in the United States and 72 percent of its worldwide sales were in that country. Yet, this did not last. In 2007, Ahold sold U.S. Foodservices to private investors for 7.1 billion dollars.[15]

By the early twenty-first century, the profile of Dutch business in America was no longer dominated by three or four giant industrial firms (two of which were shared with the British). While the layers of British-Dutch connections superimposed over U.S. business endured, German-Dutch links have not remained so prominent. The competitive U.S. market was the most serious testing ground for MNEs, as was noted in a history of Unilever in 1980: "Practical experience in

805

5

—

THE
COLD WAR
AND
BEYOND

1945-2009

—

ECONOMICS
AND
SOCIETY

America and close acquaintance with American enterprise and ebullience, to say nothing of access to American finance, are likely to remain the chief contribution made from across the Atlantic to the prosperity of Unilever worldwide, especially since America is the base for most of Unilever's international competitors...."[16]

Can one define a national style in Dutch domestic and international direct investments, particularly Dutch investments in the United States? That the Dutch had a long history as a trading, investing, and colonial nation obviously made a difference. But there is no apparent pattern whereby one nationality has consistently performed better than others through time and by industry. The specific strong British-Dutch connection (notably in Royal Dutch/Shell and Unilever) that persists throughout the history of Dutch MNEs seems to be particular to the Dutch business system. The Dutch had the upper hand in the British-Dutch collaboration that led to the creation of Royal Dutch/Shell, whereas in the case of Unilever control was shared. However, when the Germans and the Dutch collaborated the Germans almost always tried to have the upper hand. Another important aspect is that the Dutch were unique in having so few key (and large) participants in U.S. business; these participants rarely competed against each other. Only in the 1990s, with ING and Aegon, did this begin to change. In relative terms, in recent years, with Dutch direct investment lower in the United States than U.S. investment in the Netherlands, perhaps a new era has dawned.[17]

1   This article is an abridged and updated version, drafted by Giles Scott-Smith (with Mira Wilkins's approval and additions) of Mira Wilkins, "Dutch Multinational Enterprises in the United States: A Historical Summary," *Business History Review* 79 (Summer 2005): 193-273. It is published with the permission of *Business History Review.*

2   For general studies of Dutch enterprises see K.D. Bosch, *Nederlandse beleggingen in de Verenigde Staten* (Amsterdam: Elsevier, 1948); F. de Goey, "Dutch Overseas Investments in the Very Long Run (c. 1600–1990)," in Roger van Hoesel and Rajneesh Narula, eds., *Multinational Enterprises from the Netherlands,* (London: Routledge, 1999), 32-60; K. Sluyterman, *Dutch Enterprise in the Twentieth Century: Business Strate-*

gies in a Small Open Economy (London: Routledge, 2005).

3   Mira Wilkins, *The History of Foreign Investment in the United States, 1914–1945* (Cambridge, MA: Harvard University Press, 2004), chapters 8-10, especially pp. 580-581.

4   On Unilever, see C. Wilson, *The History of Unilever,* 3 vols. (New York: Cassell and Co. 1968); W. Reader, *Fifty Years of Unilever* (London: Heinemann, 1980); G. Jones, "Control, Performance, and Knowledge Transfers in Large Multinationals: Unilever in the United States, 1945-1980," *Business History Review* 76 (Autumn 2002), 435-478; G. Jones, *Renewing Unilever* (Oxford: Oxford University Press, 2007).

5   On Shell in the United States, see T. Priest, "The 'Americanization' of Shell

Oil," in G. Jones and L. Gálvez-Muñoz, eds., *Foreign Multinationals in the United States: Management and Performance* (London: Routledge, 2002), 188-206; T. Priest, *The Offshore Imperative: Shell Oil's Search for Petroleum in Postwar America* (College Station: Texas A&M University Press, 2007); S. Howarth and J. Jonker, *Powering the Hydrocarbon Revolution, 1939–1973: A History of Royal Dutch Shell,* vol. 2 (Oxford: Oxford University Press, 2007); K. Sluyterman, *Keeping Competitive in Turbulent Markets, 1973–2007: A History of Royal Dutch Shell,* vol. 3 (Oxford: Oxford University Press, 2007).

6   See I. J. Blanken, *The History of Philips Electronics N.V.*, vols. 3 and 4 (Zaltbommel: European Library, 1999); N. Faith, *The Infiltrators: The European Business Invasion of America* (London: Dutton, 1971), 80-84. It is plausible that the Shell and Lever Brothers business networks were larger. But what is most interesting is that this still means the three largest foreign-owned enterprises were Dutch.

7   *Survey of Current Business*, November 1972, 30, and February 1973, 30.

8   This was true through 2000, but from 2001 to 2006 (the latest figures available), the opposite was the case. See *Survey of Current Business,* September 2004, 94, 136 (for 1999–2003 figures) and ibid., September 2007, 68-109 (for 2002-06 figures).

9   *1976 Commerce Department Report*, vol. 5: G-125, G-129-130. A *Fortune* list of the top industrial companies in the world by sales in 1978 had only four that were not American in the top twelve. They included Royal Dutch/Shell (no. 3) and Unilever (no. 12). Philips ranked sixteen. The other two non-American companies in the top sixteen that year were British Petroleum (no. 7) and National Iranian Oil (no. 9). Unilever and Philips were the only non-oil, non-American companies in this group.

10 In October 2004, Royal Dutch/Shell announced a major corporate reorganization, creating a single company incorporated in the United Kingdom (Royal Dutch/Shell PLC) but headquartered and listed as a "tax resident" in the Netherlands. The implications for its global operations remain to be seen.

11 See Jones, "Control, Performance, and Knowledge Transfers," and Jones, *Renewing Unilever.*

12 In 2007, Philips concentrated on three core units, Philips Lighting, Philips Consumer Lifestyle, and Philips Healthcare. Late in 2006, Philips sold 80 percent of its semiconductor division and divested its U.S. television business. In 2007, however, it acquired Respironics (a U.S. medical equipment supplier) as well as a number of lighting firms, thereby participating in the move toward LEDs (light emitting diode bulbs). See *New York Times*, September 17, 2004; "Royal Philips Electronics," Hoover's Company Reports, June 15, 2008; and *Economist*, December 1, 2007.

13 Manfred Pohl, ed., *Handbook on the History of European Banks* (Aldershot: Edward Elgar, 1994); Lothar Gall et al., *The Deutsche Bank, 1870–1995* (London: Weidenfeld and Nicolson, 1995); Joh. de Vries, Wim Vrom, and Ton de Graaf, eds., *Worldwide Banking: ABN AMRO Bank, 1824–1999* (Amsterdam: ABN AMRO, 1999); "Bank of America" and "Royal Bank of Scotland," Hoover's Company Reports, July 1, 2008. In late 2008 due to the financial crisis, the takeover collapsed and ABN AMRO was effectively nationalised by the Dutch government.

14 In mid-October 2008, the ING group got a ten billion euro injection of capital from Dutch authorities, while Aegon reported expected impairments of third-quarter assets based on its U.S. exposure (Guardian.com.UK, October 19, 2008, accessed online that day, and *Financial Times*, October 10, 2008).

15 *Miami Herald*, December 1, 2007.

16 Reader, *Fifty Years of Unilever*, 95-104.

17 See note 8.

5

———

THE
COLD WAR
AND
BEYOND

1945-2009

———

ECONOMICS
AND
SOCIETY

THE BILDERBERG GROUP AND DUTCH-AMERICAN RELATIONS

———

THOMAS GIJSWIJT

Introduction

The Bilderberg Group was founded in 1954 to facilitate confidential U.S.-European dialogue on the highest level. To this day, the Group holds yearly meetings attracting some of the most influential bankers, captains of industry, diplomats, intellectuals, and politicians on both sides of the Atlantic. This article will address the question of the overall importance of the Bilderberg Group for Dutch-American and transatlantic relations. The main argument advanced is that this institution has contributed both to the cohesion and longevity of the Atlantic Alliance and to the vast increase in commerce and investment across the Atlantic in the postwar period. The Group has done so in part through the informal exchange of information, the establishment of relationships of trust among members of the transatlantic elite, and the strengthening of common values and beliefs. Just as important, however, was the Bilderberg Group's function as a safety valve for dissent and conflicting views within the pluralistic community of the West.

Particularly in the period from 1954 until 1976, when Prince Bernhard of the Netherlands was the Bilderberg chairman, Dutch involvement was considerable. This should not come as a surprise since the Netherlands was perfectly situated to "host" the Group. The traditional westward orientation of the country — exemplified by multinational firms such as Unilever and Shell — coupled with its early participation in the creation of a united Europe (Benelux, ECSC, EEC, Euratom), gave the Dutch a natural mediating role between continental Europe and the Anglo-Saxon world. Moreover, as a relatively minor power the

Netherlands was acceptable to the major powers of the alliance as a transatlantic mediator. The remarkable fact that the Netherlands has occupied the position of NATO secretary general for a total of over twenty-one years — far longer than any other NATO member — illustrates this point.

Origins of the Bilderberg Group

The Bilderberg Group was the brainchild of Joseph Retinger, a Polish-born cosmopolitan based in London.[1] During World War II, Retinger had been a close advisor to the Polish government in exile. After the war, he was instrumental in setting up various organizations promoting European unity, among them the European Movement.[2] In 1952, Retinger gave up his position as secretary general of this movement in order to devote himself to U.S.-European relations. A rising tide of anti-Americanism swept across much of Europe while Washington was preoccupied with Senator McCarthy's anticommunist witch hunts. Retinger felt that the growing lack of understanding between Europe and the United States endangered their effective cooperation. While he was convinced that building a strong Europe offered the best hope for liberating his native Poland, he also believed that the help of the United States was crucial in forging a united Europe and winning the Cold War.

In September 1952, Retinger assembled a group of leading Europeans in Paris to study the causes of anti-Americanism in Europe. The first two men he had contacted were Paul Rijkens, the Dutch chairman of Unilever, and Prince Bernhard. They both shared Retinger's concerns about the lack of unity within the West and the prince agreed to become chairman of the study group. Other members included Hugh Gaitskell, a leading Labour politician; Italian Prime Minister Alcide de Gasperi; Major General Colin Gubbins, the British chief of the Special Operations Executive (SOE) during World War II; Ole Bjørn Kraft, the Danish foreign minister; Guy Mollet, the leader of the French socialists; Antoine Pinay, France's conservative prime minister; and Paul van Zeeland, the Belgian foreign minister.

The contacts between these men mostly dated back to World War II, when London had served as a pressure cooker for ideas on remaking the postwar international order. Influenced by the 1941 Atlantic Charter, individual human rights, collective security, economic interdependence, and a minimum level of social security became staples of allied and Western thought.[3] Many early Bilderberg members belonged to the generation of internationalists that emerged from the debris of World War II.

The study group led by Retinger and Prince Bernhard produced a report on anti-Americanism in Europe, which was meant to serve as a basis for a U.S.-Eu-

809

5

—

THE
COLD WAR
AND
BEYOND

1945–2009

—

ECONOMICS
AND
SOCIETY

ropean dialogue between "men of influence." The first sentence of the report underlined its purpose: "We who have been associated in the preparation of this document are firmly convinced that the security and development of the Western world cannot be achieved unless the friendship and mutual understanding between the United States and Western Europe are maintained and expanded."[4] The report argued that anti-Americanism was the result of both structural changes in the world balance of power, long-existing cultural biases, and short-term policy differences. The fact that anti-American sentiment was strongest in France and Great Britain showed that resentment over the new status of Washington as the leader of the West was an important factor. By 1952, western Europe was no longer fully dependent on American economic and military assistance. Many Europeans expected a larger say in alliance affairs and Cold War strategy, yet American decision makers often seemed more concerned with domestic political considerations than with the interests of their European allies. However, by far the most important reason for the increase in anti-Americanism in 1952 was the overriding fear in Europe that a more aggressively anticommunist United States might turn the Cold War into a hot one. Many Europeans questioned the American capacity for responsible world leadership and feared an escalation of the war in Korea. Such reservations were reinforced by widespread stereotypes of the United States as a materialistic, culturally unsophisticated, and immature society.

Contrary to the often-heard claim that the CIA was instrumental in launching the Bilderberg Group, the American reaction to the report was slow and reluctant. Retinger traveled to the United States in late 1952, shortly after Dwight D. Eisenhower had won the presidential elections. Walter Bedell Smith and Allen Dulles, two of the first directors of the CIA, and other leading officials were too preoccupied with their jobs in the new administration to give Retinger much time. Without the persistence of Prince Bernhard—and, at least as important, his high-level contacts reaching up to President Eisenhower—the Bilderberg Group might not have come into existence.[5] As it was, the prince's perseverance and the quality of the European group that produced the report on anti-Americanism forced an American response.

The first official Bilderberg meeting, in May 1954—at its namesake, Hotel De Bilderberg in Oosterbeek, the Netherlands—was a resounding success. In the years thereafter, the Group quickly established its reputation as a valuable transatlantic meeting place. All participants took part as private citizens and were encouraged to speak freely during the confidential discussions, one of the key reasons for Bilderberg's success. Between sixty and one hundred men and women from the NATO and OEEC/OECD member states took part in the three-day meetings (the first woman to participate was Princess Beatrix of the Netherlands, in 1962, for whom the meetings formed part of her international "educa-

Prince Bernhard (with flower in buttonhole) reports to the ministerial council
of the Dutch government concerning his trip to South America, December 6, 1952 (4th
from left Sicco Mansholt, 6th from left Joseph Luns, 2nd from right Willem Drees Sr.).

5

—

THE
COLD WAR
AND
BEYOND

1945–2009

—

ECONOMICS
AND
SOCIETY

tion"). The Bilderberg steering committee, which was responsible for selecting participants, met more regularly and ensured that a carefully balanced nonpartisan group of people — including politicians from the Left and the Right and businessmen as well as trade unionists — attended. Only the steering committee members were certain of participation. The group was financed mainly by the participants themselves (or by their organizations or companies), as well as by several American foundations, such as the Ford Foundation and the Carnegie Endowment for International Peace.

Transatlantic Cohesion

What, then, held such a disparate group together? Although it is difficult to generalize given the vastly different backgrounds of the people involved, two factors are of prime importance, one ideological and the other psychological: [1] the wish for more effective international cooperation and [2] the desire for information and access; in short, influence. It is safe to say that a majority of Bilderberg participants throughout the last half century would have agreed with the statement that Americans and Europeans should work together to shape the world they were living in. In a way, therefore, the Bilderberg meetings served to keep the lessons of the failed peace of Versailles, the economic world crisis of the 1930s, and World War II alive and pass them on to new generations of foreign policy elites. Moreover, the very fact that trade unionists, businessmen, and intellectuals sat next to politicians and diplomats to discuss the international issues of the day showed that foreign policy in its broadest sense — ranging from trade, monetary rules, and human rights to military security and diplomacy — had become a concern of societies as a whole. As Roosevelt and Churchill had argued in the Atlantic Charter, economic stability and individual rights were no less important conditions for peace than the ability to deter military aggression.

In the early 1950s already, those involved in the Bilderberg Group feared that the multilateral system of institutions that grew out of World War II did not suffice to guarantee collective security, socioeconomic stability, and political freedom. Even within the community of Western democracies, differences on the aims to be pursued and methods to be employed were difficult to overcome and severely limited the effectiveness of such institutions as the OEEC and NATO. The Bilderberg Group, therefore, can be seen as part of an informal alliance, meant to round out the institutionalized Atlantic Alliance founded during the early Cold War. The Group was designed to influence patterns of thinking, rather than prescribe or promote certain policies. As Prince Bernhard said at the start of the first meeting, "Since the free countries of Europe, the United States and Canada must act as one, they will need a certain unity of outlook and they must make an effort to think in terms of Western partnership as a whole. That means that we must promote a new way of thinking, transcending the Old World mentality which often has a provincial look about it. This could help Western people realize their common interest."[6]

In its various meetings the Bilderberg Group dealt with a whole range of issues facing the West. Political and economic topics received more or less equal weight. What is more, the Bilderberg discussions highlight the extent to which many political and economic issues are closely interconnected. One of the best examples is the Group's debate on European integration in the mid-1950s. After the defeat of the European Defense Community (EDC) by the French parliament in August 1954, the future of the European project dominated several Bilderberg meetings. Proponents of European integration such as the former head of the OEEC, Robert Marjolin, Guy Mollet, and Walter Hallstein, the West German state secretary for foreign affairs and future president of the EEC Commission, used the meetings to nurture a *relance européenne*. They envisaged European integration not only as the best guarantee of binding Germany irreversibly to the West; in light of the Soviet ideological and military threat, they regarded a united Europe also as a bulwark against communist aggression and propaganda. More specifically, men such as Marjolin and Mollet portrayed the European project as a way to overcome Europe's structural socioeconomic problems by creating a larger market, thus unleashing entrepreneurial energy and modernizing European societies by encouraging more social mobility and competition. In short, a united Europe should restore Europe's faith in the future, thus undermining the ideological siren call of communism and preventing a return to the zero-sum protectionism and aggressive nationalism of the 1930s.

The Bilderberg meetings also gave American participants — among them, George W. Ball, Paul G. Hoffman, George F. Kennan, and Robert D. Murphy — the opportunity to influence the European debate on integration. Secretary of State John Foster Dulles's attempts to force the EDC upon the reluctant French — famously threatening an "agonizing reappraisal" of U.S. foreign policy — had badly backfired. Consequently, the reach of official U.S. diplomacy in the field of European integration was limited, hence increasing the importance of informal channels. Ball, Hoffman, and others used the Bilderberg meetings to argue for the advantages of a larger, more competitive European market, while American officials quietly reassured the European participants that no agonizing reappraisal had actually taken place in Washington. American experts on atomic energy, moreover, informed the Europeans on the latest developments

813

5

—

THE
COLD WAR
AND
BEYOND

1945–2009

—

ECONOMICS
AND
SOCIETY

in this emerging industry and argued for a concerted European catch-up effort. The American Bilderbergers, in a word, used the meetings to promote the self-Americanization of Europe.

Johan Willem Beyen, foreign minister of the Netherlands, strongly supported Prince Bernhard's efforts to solidify U.S.-European relations and bring about a *relance européenne*. This became evident in 1955, when Queen Juliana tried to put a halt to her husband's activities in Bilderberg. The Dutch cabinet resisted the queen, in part because Beyen felt that the Bilderberg meetings served a valuable purpose. The foreign minister no doubt realized that the prince was a considerable international asset for the Netherlands. The Bilderberg connection opened even more doors for the prince than his royal title already did. Bernhard regularly visited the White House and frequently acted as a roving economic ambassador for the Netherlands — promoting, among other things, the Dutch aircraft industry and KLM.[7] In the early 1960s, Prince Bernhard also crossed into constitutionally more hazardous territory by using his Bilderberg connections to undermine Foreign Minister Luns's position on West New Guinea. During the 1962 Bilderberg meeting in Sweden, the prince told American diplomats that Luns enjoyed limited support for his hard-line policy in the Netherlands.

Atlanticism and Its Challenges in the 1960s

In the early 1960s, the Bilderberg Group entered a more Atlanticist phase in its existence after the initial emphasis on European integration. Joseph Retinger resigned as honorary secretary general because of health problems — he died in 1960 — and was succeeded by the Dutchman Ernst van der Beugel, a high-ranking former diplomat and committed Atlanticist. Even more important than these personal developments were the long-term effects of the Suez crisis and the return to power of Charles de Gaulle in France. If most Bilderbergers had regarded European integration and Atlantic cooperation as mutually reinforcing during most of the 1950s, this became a much more difficult proposition after de Gaulle made clear his wish for a more independent Europe.

This was particularly the case for the Dutch participants. After attending his first Bilderberg conference in January 1959, Van der Beugel warned Foreign Minister Luns that the Gaullist design for a united Europe was based solely on the French desire to dominate Europe. During the Fouchet negotiations in the early 1960s, Van der Beugel was one of a group of Dutch Atlanticists who strongly and publicly supported Luns in his stubborn opposition to the de Gaulle-Adenauer design for a more independent Europe. The Dutch foreign policy elites in the early 1960s were *plus américains que les Américains* and The Hague succeeded in foiling de Gaulle's design for a French-led *Europe des patries*.

Throughout the decade, the Bilderberg meetings were an important arena for the debates between Gaullists, Atlanticists, and Europeanists. By the mid-1960s it was clear that the Gaullists had failed to convert a majority of their European partners. After de Gaulle's January 1963 veto of British entry into the Common Market — a move directed in part against the United States — the Bilderberg meetings served to rally European support for the Atlantic Alliance. The Bilderberg discussions show that one reason for the strong opposition to de Gaulle was the widely shared perception that his policies dangerously undermined the basic consensus on which the alliance was founded: that Western unity was essential in the Cold War; that the United States' presence in Europe was necessary and desirable; and, finally, that integration and cooperation were to be preferred over nationalism and unilateral action.

A different challenge to the Atlantic Alliance was posed by the protest movements of the 1960s. The Vietnam War and the civil rights question caused a severe crisis of legitimacy for the United States and other major countries of the democratic West. With the advent of modern communications technology — particularly television — this crisis developed a transnational dynamic hard to control. In 1966, Van der Beugel warned the Bilderberg steering committee that the basic assumptions of "practically every participant in the Bilderberg conferences" — namely the "need for European integration," the "need for a maximum of cohesion in the Atlantic world," and the "need for a strong defensive posture towards the Eastern Bloc" — were no longer shared by large parts of the Western publics, "especially the young people."[8] In the following years, the Bilderberg Group embarked on a sustained rejuvenation program.

Despite the generational conflicts and internal strife of the 1960s and 1970s, the Bilderberg Group continued to attract important participants, also from younger generations. Leaders of international organizations such as the OECD, the World Bank, the IMF, the European Commission, and NATO were particularly eager to participate. They saw the meetings as a key source of information and as an effective way of influencing Western policy agendas — simply because the attitudes and views of those attending were bound to be influential. In fact, all NATO secretaries general, from Lord Ismay to Jaap de Hoop Scheffer, have participated in Bilderberg meetings.

In a similar vein, smaller nations such as the Netherlands realized that they could exert influence far beyond their hard power resources through the effective use of soft power in organizations such as Bilderberg. The fact that three frequent Dutch participants simultaneously headed important international institutions in the 1970s — Joseph Luns as secretary general of NATO, Sicco

5

—

THE
COLD WAR
AND
BEYOND

1945–2009

—

ECONOMICS
AND
SOCIETY

Mansholt as president of the EEC Commission, and Emile van Lennep as secretary general of the OECD — is telling in this respect.

For bankers and captains of industry the high-level contacts and information gained at the meetings were no less important. David Rockefeller has said that up to 70 percent of his important international contacts were established at Bilderberg. It is a desideratum of research on transatlantic elite networks to trace the impact of such contacts on the economic relations between the United States and Europe. The list of Bilderberg participants does make clear that in the wake of the growing effects of globalization in the 1970s, multinationals and banks such as Ahold, Akzo, BP, Coca-Cola, Goldman Sachs, Nestlé, Paribas, Philips, and Xerox were increasingly eager to participate. At about the same time, a few members, including David Rockefeller and Zbigniew Brzezinski, decided to found the Trilateral Commission in order to include Japan in similar high-level meetings — something the Bilderberg steering committee had declined to do.

In the mid-1970s, a public scandal over Prince Bernhard's acceptance of illicit funds from the American defense giant Lockheed seriously endangered the future of the Bilderberg Group. The 1976 meeting was canceled and the members of the American steering committee reached the conclusion that Bernhard should resign. Many of the old-guard Bilderbergers thought this would mean the end of the Group. Yet, in a telling sign of the importance of the organization, a group of younger members, including German Chancellor Helmut Schmidt, insisted on continuation. Ernst van der Beugel remained secretary general — later succeeded by a Dutch professor of economics, Victor Halberstadt — and Queen Beatrix to some extent inherited her father's role by becoming a Bilderberg regular, thus ensuring a continuing Dutch flavor to the meetings.

Perhaps surprisingly, given its initial background, the Bilderberg Group has survived the end of the Cold War as well. The basic idea that the West should cooperate on the major problems facing the world remains a powerful one, even without the Soviet threat. The fact that the Group still serves as an informal meeting place for many of the leaders of the West shows the success of Retinger's and Bernhard's original idea.

Conclusion

In conclusion, the Bilderberg Group might be characterized as an attempt to "reconcile a national identity with a global one."[9] Most Bilderbergers agreed that the interwar period had proven the inability of any nation-state in isolation to provide its citizens with a minimum of security and stability, a point reinforced by the global challenges of the Cold War and decolonization. In the

Dutch-American context, the Bilderberg meetings thus tended to counter neutralist thinking in the Netherlands and isolationist traditions in the United States. However, to what extent the Bilderberg Group has been successful in its broadly defined mission of dealing with the reality of international or global interdependence remains difficult to judge. Detailed information on the discussions is available only for the period until the early 1970s and of course the impact of the meetings has been, and is, mostly indirect.

Still, the conclusion is justified that the Bilderberg Group has been part of the glue that holds the West together — however loosely at times. The active American engagement in networks such as Bilderberg has increased the legitimacy of U.S. leadership in the Atlantic Alliance, thus alleviating the inevitable tensions caused by the disparity in power between the United States and the other member states. Even if the gap between consultation and decision making is often hard to bridge, the willingness to listen has an important psychological effect. As long-time Bilderberg member Denis Healey has argued, "Nothing is more likely to produce understanding than the sort of personal contacts which involves people not just as officials or representatives, but also as human beings."[10] Likewise, the airing — and mutual understanding — of differences is as important as the more constructive task of building international consensus on important issues. The ability to deal with dissent has perhaps been the secret of the success of the Atlantic Alliance — after all, a voluntary alliance of democracies.[11]

Of course, any such conclusion needs to be tempered since there are very real limits to the influence exerted through networks such as the Bilderberg Group. From the Suez crisis to the war in Iraq, history has shown that a combination of deeply entrenched perceptions and interests, coupled with mistrust and a failure to communicate at the highest level, is very difficult to overcome. By all accounts, Secretary of Defense Donald Rumsfeld's efforts to secure wider support for military action in Iraq at the 2002 Bilderberg meeting only increased widespread European opposition. Nonetheless, despite this qualifying remark, the transatlantic proliferation of ideas, contacts, information, and trade stimulated by the Bilderberg meetings has had a cumulative impact that any serious student of transatlantic relations should at least be aware of. For a relatively small country such as the Netherlands, the potential value of these meetings was enormous, particularly with respect to its relations with the leading power of the West. As Foreign Minister Beyen already recognized in the 1950s, the contacts established at the meetings opened many doors in the United States that would otherwise have remained closed, thus offering new and important avenues of influence.

5

———

THE
COLD WAR
AND
BEYOND
1945–2009

———

ECONOMICS
AND
SOCIETY

818

1 On the early history of Bilderberg see Hugh Wilford, *The CIA, the British Left and the Cold War: Calling the Tune?* (London: Frank Cass, 2003), and Valérie Aubourg, "Organizing Atlanticism: The Bilderberg Group and the Atlantic Institute, 1952–1963," in Giles Scott-Smith and Hans Krabbendam, eds., *The Cultural Cold War in Western Europe, 1945–1960* (London: Frank Cass, 2003), 92-105. I have based this article mainly on my Ph.D. dissertation, "Uniting the West. The Bilderberg Group, the Cold War and European Integration, 1954–1968" (University of Heidelberg, 2008).

2 The European Movement was founded in 1948 after the first Congress of Europe in The Hague and served as an umbrella organization for several pro-European groups in western Europe. Funding for the European Movement came partly from Washington.

3 On the impact of the Atlantic Charter see Elizabeth Borgwardt, *A New Deal for the World. America's Vision for Human Rights* (Cambridge, MA/London: The Belknap Press of Harvard University Press, 2005).

4 Report on European American Relations, September 1952, Box 1, Bilderberg Archives, Nationaal Archief (National Archive), The Hague.

5 Stephen Gill and Richard Aldrich have based their claim that the CIA funded the first Bilderberg meeting in 1954 on an article by E. Pasymowski and C. Gilbert, "Bilderberg: The Cold War Internationale," which was put in the *Congressional Record*, vol. 117, 1971. This article, however, provides no actual evidence. The archives of the Bilderberg Group show that all funding for the first meeting came from European sources, particularly a dozen or so large Dutch firms (including Philips, KLM, and Hoogovens) that responded to an appeal made by Prince Bernhard. See Richard J. Aldrich, *The Hidden Hand: Britain, America, and Cold War Secret Intelligence* (London: John Murray, 2001), 369, and Stephen Gill, *American Hegemony and the Trilat-*

eral Commission (Cambridge: Cambridge University Press, 1990), 129.

6 Opening address by H.R.H. the Prince of the Netherlands, Box 3, Bilderberg Archives.

7 As McGeorge Bundy, national security advisor to Kennedy and Johnson, put it in 1964, "Prince Bernhard is the founding father of the Bilderberg movement, and he has always seen Presidents Eisenhower and Kennedy on his visits to the United States. The Dutch are extraordinarily good and effective allies, and a picture of the President with the Prince and the Princess [Beatrix] will be a gentle plus both here and abroad." Memorandum for Mr. Moyers, March 20, 1964, Box 2, McGeorge Bundy File, National Security Files, Lyndon B. Johnson Library, Austin, TX.

8 E.H. van der Beugel, "To the Members of the Steering Committee of Bilderberg," August 1966, Box 76, Arthur H. Dean Papers, Cornell University Library, Ithaca, NY.

9 Bruce Mazlish, "Introduction," in Bruce Mazlish, Nayan Chanda, and Kenneth Weisbrode, eds., *The Paradox of a Global USA* (Stanford, CA: Stanford University Press, 2007), 15.

10 Denis Healey, *The Time of My Life* (London: Michael Joseph, 1989), 196.

11 Note that scholars in the Gramscian tradition such as Kees van der Pijl and Stephen Gill have put more emphasis on the homogenizing effect of elite networks in building a liberal capitalist order. In contrast, John Lewis Gaddis has pointed to the consensual nature of the United States' leadership, arguing in his book, *We Now Know. Rethinking Cold War History* (Oxford: Clarendon Press, 1997), that "the habits of domestic democratic politics" helped the Americans in managing the alliance: "Negotiation, compromise, and consensus-building abroad came naturally to statesmen steeped in the uses of such practices at home" (p. 50).

THE TRANSFER OF MOBILITY: THE EMERGENCE OF A CAR SOCIETY IN THE NETHERLANDS

——

GIJS MOM

Introduction

In October 1930 automobile tycoon Henry Ford visited the Netherlands. Traveling from Cologne, where he had inaugurated the new Ford plant, and on his way to Rotterdam, he stopped in Eindhoven to meet Anton Philips. Upon arrival in Rotterdam, he refused to inaugurate the Dutch Ford factory because his local representatives had failed to follow his dictum that every Ford plant be located next to a waterway. Two years later, a Ford assembly plant opened in Amsterdam. With a market share of about one-quarter for passenger cars and nearly one-half for trucks during the 1930s, Ford was very popular in the Netherlands, certainly in comparison to most other European countries.[1]

Ford's visit can be read as exemplary for Dutch-American relations during the interwar years and beyond. Viewed from the perspective of the exchange of artifacts, technology transfer between the two countries was asymmetric in the twentieth century. Apart from some large multinational players such as Philips, Shell, and Unilever, the Netherlands was on the receiving end. This was especially true of cars: the only Dutch technical innovation worth mentioning before World War II (Spyker's four-wheel drive) was not more than a footnote in the history of international road motorization. But technology transfer is much more than the exchange of artifacts. In their material constitution they embody social relations and cultural practices that shape both their production and use.

The Netherlands, characterized by its "Western-ness" according to the Dutch historian Johan Huizinga, nonetheless formed part of a European mobility culture. It is this cultural double-bind position, this gaze to the west with the back firmly supported by a European, if not German, culture, which forms the key to understanding how the Dutch shaped their technological culture. As such, the analysis of Dutch motorization contributes to the ongoing debate on Americanization in general, and American influence on Dutch society in particular.[2]

Contrary to the diffusionist model, which emphasizes both American and Dutch exceptionalism, recent scholarship in the history of technology advocates a transnational approach in which there is room for the emergence and coexistence of "multiple modernities." And instead of following a comparative approach, which overestimates the differences among, as well as the importance of, nation-states, the study of transfer flows on both the subnational and the supranational level opens a vista upon an "Atlantic mobility culture," without losing sight of specific mobility cultures' own roads to modernity. After all, when in both countries around the turn of the century an elite started to motorize, there were for a long time significant differences among regions within a particular nation, more so than among certain regions in different countries. And when in many western industrializing countries the gestation of a car culture was really under way, international institutions of automobile and touring clubs as well as road engineering associations were at least as important in shaping local cultures as were domestic traditions.[3]

To illustrate this, this essay focuses upon two phases in Dutch road motorization that provide insight into this Atlantic interaction: the interwar years, during which the first massive motorization wave brought some one hundred thousand Dutchmen onto the roads in (predominantly American) cars, and a postwar phase when mass motorization enabled people in much greater numbers to drive on a road network designed largely after the American example by Waterstaat engineers.

Creating a Dutch Car Culture with
American Material

Initially, the Netherlands was slow to motorize. Whereas the French (mostly Parisian) urban elite initiated the craze for playing with the new toy, the British soon overtook them in terms of cars per capita. At the other end of the European spectrum of mobility culture, the Dutch followed the Germans in their reluctance to adopt the innovation, probably because in both countries the urban bourgeois elite was too small and the aristocracy, an important participant in the Parisian example, was either nonurban (in Germany) or powerless (in the Netherlands).[4] Before World War I, the Netherlands also had one of the densest railway and tramway systems in the world, and a proliferation of bicycles

---

5

—

THE
COLD WAR
AND
BEYOND

1945–2009

—

ECONOMICS
AND
SOCIETY

820

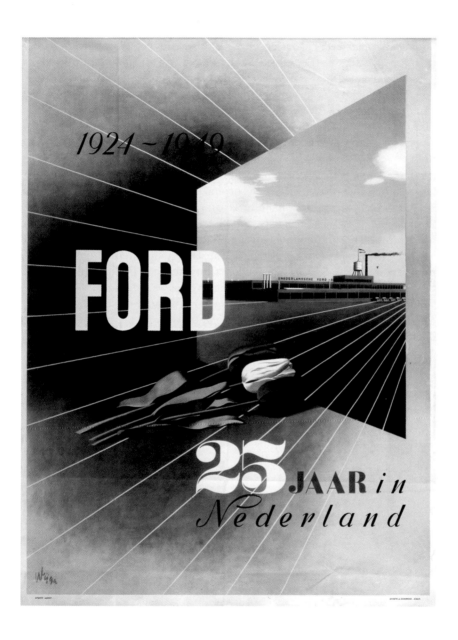

Poster celebrating twenty-five years of Ford cars in the Netherlands.

5

———

THE
COLD WAR
AND
BEYOND

1945-2009

———

ECONOMICS
AND
SOCIETY

among all social layers of society enabled those who needed and could afford them, to go wherever they wanted. Remarkably, not all small European countries followed the Dutch example: Denmark, for instance, like the Netherlands not endowed with a large domestic automobile industry, showed an eagerness to motorize only matched by France and the UK, whereas Belgium, with an even denser railway network than the Netherlands, soon developed into one of the largest car-assembling countries in proportion to the size of its population (figure 1).[5]

Remarkable in the Netherlands was the role of a "neutral" and surprisingly large touring club, ANWB, playing a societal role hardly surpassed by any other European club. An anomaly in an increasingly pillarized society of minorities (Protestants, Catholics, socialists, and liberals), ANWB initially showed hardly any interest in the automobile movement. Its leadership observed that driving a car remained an exclusively elitist pastime largely confined to the Dutch automobile club (NAC, later KNAC), which was not interested in expanding its membership as similar organizations in other countries were doing. Building or subsidizing bicycle paths, and selecting repair shops and hotels for its members, ANWB focused on the discovery of nature by tourists, on bicycles, on foot, and by motor boat, competing with travel and leisure associations related to the

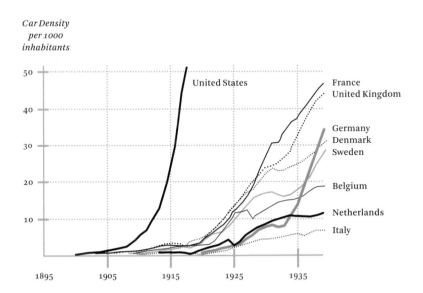

Car Density
per 1000
inhabitants

FIGURE 1
Car densities in selected European countries and the U.S.

Catholic, Protestant, and socialist pillars. In doing so, ANWB managed quite early to conquer an advisory position close to the national government, especially at the Ministry of Waterstaat, which was responsible for road building. The club also played a founding role in the international association of touring clubs LIAT (1899), which in turn influenced the debate within the international association of road building experts PIARC (1908).[6] In both associations, American clubs (LIAT) and successive governments (PIARC) were represented, but their main focus until World War II was European.

ANWB's role in transatlantic technology transfer was nonetheless important, mainly because its leaders, and especially the leading publicists in the club's weekly magazine, *De Kampioen* (The Champion), used the increasing evidence of incipient mass motorization in the U.S. to emphasize the attractiveness of the car for utilitarian purposes to the middle class, including professionals such as medical doctors, lawyers, industrialists, and the military, as well as shop owners. The United States multiplied what had been developed in Europe on a small scale, in the process transforming its shape and impact, mostly by quickly adopting the car in a wealthy, rural mobility culture, where it was reshaped into something "essential" for living a prosperous life. Whereas in other European countries medical doctors were among the first to use the car for practical purposes, in the Netherlands several of them used motorcycles instead, especially in the countryside, probably because they could not afford a car. Other European countries, too, showed a greater use of motorcycles than of cars.[7]

World War I changed all this: despite the Netherlands' neutrality, its military educated thousands of youths during and shortly after the war as truck and car drivers and as mechanics. They formed the basis for the first massive postwar wave of motorization, driving trucks or "wild," unregulated buses, or they were recruited into the fledgling garage service sector. Meanwhile, ANWB was instrumental in putting the issue of the road network not being ready for massive automobile and truck use on the national agenda, which resulted in an adjustment (broadening, straightening, paving) of this network that was largely completed by the beginning of the 1930s.

This "infrastructure" helped bring a special Dutch "flavor" to mobility culture. Before the war new social groups desiring to get motorized avoided the smallest models, and instead chose the next size. This tendency increased after the war when especially in the countryside people started buying Ford's Model T in relatively large numbers (many more per capita than in most other European countries). A German observer opined that the success of the large American cars with their powerful engines was not only due to their low price (enabled by a rather low import tax), but also because of the large Dutch family, a fact that did not escape the attention of ANWB leaders who started to build an extensive user culture around the "family car," with a remarkable high share of tourism abroad.[8]

The popularity of American makes was phenomenal: they dominated sales in 1931 with a market share of 75 percent, which was matched only in the three Scandinavian countries and Romania. Only by the end of the 1930s, when the car began to trickle down into the lower strata of the middle classes, did the American makes Ford and Chevrolet lose some popularity when some Dutch buyers turned to German makes, mainly DKW and Opel, the latter a German-American hybrid and not much smaller than its American counterparts. In 1935 sales of American makes had fallen to 66 percent, while German makes increased their joint share from 8 (1931) to 20 percent.

Prewar Americanization?

The adoption of American cars in larger numbers per capita than in many other European countries does not imply, however, that we have here a clear case of Americanization. The very non-American concept of cooperatives, for instance, also crept into the fledgling Dutch car culture, just as in many other European consumer cultures. Thus, it took the car lobby, represented by RAI (association of importers) and Bovag (association of garage owners), fifteen years of concerted efforts to fight against Dutch medical doctors who had based their car ownership on a cooperative basis, applying for discounts on cars, tires, and fuel. Conversely, America's exceptionalism as an enthusiastic and uncomplicated motorizer — traditionally cherished by automotive historiography, as opposed to the initial resistance against the car in Europe — has been convincingly questioned. Recent research shows that even in the U.S. the acceptance of the car as a part of daily life was not at all a matter of course: in the early 1920s massive local campaigns were necessary, all across the nation, to dispel the skepticism of large segments of the American urban population against what they saw as a dangerous vehicle for children and other pedestrians, and a cause of congestion.[9]

But whether Fords and Chevrolets were welcome or not, all European countries in one way or another came under the spell of American modernity. In urban planning, for instance, the same mechanism became visible as had been the case during the car's starting phase, a mechanism that has been coined "synthetic borrowing" by urban planning historian Stephen Ward. A closer look reveals that during the interwar years the contours of two quite different motorization models had become visible, although most American and European observers saw it as an issue of time (a cultural lag), rather than an issue of space and of the parallel development of distinctive cultures. Although it cannot be

5

—

THE
COLD WAR
AND
BEYOND

1945-2009

—

ECONOMICS
AND
SOCIETY

denied that the sheer size of the domestic American market led to at least two very specific characteristics (a widespread adoption of the car as a "necessity" among midwestern farmers and an urban college youth culture partially based on the automobile), most other traits long seen as characteristic of American mobility culture were also present at exactly the same time in Europe.[10] Take, for instance, the debate on the relationship between road and rail transport (with quite a different outcome on the two sides of the Atlantic), or the outcry about the increasing number of serious accidents, mainly involving women and children (with the same outcome on both continents: acceptance of the car's importance), or the adjustment and financing of existing roads and the initial rejection of building a special automobile-only network. No doubt, the exchange of ideas on a supranational level, among others in the Transit Committee of the League of Nations (standardization of road signs; facilitating border crossing in cars) but also and especially within LIAT and PIARC, did support this converging trend.

Nonetheless, the distinction between the two Atlantic cultures became visible quite literally in the cultural appropriation of two different car types: a large, heavy car with a big engine in the United States, and a smaller, lighter car with a fuel-efficient high-revving engine in Europe, developed by European manufacturers as soon as they recovered from the "American invasion" immediately after World War I. Whereas Americans preferred comfort in their cars with slow-

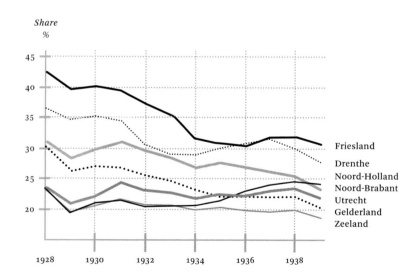

FIGURE 2
Ford's share in total registrations per Dutch province.

5
—

THE
COLD WAR
AND
BEYOND

1945–2009

—

ECONOMICS
AND
SOCIETY

turning engines, Europeans preferred sportiness with a higher rpm. While the gap between these two cultures increased, the Netherlands formed one of the bridgeheads of American car culture in Europe.[11]

For many contemporary Dutch observers, looking (or traveling) to America was looking into the Netherlands' own future, an observation that caused both disdainful resistance and admiring fascination. This, perhaps, was less the result of a cultural schizophrenia of the Dutch elite than an expression of differences in cultural orientation between this elite and an emerging urban middle class that felt a greater affinity with German culture. Although this should still be confirmed by further research, it appears that the Model T was most popular in small towns in the Netherlands, while the much larger middle-class market in the big cities only started to buy Ford cars when the Amsterdam factory began to assemble "Europeanized" Fords, such as the model Y and, later, the V8. By then, German manufacturers had recovered from the American overseas expansion and succeeded in competing effectively in this market, with their DKWs, Adlers, and Opels (figure 2). This slow shift in preference coincided with developments in the United States, where General Motors passed Ford in sales, the same General Motors that bought Germany's Opel in 1928 and managed to adjust much more effectively to European circumstances. By that time, the U.S. could already be called a society that treated cars as the very icons of a middle-class prosperity driven by consumption.[12]

Not so in the Netherlands. The German observer quoted earlier stated in 1934 that by then all Dutchmen who could afford a car already had bought one, and five years later only one hundred thousand passenger cars were registered nationwide, equally spread over the country. Although the automobile had led to a loss of first-class and other regular passengers on trains, the restructuring of the national rail- and tramway networks resulted in one of the most efficient public transport networks in the world, with some main lines already electrified and state-of-the-art diesel trains deployed on nonelectrified lines. Like the other western European countries (some more so than others), the Netherlands enjoyed modernity in mobility quite differently from the American "model." And it set itself apart from its European neighbors by its dominant bicycle culture (with more passenger kilometers than any other mode of transport), by a preference for "slow" vehicles, and overall a modest level of motorization, a process checked perhaps by its strong collective pillarized culture.

Mass Motorization and the American Example

It will not come as a surprise that Dutch postwar youths, despite their highly Americanized leisure culture, moved around on foot, on bicycles, and more and more on mopeds. American cars, after the war, did not play a role in Dutch mass motorization, although the uninterrupted preference for the German-American Opel during most of the second half of the century indicated that admiration for American products disguised under a cloak of German "robustness" was never far away. Like other European motoring novices, however, the Dutch were very reluctant to adopt a car culture of comfort, which meanwhile had developed during the American Golden Era of streamlined gas guzzlers, containing slow-revving engines coupled with an automatic transmission, and a very "soft" suspension system under a large body. It is true that the Dutch, from the launch of the Daffodil in 1958, briefly were among the top European users of a fully automatic transmission, but as soon as the novelty (and the thrill of chauvinism) had worn off, the Dutch mainstream car culture turned back to the affordable, compact family car with a "sporty" manual transmission.[13]

It was in the infrastructure rather than in its mobile artifacts, that American influence on Dutch postwar motorization became apparent. At Waterstaat, civil engineers, educated at Delft University of Technology, were among the most receptive to the American influence. In the wake of the Marshall Plan they visited Yale to study traffic engineering and in the 1960s applied this knowledge when the Netherlands started in earnest to construct its own freeway system. Waterstaat engineer Bert Beukers played a pivotal role in this: having been sent to Yale for a special course on Traffic Engineering, he designed, upon his return, a rectangular grid system that he intended to superimpose on the existing road network. Resistance to "covering the country with asphalt" and an increasing awareness of energy- and environment-related problems resulted in drastically reduced freeway planning, still largely along American lines. And although Beukers later boasted that even the lettering on Dutch road signs was copied from the American model, the resulting network was nonetheless fully integrated into the Dutch spatial tradition. Unlike the French model, for instance, it was not fully separated from a system of "national roads," resulting early on in congestion because freeway entries and exits only twenty to twenty-five kilometers apart allowed local traffic to use the system for short-range commuting as well.[14]

Despite these space-constrained adaptations of the American example, American-Dutch postwar relations in mobility matters followed Stephen Ward's model of "selective borrowing" rather than the prewar "synthetic borrowing." This selective type of transfer is more characteristic of small countries with a relatively modest domestic innovation tradition compared to larger countries such as Germany, France, and the UK. This is not to say that the Netherlands did not develop its own distinctive motorization culture. It did, but only after it had filled the void created by the war in terms of road building expertise with largely American concepts, literally paving the way for a mass motorization that in

827

5

—

THE
COLD WAR
AND
BEYOND

1945–2009

—

ECONOMICS
AND
SOCIETY

quantitative terms meanwhile easily matched car densities abroad. Thus, during the 1970s, the Netherlands became a "car country" just like the other western European countries. At the same time, however, it started to generate traffic innovations related to its long tradition of struggling with limited space, especially in its (mainly medium-sized) towns. One of these innovations, the *woonerf*, was a deliberate paradigm shift. The *woonerf* forced car drivers to slow down because its design (and the soon-to-be-introduced special traffic regulations) made it into a space where the pedestrian and the bicyclist were in charge. Meanwhile, this Dutch innovation forms part of a whole array of measures, implemented all over the world (including in the United States), aimed at redefining urban spatial structure toward a more pedestrian- and bicyclist-friendly environment.

No doubt, the motorization of other European countries provides similar stories of a common European flavor, so much so that the United States seems to have become the exception rather than the rule, since from the 1980s on it has entered what transport experts nowadays call "hyperautomobility."[15]

Conclusion

A century of American-Dutch interaction in mobility matters has resulted in a Dutch society that has developed toward a "car society" with distinct characteristics. European in the "modal split" between the use of rail, road, and waterways, the Dutch adopted many elements invented in Europe but refined in the United States and then, on their way back, adjusted to the limited space of the Netherlands. The country started its motorization in earnest with largely American cars, and grew into a postwar car society equipped with an American-inspired freeway system. Whereas, according to Stephen Ward's typology of diffusion across the Atlantic, the Dutch response to the American influence can be characterized as "synthetic borrowing" in the prewar years, the immediate postwar years were typified by the concept of "selective borrowing."

In the process, however, the Netherlands managed to maintain, and further develop, its own characteristics, such as a dominant urban bicycle culture and a waterway system that, although largely used for freight transport, also functions as an important resource for pleasure boats and sailing. While in its trade liberalism it may have been more inspired by an Anglo-Saxon culture, in its general mobility culture it maintained a mix of American and European traits, both in its infrastructure and its culture, testifying to the importance of the concept of "multiple modernities" in current scholarly debates on transnationalism.

From this perspective, there was no cultural lag between the United States and the Netherlands (or Europe, for that matter), despite some American phenomena hardly found in Europe, such as a larger motorized farmer culture as the real initial driving force behind motorization, and a prewar youth college culture based on the car. Two different models can be distinguished within an overall "Atlantic mobility culture": a car society dominated by "hyperautomobility" on the American side of the Atlantic versus a mix with collective transport, particularly in a European urban context.

Within this dichotomy, however, the Netherlands functioned as a bridgehead for an American motoring lifestyle in Europe, due to its lack of a domestic car industry, its relatively large family size until the 1960s, and its generally favorable attitude (at least among the elite) toward the United States. At the same time, its small surface placed limits on this function, in the midst of much larger car societies such as Germany, France, and the UK. The Netherlands did influence the increase in road freight transport, related to the country's bridgehead function via Rotterdam harbor and the hub function of Schiphol airport, but that is a separate story.

1   Ferry de Goey, "Ford in the Netherlands, 1903–2003. Global Strategies and National Interests," in Hubert Bonin, Yannick Lung, and Steven Tolliday, eds., *Ford, 1903–2003: The European History* (Paris: Éditions P.L.A.G.E., 2003) 2:233-265.

2   Ruth Oldenziel, "Is Globalization a Code Word for Americanization?," *Tijdschrift voor Sociale en Economische Geschiedenis* 4.3 (2007): 84-106.

3   Mike Featherstone, ed., *Global Culture: Nationalism, Globalization and Modernity* (London/Newbury Park/New Delhi: Sage, 1990).

4   James M. Laux, *The European Automobile Industry* (New York: Twayne, 1992); Mathieu Flonneau, *Paris et l'automobile: Un siècle de passions* (Paris: Hachette, 2005); Sean O'Connell, *The Car and British Society: Class, Gender and Motoring, 1896–1939* (Manchester/New York: Manchester University Press, 1998); Kurt Möser, *Geschichte des Autos* (Frankfurt/New York: Campus Verlag, 2002).

5   Gijs Mom and Ruud Filarski, *De mobiliteitsexplosie* (Zutphen: Walburg Pers,

2008); Gijs Mom, Peter Staal, and Johan Schot, "Civilizing Motorized Adventure: Automotive Technology, User Culture and the Dutch Touring Club as Mediator," in Ruth Oldenziel and Adri de la Bruhèze, eds., *Manufacturing Technology: Manufacturing Consumers. The Making of Dutch Consumer Society* (Amsterdam: Aksant, 2008), 141-160; Gijs Mom, "Mobility for Pleasure: A Look at the Underside of Dutch Diffusion Curves (1920–1940)," *Transportes, Servicios y Telecomunicaciones (TST), Revista de Historia* 12 (June 2007): 30-68.

6   Peter Staal, *Automobilisme in Nederland. Een geschiedenis van gebruik, misbruik en nut* (Zutphen: Walburg Pers, 2003); Gijs Mom, "Building an Automobile System: PIARC and Road Safety (1908–1938)," *Proceedings* of the PIARC conference (Paris, September 17-23, 2007), on CD-ROM.

7   Reiner Flik, *Von Ford lernen? Automobilbau und Motorisierung in Deutschland bis 1933* (Cologne/Weimar/Vienna: Böhlau Verlag, 2001); Helmut Braun and Christian Panzer, "The Expansion of the Motor-

829

5
—

THE
COLD WAR
AND
BEYOND

1945-2009

—

ECONOMICS
AND
SOCIETY

Cycle Industry in Germany and in Great Britain (1918 until 1932)," *The Journal of European Economic History* 32.1 (2003): 25-59; Nicolas Spinga, "L'introduction de l'automobile dans la société française entre 1900 et 1914. Étude de presse" (Master's thesis, Université de Paris X-Nanterre, Année 1972–73).

8   Gijs Mom, "Constructing Multifunctional Networks: Road Building in the Netherlands, 1810–1980," in Gijs Mom and Laurent Tissot, eds., *Road History. Planning, Building and Use* (Lausanne: Alphil, 2007), 33-62; Reinhold Stisser, *Der deutsche Automobilexport unter besonderer Berücksichtigung des niederländischen Kraftfahrzeugmarktes* (Kiel: s.n., 1938); For the next paragraph, see also Mom, "Mobility for Pleasure."

9   Victoria de Grazia, *Irresistible Empire: America's Advance through Twentieth-Century Europe* (Cambridge, MA / London: The Belknap Press of Harvard University Press, 2005); See also Marie-Emmanuelle Chessel, "From America to Empire: Educating Consumers," *Contemporary European History* 11.1 (2002): 165-175; Uwe Fraunholz, *Motorphobia: Anti-automobiler Protest in Kaiserreich und Weimarer Republik* (Göttingen: Vandenhoeck & Ruprecht, 2002); Peter David Norton, "Fighting Traffic: The Dawn of the Motor Age in the American City" (Ph.D. dissertation, University of Virginia, May 2002).

10   Stephen V. Ward, "Re-examining the International Diffusion of Planning," in Robert Freestone, ed., *Urban Planning in a Changing World: The Twentieth Century Experience* (London: E. & FN. Spon, 1991), 40-60, here 45-47; Stephen V. Ward, "Learning from the U.S.: The Americanisation of Western Urban Planning," in Joe Nasr and Mercedes Volait, eds., *Urbanism: Imported or*

Exported? (Chichester: Wiley-Academy, 2003), 83-106.

11   Gijs Mom, "Diffusion and Technological Change. Culture, Technology and the Emergence of a 'European Car,'" *Jahrbuch für Wirtschaftsgeschichte* 1 (2007): 67-82.

12   James J. Flink, *The Car Culture* (Cambridge, MA /London: MIT Press, 1975); Arthur J. Kuhn, *GM Passes Ford, 1918–1938: Designing the General Motors Performance-Control System* (University Park/London: The Pennsylvania State University Press, 1986).

13   Henk Kleijer and Ger Tillekens, "The Lure of Anglo-American Popular Culture. Explaining the Rise of Dutch Youth Culture," in Doeko Bosscher, Marja Roholl, and Mel van Elteren, eds., *American Culture in the Netherlands* (Amsterdam: VU University Press, 1996), 97-113; Gijs Mom, "'The Future is a Shifting Panorama': The Role of Expectations in the History of Mobility," in Weert Canzler and Gert Schmidt, eds., *Zukünfte des Automobils. Aussichten und Grenzen der autotechnischen Globalisierung* (Berlin: edition sigma, 2008), 31-58.

14   Gijs Mom, "Roads without Rails: European Highway-Network Building and the Desire for Long-Range Motorized Mobility," *Technology and Culture* 46.4 (October 2005): 745-772.

15   Ole O. Moen, "Mobility, Geographic and Social: The American Dream and American Realities," in Cornelis A. van Minnen and Sylvia L. Hilton, eds., *Nation on the Move: Mobility in U.S. History* (Amsterdam: VU University Press, 2002), 155-173; George Martin, "Grounding Social Ecology: Landscape, Settlement, and the Right of Way," *Capitalism, Nature, Socialism* 13.1 (March 2002): 3-30.

SUBURBIA AS THE NEW FRONTIER: A STORY OF DUTCH AND AMERICAN CONVERGENCE

——

KOOS BOSMA

Introduction

Shifts in appreciation for the paired concepts of "city" and "country" are evident across centuries of Western literature. Usually these concepts are seen as contrasting. Whereas sometimes the countryside is an arcadia and the city a stinking cesspool, at other times the city is the highest manifestation of culture and the country a place of toil, provincialism, narrow-mindedness, and stagnation.[1] During the second half of the twentieth century, however, the traditional city in America and the Netherlands alike underwent an unparalleled cultural, physical, and economic transformation that rendered this conceptual duality meaningless.

This transformation is reflected in major decentralized growth, the sharp dividing line separating functions and population and income categories, and the emergence of an alternative lifestyle. The term used to describe this rupture with the familiar urban image is "suburbia" or "suburban sprawl." For an understanding of the ideological foundation, planning, design, and marketing of this transformative built environment, whether in the United States or the Netherlands, the analysis of "suburbia" in both countries is illuminating. In the American version suburbia grew, within the space of half a century, to be the dominant cultural landscape as well as home for most families. In many instances, suburbia briefly exists as a dynamic, verdant buffer between the city and its surrounding region and is, in that sense, ambiguous: it borders pastoral nature but nonetheless has an intravenous highway hook-up with the corrupt big city. The

5

THE
COLD WAR
AND
BEYOND

1945-2009

ECONOMICS
AND
SOCIETY

Dutch version has very different origins, which are more closely linked with government initiatives. The Netherlands' postwar urban fringe spread across the rural landscape like canalized lava, creasing the face of the country.

This essay traces both variants of suburbanization — as well as their cross-pollination — along three main lines: first, the philosophical ideals giving rise to suburbia and the related debate; second, the social mechanisms in operation in suburbia; and third, the organization of suburbanization through a combination of entrepreneurship, public planning, and spatial planning.

The Roots of Suburbia

Cold War-era decentralization toward the countryside was prompted in part by a military mantra, motivated primarily by the fear that major European and American cities would be targets of nuclear bombing.[2] The American suburb of the 1950s provided an exemplary vehicle for illustrating the superiority of capitalism and the American democratic system.[3] It was from this perspective that the private, detached home with its own yard — the key to what lent middle-class homeowners a special position on the social ladder — came to be presented as a bulwark against communism. At the same time, however, suburbia provided fertile ground for myth formation.

The ideological foundation of the American suburb was formed by notions of the Enlightenment: freedom, personal property, entrepreneurial spirit, and the right to the pursuit of happiness. In its American incarnation this ideal is hyperindividualistic: everyone has the potential to be a self-made man or woman. The suburbanites' ambition is to have unlimited opportunities to climb to the top of the social ladder and to strike it rich. Theirs is a search for space, privacy, consumer goods, and a better life for their children. By purchasing a new home they are not only changing their address, but buying into a frontier dream, which has three themes: escape from the congestion and corruption of urban life, self-development ("private fiction"), and a higher social status.

Dutch dreams of life outside the city were quite different. Their ideological foundation fit within a more general model of European collaboration that was manifested in public housing. It was the government, therefore, that took the leading role, operating in an investment climate that was more egalitarian and in which the idea of the "state contribution" occupied a key position. Postwar Holland had no leisure class. Reconstruction and, later, the welfare state took first priority. In the Netherlands, hard work would only effect a slight rise on the social ladder.

Fear and uncertainty about the future helped foster the Dutch dream of equality during the Cold War. These feelings were neutralized somewhat by the

Marshall Plan, which in its wake imported a carefree kind of consumerism embedded in a comfortable and adventurous lifestyle.[4] Media interest focused on new trends, inventions, and fashions: T-shirts, sexy bikinis, limousines, jazz improvisations, and luxury mansions with swimming pools. The architectural modernism of the International Style seemed a tailor-made cocoon for this new culture. Its propaganda advocating an optimistic lifestyle and happy-go-lucky consumerism as the engine that would power the welfare state stood in sharp contrast with the socialist realism of the Soviets and the disciplined collectivism of the communist regimes.

Clearly, the impetus for suburbanization in the U.S. and the Netherlands was considerably different. Whereas Dutch outlying neighborhoods fostered community ideals in the evenly distributed composition of row houses or apartment buildings, straight streets, and regimented vegetation, the meandering American suburb revolved around the interior of the single-family home — the "indoor arcadia" — whose marketing proposition focused on "living the American dream." The Dutch dream, by contrast, centered on collaboration and group processes; marketing was superfluous, since ultimately it was the state that owned the land and was responsible for its development. It was the state, therefore, that would make the dream come true and offer equal opportunities for all.

Suburbia in the Cultural Debate

Though drenched in social and ethical moralism, the — often fierce — criticism of American suburbia never really managed to broach the foundations of the American dream. Elitist critics like Lewis Mumford objected to suburbia on social grounds, arguing that the consumer-product culture would lead to a decline of American society. The legions of suburbanites who were toasting their freedom were destined to suffer from a hollow individualism that would endanger society as a whole. Their cookie-cutter homes were paving the way for the slums of the future, according to many a cultural pessimist. A more aesthetically motivated objection was that the highly personal manifestation of the democratic dream was diametrically opposed to its material attainment in a stereotyped design and mass-produced dwellings.

Despite the enormous architectural differences, similarities did exist in the industrialization of building processes in both countries, specifically with regard to attempts to minimize overall costs (for private homes in the U.S. and rental homes in the Netherlands) in order to put a home within reach of large segments of the population. American standardization resulted in a uniformity of traditional building styles embellished with bay windows, porches, and ga-

833

5

————

THE
COLD WAR
AND
BEYOND

1945–2009

————

ECONOMICS
AND
SOCIETY

rages. The architectural essence of the standardized Dutch home was, and still is, a series of stacked hollow drums with unadorned façades tacked on on either side. In both countries, the market for mass-produced, cheap consumer goods provided an imperative for repetition. The contribution of landscape architects and urban planners merely consists of fiddling within its dictates and introducing thematic types and variations. The composition and architecture of suburbia are continually being accommodated to the ideological framework, while it is the individual who — despite the standardized dwelling and with certain preconditions — adapts it all to suit personal taste. A lingering problem in the Netherlands and America alike is the difficulty of understanding how this far-reaching standardization bears on the individual's aspirations (to experiment, innovate, and personalize). And this begs the question: is the consumer simply the helpless victim of clever marketing ploys?

Whereas in the American suburbia debate criticism centered on its visual (standardization of dwelling types) and social (conformism and hyperindividualism) effects, Dutch suburban districts met with no such criticism initially, apart from the occasional attack from within professional circles on the underlying planning concept. The social sciences were still developing in the Netherlands and would not really take off until the 1960s. The traditionally Protestant and Catholic Dutch culture regarded unfettered consumerism seeping into the nation's suburbs as the silent killer of moral standards. In the pillarized Dutch society, consumption belonged to the same category as hedonism and excessive behavior. Modernization was therefore supervised by social scientists, church leaders, and social workers.

As the 1960s progressed, it became clear that the Dutch welfare state had brought about certain changes in society. An extended education system and increase in prosperity and leisure time contributed to a generation gap between the hardworking, religious, postwar reconstruction generation, which knew the meaning of hunger and poverty, and the easygoing youth plucking the fruits of older people's labors but showing little gratitude for their own socioeconomic security. When viewed through the eyes of its artists, the Netherlands of the 1950s is invariably depicted as a country of oppressive petty-bourgeoisism, with its anticommunism, staunch support of America, large-scale church attendance, and high birth rate.

Toward the end of the 1960s, both America and the Netherlands were coming to harsh terms with established moral codes, opening the floor for discus-

A typical American landscape, dominated by endless highways and suburbs stretching to the horizon. The Netherlands also went through a dramatic expansion of urban areas in the post-World War II period, but space restrictions and different social expectations produced quite different results. ➤

5

—

THE
COLD WAR
AND
BEYOND

1945-2009

—

ECONOMICS
AND
SOCIETY

sions on authoritarian government systems, exploitation of the working class, and the fate of the oppressed. The architectural elite was at loggerheads with the public at large. Architecture had to be liberated from the chains of capitalism and its design tailored to the needs of residential housing—giving rise to the reemergence of community planning.

Countless sociologists denounced the "inhospitality" of the big city and condemned new large-scale traffic networks, blaming it partly for the exodus of city dwellers to the suburbs, which—according to the same elite—represented a means of escape. "Alienation" was the buzzword; personal identity was at stake. Within this climate of political consciousness raising, criticism of the way in which postwar urban design was functioning also grew to unexpected proportions. The classic and extraordinarily influential prototype of such criticism was Jane Jacobs, whose 1961 book *The Death and Life of Great American Cities* created an international furor. The time was ripe for a new dream. Criticism of the deterioration of large cities and the suburban migration with which it was linked, and also of the one-dimensionality of the residential districts, eventually led each country to respond in ways that caused the respective American and Dutch suburban variants to converge.

Planning Suburbia

Implicit in the collaborative model conceived for the reconstruction of postwar Europe was a lengthy period of government involvement. Large-scale government projects were driven by socioeconomic objectives (industrialization policy and a guided economy) and scientific management of design and production processes. In the Netherlands, structural realignment went hand in hand with increasing demands on space, particularly for metropolitan growth and the expansion of rail, water, and highway networks. The Dutch "wage explosion" and skyrocketing prosperity of the 1960s that put car ownership within everyone's reach resulted in rapid expansion and modernization of the national road network. With the country reframed as an infrastructural composition, highways became the carriers of the processes of urbanization, their positioning on the map an increasingly important determinant for where outlying residential neighborhoods were to be built.

State-directed, driven by a combination of national legislation, spatial planning, fiscal aid, and government contributions, suburbanization in the Netherlands differed from that in the U.S. The looming specter of megacities and congestion in the urban agglomeration of the Netherlands' western part propelled the government to develop a vigorous program aimed at decentralizing the country's population and businesses. The residential housing sector grew to be one of the key forces driving the economy, and some 80 percent of all homes in modern-day Holland were built after World War II. The importation of foreign architectural systems — and subsequent development of Dutch systems — that allowed building segments to be prefabricated and then be assembled on the building site using advanced techniques (including gantry cranes, construction elevators, and standardized forms for pouring cement) led to the modernization of Dutch residential and public-building construction. This form of industrial mass-produced construction gave rise to a new urban landscape, in which standardization was elevated to the level of a great virtue.

Central in the discussion surrounding suburbia in both countries was the notion of the neighborhood. The ongoing segmentation of the family and individuals notwithstanding, a steady stream of praise was heard concerning the vital and positive role of community building, or the "neighborhood concept" (*wijkgedachte*, as it was referred to in the Netherlands). Dutch suburban modules for standardized rental housing presupposed self-sufficient districts with neighborhoods whose two to four thousand residents would be knit into a tight social network secured on the basis of a range of community services and a stimulating residential environment. "Initially, the look of postwar residential zones was defined by their repetition of identical compositions of various independent building complexes linked by a large patchwork of rectangular allotments. Defining elements at the level of the residential district were the broad through-roads, urban infrastructure zones, and green belts. At the neighborhood level it was the local street plan, parking provisions, public green spaces, front and backyards and property blocks of alternating heights that determined its appearance."[5] This design ideal cultivated an aesthetic of rectangularity, transparency, organizational clarity, and openness, together with a moralizing drive toward modernization of home life and interior design. It was an aesthetic steeped in a medical asceticism of hygiene, health, discipline, and efficiency, and expressed in light colors, portable furniture, large expanses of glass, smart kitchens and bathrooms and household equipment. This self-contained formulation could in theory be repeated endlessly.

In practice, however, the quality of this residential environment fell short. The intended facilities usually did not materialize and, moreover, when it came to social networks, it turned out that occupation, religious and political views, and mobility were stronger than any designer-imposed territorial compartments. These failings were to some extent corrected during the prosperous 1960s, when residential building projects could count on government contributions aimed at keeping suburbs from turning into bedroom communities, with funding for infrastructure and employment opportunities, multipurpose facilities, schools, regional care centers, and recreational and medical facilities.

5

—

THE
COLD WAR
AND
BEYOND

1945–2009

—

ECONOMICS
AND
SOCIETY

The American suburb could hardly have differed more. Meandering suburban street patterns, with their cul-de-sacs ending in paved circles, presented a sharp contrast to the classic American city grid. Public green space was minimal and the creation of infrastructure hinged on resident initiative. Its landscape was defined by the archetypal detached private home. The first great wave of migrants to this new frontier began in the 1950s: whereas no more than 144,000 urbanites moved to the countryside in 1944, that number had grown to 1.7 million around 1950.

Thus, while the 1950s suburb took on vastly different guises in the U.S. and the Netherlands, cross-pollination in their underlying concepts during the 1930s had nevertheless yielded certain similarities. Architects and urban planners working in postwar Holland had been inspired by planning concepts advanced in connection with the New Deal — for example, in the design of twenty-five garden cities, three of which were actually built.[6] Their designers were members of an international planning community linked by informal meetings and international conferences. The garden city — consisting of low-density construction within bounded satellite cities — formed the international template on which many European urban expansion experiments came to be based. The largest of these Dutch projects, which included Vreewijk in Rotterdam (designed and completed by Granpré Molière, Verhagen and Kok between 1915 and 1940) and Amsterdam South (designed by Berlage and completed between 1915 and 1940), grew to be famous around the world, not least for their brick architecture. Lewis Mumford visited the Dutch districts and propagated them in the U.S., and his criticism of American 1950s and 1960s suburbia was in fact based in part on the community-building and aesthetic qualities of these very districts.

Another direct inspiration from the 1930s was the New York suburb of Radburn — dubbed "a town for the motor age" — which represented a marriage of American and European models.[7] Through traffic was kept strictly separate from local traffic in Radburn, and pedestrians were given their own safe walkways. Public space between the residential rows was conceptualized and designed as a community park, while the rows themselves were laid out in an almost European style. The neighborhood unit of Radburn remained an exception in New York, but became a huge success all across the European continent. When reconstruction plans for Europe were drawn up during the war, the Radburnian neighborhood unit and spatial plan provided the basic blueprint. In the Netherlands, Radburn served as an urban development model for various neighborhoods in the new towns of Emmen and Almere. This model underwent further refinements in the 1950s to yield the restricted-traffic residential zone, which integrated pedestrians and motorists into a community where safe streets functioned as an extension of the individual home's entrance.[8] For the

Netherlands this model was the sought-after ideal that in the 1970s provided an alternative to the country's rigid and reserved reconstruction districts.[9]

Led by activists, newly minted left-wing architects flooded residential neighborhoods to get a good look at urban institutions. Residents were to be cured of their "sensory deprivation" through injections of verdure, playground equipment, modernized housing, and, above all, opportunities for social encounters. A new version of the Dutch dream would finally be achieved.

Arguments in favor of variation in housing developments and façade design, scaled-down proportions, and traditional references found much support and were to determine suburban development in the 1970s. Architectural and urban-planning designs reached back to traditional elements connoting the coziness, intimacy, and security of group life, with warm, natural colors, wood and masonry work, red- and brown-tiled roofs, bay windows, balconies, front-door awnings, and lots laid out in short streets — where no cars were allowed — with gates, small squares, public green space, and different silhouettes for homes and rooflines that offered a great variety of perspectives.

Given the 1970s' metamorphosis of Dutch suburbia, it is remarkable that the American version underwent hardly any significant changes during this time. Though odd, nonconformist settlements certainly cropped up, these were usually short lived and left no lasting impact on suburbia. Critics who had decried America's suburban landscape as a conformist cultural desert fell silent without further fresh evidence of negative trends.

Suburbia and Generic Sprawl

By 1980, some sixty million Americans had moved to suburbs. This was a scale of decentralization so immense — and one that has continued unabated over the past twenty years — that it came to represent an ever-growing problem. The most rapidly expanding suburbs typically passed through a number of specific stages. From the 1970s onward, the suburban concept began to include more than houses alone. Metropolitan areas experienced a parallel process of corporate suburbanization, in the form of extended conglomerations of commercial and industrial zones, shopping malls, and office parks. Sooner or later the suburb was swallowed up by the city, suffered a decline, and was claimed by low-income and ethnic-minority residents. In the final stage, city, suburb, and countryside melted into a single polycentric, heterogeneous network of variable land use, distinct classes, diverse ethnicities, and different households.[10]

In the Netherlands, the final decade of the twentieth century brought a paradigm shift that, among other things, cemented the decentralization process

839

5

—

THE
COLD WAR
AND
BEYOND

1945–2009

—

ECONOMICS
AND
SOCIETY

discussed above. Up until then, the single-family home had been the exception; the run-of-the-mill Dutch suburb was a market segment geared toward public housing, with 70 to 80 percent consisting of rental properties and an outer fringe of private properties. Such an uneven distribution was in fact unique in Europe. But following the euphoric 1970s, with their emphasis on scaled-down proportions, the economic downturn of the 1980s marked a return of the familiar standard suburban building complex. These changes were the run-up in a major shift toward American models in the 1990s.

The exodus to suburbia had left many an "old" city sinking into a state of impoverishment. Midway into the 1980s, urban renewal gained a new, ideological, momentum in the form of so-called cultural renewal. Its aim was to curb the exodus by addressing the architectural appearance of not only residential buildings, but the city center as a whole. Urban renewal—a process that continues to this day and increasingly is carried out by private parties with ready capital—went hand in hand with the withdrawal of government involvement, also in the suburbs. The Netherlands once again turned an eager and optimistic eye to the American market approach, leading to a construction boom (particularly in office space) and a wave of high-rise building. Public housing—a system that had represented the status quo for no less than ninety years—came to an abrupt end and, from 1990 onward, the private housing market became accessible to all. Suburban development now progressed without state support, taking as its basic unit the privately owned home fitted with all the latest novelties but devoid of any cohesive standard of architectural or urban development quality. Market trends fueled the Dutch adoption of American real estate rhetoric. In fact, American and Dutch suburban expansion displayed more visual similarities than ever before. Low-rise property evolved as a status symbol in the Netherlands, too, with location serving as an affirmation of one's highly individual identity vis-à-vis society. The "housing consumer" preferred a suburban, park-like living environment with broad streets and a spacious yard. Given this context, the application of American models found a ready reception.

In America, the rhetorical alliance between suburbia, indoor arcadia, and the American dream experienced a 1980s revival. In 1987, law-firm employee Faith Popcorn labeled the suburban dream as an example of "cocooning": "insulating oneself from the harsh realities of the outside world, and building the perfect environment to reflect one's personal needs and fantasies."[11] City dwellers with any capital were lured to the cocooning suburbs by low property prices and advantageous loans to purchase homes and consumer goods. Renewed attacks on widespread generic suburban sprawl now aimed not only at the homogeneity of the living environment and absence of any features allowing residents to relate to its history, but also at the dearth of public services and poor public transportation; even bowling alleys and clubs had become rare. All that

remained amidst the ever-present sprawl were stores. Thanks to mass-production methods applied by residential construction companies, which operate
under extreme pressure to make high profits while selling standard products
with a low profit margin, the life expectancy of buildings has shrunk to fifteen
years. Generic building is an inescapable fact, since it alone offers the fastest
ticket to realizing a high return on an investment. And so the American model
is being propagated to its extremes.

At the same time, however, a counter movement has emerged in America
as well — one bearing comparison with Dutch practices. This so-called New
Urbanism does more than simply denounce the "degeneracy" of the suburb;
it has been seeking alternatives. Its advocates were, and are, urban and other
planning professionals who endeavor to reintroduce land-use plans as part of
the planning process, together with building codes, financing procedures, and
traffic and parking regulations. In short, they envision a return to traditional
urban planning strategies, durable building types, and local landmarks. New
Urbanism's neotraditional private and public housing relies on uniform architectural styles as a deliberate means of stimulating economic allegiance to the
neighborhood. This alternative approach displays marked similarities to the
way in which the Netherlands has sought to shape traditional town and village
landscapes and to define public space, of which the suburban neighborhoods
designed by Rob Krier and Sjoerd Soeters serve as good examples.

Prognosis

The past half century has shown that neither the American nor the Dutch dream
is static: rather, it is an ideal in flux that has expanded almost beyond definable
limits. The general template for the proliferating suburban landscape — the
home with its attendant conventions — is at the macro level nothing more, nor
less, than a ticking ecological time bomb, with its massive demands on space,
energy-intensive residential conveniences, and exponential increase of automobile traffic.[12]

In his pseudo-ironic hymn to "The Generic City," Dutch architect and one-
time Harvard University professor Rem Koolhaas praises the serenity of suburban fragmentation. He points out our modern-day conditions of personal freedom, short-term investments, postindustrial technology, and globalization,
and then draws his alarming conclusions. The generic city of the future will
have banned all forms of authenticity, relegated planning to the sidelines, and
abandoned the public domain to exist as an infinite repetition of the same simple suburban module.[13] The only context will be a "free-style" amalgam of infrastructure, buildings, and nature. Objects in the generic city do not exist in any

841

5

—

THE
COLD WAR
AND
BEYOND

1945–2009

—

ECONOMICS
AND
SOCIETY

formal relation to one another. The image we are left with is of a disconnected metropolis without a center and lacking any historically stratified foundations. The single point of orientation is the central airport. "Generic City" is devoid of features. Will Koolhaas's spectral vision of a world of unrestrained consumption and nonexistent cultural ambitions shape the face of twenty-first-century sprawl? If we are to believe him, we are facing a decision of historic importance and utmost urgency: do we side with America's hyperindividualistic, short-term capitalism or with the more community- and sustainability-oriented European collaborative model?

1   R. Williams, *The Country and the City* (London: Chatto and Windus, 1973).

2   Koos Bosma, *Schuilstad. Bescherming van de bevolking tegen luchtaanvallen* (Amsterdam: SUN, 2006), 358-378.

3   John Archer, *Architecture and Suburbia. From English Villa to American Dream House, 1690–2000* (Minneapolis: University of Minnesota Press, 2005), 292ff.

4   Cor Wagenaar, "Modernism, Americanism and Historiography," *Architecture Bulletin* 1 (2006): 2, 11-18.

5   Noud de Vreeze, "Woningbouw: massaproductie van individuele idealen, 1945–2000," in Koos Bosma et al., eds., *Bouwen in Nederland 600–2000* (Zwolle: Waanders, 2007), 606-607.

6   Koos Bosma, *J.M. de Casseres. De eerste planoloog* (Rotterdam: 010 Publishers, 2003), 33-40.

7   Clarence S. Stein, *Towards New Towns for America* (Liverpool: University Press of Liverpool, 1951).

8   Evelien van Es, "Het veelzijdige woonerf als toonbeeld van democratische ruimte," *Architecture Bulletin* 3 (2008): 4, 21-29; Koos Bosma and Helma Hellinga,

eds., *Mastering the City: North-European Planning 1900–2000* (Rotterdam: NAi, 1997), 310-315, 338-345.

9   Rather, the American models harked back to Frank Lloyd Wright's *Broadacre City* and Norman Bel Geddes's *Futurama*. Astrid Böger, "Die Zukunft der Vergangenheit: General Motors' Futurama (1939) im Kontext urbanistischer Modelle" and Christoph Asendorf, "Verkehrsfluss und Gesellschaftsform. Reichsautobahn und Highway im Konzeptvergleich," in Anke Köth, Anna Minta, and Andreas Schwartung, eds., *Building America. Die Erschaffung einer neuen Welt* (Dresden: Thelem, 2005), 285-302, 271-284.

10 Thomas Hine, *Populuxe* (London: s.n., 1987), 177.

11 Archer, *Architecture,* 297.

12 Ellen Dunham-Jones, "Capital Transformations of the Post-Industrial Landscape," *Oase* 54 (2001): 9-35.

13 Rem Koolhaas, "The Generic City," in O.M.A., Rem Koolhaas and Bruce Mau, *S,M,L,XL* (Rotterdam: 010 Publishers, 1995), 1238-1264.

AMBIVALENT SOLIDARITY: SIXTY YEARS OF DUTCH-AMERICAN TRADE UNION RELATIONS

———

TOM ETTY

The standard version of post-World War II international trade union relations runs according to the stereotype that the Western unions, under U.S. leadership, united around the common cause of opposing their Soviet-backed communist alternatives. According to this cliché, American and Dutch unions worked closely together in the anticommunist cause, and one would also expect the smaller Dutch unions to have consistently been the junior partner, complementing but certainly following the American lead. However, reality was more complex than this simple narrative suggests. Direct bilateral relations between the unions in the United States and the Netherlands were generally the exception, since most international union business was carried out within a multilateral context set by the International Confederation of Free Trade Unions (ICFTU) and the International Labour Organisation (ILO). The complexity of the Dutch-American union relationship will be illustrated through three examples covering the struggle against apartheid, workers' and trade union rights in Indonesia, and joint actions against multinational companies. Overall, the picture that emerges suggests that the Dutch were not only a full partner with the Americans but that they also took a completely different course of action in certain key fields of activity.

Anticommunism as a Common Cause

There is no doubt that the cause of anticommunism did unite Dutch and American unions early on in the Cold War.[1] In 1947 the Nederlands Verbond van Vak-

5

———

THE
COLD WAR
AND
BEYOND

1945–2009

———

ECONOMICS
AND
SOCIETY

verenigingen (NVV, the social democratic trade unions), the largest Dutch trade union confederation, still recovering from the damage done by World War II, received one hundred thousand dollars from the American Federation of Labor (AFL) to assist in its postwar recovery. A year later the communist Eenheids Vakcentrale (EVC) exposed this support and criticized in particular the "ideological grounds" behind the assistance, meaning the AFL's determined anti-communism. The sum was considerable for the Netherlands of 1947, although it was far less than other amounts given by the AFL in that period to other anticommunist unions in Europe. The AFL was at the time aiming to undermine the World Federation of Trade Unions (WFTU), set up in 1945 to unite the major trade unions in the world. The AFL's main rival in the U.S., the Congress of Industrial Organizations (CIO), was a member. According to the AFL, many affiliates of the WFTU were close allies of communist parties and several of them were not trade unions at all but mere communist fronts. To pursue its aim, the AFL cooperated not only with the State Department but also with the CIA.[2] The NVV, at the time also a member of the WFTU, was embarrassed by the EVC revelations, claiming that it was no more than a loan for humanitarian reasons to the railway workers' union, that it was less than the amount stated, and that it had since been repaid. Ideological reasons had nothing to do with it.[3]

What is certainly clear is that the NVV needed no extra American encouragement or inspiration to fight Communist Party-inspired action in its own ranks and, more generally, in the Dutch trade union movement as a whole. The NVV was active on that front before 1947, and continued to be so afterward. Several of its affiliated unions were still screening members and staff, in collaboration with the Dutch intelligence services, up to the early 1970s. Lodewijk de Waal, president of the Service Employees Union and later, from 1997 until 2005, president of the Federatie Nederlandse Vakbeweging (FNV), was himself a Communist Party member in his late teens and early twenties. He subsequently claimed that it was only because the screening system was so inefficient that he was hired for a staff job by the Service Employees Union and could begin his trade union career. His union did not abolish the screening practice officially until the early 1970s. Such practices were initiated for NVV interests, so perceived, and not because of U.S. demands. In fact, the NVV had a long record of being critical of AFL-CIO anticommunism and the methods applied by that federation to achieve it.

The Multilateral Framework: ICFTU and ILO

Practically all Dutch-American trade union contacts took place within the framework of the international organizations to which the AFL, the CIO (and after their merger in 1955 the AFL-CIO), the NVV/FNV, and their affiliated unions belonged, namely the ICFTU and the international federations covering sectoral activities such as food and agriculture, metal, and textiles/garments. Another important place of contact was the ILO, the specialized agency of the United Nations dealing with labor and socioeconomic policy questions. The ILO is the only UN institution that is not purely intergovernmental. Workers' and employers' representatives are full members, on an equal footing with and independent of their governments. Since its inception the ICFTU has played the leading role in the Workers' Group in the ILO.

Major trade union policies concerning economic questions, trade, sustainability, migration, development cooperation, environment, and workers' and trade union rights are jointly developed in these multilateral settings. The Dutch have, traditionally, been active members and, on the whole, the same can be said for the Americans. It should be noted, however, that the AFL and later the AFL-CIO have from the start operated outside the fold of the ICFTU and the ILO, developing their own policies and sometimes going against the views of the majority in the free trade union movement. This occurred especially during 1969–82 when they stayed outside the ICFTU and the ILO, but it was also apparent when they were active members.[4]

The Dutch NVV/FNV has on the contrary been relatively steadfast in its multilateralism. Whenever it had differences of opinion with fraternal unions, the ICFTU executive bodies, or the ICFTU secretariat in Brussels, it fought these battles from the inside and abstained from tactics practiced by the Americans, such as blackmail and withholding affiliation fees. It never contemplated breaking away and steering its own course. Only more recently, since the early 1990s, has it largely withdrawn from contributing to the ICFTU's development cooperation efforts, continuing to work instead through the sectoral Global Union Federations. The Scandinavian unions, which, like the Dutch, receive substantial development cooperation funds from their governments to help strengthen trade unions in developing countries, have followed a similar path. This withdrawal has undoubtedly weakened the ICFTU's role in this important policy area, and in this respect it is somewhat comparable to the damaging effects of the AFL-CIO's separate Free Trade Union Institutes in Latin America (AIFLD), Africa (AALC), Asia (AAFLI), and Europe (FTUI) from 1962 onward.

Today, the AFL-CIO and many of its unions have clearly lost the leading role in the international trade union movement that they held in the late 1940s and 1950s. Their prominent position was undermined early on by their obsession with anticommunism. With this as the driving force behind their international work, the American unions became allies of the U.S. government, getting involved in overt and covert operations that had more to do with global power politics than with the representation of workers' interests. European unions,

5

—

THE
COLD WAR
AND
BEYOND

1945–2009

—

ECONOMICS
AND
SOCIETY

including the Dutch, grew more and more embarrassed and irritated when confronted with these activities. The Americans, in particular the AFL, were deeply suspicious of and disappointed by their European counterparts when the latter started making contacts with trade unions in Soviet-dominated central and eastern Europe. Although there could be no misunderstanding about the strongly anticommunist attitude of most of the ICFTU's European affiliates, the Americans duly accused them of appeasement and being soft on communism. The Europeans pointed out that they hoped these bilateral contacts could make a contribution to détente and security. The ICFTU itself, criticized by the Left in Europe (and by many unions and politicians in the developing countries) for being an agent of imperialism and a willing tool of U.S. Cold War policies, was publicly vilified by AFL-CIO President George Meany. The NVV/FNV strongly disagreed with the Americans, particularly concerning the role of the free trade union movement in the Cold War, contacts with the party- and state-controlled "unions" in central and eastern Europe, assistance to trade unions in developing countries, and the emergence of an independent European Trade Union Confederation (ETUC) as part of the process of European integration. The ETUC, which was outside the ICFTU, was relevant for the Americans only in the sense of how it might affect policies in the East-West conflict.

High-level contacts between AFL-CIO and NVV/FNV did not take place during the presidency of George Meany (1955–82), and only incidentally and informally under Lane Kirkland/Tom Donahue (1979–95) and John Sweeney (1995-present). There were no exchanges of delegations as, for instance, in the case of the British TUC, the German DGB, or the Nordic unions. Discussions on major policy issues were mainly the responsibility of representatives of the international departments (and in the AFL-CIO's case the director of the European Office in Paris), during ICFTU meetings, missions to problem areas, and in the ILO. Usually, these only served the purpose of clarifying positions, defining policy views in controversial debates, and, whenever possible, forging supportive coalitions. On the main general policy issues, there were no spectacular differences of opinion, with the exception of those already mentioned. Nevertheless, after the 1950s the continuing U.S. insistence that anticommunism be the central purpose of the union movement began to cause frictions between the AFL-CIO and its international partners. In some cases, where the Americans and the Dutch were key actors, uneasy and ambivalent forms of cooperation did emerge that influenced the course taken by the ICFTU and its relations with unaffiliated trade unions. But there were clear differences of opinion on the main goals to be reached. Two examples of this awkward relationship will be given here, concerning South Africa and Indonesia during the 1960s and 1970s.

The Struggle against Apartheid

At an early stage the FNV strongly supported the independent unions formed by black workers opposing the South African regime. This support was given in the context of the Coordinating Committee on South Africa, which the ICFTU and the international sectoral federations had set up in 1974. Work in the committee and cooperation between the committee and the new South African unions were not easy for several reasons, one of the main problems being that the latter had difficulties with some ICFTU affiliates. They had even greater difficulties with the AFL-CIO, which, although outside the ICFTU during this period, was not acceptable as a partner to most of the South Africans. These difficulties were caused by the Americans' obsession with communism. The South African Congress of Trade Unions (SACTU), operating in exile, was very close to the African National Congress (ANC) and the South African Communist Party (SACP). The same was true for leaders of the independent (black) trade unions that emerged within the country, like FOSATU and COSATU. Many of them saw the ICFTU as little more than an instrument of AFL-CIO foreign policy, and this created a difficult relationship with the Coordinating Committee. Eventually, they preferred working exclusively with a "consortium" of donor organizations (consisting of the Nordic trade union centers and the FNV) belonging to the ICFTU Coordinating Committee. This caused considerable irritation among other ICFTU members. The Dutch/Scandinavian answer to the critics was that they had not chosen this situation and they were trying to function as ICFTU ambassadors while helping the South African unions grow under difficult conditions. In the end, this approach seems to have worked and contributed to clearing the air between the South African unions and the ICFTU/AFL-CIO. Anti-American sentiments in the major South African Confederation COSATU did last for a long time and the suspicion against the ICFTU possibly even increased after the AFL-CIO's reaffiliation with the ICFTU in 1982. Nevertheless, COSATU did join the ICFTU in 1998, dropping initial ideas to cofound an alternative "progressive" trade union international led by themselves, the CUT (Brazil), the KCTU (South Korea), the CGIL (Italy), and the CGT (France). The normalization of the relationship between the Americans and the South Africans was helped considerably by the intensive mediation of the "chosen five" (the Dutch and the Scandinavians), as they were sneeringly called in the ICFTU.

NVV (Nederlandse Verbond van Vakverenigingen or Netherlands Association of Trade Unions) conference on the struggle for freedom and workers' rights in South Africa, held in Amsterdam in 1974.

Trade Union Rights in Indonesia

Another example of FNV/AFL-CIO dissonance in the international labor field was the issue of workers' and trade union rights in Indonesia. After the bloody 1965 military coup in that country, which was supported by the U.S., the new Suharto regime had broken up the strongest, communist-dominated trade union center, SOBSI, and brought the rest of the deeply divided trade union movement under its full control. It forced a unitary confederation upon the workers and kept it under close supervision by appointing a large number of retired military personnel at different levels of the organization. The FNV, which for many years had not shown a special interest in the trade union situation in the former Dutch colony, took an interest in the early 1980s. When the role of the military in the trade union movement and the extremely repressive trade union and labor legislation were exposed a few years later by the FNV in ICFTU Executive Board meetings and the ILO, initial reactions from the secretariat and fraternal organizations were not very positive. Some even echoed the Indonesian government in the ILO, accusing the FNV of using claims of trade union rights violations as a postcolonial grudge. The ICFTU leadership was irritated, as it had allowed the president of the unitary Indonesian confederation FBSI to sit on the ICFTU Executive Board, despite the fact that this organization was not even affiliated. The Indonesians were also represented in the Workers' Group of the ILO's Governing Body, with the active support of the ICFTU. In the late 1980s the ICFTU even tried to arrange a formal affiliation for the FBSI (which had meanwhile been renamed SPSI by the Indonesian minister of manpower), notwithstanding all the evidence of its questionable credentials accumulated by the FNV. However, the Dutch eventually won the debate, and the ICFTU at long last lodged a complaint at the ILO against Indonesia's violations of basic workers' and trade union rights, both in law and in practice.

During all these years the AFL-CIO, which had an AAFLI office in Jakarta from 1962 onward and knew exactly about the practices denounced by the FNV, kept this information to itself, did not use it as ammunition in the ILO debates to silence the angry denials of the Indonesian government and the state-controlled unions, and did not object to the idea that this very peculiar species of free and democratic trade unionism should be admitted to ICFTU membership. On the contrary, for some time it supported the affiliation request. In the 1990s the AFL-CIO/AAFLI did change its policies toward Indonesia, comparing notes regularly with the FNV and cooperating in the ILO's Conference Committee on the Application of Standards. Eventually it even started to support the dissident trade unions that emerged during that decade.

849

5

—

THE
COLD WAR
AND
BEYOND

1945–2009

—

ECONOMICS
AND
SOCIETY

850

Joint Actions against Multinational Companies

South Africa and Indonesia are not so much examples of straightforward co-operation but, rather, examples of strong differences of opinion (initially at least) as to what the international union movement should be aiming for. Joint approaches were eventually developed via the ICFTU and the ILO, but there were many tensions along the way. The initiatives for such processes usually came from the Dutch, not from the Americans. Moving into the 1980s and 1990s, more clear-cut forms of cooperation have only occurred concerning the defense of workers' and trade union rights in multinational companies. The main tool that trade unions have in this area is the OECD document *Guidelines for Multinational Enterprises* from 1976. It spells out which rules of the game companies should respect in employment and industrial relations issues. The guidelines are not a binding instrument, but a set of recommendations from the OECD member states to the business community. There is a (rather weak) supervisory system, underpinned by so-called National Contact Points (NCPs) that can handle trade union and NGO complaints.

The FNV has been one of the main producers of complaints since 1976 and it has found more effective ways and means to activate the Dutch NCP than most other unions in the OECD area. On numerous occasions the American unions have also tried to use the guidelines, in particular in freedom of association cases. These usually concern unions trying to organize a plant against strong opposition from the employer, who is prepared to use all possible means to prevent this. Virtually all NCPs are less than keen to take on multinational companies, including in the Netherlands, but the American NCP is especially resistant to union efforts to get it involved.

In the Netherlands, there have been several cases of alleged violation of the OECD guidelines by subsidiaries of multinational corporations based in the U.S. One of the earliest that the FNV raised with both the Dutch NCP and the OECD was the closure in 1981 of a large Ford plant in Amsterdam. The FNV discussed the chances and the potential positive impact of a supportive complaint of the AFL-CIO and the United Automobile Workers with the American NCP, but soon realized that this would not achieve very much due to the latter's passivity. Consequently, in other cases of alleged violations by subsidiaries of American multinationals in the Netherlands that the FNV presented to the Dutch NCP (involving Hyster Company, 1983, and Hewlett Packard, 2002), the FNV only informed the AFL-CIO and did not request support.

For their part, the AFL-CIO and some of their affiliated unions have solicited FNV support in a number of cases involving subsidiaries of Dutch multinationals that they tried to raise with the American NCP. They were hoping that their Dutch colleagues would use their contacts with the company's head office (which are usually much better than the equivalent contacts between American unions and the management of U.S. subsidiaries). Such an intervention, possibly a joint one with a delegation from the American union, might induce the Dutch head office to resolve the dispute in the U.S. They also expected that an FNV intervention with the Dutch NCP, calling upon it to contact the American NCP with a request to take the case on board and approach the company in the U.S., might put some useful pressure on the U.S. employer. The most recent example is a conflict in a subsidiary of Dutch-based Gamma Holdings, National Wire Fabric, based in Star City, AR. This case involved the dismissal of striking workers, members of the United Steelworkers of America (USW), in a wage dispute, and their replacement by management with non-union strike breakers. The conflict produced the longest strike in the history of Arkansas (February 2006–May 2007) and it was eventually solved in a way satisfactory to the workers and their union. Direct intervention with the board of Gamma Holdings by FNV Bondgenoten, the largest FNV affiliate, proved to be of crucial importance, according to the Steelworkers. The Dutch NCP, reluctantly and only after strong FNV insistence, also spoke to the company in the very last stage of the dispute, when the crucial intervention had already been made by the unions. However, the Dutch NCP refused to try to activate their colleagues in Washington, who had limited their own involvement to asking the Dutch NCP for information (which was not delivered) and to following events as they occurred.

In addition to the "guideline cases," the FNV (affiliates) and the AFL-CIO (affiliates or former affiliates) have cooperated on "right to organize cases" in the U.S. Since 1990 there have been seven such cases. One of them concerned a bitter conflict at Ravenswood Aluminium Company in Charleston, WV, with seventeen hundred workers locked out, and another covered prejudicial actions against the Steelworkers. The "Dutch connection" here was not a Dutch parent company, but a Dutch bank servicing the American enterprise. The FNV tried to use its influence with the bank in the Netherlands and arranged a meeting between a USW delegation and the board of directors. In general, it is difficult to say how much such interventions contribute to finding a solution, but the result in this case was positive. After an agonizingly long dispute of seventeen months, the union and the company reached an agreement in May 1992. Ravenswood chairman Boyle, who had sought the confrontation with the union, was fired. However, this was an exceptional outcome, since in similar cases elsewhere no such tangible result has been reached.

Practical forms of cooperation over basic workers' and trade union rights at the workplace level have also taken place through efforts of the AFL-CIO and some of its affiliates (or former affiliates) to use the influence of FNV unions in Dutch pension funds. For instance, the U.S. Service Employees Internation-

5
—

THE
COLD WAR
AND
BEYOND

1945–2009

—

ECONOMICS
AND
SOCIETY

al Union (SEIU) tried to involve its Dutch colleagues in its organization drives among janitors. In 1991, 1992, 1993, and 1996 it sought support in actions against Apple Computers in Silicon Valley, CA and John Akridge Corp., a big developer of office buildings in Washington, DC. Here, the Dutch unions have not always delivered what the Americans had hoped for. While they discussed the cases at length and arranged meetings between SEIU delegations and union representatives in some large pension funds investing in the targeted companies, in the end there was no pressure brought to bear on the American firms. This had partly to do with the employer representatives in the pension funds not being ready to cooperate. But the union representatives also showed reluctance. Potential financial consequences for their members were one reason given. Another was that there are hundreds of these recognition cases in the U.S., and that it would not be feasible to mobilize the pension funds weapon in each and every instance. Moreover, the American union representatives have not always been very careful in the preparation of their cases, leading their Dutch counterparts to question the value of making an extra effort to support them. The opinion of the FNV was, and is, that their American colleagues should make a strategic selection of a few cases of gross violation of fundamental rights in order to organize, bargain collectively, and push them through as test cases. The chances of success would be higher in a well-prepared national and international campaign, including trade union action in pension funds in the Netherlands and elsewhere. The use of pension fund influence has been given a lot of attention in the ICFTU since the early 1990s, driven forward by the AFL-CIO and dealt with by a special Committee on Workers' Capital, presently chaired by the president of the Canadian confederation, CLC. The FNV is an active member in this committee, making available both intellectual and financial resources.

Conclusion

Since World War II, the record of Dutch-American trade union solidarity has often been ambivalent, and at times awkward. The American insistence on opposing communism in every case and at any price, regardless of the particular needs of local workers, did not always make cooperation easy, as the cases of South Africa and Indonesia demonstrate. It is therefore important to recognize the special contribution the Dutch unions have made to the international union cause, often in alliance with their colleagues in Scandinavia and against the views of their colleagues from across the Atlantic. The Dutch particularly were able to "sell" the policies of the ICFTU and the ITS/GUF in countries where these met with suspicion or even hostility due to the activities of the American unions. Nevertheless, the Dutch — like many other Europeans — have always been convinced that an American presence in the trade union internationals is an essential precondition for a strong and authoritative international movement. Both countries can make important contributions to the success of the new ITUC, particularly through stronger coordination in development cooperation activities. Both the Dutch and the Americans are large donor organizations for development projects. Indeed, the combined funds for trade union projects that these organizations (together with the Scandinavian trade unions) control make the total ITUC budget look meager.

1   This essay concentrates on the activities of the NVV/FNV and the AFL or, after 1955, the AFL-CIO. The other main Dutch union confederations, the CNV (Protestant) and the NKV (Catholic, which joined with the NVV in 1976 to form the FNV), had fewer contacts with the main American unions. The NKV and CNV were founding members of the International Federation of Christian Trade Unions (IFCTU), which changed its name in 1969 to the World Confederation of Labour (WCL). In 2006 WCL and ICFTU, together with some other national trade union centers that had up to that point not been affiliated internationally, founded the new International Trade Union Confederation (ITUC).

2   On the AFL and the CIA see A. Carew, "The American Labor Movement in Fizzland: The Free Trade Union Committee and the CIA," *Labor History* 39.1 (1998): 25-42.

3   Henk Sporken, "Een trouwe bondgenoot van de 'vrije wereld': het NVV, het Marshall-plan en de internationale vakbeweging," *Cahiers voor de politieke en sociale wetenschappen* 2.1 (February 1979): 49-93. Sporken also reports that the AFL had already funded the NVV in 1945 with a sum of 135,000 guilders, of which 50,000 was earmarked for "the financing of the press" (p. 53). However, the exact sums, and their timing, are still difficult to clarify precisely.

4   See A. Carew, M. Dreyfus et al., eds., *The International Confederation of Free Trade Unions* (Berne: Peter Lang, 2000), 187-339, 341-517.

5

THE
COLD WAR
AND
BEYOND

1945-2009

ECONOMICS
AND
SOCIETY

854

CORPORATE GOVERNANCE: THE POLDER MODEL AND THE ANGLO-SAXON MODEL

JOHN GROENEWEGEN

Introduction

The socioeconomic systems of the Netherlands and the United States of America are known for their significant differences: the former is based on the principles of consultation between interest groups and government (Rhineland model, or specifically for the Netherlands: the Polder model), while the latter relies more on market principles, with government at arm's length (Anglo-Saxon model).[1] In this essay we explore the characteristics of the Dutch and American socioeconomic models and the changes that have occurred over time. Specifically, we focus on the issue of corporate governance — the question of who controls the firm. According to the *OECD Principles*,[2] corporate governance refers to the "set of relationships between a company's board, its shareholders and other stakeholders." A system of corporate governance determines who makes investment decisions in corporations, what types of investments are made, and how returns from investments are distributed. Control should be organized in such a way that investors, managers, employees, and other stakeholders commit resources to firms with the expectation of a return.[3] Since the mid-1980s a debate on the nature and development of corporate governance in the Netherlands has been taking place, and the central question has been whether the Dutch system is converging more and more with the American system. Does the Dutch system resist international pressures and continue along its own specific path of development, or should we conclude that the United States dominates developments in the European Union in general and in the Netherlands in particular? After a characterization of the Anglo-Saxon model and the Polder model, we will discuss in more detail the characteristics of the systems of corporate governance in the U.S. and the Netherlands. We will conclude that from the 1980s onward the Dutch system has moved in the direction of the Anglo-Saxon model, but that for the time being the basic characteristics of the Dutch model continue to determine its own specific path of evolution.

The Anglo-Saxon and Rhineland Models

In this section we discuss the "ideal types" of the Anglo-Saxon and Rhineland models. A system of corporate governance is embedded in a broader cultural and judicial system. Therefore, we briefly discuss the elements of culture, law, and corporate governance in the models of the United States and the Netherlands, respectively.

1 With respect to culture, the Anglo-Saxon model is based on individualistic values, whereas the Rhineland model has a more collectivistic nature.[4] In the one system the role and responsibilities of the individual are highly valued, whereas in the other great value is placed on the collectivity of the firm, the industry, the region, or the nation. In the literature the roots of a value system are often traced back to a country's geographical location and to its natural resources (e.g., pioneers in the United States and defenders against water in the Netherlands).

2 With respect to laws and regulations, the two models differ in terms of the nature and role of the market and government. In the Anglo-Saxon model the government is at a distance but plays an important role in the introduction and enforcement of laws. Crucial in this regard is a clear allocation of property rights to stimulate the individual. When the individual bears the costs and reaps the benefits, the incentives are present for an optimal allocation of the production factors in an economy. The individualistic values of freedom and free markets are translated into a strict law of competition that forbids basically any type of collusion among firms. The rationale is based on the idea that markets produce the right competitive pressures that compel all actors to be efficient. This means that markets should be perfectly transparent (so consumers and shareholders have all information necessary to make choices for their own benefit) and also perfectly flexible (when a new technology offers a more efficient allocation of labor, that production factor should be allocated without any delay). Government in the Anglo-Saxon model should be strong and active to safeguard the right functioning of the market, yet always at arm's length: that is to say, government does not interfere in the market process in order to realize certain outcomes in terms of industrial structure or size of firms. An Anglo-Saxon government does not, for example, intervene to orchestrate a merger between "national champi-

855

5

———

THE
COLD WAR
AND
BEYOND

1945-2009

———

ECONOMICS
AND
SOCIETY

ons," or to prevent a takeover by a foreign firm. As long as the rules of the game are clearly set and enforced, individual actors can coordinate their transactions in contracts and organizations as they please. Employers and employees conclude in contracts the conditions they consider relevant and reasonable. Firms merge or are subjected to hostile takeovers when efficiency so dictates.

3 The characteristics of the Rhineland model, and of the Polder model, are more or less the opposite of the Anglo-Saxon model. Collective values are dominant. Long-term perspectives and stability for the individual actors are central. In the Rhineland model these collective values are translated into laws and regulations that recognize the importance of the collectivity and allow individuals to act in concert, in order to optimize the performance of the larger unit. This reflects a fundamentally different value attached to the capabilities of "free markets" to serve the interest of all members of society. The consultation process, in which a variety of stakeholders participate, is a central characteristic of the Rhineland model; consultation is considered crucial for both the production and dissemination of information and for the legitimization of the (macro-) objectives, which government explicitly specifies in plans at the level of industries and regions.

With respect to laws and regulations, the Rhineland model offers more possibilities for the various parties to "organize" the market. The representatives of labor unions and employer associations often negotiate with government (tri-partite negotiations, at the national level) on the development of macroeconomic indicators, like the general wage level, inflation, investments, and employment. The results are formulated in a national plan or national agreement that serves as a guideline for the negotiations at lower levels in the system. This consultation is typical of the Rhineland model.

With respect to contracts and organizational structures, which individual actors establish among each other, the Rhineland model allows and stimulates long-term contracting and forms of organization that create long-term stability for individuals — a basic value of this model.

In short: the Anglo-Saxon model puts the market center stage and regulates the socioeconomic system in such a way that competition among independent individual actors results, whereas the Rhineland model emphasizes the importance of agreements between the parties involved about the outcomes of the economic processes and guides the market toward those objectives. This fundamental difference can be illustrated with the history of the systems of corporate governance in the Netherlands and the United States.

The American System of Corporate Governance

In the United States the system of corporate governance has evolved from a situation in the early 1900s where the manager and owner were the same person, to a situation of separation of management and ownership in the first half of the twentieth century.[5] In the days of owner control, firms were in the hands of individuals and families who had a large stake in the firm and made long-term investments, which were intended to be in the firm's interest as well as their own. Technological developments put pressure on firms to grow to a large scale in order to produce at minimum cost per unit and to survive the competition.[6] Technological development implied investments with high fixed costs in human, physical, and distribution assets. The required type of investment, the scale of finance and production, and the scale of organization all demanded management control by professionals. The need for firms to grow resulted in merger waves and offerings of shares on the public markets, resulting in a separation of ownership (dispersed shareholders) and professional management (known as the "managerial revolution"). This separation of ownership and control created coordination problems between the shareholders and management. How to discipline management in such a way that they would serve the shareholders' interests? The American answer is about strict rules of information disclosure, non-executives on the board of directors, and the creation of a market for corporate control.

Changes took place in the United States in the composition of shareholders: from 1955 to 1990 the share of households fell (from 91 percent of all outstanding equity to 47 percent), whereas the share of pension funds grew from to 2 to 28 percent. This development continued after the 1990s. Concentrated shareholding replaced fragmented shareholding. The portfolio managers of the pension funds focused on quick capital gains and high levels of dividend. This was reinforced by "financial innovations" such as junk bonds in the 1970s, which put pressure on the market to generate higher short-term returns. In the 1980s, developments on the capital market stimulated the appearance of the so-called corporate raider, who monitored firms and launched a hostile takeover bid when the price of a firm's shares was underperforming compared to the short-term potential. Being then the new owner, the raider reorganized the firm, increased short-term profits that drove up the stock price, and sold the firm for a profit. This "market for corporate control" approach reduced the long-term financial commitment of the American shareholder. At the same time, the compensation of top managers became increasingly dependent on stock-based rewards, which also stimulated short-term strategies to influence stock prices.[7]

5

—

THE
COLD WAR
AND
BEYOND

1945–2009.

—

ECONOMICS
AND
SOCIETY

By boosting short term profits, top managers saw the value of their shares rise, which in turn justified increasing dividends to maintain yields and which in turn reduced the retained earnings available for investments in organization and technology.[8]

In the United States management should be controlled by the non-executives on the board of directors. However, the problem is that the CEO dominates this board in terms of providing information and strongly influences the appointment of board members. Moreover, like shareholders, the non-executives often lack sufficient time and expertise to really control the CEO. When the checks and balances fail, the autonomy of the CEO grows too large. Recently, a number of scandals have demonstrated the failure of the American system of corporate governance. Enron is a case in point.

In 2001 the Enron Corporation — an energy company in Houston, TX — went bankrupt and collapsed. It was a large, leading firm (twenty-one thousand employees and a turnover of 101 billion dollars in 2000), whose management was accused of deliberately misleading people by manipulating the firm's financial statements in order to increase the stock price. People were led to believe that the assets and financial resources were far greater than they actually were. Moreover, several managers sold their shares immediately before disclosing the real situation to the public: a typical case of lack of morality in management. Around that same time, more scandals became public (WorldCom, Tyco), and not only in the United States (Ahold in the Netherlands). Enron's fraud had been covered up by one of the top five U.S. accounting firms, Arthur Andersen. The public's confidence in the management of large firms and the role of accounting firms was profoundly shaken. To restore trust in the financial and accounting system Congress passed a new law: the Public Company Accounting Reform and Investor Protection Act of 2002, also known as SOX (the Sarbanes-Oxley Act, named after its initiators, Paul Sarbanes and Michael G. Oxley). SOX contains a number of measures to enhance corporate responsibility and financial disclosures, and offers the possibility to combat fraud. It also created the Public Company Accounting Oversight Board (PCAOB) to oversee the activities of accounting firms.

Corporate Governance in the Netherlands

The development of the Dutch system of corporate culture reflects the stock exchange culture of the seventeenth century, the legal system that the French introduced during a short but important period of occupation at the end of the eighteenth century, and more recently the influence of the EU and the U.S.

There is no doubt that the Dutch system has changed over time, and that it has changed quite fundamentally during the last two decades. Yet, historians generally argue that these changes fit in a specific Dutch path of development.[9] In the Polder model the firm is characterized as a coalition of stakeholders and there is recognition that all stakeholders, especially labor, should have a say in the firm's strategy. This is reflected in a central role for the supervisory board and the position of the workers' council, a relatively strong position of management vis-à-vis other stakeholders, a relatively strong protection of firms against hostile takeovers, and a role for government as facilitator of what private parties agree upon. Systems of corporate governance do change over time, including the Dutch one. The first big change took place during the 1960s and 1970s when the role of banks in the economy grew to such an extent that the relationship between banks and industry started to become as tightly interwoven as the German model. Behind strong protection walls, top management of large Dutch firms developed their growth strategies and through a series of mergers and takeovers financial giants emerged, such as ING, ABN AMRO, and the Rabobank.

> Through interlocking directorates—managers of the big banks became members of the boards of supervisors of business firms and vice versa—buffers between the big companies and the capital market were created.[10]

A tight old boys network developed that facilitated the exchange of crucial information, reduced uncertainties, and in that way stimulated investments, innovation, and economic growth in general. The downside was the concentration of power in the hands of a few.[11]

In 1971 the idea of the firm as a coalition of stakeholders was legally formalized as the *structuurregeling* (structured regime). The larger firms—those with at least one hundred employees—were required to install an *ondernemingsraad* (company council), which had to be consulted for a number of decisions that management wished to make. These firms and the ones with capital and reserves of at least twenty-five million guilders were also required to install a so-called supervisory board. The creation of such boards limited the powers of the shareholders substantially. Thus, since 1971 the Dutch corporate system has had a two-tier system, in which management is monitored by a board of supervisors. That board is powerful because it appoints the management board and approves the accounts. Moreover, the members of the supervisory board are appointed by cooption: new members are elected by current members.

The supervisory board monitors management especially with respect to how it weighs the interests of the different stakeholders and how it guarantees the continuity of the firm. Related to this view on the firm is the special posi-

Denver Summit of the Eight

President Clinton leads the way to the opening of the "Summit of Eight" in Denver on June 20, 1997. Dutch Prime Minister Wim Kok is in the background, 2nd from right. Clinton invited Kok to the G8 meeting to talk about the merits of the Dutch "polder model" for economic management. Clinton: "This economic policy that we are introducing in the U.S., you have been doing all along, Wim, in the Netherlands."

tion of the market for corporate control in the Netherlands. The Dutch system provided instruments to corporations to protect themselves effectively against hostile takeovers. Because of the restricted power of shareholders the interest in taking over a Dutch firm was limited anyway, but firms could make it even less attractive by means of special protection measures, such as preference shares (registered shares in friendly hands with limited dividend and liquidation rights) and priority shares (with statutorily defined extra powers — for instance to make a binding proposal concerning the appointment of members of the management board). Another popular protective measure was the issue of certificates, which created shares without voting power. An "administration office" was then created: a foundation that owned all or a large part of the shares and issued certificates without voting power to the general public.

The second big change started in the mid-1970s and pushed the Dutch system more in the direction of the Anglo-Saxon model: more power was given to the chairman of the management board, as well as to the shareholders, implying less power for the other stakeholders (especially labor). The position of the supervisory board also changed: less power was given to that board, which benefited the shareholders, and more explicit accountability was demanded for the behavior of its members. In the meantime, the "old boys network" fragmented because of the declining role of the banks on the supervisory boards.[12] Pressure to make additional changes toward the Anglo-Saxon model came from both inside the Netherlands (the Amsterdam Stock Exchange performed badly because of the limited influence of shareholders), and from outside (especially from Brussels). The EU, which attempted to harmonize the systems of corporate governance in Europe, followed largely the characteristics of the Anglo-Saxon model in putting more power in the hands of shareholders, but left room for country-specific characteristics.

During the 1980s the conviction grew that the open Dutch economy suffered increasingly from the high level of protection of firms. More and more politicians were convinced that foreign firms should not only be able to enter Dutch markets, but should also be allowed to merge with or take over Dutch firms, and vice versa. It is striking that these changing opinions did not lead to a change in the stakeholders' role in the Dutch model and the related structured regime with its two tiers. This specificity of Dutch firms was confirmed in the report on the Dutch Corporate Governance Code presented by the Committee Tabaksblat in December 2003:

861

The code is based on the principle accepted in the Netherlands that a company is a long-term form of collaboration between the various parties involved. The stakeholders are the groups and individuals who directly or indirectly influence (or are influenced by) the achievement of the aims of the

5

—

THE
COLD WAR
AND
BEYOND

1945–2009

—

ECONOMICS
AND
SOCIETY

company. In other words, employees, shareholders and other providers of capital, suppliers and customers, but also government and civil society. The management board and the supervisory board have overall responsibility for weighing up the interests, generally with a view to ensuring the continuity of the enterprise.

The Committee Tabaksblat had representatives of all parties involved (which was consistent with the Polder model) and its recommendations apply to all listed firms. The Code offers "principles and best practice provisions" aiming to regain confidence in Dutch management and supervisors. Integrity, transparency, and accountability are the key concepts. Recently the recommendations have become "law" (statutory basis in book 2 of the Civil Code).

Conclusion

Over the centuries the Dutch firm has evolved into an institution with specific characteristics. In these firms the focus is on stakeholder concern, whereas the American firm is based on shareholder concern.

In this essay we showed how the Dutch system of corporate governance evolved over time under the influence of international developments. It has been argued that the Dutch system fits the Rhineland model and that a strong Anglo-Saxon influence can be discerned in the last two decades. It is difficult, though, to draw conclusions about the strength of that influence. In most of the popular newspapers and management magazines the conclusion is that "we are all Americans now." Stock options, hostile takeovers, more rights for the shareholder, high rewards for management, flexibilization of the capital and labor markets, are all examples to illustrate that conclusion. Indeed, many Anglo-Saxon elements are nowadays present in the Dutch system of corporate governance, but at the same time the fundamental values in society and the roles of stakeholders have been maintained, at least in formal laws and codes. Today, the Anglo-Saxon way of thinking certainly has a strong impact on how the Dutch perceive "good governance." It is too simple, however, to conclude that the Anglo-Saxon model prevails. It is a more complicated issue of importing Anglo-Saxon influences and molding these into the Dutch model's own path of development.

1   See Jelle Visser and Anton Hemerijck, *A Dutch Miracle* (Amsterdam: Amsterdam University Press, 1997).

2   *OECD Principles of Corporate Governance* (May 1999).

3   See John Groenewegen, "Who Should Control the Firm? Insights from New and Original Institutional Economics," *Journal of Economic Issues* 38 (June 2004): 1-9.

4   See John Groenewegen, "Institutions of Capitalism: American, European, and Japanese Systems Compared," *Journal of Economic Issues* 31 (June 1997): 333-347.

5   See William Lazonick, *The Anglo-Saxon Corporate System*, in Piet Hein Admiraal, ed., *The Corporate Triangle: The Structure and Performance of Corporate Systems in a Global Economy* (Oxford: Blackwell Publishers Ltd., 1997).

6   See Alfred Chandler, *The Visible Hand: The Managerial Revolution in American Business* (Cambridge, MA: Harvard University Press, 1977).

7   See Ronald Dore, *Stock Market Capitalism: Welfare Capitalism* (Oxford: Oxford University Press, 2000).

8   Lazonick, *The Anglo-Saxon Corporate System*, 16.

9   See Jan Luiten van Zanden, "Post-War European Economic Development as an Out of Equilibrium Growth Path. The Case of the Netherlands," *De Economist* 148 (2000): 539-555.

10 Ibid., 551.

11 See Eelke Heemskerk, *Decline of the Corporate Community* (Amsterdam: Amsterdam University Press, 2002).

12 Ibid.

5

THE
COLD WAR
AND
BEYOND

1945–2009

ECONOMICS
AND
SOCIETY

THE NETHERLANDS, THE UNITED STATES, GERMANY, AND EUROPEAN INTEGRATION IN THE 1950S AND 1960S

JOOST KLEUTERS & MATHIEU SEGERS

In the spring of 1949, the Dutch foreign policy elite came under the spell of economic pragmatism. The cold facts concerning the deplorable structural situation of the postwar Dutch economy led Hans Max Hirschfeld, head of the Commissariat for German Affairs, and his colleague Max Kohnstamm to the conclusion that a revival of the German economy was of existential importance for the recovery of the Netherlands. In the extensive and influential "Hirschfeld Memorandum" they made a strong case for a policy based on economic rationality. Within the context of the Cold War, an economically strong West Germany was crucial for western European stability and security. For the structurally weakened Dutch economy the reemergence of West German economic power represented a life line to fundamental recovery and welfare.[1]

In key areas like the normalization of trade with Germany, the Dutch government could achieve nothing without American backing. The "Hirschfeld Memorandum" should be seen in the context of the Marshall Plan, which was already in progress by 1948. The American program for the economic recovery of western Europe also led U.S. policy to promote the reintegration of West Germany into a western European community, "which might develop into a 'third force' capable of withstanding Soviet pressure without direct American involvement."[2] Moreover, such a system would limit Germany's freedom of action and thereby prevent it from once again threatening international stability.

The Dutch government consistently defined its position by referring to a robust and apolitical economic rationale, representing free trade, currency convertibility, budgetary discipline, and monetary prudence. However, in the political process of European integration during the 1950s and 1960s the Dutch

could not maintain a strict technocratic stance. The economic rationale was often overruled by political considerations stemming from Franco-German compromising and/or American geopolitical considerations.

In this article we deal with Dutch-German-American relations during the
first decades after World War II, primarily focusing on economic and monetary
policy and the European integration process until the end of the 1960s. The
Hague summit of 1969 marks a last instance of transatlantic convergence regarding European integration against the background of the Bretton Woods
system, before the latter collapsed in the early 1970s. In the first section we
sketch the broader background of the economic difficulties of the first postwar
years in the Netherlands and the importance of West Germany for the Dutch recovery (1945–51). During this period European integration was realized through
the European Coal and Steel Community (ECSC). In the following sections we
emphasize two crucial formative phases in the history of European economic
and monetary integration: the creation of the European Economic Community
(EEC) during the years 1955–57 and the "Hague compromise" on Economic and
Monetary Union (EMU) in 1969. In both cases, political calculus in Bonn, Paris,
and Washington eventually forced the Dutch government to subordinate economic rationality to political reality.

The Multilateral Dimension of Dutch Recovery

In the first years after the war Dutch recovery struggled against the enormous
damage the war had caused to the country's economic structure. Regarding
production, infrastructure, and housing stock the Dutch had to deal with major problems. The German defeat deprived the Netherlands of its most important consumer markets and supplies. Dutch exports, consisting mainly of agricultural and luxury goods, were out of sync with an international market that
demanded capital and raw materials. As a result, the Netherlands had to cope
with tremendous financial shortages and Dutch imports were almost fully dependent on foreign credits. It was the signing of the postwar trade treaty with
the Federal Republic of Germany (FRG) in November 1949 that signaled a definitive turning point. In addition, restrictions regarding international trade and
capital flows were gradually lifted. As far as international trade was concerned,
bilateralism was to a large extent replaced by negotiations within the multilateral framework of the General Agreement on Tariffs and Trade (GATT).

Transatlantic multilateralism was the essential pillar under the somewhat
late but very strong Dutch recovery from 1951 onward. For this traditional trading nation the Marshall Plan not only meant financial support, but a multilateral process of liberalization of trade and capital flows as well. In economic mat-

865

5

—

THE
COLD WAR
AND
BEYOND

1945–2009

—

ECONOMICS
AND
SOCIETY

ters, the goal of Dutch foreign policy was to facilitate and speed up this process as much as possible by positioning itself as a true ally of the United States and the United Kingdom.

In 1944, the Dutch had actively supported, and participated in, the successful American-British initiative to establish the Bretton Woods system, which, based on global American economic predominance, was designed to stimulate economic growth, employment, price stability, and free trade. In Bretton Woods exchange rates were kept within a narrow band of the dollar. Furthermore, nations should restore the convertibility of their currencies. The leading conviction behind Dutch policy was that a recurrence of the flagrant inflation of the 1930s had to be avoided at all costs. The key was to be found in multilateral *economic* cooperation within a transatlantic framework.

In every single Dutch plan for multilateral cooperation, attention focused on maintaining and developing the bond with the United States, but during the early stages of European economic cooperation within the framework of the Organisation for European Economic Co-operation (OEEC), the Dutch government had to conclude that Washington was unable to dictate either the pace or the form of European cooperation.[3] Furthermore, the establishment of Bretton Woods could not protect postwar Europe from a number of pressing economic problems. In particular, the so-called dollar gap — the urgent shortage of dollars caused by the inconvertibility of all currencies except the U.S. dollar — hampered efforts to rebuild Europe. To counter these problems, the European Cooperation Administration (ECA) initiated the establishment of the European Payments Union (EPU) to facilitate interstate trade payments and, in time, the development of a full-fledged monetary union.[4] EPU was launched in December 1949. Its main goal was to provide a basis for currency convertibility in Europe by establishing an automatic mechanism for the settlement of net surpluses and deficits on the balance of payments of its members.

During the early 1950s, however, the successful establishment of the ECSC pushed the OEEC model of free trade into the background as a secondary "British" alternative. Nevertheless, the principles that were central to the Dutch endeavor for economic multilateralism did not change. Transatlantic economic partnership, liberalization, and monetary prudence — at the core of the Dutch doctrine of multilateral cooperation — remained unchallenged. From the beginnings of the ECSC, the Netherlands combined its ideas concerning European economic and monetary unification with ardent support for the primacy of economic over political considerations. Especially in the monetary field, Dutch policymakers were very reluctant to engage in monetary cooperation with nations that did not share their prudent monetary and economic ideas, France in particular.

The Dutch position was essentially Atlanticist, based on the model of the gold standard, and was fully shared by the West German financial-economic policy elite, who feared 1930s inflation even more. However, under pressure from the political implications of the process of European integration in the 1950s and 1960s, the "iron" Dutch and West German economic values led to fundamental controversies between so-called Atlanticists and Europeanists in both The Hague and, especially, Bonn.

The Arrival of the EEC

The most prominent representative of the liberal Atlantic approach to international economics in the history of European integration is the first West German minister of economic affairs, Ludwig Erhard, according to whom in 1953 the ECSC was only a first and inadequate step.[5] The German minister wanted to go beyond economic sector integration in line with the ECSC model and construct a "functionalist" economic integration in a broader western zone that included the United Kingdom. Like the Dutch, Erhard opposed European monetary integration without "parallel ... economic integration,"[6] which contrasted with contemporary Keynesian reasoning. According to Erhard, currency convertibility and trade liberalization had to be the new principles of European integration, taking the Havana Charter as its guideline.[7] This view, which was central to German and Dutch economic policy making, supposed a multilateral "one-world approach" based on a liberal economic transatlantic core.

In 1952, Johan Willem Beyen became minister of foreign affairs in the Dutch government, charged with multilateral relations and, especially, European integration.[8] In this role the former IMF executive director was responsible for the 1952 Dutch initiative to turn the plans for a European Political Community (within the framework of the European Defence Community) into schemes that included an economic organization as well. During the war he had concluded that "cooperation between nations" was "an inescapable necessity as long as the war lasts," but at the same time "no less essentially a condition for 'winning the peace.'"[9] Beyen took a clear-cut position in favor of regional cooperation in western Europe, considering it perfectly compatible with the so-called one-world approach.

With regard to the question of ECSC versus OEEC integration, Beyen was convinced that the former model was a necessity in postwar western Europe, all the more since regional cooperation was the more realistic alternative for a "Europe threatened externally by military pressure and internally by communism and fascism." Europe would only be able to survive by increasing production and

5

—

THE
COLD WAR
AND
BEYOND

1945–2009

—

ECONOMICS
AND
SOCIETY

productivity, which was impossible as long as it was splintered into small markets. As a result, he was a convinced supporter of the *relance européenne*, the follow-up initiatives to the ECSC, such as EEC and Euratom. This was in sharp contrast to Erhard, who became the strongest opponent of the *relance*. In a way, this divergence foreshadowed the deep-rooted tensions between Atlanticists and Europeanists that shaped political dynamics between The Hague, Bonn, and Washington.

In the spring of 1955, Beyen, together with his Belgian counterpart Paul-Henri Spaak, drafted a memorandum combining the new initiatives for European integration: a nuclear community and a common market. Beyen managed to convince the predominantly skeptical Dutch government to adopt a pro-*relance* position in the negotiations on EEC and Euratom. Although he shared Erhard's ambitions with regard to convertibility, he rightly feared that the geographical reach of the OEEC and the one-world approach of the West German minister would raise fierce opposition, for example from economically less competitive European partners like France and Italy. An "OEEC overstretch" would probably wreck the *relance* altogether and, most crucially, would put Western unity under pressure against the Soviet threat. It was precisely this geopolitical perspective that was of the utmost importance in the American position regarding issues of European cooperation, and as a result Washington, time and again, was prepared to intervene in European negotiations to promote European integration.

Eventually, during the final phase of the treaty negotiations on EEC and Euratom — only a few days before Chancellor Adenauer's crucial meeting with his French counterpart Guy Mollet on November 6, 1956 at the climax of the Suez Canal crisis — the Europeanists got the upper hand, to a large extent thanks to the geopolitical calculations of Chancellor Adenauer in reaction to the lack of American support for the British and French. Paradoxically, Adenauer's position was informed by both his uncertainty over U.S. security commitments toward Europe — Eisenhower's New Look — and by the American-sponsored Euratom lobby of the Jean Monnet Action Committee. The subsequent Adenauer-Mollet agreement ultimately paved the way for the Treaties of Rome, signed in March 1957.[10]

By that time Beyen was no longer minister, but it had been at his insistence that the Dutch government made important adjustments to its traditionally prudent liberal economic principles. Beyen represents a rather exceptional episode in Dutch European policy. His famous proposals for "general European integration," eventually leading to the Common Market, were drawn up largely against the prevailing sentiments in the Dutch cabinet. First and foremost, however, Beyen was prepared to make concessions to strict economic reasoning for the greater good of European integration, as was Adenauer, for whom the question was whether West Germany should be prepared to make sacrifices for its economically weaker neighbor (France) as the ultimate proof of its commitment to European integration. This matter divided Bonn into two camps. On the one hand, Erhard and his advisors refused to make accommodations for France's economic weakness. On the other hand, West Germany's Europeanists in the Ministry of Foreign Affairs and the High Authority of the ECSC were prepared to make concessions in order to help the Fourth Republic overcome its economic problems "through Europe." Ultimately, Adenauer's decision to side with the latter was decisive.

Ironically, in placing political arguments above economic rationale, Beyen and Adenauer more closely followed the priorities of Washington than the arch-Atlanticists in The Hague and Bonn. By mollifying the French and enabling the next step in European integration, Beyen and Adenauer were more pro-Atlantic than the ardent proponents of European integration modeled on the American example (OEEC), like Erhard and the Atlanticists within the West German and Dutch governmental organizations.

The Compromise of The Hague

By the late 1950s West Germany began to emerge as western Europe's leading economic power. At the same time, the growing American balance-of-payment deficits began to strain the Bretton Woods system and the leading position of the dollar, a problem that worsened as the costs of the war in Vietnam exploded in the second half of the 1960s. American allies in western Europe reacted with alarm to this development. Not only did the Vietnam War divert American foreign policy efforts from Europe, it also had serious consequences for the transatlantic monetary system.[11] Inflation started to undermine the position of the dollar and the dollar reserves of the western European allies. How to deal with the ensuing European insistence on a greater voice in the creation and management of international reserves became one of the central issues in transatlantic relations in the 1960s.

The United States government put strong pressure on West Germany to support the Bretton Woods system. Since the early 1960s the so-called offset agreements formed a crucial mechanism for West German monetary help to the United States: Bonn would purchase American weapons to offset the foreign exchange losses occasioned by the American military presence. Furthermore, the Johnson administration pushed for a West German pledge not to exchange dollars for gold. In 1967, the West German government pressured Bundesbank President Karl Blessing to promise to continue to support the dollar.

The West German government was not only worried about America's monetary policy, but even more so about the rigid French policy. In February 1965,

869

5

———

———

French President de Gaulle, in his campaign against American monetary domination, denounced the Bretton Woods system as unfair because it allowed Washington to finance its foreign and economic policy simply by printing dollars. De Gaulle's call upon all industrial countries to follow France in challenging the system by exchanging dollars for gold was not successful. The political implications of this largely symbolic suggestion, however, were sure to set the tone in transatlantic relations. De Gaulle's power politics also led to stagnation in the process of European integration because of his refusal to accept British membership in the EEC and the "empty chair" politics that thwarted Commission proposals for majority voting.

As a result of increased economic competition and monetary problems between the Western allies, American support for European integration decreased. Both Washington and The Hague shared a distrust of the Gaullist interpretation of Europe as a French-led independent "third force" between the superpowers. The Dutch distrust was triggered by de Gaulle's attempt, in 1960, to establish a European Political Union and West German Chancellor Adenauer's willingness to cooperate. Although de Gaulle's plan failed to materialize because the Dutch and Belgians insisted that the United Kingdom must first become an EEC member, the president did succeed in persuading Adenauer to sign the 1963 Franco-German Treaty. This provoked a storm of protest in the United States, the United Kingdom, and the Netherlands, but also in West Germany. Eventually, at the urging of Atlanticists within Adenauer's own Christian democratic party, the West German parliament was able to agree on a preamble as a precondition to the ratification of the treaty, in which the Atlantic Alliance and the development of the European institutions were reconfirmed as the guiding principles of West German foreign policy.

While the West German government was split between Atlanticists and Europeanists, the Dutch government remained largely Atlanticist in the 1960s. It was the long-time and influential Minister of Foreign Affairs Joseph Luns (1952–71) who was largely responsible for this position of the Dutch government.[12] Yet, tensions between transatlantic loyalty and regional economic integration eventually became more prominent, especially in the field of agriculture. In contrast to Luns, Agricultural Ministers Barend Biesheuvel (1963–67) and Pierre Lardinois (1967–73), together with the Dutch EEC agriculture commissioner, Sicco Mansholt, promoted European economic bloc-building and emphasized the positive effects of the EEC Common Agricultural Policy (CAP) for the Dutch economy.[13]

Regarding the mode and scope of European integration, the Dutch government strongly favored British accession as well as a strengthening of the Community institutions. Despite the dubious commitment of the British to European institution building, Franco-German dominance over western Europe had

Dutch Prime Minister De Jong (left) with West German Chancellor Brandt at
the Hague Summit of December 1969. During the summit the member-states
of the European Community decided to grant membership to Great Britain
(something long desired by the Americans), but also took important first steps toward
increasing their monetary and political independence from the United States.

5

—

THE
COLD WAR
AND
BEYOND

1945–2009

—

ECONOMICS
AND
SOCIETY

to be countered. For this reason both the Dutch and the American governments were in strong support of British entry into the EEC.

After de Gaulle's resignation in April 1969, his successor Georges Pompidou immediately showed a readiness to move European integration along. He announced a plan for a European summit in the fall of 1969 that would fall under the auspices of the Dutch presidency of the Council of Ministers. The French government was concerned about the financing of the CAP and recurring monetary problems. The French franc was under great pressure, leading to a unilateral devaluation in August. Whether France would be willing to commit itself to British membership of the EEC as a quid pro quo in the context of a new step in the process of European integration remained unclear.

In West Germany, after Willy Brandt became chancellor in October 1969, the Bonn government announced new ambitions regarding East-West relations and the process of international détente, focusing not only on cooperation with the West but on reconciliation with the East as well. The plans for a new *Ostpolitik* led to traditional French fears about German relations with the East, which Brandt was eager to dispel by supporting further steps in the European integration process.[14] Especially regarding economic and monetary union, he proved willing to make groundbreaking proposals that overcame the prudent liberal economic principles of the West German financial elite.

At the Hague summit of December 1 and 2, 1969, the EEC member states agreed on talks with the United Kingdom about membership, decided to work on the establishment of European Monetary Union (EMU), agreed on renewed financing of the CAP, and pledged to take steps to strengthen the role of the European Commission and the European Parliament. This outcome reflected a political compromise serving both Atlanticists and Europeanists in The Hague and Bonn. The Atlanticists could proclaim British accession to the EEC, whereas Europeanists could celebrate continuation of the CAP and a first step toward EMU.

Regarding EMU, the Dutch government once again had to subordinate prudent economic liberalism to the political dimension of the process of European integration. With the Hague compromise, the Dutch government effectively abandoned its traditional reluctance to monetary cooperation outside the Bretton Woods institutions.

Conclusion

It is clear that West Germany played a central role within Dutch-American economic and political relations during the 1950s and 1960s. Both during the negotiations over the EEC and at the Hague summit, the Dutch and the Ameri-

cans were faced with a political agreement that put regional cooperation before the creation of a liberal transatlantic economic space. In the former case,
the Dutch position was relatively pro-European thanks to the atypical position
of Foreign Affairs Minister Beyen. In the Hague compromise, it was Chancellor
Willy Brandt who was willing to make innovative proposals despite the liberal
economic principles of the West German financial elite. As far as the Dutch government was concerned, the Atlanticists (along with the U.S.) finally obtained
British EEC membership, while the Europeanists gained structural financial arrangements for the CAP and a new effort toward strengthening EEC institutions.
In both cases, the Americans and the Dutch were dependent on the willingness
of the West Germans to come to a political arrangement with the French at the
cost of giving up some of their own economic principles for the sake of European cooperation. Therefore, Dutch-American diplomats in this period often had
to go via Bonn and Paris in order to find the most accommodating policies for
the postwar transatlantic environment.

1   Friso Wielenga, *West-Duitsland: Partner
    uit noodzaak. Nederland en de Bondsre-
    publiek 1949–1955* (Utrecht: Het Spec-
    trum, 1989), 231-233, 266-267; Walter
    H. Salzmann, *Herstel, wederopbouw en
    Europese samenwerking* (The Hague:
    SDU uitgeverij, 1999), 185.
2   Marc Trachtenberg, *A Constructed Peace.
    The Making of the European Settlement
    1945–63* (Princeton, NJ: Princeton
    University Press, 1999), 62.
3   Albert E. Kersten, "Oorsprong en inzet
    van de Nederlandse Europese integra-
    tiepolitiek," in E.S.A. Bloemen, ed.,
    Het Benelux-Effect (Amsterdam: NEHA,
    1992), 10.
4   M.M.G. Fase, *Tussen behoud en vernieu-
    wing. Geschiedenis van de Nederlandsche
    Bank 1948–1973* (The Hague: SDU
    uitgeverij, 2000), 170.
5   Ludwig Erhard, *Deutschlands Rückkehr
    zum Weltmarkt* (Düsseldorf: Econ, 1953),
    146.
6   A. Szász, *The Road to European Monetary
    Union* (Basingstoke: Palgrave Macmillan,
    1999), 9.
7   The United Nations Conference on
    Trade and Employment, held in Havana,
    Cuba, in 1947, adopted the Havana
    Charter for the International Trade
    Organisation, which was meant to
    establish a (full-fledged) multilateral
    trade organization. For various reasons,
    the charter never was enforced. Mean-
    while, a mechanism was needed to
    implement and protect the tariff
    concessions negotiated in 1947. To do
    so, it was decided to take the chapter on
    Commercial Policy of the Havana
    Charter and convert it, with certain
    additions, into the General Agreement
    on Tariffs and Trade. To implement the
    GATT quickly, a Protocol of Provisional
    Application was developed.
8   From 1952 to 1956 Beyen shared this
    position with Joseph Luns, who was
    responsible for relations with the United
    Nations and bilateral relations outside
    Europe.
9   W.H. Weenink, *Johan Willem Beyen.
    Bankier van de wereld, bouwer van
    Europa* (Amsterdam: Prometheus, 2005),
    229.
10 Mathieu Segers, *Deutschlands Ringen
    mit der Relance* (Frankfurt am Main:
    Peter Lang, 2009).

5

———

THE
COLD WAR
AND
BEYOND

1945-2009

———

ECONOMICS
AND
SOCIETY

11 Alfred Grosser, *The Western Alliance:
European-American Relations since
1945* (London: Macmillan, 1980), 237-
243.

12 See Albert Kersten, "De langste. Joseph
Antoine Marie Hubert Luns," in Duco
Hellema et al., eds., *De Nederlandse
ministers van Buitenlandse Zaken in
de twintigste eeuw* (The Hague: SDU
uitgeverij, 1999), 224-226.

13 Anjo Harryvan and Jan van der Harst,
"Swan Song or Cock Crow? The Nether-
lands and The Hague Conference of
December 1969," *Journal of European
Integration History* 9.2 (2003): 31.

14 A. Wilkens, "Westpolitik, Ostpolitik and
the Project of the Economic and Monetary Union. Germany's European Policy
in the Brandt Era (1969–1974), *Journal of
European Integration History*, 5.1 (1999).

THE DUTCH AND THE AMERICANS IN THE BRETTON WOODS INSTITUTIONS

——

AGE F. P. BAKKER

Introduction

The Netherlands and the United States both belong to the forty-five founding nations of the International Monetary Fund (IMF) and the World Bank. The Bretton Woods institutions were established at a time when there was consensus among countries about the desired shape of the international monetary system. As an open economy, dependent on international trade, the Netherlands has been interested in arrangements that maintain global economic welfare and foster international trade. Over the years the Netherlands has taken a fairly consistent approach toward the Bretton Woods institutions. Dutch experts helped shape the IMF's approach toward balance-of-payments adjustment. Conversely, the U.S. has changed its attitude over time as it turned from a surplus into a deficit country and did not want to adjust its own domestic policies. Recently, the positions of both countries have become more aligned as the focus has shifted from monetary to financial stability issues under the influence of globalization.

The Negotiations in Bretton Woods

During World War II the United States and the United Kingdom worked out the basic outlines of a postwar monetary system that would avoid the recurrence of competitive devaluations as had occurred during the Great Depression of the 1930s. At the same time, the U.S. was keen to prevent that the rather far-reaching proposals of Keynes, the British spokesman, for international monetary re-

875

form might lead to the United States providing practically unlimited financing to the rest of the world.[1]

The cautious U.S. attitude appealed to the Dutch delegation — headed by Johan Willem Beyen, the former president of the Bank for International Settlements — at the 1944 Bretton Woods conference where the outlines of Fund and Bank were agreed upon. Beyen was somewhat skeptical about the proposals and favored regional solutions to monetary problems, as evidenced by his personal involvement with the monetary Benelux agreement of 1943.[2] However, at Bretton Woods radically different proposals were not on the table and Beyen had no way of pushing his own ideas as he had to operate under instructions from The Hague.

The Netherlands delegation realized that the direct advantages that the IMF and World Bank could offer to the open Dutch economy were rather limited, but that their main advantage lay in their mission to improve the global economic situation and foster world trade. The Netherlands had been active in promoting international monetary arrangements in the 1930s and it was no coincidence that it had been the last country to leave the gold standard, in 1936. Therefore, it was attracted to any disciplinary mechanisms that the envisaged monetary system could provide. It shared with the U.S. a firm belief in fixed exchange rates. In the Dutch view, too much flexibility in exchange rate arrangements would provide too much freedom to shift the adjustment burden to other countries. The preference for disciplinary mechanisms that would force countries to adjust, would be a constant theme in the postwar position of the Netherlands.

However, the major theme of the Dutch delegation at Bretton Woods was that Fund and Bank should be established in a financially sound way. For the IMF this implied that the use of its resources should be safeguarded from undue use. In the informal preparatory meetings the Netherlands was among the countries that suggested that greater pressure be exerted by the Fund on debtors and that the use of credit be circumscribed for specific purposes.[3] Whereas other countries were rather lenient as they themselves expected to benefit from Fund drawings, the Netherlands delegation emphasized financial discipline and, therefore, was a natural ally of the Americans in creating safeguards to prevent the usable resources of the IMF — in the initial years mainly consisting of U.S. dollars — from being depleted too quickly.

For the World Bank the Dutch similarly pressured for strict caps on the amounts it could lend, in order to preserve its good standing in global capital markets. The Dutch delegation was composed of experienced practitioners. They were aware of the large losses American institutional investors had incurred on defaults of foreign entity loans in the 1930s. It was clear that the World Bank could only become a success if American investors were absolutely sure of the soundness of the claims on this new institution.

5

—

THE
COLD WAR
AND
BEYOND

1945–2009

—

ECONOMICS
AND
SOCIETY

The participants at the international financial conference at Bretton Woods, NH, that took place from July 1 to July 22, 1944.

5

—

THE
COLD WAR
AND
BEYOND

1945–2009

—

ECONOMICS
AND
SOCIETY

Unlike other countries, such as France and the Soviet Union, the Dutch did not push to increase their relative share in the institutions. The Netherlands authorities were reluctant to deposit too much of their gold holdings at the IMF, quota payments being made partly in gold. Neither did they want to assume large risks of losses in case the IMF were to be a failure or if guarantees for the World Bank would have to be invoked.

The Early Years

There were relatively few transactions at the Bretton Woods institutions in the initial postwar years as they had to get organized and work out their proceedings. The IMF was primarily involved in establishing the right par values for the exchange rates of its members, which did not come to a resolution until European countries devalued vis-à-vis the U.S. dollar in 1949. In the meantime, the Marshall Plan (1948–51) provided the principal flow of finance to Europe. The U.S. Treasury was unwilling to grant any IMF credit to countries that received Marshall aid.[4] Ironically, the Netherlands, which had been such a staunch supporter of financial discipline at Bretton Woods, was to be the first country to suffer from this attitude.

In May 1947, the Netherlands was the second country after France to use the Fund's resources, albeit for a minimal amount. However, a second request in 1948 got a frosty reception from the U.S. executive director who questioned whether the use of the Fund's resources would be temporary, as the Netherlands had a large budget deficit and was experiencing inflationary pressures. Eventually the loan was approved, but staff were sent to the Netherlands to examine the economic situation.[5] A third request gave rise to the first systematic discussion in the board on the use of IMF resources, in which the U.S. executive director formulated criteria that would assure that credit would be temporary. These criteria foreshadowed the principle of conditionality that has governed IMF credits ever since.[6]

The dissuasive U.S. position was also inspired by increasing doubts about the appropriateness of the exchange rates set after World War II. When the Netherlands in 1949 again applied for a loan, the U.S. director objected and the decision was postponed time and again. Eventually the Dutch request was withdrawn and the guilder was devalued by 30 percent vis-à-vis the U.S. dollar, along with other European currencies. In 1951, another loan to the Netherlands was refused because the financial position was not deemed safe enough.[7] In December 1958 the convertibility of the guilder was restored, along with that of other European currencies. From this time on, the Netherlands took up a creditor position in the IMF.

For postwar reconstruction the Netherlands received a number of loans from the World Bank. These did not meet with the resistance experienced at the IMF. However, an application in 1947 brought with it a barrage of protest letters against granting a loan to a country that did not wish to give independence to its colonies (Indonesia). World Bank President McCloy, an American, withstood this pressure (including a protest letter from his mother) and defended the institution's nonpolitical nature.[8] Moreover, Finance Minister Lieftinck convinced the American bankers that plans to nationalize Dutch enterprises, as advocated by his own Socialist Party, would not materialize. The World Bank loan helped the Netherlands accept a ceasefire in Indonesia and start negotiations under the auspices of the Security Council. Lieftinck later joined the World Bank and IMF executive boards for a prolonged period.

A Dutch Approach in the IMF

Among the members of the original Dutch delegation at Bretton Woods was J.J. Polak, who later became the director of the IMF's Research Department. Polak became one of the intellectual heavyweights in the IMF and his name is associated with the analytical framework for the Fund's financial assistance.[9] He had worked at the League of Nations in Geneva, where together with (future) Nobel laureate Jan Tinbergen he coauthored an econometric macro model of the U.S. economy. Tinbergen had been a major force in the transformation of economics into a model-building discipline and Polak was to build on this experience at the IMF by incorporating a distinctive monetary dimension in the models.

At the same time, the monetary approach to balance-of-payments problems was developed at the Nederlandsche Bank, the Dutch central bank. Governor Holtrop was a proponent of a monetary approach to economic problems in which a clear distinction is made between domestic and foreign sources of liquidity creation.[10] As early as 1950 he observed that balance-of-payments deficits that led to reserve losses always coincided with inflationary domestic financing. In the early 1960s Polak and Holtrop intensively debated the merits of the monetary models used in both institutions. The approach gained recognition when successfully applied in 1969 in an IMF program for the United Kingdom.

879

From Dollar Shortage to Dollar Glut

The United States for a long time could ignore its own balance-of-payments position because the rest of the world had a thirst for dollars. Around 1960, howev-

5

—

THE
COLD WAR
AND
BEYOND

1945–2009

—

ECONOMICS
AND
SOCIETY

er, when European economies had recovered significantly and the dollar shortage was long over, observers started to talk of a dollar "glut." European central banks began to worry about the quality of their dollar reserves and converted them into gold. The U.S. reacted, not by adjusting domestic policies, but by organizing bilateral swap arrangements with other central banks, including the Nederlandsche Bank, in order to counter speculative flows that might destabilize major currencies. Eventually, the General Arrangements to Borrow (GAB) were developed to enlarge the potential resources of the IMF, should the U.S. need assistance, and the SDR was promoted as a supplementary reserve currency to the dollar.

The Europeans, however, were not prepared to lend passively to the IMF, which they felt was U.S.-dominated, and insisted on procedures under which they themselves could decide upon a proposal of the IMF managing director. This gave birth to the Group of Ten and a period of intensive transatlantic consultations. Although there was criticism from nonparticipating countries Lieftinck, the Dutch executive director, described the GAB as a "compromise between the ideology of the Fund as a global monetary institution and a newer ideology which sought solutions by closer cooperation between the main industrial countries."[11] From this time there was regular attendance by Federal Reserve officials at the monthly BIS meetings, chaired by Governor Holtrop in his capacity as president of the BIS.

The dialogue between Europe and the United States was diverted from the executive board rooms in Washington to smaller groupings. At the initiative of President Kennedy Working Party 3 was established at the OECD, comprising the Group of Ten countries, and Dutch Treasurer General Emile van Lennep was chosen as its chairman. A major issue was the distribution of the burden of adjustment over deficit and surplus countries. The U.S. had become a deficit country and it wanted surplus countries to adjust by stimulating their economies. U.S. adjustment was deemed out of the question as this would be tantamount to "the tail wagging the dog." However, the Dutch, like many other European countries, feared the inflationary consequences of stimulatory policies in surplus countries and thought that the U.S. should also play its part.

The conflict escalated when surplus countries continued to convert dollars into gold in the expectation that this would force the U.S. to adjust. Toward the end of the 1960s Dutch official reserves consisted of 85 percent of gold and only 15 percent of U.S. dollars. When the U.S. deficits continued to soar, surplus countries were implored to no longer convert their dollar holdings into gold. To this effect a high-level U.S. delegation, including Paul Volcker, visited the Dutch central bank in July 1971 in an attempt to discourage the conversion of two hundred fifty million dollars. When Governor Zijlstra refused, Volcker warned him that he was rocking the boat. Zijlstra's reaction was that if such a small transaction could rock the boat, the boat had already sunk.[12] A few weeks later, on August 15, 1971, President Nixon withdrew gold convertibility, thus initiating the eventual demise of the Bretton Woods system of stable exchange rates.

A New Mission for the IMF

Flexible exchange rates gave large and relatively closed countries like the United States and Germany greater room to maneuver in favor of domestic economic policies. Small open economies were, however, less enthusiastic and the Netherlands became an ardent proponent of regional exchange rate arrangements, like the European Monetary System that was established in 1979. As central bank Governor Zijlstra phrased it, exchange rate flexibility would give small open economies the freedom of a slide as exchange rate depreciation would lead to increased inflation through inflated import prices, in turn leading to further depreciation. Therefore, the Netherlands would continue to advocate rules for internal adjustment, just as it had done under the Bretton Woods system.

In the meantime, international monetary cooperation gradually shifted from the IMF to the G7, which was created as a political forum in the mid-1970s but increasingly focused on economic and financial matters. Although there were successes like the Plaza and Louvre accords in the mid-1980s, international coordination proved difficult as it easily trod on politically sensitive areas. Over these years the Netherlands was a strong supporter of German policies aimed at maintaining price stability. From this, the Netherlands gradually derived the reputation of a hard-currency country.

A new mission for the IMF developed in the wake of the debt crisis in the 1980s and the new membership of former communist countries. Increased emphasis was put on structural adjustment with the aim of reforming domestic policies and creating the basis for sustainable growth. The Fund and the World Bank came to the assistance of countries with large external debts by providing expertise and mobilizing the international banking community as well as official creditors. The enlarged access to IMF's resources — emerging economies received large credit packages — did strain its financing capacity, and the Netherlands played an active role trying to preserve the Fund's monetary character.

Although the IMF and the World Bank try to be nonpolitical and technical, in practice it is difficult to avoid political influences in their executive boards. The U.S. executive director receives strict instructions from the U.S. Treasury, which in some matters is bound by Congressional legislation, and can veto substantive policy matters. From the American viewpoint, the IMF and the World

5

—

THE
COLD WAR
AND
BEYOND

1945-2009

—

ECONOMICS
AND
SOCIETY

Bank can provide substantial leverage for U.S. financial resources. For example, the Netherlands adds approximately 20 cents to every U.S. dollar in the IMF and the World Bank, which is quite impressive as Dutch GDP is 5 percent of U.S. GDP.

The Netherlands is one of only a few countries to have adhered to the United Nations target of development assistance of 0.7 percent of GDP (it actually gives 0.8 percent). Its generous aid policies explain the keen interest the Netherlands takes in World Bank policies. Although the Bank increasingly has focused on poverty reduction, Jan Pronk, Dutch minister for development affairs during the 1970s and 1990s, has continued to press for reforms. Over the years, however, Dutch development assistance has become more closely aligned with World Bank policies as the institution has put greater emphasis on the environment and on governance.

The Dutch Money Masters

International monetary relations have always been very important for an outward-looking country such as the Netherlands with its open economy and its strong banking and insurance sectors. Because of the country's impressive monetary tradition it is not surprising that a number of Dutchmen have left their imprint on international monetary relations. The Netherlands has appointed high-level officials to the IMF and Bank boards. Apart from Beyen, other names have included Pieter Lieftinck and Onno Ruding, both of whom also served as Dutch minister of finance. At the Bank, former ministers like Eveline Herfkens and Ad Melkert were appointed as executive director. Jacques Polak was elected as executive director for the Netherlands after retiring from the IMF staff. Johannes Witteveen was managing director of the IMF from 1973 until 1978. His constructive approach as minister of finance to the problems in the Bretton Woods system had impressed the Americans. Polak and Witteveen also played a role in the influential Group of Thirty, which studied international economic issues.

Dutch staff have held high positions in the Bretton Woods institutions from the start. At the World Bank Aron Broches, who had been at the Bretton Woods conference, joined the Bank from its inception and had a distinctive career as general counsel and eventually vice president of the Bank. Siem Aldewereld joined the Bank in 1946 and also became a vice president. Another Dutchman, Frans Keesing, was the first director of the IMF Institute.

At a certain time Dutch economists played such an influential role that *Business Week* carried an article referring to the Dutch Money Masters. Dutch central bank presidents have led the Bank for International Settlements in one out of every two years. Among them, Willem Duisenberg became the first president of the European Central Bank. Emile van Lennep, secretary general of the OECD from 1969 until 1984, was closely involved in international monetary negotiations as chairman of the EC Monetary Committee and the influential Working Party 3 of the OECD.

It is no coincidence that Dutch-American relationships have been closest among the monetary authorities. The central bank governors meet in Basel in the framework of the Group of Ten, among them the chairman of the Federal Reserve System and the president of the New York Fed. Both the Federal Reserve Bank and the Nederlandsche Bank have important supervisory responsibilities in the financial sector, and the Americans trust the Dutch as guardians of financial stability. For the Basel Committee on Banking Supervision three out of nine chairmen have come from the Nederlandsche Bank.[13]

In the course of the 1990s the Americans increasingly pushed to diminish the influence of the Group of Ten and involve emerging and developing countries in the discussions on the monetary system outside the IMF. A major American motive was that greater support from emerging countries was expected to put pressure on surplus countries like Japan and some in continental Europe. In 1999, on the initiative of the Americans, the G7 established the Group of Twenty as an informal forum for discussions between the G7 and emerging countries.[14] The Netherlands was not invited as membership for advanced countries was limited to the G7 and Australia. At the same time the global Financial Stability Forum was established, in which the Netherlands does participate together with Australia, Hong Kong, Singapore, and Switzerland. This development underlines the shift in the Dutch emphasis from international monetary issues to financial stability issues.

Despite European monetary integration, the interest of the Netherlands in the Bank and the Fund has continued due to their increased emphasis on financial stability. The Netherlands occupies the sixth position as a global financial center worldwide (based on external financial assets and liabilities) and its strong financial sector has a global presence. The Netherlands also takes a strong interest in international development assistance; it is the sixth-largest provider in absolute terms and therefore has a key stake in the World Bank.

The IMF and World Bank boards are comprised of twenty-four executive directors, eight of whom represent a single country, whereas the other sixteen represent country groupings, so-called constituencies. The Netherlands-led constituency has grown over time as membership of Fund and Bank grew. It now comprises thirteen mainly eastern European countries, the largest being Ukraine.[15] As one of the mixed constituencies the elected executive director can mediate between large advanced countries and emerging and developing countries.

5

——

——

Conclusion

As a small, open country, the Netherlands has been a proponent of efficient and effective international monetary cooperation, partly out of fear that the large industrial countries would make a deal among themselves. The Dutch favor a central role for the IMF in discussions on the international financial system and would like the Fund to take a proactive stance. Over the years the Netherlands has maintained a fairly consistent approach toward the Bretton Woods institutions, characterized by a firm belief in international disciplinary mechanisms that promote adjustment.

In contrast, U.S. attitudes vis-à-vis the IMF and the World Bank have changed over time and the United States has increasingly focused on the IMF's financing role in financial crises. As the largest member and the provider of the key reserve currency, it believed that it was entitled to different rules and that it was justified in having its national interest come first. In recent years, the U.S. has increasingly tried to influence policies and force the institutions to align themselves with domestic policy priorities. Also, presidential administrations have taken diverging views, and there have been differences of opinion between the principal agencies involved, such as the U.S. Treasury and the financial establishment in New York. At the same time, it is clear that the multilateral institutions cannot function without continued U.S. support.

Even within the context of the Economic and Monetary Union the Netherlands continues to be an interesting partner for the United States. It is small enough to know that it has to accept international compromises, yet it is financially and economically important enough to make a difference, especially when major countries have disagreements. Among continental European countries the Netherlands has a distinct Anglo-Saxon outlook and it can prove to be an interesting mediating partner with the larger, more regulation-oriented, Rhineland countries such as France and Germany. As the focus in the international discussions has shifted from monetary to financial stability issues, the former Dutch Money Masters now can position themselves as guardians of financial stability.

1   Robert Solomon, *The International Monetary System, 1945–1981* (New York: Harper and Row, 1982), 11.

2   Jan Willem Beyen, *Het spel en de knikkers. Een kroniek van vijftig jaren* (Rotterdam: Donkers, 1968), 158; Jacques Polak, "Financial Relations between the Netherlands and Belgium: 1943 to 1993," in Age Bakker et al., eds. *Monetary Stability through International Cooperation* (Dordrecht: Kluwer Academic Publishers, 1994), 185-186.

3   Keith Horsefield, *The International Monetary Fund 1945–1965,* vol. 1, *Chronicle* (Washington, DC: IMF, 1969), 35.

4   Beyen, *Het spel,* 190.

5   Horsefield, *The International Monetary Fund,* 227.

6   Ibid., 245.

7   Beyen, *Het spel,* 191.

8   Ibid., 183.

9   Jakob Frenkel and Morris Goldstein, eds., *International Financial Policy. Essays in Honor of Jacques J. Polak* (Washington, DC: IMF, 1991), 20-27.

10 Age Bakker, *The Liberalization of Capital Movements in Europe. The Monetary Committee and Financial Integration, 1958–1994* (Dordrecht/Boston/London: Kluwer Academic Publishers, 1996), 37-38.

11 Horsefield, *The International Monetary Fund,* 514. The Group of Ten is composed of the United States, Japan, Germany, France, Italy, the United Kingdom, Canada, the Netherlands, Belgium, Sweden, plus Switzerland (which joined later, making the G10 consist actually of eleven countries).

12 Cited in André Szàsz, *Monetaire diplomatie. Nederlands internationale monetaire politiek, 1958–1987* (Leiden: Stenfert Kroese, 1988), 71.

13 Huib Muller (1988–91), Tom de Swaan (1997–98), and Nout Wellink (2006-present).

14 As the membership of the G20 is mostly the same as that of the twenty-four-member IMFC, which is appointed by the IMF's Board of Governors, its establishment can be seen as another step in undermining the legitimate governing bodies of the IMF.

15 The constituency now is comprised of the Netherlands, Ukraine, Romania, Bulgaria, Israel, Cyprus, Croatia, Macedonia, Armenia, Georgia, Bosnia and Herzegovina, Moldova, and Montenegro.

5

—

THE
COLD WAR
AND
BEYOND

1945–2009

—

ECONOMICS
AND
SOCIETY

THE ECONOMIC INFLUENCE OF THE UNITED STATES IN SURINAME

—

JEROME EGGER

In an article published in a local newspaper, *Suriname*, a journalist pointed out that the country was becoming more and more American. The date was January 7, 1950, five years after World War II. The article made clear that American capital played a major role in the economy, because bauxite was mined by the Aluminum Company of America (ALCOA) and trade between the two countries had increased rapidly. In that same year Suriname had been granted home rule, with the exception of foreign affairs and defense, which remained the responsibility of The Hague. The Dutch scoffed at the idea that their colony was turning into an American enclave, but reality was there to see, according to the newspaper. This probably did not come as a surprise to Surinamers. It had been obvious that the economy depended on American capital and know-how. Particularly during the war, the bauxite deposits of the country had made it a coveted territory. The country contributed significantly to the Atlantic war effort, and this had brought a certain amount of prosperity to the people. The Netherlands had traditionally not been much involved in the Caribbean because the Dutch East Indies (present-day Indonesia) attracted most of the interest and had paid a higher dividend.

This essay answers the question whether the United States has dominated Suriname's economy since 1945 even though it was a Dutch colony until 1975. The answer lies in the importance of one mineral: bauxite. The other Dutch Caribbean possessions — six islands united under the name Dutch Antilles (Curaçao, Aruba, Bonaire, Saba, St. Eustatius, and part of St. Martin) — did not carry as much economic weight. A few lines at the end will highlight developments in their economic ties with the United States.

Increasing U.S. Influence

In the late 1940s the high output of the bauxite industry in Suriname continued even though the war had ended. This was directly linked to the global political situation. The United States and the Soviet Union began their long rivalry. They created a bipolar world in which the Dutch Caribbean belonged to the Western world and was firmly brought within the American orbit despite official Dutch rule. The weapons industry needed large amounts of bauxite to produce aluminum and Suriname provided the raw material. This clearly illustrated how the international context influenced the direction of the Surinamese economy. Thus, Alcoa began to dominate in Suriname, although the Dutch mining company Billiton continued to operate there as well.[1] The growing American activities also translated into cultural influences. Hollywood movies, music, and fashion all entered daily life in the country.

After the war, Suriname tried to diversify its economy so that it could decrease its dependency on just one product. This is where the Dutch still showed their responsibility toward the colony. For the first time long-term development plans were written. The Dutch made some funding available, known as the Welvaartsfonds (prosperity fund). However, when the Dutch devalued their currency in the late 1940s the value of the fund decreased because Suriname saw no reason to do the same. Its economy was firmly tied to the United States, so devaluation would lead to less income from the bauxite industry. This case exemplified the way in which a colony was linked to outside economic forces and had to make a choice that best suited its own economy. The fund did have an impact. The agricultural sector was modernized — one of the priorities — and rice quickly became another important export product. A Dutch company developed the lumber industry. Fishing and animal husbandry also received attention. Americans participated in these attempts when a company invested in the fishing industry, in particular shrimp. However, most of the money provided by the Welvaartsfonds went into the infrastructure and also contributed to making an inventory of minerals, both in the coastal area and in the hinterland. This was certainly good news for the bauxite companies because they learned more about the possibilities for new mining deposits. The Surinamese government developed other economic sectors, but these were not able to replace bauxite as the most important and most profitable foreign currency earner.

In the 1950s Alcoa continued its dominance over the Surinamese economy, increasing its influence with the Brokopondo agreement in 1958. This made the local economy more dependent on this one product and was also significant because an American multinational agreed for the first time to build a fac-

887

Moenga, the center of the bauxite mining operation of Suralco
(the Surinamese subsidiary of Alcoa).

tory to make aluminum — the end product in the processing of bauxite — in a developing nation.

Alcoa, the Surinamese Government, the Dutch, and the Brokopondo Agreement

The Brokopondo agreement turned out to have far-reaching consequences. Suriname gained a factory and a major hydroelectric dam on one of its rivers, but it also lost control over its only major industry.

In the early 1950s some of the money from the Welvaartsfonds had been used to do research on the possibility of establishing an integrated bauxite-alumina-aluminum industry in Suriname, which would generate enormous profits for the country. The only problem was how to get cheap energy. A Dutch engineer suggested a project in which hydroelectricity could be used in the factories, but the initial costs were high, and Billiton was not willing to make the investment on its own. Nevertheless, the Surinamese government became very interested in the project and explored alternative financing possibilities. The World Bank did a preliminary study. In the end, experts agreed on the feasibility of the dam and the bank expressed a willingness to finance the plan. The only demand was that the mother country underwrite the loan. This is where the problems started. The Dutch refused and the whole project ended up on the doorsteps of Alcoa.

Authors have speculated why the Dutch did not underwrite this loan. The plan itself made sense. Bauxite was worth approximately 6 U.S. dollars per ton in those days, but aluminum brought in 125 dollars.[2] Some commentators have pointed out that the Dutch wanted to produce aluminum themselves, using energy from natural gas. Hydroelectricity would allow aluminum to be produced more cheaply, and this would make Suriname more competitive on the lucrative European market.[3] Some official Dutch documents suggest another reason. Officials may simply have doubted the feasibility of the project and Surinamese optimism that the economy would benefit from increased American participation. The Dutch governor in Suriname in the late 1950s, J. van Tilburg, did not help matters either with his dispatches — sometimes very disrespectful toward elected politicians — which did not paint a favorable picture of local circumstances and downplayed the need for the Dutch government to get involved.[4] This is important because Dutch politicians in general did not pay much attention to the Caribbean. Most had never visited the region, and since the Dutch economy would receive no significant benefits it is not difficult to understand the refusal to underwrite the loan.

In the end, the Dutch denied the colony the possibility to reap more benefits from bauxite. They left the country no option but to discuss the matter with

5

THE
COLD WAR
AND
BEYOND

1945–2009

ECONOMICS
AND
SOCIETY

Alcoa. Negotiations resulted in a letter of intent in 1957, and in January 1958 the Brokopondo agreement was signed. As Girvan put it, "Dutch and American pressure had converted what should have been a public national developmental project into one that was private and foreign."[5]

The Brokopondo agreement was a watershed in Surinamese-U.S. relations, but it came at a price. Alcoa was given major bauxite concessions for seventy-five years to enable it to recoup the costs of building the dam, but the company also owned the power generated by the dam itself, placing it in a very dominant position. All materials used to construct the dam were imported free of tariffs. The large-scale Surinamese investments in the project, such as the preliminary research into its feasibility, logistical developments (roads, land), and the costs of resettling the Maroon community (runaway slaves living in the interior) away from the area to be flooded for the dam were neither categorized nor acknowledged in the plan.[6] Opposition was widespread, and eight out of twenty-one members of parliament voted against the bill even though the letter of intent a year earlier had been accepted unanimously. But this episode remained contentious, since others regarded it as an insult to Alcoa's large-scale investment that such opposition was expressed in public.[7]

All successive governments after 1958 abided by the agreement and Alcoa was able to control most of the then known bauxite reserves in the country. Without the slightest irony, over the following years politicians almost always brought foreign dignitaries to pay a visit to the lake and the dam. They saw it as a proud achievement of the country. Only much later, when oil-based energy became more and more expensive (by which time Alcoa had closed its aluminum plant and did not need the dam's electricity), was Suriname able to profit from this relatively cheap resource.

After Brokopondo

After the Brokopondo project was completed, Suriname began to produce aluminum. From an economic point of view the integrated bauxite industry did not perform badly. The Surinamese economy grew in the 1960s and trade flourished. A good indication is a report that the American consulate submitted to Washington in 1970. In 1968, 37 percent of all Surinamese trade was with the United States, while one year later it increased to almost 40 percent. Although the European Union offered some advantages because Suriname was a Dutch colony, familiarity with U.S. lines of goods and their preferred quality explains the predominance of American goods. It is also important to remember that in 1965 television arrived in Suriname. Most programs came from the United

States and popular American culture became ever more pervasive in Surinamese society.

The consulate's report went even further, advising American businessmen to be more aggressive on the Surinamese market. The example was given of a representative of American manufacturers who was able to do business to the amount of ten thousand dollars a day. Moreover, the report praised Suriname's good record in fulfilling its commitments and went on to say that the country "[offered] highly advantageous tax benefits and unrestricted remittance of profits."[8] If that was not enough, the report also made clear that the local government provided the infrastructure. The consulate did not state that Suriname's wealth was based on just the bauxite industry. As long as factories in the United States and Europe produced machinery using this metal, things would be fine. But competition on the world bauxite market was growing.

After World War II Suriname was the most important high-grade bauxite producer in the world. But slowly other Caribbean nations such as Jamaica, Haiti, and the Dominican Republic started producing this raw material. Different players on the world market such as Alcan, Kaiser, and Reynolds set up their operations in these countries. Although the military budgets of the Cold War ensured a continuous need for aluminum, Suriname could not claim to be the sole player close to the United States forever. Neither did the bauxite industry create large employment opportunities. An exchange between the Surinamese and U.S. governments in the early 1960s provides interesting insights in this regard. Washington was concerned that communist-inspired political instability in neighboring British Guiana would lead to unrest in Suriname as well.[9] One million dollars for technical assistance was allocated in 1963, but Mr. Pengel, the Surinamese prime minister, wanted the money for social projects to alleviate unemployment. His argument was that this would help maintain political stability. Despite the political concerns, the U.S. government refused to give in and the money was not transferred.[10]

Surinamese Independence and Economic Setbacks

In the 1970s and 1980s increasing bauxite supplies from West Africa and Brazil made it more difficult to stay competitive. The rise in oil prices after 1973, and the slower growth of the world economy in the 1970s and in particular in the 1980s led to a decrease in the demand for aluminum. At first Suriname did not seem to feel the growing economic problems. To ease its path to independence on November 25, 1975, the Netherlands transferred 2.7 billion guilders to the Paramaribo treasury. Independence had come relatively easy. The lead-up to in-

891

5

———

THE
COLD WAR
AND
BEYOND

1945–2009

———

ECONOMICS
AND
SOCIETY

dependence was marked by opposition to the government in Paramaribo and there were concerns that racial tensions might explode into violence. However, an agreement between government and opposition leaders a few days prior to independence calmed things down, and on the day itself remarkable unity was demonstrated to the world. Nevertheless there was concern in the United States about Suriname becoming an additional problem in the region. Moreover, Secretary of State Kissinger stated clearly that the U.S. had no intention to contribute to development programs for Suriname. The Dutch had asked for a U.S. military presence to ensure a peaceful transition of power, but plans to send a large naval vessel were canceled because the coastal waters were too shallow and muddy for it to dock in Paramaribo. On independence day itself only regional powers such as Brazil were present with military regalia.[11]

Another positive development was the fact that Suriname received a better deal from Alcoa in the 1970s, so that the country could generate extra income. This was partly due to some of the major bauxite producers creating their own cartel, the International Bauxite Association (IBA). Influenced by the success of OPEC in 1973 in raising the price of crude oil, other producers of raw materials tried to do the same. For a while IBA was able to negotiate better prices, but as more bauxite was found in other locations the association became less effective and eventually collapsed in the 1980s.

During the first years of independence there was a flurry of socioeconomic development across the country. Major infrastructural works were carried out, but there also was money for social and other noneconomic programs. Nevertheless, in the end the bauxite sector would continue to dominate the economy because one of the projects was to exploit major bauxite depositories in the western section of Suriname. The government used part of the development aid from the Netherlands to invest in the infrastructure of that area. In fact, it continued the traditional role the government had assigned itself, namely to build the (rail) roads and harbors. Foreign companies would then do the mining. Alcoa looked on without committing itself to exploiting the bauxite deposits in western Suriname. This was understandable because after the second oil crisis in the late 1970s world trade had decreased. Slowly Suriname began to feel the economic woes that it had long avoided. Gambling on just one major export product came to haunt the country and Dutch aid could not carry the whole economy. But political developments in the country also help explain why the economic situation worsened.

In February 1980, a military coup led by Desi Bouterse took place. Less than five years after independence noncommissioned soldiers of the newly created defense force removed the elected government and controlled all aspects of life in the next seven years. However, this led to resistance from the interior. In 1986 skirmishes between the army and one of the Maroon cultural groups turned into a guerilla war that lasted more than six years until an official peace treaty was signed in 1992, after the return of democracy. Compared to other wars in the Latin American region this was small scale, but it had a tremendous effect on the bauxite industry. All of the mines were in the interior and it became difficult to get to the supplies. But more important were guerilla attempts to disrupt the economy. They succeeded in destroying the connection between the hydroelectric dam and the factories that were closer to the capital. Aluminum production had to be suspended. A few years later this postponement of production became permanent. Alcoa decided it was not worth restarting the plant. From then on Suriname exported only bauxite and alumina.[12]

During the military period the political relations with the United States were not as friendly as before. Moreover, Ronald Reagan was elected in 1980, and when the military leadership took a turn to the left in early 1981, the United States did not look kindly upon these developments. The killing of fifteen opponents to the Bouterse regime in December 1982 was a low point not only for Surinamese society as a whole but also in its relations with other — up to then — friendly countries such as the Netherlands and the United States. The Dutch suspended development aid and the U.S. sent strong signals indicating that the situation was unacceptable. Plans were even made by the Reagan administration to topple the Bouterse regime after 1982, but they were canceled due to opposition from the Senate committee responsible for overseeing CIA foreign operations.[13] One should also keep in mind that in the 1980s Suriname was not a major player anymore in the aluminum world. The economy went from bad to worse. Trade collapsed, shops were empty, inflation skyrocketed, and salaries amounted to next to nothing for the average Surinamers. American businessmen were certainly not interested in the country anymore. Eventually, however, elected Surinamese governments turned the economy around.

Conclusion: New Millennium, New Opportunities?

In the twenty-first century the Surinamese economy slowly picked up. In 2004 the Central Bank of Suriname introduced a new currency, the Surinamese dollar, to replace the guilder. At the same time, the exchange rate was simplified. The U.S. dollar now was worth 2.75 to 2.80 local dollars instead of the previous 3,000 guilders. Inflation went down and this helped stimulate more trade. The arrival of the annual U.S. Products and Trade Fair indicated that Suriname, however small, might be of some interest again to businessmen from the United States. Newspapers reporting on the opening of the seventh fair in 2007 had some interesting figures. In 2006 Suriname exported goods worth 134 million U.S. dollars to America, while imports of manufactured goods were much high-

5

———

THE
COLD WAR
AND
BEYOND

1945-2009

———

ECONOMICS
AND
SOCIETY

er at 303 million dollars. In his speech to open the fair, the Surinamese minister of trade and industry emphasized that he considered the United States one of the important trading partners. The Surinamese market had been flooded by cheap Chinese products, but high-quality goods still came from the United States.[14] In the bauxite industry, America's influence remained significant. It shared all the operations in the country with Billiton, now merged with the Australian mining conglomerate BHP. One of the interesting questions is which company will decide the future of the bauxite industry in Suriname. In early 2008, negotiations with the companies that will exploit the major depositories in the western part of the country had not been concluded. Their outcome will decide whether American control over bauxite mining will continue long into the twenty-first century.[15]

The economies of Suriname and the islands of the Dutch Caribbean were brought fully into the U.S. sphere of influence after World War II. During World War II Curaçao and Aruba were important locations because their refineries processed crude oil from Venezuela, and this role continued through the postwar decades, with Shell in a prominent position. In those years the Netherlands maintained an important influence in the island economies. Gradually, this changed when the tourist industry brought growing numbers of Americans to the islands, and during the 1990s tourism became the major foreign currency earner. Shell has now sold all its operations on the islands, but special economic zones have generated jobs for the local population and the Dutch government has been willing to give a helping hand in solving budget deficits. A new political relationship will come into effect in the next few years tying some of the smaller islands more strongly to the Dutch, while leaving Curaçao and Aruba more room to maneuver. Thus, the problems of the 1980s and early 1990s — low prices for raw materials, high public debt, and political instability in Suriname — have disappeared. Americans have contributed to this development with their presence on the beaches.[16]

1   Billiton began its operations in Suriname in 1940, but it remained a minor company compared to Alcoa.

2   Norman Girvan, *Corporate Imperialism: Conflict and Expropriation, Trans-national Corporations and Economic Nationalism in the Third World* (New York/London: Monthly Review Press, 1976), 129.

3   Ruben Kalpoe, *De bauxietsector en haar effecten op de Surinaamse economie*

(Paramaribo: Universiteit van Suriname, 1983), 25.

4   Gert Oostindie and Inge Klinkers, *Knellende Koninkrijksbanden: Het Nederlandse dekolonisatiebeleid in de Caraïben, 1940–2000*, vol.2, *1954–1975* (Amsterdam: Amsterdam University Press, 2001), 36-37.

5   Girvan, *Corporate Imperialism,* 129.

6   Kalpoe, *De bauxietsector,* 29.

7   See Edward Dew, *The Difficult Flowering*

of Surinam: Ethnicity and Politics in a Plural Society (The Hague: Martinus Nijhoff, 1978), 117.

8   U.S. Department of Commerce, *Foreign Economic Trends and Their Implications for the United States: Suriname* (Washington, DC: Government Printing Office, 1970), 11.

9   "Relations between Pro-Communists in British Guyana and Surinam," March 23, 1964, and "Political and Sociological Conditions in Surinam," July 27, 1964, Declassified Documents Reference System (hereafter DDRS), Roosevelt Study Center, Middelburg, the Netherlands.

10 "US Million Dollar Loan Offer to Surinam," April 10, 1964, DDRS.

11 See Ko Colijn, "Onneembaar Paramaribo," *Vrij Nederland* 68.48 (December 2007): 28.

12 Bauxite found in the interior is first washed. Then it is reduced to alumina, which is a powdery substance. This is further reduced to aluminum, which can be worked and shaped into cans, building material, and so on.

13 Bob Woodward, *Veil: The Secret Wars of the CIA, 1981–1987* (New York: Pocket Books, 1988), 264-265.

14 *De West*, June 2, 2007.

15 On December 1, 2008, BHP-Billiton announced it would cease all mining activities in Suriname by 2010. However, the Swiss Company Glencore and the Chinese state-owned company Chalco have expressed interest in investing in the bauxite sector.

16 Some of the general histories of the islands with an overview of developments from the first European encounters to the present are F.E. Gibbens, N.C. Römer-Kenepa, and M.A. Scriwanek, *De bewoners van Curacao: Vijf eeuwen lief en leed, 1499–1999* (Willemstad, Curaçao: Nationaal Archief, 2002), and Luc Alofs and Leontine Merkies, *Ken ta Arubiano? Sociale integratie en natievorming op Aruba, 1924–2001* (Oranjestad, Aruba: Vad/De Wit Stores, 2001).

5

—

THE
COLD WAR
AND
BEYOND

1945–2009

—

ECONOMICS
AND
SOCIETY

896

U.S. IDEOLOGY AND THE FOUNDING OF BUSINESS SCHOOLS IN THE NETHERLANDS

—

PETER VAN BAALEN

Why Business Schools?

In their well-received study, *Management in the Industrial World*, Frederick Harbison and Charles Myers asserted in 1959 that the professionalization of management was a "logical" consequence of the ongoing industrialization of the business sector. The emergence of modern business schools played a crucial and inevitable role: "education and training rather than family ties or political connections, *must inevitably* become the principal avenue of access to its ranks" [italics added].[1] While the authors conceded that delayed effects and variances in tempo might arise due to cultural, institutional, and political circumstances, they believed that every industrialized country would ultimately evolve according to the "logic of industrialization" — with America's position as the most industrialized nation according it a "reference society" status.

In contrast, the U.S. historian Robert R. Locke has argued against any such logical and necessary link between a country's economic success and the existence of American-style business schools. To prove his point he referred to the successful development of post-World War II economies in Germany and Japan, neither of which had business schools based on the American model. As such, Locke concluded, "we are left with the fact of postwar economic recovery, growth, and prosperity and solid evidence of the spread of American managerialism, but with no sure way to establish a causal link between them."[2] Instead, Locke offered an alternate hypothesis. The widespread dissemination of American management thinking and, in its wake, of the business school model, represented the triumph of American ideological management rhetoric. Initially wielded as a weapon in the battle against the collective enemy — communism — this rhetoric gradually lost force during the 1980s, when it made way for admiration for the Japanese brand of management thinking. Other authors have likewise pointed to the ideological character inherent in the broad geographical dissemination of the American business school model. Those working at the Ford Foundation, which played a key role in advancing the American model in western Europe during the 1960s, were heard to remark that "the United States are the *ideological* center of management education empire" [italics added].[3]

In part because of its highly divergent traditions in higher education, western Europe never mindlessly copied the American business school model, adopting instead a "selective appropriation" of U.S. methods within existing educational systems. Given this background, what was the specifically Dutch response to postwar American business school "imperialism," and what was the role of the traditional Dutch system of higher education in this response?

Pre-World War II American and European
Business School Movements

Initially, business schools in the U.S. and Europe evolved along parallel lines. In Germany, the Deutsche Verband für das Kaufmännische Unterrichtswesen (German association for commercial education) initiated the so-called *Handelshochschulbewegung*, a movement that provided the major impetus for the establishment of undergraduate-level management schools (*Handelshochschulen*) in Berlin (1906), Mannheim (1907), Munich (1910), Königsberg (1915), and Nuremberg (1919). In America, too, a business school movement took shape during this period. Driven in part by the business community, it provided the stimulus for founding schools in, for example, Chicago (1898), California (1899), New Hampshire (Amos Tuckschool, 1900), Wisconsin (1900), Illinois (1902), and Boston (Harvard Business School, 1908). A key difference between schools in these two countries was that American business schools were generally set up within a larger university, whereas in Germany they were organized as independent institutes. Given the fact that both German and American business schools faced the initial difficulty of embarking in an as yet nonexistent field of scholarly study and teaching, their curricula were by and large conceived as a combination of practical and general training courses.

The Netherlands, much like Germany, established its business colleges as independent entities, the first being the Nederlandsche Handels Hoogeschool (Netherlands School of Commerce), set up in 1913 and modeled to a large extent on the business school in Berlin. Dutch higher education in business would lat-

897

5

—

THE
COLD WAR
AND
BEYOND

1945–2009

—

ECONOMICS
AND
SOCIETY

er be expanded with the addition of the Faculty of Economics and Business at the University of Amsterdam in 1922 and the School of Economics in Tilburg in 1927.

Despite these early similarities, however, American and European business schools were to develop in very different directions. Dutch higher education in general was influenced by trends in Germany, which placed a heavy emphasis on scientific training, academic freedom, and the integral connection between research and teaching. Professional training was far less a concern in this context, which, described by Locke as the "German Wissenschaft Paradigm," dictated that "no discipline in a German university could have any ambition other than a scientific status."[4] This primacy of scientific training held equal sway in Dutch academia. Amsterdam's Faculty of Economics and Business stated unequivocally that "the future businessman" must be "equipped with a training that was purely theoretical, or indeed, scientific."[5] Practical courses were cut from the curriculum not long after the Nederlandsche Handels Hoogeschool welcomed its first students, and the program was lengthened from two years to five. In Amsterdam and Tilburg, much as in Germany, business and management subjects were transformed into the coherent scientific discipline of business economics.

American business schools progressed along an entirely different course. Many of them embraced the emerging field of scientific management, but almost no attempts were made to mold it into a "management science." The development of the case study method at the Harvard Business School led to teaching innovations, yet this method had primarily been designed to improve management-level decision-making processes, rather than to contribute to any kind of management science. Unlike their counterparts in the Netherlands and Germany, U.S. business schools failed in their attempts to create an integral, clearly circumscribed field of knowledge capable of countering increasing fragmentation.

Nevertheless, American business schools were immensely successful. Student enrollment grew from 36,456 to 67,496 between 1920 and 1929 alone. The number of business schools went from 12 in 1912 to 120 in 1930.[6] Yet the combination of powerful growth with poor quality of education and mediocre teachers at most business schools aroused sharp criticism from universities and the business community alike. The many attempts at improving education notwithstanding, the prewar American business school remained, according to the historian Rakesh Khurana, "a very ill-defined institution."[7]

The Dutch therefore took little notice of American business schools up to 1940. Harvard's famous case study method, too, was found to be lacking, and was considered a low-level, nonscientific treatment of business issues at universities.

Business and Higher Education after 1945

The notion that those filling management positions needed a full-fledged, scientific education underwent a sudden turnaround in the Netherlands soon after 1945. World War II had inflicted serious damage on national production processes, and major Dutch companies that had rarely taken an active interest in higher education before 1940 now became outspoken in their criticism of the economic and technical academic programs that, in their view, took theoretical and specialist training too far. They held the existing lengthy programs responsible for creating a business-sector labor pool of relatively older graduates whose theoretical training left them utterly "immalleable." The Contactcommissie Industrie-Hoger Onderwijs (Liaison committee for industry and higher education), established in 1954, proposed the development of a business school that would offer a shorter course of study, similar to a bachelor's program, where students explored management and organizational questions and developed their leadership capacities. Case studies were also to be included in the curriculum, as was common at many American business schools. These proposals were tested in an experimental bachelor's program in Rotterdam, but the experiment quickly proved a failure, suffering from connotations of furnishing a "degree for dummies."

Dissatisfaction with existing higher education programs also resulted in a 1946 initiative to found the Nederlands Opleidings-Instituut voor Dienst in het Buitenland (NOIB, the present-day Nyenrode Business University). Leading this initiative were several eminent industrialists and the then minister of education, arts, and sciences, Gerrit Bolkenstein. Their primary motive in founding the school was to restore and renew Dutch international trade relations after the war. British educational ideals served as a point of orientation from the very beginning, with an emphasis on character formation, athletic development, and "social virtues." Nyenrode was not easily accepted by Dutch academia. Jan Goudriaan, a prominent professor of business economics, called it an example of Anglomania that had failed to recognize the true value of Dutch national educational traditions. The NOIB, he concluded, was "a terrible misunderstanding...."[8] Gradually Nyenrode developed into a typical American business school, and as this type became more accepted in the Dutch higher education system Nyenrode established itself as one of several prestigious schools in this field.

Nyenrode, where the Nederlands Opleidings-Instituut voor Dienst
in het Buitenland (Netherlands Training Institute for Serive Abroad or NOIB)
was founded in 1946, and where the current Nyenrode Business University
is still located.

Marshall Aid and the Push for Management Education

In the period immediately following World War II, the Netherlands initiated — as indicated above — a reassessment of its higher education objectives and structures. A stronger orientation toward American (instead of German) models from 1945 on contributed to a "climate of change" that set the stage for the emergence of business schools in the 1960s and 1970s. Initially, Marshall Plan aid (1948–51)[9] provided the broad context for a large-scale transfer of knowledge regarding management and management education from America to western Europe. Boosting productivity was one of its key aims. Support was coordinated by the Economic Cooperation Administration, with the Technical Assistance Productivity Program (USTAP) being launched to promote the productivity gospel throughout western Europe. The initial focus was on technical fields; later the accent shifted to management education, where an express emphasis was placed on management's key role in enhancing productivity levels. Financial and intellectual support was provided for new management training programs and for National Productivity Centers that, from 1953 on, were coordinated by the Paris-based European Productivity Agency (EPA), which would come to play a central role in the advancement of management education concepts in Europe.

The Netherlands proved highly receptive to American ideas and, most particularly, to the explicit correlation between enhanced productivity, management, and management education. By the end of 1959, 170 study trips had taken place within the Marshall Plan framework, in which over 1,100 Dutch participants had been involved. Several of these trips were directly related to the issue of management education, and the 1953 report "Wie volgt ons op?" (Who will succeed us?) established a clear link between the success of American enterprises and the energy that businesses and universities devoted to management training. Yet, quite remarkably, this observation did not actually generate any proposals for changing standard economics and technical higher education; instead, participants focused on the idea of organizing a postacademic study program to provide additional training for existing managers. Other reports likewise reveal an unfeigned admiration for the American approach to management education, yet the organization of an independent university business school was deemed unnecessary. Why? To begin with, there was a severe shortage of managers. Opting for a full-fledged university program would mean a wait of five years at the very least before the first graduating class would emerge with their degrees. A second key factor was the assumption that a program of this type would have to fight off too many objections from the academic world.

901

The organization of a true university-level management program in a field with no disciplinary foundation was regarded as an impossible task.

However, the Marshall Plan succeeded in fostering an awareness of the connections between productivity, professional management, and management education. In his influential 1951 speech, "Verhoging van de productiviteit" (Raising productivity), Unilever executive Paul Rijkens emphasized the need for applying modern, rational management concepts in Dutch business and argued in favor of creating postacademic institutes to train efficiency consultants and leaders in enterprise.[10] Eventually two key national training initiatives were begun, the Nederlands Studiecentrum voor Doelmatige Bedrijfsleiding (Dutch center for effective management, NSDB) and the Inter-University Centre for Organisational Change and Learning (SIOO). The NSDB was by and large modeled on the Harvard Business School's advanced management program and the postexperience training offered at the Henley Management College in the UK. Both the NSDB and the SIOO were indebted to the new, intensified collaboration between the business community and higher education. The establishment of these two training programs was financed in part by Marshall Plan counterpart funds.

The European Movement for Management Education

Dutch professors were exceptionally active in the European management education movement. In 1952, the TU Delft professor and organizational advisor B.W. Berenschot joined with several of his colleagues from other European countries to found the International University Contact for Management Education (IUC) to facilitate the exchange of management-education-related knowledge and experience in the academic field of engineering. The IUC worked in close cooperation with the EPA in Paris and with other organizations engaged in advancing management-education thinking in Europe, and it ultimately paved the way for acceptance of the business school concept throughout Europe.

The EPA ceased its operations in 1961, its tasks being taken over by the newly created Organisation for Economic Cooperation and Development (OECD). Yet by 1964 the OECD itself had opted to discontinue operational activities in the area of management education, thus dissolving what had been a cohesive force within the European management education movement and transferring most of the responsibility for its advancement to the national level.

The Fisher and Platt reports (1962 and 1963, respectively) that were initiated by the EPA, presented an analysis of the state of management education in Europe. Both reports contained pleas in favor of an independent European policy, arguing that "the path of progress … in each country [lay] in adapting and devel-

5

—

THE
COLD WAR
AND
BEYOND

1945–2009

—

ECONOMICS
AND
SOCIETY

oping management education in conformity of its own particular culture, educational pattern and business needs."[11] Simply adopting an American model was out of the question, both in terms of viability and desirability. First, the American university system was too different from that in Europe. Moreover, from the second half of the 1950s onward American business schools had themselves come under heavy fire from critics in business and academia alike. Corporate America was experiencing rapid growth and modernization, creating a huge demand for professionally educated managers. Meanwhile, there was a demand for the application of "new management sciences," a field that traced its roots to the war years when the American economy and war industry had been confronted with unprecedented, complex managerial problems for which new solutions were needed. The large-scale demands of running a war economy had led to the emergence of new areas of management knowledge, such as operations research, linear and dynamic programming, decision-making theory, probability theory, game theory, and systems theory. As such, the new management sciences united mathematical, economic, behavioral, and social science theories and lifted management from an area of application and practice to that of an entirely new scholarly discipline. The emergence of leading journals such as *Management Science* (1954) and *Administrative Science Quarterly* (1956) solidified this transformation.

American business schools had no ready answer for management's rebirth as a scientific field. Both the Ford and Carnegie foundations issued reports in 1959 that concluded that education at U.S. business schools was fragmentary and below par, recommending a greater emphasis on research (in the social sciences especially), developing students' analytical skills, offering fewer undergraduate and more graduate courses (MBA and Ph.D.), and reducing the number of courses with a functional and markedly professional orientation.[12] This "New Look" perspective led the Ford Foundation to sponsor select business schools as centers of excellence that would come to supply the model for later developments in America and Europe alike.[13]

The Ford Foundation and the European Management Education Program

During the 1960s European criticism of the American business school model faded away. A key factor in this was the debate surrounding the publication of French journalist Jean-Jacques Servan-Schreiber's *Le défi américain* in 1967. According to its author, corporate America was slowly but surely penetrating Europe, with a total takeover by the U.S., in the form of technological colonization, being the inevitable result. Servan-Schreiber's book launched a wide-ranging

5

—

THE
COLD WAR
AND
BEYOND

1945-2009

—

ECONOMICS
AND
SOCIETY

debate about the so-called technology gap between the U.S. and Europe. In his famous speech of 1967, American Secretary of Defense Robert MacNamara was to emphasize that "the technology gap is misnamed. It is not so much a technology gap as a managerial gap." The emphasis was therefore placed on the lack of professional management knowledge, highlighting along the way the absence of a management education system in Europe. Hence the crux of the problem for some lay in the shortage of middle managers, since "they are the basic products of the American business schools, and it is their absence that in large measure creates and defines the gap."[14] The management gap discussion played an important role in the Dutch pro-business school rhetoric, and it became the main reason for founding a business school in the Netherlands.

Following the termination of its New Look program for the reform of American business schools in 1965, the Ford Foundation turned its attention to the management gap discussion, with the intention of advancing management education in Europe. In 1967, it launched the European Management Education Program, investing a total of 10.8 million dollars, primarily to introduce the American business school model (the MBA model) in Europe, albeit in a modified version to reflect European needs and experiences.[15] The program framed five key objectives: [1] to recruit a corps of European management educators and researchers, [2] to improve management education by utilizing case studies and by funding American guest lectureships and American and European teacher exchange programs, [3] to propagate business school thinking, [4] to simulate specifically national management education strategies, and [5] to institute an enduring European management education movement.

Toward a Dutch Business School?

The Netherlands, which had led the movement for management education in the Marshall Plan era, ultimately gained little from this stimulus program. The country did not have any business schools, and therefore Ford Foundation stimulus measures such as the design of educational materials and gathering a corps of educators and researchers served little purpose. Using the American business school as a template had not been widely accepted. Instead the emphasis was placed on postacademic and postexperience training. However, American business school reform, the debate about the management gap, and the Ford Foundation stimulus program provided sufficient evidence that a Dutch business school was both desirable and necessary. By the mid-1960s, therefore, the question was not so much whether to found a school as which model to use in doing so. The Dutch business community had a definite preference for the MBA model, but there was no consensus.

In 1965, Royal Dutch/Shell decided to intervene in the difficult deliberation process by donating 2.5 million guilders to the Netherlands School of Economics (NEH) in Rotterdam for the foundation of a Dutch business school. Shell's support came with the proviso that the school be designed as a postgraduate institution (requiring a *postkandidaatsopleiding*, a degree roughly equivalent to the modern-day master's degree) and a stated preference for its realization as part of a national initiative. In 1970 a postgraduate program in business administration was finally begun, run jointly by the NEH and the Delft Institute of Technology. The University of Groningen followed in similar fashion with its own program in 1975.

This kind of postgraduate program was unique in higher education, and it was phased out by the introduction of the higher education reforms in 1982. Under the new structure, business administration took its place among the full-fledged, four-year degrees offered in regular higher education. Demand for MBA programs grew at a rapid pace, however, leading to the widespread development of master's-level programs outside the parameters of regular higher education, not only in the Netherlands, but throughout much of Europe. These private MBA programs have been purposely designed to follow the American (New Look) model to a far greater degree. With the recent implementation of the bachelor-master structure in Dutch higher education, regular business administration programs have now come to reflect quite closely the structure of the Netherlands' former *postkandidaatsopleiding* and of the business school as it exists in America.

Conclusion

Just as in the U.S., the Dutch academic degree programs in business administration have proved an immense success. Currently there are eight universities (12,000 students), three technical universities (1,000 students) and twenty-five colleges of applied science (115,000) that offer MSc and BA programs in business administration, as well as a wide range of MBA degree programs.

On the whole, the Netherlands has in large measure adopted the American business school model. This is not to say that the emergence of the Dutch business school should be interpreted as simply the unavoidable consequence of a modernizing business community's demand for professional managers, or that there was ever any blind imitation of the American model. America's role in the dissemination of business school thinking in Europe can best be characterized as that of an "active reference society": the Dutch search for solutions in the postwar period was met by very active proposals from the U.S. Yet, however true it may be that the Dutch business school more or less adopted the Ameri-

5

—

can model, there is no clear indication that the schools have become fully embedded into the fabric of Dutch society.

Between 1980 and 1995, American business schools again suffered an avalanche of criticism. Some critics held them responsible for the unfolding economic crisis and the absence of any effective strategy in the face of Japan's economic success. Implicit in such criticism is a deep-rooted conviction that education and economic and social success are directly linked. In the Netherlands, however, the continuing lack of any major interest in the development of a national system of management education suggests that the professional manager and the business school are still not taken for granted as basic institutions in Dutch education and society.

—

1   F. Harbison and C. A. Myers, *Management in the Industrial World. An International Analysis.* (New York / Toronto / London: McGraw-Hill, 1959), 81.

2   R. R. Locke, *The Collapse of the American Management Mystique* (Oxford: Oxford University Press, 1996), 53.

3   G. Gemelli, "From Imitation to Competitive-Cooperation: The Ford Foundation and Management Education in Western and Eastern Europe (1950's–1970's)," in G. Gemelli, ed., *The Ford Foundation and Europe (1950's–1970's). Cross-Fertilization of Learning in Social Science and Management* (Brussels: European Interuniversity Press, 1998), 167-305, here 168.

4   R. R. Locke, *Management and Higher Education since 1940. The Influence of America and Japan on West Germany, Great Britain, and France* (Cambridge: Cambridge University Press, 1989), 89.

5   Th. Limperg, "De Faculteit der economische wetenschappen der universiteit van Amsterdam." Reprint from Jaarboek van de Gemeente Universiteit van Amsterdam 1946–1947 (Amsterdam: University of Amsterdam, 1947), 7.

6   R. A. Gordon and J. E. Howell, *Higher Education for Business* (New York: Columbia University Press, 1959).

7   R. Khurana, *From Higher Aims to Hired Hands* (Princeton, NJ: Princeton University Press, 2007), 137.

8   J. Goudriaan, "Productivisme en democratie." *Afscheidscollege* [last professorial lecture], January 18, 1950 (Delft: s.n., 1950), 19.

9   The Marshall Plan, or European Recovery Plan (to use its official reference), was succeeded as of January 1952 by the Mutual Security Program. See John Killick, *The United States and European Reconstruction, 1945–1960* (Edinburgh: Keele University Press, 1997), 96.

10 P. Rijkens, "Verhoging van de produktiviteit. Pre-advies," *Maatschappijbelangen. Maandblad van de Nederlandsche Maatschappij voor Nijverheid en Handel* (June 1951), 132-142.

11 OECD, *Management Education* (Paris: OECD, 1963), 57.

12 Gordon and Howell, *Higher Education for Business*, and F. C. Pierson et al., *The Education of American Businessmen. A Study of University-College Programs in Business Administration* (New York/Toronto/London: McGraw-Hill, 1959).

13 S. Schlossman, M. Sedlak, and H. Wechsler, "The 'New Look': The Ford Foundation and the Revolution in Business

Education," *Selections. The Magazine of the Graduate Management Admission Council* (Winter 1987), 11-31.

14 E.F. Cheit, "Review of the European Management Education Program." Internal report of the Ford Foundation

(New York: Ford Foundation, 1982), 4, 37.

15 See P.J. van Baalen, *Management en hoger onderwijs. De geschiedenis van het academisch-management onderwijs in Nederland* (Delft: Eburon, 1995), 301.

5

THE
COLD WAR
AND
BEYOND

1945–2009

ECONOMICS
AND
SOCIETY

908

U.S. ADVERTISING STRATEGIES IN THE NETHERLANDS

WILBERT SCHREURS

Ever since the beginning of the twentieth century, the Dutch advertising world has perceived the United States as the birthplace of advertising. America formed a touchstone for Dutch advertisers and ad agencies, and its impact was considerable. Nevertheless, up until the 1960s there also was unmistakable resistance within the ad industry to the espousal of American practices, and their desirability for the Netherlands was questioned on a regular basis. This article posits that the Dutch attitude of reserve toward American advertising was rooted in a combination of factors. It was linked not only to an underlying anti-American sentiment, but also to the fact that the creators of Dutch ads considered circumstances in the Netherlands to be so different from those in the United States that it seemed unwise to them to rely too heavily on American models. Another factor was the lack of any sense of urgency: until the 1960s, the Dutch advertising industry was primarily concerned with consolidation and felt little incentive for change. The result was that new insights in areas such as marketing were adopted with some delay.

All this was to change in the 1960s, when Dutch receptiveness to new insights gleaned from the American ad steadily began to grow. This change was inextricably linked to the "invasion" of American ad agencies in the Netherlands, though it can also be ascribed to the "creative revolution" that found its expression in American advertisements around that time and likewise found a ready audience in the Netherlands, which, emerging from a period of consolidation, finally experienced a drive for renewal.

From the early 1970s onward, U.S. influence on Dutch advertising began to wane, while a corresponding, albeit modest, current was moving in the opposite direction: there was a slow but steady rise in U.S. recognition of the quality of Dutch advertisements. Toward the end of the twentieth century this one-way traffic, in either direction, definitely became a thing of the past.

From the 1930s Onward: Early Ambivalence

Countless Dutch magazines of the 1930s featured advertisements published in a comic strip format. By and large, these ads promoted brands that originated in the United States, such as Lux and Colgate, and generally followed a fixed formula using four to six pictures in which a story was told. The plot typically centered on a person who was struggling with some problem. Sometimes it was a woman failing to attract the attention of the man she had an eye on, at other times it was an unemployed man unable to find a job no matter how hard he tried. The product invariably provided the solution. By using the right brand of soap or toothpaste, the main characters in the ads saw their lives turn around.

Such comic strip ads were borrowed directly from American examples. The comic book-based form of advertising had been introduced in the U.S. in the early 1930s and proved exceptionally successful. In the Netherlands, however, it quickly came under fire from advertising professionals. These ads clashed with generally held notions about the Dutch consumer and, according to the secretary of the Nederlandse Periodieke Pers (Dutch periodical press), J. Tersteeg, "underestimated the common sense of their intended audience, and in a highly insulting manner to boot." Nevertheless, as gradually became clear, this type of ad was effective in the Netherlands, too. In 1937, agency director and advertising publicist W.N. van der Sluys confirmed that "balloon advertising has been fully assimilated as a publicizing tool." He compared its achievement with the success of Hollywood movies in the Netherlands, which likewise catered to the public's desire to trade reality for fantasy. According to the ad industry journal *Meer Baet*, it was understandable that advertising professionals might view the comic strip ad as "awfully childish," but then went on to point out that advertisements were not developed for the gratification of their makers but, rather, to deliver results. And that was something comic strip ads did do.[1]

These diverging responses to the comic strip ad were indicative of the ambivalence that characterized Dutch attitudes toward American advertising in the years leading up to World War II. The United States was the country that advertisers imitated in myriad ways, be it for the level of professional training programs, the use of psychological insights by advertising copywriters, or familiarity with one's target audience — America could serve as an example in each of these areas. Yet, at the same time there definitely also was reticence. The "omnipresence of advertising" in the U.S. was one of the motivations — particularly

909

5
—
THE
COLD WAR
AND
BEYOND

1945–2009

—

ECONOMICS
AND
SOCIETY

in intellectual circles—for assuming a critical attitude toward America.[2] The echoes of such criticism filtered through to professional circles as well. Doubts were raised as to what was really being gained by Dutch ad makers' U.S. orientation. In his 1939 book *Grondslagen der moderne reclame*, Philips advertising director E.B.W. Schuitema asserted that "Dutch advertising require[d] a personal identity." Advertising consultant Hans Vollenga regarded "Americanism" as the key spoke in the wheel of Dutch advertising, commenting in the *Revue der Reclame* in 1930 that "we are looking at precisely those countries where the general level of development and civilization of those engaged in making the advertisements there is so supremely inferior to that of us Netherlanders." Resistance to foreign influences resulted in chauvinism being granted free reign.

Despite the objections voiced against an American orientation, professional circles in the Netherlands continued to watch developments in the U.S. ad industry with intense interest and professional journals published countless articles on the subject. The total 1952 tally for the monthly *Ariadne* journal was characteristic: seventeen articles about advertising in America appeared that year, but only four on English and two on German ad industry topics. And yet, reservations remained. As one member of the *Ariadne* staff remarked in 1950, following the publication in *Fortune* of an article about posters in the U.S., "in the domain of poster art, America has nothing—quite literally nothing—to teach us. ... Each outdoor poster is just one Coca-Cola production line reflection of every other: sweet, sticky, oversexed, under-spirited, photographically precise, uninspired, entirely deculturized—but tested inch by inch and color by color via mechanized means for its ability to hit the target."

First-hand observation of the U.S. advertising business was arranged through study trips organized in the 1950s by the Contactgroep Opvoering Productiviteit (COP). This organization was established in the framework of Marshall Plan aid and provided opportunities for members of Dutch trade and industry to become acquainted with American business methods, the objective being that the Dutch visitors would themselves apply the lessons thus learned and disseminate them further. The study trips resulted in a number of reports that were to serve as an important source of information and inspiration for Dutch business owners. The report "Verkopen volgens plan" (Selling by design), which appeared in 1954, described the way in which turnover policy in American business formed "one single organic and cohesive whole of market research, product development, advertising, sales activity and all associated public relations. The interconnectedness of each of these elements with one another is epitomized in the brand Marketing Mix, which has already won general acceptance." Marketing, by definition, allotted a clearly circumscribed role to advertising, whose primary function was to communicate the sales pitch. Those who drafted the report attested to their admiration for the American method and empha-

A Dutch advertisement for Colgate toothpaste from 1940, making use
of the American comic-strip technique. This was an almost exact copy
of an American advertisement for the same product.

5

—

THE
COLD WAR
AND
BEYOND

1945–2009

—

ECONOMICS
AND
SOCIETY

sized that the Netherlands could learn a great deal from this example. But initially the response to the authors' message was only lukewarm, and it was not until the 1960s that the "marketing approach" would truly make its mark in the Netherlands.[3]

Dutch hesitancy regarding the U.S.'s role model status was evidenced by pieces contributed to the *Revue der Reclame* by several of the individuals who had participated in COP study trips and who themselves were advertising professionals. A. Borstlap, who worked for a retail purchasing enterprise, asserted that the situation in the United Sates was so completely different from that in the Netherlands that the adoption of American methods would serve no purpose. The difference was not only one of scale, but also of audience mentality, which in the Netherlands was considerably more "down to earth."[4] A. Trel, advertising director of the grocery chain Végé, noted that advertisements used, for instance, by supermarket chains were of a much lower level, "usually a bit of chitchat about dollars and a summary of items," leading him to conclude: "We have nothing to gain by a mad dash for America."[5]

Other Dutch reactions reflected an attitude of complete aversion. The discussion that arose in connection with advertising's application of insights yielded by depth psychology is well known. Following the 1957 publication of *The Hidden Persuaders* by the American journalist Vance Packard (with a Dutch translation appearing only one year later), countless warnings were sounded in the Netherlands against the "advertising superexperts" from the U.S. Television ads elicited a similar response. The phenomenon of commercial television, which had been established in the Netherlands in 1951 and offered a modest selection of programs, was a hotly discussed topic during the 1950s. One point in the discussion focused on the — according to the majority of Dutch commentators — excessive amount of advertising shown on American television; this became the frequently cited example of how things ought not to be done.[6] The United States was the "counterexample" that served to confirm the necessity of developing an identity unique to the Netherlands.

What lay behind the Dutch ad agencies' continued resistance to the United States, which persisted throughout the 1950s? The reasons were in part the same as before the war. Not only was there a general consensus that situations in the two countries were considerably different, but there was also a tendency to look down on the United States in certain ways. Equally important was the lack of any urge to change. The world in which Dutch advertising agencies operated comprised a sector that was closed to outsiders and featured cartel-like traits — hardly the ideal climate for innovation. Add to this the fact that the Dutch ad industry, which during the first half of the century had never enjoyed much prestige, began, from the 1950s onward, to win increasing social and political recognition. "It is conceivable that the recognition eventually gained had made many advertising practitioners blind to developments in the business-enterprise arena, with the result that people failed to take proper account of the pace and the consequences of the innovations," Esther Cleven wrote in her dissertation "Image bedeutet Bild."[7] A final significant factor in this context was the economic situation. Through the 1950s the demand for goods was high in the Netherlands, and as a result the effort that most advertisers and ad agencies needed to expend in order to sell their products was nominal. Why, then, would they change their approach?

The "Invasion" of the American Advertising Agency

The year 1958 saw the opening of a branch of the American J. Walter Thompson ad agency in Amsterdam. JWT had already made one previous attempt to get a foothold in the Netherlands, but World War II forced the agency to close its doors, and its success had been only marginal. There was a consensus in Dutch professional circles all through the 1950s that American businesses operating in the Netherlands were better served hiring local agencies for their advertising work — after all, they knew the market. But JWT quickly proved itself adept at winning over countless American clients, and soon Dutch companies began turning to the renowned American firm as well. The opening of JWT was followed over the course of the 1960s by the arrival of other large American agencies, including McCann-Erickson, Young & Rubicam, and Foote, Cone & Belding. Each of the American agencies that opened an office in the Netherlands elected to proceed via the takeover of a Dutch competitor. The maneuver was essential to their earning an *erkenning* (recognition), a designation granted by the Vereniging voor Erkende Advertentiebureaus or VEA (Association of Recognized Advertising Agencies), whereby an agency became eligible to demand a 15 percent discount in media placements of print and other forms of advertising. The 15 percent provision formed the basis of the payment system applied for Dutch ad agencies and additionally served to more or less shield the market from foreign competition. The takeover of a Dutch agency furthermore assured the American newcomers of an existing network of Dutch clients and staff. Far from being confined to the Netherlands, this was a development that affected numerous countries in Europe, which from the 1950s onward was confronted with an influx of American ad agencies.

American advertisers operating in Europe preferred to work with their own agencies because the level of professionalism among European colleagues was considered too low. But there were other reasons for American agencies to open offices across the Atlantic after World War II. Partly it was a defensive move against losing important U.S. clients to overseas competition. Partly it was due

913

5

——

THE
COLD WAR
AND
BEYOND

1945–2009

——

ECONOMICS
AND
SOCIETY

to Dutch agencies willingly being sold to the Americans, both for financial gain and for the benefits associated with involvement in a growing international market.[8] Nevertheless, Dutch reactions to the American "invasion" were mixed. "Ad branch pocketed by Americans," announced a headline in the daily newspaper *De Telegraaf*. The *Revue der Reclame* became the arena for a heated debate about the "ugly American" — a notion that referred to American agency directors who were perceived to be running their operations without any respect for the nature of the Dutch market. Reactions in professional circles were not wholly favorable either. Client companies were critical of the manner in which American agencies conducted their activities. Dutch staff members employed at agencies that had been taken over, were unhappy having to work toward objectives dictated by head offices in the U.S. Differing mentalities formed the crux of the problem. Whereas the Dutch approach to doing business had traditionally been rooted in personal relationships, the American way was more formal. But such disapproving attitudes also seem to have reflected a certain unwillingness to be swept up in the heightened professionalization of the American agencies. There was simply too little desire to change.

Nevertheless, this wariness did not preclude Dutch ad makers from learning several things from their American associates. In hindsight, U.S. influence was unmistakable in matters of financial responsibility, setting targets, and ad agency structure; the same was true of marketing — an area in which Dutch agencies found there was a great deal they could learn.[9] Creative development took longer, however, and it was not until the mid-1960s that American influences would manifest themselves in this domain.

The Creative Revolution of the 1960s

The most important figure behind the "creative revolution" was the American cofounder of the Doyle Dan Bernbach (DDB) advertising agency, William Bernbach. It was Bernbach who introduced 1950s America to a new style of advertising, one that diverged sharply from the existing mainstream practice of the "hard sell," which convinced consumers to buy a product by hammering home a product's strong points. Ads were not meant to leave anything up to the consumer's imagination; rather, their purpose was to make it as clear as possible to the consumer why he should want to buy that one particular product. Repetition was key. Bernbach, by contrast, assumed that an ad should appeal to the consumer's intelligence and imagination. Advertisements and commercials that incorporated humor and an element of surprise and showed a bit of irony and self-mockery, would be more successful in helping the advertiser win a consumer's trust. DDB's "soft sell" technique was particularly evident in their

914

legendary campaigns for Volkswagen and Avis. DDB was a revolutionary force not only in their strategies for addressing the consumer, but also with regard to the agency's internal organization. Whereas agency operations in the 1950s had usually centered on the copywriter, who was responsible for determining the ad line to which the designer was subsequently assigned to append an illustration, to Bernbach and his partners text and image were in fact equal. Campaigns were created by teams of copywriters and art directors working together to develop an advertising concept.

Bernbach's ideas caused a complete overhaul of advertising methods in the United States, and from the beginning of the 1960s Dutch industry publications ran extensive reports on new developments in America. The previous nearly universal reluctance to adopt American influences now made way for an open display of admiration for and curiosity about American advertising. Leading professionals such as Dimitri Frenkel Frank and Hans Ferrée published enthusiastic reflections on the new style of ad creation in the U.S. But the impact was far deeper. Even such new, successful advertising agencies as Franzen, Hey & Veltman and Kirschner Vettewinkel Van Hees were influenced profoundly. The decision to advertise in a different, more soft-sell-oriented mode, the new focus on creative aspects of advertising practice, the introduction of a creative team operating within the agency, the targeting of youth, and the leeway given to nonconformity were all initiatives borrowed from American examples that redefined Dutch advertising after 1960.

Clearly, the creative revolution met with fewer reservations in the Netherlands than previous U.S. influences. As the decade progressed, the Dutch ad industry began to recognize the need for innovation, impelled by the new generation of professionals filing into the offices of advertisers and ad agencies alike —a generation unwilling to apply what it considered the outdated techniques of the 1950s. Increasing prosperity had now made it more difficult for businesses to achieve turnover and, with competition on the rise, it was becoming ever more important for brands to distinguish themselves on the market. This was the role of advertising. Moreover, the paternalistic techniques used for so long were now beginning to elicit an adverse response. The Bernbach School tuned into this trend and was itself steeped in the critical mindset that started to take shape during the 1960s.

From the 1970s Onward: A Waning Influence?

The force of the creative revolution began to wane after 1970. Driven in part by an economic recession, U.S. advertisers reverted to their trusted hard-sell approach, under the motto, "hard times need hard sell."[10] Around the same

5

—

THE
COLD WAR
AND
BEYOND

1945–2009

—

ECONOMICS
AND
SOCIETY

time, interest in American ads gradually began to ebb away in the Netherlands. While America had been regarded as an important and inspiring teacher during the 1960s, the advent of the 1980s marked a shift in opinions. According to the Dutch agency director Wim Slootweg, Dutch advertising had evolved to the point where it was now the Americans who could profit from the Netherlands' example. In an article published in the *United States-Netherlands Economic Yearbook 1984–85* (and, in a revised translation, in the Dutch trade journal *Adformatie*), Slootweg — who during the 1980s was general manager of Ogilvy & Mather in Chicago — asserted that it was not so much at the professional level that American and Dutch advertising diverged, but more at the level of their respective ads' tone and style of presentation. Whereas humor and taking things with a grain of salt were strategies of choice in the Netherlands, in the United States it was again the hard sell that dominated. He suggested that if American advertisers wished to avoid irritating their audience, they would do well to take a leaf out of the Dutch advertising book. Slootweg was not alone in his assessment: as was evident from the critical commentaries that began to appear in large numbers during the early 1990s, the supremacy of American advertising was over. Thus, in his 1991 book *Whatever Happened to Madison Avenue?*, Martin Mayer would be led to wonder "why European advertising [had] been on the whole more imaginative than American advertising in the past fifteen years." And William Leiss would later describe the 1980s as the period in which the "image of advertising — and especially international advertising — as a characteristic American institution" came to an end.[11]

Slootweg was not the only Dutch advertising professional to make the move to the United States; over the past few decades various other figures in Dutch advertising have spent time working in the U.S. The celebrated Dutch creative mind Paul Meijer, for example, accepted a position as creative director of Young & Rubicam in New York in the 1990s. A more recent trend has seen several American agencies transfer their head offices to the Netherlands, most notably Wieden & Kennedy (responsible for global campaigns for Nike and Coca-Cola, among others), Strawberry Fox, and 180. These shifts have doubtless contributed to a growing U.S. interest in Dutch advertising. The 2003 edition of the *Encyclopedia of Advertising*, published by the American ad industry journal *Advertising Age*, cites the Netherlands as an example of a European country whose brand of advertising "has earned respect for its creativity and humor."[12]

916

Conclusion

The United States has exerted considerable influence on the development of the Dutch ad over the course of the past century. In the application of scientific insights and the marketing approach, in the organization of agency structure and in its focus on creativity, as well as in many other areas, the American ad industry has had a far-reaching impact on advertising in the Netherlands. And yet, initially, there was a general consensus in professional circles that simply transplanting American methods onto Dutch soil was out of the question. The advertising sector wished to develop a unique, national identity and there was no impetus for change. Before the 1960s the Dutch advertising world remained relatively conservative and pedantic, determined to gain a higher social status and respect through stability instead of innovation. Moreover, advertisers were convinced that circumstances in the Netherlands were simply too far removed from those characterizing the United States, making adoption of their methods impossible. With less competition in the Netherlands, there was no real need for brands to distinguish themselves by means of original campaigns.

From the late 1950s and early 1960s onward, however, the climate in the Dutch advertising world began to change. There was a growing receptiveness to influences from abroad and, equally important, American ad agencies actually came to the Netherlands. While there was predictable resistance, these changes initiated innovations in advertising as a profession. The spread of the marketing approach — which represented one of the most important changes to affect advertising in the years since World War II — received an additional impetus with the "invasion" of the American ad agency.

The creative revolution, by contrast, met with scarcely any such resistance. Various factors contributed to its positive reception in the Netherlands, including changes in the economic landscape (heightened competition to lure consumers), increasing interest in the younger generation, and the cultural innovations of the 1960s. Equally important was the arrival of a new generation of advertising professionals, whose entry into the workforce contributed to the realization that Dutch advertising strategies had to change. During this process the United States provided the main inspiration. But this leading role did not last. The 1970s saw American influences on Dutch advertising move into a gradual decline as the level of professionalism achieved in Dutch advertising all but eliminated the need for outside models. The one-time apprentice had slowly but surely emerged from the shadow of its teacher.

1   W. Schreurs, *Geschiedenis van de reclame in Nederland* (Utrecht: Het Spectrum, 2001), 113-115.

2   M. van Elteren, *Americanism and Americanization: A Critical History*

of Domestic and Global Influence (Jefferson, NC: McFarland, 2006), 24.

3   L. Soeterboek and J.-W. van der Hoek, "Marketing-Geschiedenis Nederland," *Encyclopedie voor Reclame en*

Marketing (Deventer: Kluwer, 1981–83).

4   A. Borstlap, "Een nuchtere kijk op Amerika: Het is niet alles goud wat blinkt," *Revue der Reclame* 12 (1954): 431.

5   F. van der Molen, "Reclamemensen over Amerika: Het is niet alles goud wat blinkt," *Revue der Reclame* 12 (1954): 327.

6   W. Schreurs, *Leuker kunnen we 't niet maken: Televisie en Radioreclame 1965–2005* (Hilversum: Ster, 2004), 13.

7   E. Cleven, "Image bedeutet Bild. Eine Geschichte des Bildbegriffs in der Werbetheorie am Beispiel der Niederlande, 1917–1967" (Ph.D. dissertation, University of Utrecht, 1999), 249.

8   M. Ackermans, *De veranderingen in de Nederlandse reclamebedrijfstak in de jaren zestig* (Master's thesis, Erasmus University Rotterdam, 1985), 39-41; M.J. Rechsteiner, *De geest van de goeroes.*

Amerikaanse invloed op reclamebureaus in Nederland (Master's thesis, University of Amsterdam, 1987), 49-50.

9   L. Soeterboek, "Amerikaanse reclamebureaus in Nederland," *Encyclopedie voor Reclame en Marketing* (Deventer: Kluwer, 1981–83).

10   S. Fox, *The Mirror Makers. A History of American Advertising and Its Creators* (New York: Vintage Books, 1985), 323-328.

11   W. Leiss, S. Kline, and S. Jhally, *Social Communication in Advertising*, 2nd edition (New York: Routledge, 1997), 172; M. Mayer, *Whatever Happened to Madison Avenue? Advertising in the 90's* (Boston/Toronto/London: Little, Brown, and Company, 1991), 212.

12   J. MacDonough, "The Netherlands," in John MacDonough, Karen Egolf, and Jacqueline V. Reid, eds., *The Advertising Age Encyclopedia of Advertising*, vol. 2, *F-O* (New York: Fitzroy Dearborn, 2003).

DUTCH-AMERICAN COOPERATION IN WATER MANAGEMENT

—

DIRK DEKKERS & TACO WESTERHUIS

Just as he was bracing himself for a run, he was startled by the sound of trickling water. Whence did it come? He looked up and saw a small hole in the dike through which a tiny stream was flowing.[1]

Any child in Holland will shudder at the thought of A LEAK IN THE DIKE! The boy understood the danger at a glance. That little hole, if the water were allowed to trickle through, would soon be a large one, and a terrible inundation would be the result.

Quick as a flash, he saw his duty. Throwing away his flowers, the boy clambered up the heights until he reached the hole. His chubby little finger was thrust in, almost before he knew it. The flowing was stopped! Ah! he thought, with a chuckle of boyish delight, the angry waters must stay back now! Haarlem shall not be drowned while I am here![2]

When Mary Mapes Dodge wrote these passages in her book, *Hans Brinker, or the Silver Skates,* she created a caricature of the Netherlands that to some extent still holds today, and introduced the Netherlands as a land of water to many Americans who were unfamiliar with this small country on the North Sea. Although entirely fictional and based only upon Dodge's second-hand knowledge of the country, the book created an idealistic picture of the Dutch that appealed to Americans at the time: conservative, hard working, God fearing, honest, clean, and well organized — a picture that resembled conservative Americans' self-image.

The Dutch and the Americans shared then, and still share today, a belief that nature can be shaped to their wills. Ingrained in them is the conviction that a wild, uninhabitable environment can be overcome, notwithstanding seemingly impossible obstacles and hostile forces. Americans went westward and created a successful, pioneering society. Dutch fishermen and traders dredged

5

—

THE
COLD WAR
AND
BEYOND

1945-2009

—

ECONOMICS
AND
SOCIETY

watery swamps and inland lakes, doubling the country's size. The land thus discovered became one of the most densely populated places on earth, and enabled a productive society, both in economic and political terms. To this day, some two-thirds of the Netherlands is at or below sea level.

In their respective fights against the water, the Dutch and Americans often came together. In the nineteenth century, Pieter Justus van Löben Sels, a Dutch diplomat posted in San Francisco, oversaw the construction of the first levees built in the Californian Bay delta. He did this to protect the growing cities in the area, including the booming gold-mining outpost later known as Sacramento, the state capital. Löben Sels settled in California, where some of his descendants became prominent members of society and important engineers of the Bay delta region's flood protection system.

Water Management in the Netherlands

The area of the Netherlands has always been notorious for its flooding. The first reports of floods date to 250 AD, and major disasters are known to have occurred in 1287, 1421 (Saint Elisabeth's flood), 1516 (Saint Catharine's flood), 1530 (Saint Felix's or Evil Saturday's flood), 1570 (All Saints' flood), 1686, 1775, 1825, 1916, and 1925.[3] In the Middle Ages the Dutch started to organize their flood protection in the *waterschappen* (water boards), the first of which was established in 1255. These boards brought together everybody who had a stake in protecting what was behind the dikes — people, agriculture, towns. The *dijkgraven* (chairmen of the water boards) were elected directly by the stakeholders — making the water board one of the first democratic institutions in the world — and the boards were empowered to levy taxes and fees to plan, develop, and maintain the "water system," both in terms of water quality and quantity.[4]

The most damaging flood in recent Dutch history occurred in 1953 when, in the middle of the night of February 1, a combination of rising sea levels, a spring tide, and a powerful northwestern storm caused extremely high waves. Many dikes in the Netherlands had been damaged or poorly maintained during World War II, and in the postwar years recovery and rebuilding were proceeding slowly due to lack of funds and priority. As many as 1835 people died, and the material damage was likewise enormous: fifty thousand homes were destroyed, two hundred thousand livestock were killed, and thousands of acres of rich agricultural land were inundated and salinated.

Offers from abroad to assist with evacuation and recovery poured in, and the United States was at the forefront. The U.S. Army immediately sent troops from Germany, including West German soldiers under American command. U.S. helicopters and amphibious vessels arrived within forty-eight hours. The psychological effect of U.S. Bell and Sikorsky helicopters flying over the devastated countryside was huge, reminding many of the liberation of the country by the Allied forces only a few years before. The United States Army Corps of Engineers donated one hundred pumps (some twenty-five of which were still in use in the Netherlands fifty years later).

Immediately after the disaster the Delta Commission was established to consider how to protect the Netherlands from such large-scale floods in the future. The subsequent Delta Plan led to a moveable storm surge barrier in the Hollandse IJssel River, completed in 1958, followed by the closure of two other major estuaries in the province of Zeeland in 1961 with dams able to mediate the tide with sluice gates. The closure of the last open estuary, the Eastern Scheldt, was rejected due to damage to fisheries and the environment, and a compromise led to the construction of a 5.5-mile-long storm surge barrier that can be closed in the event of coastal storm surge. The final piece of the Deltawerken (Delta Works), completed in 1997, was an ingenious moveable storm surge barrier in the Nieuwe Waterweg, which is the main navigable inlet into the port of Rotterdam. It has two vast gates — each the size of the Eiffel Tower — that are closed when a big storm is expected.

These efforts reduced the "exposed" Dutch coastline by two-thirds, and overall flood protection was thus greatly enhanced. But this only solved the problem of flooding from the sea. In 1993 and 1995 snowmelt from the Swiss and French Alps, combined with heavy rainfall over northwestern Europe, sent water cascading downstream into the Dutch delta. Levees along the Rhine and Maas rivers almost collapsed and more than two hundred thousand persons were evacuated. These "near-disasters" led to the drafting of a new Delta Plan for rivers, which aimed to create more space (bypasses and overflow areas) in the old flood plains, while also raising the height of the primary river dikes.

Water Management in the United States

Floods have been known to occur ever since recorded history in the United States and have been a regular phenomenon, but the Mississippi has been particularly vulnerable, most recently with its river basin flooding in 1993 and again in May-June 2008. An array of federal, state, and local government services have a role in the prevention of and recovery from flooding. The most important federal agency in U.S. water management is the Army Corps of Engineers (USACE). The Corps is similar to Rijkswaterstaat, the primary government water management agency in the Netherlands.[5] Since the early twentieth century, the USACE has been responsible for most large flood-protection projects, particularly along the Mississippi and Tennessee rivers. Looking to enhance the energy potential

921

The closing of the Veerse Gat in 1961. This was the first major closure of a waterway in the province of Zeeland, as part of the Delta Works project to protect the Dutch coastline against storm flooding.

of these rivers, the USACE built many dams and related hydroelectric plants in Maine, along the Columbia River in the Pacific Northwest, and along the Missouri River, as part of President Franklin Roosevelt's New Deal.

By the early twentieth century, it was apparent that many U.S. flood defenses, particularly along the major rivers and basins, were inadequate. After yet another disastrous flood in 1916, Congress adopted the Flood Control Act for the Mississippi and Sacramento rivers and sanctioned the improvement of the levees. Nevertheless, the devastating 1927 Mississippi River flood followed, and in 1936 flood control was placed under federal authority. The USACE was given responsibility for reservoir construction and for close coordination with local authorities. The Flood Control Act of 1944 (Pick-Sloan Plan) was designed primarily for flood control along the Missouri River, but it also enabled the U.S. secretary of the interior to sell energy produced at Corps projects, thereby directly linking water management to power generation. Subsequently, several huge dams were built on the main stem of the Missouri River, providing flood control, water supply, irrigation, navigation, and hydropower. In the years after World War II, the multipurpose approach became even more popular. Although costly, these massive projects contributed significantly to regional economic growth, providing cheap electricity for business and households.[6]

American-Dutch Cooperation and the Impact of Katrina

The connection between the U.S. and the Netherlands did not end after the 1953 flood in Zeeland. When the Dutch started the Delta Works, they were aware that an engineering project on this scale had never been attempted before. The planners found it difficult to predict the potential consequences in terms of coastal dynamics, erosion, or ecology. Mathematical models, provided by the American RAND Corporation, were used to help optimize the project designs in addition to physical scale models. During the project's thirty-year time span these mathematical models were elaborated and refined by Dutch scientists and engineers at Delft University and WL Delft Hydraulics.[7] The models are now regarded as among the best in the world and are also being used to advise American authorities on a wide range of water management issues.

The Delta Works have design safety standards set in law that mandate protection against flooding from storms that should theoretically occur once in 10,000 years in built-up areas and once in 1,250 years in rural areas. One negative result, however, is a reduced awareness of the fact that even the strongest flood protection does not guarantee absolute safety from flooding. Increasingly, politicians, developers, and citizens expect the government to provide this absolute safe-

923

5

—

THE
COLD WAR
AND
BEYOND

1945-2009

—

ECONOMICS
AND
SOCIETY

ty, even in coastal towns in front of levees or in developments within the natural riverbed. In an attempt to raise awareness, the Dutch government turned to the U.S. Because America has to cope with a wider variety of more frequent and more severe natural disasters than the Netherlands, U.S. culture is generally more focused on risk management than on risk avoidance. While some coastal states actively discourage development of high-risk zones, others combine development with well-practiced communication, disaster management, and recovery plans. This diversity provided a valuable study area for Dutch policymakers. In the first week of August 2005, officials of the Ministry of Transport, Public Works and Water Management were assisted by experts from the USACE and the Federal Emergency Management Agency (FEMA) in a comparison of communication and emergency management plans for the regions of New Orleans and Houston.

On August 29, 2005, hurricane Katrina crashed into the U.S. Gulf Coast and devastated Alabama, Mississippi, and Louisiana. While Katrina narrowly missed New Orleans proper, the storm damaged crucial levees to the east and north of the city, allowing water from the Gulf and Lake Pontchartrain to flood residential areas. Secondary levees were also weakened, and then failed, followed by many of the pump stations. The disaster—particularly the destruction of the Lower Ninth Ward, St. Bernard Parish, Lakeview, New Orleans East, and other flooded parishes—was televised around the world. The Dutch Rijkswaterstaat immediately dispatched three large mobile pumps and an emergency team to drain greater New Orleans and St. Bernard Parish. The Netherlands Royal Navy ship *Van Amstel,* based in the Caribbean, was sent to the Gulf Coast to assist the local population and emergency workers. Together with Mexican colleagues, Dutch marines were active for weeks in and around Biloxi, MS, helping people living on the coast recover somewhat, and providing medical services and clean water.

Within days after Katrina, a task force was established in the Netherlands with representatives of the Ministry of Transport, Public Works and Water Management, the Ministry of Economic Affairs, private sector engineers, and representatives of the Netherlands Water Partnership (NWP).[8] Together with the Dutch diplomatic network in the U.S., the task force put together a plan for short- and long-term assistance. The Royal Netherlands Embassy in Washington, DC, became the locus for a coordination team to promote a more durable outreach from the Netherlands to Louisiana and to federal officials in Washington. In the first few months after the disaster, the Dutch private water sector—often through its American branches—delivered crucial services. Heavy-machinery specialist Mammoet restored bridges, while Smit Internationale and Svitzer Wijsmuller took care of salvage operations along the coast. Den Boer, a company specializing in the production of tents, delivered several of its products, including a temporary shelter that served as a morgue. Other companies that were immediately involved and delivered their specific services, were Geodelft, Alterra, TNO, Terratech , BAM, DHV, and Boskalis.[9]

Several Dutch experts were involved in the first evaluations, responding to the many calls to "bring in the Dutch." The former head engineer of Rijkswaterstaat, Jan Hoogland, spoke to the U.S. House of Representatives about Dutch flood protection and gave his views on the future protection needs along the U.S. Gulf Coast. A former professor of civil engineering at Delft University, Jurjen Battjes, was invited to take a seat in the External Review Panel that investigated the functioning of the water barriers in New Orleans. Jos Dijkman of WL Delft Hydraulics, formerly involved in projects in Mississippi, Illinois, and Missouri, sat on a research committee of the U.S. National Academy of Sciences.

Many U.S. politicians from Louisiana and Mississippi, but also others involved in oversight of the USACE and public works projects, contacted their Dutch counterparts to discuss durable forms of cooperation. Senators Mary Landrieu and David Vitter, Governor Kathleen Babineaux Blanco, and another forty-five local officials from Louisiana, visited the Netherlands in January 2006.[10] The Louisiana delegation was welcomed by Crown Prince Willem-Alexander and received a crash course on Dutch water management policy and practice. In the meantime, the USACE looked for, and received, support from the Netherlands to better estimate damage to the flood protection infrastructure, to assist in studying the causes of the flooding, and to look at preventive measures.[11]

The scale of hurricanes Katrina and Rita acted as a wake-up call in Dutch politics as well. A national Task Force for Flood Emergency Management was established in 2007 to coordinate the first national flood emergency management exercise. The task force visited federal agencies in Washington, DC, and state and local emergency management agencies in Florida and Louisiana. Special attention was paid to the medium- and long-term recovery process, in which the U.S. has gained much expertise. The 2005 hurricanes have further stimulated Dutch discussions about how potential consequences of a flood should be taken into account in decisions on where (and where not) to build. The discussion on the recovery of the Louisiana coast and New Orleans is seen as a great learning opportunity for staff and leaders of the Ministry of Transport, Public Works and Water Management and the Ministry of Housing, Spatial Planning and the Environment.

5

—

THE
COLD WAR
AND
BEYOND

1945–2009

—

ECONOMICS
AND
SOCIETY

Continuing Cooperation between the Netherlands
and the United States

The Dutch outlook on flood management has been changed by the Gulf Coast disaster. The tiny country of the Netherlands is used to defending itself against storm surges from the North Sea. Not to protect inhabitable land because it is below sea level (part of the discussion concerning the rebuilding of New Orleans) is no option for the Netherlands. For the Netherlands, Katrina was evidence of the need to think more about the dangers of minimal awareness with regard to natural disasters, and of the need to think clearly about "what if" scenarios and large-scale evacuation plans. Although 9/11 has certainly contributed to a greater alertness with regard to the consequences of terrorist activity, the risks and consequences of natural disasters are believed to be much larger.

The exchange of expertise and lessons learned from experiences such as Katrina are of the utmost importance for both countries. Not surprisingly, therefore, Dutch-American cooperation on water management issues has been expanded. Dutch techniques and innovations are in demand, and talks are under way about involvement of experts from the Netherlands in Florida, where authorities are looking for ways to restore the Everglades and further protect the Florida Keys. U.S. conferences on water management regularly have Dutch guest speakers. Together with American partners, a number of Dutch firms are involved in different projects in several states. The Dutch water management sector is quite diverse indeed. Dozens of large and smaller water engineering and consultancy firms, public-private partnerships, government agencies, universities, and knowledge institutes are involved in "delta technology," as it is called in the Netherlands.

The NWP brings everybody involved together, thus presenting the Dutch sector as one when active abroad. The firms involved assess on a case-by-case basis how to deal with the different projects they might be involved in, be it separately or through consortia with or without American partners. Through subcontracting, there often are opportunities to involve smaller, more specialized firms that would find it difficult to work and position themselves abroad on their own. The engineering and consultancy firm Arcadis, for instance, was able to gain a major framework contract for the delivery of design services, consultancy, and implementation guidance for the protection of New Orleans areas against future floods. Together with WL Delft Hydraulics, Arcadis designed two storm surge barriers for the canals of New Orleans. Another result of NWP representation in Louisiana is the "Dutch Perspective," a plan developed by a consortium of the firms that first traveled together to the Gulf Coast in 2005: Arcadis, Royal Haskoning, DHV, Fugro, and Deltares (WL Delft). The perspective includes alternative planning of protection against future flooding for the city of New Orleans.

On the American side IBM, already active in water-related projects in New York (Hudson River), is opening a Global Center of Excellence in Amsterdam. One of its first projects will be to utilize its digital knowledge for models and simulation of flood prevention. Since the Dutch government is working on new plans for its coastal defenses, called "Flood Control 2015," the center will be a major new asset for Dutch water management. Climate change is expected to have a major impact on the cooperation. Adaptation to rising sea levels poses great challenges to both parties. New York and Florida, for instance, are faced with the same challenge of "climate proofing" their coastal defenses in order to prevent their major urban and economically valuable areas from flooding.[12] Because of this, and also to celebrate four hundred years of Dutch-American contacts, the NWP and the New York Metropolitan Waterfront Alliance are together planning a major bilateral water conference in 2009, along with a host of meetings between American and Dutch experts from both the public and private sectors.

For both sides, working together means mutual benefits from new and different perspectives, access to innovative technologies, and information about water management methods. In that sense, not much has changed since the first cooperation in the nineteenth century. In 2006 and 2007 Dutch policymakers and engineers visited the Bay delta area in California several times to discuss the levee problems. One of the experts who hosted the group and explained the local situation was James van Loben Sels, retired major general of the USACE, and a direct descendant of the Dutch diplomat who directed the design and construction of levees in northern California some 150 years earlier.

1   The authors work, respectively, for the Netherlands Ministry for Transport, Public Works and Water Management, and the Netherlands Ministry of Economic Affairs. The views laid down in this article are entirely their own. They would like to thank Hans Balfoort of the Ministry of Transport, Public Works and Water Management and Dale Morris of the Royal Netherlands Embassy in Washington, DC, for their valuable comments and corrections. Both were in the forefront of the establishment of Dutch-American cooperation after hurricanes Katrina and Rita hit the Gulf Coast.

2   Mary Mapes Dodge, *Hans Brinker, or the Silver Skates*, http://www.worldwideschool.org/library/books/youth/classic/HansBrinkerOrtheSilverSkates/chapt18.html.

3   Kees Slager, *De Ramp. Een reconstructie van de watersnood van 1953* (Goes: s.n., 1992), 7.

4   Water boards (*waterschappen*) are decentralized public authorities on an equal standing with the national, provincial, and local governments in

5
—

THE
COLD WAR
AND
BEYOND

1945-2009

—

ECONOMICS
AND
SOCIETY

the Netherlands. They are responsible for flood control, management of water resources (quantity and quality), and treatment of urban wastewater in the specific areas under their control. Nowadays twenty-seven water boards govern daily water management in the Netherlands. Nearly all are also involved in international activities.

5   Rijkswaterstaat is an agency within the Ministry of Transport, Public Works and Water Management. In 2002 Rijkswaterstaat and the USACE decided to work together on water management issues, and they formalized this cooperation through a memorandum of agreement (MoA).

6   By 1975, the USACE projected that the dams on the Columbia and Snake rivers provided 27 percent of the total U.S. hydropower and 4.4 percent of all electricity output.

7   Founded in 1929 as a nongovernmental organization, WL | Delft Hydraulics, together with GeoDelft, the subsurface and groundwater unit of TNO, and parts of Rijkswaterstaat, on January 1, 2008 became Deltares, an independent Dutch institute for national and international delta technology.

8   The Netherlands government and the private water sector share a long tradition of cooperation in water management issues. The Netherlands Water Partnership (NWP) is a public-private partnership of companies, government agencies, water boards, universities, and nonprofit organizations that collaborate in international projects. Before Katrina, the NWP mainly focused on water management issues in developing countries. When the hurricane struck, however, it was decided that the NWP was well positioned to organize Dutch public and private expertise to assist the states on the U.S. Gulf Coast in their short-term and future water management and protection projects.

9   Initially, Dutch maritime firms were hesitant to become involved because of the restrictions imposed by the Jones Act. The act is a federal law that regulates shipping in the U.S. The proper name is the Merchant Marine Act of 1920. It prohibits maritime activity in the U.S. by foreign vessels, thus fending off foreign competition. In the past, Dutch dredging firms have strongly objected to this legislation and to terms of the U.S. Dredging Act.

10   Referring to the Delta Plan, Senator Landrieu praised the Netherlands as an example of how to deal with reconstruction after a major disaster and prevention of other such catastrophes. In her words: "If the Netherlands, at half the size of Louisiana, can protect itself from North Sea storms so strong they occur but every 10,000 years, surely the United States of America can protect its own citizens from a lake."

11   The first estimates of the total economic damage were calculated at 125 billion dollars. See M. Kok, R. Theunissen, B. Jonkman, and J. K. Vrijling, *Schade door overstroming: Ervaringen uit New Orleans* (Delft: TU Delft and HKV *lijn in water*, 2006), 24.

12   See, for instance, http://www.giss. nasa.gov/research/news/20050520/. The chances that New York City (including Manhattan) and Florida will, as a result of global warming, be hit by floods are even higher than for the Netherlands because of the predicted increase of hurricanes on the U.S. East Coast.

6

THE
COLD WAR
AND
BEYOND

1945-2009

CULTURE

6

THE
COLD WAR
AND
BEYOND

1945–2009

CULTURE

INTRODUCTION

———

CULTURAL DEVELOPMENTS IN THE DUTCH-AMERICAN RELATIONSHIP SINCE 1945

———

JAMES C. KENNEDY

Since 1945, the Netherlands is not only one of the most strongly pro-American countries in Europe, but also a country with demonstrably strong cultural ties to the United States. Its notable Anglophone cultural orientation, while obviously not aimed exclusively at America, has nevertheless drawn much of its inspiration from American influences and American examples. This orientation seems part and parcel of its postwar geopolitical position and culturally "open" tendencies. The Netherlands is, after all, a small decolonized maritime country that historically has had more confidence in a transatlantic American political leadership than in that of its larger continental rivals. It is a country, moreover, historically disposed to extensive cultural borrowing from the most dominant of its geographical neighbors — France, Britain, Germany and, after 1945, from a country farther off: the United States. Perhaps the Netherlands is, in its American cultural orientation, not unlike other countries on the northwestern edges of Europe, like Norway or Britain, though perhaps some eastern European countries have surpassed them in looking to the U.S. for political leadership. But for the last two-thirds of a century, there has been — to varying degrees — a Dutch fixation on the United States that has helped create a society that is, perhaps in all of continental Europe, the one that feels the closest culturally to the United States. The U.S. embassy in The Hague, Giles Scott-Smith reports in this volume, suggested back in 1952 that the Dutch were "perhaps closer ideologi-

6

—

THE
COLD WAR
AND
BEYOND

1945–2009

—

CULTURE

cally to the United States than any people in Europe" — an assertion that may be as true today as it was then.

But which contours did the cultural dimensions of this relationship take? Scholars no longer subscribe to the notion of an American cultural juggernaut crushing everything European (or Dutch) before it, or of an American government powerful enough to assert a form of cultural imperialism over its Western European subjects. We understand now that Europeans (including the Dutch) did not swallow American cultural products hook, line and sinker but "mediated" them, "creolizing" American products and making them identifiably Dutch.[1] The United States may have been, as Mel van Elteren has noted, "the society of reference" for the Netherlands, but that did not, of course, mean that all things American were accepted; Europeans often found America most arresting as counterpoint, a society they were not, and would never want to be.[2] Indeed, the mediated acceptance of American products being anything but guaranteed, the appropriation of "America" varied from country to country, from decade to decade, from cultural sector to cultural sector. "Americanization" — understood here as the conscious borrowing of American cultural products[3] — was moreover a process that began at various levels, both "top down" (government) and "bottom up" (from the grassroots),[4] and I would argue, from the middle: cultural brokers in charge of important institutions.

These insights and others, articulated by scholars in the last twenty years, have made it more difficult than before to trace Dutch-American cultural relations in straight lines, in which ideas and practices emanating in the United States were culturally transferred to the Netherlands to be applied there. The reception of American cultural products is simply too uneven a process to be described this way. Moreover, postwar cultural relations were not only a one-way street; in a modest way Dutch cultural products traveled in the other direction, and in any event, European and American institutions came to cross-pollinate one another. In some cases one could speak of a "double creolization": the diary of Anne Frank was Americanized (as David Barnouw shows below) for U.S. theater audiences in the 1950s, only to be imported back to a rather different Dutch context, which would in turn develop its own relationship to her legacy. Cultural refraction, the multiple transfer of ideas, and the diffusion and fragmentation of cultural sectors have made it all the more difficult to trace patterns of influence.

Given all of this, it has become, furthermore, problematic to discuss transatlantic cultural relations in bilateral terms. Cultural ties between the two countries were often enough linked to other parties, and over time it has become more difficult to talk about ties between the Netherlands and the United States without talking about Europe as an entity with its own cultural policies and its own transnational cultural institutions.

Having said all of this, however, it is important to offer a sketch of postwar Dutch cultural relations, at three distinct levels: government policy, "high" culture, and broader forms of cultural expression, from rock 'n' roll to religion. This is important for several reasons. In the first place, it is illuminating to see in *concrete* form how cultural ideas and practices traveled the Atlantic. Many of the subsequent essays offer relatively short sketches of how American cultural expression came to be appropriated in the Netherlands, offering us critical insights into the when, how, and where of cultural exchange. In a word, these contributions are a critical antidote to the amorphousness of cultural interaction that one sometimes encounters in broader overviews of the subject.

Second, and more important, is another pattern that emerged out of the postwar relationship: the strong but uneven presence of American cultural influence has always depended on the good offices of organizations, networks, and persons — sometimes the conscious product of government policies, sometimes not — that to a very significant extent have determined the vitality of cultural exchange between the two countries. Nor is this vitality simply dependent on American cultural products being adopted by Dutch artists and by Dutch consumers; it also has, in the widest sense, necessarily relied on Dutch cultural investment in the United States. The exchange has not been — could not be — exclusively one-sided, but has depended on cross-border traffic moving in both directions. Without active Dutch initiatives in the cultural sphere, whether on the governmental level or through private initiative, the American cultural presence in the Netherlands would have been more superficial and less culturally significant than it has been. In a word, even an asymmetrical relationship such as the one between the United States and the Netherlands has depended to a significant extent on mutual investment and reciprocity, not only through impromptu and personal channels of cultural exchange, but through the structured policies of institutions.

Third and last, it is important to track this cultural relationship over the decades since World War II to show critical changes over time: the level of acceptance and appreciation for American cultural products, the forms in which they were mediated, and the kinds of sponsors involved. It seems true enough that Dutch society "Americanized," as it consciously took its cue from the United States on a broad range of cultural, economic, and political tastes and practices. This process was most clearly seen in the first half of the postwar period, especially in the period from the late 1950s until early in the 1970s, the period between an initial inertia and skepticism toward the legacy and more critical distance from America in the wake of the Vietnam War. In this "golden age" of American influence, it is often not very hard to point to American ways of thinking that were consciously adopted by the Dutch. Indeed, one could argue — on the basis of the contributions offered in this section — that the 1960s roughly

933

6

—

THE
COLD WAR
AND
BEYOND

1945-2009

—

CULTURE

constituted the decade when discernibly *American* cultural products had their most demonstrable impact on Dutch cultural life. Since then, American cultural influences may be said to have declined, at least in relative terms, or perhaps better said: they became more diffuse. For example, the European (including the Dutch) cultural life, having drawn earlier from American sources for inspiration and revitalized from it, no longer needed to look much to the United States at all in the search for new vistas. In a more multipolar cultural world, the U.S. simply counted for less from the 1970s on; it has become just one player, although an admittedly still important one, in a global cultural field. But the relative decline may not in fact express the most important trend of the last thirty years in Dutch-American cultural ties. Seen this way, American influence in the Netherlands has remained significant but is less likely to be experienced as such, and, indeed, the initial influences have often become so "Dutchified" that one could not speak easily of them as American.[5]

The diffusion and fragmentation of transatlantic cultural relations may characterize the current situation as impossibly fluid, a swirling mix of currents and eddies that defies any rational ordering. It may then seem that the Dutch-American relationship will sustain itself by the countless connections that travel, the market, and the new media afford. But that may be too facile a conclusion. The constantly changing dynamics of the cultural relationship between the Netherlands and the United States raise at least one pertinent question for the present: who can and who will sustain vital cultural ties between the two countries in a time of cultural fragmentation and of, it seems, political indifference? As noted above, the ability and the willingness of various actors to sustain the cultural relationship in the past has played a decisive role, and this may be true even now.

This introductory essay will explore these themes, systematically drawing on the fifteen essays written by a wide assortment of experts who, in their respective studies, have observed and analyzed aspects of the Dutch-American cultural relationship. The arts are relatively well represented in this section; sport, unfortunately is not, and aspects related to the media, effectively covered elsewhere, are, with the exception of film, not analyzed here. But the range is wide and varied enough to sketch a picture of a relationship that has changed much since the first years after World War II.

The Cultural Initiatives of Two New Allies (1940s)

Neither the Americans nor the Dutch were prepared for the closer cultural, economic, and political relationship they were to develop in the course of World

War II. Yet both the Dutch and American governments soon felt the need to solidify the ties between the two nations; both thought they politically had much to gain from proactively seeking to shape public opinion in the other country in a favorable way. In one case, government policy would, in the postwar period, be employed to save a threatened colonial empire; in the other, it would be to create and sustain a new alliance system headed by an emerging superpower.

The Dutch government in exile was the first to act, establishing in 1941 —before the entry of the United States into the war—the Netherlands Information Bureau (NIB), which sought to channel the right kind of information of the Netherlands into the American media. After 1945, the NIB would vainly seek to gain, through the funneling of information and through traveling exhibits to mobilize American opinion in support of the Dutch presence in Indonesia. But even after the Dutch recognized Indonesian independence in 1949, the NIB (now the Netherlands Information Service) would seek to familiarize Americans with Dutch culture through the sponsoring of visits of Dutch artists to the United States. American initiatives in Europe—including the Netherlands—started later and would also reach their height of engagement in the 1960s. But already in 1946, the American government funded through the Fulbright Educational Exchange Program the beginnings of a cultural program that included the dissemination of information about the United States and enabled scholars from Europe and the United States to make transatlantic visits. Prewar programs for European scholars to visit the United States had existed, of course, but this was the first time the government made a structured commitment to cultural exchange. It would turn out to be a long-term commitment in the first decades of the Cold War, when the political and military ties of the Atlantic Alliance seemed to require parallel cultural ties.

None of this should suggest, however, that the government had the monopoly on cultural ties between the two countries in the 1940s. There were "natural constituencies" that helped strengthen contacts between the two countries. Starting in the 1920s but culminating in the 1940s and 1950s, Dutch artists like Willem de Kooning, Piet Mondrian, and Karel Appel would be active, among elsewhere, in New York, where they had a profound influence on other artists, on modern art museums, and on the world of the art dealers, as Gail Levin shows. In doing so, they internationalized the art world and also ensured for a time that that world had its center in New York. Not only Dutch artists would feel the pull of New York and of America, but Dutch museum directors would as well. Willem Sandberg of the Stedelijk Museum was relatively early in developing contacts with the American art world; Jan van Adrichem suggests that Sandberg may have developed contacts with Peggy Guggenheim as early as 1948, and advised her in setting up her first traveling exposition, which included American

6

—

THE
COLD WAR
AND
BEYOND

1945-2009

—

CULTURE

art. The shift toward a more American orientation among Dutch artists and observers was already evident by the 1940s, and was not chiefly the result of either
the war or of government policy.

But in other areas the war did serve as a catalyst for new transatlantic ties.
That was the case not only in new forms of economic, military, or political cooperation, but in the religious sphere as well, where new forms of American cultural entrepreneurship were developed. American missionaries found in Western
Europe a new field for activity, and this included the evangelical Youth for Christ
(YFC). The early postwar presence of YFC in the Netherlands (1946) was made
possible by Dutch Protestant immigrants in the American Midwest, who were
keen to see "revival" in the Netherlands as much as in the rest of Europe.

In summary, the desire by both the Dutch and the American governments
for new cultural ties between the two countries was partially sustained by a
collection of other parties who in their way strengthened these ties after the
war, from missionaries to artists. But these people were, in the 1940s, only har-
bingers of things to come. The Netherlands in the 1940s was not yet ready for
an extensive counter for America, and the vehicles for American cultural influence were not yet fully developed. To be sure, American cultural influences
that had made themselves felt long before World War II, such as Hollywood
and jazz, also reasserted themselves after 1945. But the war did not result in a
sudden cultural reorientation by the Dutch toward the United States. The elite
of the country retained a deep ambivalence about America, not least on the cultural front. The level of cultural contacts between the countries remained modest. The Dutch knew nothing of nor cared for American literature, for instance.
Intellectuals, including those in the social sciences (as Tity de Vries shows),
paid little attention to American intellectual developments, and many Dutch
clergymen and laity remained suspicious of American evangelism techniques.
And even someone like Sandberg was not really a seer when it came to American art; he was slow, as Van Adrichem shows, to recognize the value in the work
of someone like Jackson Pollock in particular or American abstract art in general. In this, he was like other Europeans who only by the late 1950s came — rather suddenly — to an appreciation of such art. Indeed, as the Sandberg example
shows, attention to American cultural products would grow only in the course
of the 1950s, partly as the conscious result of American policy, partly through
important private initiatives.

The Take-Off Period of Cultural Exchange (1950s)

It was not until the 1950s that American influences made more of a systematic impression on the Netherlands. That had something to do with government policy; the American government helped establish an American library in the Netherlands, and the United States Information Agency systematically presented material about the United States for the Dutch public. By the early 1950s, too, the Netherlands-America Institute had become the primary organization for educational exchange between the two countries, according to Scott-Smith. But it had even more to do with the rising interest among Dutch artists and intellectuals in cultural and intellectual developments in the United States. American influences probably made themselves most felt in areas where the Dutch (or the Europeans) had the thinnest traditions. This is exemplified, perhaps, in the postwar history of Dutch dance. As Onno Stokvis has illustrated, Dutch dance really needed to be built from the ground up after the war, and the founder of the Nederlands Ballet, Sonia Gaskell, looked to the United States for both inspiration (in the persons of Balanchine and Graham) and for her dancers. But in the Dutch social sciences, too, American influences were consciously copied from the mid-1950s on. Dutch sociology had been relatively weak as both a separate and socially influential discipline, taking much of its cue from Germany. But as the discipline was increasingly employed to assist in policies guiding the modernization of Dutch society, it developed the functionalist approach of the American social sciences, a trend that would continue until the end of the 1960s, according to De Vries. In more traditional fields, such as literature, poetry and, as noted above, art, a structural and sustained interest in American developments would have to wait until the end of the decade, when leading journals began to devote systematic attention to American writers and artists. In art, New York became, in the third quarter of the twentieth century, the center of the world, and this was recognized by Dutch artists and museums.

American cultural influences made themselves felt earlier in less highbrow forms of culture. The cinema and jazz have already been mentioned, but the same can be said of rock 'n' roll, which made quick inroads from its inception in the mid-1950s. The electric guitar bands in particular became popular, largely in the first years through the inspiration of "Indo-bands," as Lutgard Mutsaers summarizes here. Even though it would not be until the 1960s that this new musical form would find a place in Dutch media, it was an early indication of youth interest not only in American music but in (ostensible) American ideals of freedom and of individualism. American cultural forces, then, could also be regarded as subversive in their significance, undermining the structures of authority. This was a fear expressed not only of rock music but of American

937

6

———

THE
COLD WAR
AND
BEYOND

1945–2009

———

CULTURE

evangelical religion. The coming to the Netherlands of the Billy Graham Crusades in the mid-1950s heralded a new kind of religious engagement — more individualistic in its piety and less beholden to the former structures of the church than had traditionally been the case in the Netherlands, as Hans Krabbendam shows in his article.

But American cultural influence was not only for those seeking, in their own way, to subvert the moral or the religious order. It also expressed itself in commercial terms, in which American goods — and American tourists — became an increasing part of the Dutch economy (see the section on economics). The American tourist came over in increasing numbers — and often by commercial airplane — in the course of the 1950s; American travel to Europe doubled between 1953 and 1959, as Marc Dierikx outlines in his contribution. This number swelled after the introduction of the economy fare in 1958. Transatlantic travel and tourism thus brought the two countries closer together as millions of Americans experienced firsthand the sights of Europe, and of the Netherlands.

Transatlantic travel, incidentally, went not only in the direction of Europe, but included the some seventy-five thousand Dutch citizens who immigrated to the United States in the period from 1947 to 1963. That was a modest 18 percent of the total emigration in those years, Enne Koops has determined, but these immigrants often served to revitalize the bonds between the Dutch communities in the United States and those at home, particularly in the religious enclaves of the Midwest. For a time, and on a more modest scale, Dutch immigration to the United States provided another important set of ties between the two countries.

In the 1950s, then, the United States and the Netherlands were, culturally speaking, bound more closely than they ever had before. But convergence, of course, obviously had its limits. This is poignantly exemplified in the diary of Anne Frank, published in Dutch as early as 1947 but destined to become more popular in the United States, where it was transformed into a Broadway play in 1955. A year later, the play was performed in Amsterdam and served as the basis for the diary's continued publishing success in the Netherlands. Nevertheless, the "American" Anne Frank generated some resistance among Dutch commentators, as David Barnouw has observed, and her hiding place would largely attract foreign visitors until the 1990s. Anne Frank had become, already in the 1950s, a shared heritage of the Americans and the Dutch (not to mention others), but Dutch appropriation of Anne Frank was slower in coming. And even as the two countries drew closer to each other culturally, the Dutch would necessarily negotiate the legacy of Nazi occupation somewhat differently from the liberators of Western Europe.

The Heyday of Americanization (1960s)

In hindsight, American cultural influences in the Netherlands were at their visible height during the 1960s. This was true at the level of popular culture, where American tastes in film, popular music, clothes, and other consumer items were widely appreciated and imitated. And it was true at the level of "high" culture as well, where the Dutch looked more to the United States than ever before for inspiration. Growing political criticism of the United States as a result of its superpower policies in general or its role in the Vietnam War in particular did not preclude a cultural appreciation of the country, as Rob Kroes notes in his contribution. Indeed, this attitude of cultural esteem and political critique became part of a predictable leftist stance toward the United States (in contrast to a more right-wing "anti-Americanism," which appreciated America's political role but decried its cultural philistinism).

Nowhere was the American cultural presence more evident, of course, than in rock music — the dominant British influence of the Beatles and the Rolling Stones in the mid-1960s notwithstanding. As Mutsaers sketches developments in her article, American music made its mark on the dance floor in the early 1960s but was especially influential through rising Dutch interest in American folk music and, by the end of the decade, a variation on this folk music — West Coast rock. Dutch bands began, she writes, to produce their own English-lyrics music influenced by the blues and by folk rock. But in contrast to the early 1960s, she continues, Dutch makers and lovers of rock 'n roll no longer looked exclusively to the United States for inspiration. It was a sign that the genre had been internationalized and that the Dutch could increasingly build on their own musical traditions.

American literature and poetry had begun to draw the systematic attention of Dutch literati by the end of the 1950s, a development that would discernibly continue until the early 1970s, as Jaap van der Bent and Bertram Mourits make clear in their contribution. The American Beat writers of the 1950s strongly influenced Dutch 1960s writers like Simon Vinkenoog, Jan Cremer, and Cornelis Vaandrager, and Dutch literary journals like *Barbarber* were strongly oriented toward American poets. At the Stedelijk Museum of Amsterdam, the tenure of director Edy de Wilde in the 1960s and 1970s would generate an extensive buying program of American modern art (made possible by Dutch prosperity) and some forty exhibitions of U.S. contemporary artists, as Van Adrichem has shown. By the 1960s, Stokvis writes, Dutch dance "came into its own," but its gaze remained fixed on international — and particularly — American developments, not least in fields such as show and jazz dance. In sociology, too, American influence would reach its greatest level of influence in the 1960s, when in-

939

6

—

THE
COLD WAR
AND
BEYOND

1945–2009

—

CULTURE

940

fluential works like Johan Goudsblom's *Dutch Society* would show, among others, an American approach to social science.

The breadth of American influence obviously had much to do with developments within Dutch society. Not only were the Dutch exposed to more and more elements of American culture on television, but they were, like other Europeans, increasingly experiencing the United States firsthand. A decade later than Americans, in the course of the 1960s, Europeans began to explore the United States in large numbers. More important, this had to do with the consciously democratizing and individualizing trends in Dutch society. Both American rock music and American religion, most notably its evangelical form, challenged the social order, as noted above, and this was a trend that only grew during the 1960s. The creation of the Evangelische Omroep in the late 1960s, borrowing from American ideas and American advice, was one sign of a new religious dynamic in the Netherlands, as Hans Krabbendam shows. The civil rights movement made a great impression and would inspire new forms of political protest like civil disobedience, first evident in protests against the Vietnam War but later to be employed in a variety of different progressive causes. Dutch parliamentary politics, too, would find American inspiration: in founding the new party D66 Hans van Mierlo consciously looked to the United States, for both its personality-driven politics and for its, as Van Mierlo then saw it, more democratic electoral system.

In summary, the 1960s constituted the high-water mark of American influence in the Netherlands. A modest part of that influence had to do with a conscious American government policy, which — in addition to maintaining its information programs — systematically established and funded chairs in American studies in the course of the 1960s, as Scott-Smith reports. But American influence, of course, went further and deeper than any government policy could direct. In respect to both its high culture and pop culture, to both commercial and to what one might call counterculture, to ideas associated both with the radical Left (such as new protest repertories) and with conservative Christianity (the new evangelicalism), American influences changed Dutch society through Dutch actors consciously emulating American examples. That the Dutch increasingly became divided in the course of the 1960s over the political legacy of the United States did little as such to reduce American influence; the models that the country offered were so wide and so diffuse that the Dutch could utilize these models as they themselves chose to do.

Political Ambivalence and Cultural Fragmentation (1970s)

The cultural influence of the United States remained strong in the Netherlands, but after 1970 began to suffer from a series of partially unrelated factors. Taking the articles of this section into account, it seems safe to say that Dutch-American cultural relations entered a new phase in the 1970s, in which American examples were less consciously and eagerly incorporated by the Dutch. There are various discrete, if related, reasons for this development: the background was the decline, real and perceived, of American power and prestige, visible not only through the Vietnam War and its aftermath but in the decline of the dollar and the rise of Europe (and Japan) as economic competitors with the United States.

In this context, both the American and Dutch governments saw less need to maintain intensive cultural programming in the other country. This was evident in Dutch cultural policy in the 1970s, which ended the Netherlands Information Service in 1974. Although not very anti-American, Dutch elites distanced themselves from the United States in ways perhaps reminiscent of their earlier reticence toward American culture. But the American government, too, was disinvesting in the Netherlands; the Netherlands-America Institute, too, closed its doors in 1974. Both David Snyder and Giles Scott-Smith see the 1970s as a time when formal, government-sponsored exchange was at low ebb, even as exchange and cultural programs were continued in other organizational forms. Anti-American sentiments did make a difference in diminishing student interest in American studies and in study in the United States. Both governments saw the value of celebrating the American Bicentennial of Independence in 1976. But in a period where détente had temporarily eased the tensions of the Cold War, where the U.S. was investing in more strategic alliances elsewhere, and where Western Europe felt less beholden to the United States, both governments did not give cultural exchange the same high priority as previously had been the case.

But the reason why the United States did not enjoy the same level of cultural interest in the 1970s as it had in the 1960s probably chiefly had to do with reasons other than anti-Americanism or the retrenchment of government policy. Two related factors must also be considered. In the first place, Western European cultural life in general and Dutch cultural life in particular had been revitalized after the war, partly through American inspiration. Now Europeans could contribute again on the same level as the Americans on the cultural world stage — or surpass them. This is an essential point that Stokvis makes. By the 1970s, it had become clear that European governments — including the Dutch one — were far more willing to financially support dance than their American coun-

6

—

THE
COLD WAR
AND
BEYOND

1945–2009

—

CULTURE

terparts, resulting in talent moving from the United States to Europe. Dutch dancers and choreographers looked to West Germany, not to the United States in the 1970s.

Accompanying this reason was a second and related factor: cultural life had become too diffuse and too fragmented for any cultural actor to draw from just one or two traditions of from primarily a single country, even an influential one like the United States. In the first place, the age of grand theory and "great movements" (to cite Van der Bent and Mourits) was over; Dutch social scientists did not look for an overarching model to understand the world, and Dutch writers and poets no longer sought a vision, modernist or otherwise, to inspire them. The move toward a greater eclecticism meant that Dutch — or, for that matter, American — artists, writers, musicians, and intellectuals drew their information and inspiration from an increasingly wide range of sources and material. "New York" was still the "normative" center of modern art in the 1970s, Van Adrichem writes, but not for much longer. In a cultural field that had become more diffuse and polycentric, American influence competed with other sources, and was itself increasingly influenced by these sources. If the lines of influence had been relatively unidirectional and relatively straightforward, that was no longer the case. American influences continued apace — in music, in the media, in scholarship and the sciences, and to a lesser extent in the arts — but at the same time they seemed to have lost the leading role that many Dutch had once assigned to them. Seen one way, American cultural expressions had become so internalized that they were experienced as universal or belonging to one's own nation.[6]

Cultural Reconvergence (1980s)

These factors were for the long term, and the Dutch fascination with the United States, and willingness to be inspired by American influences culturally, never returned to what they had been in the 1960s. Nevertheless, there were reasons the Dutch-American relationship revived, also culturally, in the 1980s. Here, too, larger political developments played a role. The intensification of the Cold War and the NATO decision to place cruise missiles on Dutch soil generated much opposition among the Dutch public. That required a more intensive cultural diplomacy on the part of the United States, and, as Scott-Smith outlines, led a series of new initiatives to cement the cultural relationship. The celebration of two hundred years of Dutch-American relations in 1982 had already enjoyed the support of both governments, but with the arrival of Ambassador Paul Bremer in 1983 a number of new initiatives were taken to, above all, solidify ties in the humanities in general and American studies in the Dutch universities in particular. The Dutch government also undertook new, more focused initiatives in the United States during the 1980s (such as the not very successful Texas Project, as Snyder relays). One could very well argue that, as in the 1940s and 1950s, the need to (re)seal the Atlantic military and political alliance helped relaunch cultural ties between the two countries.

For the first time, too, Americans in the 1980s became interested in Dutch society and culture as an alternate model to their own. Their first motivation for doing so was the cruise missile debate, in which critics like Walter Laqueur saw a neutralist, pacifistic "Hollanditis" returning to the Netherlands — and to Western Europe. Through the course of the 1980s and 1990s, Americans would become fascinated with the vicissitudes of Dutch tolerance, with its acceptance of homosexuality, its soft and hard drug approaches, and, by the mid-1980s, euthanasia policy. Dutch needle policy and forbearance toward cannabis drew the most attention, though later, in the 1990s, conservatives became concerned with what they saw as the "culture of death" in Dutch euthanasia practice. These were highly controversial topics about which Americans thought differently, but for the first time 'liberal' Dutch society functioned for some Americans as an alternative vision to the one offered by their own country. This emergent image of a freewheeling, libertine Holland came to exist uneasily next to the more traditional American view of the country that celebrated Dutch tulips, cheese, and windmills, and which — presumably — continued to attract the lion's share of the 570,000 Americans who came annually to the Netherlands in the 1970s and the 1980s (Dierikx).

By the mid-1980s, Dutch public opinion was no longer as critical of the United States. Many Dutch had developed a critical but real appreciation of American culture, which found an important outlet in tourist travel: since the late 1970s, about 9 percent of Dutch travel has been directed toward American destinations, Dierikx reports. People's particular travel choices had much to do with the media images of the United States, most preferring New York and the West Coast. Media impressions and tourist travel thus came mutually to reinforce Dutch cultural visions of America, generating in their own way an important nexus with the United States.

The third focal point of Dutch travel to the United States was the Great Lakes region, which, in addition to West Coast settlements, was home to many Dutch immigrants. Émigré ties between the United States and the Netherlands began to fade in the 1980s, as the immigrating generation gave way to a more Americanized generation. In some Calvinist circles, a transatlantic divide also became apparent in a theological sense, as the once orthodox Reformed churches in the Netherlands adopted stances (perhaps most notably in respect to sexuality) that alienated their more traditionally minded coreligionists in North America. Dutch communities in the Midwest — and elsewhere — continued to celebrate

943

6

—

THE
COLD WAR
AND
BEYOND

1945–2009

—

CULTURE

944

their ethnic heritage, and Queen Beatrix celebrated with them in 1982. But the absence of any new influx of Dutch immigrants served in effect to diminish the importance and vitality of these ties.

Yet, this gradual distancing could not counter a larger trend in American-Dutch cultural relations. Precisely because of the extent of cultural Americanization in Western Europe and in the Netherlands more particularly, the Dutch and Americans increasingly shared discourses about social and cultural ideals, largely shaped by democratic ideals, consumerism, and individual notions of freedom — however much some Americans viewed Dutch drugs and euthanasia policies with suspicion. As the Cold War faded away, in fact, the Dutch arguably became even more influenced by American cultural ideals, though less in "high" cultures of the arts, literature, and the social sciences than in more popular outlets such as media and tourism.

A Sustained but Diffuse Interaction (1990s)

The fall of the Berlin Wall and the collapse of the Soviet Union had profound effects on Dutch-American cultural relations, for it also meant, though not so dramatically, a slow implosion of the Atlantic Alliance. The energy that the American government had given to strong cultural ties with the Netherlands in the Reagan years now had lost its rationale; the common enemy had been defeated. As Scott-Smith notes, the USIA was disbanded in 1999, and American cultural diplomacy in Europe flagged as Americans cast their eyes on China and the Pacific Rim. The creation of the European Union in 1992 further prompted the Dutch, for all their continued Atlanticism, to invest more in Europe.

At the same time, the end of the Cold War removed many of the tensions between the United States and Western Europe. The slow receding of the welfare state, coupled with a neoliberal embrace of the market in many countries of Western Europe, helped bring the Netherlands and the United States even more closely together, politically, economically, and culturally. McDonalds and Disney, two symbols associated with America, made further inroads into European societies in this decade. The end of the Soviet Union further enhanced the use of English in commerce and intellectual life, a trend in which the Dutch, already used to speaking English, actively participated. Within the Netherlands, English became more pervasive than ever before, not only on television and in new media such as internet, but also in the literature that the Dutch purchased. Hollywood became even more dominant than it had been; American films took some 80 percent of the Dutch movie market in recent decades.

But these two examples — the widespread use of English and the dominance of Hollywood — illustrate the problem in identifying the cultural trends of the last two decades as *American* influences. "There is hardly a non-English-speaking country where as many English-language books are sold as in the Netherlands," Van der Bent and Mourits conclude, "[but] it is the *language* that is the factor, not the country of origin." American authors have had to compete with other Anglophone writers in the Dutch market. In a similar vein, Dutch film in particular and European film in general should not be seen in opposition to Hollywood, but as a cinema that views "Hollywood [as] its principal frame of reference," Jaap Kooijman writes, a reference that "can be mimicked or mocked, reinforced or challenged." Seen this way, Dutch film is itself transnational or, for the sake of this volume, transatlantic, itself selectively appropriating "Hollywood." Like Dutch pop music, Dutch filmmaking produced its own sort of music all the while relying on American elements.

In summary, one may say that American influence has come to take a central place in Dutch artistic and commercial culture, as is certainly evident in the mass media. But what did this mean in fields where ideas and practices could no longer identifiably be tied to a point of origin? At the very least, the Dutch had appropriated forms of thought and practice that were amalgams of concepts drawn from multiple sources.

And none of this meant that the cultural convergence was total, of course. Americans remained astonished at what they saw as freewheeling Dutch ways; Jonathan Blank's *Sex Drugs and Democracy* (1994) was lyrical over libertine Holland; more conservative critics were just as critical. There were a couple of ways in which the two countries were particularly estranged from each other in the 1990s, namely in the role of religion and ethnicity. Until the 1960s, Dutch church-going rates had been somewhat higher than those of the Americans, but the rapid decline of religion in the Netherlands and other parts of Western Europe thereafter led to the broad perception that Americans were too religious, a critique that had existed for longer among secular leftist intellectuals. "Christian America" was not a part of the United States that most Dutch felt much sympathy for, particularly its more political manifestations. But Dutch orthodox Protestants, now long influenced by American evangelicalism, continued to look to the United States for models, including those of "church growth," which some hoped to apply in the Netherlands. But here, too, as in cinema, Dutch evangelicals were developing their own paths and their own styles, borrowing not only from American but from British evangelicalism as well — an indication that American sources of inspiration had become more diffuse.

Race and ethnicity long had been preoccupying concerns for Americans, and the eruption of "culture wars" in the 1980s but especially the 1990s was a seemingly unending debate over the merits of "multiculturalism," as Jaap Verheul outlines. It was also a debate that did not in those years find much resonance in the Netherlands, Verheul remarks, showing that "multiculturalism"

945

6

—

THE
COLD WAR
AND
BEYOND

1945–2009

—

CULTURE

in the Netherlands looked very much like the pillarization of foregone years, in which each subgroup was accorded subsidies to maintain its own subcultural life. The conflicts in the United States over such matters were hardly attractive in the Netherlands, where — at least in the eyes of many — immigration and integration were better regulated. There was, however, growing dissent over the Dutch approach, but the political and cultural effects of this dissent would largely express themselves in the new century.

A Relationship Requiring Reinvestment
(Early Twenty-First Century)

The attacks on the Pentagon and on the World Trade Center in 2001 seemed initially to galvanize Western Europe and North America together, bound together in the War on Terror. But soon political divisions erupted over the course of that struggle, and though there was an intensified intergovernmental cooperation, many Americans and many Dutch saw the political divisions as rooted in a cultural divide. As Kroes argues, the Dutch could not be classified in the early years of this century as "anti-American" though their disapproval of the United States went beyond their dislike of George Bush; they thought, for example, the Americans too religious — an increasing and structural cultural source of attention between the United States and Europe.[7] Americans in turn had their suspicions of Dutch resolve in the face of radical Islam, as Verheul outlines in his contribution. The murder of Theo van Gogh by an Islamic radical and perceived Dutch indifference toward the plight of Ayaan Hirsi Ali, the Dutch parliamentarian who warned the public about the ostensible dangers of Islam, seemed to underscore this suspicion among many Americans.[8]

In some ways, the new century seemed to usher in a new isolationism in both countries, as both the Dutch and the Americans focused on problems within their societies. Certainly it seems plausible to argue that the Dutch, more than they had for a long time, chose to focus on social and moral cohesion in their own country, and on the question of how to order Islam within Dutch society. At the same time, many Dutch felt that they might have something to learn from the United States, where, at least in the view of influential observers like Paul Scheffer, immigrants had been successfully "integrated" into society.[9] Now uncertain of their own model, Verheul notes, the Dutch looked to American models for answers. But Americans were not only critical of the Netherlands, but interested to see whether European countries — and perhaps most particularly the historically "tolerant" Netherlands — would successfully be able to negotiate the new social challenges that beset them. More than had been the case in the 1990s, when Dutch drugs and euthanasia policy drew the attention, American social scientists poured into the Netherlands, eager to investigate how the Dutch were coping with these challenges.

One might well wonder how important this new interest was in a context where the two countries (and the two continents) seemed to be drifting further apart. Immigration to the United States had for some decades no longer primarily come from Europe, but from other parts of the globe. Dutch towns in the American Midwest received plenty of new immigrants, but they were now not from the Netherlands, but from Mexico or further south. The focus for most Americans, Latino or non-Latino, was not aimed at Europe; the arrival of immigrants to the Netherlands from Asia and Africa arguably had the effect of making the Dutch cultural gaze less transatlantic. At the very least, it was another important indication that the cultural exchange between the United States and the Netherlands was itself subject to new influences and traditions that extended far beyond the relationship as defined by Western European and European-American cultural exchange.

In any event, this continental drift was also expressed by other developments. The European Union offered financial inducements for international cultural activity within Europe at a scale that dwarfed cultural ties across the Atlantic. This dynamic was worsened by the continued lack of American government support for cultural exchange; U.S. government cultural programming for Europe was slashed, and the American studies programs were ever more dependent on the whims of university policy, universities that for decades had regarded them with some ambivalence, as Scott-Smith notes. But the problem of maintaining a healthy cultural exchange was not only dependent on American foreign policy. As Stokvis shows in his essay on dance, the unwillingness of the American government to financially underwrite its own cultural institutions (such as dance ensembles) has made it difficult for better-financed Dutch organizations to maintain structured ties with their American counterparts. In this way, the problem of maintaining close transatlantic cultural ties is a deep one, dependent as it is on the willingness of government and private donors to support cultural initiatives in general. The arrival of the Henry Hudson year in 2009 was impetus to renew cultural and economic ties between the two countries, but the more important question is to what extent such an impetus will lead to lasting, revitalized cultural connections.

No one can deny that American cultural influence on the Netherlands has been significant, and no one can deny that the cultural ties between the two countries have generated a long legacy. But who, or what, will carry these ties into the future? In some ways, both nations are less interested in sustaining the old transatlantic connections, an ambivalence possibly heightened by critical Dutch views of their American ally. Perhaps the Dutch have Americanized enough on their own without necessarily having to look to the U.S. for further

947

inspiration, even if "America" as a cultural ideal remains alive. In any event, the financial supports for giving structure to the cultural relationship have fallen on hard times, certainly in respect to American investment in transatlantic exchange. The relationship will continue to be forged by countless networks, by the popular media, by millions of travelers, and by an Anglophone Dutch society. But the tight, structured relationship of a superpower and a willing ally seems a thing of the past.

6
———

THE
COLD WAR
AND
BEYOND

1945–2009

———

CULTURE

1 See, for a discussion of both Ulf Hannerz's notion of creolization and Reyner Banham's notion of mediation Rob Kroes, *If you've Seen One, you've Seen the Mall: Europeans and American Mass Culture* (Urbana: University of Illinois Press, 1996), 162-178.

2 Mel van Elteren, "Werken op zijn 'Amerikaans.' Anglo-Amerikaanse invloeden op de arbeids- en organisatie-wetenschappen in Nederland (1945–1980)," *Sociale Wetenschappen* 4 (1993): 7; David W. Ellwood, "Introduction: Historical Methods and Approaches," in David W. Ellwood and Rob Kroes, eds., *Hollywood in Europe: Experiences of a Cultural Hegemony* (Amsterdam, vu University Press, 1994), 13.

3 Frank Inklaar, "Veramerikaniseert Nederland?," in Frank Inklaar et al., *Kijken naar Amerika. Twintigste-eeuwse Amerikaanse cultuur in de Verenigde Staten en in Nederland* (Heerlen: s.n., 2000), 98.

4 Natalie Scholz, 'The "Modern Home" during the 1950s: West German Cultural Reconstruction and the Ambivalent Meanings of Americanization," *Tijdschrift voor Geschiedenis* 121.3 (2008): 298-299.

5 Inklaar, "Veramerikaniseert Nederland?," 111.

6 Tity de Vries, "Hoe Nederland in de ban van Amerika raakte," in Inklaar et al., *Kijken naar Amerika*, 90-91.

7 Ronald Havenaar, "Religie en moraal. Amerika en Europa van de 20ste naar de 21ste eeuw," *Tijdschrift voor Geschiedenis* 121.3 (2008): 271-283.

8 Bruce Bawer lived in Amsterdam for a while and became alarmed at what he saw as the soft stance of the Dutch toward radical Islam; See his *When Europe Slept: How Radical Islam is Destroying the West from Within* (New York: Random House, 2006).

9 Paul Scheffer, *Het land van aankomst* (Amsterdam: De Bezige Bij, 2007).

DUTCH IMPRESSIONS
OF AMERICA

——

ROB KROES

In a 1941 editorial in *Life* magazine, Henry Luce heralded the American Century, presaging a period of United States international preeminence in pursuit of a mission with the "triumphal purpose of freedom."[1] The term he coined for a new era in history was universally adopted to refer to America's place on the global stage after World War II. Militarily, economically, and culturally, America had become a world power with a profound influence on other countries. The neo-conservative foreign policy wonks who formed the Project for a New American Century think tank in the 1990s were set on prolonging their country's role in the world into the twenty-first century. Their voice rang out in George W. Bush's administration, not least in the president's vaunted claim that "freedom is on the march" in Iraq, thanks to the American invasion.[2] But what the American intrusion in the Middle East has set in motion might not be quite the same as a triumphal advance of freedom. Around the world, America's plummeting reputation has resembled a stock market crash. The U.S. has unceremoniously jettisoned much of the symbolic capital it accumulated through the years of the Cold War, and which, to use Joseph Nye's term, it had used in wielding its "soft power,"[3] i.e., its capacity to provide an enlightened example to others so that they then voluntarily wanted what the U.S. wanted. However, the Bush administration's actions have served to revive anti-Americanism worldwide.[4] Instead of the American Century, some are now seeing the prospect of an Anti-American Century.[5]

There has been a flood of books about anti-Americanism in recent years. Stunned by the September 11 terrorist attacks on U.S. targets in 2001, there was initially much searching for an answer to "why do they hate us?" The question acquired new urgency after America responded to Islamic terrorism by invading Afghanistan and, shortly afterwards, Iraq. These actions stirred up ill feeling well beyond the Islamic world. Both the high-handed, unilateral push for the invasion of Iraq, disregarding allies, international law, and international organi-

6

———

THE
COLD WAR
AND
BEYOND

1945–2009

———

CULTURE

zations such as the UN, and the lawlessness apparent in the treatment of opponents who were humiliated in Abu Ghraib or detained without trial in Guantánamo and elsewhere, have persuaded many that America has come adrift from its moral anchor. Despite the high-minded rhetoric of spreading democracy and freedom, America's actual performance appeared to many to exhibit an unbridled exercise of power: self-willed, and unconstrained by law, constitution, or international treaties.

Is it actually always valid to view international protests against these tendencies as signs of anti-Americanism? The protest can be gauged in terms of expressive action, such as burning the American flag, demonstrations, kidnapping and murdering American citizens, and storming U.S. consulates and embassies. And for feelings that remain unexpressed, we have for many years been able to estimate international disapproval through opinion polls. But often, regardless of whether actions or passive opinions are involved, the expressions of indignation have a precise cause, and a specific address. Longitudinal surveys in particular, such as the admirable Pew Global Attitudes Survey, show that recent indignation focuses on the actions of the Bush administration. Opinions about America and the American people appear to be surprisingly untainted by the U.S. government's actions. A different president and a different foreign policy could persuade many to change their minds on American politics, as demonstrated by the enthusiastic reactions to the election of Barack Obama. In such cases anti-Americanism is a misleading term. To the extent that it is used, it often serves an argumentative purpose to dismiss protest and accusation as predictable emotional outbursts from people for whom America never can do anything right anyway.

Researchers seeking a more refined understanding of censorious or critical attitudes vis-à-vis the United States, and of the resilience of these attitudes, would be well advised to avoid reference to anti-Americanism. The term has the inherent danger of reification, suggesting that it is an unvarying phenomenon wherever in the world it appears. According to scientific research, a favorable consequence of the upsurge of protest against and resistance to America's foreign policy since 9/11 is the view that the country's current loss of global status is just an episode in a longer history of assimilating U.S. conduct in the world. This assimilation displays a pattern of rational and understandable response. Recent studies by sociologists and historians make us aware that attitudes toward America differ consistently in accordance with the specific historical context in which America's power and influence were experienced. Latin America's collective memories of U.S. conduct in the region are different from those of countries in the Far East, the Middle East, the former Soviet Union, or Western Europe.

Another systematic insight that is emerging more clearly from recent studies pertains to the multidimensional nature, or the semantic polyvalence, of impressions of America and its influence on and power over others. This influence or power affects spheres of culture, economics, politics, and military potential. Certainly since World War II, with America's rise as a world power, people throughout the world have been confronted with these aspects of America's presence and have questioned its justification. Some have done so through systematic rejection, allowing cultural repertoires to develop to help people define their national identities as a counterpoint to aspects of the U.S.'s unfurling across the world. But by no means all reactions were simply about nations forming closed blocks against undesirable aspects of America's influence. Internal fault lines invariably appear on the receiving side, between generations, classes, or minority groups who tend to polarize in internal debate, claiming America's presence to be desirable or undesirable. Young people in Europe, for instance, in their emancipation from parental authority, embraced some forms of American mass culture in opposition to established guardians of culture. But at the same time, wearing T-shirts and jeans, they would demonstrate against an American foreign policy in which they detected signs of political imperialism. Thus, they were culturally pro-American and politically anti-American.[6]

Although the word anti-Americanism suggests that the observations and judgments are concerned with all of America, as a homogenized notion, subtle questioning in international comparative opinion polls conducted in recent years shows that people are perfectly capable of distinguishing between American thinking, the Americans as a people, and American government action. Furthermore, recent international comparative historical surveys have shown that large groups within American society often share critical opinions held by foreigners about America. Sometimes, as in the international anti-Vietnam protests, demonstrators may be aware of this fact and derive a campaigning style and slogans directly from the American example. In other cases, as is now common in expressions of indignation about the war in Iraq, this aspect tends to be forgotten and all Americans are viewed as tarred with the same brush. This is a bias on which serious observers of anti-American expression cannot focus too much attention.

Longer Lines of "Anti-Americanism" in the Netherlands

If anti-Americanism is a multidimensional phenomenon, it has become so largely since World War II. Only then did the United States emerge as a world power, while other countries found themselves outclassed in power. European countries, once prominent on the world stage, were obliged for the first time to adopt a dependent stance in a new international order called the *Pax Ameri-*

951

cana. This new experience of America's power added a political dimension to the image being formed about the country. Resentment of these trends was translated into a discourse of political anti-Americanism. In an economic sense as well, former superpowers were pushed aside to make way for America's advance. Sometimes, out of enlightened self-interest, they would willingly accede to the new economic order and gratefully accept the new American leadership, as they did with the Marshall Plan. But in this respect, too, a critical discourse has developed, which might be called economic anti-Americanism.

We also encounter an aspect of European anti-Americanism — resistance to the threat of cultural Americanization — that before the war had actually been the main theme in European thinking about America's significance. Cultural anti-Americanism had already developed in the nineteenth century in prominent European intellectual circles.[7] Their objections might involve harsh denigration, as repeatedly exemplified by France, but more usually they were balanced assessments of American cultural "difference."[8] The Netherlands occupies a place of its own in this European pattern. Even before World War I, many Dutch people had traveled to America and reported their findings in a mixture of admiration, astonishment, and aversion.[9] Dutch thinking about America in the interwar years was expressed pointedly in the work of Menno ter Braak and Johan Huizinga.[10]

Against the background of all the social and political disruption, the concept of Americanism came into vogue as a tool for diagnosing Europe's situation. The instinct for self-confirmation in a focused attempt to find sense and meaning in the stained pages of European history was cultural and conservative. It was also an expression of challenging protest. The discussion in nearby European countries became more heated than in the Netherlands, with Germans even engaging in what they called an *Amerikanismus Debatte.*[11] But in all these countries the cultural criticism of the United States was supported by a culturally conservative elite. Other circles meanwhile entertained a cheerful acceptance of many forms of American mass culture in its initial triumphal advance in Europe. It was actually this breakthrough that formed a potential threat, prompting cultural guardians to reflect urgently on America as a cultural counterpoint. Even then, young people in European countries could serve as a Trojan horse for America's mass-culture invasion, soon forming camps with conflicting orientations on America that are still discernible today.

If we were to draw a diagram, we would see two pairings of pro and anti sentiment. One is an anti-Americanism that rejects cultural developments under

953

◄ Pro-America demonstration in 1968 [top]. Anti-America demonstration in the 1980s [bottom].

American auspices, combined with respect for America's energy, refreshing zest, "can do" attitude, and democratic vitality. Then there is a contrasting anti-Americanism that rails against an American political messianism that, despite its fervor, cannot avoid being perceived as imperialistic and oppressive, while simultaneously valuing America's culture, in all its variants from "highbrow" to "pop." Especially after World War II, when America emerged more clearly as a political power factor in Europe, these two anti-Americanism varieties could be seen to turn somersaults. As was pointed out, the cultural anti-Americanism of the interwar years was typically a conservative position, and would remain so, whereas the political anti-Americanism was typically a left-wing position after the war. On the right we find support for America's new role on the world stage as political orchestrator combined with an elitist contempt of America's culture, while on the left there is resistance to an America that preceded Europe in its Cold War policy, accompanied by receptiveness for America's mass culture.

This reordering in the Atlantic world took place in the late 1940s and 1950s, in what could be called the honeymoon in the relationship between America and western Europe. However, the complete reorientation in this period forced groups on the left in the Netherlands to make an "agonizing reappraisal," leading to yet another ambivalent anti-Americanism variant. These groups refused to go along with the emerging Cold War thinking, nostalgically recalling the anti-Nazi alliance with the Soviet Union. This was a company of "fellow travelers," supporters of the "Third Way," and Christian pacifists, who united in their orientation to America with like-minded people in the United States, themselves branded as "un-American" and liable to be put on trial in the McCarthy years. The solidarity felt by the Dutch groups with these persecuted people was the final thread binding them in their anti-Americanism with America.

The historian Jacques Presser tellingly exemplifies this intellectual balancing act. As a Jew who had gone into hiding during the war he wrote the first draft of *Amerika: Van kolonie tot wereldmacht* (America: from colony to world power), even though he did not have the necessary research tools at his disposal. The first edition appeared in 1949, displaying an America viewed through a picaresque lens, as a country of cheerful crooks and villains. It is evident nonetheless that America must have been a source of hope and inspiration for Presser in hiding, and there is repeated praise for the ideals that inspired these Americans. He would not lose this affinity with a high-minded America, even after the painful witch-hunt of the McCarthy years. He did not go so far as to deny his affinity with the American Dream, but merely placed it with those who had disowned America, a trick that turned the accusation of "un-Americanism" against America itself. In Presser's view, people such as the Rosenbergs now represented the American cultural inheritance, which for them — and Presser quotes them literally —

954

meant "freedom, culture, and human decency." Presser thus preserved a precarious balance in his feelings for America and was also able to conclude the later edition of his popular book with praise for the American Dream, as threatened, in peril, and even impossible, as it might be.

Presser and this Atlantic-spanning league of radical dissenters were a minority. As a whole, the Netherlands at the time had no need for their tricks. The American Committee for Cultural Freedom in 1952 assessed the Netherlands as the most pro-American country in Europe.[12] Within the North Atlantic Treaty Organization (NATO), the Netherlands was the most faithful ally, with broad support across the political spectrum from social democracy to right-wing liberalism.[13] It was not until the late 1960s that the critical stance of a left-wing minority of "radical dissenters" became commonplace and set the tone in the media, public opinion, and public expressions of anti-American protest. The Vietnam War was the most important catalyst.[14] Measured against its lofty ideals of freedom and democracy, America in its internal affairs and foreign policy was considered substandard. The Nixon era and the Watergate scandal confirmed this critical view. Gradually, people in the Netherlands and elsewhere in Europe started to perceive links with America as onerous, and a need arose to establish a clearer profile for national and European interests.

This was evident most plainly in the cruise missile debate around 1980. By deploying cruise and Pershing II missiles, NATO had responded strategically to the Soviet Union's targeting of Europe with medium-range missiles. Originally, European politicians pressed President Carter to act, and his assent was wavering. But the public perception was of an American initiative, with the suspicion that it was a ploy to deflect the threat of nuclear war from America to Europe. Broad-based anti-cruise-missile and peace movements rapidly formed in the Netherlands, and they organized demonstrations in 1981 and 1983 that attracted approximately half a million people, followed in 1985 by a public petition with four million signatures. Some American observers interpreted this as a trend toward neutralism and an expression of anti-Americanism. Yet, figures on public opinion gathered at the time by market research institute NIPO do not confirm that view, even though more than half the respondents saw themselves in 1983 as neutral rather than pro- or anti-American. Only after some urging ("If you had to choose, which option would it be: pro- or anti-American?") did 71.5 percent say they were pro-American.[15]

Also in 1983, the Netherlands Foundation for Statistics (NSS) published figures that could augment this view.[16] As a group, young people (from eighteen to thirty years of age) at the time had a more negative image of America than people over the age of thirty. There was a general awareness that attitudes of the Dutch toward the United States had recently turned more negative. This was mainly attributed to American policy in the areas of peace and security.

955

6

—

THE
COLD WAR
AND
BEYOND

1945–2009

—

CULTURE

Dutch people had a pronounced preference for countries in Europe that were neutral, such as Switzerland, Sweden, or Austria. The sense of involvement in American policy was relatively low and had not increased since 1981. The NSS concluded that this was a sign that the measured opinions were fairly superficial and unstable. Those who felt more involved (a minority of 15 percent) were substantially more negative in their attitudes toward the United States. They might have been a group in which anti-Americanism was more firmly anchored.

Answers to one question in particular appeared to support the view that Europe and America were drifting apart psychologically in the early 1980s. When asked to rank America, the Soviet Union, and the Federal Republic of Germany according to a number of criteria (peace policies and disarmament, human rights, foreign policy, and the social climate in each of the three countries), respondents presented the following picture. For each criterion, half of the response was favorable toward the Federal Republic of Germany, while both the United States (with scores varying from 19 to 31 percent) and the Soviet Union (with scores between 2 and 14 percent) lagged far behind. The respondents were able to identify with the Federal Republic of Germany, but not, or no longer, with the United States or the Soviet Union. It was as if there had been a kind of mental separation from the United States, along with a need for a new solidarity with countries closer to home: a new Europe groping to find its own identity (which it still is). Opinion figures mentioned at the beginning of this article still reflect this need for distance from America. There is more room now for critical public debate on what America means for the Netherlands and Europe, but there is no reason to see this as a sign of anti-Americanism.

The Netherlands in the Picture

Recent research has shown that the Netherlands, in its current patterns of perception of America, illustrates this more balanced image well. Although in individual cases aversion to America's actions in its self-chosen War on Terror may color the overall perception and possibly lead to a more general rejection, statistics do not suggest that this is happening across the board.[17] In 2005, 45 percent of the Dutch population had a favorable image of the United States, which is a slightly higher proportion than for the populations of France, Germany, or Spain, but about 10 percentage points lower than in the United Kingdom. This is a low figure historically, which, as elsewhere, is attributable to the actions of the Bush administration. The Dutch viewed countries such as Germany, France, Japan, and China (in that order) considerably more favorably. When asked how well, in their opinion, American foreign policy took the interests of others into consideration, only 20 percent of Dutch persons gave a favorable rating, which is comparable with the low scores in Canada, France, Spain, Russia, and Poland, but lower than those in the United Kingdom and Germany. When questioned about their impressions of Americans, a large majority in the Netherlands considered them to be hard workers, resourceful, violent, greedy, and fewer than half thought Americans were honest, coarse, or immoral. A majority, as in France, considered them to be excessively religious; the figure for other countries in Europe was not higher than 40 percent. When asked what exactly America's problem is, 63 percent of Dutch persons stated that it was "mostly Bush," with 30 percent saying "America in general," which are figures that are consistent with the measurements in Germany, France, and the United Kingdom. A minority of Dutch people (39 percent) expressed confidence in Bush, compared with 65 percent for Blair and 67 percent for Chirac. To the question "where to go to lead a good life," the United States came in first only in India. The Dutch preference was for Australia or Canada.

Compared with the image of the United States as a political power, the Dutch appear to attach a substantially higher value to Americans as a people (66 percent). This proportion is consistent with that in other European countries. No statistics are available for the Netherlands in earlier years. For the other countries investigated, the measured assessment of the American people has exhibited a decline since 2002, even in comparison with the years before 9/11. Therefore it is not inconceivable that the figure for the Netherlands has fallen likewise. Regarding opinions on the formation of America's foreign policy, there appears to be a dearth of democratic expectations among respondents in all investigated countries. The Netherlands still has a relatively high score, with 14 percent attributing influence to "ordinary Americans" on U.S. foreign policy. Aside from differences of emphasis, other European countries, like the Americans themselves, appear to be in step in terms of influence on American foreign policy. Americans achieve the highest score for the influence of news media (40 percent), while only 13 percent attribute influence to average Americans.

Sober images of this kind do not appear to have prevented a majority of the Dutch population (59 percent) from concluding in 2005 that the use of armed force was justified in the war in Iraq, or, more generally, in the War on Terror. At the same time, however, 62 percent considered the world to have become more dangerous without Saddam Hussein. Nonetheless, the American-led War on Terror could count on the support of 71 percent of the Dutch population, which was by far the highest score in Europe, and only 5 percent behind support for the war from Americans themselves.

The most surprising refutation of common misconceptions about widespread anti-Americanism in the Netherlands, as a country that has lost all confidence and withdrawn all support for any U.S. action, is provided by the follow-

957

6

———

THE
COLD WAR
AND
BEYOND

1945–2009

———

CULTURE

958

ing figures. The 2005 parliamentary elections in Iraq led to a more favorable image of American policy in hardly any of the investigated countries. Only in the Netherlands and Germany did 55 and 50 percent, respectively, say that they had had a positive influence. Again, the only countries in Europe in which a majority was favorably inclined toward America's actions after President Bush's repeated calls for more democracy in the Middle East were Germany (50 percent) and the Netherlands (55 percent). The conclusion is plain: even in these early years of what some are labeling the "Anti-American Century," Dutch people's views about America's intentions and actions appear too well balanced to justify viewing the Netherlands as an anti-American country.

1   This article has been adapted from a larger version published in Dutch: "Antiamerikanisme in Nederland," *Sociologie* 4.2/3 (2008): 271-285. For the quotation see H.R. Luce, "The American Century," reprinted in M.J. Hogan, ed., *The Ambiguous Legacy* (Cambridge: Cambridge University Press, 1999).

2   http://www.defenselink.mil/news/newsarticle.aspx?id=24241.

3   Joseph S. Nye, Jr., *Soft Power: The Means to Success in World Politics* (New York: Public Affairs, 2004).

4   For comprehensive information on this subject, see The Pew Global Attitudes Project, June 23, 2005, www.pewglobal.org.

5   Ivan Krastev, "The Anti-American Century?," *Journal of Democracy* 15.2 (April 2004): 5-16; Julia Sweig, *Friendly Fire: Losing Friends and Making Enemies in the Anti-American Century* (Washington, DC: Council on Foreign Relations, 2006).

6   Recent studies include Peter J. Katzenstein and Robert O. Keohane, eds., *Anti-Americanisms in World Politics* (Ithaca, NY: Cornell University Press, 2007); David Farber, ed., *What They Think of Us: International Perceptions of the United States since 9/11* (Princeton, NJ: Princeton University Press, 2007); Andrew Ross and Kristin Ross, eds., *Anti-Americanism* (New York: New York University Press, 2004); Toni Judt and Denis Lacorne, eds., *With Us or Against Us: Studies in Global Anti-Americanism* (Basingstoke: Palgrave MacMillan, 2005).

7   R.W. Rydell and Rob Kroes, *Buffalo Bill in Bologna: The Americanization of the World, 1869–1922* (Chicago: University of Chicago Press, 2005).

8   Philippe Roger, *L'ennemi américain: Généalogie de l'antiaméricanisme français* (Paris: Editions du Seuil, 2002).

9   A. Lammers, *Uncle Sam en Jan Salie: Hoe Nederland Amerika ontdekte* (Amsterdam: Balans, 1989).

10   As described in Cornelis A. van Minnen's article, elsewhere in this volume, in the section on the interwar years.

11   For a survey of the points of view in these discussions, see Rob Kroes, *If You've Seen One, You've Seen the Mall: Europeans and American Mass Culture* (Urbana/Chicago: University of Illinois Press, 1996), 1-42; Rob Kroes, "French Views of American Modernity: From Text to Subtext," in Michael Kazin and Joseph A. McCartin, eds., *Americanism: New Perspectives on the History of an Ideal* (Chapel Hill: University of North Carolina Press, 2006), 221-242; Unlike what Philippe Roger would have us believe, French intellectuals were not universally inclined to anti-American views.

12 See Marja Roholl, "Uncle Sam: An Example for All? The Dutch Orientation towards America in the Social and Cultural Field, 1945–1965," in Hans Loeber, ed., *Dutch-American Relations, 1945–1969* (Assen/Maastricht: Van Gorcum, 1992), 147.

13 Alfred van Staden, *Een trouwe bondgenoot: Nederland en het Atlantisch Bondgenootschap (1960-1971)* (Baarn: Anthos, 1974); See also the articles by Rimko van der Maar and Hans Righolt, elsewhere in this volume.

14 For a summary of the changing attitude to America in the press, see Rob Kroes, "The Great Satan versus the Evil Empire: Anti-Americanism in the Netherlands," in Rob Kroes and Maarten van Rossem, eds., *Anti-Americanism in Europe* (Amsterdam: Free University Press, 1986), 42-46.

15 Koen Koch, "Anti-Americanism and the Dutch Peace Movement," in ibid., 97-112.

16 *Opinie-analyse: Hoe anti-Amerikaans zijn wij?* (The Hague: Nederlandse Stichting voor Statistiek, 1983).

17 R. Kroes, "European Anti-Americanism: What's New?" *The Journal of American History* 93 (September 2006): 417-432.

6

—

THE
COLD WAR
AND
BEYOND

1945–2009

—

CULTURE

960

ANNE FRANK IN THE UNITED STATES AND IN THE NETHERLANDS

—

DAVID BARNOUW

Introduction

The diary of Anne Frank should be regarded as the first link between Europe and the United States as the two continents came to terms with the Holocaust. Thanks to the American dramatization of her diary in 1955, Anne Frank became both an international icon and a kind of honorary American.

Anne Frank plays an important cultural role in the international memory of World War II, first as a symbol of suffering in general, later as a symbol of the extermination of six million Jews.[1] In addition, she was deployed as an instrument in bringing disparate social groups together. A case in point was the New York film premiere of *The Diary of Anne Frank* in April 1959, attended by important members of the African-American community as a means of signaling their solidarity with the Jewish community that had invested so much effort on their behalf in the American civil rights movement.[2]

For millions of Americans from the 1950s onward, the autobiography of Anne Frank as related in *The Diary of a Young Girl* was the first and sometimes only book they read about the persecution of the Jews. Most read the book as teenagers, for whom it represented the story of a high-spirited girl whose energetic personality pulled her through moments of despondency. With a main character like this, a supporting cast of self-sacrificing helpers, and the setting of a small, innocent country that was being assaulted and subjugated by its big, bad German neighbor, the book became a standard of juvenile literature and found its way into many school curricula.

The uplifting message was even more pronounced in the play. In a narrative that intermingled the good and the bad, theater audiences ultimately saw goodness prevail. At the end of the play, the character of Anne Frank pronounces that "[in] spite of everything, I still believe that people are really good at heart." This dramatized ending was a far better fit for the typically optimistic Broadway script than her incomplete diary or an accurate rendering of her death would have been.

The Broadway Anne would continue to have a definitive impact on understanding the real Anne up until the end of the twentieth century; the play was to be performed by thousands of high school students, and millions of Americans would pay a visit to "the place where it all happened" in Amsterdam. And it is thanks to this Broadway version, too, that Anne Frank assumed a prominent position in the United States long before she attained a similar status in the Netherlands.

Anne Frank's Position in the Netherlands

Until the 1980s, Anne Frank's role in the Dutch memory of World War II was all but nonexistent. The country was preoccupied with postwar reconstruction efforts and decolonization, and had to come to terms with its new position in a changed international context that required it to shed its neutrality and become an active Atlantic ally. On the one hand, many people simply wanted to put the war as far behind them as possible, as was obvious in a January 1947 protest published in the former resistance newspaper *Het Parool* against a discount offer of "a full fifty percent" on antiwar publications.[3] On the other hand, the memory of the war was still so fresh that those who wanted to learn more only had to ask their parents or grandparents; they did not need *Het Achterhuis* (the secret annex), as Anne Frank's autobiography was entitled in Dutch.

Initially this book functioned in the Netherlands, too, to fulfill a psychological need to remember "the gruesome choice faced by so many Jewish families: to let themselves be deported like sheep following a 'call,' or to go into hiding," as described in the introduction to the first edition in 1947. The diary was "a war document also, a document of the savagery and awful misfortune of the persecution of the Jews, of human charity and betrayal ... ." More important, however, was "that single vital quality of the great writer ... : an open mind."

The first critical reviews of the diary were positive, calling it "a *document humain* of great lucidity and honesty" and "a moving human document." And yet it was "in no way a war document as such ... but purely and simply the diary of an adolescent girl." Another critic saw in her "the symbol of her and those like her, who were murdered by the Germans." Of course for "her and those like her" we should read "Jews," but this term, like "persecution of the Jews," remained unspoken; these were words that belonged to that particularly pitch-black period of the occupation that had just passed and could not quite yet be named.

961

6

THE
COLD WAR
AND
BEYOND

1945–2009

CULTURE

The persecution of the Jews merely set the scene in which the youthful writer operated.

This categorization helped ensure that *Het Achterhuis* for decades remained — in the Netherlands at least — a girls' book with only limited distribution: with two editions published in 1947, another two in 1948, and one in 1949 and 1950 each, demand for the book was filled for five years. From 1955 onward, however, came a never-ending series of reprints — a development that was directly attributable to the phenomenal success of the play produced in America. Nevertheless, the book was still read primarily at home by teenage girls, who recognized a fellow adolescent in the person of Anne Frank. A special committee proposal to establish an Anne Frank monument was promptly rejected by the Jewish community, which saw no reason to place on Anne's shoulders "the full weight of Judaism in the Netherlands," as the Jewish weekly paper *Nieuw Israëlitisch Weekblad* wrote on November 23, 1956. In a footnote to the report, the paper added that committee members included "Stalinist communists" — reason enough, therefore, to be cautious. The monument came nonetheless: the Anne Frank Museum opened its doors at number 263 on the Prinsengracht in Amsterdam on May 3, 1960. For a long time, however, it remained by and large a destination for foreign tourists.[4]

From Book to Script

The intense American interest in Anne Frank resulted from positive reviews of *Het Achterhuis* and the successful stage adaptation of the book. While the book lent itself to subjective interpretation, the play represented a radical intervention that molded Anne into a collective image. A progressive series of scripts reflected changing perceptions of the fate that befell the Jews during World War II. The American novelist Meyer Levin (1905–81) took the initiative in creating the first stage adaptation. Working as a correspondent in Europe at the end of World War II, he had produced a report for the *Overseas Agency* in which he described what he had seen in the concentration camps of Dachau and Buchenwald. His subsequent conversion to Zionism owed much to these experiences. In addition to his journalistic activities, Levin wrote a large number of novels, several of which were made into movies. The position of the Jew in the Diaspora was a key theme in his work. In 1950–51 he read the then recently published French translation of *Het Achterhuis*. The book made a deep impression on him, and Anne Frank was to haunt him for the rest of his life.[5] In the November 13, 1950 review of J. Hersey's book *The Wall*, written for the American Jewish Congress publication *Congress Weekly*, he spoke of Anne Frank with great admiration. He told readers that he had contacted Anne's father: "Her father informed me that the book had been rejected by a whole series of eminent American publishers. ... Finally, one American publisher offered to bring out the Journal if a British publisher could be found to share translation and typesetting costs." The English translation of *Het Achterhuis* was published for the American market by Doubleday, where it was released under the title *Anne Frank: The Diary of a Young Girl*. The introduction was written by none other than Eleanor Roosevelt, the former U.S. first lady who had herself taken steps to strengthen ties with the Netherlands. Her introduction resonates with optimism:

> ... one of the wisest and most moving commentaries on war and its impact on human beings that I have ever read. Anne Frank's account of the changes wrought upon eight people hiding out from the Nazis for two years during the occupation of Holland, living in constant fear and isolation, imprisoned not only by the terrible outward circumstances of war but inwardly by themselves, made me intimately and shockingly aware of war's greatest evil — the degradation of the human spirit. ... Anne's diary is a fitting monument to her fine spirit and to the spiritual powers who have worked and are working still for peace. Reading this book is a rich and rewarding experience.[6]

Words and phrases like "Jewish" and "persecution of the Jews" appeared nowhere in this text: in the United States, as in the Netherlands, the persecution had not — or had not yet — assumed a pivotal place in the memory of the war.

Though the publisher was highly confident of the book's success, the first edition had a print run of a modest five thousand copies. This hesitancy was overturned with the critical acclaim the book received in Meyer Levin's review for the authoritative *New York Times Book Review*, on June 15, 1952. His characterization stating that "Anne Frank's voice becomes the voice of six million vanished [Jewish] souls" found a ready reception and soon made a second edition with a print run of fifteen thousand necessary, with a third edition issued in forty-five thousand copies following several days later.

In a second review, this time for *The National Jewish Post*, on June 30, 1952, Levin emphasized the imperative of dramatizing the book for the stage and cinema. Thanks in part to Levin's success in convincing Anne's father of his own single-handed role in effecting the book's publication in English, which was patently false, Otto Frank authorized Levin to act as his literary agent in getting a stage adaptation written for the American theater. Levin envisioned himself as more than a mere literary agent, however, and proceeded to write this adaptation himself. Yet when the time came to produce the play, he was forced to accept no more than a mediating role in its realization.

963

The Performance

6

————

THE
COLD WAR
AND
BEYOND

1945–2009

————

CULTURE

Kermit Bloomgarden, a producer who had won acclaim for his productions of works by the American writer Arthur Miller, among others, approached the husband and wife team Frances Goodrich and Albert Hackett in 1953 about creating a stage adaptation. The MGM film studios, where they were employed at the time, granted them a leave in order to write the script. It took eight versions before all eight of the story's characters in hiding were sufficiently fleshed out and before all parties concerned, including Otto Frank, were satisfied. Though Frank would later deny any direct involvement in the play's creation—he also claimed never to want to see the piece performed—he was in fact very much involved.[7] To enable them to get a direct sense of the surroundings, the writers and prospective director Garson Kanin traveled to Amsterdam, where they were given a tour of "the secret annex" in the Prinsengracht house. Furthermore, photographer Maria Austria was charged with documenting the whole of the interior on film. Discussions were held with the director of the Netherlands Institute for War Documentation, Dr. Lou de Jong, to prevent inadvertent historical errors.

On October 5, 1955, the play officially premiered in the Cort Theater in New York and proved a huge success, with 717 Broadway shows and much critical acclaim. The cast, the director, and Goodrich and Hackett raked in almost all the drama awards for the 1955–56 season. Critics writing in Dutch newspapers praised the play as well.

The diary's adaptation diverged considerably from the original. Hitler, national socialism, anti-Semitism, and Anne's Jewish background disappeared into the sidelines. Into central position came Otto Frank, whose role in the play exceeded what it had been in Anne's diary. The most negative role in the book had been reserved for Mr. van Pels, changed by Anne into Van Daan. In the play, this companion in the Franks' hideaway is caught stealing food on the eve of the Allied invasion of Normandy, upon which Anne's mother calls for him to leave. This scene occurs nowhere in the diaries and is in fact a dramatic addition concocted by the writers to enhance the contrast between the good and the bad guys living inside the secret annex, rather than between them and the evil world outside. European interest in the play grew in the wake of its New York success, with Sweden hosting the European premiere and Germany (West and East) following shortly thereafter. "The Diary of Anne Frank conquers Germany," announced a headline in the newspaper *Trouw*. Reactions varied from one place to another. The Berlin public filed from the theaters in silence, but in Karlsruhe and Dresden audiences clapped longer than for any other play ever, as an October 6, 1956 headline in the Dutch *Algemeen Handelsblad* newspaper reported almost triumphantly.

Reception in the Netherlands

The Dutch premiere came at the end of November 1956, in the De la Mar Theater in Amsterdam. The press raved, with headlines announcing: "Masterful interpretation by the Toneelgroep Theater," "Affecting performance," "Solemn premiere," and "Disquieting drama." The *Het Parool* critic stated on November 28, 1956, "I must confess that I have never before experienced such great and encompassing emotion in a playhouse before. There was no applause. The public, which included Queen Juliana and Prince Bernhard, Mayor d'Ailly and many other persons of authority, parted company without a word." The Dutch performance was acclaimed on all sides, its significance assuming all but sacred proportions. Anne had found a new public. Not only professional drama companies now organized performances every several years (May 4 being the favored date), but among amateur groups and at schools and universities around the world it ranked among the select group of most-frequently staged plays, though the cerebral character of the performances faded somewhat over the years.

The play was considered a monument—like Anne herself—and the Netherlands saw itself validated, also in the eyes of the world, as a brave nation. The version of Anne promulgated in the Netherlands from the mid-1950s on was the optimistic Broadway Anne. Otto Frank, resident of Switzerland since 1952, was undisturbed by this development; he was himself an advocate of emphasizing the good in people. The house on the Prinsengracht had become a destination for foreign visitors, who contributed little to Anne Frank's "Dutch" identity. And when public memory of the war resurfaced in the Netherlands of the 1960s, Anne Frank's role was of little note. From 1960 until 1965, Dutch television broadcast a series entitled *De Bezetting* (The occupation). The program, which drew huge audiences, had a script written by Dr. Lou de Jong and portrayed a small yet brave nation that suffered war and strife but always emerged on its feet. De Jong himself was the series' presenter and conducted interviews with many of the leading figures from the period of the German occupation, thereby stimulating widespread public interest in the topic. This interest intensified still further with the 1965 publication of the book *Ondergang: De vervolging en verdelging van het Nederlandse Jodendom, 1940–1945* (Destruction: The Persecution and Extermination of Dutch Jewry), written by the historian Jacques Presser and issued in high print runs. It was only now, twenty years later, that the full scope of the disaster was widely recognized by a larger public.

965

Queen Juliana, Prince Bernhard and actor R. de Vries at the premiere
of the *Diary of Anne Frank* in the Nieuwe de la Mar Theater in Amsterdam
on November 27, 1956.

The play's success led to the creation, in 1957, of the Anne Frank Foundation. Initially the foundation's main concern was to save the site of the secret annex on the Prinsengracht from collapse, though working to spread "the ideals of Anne Frank" was also an express motive. The dilapidated building on the Prinsengracht was purchased, using considerable private funding, renovated, and opened to visitors. But the Anne Frank Foundation envisioned something more and decided to commemorate its ten-year anniversary with the founding of the Anne Frank Academy, whose mission would be "to engage in international political training and international psychology." Finding the correct balance turned out to be a thorny issue, with an internal conflict arising over the question of the organization's identity — "pilgrimage site or training center" — early in 1969.

There was an ever-growing tendency to "flesh out" the pilgrimage site with exhibitions about race discrimination and contemporary injustice. The foundation itself was actively involved in the Netherlands' leftist movement, and thereby gained the reputation of being an ultra leftwing, antifascist organization. Its attitude toward the state of Israel proved another sensitive issue. In 1976 Amsterdam's Protestant Youth Council sought to organize a meeting in the Anne Frank House, to which the Palestina Komitee (Committee on Palestine) was invited, but the Werkgroep Israël (Working group Israel) was not. The board of directors of the Anne Frank Foundation intervened to prohibit the meeting, and though it subsequently was held elsewhere, the incident made it plain that the board, the trustees, and the staff did not see eye to eye. Yassar Arafat's visit to the house on the Prinsengracht with the mayor of Amsterdam more than twenty years later, by contrast, was no problem at all.

Incidents such as these made headlines, but formed no impediment to foreign tourists visiting the house. From 1979 onward an annual Anne Frank newspaper was distributed to tens of thousands of Dutch school children, its purpose being to bolster the "Dutch" side of Anne Frank. Her international side received a boost by means of various exhibitions presented in hundreds of countries. Only with the publication of an unabridged edition of her diaries in 1987 did people begin to take a greater interest in what Anne herself had actually written. Scholarly studies — originating in the U.S. in particular — considered such themes as the stage dramatization and Anne Frank's impact on conceptions of the Holocaust.[8] For half a century it was the "stage Anne" — more American and universal than Dutch — who would predominate, and it was not until the end of the twentieth century that she, very gradually, was "Dutchified." Dutch visitor numbers at the Anne Frank House increased considerably and contributed to the total of one million visitors in 2007.

967

6

—

THE
COLD WAR
AND
BEYOND

1945-2009

—

CULTURE

Shifting American Representations of Anne Frank

Meanwhile, Meyer Levin continued to insist that his dramatization had been rejected because it was "too Jewish" and contained too many religious Jewish and Zionist elements. Certainly these elements would have appealed little to Otto Frank. More to the point, however, they had played almost no part at all in the original diary. Levin's criticism concerning Goodrich and Hackett's "de-Judaization" and "universalization" of the diary was — and still is — shared by many, but whether his version would have come any closer to the original and would have enjoyed as much success on stage was considered questionable.

The American publication of the "new" *Diary of a Young Girl* in 1995 generated renewed interest in the play. The Goodrich-Hackett version was partially rewritten and had its premiere in 1997. The narrative was now more firmly situated in the historical context and Otto's role was diminished somewhat in favor of Anne's. Moreover — the advance publicity announced — the so-called de-Judaization of the 1950s would be undone in this new version. The Chanukah song was now sung in Hebrew, for example, whereas Goodrich and Hackett had opted for an alternate song in English in order to avoid confronting American audiences with something they were unable to understand. Doctor Pfeffer, the dentist sharing the secret annex with the Frank family, was now even shown in prayer and wearing a prayer shawl. The new version of the play portrayed an explicit Judaism, characteristic of the United States in the 1990s but which would have been impossible to put on in the 1950s when any form of "un-American behavior" was regarded with suspicion.

Anne Frank's popularity grew in the Netherlands, too. In 2004, Anne was eighth in a TV competition held to establish the most noteworthy Dutch person in the nation's history. When it emerged that she was in fact stateless, there was a brief ensuing flare of interest — also among Dutch parliament members — in granting Anne Frank posthumous citizenship, but ultimately nothing came of it. When an official canon of Dutch history was formulated in 2007, she was included as a symbol of the persecution of the Jews.

Yet the American public by no means intended to let Anne Frank go without a fight, and in February 2007 the Democratic representative from Long Island, Steve Israel, proposed to confer honorary U.S. citizenship onto Anne Frank. His proposal was motivated by the fact that Otto Frank and his family had made a failed attempt to flee to the United States in 1941; the rediscovery in an all but forgotten American archive of three emigration application letters sent by Otto Frank brought this fact back into the public eye.[9]

Will the United States continue to invest in Anne Frank the symbolic value she has today? There is no reason to presume otherwise, since hers is the most clear and direct voice of the Holocaust that history has given us thus far. Primo Levi, Elie Wiesel, and Etty Hillesum are too intellectual to appeal to a broad public. Only Hollywood poses a threat, with Steven Spielberg's *Schindler's List* (1993) serving as a prime example. In the Netherlands, however, Anne Frank's symbolic value never reached such great heights, and discussion has centered more on whether *Het Achterhuis* should be classified as "real" literature. The U.S. has tended to accord the words of Anne Frank the status of absolute truth — because, "after all, it's a diary" — and she is regarded, erroneously, as a chronicler of the Holocaust. Americans are also inclined to see only the self-sacrificing aspect of Miep Gies and the other helpers, and in the process forget that the Netherlands had its fair share of German collaborators, too. The fact that the Netherlands has such a good reputation in the U.S. regarding its role in World War II is therefore due in part to Anne Frank.

Anne Frank was abducted by America, there to be transformed into a victim of evil who all the while cherished a belief in the goodness of man. Once returned to the Netherlands and the rest of the world, this image of her continued to be projected for decades. Anne Frank had an immense influence on America from the very outset, whereas her influence in the Netherlands was limited. Yet thanks to America's unabating interest, the theatrical adaptations, and training activities, her influence has now grown in the Netherlands, too.

1   Of course Anne Frank was not alone in fulfilling this role: see for example Peter Novick, *The Holocaust in American Life* (Boston/New York: Mariner, 2000).

2   David Barnouw, "Anne Frank and Film," in Hyman A. Enzer and Sandra Solotaroff-Enzer, *Anne Frank: Reflections on Her Life and Legacy* (Chicago: University of Illinois Press, 2000), 165-173.

3   A.G.H. Anbeek van der Meijden, "De Tweede Wereldoorlog in de Nederlandse roman," in D. Barnouw a.o., *1940–1945: Onverwerkt verleden?* (Utrecht: HES, 1985), 73-87.

4   See James E. Young, "The Anne Frank House: Holland's Memorial Shrine of the Book," in Enzer and Solotaroff-Enzer, *Anne Frank*, 223-229.

5   See not only his book *The Obsession* (New York: Simon and Schuster, 1973), but also the one published by his wife: *Les Maisons hantées de Meyer Levin* (Paris: Editions Denoël, 1991).

6   The true author was Barbara Zimmerman of Doubleday; Lawrence Graver, *An Obsession with Anne Frank. Meyer Levin and the Diary* (Berkeley: University of California Press, 1995), 24.

7   Ralph Melnick, *The Stolen Legacy of Anne Frank: Meyer Levin, Lillian Hellman and the Staging of the Diary* (New Haven, CT: Yale University Press, 1997).

8   *De Dagboeken van Anne Frank* (The Hague: Staatsuitgeverij; Amsterdam: Bert Bakker, 1986); See note 7 and Alvin Rosenfeld, "Popularization and Memory: The Case of Anne Frank," in Peter Hayes, ed., *Lessons and Legacies: The Meaning of the Holocaust in a Changing World* (Evanston, IL: Northwestern University Press, 1991).

9   *The New York Times*, February 26, 2007.

969

6

DUTCH CULTURAL POLICY
IN THE UNITED STATES

—

DAVID J. SNYDER

Dutch-American cultural ties enjoy a long history. Most such contact between the Netherlands and the United States occurred privately, however, through commercial and financial links or in the realm of popular culture. Governments remained largely aloof from cultural relations until the trauma of World War II made cultural policy necessary. As it did for most Western nations, the war altered the foreign policy of the Netherlands. Homeland occupation by German armies and Japanese occupation of the Dutch East Indies dissipated the country's military and economic power. Maintaining influence in the postwar world would require a new emphasis on alliances, collective security, and what came to be known as "public diplomacy," understood here to include both cultural relations as well as information and propaganda programs.[1] This public diplomacy aimed to reconcile a number of cultural, ideological, and political asymmetries confronting postwar Dutch foreign policy, chief among which were the frictions arising when Dutch interests clashed with American hegemony during the Indonesian crisis of 1947–49. While Dutch cultural policy rarely achieved the foreign policy goals it sought, it did leave an enduring, if partial, legacy of Dutch culture in the United States.

The Birth of the Dutch Government
Information Service

Twentieth-century Dutch cultural policy in the U.S. grew from wartime necessity. Virtually within hours of the establishment of the government in exile in May 1940, Foreign Minister Eelco N. van Kleffens established the Regeringsvoorlichtingsdienst (RVD; Government Information Service) as a communications hub between the occupied Netherlands, the London government, and the outside world. The RVD maintained Radio Oranje, as well as contacts with the illegal and underground press. The organization also established press offices in Lisbon, Berne, Pretoria, and Stockholm, with other offices in smaller cities. By the end of the war, nearly 10 percent of Dutch government personnel in London worked for the RVD.[2]

In March 1941, with the United States still officially neutral, the RVD introduced its most important asset, the Netherlands Information Bureau (NIB) to promote Dutch affairs within the U.S. The NIB's main New York office established subsidiary branches in Holland, MI, and San Francisco, with lesser stations in Boston, Washington, DC, Buenos Aires, and Montreal. NIB's field of operations included the entire western hemisphere, save the Netherlands Antilles, which were connected directly to London. The NIB answered to the RVD and to the press section of the Foreign Ministry. The East Indies connection made the NIB a paramount news source about the Pacific theater in the early days of the war with NIB/San Francisco playing an important role as a cable terminus.[3] N. A. C. Slotemaker de Bruïne headed the NIB, a theologian by training who had been in the East Indies since the 1920s, first as a missionary and then in 1937 as managing director of the Algemeen Nieuws en Telegraaf Agentschap (Aneta), the wire service that operated out of Batavia. NIB's assistant director was J. H. Huizinga, son of the great Dutch historian.

Housing a press section, a film division, a radio and broadcasting operation, a full-service reference library, and later a special Indonesian department, the NIB sought to elicit the sympathy of the still neutral Americans for the plight of the occupied Netherlands. Isolationism, accompanied by general anti-European sentiment, was particularly pronounced in the Midwest, which, along with the large Dutch émigré population in western Michigan, accounts for the placing of an NIB bureau in the small town of Holland.[4] The NIB, like most Western public diplomacy agencies, followed two main lines of work: cultural diplomacy and information programming. The first effort consisted of building goodwill and long-term cultural affinity with the Americans through art exhibitions, performances, educational programs, films, radio scripts, and the like. The information programming, or propaganda, promoted the government's foreign policy goals more directly. A deluge of NIB press services, wire releases, magazines and news bulletins, lecture tours, and speeches by prominent officials ventured to counter American neutralism and to keep the American public informed of Dutch wartime activities. NIB officials both in New York and in the regional bureaus kept a close watch on all newspaper and periodical coverage of the Netherlands and mobilized quickly to counter unflattering portraits. Critical stories, for instance about Queen Wilhelmina's flight to London, the quick surrender of the Dutch army, and the disastrous Battle of the Java Sea, could expect a reply from the NIB or from bureau directors within their jurisdictions.

971

6

—

THE
COLD WAR
AND
BEYOND

1945-2009

—

CULTURE

One important propaganda theme in this regard was to showcase Dutch hardiness and the ongoing commitment of Dutch resources to the war. Books appeared with NIB assistance, such as Van Kleffens' *Juggernaut over Holland* (1941), which sought to counteract American criticism by noting the insuperability of the Nazi blitzkrieg. The NIB collaborated with both in-house and outside authors on books relating to the Netherlands and the Dutch East Indies at war, supplying data and photographs, as well as helping to arrange for publication, distribution, and publicity. Such books, written for information purposes, also advanced scholarship, such as NIB library section chief B. Landheer's still useful 1943 anthology, *The Netherlands*.[5]

After Pearl Harbor, American isolationism gave way to recurrent charges that the Dutch were not shouldering enough of the burden, that Americans were sacrificing too much on behalf of Dutch liberty. Here the training of Dutch pilots in Jackson, MS, offered fertile propaganda opportunities. Arguably the most sensational of all NIB's wartime activities, a squadron of Dutch B-25s toured midwestern cities including Minneapolis/St Paul, Des Moines, Chicago, Omaha, and Grand Rapids, in addition to New York, in June and July 1943. Local VIPs enjoyed flights on the bombers, which simulated bombing runs to allow local air raid systems to practice.

A key part of this Holland-carries-on theme highlighted the importance of the Dutch East Indies to the war effort. The NIB sought to draw attention to the economic and strategic importance of the archipelago while countering the allegation, again often expressed in the Midwest, that Indonesians welcomed the Japanese as liberators. NIB materials defended against the charge that American blood and treasure was being expended for the sake of Dutch colonial interests, and depicted Dutch colonialism as munificent, enlightened, and technically advanced. A 1945 *Chicago Tribune* editorial, "The Trusteeship Hoax," which alleged that a "Dutch communications monopoly" kept Indonesian voices from being heard, was condemned by NIB authorities as "a lie from beginning to end."[6]

Anti-Dutch editorials frequently appeared in the *Tribune*'s pages throughout the war, and NIB/Holland would keep up a running battle against the *Tribune*'s shrill isolationism. One especially incendiary editorial appeared in August 1944, "The First Communist Queen," which opined that calls from the resistance for the participation of Dutch labor in key policymaking bodies heralded the emergence of Dutch communism. The editorial was based on material published by the Dutch resistance, specifically a famous April 1944 joint statement by underground newspapers that demanded the democratization of postwar Dutch economic policymaking. The NIB had actually released this communiqué to the American press, but based on the *Tribune*'s highly tendentious interpretation, it was a decision Slotemaker came to regret. He insisted that the Americans lacked the requisite political and cultural context in which Dutch resistance leaders formulated such calls.[7] The existence of information from the resistance constituted yet another part of the wartime cacophony of information that led to discomfort within the NIB about controlling information flows. The bureau's preference, following the lead of the London government more generally, was that the resistance should fight, expressing Dutch gallantry, but not actually speak.

Between Objectivity and Propaganda

The NIB, in other words, chiefly operated as an information manager rather than as an information generator. A crucial part of this program was the NIB's direction of what the Dutch newswire service, Aneta, syndicated over its nominally objective wire service. Unknown to the public, Slotemaker had been entrusted as managing director of Aneta after the Japanese occupation forced the liquidation of the agency's main headquarters. Slotemaker's responsibility was to ensure that Aneta would not release stories injurious to the Dutch cause. Because NIB's own press releases came from Aneta, these releases enjoyed the imprimatur of objectivity.[8]

As the relationship with Aneta illustrates, the NIB was more concerned to promote the cause of the occupied Netherlands than to maintain the distinction between objective journalism and state propaganda. NIB releases consistently overestimated the number killed in the Rotterdam bombing of 1940, for instance, or downplayed the military importance of the city prior to its destruction, in each case heightening the sense of Nazi brutality.[9] Nevertheless the NIB remained cautious in the material it produced lest the Americans perceive it as just another propaganda ministry. It was one thing, for example, if a local newspaper story wished to draw a "laudatory" portrait of a Dutch official on a local speaking tour. The NIB should avoid, however, as the Netherlands embassy pointed out, biographical sketches dripping with "honey, sweetness, and praise."[10] No published material that addressed the Netherlands in any substance went unreviewed by the NIB. It is fair to conclude that the bureau helped shape Americans' image of the Netherlands in these years by acting as a clearing house for the preponderance of Dutch-related information in the U.S.

The NIB's second line of action consisted of cultural diplomacy, the sponsoring of art and technical exhibits, academic exchanges, performances, lecture tours, and other such activities. Americans generally flocked to exhibitions of Dutch art, especially the great masters. One early exhibit that visited Dayton, Kansas City, St Louis, Toledo, and elsewhere paired an exhibition of

973

6

———

THE
COLD WAR
AND
BEYOND

1945–2009

———

CULTURE

paintings with an appearance by J. H. Geys, commander of a Dutch submarine in the Battle of Java Sea. It was hoped the combination would serve political purposes by highlighting the damage inflicted on the great Dutch artistic tradition by the occupation forces.

Internal Tension

Common to all public diplomacy programs, cultural challenges persisted throughout the life of the NIB. It was difficult, for example, to transmit to Americans the idea of Dutch patriotism, symbolized as it was by loyalty to the House of Orange. Even greater difficulties would arise after the war, in connection with the "Indonesian question," as NIB officials attempted to promote two opposing views of the Netherlands, one emphasizing the destruction and vulnerability of the country in the war and hence the need for the retention of the Indies, the other suggesting Holland's great-power claims by virtue of that same colony.

This tension between "little Holland" and "big Holland" persisted throughout the life of the NIB. The "little Holland" of tulips, dikes, and windmills often served as the focal point for American interest in NIB material and exhibitions. It fetched audiences and provoked sympathy for the plight of Dutchmen living under occupation in the Netherlands and the East Indies. But a foreign policy that sought a continuing role for a powerful Kingdom of the Netherlands was difficult to weave into exhibitions focusing on "little Holland." The East Indies were showcased as central to the power of "big Holland," whose imperial expertise, benevolence, and long experience in the region were promoted as key to unlocking Indonesia's contribution to Free World defense. The NIB, however, could never discern how to employ the trope of "little Holland," successful as it may have been as a national "brand" that attracted audiences, to persuade the Americans to use their military and economic power on behalf of an imagined "big Holland" that no longer existed in the postwar world.

Postwar Reconstruction

Emerging concerns about propaganda, arising especially after the encounter with the malicious Nazi type, coupled with the expectation that the American public would lose interest in the Netherlands after the liberation, led to a reshaping of NIB work as the war drew to a close. Budgets were slashed and plans were generated to convert the NIB into a passive information supplier and promoter of Dutch-American business. At the same time the postwar environment presented fresh obstacles to cultural programming. The NIB broadened

974

its exhibition offerings to include Dutch architecture, city planning, and water management technologies. But the wartime cultural environment in which the *esprit de corps* of alliance made Americans receptive to Dutch exhibits was already beginning to dissipate. Most of the postwar exhibitions did not reckon with fast-changing and discriminating tastes. This problem was aggravated by deteriorating American attitudes toward the Netherlands during the Indonesian crisis.

No matter occupied the postwar NIB more than Indonesia. During the war, the bureau had made the strategic importance of Dutch holdings in Asia a cornerstone of its effort to promote the value of Dutch military contributions to the Allied cause. Following the Atlantic Charter of 1941, however, and before the full weight of the Cold War determined that U.S. foreign policy would look on nationalist movements with suspicion, postwar U.S. foreign policy made anticolonialism a key principle. A steady stream of anti-Dutch stories appeared in the American press in the years after the war, and it was to these that the NIB machinery bent its efforts. Moreover, the free movement of correspondents now meant that the NIB could not control the information flow as before. Despite sustained efforts to imprint an image of benevolent rule, most U.S. press accounts continued to emphasize the repressiveness of Dutch colonialism.

The information program highlighted the positive aspects of Dutch rule, the shared Dutch-Indonesian sacrifice against Japanese aggression, the role of Dutch investment in the region, or the importance of the Indies to the ravished postwar Dutch economy. The NIB also attempted to discredit the Indonesian nationalist movement by associating it with the imperialist Japanese government of the war years, and then later by claiming it was tainted with communism. In neither case were American officials convinced, and none of the broader themes addressed the fundamental point of U.S. anticolonialism.[11] The Americans remained unwilling to venture American blood and treasure on behalf of Dutch colonial interests so soon after the tremendous sacrifices of World War II, and, as NIB assistant director Huizinga pointed out, exhibitions on Balinese art were unlikely to reverse this position.[12] NIB's information counteroffensive was also significantly damaged in July 1949 when a NIB-arranged press tour of Indonesia ended in tragedy outside Bombay. When the KLM airliner *Franeker* crashed on final approach, thirteen prominent American journalists were lost as well as the generally pro-Dutch stories they carried on board and would have filed with their news bureaus.

By the early 1950s, the Indonesian crisis had run its course. In 1951 the new NIB director, Jerome Heldring, changed the agency's name to the Netherlands Information Service (NIS), highlighting a more routine informational orientation. NIS fielded requests for information about the commercial environment in the Netherlands and tried to demonstrate to the Americans that the country

975

Dutch pavillion at a wartime state fair in Minnesota.

was shouldering its share of the NATO burden. Dutch high culture continued to be a perennial audience favorite and NIS arranged for art and music exhibitions to tour major American cities throughout the 1950s and 1960s, including the 1961 tour of famed Dutch jazz pianist Pia Beck. The Hague Philharmonic, to cite another example, toured in 1963 and again in 1965. Challenges still occasionally flared. Queen Juliana's celebrated 1952 visit caused a stir within the NIS (and throughout the Dutch government) when the queen offered remarks in her speech to Congress denouncing the Cold War and, by extension, many of the foreign policy premises of her hosts. Yet lacking the direction imposed by wartime and early Cold War crises, Dutch cultural policy tended to drift.

Private Initiatives and the End of the NIS

Shrinking budgets made the initiative of officials on the ground crucially important to Dutch cultural policy. No better example of this exists than the career of Willard Wichers, longtime director of NIB/Holland. Wichers was the driving force behind one of the bureau's most enduring legacies, the revival of the annual Tulip Time Festival in Holland, MI. This week-long celebration featured hundreds of thousands of planted tulips, traditional Dutch food and crafts, and local schoolchildren performing *klompen* dances generally unknown in the modern Netherlands. "Tulip Time" continues to attract crowds eager to sample what they imagine to be an authentic "little Holland."

In like manner the constellation of Dutch academic studies in the United States grew both as a legacy of the information program and from the commitment of dedicated individuals whose support from the Netherlands government has often been lacking. The short-lived chair at the University of Chicago, and the Queen Wilhelmina Chair in Dutch Literature at Columbia University founded in 1913, dominated by two figures, B. Hunningher (1948–64) and J.W. Smit (1965–2006), were the precursors to a greatly expanded network of Dutch studies after World War II.[13] In 1952 the second chair in Dutch studies was established at Calvin College, in Grand Rapids, MI. Intended to honor Juliana on her 1952 visit to west Michigan, the Queen Juliana Chair of the Language and Culture of the Netherlands received no financial support from the Dutch government. Perhaps the most vibrant of the Dutch studies programs in the U.S. is also the most recent, the Dutch Studies Program and the Queen Beatrix Chair in Dutch Language, Literature and Culture, established in 1971 at the University of California, Berkeley. Largely the initiative of the vice-consul in San Francisco and director of NIS/San Francisco, H.F. van den Broek, who secured some financial backing for the chair's endowment from the Dutch government, the Beatrix Chair was the longtime post of Professor Jo-

977

6

—

THE
COLD WAR
AND
BEYOND

1945–2009

—

CULTURE

han Snapper. Other academics who contributed substantially to the promotion of Dutch studies in the U.S. include Professor William Shetter at Indiana University, Professor Walter Lagerwey at Calvin College, and Professor Robert Swierenga at Kent State University, whose work in Dutch-American immigration has been seminal. Furthermore, the Association for the Advancement of Dutch-American Studies (which focuses on immigration topics) and the multidisciplinary American Association for Netherlandic Studies have, since the early 1980s, established nationwide academic networks in the U.S. and organize biennial conferences.

One more recent important source of support for Dutch studies in America, which grew independently of the NIS, has been the Nederlandse Taalunie (Dutch Language Union). Established in 1980 as a joint Belgian-Dutch initiative, the Taalunie continues to provide key logistical, curricular, and financial support to Dutch language studies in the U.S. (and elsewhere). Besides the programs at Berkeley and Calvin, several prominent American institutions, including the University of Michigan, Indiana University, the University of Minnesota, and the University of Wisconsin, offer Dutch language courses. Much like Dutch cultural policy more broadly, the terrain of Dutch studies in the U.S. is thus both rich and patchy, with well-developed English-language literatures in the history of the Golden Age, Dutch language and linguistics, the colonial history of the East Indies, Dutch political science, and the Netherlands under German occupation. There remains a great dearth, however, of English-language scholarship in nineteenth- and twentieth-century Dutch social and political history. American scholars are selectively drawn to Dutch-related subjects, and seem unwilling to address topics beyond certain well-traversed areas.

The proliferation of Dutch academic studies in the 1960s and 1970s occurred as state support for cultural diplomacy waned and other avenues of cultural contact increased. Still, the NIS remained active in all manner of cultural and political exchanges. The royal family remained a perennial focal point, as the NIS helped arrange Prince Bernhard's 1965 visit, or scheduled events to celebrate important milestones including the wedding of Princess Beatrix in 1966 and Princess Margriet's 1965 engagement. The NIS also continued to issue radio scripts and concert recordings to stations in regions with significant concentrations of Dutch-American populations. By the 1970s, costs had lowered sufficiently to allow the NIS to distribute programs produced by Radio Nederland Wereldomroep in Hilversum. The NIS promoted exhibitions too, helping to arrange for a "Netherlands Week" in March 1968 in New Orleans to commemorate the 250th anniversary of the founding of that city. "The Dutch Republic in the Days of John Adams, 1775–1795" toured the U.S. from 1973 through 1979.

By the mid-1960s, NIS/NY had moved its operations to the press section of the Netherlands embassy in Washington, DC, to save costs. Mounting popular discontent in the Netherlands over the U.S. role in Vietnam coupled with strict budgetary constraints led to a dwindling of official sponsorship for Dutch culture in the U.S. NIS publications such as *Holland Herald* continued through the 1970s, as did the long-running *Feminine Vignettes*, a radio program and bulletin that had run from the late 1940s through the early 1970s. But the NIS of this era never enjoyed the clear mandate of the first generation of Dutch cultural policy, and swimming against a popular Dutch anti-Americanism associated with the Vietnam era, officials within the embassy argued that necessary public relations work could now be accomplished by its press section and the consulates general in large American cities. The NIS shut its doors in 1974, with select assets apportioned to the embassy, the Permanent Mission to the United Nations, and the consulates general in Chicago and San Francisco.

Contemporary Challenges after the NIS

With the demise of the NIS, Dutch cultural policy lacked definition, if not substance. The Netherlands government was active in the bicentennial celebrations of 1976, but it was the 1982 anniversary of two hundred years of formal ties between the Kingdom of the Netherlands and the independent United States that witnessed a much stronger recognition of the Dutch-American cultural heritage. The year-long celebrations were developed independently at the community level or in conjunction with the largely privately funded Netherlands-American Bicentennial Commission (NABC), and included scores of events at both the national and local levels featuring exhibitions of art, film, and music, royal visits, business and technological displays, and conferences and symposia, of a kind that had marked Dutch cultural policy since the beginning of the Cold War. Again the trivializing discourses of "little Holland" were on full display: the NABC's prize-winning float in the 93rd Tournament of Roses Parade featured windmills, tulip fields, and wooden shoes for each of the float's riders. Of a more enduring legacy were the dozen or so books published in 1982 that explored various aspects of Dutch history and U.S.-Netherlands relations, the most important of which was *A Bilateral Bicentennial: A History of Dutch-American Relations*, edited by the esteemed scholars J.W. Schulte Nordholt and R.P. Swierenga.

Despite such successes, critics within parliament and elsewhere increasingly complained of the uncoordinated drift and "hobbyism" of Dutch cultural relations. They began to press for greater activity and greater coordination. The legacy of postwar information programming, the stereotypes of tulips and windmills that dominated American perceptions of the Netherlands, did not serve the requirements of an age in which increased communications and trav-

6

THE
COLD WAR
AND
BEYOND

1945–2009

CULTURE

el possibilities allowed for more sophisticated international cultural under-standing. In response to such criticism, a new Foundation for Dutch-American Cultural Exchange (Stichting Culturele Uitwisseling Nederland-Verenigde Sta-ten), housed in the Ministry of Welfare, Health, and Culture (WVC), formulated the so-called concentration policy, which recognized that limited funds were better spent focused on achievable goals. The flagship project of this policy was the Texas Project, which identified the emerging arts scene in and around Houston, fueled by a burgeoning oil economy, as the site of primary attention. The project would be bedeviled by penurious budgets and administrative in-fighting and closed by 1990.

The failure of the concentration policy reflected the challenges of a cultur-al policy that lacked a clear ideological mandate and an unquestioned orga-nizational center. But it did spawn two primary debates over cultural policy of lasting significance. The first concerned the question whether limited funds should be spent focusing on priority regions and nations, or whether funds should be spent only within arts sectors that promised a reasonable return of goodwill for the investment. In this case, administrators attempted to have it both ways, directing the policy toward what was perceived at the time as a promising region in a high-priority nation, and also focusing primarily on high culture, such as painting and symphonic music. This gave the overall program a decidedly elitist flavor. A more interesting debate, still largely unexplored by the current scholarship, occurred in the run-up to the concentration policy be-tween advocates of the traditional view — cultural programs should support essential Dutch political and commercial policies — and the new progressive internationalists who argued that international cultural relations should stim-ulate the aesthetic and creative aspects of domestic culture itself. While the Texas Project closed down before the full direction could be determined, the very existence of the debate points to the potentially greater flexibility and cre-ativity of cultural policy in nonhegemonic states. The United States, with its vastly greater resources and exponentially larger cultural relations machinery, never posed the question whether any of this ought to be directed toward stim-ulating American culture.[14]

Clearly much research on cultural relations remains to be undertaken. Nev-ertheless certain conclusions seem warranted. Thanks to Dutch cultural policy, American audiences learned, many for the first time, about Indonesia or Dutch architecture, or received a political, sociological, and cultural education about the Netherlands and its regional cultures. Information officers struggled to dis-cern whether any of this had the desired political effect and generally conclud-ed that audiences were perfectly capable of forming their own impressions as to the moral and political values on display. Limited budgets plagued informa-tion and cultural efforts, yet energetic officials in the United States nevertheless offered creative and compelling introductions to Dutch art and culture, and in so doing began to rethink the premises of international cultural policy itself. While Dutch cultural policy never quite achieved political support among the Americans for the foreign policy goals of "big Holland," the image of picturesque "little Holland" and a productive, if fragmentary, Dutch studies network survive as enduring legacies.

1   J.J.C. Voorhoeve, *Peace, Profits and Principles: A Study of Dutch Foreign Policy* (The Hague: Martinus Nijhoff, 1979).

2   Bert van der Zwan, "De Regerings Voorlichtingsdienst (RVD) te London, 1940–1945," in Bert van der Zwan et al., eds., *Het Londens archief: Het Ministerie van Buitenlandse Zaken tijdens de Tweede Wereldoorlog* (Amsterdam: Boom, 2003), 39.

3   Jan van de Ven, "De Regeringsvoorlichtingsdienst in London, 1940–1954" (Ph.D. dissertation, Katholieke Universiteit Nijmegen, 1988), 42.

4   For NIB's cultural influence in west Michigan, see David Zwart, "Constructing the Homeland: Dutch Americans and the Netherlands Information Bureau during the 1940s," *Michigan Historical Review* 33 (Fall 2007): 81-100.

5   Published by Columbia University Press in New York and University of California Press in Berkeley, respectively.

6   Slotemaker to Wichers, May 25, 1945, Archief van het Nederlands Informatiebureau, collectie 243 b, inv. no. 202, Nederlands Instituut voor Oorlogsdocumentatie, Amsterdam.

7   Slotemaker to Wichers, August 18, 1944, ibid.

8   David J. Snyder, "The Problem of Power in Modern Public Diplomacy: The Netherlands Information Bureau and the United States in World War II and the Early Cold War," in Kenneth Osgood

and Brian Etheridge, eds., *The United States and Public Diplomacy: Toward an International History* (Leiden: Brill, forthcoming).

9   Van der Zwan, "De Regerings Voorlichtingsdienst," 40.

10 H.R. van Houten, Counselor of Netherlands Embassy, to Mr. Orbaan of the NIB/New York, March 1, 1943, Papers of Willard Wichers, box 2, folder "Wichers/1942–1943 Projects, Ambassador's Tour, 1943," Holland Museum, Holland, MI.

11 David J. Snyder, "Representing Indonesian Democracy in the U.S., 1945–1949: Dutch Public Diplomacy and the Exception to Self-Determination," in Charlotte Wallin and Daniel Silander, eds., *Democracy and Culture in the Transatlantic World* (Växjö, Sweden: Växjö University Press, 2005), 35-48.

12 James Huizinga, "Memorandum on N.E.I. Propaganda in the USA," October 1942, Londens Archief, inv. nr. 5728, Nationaal Archief (National Archive), The Hague.

13 The Queen Wilhelmina Chair at Columbia became a visiting position in 2006.

14 Robbert Veltman, "Het Texas-project en het Nederlandse buitenlands culturele beleid," in F. van den Burg et al., eds., *Kunst en beleid in Nederland* (Amsterdam: Boekmanstichting/Van Gennep, 1993), 113-150.

AMERICAN STUDIES IN THE NETHERLANDS

—

THE
COLD WAR
AND
BEYOND

1945-2009

—

CULTURE

GILES SCOTT-SMITH

Since World War II the promotion of American studies — that is, "the study of the past and present civilization of the United States through specific courses in academic departments (such as literature, history, geography, government, et cetera)"[1] — has been one of the prime activities of U.S. public diplomacy around the world. A greater cultural affinity and knowledge of all things American was a necessity for strengthening the legitimacy of U.S. power abroad, and all the more so amongst those allied nations that were required for the common (anti-Soviet) enterprise under U.S. leadership. The history of American studies in the Netherlands reflects this large-scale U.S. investment.

From the perspective of the United States, the Netherlands was an ideal postwar ally. By 1949 the Dutch had abandoned neutrality, joined NATO, and aimed to anchor themselves within the transatlantic alliance. They were close politically to the UK and opposed to European affairs being dominated by either a renewed France or a resurgent Germany. The Netherlands was also positive toward a U.S.-led free trade regime, and during the Cold War was wholly committed to building a managed postwar economic and political order based around international organizations such as the IMF, the World Bank, and the OECD. Furthermore, the Netherlands was a site of high-quality research in strategic sectors such as nuclear physics, mathematics, and aerodynamics, fields that the United States wanted to secure within its own sphere of influence. Due to the long tradition of democratic rule, free market economics, and intellectual exchange, the U.S. embassy in The Hague could report in 1952 that the Dutch were "perhaps closer ideologically to the United States than any people in Europe."[2] Since U.S. strategy was based on the need to secure close political and military allies in western Europe, it was logical that the already existing cultural affinity between the Dutch and the Americans be extended and reified through educational exchange. The broad basis for this approach, around which a positive atmosphere of academic socialization could be promoted, was the development of American studies within the Dutch university system. As J. Manuel Espinosa of the State Department's Bureau of Educational and Cultural Affairs stated in 1961:

> The study of American subjects in the educational systems of other countries strengthens the basis for a better understanding of American life and institutions on the part of those elements of the population that shape public opinion and give direction to national policy—through educators, students, intellectuals, serious writers, and other leadership elements.[3]

A prime means to achieve this was through the fostering of local "opinion leaders" who would act as guides and interpreters of American culture within their own national communities. In order to make American history and literature a permanent feature of European curricula, it would be necessary "to recruit and train a cadre of Americanists in Britain and on the Continent."[4] The promotion of American studies abroad was sanctioned by three pieces of legislation. The Fulbright Act of 1946 granted the use of funds gained from the sale of surplus military equipment for "financing studies, research, instruction, and other educational activities" to establish reciprocal exchanges between the United States and other nations. It was followed by the Information and Educational Exchange Act of 1948 (Smith-Mundt), which authorized in global terms "an information service to disseminate abroad information about the United States, its people, and policies," and allowed the secretary of state "to provide for assistance to schools, libraries, and community centers abroad...[that serve] as demonstration centers for methods and practices employed in the United States." In 1961 this was formalized by the Mutual Educational and Cultural Exchange Act (Fulbright-Hays Act), which explicitly included the "fostering and supporting" of American studies abroad as one of its central goals. To this end, the Act aimed to encourage "professorships, lectureships, institutes, seminars, and courses in such subjects as American history, government, economics, language and literature, and other subjects related to American civilization and culture."

The 1950s: The First Phase

Although a Fulbright agreement was signed between the two governments in January 1949, Dutch complaints over the lack of equal provisions (Dutch participants obtained only travel grants, while Americans coming to the Netherlands received a more generous financial package) led the U.S. embassy to report in early 1950 that "it is not thought that the Program has been received

6

———

THE
COLD WAR
AND
BEYOND

1945-2009

———

CULTURE

with particular enthusiasm." Other initiatives were more successful. In 1946 the sociologist Arie N.J. den Hollander was appointed professor at the University of Amsterdam and began lecturing on U.S. culture and society. Den Hollander had received a Rockefeller Foundation scholarship to study in the U.S. during 1930–32, and had written his dissertation on poor whites in the Deep South. Over the next few years he worked toward broadening the study of the United States through the establishment of an Amerika Instituut.[5] In 1952, having received further financial and logistical support from the Rockefeller Foundation and the U.S. embassy, the Amerika Instituut was officially opened, effectively providing an extra outlet in Amsterdam for the embassy's information services. A key ally of Den Hollander's in this early period was Professor R.W. Zandvoort, head of the Anglo-American Institute (which he had created in 1937) at Groningen University, then the only other American studies-related center outside Amsterdam. Both Den Hollander and Zandvoort were active in establishing the European Association of American Studies in 1954. Further transatlantic contacts were developed via the Harvard-Leiden Foundation, set up in 1945 to assist with an annual exchange of professors and students between the two prestigious universities. Several prominent figures, including Arthur Schlesinger, Jr. (1948–49) and Perry Miller, a Harvard history professor, came to study and teach in Leiden for an academic year. Finally, in 1946 the Netherlands-America Institute (NAI) was created by a group of Amsterdam businessmen keen to establish opportunities for apprenticeships in the United States. By the early 1950s the NAI, working closely with the U.S. embassy, had become the principal channel for selecting and arranging transatlantic educational exchanges as sanctioned by the Fulbright and Smith-Mundt Acts.

Despite these local initiatives and despite the close alignment of the Netherlands with the United States in international affairs generally, by the end of the 1950s American studies remained no more than the interest of a select elite and lacked deep roots in the Dutch education system. Several reasons for this can be found. Sigmund Skard posited that the long history of commercial links with North America had led to no more than a predominantly economic interest among the Dutch in the transatlantic relationship, a supposition that fitted with the origins of the NAI. Dense traditional curricula, as a 1957 report stated, meant that "there is really no opportunity for American Studies at the secondary school level," and the universities operated according to a specialized division of study that excluded a more multidisciplinary approach. If courses were provided by visiting Fulbright lecturers, they were not compulsory and so unable to attract committed students. In general, USIS also had to overcome the long-standing dominance of British cultural influence, not an easy task considering the resistance of English departments toward the recognition of American literature as a separate field. Not for nothing did Eric

Mottram, in 1955 the new lecturer in English literature at Groningen University, speak of "the almost universal academic suspicion and ironic disdain of American Studies" that he had encountered in the Netherlands.[6]

Public-Private Coordination:
The Second Wave of the 1960s

In December 1960 the Ford Foundation announced a 2.5 million dollar grant to the American Council of Learned Societies (ACLS) to be spread out over the following five years specifically for the expansion of American studies programs in European universities. Meanwhile, to compensate for cutbacks in USIS operations in western Europe due to the reallocation of funds to the Third World, local currencies generated via the 1954 P.L.480 Agricultural Trade Development and Assistance Act were made available specifically for long-term American studies development. With legislative impetus also provided by the passage of the Fulbright-Hays Act in 1961, public and private initiatives merged within a coordinated campaign to build on the foundations created during the 1950s.

By 1960 the temper of Dutch-American relations had changed. The importance of the Netherlands had increased due to its place as one of the original Six of the EEC. From this position the Dutch argued in favor of holding the Community open to world markets and opposed de Gaulle's vision for French political dominance via the Fouchet Plan. During the 1960s the Dutch also proved themselves as a vital U.S. ally within NATO. Yet areas of friction with the U.S. did appear. The Dutch elite, particularly in the Ministry of Foreign Affairs under Joseph Luns, were offended by American determination that the Netherlands should hand over control of its last colony in the Far East, New Guinea, to the Indonesians. The failure to arrange a deal on increased landing rights for KLM within the United States was also taken badly by the Dutch. Within broader Dutch society the founding of the Pacifist Socialist Party in 1958 signaled the arrival of an antinuclear left opposition to the pro-NATO Labor Party. Although it was small and politically insignificant at the time, the danger existed of a united, morally driven, antinuclear platform among Christian and socialist political groups. In response, every effort had to be made to maintain the Netherlands as an Atlanticist bulwark within continental Europe, a vital ally for U.S. foreign policy interests.

In answer to these circumstances, a long-term strategy was duly crafted by USIS to promote the entrenchment of Dutch-American university contacts and so solidify positive opinion on relations between the two countries. U.S. embassy public affairs officer Patricia van Delden was adamant that "the continuing stream of exchange in the educational institutions of both countries is a highly effective means of counter-acting" problems in U.S.-Netherlands relations, and that "the most vital element of the program remains academic: students, teachers, lecturers, research scholars."[7] The U.S. embassy's 1965 Country Plan focused on Dutch education:

> Develop chairs, lectureships, and courses in American Studies in specific Dutch universities, particularly in the key faculties of Law, Letters, and Economics where most of the future leaders in government, the mass media, and the political parties are trained. Purpose: [1] to foster an understanding of US policies and confidence in US leadership of the Atlantic Alliance among future Dutch leaders and [2] to establish within the Dutch educational system a group of professors, writers, and teachers who will function as important interpreters of America and its policies to target audiences.[8]

Leiden University was the principal focus for the USIS-ACLS American studies drive, and in particular Dr. Jan Willem Schulte Nordholt. A lecturer in history, Schulte Nordholt was highly recommended to the U.S. embassy for a Fulbright research grant in 1954. The result of this trip was one of the best-known Dutch books on the United States, *Het volk dat in duisternis wandelt* (*The People That Walk in Darkness*), published in 1956. Although he presented the topic in an optimistic light, USIS cultural affairs officer Earl Balch complained that the book "so slighted the past fifty years that it gives an unbalanced picture of the situation which does us no good."[9] Over the following years USIS employed a potent mix of persuasion and patronage to sway Schulte Nordholt's opinion. A yearlong guest lectureship in New York was arranged to secure his second trip to the United States in 1962–63. Trading between the rivalries of Utrecht and Leiden, USIS was able to encourage the creation of a chair in American history at Leiden for Schulte Nordholt. In 1965 the U.S. embassy reported that "USIS officers spent considerable time developing close personal contact with Dr. Schulte Nordholt because he is no doubt the single most important and influential person among the target audiences."[10] Following on from Leiden, USIS looked to broaden the American studies network across the Netherlands:

> The Post believes that the University of Groningen may be interested in the establishment of a Chair of American Law.... The University of Nijmegen has shown interest in a Chair in Political Science and the University of Utrecht in a Chair of American Literature.[11]

ACLS duly provided a five-year grant for a guest professor position in Utrecht, with the aim being that by the fifth year the university would take over the fi-

6

——

THE
COLD WAR
AND
BEYOND

1945-2009

——

CULTURE

986

New York Governor Nelson Rockefeller speaking at a Europe-America Conference
in Amsterdam in 1973.

6

—

THE
COLD WAR
AND
BEYOND

1945–2009

—

CULTURE

nancing for a permanent post. The first chair in American literature in the Netherlands, it was occupied by Seymour Betsky (whose wife, Sarah Betsky-Zweig, later became professor of English and American literature at Leiden). Using this as an initial platform, further efforts were made to stimulate the development of American history at Utrecht with the final goal being another chair. USIS gave further stimulus to establish chairs in American literature at both Nijmegen and Groningen universities, and by 1965 they could report that "all Dutch universities recognize American literature as an official subject and future teachers of English are beginning to be trained in this field."[12]

Yet the 1970s were to be a difficult decade for this subject field. U.S. funding dried up and there was no local support to replace it. The radical wave that went through Dutch universities from 1968 onward also had a major effect, as criticism of the Vietnam War led American social science in general and American studies in particular to be singled out as no more than tools of U.S. hegemony. Student participants in the Fulbright Program declined from an annual average of sixty-one during 1950–59 to forty-eight in 1960–67 and thirty-three in 1968–75 (although a new Fulbright agreement was signed in 1972 that increased the Dutch share of both funding and board members to 50 percent). In 1974 the NAI closed its doors due to cutbacks in the U.S. embassy's cultural affairs budget, and while its exchange functions were taken up by the newly formed Netherlands America Commission for Educational Exchange (NACEE), its closure meant the end of a significant fixture of U.S. cultural diplomacy in the Netherlands. Political wrangling caused major difficulties in maintaining the chairs at Leiden and Amsterdam, and Groningen even abandoned its focus on American literature in 1980.[13] In these difficult circumstances it was opportune for a regrouping of the American studies community to bolster its faltering position. Schulte Nordholt attempted to form a Netherlands Association for American Studies in 1971-72, but the personal rivalry with Den Hollander meant there was no cooperation from the Amerika Instituut and it never got off the ground. A second attempt in 1977, this time under the leadership of Den Hollanders' successor as director of the Amerika Instituut, Rob Kroes, did lead successfully to the formation of the Netherlands American Studies Association (NASA).

The Return of U.S. Patronage:
The Third Wave of the 1980s

The increase in U.S. support for American studies in the Netherlands during the 1980s was wholly related to concerns over the level of anti-Americanism in Dutch society at large. The decision to modernize NATO nuclear forces in response to the Soviet nuclear build-up, and the subsequent aim to place cruise missiles on Dutch soil, triggered widespread public and political protest in the Netherlands during 1979–85. In 1985 a public petition against this policy drew a total of 3.7 million signatures (although opinion polls at the time indicated the Dutch were on the whole still in favor of NATO). For the United States (and for many Dutch elites) the extent of public resistance in the Netherlands was a matter of major concern, and efforts were coordinated to highlight the continuing close relations between the two countries. The best example is the celebration of the bicentennial of Dutch-American diplomatic relations in 1982, which was marked by a whole array of cultural activities, including the state visit of Queen Beatrix to the United States. One public-private initiative stemming from the bicentennial celebrations concerned the establishment of the Roosevelt Study Center (RSC) in Middelburg. The year 1982 was also the centennial of the birth of Franklin Roosevelt, and the fact that the Roosevelt family originally emigrated from the province of Zeeland to the New World in the seventeenth century led the Franklin Roosevelt Four Freedoms Foundation to issue the Four Freedoms Awards in Middelburg for the first time. Out of this came a proposal, negotiated between the province of Zeeland, the Four Freedoms Foundation, and the Franklin and Eleanor Roosevelt Institute in Hyde Park, NY, to establish a permanent library and archive for the study of American history in the Netherlands, and the RSC opened in September 1986.

When U.S. Ambassador Paul Bremer arrived in The Hague in late spring 1983, revitalizing the Fulbright Program became one of his many goals for improving the image of the United States and the opportunities it could offer in Dutch academia. In January 1984 the inspector general of education, Jan Veldhuis, was appointed to the NACEE board. During June-July 1983 he had undertaken a study tour as part of the U.S. State Department's International Visitor Program, visiting various American universities and compiling a report on their methods, approaches, and quality-control systems. On the NACEE board Veldhuis initiated a program that aimed to shift grant resources to the humanities and social sciences ("most conducive to mutual understanding"), to expand its network beyond the universities of Leiden, Amsterdam, and Wageningen, and "to focus on the members of the successor generation: graduate students, teachers and young scholars."[14] Funding was also increased to expand the range of scholarships on offer, with American studies and the social sciences being emphasized. In particular, a renewal of teacher exchanges helped expand interest at the secondary school level. With the NACEE back on track, a determined effort was made to build on the achievements of the 1960s and finally ensure a permanent presence for American studies at major Dutch universities. To secure the regular presence of a recognized American lecturer in Dutch undergraduate courses, in 1983 the first of a series of prestigious chairs,

989

6

———

THE
COLD WAR
AND
BEYOND

1945–2009

———

CULTURE

the John Adams Visiting Scholar in American Civilization (now American History) was established at the University of Amsterdam. This was followed in 1985 by the Walt Whitman Chair in American Culture Studies (originally linked with Leiden) and in 1990 the Thomas Jefferson Chair in American Social Studies (originally linked with Utrecht). Cooperation with other USIS offices across western Europe, encouraged by USIA in Washington, enabled a sharing of costs for bringing speakers over and organizing multinational events. By the end of the Cold War, therefore, American studies had been established as a prominent feature in the world of Dutch higher education, thanks to the efforts of both U.S. public diplomacy and American studies advocates in the Netherlands itself.

The Future

In the early twenty-first century American studies in the Netherlands is not in a strong position, struggling to maintain its presence in a rapidly changing academic environment. There is no doubt that the influx of U.S. funding via USIA and the private foundations assisted in the establishment of several positions for American history and American literature across the Dutch university landscape. However, the main problem has been to sustain these positions once the American patronage has expired. Resistance to the introduction and maintenance of American studies both from a scholarly perspective (the lack of recognition for American literature as opposed to English literature) and from an institutional perspective (the uneasy fit of American studies among more established disciplines) has been a constant factor. These obstacles are ever present in any university context and the experience in the Netherlands is similar to other countries in western Europe.[15]

Alongside this is the impact of a changed transatlantic relationship since the end of the Cold War. With the increase in opportunities for travel and study across the Atlantic, the Fulbright Program was unable to develop a new *raison d'être* and U.S. funding gradually declined during the 1990s, a situation propelled by the dissolution of USIA in 1999. Between 2001 and 2006 the U.S. share of funding for Fulbright in the Netherlands was again halved as the Bush administrations shifted post-9/11 public diplomacy funds to the Middle and Far East. Coupled with this retreat of U.S. patronage has been the restructuring of Dutch higher education and a more competitive distribution of research funds. As a result, American studies, often operating across departmental lines, has suffered. The Amerika Instituut was duly absorbed into the History Department in Amsterdam, and similar retrenchment has occurred in Leiden and Utrecht. Although a professorship in American culture was secured at Groningen University in 2004, the failure of any Dutch university to establish a two-year research master's program since the introduction of the European Union's Bologna reforms has exposed the fact that American studies (and its main components American history and literature) is institutionally weak and struggling to generate or maintain its own postgraduate community. The move of the Fulbright Program in 2007 to open up the Adams, Jefferson, and Whitman chairs to a broader range of subjects, thereby loosening slightly their original role in support of American studies, is a further illustration of this. The impulses that led to the foundation of American studies in the Netherlands — U.S. strategic interest and patronage, and Dutch initiative — have moved on to focus on other targets. As it is, the field as it was built up during the Cold War will now have to adapt to survive.

1 Walter Johnson, *American Studies Abroad: Progress and Difficulties in Selected Countries.* Special Report from the U.S. Advisory Commission on International Educational and Cultural Affairs, July 1963, 6-7.

2 Country Plan for USIS The Hague, January 30, 1953, 511.56/1-3053, RG 59, National Archives, College Park, MD (hereafter NA); See also Jan C. C. Rupp, *Van oude en nieuwe universiteiten. De verdringing van Duitse door Amerikaanse invloeden op de wetenschapsbeoefening en het hoger onderwijs in Nederland, 1945–1995* (The Hague: SDU uitgeverij, 1997), 214-216.

3 "American Studies Abroad: The Role of the Educational Exchange Program of the Department of State," 1961, archive of the Bureau of Educational and Cultural Affairs (hereafter CU), Group 4 Series 7 Box 166 Folder 10, Special Collections, University of Arkansas, Fayetteville, AR.

4 Richard Pells, *Not Like Us* (New York: Basic Books, 1997), 104.

5 U.S. Embassy at The Hague to State Department, February 15, 1950, USEF Netherlands: Annual Reports 1949–63, Archive of the Netherlands America Commission for Educational Exchange, Amsterdam (hereafter Fulbright); On

Den Hollander see Alfons Lammers, "Amerikanist van het eerste uur: A. N. J. den Hollander," in Klaas van Berkel, ed., *Amerika in Europese ogen* (The Hague: SDU uitgeverij, 1990), 161-170; Peter Knegtmans, *Een kwetsbaar centrum van de geest. De Universiteit van Amsterdam tussen 1935 en 1950* (Amsterdam: Amsterdam University Press, 1998), 276-278.

6 "Netherlands: General Status of American Studies Program," November 1957, Group 4 Series 7 Box 166 Folder 9, CU; E.N.W. Mottram, *American Studies in Europe* (Groningen: Wolters, 1955), 3; See also Doeko Bosscher, "The Study of U.S. History in the Netherlands," in Cornelis A. van Minnen and Sylvia Hilton, eds., *Teaching and Studying U.S. History in Europe: Past, Present and Future* (Amsterdam: VU University Press, 2007), 175-193.

7 "Recommended Country Program Plan for FY 1962," March 23, 1960, and "FY 1963 Proposed Educational Exchange Program," March 29, 1961, Country Files 1955–64, Lot File 66D499, Entry 5118, RG 59, Boxes 212-218, NA.

8 "Revised Section V of the Country Plan for the Netherlands," November 7, 1963, Country Files 1955–64, Lot File 66D499, Entry 5118, RG 59, Boxes 212-218, NA.

6

—

THE
COLD WAR
AND
BEYOND

1945-2009

—

CULTURE

9   Menno Steenhuis, *Voor de vrijheid geschapen. Flitsen uit het leven van Jan Willem Schulte Nordholt, historicus en dichter* (Zoetermeer: Meinema, 2001), 27; "Annual Report on the International Educational Exchange Program," July 31, 1958, 511.563 1955-59, Box 2/63, RG 59, NA.

10 See Giles Scott-Smith, "The Ties That Bind: Dutch-American Relations, U.S. Public Diplomacy, and the Promotion of American Studies since the Second World War," *The Hague Journal of Diplomacy* 2 (2007): 283-305; "Country Assessment Report," February 1, 1965, Country Files 1955-64, Lot File 66D499, Entry 5118, RG 59, Boxes 212-218, NA.

11 "Annual Report on the Educational and Cultural Exchange Program FY 1963," September 7, 1963, Country Files 1955-64, Lot File 66D499, Entry 5118, RG 59, Boxes 212-218, NA.

12 Ibid.

13 Rupp, *Van oude en nieuwe universiteiten*, 242-243, 248. The only positive signs in this period were the creation of a professorship of English and American literature at Nijmegen in 1975 and the appointment of the American Paul Sellin as professor of English literature at the Free University in 1981.

14 NACEE Annual Report 1983–84 and 1984–85, File: Annual Reports 1969–86, Fulbright; On the 1980s and Bremer see Doeko Bosscher, "The Nadir of Dutch-American Relations: Ronald Reagan, El Salvador and Cruise Missiles," in Tity de Vries, ed., *Dynamics of Modernization: European-American Comparisons and Perceptions* (Amsterdam: Free University Press, 1998), 67-83.

15 See Giles Scott-Smith, "Laying the Foundations: U.S. Public Diplomacy and the Promotion of American Studies in Europe," in Van Minnen and Hilton, *Teaching and Studying U.S. History in Europe*, 47-61.

AMERICAN PRACTICES IN DUTCH SOCIOLOGY, 1945-1968

———

TITY DE VRIES

During the 1950s and 1960s Dutch society modernized at a fast pace. Reconstruction after the damages of war and German occupation accelerated the processes of industrialization and urbanization and their related consequences for the nation's social order. Increasing secularization enforced a decline of the power of the churches and their organizations. The traditional Dutch capitalist state rapidly transformed into a welfare state, with changed labor relations and more responsibilities and duties for the state. The welfare state was considered to improve the quality of life and work for everyone and to solve social problems. Welfare state policies were to result into a harmonious society with a content population that was more than willing to conform to the status quo. In modern Dutch society everyone would enjoy increasing material comfort and be free from fear of the future. Organizations and institutions on national, provincial, and local levels, led by professional managers, were responsible for streamlining these processes. Designing a modern Dutch society was a rational process of planning and organization, resulting from a belief in social engineering that was based on scientific research. Social sciences, in particular sociology, were considered to be suited to support policymakers with data and studies. This postwar modernization of Dutch society coincided with a shift in orientation of the Dutch academic world, from a German or European focus toward an orientation on the United States. The social sciences in particular benefited from this shift, which resulted among other things in the adoption of American scientific research methods and theoretical approaches. This reorientation in combination with the needs of Dutch postwar society turned out to be especially beneficial to Dutch sociology. Together with the rise of a new generation of scholars, sociology was able to develop from a one-

6

—

THE
COLD WAR
AND
BEYOND

1945–2009

—

CULTURE

sided and limited academic field into a full-grown and highly valued discipline with assumed qualities for the social engineering of a modern Dutch society. In this essay the focus will be on the smooth and successful adoption of American sociological practices, in particular that of the structural-functional approach. This made-in-America approach proved to be instrumental in establishing and strengthening the belief in science as a foundation for policies in the Netherlands. Structural functionalism had a dominant position until the late 1960s, when the emergence of new theories and approaches, together with an increasing dislike for "grand theories," caused its rapid decline.

A Prewar European Focus

Social engineering was not a new element in Dutch sociology. In the 1920s and 1930s the discipline already had such a tradition since it was dominated by sociography, a "mixed marriage of geography and sociology" that focused on the detailed description of social life, usually in small-scale communities. Sociographers denied having a normative ideology. Instead, they liked to present themselves as social engineers or social analysts who were able to determine the core elements of social problems and subsequently, as social inventors, offer solutions or improvements. Their technical-empirical and descriptive methodology, with concepts like "society as a social enterprise," "social efficiency," and "rational social planning" (for example for the new reclaimed lands in the Zuiderzee in the 1930s), created an impression of value-free research, even though these studies were often very moralizing.[1] Its leading practitioners, S.R. Steinmetz (the "father of Dutch sociology") and H. ter Veen, had mainly been influenced by German sociologists like F. Tönnies and L. von Wiese. Surprisingly, these Amsterdam sociographers had very little interest in the work of their American colleagues of the Chicago School, which had many topical and methodological similarities with their own research. Both schools had a positivist outlook based on a strong belief in progress, and both considered empirical research the best scientific method for sociology. However, the Dutch orientation toward Germany was very strong and even though every now and then the social science journal *Mensch en Maatschappij* (Man and Society) published reviews of American sociological studies, these were not acknowledged as useful and important contributions to the discipline.[2]

Americans showed more initiative regarding transatlantic intellectual exchange. From their perspective, the social sciences had been one of the main original and successful American contributions to international academics and science. More than other disciplines, the social sciences were considered to be "authentically" American. Due to a pragmatic belief in the perfectibility of human life, American social scientists were convinced of the usefulness of knowledge and technology in the improvement of human life. The Rockefeller Foundation (RF), by way of the Laura Spelman Rockefeller Memorial Fund (LSRMF), supported and exported their views by funding visits, fellowships, and foreign research institutions and projects. Thanks to these subsidies approximately twenty Dutch social scientists, including the historian Johan Huizinga in 1926, visited social science research centers of American universities during the 1920s and 1930s.[3] Huizinga also was the LSRMF's representative in the Netherlands. Many leading scholars, chiefly Rotterdam economists like Jan Tinbergen, but also sociologists like A.N.J. den Hollander from Amsterdam, visited the U.S. on an RF fellowship and this usually turned out to be a good investment in their postwar careers. Tinbergen was appointed director of the Dutch Central Bureau of Statistics and Den Hollander became the first director of the Amsterdam Amerika Instituut and subsequently the nestor of American studies in the Netherlands. In addition to these travel grants, the RF provided substantial funding for the Netherlands Economic Institute (NEI) in Rotterdam from 1931 until 1940, considering this institute to be the best "university in Holland on the social science side."[4]

However, these RF efforts to create international expansion of American social sciences had little effect on the development and institutionalization of Dutch sociology in the 1930s. "Too little and too late" has been the general (although not in all respects correct) opinion on Dutch sociology in the first half of the twentieth century.[5] Sociological practice in the Netherlands was small and, as noted above, almost completely limited to sociography. Academic institutionalization was slow: the first chair in sociology, occupied by W.A. Bonger, was established only in 1921 at the University of Amsterdam. The journal *Mensch en Maatschappij* (M&M; as of 1947 *Mens en Maatschappij*), founded four years later, was not particularly dedicated to sociology, and the Dutch Sociological Association was established in 1936. It was only after the war, in 1949, that the Instituut voor Sociaal Onderzoek van het Nederlandse Volk (ISONEVO; Social Research Institute of the Dutch People) was founded.

Postwar Explosion

This situation of limited sociological practice changed fundamentally in the postwar years. Interest grew explosively and hundreds of sociology students flocked to the universities where new chairs in sociology were rapidly created and young sociologists occupied new positions.[6] The establishment of a separate College (*Faculteit*) of Political and Social Sciences at the University of Amsterdam in 1947 contributed to further recognition of sociology as an au-

6

—

THE
COLD WAR
AND
BEYOND

1945-2009

—

CULTURE

tonomous discipline. Expansion went along with a process of reorientation in methodology and approach, which would bear fruit during the 1950s. Fundamental to this process was the positivist climate of opinion after the war: the reconstruction and modernization of Dutch society were founded on a strong belief in a better future. In this climate of opinion the American perception of the social sciences as instrumental for human progress offered excellent opportunities for sociologists to join policymakers in modernizing Dutch society. Modernization was considered to be a rational process that could be planned and controlled if the right data and instruments were available. Sociologists could provide these.

Initially and because of its prewar dominance, the sociographic tradition with its technical-descriptive approach continued to be one of the main directions in Dutch sociology, together with the so-called cultural sociology with its often moralizing and patronizing outlook. The influence of American sociology remained quite limited. Dutch cultural sociology with its roots in the 1930s was mainly based on the work of Karl Mannheim, in particular his *Mensch und Gesellschaft im Zeitalter des Umbaus* (1935). This classic study was greatly admired in social democratic circles for its analysis of the problems of modern mass society and for its proposed solutions to the alleged crisis and decay of Western civilization. In Mannheim's perception a planned, regulated society would offer the best opportunities for individual self-development and this could prevent modern man from becoming alienated and socially isolated. In their often broad and ethically engaged studies on problems of modern mass society (lack of social cohesion, standardization, secularization, and massification), Dutch cultural sociologists W. Banning, C.S. Kruijt, P.J. Bouman, and others proposed participation in community activities as the best strategy for creating a healthy, modern society. They considered their work to be the expert foundation for social policymaking, in particular because of their ethical, often religiously informed approach. Obviously they had no affinity with the much more theoretical and empirical approach of American sociologists. In this respect P.J. Bouman (University of Groningen), author of the 1953 bestseller *Revolutie der Eenzamen* (*Revolution of the Lonely*), is exemplary. In his work Bouman emphasized the negative side of progress and modern mass society like materialism, loneliness, and mechanization of culture. American influences on his landmark work are hard to find. Although his trip to the U.S. in 1950 on a Fulbright fellowship had increased his appreciation for the dynamics and flexibility of American society and the position of the social sciences, it did not affect his own cultural approach to sociology. The same can be said of Rotterdam sociologist F.L. Polak, who spent almost a year in California at the Center for the Advanced Studies in the Behavioral Sciences in Palo Alto, in 1954–55. Polak (whose *The Image of the Future* became one of the pioneering classics of American Futures studies) had daily opportunities for discussions with famous social scientists like Paul Lazarsfeld and William Kornhauser, but his own approach stayed the same.[7]

This was different for the third sociological tradition that from the early 1950s on rapidly gained ground among a new generation of sociologists. Educated in the sociographic tradition of their professors they were trained in empirical social research with few theoretical notions. Eager for new directions and stimulated by the increase of information on American developments in sociology they turned to the functionalist-theoretic perspective that had been introduced by Talcott Parsons in his 1937 *The Structure of Social Action*. Structural functionalists considered society as an almost organic system that was constructed from a variety of coherent social units or subsystems. If there was no malfunctioning in the subsystems, society was balanced and harmonious, which was the ultimate goal. By analyzing social behavior, the roles of institutions, and the way in which these were related to other social features, functionalists developed explanations of malfunctioning elements and offered policymakers opportunities for improvements. They conceived of their work as value-free since their instruments for research and analysis were rational and scientific, but in fact they aimed at the protection and support of existing values and social structures.

The functionalist focus on empirical social research facilitated the adoption of this American practice by Dutch sociologists because it created a certain continuity with the Dutch sociographic tradition. At the same time, it answered the young generation's need for a different, more theoretical approach that characterized this generational rotation. The growing complexity of the Dutch welfare state and society was also a stimulating force in this process.

In 1945 the Leiden sociologist F. van Heek published a study on social stratification and social mobility, *Stijging en daling op de maatschappelijke ladder* (Rise and fall on the social ladder). His methodology in determining the social ranking of individuals was adopted from Talcott Parsons and became the start of the successful advance of functionalism in 1950s Dutch sociology.[8] Among other things, this advance resulted in a 30 percent increase, between 1951 and 1957, of so-called Parsonian dissertations with a strong theoretical approach. Modern sociology had entered the Dutch university and was there to stay until the late 1960s.

Modern Sociology

997

In the modern, analytical approach the prewar subservience to solving social problems was gone: sociology became an academic discipline based on a sci-

6

—

THE
COLD WAR
AND
BEYOND

1945-2009

—

CULTURE

entific methodology in which theory and empirical research were considered to be a unity. Research projects were expected to be based on the formulation of a problem or a hypothesis and on theoretical concepts. The sociologist's outlook on the future was optimistic and self-conscious. This new generation no longer considered modernization as a threat to traditional Dutch values and moral standards but as a challenge that offered new opportunities for research. They fully accepted the process of modernization and its various manifestations. They aimed at an open society in which independent individuals, untroubled by class distinctions, could make their own choices in arranging their lives. Next to Parsons' structural functionalism, Robert K. Merton offered ample tools to practice this new outlook. With his "theories of the middle range," which might explain a limited number of social phenomena, Merton had developed an approach between grand theoretical, speculative system building and hairsplitting empiricism. Dutch sociologists, with their traditional dislike for general system theory and large research themes, found this approach very attractive and fitting for research on Dutch society. It resulted in a preference for limited topics, for example in studies on secularization in the Catholic city of Tilburg, or juvenile delinquency in the industrial town of Oss, or social relations in new settlements in reclaimed land or polders. Such research topics created continuity between pre- and postwar sociology, notwithstanding differences in approach and methodology.[9] In 1963 Merton was awarded an honorary doctorate from the University of Leiden for his pragmatic contributions to sociology.

A relatively new and American-inspired field of research was social relations within businesses: studies on management and labor relations, professional satisfaction, rationalization of production, wage systems, and shifts became increasingly popular. Internationally the American impact on this so-called business sociology had been very strong since the 1920s, so it was not surprising that Dutch sociologists turned to the work of their American colleagues when Dutch industrialization took a spurt.

It took less than a decade (and surprisingly little debate) before the modern, functionalist approach had settled as a leading direction in Dutch sociology. In 1959 J.A.A. van Doorn and C.J. Lammers published the first edition of their *Moderne Sociologie. Systematiek en analyse* (Modern Sociology. Systematics and Analysis). Very soon this introduction to sociology became the compulsory textbook for generations of students, not just in the social sciences but also in academic fields that required some basic knowledge of sociological processes and research. *Moderne Sociologie* was a milestone in the history of Dutch sociology. In twenty years the book went through fourteen editions. Its publication and success signified the victory of the new approach within the

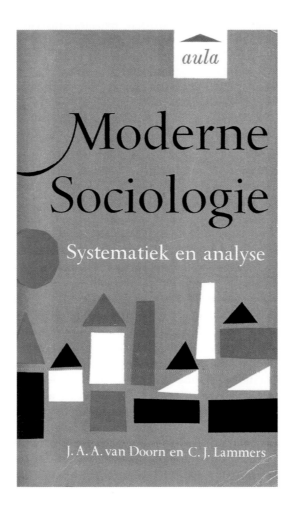

aula

Moderne
Sociologie

Systematiek en analyse

J. A. A. van Doorn en C. J. Lammers

Cover of the first edition (1959) of the book that helped the functionalist approach break through in Dutch sociology, *Modern Sociology* by J. A. A. van Doorn and C. J. Lammers. It was pusblished in a paperback edition by publisher Het Spectrum.

6

———

THE
COLD WAR
AND
BEYOND

1945–2009

———

CULTURE

1000

discipline that would dominate its research and debates until the late 1960s. Yet, Dutch sociology remained a diverse discipline during the 1950s and 1960s in which different approaches coexisted, reflecting the cultural context in which it operated.[10]

Instruments and Tools

H.P.M. Litjens' 1953 study on maladjusted families in the city of Maastricht is an early example of adoption of American methodology. Litjens referred explicitly to American research and his bibliography showed a rather impressive list of American methodological publications. Maladjusted behavior was a popular research topic for postwar sociologists. Local and national administrations showed great concern for the effects of asocial families, juvenile delinquents, and other maladjusted groups and individuals that might undermine Dutch social order. Litjens' Maastricht study was one of many that analyzed this phenomenon in a "modern" empirical way (using a large-scale survey to collect data on the social situation of families) while at the same time applying a highly subjective and normative definition of what it meant to be "well adjusted."

As Litjens' study showed, the new approach involved the application of very technical American methods of research that had rapidly become popular among Dutch sociologists. The number of "Methods and Techniques" departments at colleges of social sciences increased, especially after the introduction of the computer for statistical calculations in the early 1960s. According to some, fascination with technical skills and tools often exceeded the contents of research projects.[11] American methods like participatory observation, large-scale polling, and statistical analysis of data became standard for empirical research. In particular the large-scale survey questionnaire grew very popular with researchers: it supposedly provided them with representative data for making generalizing statements that explained cultural changes. In adopting these survey techniques, sociologists also confirmed the increasing individualization of Dutch society: individual opinions were more important than the group opinions of traditional organizations, professions, or social classes. In this way American sociology contributed to a significant element of the Dutch modernization process.

Large-scale surveying was also considered to be an effective instrument for assessing the progress of modernization of daily life, for instance among farming communities. The then Agricultural College of Wageningen, for example, used surveys to assess farmers' readiness to apply modernization strategies in the management and financing of their farms, to enlarge their enterprise, or to start using artificial fertilizer. Wageningen sociologists often applied the "two-step flow of communication" of their American colleagues Paul Lazarsfeld and Bernard Berelson: officials who, instead of addressing the population directly, used local opinion leaders to distribute new information had a better guarantee that it would reach the population. Surveying also stimulated gender-based research. Studies of housewives as "social pace setters" in the family, or the revelation of gender differences in migrants' experiences were the results of applying survey and interview techniques.

Adoption of American research techniques is shown very clearly in the study on the social effects of the February 1953 flood disaster. A huge storm combined with spring tides caused the destruction of the dikes in the southwestern parts of the Netherlands, in particular in the province of Zeeland. Towns and villages were flooded, farms and farmland were destroyed, animals and people drowned. After the worst was over, a delegation of the Committee on Disaster Studies of the U.S. National Academy of Sciences initiated and funded a study of the social and psychological aspects during and after the disaster. For five months, from April until September, students polled and interviewed evacuated victims, rescue workers, and people involved in reconstruction activities on their experiences. Participatory observation was another of their research techniques. A systematic analysis of the acquired sociological and psychological data resulted in a final report that concluded with some "miniature hypotheses."[12]

Transfer and Reception

How did the above transfer of American sociological practices take place during the first postwar years? Most Dutch university libraries had a subscription to the American Sociological Society's journal, the *American Sociological Review*, which was a rich resource for new studies and publications. The newly established sociology departments quickly adopted American textbooks for their programs, and most Dutch sociologists who visited the U.S. returned home with suitcases filled with books. Between 1945 and 1949 four Dutch social scientists went to the United States on a Rockefeller Foundation grant, and in the following ten years five sociologists and nine students in sociology traveled to America on a Fulbright scholarship. In the same period ten American sociology Fulbrighters stayed in the Netherlands, mostly in Amsterdam or Groningen.[13] In 1970, one of the tangible results of these intellectual exchanges and encounters was the establishment of the Netherlands Institute for Advanced Study (NIAS) in the Humanities and Social Sciences in Wassenaar. NIAS's aims and organization were based on those of the Center for Advanced Study in the Behavioral Sciences, which had been successful as a center for American and international social scientists since 1954.

6

——

THE
COLD WAR
AND
BEYOND

1945–2009

——

CULTURE

For most sociologists the two main Dutch academic journals together with its American counterparts have been their major sources of information. Except for an occasional article, like P.J. Bouman's 1950 report on the social sciences in the United States, the traditional journal *Mens en Maatschappij* did not pay much attention to American sociology. But in 1955 this stance changed, starting with an article, "American Sociology, Seen from a European Viewpoint," in which B. Landheer offered his readers a critical insight into the origins and characteristics of American sociology, juxtaposing the more philosophical European approach with the scientific, mathematical American approach: "While European social thinking is generally thinking about society in its entirety, we find that American sociology is less concerned with general philosophies about society than it is with scientific analysis of existing society."[14] Landheer's article was the beginning of increasing attention for American developments in M&M, obviously also in reaction to the creation, in 1953, of a new journal of sociology, the *Sociologische Gids* (SG; Sociological Guide). Dissatisfaction with the contents and policy of M&M, together with the rise of modern sociology, had resulted in this new periodical. From the start it had an international orientation with its column Vensters (Windows), in which international sociological research centers, conferences, and publications were discussed. In particular American publications (e.g., by Lewis Coser, S.M. Lipset, and Robert Merton) were regularly reviewed and discussed, while Dutch sociologists often published articles on American theories and methodologies. In 1960, for example, SG readers had access to several analyses of the method of participatory observation. A year later, the pages of the journal offered an extensive theoretical discourse on (structural) functionalism as a theoretical approach to sociology with H.P.M. Goddijn and J.E. Ellemers as the main participants. The debate itself and its intellectual level showed indeed how familiar Dutch sociologists had become with American theoretical notions. They were, in this sense, no longer out of touch.

Epilogue

In 1967 Random House published the first volume in a new series of studies on the social and cultural systems of national societies, *Dutch Society*, written by Amsterdam sociologist Johan Goudsblom. The series was aimed at a wide audience ranging from undergraduate students to foreign visitors. In fact, very soon every American Fulbright scholar heading for the Netherlands received a copy of *Dutch Society* as a preparation for his or her temporary residence. It was no coincidence that this first volume in the new series dealt with the Netherlands: "... although the Netherlands is a small country, within its limited area and population have emerged most of the dominant structural and cultural features of advanced 'modernization': large-scale urbanization and suburbanization, industrial and technological sophistication, a rapidly changing class structure marked by considerable social mobility, multi-associations and a system of 'countervailing power,' widespread education and mass media, nucleation of the family and decline of the functional significance of the small community. These are familiar phenomena to American readers; *Dutch Society* shows how and why they have come about in a smaller nation with a far different economic, political, and cultural legacy,"[15] editor Charles H. Page wrote in his introduction.

In more than one way *Dutch Society* was a significant publication. Apart from being the first comprehensive sociological study of modern Dutch society, inspired by existing similar studies on American society, it was also an excellent example of Dutch applications of American sociological approaches. Goudsblom discussed the modernization of Dutch society as a gradual process of change, emphasizing continuity and social cohesion and creating an image of a harmonious and consensual Dutch society in the 1950s and early 1960s. References to American publications (Merton again!) show the American structural-functionalist inspiration for this perception. However, Goudsblom integrated this with the modernization theory of the German-British sociologist Norbert Elias. In fact, the prominent presence of Elias in *Dutch Society* can be seen as an indication that the American functionalist dominance in Dutch sociology was now compelled to make room for different orientations and approaches. This became most obvious in the post-1968 era when, inspired by C. Wright Mills's criticism on the "abstractness" of structural functionalism and by the Marxist sociologists of the Frankfurter Schule, a new generation of scholars replaced the consensual functionalist approach with a critical sociology that aimed at being useful for emancipating groups in society.

By then, American sociology had made an enduring mark on the development of its Dutch counterpart. In postwar Dutch society sociology was looked upon as a valuable, rational instrument to monitor the transition from a traditional into a modern society. A new generation of sociologists, in need of new directions for their still young discipline discovered American approaches and methods to be excellently suited for this aim, in particular because it was not too hard to integrate these with elements of traditional Dutch sociology. In fact, in applying the American functionalist approach within the Dutch cultural setting, modern sociology in the Netherlands became one of the cornerstones of the predominantly harmonious social-political climate of opinion of the 1950s and early 1960s.

1   Marja Gastelaars, *Een geregeld leven. Sociologie en sociale politiek in Nederland 1925–1968* (Amsterdam: SUA, 1985), 239.

2   Frank Bovenkerk and Lodewijk Brunt, "De sociografieën van Chicago en Amsterdam in de jaren '20 en '30," in F. Bovenkerk et al., eds., *Toen en thans. De sociale wetenschappen in de jaren dertig en nu* (Baarn: Amboboeken, 1978), 68-78, here 76.

3   J.C.C. Rupp, *Van oude en nieuwe universiteiten. De verdringing van Duitse door Amerikaanse invloeden op wetenschapsbeoefening en het hoger onderwijs in Nederland, 1945–1995* (The Hague: SDU uitgeverij, 1997), 95-96.

4   Ibid., 93. Economics was part of the social sciences at that time.

5   Ed Jonker, *De sociologische verleiding. Sociologie, sociaal-democratie en de welvaartsstaat* (Groningen: Wolters-Noordhoff, 1988), 81.

6   In 1950 each of the six Dutch universities and the two schools of economics possessed a chair in sociology. J.A.A. van Doorn, "The Development of Sociology and Social Research in the Netherlands," *Mens en Maatschappij* 31 (1956): 189-229, here 216.

7   Tity de Vries, "Crossing the Frontiers of the Unknown: Fred. L. Polak's Road to Pioneer of Futures Studies in the United States," in Joyce D. Goodfriend et al., eds., *Going Dutch: The Dutch Presence in America 1609–2009* (Leiden: Brill, 2008).

8   Jonker, *De sociologische verleiding*, 134.

9   J.A.A. van Doorn, *Beeld en betekenis van de Nederlandse sociologie* (Utrecht: Bijleveld, 1964), 74.

10 J. Berting, "De sociologie tussen universalisme en specificiteit," *De Sociologische Gids* 51 (2004): 473-481.

11 Gastelaars, *Een geregeld leven*, 208.

12 J.E. Ellemers, *De Februari-ramp: Sociologie van een samenleving in nood* (Assen: Van Gorcum, 1956), 3.

13 J.C.C. Rupp, *Het Fulbright Programma Nederland: Een hoofdstuk uit de geschiedenis van de academische betrekkingen tussen Nederland en de Verenigde Staten, 1945–1995* (Amsterdam: Amsterdamse School voor Sociaal-Wetenschappelijk Onderzoek, 1996), 53.

14 B. Landheer, "American Sociology, Seen from a European Viewpoint," *Mens en Maatschappij* 30 (1955): 34-48, here 38.

15 Johan Goudsblom, *Dutch Society* (New York: Random House, 1967), vii.

6

THE
COLD WAR
AND
BEYOND

1945–2009

CULTURE

DUTCH EMIGRATION TO THE UNITED STATES

ENNE KOOPS

This article provides an overview of postwar Dutch emigration to the United States from a political, religious, and cultural perspective. Two questions will be answered. Was the limited size of the Dutch trek to the United States after World War II related to a lack of interest from the sending country or mainly to restrictive American immigration policies? And to what extent did the trek strengthen the cultural bonds between the countries? These questions will be answered within a broader transnational framework that includes Canada.

Incantation of Modern Times

In 1953 the journalist H.M. Bleich wrote: "Emigration has become the incantation of modern times. Tens of thousands of people are considering emigration. Dutch newspapers are writing about this topic every week." Bleich was not exaggerating. Soon after World War II, a dynamic emigration climate had developed, which resulted in the exodus of 409,000 Dutchmen in the period of 1947 to 1963. Of these, 18.5 percent settled in the United States, while 36 percent ended up in Canada. The remaining 45 percent chose other destinations.

From 1947 to 1963 an average of 24,000 persons a year left the Netherlands. During the much longer period from 1840 to 1910 about 230,000 people had moved overseas, a yearly average of 3,200 persons.[1] A combination of push and pull factors explains why Dutch emigration after 1945 was so extensive. Five years of Nazi occupation had devastated the Dutch economy and prolonged the idea of a permanent economic crisis since the 1930s. The destruction of the German hinterland meant that the Netherlands had lost a substantial outlet for its export. Combined with the loss of the Dutch East Indies economic prospects looked bleak. Furthermore, the lack of proper housing and agricultural land stimulated interest in emigration. Additional push factors were the widespread fear of a third world war and the growing state intervention in economic life. Finally, from 1949 to 1962, the Dutch government had an active emigration policy, among other things by granting subsidies to prospective emigrants. This policy was aimed at relieving population pressure and reducing mass unemployment.[2]

The opportunities and freedom in North America contrasted sharply with the depressed situation in the Netherlands. The United States and Canada had a substantial share in the liberation of the Netherlands, which generated feelings of gratitude. The positive image of both countries was further strengthened by enthusiastic letters from relatives who had emigrated before, Hollywood films that promoted "the American way of life," and the Marshall Plan.

Four Stages of Emigration

Although until the 1960s the reputation of the United States was excellent and most aspiring emigrants showed a preference for this country, Canada and Australia surpassed the U.S. as popular destinations. While the desire to emigrate was caused by economic and political pressure in the Netherlands, the volume and direction were mainly shaped by American immigration policies. After World War II four stages of emigration to the U.S. can be discerned: a period of restricted admission (1947–52), the entrance of Dutch refugees and expatriates under special legislation (1953–62), limited emigration due to the economic recovery of the Netherlands (1963–79), and, lastly, a revival of Dutch agrarian emigration (1980–present).

TABLE 1
Emigration from the Netherlands, 1947–63[3]

	Canada		Australia		U.S.		South Africa	
	Abs.	%	Abs.	%	Abs.	%	Abs.	%
1947–52	62,406	43.8	38,171	26.8	16,423	11.5	13,341	9.4
1953–57	61,983	37.7	50,140	30.5	27,857	16.9	12,589	7.6
1958–63	23,137	22.6	32,004	31.2	31,570	30.8	5,592	5.4
Total	147,526	36.1	120,315	29.4	75,850	18.5	31,522	7.7

During the first period the quota system dating from 1929 was still operative and restricted Dutch emigration to an annual maximum of 3,136. However, according to Dutch statistics, a yearly average of only 2,700 Dutch emigrants arrived in the United States during the period from 1947 to 1952, while at the same time the Dutch waiting list for admission to this country stood at 40,000.[4] It seems that not all quotas were utilized. A plausible explanation is that about 14 percent of all available visas for the Netherlands were sent to Dutch consulates in foreign countries, giving residents outside the Netherlands the opportunity to emigrate as well.[5] These emigrating expatriates are presumably absent in the Dutch statistics.

The Dutch trek during this period had three other characteristics. First, it was almost exclusively relation migration, because emigrants needed a so-called affidavit of support, which guaranteed that a sponsor would provide work and housing. For Canada, emigrants also needed sponsors who would assure housing and a minimum wage for one year. Second, Dutch emigration initially had a strong agrarian character, a continuation of the prewar pattern. In 1948, the share of farmers among Dutch emigrants to the United States amounted to 48 percent. This percentage declined from 21 percent in 1950 to 15 in 1953.[6] In the third place, there was a striking difference regarding the religious affiliation of Dutch emigrants who moved to North America. Orthodox Calvinists, members of different churches in the Netherlands bearing the name *Gereformeerd*, only made up 9.6 percent of the Dutch population, but constituted 19.8 percent of all Dutch emigrants settling in the United States between 1947 and 1952. About 85 percent were members of the Gereformeerde Kerken in Nederland (Reformed Churches in the Netherlands), because this church had a long

New Zealand		Brazil		Other		Total
Abs.	%	Abs.	%	Abs.	%	
8,469	6.0	1,450	1.0	1,981	1.5	142,241
7,009	4.3	2,128	1.3	2,859	1.7	164,565
7,142	7.0	1,281	1.3	1,702	1.7	102,428
22,620	5.5	4,859	1.2	6,542	1.6	409,234

6

—

THE
COLD WAR
AND
BEYOND

1945–2009

—

CULTURE

1008

emigration tradition, a positive view of emigration, and an experienced organization—the Christelijke Emigratie Centrale (Christian Emigration Center)—to support its emigrants. The share of Calvinists in the trek to Canada during this period was even more spectacular with 41.2 percent. The Canadian contingent was overrepresented because Calvinists employers and employees had a relatively high share in the agrarian sector. Until 1950, only agrarians were welcome in Canada, and consequently most Calvinists ended up there. Compared to the Calvinists, emigrants from the Nederlandse Hervormde Kerk (Dutch Reformed Church) and Catholics lagged behind. The Dutch Reformed Church made less of an effort to stimulate and organize emigration.[7] Furthermore, a part of the Catholic clergy was reluctant to promote emigration because North America was seen as a threat to the religious well-being of Catholics. Consequently, many of them did move to Australia because the Catholic Church was well organized there.[8]

The second stage ran from 1953 to 1962. In this period several American immigration acts opened the doors to European refugees and repatriates. In August 1953, Congress enacted the Refugee Relief Act (RRA), which allowed seventeen thousand Dutch refugees into the United States until January 1, 1957. Two thousand visas were allocated to prospective emigrants with relatives in the country and fifteen thousand to special groups. Persons who received consideration for extra visas included three categories: victims of World War II, refugees from the flood disaster that had struck the Netherlands, and repatriates from the Dutch East Indies. The RRA was realized against the background of the Cold War atmosphere. In the early 1950s, Robert West, special consultant on migration affairs under the Truman administration, feared that unproductive people would undermine the stability in Europe and therefore he argued for special immigration legislation. It took a while before Truman was convinced of the seriousness of European overpopulation, but appeals from Queen Juliana and Prime Minister Willem Drees helped convince him.[9] Under the RRA 15,162 Dutchmen, including 7,000 repatriates from Indonesia, emigrated to the U.S. For three reasons, the enforcement of the RRA program proceeded with difficulty. First, most applicants from the Indies did not have relatives in the United States. However, a sponsor was required, so they had to contact so-called voluntary agencies (international or American organizations that helped solve the refugee problem). This resulted in a bureaucratic procedure that led to much delay. The waiting list of forty thousand Dutchmen who were eager to start a new life in the United States, further hampered the administration. Finally, strict entry requirements handicapped the implementation of the RRA. Not only was there much confusion about the interpretation of the term "refugee," but aspiring emigrants were also screened carefully regarding their political convictions, their status vis-à-vis the law, and their ethnic origin.

Emigrant ship Willem Ruys, in the port of Vlissingen, 1958.

6

———

THE
COLD WAR
AND
BEYOND

1945–2009

———

CULTURE

The United States only accepted politically reliable repatriates and people of Dutch ethnic origin, not those of pure Indonesian descent. In 1956 these regulations were made less rigid. However, when the RRA expired in January 1957, fourteen hundred visas remained unused. To fill this gap, President Dwight D. Eisenhower adopted the so-called 85-316 Act on September 11, 1957, which allowed an additional sixteen hundred Netherlanders to emigrate.

On September 2, 1958, the U.S. Congress accepted another immigration act for Dutch expatriates, the Pastore-Walter Act (PWA), which enabled another 8,956 repatriates from Indonesia to emigrate to the United States, until June 30, 1960. The PWA was implemented because in 1957 Sukarno had nationalized all Dutch businesses in Indonesia, which had caused a mass repatriation. Because the PWA proved successful, the United States decided to extend the program for two years. Ultimately, another 8,876 Dutch Indonesians settled in America under the Pastore-Walter Act II.[10]

Dutch emigration to the U.S. between 1953 and 1962 was different in sociological terms from emigration to Canada and Australia. The high proportion of people from the former Dutch East Indies had consequences for the composition of the group going to the United States. A comparative survey pointed out significant differences between the groups. A relatively high percentage of the Dutch who went to the United States were married and not affiliated with a church. A large share of them worked in the service sector and came from North and South Holland, a consequence of the fact that many repatriates lived in these provinces.

Between 1953 and 1962, the share of Calvinists in the trek to the United States dropped from 14 to 6 percent. The portion of Catholics increased remarkably from 26.5 to 35 percent. The share of emigrants belonging to the Nederlandse Hervormde Kerk rose from 27.5 percent to 36. This shift in terms of religious af-

TABLE 2
Composition of Dutch Emigrant Groups, 1955–56[11]

	Australia	Canada	U.S.
	%	%	%
Married	66	69	90
Employed in services sector	39	33	51
Income of fl.80 a week or more	21	20	43
Originating from North and South Holland	48	47	64
No religious denomination	18	13	28

filiation can be explained by the fact that Catholics and Dutch Reformed were highly overrepresented among the group of repatriates who transmigrated to the United States. Catholics and Dutch Reformed had a share of 50 percent and 35 percent respectively in this group. Only 2.5 percent of the repatriates belonged to the Gereformeerde Kerk (the Calvinist Church). However, when we exclude the emigration of Dutch Indonesians and only take into consideration Dutch emigration under the normal quotas, the Calvinists had an average share of 15.2 percent, instead of 10 percent. This justifies the conclusion that the emigration of Calvinists to the United States remained relatively strong between 1953 and 1962.

The third stage of Dutch emigration, from 1963 to 1979, was characterized by its limited size and non-agrarian character. Emigration to the United States fell from a yearly average of 3,100 emigrants during the 1960s to 340 during the 1970s. The trek to Canada also dropped considerably, from an average of 2,800 to 1,200 Dutch newcomers a year.[12] The economic restoration in the Netherlands and the drop of birthrates led to this sharp decline. Furthermore, in 1962 the Dutch government abandoned its active emigration policy and gradually curtailed related subsidies. Even the implementation of the Hart-Cellar Act (1965), which put an end to the quota system, did not lead to an increase in Dutch emigration to America. While the contingent of farmers who moved to the U.S. fell to 1 percent in 1966, the share of factory laborers, administrative personnel, skilled workers, and emigrants occupied in the services sector rose significantly. A similar process took place in Canada and Australia, where only 5 percent and 1 percent respectively of Dutch emigrants in the period 1962–66 had jobs in the agrarian sector.[13]

While emigration generally dropped during the 1970s and also during the 1980s, the trek of agrarians to the United States and Canada started to intensify during the fourth distinguishable period, from the 1980s to the present. Several factors increased the interest to emigrate among farmers: the high prices of land in the Netherlands, the poor economic performance (1979–86) resulting from the 1979 oil crisis and from tax pressures. The northern part of Texas was especially popular among Dutch dairy farmers. From 1979 to 1987 about fifty Dutch families settled in this state to start a dairy farm. From the mid-1980s onward the Dutch economy enjoyed a recovery, but farmers nevertheless faced growing problems and agrarian emigration rose strongly, especially to the Canadian province of Ontario. A couple of factors contributed to this development. In 1984, Dutch politicians, following European policies, introduced quotas to restrain the overproduction of milk. The new policies also restricted the disposal of liquid manure and farm expansion, and enlarged wetland preservation in the Netherlands. In contrast, the Canadian government paid farmers to spread manure on their neighbors' fields for fertilization. Finally, chang-

1011

6

——

THE
COLD WAR
AND
BEYOND

1945–2009

——

CULTURE

es in Canadian immigration policy in 1978 had made it easier for newcomers to set up farm enterprises. In 2000, almost 90 percent of the Dutch newcomers in Canada were dairy farmers or owners of mixed farms. Throughout the 1990s the United States had become a more popular immigration country for Dutch farmers than Canada. From 1991 to 2002 the U.S. received more than fifteen thousand Dutch emigrants. It was mainly the absence of milk quotas and the relatively cheap land prices that exerted attraction on dairy farmers (Texas) and horticulturists (California). Furthermore, the new Immigration Act of 1990 allowed more Dutch emigrants into the U.S.

Settlement, Integration, and Religious Bonds

Before the variety of cultural bonds between the Netherlands and North America — as a consequence of emigration — can be discussed, it is necessary to elucidate the settlement patterns and the integration of three significant groups (Dutch Indonesians, Catholics, and Protestants) in the host society, especially during the period of mass emigration from 1947 to 1963.

In the United States a process of concentration took place. In the first postwar years, the already established Dutch-American communities in Michigan attracted most emigrants. The direction of the emigrant stream gradually changed. In 1960 Michigan was surpassed by California, where the dairies east of Los Angeles became popular destinations. Cities on the East and West Coast and in the Midwest also exerted attraction, e.g., Seattle, Chicago, Washington, DC, and New York. The traditional rural districts in the Midwest — Michigan, Illinois, and Iowa — lost more and more ground in the 1960s. Three explanations for this shift can be provided. First, urbanization had become a general trend in both the United States and the Netherlands. Second, among the Dutch emigrants many had been repatriated from the Indies and this group in particular had a preference for California: 65 percent of the Dutch Indonesians ended up in this state, because of its climate and good employment and housing opportunities. In the third place, there were established Dutch communities in the Los Angeles and San Francisco areas, which was attractive to newcomers. A similar process of concentration occurred in Canada, where in 1971 almost 50 percent of the Dutch population resided in Ontario, 17 percent in British Columbia, and 14 percent in Alberta.[14]

To what extent did Dutch Indonesians, Catholics, and Protestants adjust to American society and how did this process influence the cultural alliance with the Netherlands? The integration of the Dutch Indonesians went relatively smoothly. They rapidly adapted and rarely congregated in separate communities or organizations like Dutch social clubs. Because most of them had lived in the Netherlands only temporarily, transnational cultural bonds with the Netherlands remained weak after their emigration.

Upon arrival in North America, Dutch Catholics joined existing national churches, mostly in urbanized areas. Because of the international character of the Catholic Church the newcomers soon interacted with other nationalities, which hastened the process of adjustment. The English liturgy used during worship stimulated Dutch Catholics to make the language adjustment quickly. On the organizational level, the Dutch contribution regarding the integration of emigrants in the United States was minimal. The Dutch Katholieke Centrale Emigratie Stichting (KCES; Catholic Central Emigration Foundation) left this work almost completely to an American "voluntary agency," the National Catholic Welfare Conference, and, on a broader level, to the International Catholic Migration Commission, which was founded in 1951 by Pope Pius XII.[15] The clergy in the Netherlands mostly relied on existing international organizations to welcome emigrants to their new country. Only occasionally were Dutch clergymen sent over to support emigrants in North America. This strategy stimulated the integration process of the emigrants who, consequently, quickly lost their Dutch mentality. Despite their quick integration, the cultural bonds of Catholics with the Netherlands remained fairly strong. They mainly kept in touch by joining Dutch-American or Dutch-Canadian social clubs and through family visits.

The integration process of Protestant emigrants was different. They were the only Dutch group that tended to isolate in its own religious organizations. Many Protestants joined already existing immigrant churches in North America, which consequently grew fast in the first postwar period. The Christian Reformed Church in the United States—a sister church of the Gereformeerde Kerken—grew from 128,000 members in 1945 to 268,000 in 1965. The Reformed Church in America—which was close to the Nederlandse Hervormde Kerk—also grew, although proportionally less than the Christian Reformed Church, from 233,000 in 1945 to 386,000 in 1965. Both churches functioned as stepping stones for newcomers and stimulated adjustment to the new country. So-called fieldmen, for example, helped Dutch emigrants find sponsors, housing, and jobs, which contributed to the integration process. A second example is that as early as the 1940s newly established Canadian churches organized alternately Dutch and English worship services.

Protestant immigrant churches not only hastened integration processes, but at the same time stimulated transnational religious interaction, especially during the first two stages of Dutch emigration, from 1947 to 1962. Between 1948 and 1956, 103 Dutch ship's chaplains traveled on emigration ships, most of them (53 percent) to Canada. These ministers often combined their voyage with visits to Canada and the United States. Consequently, bonds between

1013

6

——

THE
COLD WAR
AND
BEYOND

1945-2009

——

CULTURE

the churches in the three countries were intensified. Another example is that during the 1950s twenty-one American pastors from the Christian Reformed Church served in Canada as home missionaries. The strategy of establishing churches in a new country — which had been practiced by Dutch immigrants in the United States in the period of 1847 to 1940 — was thus transplanted to Canada. Between 1952 and 1961 the Christian Reformed Church in Canada also welcomed forty-three ministers from the Netherlands.

Transnational Contacts

Besides religious interaction, postwar Dutch emigration also led to cultural contacts on other levels. Roughly three periods of transnational cultural interaction can be discerned: 1947–62, 1963–90, and the period of the 1990s to the present.

During the first stage transnational contact was mainly stimulated by Dutch emigrants moving to North America. The emigration wave during these decades had a multiplier effect in the sense that it encouraged more emigration from the Netherlands. A good example is the fact that in 1947 Canada received 32,000 kilograms of mail from the Netherlands and in 1954 369,000, which was an increase by a factor of 11.[16] This growing flow of paper presumably stimulated further emigration: for 70 percent of all Dutch emigrants correspondence with relatives played a crucial role in the decision-making process. During this period, emigration to North America already had important economic effects. From 1947 to 1958, for instance, Dutch businesses established about forty subsidiaries in the U.S. as a result of contacts with Dutch emigrants. Another result was that thousands of Dutch agrarians participated in work placements overseas, mostly on farms in Canada, New Zealand, and the United States, especially after 1958, when the Dutch Young Farmers Program (Jonge Boeren Programma) was established.

Transnational contact during the second period (1963–90) was predominantly determined by initiatives to maintain contact with former countrymen, and not by actual emigration. The commercialization process of the aviation industry led to a sharp decline of ticket prices, which stimulated prominent Dutch clubs, e.g., AVIO in California and the Dutch Immigrant Society (DIS) in Michigan, to organize inexpensive charter flights to the Netherlands. In 1972 about six thousand DIS members — more than half of the total — took these flights. A questionnaire held in the early 1980s among 261 DIS members pointed out that the average member had returned to the Netherlands six times.[17] Vice versa, Dutch emigration strongly stimulated transatlantic tourism as well. The number of Dutch travelers who paid a visit to the United States rose significantly from 20,000 in 1963 to 44,000 in 1969, 74,000 in 1975, and 141,000 in 1978. In a 1976 survey, 55 percent of the tourists stated that visiting relatives was their main motive.[18]

It seems that since the 1990s, emigrating Dutch agrarians—in particular dairy farmers and horticulturists—have become the main intermediaries of transnational interaction again, as was the case in the first postwar years. A recent development is that the paper flow is drying up, not only because the first generation of Dutch emigrants is aging, but also because the rise of the internet and e-mail has made letter writing too slow for many, and even superfluous. Thus, it is clear that contacts between Dutch emigrants and their former homeland continue to adapt to new circumstances and opportunities, just as has been the case since the very beginning of the period discussed in this article.

1   P. Stokvis, "Nederland en de internationale migratie, 1815–1960," in F. L. van Holthoon, ed., *De Nederlandse samenleving sinds 1815. Wording en samenhang* (Assen: Van Gorcum, 1985), 71-92, here 72.

2   Marja Roholl, "Emigration Policy versus Emigrants' Policy: The Struggle between the Government and the Social Emigration Organisations in the Netherlands, 1945–1962," in Rob Kroes and Henk-Otto Neuschäfer, eds., *The Dutch in North-America: Their Immigration and Cultural Continuity* (Amsterdam: VU University Press, 1991), 57-79.

3   J. H. Elich and P. W. Blauw, *Emigreren* (Utrecht: Het Spectrum, 1983), 22.

4   Herbert Brinks, "Recent Dutch Immigration to the United States," in D. L. Cuddy, ed., *Contemporary American Immigration. Interpretive Essays* (Boston: Twayne, 1982), 136-154, here 144.

5   "Jaarverslag Stichting Landverhuizing Nederland, 1949," page 8, Archives, Koninklijke Rotterdamsche Lloyd: correspondentie 1929–1976 (entr. no. 454.05), inv. no. 826, Gemeentearchief Rotterdam (hereafter GAR).

6   Gerald DeJong, *The Dutch in America, 1609–1974* (Boston: Twayne, 1975), 185.

7   N. J. Prinsen, *De Nederlandse Hervormde Kerk en de emigratie naar Canada en Australië na de Tweede Wereldoorlog* (Bunnik: Libertas, 2005), 10-19.

8   B. P. Hofstede, *Thwarted Exodus. Post-War Overseas Migration from the Netherlands* (The Hague: Martinus Nijhoff, 1964), 125.

9   Jay Weessies, "Dutch-American Immigration Issues during the Truman Administration," *Origins* 17.2 (1999): 29-42, here 35-38.

10 H. van Stekelenburg, *De Grote Trek. Emigratie vanuit Noord-Brabant naar Noord-Amerika, 1947–1963* (Tilburg: Stichting Zuidelijk Historisch Contact, 2000), 50.

11 Hofstede, *Thwarted Exodus*, 4.

12 Figures from the Nederlandse Emigratie Dienst; See L. de Graaf and A. Kappeyne van de Coppello, *Advies over het emigratiebeleid* (The Hague: Sociaal-Economische Raad, 1985), 80.

13 "Ontwikkeling v/d emigratie," box 83, class.no. 07.77: "Statistieken emigratie, 1954-1960," Archives, Nederlandse Emigratie Dienst (hereafter NED), Ministerie van Sociale Zaken (Ministry of Social Affairs), The Hague.

14 Janny Lowensteyn, "Cultural Continuity

1015

6

———

THE
COLD WAR
AND
BEYOND

1945–2009

———

CULTURE

and Adaptation among Dutch Immigrants in the Province of Quebec," in Kroes and Neuschäfer, *The Dutch in North America*, 259-281, here 279.

15 "Letter ICMC to Dutch Ministry of Social Affairs, March 5, 1954," page 1, box 25, "Samenwerking met derden," class.no. 1.839.621/07.23, "International Catholic Migration Commission," NED.

16 "Toeneming postverkeer," box 124, class. no. 08.84, "Contacten immigranten-moederland, 1947-1957," NED.

17 Brinks, "Recent Dutch Immigration," 147.

18 Marc Dierikx, "In Pursuit of the American Dream. The Spread of the Televised American Image and the Rise of European Tourism to the United States," in Doeko Bosscher, ed., *American Culture in the Netherlands* (Amsterdam: VU University Press, 1996), 114-132.

BEYOND THE BLUE HORIZON: TOURISM AND TRAVEL

——

MARC DIERIKX

Tourism as a Political Tool

"America's most democratic weapon against communism"[1] — that was the political context in which transatlantic tourism, based on air travel, began in the years following the return of peace in 1945. In an era dominated by the emerging Cold War, even tourists featured on the political agenda. This was new. As citizens of the richest nation, Americans were front-runners in intercontinental travel. Air tourism to Western Europe originated toward the end of the 1940s with ex-servicemen who wished to recapture some of the memories of a Europe they had left in 1945. Air travel made such new encounters possible. Whereas an Atlantic crossing by ship took five to eight days each way, an airplane covered the distance in one.

In the second half of 1945 American decommissioned servicemen were the first to get a taste of transatlantic air travel, when some thirty thousand of them were ferried home monthly on board military transport aircraft. Civilian flying was initially limited to priority passengers who had been approved by their respective governments. This continued in 1946, but thereafter the numbers of other passengers began to rise. In 1947 already, some 194,000 people traveled the Atlantic air route, 85 percent more than during the previous year. In 1948 the start of the American Marshall Plan in Western Europe accounted for yet another 30 percent increase. Americans made up approximately two-thirds of all embarkations. While many of these were work related, leisure travel was also on the rise. Washington actively encouraged this development.

The federal government created a separate Travel Development Section within the Economic Cooperation Administration (ECA) of the Marshall Plan. The idea was to enable average Americans to participate in transatlantic group tours, for which reduced fares were negotiated with the airlines. For American officials the promotion of tourism to Europe meant a contribution to the fight

6

—

THE
COLD WAR
AND
BEYOND

1945–2009

—

CULTURE

1018

against communism, strengthening Western cooperation in the Cold War. The exposure of Europeans to American tourists, and more generally to the "American way of life," would, it was believed, help secure a lasting allegiance to the United States and bolster the sense of a transatlantic culture embedded in the Marshall Plan and in the newly founded NATO alliance.[2] At the same time, American tourist spending would contribute to the costs of European reconstruction. By one estimate, these tourists provided as much as one-quarter of all Western European dollar earnings in 1949. Paris, or France in general, was a preferred destination. Tourism brought the U.S. and Europe closer.

Impact of Fare Reductions

The 1950s produced a veritable travel boom. Growing prosperity and reduced air fares made this possible. Another factor was the rise of consumer credit, which allowed people to pay for their vacations in installments. American airline companies, particularly Pan American World Airways, played an instrumental role in developing international air tourism. Since 1946 it had been pressing for international agreements on fare reductions,[3] but in the International Air Transport Association (IATA) European carriers opposed these proposals for years. It was not until May 1, 1952 that the first tourist class flight, with its reduced rates, left New York, in a reconfigured Pan Am Douglas DC-6. It had thirty more seats than usual and passengers were only served sandwiches. The cost of a roundtrip ticket between New York and London went from $711 to $486.[4] In general, the new tourist class fares were 32 percent below standard costs. This turned out to be a golden idea: in 1953, the first full year in which the new tickets were sold, the IATA airlines already had 53 percent more passengers than in 1951, the last full year before the fare reductions. But even so, tourists essentially were American tourists. With a very expensive dollar at international exchange rates and currency restrictions in force in most European countries, few Europeans could afford even these lower fares. Nonetheless, the tourist class gave rise to a new phenomenon: the holiday break, in which those who could afford the price could go on a vacation that took no more than a week or two. American trips to Europe went up from 376,000 in 1953 to double that number in 1959.[5]

In 1958 a second, bigger step was taken by introducing the economy class fare, which was another 20 percent below the earlier tourist class. This new reduction brought American destinations also within reach for tourists from Europe, as shown in embarkation records. In 1963 the number of European visitors to the United States climbed to 325,500. The Organization for Economic Cooperation and Development (OECD) ascribed it to the combination of cheaper tickets and special discounts on domestic connections for foreign visitors, as well as simplified customs formalities.

Apart from this, the legal regime under which air travel took place also had an impact. International air transport required bilateral diplomatic agreement prior to the opening of any scheduled service. This had been agreed to in December 1944, when an international convention was signed establishing conditions for postwar worldwide air transport. The Chicago Convention instituted separate legal regimes for scheduled air transport (i.e., flights carried out according to a published timetable and accessible to the general public) and unscheduled carriage (i.e., charter flights). The formal bilateral exchange of landing rights was a precondition for the operation of scheduled services. It was a disconcerting experience for European nations to find that their American ally conducted a very restrictive policy toward such exchanges. Airlines from the smaller, strategically less important European countries in particular, such as the Dutch KLM, had a hard time securing more liberal access to the U.S. market. Negotiations dragged on for decades and put a strain on bilateral relations generally.[6] In 1956, The Hague even made threats not to ratify the Treaty of Friendship, Commerce and Navigation between the U.S. and the Netherlands and possibly reevaluate participation in NATO.[7] Charter flights, however, did not require prior bilateral agreements and were left at the discretion of the airlines, provided certain safety standards and procedures were met. In the 1960s low-priced charter travel effected a considerable expansion of the air travel market.

The development of aviation as a means of mass transport had been a long time in coming. Anticipation about the great future for air transport had been strong from its very early days in the months following the end of World War I. Yet the technological developments that made it possible to open up a worldwide market for travel and tourism only really took flight after 1945. In the Netherlands the national airline, KLM, was founded in October 1919 — not with the idea of using it as a means to bridge the Atlantic and connect the Old World and the New, but to bridge the distance that separated the mother country from its overseas territories in Southeast Asia. In 1919, the notion that air transport might be used for anything other than strengthening such colonial bonds, was no more than a vague hope shimmering on the horizon — the realm of visionaries and romantics hoping aviation would change the world for the better. Until the end of the 1930s America could only be reached by ship. Nonetheless, travel between the Old World and the New was substantial even then: between 1919 and 1939 over nineteen million passengers undertook the sea voyage.[8] Emigrants largely made up these numbers; only those who were able to invest the combination of time and money traveled for pleasure. The eastbound voyage, with the attractions of European history and cul-

1019

6

—

THE
COLD WAR
AND
BEYOND

1945–2009

—

CULTURE

ture, offered better prospects for tourism than sailing west, where America as a tourist destination awaited discovery.

World War II changed this situation dramatically. The outcome of the war brought to Europe a fascination for all things American. In the years that followed, America changed from a land of dreams where life offered prospects not elsewhere available, to a country one might sample as a tourist. Still, it was only in the 1960s that larger numbers of tourists began to flock westward across the Atlantic to balance the flow of Americans who came to admire history and heritage in Europe. In this development, rising disposable incomes — in 1963–64 the Netherlands and other European countries saw rapid wage increases — and reductions in air fares came together to create a growing market. But why did so many people want to travel to the U.S. in the first place?

Fascination with the "American Way of Life"

The attractiveness of the United States as tourist destination differed from that of Europe's primary air travel destination, Spain. The latter's tourist attractions could, perhaps, best be summarized as sun, sea, sand, and low prices. Tourism to the U.S. was mainly driven by curiosity about American stereotypes that had come to permeate European consciousness. Particularly from the mid-1940s onward such stereotypes became part of the European picture of things American: skyscrapers, consumerism, prosperity, car culture, the Wild West, crime and violence, fast food.

In the Netherlands, as in most European countries, the media were quick to pick up on the newborn fascination. Establishing their own correspondents in the U.S., they devoted increasing attention to life and culture in America, the country many postwar adolescents dreamed about. To many young Europeans American movies in particular seemed to depict a society in which happiness lay just around the corner (or was even on sale). An impoverished Europe, kept on its feet by Marshall aid, and sheltering under the American nuclear umbrella against the perceived threat from the East, was beguiled by the Hollywood version of the American way of life.

"Americanization" was the word that came to be used to describe the general phenomenon of increased cultural penetration of Europe. And while the material expressions of American consumer culture could be found only in prime destinations for American tourists, like Paris, their lure was universal. The Netherlands formed no exception. The fascination for things American was there, even if they could only be seen on paper or on a movie screen. America featured as the example where everything seemed to be bigger and better than in the Low Countries.

It was only in the 1960s that Dutch tourism to the U.S. came into its own. Apart from growing disposable income, its rise was linked to television. By 1960 no more than one out of every five Dutch households owned a TV set. Yet an explosive proliferation was about to take place: in 1964 the density was already over 50 percent; by 1968 four out of every five Dutch households had a set.[9] Television programs went from occasional showings of old Hollywood movies in the late 1950s to daily TV shows in the 1960s. By the middle of the decade hardly an evening went by without American programming. American serials were often the most popular of what television had to offer. The strong presence of American imagery ensured that the U.S. became the best-known foreign country, where life might be a bit tougher, but could also be more adventurous, luxurious, and where health and justice were at least as well protected as in Europe. America's exported self-images acted as a magnet attracting those who wanted (and could now afford) to taste the American Dream temporarily, for nothing more than curiosity's sake. The younger generation in particular developed a direct and deep affection for American cultural exports. Europe's teenagers, a term itself imported from America, not only consumed the American imagery, but paraded the ingredients that began to make up an emerging transatlantic youth culture: film, pop music, television series, (blue jeans) fashion. The success of commercial imagery created a number of easily recognizable American icons that were embraced by the younger generation and developed into a lingua franca understood around the world.[10]

Tour operators and airlines responded to the growing popular interest in America by offering all manner of special offers and reduced fares. Cheap charter flights, for example, proved particularly popular among young travelers. These flights proliferated in the 1960s, opening up a whole new travel market that catered to less affluent, but nonetheless travel-eager Europeans, like students. Initially aircraft could be chartered only by travel agents, or groups of people who showed a distinctive common "affinity" that justified their wish to travel together. Throughout the 1960s a gradual relaxation of the rules vastly increased the popularity of this travel mode. Before long "affinity" could mean anything, the extreme example being the American "Left Hand Club," which attracted its members with cheap air tickets until the club was exposed as fraudulent and its travelers taken off a transatlantic flight in 1971. Because of the substantially lower fares, it was not surprising that the charter concept met with growing success. If total world air transport tripled between 1963 and 1973, the share of charter airlines increased tenfold, from 2 to 20 percent. Chartered air travel increased to some 2.9 million passengers in 1970, while during that same year total airline embarkations on the transatlantic route reached 7.2 million, according to the International Air Carrier Association. Protecting the interests of its scheduled domestic carriers, U.S. aviation policy sought to ensure that all

1021

6

———

THE
COLD WAR
AND
BEYOND

1945-2009

———

CULTURE

European air travel to the United States would be restricted to a few designated gateways on the eastern seaboard, New York in particular.

In 1961 the U.S. Commerce Department started a "Visit the U.S.A." campaign to boost European tourism. Moreover, the airlines did their best each year to make their scheduled flights more attractive by marketing them in combination with cheap domestic connections and low-budget hotel accommodations. In an advertisement published in the fall of 1960, KLM proudly announced that travelers could easily save as much as 500 guilders on a regular economy-class fare of 2,015 guilders by buying one of these combined tickets. Trans World Airlines had its "Discover America" campaign, combined with a "Modern and Industrial America Tour," a fifteen-day coach trip that stopped at the major eastern seaboard cities for just $219.[11] These were special offers from which the twenty thousand or so Dutch tourists who visited the United States also benefited. And so it was that in the first half of the 1960s developments in air travel and burgeoning Americanization in Europe combined to generate a growing flow of tourist traffic to the United States. While 288,000 Europeans traveled to America in 1961, that figure more than doubled within four years. Between 1960 and 1976 the number of foreign visitors grew almost twice as fast as the international travel market as a whole: 13.6 percent per year on average. According to the OECD, tourists accounted for about 70 percent of this traffic.[12]

With public opinion in Europe turning increasingly critical toward America, the U.S. federal government was keen to present European tourists with a favorable impression of the country. In June 1966 the deputy head of the U.S. Travel Service, Sylvan Barnet, said: "We're in a hurry. We're in a particular hurry to improve our popular image. The most important finding of all the surveys we have conducted is that tourists think Americans are friendly people. And what they are saying, specifically, is that people are much friendlier here in the States than in Europe, for example."[13] It was with this element in mind that a program called "Americans at Home" was designed specifically for European visitors, allowing them to find out for themselves whether the image of America that was projected day in day out on television genuinely reflected the truth. The airlines launched massive advertising campaigns to tie in with the program. Rising criticism of the United States in the 1960s, originating in perceptions about the Vietnam War and American social problems, did not have any marked impact on the growth of European tourism to the U.S.

Of course tourists continued to travel in the opposite direction, too, and the number of their trips was not without consequence either. In 1965, and again in 1968, President Lyndon Johnson actually tried to curb foreign tourist travel as it had become an economic liability, and called upon Americans to refrain from flying abroad. On January 1, 1968 he proposed a two-year restraint program on all "nonessential" foreign travel to help cope with the American balance of payments deficit that had been running up with the costs of the Vietnam War. American airline companies were strongly opposed to the measures and made sure that the legislation that accompanied the plea — a 5 percent tax on international air travel and a levy on each day spent abroad — failed to make it through Congress. Their cooperation did not extend beyond emphasizing the desirability to travel abroad on American carriers. Figures suggest that about 50 percent of Americans traveling abroad departed on foreign carriers, mostly scheduled airlines.[14]

An annual average of some 570,000 Americans visited the Netherlands in the 1970s and 1980s. The country was often advertised as a gateway to Europe, and Amsterdam and its canals were the prime attractions. Typically, such a visit would be followed by a quick peek at Dutch windmills or the Alkmaar cheese market. Most visits were short: two days on average. More than 50 percent of these tourists left after three or four days; fewer than 20 percent stayed a week. American tourists generally belonged to higher income, education, and age groups and until the mid-1980s preferred to travel on package tours.[15]

Most Popular U.S. Destinations

In the opposite direction, tourist numbers were smaller. Between 1960 and 1980 over a million Dutch tourists visited the U.S. — that is to say, people who mentioned tourism as their prime reason for travel on their American landing card. Between 1961 and 1969 annual Dutch tourist arrivals tripled, and again between 1970 and 1979. The actual number of tourist encounters was higher, but lack of available data prevents a fully accurate reconstruction. In a 1976 survey a mere 36 percent stated tourism as their sole motive for travel; 55 percent indicated they were visiting family and friends.[16]

Most Dutch tourists first set foot on American soil in New York. This was not only the result of the almost magical attraction of this metropolis, but also because KLM had landing rights in only a few destinations in the U.S. Until 1970 New York and Houston were the only gateways assigned to the Dutch. America's refusal to grant scheduled air service to Los Angeles remained a source of friction on the bilateral agenda of the U.S. and the Netherlands until Washington finally gave in in 1979. New York in particular, with its traffic, noise, crowds of people, and sheer scale, proved something of a culture shock to newcomers. Many had a hard time when they abandoned their familiar, two-dimensional, black-and-white picture of America and stepped into what was in fact an unknown, three-dimensional world full of sound, movement, and color.

But which American symbols continued to attract tourists? General studies of the reasons for travel conducted by sociologists and psychologists usu-

1023

Advertisements for KLM's service to the United States.

ally pointed to expectations about natural features and beautiful scenery as the dominant factors underlying the choice of a particular destination. America was the exception to the rule. Here, cities were perceived to be the most attractive feature. Despite the fact that large numbers of people returned to their home countries claiming that there was not a great deal to see or do in the cities they had visited, the average European tourist nevertheless preferred to have his or her picture taken in a metropolitan setting, standing next to a limousine, with a huge skyscraper in the background. After all, these were the stereotypes of America's wealth that were easily recognizable to the folks back home. Over the years Dutch visitors to the United States largely stuck to the urbanized East Coast, about half of them venturing no farther than New York. California (i.e., San Francisco, Los Angeles, and Disneyland) came in second, attracting 23 percent, while the area around the Great Lakes, the vicinity of Chicago, was third. The younger generation, which had been submerged in the first wave of American culture in the 1950s, accounted for relatively large numbers: in 1976 the majority of Dutch tourists visiting the United States were still under the age of forty-five. While studies confirmed that tourists regarded the beauty of the landscape as a key attraction, areas of great natural beauty to which relatively little television time had been devoted, such as the Grand Canyon and Yellowstone National Park, attracted correspondingly low numbers of foreign visitors. In fact, they were the destinations of just 3.5 percent and 2 percent, respectively, of Dutch tourists. Not that the Dutch were particularly atypical in their behavior. A study of British tourists revealed a similar pattern. After all, foreign tourists in the U.S. went looking for the sort of urban images they knew best from the home television screen. Thus, cities with a high media profile (New York, Chicago, Los Angeles, San Francisco) were most popular.

Since the end of the 1970s, American destinations have continued to account for around 9 percent annually of the aggregate Dutch market for foreign travel, irrespective of changes in political perception of the U.S.[17] By comparison, the Netherlands has on average attracted approximately 5 percent of U.S. citizens traveling to Europe. Beyond the blue horizon, the American Dream has kept its universal appeal despite the ups and downs in public appreciation of the United States.

1   Christopher Endy, *Cold War Holidays: American Tourism in France* (Chapel Hill: University of North Carolina Press, 2005), 123.
2   Ibid., 33-35, 42-50, 54, 84-85, 100-103.
3   Telegram, U.S. Embassy in London to State Department, December 1, 1945, Record Group 59, State Department, Decimal Files, 711.4127/12-145, U.S. National Archives, College Park, MD.
4   Roger Bilstein, "Air Travel and the Travelling Public: The American Experi-

6

—

THE
COLD WAR
AND
BEYOND

1945–2009

—

CULTURE

1026

ence, 1920–1970, in *From Airships to Airbus: The History of Civil and Commercial Aviation*, vol. 2, William F. Trimble, ed., *Pioneers and Operations* (Washington, DC: Smithsonian Institution Press, 1995), 91-111; David Courtwright, *Sky as Frontier. Adventure, Aviation, and Empire* (College Station: Texas A&M University Press, 2005), 130-131; Endy, *Cold War Holidays*, 125.

5   Endy, *Cold War Holidays*, 128.

6   Marc Dierikx, *Clipping the Clouds: How Air Travel Changed the World* (Westport, CT: Praeger Publishers, 2008), 51-52.

7   Minutes of a meeting of representatives of the various ministries involved and KLM, September 5, 1956, Code 5, 1955-1964, 554-1, NL-U.S., part 7, Dutch Ministry of Foreign Affairs Archive, The Hague.

8   G. Besse and G. Desmas, *"Conjoncture" of Air Transport: The General Interaction between Air Transport and General Technical, Economic and Social Trends: Air Transport, Its "Conjoncture" and the General "Conjoncture" — Past Experience and Lessons for the Future*, for the 2nd Institut du Transport Aérien International Symposium (Paris: Institut du Transport Aérien, 1966), 119 (= IATA Bulletin nr. 21).

9   Jan Bank, "Televisie in de jaren zestig," *Bijdragen en Mededelingen betreffende de Geschiedenis der Nederlanden* 101.1 (1986): 52-75.

10 Rob Kroes, "The Commodification of American Icons," in William L. Chew III, ed., *Images of America: Through the European Looking-Glass* (Brussels: VUB Press, 1997), 25-36.

11 Michel van der Plas, "Amerika is anders," *Elsevier's Weekblad*, June 4, 1966.

12 OECD, *Tourism in OECD Member Countries*, 1964 (Paris: OECD, 1965), 10.

13 Quoted in Marc Dierikx, *An Image of Freedom: The Netherlands and the United States, 1945 to the Present* (The Hague: SDU uitgeverij, 1997), 74.

14 Endy, *Cold War Holidays*, 11, 182-183, 191-192.

15 P. A. Beukenkamp, *South-East U.S. Tourism to Europe and Holland: Some Characteristics of the South-East U.S. Tourists Using the Amsterdam Gateway: An Exploratory Study* (Breukelen: Nyenrode School of Business, 1989), 2:9, 10, 15-17, 30; 3:11.

16 U.S. Department of Commerce, *Summary and Analysis of International Travel to/from the United States: Calendar Year 1976 and Historical Series from 1960* (Washington, DC: U.S. Department of Commerce [United States Travel Service Research and Analysis Division], undated), 15-16; OECD, *Tourism Policy and International Tourism in OECD Member Countries - 1980* (Paris: OECD, 1981), 134. In 1969 arrivals of Dutch tourists in the U.S. stood at 44,218; in 1978 they amounted to 141,021. U.S. Department of Commerce, *Netherlands: A Study of the International Travel Market. (Results of a Sampling Survey among Residents of the Netherlands, Indicating Their International Travel Habits and Patterns, Attitudes and Preferences for Foreign Travel, and Their Demographic and Trip Characteristics)*, (Washington, DC: U.S. Department of Commerce [U.S. Travel Service Research and Analysis Division], 1978), 5-6.

17 U.S. Department of Commerce, *Netherlands*, 5; U.S. Department of Commerce, *United Kingdom: A Study of the International Travel Market* (Washington, DC: U.S. Department of Commerce [United States Travel Service Research and Analysis Division], 1978). For recent trends, see http://www.unwto.org.

THE AMERICAN IMPACT
ON DUTCH RELIGION

——

HANS KRABBENDAM

After World War II an increased mobility, the communications revolution, and a revived missionary impulse enabled American religion to spread over an unprecedented number of places in the Netherlands, both within the churches and without. At one end of the spectrum, easily accessible and simple self-help literature from religiously motivated "positive thinkers" such as Norman Vincent Peale and Robert Schuller found a broad market in the Netherlands. At the other end, distinct cults such as the Church of Jesus Christ of the Latter-day Saints or Mormons, and the members of the Watchtower Society, the Jehovah's Witnesses, recruited a small but committed band of followers. These new religious groups came most explicitly from America and had been active in the Netherlands since the second half of the nineteenth century.[1]

In between these two poles, numerous Protestants belonging to established Dutch churches also took inspiration from American sources. The main feature of this impact was the strengthening of a democratic trend, which had swept the United States since its independence. Historian Nathan O. Hatch indicated this quality as the main distinction between religion in the United States and in other modern industrial democracies.[2] The democratic ideal had emerged during the early republic and pursued three goals. The first purpose was a passion for equality and a rejection of the powers of the clergy, learning, and tradition. The second aim was to empower ordinary people with the authority of their own spiritual intuition. And the third goal was to liberate those who were suppressed elsewhere. These ends could be achieved by a variety of means, and sometimes replaced one old authority with a new one, but they all aspired to a prominent place for common men and women. This essay will show how activities of Americans led to democratization of Protestantism in the Netherlands by challenging traditional ecclesiastical authorities, empowering common believers, and spreading this liberation in society. During the pioneering phase, between 1945 and 1965, young believers and the unchurched were mobilized, which caused some tensions with both liberal and traditional theologians. During the second phase, from 1965 until 1990, these skills were used in efforts to counter secularizing trends both within and outside the churches. Since 1990 a new phase seems to have begun in which established churches accept this American influence without hesitation. A clear sign of this new trend is the development of a Baptist church into the first Dutch megachurch: Bethel in Drachten, hosting three thousand visitors each Sunday.

The focus of this essay is primarily on the foundational period of the so-called evangelical movement immediately following World War II, exemplified by an organization that carried its American origin explicitly in its Dutch name: Youth for Christ (YFC). This organization was (and is) a model of American inspiration and Dutch adaptation. It became one of the central institutions around which a Dutch evangelical subculture emerged. Before focusing on the receiving end, however, the motives of the senders need to be explored.

6

——

THE
COLD WAR
AND
BEYOND

1945–2009

——

CULTURE

1028

The American Missionary Impulse

Interdenominational social reform movements and an egalitarian tradition in America stimulated the mainline churches to seek interdenominational cooperation, a trend that continued when the U.S. became engaged in other parts of the world in the late nineteenth and early twentieth centuries. Protestant leaders and especially the chairman of the Young Men's Christian Association, John R. Mott, encouraged and prepared young Americans to redeem the world, including Europe. American money, manpower, and the notion of America's Manifest Destiny strengthened the global missionary enterprise. Americans took over the leading position from a Europe that, weakened by World War I, lacked energy, was stifled by slumbering state churches, and was too preoccupied with its own empires to assume this task on the mission fields. However, after 1925 the missionary zeal in America and Europe waned.

During and following World War II, a new impetus emerged among American evangelicals. Some of them attempted to transcend their defensive fundamentalism and sought to restore the central position they had occupied in the nineteenth century. In 1942 they founded a platform, the National Association of Evangelicals (NAE), which became an alternative to the more liberal Federal Council of Churches (1908). Evangelicals emphasize four basic beliefs, all of which have a socially leveling effect: a personal and explicit conversion experience; active involvement in the organization of revival meetings and the development of social programs; a strong attachment to the Bible as God's authoritative revelation, free of human devices; and a firm belief that Jesus Christ's death on the cross is the crucial event in history. Additional features include an urgent expectation of the end of times and an emphasis on the special gifts of the Spirit. In comparison, Dutch orthodox Protestants shared the centrality of Jesus' atonement and the strong authority of the Bible, but tied its interpretation to historic confessional standards. The emphasis on a conversion experience was strong only among pietist believers who kept their distance from those evangelicals recognizing free will.[3]

The Dutch discovered American religious events in the mid-nineteenth century, borrowing practical aspects from American Protestants such as temperance campaigns, gospel songs, and stimulating attention for the inner working of the Holy Spirit. Dutch observers were familiar with mass evangelism campaigns of Dwight L. Moody in England in the 1870s, marveled at former baseball hero turned evangelist Billy Sunday in the early 1900s, and a few of them briefly embraced the pietist Oxford Movement, which led to the Moral Rearmament Campaign of Frank Buchman in the 1920s and 1930s. These incidents did not structurally change the Dutch religious scene, but proved to be reminders of the promise of spiritual injections from America, which did become structural after World War II.

Youth for Christ: A Bridgehead

Youth for Christ originated in a series of local youth rallies in the United States during World War II. These meetings were set up by fundamentalist ministers as alternatives to the worldly and "cheap" forms of entertainment frequented by teenagers and young service men and women who were off duty. The programs were lighthearted, with easy-listening gospel songs, testimonies by entertainers, athletes, businessmen, and military heroes, and short sermons tailored for the young generation and addressing their concerns and problems. Its style has been described as "evangelical vaudeville," which caught the attention of a young audience and showed that traditional Christianity need not be dull and stale.[4]

It was Torrey Johnson, Baptist pastor, initiator of Christian radio programs in the Chicago area, and a delegate to the still young NAE, who brought the idea to Chicago and recruited Billy Graham for his radio work and youth rallies. After the war, many Americans volunteered to help Europe back on its feet. The goals of the American nation and its churches were compatible: both urgently resisted the threat of the materialistic and godless Soviet Union. While the mainline denominations continued to provide relief, evangelicals and new religious movements were directly concerned with the spiritual dimension, even though they also provided humanitarian aid. Their vocal anticommunism, the celebration of economic freedom in the U.S. and of old-fashioned values se-

6

—

—

cured the support of wealthy American businessmen and established a sound financial basis for this type of ministry. They succeeded in pairing their contagious enthusiasm with great organizational skills. Graham and his associates secured a clean reputation by creating a code that included never being alone with a woman, checking one another's pastoral contacts, depositing finances in a separate and accountable fund, letting civil authorities estimate attendance, and meeting with critics in person.

The successes in America stimulated the young YFC organization to send a team to Europe in March 1946. Their intention to reach the masses was clear from the services of Wesley Hartzell, a Christian newspaperman from the Hearst concern who proved his value in securing professional coverage for the activities of this mission. He gave the serendipities of the improvised tour a spiritual meaning.[5]

The democratizing effect of YFC was visible in its efforts to reach the masses of Dutch youths. YFC president Torrey Johnson justified this mission to the Netherlands, where he had found "a church paralyzed by formal fundamentalism and dead orthodoxy … a nation recovering from the gaping wounds of a bloody war … young people hungry for God and the Gospel — moral casualties of World War II reaching out for reality."[6] As in other European capitals, the team in Amsterdam solicited support from local youth ministers and theologians, linked up with existing groups, addressed them in English, and left instructions for a more permanent organization.[7]

YFC received strong support for its mission plan from volunteers among the Dutch-American community in the Midwest. Joseph Biegel, a Dutch-American baker on Chicago's South Side, mobilized the Dutch-American business community to underwrite a team for the Netherlands at five thousand dollars per year. It proved a mutually profitable combination for YFC. The Dutch Americans supported YFC's work in Europe and reports about a worldwide revival in the making gave the organization an enormous boost at home.

The Dutch-American team came to the Netherlands in October 1946 to hold meetings in the major cities and set up a permanent organization in two months' time. The team members were recruited for their practical experience in YFC. Their official ministry, however, helped them assuage the criticism of the Dutch clergy, whom they met in special meetings. They also met with key leaders, such as the world-famous missiologist Hendrik Kraemer and the aged evangelist and song writer Johannes de Heer. They reached a broad audience through mass distribution of three hundred thousand pamphlets, recruiting many volunteers, delegating authority to local leaders, encouraging spiritual growth, and organizing social events. The spokespeople denied negative stories about YFC rallies being an excuse for drinking, dancing, and jazz music, even as these rumors inadvertently suggested that they were hip events.[8]

The motive of liberation became visible in the team's conviction that it took part in a spiritual battle, pitching Youth for Christ against communism. This generated the energy necessary to hold forty-two meetings in twenty-four cities on thirty-seven evenings, and to travel in minimal comfort and sleep in hotels and private homes. The communists confirmed this spiritual dimension by their failed efforts to disrupt meetings in Amsterdam and Utrecht.[9] The team reports testified that they had addressed fifty-six thousand people, of whom thirty-five hundred had indicated wanting to accept Christ as their Savior. On an average night between eight hundred and two thousand attended, often overflowing the venue's capacity.[10] This unexpected response proved that mass evangelism could work in the Netherlands, and that a parachurch organization was much more effective and efficient than church agencies.[11] Despite much criticism by ministers, YFC was accepted by prominent church leaders and lay people. A national board, led by the head of an efficiency agency, solved the main problem of organizing mass evangelistic meetings without entanglement in church politics. The strict Calvinist churches, however, rejected the Arminian free-will character of the evangelicals; the small Protestant groups, such as the Salvation Army, Baptist and Pentecostal churches, lacked the resources to help; and the big Protestant churches kept their youth programs in their own professional hands. Meanwhile, the sense of urgency remained. The YFC team fervently prayed for access to Germany, believing that "only a spiritual revival [could] save Germany and Europe."[12]

The Development of an Alternative Youth Movement

The passion for equality among American evangelicals did not lead to a frontal attack on the church authorities — far from it — but it did so indirectly by the explicit call for conversion, there and then. One became a Christian through a spontaneous response based on a religious experience, instead of a confession of faith after years of catechism lessons. This "lived religion" presented faith as an adventure and not merely a tradition. Of course, the emotional response was not entirely spontaneous, because it was evoked through a time-tested program of harmonic music and a captivating exhortation. All of this happened in civic auditoriums or in rented church buildings, but outside the authority of established institutional religion. The self-assured young Americans had a clear understanding of the contents of their faith and were able to communicate a well-structured and straightforward message to a broad audience. While many established religious authorities rejected the YFC approach as Methodist, they had to admit that YFC succeeded where they failed: in reaching large numbers of the young generation with the gospel message. Meanwhile, the official

1031

6

—

THE
COLD WAR
AND
BEYOND

1945–2009

—

CULTURE

Christian youth work lost itself in the jungle of government subsidies and bureaucracies, and neglected the spiritual aspect of its work through its emphasis on development of creative abilities, ecumenical contacts, and social action instead of basic evangelistic outreach.

The democratizing effects of Youth for Christ nicely fit in historian Peter van Rooden's characterization of the postwar change in Dutch society and religion, as a shift from ritualized and collective experiences to individual expression and the development of a reflective self. The rallies taught the teenagers and young adults to appropriate their faith through a simple song sung both in English and in Dutch: "Jesus Christ is the Way, Jesus Christ is the Truth, Jesus Christ is the Life, and He's mine, mine, mine." They did not need a blessing from a minister, but experienced it among themselves. Before, during, and after the meetings people prayed spontaneously for the cause and for one another. The spectacular results helped connect personal activity and divine blessing, confirming that faith was an action, not a passive adherence.

The American team quickly taught the Dutch how to proceed, with literature and training models, offering training sessions to individual staff, and injecting seed money from the United States. After the absorption of a number of local organizations for evangelism, the Dutch YFC began to train its own leadership in impromptu courses and camps, and at the Nederlands Bijbel Instituut in Doorn, established in 1948. Churches modeled their evangelistic meetings after YFC. Local chapters organized rallies, which met an interest until the 1950s, but the truly big mass events were only possible when the Americans came to town.[13]

This opportunity arose in 1954 when Billy Graham, now independent from the American YFC, embarked on a British and continental tour. On June 22, Graham addressed a crowd of thirty thousand people in Amsterdam's Olympic Stadium, after meeting with eighteen hundred ministers and volunteers during the day. The Billy Graham organization prepared well for this visit. It assessed the spiritual situation in the Netherlands as weakening, caused by a decline in the Protestant proportion of the population, a strong formalism, and an impressive (Barthian) theology, which obstructed a simple straightforward presentation of the gospel. However, it also recognized a growing interest in evangelism and a crucial role for the Dutch in tying evangelicals in western European countries together. In 1955 Graham returned to address an even larger crowd in the Rotterdam soccer stadium De Kuip on June 30.

These mass meetings, which drew national attention and effectively used modern communications technology, were soon copied by American faith healers. In 1958 T. L. Osborn drew at least as much attention as Billy Graham had gathered. With a campaign in late August in The Hague and Groningen he gave an enormous boost to the Pentecostal Movement in the Netherlands and

Billy Graham and representatives of the Salvation Army at his rally
in Amsterdam, 1954.

6

———

THE
COLD WAR
AND
BEYOND

1945–2009

———

CULTURE

inspired the Dutch Pentecostal pioneers Johan Maasbach and Ben Hoekendijk to expand their ministries. These new religious leaders followed American examples by advertising their ministries and using their own names, and challenged the churches by founding new congregations.

YFC appeared at the right time. In America it benefited from a restoration of respect for religion and national destiny, a return to basic values, and a concern with juvenile morality. In the Netherlands YFC was aided by the positive image of American liberators, reinforced by private American relief and the public Marshall Plan. A combination of feelings of relief after the war horrors and concern for the moral future of the next generation created a receptive audience.

The plain message enabled the young to fully participate and assume responsibility, and the first fruits encouraged them to pursue their aims. The permanent campaign kept them committed to practical local activities and connected with the larger world. The emphasis on personal conversion constituted a key part. To American evangelicals, the truth of their beliefs is established by visible transformations of individual lives. A lack of converts would weaken the validity of the gospel. Though in theory many Protestant ministers acknowledged these conversions, they were not convinced that conversion changed people on the spot and questioned the pressure put on people. They were also a bit shy with the new converts, who themselves missed the spiritual space, the emotions, spontaneity, relevance of sermons, and the singing, and were drawn to Baptist, Pentecostal, and Full Gospel churches.[14]

In the late 1950s the YFC organization stagnated. It was torn between those who wanted to continue the rallies and those charmed by the Pentecostal wave of faith healers, who jeopardized the fragile contacts with the established churches. The founding members left the leadership, local chapters disbanded, and those remaining turned inward. The emerging youth culture asked for a new approach.

Toward a Movement, 1965–90

The prosperity of the 1960s, with a 3.5 percent annual growth of income enabled expenditures for individualized mobility, physical and emotional pleasures, and popular entertainment. This trend contrasted with the collective and ritualized forms of organized religion, which seemed to lose their relevance for everyday life. While progressive Dutch theologians sensed the new demands of the era, they remained elitist and replaced one brand of conformity with another, despite the promises of liberation. Moreover, they were inexperienced in marketing their ideas.[15]

In the late 1960s YFC found the right answer in the coffee bar: a safe ("dry") cozy place for conversation, a speaker, or a gospel artist with a testimony. In addition, it developed the first Christian rehabilitation program for drug addicts. Like-minded organizations from America joined in. Reports about the rapid secularization of the Netherlands in the mid-1960s triggered the founding of a number of specialized evangelistic bodies: in 1968 Campus Crusade for Christ (later called Instituut voor Evangelisatie), in 1969 Continental Sound, which organized gospel concerts as outreach. Teen Challenge and a number of local Jesus People communes in the 1970s took pity on drug addicts and modeled their cure after American examples. Youth for Christ had connections with many of these organizations, which shared the same concerns, aims, methods, and styles. In the 1970s more than one hundred local chapters organized activities, while its magazine had a circulation of eight thousand.

The established churches showed mixed reactions to these eruptions of spiritual renewal. Initially they were curious, giving these groups the benefit of the doubt, until they presented themselves as competitors to the church by baptizing adults, many of whom had been baptized as children, and sharing the sacraments. Many saw the evangelical operations as a return to old (and abandoned) certainties. The evangelicals blamed the modernist theology of the mainline churches for the decline of organized religion. They took to founding practical Bible Schools for training evangelists, which had a multiplier effect on evangelical initiatives. In 1967 the Pentecostals founded a seminary modeled after the American Assemblies of God. The charismatics of Youth With a Mission began a commune in Amsterdam and soon opened training facilities for various missionary jobs in other places in the Netherlands.[16] From 1973 on, the Evangelical Missions Alliance assisted an ever-growing number of private missionary organizations in their professionalization efforts and became an alternative to the official mission societies of the churches.

All these organizations gradually contributed to an emerging evangelical network that circulated ideas and personnel. They collectively challenged the traditional institutions and equipped their supporters with skills and knowledge to create an alternative. These parachurch organizations were the real innovation. A survey of the most important evangelical organizations in 1984 counted three evangelical denominations and twenty-nine parachurch organizations, all of which had interlocking contacts. Four of them could trace their lineage directly to the United States, while many others had close inspirational ties with American evangelicals. The flow of American resources was channeled by new communication initiatives. Among these was the publishing firm of Gideon, which translated a large selection of American authors into Dutch, but the key player in the formation of an evangelical movement was the Evangelical Broadcasting Company (Evangelische Omroep or EO), founded in 1967.[17]

1035

6

———

THE
COLD WAR
AND
BEYOND

1945–2009

———

CULTURE

The impetus for the EO came in 1965 when the Protestant broadcasting association NCRV canceled its devotional program. American experts helped prepare the first EO broadcasts in 1970.[18] The organization grew rapidly from the initial twenty thousand supporters to one hundred thousand in 1971, three hundred thousand in 1983, and six hundred thousand in 1997. Its success in drawing tens of thousands of young people to its annual rally served as a symbol for the vitality of religion in a secularized society. The EO became the hub for many new initiatives among Dutch evangelicals. This cooperation triggered the founding of an Evangelical College in 1977, which prepared college students for an atmosphere challenging their faith at the universities and specifically tried to defend creationism and challenge evolution. In 1981 a former EO reporter became the first member of parliament for a new political party, the Reformatorische Politieke Federatie (RPF). The RPF was founded in 1975 in response to the liberalizing trend in abortion rules and the pressure to make Christian institutions conform to nondiscriminatory legislation relative to gay employees. A new democratic outlet for orthodox Christians took shape.

Not all efforts were successful. A national outreach campaign in 1982 following American examples by distributing 5.2 million tracts door to door in the Netherlands alienated the established churches and overextended the organizers' financial means. The evangelicals survived a brief spell of anticult sentiment in the early 1980s, when the more radical evangelical groups such as the Jesus People were considered suspect.

Conclusion

In the United States, YFC had contributed to, and represented, the public acceptance of orthodox Christianity. American evangelicals had jointly turned wartime anxiety into a nationwide revival, and this success had brought them close to the heart of the nation. They were accepted when they muted their distinct message and shared the celebration of America's goodness until their fundamentalist brethren, who had stayed behind, came forward and entered the public sphere in the late 1970s. The situation in the Netherlands was quite different. There, evangelicals were only a small minority and did not inherit the role of being the source of traditional values for the nation. But over the years they proved to offer an alternative path for orthodox Christians to participate in a modernizing society.[19] In the 1980s, YFC leaders rose to national and international positions in evangelical and ecclesiastical organizations.

The democratizing effects of American volunteers helped emancipate orthodox believers in the Netherlands at a time when the pillarized society crumbled. They familiarized the Dutch with parachurch organizations, which allowed cooperation with fellow believers without the strain of defining formal relations to the churches. Subsequently, these models encouraged orthodox Protestants confronted with the rapid process of unchurching, to find innovative cultural means as an alternative to the less effective outreach practices by church agencies. The latest trend is to emphasize the missionary practice of local churches by making evangelism and outreach their first priority. What cemented the contact was a frank spirituality maintained by and in small groups. These trends increased commitment to the church through an experienced relevance of faith. The frank showing of emotions strengthened subjectivity and the voluntary character of the groups made ties informal and membership flexible. The optimism of American evangelicals encouraged the Dutch orthodox believers to become active again: they were not predestined to decline. The evangelicals added personal experience as a source of authority, without rejecting the authority of the Bible. This met the need for authenticity that had begun to surface in the 1960s. Many orthodox believers experienced that liberal theology increased the distance to God and that religion declined. The evangelical tradition helped them keep their faith, independent of theologians, and reclaim part of their domain.

A reported eight hundred thousand Dutch believers identify themselves today as evangelicals and many experts predict that they will soon dominate the Protestant churches. Whatever the future may bring, Dutch evangelicals owe much to the democratizing tools of their American kin.

1   Other small groups with American origins are the Christian Scientists and the Adventists.

2   Nathan O. Hatch, *The Democratization of American Christianity* (New Haven, CT: Yale University Press, 1989), 5.

3   David Bebbington, "Evangelicalism in Its Settings: The British and American Movements since 1940," in Mark Noll, David W. Bebbington, and George A. Rawlyk, eds., *Evangelicalism: Comparative Studies of Popular Protestantism in North America, the British Isles, and Beyond, 1700–1990* (New York: Oxford University Press, 1994), 365-388.

4   William Martin, *A Prophet with Honor: The Billy Graham Story* (New York: Morrow, 1991), 93.

5   *Youth for Christ Magazine*, September 1946, 31.

6   *Youth for Christ Magazine*, November 1946, 4-5; Spencer C. De Jong, "YFC Holland Report," brochure in Stratton Shufelt Papers, box 1, folder 17; Douglas Fisher, "The Holland Story," in The Papers of Torrey Maynard Johnson, Sr. (hereafter TMJ Papers), 1919-2001: box 27, folder 5, Holland (1946-1949), Collection 285 of the Billy Graham Center Archives, Wheaton College, Wheaton, IL (hereafter BGCA).

7   Lesley Hartzell, "Fourth and Fifth Week YFC Itinerary," in J. Stratton Shufelt Papers, 1930-1979, Collection 224, box 1, folder 17, Youth for Christ, European Teams: Letters and Reports; March-April 1946; May-June, 1947, BGCA.

6

—

THE
COLD WAR
AND
BEYOND

1945–2009

—

CULTURE

8   "YFC Holland Report" and News Letter by S. De Jong (October 2, 1946), TMJ Papers.

9   De Jong to Torrey, early November 1946; Transcript of telephone conversation, October 5, 1946, TMJ Papers.

10 *Youth for Christ Magazine*, February 1947, 4-5, 54.

11 De Jong, "Special News Report," TMJ Papers (October 16, 1946), and published report in *Youth for Christ Magazine*, January 1947, 54.

12 News Letter no 2, May 31, 1947, Shufelt Papers, BGCA.

13 Jan van Capelleveen et al., *De story van Youth for Christ* (Kampen: Kok, 1977), 41.

14 Sipco J. Vellenga, *Een ondernemende beweging. De groei van de evangelische beweging in Nederland* (Amsterdam: VU Uitgeverij, 1991), 106.

15 Peter van Rooden, "Long-Term Religious Developments in the Netherlands, ca 1750–2000," in Hugh McLeod and Werner Ustorf, eds., *The Decline of Christendom in Western Europe, 1750–2000* (Cambridge: Cambridge University Press 2002), 113-129.

16 C. and P. N. van der Laan, *Pinksteren in beweging. Vijfenzeventig jaar pinkstergeschiedenis in Nederland en Vlaanderen* (Kampen: Kok, 1982), 57-62, 69, 79; Vellenga, *Een ondernemende beweging*, 28-36.

17 Hijme C. Stoffels, "Wegwijzer in evangelisch Nederland," *Religieuze Bewegingen in Nederland* 9 (Amsterdam: VU Boekhandel/Uitgeverij, 1984): 101-152.

18 *Altijd goed voor... Hartkloppingen* (Hilversum: Evangelische Omroep, 2007), 20-25, 167.

19 Joel Carpenter, "Youth for Christ and the New Evangelicals' Place in the Life of the Nation," in Rowland A. Sherril, ed., *Religion and the Life of the Nation: American Recoveries* (Urbana: University of Illinois Press, 1990), 128-151.

AMERICANIZING TRENDS IN DUTCH PROSE AND POETRY

—

JAAP VAN DER BENT & BERTRAM MOURITS

In the years preceding World War II there was not a great deal of Dutch interest in English and American literature. The writers of the so-called *Forum* generation (named after an influential literary magazine published in the Netherlands between 1932 and 1935) tended to look to France and sometimes to Germany for inspiration. *Forum* author Menno ter Braak, who despised America, would only refer to the country in quotation marks. This changed in the postwar period. As critic Kees Fens once wrote, English was the language associated with the liberation; for him it became the most beautiful language he had ever read.[1] Fens was not the only one to think so, as is illustrated by the fact that around 1950 a number of Dutch literary magazines did not hesitate to publish contributions in English: the February 1950 issue of *Podium*, for instance, contained two poems by the American author Elliott Stein, and in 1951 the first twelve pages of the final issue of *Braak* were even entirely in English.

This affinity with the English language was in line with the eagerness of writers and critics, but also of readers in general, to find out what had been going on in English and American literature, especially in the most recent period. First, discoveries were made by critics like Paul Rodenko and Jacques den Haan. Along with the Dutch novelist Willem Frederik Hermans, both were impressed by the work of Henry Miller and both found an outlet for their reviews and articles on Miller (as well as other American writers) in *Litterair Paspoort*. This magazine was founded by Den Haan and the poet Adriaan Morriën in 1948 in order to acquaint Dutch readers with what had been happening in foreign literature during and immediately after the war. *Litterair Paspoort*, which continued to appear until the early 1970s, and later *Randstad*, a magazine published in book format between 1961 and 1969, played an important role in making Dutch readers aware of literary developments in the United

6

———

THE
COLD WAR
AND
BEYOND

1945–2009

———

CULTURE

States. *Randstad* was closely modeled on American examples such as *Big Table* and *City Lights Journal*. The magazine's range of topics was wide: it contained poetry, essays, art, and photography from all over the world, but its American focus was obvious from commentaries on American politics and several articles in the vein of New Journalism (translated as well as originally written in Dutch). *Randstad* helped make American popular culture more widely known, also among Dutch authors, and as a result the influence of popular culture became increasingly prominent. While poets in the 1960s were influenced by William Carlos Williams and Marianne Moore and by contemporary authors like Frank O'Hara and John Ashbery, at the same time jazz, pop music, television, and advertising also found their way into the literary domain.

Prose

As is suggested by the relatively late Dutch reception of Henry Miller, whose work already had been published in the 1930s, readers and writers in the Netherlands were sometimes rather slow in their discovery and appreciation of new American novelists. In Miller's case the intervening war, of course, served as an excuse, but in the following decades it usually took a number of years as well before the work of groundbreaking new American writers was discovered in the Netherlands and incorporated into literary life to such an extent that it could begin to affect the work of Dutch authors. Two of the most important Dutch authors who began to write in the 1950s, Jan Wolkers and Remco Campert, were influenced not by recent authors but by earlier American fiction. Wolkers' work owes much to the stance and tone of Ernest Hemingway's novels, although Wolkers combines Hemingway's stoicism with a much more baroque use of language; as far as Campert is concerned, it is easy to see that his wistfulness and his sharp eye for detail can to a large extent be attributed to the influence of F. Scott Fitzgerald and to the kind of writing that was popularized by *The New Yorker* since its inception in the mid-1920s.

To be sure, this lag time was becoming much shorter. When the Beat Generation appeared on the American literary scene in the 1950s, this new development was closely observed in *Litterair Paspoort*. Especially after poets Allen Ginsberg, Gregory Corso, and Peter Orlovsky had temporarily settled in Amsterdam in 1957, *Litterair Paspoort* regularly paid attention to the Beats. The magazine not only reviewed books by Beat writers, but in November 1957 it also published the essay "The Literary Revolution in America," written by Corso and Ginsberg at the request of Adriaan Morriën, which was one of the first essays in which the Beat movement was discussed by two of its own members. Still, it took a number of years before the echoes of Jack Kerouac's fiction and Allen

Jan Cremer (left) and Frank O'Hara eating
raw herring in Amsterdam, in 1963.

6

—

THE
COLD WAR
AND
BEYOND

1945–2009

—

CULTURE

Ginsberg's poetry could be detected in the work of Simon Vinkenoog and other literary rebels. Vinkenoog's third novel in particular, *Hoogseizoen* (1962), while also referring to Ginsberg and Corso, is a spontaneous account of bohemian life in Amsterdam in the early 1960s that is frequently reminiscent of Kerouac. Another Dutch writer often associated with the Beats is Jan Cremer. His autobiographical novel *Ik Jan Cremer* exploded like a bombshell on the Dutch literary scene in 1964 and even created minor ripples abroad in its English translation, and Cremer spent much of his time in America in the 1960s and afterwards. While Henry Miller and Kerouac can be mentioned as influences on Cremer's first novel, the influence of the Beats and of various aspects of American society are especially noticeable in *Jan Cremer 2* (1966) and in his third novel, *Made in U.$.A.* (1969). The more experimental fiction of Beat writer William Burroughs left a strong mark on the two novels that Cornelis Bastiaan Vaandrager published in the early 1970s: *De Reus van Rotterdam* (1971) and *De Hef* (1975). Both have a mosaic-like structure and a drug-related subject matter that owe much to the American author.

By the early 1970s, the American literary scene had moved from the Beats to the postmodernists and to neorealist writers like Raymond Carver and Richard Ford. American neorealism found fertile soil in the Netherlands, which has always had a strong realist tradition; in the 1970s (and later) its influence is clearly seen in the work of, for instance, Jan Donkers, whose fascination with American culture and society is evident both in his short stories and in his nonfiction. Johnny van Doorn is another example: his poetry was heavily influenced by Beat literature, but as a prose author he would develop into a Dutch "dirty realist" with several short-story collections.

The acceptance of American postmodernism, however, was slow and again suggests that it sometimes takes time for Dutch readers and writers to familiarize themselves with literary developments shaking other parts of the world. Frans Ruiter corroborates this in an essay in which he tries to find reasons why "postmodernism as a label became accepted in The Netherlands only in the second half of the eighties."[2] Attempting to penetrate the workings of the Dutch literary and academic world, Ruiter uses the case of the American literary scholar Leslie Fiedler, whose radical ideas on postmodern and popular literature had regularly been featured in *Litterair Paspoort,* without making much of an impression. After Fiedler had been invited in 1967 as a visiting professor by the University of Amsterdam, the invitation was quickly withdrawn when it became known that in the United States Fiedler had been prosecuted on the charge of maintaining premises where drugs were being used. The university's hasty decision led to much controversy, in which the originality of Fiedler's ideas hardly played a role. At the same time those ideas were considered highly relevant in Germany. Ruiter's explanation of this difference in Fiedler's reception is that in the Netherlands "the political turmoil at the end of the sixties was less linked to literary issues than in Germany." As a consequence, in the Netherlands the debate about Fiedler focused on a political issue and overlooked the value of his literary views, including his ideas on postmodernism, which fell on much more fertile ground in Germany.[3]

According to many, the gap in Dutch literature between politics and literature, between society and fiction, still existed at the beginning of the 1980s. In 1981 Dutch literary historian Ton Anbeek published an essay about American and Dutch literature that caused quite a stir and is still regularly mentioned. In "Aanval en afstandelijkheid: Een vergelijking tussen Nederlandse en Amerikaanse romans" (Attack and Detachment: A Comparison between Dutch and American Novels), published in the leading Dutch literary magazine *De Gids*, Anbeek made a comparison between two recent, bestselling Dutch novels and three slightly less recent American novels. What he found attractive about the American novels — the extravagance of their plots, their energetic tone, and, especially, their authors' willingness to take on relevant social issues — he found sadly lacking in recent Dutch fiction. In Anbeek's view, Dutch fiction was especially in need of more "street noise," which quickly became the term that was used whenever Dutch writers were asked to include more social issues in their work. Whether or not they heeded Anbeek's call, in the 1980s and 1990s Dutch novelists like Joost Zwagerman en Leon de Winter — inspired by American authors ranging from Bernard Malamud and Saul Bellow to Jay McInerney and Bret Easton Ellis — did find room in their work for some of the forces and events that in their view defined the last two decades of the twentieth century. It probably has as much to do with changes in Dutch society — immigration especially, and the backlash against it, have changed the nature of social exchange — as with American influences, but it cannot be denied that in recent years many of the social and ethnic issues that have come to dominate the Dutch political debate have found their way into the work of, for instance, Marja Brouwers, Abdelkader Benali, and Robert Anker. The popularity of New Journalism in the Netherlands (which is usually called "literary nonfiction") also indicates an increasing interest in political and social matters.

Poetry

1043

After World War II, Dutch poetry went through a period of reconstruction; traditional forms and themes were prominent until the *Vijftigers* entered the scene, a group of young poets who wanted to break free from formal traditions

6
—
THE
COLD WAR
AND
BEYOND

1945–2009
—

CULTURE

and drew their inspiration in particular from the European avant-garde. The only aspect of American culture that appealed to this group was jazz music, mainly discovered in Paris.

There were some exceptions: Hans Lodeizen was a friend of the American poet James Merrill, and he wrote some (mediocre) poems in English. The time he spent at Amherst College, in Massachusetts, in the second half of the 1940s helped him come into his own as a poet and as a person. Simon Vinkenoog translated, and was inspired by, the work of Allen Ginsberg. And Jan Hanlo was one of the first poets to openly appreciate American popular culture. In a 1954 interview Adriaan Morriën asked Hanlo which poets he read. The answer was evasive: "One of the few things I read is Donald Duck. I think Walt Disney is very good."[4] Although Hanlo might not be typical of his contemporaries, his preference for the comic book shows a changing position in favor of American popular culture from a man who wrote about jazz music and comics, especially Charles Schultz's Peanuts strip. With these interests, he fit in very well with people associated with the literary journal *Barbarber*. From 1958 until 1971 this was one of the places where young Dutch poets reported their discoveries of American culture. There was a special issue about America, with poetry by Robert Lowell, the credits from the movie *The Fortune Cookie*, and essays about Charles Ives and Hoagy Carmichael.

J. Bernlef, one of the editors of *Barbarber*, introduced several American poets to the Netherlands: Marianne Moore, William Carlos Williams, Weldon Kees, Elizabeth Bishop, and others. Bernlef learned from them as well: he used the colloquial language and the collage technique employed by some of them, for several long, epic poems—which he would later disown.[5] He was not the only one to apply this technique: Leo Vroman's "Over de dichtkunst" (On Poetry) is a long poem that describes how Vroman uses text fragments, newspaper clippings, and inspiration from other everyday sources to create a deliberately imperfect work, protesting against "that damned divinity of the perfect poem," as he wrote in a letter to Bert Voeten, editor of *De Gids.*

The poets of the 1960s were not on a mission when they introduced American art to the Dutch public. They were looking for similar work and a sounding board, and they found it in American popular culture and in its anti-academic attitude. In doing so, they found the same "godfather" as their American contemporaries: William Carlos Williams, and especially his epic work *Paterson*, with the credo "Anything is good material for poetry. Anything. I've said it time and time again." This refreshing idea, taken from Dada and the avant-garde, resonated through the 1960s, and when Dutch poets discovered American literature the prewar William Carlos Williams was among their first finds.

The discovery of America in Dutch poetry took place in the 1960s and coincided with the last stage of literary history that can be described with any coherence, since from the 1970s on there no longer have been any leading groups or schools. Rather, movements now exist next to each other, and they are often called "neo something": neosymbolist, neo-Romanticist, neorealist, all drawing upon older traditions but not "advancing" the history of poetry, and all of them mostly working in the lyric tradition. America's strong anti-academic outlook would only come to the surface again with the so-called *maximale poëzie*, written by a group of poets who leaned heavily on the rhetoric and style of the *Vijftigers*, without referring to either the U.S. or to previous poets. With the *Maximalen* the development from the 1930s (anti-America), through the 1940s (reconstruction) and the 1950s (early adopters), and ending in the 1960s (genuine discovery) comes to a grinding halt. Dutch poetry is very much alive and very versatile, but "the era of the great movements has passed" (as Elly de Waard put it)[6] and poetry borrows from various sources, as is illustrated also by what happened on stage and in songs.

In June 1965, Simon Vinkenoog attended an international poetry festival at the Royal Albert Hall in London, organized by Allen Ginsberg. He was impressed and managed to organize something similar in Amsterdam in record time: Poëzie in Carré (Poetry in Carré), a gathering of twenty-six Dutch poets who read their work to an audience of two thousand people in the Carré Theater. This major event in the history of performance poetry in the Netherlands, held in February 1966, was the blueprint for the highly successful Nacht van de Poëzie (Night of Poetry) in Utrecht, now an annual event, not to mention numerous other poetry festivals all over the country. This was the period during which poetry descended from its ivory tower, as literary history would have it. Vinkenoog (a fan of the Beat poets) was instrumental in this development. He could have been writing about himself when he described Ginsberg's work as stemming from "a protest attitude against existing perceptions of poetry, and associative and irrational impulses all contributed to the Celebration of the Word."[7] This resulted in long poems, with many personal associations, inspired by drugs, jazz music, or both. Spontaneity was the key word: "type writer jazz," in the words of Lawrence Ferlinghetti.[8] Poëzie in Carré was the beginning of a long tradition of spoken poetry, but it was quickly adopted by the establishment.

The performance tradition was rejuvenated by yet another American invention, the slam. In the mid-1980s, poetry slams had become increasingly popular in the U.S. These are open-mike events for poets who compete for attention and applause, thus mocking the idea of poetry as a genre of subtle reflection. The influence of rap culture—where dissing and bragging are standard procedure—is obvious, the winning poet often being the one who best manages to move away from the word on paper. Poet Ron Alcalay sees slam as an extension of the Beat tradition: social awareness and spontaneity are combined and "poet-

1045

6

—

THE
COLD WAR
AND
BEYOND

1945-2009

—

CULTURE

ry flourishes unexpectedly, like those brilliant sunflowers Allen Ginsberg plant-ed years ago, when the world also seemed to many interminably grey."[9]

The poetry slam has found its place in the Netherlands. There is a more or less official "championship" and the prestigious Poetry International festi-val in Rotterdam also has slam evenings. Influence here is limited to appear-ances, though: when they are published on paper, the poems show no distinct American influence. Still, the spirit of slam does seem related to early Ameri-can postmodernism: Charles Olson (one of the first poets to use this term) only saw relevance for poetry if it would conform itself to the rhythm of breathing: "Verse now, 1950, if it is to go ahead, if it is to be of *essential* use, must, I take it, catch up and put into itself certain laws and possibilities of the breath, of the breathing of the man who writes as well as of his listenings."[10] The communi-cative situation for Olson is the primal form of poetry: the gap between artist and public must be bridged, to use the terms in which Leslie Fiedler described art in the 1960s.

Conclusion

How can the similarities between Dutch and American literature be explained if not in terms of influence? Dutch and American society are hardly identical, but some changes were not limited to national borders. All over the Western world, the end of the war had brought about unparalleled economic prosper-ity. The rise of television and pop culture made the youngest Dutch generation culturally independent in a way similar to American adolescents. Modernity and prosperity went hand in hand, and the media focused more on the young-er generation, following the money.

These developments contributed to a changing view of art and poetry, which were now seen as less loaded with relevance and responsibility and were looked at increasingly in terms of entertainment. The function of literature in this soci-ety has changed: literature has become less important in the political and social debate, which is even more true of poetry. Modernist literature had been part of a Great Narrative, but that notion is disappearing quickly, let alone that poetry could be a part of it. "Hello wealth, goodbye poetry," Jan Elburg says — and he laments this situation. But he is one of the *Vijftigers*, the last romantic school in Dutch poetry. The view of the poet as a struggling loner is disappearing — and even if the idea that poetry is without much power in society is not new, what ís new is the fact that poets are happy to "give up" their role as opinion leaders and focus on entertainment and popular culture instead.

When literature loses its ambition to change the world, the risk of super-ficiality lies around the corner, and the experimental prose and poetry of the

1960s will continue to be characterized as an antisocial, language-focused, and empty form of play. But another viewpoint is possible: if literature no longer tries to contribute to a Great Narrative, it can still be part of a much smaller, everyday narrative. Frank O'Hara's *Lunch Poems* (1964) is an example, while in the Netherlands Cees Buddingh' and Cornelis Bastiaan Vaandrager often refer to their own lives and circumstances.

Most of these tendencies have one thing in common: democratization. This happened in society, in literature, and also in the market place. In the early 1960s, the Dutch publishing house De Bezige Bij was among the first to publish new literary novels in "trade paperback" format, an idea taken from American publishers. Harry Mulisch's and Jan Cremer's novels became huge bestsellers in a way the Dutch market had not known until then. Books became inexpensive, and at the same time adolescents had more money to spend. When other publishers copied this format, literature was able to reach a much bigger and younger audience.

Indirectly, education was a factor as well. Not only because American literature was taught more often in the classroom, but also because every youngster learned to speak English. Combined with an increasing presence of popular American culture on radio and television, this led to a better command of the language. As a result, English-language books became increasingly popular. This phenomenon also started in the 1960s, as was apparent in an advertisement in *Randstad*: in 1962 De Bergensche Boekhandel promoted its store with advertisements that mentioned Allen Ginsberg, Kenneth Patchen, Gregory Corso, and Lawrence Ferlinghetti, among others. The Dutch market was indeed receptive to American literature: "Grove Press sells more books in Amsterdam than in Cincinnati, Kansas City and Detroit combined," publisher Barney Rosset told *Randstad* in a 1962 interview."[11] In the 1960s, the cultural avant-garde did not mind buying poetry in English and the rest of the public would follow suit: there is hardly a non-English-speaking country where as many English-language books are sold as in the Netherlands. American literature has become part of the Dutch literary conscience, even to the extent that it has become impossible to view it as an influence: it has become a presence. Dutch publishers often try to compete by publishing Dutch translations before the original.

But the fact that the Dutch reading public does not shy away from buying books in English has its consequences for translations. It is very well possible for American books to play a role in the Dutch literary system without being translated, and the availability of a Dutch translation is not an indication per se of the importance of that book. For instance, David Foster Wallace and William T. Vollmann currently do not have Dutch publishers, but they do have Dutch followings. Remarkably, John Irving's Dutch publisher even bought the

1047

6

—

—

English-language rights for the Dutch market. But it is the *language* that is the factor, not the country of origin. American authors compete in an English-language market with Donna Tartt, for example, or with J.M. Coetzee and Salman Rushdie, among others.

In the end, this is the story of a one-way street: there is no Dutch influence on American literature to speak of. Dutch storytellers like Jan de Hartog and Janwillem van de Wetering work(ed) and write/wrote in the U.S, but they are not part of the Dutch republic of letters. There have been occasional translations of Dutch novels and poems (e.g., Harry Mulisch, Hella S. Haasse, Margriet de Moor), but these are considered part of European, not Dutch letters. Occasionally, an adventurer like Jan Cremer will manage to date Jayne Mansfield and impress Frank O'Hara. And when the latter started working on a collection of poems he was going to call "The New York Amsterdam Set," there it was, finally: some actual Dutch influence on American literature.

1   H.J.A. Hofland and Tom Rooduijn, eds., *Dwars door puinstof heen: Grondleggers van de naoorlogse literatuur* (Amsterdam: Bas Lubberhuizen, 1997), 103.

2   Frans Ruiter, "The Reception of Postmodern American Fiction in the Netherlands," in Theo D'haen and Hans Bertens, eds., *"Closing the Gap": American Postmodern Fiction in Germany, Italy, Spain, and the Netherlands* (Amsterdam: Rodopi, 1997), 206.

3   Ibid., 212.

4   Adriaan Morriën, "Gesprek met Jan Hanlo in mei 1954," in Jan Hanlo, *Mijn benul* (Amsterdam: Van Oorschot, 1977), 11.

5   *De schoenen van de dirigent,* "Bermtoerisme," and *De Vliegende Hollander.*

6   *De Revisor* 26 (1999): 5.

7   Allen Ginsberg, *Proef m'n tong in je oor,* trans. Simon Vinkenoog (Amsterdam: De Bezige Bij, 1966), 124.

8   Richard Gray, *American Poetry of the Twentieth Century* (London/New York: Longman, 1990), 291–292.

9   Ron Alcalay, "Confessions of an American Poetry Slammer," *Bad Subjects* 2 (1993): 8.

10 Charles Olson, "Projective Verse," in Paul Hoover, ed., *Postmodern American Poetry. A Norton Anthology* (New York/London: W.W. Norton, 1994), 613.

11 Henk Leffelaar, "Barney Rosset — Grove Press," *Randstad* 3 (1962): 131.

AMERICAN POPULAR MUSIC IN THE NETHERLANDS

—

LUTGARD MUTSAERS

Introduction

From the late nineteenth century onward, American popular songs and dance tunes found their way into the Dutch commercial realm of sheet music and record stores, the entertainment stage, public dancing facilities and private schools, clubs, and homes. Consecutive American popular song and dance genres invaded Dutch culture as the passing fads that the music industry thrives on, and, more important, as the agents of profound change. The new mass media of radio and film stimulated the intensity and pace of this process. Between the two world wars, American popular music represented modernity, urbanity, and vitality, and became increasingly important as dance music.

The direction was one way; yet, a tiny Dutch touch within American pop culture can be ascertained. Bing Crosby's "Little Dutch Mill" was a number-one hit in 1934, and Glen Miller's "In an Old Dutch Garden by an Old Dutch Mill" was a popular recording in 1938.[1] The family names of Dick Jurgens, Bob Haring, and Don Voorhees, American-born big-band leaders who made recording history, suggest Dutch ancestry. Richard Hageman, born in 1882 in Friesland's capital city of Leeuwarden, moved to the United States, where he became a pioneering Hollywood film music composer and a key figure in music scoring for westerns. His music for John Ford's *Stagecoach* (1939) was awarded an Oscar.[2]

The American musical impact on Dutch culture after World War II became even more sustained and structural, not least through rock'n'roll, strictly speaking an updated type of dance music with dominant African-American roots (jazz, blues, rhythm and blues) that had left a deep imprint in the United States before it was exported to all corners of the world. The immediate target group of rock'n'roll in the Netherlands eagerly and quickly welcomed and adopted the new style.

6

―

―

When in the mid-1950s rock 'n' roll took over as the leading trend in the music industry, the viability of a career in popular music underwent drastic changes for everyone involved.[3] Rock 'n' roll catered to the teenage consumer, regardless of place, race, gender, and class. It created and developed its own aesthetics in close relation to a handful of local, regional, and national musical traditions. Rising from the grassroots where musical cross-fertilization already was paramount, it favored personal performance styles not taught at school. Rock 'n' roll deeply challenged the major music industry and related media conglomerates. No wonder that the new hit sound caused a stir, first in the United States, and then everywhere else where it landed.

In the Netherlands, rock 'n' roll occurred in a context and on a scale that were different from the American scene. It was equally disliked by the older generation in charge of raising and educating the young, guiding the religious, running society in general, and controlling the media. But young urban working-class people welcomed it with great enthusiasm. The adversaries of rock 'n' roll tried everything, even brushed up old racial stereotypes, to put the music and its performers down, but to no avail. Times had changed and Dutch home-grown entertainment music was already losing ground rapidly with the young generation. Rock 'n' roll and the music that followed within this newly created cultural space with its own aesthetics and forms of communication, remained the standard in an expanding youth market for a long time to come.

Three aspects of the reception and appropriation of American popular music genres of the 1950s and 1960s will be examined more closely in this article: first, the novelty of the electric guitar band, which revolutionized the sound of popular music; second, the social dance revolution called "the twist" that immediately followed in the footsteps of rock 'n' roll; and third, the craving among young musical trendsetters for a seriously listenable music to actively share with like-minded souls, which they found in American folk music. Finally, a concise assessment of the long-term impact of these American influences will be made.

A Flying Start

The actual introduction of rock 'n' roll in the Netherlands happened at the unique American enclave in the heart of the country, the air force base at Soesterberg. Nicknamed Camp New Amsterdam (CNA), it opened in November 1954[4] and expanded considerably during the Cold War. The latest American popular music in the form of 7-inch 45 rpm records (singles) was flown in directly from the United States, as were all goods necessary for daily life at CNA.

Professional pilots, trainees, and technicians who worked on the base sought their weekend entertainment in the nearby cities of Amersfoort, Utrecht, and Amsterdam. Before long, they made Dutch friends and shared interests. Music often is a favorite topic for conversation, and, not surprisingly, rock 'n' roll was hot news. When the first Hollywood rock 'n' roll movie, *Rock Around the Clock*, came to Dutch cinemas in the fall of 1956, the seed had already been sown.

The immediate appeal of rock 'n' roll was its hard driving beat and rough-edged sound. While Dutch radio shunned rock 'n' roll completely, enthusiasts discovered the wavelengths of the foreign commercial station Radio Luxembourg and of the American Forces Network (AFN), broadcasting to a large number of military bases in West Germany. These stations were instrumental in distributing both country and western music and rhythm and blues, the main highways to rock 'n' roll for new artists on the popular music scene. Through radio, the new sound of the electric guitar band caused a sensation. Before long, imported rock 'n' roll singles were sold in Dutch record stores.

Rock Around The Clock, the Movie

Dutch popular music magazines — *Tuney Tunes*, *Muziek Parade*, and *Muziek Expres* — had paid some attention to Bill Haley and the Comets, the stars of *Rock Around The Clock*, even before their 1955 U.S. number-one hit with the same title, but they had hardly made any critical comments. However, when rock 'n' roll proved to be more than a passing fad, the middle-aged editors of these Dutch magazines started to vent their bias. When *Rock Around The Clock* opened in Dutch cinemas, media comments expressed apprehension and referred to the stir the film had caused in Great Britain, where heated crowds had been dancing inside the theaters and out in the streets. In order to prevent rioting, several Dutch city councils refused permission to show the film, others ordered it shown without sound. But even as a silent movie it was useful, as it gave important information about how to dance to the hit records already in circulation. The movie ran for a few weeks only, but it reached every large city and most smaller towns. The news spread by word of mouth in a country too small to keep eager teenagers ignorant for long.

Electric Guitar Bands

Bill Haley was a big name in the music business in 1956. However, it was the film's prototypical rock 'n' roll band, Freddy Bell and his Bellboys, that captured

6

———

THE
COLD WAR
AND
BEYOND

1945–2009

———

CULTURE

the imagination of aspiring musicians in the Netherlands most. Freddy Bell and his mates were young, while Bill Haley was already in his early thirties. Freddy and the Bellboys had sharp outfits, whereas Bill and his men dressed in cowboy gear or old-fashioned tuxedos. The Comets had a pedal steel guitar and an upright bass, associated with older mainstream styles, whereas the Bellboys had the novel solid-body electric guitars and an electric bass guitar.

The appeal of the electric guitar band was strongest among young men who had grown up with the guitar as their household instrument in the Dutch East Indies, where people had long been aware of popular music genres played by American radio stations broadcasting from the Philippines (at the time an American colony).[5] Thus, when Indonesia became independent several migration waves resulted not only in new and visible subcultures in the Netherlands, but also in a new pool of young musicians already familiar with American popular music. The fascination for this music, played live by local dance bands and also heard on gramophone records, had pervaded the Dutch East Indies' upper layers of colonial society early on.

Aspiring rock'n'roll musicians fresh from Indonesia—who chose the epithet "Indo" as their in-group nickname—had trouble finding the right equipment, though. The solid-body electric guitar and bass guitar, still unavailable in the Netherlands, had to be made by hand. A strip of hardwood, taken from furniture such as beds and cabinets, was cut out to size and shape. The electronics were figured out by family and friends who knew basic radio technology. Guitar strings made of steel were available in Dutch music shops, because of the longstanding popularity of Hawaiian music and its metal-stringed lead instrument, the steel guitar.[6]

The solid-body electric guitar, the symbol of rock'n'roll and its defining icon, soon became the new affluent generation's plaything. Around 1960, the Dutch guitar manufacturing company Egmond started to produce several solid-body electric guitar and bass guitar models. Cheaper and easier to come by than the American Telecaster (Fender, 1952), Stratocaster (Fender, 1954), Les Paul (Gibson, 1952) and their solid-body bass guitar equivalents, the Egmond electric guitars sold like hot cakes.

At least one professional rock'n'roll band took the name Bellboys after seeing Freddy Bell and his musicians in *Rock Around The Clock*. For legal reasons renamed the Black Dynamites, this Indo-rock band from The Hague was the first of a large number of Dutch-based rock'n'roll showbands to tour the West German nightclubs and American military bases professionally, thus bringing American expats and their German friends and neighbors the live entertainment that was so close to their hearts and tastes. The temporary presence of private Elvis Presley in West Germany gave an extra touch of authenticity and excitement to rock'n'roll in the region. At the 1958 World Fair in

Brussels, another Dutch-based Indo band working in Germany, the Tielman Brothers, played rock 'n' roll to packed houses in the Dutch pavilion. Ironically, on this occasion they recorded what has gone into history as the first original rock 'n' roll single "from the Netherlands."

After approximately five years of Indo-rock dominance, native Dutch musicians started forming their own bands.[7] By then rock 'n' roll had lost its edge and had turned into a smoother type of teenage music. In September 1959 Dutch public radio introduced two separate one-hour programs a week to spin the latest hits. Elvis Presley was only just beginning to sell in the Netherlands. Dutch bands in the meantime had turned to British beat music. Popular music, narrowly defined as "rock music by guitar bands" — *popmuziek* — had ceased to be exclusively American.

Revolution on the Dance Floor

In 1961, a social dance revolution that had originated in the United States, hit the Netherlands.[8] The twist craze imposed a fundamental change upon Dutch social dancing as an integral part of middle-class education. "The Twist" (1959, Hank Ballard and the Midnighters, U.S.) was covered in 1960 by the African-American artist Chubby Checker, who had a monster hit with it. At the height of his popularity he married Rina Lodders, Miss World in 1962, from Haarlem. Checker's visits to the Netherlands and his presence in the Dutch media sparked lively discussions about the sorry state of American race relations. The positive reactions in the Netherlands to the biracial marriage of Chubby and Rina added to the Dutch image of liberalism.

The twist craze caused some major changes. Anyone could now start dancing at will, alone, or as a duo, facing one another without touching, in groups, lines, circles, or crowds, and stop whenever one felt like doing so, even in the middle of a song. The twist was wholly democratic, anyone could do it, and did, even people who had never been on a dance floor before. Chubby Checker had shown the basic rules. "It's hips," he used to say.

Twist music was the epitome of rock 'n' roll. It repackaged existing tunes for a new purpose, while adding original items to the repertoire. Rock 'n' roll bands smoothly adapted to the twist craze, as twist music stuck to the sound of the electric guitar band. Amsterdam became the twist capital. The later rock guitar hero Jan Akkerman emerged then and there. Soon there were national twisting contests and Dutch names were added to the roster of youth idols.

The twist craze in the Netherlands (1961–63) enlarged the numerical presence of electric guitar bands in the cultural sphere. Suddenly, adults started to embrace twisting. This turned inquisitive teenagers off from a form of music

1053

THE
COLD WAR
AND
BEYOND

1945–2009

CULTURE

now stripped of generational codes. They were eager to explore other American music that was new to them, preferably styles not designed for dancing, as they were tired of the worn-out beats of the twist craze. While American popular dance music continued to be relevant as a functional force, it was the idea of *listening* and paying serious attention to musical and lyrical content that interested these trendsetters.

An Alternative Popular Music

American folk music was the alternative choice made by well-educated Dutch adolescents who were inclined to have left-wing political sympathies and anti-commercial attitudes.[9] Their interest in a deeper engagement with American music "of the people" as opposed to music produced "for the people," took off when the Kingston Trio from the U.S. became number one in the Netherlands in 1959 with their newly arranged folk song, "Tom Dooley." It remained in the Dutch charts for five months. No romance, no dancing were involved. A new field had opened up.

The Kingston Trio alerted new audiences to an important strain of American music. Historically, American folk music was a form of community music that deliberately shunned commercialism and media promotion. In the early 1960s, this rediscovered strand was woven into the musical and lyrical fabric of American popular songs fit for the charts. During the early 1960s the U.S. folk act Peter, Paul and Mary inspired a budding Dutch folk scene further to discover its own investment in this new area.

Bob Dylan's rise to the frontline of folk music and, by 1965, folk rock, was the decisive impulse for the Dutch folk movement to emerge. In 1966, so-called hootenannies — a longstanding American format of folk music meetings where audiences could actively join in — were organized by youth clubs in several cities. Bob Dylan had by that time been dismissed by folk purists for his embrace of the electric guitar and the rock sound. As usual, though, the music enthusiasts outnumbered the purists by far. The folk interest Dylan had raised, inspired self-taught Dutch musicians to try their hand at this diverse musical tradition.

CCC Inc., founded in 1966 by an all-male group of friends living in Amsterdam, was the first band to tour the Netherlands professionally with American folk tunes and songs. Their set of instruments included the banjo, the violin, and the washboard. CCC's repertoire consisted of Leadbelly and Woody Guthrie songs, traditionals and bluegrass tunes, and the occasional composition of their own. The band performed at the first Dutch Folk Festival, held at a students' club in Utrecht in 1967, where it caused a sensation.

CCC Inc. continued to dominate the developing folk scene. It was the only Dutch act on the international bill of the first Dutch outdoor rock festival at Kralingen (Rotterdam) in 1970. In 1974 CCC Inc. split up as a professional touring act. Several of its members went on to improve the status of noncommercial popular music by founding Stichting Popmuziek Nederland (Dutch Rock Music Foundation) in 1975. Others continued to make their mark musically.[10]

Popular Music Media

By the mid-1960s popular music genres of American origin had marginalized, and among young audiences virtually wiped out, older types of Dutch popular music. Dutch pop radio began as a pirate enterprise called Radio Veronica, broadcasting from the North Sea in 1959. Radio Veronica worked exactly like American pop stations, with its own printed weekly hit list ("Veronica Top 40" first appeared in January 1965), personality disk jockeys, jingles, games, phone-ins, and commercial breaks. Pirate stations dominated the 1960s in their constant search for new sounds and songs, largely unhindered by government and public media restrictions.[11] In 1974 the Dutch government implemented the heralded ban on piracy, in compliance with international treaties.[12] By that time, transnational popular music was firmly rooted in Dutch culture. By hiring former pirate radio personnel, public radio took a giant leap forward in its quest for pop audiences. Public radio itself, while remaining divided along traditional lines of pillarization, had opened up to commercial funding.

Meanwhile, British beat music had interrupted the steady flow of predominantly American popular songs and dance genres to the Netherlands. In the mid-1960s, British pop was the dominant sound. This sparked a considerable wave of beat groups, the crest of which started producing their own songs. The first nationally distributed printed medium by and for the Dutch beat generation was *Hitweek*, first issued in September 1965. It soon redirected the fans' attention toward the United States.

When the 1960s decade closed, American popular music had regained a dominant position through the genre of West Coast rock. Dutch interest indeed refocused on the United States, though never again exclusively so. Popular music in the narrow sense of the word (*popmuziek*) by that time became synonymous with the aesthetically high-ranked rock music that moved from the single to the long-playing album. The late 1960s brought an ever wider spectrum of Dutch-origin blues and folk influenced rock music. The English language remained paramount.

Serious rock music journalism in the Netherlands copied its scope and tone and, more often than not, content, from the American rock magazine *Rolling*

1055

6

Stone, first published in 1967 and produced in New York. Its rock journalists were researchers, critics, and fans at the same time. *Oor*, first published in 1971, copied the American standard of rock journalism rather than the British style of a more tongue-in-cheek and gossipy approach toward popular culture. Parallel to what happened at *Rolling Stone*, the first wave of Dutch rock historians emerged from the ranks of *Oor*.

Apotheosis of an Era

The 1960s ended with the first Dutch chart topper in the American *Billboard* Hot 100: "Venus" by Shocking Blue reigned supreme for one week in February 1970.[13] The rock band from The Hague was, uncharacteristically, fronted by a female singer, Mariska Veres (1947–2006). The song, written by the band's guitarist Robbie van Leeuwen and released in the fall of 1969, surprisingly halted at number three in its home territory but topped the charts in many other countries.

"Venus" is the proverbial exception to the rule that Dutch-made popular music is predominantly aimed at the home market. The global picture of the popular music industry and its media has undergone truly profound changes since the close of the 1960s, but because of its history and creative output the United States has remained the ultimate paradise of pop.

Conclusion

Three aspects of American-Dutch musical relations during the 1950s and 1960s have been singled out here: the electric guitar band, the twist craze, and the emergence of the folk scene.

The overall conclusion is that the newly defined musical relationship between the United States and the Netherlands as one predominantly concerning the youth market was forged ever so tightly. Ranging from its mainstream pop mediated by the major entertainment corporations to its roots genres mediated mostly by alternative networks, American popular music became firmly woven into the Dutch cultural fabric. Songwriters, musicians, and producers in the Netherlands made American popular music of the 1950s and 1960s audible in their sounds, beats, and choice of language, and visible in their performance styles.

The members of the Dutch band Shocking Blue show the golden record for their number 1 hit "Venus".   ➤

6

———

THE
COLD WAR
AND
BEYOND

1945–2009

———

CULTURE

The electric guitar band was the chosen format of professionals and amateurs alike — note that in the Netherlands professionalism in popular music is defined by dedication, time investment, and creative output, rather than by financial aspects. A diverse roster of Dutch artists actively acknowledges indebtedness to American popular music to this very day. For instance, hip hop artists appropriated the American genre as the same kind of bridge builder between young urban people of different ethnic and cultural background as the Indo-rockers had achieved by playing rock'n'roll.

The twist craze of the early 1960s epitomized the first phase of youth-oriented American pop invading the world market. Resulting from a long line of African-American dance music and practice, the twist craze loosened up Dutch dance culture to the extent that social dancing in general became a favorite pastime. Disco, the American dance craze of the 1970s that was also mass-mediated by a Hollywood movie (*Saturday Night Fever*, 1977), was the immediate forerunner of innovative computer-generated Dutch dance music in the 1990s. Vengaboys and 2 Unlimited, to name only the absolute top acts, brought fresh sounds, beats, and performance styles to the international stage. Dutch dance music became the nation's biggest cultural export product, while its creative DJs such as Tiësto and Armin van Buuren rank among the world's award-winning best. Amsterdam Dance Event developed into a globally important dance-music trade fair and expert meeting. Former rock guitarist and DJ Tom Holkenborg (also known as Junkie XL) created the remix track that put Elvis Presley posthumously back on top ("A Little Less Conversation," 2005), and went on to write for Hollywood movies and produce for Madonna (2008).

What happened in folk music is yet another story of Dutch interest in American music as an inspiration for developments at home. To become aware of folk music as a unique source of historical knowledge and expression of personal experiences was a newly gained insight. American folk music, as it evolved into folk rock and singer-songwriter music, remained a major influence in Dutch music making. Its critical agenda, its foregrounding of meaningful lyrics, its musical freedom in terms of form, structure, and sound, its home in independent record companies and media niches, its credibility as a serious artistic expression of intimate thoughts and feelings, are all elements that enhanced the quality of Dutch popular music, live and on record.

Under the umbrella term "Americana" — usually excluding the blues that has its own niche in festival land — American artists regularly perform at Dutch festivals, for instance at the Blue Highways festival (Utrecht, since 2000) and Take Root (Assen, since 1998; Groningen, since 2007). At these events, Dutch audiences check out "the real thing," straight from the United States. Inspired by these festivals and the availability on record, local Americana scenes and venues were developed, away from the spotlights of mainstream pop, but attended by considerable crowds of aficionados beyond generational lines.[14] Dutch groups, such as the Bluegrass Boogiemen, in turn found their way into Americana festivals in the United States.

Finally, the Netherlands during the 1950s and 1960s was a fantastic sponge for American popular music and its roots genres. It had functioned as such well before, but most notably after the two musically defining decades. For American artists the Netherlands is their critical and concrete gateway to continental Europe, via the Dutch rock press and internationally renowned venues such as Paradiso in Amsterdam. The connection with the young Dutch audience that was established in the 1950s through rock'n'roll movies and records, has remained strong over the decades and beyond generations. The relevance of American popular music to Dutch culture at large has a long history and is immense. One nowadays cannot begin to imagine a popular music culture without the American element towering over all other influences.

1   Joel Whitburn, *Pop Memories 1890–1954: The History of American Popular Music* (Menomonee Falls, WI: Record Research Inc., 1986).

2   Aat C. Swart, *De lichte muziek van A–Z* (Hilversum: International Musicals, 1957), 81-82.

3   Colonel Parker, born in Breda and manager of Elvis Presley, denied his Dutch heritage, never returned to the Netherlands, and kept his major star from performing in Europe.

4   Lutgard Mutsaers, "Door het geluid. De muzikale impact van Camp New Amsterdam op Soesterberg en omgeving," *Jaarboek Oud-Utrecht* (Utrecht: Vereniging Oud-Utrecht, 2005), 154-181.

5   Lutgard Mutsaers, *Rockin' Ramona. Een gekleurde kijk op de bakermat van de Nederpop* (The Hague: SDU uitgeverij, 1989).

6   Lutgard Mutsaers, *Haring & Hawaii. Hawaiianmuziek in Nederland 1925–1992* (Amsterdam: SPN/Mets, 1992).

7   The term Indo-rock was introduced by record collectors in the 1970s.

8   Lutgard Mutsaers, "Beat Crazy. De impact van de transnationale dansrages twist, disco en house in Nederland" (Ph.D.

dissertation, Universiteit Utrecht, 1998).

9   Jos Koning, "De folkbeweging in Nederland. Analyse van een hedendaagse muziek-subcultuur" (Ph.D. dissertation, Universiteit van Amsterdam, 1983), 48-54.

10 *CCC Inc. Het Verzameld Werk 1967–2007* (eleven CDs and one DVD).

11 Television, when it was a new medium, was not of great consequence for popular music in the Netherlands. This situation took a turn with the founding of MTV Europe in 1987, the rise of commercial television in the late 1980s, and the founding of Dutch clip station The Music Factory (TMF) in 1995.

12 Auke Kok, *Dit was Veronica. Geschiedenis van een piraat* (Amsterdam: Thomas Rap, 2007).

13 Fred Bronson, *The Billboard Book of Number One Hits*, revised and updated 4th edition (New York: Billboard Books, 1997), 268, 646. The 1986 cover version of "Venus" by the British girl group Bananarama also reached the top spot in the U.S.

14 Herman van der Horst, "Binnenwegen," in Lutgard Mutsaers, ed., *Van The Black Rocking Cats tot Spinvis. Een halve eeuw popmuziek in & uit Utrecht* (Utrecht: Villa Utapio, 2007), chapter 22.

6

THE
COLD WAR
AND
BEYOND

1945-2009

CULTURE

1060

CONTEMPORARY DUTCH CINEMA AND HOLLYWOOD

JAAP KOOIJMAN

Like most non-English European cinemas, Dutch cinema cannot really be compared to Hollywood and American independent cinema. European cinema constitutes only a small part of the global film market, whereas Hollywood is dominant worldwide. In the U.S., European cinema constitutes a niche market, serving a specific and relatively small segment of the American public that is interested in an alternative to Hollywood and is not put off by cultural barriers such as the use of subtitles.[1] In the Netherlands, the large majority (roughly 80 percent) of the feature films watched in movie theaters are subtitled Hollywood genre movies, making Hollywood the principal frame of cultural reference not only for Dutch audiences but also for Dutch directors of feature films. Even when compared to other European cinemas, Dutch cinema as a clearly defined entity does not stand out, although some of its traditions and directors have been recognized internationally, such as the documentaries of Bert Haanstra and Johan van der Keuken, the Dutch feature films of Paul Verhoeven, and the so-called Dutch School cinema by directors Jos Stelling and Alex van Warmerdam. Sometimes, Dutch films are linked to films from Belgium and Luxembourg as "the cinema of the Low Countries," and in international DVD stores they also end up, from time to time, in the Scandinavian section.[2]

This does not mean, however, that Hollywood has always been dominant in the Dutch cinematic landscape. From the first days of silent film through World War II, German cinema was far more popular than Hollywood and even after the war, when Hollywood's popularity increased, other European cinemas (particularly the French and the Italian) continued to attract Dutch viewers, remaining popular up to the late 1970s. Throughout the twentieth century the production of Dutch films was limited to a handful annually[3] and depended in most cases on funding by the state-financed Dutch Film Fund, which was founded in 1956 and tended to evaluate proposals on their artistic and cultural (rather than their commercial or entertainment) merits. Since 1999, however, a new tax subsidy program to promote private economic investment in film production has drastically increased the number of Dutch films.[4] Moreover, the Dutch Film Fund and the television broadcasting companies have changed their policies and no longer look only at a film's artistic quality but also take its commercial feasibility into account.[5] As a result, there has been a large increase in commercial "feel good" cinema consisting of Dutch popular movies that follow Hollywood genre conventions, are targeted at the teenage audience, and claim no "artistic" pretensions.

Instead of providing a comprehensive overview of Dutch cinema since 1945, or attempting to categorize or essentialize it, this article focuses on how the case of Dutch cinema questions the rigid distinction between Hollywood and definitions of European cinema, thereby focusing on Dutch cinema's use of Hollywood as its principal frame of cultural reference, rather than on the insurmountable differences between the two. First, I will place Dutch cinema within the broader discussion of defining European cinemas as national cinema in relation to Hollywood. Second, I will discuss four significantly different yet renowned Dutch feature films that all highlight aspects of the imbalanced relation between Dutch cinema and Hollywood: *Turkish Delight* (Paul Verhoeven, 1973), *The Vanishing* (George Sluizer, 1988), *Antonia's Line* (Marleen Gorris, 1995), and *Costa!* (Johan Nijenhuis, 2001). They will be presented in chronological order to emphasize the general shift from artistic to commercial "feel good" cinema, yet without suggesting that the latter has replaced the former. Focusing on specific films avoids the trap of discussing cinema without including the films themselves.[6]

European Cinema as National Cinema

Dutch cinema cannot escape from the shadow of "big brother" Hollywood, a cinema that is both its main competitor and its main inspiration. Moreover, Dutch cinema cannot be separated from the whole of European cinema, particularly in the way in which it relates to Hollywood. In his book *European Cinema: Face to Face with Hollywood*, Thomas Elsaesser effectively goes beyond the conventional binary oppositions that mark the Europe-America divide, which is based on the contrast between European highbrow state-sponsored "auteur" cinema (film as an artistic expression of one individual director) on the one hand, and American lowbrow studio-based commercial Hollywood blockbuster cinema on the other. As Elsaesser shows, this seemingly antagonistic dichotomy is not a contradiction, but actually a mutually beneficial arrangement

6

———

THE
COLD WAR
AND
BEYOND

1945-2009

———

CULTURE

that helps each cinema define its identity in opposition to the other, thereby securing its position within a global film market, with the result that the film industries on both sides of the Atlantic are strengthened.[7]

The easily recognizable and thus compelling distinctions between European cinema and Hollywood echo conventional dichotomies not only along the lines of Europe versus America, but also of highbrow art versus lowbrow pop culture. In such dichotomies, Europe tends to be equated to artistic traditions rooted in history, connected to cultural elites, whereas America equals freedom from such constraints, thereby providing space for popular taste. As I have discussed elsewhere, Hollywood, although often explicitly identified as "American," can present itself (as can other forms of American popular culture) as being universal, easily appropriated within other cultures around the globe. European cinemas, on the contrary, tend to be defined by their national character (even when such identification tends to be limited to one particular cinematic "wave" or period, such as Italian neorealism or French *nouvelle vague*), most often exemplified by the work of renowned directors.

In his article "The Concept of National Cinema," British film scholar Andrew Higson explores some of the implications of using the term "national" when defining European cinemas. Most commonly it refers to films produced within a particular nation-state. However, Higson's objective is to arrive at definitions that take into account not only film production but also film reception (both critical and popular). Based on Higson, yet applied to the Dutch situation, the following four approaches can be recognized: [1] an *economic approach* in which Dutch cinema consists of the films that are produced and financed by parties in the Netherlands and/or are directed by Dutch filmmakers; [2] an *exhibition- and consumption-based approach* in which Dutch cinema consists of the films that are watched by and popular with Dutch audiences, thus including those produced in Hollywood and other popular international cinemas; [3] a *cultural-heritage- and identity-based approach* in which Dutch cinema consists of nationally produced films that explicitly deal with Dutch cultural and national identity, often adaptations of the classics of Dutch literature and focusing on "typically Dutch" themes, such as Calvinist culture, water, or World War II; [4] a *criticism-based approach* in which national cinema is reduced to the terms of quality art cinema, a cinema rooted in the highbrow modernist heritage of a particular nation-state, rather than one that appeals to the desires and fantasies of popular audiences.[8]

Although Higson himself and others have questioned the validity of these specific categorizations, the four approaches taken together broaden the discussion of what "national" cinema might mean even as it problematizes the concept. The approaches help reveal that definitions of national cinema tend to favor one category over another. Most often, national cinema is limited to films that are produced by an artistic director from one specific country and subsequently are interpreted along the lines of nationalist themes. By applying the different approaches to the notion of national cinema, important questions are raised. If Hollywood films tend to be far more popular than most Dutch films among Dutch audiences, should Hollywood not be included within a definition of Dutch cinema, either as part of its cinematic content or at least as its main inspiration? In this way, the dominant perspective of Dutch (and European) cinema as a form of artistic expression by an individual director is problematized. Moreover, the shift toward perceiving Dutch cinema as a commercial commodity to entertain a popular audience, rather than as a work of art, fits within such a broader and more inclusive approach to Dutch national cinema.

The discussion then should move beyond reductive notions of national identity that are based on how Dutch cinema differs from other European cinemas and Hollywood. Instead, the focus should be on how Dutch cinema has appropriated Hollywood within its local and national context, emphasizing the interaction rather than a static dichotomy. This does not mean that there are no distinctive differences between Hollywood and Dutch cinema but, instead, that the differences should not be overemphasized, reinforcing the America-Europe divide, while similarities are overlooked. To do so, I will present four snapshots of Dutch feature films that all, in one way or another, can be connected explicitly to Hollywood, thereby providing some insight into the complex interrelation between Hollywood and Dutch cinema along the lines of production, content, and critical reception.

Turkish Delight (Paul Verhoeven, 1974)

Turkish Delight—director Paul Verhoeven's second feature film—has been widely recognized as the main representative of a "new wave" in Dutch cinema, in which explicit depictions of sex, bodily functions, and violence were used to attack the restrictions of Dutch bourgeois culture.[9] After *Turkish Delight*, Verhoeven continued to make popular feature films in the Netherlands, including *Soldier of Orange* (1979), *Spetters* (1980), and *The Fourth Man* (1983), but eventually he moved to Hollywood to make blockbuster productions such as *Total Recall* (1990), *Basic Instinct* (1992), and *Starship Troopers* (1997), only to return to the Netherlands to shoot *Black Book* (2006). Here the problem of the auteur as marker of national cinema becomes apparent. Do Verhoeven's Hollywood films also belong to Dutch cinema, based on the nationality of the director, or are they distinctively different from the ones he directed in the Netherlands?

Based on the best-selling novel by Jan Wolkers, *Turkish Delight* is considered the most popular Dutch film of all time, starring Rutger Hauer as the bo-

1063

hemian artist Erik Vonk who falls in love with Olga (Monique van de Ven), the young daughter of a bourgeois family. In one of its most famous scenes, Erik bikes through Amsterdam with Olga on the backseat, joyfully playing a cat-and-mouse game with a car that is trying to pass them. In addition to its celebration of romance, the bicycle scene emphasizes the film's contrast between the bohemian lifestyle of artistic and sexual freedom and bourgeois small-mindedness as represented by Olga's family.

From an auteur film perspective, Verhoeven's *Turkish Delight* has been compared to other European films such as Pier Paolo Pasolini's *Theorem* (1968) and Bernardo Bertolucci's *Last Tango in Paris* (1972), all fitting within a tradition of *épater les bourgeois* through sexual liberation. Yet, *Turkish Delight* can also be perceived as a raunchy version of the Hollywood melodrama *Love Story* (Arthur Hiller, 1970). Like Oliver (Ryan O'Neal) and Jennifer (Ali MacGraw), Erik and Olga fall in love in spite of their different social backgrounds, and like Jennifer, Olga dies of cancer in the end. Moreover, both movies were extremely popular and have become iconic representations of the early 1970s. If one views *Turkish Delight* as "the other face of *Love Story*," as one American critic did, it is tempting to overemphasize the differences between these two popular love stories as part of the traditional divide between Hollywood and European cinema.[10] Accordingly, as a product of the American studio system, *Love Story* is a tear-jerker made to move the audience along the lines of predictable genre conventions, whereas *Turkish Delight* is the artistic expression of one individual director, intended to confront rather than to please the audience.

However, as Elsaesser also points out, these two seemingly antagonistic poles actually complement each other, as two sides of the same coin. European national cinemas have developed not so much in opposition to, but in relation to Hollywood, "existing in a space set up like a hall of mirrors, in which recognition, imaginary identity and mis-cognition enjoy equal status, creating value out of pure difference."[11] Thus, one can also focus on similarities — for example, how the bicycle scene in *Turkish Delight* evokes the romantic sentiment of that other famous scene in *Love Story* with Oliver and Jennifer throwing snowballs in New York's Central Park.

The Vanishing (George Sluizer, 1988)

Based on a short Dutch novel by Tim Krabbé, *The Vanishing* is a psychological thriller centered around the obsessive search by a young Dutchman, Rex Hofman (Gene Bervoets), for his missing girlfriend Saskia (Johanna ter Steege), who disappears at a gas station in France during their summer vacation. When, three years later, Saskia's abductor Raymond Lemorne (Bernard-Pierre Donna-

6

———

THE
COLD WAR
AND
BEYOND

1945–2009

———

CULTURE

dieu) makes contact with Rex, the two men meet and slowly Saskia's horrifying fate is revealed. Both a critical and a commercial success, the film has been widely considered as Hitchcockian in the way it focuses on the complex psychological relationship between the boyfriend and the abductor, rather than merely on the sensational effects evoked by the thriller's genre conventions. *The Vanishing* has been compared to other Dutch thrillers such as *The Fourth Man* (Paul Verhoeven, 1983) and *The Lift* (Dick Maas, 1983), not only in how they deal with male anxiety about sexuality, fidelity, and commitment, but also in how, as auteur films, they break with genre conventions, arguably sharing a specifically Dutch appropriation of the thriller genre.[12]

The distinction between the Dutch appropriation and the American "original" became even more apparent in the American remake of the film, which — significantly — was also directed by George Sluizer. This remake, also entitled *The Vanishing* (1993), differed greatly in the final scene. The horrifying ending was replaced by a happy ending that Hollywood allegedly required. It disappointed many viewers for being "laughable, stupid and crude."[13]

It is tempting to see the American remake of a European original by the same Dutch director as a reinforcement of the conventional Europe-America divide. To attract an American mainstream audience, *The Vanishing* was "Americanized" through the use of clichéd Hollywood horror genre conventions, including a thrilling yet happy ending. However, the disappointing fate of the American version of *The Vanishing*, critically as well as commercially, suggests instead that such a divide was being challenged. Obviously, there are many reasons for a film's commercial failure, but in this case the lack of success may be explained by the almost desperate attempt to transform the European original into what was believed to be a standard Hollywood film.

Antonia's Line (Marleen Gorris, 1995)

When *Antonia's Line* was first released in the Netherlands in 1995, the film received negative reviews. *Antonia's Line* celebrates female independence by telling the story of four generations of women living in a small Dutch village. Dutch film critics expressed their amazement that Marleen Gorris, the critically acclaimed director of classic Dutch feminist films such as *A Question of Silence* (1982) and *Broken Mirrors* (1984), could make such a "superficial" film. Then, one year later, *Antonia's Line* won the Academy Award for best foreign-language film, the second Dutch feature film to win in that category. In spite of the earlier nominations of *Village on the River* (Fons Rademakers, 1958) in 1960 and *Turkish Delight* in 1974, the first Dutch feature film that actually won an Oscar was *The Assault* (Fons Rademakers, 1986) in 1987. Two Dutch Academy Award-win-

1065

6

—

THE
COLD WAR
AND
BEYOND

1945–2009

—

CULTURE

ning films were added in the next decade: *Antonia's Line* in 1996 and *Character* (Mike van Diem, 1997) in 1998.

In an interview with *Salon.com* magazine, Mike van Diem expressed his amazement at the critical success of *Antonia's Line* in the United States: *"Antonia's Line* is not a very popular [film] back home. The Oscar came as a shock to us. We thought it was a good film, but nobody thought it was *that* good. There was a cultural difference that made the English-language audience appreciate that film so much more than we did."[14] Obviously Van Diem was not surprised by the American success of his own film *Character*, which, much more than *Antonia's Line*, fits within the category of the typical Dutch cultural heritage film: highbrow drama based on a classic Dutch novel set in the early twentieth century and focusing on the "coming of age" of its male protagonist. In other words, *Character* was considered by many a logical winner of the Oscar, as the film, in contrast to *Antonia's Line*, seemed to reconfirm the conventional characteristics of European cinema in opposition to Hollywood.

The conventional Europe-America divide came to the foreground in the critical reception of *Antonia's Line* in both the U.S. and the Netherlands. American film critics tended to perceive *Antonia's Line* as a European art film. *The Boston Review*, for example, recognized the film as "Mozartian in its beauty — so artfully made that we are carried along by the surprising flow of the narrative without being forced to recognize the intellectual daring and craft of the filmmaker."[15] Dutch film critics, on the contrary, and writing after the film had won, accused director Marleen Gorris of having made a Hollywood movie. In his article "Why Americans love *Antonia's Line*," Hans Kroon suggested that Americans loved the escapism provided by *Antonia*, as its simplistic and folkloric portrayal of life in an imaginary countryside enabled its spectators to find temporary relief away from their own hectic existence. Tom Ronse saw the American popularity as proof of *Antonia*'s American shallowness, claiming that its one-dimensional character made the film "ready to eat, easily digestible." According to Ab van Ieperen, *Antonia's Line* was a Dutch feminist version of the American pioneer western, including its convention of letting the plot prevail over character development.[16] Regardless of whether these film critics, both the American and the Dutch ones, were correct in their judgments, they all reinforced the traditional distinction between America and Europe. However, they also revealed its limitations, as *Antonia's Line* embodied, on the American side, European depth, and, on the Dutch side, American shallowness. In other words, the American critics emphasized the film's artistic quality as the expression of an individual auteur, while the Dutch critics focused on the film's formulaic genre conventions based on the Hollywood example.

Costa! (Johan Nijenhuis, 2001)

The romantic comedy *Costa!*, which was the Dutch blockbuster hit of 2001, takes place in Spain, telling the story of a group of Dutch youth who work at Costa, a trendy disco that primarily caters to Dutch teenage tourists. *Costa!* was one of many Dutch commercial films that appropriated the genre conventions and audiovisual language of Hollywood. Some of these films were explicitly targeted at an international mainstream audience, such as *Do Not Disturb* (1999) and *Down aka The Shaft* (2001), both directed by Dick Maas and starring Hollywood actors like William Hurt and Naomi Watts, and the films by Roel Reiné, *The Delivery* (1999) and *Adrenaline* (2003). As Elsaesser points out, only a few European films have "the budgets, stars and production values even to try to reach an international mainstream audience," concluding that "often enough these films fail in their aim, not least because they have to disguise themselves to look and sound as if they were American."[17] That these films by Dick Maas and Roel Reiné turned out to be commercial and critical failures may be explained by the plausible factor that their disguises as "real" American movies were obvious to such an extent that the films became less convincing to audiences and critics alike. The Dutch self-acclaimed "feel good" movies like *Costa!*, on the contrary, were targeted at a national and often younger audience and tended to be commercially successful, including romantic comedies like *Phileine Says Sorry* (Robert Jan Westdijk, 2003) and *Schnitzel Paradise* (Martin Koolhoven, 2005), teenage comedies such as *All Stars* (Jean van de Velde, 1997) and *Shouf Shouf Habibi!* (Albert ter Heerdt, 2004), and action films such as *Leak* (Jean van de Velde, 2000) and *Too Fat Too Furious* (Tim Oliehoek, 2005). Even though these films also heavily relied on the often clichéd genre conventions of Hollywood cinema, they did not disguise themselves as American, but explicitly emphasized their national or local character, often using well-known actors from national television. In this way, these films have appropriated Hollywood within their own national context, rather than being mere imitations of the American original.

Although also referring to popular American films like *West Side Story* (Jerome Robbins and Robert Wise, 1961) and *Grease* (Randal Kleiser, 1978), *Costa!* was most of all a Dutch adaptation of *Dirty Dancing* (Emile Ardolino, 1987), the latter being the romantic story of a shy teenage girl, played by Jennifer Grey, who, while on vacation, experiences her sexual awakening and becomes a confident woman after competing in a dance contest with her hunky lower-class dance instructor, played by Patrick Swayze. In *Costa!* the shy teenage girl Janet, played by former soap-opera actress Georgina Verbaan, is on vacation in Spain, where she meets Rens (Daan Schuurmans), the leader of the Costa danc-

1067

Katja Schuurman as Frida, one of the main characters
in the film *Costa!*

ers. Similar to the plot of *Dirty Dancing*, their romance blossoms when Rens's regular dance partner cannot perform and is replaced by Janet, who is transformed into a wonderful dancer. Particularly the scene in which Rens, like Patrick Swayze's character, teaches Janet the dance's choreography in the water at a desolated beach, is almost identical to the *Dirty Dancing* original. Though clearly inspired by *Dirty Dancing*, *Costa!* appropriated the Hollywood example by translating the story into a local and contemporary context — Dutch tourists on a summer vacation in Spain — thereby enabling young Dutch viewers to incorporate the movie within their own experience of everyday life. Moreover, the film defied the conventional America-Europe divide by clearly favoring commercial feasibility and popular taste over the artistic pretensions of the cultural elites.

Conclusion

This eclectic collection of four significantly different Dutch feature films obviously does not cover the wide range of films that constitute Dutch cinema. However, they do — each in its own way — challenge the conventional distinction between European auteur cinema on the one hand and Hollywood genre film on the other. It may be compelling to perceive the imbalanced relationship between European cinemas like the Dutch one and Hollywood as antagonistic, yet in actual practice the relationship is mutually beneficial. Differences are overemphasized to capitalize on the America-Europe divide, whereas similarities tend to be overlooked. In Dutch cinema, Hollywood is its principal frame of cultural reference, providing the genre conventions that can be mimicked or mocked, reinforced or challenged. Dutch cinema appropriates Hollywood within a local and national context of meaning. This is not to suggest that "typically Dutch" films do not exist, or that specific traditions within Dutch cinema cannot be recognized. The national character of Dutch cinema can be based on a film's production, content, and both critical and popular reception. However, as the snapshots of the four films show, such national identification is not clear cut, as categorization can be contested along different lines. Instead of reducing it to one essentialist characteristic of national identity, Dutch cinema should be seen as part of an evolving transnational cinematic culture, defined not in opposition to but in continuous interaction with Hollywood.

6

——

THE
COLD WAR
AND
BEYOND

1945–2009

——

CULTURE

1   Parts of this article are based on Jaap Kooijman, *Fabricating the Absolute Fake: America in Contemporary Pop Culture* (Amsterdam: Amsterdam University Press, 2008). See Geoffrey Nowell-Smith, "Introduction," in Geoffrey Nowell-Smith and Steven Ricci, eds., *Hollywood & Europe: Economics, Culture, National Identity, 1945–95* (London: British Film Institute, 1998), 1-16.

2   Ernest Mathijs, ed., *The Cinema of the Low Countries* (London/New York: Wallflower, 2004).

3   Bart Hofstede, *In het wereldfilmstelsel: Identiteit en organisatie van de Nederlandse film sedert 1945* (Delft: Eburon, 2000), 247.

4   The tax subsidy program revealed an important shift in Dutch policy, as the program was introduced by the Ministry of Economic Affairs rather than the Ministry of Education, Culture, and Science, which before had been the only ministry involved in Dutch cinema.

5   Bart Hofstede, *Nederlandse cinema wereldwijd. De internationale positie van de Nederlandse film* (Amsterdam: Boekmanstudies, 2000).

6   As Ernest Mathijs has pointed out (in Mathijs, *The Cinema*, 1), discussions of Dutch cinema often "hardly care about the films themselves, often reducing cinema to a sociological phenomenon (a curiosity), an economic enterprise (a commodity) or a source of concern (a threat). ... It almost seems as if film discourse in the Low Countries could do away with discussion of what actually happens on the screen."

7   Thomas Elsaesser, *European Cinema: Face to Face with Hollywood* (Amsterdam: Amsterdam University Press, 2005).

8   Andrew Higson, "The Concept of National Cinema," *Screen* 30.4 (Autumn 1989): 39-47.

9   Hans Schoots, *Van Fanfare tot Spetters: Een cultuurgeschiedenis van de jaren zestig en zeventig* (Amsterdam: Bas Lubberhuizen/Filmmuseum, 2004), 99-102; Xavier Mendik, "*Turks Fruit/Turkish Delight*," in Mathijs, *The Cinema*, 109-118.

10 Mendik, "*Turks Fruit/Turkish Delight*," 112.

11 Elsaesser, *European Cinema*, 47.

12 Steven Jay Schneider, "*Spoorloos/The Vanishing*," in Mathijs, *The Cinema*, 177-185.

13 Roger Ebert, "*The Vanishing* [review]," *Chicago Sun-Times*, February 5, 1993, http://rogerebert.suntimes.com/apps/pbcs.dll/article?AID=/19930205/REVIEWS/302050304/1023.

14 Cynthia Joyce, "A Director of 'Character': An Interview with Academy Award-Winning Director Mike van Diem," *Salon.com*, April 3, 1998, http://www.salon.com/ent/int/1998/04/03int.html.

15 Alan A. Stone, "A Second Nature: *Antonia's Line* Re-imagines Life, after Patriarchy," *The Boston Review*, Summer 1996, http://bostonreview.mit.edu/BR21.3/Stone.html.

16 Hans Kroon, "Waarom Amerikanen van *Antonia* houden," *Trouw*, March 28, 1996; Tom Ronse, "*Antonia* in Oscarland," *De Groene Amsterdammer*, April 3, 1996; Ab van Ieperen, "*Antonia*: Een echte Amerikaanse pionierswestern," *Vrij Nederland*, March 30, 1996, 17.

17 Elsaesser, *European Cinema*, 76.

THE PRESENCE AND IMPACT OF DUTCH PAINTERS IN TWENTIETH-CENTURY AMERICA

——

GAIL LEVIN

"We never heard in Holland that there were artists in America. There was still the feeling that this was where an individual could get places and become well off, if he worked hard; while art, naturally, was in Europe," said Willem de Kooning in a 1963 interview with David Sylvester, a distinguished art critic.[1] De Kooning's remark, stereotypical and reductive though it sounds, reflects a common tendency to limit Dutch cultural input in America to seventeenth-century New Amsterdam or to the artists of the Golden Age of Dutch painting — Rembrandt, Hals, or Vermeer — and their influence on later American art, from Edward Hopper to Larry Rivers. Although another Dutch-born artist, Vincent van Gogh, has captured the American imagination, he never came to the United States and his tormented life took place mainly in France at the end of the nineteenth century.

A number of artists born and raised in the Netherlands actually came to America during the twentieth century and made their presence felt. Three in particular — Piet Mondrian, Willem de Kooning, and Karel Appel — won international fame and had an impact on postwar U.S. culture. While this essay will discuss other Dutch visual artists whose influence may not yet be fully understood, its scope does not allow an encyclopedic survey of all artists from the Netherlands who have worked or now work in America.

Adriaan Lubbers

6
—
THE
COLD WAR
AND
BEYOND

1945–2009

—

CULTURE

Although Piet Mondrian's paintings inspired by New York City are now world famous, those of Adriaan Lubbers (1892–1954) merit attention both for their quality and because he was probably the first Dutch painter to work in twentieth-century New York and attract significant notice. He first arrived in 1916 and worked at odd jobs in the city and across the Hudson River, in Hoboken, NJ, a settlement that had long attracted Dutch sailors. In Amsterdam he had trained as a mechanical engineer and was largely self-taught as an artist. When he insisted on pursuing a career in the arts, his well-to-do father disinherited him. Lubbers returned to the Netherlands in 1919 and settled in Bergen.

After more travel in Europe, Lubbers returned to New York, arriving on September 30, 1926. The next day he was interviewed by the *New York Times* in a feature that identified him as "an ex-immigrant, who fought off starvation here ten years ago by taking odd jobs as chauffeur, factory hand and singer in seaman's restaurants." He told the reporter that "[it] was while I was in Europe that I came to realize what a great subject for a painter New York is and made up my mind to return when I could."[2] He drew, painted, and produced lithographs, capturing the energy of Wall Street and the distinctive skylines with their bold skyscrapers. In the spring of 1927, Lubbers showed his new work at the Kraushaar Galleries, a major commercial venue on Fifth Avenue. "Mr. Lubbers is able to carry out his conceptions of the Titan city with power and dramatic intensity," wrote the critic in the *New York Evening Post*.[3]

"I want my pictures to be strong. I want them to show this city with its tremendous tragedy and its pulsing energy as it really is," said Lubbers, who stayed in the United States until the spring of 1928.[4] He then left for Paris, where he met Piet Mondrian, whose portrait he painted in 1931. Lubbers later settled in the Netherlands, but revisited the United States, traveling in 1934 to Chicago, where he painted the World's Fair (A Century of Progress International Exposition), and to New York again in 1937; he returned for the last time in 1954.

In 1937 Lubbers was honored with an exhibition held, under the auspices of the Netherlands-America Foundation, at New York's Rockefeller Center. The exhibition's honorary committee included such notables as First Lady Eleanor Roosevelt, and Willem de Vlugt and Fiorello La Guardia, the mayors of Amsterdam and New York. Featured were two murals, both panoramas of New York, painted for the Holland America Line ship *Nieuw Amsterdam*. "Except Ernest Fiene [a German immigrant]," wrote the critic Howard Devree, "it is doubtful if any American has devoted as much attention to the New York waterfront as this Dutch artist. The whole show is New York: bridges, skyscrapers, street vistas, nocturnal panoramas. Lubbers has painted the city with the fervor of a convert."[5] Lubbers' work attracted a remarkable amount of attention in the press. The idea of painting New York in murals was then in vogue since it was the time of the Federal Arts Project — under the Works Progress Administration (WPA), a part of Franklin Roosevelt's New Deal. Murals for schools, post offices, libraries, and other public buildings were going up in record numbers.

Willem de Kooning

By October 1926, when Lubbers was first getting interviewed in the press, Willem de Kooning (1904–97) had just arrived from his native Rotterdam and taken refuge in Hoboken, the same New Jersey shipping town where Lubbers had worked a decade earlier. De Kooning, who had fled poverty and arrived in the United States as a stow-away on a freighter, initially boarded at the Dutch Seaman's Home there. In Rotterdam he had apprenticed with commercial artists in a design firm and then studied at the Academie van Beeldende Kunsten. In America he proved adaptable, working at first as a house painter in Hoboken for nine dollars a day, and then in commercial art in Manhattan. After a year, de Kooning discovered a lot of other artists and an entire community of painting and poetry in Greenwich Village. By the mid-1930s, he was working on abstract murals for the Federal Arts Project and later in Queens for the New York World's Fair of 1939. The Depression years were a time of enormous socializing and solidarity among artists and writers, who were all suffering through the tough times.

After years of struggle, de Kooning began to obtain recognition during the late 1940s. Important American critics, especially Harold Rosenberg and Tom Hess, promoted him as a leader among abstract expressionist painters, just as the reputation of his friend and American contemporary, Jackson Pollock, began to decline as a casualty of alcoholism. De Kooning shared with Pollock and other contemporaries a love of jazz, and in the early 1940s he used to go to jazz clubs in New York, together with the composer Aaron Copland and Max Margolies, a vocal coach, writer, and the cofounder of Blue Note Records, whose portrait he sketched about 1944.[6] Like Lubbers and Mondrian before him, de Kooning painted some important pictures inspired by New York City, such as *Gotham News* (1955–56) or *Police Gazette* (1954–55), the latter title calling to mind famous crime-scene photographs of the city by the photojournalist Weegee (Arthur Felig).

Some of de Kooning's abstract images, especially those of women, took inspiration from tooth paste advertisements and anticipated developments in

1073

6

—

THE
COLD WAR
AND
BEYOND

1945–2009

—

CULTURE

pop art of the 1960s. Though de Kooning did not embrace the pop aesthetic, Robert Rauschenberg (1925–2008) famously convinced him in 1953 to hand over one of his drawings so that he could erase and exhibit it as a neo-Dada joke. Another pop artist, Roy Lichtenstein (1923–97), produced a series of ironic parodies of a giant de Kooning-like gestural brushstroke, in his own crisp, hard-edge style. De Kooning's impact, however, was much broader than such direct challenges, and in the early 1950s his influence was so prevalent that it seemed contagious. It was then that Jack Tworkov (1900–82), who had met de Kooning while both were working on the WPA in the mid-1930s, seemed to come under his spell; the two had adjoining studios and met at The Club at 39 East 8th Street, where hip artists congregated in the 1950s.

We can easily see de Kooning's hold on younger contemporaries such as Milton Resnick (1917–2004) or the early work of Al Leslie (b. 1927). Both hung out with him at the notorious Cedar Tavern and also participated with him in the famous 9th Street Show, which members of The Club organized in 1951. At that time, de Kooning's example held sway, though some of these young artists later gave up the abstract expressionist style and moved on, in Leslie's case returning to realism.

Another painter who came under de Kooning's spell and formed an interesting link to his Dutchness is Joop Sanders (b. 1921 as Joan Alfred Levy in the Netherlands), who arrived in New York in 1939, having already studied in Amsterdam with Theo Ortmann. After a brief formal study with the German immigrant George Grosz at the Art Students League, Sanders worked informally painting still life in de Kooning's studio in the early 1940s. The two Dutch artists had met by chance one evening in a loft where the music of Virgil Thomson, Aaron Copland, and Samuel Barber was being performed. Sanders and de Kooning's wife, Elaine (Fried), also painted each other's portraits. Both she and Sanders were among the younger artists showing with de Kooning in the 9th Street show, nor would she be the last young woman painter to respond to her husband.

The metal expressionist sculpture of John Chamberlain (b. 1927), where those bold, gestural brushstrokes are transformed into three dimensions, also reminds us of de Kooning, whose influence is indeed so vast that a multitude of younger artists either continue to imitate his gestural style or experimented with some aspect of his work and then moved on. The continuing vitality of de Kooning's influence is evident in America in the work of the British-born painter Cecily Brown (b. 1969), who moved to New York after graduating from the Slade School of Art in London in 1993. Like de Kooning, whose work she credits as influencing her, she delves into sexuality and attraction. Her output, like much of his, is semi-figurative. She must have encountered de Kooning's work at an early age since she is the daughter of the same David Sylvester who interviewed the artist and has written about his work.

De Kooning's influence was such that he eventually received two Presidential Medals of Freedom and, to commemorate his seventy-fifth birthday, was named an officer of the Order of Orange-Nassau. In 1982 he was invited to a dinner at the White House in honor of Queen Beatrix during her state visit. The year after his death, the Academie van Beeldende Kunsten that de Kooning had attended in Rotterdam was renamed the Willem de Kooning Academie.

The painter Al Held (1928–2005) once commented in an interview: "[T]hings from de Kooning could be lifted because it came from a lineage…. It wasn't so much that de Kooning's style didn't refer back to de Kooning so much as that it was a broader language."[7] Art critic Michael Kimmelman wrote of Held: "Inspired by Mr. de Kooning and Hans Hofmann, Mr. Held also looked with admiration at the works of Piet Mondrian, and he achieved in these canvases an extraordinary balance between seemingly contradictory elements."[8] Held soon abandoned abstract expressionist gesture to make geometric hard-edged paintings with a distinct link to Mondrian's reductive aesthetic. The intermediate works, his "Taxi cab" paintings, were a response both to the pace of New York streets and to Mondrian's painting *Broadway Boogie Woogie*, an homage in 1942–43 to both jazz rhythms and the city, that the Museum of Modern Art acquired soon after its completion.

Piet Mondrian

Piet Mondrian (1872–1944) was already famous in New York before he took refuge there during World War II. Living in Paris since 1919, he had had to abandon paintings there during World War I, and not long after Hitler's rise to power in the 1930s he found himself on the Nazi's list of "degenerate modern artists" (those whose work was considered *entartete Kunst*). When the Spanish Civil War was raging and wider conflict seemed inevitable, he departed for London in September 1938. But when a bomb exploded in the building next to his studio, Mondrian urgently decided to flee to New York, where he arrived, at the age of sixty-eight, on October 3, 1940. He had won praise as "the architect of modern painting" from one of American art's most influential teachers, Hans Hofmann, himself a German émigré.[9] Mondrian was also a favorite of the American Abstract Artists, a group founded in 1936 to exhibit the new art. Several of the group's members responded to the influence of his art and theory, including Harry Holtzman, Lee Krasner, Carl Holty, George L. K. Morris, Balcombe Greene, Albert Swinden, Ilya Bolotowsky, Burgoyne Diller, Fritz

6

—

THE
COLD WAR
AND
BEYOND

1945–2009

—

CULTURE

Glarner, and Charmion von Wiegand. Some, like Diller, were introduced to the De Stijl movement through Mondrian and then went on to explore the work of other De Stijl artists, such as Theo van Doesburg and Georges Vantongerloo.

Mondrian's paintings on exhibition in the Museum of Living Art (housing the collection of Albert Gallatin), then located at New York University, had attracted many American fans during the 1930s. Among them was Harry Holtzman, a founding member of the American Abstract Artists and a former student of Hofmann. Holtzman had felt so inspired that he had gone to meet Mondrian in Paris in 1934. The two men, four decades apart in age, developed a close friendship. Thus it was Holtzman who, financed by his wife's money, was able and eager to help Mondrian emigrate to the United States and find him a New York studio (near his own) in which he could live and work.

The American Abstract Artists voted in November 1940 to invite both Mondrian and the French refugee Fernand Léger to join their organization. Mondrian accepted with pleasure and even volunteered to pay the annual dues of four dollars, a gesture welcomed by the young American artists, who considered him their idol. When a reception was held to welcome the two European artists, Mondrian, who had just recovered from the month-long journey by convoy ship across the Atlantic in wartime, turned out to be "the life of the party."[10] He had such a good time that he made a date for a few nights later to go dancing with other members, including the artist Lee Krasner, who remarked: "I met Léger; but he was not one of my gods as Mondrian was." Mondrian not only showed his work in the annual exhibitions of American Abstract Artists; he socialized with the younger members. "Mondrian I saw on many occasions," Krasner recalled. By the time she met the older Dutch artist, her own abstract paintings had already reflected the influence of his work. Thus, she relished the opportunity to socialize with him: "We were both mad for jazz, and we used to go to jazz spots together."[11] "We discovered that we liked to listen to jazz and we used to go to a Café Uptown or Café Downtown, I can't remember now, and dance." She considered Mondrian one of her most outstanding partners for dancing. "I was a fairly good dancer, that is to say I can follow easily, but the complexity of Mondrian's rhythm was not simple in any sense."[12]

Mondrian's influence on American artists continued long after his death. These artists, who tend to paint hard-edged, geometric abstraction that is reductive, include Leon Polk Smith, Charles Biederman, Ad Reinhardt, and Barnett Newman. Smith was actually so thrilled to meet Mondrian at an exhibition opening in New York that he openly acknowledged this influence and eventually painted *Homage to "Victory Boogie Woogie" No. 1* in 1946–47. Mondrian's legacy continued in the late 1960s and early 1970s in the work of minimalist artists, whose work is stripped down to its basic features. Minimalism includes artists as diverse as Frank Stella, Peter Halley, Brice Marden, and Agnes Martin, all of whom might be said to owe a debt to Mondrian.

Although previously associated with abstract expressionism, Barnett Newman became another figure important for minimalist artists. His four *Who's Afraid of Red, Yellow and Blue* paintings, produced from 1966 to 1970, make reference to Mondrian's focus on primary colors, but the provocative title also challenges Mondrian. Nonetheless, Newman even employed tape, as had Mondrian, and also adapted his flat planes of pure color and vertical lines. His critique suggests the important position that the Dutch painter held for him. People often perceive spiritual qualities in the work of both artists. Newman found his spirituality in a secular existence; his Jewish agnosticism encompassed reading the Kabbalah, which he mined for some of his titles.

In contrast to Newman, Mondrian's spiritual quality derived from his long-held belief in Theosophy, which combines Christian and Eastern religious ideas. For some of his followers, it was his spirituality that appealed above all else. This was true for the Chicago-born Charmion Von Wiegand, who is said to have wept at Mondrian's funeral and who pursued Theosophy herself. While several first met him in Paris, including the Swiss-born Glarner and Holtzman, they did not become close to him until his years in New York. With Mondrian, many different aspects appealed to the diverse artists who met him or got to know his work.

Karel Appel

Like de Kooning and Mondrian, Karel Appel (1921–2006) fell in love with American jazz. Born in Amsterdam, Appel studied there at the Rijksakademie van Beeldende Kunsten (National Academy of Fine Arts). In 1946 he had his first solo show at the Beerenhuis in Groningen and was chosen for the *Young Artists* show at Amsterdam's Stedelijk Museum. By 1948, Appel had joined with Constant and Corneille to found the Dutch group Reflex in Amsterdam, which then became part of the international Cobra group founded in Paris, where he moved in 1950.

In 1954, Appel's reputation was such that he attracted the New York dealer Martha Jackson, who gave him his first solo show in America. In 1957 Appel went to New York and took over a studio on 66th Street that had been used by the abstract painter Sam Francis. Appel immersed himself in the milieu of jazz, appreciating the value of improvisation in both music and abstract expressionist painting. He also began to spend time in California, but New York held more of his attention. A banner year was 1960: he won the Guggenheim

1077

Willem de Kooning (left) and Karel Appel at an award ceremony, in 1968.

International Award, showed paintings and sculpture in a second solo show with Martha Jackson, had a show in Los Angeles at the Esther Robles Gallery, and displayed one of his graphics at the David Anderson Gallery in New York. Thereafter, Appel showed frequently around the United States, including in a major retrospective exhibition that began at the San Francisco Museum of Modern Art in 1961 and toured a number of museums in the West. In 1970 he collaborated in San Francisco on jazz recordings with Chet Baker, Merrill Sanders, and other musicians.

Ever restless, Appel moved about and won much recognition in the Netherlands and elsewhere in Europe, returning to New York in 1971, where he began a series of large-scale sculptures in polychrome aluminum. By the next year he had begun to live part-time in New York, where he felt the streets inspired both the objects he made and his subsequent paintings: "My eye is drawn to a pile of discarded objects. Sometimes I feel extra-lucid, sometimes dreamy. What I discover is what any New Yorker can see in the street: old beds, mattresses, lamps, pieces of magnetic tape, kitchen utensils, advertising throw-aways. ... And just as in Amsterdam after the war, the street becomes my studio and the place to recharge my batteries."[13] In 1976 he wrote about New York in a poem: "City of the world, I sniff you, I see you, I feel you."

Appel's street art appears to have influenced the constructions of the artist and art dealer Betty Parsons, among others. His reputation continued to flourish with another retrospective that toured American cities in 1973–74, including New York, Miami, Oklahoma City, Ft. Lauderdale, and Phoenix. By 1985 more than a dozen major American museums had Appel's work in their permanent collections. Alfred Frankenstein's monograph on Appel appeared in 1984.

As early as the 1970s, Appel had taken the initiative to make contact with the Beat poet Allen Ginsberg and suggested that they collaborate. Beginning in 1957, Ginsberg had made many trips to the Netherlands, meeting Dutch poets such as Simon Vinkenoog. Now Ginsberg and Appel arranged to meet. The latter was accompanied by other Dutch poets, such as Bert Schierbeek and Jules Deelder, in 1982 at the Naropa Institute of the Boulder Center for the Visual Arts in Colorado. The occasion was the preparation for a Jack Kerouac festival to celebrate the twenty-fifth anniversary of *On the Road*, and Appel was asked to design a poster. To Ginsberg's surprise, after Appel produced a couple of bold, colorful images, he handed him the paintbrush and encouraged him to "put on words." This spontaneous collaboration led to a series of paintings and visual poems. "With each succeeding improvised work," Ginsberg later wrote, "Karel left space open to me to make up words and put them in all over, big, right on top of his spaces. Sometimes he'd suggest a color, sometimes a space, other times encourage me to make up my own mind, go ahead. Finally I realized he was actually free of shame and proud to let everything happen ... ."[14]

1079

6

THE
COLD WAR
AND
BEYOND

1945–2009

CULTURE

Once again working across media, Appel collaborated on a theater piece, "Can we Dance a Landscape?," a ballet performed in the fall of 1989 at the Brooklyn Academy of Music. He came up with the design, which consisted of nonrepresentational backdrops evoking hilly landscapes, and the theatrical concept, working together with Japanese choreographer and dancer Min Tanaka and the Vietnamese composer Nguyen Thien Dao. The publicity called Appel's design "Surrealist" and identified Tanaka's choreography as in the Japanese Butoh style, an experimental dance form emphasizing the grotesque.[15] Appel also created sculptural shapes that descended from above, including the head of a beast and a wreath.

More recently, many Dutch artists have been able to work for a year in New York as residents in the studio at the Museum of Modern Art's PS 1 in Queens, which is run by the Stichting Fonds voor Beeldende Kunst, Vormgeving en Bouwkunst. A second studio for Dutch artists has been added in the Tribeca neighborhood of Manhattan. Such support for this American experience may reflect the prestige that Dutch visual artists have garnered for their work in the United States. Perhaps the next de Kooning is waiting to be discovered.

1 Willem de Kooning to David Sylvester, quoted in Clifford Ross, ed., *Abstract Expressionism: Creators and Critics: An Anthology* (New York: Harry N. Abrams, 1990), 43.

2 "Ex-Immigrant Back As Famous Artist," *New York Times*, October 2, 1926, 33.

3 *New York Evening Post*, April 2, 1927, quoted in *Adriaan Lubbers… zie hier mijn nieuw adres…* (Amsterdam: Gebr. Douwes Fine Art, 1988), 9.

4 "Once A Peddler Now to Show Art," *New York Times,* March 20, 1927, E4.

5 Howard Devree, "A Reviewer's Notebook," *New York Times,* November 7, 1937, 191.

6 See Gail Levin, *Aaron Copland's America: A Cultural Perspective* (New York: Watson-Guptill Publications, 2000), 75.

7 Al Held to Paul Cummings, interview of December 12, 1975, Archives of American Art (hereafter AAA), Smithsonian Institution, Washington, DC.

8 Michael Kimmelman, "Al Held's Passage in the 50s From Action to Abstraction,"

New York Times, January 12, 1990.

9 Hofmann left an undated essay, "Toward the True Vision of Reality," in Hans Hofmann papers, box 7, reel 5808, AAA.

10 Virginia Pitts Rembert, *Mondrian in the USA* (New York: Parkstone Press USA Ltd., 2002), 56.

11 Lee Krasner to Barbara Rose, interview of March 1972, reel 3774, AAA.

12 Lee Krasner to Barbaralee Diamondstein, interview of 1978, AAA reel 3774 sent to Krasner by the Columbia University Oral History Program.

13 Karel Appel, quoted in Pierre Restany, "Street Art," in *Karel Appel: Street Art, Ceramics, Sculpture, Wood Reliefs, Tapestries, Murals, Villa el Salvador* (Amsterdam: H.J.W. Becht, 1985), 7-8.

14 Karel Appel, quoted in Allen Ginsberg, "Playing with Appel," in *Karel Appel: Street Art,* 248.

15 Jack Anderson, "Some Cows, A Goat and (So to Speak) Real Hoofers," *New York Times,* October 20, 1989, C3.

AMERICAN MODERN ART IN THE STEDELIJK MUSEUM AMSTERDAM

—

JAN VAN ADRICHEM

As a trading nation and place of transit, the Netherlands has become particularly adept at signaling trends abroad, adopting them, and passing them on —much to its own advantage. This national trait has also manifested itself in certain Dutch museums of modern art. In the decades following World War II, Amsterdam's Stedelijk Museum (with the Gemeentemuseum of The Hague and the Van Abbemuseum in Eindhoven not far behind) molded itself into a "transit hub" for international contemporary art. From 1950 onward, the Stedelijk developed a reputation for having an independent-minded and progressive exhibitions and acquisitions policy, aimed at international modern art and design. Together with a handful of museums in Scandinavia, Switzerland, and Germany's Ruhr area, these three Dutch museums were the first to show and collect visual art from the U.S., thus introducing it to western European audiences. Between the mid-1960s and mid-1980s, the Stedelijk acquired an ensemble of American visual art of exceptional quality, comprising some 80 paintings, 100 sculptures, reliefs, installations, objects, and neon works, and 115 films and videos. That the museum thus distinguished itself in the international art world early on was the result of policies pursued by its directors Willem Sandberg (1945–63) and Edy de Wilde (1963–85). Yet, how exactly did the presentation—and, later, acquisition—of American modern art by the Stedelijk take shape under their leadership, and to what extent did the museum give American art a foothold in western Europe?

6

—

—

Growing Importance of American Art

To answer these questions it is necessary to review how the significance and appreciation of American modern visual art changed over time. Until approximately 1950, its importance was considered limited: American artists followed the visual experimentation taking place in European artistic centers, and generally offered little to arouse international interest. The change in perception came after 1950, with abstract expressionists such as Arshile Gorky, Willem de Kooning, and Jackson Pollock. It was during the third quarter of the twentieth century that the authenticity, quality, and variation — and, hence, status and reputation — of American art reached such great heights that New York replaced Paris as the art capital of the Western world, with American art of the early 1970s even assuming a normative role. Since then, history has turned another page: internationalization and decentralization in the art world during the 1970s created a scattering of local artistic centers and, with the market's globalization in the decades that followed, New York lost some of its status and fame.

New York's emergence as an artistic center, and the rising quality of artistic production there, was the result of a slow process in which American artists, art dealers, collectors, and people affiliated with museums all played their part. Even before World War I some of them had already turned to the work of the European avant-garde and brought it to the U.S. stage.[1] Moreover, educational policies in the larger museums had, by the late 1930s, created an audience for whom European modern art (geometric abstraction and surrealism) was the norm — often in advance of its popular acceptance in Europe. Interest among artists in America in the latest European modern art in the 1930s and 1940s served as a further stepping stone toward American artistic innovation. A strong need for an independent artistic program and a visual language of its own was developed during World War II. Additional stimuli arrived with the emigration of a large number of European artists to the U.S. between 1933 and 1943. While Europe's totalitarian regimes were declaring modern art degenerate, personal links were now being formed between European artists and a young, ambitious generation of New Yorkers — artists who subsequently emerged as the best-informed in the Western world. Among them were Gorky, Pollock, de Kooning, and Rothko. Each of them had begun to frame an individual approach toward painting by 1943 and within several years arrived at abstract expressionism — an art form that sought to manifest both the sublime and the tragic in the human condition. Their art, which slowly gained recognition among a wider American public in the 1950s, was rooted in a pessimistic, leftist political outlook, a personal response to the 1940s and 1950s, when the threat of weapons of mass destruction and the Cold War filled them with somber premonitions. Abstract expressionists often felt alienated in an imperialist America, whose repressive attitude toward progressive artists, writers, and thinkers at home, as well as toward the world at large, was juxtaposed with national cultural policies that sent work by those very same artists onto the international exhibitions circuit. Large-scale paintings employing exceptional all-over techniques and an abstract visual language were thus held up as typical expressions of the ideology of the Free World. Although abstract expressionists certainly enjoyed an enhanced status, the U.S. political agenda ran counter to their critical stance and often left them feeling misunderstood and used.

The first limited European recognition of this American "heroic generation" came at the end of the 1950s, and led to the accelerated acknowledgement of American pop art later on. Pop art was winning admirers in western Europe as early as 1964, in part because it offered an accepting, ironic commentary on the visual aspects of modern consumer culture. From 1966 onward, cutting-edge museums in western Europe — taking their cue from progressive galleries in Paris, Cologne, Düsseldorf, and New York — also began to pay attention to postpainterly abstraction. Western European interest in innovative American trends continued with a further shift in focus to minimal art around 1968 and, even before 1970, to American postminimal and conceptual art. The latter were centered on dematerialization and on the artistic process itself, on experiments in various new media, and on modes to formulate new approaches to artistic means and methods, ranging from film and video to text, ideas rendered in graphical statements and diagrams, and performances.

Differing outlooks, ambitions, and objectives in the U.S. and Europe meant that Western European recognition of New York's leading role, and of the quality of the art being produced there, did not come about easily. While MoMA director Alfred Barr could comment as early as 1949, "I would say that American painting 'stacks up against the Old World' very well indeed. American painting seems to me more vigorous and original than that of any single European country," such statements by in-the-know New Yorkers were hardly representative of general public opinion in the U.S., or in western Europe, where Paris had resumed its reign as cultural capital in 1945.[2] Moreover, western European leftist circles regarded U.S. international cultural policy as an integral component of the foreign policy of an imperialist nation. While certain products of American culture such as movies, literature, jazz (which had already gained a following in Europe during the interwar years), comics, and other mass-cultural output won easy acceptance after the war among general audiences in western Europe, and after 1964 even helped do the same for American pop, an earlier and similar appreciation for abstract expressionism was, by contrast, very slow in coming. Western Europe in the 1950s had hardly any notion of the highly per-

6

—

—

sonal and socially critical attitude that the abstract expressionists' work represented, an attitude that had as little to do with American mass culture as it did with any conception of a "national" art. In the large dimensions and particular treatment of their works, these American artists were too far removed from European progressive art, where the focus lay on more limited dimensions, an informal art, and on the energetic painterly style of the Cobra and post-Cobra schools. It was not until 1964 that attitudes toward contemporary American art definitely began to change; proto-pop-art artist Robert Rauschenberg's Grand Prize award for painting in that year's Venice Biennale sent the clear signal that American art could no longer be ignored. Among the Western European museums interested in contemporary visual art, a few now began to pursue a more emphatic program of purchasing U.S. art, acquiring seminal works in the process. A full decade and a half had passed, however, between claims asserting the primacy of American art, such as Barr's in 1949, and the 1964 watershed among European museums.

The Stedelijk's Early Role

Comparison with early initiatives for American visual art throws an interesting and more nuanced light on the Stedelijk's role as its Western European advocate. The painter Georges Mathieu, for example, organized several Paris gallery exhibitions between 1948 and 1960 where work by U.S. artists such as Arshile Gorky, Willem de Kooning, Jackson Pollock, Ad Reinhardt, Marc Rothko, and Mark Tobey was featured side by side with paintings by artists working in France, including Hans Hartung, Wols, Jean-Paul Riopelle, Pierre Soulages, and Mathieu himself. At the Basel Kunsthalle, Arnold Rüdlinger, director since 1955, was in contact with the young American painter Sam Francis, who was living in Paris. In 1957 Francis convinced Rüdlinger to go to New York and witness the latest painting trends there in person. The Kunsthalle director was so impressed with what he saw that he proceeded in 1959 to purchase, using special Swiss acquisition funds, one work each by Kline, Newman, Rothko, and Still. These were donated to Basel's Kunstmuseum, where they are among the most important works in the collection to this day. These acquisitions represent the first major purchase of contemporary American art by a prominent European art official.

Running alongside these early connections between American artists and Europeans were institutional channels established by the U.S. From 1953 onward, the MoMA organized traveling exhibitions of contemporary American art.[3] Dutch museum directors used their own discretion in selecting which to show. Among them was the Stedelijk's presentation in 1956 of the traveling photo exhibition "The Family of Man," under the Dutch name of "Wij Mensen." This was followed in 1958 by the MoMA's "The New American Painting," or "Jong Amerika schildert," with works by Pollock, Newman, de Kooning, and others, and, in that same year, the MoMA's solo show "Jackson Pollock." Both these latter exhibitions had their European premiere in the Basel Kunsthalle in 1958, proceeding from there to cities throughout Europe. Basel owed its preferential position to Rüdlinger's determination — following his first visit to New York — to set up his own group exhibition of U.S. contemporary artists. Lacking the necessary financial means, he had joined with the MoMA in planning these exhibitions. In addition to these traveling shows of American modern art (which exhibited, in the course of several years, work by several artists), the Stedelijk Museum hosted in 1961 the MoMA's traveling solo show of Rothko's work (from which Sandberg hoped to buy a painting that, in the end, proved too expensive), which also made stops at Basel, Brussels, London, Paris, and Rome.

Willem Sandberg

The Stedelijk's contribution to the introduction of American art in western Europe was, however, also spearheaded early on by the museum itself. In June 1950, director Willem Sandberg teamed up with the Dutch-American collector Jack Vandenbergh to organize a retrospective of two centuries of American painting, entitled "Amerika schildert" (America paints). Works by older U.S. modernists like Feininger, Hartley, and Shahn were featured prominently, but four paintings by Pollock were also included. Of key importance, moreover, was Sandberg's association, from as early as 1948, with Peggy Guggenheim. She had just closed her gallery, Art of the Century, in New York (1942–47) in order to move to Europe, taking with her a collection of modern art that included a great many prewar European avant-gardists, as well as works by Gorky, Pollock, and Rothko. At the 1948 Venice Biennale she presented her collection and Venice now became the city where she wanted to settle and house her collection. She also wanted a more favorable import tariff, which meant she would have to convince the Italian government of the collection's value. Acting on Sandberg's advice, she took it on tour to several European museums, the Stedelijk among them, where the collection was presented as "Surrealisme + abstractie" (Surrealism + abstraction) in February 1951. As a token of thanks to Sandberg, Guggenheim subsequently donated three paintings to the Stedelijk Museum, including Pollock's *The Water Bull* (circa 1946) and *Reflection of the Big Dipper* (1947). Guggenheim, whose New York gallery had represented Pollock and who in 1950 owned some twenty works by the artist, was fully aware of

6

—

THE
COLD WAR
AND
BEYOND

1945–2009

—

CULTURE

the value of her gift. Yet, her immense faith in Pollock notwithstanding, Sandberg was not really receptive to his work at that time. In July/August 1950 the Stedelijk lent the two paintings to Venice's Museo Correr for inclusion in Pollock's first western European museum solo show, but once back in Amsterdam and for much of the rest of the decade, the works were all but ignored. Nevertheless, Guggenheim's gift at this early date was an exceptional one, arriving at the Stedelijk several years in advance of Rüdlinger's purchases for Basel.

By 1950 Sandberg was also acquainted with de Kooning's work, which he had seen in the MoMA's American pavilion at the Venice Biennale: it, too, failed to impress him. This artist, who had emigrated from Rotterdam to the U.S. in 1926 and who by 1950 had risen to become one of New York's leading abstract expressionists, was not included in the Stedelijk's "American Painting" exhibition of 1950. In fact, it was not until 1958, when the museum showed "The New American Painting," that Sandberg became interested in de Kooning's work and incorporated it into various group exhibitions. Yet, he never managed to acquire any of the artist's works, despite continued attempts since 1958; by that time, de Kooning himself was no longer interested, having judged Sandberg a self-serving man who had failed to back him when it mattered most.

Thus, while Sandberg's pursuit of American art did generate exhibitions, it yielded hardly any acquisitions. His approach to art from the U.S. reflects that of other forward-looking museum directors in Europe — not taking any particular interest until 1958, and then remaining unprepared to pay what abstract expressionist works commanded on the American market. His interest in presenting American art in the museum had more to do with its topical value than with having it represented in the collection: he considered it primarily *as information*, and not until it was too late did he perceive anything inherently exceptional in the work. That the Stedelijk Museum can now boast not only two Pollocks but also a collection of works by de Kooning comprising eight paintings dating between 1963 and 1983, thirteen sculptures (donated by the artist), and many works on paper, is thanks to director De Wilde. His 1964 purchase of de Kooning's painting *Rosy Fingered Dawn at Louse Point* (1963) was the first step toward assembling an overview of the artist's later period; he also organized two important solo shows of de Kooning's work at the Stedelijk in 1968 and 1983, respectively.

Sandberg's strongly exhibitions-oriented approach to, among others, American art is confirmed by several shows that he put on toward the end of his professional career (some of them organized together with director Pontus Hultén of the Moderna Museet in Stockholm and the artists Spoerri and Tinguely), which included ground-breaking works by Kaprow, Johns, and Rauschenberg. They presented, for instance, moving objects as part of a 1961 exhibit on kinetic art entitled "Bewogen beweging" ("Moving Movement"). Rauschenberg

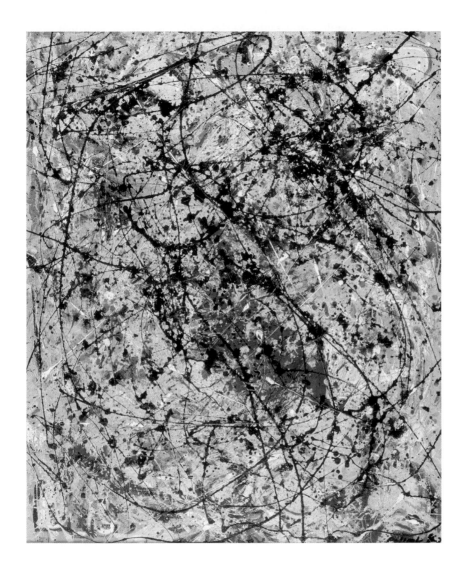

Jackson Pollock, *Reflection of the Big Dipper*, 1947.

THE
COLD WAR
AND
BEYOND

1945–2009

CULTURE

was among the six artists whose work was used to create a total environment in the 1962 "Dylaby (Dynamic Labyrinth)" exhibition, and he figured also in "4 Americans" (together with Johns, Lesley, and Stanciewicz), in which Sandberg presented paintings, assemblages, and installations earlier that same year. This trio of exhibitions, together with the 1964 "American pop art" (shown under De Wilde), introduced a new, theoretically founded, playfully experimental, neo-avant-garde conception of art. Even with canonical works within such easy reach, however, Sandberg made no move to purchase. Not until "American pop art" — featuring works by Dine, Lichtenstein, Oldenburg, Rosenquist, Segal, and Warhol in an exhibition that De Wilde took over from the Moderna Museet, which effectively introduced pop art in western Europe — did the Stedelijk's acquisitions practices change: now definitive works by artists including Oldenburg, Lichtenstein, and much later on Warhol, were purchased. In 1965 and 1966, moreover, De Wilde acquired Rauschenberg's assemblage *Charlene* (1954) and Johns's triptych-and-a-half *Untitled* (1964–65) for the museum.

Edy de Wilde

De Wilde first visited the U.S. in 1962 while still serving as director of the Van Abbemuseum. As Sandberg's successor at the Stedelijk he continued the latter's dynamic-denotative exhibitions policy, but also used acquisitions to spotlight, among others, contemporary American works of art. Early in 1967 he sent the MoMA a list of the more than thirty exhibitions between 1958 and 1966 in which the Stedelijk had shown work by young American artists, to emphasize the museum's vital role in introducing that work to European audiences.[4] In fact, during De Wilde's tenure (1963–85) the Stedelijk would ultimately host a total of over forty monographic exhibitions of contemporary American artists.

De Wilde's fascination with contemporary American art was based on more than just the conviction of its value. Since 1930, a collection of the Van Gogh family containing many works by Van Gogh and his artistic circle had been on permanent loan in the museum and contributed in large measure to the Stedelijk's international renown. Toward the end of Sandberg's term as director it became clear that the collection would in due time move to the new Van Gogh Museum, next to the Stedelijk. The relocation came in 1973. De Wilde was fully cognizant of losing a major crowd puller so, to fill the gap, he promoted art from after 1960 — and American art in particular — as the museum's new specialty. In a 1973 letter to Amsterdam's alderman for the arts he wrote: "The Van Gogh collection has left the Stedelijk Museum. This forces us to assemble a collection of the highest caliber. ... We are chiefly collecting art made since

1960. ... The Stedelijk Museum possesses the most important collection of post-1960s art in Europe. Its reputation is not determined by numbers, but by its design (homogenous parts) and the qualitative level of the individual art works."[5] He went on to name seven purchases that stood out in the collection, five of them of U.S. artists: Rauschenberg, Johns, Lichtenstein, de Kooning, and Newman. There can be no doubt of the centrality of contemporary American art in De Wilde's collections policy, and in the reputation that the museum was to build for it in Western Europe.

The Netherlands' explosive economic growth and prosperity during the 1960s gave De Wilde access, until well into the 1970s, to larger acquisitions and exhibitions budgets than had been available to Sandberg. He also managed to cut shipping costs by negotiating sponsorship arrangements with the Holland America Line, thus making it easier for the Stedelijk than for other museums to transport works from the U.S. He relied on talented curators to organize revolutionary shows featuring the very latest American art. An exhibition such as "New Shapes of Colour" (1966) traced a particular twentieth-century painting's evolution into a large, abstract, flat field of color, thereby endowing it with a distinct and concrete object status in the here and now. This exhibition, which also traveled to Stuttgart and Berne, encompassed European art, but also American pop art, postpainterly abstraction, shaped canvases, and minimalism — artistic trends that had not yet been defined as such in Europe. The Stedelijk, with its progressive collections policy and traveling shows such as "New Shapes of Colour," had launched itself as a showcase for new American art, thus also picking up the tradition begun with the MoMA's tours of the 1950s.

Exhibitions and acquisitions fed into one another under De Wilde's guidance. In the years before and after "New Shapes of Colour," for example, the museum acquired many works by artists represented in that exhibition — often the first step toward gathering an ensemble of works by a particular American artist that was subsequently presented in the Stedelijk's galleries as a unified whole.[6] These ensembles and flanking (solo) shows of the 1960s and 1970s allowed the Stedelijk to send a clear signal about its own position and, at the same time, reap international appreciation for its policies aimed at denoting successive new trends in U.S. and Western European art.[7] But De Wilde's aim was not art-historical encyclopedic inclusivity; rather, his affinities and contacts led him to gravitate toward certain artistic personalities. Summing up his acquisitions policy in a 1984 statement, he said: "Consistency of vision has greater persuasive power than a broad scope of the setup."[8]

One artist whose work would have been included in "New Shapes of Colour" had transportation difficulties not stood in the way, was Barnett Newman. His *The Gate* (1954) was purchased by the museum in 1967. If Newman's color-

1089

6

——

THE
COLD WAR
AND
BEYOND

1945–2009

——

CULTURE

field work had been in the exhibition it would hardly have been understood as abstract expressionism at all, but rather as painting in expanses of color on a monumental scale. De Wilde developed a great affinity for Newman's work, such that the Stedelijk Museum now owns four of his paintings and dedicated a large solo exhibition to him in 1972. In Newman De Wilde perceived an artist who had already turned away from de Kooning's gesticulative work in the 1950s and had recreated himself — yet still within the ambit of abstract expression-ism — as the latter's counterpoint. As such, the museum director saw Newman as having laid the foundations for the new, large-scale, coolly abstract art of Kelly and Stella. Newman's work thus came to represent the essential link be-tween the collection's abstract expressionists on the one hand, and, on the oth-er, its postpainterly abstract art — and hence, later on, minimalism and con-ceptualism, as per De Wilde. The director's collections policy, in the late 1960s and early 1970s bent on contemporary abstract-reductive painting, was rooted in his appreciation for Newman's work, as is reflected in the deliberately cho-sen ensembles of works by Mangold, Marden, Martin, and Ryman that arrived to augment the Stedelijk's collection from 1970 on (after several years of many kinds of contemporary art that in its neo-avant-garde experimentation tried to break free of all sorts of artistic conventions). These ensembles testified to De Wilde's preference for a rational art rooted in basic principles of painting — a preference that was further crystallized in the exhibition "Fundamental Paint-ing" (1975).

De Wilde's personal affinities were not the only determinants at work; there was room for experimentation and contrast too, such as in head curator Wim Beeren's ground-breaking 1969 neo-avant-garde exhibition, also shown in Ger-many, "Op losse schroeven/Square Pegs in Round Holes." This exhibition de-fined a new kind of collaboration between organizers and artists, with free-form museum installations and process-oriented works by such Americans as Andre, De Maria, Heizer, Huebler, Morris, Nauman, Oppenheim, Serra, Smith-son, Sonnier, and Weiner (and several of their western European peers). It also marks the Stedelijk's early receptivity to the emerging antipainterly trends of minimalism, conceptualism, and postconceptualism.

In the politicized, critical, and for the Stedelijk difficult stretch of the 1970s, De Wilde acquired a reputation for clinging to his preference for painting at a time when this type of art's significance as a mode of artistic expression was on the wane, and for not giving minimal and conceptual art the attention they deserved. More and more, he was deemed the authoritarian and old-fashioned director of a stagnating museum where recognition of innovative visual art forms — such as performance — came too late. Yet, the arguments against this perception are many. The Stedelijk's exhibitions and acquisitions policy after

A room in the Stedelijk Museum (1978), showing from left to right:
Willem de Kooning's *Two figures in a Landscape* (1967), *Montauk IV* (1969), *Untitled IX* (1975),
Rosy Fingered Dawn at Louse Point (1963) and *Cross Legged Figure* (1972/1979).

6

—

—

"Square Pegs in Round Holes" testifies to its interest in work by American light artists from the West Coast, in Serra's new sculptures, Serra and Nauman's postconceptual films and videos, and in Nauman's neon text pieces, which the Stedelijk began collecting as early as 1969. When it came to acquisitions of contemporary American art, the museum continued to pursue a policy of diversity; just witness its enduring positive response (by acquiring many films and videos) when the neo-avant-garde's freeing and expanding of traditional notions about art became increasingly important around 1970.

Yet, the acquisition of art forms other than painting was the exception that proved the rule: De Wilde never veered from a course that placed painting—1960s and 1970s American neo-avant-garde painting in particular—front and center. The final years of his directorship were characterized by a shift in contemporary artist production—and public appreciation—toward paintings that were free, figurative, regionally specific, stylistically diverse, and highly subjective in their iconography. Around 1980 this emerged as the dominant trend, and De Wilde responded, in 1981 and 1982, by purchasing pieces of the American Julian Schnabel, whom the Stedelijk also gave a solo show in 1982, and by training an eye on the older generation of U.S. artists whose work had taken on fresh relevance in the wake of the new trend. Philip Guston, who had already enjoyed a solo show of his abstract expressionist paintings at the Stedelijk in 1962, returned to the museum in 1983 with his later, somber, cartoon-like canvases, of which the Stedelijk purchased two in 1984.

The Stedelijk's interest in Guston's later work was indicative of its tendency at that time toward reaching back to former contours of American modern art, as is also evident in the retrospectives it held of drawings by Jackson Pollock and Barnett Newman in 1979 and 1980, respectively. More evaluative in character were the three major retrospective exhibitions organized during the early 1980s: "'60'80. Attitudes/Concepts/Images. A Selection from Twenty Years of Visual Arts" (1982), "20 Years of Collecting. Acquisitions Stedelijk Museum 1963–1984" (1984), and "La Grande Parade. Highlights in Painting after 1940" (1984–85). This last one was a veritable procession of De Wilde's favorites. Of the forty painters represented, one-third were Americans. While this may seem a modest proportion, the retrospective also included later works by European modernists like Beckmann, Braque, Léger, Matisse, Mondrian, and Picasso, along with postwar European painters. As such, American work formed a considerable presence, with highlights including pieces by Pollock, de Kooning, Rothko, Newman, Kelly, Mangold, Marden, and Ryman. And of the 110 artists represented in the "'60'80" show, as many as 40 came from the United States.

Conclusion

The Stedelijk was clearly a Western European frontrunner in presenting exhibitions of contemporary American art, whether they were traveling shows or were organized by the museum itself. It also got an early start with the acquisition of two exceptional Pollocks, while the ensembles of American art collected from 1964 onward served — together with the exhibitions — to single out individual artistic personalities, to lend support early on to certain artistic forms and artists from the U.S., to circumscribe a signature identity for the museum itself, and to define a context in which specific American artists would feel at home. Precisely the circumscribed character of its collection and shows engendered general recognition at an early date of its special contribution to growing western European appreciation for American art. While one may argue that the Stedelijk's pursuit of American art from the third quarter of the twentieth century on was "cultural subservience" to a superpower, at the same time its recognition of American art's high quality was in fact commendable. This interest was certainly welcomed in the U.S.; it was not a coincidence that, at the end of De Wilde's term, two donations arrived at the museum from the United States: Rothko's *Untitled (Umber, Blue, Umber, Brown)* of 1962, which had been included in "La Grande Parade," and, from Newman's widow, that artist's *Right Here* of 1954.

1   Via exhibitions (the Armory Show, 1913), New York galleries (Stieglitz's 291 and De Zayas' The Modern Gallery), private collectors (the Arensbergs, Albert Barnes, the Cone sisters, John Quinn, Katherine Dreier, and Solomon R. Guggenheim), and acquisitions and exhibitions of the Société Anonyme (founded in 1920 by Duchamp, Man Ray, and Dreier), the Museum of Modern Art (MoMA, from 1929), and the Solomon R. Guggenheim Museum (from 1939).

2   A. Barr, "A Symposium: The State of American Art," in I. Sandler, ed., *Defining Modern Art: Selected Writings of Alfred H. Barr, Jr.* (New York: s.n., 1986), 211-213, here 212.

3   For example, in addition to the pavilion at the Venice Biennale (1948) and work by Gorky, de Kooning, and Pollock, presented in the same city two years later, the MoMA showed work by contemporary American artists at the 1959 "Documenta II" in Kassel.

4   For exhibitions of U.S. art in the Stedelijk between 1960 and 1980, see exh. cat. *'60'80. Attitudes/Concepts/Images: A Selection from Twenty Years of Visual Arts* (Amsterdam: Stedelijk Museum, 1982), 12-43; acquisitions from the U.S. in exh. cat. *20 Years of Collecting. Acquisitions Stedelijk Museum 1963-1984. Painting and Sculpture* (Amsterdam: Stedelijk Museum, 1984), 150-323; On De Wilde's letter to the MoMA, see J. van Adrichem, *De ontvangst van de moderne kunst in Nederland 1910-2000. Picasso als pars pro toto*

6

—

THE
COLD WAR
AND
BEYOND

1945-2009

—

CULTURE

(Amsterdam: Prometheus, 2001), 533, note 65.

5   Letter dated October 4, 1973 from E. de Wilde to H. Lammers, copy in the Stedelijk Museum Archives.

6   Purchases from artists such as Indiana included in 1966 *Six* and *Eight* (dated 1965), from Kelly in 1967 *Blue Red Rocker* (1963) and *Blue Green Red* (1964–65), from Louis in 1966 *Unfolding Light* (1961), from Noland in 1968 *Trans West* (1965) and *Wide Spread* (1968), from Stella in 1968 *Newstead Abbey* (1960) and his *Les Indes Galantes*, soon after it was completed in 1967.

7   Art historian Benjamin Buchloh pointed to the 1964 pop art exhibition and to purchases made by the museum of works by Kelly and Newman as having influenced German artists like Palermo and Genzken; See B. H. Buchloh, "Interview mit Benjamin H. Buchloh 1986," in H.-U. Obrist, ed., *Gerhard Richter. Text. Schriften und Interviews* (Frankfurt am Main/Leipzig: s.n., 1993), 122-155, here 128; B. H. Buchloh, "Isa Genzken: The Fragment as Model," in exh. cat. *Isa Genzken* (Chicago/Frankfurt am Main /Brussels/Munich: s.n., 1992–93), 135-141.

8   A. van Grevenstein, J. Joosten, and K. Schampers, "20 Years as an Art Collector. An interview with Edy de Wilde," in exh. cat. *20 Years of Collecting*, 6-37, esp. 15.

NORTH ATLANTIC DANCE RELATIONS

——

ONNO F. STOKVIS

Dance had been all but driven from the Dutch stage during the German occupation. The chaos of the war's closing years made it almost impossible to put on performances and kept dancers from maintaining their technique. It was to be expected, then, that the first dance performance to be held after May 1945 would offer little in the way of elevated artistry. It was precisely for this reason that many dancers and choreographers left the Netherlands during the early postwar period, turning to the urban dance centers of Paris and London to regain lost ground. There, mostly Russian ballet instructors — connected with Les Ballets Russes — passed on the traditions of classical ballet to a new and hungry generation.

The most important influence on post-1945 Dutch dance, however, came from the United States, which, together with the Soviet Union, had emerged as the major winner after the war. Through the Marshall Plan the U.S. provided a great boost to Europe's reconstruction, and it was not long before America became the dominant player in the Western financial and cultural world. To the hardworking Europeans the U.S. was a shining example, and everything American was intrinsically good. Whereas in the years before World War I it had been the emergence of Les Ballets Russes that radically redirected the future course of European dance, after World War II it was the Stateside New York City Ballet (NYCB) and the Martha Graham Dance Company that offered new perspectives to artists working in Europe.

The NYCB, led by the Russian-American choreographer George Balanchine, first toured Europe in 1950, followed by performances in the Netherlands in 1952. The company's 1950 tour was a revelation to its European public: here was dance that, with its abstract yet highly accessible style of movement, modest staging, and reserved costuming and décor, presented the perfect medium for the dancers' technique.

1095

Eyes on America

6

—

THE
COLD WAR
AND
BEYOND
1945–2009

—

CULTURE

1096

The first person to recognize the key significance of American ballet for the future of Dutch dance was the Lithuanian-born dancer and ballet instructor Sonia Gaskell. After living in Palestine and then Paris, she emigrated to the Netherlands in 1939, where she founded the Nederlands Ballet (Dutch Ballet) after the war. She established her company in Amsterdam and, in 1953, managed to obtain a government subsidy to fund it. It was from the Nederlands Ballet that, following a series of mergers and divisions during the 1950s, the Netherlands' two most important dance companies would later emerge: The Hague's Nederlands Dans Theater (Dutch Dance Theater; NDT) in 1959 and Amsterdam's Het Nationale Ballet (Dutch National Ballet; HNB) in 1961. Gaskell's primary aim was to gain recognition for dance as a full-fledged art form. To achieve her objective, she worked at improving the dancers' technique and developed a repertoire that comprised nineteenth-century classical masterpieces, modern twentieth-century work by internationally renowned choreographers, and work by contemporary Dutch choreographers.[1]

To help her realize these goals, Gaskell turned to Balanchine as her model. She was clearly very much in awe of his work, as is evident in an article she penned for the Dutch newspaper *Het Vrije Volk* in response to a performance of Balanchine's *Episodes* in New York in 1959. What she had seen left her stunned: Balanchine is a genius, she wrote, and one hundred years ahead of his time.[2] In fact, the extent of her admiration was apparent even earlier, when the Nederlands Ballet added Balanchine's choreography of *La Somnambule* to its repertoire in 1955.

Three years later she recruited the American ballet master and choreographer Benjamin Harkarvy. He had trained as a dancer at the School of American Ballet — the NYCB's official training program — and was to become a key figure in the developmental phase of Dutch dance. He was given responsibility for training the dancers and was subsequently among the founders and artistic directors of the NDT. When Harkarvy stepped down as the company's ballet master in 1959, Gaskell appointed Karl Shook at Balanchine's urging, and at the same time added one of the latter's newly choreographed pieces to the repertoire of the Nederlands Ballet.

Acting again on Balanchine's advice, Gaskell next engaged two young black soloists: Billy Wilson in 1959 and Sylvester Campbell one year later. Balanchine himself had had the black dancer Arthur Mitchell in his company since 1956, but the course of Mitchell's career was anything but smooth. American public opinion held that ballet was the exclusive domain of whites and that black dancers were better suited for more light-hearted genres like shows and tap dance.[3] Mitchell was therefore to remain the NYCB's sole black dancer up until 1970, dancing in more abstract ballets such as *Agon* or in character roles like Puck in *A Midsummer Night's Dream*. And it was for this very reason, too, that Balanchine advised talented young black dancers in his academy to set their sights on Europe, where racial bias was less of an issue. Thus, Gaskell — who had become artistic director of HNB in 1961 — was able to give Sylvester Campbell a leading role in her staging of the nineteenth-century ballet *La Bayadère* in 1964 and, one year later, as Prince Siegfried, the male protagonist in *Swan Lake*.[4]

The impact of American dance on developments in the Netherlands was by no means restricted to ballet. Taking their cues from Isadora Duncan, a number of innovators on the American dance scene were continuing to extend the limits of modern dance ever farther. The most important among them was the choreographer Martha Graham, who led her Martha Graham Dance Company in a 1954 performance in Amsterdam's Carré Theater. Her psychologically and emotionally charged dance dramas, based on themes borrowed from classical antiquity, deeply impressed the public. Even more important in terms of influencing Dutch developments was the workshop on the "Graham technique" after the performance. This technique was a departure from the lofty and ethereal silhouettes of ballet, which she countered with the struggle of the dancer's body against gravity, anchoring her dancers to the ground while tapping a wealth of expressive potential. The Graham technique was an assurance to dancers that dance was indeed a "contemporary" art form with ties to other avant-garde currents in art. Sonia Gaskell was characteristically quick to grasp the significance of this vision, and had soon contracted the Graham dancer Pearl Lang to teach at HNB.

Graham was also to influence the younger generation of choreographers whom Gaskell sought out to create new repertoires for her company during the 1950s and 1960s. The most important one was Rudi van Dantzig. From 1965 onward he shared HNB's artistic directorship with Gaskell, continuing after her departure in 1969 and remaining in the position until 1991. Much of Van Dantzig's work carries a social charge, manifest in such early work as his 1964 *Monument for a Dead Boy*, a piece in which the deepest stirrings of a homosexual young man's soul are bared in a style strongly reminiscent of a Graham ballet.

A third American trend to exert its influence on Dutch dance had a much more playful character. Running parallel to the serious work of Balanchine and Graham was the entertainment-oriented show and jazz dance genre, which had carved out an important niche for itself on stages in the U.S. Major theaters on Broadway and elsewhere in Manhattan staged nightly shows and musicals that attracted large audiences. The genre made its international breakthrough in 1957 with the musical *West Side Story*. This song and dance adaptation of

1097

6

—

THE
COLD WAR
AND
BEYOND

1945–2009

—

CULTURE

Shakespeare's *Romeo and Juliet* featured a musical arrangement by New York-based composer Leonard Bernstein and choreography by Jerome Robbins, who also served as its director. *West Side Story* was years ahead of its time, combining narrative, song, dance, and acting into a single unified whole. After its release as a movie in 1961 the musical won accolades and admiration around the world. This spirited piece of performance art made a profound impression on Holland's foremost choreographer, Hans van Manen, who adapted his own version for the NDT, entitled *Feestgericht*. Van Manen choreographed additional jazz ballets during this same period, for example for the weekly television show hosted by singer and presenter Teddy Scholten.

Blending Classical and Modern Dance at the Nederlands Dans Theater

Having absorbed these models and inspiration over the course of the 1950s, the 1960s would mark the period when Dutch dance came into its own. While interest in developments abroad—and in the U.S. especially—continued unabated, dancers and choreographers now adapted models to fit their own ends, making their first venture onto the international stage in the mid-1960s. The NDT, which in the early 1960s was operating under the codirectorship of Benjamin Harkarvy and Hans van Manen, played a key role in these developments. In addition to being artistic director of the NDT, Van Manen was at this time building his reputation as a choreographer of international standing. For his inspiration he was not only indebted to Robbins, but especially to Balanchine. His succinct statement describing his approach to dance is often quoted: "All of my dance is about dance, and about nothing else."[5] Van Manen creates ballets devoid of narrative themes or deep spiritual meanings; his choreography consists of series of movements in their purest form, danced by virtuoso dancers. Precisely this relationship to dance is what reveals Van Manen as a kindred spirit of the master of neoclassical ballet, George Balanchine.

Harkarvy and Van Manen engaged two choreographers from New York for the NDT: John Butler and Glenn Tetley. The latter in particular was to be important in directing the course of the company in these early years. He came to The Hague in 1962 after having seen the NDT performance of American choreographer Anna Sokolow's *Rooms*. Though Tetley had his own company in New York, he asserted that he was keen to work for the company capable of dancing *Rooms* so well and—an equally important consideration—one that received government subsidies and could therefore afford to pay him a reasonable salary. Certainly this was not, and still is not, the case in the harsher American art world. Tetley instructed the dancers of the NDT in the Graham technique and

Scene from Hans van Manen's *Feestgericht*, at the NDT.

6

—

THE
COLD WAR
AND
BEYOND

1945–2009

—

CULTURE

put on box office hits like *Pierrot Lunaire* and *The Anatomical Lesson*, in effect marking out parameters, together with Van Manen, that were to be of the very greatest importance for the further development of dance in the Netherlands. After all, these two choreographers shared not only their interest in classical dance, but also in Graham and jazz dance, and sought to combine the best of both worlds in their work. The undogmatic and eclectic attitude toward dance being pursued by the NDT was entirely unique in Western theater dance and would in time effect astonishing results. In 1965 the NDT took Tetley and Van Manen's work to the summer dance festival Jacob's Pillow in the Berkshires (in Massachusetts), a three-hour drive north of New York City. The group subsequently appeared in New York itself in 1968 and toured the U.S. very successfully in 1973.

Social Criticism and Radical Innovation in Dance

Apart from the NDT's successes, Dutch dance was making additional important strides during the 1960s. These were closely linked with the wave of protests shaking the very foundations of Western society, with the younger generation criticizing the 1950s' materialism of their parents and putting long-standing political, societal, and social relationships under pressure. The changes of the 1960s found clear expression in a drive for independence manifested by several revolutionary and radical innovators of dance. These individuals resisted the large, hierarchically organized ballet companies like the NDT and HNB, in which they felt themselves unable, as well as disinclined, to function. They made a radical break with the classical ballet tradition and created dance that was based on previously unknown concepts and techniques. Yet despite the increasingly critical attitude of the younger generation vis-à-vis U.S. foreign politics, this group of rebels, like their colleagues in the large dance companies, also looked for their inspiration and models to Manhattan, the mecca of dance.

It was in Manhattan that the shift toward greater abstraction in choreography and concentration on pure dance movements, as applied by Balanchine, was picked up and further exploited by the dance innovator Merce Cunningham. Under his influence the 1950s and 1960s became a period of exploring the abstract and formal character of dance and the relationships between dance and other art forms. Concepts with their roots in music, such as "chance," were introduced into dance, resulting in pure motional compositions enacted by dancers making such commonplace movements as walking and rolling, or just standing.[6] Nevertheless, Cunningham was in fact a moderate modernist when compared to the group of young dancers and choreographers who worked in the latter half of the 1960s in Manhattan's Judson Memorial Church and who used the offered space for artistic group work. They likewise sought to free themselves of every reference to the ballet tradition, asserting that dance technique was not a prerequisite for being a dancer. And they, too, addressed the fundamental question of what dance really is. Their approach engendered a playful environment that gave rise to new definitions of dance based on other uses of time, space, and the body. Shows were created in which a performer might stand on the stage naked without moving for half an hour. Small, out-of-the-way Manhattan theaters formed venues for conceptual presentations with clear links to performance art and happenings in which the divisions separating dancers, visual artists, composers, and painters melted away.

This group of artists is collectively referred to as the Judson Dance Theater.[7] The first person in the Dutch dance world to take an interest in their radical innovations was Pauline de Groot. She left for the United States in 1957 and studied there with Erick Hawkins, who was among those active in the Judson Dance Theater. Upon her return to the Netherlands she founded her own dance group and in 1974 became artistic director of the newly established School for New Dance Development at Amsterdam's Theater School. This school gained international fame and many of its pupils and teachers, such as Ineke Sluiter, Bianca van Dillen, and Krisztina de Châtel, would go on to form their own dance companies and have a major impact on the evolution of dance in the Netherlands. De Groot continued to pursue her connections in the U.S., performing and teaching on a regular basis, but in her own country her importance faded as the 1980s progressed. In the Netherlands, moreover, where conditions were ripe for acceptance of Balanchine and Van Manen's style of dance — with their preference for abstract ballet and emphasis on the virtuosity of the dancers — interest in the conceptual dance of the Judson Dance Theater would always remain limited. This circumstance would also affect the career of a second radical Dutch dance pioneer, Koert Stuyf. As a student he had come into contact with Lucas Hoving, who for many years had worked as the soloist in the Mexican-American choreographer José Limón's dance company and would later go on to become artistic director of the Rotterdam Dance Academy. Acting on Hoving's advice, Stuyf left for New York in 1959, where he trained with such choreographers as Limón, Graham, Cunningham, and others. Upon his return to the Netherlands Stuyf joined legendary dancer Ellen Edinoff for performances that created a stir among audiences, such as *A Person of the Place* and *Within Pale Silence*, both staged at the Carré Theater in 1964. Both of these pieces were clearly indebted to the style of Cunningham. In addition to establishing his own company — the Stichting Eigentijdse Dans (Contemporary Dance Foundation), which engaged such dancers as Krisztina de Châtel — Stuyf set up a dance academy at the Amsterdam Theater School. His personality being unsuited to

6

———

THE
COLD WAR
AND
BEYOND

1945–2009

———

CULTURE

the bureaucratic structures of an official training program, however, the 1970s saw Stuyf's and his wife Edinoff's importance slowly fade away.

As loyal adherents of the ideology of the Judson Dance Theater, De Groot and Stuyf were never to create any established institution; rather, they would always continue to work in the margins. This was different for the Graham dancer and choreographer Ineke Sluiter. In 1968 she set up the Rotterdams Danscentrum (Rotterdam Dance Center), which continued as the Werkcentrum Dans (Dance Works Center) after 1974 under the directorship of NDT dancer and choreographer Käthy Gosschalk. Gosschalk had a good eye for talent and during her study trips to New York she contracted a number of world-class choreographers, including David Gordon, Bill T. Jones, Tere O'Connor, Denis O'Connor, Steven Petronio, Randy Warsaw, and Amanda Miller.[8] Gosschalk also kept in touch with the New York dance scene via Ton Simons. Simons had studied at the Rotterdam Dance Academy, where Lucas Hoving served as director, and had completed his training with Merce Cunningham in New York. In 1978 he settled in New York and established a company, Ton Simons and Dancers. Gosschalk also engaged Simons as her own in-house choreographer, and in 1999 he succeeded her as artistic director of what had by then become the Rotterdamse Dansgroep (Rotterdam Dance Group) — today known as Dance Works Rotterdam.

Shifting from the United States to Europe

While the Rotterdamse Dansgroep was certainly very focused on the United States, it also had a role in plotting the new course that Dutch dance was to take from the 1970s onward. In 1970 the then unknown German choreographer Pina Bausch debuted her work *Im Wind der Zeit* for the Rotterdams Danscentrum. This piece heralded the growing importance of western European dance currents in the Netherlands. After all, the dance revolution that left its mark on the Netherlands during the 1950s and 1960s had swept the rest of Europe, too, and had led, by the 1970s and 1980s, to the emergence of new, small-scale, modern dance initiatives for which — albeit with occasional reluctance — government subsidies were made available.

Developments in the U.S. dance sector, by contrast, began to stagnate during this period. Availability of stimulus funding from the government or other sponsorship sources was little to nonexistent for any but a handful of major and well-established companies like the NYCB, the Graham Company, and the Merce Cunningham Dance Company. Moreover, in Manhattan the cost of living and studio rentals skyrocketed to the extent that many artists were compelled to pack their bags and resettle in cities like San Francisco. Others chose a nomadic existence, working in the U.S. as well as Europe. The straw that broke the camel's back was the outbreak of the AIDS epidemic at the beginning of the 1980s, which had terrible consequences for the New York dance community. Little was left of the energetic dance center that Manhattan had been in the 1960s and 1970s. While Graham's and Cunningham's dance studios continued to attract a large number of young dancers from all over the world, these dancers returned to their home countries once their training was complete; there was simply not enough work available in the U.S.

Characteristic of the shift in orientation from the U.S. to Europe were developments like the appointment of Jiri Kylian as artistic director of The Hague's NDT in 1975. Rather than engaging a Dutchman or an American, it was a Czech without any claim to fame whatsoever who was placed at the head of the Netherlands' preeminent dance company. Kylian had completed his training in Prague and London and was subsequently engaged as a dancer with the German Stuttgarter Ballett, then under the artistic directorship of John Cranko. In 1973 he created *Viewers* for the NDT and, after agreeing to return for the following season, was employed by the company under permanent contract. Kylian's work distinguished itself from that of Van Manen in that it consisted not solely of purely aesthetic dance movements, but incorporated dramatic content and theatricality as well.[9]

The Dutch dance world's focus on Germany became even sharper following the Wuppertaler Tanztheater's groundbreaking performances of work by the aforementioned Pina Bausch. When she brought her neoexpressionistic Tanztheater to the 1978 Holland Festival, the performances caused a sensation. Her pieces were framed as commentaries on societal relations, with her dancers contributing in significant measure to the performances' conception. Dancers were selected not on the basis of the quality of their technique, but for their dancing and acting skills and their personalities. Each performance consisted of a succession of scenes that typically revolved on improvisation and associative links, rather than on a prearranged linear narrative — techniques that not only enabled Bausch to make revolutionary dance, but that also left a considerable mark as theater.

Another person who stimulated Dutch interest in German dance — and whose career also serves to illustrate the altered situation in the United States — is the American William Forsythe. Having trained in the U.S., where he specialized in the dance techniques of Balanchine and Graham, Forsythe left to join the Stuttgarter Ballett as a dancer in 1974. There he was encouraged by Cranko to try his hand at choreography, like Kylian before him. In 1984 he established the Frankfurt Ballett, whose performances of his choreographies, such as *Artifact* and *Impressing the Czar*, sent shock waves throughout the international dance world, the Netherlands included. Unlike Bausch, Forsythe continued to

6

—

THE
COLD WAR
AND
BEYOND

1945–2009

—

CULTURE

apply the techniques of classical ballet, but enriched them with his own style of improvisation, thereby infusing the heritage of Balanchine's ballet with surprising new aesthetic and expressive possibilities.

And so it happened that forty years later the roles were reversed. While the America of 1934, and New York in particular, had represented an opportunity to escape Europe's struggle with economic recession and descent into World War II, thus making it possible for George Balanchine to continue to develop his ideas, by 1974 the cultural climate in Europe was so much more attractive than in the U.S. that a world-class choreographer like Forsythe left America for Europe in order to be able, like a new Balanchine, to create pioneering work in dance.

A New Balance

To this day the situation has not changed. Europe has now developed a multifaceted artistic ballet and dance culture — nourished at first on American models but continuing ever more independently since the 1970s — consisting of major, established companies allied to particular cities at the top, an intermediate tier of smaller and upcoming talents, and a base of small experimental dance clusters. Whereas government funding ensures the continued existence of groups at each of these levels in Europe, the almost complete lack of such support in the U.S. has meant that there are only a handful of major, established companies (including some founded in the 1950s, such as the NYCB and the Graham and Cunningham companies) and a large number of small experimental groups. Since the intermediate tier is virtually nonexistent, choreographic talent in America has few avenues along which to advance and develop. Some of that talent has even left the U.S. to seek refuge in Europe; in the Netherlands with companies like the Rotterdamse Dansgroep, which commissions such choreographers as Tere O'Connor, Denis O'Connor, Steven Petronio, Randy Warsaw, and Amanda Miller.

The U.S. government's lack of interest in the culture of dance is likewise manifested in the dwindling number of dance groups still prepared to bring their performances to Europe. Travel subsidies are difficult to obtain, and consequently only major names like Cunningham, Graham, and Bill T. Jones are capable of gathering the necessary funds. Groups from Europe, including from the Netherlands, are much more active in America by comparison. In recognition of the important position that the U.S. occupies in Dutch foreign politics and trade relations, and of the need to serve the interests of the dance companies themselves, the Dutch government has lent its support to a number of promotional and cultural exchange programs. It was this support that enabled the Theater Instituut Nederland (Dutch Theater Institute), for example, to realize its so-called U.S./Netherlands Touring & Exchange Project between 1992 and 2000, with the Netherlands-American Dance & Theater Project (NA-DTP) as a sequel from 2004 until 2007. Programs like these have greatly enhanced U.S. recognition of and appreciation for Dutch dance in general, and youth dance in particular. Dutch groups have toured the U.S. extensively, and Dutch directors and choreographers have been invited to create performances for American companies and have won awards at important U.S. festivals.

Yet whether such initiatives will have any lasting effect remains to be seen. The lack of funding options for these projects on the American side means that reciprocity has been difficult to arrange, thus sidelining any true form of cultural exchange and ultimately making it impossible for sustainable exchange projects to get off the ground. At the same time, the emergence of China and India as formidable economic competitors on the world market has made these countries the focus for a growing number of cultural projects initiated and directed by the Service Centre for International Cultural Activities (SICA), a foundation that works in close cooperation with the Dutch government.

The future of dance relations between the Netherlands and the United States now hangs in the balance. Given the waning interest in investing in this relationship on the Dutch side, and the very absence of investment opportunities within the U.S. dance sector, much will depend on the involvement of the artists and companies themselves — and also, of course, on the presence of exceptional talent, which, as the careers of figures like Balanchine and Forsythe demonstrate, will always find a way to express itself, with or without government support.

1   Eva van Schaik, *Op gespannen voet. Geschiedenis van de Nederlandse theater-dans vanaf 1900* (Haarlem: De Haan, 1981), 78.

2   Conrad van de Weetering and Luuk Utrecht, *Sonia Gaskell* (Zutphen: Walburg Pers, 1976), 55.

3   Edward Thorpe, *Black Dance* (Woodstock, NY: The Overlook Press, 1990), 164.

4   Luuk Utrecht, *Het Nationale Ballet, 25 jaar* (Amsterdam: Het Nationale Ballet, 1987), 30-33.

5   Coos Versteeg, ed., *Dancing Dutch* (Amsterdam: TIN, 2000), 32.

6   Sally Banes, *Terpsichore in Sneakers: Post-Modern Dance* (Middletown, CT: Wesleyan University Press, 1987), xvi.

7   Deborah Jowitt, *Time and the Dancing Image* (New York: William Morrow and Company, 1988), 323.

8   Käthy Gosschalk, *Moed en avontuur* (Amsterdam: TIN, 1999), 44.

9   Jochen Schmidt, *Tanzgeschichte des 20. Jahrhunderts* (Berlin: Henschel Verlag, 2002), 198.

6

—

THE
COLD WAR
AND
BEYOND
1945–2009

—

CULTURE

1106

A TRANSATLANTIC DEBATE ABOUT DIVERSITY AND NATIONAL IDENTITY

—

JAAP VERHEUL

If the debate about multiculturalism in the Netherlands had an obvious turning point, it was not 9/11 or the domestic political murders and upheavals in the years that followed. It was a 2000 newspaper article by Labor Party member and sociologist Paul Scheffer, who defined the Dutch immigrant experience as "a multicultural tragedy," which sparked a heated national discussion and led to the demise of the ideal of Dutch multiculturalism. He compared the failed integration of immigrants into Dutch society unfavorably to the successful social emancipation of the working classes at the end of the nineteenth century, and argued that the Dutch elites, who had energetically invested in that earlier social emancipation, had utterly failed to recognize the urgency of the immigrant question because they were blinded by a "lazy multiculturalism." The resulting levels of unemployment, poverty, crime, and truancy among immigrant groups had effectively created an ethnic underclass, Scheffer warned, which formed the single most dangerous threat to civil order in the Netherlands.

When Scheffer tried to formulate a solution for the impending ethnic crisis, he firmly rejected multiculturalism as a meaningful way to deal with the Dutch immigrant experience, but instead called upon Norman Podhoretz, the neo-conservative commentator and editor of the equally conservative magazine *Commentary*. As a son of Polish immigrants who had successfully climbed the American educational and social ladder, Podhoretz had famously described as "a brutal bargain" the painful but necessary step to sever ties with his immigrant background in order to open the way to assimilation. It was this bargain of ethnic disconnection and high-cultural inclusion that Scheffer now prescribed to the Dutch immigrant populations, especially those who hailed from Muslim countries such as Morocco and Turkey. As Podhoretz had done, these immigrants should discard values and practices incompatible with those of

Dutch society and embrace the culture of their newly adopted country. Dutch elites, for their part, should promote this inclusion by assuming a civilizing mission and strongly affirming a shared Dutch national culture. In short, if the United States offered a narrative that was relevant to the Netherlands, Scheffer seemed to suggest, it was the classical assimilationist model of the melting pot, instead of the multicultural salad bowl.[1]

This intellectual rallying cry against multiculturalism was to become a highly significant turning point in the debate about immigration and national identity in the Netherlands. It also marked a meeting point between two different but comparable trajectories at the opposite sides of the Atlantic. It was not so much in the celebration of ethnic diversity, as in the shared concern about the multicultural ideal that the United States and the Netherlands found common ground at the beginning of the twenty-first century.

Multicultural Trajectories

When in early 2001 a government think tank published a study on immigration and diversity in the Netherlands, its programmatic title *The Netherlands as an Immigration Society* reflected the element of surprise and self-discovery that marked the public debate at the turn of the century. In spite of the successive waves of postwar immigration from former colonies and the Mediterranean, the Dutch had overlooked the fact that their country was becoming a nation of immigrants. For a long time, the immigrants and asylum seekers who had reached the Low Countries had been viewed as temporary or accidental visitors. After all, almost all repatriated persons from the former Dutch East Indies were eligible for Dutch citizenship or already carried Dutch passports, as did most immigrants from Suriname and the Antilles. And the laborers who were recruited from Morocco and Turkey in the 1970s were labeled migratory "guest workers" to underscore their transient status.[2]

Although immigration did not seem a pressing issue, at the turn of the century the number of foreign born living in the Netherlands had risen to 9 percent. In fact, 17 percent of the population was either foreign born or had one or two foreign-born parents. These numbers were comparable to those of the United States.[3] However, whereas the U.S. had accepted immigration as part of its self-image, mythology, and popular culture, the Dutch lacked such a national immigration narrative. Therefore, it was not until they suddenly began to recognize their own ethnic diversity that the narrative of the United States became relevant.

When the skirmishes about the United States' multicultural identity first erupted into a full-scale culture war in the 1980s, the Dutch observed the Amer-

6

—

THE
COLD WAR
AND
BEYOND

1945–2009

—

CULTURE

1108

ican debate from afar with benign amusement and surprise. The term "multi-culturalism" was used to describe a society in which cultural minorities inter-act and influence each other but also are free to maintain their own cultural identities. It was in this debate that the concepts of national identity and multi-culturalism were firmly developed as mutually exclusive opposites. It is no coin-cidence that in the same period new calls for national identity and exceptional-ism were formulated. More interestingly, the term "multiculturalism" entered the public debate mainly with a highly derogatory meaning, as it was primarily articulated by its critics. They feared that it would lead to an ethnic balkaniza-tion that could well herald, as Gitlin ominously phrased it, the "twilight of com-mon dreams."

Dutch newspapers dutifully reported the ongoing battle, and from the early 1990s on began introducing the terms "multiculturalism" and "affirmative ac-tion" to their readers with superior aloofness. "Americans are confused," one foreign correspondent gleefully summarized the Dutch perception.[4] Mean-while, further away from the public gaze, the many government reports and ac-ademic surveys of the 1980s and 1990s recognized that most immigrants were in the country to stay and that the government should develop what was called a "minority policy." It was in these policy debates about immigration and diver-sity that the Netherlands first began to be recognized as a "multicultural soci-ety." Even if the term "multiculturalism" was rarely used explicitly, one could argue that acceptance of the related term "cultural pluralism" was a guiding principle of Dutch government policy toward its ethnic immigrant minorities. Although the government now started to stimulate institutional integration of immigrants in work, housing, and education, and also offered civic integration and Dutch language courses, minorities were expected to preserve their own cultural identities.[5]

Yet, the new Dutch minority policy was a far cry from American-style multi-culturalism. If the official government position suggested a "cultural relativ-ism" of mutual acceptance, policymakers left no doubt about the dominance of Dutch cultural values. In spite of the multicultural tone in terminology, their model of Dutch plurality foremost recalled the well-established principles of pillarization, the system of segregation along religious and social fault lines that had dominated Dutch society until the 1960s. Ironically, it was as if the Dutch government revived that largely obsolete arrangement of cultural segre-gation by placing immigrant minorities once more inside a "pillar," assuming that they would be able to emancipate themselves from their own station, just as other minorities had done in the past century.[6]

In contrast to the United States, the public debate about immigration and diversity in the Netherlands was still very much optimistic, if not utopian, in tone. The few detractors were either ignored or quickly forgotten. When conservative party leader Frits Bolkestein in 1991 openly argued that Islam was incompatible with essential values of Western culture such as freedom of expression and the separation of church and state, he was met with widespread criticism and skepticism. It was only when this climate of utopian consensus about the peaceful homogeneity of Dutch society abruptly disappeared after the turn of the century that the Dutch and American trajectories began to converge.[7]

American Models

When the Dutch government realized that the Netherlands had "developed into an immigration country" it began to look with renewed interest at the United States. A striking example is a study that the Scientific Council for Government Policy (Wetenschappelijke Raad voor Regeringsbeleid; WRR) commissioned from the RAND Corporation. The council asked the American think tank to examine "whether the Netherlands could gain some insights from the United States, being a country that has a lot of experience with immigration processes." The report, which the council published in May 2001, carefully compared the approaches of the two countries by looking at admission policy, asylum seekers, illegal immigration, naturalization, and return migration, and in order to assess integration it discussed how immigrants fared in education, the labor market, social welfare, and housing. In spite of the wide range of aspects it discussed, the report could identify only a few elements in U.S. policy that it considered relevant for the Netherlands. Most controversial was its discussion of welfare programs, which were not offered to newcomers in the United States but were readily available to immigrants in the Netherlands. When the report concluded that the Dutch lagged behind the Americans in actual integration of immigrants in spite of the many welfare programs, it clearly suggested that the soft cushion of social benefits in the Netherlands actually prevented the integration of immigrants. The report also concluded that the Dutch lacked sufficient data to assess the economic costs and benefits of immigration, and suggested that the country should ease some of its restrictions on obtaining citizenship to attract skilled laborers. These kinds of recommendations supported the more pragmatic and business-like approach to immigration that was associated with the United States.[8]

A number of Dutch conservatives who started to participate in the immigration discussion after 2000 were also informed by American ideas. Most prominently, the small group of conservative intellectuals who founded the Edmund Burke Foundation in 2000 "to conserve the virtuous elements of Dutch society," was inspired by American conservative thinkers such as Leo Strauss, Francis Fukuyama, and Samuel P. Huntington. This foundation was affiliated with the

6

——

THE
COLD WAR
AND
BEYOND

1945–2009

——

CULTURE

conservative Intercollegiate Studies Institute of William F. Buckley, Jr., maintained contacts with conservative American think tanks such as the Heritage Foundation and the American Enterprise Institute, was reportedly funded by large American multinationals, and promoted a Dutch version of neoconservatism. Its members not only resisted government interference and taxation, but also echoed their American examples in strongly promoting Western civilization and the classical tradition of Great Books. They routinely compared "the political theology of Islam" with fascism and called for limits on immigration. Furthermore, they strongly supported the American war against Iraq. Although the Burke Foundation was never able to build the infrastructure it envisioned, these American-inspired neoconservatives added a distinctively assimilationist voice to the debate about multiculturalism in the Netherlands.[9]

A new discourse about Dutch identity and the multicultural society had already emerged at the beginning of the twenty-first century that emphasized national core values and the need for assimilation, as Scheffer's important article also illustrates. But the Dutch public discussion about diversity took an especially radical turn after the terrorist attacks that hit the United States on September 11, 2001. First there was a strong—if short-lived—surge of support for American society, which led Prime Minister Wim Kok to emphasize that "[t]he Netherlands and the United States share the same fundamental values." As the U.S. responded to the attack by Muslim fundamentalists with a War on Terror, many people in the Netherlands began to look at Muslim minorities with different eyes. This already volatile climate soon turned combustible after the two political assassinations that not only led to a painful political shakeup, but would also change transatlantic relations. Although politician Pim Fortuyn was murdered by an animal rights activist in 2002, it had been his strongly voiced protest against cultural relativism and what he called the "islamification" of Dutch culture that turned him into a controversial populist. That the anti-immigration position of his newly founded party proved stunningly successful pointed at cultural divisions within Dutch society that other politicians had neglected.

Dutch filmmaker Theo van Gogh, who shared Fortuyn's fondness for provocation and media appearances, had also caused controversy by deriding radical Islam in his films and columns. He was murdered in 2004 by a Dutch radical Muslim who had been enraged by the short video Van Gogh had made for the ex-refugee member of parliament Ayaan Hirsi Ali, one of the most outspoken critics of Islam in the Netherlands. The video, *Submission, Part One*, which criticized the oppression of women under Islam, caused immense resistance within the Islamic community. Hirsi Ali has lived under twenty-four-hour police protection ever since and in 2006 decided to leave the Netherlands to join the American Enterprise Institute after her Dutch citizenship was questioned. Both political assassinations and the ensuing political confusion radically ended the utopian tone that had marked the Dutch debate about integration for so many years. The unquestioned dominance of Dutch-style multiculturalism was over.[10]

A Dutch 9/11

As the Dutch began to rediscover the United States, they also became a focal point of the American multicultural debate. After the assassination of Fortuyn, the Netherlands became front-page news for all major U.S. newspapers. Three themes dominated the American interpretation of the assassination. The first was, not surprisingly, the motive of a paradise lost. This was a compelling story line that would dominate the American image of the Netherlands for years. Readers were persistently reminded that the Netherlands traditionally had been one of the most civil and tolerant countries in the world. It was, as one commentator noted, "[a] bourgeois and orderly country that prides itself on tolerance."[11] Because it had mostly welcomed and accommodated foreigners, the Netherlands had become a case study of utopian multiculturalism. Of course, as American readers now learned, dark forces had been lurking in this paradise. The sudden success of Fortuyn's party had shown that even the "Dutch tradition of tolerance" had reached its limits. In fact, as readers were told, for many years the integration of immigrants had led to problems that had been largely ignored by the political elites, both right and left.[12]

A second theme was a concern about transatlantic relations after 9/11. Many commentators argued that Fortuyn, who had entered politics shortly before the terrorist attacks, had risen to prominence because of sudden concerns over Muslim extremism in Europe. Even though Fortuyn was not killed by a Muslim extremist, most articles connected his rise with the changed political climate since 9/11. It was as if American commentators wanted to emphasize that Europe, too, was now feeling some of the same pain. The notion of a "Dutch 9/11" would be more strongly developed after the Van Gogh murder.

The most ironic aspect of the U.S. reactions to the Fortuyn murder, however, was that he was suddenly embraced by conservative journalists and commentators as a martyr for libertarianism and freedom of speech. Somewhat surprisingly, American conservatives and neoconservatives posthumously celebrated Pim Fortuyn, that maverick, gay ex-Marxist, as one of their own. Two of Fortuyn's ideological positions in particular enthralled these commentators: his stance against multiculturalism and his open attack on the European elites. Hence, Fortuyn was craftily reinvented as a monoculturalist, a liberal nationalist, a patriotic modernist, and a libertarian populist who had attacked what was called "Europe's multicultural establishment."

Artwork *De schreeuw* (*The scream*), commemorating the murder
of Theo van Gogh in Amsterdam, in 2004.

When filmmaker Theo van Gogh was murdered in 2004 the U.S. media immediately picked up the story. CNN sent film crews to Amsterdam and reporters were flown in, visiting inner cities and immigrant neighborhoods, and interviewing every Dutch pundit, commentator, and academic they could find. Much of the reporting was matter of fact, informative, balanced, sensible, and emphatic. But conservative media in particular jumped on the story. Conservative newspapers such as the *New York Sun* and *The Washington Times*, and neoconservative magazines such as the *Weekly Standard* and the *National Review*, each published a series of stories and analytical articles, and sent reporters to the Netherlands to offer firsthand reporting and inside information. Some of these alarmist reports were later collected in best-selling books. They also found a new hero in rebel member of parliament Geert Wilders, who broke with the conservative VVD Party because of his stubbornly hostile position toward immigration. Wilders, who was sympathetically described as a "Tocquevillian conservative" was praised for "asking the right questions, something that few in Holland have been brave enough to do." The conservative press was particularly enamored with Ayaan Hirsi Ali, who had become a vocal critic of Islam from within the VVD, and who was hailed as "a daughter of the Enlightenment" who "has been dealt with a full house of the royal virtues: courage, intelligence and compassion."[13]

The theme of a "Dutch September 11" was especially appealing to the conservative commentators because it showed how the United States had been right about its war against radical Islam. They fell over each other to explain how the Dutch finally had lost their innocence and had woken out of their "cultural naivete." More important, they felt that this rude awakening opened possibilities of Europe finally joining in the struggle. "This Christmastime," *The Washington Times* almost cheered, "would be the moment when Western Europe finally joins our war on terrorism." Although it was convinced that the population of Europe had long been eager to do so, *The Washington Times* pointed out that the European elites had been in full denial about who the true enemy was. But now, the newspaper gleefully reported, the murder of Van Gogh and the subsequent violence against Muslim mosques and schools "have forced high European leaders and news outlets to begin to publicly face up to the implications of September 11, 2001 and the migration of Muslims in large numbers into the heart or Europe."[14]

Christopher Caldwell of the *Weekly Standard* found that the murder of Theo van Gogh, exactly 911 days after that of Pim Fortuyn, "[was] described by people in Holland as having had the same effect on their country as the attacks that killed nearly 3,000 in the World Trade Center Towers." The Dutch, he explained, used to have "a generous, no-questions-asked welfare state" but were having second thoughts once they discovered that many Muslims in their country sym-

6

—

THE
COLD WAR
AND
BEYOND

1945–2009

—

CULTURE

pathized with the 9/11 terrorists, that Van Gogh's assassin was a member of an extensive terrorist network, and that a series of "American-style shootouts" took place in schools populated by immigrant children. With unveiled empathy Caldwell observed that the Dutch Minister of Justice Piet Hein Donner was planning "something like the Patriot Act in the Netherlands."[15] In short, the two political murders brought the Netherlands closer to the United States both in its experience with radical Islam and in its responses to it.

The second theme in conservative reporting on the Van Gogh murder was that of the failings and dangers of multiculturalism. Moreover, it was argued that the Dutch population always knew this, but was kept from openly expressing its opinion by the "multicultural elites from The Hague and Brussels."[16] By emphasizing this connection the neoconservatives opened a two-pronged attack on the multicultural ideal and on European leaders.

It is remarkable that almost all of these critics described multiculturalism as an experiment, a dogma, a mantra, a utopian dream, forced upon an unwilling population by a hardheaded, haughty, and undemocratic elite. Obviously, American neoconservative commentators had started to project their worst nightmares on the Netherlands. When they described how Fortuyn, Van Gogh, and Hirsi Ali heroically attacked the "intolerant left-wing hegemony of political correctness," they first and foremost had the United States in mind. Everything they abhorred in post-1960s America suddenly seemed to have made its way to the Netherlands. What they were really trying to do, was to enlist the Netherlands in their own ideological struggle.

The sudden neoconservative interest in the Netherlands opened a new chapter in the meandering chronicle of American utopian and dystopian depictions of Dutch society. The dreams of nineteenth-century Holland mania that had lingered in the American mind for a long time were finally shattered after the 1960s when Holland became a byword for a welfare state gone awry and permissiveness gone too far. "Hollanditis" had been discovered as a contagious disease of pacifism and anti-Americanism that threatened to infect all of Europe and could sour the long-standing transatlantic relationship. At the end of the twentieth century, however, a brief interlude of utopian bliss occurred when the consensual *poldermodel* stirred American hopes that the Dutch had found a way to combine economic prosperity, labor stability, and welfare reform. The "Dutch 9/11" at the beginning of the twenty-first century marked a new downward curve that shed the impression of peaceful diversity and undisturbed concord. It should be noted, however, that these images are projections of national identity, representations of national character. Put differently, the Dutch society of these discourses is an imagined community—imagined, not by itself, but by others.

The Rediscovery of America

When Paul Scheffer looked back on the multicultural debate in the Netherlands in which he had so actively participated, he pulled his views on immigration and integration together in a comprehensive, evocative study. Although he discusses many perspectives on immigration and vividly sketches many compelling vignettes from all over the world, Scheffer considers himself most strongly inspired by one single work, Oscar Handlin's 1952 Pulitzer Prize-winning classic *The Uprooted*, about the American immigration experience. Scheffer emphatically shares Handlin's view that "[t]he history of immigration, is the history of alienation and its consequences." He is convinced that this painful, but ultimately successful, immigration history of the United States will be repeated in Europe. "The United States," he argues "proves that a society of newcomers can bring forth a vigorous economy and culture."[17] In this respect, Scheffer's book also illustrates, as the title of one of his chapters suggests, the "Rediscovery of America." For over four centuries, the Netherlands and the United States served as a useful touchstone for each other when discussing their constitutional framework, system of political representation, foreign policy, economic prospects, or cultural achievements. Not surprisingly, both nations also looked askance at each other when the very idea of their national identity became a topic of national discussion and collective soul searching. In the end, both nations ultimately were fighting their internal cultural wars. Much of what observers across the Atlantic wrote about the other reflected their own domestic concerns more than anything else. Yet, even in that respect the transatlantic multicultural debate illustrated something valuable: a history of mutual relevance.

1 Paul Scheffer, "Het multiculturele drama," *NRC Handelsblad*, January 29, 2000; Norman Podhoretz, "Making It: The Brutal Bargain," *Harper's*, December 1967; Fleur Sleegers, *In debat over Nederland. Veranderingen in het discours over de multiculturele samenleving en nationale identiteit* (Amsterdam: Amsterdam University Press, 2007).

2 Wetenschappelijke Raad voor het Regeringsbeleid, *Nederland als immigratiesamenleving* (The Hague: SDU uitgeverij, 2001).

3 Han Entzinger, "The Rise and Fall of Multiculturalism: The Case of the Netherlands," in Christian Joppke and Ewa Morawska, eds., *Toward Assimilation and Citizenship: Immigrants in Liberal Nation-States* (Basingstoke: Palgrave Macmillan, 2003); Han Entzinger, "Changing the Rules While the Game Is On: From Multiculturalism to Assimilation in the Netherlands," in Y. Michael Bodemann and Gökçe Yurdakul, eds., *Migration, Citizenship, Ethnos* (New York: Palgrave Macmillan, 2006).

6

—

THE
COLD WAR
AND
BEYOND

1945-2009

—

CULTURE

4   Ben Knapen, NRC Handelsblad, May 4, 1992.

5   Entzinger, "Changing the Rules," 125-127.

6   Sociaal Cultureel Planbureau, "Naar een multi-etnische samenleving." Chapter 9, Sociaal en Cultureel Rapport. 25 Jaar Verandering (Rijswijk: SCP, 1998); Sleegers, In debat over Nederland.

7   Frits Bolkestein, "Integratie van minderheden moet met lef worden aangepakt," de Volkskrant, September 12, 1991.

8   Mirjam van het Loo et al., A Comparison of American and Dutch Immigration and Integration Experiences. What Lessons Can Be Learned? The Multicultural Society (The Hague: WRR, 2001).

9   Bart Jan Spruyt, De verdediging van het westen: Leo Strauss, Amerikaans neoconservatisme en de kansen in Nederland. Rooseveltlezing, April 12, 2006 (cited March 19, 2008), www.burkestichting.nl/nl/actueel/rooseveltlezing.pdf.

10 Ian Buruma, "Final Cut: After a Filmmaker's Murder, the Dutch Creed of Tolerance Has Come under Siege," The New Yorker, January 3, 2005; Ian Buruma, Murder in Amsterdam. The Death of Theo Van Gogh and the Limits of Tolerance (London: Atlantic Books, 2006); Galen A. Irwin and Joop J. M. Van Holsteyn, "Never a Dull Moment: Pim Fortuyn and the Dutch Parliamentary Election of 2002," West European Politics 26.2 (2003).

11 Rod Dreher, "Murder in Holland," National Review Online, 2002.

12 See for instance Keith B. Richburg, "Key Dutch Rightist Is Shot Dead; Anti-Immigrant Stance Was Attracting Support," The Washington Post, May 7, 2002.

13 Bruce Bawer, While Europe Slept: How Radical Islam Is Destroying the West from Within (New York: Doubleday, 2006); Tony Blankley, The West's Last Chance. Will We Win the Clash of Civilizations? (Washington, DC: Regnery, 2005); Andrew Stuttaford, "Yelling Stop: Geert Wilders, Who Lives in a Prison, Tries to Save Holland," National Review, April 25, 2005; Christopher Caldwell, "Daughter of the Enlightenment," The New York Times, April 3, 2005.

14 Dan Dilanian, "Death Highlights Segregation of Dutch Muslims: Theo Van Gogh's Slaying Sparked More Ethnic Violence," The Philadelphia Inquirer, November 22, 2004; William Pfaff, "Europe Pays the Price for Cultural Naivete," International Herald Tribune, November 11, 2004; Tony Blankley, "Europe to the Barricades," The Washington Times, November 24, 2004.

15 Christopher Caldwell, "Holland Daze: The Dutch Rethink Multiculturalism," Weekly Standard, December 27, 2004.

16 John O'Sullivan, "The Islamic Republic of Holland. How One Nation Deals with a Revolutionary Problem," National Review, July 18, 2005.

17 Paul Scheffer, Het land van aankomst (Amsterdam: De Bezige Bij, 2007), 15. Quotation translated by Jaap Verheul.

LIST OF MAPS AND GRAPHICS

1119

LIST OF CONTRIBUTORS

JAN VAN ADRICHEM is Head of Collections at the Stedelijk Museum in Amsterdam, the Netherlands.

PETER VAN BAALEN is Associate Professor of Knowledge, IT and Organization at Erasmus University Rotterdam, the Netherlands.

PETER R. BAEHR is Professor of Human Rights Emeritus at Utrecht University and Leiden University, the Netherlands.

HANS BAK is Professor of American Literature and American Studies at Radboud University in Nijmegen, the Netherlands.

AGE F. P. BAKKER is Executive Director of the International Monetary Fund, representing thirteen countries in the Netherlands Constituency.

DAVID BARNOUW is a researcher at the Netherlands Institute for War Documentation in Amsterdam, the Netherlands.

FLORIBERT BAUDET is Associate Professor of Strategy at the Netherlands Defence Academy in Breda, the Netherlands.

JAAP VAN DER BENT is Assistant Professor of American Literature at Radboud University in Nijmegen, the Netherlands.

HERMAN VAN BERGEIJK is Architectural Historian at Delft University of Technology, the Netherlands.

KOOS BOSMA is Professor of History of Architecture and Heritage Studies at the VU University in Amsterdam, the Netherlands.

DOEKO BOSSCHER is Professor of Contemporary History at the University of Groningen, the Netherlands.

BRAM BOXHOORN is Director of the Netherlands Atlantic Association in The Hague, the Netherlands.

WAYNE TE BRAKE is Kempner Professor of History at Purchase College of the State University of New York in Purchase, NY.

HARRY P. VAN DALEN is Associate Professor of Economics at Tilburg University, and Senior Research Associate at the Netherlands Inter-disciplinary Demographic Institute in The Hague, the Netherlands.

DIRK DEKKERS is an advisor in the Inter-national Affairs Directorate of the Ministry of Transport, Public Works and Water Management in The Hague, the Netherlands.

KAREL DIBBETS is Lecturer in Media History at the University of Amster-dam, and Editor of Cinema Context (www.cinemacontext.nl), the online encyclopaedia of film culture in the Netherlands.

MARC DIERIKX is Project Manager of European Integration Studies and Development Cooperation Studies at the Institute of Netherlands History in The Hague, the Netherlands.

WIM VAN DEN DOEL is Professor of
Contemporary History and Dean of
the Faculty of Arts at Leiden University,
the Netherlands.

MICHAEL DOUMA is a Ph.D. candidate
at Florida State University in Talla-
hassee, FL.

J. W. DRUKKER is Professor and Chair
of the Department of Design History
at Twente University in Enschedé,
the Netherlands.

JEROME EGGER is affiliated with the
History Department at the Anton
de Kom University in Paramaribo,
Suriname.

TOM ETTY was Senior Advisor on international affairs at the Confederation
of Netherlands Trade Unions (FNV)
between 1978 and 2007, representing
the FNV at the International Confederation of Free Trade Unions (ICFTU)
and the International Labour Organisation (ILO).

FIRTH HARING FABEND is an independent historian and a novelist.

MARC FREY holds the Helmut Schmidt
Chair of International History at
Jacobs University in Bremen, Germany.

WILLEM FRIJHOFF is Professor of History
Emeritus at the VU University in
Amsterdam, the Netherlands.

CHARLES T. GEHRING is Director of the
New Netherland Project at the New
York State Library in Albany, NY.

THOMAS GIJSWIJT is Assistant Professor
of American History and American
Politics at Radboud University
in Nijmegen, the Netherlands.

FERRY DE GOEY is Assistant Professor
of History at Erasmus University
Rotterdam, the Netherlands.

JOYCE D. GOODFRIEND is Professor
of History at the University of Denver
in Denver, CO.

FRANCES GOUDA is Professor of History
and Gender Studies at the University of
Amsterdam, the Netherlands.

BOB DE GRAAFF is Professor of Terrorism
and Counterterrorism Studies and
Director of the Center for Terrorism
and Counterterrorism at Leiden
University's Campus The Hague,
the Netherlands.

JOHN GROENEWEGEN is Professor of
the Economics of Infrastructures
at Delft University of Technology,
the Netherlands.

MICHIEL VAN GROESEN is Assistant
Professor of Early Modern History
at the University of Amsterdam,
the Netherlands.

GEORGE HARINCK is Professor of History
and Director of the Historical Documentation Centre for Dutch Protestantism at the VU University in
Amsterdam, and Professor of History
at the Theological University of the
Reformed Churches in Kampen, the
Netherlands.

JAN VAN DER HARST is Professor of the
History and Theory of European Integration at the University of Groningen,
the Netherlands.

DUCO HELLEMA is Professor of the
History of International Relations at
Utrecht University, the Netherlands.

LINDA HEYWOOD is Professor of African
American Studies and History at
Boston University in Boston, MA.

PIETER HOVENS is Curator of the North
American Department of the National
Museum of Ethnology in Leiden,
the Netherlands.

1121

FRANK INKLAAR is Assistant Professor of Cultural Sciences at the Open University in Heerlen, the Netherlands.

JAAP JACOBS is an independent researcher and has taught at universities in the Netherlands and the United States.

MAARTJE JANSE is a postdoctoral researcher at Leiden University, the Netherlands.

JANNY DE JONG is Senior Lecturer in Modern History at the University of Groningen, the Netherlands.

JAMES C. KENNEDY is Professor of Contemporary History at the University of Amsterdam, the Netherlands.

ALBERT KERSTEN is Professor of Diplomatic History Emeritus at Leiden University, and Honorary Historical Advisor to the Minister of Foreign Affairs in the Netherlands.

ARJO KLAMER is Professor of the Economics of Art and Culture at Erasmus University Rotterdam and Dean of Academia Vitae in Deventer, the Netherlands.

CHRIST KLEP is Lecturer in History at Utrecht University, the Netherlands.

JOOST KLEUTERS is a Ph.D. candidate and Junior Lecturer at Radboud University in Nijmegen, the Netherlands.

WIM KLINKERT is Professor of Military History at the University of Amsterdam, and Associate Professor of Military History at the Netherlands Defence Academy in Breda, the Netherlands.

WIM KLOOSTER is Associate Professor of History at Clark University in Worcester, MA.

PAUL KOEDIJK is Historian and Consultant and Investigator with Integis B.V. in Haarlem, the Netherlands.

JAAP KOOIJMAN is Associate Professor of Media and Culture and American Studies at the University of Amsterdam, the Netherlands.

ENNE KOOPS is a Ph.D. candidate at the Roosevelt Study Center in Middelburg and the Theological University in Kampen, the Netherlands.

HANS KRABBENDAM is Assistant Director of the Roosevelt Study Center in Middelburg, the Netherlands.

ROB KROES is Professor of American Studies Emeritus at the University of Amsterdam, the Netherlands.

GAIL LEVIN is Professor of Art History at Baruch College and the Graduate Center of the City University of New York, in New York, NY.

FRED VAN LIEBURG is Professor of the History of Dutch Protestantism at the VU University in Amsterdam, the Netherlands.

RIMKO VAN DER MAAR is Lecturer in History at Utrecht University, the Netherlands.

CATHY MATSON is Professor of History and Director of Graduate Studies at the University of Delaware in Newark, DE.

INE MEGENS is Senior Lecturer in Contemporary History at the University of Groningen, the Netherlands.

SIMON MIDDLETON is Senior Lecturer in Early American History at the University of Sheffield, United Kingdom.

CORNELIS A. VAN MINNEN is Director of the Roosevelt Study Center in Middelburg, the Netherlands, and Professor of American History at Ghent University, Belgium.

NANCY T. MINTY is Lecturer at the Metropolitan Museum of Art in New York, NY.

GIJS MOM is Assistant Professor of Industrial Engineering and Innovation Sciences at Eindhoven University of Technology, the Netherlands.

BERTRAM MOURITS is an editor at Contact Publishers in Amsterdam, the Netherlands.

LUTGARD MUTSAERS is Assistant Professor of Media and Culture Studies of Utrecht University, the Netherlands.

JAN NOORDEGRAAF is Associate Professor of Dutch Linguistics at the VU University in Amsterdam, the Netherlands.

THUNNIS VAN OORT is Assistant Professor of Film and Television Studies at Utrecht University, the Netherlands.

PAUL OTTO is Professor of History at George Fox University in Newberg, OR.

BOB REINALDA is Senior Lecturer in International Relations at Radboud University in Nijmegen, the Netherlands.

MICHAEL RIEMENS is Assistant Professor of History at the University of Groningen, the Netherlands.

HANS RIGHOLT is a Ph.D. candidate at the Roosevelt Study Center in Middelburg and Utrecht University, the Netherlands.

TIMO DE RIJK is Associate Professor of Design History at Delft University of Technology, the Netherlands.

WILBERT SCHREURS is a historian of advertising in the Netherlands and teaches advertising history at the VU University in Amsterdam, the Netherlands.

GILES SCOTT-SMITH is Senior Researcher at the Roosevelt Study Center and Associate Professor of International Relations at the Roosevelt Academy in Middelburg, the Netherlands. He is also the Ernst van der Beugel Chair in Transatlantic Diplomatic Relations at Leiden University.

MATHIEU SEGERS is Assistant Professor of International Relations and European Integration at Utrecht University, the Netherlands.

MARTHA DICKINSON SHATTUCK is an editor and researcher at the New Netherland Project at the New York State Library in Albany, NY.

DAVID J. SNYDER is Instructor of History at the University of South Carolina in Columbia, SC.

ONNO F. STOKVIS has worked at the Theater Instituut Nederland in Amsterdam, the Netherlands, and is now an independent writer.

ANNETTE STOTT is Professor of Art History and Director of the School of Art and Art History at the University of Denver in Denver, CO.

ROBERT P. SWIERENGA is Professor of History Emeritus at Kent State University in Kent, OH, and A.C. Van Raalte Research Professor at the A.C. Van Raalte Institute of Hope College in Holland, MI.

JOHN THORNTON is Professor of African American Studies and History at Boston University in Boston, MA.

1123

JEROEN TOUWEN is Lecturer in Economic and Social History at Leiden University, the Netherlands.

HUBERT P. VAN TUYLL is Professor and Chair of the Department of History, Anthropology, and Philosophy at Augusta State University in Augusta, GA.

AUGUSTUS J. VEENENDAAL, JR. is Senior Research Historian (retired) at the Institute of Netherlands History in The Hague, the Netherlands.

JAAP VERHEUL is Associate Professor of American Studies at Utrecht University, the Netherlands.

DAVID W. VOORHEES is Director of the Papers of Jacob Leisler Project at New York University and Managing Editor of *de Halve Maen* at the Holland Society of New York in New York, NY.

TITY DE VRIES is Associate Professor of Contemporary and American History at the University of Groningen, the Netherlands.

TACO WESTERHUIS is Senior Policy Advisor in the Directorate-General for Foreign Economic Relations of the Ministry of Economic Affairs in The Hague, the Netherlands.

MIRA WILKINS is Professor of Economics at Florida International University in Miami, FL.

KEES WOUTERS is an independent historian.

BEN WUBS is a researcher at Erasmus University Rotterdam, the Netherlands.

FRANK ZUIJDAM is Senior Consultant with the Technopolis Group in Amsterdam, the Netherlands.

BERT VAN DER ZWAN is the historian of the Dutch Ministry of Foreign Affairs.

FRITS ZWART is Director of the Netherlands Music Institute in The Hague, the Netherlands.

COPYRIGHT OF ILLUSTRATIONS

The publisher has made every effort to contact all those with ownership rights pertaining to the illustrations. Nonetheless, should you believe that your rights have not been respected, please contact Boom Publishers, Amsterdam.

INDEX

Page numbers in italic refer to illustrations, maps or figures.

1161